DR. Z's
BEAT THE
RACETRACK

Other books by *WILLIAM T. ZIEMBA*
and *DONALD B. HAUSCH*

Betting at the Racetrack

Efficiency of Racetrack Betting Markets

Other books by *WILLIAM T. ZIEMBA*

Stochastic Optimization Models in Finance

Turkish Flat Weaves

Energy Policy Modeling: United States and Canadian Experiences, Vols. I and II

Generalized Concavity in Optimization and Economics

Dr. Z's 6/49 Lotto Guidebook

Economics of Information and Contracts: Essays in Honor of John E. Butterworth

Strategies for Making Excess Profits in the Stock Market

DR. Z's BEAT THE RACETRACK

Revised Edition

William T. Ziemba and Donald B. Hausch

With a Foreword by Edward O. Thorp

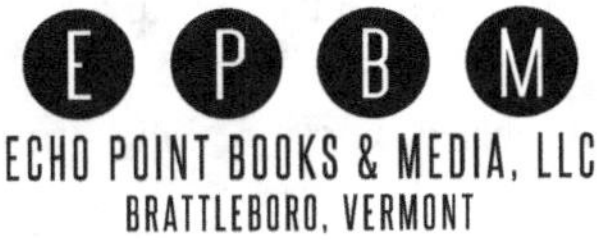

To Rachel, who likes the horses
but loves the popcorn
—W. T. Z.

To my parents, Robert and Margret Hausch
—D. B. H.

Published by Echo Point Books & Media
Brattleboro, Vermont
www.EchoPointBooks.com

Dr. Z's Beat the Racetrack
ISBN: 978-1-63561-749-8 (paperback)

Interior design by Bernard Schleifer

Cover design by Alicia Brown

Front cover images:
horse-riding-school-jockey vector art, by Gocili, courtesy of Shutterstock
one-9-horse-races-that-passed, by Sukhanova Daria, courtesy of Shutterstock
Back cover image:
bet-ticket-male-female-hands, by ABB Photo, courtesy of Shutterstock

Foreword

The publication of this book is a rare event in the world of gambling because it presents one of the few betting systems ever discovered that really works. It is the only system for betting on horse races which has enough scientific analysis to persuade me that it is valid.

The system is easy to understand and use, which makes it appealing to readers and bettors. The basic ideas behind it are simple ones:

1. The crowd is good at picking a winner—so good, in fact, that the relative amount bet on a horse to win corresponds closely to its actual chances of winning.
2. In the same way, the amount the crowd bets on horses to place and show should be distributed in approximately the same proportions as the amounts bet in the win pool.
3. But sometimes—in about two to four races a day—the place and show pools are considerably "off" from the proportions in the win pool. When that happens, the place and show bets give the player an edge of as much as 20% or even more. This phenomenon is an example of an "inefficient market," and it is the basis of the Dr. Z system.

It took two good scientists, Professor William Ziemba and his student Donald Hausch, to back up these ideas with solid analysis. They set out to develop a precise method to measure just how good a bet is, one that would show you both when to bet and how large a bet it should be. Bill Ziemba is an expert in operations research and portfolio management and in the theory and practical applications of gambling. He has long had an active interest in gambling games and systems and has served as a consultant for the Canadian government. His main area of academic expertise, operations research, is concerned with the application of mathematics to the real world. Donald Hausch is an expert economic modeler and computer analyst. All this provides them with the perfect background for what they have done in this book.

Besides the mathematical and scientific analysis, the development of the Dr. Z system required verification using historical data from past races, and it needed to be tested by actual play. The authors did all these things. *And* they won money at the track using their own system. The book presents all the details necessary to make a careful, intelligent, and profitable application of their system. Beyond this, it is also an entertaining introduction to the lore of the track.

This book is for people who want to win. The gambling system it presents is one of the few I have ever seen that I think really works. I am convinced enough to bet my own money on it.

EDWARD O. THORP

Newport Beach, California
April 1987

Acknowledgments

In the course of our research and the preparation of this book, we have received the aid and support of a number of colleagues and friends. Without implicating them for any possible errors in this book, we would especially like to thank Mukhtar Ali, Michael Brennan, Brian Canfield, Robert Cheung, Tom Cover, Bruce Fauman, Peter Griffin, Dick Mitchell, James Quinn, Fraser Rawlinson, Jay Ritter, Jerry Rosenwald, Mark Rubinstein, Richard van Slyke, Nancy Thompson, Edward O. Thorp, and John Woods. Jenny Russell, Linda Stewart, Marilyn Withers, and Evelyn Fong did a marvelous job of typing and checking the various drafts of the manuscript. Sandra Buckingham and Ulrike Hilborn did the artwork. It is our hope that this book will follow proudly in the tradition of Ed Thorp's books *Beat the Dealer* and *Beat the Market* as a scientifically proven system to exploit an existing market inefficiency. We are pleased that Dr. Thorp has written the foreword to the book.

Contents

FOREWORD BY EDWARD O. THORP 7

ACKNOWLEDGMENTS 9

INTRODUCTION 17

1 **Discovery of the Dr. Z System** 19

The lure of racing. The difficulty of actually winning at the racetrack. Putting together the concepts for a winning system.

2 **Betting at the Races** 27

Reading the program and the *Daily Racing Form*. The various types of bets. How the odds are determined: The track take and breakage.

3 **Applying Stock Market Efficiency Concepts to Horseracing Betting Markets** 35

The crowd is very good at estimating the true probability of winning: Efficiency of the win-betting market. Can you win by betting on only the very best horses? How accurate is the morning line? The need to look for special situations to avoid betting on all races and on inappropriate days.

4 **Finding Profitable Place and Show Bets** 56

Understanding the win, place, and show payoffs. Why place and show betting can yield positive profits. Expected return per dollar

bet. Determining when there is an inefficiency in the betting pools and thus a good opportunity to bet. Formulas for determining the expected value per dollar bet.

5 **How Much Should You Bet?** 88

Why you need to have a good money management system. Using the Kelly criterion to maximize the long-run growth of your betting fortune. More on the Kelly criterion: Good properties, bad properties. Betting simulation. Assumptions of the Dr. Z system. Steps in applying the Dr. Z system. The First Race, Churchill Downs, Louisville, Kentucky, May 6, 1983. The Sixth Race, Hollywood Park, Inglewood, California, June 5, 1982. The King's Favor Purse, Longacres, Renton, Washington, August 14, 1983. The Beat the Racetrack Calculator™.

6 **Using the Dr. Z System at the Racetrack** 130

The Sixth Race and the Triple Bend Handicap, Hollywood Park, Inglewood, California, May 8, 1982. The Whitney Handicap, Saratoga Racetrack, Saratoga, New York, August 1, 1981. The Santa Ynez Stakes, Santa Anita, February 2, 1983. The Seventh Race, Exhibition Park, Vancouver, British Columbia, April 13, 1983. The Kentucky Oaks, Churchill Downs, Louisville, Kentucky, May 6, 1983. The chance of collecting place and show wagers on various odds horses. The Matinee Handicap, Hollywood Park, Inglewood, California, April 24, 1982. The Longacres Derby, Longacres, Renton, Washington, August 14, 1983.

7 **Using the Dr. Z System in Other Situations** 174

The Belmont Stakes, June 5, 1982: Other-track betting at Golden Gate Fields, Albany, California. The Clout Handicap, Aqueduct, November 12, 1981: A visit to Teletrack, New Haven, Connecticut. The growth of intertrack wagering. Multiple track betting on the classic races.

8 **A Great Race: John Henry versus Lemhi Gold in the Oak Tree Invitational at Santa Anita, October 31, 1982** 194

The field. The evolution of the odds. What if Lemhi Gold had been in the money?

9 **Results of Computer Studies Using the Dr. Z System over Long Periods** 205

Exhibition Park: The 1978 summer season. Santa Anita: The 1973–74 winter meeting. Aqueduct: The 1981–82 winter season. How important is the track take? How important is breakage? The two-minute problem: Bets at Exhibition Park in 1980. Characteristics of Dr. Z system bets.

10 **The Kentucky Derby: The Most Exciting Two Minutes in Sports** 221

The pageantry. The spectacle. The Dr. Z system bets. Proud Appeal versus Johnny Campo in the 107th Kentucky Derby.

11 **A Great Day for Canada: Sunny's Halo Wins the 1983 Kentucky Derby** 245

The Kentucky mood. A Mexican filly is the first Dr. Z system bet. Chris McCarron steals the race. Two Dr. Z system bets in the Bold Forbes. Just call me George. The Dreadnought. The Twin Spires: Almost Derby horses. The 109th Kentucky Derby. It was never like this in Louisiana.

12 **Derby Day 1982, 1984, 1985, and 1986** 273

Kentucky Derby Day 1982. Alzabella is the first Dr. Z system bet. A late scratch. Baraco in the fifth. The Demolition Derby: The 108th run for the roses. Dual tracks in the ninth.

Kentucky Derby Day 1984. A loser after a four-race wait. The Bay Phantom Allowance. Duped in the Seventh. Althea dies in the stretch: A lesson in dosage analysis.

Kentucky Derby Day 1985. The first bet was on Danceman. Smokey Sherry gets us going. Clouhalo charges to win the fourth. Flying Rumor gets us back in the black. Bold and Vibrant wins the sixth and we pass in the seventh. The 111th Kentucky Derby. Turn Here is the final Dr. Z system bet.

Kentucky Derby Day 1986. Others are playing the Dr. Z system. Eddie Delahoussaye wins for me in the third. The WHAS Stakes. Son of the Desert in the fifth. Six winners in a row for the Dr. Z system. Betting the favorite to show in the Kentucky Derby.

13 Betting on Favorites 338

Betting to win may be profitable with good handicapping. Betting the favorite to place or show. Betting extreme favorites: The Ballerina, Exhibition Park, October 11, 1982. Betting all extreme favorites to place and show. Betting overwhelming favorites in major stakes and futurity races. The Longacres Mile, Longacres, Renton, Washington, August 21, 1983.

14 A Typical Day at the Races: Making the Best Bet in Each Race, Hollywood Park, May 30, 1982 357

Betting on all the races. Useful betting rules. The Results. Betting at Louisiana Downs and Churchill Downs.

15 Minus Pools 388

Eliminating possible minus pools: The Kentucky Oaks at Churchill Downs, May 1, 1981. An extraordinary show pool: The Coaching Club American Oaks at Belmont, June 27, 1981. An exception to the rule to not bet on minus pools. A typical minus pool: The San Juan Capistrano Invitational Handicap at Santa Anita, April 18, 1982.

16 Refinements to the Basic Dr. Z System 409

Dangers to look for, when not to bet and horses to avoid, conservative versus risky use of the Dr. Z system, and hints on good betting techniques at the racetrack. Regression equations based on differing wealth levels and track handle. Adjusting the optimal bet size for differing track paybacks. Adjustments for coupled entries. Adjustments for making more than one bet. Flow chart of the betting rules for a single bet to place or show. Using fundamental information to improve the Dr. Z system. Recommended handicapping books.

17 Epilogue 428

Why are we making the Dr. Z system public? Will the market become efficient: How much can be bet by all Dr. Z system bettors? Advice and conclusions. Using the Dr. Z system for harness racing. Using the Dr. Z system at Stampede Park's harness-racing track. Using the Dr. Z system in England.

Introduction

This book is about the Dr. Z system, a method that should actually enable you to beat the races. We have used the Dr. Z system at racetracks in California, Florida, New York, Kentucky, Washington, and British Columbia. Others have used the approach at racetracks all over North America. When properly applied, its average profit per dollar wagered is about 10%.

The Dr. Z system is based on an inefficiency in the place- and show-betting markets. The inefficiency is similar to that which occurs in stock option markets and warrant trading, and casino card games such as blackjack. Simply put, the bet or investment will return, on average, substantially more than its purchase price with only a small risk. The inefficiency is large enough to yield profitable bets about two to four times per average racing day. The inefficiency occurs because of the betting habits of the public—in particular, because of their greed for large profits—and because it is difficult for them to estimate the true worth of place and show bets.

We have used a sophisticated mathematical model that selects those profitable bets and determines how much should be wagered to maximize the long-run rate of growth of the bettor's fortune.* The model is solved using a mainframe computer. To make the Dr. Z system operational at the racetrack, we have developed simple approximations that provide you with easy-to-follow rules. The rules indicate how good a possible bet is, whether or not it is advisable to place a wager, and how much should be wagered given your particular betting fortune.

Charts are provided in the book for actual application of the Dr. Z system at a racetrack. The Beat the Racetrack Calculator™ is also available for those wishing the simplest, most accurate application of the Dr. Z system.

---

*Some of the research that made this book possible is based in part on stochastic mathematical optimization research supported in part by the Canadian Natural Sciences and Engineering Research Council.

We have read dozens of books and investigated numerous systems for handicapping and racetrack betting. We believe that the Dr. Z system is the first scientifically proven method for the average person to obtain consistent horse-race betting profits. Though it is difficult to find hard evidence, no doubt handicapping systems exist that yield profits upon proper application of their methods. These systems, however, usually require extensive knowledge that borders on expert handicapping. The aim of the Dr. Z system is to provide the average nonexpert with a simple, easy-to-use procedure for making modest short-run rates of return that yield substantial long-run profits. To apply the Dr. Z system you need only to follow a few key rules and to be patient, betting only when the wager is really worth making and avoiding the temptation of betting too much or too soon. The Dr. Z system tells you how much of your betting fortune to wager on each profitable situation. You do not have to become an expert handicapper to apply the Dr. Z system and win with it. It should provide slow, steady profits with small risk. At the very least, we hope it will teach you why most racetrack bettors lose and how you can avoid being one of them.

1

Discovery of the Dr. Z System

THE LURE OF RACING

People have been interested in horse races and betting on their outcome for several thousands of years. The Hittites, Greeks, and Romans all had horse races, as well as track-and-field competitions among human athletes.

The horses we call thoroughbreds are descended from three Near East stallions, the Byerly Turk, the Darley Arabian, and the Godolphin Barb, which were bred to English mares in the seventeenth and eighteenth centuries. Of some two hundred sires listed in the first stud book, which was published in 1793, only these three developed breeding lines that exist today. Matchem, foaled in 1748, became the only stallion to continue the Godolphin Barb's line; Herod, foaled in 1758, continued the Byerly Turk's line, which began in 1686; and Eclipse, foaled in 1764, continued the Darley Arabian line. Every thoroughbred racing today is a direct descendent of one of these three lines. It is these thoroughbreds in the North American setting with which we are concerned in this book. However, the Dr. Z system also applies to standardbreds running in harness races, quarter horses, greyhounds, and racing situations involving thoroughbreds in England and other countries (see Chapter Seventeen).

Thoroughbred horse racing is a very popular sport. Indeed, about the same number of people in North America attend the track each year as attend professional and college football and baseball games combined. There are about a hundred thoroughbred tracks in North America, with seasons running from just a few days to nearly half the year. (A current listing of these tracks and their handles appears in Appendix A.) Racetracks are big business: In 1985, 55 million people bet $8.2 billion at racetracks and legalized off-track betting shops in North America. Many more billions were bet with illegal bookies.

People go to the track for several reasons. Among these are the beauty and excitement of the sport. Eight or ten one-thousand-pound animals piloted by hundred-pound jockeys in colorful silks vying to win a race are quite a sight. It is hard to beat the thrill of a horse coming from far off the pace to mount a late charge and nip the leader at the wire. Even more exciting is the challenge of picking the winner. It is a very demanding task, which has its high and low moments. After each race you see countless bettors with long faces tearing up their tickets and rushing to look at the *Daily Racing Form* in an attempt to recoup their losses in the next race. A few winners will be telling their friends about the intricate analysis they used to pick the winner. The longer the odds the horse had, the greater these "bragging rights." Then there is the sheer greed of many bettors. They want to pick up easy winnings. For some bets, like the triactor and pick six, payoffs can be in the thousands or even hundreds of thousands of dollars. There is even a chance a big win will change a person's whole life.

Myriad factors can influence the performance of an individual horse and the outcome of a particular race. Some are analyzable and some are due to pure chance. Trying to pick the winners and the in-the-money finishers in a horse race is an intense intellectual challenge that draws the interest and talents of millions of people each year. Their attempts to put together all the relevant factors—the condition of the horses, the track, the skill of the jockeys, the trainers' and owners' intentions, the length of the race, the weights carried by the various horses, and so forth—is an irresistible challenge. One measure of the difficulty of this task is the number of people who can do it successfully. How many people do you know who go to the races? Quite a few, probably. How many win each year? Not many, right? That's what makes it so interesting and challenging.

I have been interested in horse racing for a long time. As a youth I spent many hot summer days at Saratoga analyzing racing forms. Having an analytical mind, I reasoned that I just needed to figure out which factors were really important, and when, in order to have the basis of a winning system. I spent quite a bit of time and energy trying to isolate the factors that determine the chances of a particular horse's winning a given race. One can develop such prediction equations that work reasonably well, but is it possible to beat the races with them? I concluded that you could beat the races with handicapping systems only if you were an expert, one willing to keep abreast daily of all relevant happenings in a given meet.

But I was searching for something simpler that could be applied in a systematic fashion without an intimate knowledge of recent racing results. This required a different approach. Rather than trying to pick the winner and the in-the-money finishers in a given race, I needed to concentrate on how to manage my money and to determine when there are bets that, on average, return significantly more than their costs. I found a good predictor of the actual probability of winning was the amount bet by the crowd.

In aggregate, all the experts and others betting on a particular day generated odds. Those odds, on average, were excellent predictors of the actual chances of each horse's winning. This is not surprising; it is the way most security markets work. Financial analysts call them *efficient markets*. This suggested to me that the best bets were really to place and show.

On the basis of financial markets, I realized that it was best to use the efficiency in the win pools to isolate inefficiencies in the place and show pools. Then I needed to develop sophisticated betting procedures that are easy to use. The idea is to bet more the more advantageous the situation is. That way, your betting fortune grows as fast as possible. Most bettors bet the win pools, since they appear to provide the highest payoff and are the easiest to understand. Place and show betting is considered less profitable and much harder to understand. For example, the exact payoff on place and show bets depends upon which three horses finish in the money. This book is concerned with the use of the Dr. Z system for making bets on outstanding place and show opportunities. Before we begin, let's look at why it is so difficult to win at the racetrack.

THE DIFFICULTY OF ACTUALLY WINNING AT THE RACETRACK

Studies of betting behavior show that fewer than one out of every hundred racetrack bettors is actually ahead over a long period of time. Why is it so difficult to win? In the parimutuel system of betting, you must be just a little more clever than the other bettors in the crowd, since you are betting against them. But how much better do you have to be to win? The hidden difficulty is the track commission, which consists of two parts: the *track take* and the *breakage*. The track take is the normal commission that the track subtracts from the total betting pool to make its profit and to pay its expenses. It varies from a low of 14.8% in Ontario and 15.33% in California and 15% in Kentucky to a high of 22.1% in Saskatchewan. The rates tend to be lower in states and provinces where the volume of betting is larger. Table A.6 in Appendix A lists current track takes in the major American states and Canadian provinces. These rates are periodically changed. Call your local jockey club for the latest information if you don't find it listed in the program.

The track take is enormous! In the 1983 Kentucky Derby, 134,444 people bet $5,546,977, so the 15% track take in Kentucky amounted to $832,046—a handsome payoff for the track and a large amount not returned to the winning bettors. Over the full day, $11,851,527 was bet, for a commission of $1,777,729.

The second part of the track's commission is the breakage, which is the rounding down of the winnings to common payoff amounts. For example, suppose a horse pays $12.77 for each $2 bet. That $12.77 represents the total bet on all the horses less the track take divided by the number of tickets sold on the winning horse. The actual payoff will be either $12.70 or $12.60, depending on whether the track uses 5¢ or 10¢ breakage to the dollar.

At first glance this 7¢ or 17¢ does not seem like much. After all, with a $2 bet 7¢ is a mere 0.65% of the potential profit, and 17¢ is only 1.58% of the profit. But suppose the parimutuel payoff should be $2.78, with the winning bettors getting $2.70 or $2.60. Now the effect on profits is much more substantial. In the 5¢ case it is 8¢/78¢, or 10.3%, and in the 10¢ case it is 18¢/78¢, or 23.1% of the potential profit. Thus the effect of breakage depends upon the type of bets being made. Ten cent breakage is always at least as large as 5¢ breakage and is often more than double. You can find out which type your track uses by looking at the payoffs in your local newspaper. If all the payoffs are numbers that are multiples of 20¢, like $6.40, $12.80, and $4.20, then it's the 10¢ variety. If you see payoffs that are multiples of 10¢, like $5.10, $8.30, and $13.30, then you are fortunate to have 5¢ breakage. Typically, breakage amounts to an added commission of about 1%–3% on the amount bet for wagers to win. So the total commission of a typical track might be 17% + 2%, or 19%.

Figure 1.1 indicates how two typical bettors, Handicapper Hal and Number-picker Ned, might do in comparison with the average bettor if the total commission is 19%. It is assumed that each bettor begins with $1,000 and bets $20 on average on each of the ten races each day over a twenty-day period.

The average bettor wagers $200 each day and loses $38 (0.19 × $200) plus his or her admission ticket, program, racing form, parking, gas, food, and so forth. So after twenty days his or her $1,000 betting stake has dwindled to $240. Handicapper Hal has studied a number of handicapping books, and when he was on vacation in Las Vegas two years ago, he took a one-day seminar that featured several of America's top handicappers. He prides himself on the fact that he knows a lot about speed horses. He always bets each race, although he might double up on horses he thinks are overlays (that is, the odds are better than the chances of winning), and bets less when the race looks very tough. Hal does better than most of his friends who frequently seek out his advice. Hal goes to the track both Saturday and Sunday, since he is too busy driving his cab during the week. He often breaks even or has small winnings. He thinks that if he can eliminate a few more bad bets he will be an overall winner. Hal gets a lot of enjoyment from analyzing the *Daily Racing Form*, and he studies it for about two hours the evening before a day's races. The $355 loss that he had over the twenty days was more than compensated for by Hal's enjoyment of the races. He is sure that he will do better next year and likely be ahead at the end of the season.

Ned works as a cashier for a big food market that is several miles from the local racetrack. He likes to go to the track Wednesday evening with several of his pals. On Fridays they play poker. Ned is too busy to spend time studying the racing form. In fact he never buys it. Instead he relies on the picks in the program and often buys one of the tipster's pick sheets. He likes to bet on horses that look good. So gray horses, those with bandaged legs, and those ridden by jockeys he doesn't like are out. He always bets on number 7 in the seventh and number 6 in the ninth, since it was a lucky day when his son was born on the sixth day of September. Ned and his pals sometimes share bets. They like to bet to win and love the exotic pools. One of Ned's friends won $1,400 on the triactor last fall. Ned does not really expect to win, but he thinks that someday he'll get lucky and make a killing. He thinks of his $770 losses this year as an investment and maybe he'll get it all back if he wins the triactor next year.

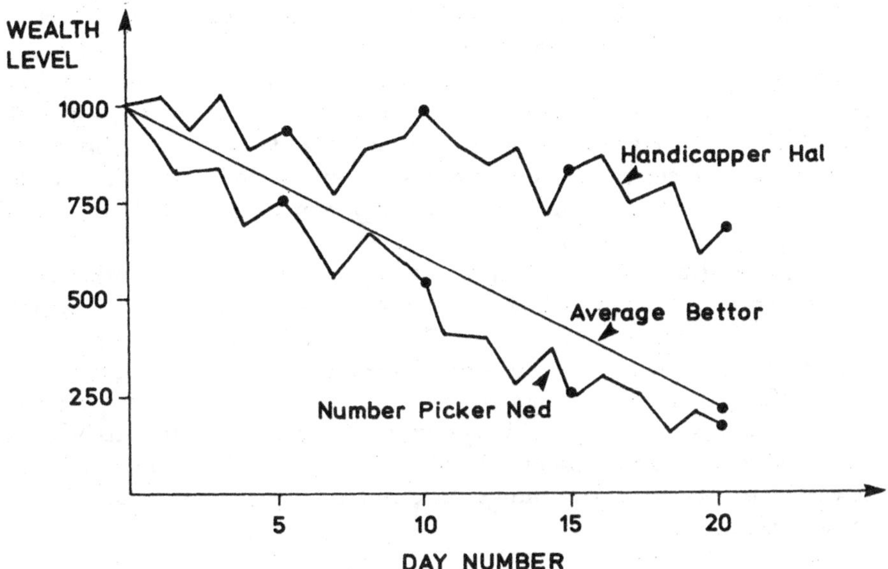

Figure 1.1 Typical behavior of the betting fortunes of three bettors

The crowd is composed of many different types of bettors, although many of them are like Hal and Ned. On average they lose 19% of what they bet because of the track take and breakage. Ned might conceivably win a large triactor and come out ahead, but it is unlikely. Most bettors like Ned will continue to lose a little bit more than the average bettor. Hal is pretty good at handicapping. He might be able to turn himself into a winner. If he can improve his handicapping a little and learn to bet more wisely, maybe this will happen.

But just how much better than the average bettor would Hal have to be to break even? Suppose Hal decides to concentrate on the top horses. Studies show that the top choices of the betting public win about a third of their races. The typical person betting favorites in a nine-race card might pick the winner in three of the races on average. I say on average, because he or she might pick six Monday evening, two Wednesday afternoon, one on Saturday, and so on, to average three per day. These winning horses pay about $5.22 per $2 bet, since $(3/9)x = 0.87$ gives $x = \$2.61$ per dollar bet (the 0.87 is 100% minus the track take and breakage of 19% plus the favorite bias of about 6% [see Table 3.1]). To break even, Hal has to pick about 38.3% winners, since $(2.61)y = 1.00$ gives $y = 0.383$. Thus Hal has to be about 15% better than the average bettor just to break even betting favorites. This situation is worse if Hal is picking medium-priced horses that are winning about 15–20% of the time or long shots that win 2–6% of their races. For example, with 5–1 shots the winning horses pay about $12 per $2 bet and win about 12.8% of the time. To break even Hal must win about 16.7% of the time, or 30.4% more often than the average bettor. With 20–1 shots the winning horses pay about $42 and win about 3.2% of the time. To break even with long shots Hal must win about 4.8% of the time, or about 50% more often. Hal simply must be at the least 15% better than the average bettor just to break even. Hal does not think this will be that difficult. After all, he knows so much more than the Neds of the world. Hal will be as surprised as we hope you are when he learns about the efficiency of the win market.

The evidence shows that even though the average bettor is losing 19% of the bet with every wager, he or she is actually quite good at picking winners and establishing fair odds. The average bettor is a composite of experts, those following the consensus, those following the betting patterns, those following their instincts, those who pick gray horses and popular numbers, and so forth. Roughly speaking, on average, their betting odds are a pretty good indication of the true probability of each horse's winning. It will be tougher than Hal thinks. In Chapter Three we take a careful look at this evidence.

PUTTING TOGETHER THE CONCEPTS FOR A WINNING SYSTEM

Beating the races is an intellectual challenge. To have a winning system means that you must be a good handicapper and a good money manager. You need to have an accurate method of predicting not only the probability that each horse will win a given race, but the probabilities of all possible 1-2-3 finishes. Then you need a way to determine when a given bet will return significantly more, on average, than it costs. Finally, you need to determine how much to bet, taking into account the effect of the bet on the odds, the worthiness of the particular bet, and the amount of betting wealth available for wagering. Since the betting pools and the odds are constantly changing, the procedure must be simple enough for it to be applied quickly just prior to the closing of the mutuel windows and the running of the race. That is the challenge.

We think that we have developed such a system for beating the races. It is called the Dr. Z system, and you should be able to apply it successfully at the racetrack. Although some of the ingredients in the winning mix are complicated, the Dr. Z system is easy to use. You do not have to be an expert handicapper. On the contrary, you need only to follow a few rather simple rules. You need to be patient and bet only when the conditions are right and when the bet is really good enough. To determine whether to bet or not, you'll simply watch the tote board and then use the charts provided in this book or the calculator discussed in Chapter Five.

Before we go on, it's time to tell you how we discovered the various ingredients that make up the Dr. Z system and who your guides are. The emphasis in this book is on the efficiency-of-market approach. It has been used by financial analysts to extract excess returns from various security, financial, and commodity markets whenever this is possible. See Malkiel (1985), Sharpe (1985), Thorp and Kassouf (1967), and Ziemba (1988).* In stock market jargon, it is a technical system based on relative prices rather than on a fundamental system based on intrinsic values. A key to the analysis is the notion that the public, in aggregate, knows pretty well what the chances are of particular horses' winning a given race. However, their greed to make a big killing at the track and the boost to the ego that goes with it make long shots very popular, while favorites are shunned. This makes the favorites relatively better bets. This bias is not enough, however, to produce a winning system for bets to win. But it is a key ingredient in the Dr. Z system for place and show bets.

The efficiency of the win markets has been known for some time. Studies by psychologists, such as Griffith (1949), pointed this out over thirty years ago. We were forcefully reminded of the principles of efficient win markets by the significant study by Snyder (1978). All that needed to be done was to find a good way to estimate the probability of each horse's winning. And that is amazingly simple to do. You need only to find the ratio between two numbers—the amount bet on each horse to win divided by the total win pool. It is quite accurate.

While I was a visiting professor at the University of California at Berkeley in 1978, I had a number of discussions about racetrack market efficiency with Professor Mark Rubinstein. He has a background in financial markets and he, too, was looking for a way to use the tote-board information to yield a profitable betting system. He told me about his work with his student King (1978) and the similar ideas of Harville (1973). As you will see in

*We will cite references, which are listed on pages 511–518, by the author's name and year of publication.

Chapter Five, the Harville formulas combined with the efficiency of the win-market estimates of the probability of winning, generate the probabilities of all possible 1-2-3 in-the-money finishes. This early advice proved invaluable. The key step was to combine these ideas with that of optimal investment over time, a subject in which I have expertise. Doing the actual calculations, developing and testing the Dr. Z system required many refinements. Don Hausch, a former student of mine, and I have been working on this together for the past nine years.

Along the way, we have benefited from a number of sources and people mentioned in the acknowledgments. We have also found useful and supportive the work of several people who have investigated ideas associated with the Harville formulas, the favorable favorite bias, or place and show betting. These include Harville (1973), Humber (1981), McCleary (1981), King (1978), Ritter (1978), and Yass (1980). These authors point to possible good bets, although they do not go so far as to tell you when a particular bet is really good enough to bet, nor do they discuss how much the bet should be.

In writing this book, Don and I have drawn on several aspects of our background and expertise. Don is an expert computer analyst, and he developed all the computer programs needed for our work, as well as performed the calculations you will find here. He is also an expert in model formulation and worked closely with me in developing the Dr. Z system. I have been interested in horseracing for over twenty years and have followed it over this period, quite intensely since 1978. As a professional researcher and editor in the areas of optimization, financial markets, and investment strategies, I saw the potential of combining the efficiency of the win market and the Harville formulas with proper betting models. Finally, Don and I have been successful appliers of the Dr. Z system at racetracks all over North America.

Let's begin with a general discussion of betting at the races.

2

Betting at the Races

READING THE PROGRAM AND THE DAILY RACING FORM

When you go to the racetrack you need to buy a program. It costs about 50¢ to 75¢. The program is published by the racetrack and gives the latest information on which horses are scheduled to run in each race. It also provides you with other useful information, such as the names of the jockeys, owners and trainers, the father (sire) and mother (dam) of each horse running, the morning line odds, the weight carried by each horse, the post positions, the value of the race's purse, the eligibility conditions for entering the race, the track record at this distance, and the colors of the jockeys' silks so that you can recognize the various horses during the running of the race.

A sample program for a mythical dream race involving many famous Kentucky Derby winners appears on page 28. Notice that there are two entries for numbers 1 and 2. Imagine getting Whirlaway and Citation together at 5–1 odds! In the next section we discuss more fully the way the odds are determined, but 5–1 means that if either of these horses were to win, the payoff would be a $5 profit plus the return of the $1 for each dollar bet. So a bet of $10 would return $60. The favorite is the great Secretariat at 3–2, so a winning $10 ticket would pay $25.

Entries are formed when two or more horses are entered from the same stable or by the same trainer. They are coupled to avoid any irregularities arising from the fact that they are running for the same people. An exception is in stakes and some allowance races (at all Thoroughbred Racing Association tracks, which include about 99% of all North American tracks) in which case a trainer can run horses from different owners as separate betting interests. The *field*, on the other hand, generally puts weaker horses together so that there are no more than twelve separate bets, since that is all that racetrack totalizator boards can usually accommodate. In races such as the

Kentucky Derby, with up to twenty starters, the field may contain as many as nine separate horses. Each day the track announcer provides additional information regarding such items as late scratches, jockey changes, or overweights. It is easy to mark these changes on your program. Most races have about six to ten horses and do not have entries or fields. In most races if a horse is, for instance, number 3, he will run in post position 3. However, when there are entries or fields, the post position order is usually altered.

The program often provides you with information about the jockey and trainer standings and post position statistics of the current meet. The following reprint is from a 1983 Exhibition Park program.

It is a good idea also to buy the *Daily Racing Form*. It now costs $2. It contains a tremendous amount of information about the past performances

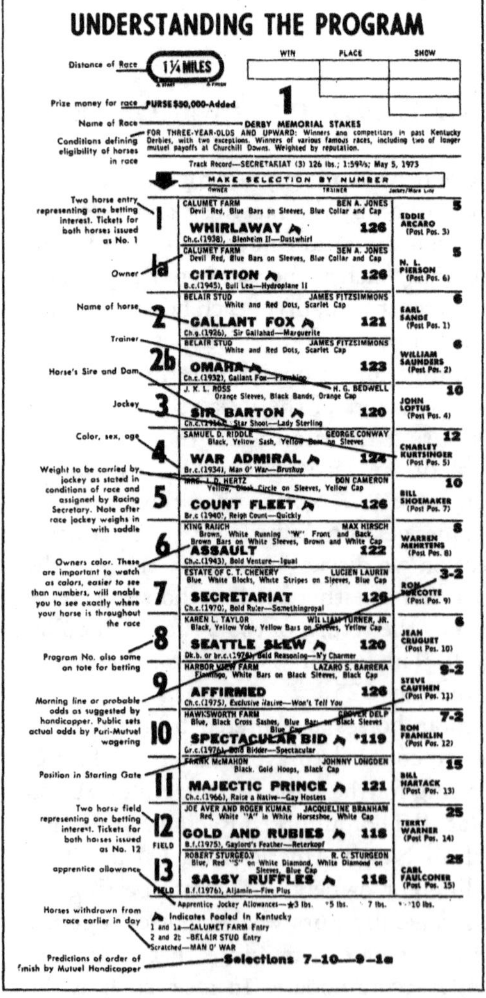

RACING STATISTICS—JOCKEY STANDINGS
(Up to and including May 18)

	Mts.	1st	2nd	3rd	Win%
C. Loseth	150	26	19	16	17.3
M. Walker	137	24	13	22	17.5
S. Krasner	156	23	16	18	14.8
R. Creighton	131	20	14	20	15.2
D. Rycroft	140	17	21	10	12.1
B. Johnson	156	17	15	30	10.9
M. Patzer	141	15	26	11	10.6
K. Skinner	108	12	19	11	11.1
D. Zook	104	8	8	14	7.6
A. Smith	62	7	3	2	11.2
C. Hoverson	70	7	8	7	10.0

TRAINER STANDINGS

	Sts.	1st	2nd	3rd	Win%
H. Barroby	69	18	8	10	26.0
G. Cummins	55	10	9	7	18.1
H. Johnson	59	10	8	8	16.9
H. Clyde	33	8	1	6	24.2
E. Thompson	28	7	4	2	25.0
E. Garcea	34	6	2	7	17.6
R. Crawford	15	5	2	1	33.3
R. Wood	21	5	3	3	23.8
D. Hannah	30	5	2	4	16.6
D. Forster	46	5	8	4	10.8

POST POSITION STATISTICS
(Up to and including May 18)

P.P.	1	2	3	4	5	6	7	8	9	10
Starts	225	223	224	227	224	223	209	188	171	141
Wins	38	28	36	16	31	23	18	14	12	11
% Wins	16.88	12.55	16.07	7.04	13.83	10.31	8.61	7.44	7.01	7.80

of the horses running in each race, as well as an analysis of each race by the *Form*'s consensus experts. Samples of the *Daily Racing Form*'s consensus selections appear in many places in this book, such as in the discussion of the Kentucky Oaks in Chapter Six beginning on page 150. A guide to reading the *Daily Racing Form* past performances appears on pages 29–30. Try applying this guide to the horses running in the Kentucky Oaks to familiarize yourself with how to read these past performances.

As we have mentioned, the goal of this book is to help you to master the Dr. Z system for beating the racetrack without ever having to become an expert handicapper. We utilize the handicappers' vast knowledge in a very precise way when we discuss the Dr. Z system in Chapters Four and Five. But you will be able to apply the Dr. Z system without referring to the *Daily Racing Form*. The *Form*'s main advantage is to give you a deeper understanding and confidence in what you are doing and, most importantly, to provide a quick way to look up information that allows you to eliminate potentially bad bets. We discuss this more fully later in Chapters Five, Fourteen, and Sixteen. For now we suggest that you use extreme caution in betting on horses that have not run recently, are running for the first time, or have extremely mediocre records and whenever the track conditions are not ideal—that is, when the track is not fast. The best bets you can make are those on outstanding horses, when the odds as measured by the Dr. Z system are good, and when the track conditions are ideal. We supply you with numerous examples to study for full details on how to apply the Dr. Z system.

HOW TO READ DAILY RACING FORM PAST PERFORMANCES

Past Performances include cumulative statistics for every horse who has raced on the grass in the U.S. and foreign countries; a symbol Ⓢ pointing out restricted races (not for open company) as well as races for horses bred in a specific state, and a "bullet" ● denoting superior workouts (the best workout of the day at that track for that distance).

FOREIGN-BRED: An asterisk preceding the horse's name indicates he was bred in a foreign country. The country of origin (abbreviated) appears after the breeder's name, as does the state or place and Canadian province of all horses foaled in the United States, Puerto Rico or Canada.

MUD MARKS: One of the following symbols after a horse's name reflects an expert's opinion of his ability on an off track:

*** Fair Mud Runner   X Good Mud Runner   ⊗ Superior Mud Runner**

RECORD OF STARTS AND EARNINGS: Each horse's lifetime statistics are given as well as his complete racing record for the current and prior year, or the last two years in which he competed. The letter M in the current year's record indicates the horse is a maiden. M in the previous year's record indicates the horse was a maiden at the end of that year. TURF RECORD shows his lifetime starts, wins, seconds, thirds and earnings on the grass.

Horse	Mud Mark	Today's Weight	Color Sex Age Pedigree	Today's Claiming Price	Earnings Record					
			Ch. f. 4 by Ridan—Miss Hopes, by Jet Pilot							
Good Hopes	*	117^{5}	Br. Jones H G (Cal)	$12,000	1981	12	3	2	1	$20,280
Own.—Good Hope Farm			Tr. Jones H G		1980	4	M	0	2	$1,100
			Lifetime 20 3 3 4 $23,600		Turf	4	1	0	1	$6,500

30Jun81-6Hol 6f :22^{4} :46 1:11^{3} ft *6-5e 117^{5} 3^{3} 3^{2} 2^{1} 1no SmithT^{3} Ⓕ Ⓢ c12000 81 GoodHpes,LionTmr,HppyDys 12
Jly 28 Dmr 3f ft :37b ●Jun 25 Hol 4f ft :46h ●Jun 30 Hol 3f ft :36^{2}h May 25 Hol 4f ft :49b

NOTE: Latest workouts are printed under each horse's past performances when they are available. The "bullet" ● indicates it was the best workout of the day at the track and distance.

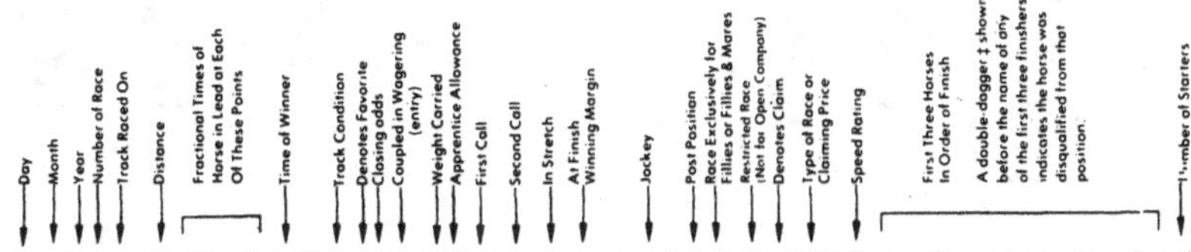

KEY TO SYMBOLS, ABBREVIATIONS IN PAST PERFORMANCES

FOREIGN-BRED HORSES
An asterisk (*) preceding the name of the horse indicates foreign-bred. (No notation is made for horses bred in Canada and Cuba.)

MUD MARKS
✱—Fair mud runner ✕—Good mud runner
⊗—Superior mud runner

COLOR
B Bay Blk—Black Br—Brown Ch—Chestnut Gr—Gray
Ro—Roan Wh—White Dk b or br—Dark bay or brown

SEX
c colt h horse g—gelding rig—ridgling f—filly m—mare

PEDIGREE
Each horse's pedigree lists, in the order named, color, sex, age, sire, dam and grandsire (sire of dam).

BREEDER
Abbreviation following breeder's name indicates the state, Canadian province, place of origin or foreign country in which the horse was foaled.

TODAY'S WEIGHT
With the exception of assigned-weight handicap races, weights are computed according to the conditions of the race. Weight includes the rider and his equipment; saddle, lead pads, etc., and takes into account the apprentice allowance of pounds claimed. It does not include a jockey's overweight, which is announced by track officials prior to the race. The number of pounds claimed as an apprentice allowance is shown by a superior (small) figure to the right of the weight.

TODAY'S CLAIMING PRICE
If a horse is entered to be claimed, the price for which he may be claimed appears in bold face type to the right of the trainer's name.

RECORD OF STARTS AND EARNINGS
The horse's racing record for his most recent two years of competition appears to the extreme right of the name of the breeder and is referred to as his "money lines". This lists the year, number of starts, wins, seconds, thirds, and earnings. The letter "M" in the win column of the upper line indicates the horse is a maiden. If the letter "M" is in the lower line only, it indicates the horse was a maiden at the end of that year.

TURF COURSE RECORD
The horse's turf course record shows his lifetime starts, wins, seconds, thirds and earnings on the grass and appears directly below his money lines.

LIFETIME RECORD
The horse's lifetime record shows his career races, wins, seconds, thirds and total earnings. The statistics, updated with each start, include all his races—on dirt, grass and over jumps—and are located under the trainer's name.

DISTANCE
a—preceding distance (a6f) denotes "about" distance (about 6 furlongs in this instance.)

FOREIGN TRACKS
♦—before track abbreviation indicates it is located in a foreign country.

RACES OTHER THAN ON MAIN DIRT TRACK
[i]—following distance denotes inner dirt course.
Ⓣ—following distance indicates turf (grass) course race.
[T]—following distance indicates inner turf course.
[S]—following distance indicates steeplechase race.
[H]—following distance indicates hurdle race.

TRACK CONDITIONS
ft—fast fr—frozen gd—good sl—slow sy—sloppy
m—muddy hy—heavy
Turf courses, including steeplechase and hurdles:
hd—hard fm—firm gd—good yl—yielding sf—soft

SYMBOLS ACCOMPANYING CLOSING ODDS
* (preceding)—favorite e (following)—entry
f (following)—mutuel field

APPRENTICE OR RIDER WEIGHT ALLOWANCES
Allowance indicated by superior figure following weight—117[5].

ABBREVIATIONS USED IN POINTS OF CALL
no—nose hd—head nk—neck

DEAD-HEATS, DISQUALIFICATIONS
•—following the finish call indicates this horse was part of a dead-heat (an explanatory line appears under that past performance line).
†—following the finish call indicates this horse was disqualified. The official placing appears under the past performance line. An explanatory line also appears under the past performance of each horse whose official finish position was changed due to the disqualification.
‡—before the name of any of the first three finishers indicates the horse was disqualified from that position.

POST POSITION
Horse's post position appears after jockey's name—Smith T[3]

FILLY OR FILLY-MARE RACES
Ⓕ—preceding the race classification indicates races exclusively for fillies or fillies and mares.

RESTRICTED RACES
[S]—preceding the race classification indicates races that are not for open company, in addition to those for state-breds.

RACE CLASSIFICATIONS
10000—Claiming race (eligible to be claimed for $10,000). Note: The letter c preceding claiming price (c10000) indicates horse was claimed.
M10000—Maiden claiming race (non-winners—eligible to be claimed).
10000H—Claiming handicap (eligible to be claimed).
°10000—Optional claiming race (entered NOT to be claimed).
100000—Optional claiming race (eligible to be claimed).
Mdn—Maiden race (non-winners).
AlwM—Maiden allowance race (for non-winners with special weight allowances).
Aw10000—Allowance race with purse value.
HcpO—Overnight handicap race.
SplW—Special weight race.
Wfa—Weight-for-age race.
Mtch—Match race.
A10000—Starter allowance race (horses who have started for claiming price shown, or less, as stipulated in the conditions).
H10000—Starter handicap (same restriction as above).
S10000—Starter special weight (restricted as above). Note: Where no amount is specified in the conditions of the "starters" race dashes are substituted, as shown below:
A—— H—— S——
50000S—Claiming stakes (eligible to be claimed).

STAKES RACES
In stakes races, with the exception of claiming stakes, the name or abbreviation of name is shown in the class of race column. The letter "H" after name indicates the race was a handicap stakes. The same procedure is used for the rich invitational races for which there are no nomination or starting fees. The letters "Inv" following the abbreviation indicate the race was by invitation only.

SPEED RATINGS
This is a comparison of the horse's final time with the track record established prior to the opening of the racing season at that track. The track record is given a rating of 100. One point is deducted for each fifth of a second by which a horse fails to equal the track record (one length is approximately equal to one-fifth of a second). Thus, in a race in which the winner equals the track record (a Speed Rating of 100), another horse who is beaten 12 lengths (or an estimated two and two-fifths seconds) receives a Speed Rating of 88 (100 minus 12). If a horse breaks the track record he receives an additional point for each one-fifth second by which he lowers the record (if the track record is 1:10 and he is timed in 1:09⅘, his Speed Rating is 102). In computing beaten-off distances for Speed Ratings, fractions of one-half length or more are figured as one full length (one point). No Speed Ratings are given for steeplechase or hurdle events, for races of less than three furlongs, or for races for which the horse's speed rating is less than 25.
When Daily Racing Form prints its own time, in addition to the official track time, the Speed Rating is based on the official track time.
Note: Speed Ratings for new distances are computed and assigned when adequate time standards are established.

WORKOUTS
Each horse's most recent workouts appear directly under the past performances. For example, Jly 20 Hol 3f ft :38b indicates the horse worked on July 20 at Hollywood Park. The distance of the work was 3 furlongs over a fast track and the horse was timed in 38 seconds, breezing. A "bullet" ● appearing before the date of a workout indicates that the workout was the best of the day for that distance at that track.
Abbreviations used in workouts:
b—breezing d—driving e—easily g—worked from gate h—handily bo—bore out Ⓣ—turf course Tr—trial race
tr.t following track abbreviation indicates horse worked on training track.

POINTS OF CALL—PAST PERFORMANCES

The points of call in the past performances vary according to the distance of the race. The points of call of the running positions for the most frequently raced distances are:

Distance	*1st Call*	*2nd Call*	*3rd Call*	*4th Call*
2 Furlongs	Start	—	Stretch	Finish
5/16 Mile	Start	—	Stretch	Finish
3 Furlongs	Start	—	Stretch	Finish
3 1/2 Furlongs	Start	—	Stretch	Finish
4 Furlongs	Start	1/4 Mile	Stretch	Finish
4 1/2 Furlongs	Start	1/4 Mile	Stretch	Finish
5 Furlongs	3/16 Mile	3/8 Mile	Stretch	Finish
5 1/2 Furlongs	1/4 Mile	3/8 Mile	Stretch	Finish
6 Furlongs	1/4 Mile	1/2 Mile	Stretch	Finish
6 1/2 Furlongs	1/4 Mile	1/2 Mile	Stretch	Finish
7 Furlongs	1/4 Mile	1/2 Mile	Stretch	Finish

Distance	*1st Call*	*2nd Call*	*3rd Call*	*4th Call*
1 Mile	1/2 Mile	3/4 Mile	Stretch	Finish
1 Mi., 70 Yds.	1/2 Mile	3/4 Mile	Stretch	Finish
1 1/16 Miles	1/2 Mile	3/4 Mile	Stretch	Finish
1 1/8 Miles	1/2 Mile	3/4 Mile	Stretch	Finish
1 3/16 Miles	1/2 Mile	3/4 Mile	Stretch	Finish
1 1/4 Miles	1/2 Mile	1 Mile	Stretch	Finish
1 5/16 Miles	1/2 Mile	1 Mile	Stretch	Finish
1 3/8 Miles	1/2 Mile	1 Mile	Stretch	Finish
1 1/2 Miles	1/2 Mile	1 1/4 Miles	Stretch	Finish
1 5/8 Miles	1/2 Mile	1 3/8 Miles	Stretch	Finish
1 3/4 Miles	1/2 Mile	1 1/2 Miles	Stretch	Finish

NOTE: The second call in most races is made 1/4 mile from the finish; the stretch call 1/8 mile from the finish.

THE VARIOUS TYPES OF BETS

Wagers at the racetrack are of two types, straight bets and so-called exotic, or gimmick, bets. The straight bets are to win, place, and show. It is these bets that we are concerned with in this book. Specifically, the Dr. Z system determines when good place and show bets exist and how much should be bet on them. Exotic bets combine the outcomes of two, three, or six horses. It is unlikely that a given ticket will win, which is why they have such high payoffs. We describe these bets here for your information. There is one important point to remember about them in case you do play them: Although breakage is minimal, the track take is generally higher by 2% or more on exotic wagers than on straight bets. Therefore, on average, it is more difficult to beat the racetrack by betting in exotic pools than in straight wagering. Now let's describe the various types of bets.

Type of Bet	You Choose	You Win Only When
Win	One horse	This horse is first.
Place	One horse	This horse is first or second.
Show	One horse	This horse is first, second, or third.
Quinella	Two horses	These two horses finish first and second, in either order.
Exactor (Perfector)	Two horses	These two horses finish first and second in the exact order that you specified.
Triactor (Trifector)	Three horses	These three horses finish first, second, or third in the exact order that you specified.
Daily double	One horse in one race and a second horse in another race (usually races 1 and 2)	Both horses finish first.
Pick six (Sweep six)	One horse in each of six consecutive races	All six horses finish first. Consolation prize is often available for five winners.

HOW THE ODDS ARE DETERMINED: THE TRACK TAKE AND BREAKAGE

There are two basic systems for setting the odds in horse races: *fixed* and *parimutuel* odds. Legalized bookmakers may set their own odds. These odds may be different at various points in time as more information becomes available and bets are made. Fixed means that once a wager is placed, its odds are specified and will not change, even though one might be able to place another wager later at different odds. For example, months before the

Kentucky Derby, such odds are available at various legalized betting establishments for most of the possible contenders and entrants in this race. Since many horses are on the list of Derby hopefuls, a considerable number of which will not even run in the race, these odds are quite high. The 1983 Kentucky Derby winner, Sunny's Halo, went off at 5–2 at Churchill Downs on Derby Day, paying $7 for each $2 bet to win—$5 profit and $2 return of the wager. Sunny's Halo was a 100–1 shot in the Las Vegas winter book. The wife of David Cross, Sunny's Halo's trainer, bet $200 at those odds and received a $20,000 profit plus her $200 bet.

Fixed betting is used very extensively at racetracks in many British Commonwealth countries, such as Australia, Great Britain, and Hong Kong. It is not used at North American racetracks. Here the parimutuel system is used. The essence of the fixed-odds system of betting is that you are wagering against the bookmaker. One of you will lose. He or she must therefore set odds on the various horses that will turn a profit for him or her. To do this the bookmaker sets odds that pay you less than what he or she thinks the true chances of each horse's winning are. For example, if Larry thinks a particular horse has a 25% chance of winning, he might offer you odds of 5–2. Then if the horse wins, he will pay you $7 instead of $8 for your $2 bet. The extra $1 is Larry's expected profit. To make actual profits rather than the expected average profits, he will try to balance the bets so that he has an amount of money inversely proportional to the payout he is giving on each horse. In that way he is assured of making a profit. If too little money is bet on a particular horse, Larry can attempt to generate more bets by raising the odds. This cat-and-mouse game continues until the race is run.

Let us see how it works with an example. For simplicity, suppose there are three horses—A, B, and C. The bookie thinks A has a 50% chance of winning, B has a 30% chance, and C has a 20% chance. True odds are then 1–1 for A, 7–3 for B, and 4–1 for C. These odds are set so that the average return is the amount bet, so there are no profits. For example, with A the average return is $0.5(1 + 1) = 1$. (Recall that with 1–1 odds, the return is the $1 profit plus the return of the original $1 bet.) For B and C it's similar, since $0.3(\frac{7}{3} + 1) = 0.2(4 + 1) = 1$. Hence to make a profit, the bookie might quote 4–5 for A, 2–1 for B, and 7–2 for C. For Larry to be guaranteed a profit, he needs bets roughly in the ratio of 50% bet on A, 30% bet on B, and 20% bet on C. If too little money is bet on A, he might increase the odds to 9–10 or even 1–1. In this way he can balance his books and still guarantee his profit. He will not be able to do this in all cases. Hence he needs to ensure a reasonable profit by taking a sizable commission. The commission plus his winnings then outweigh his losses. This is where the parimutuel system comes in.

Pierre Oller was a perfume shop owner who played the horses in the 1850s in Paris. After a while he felt that the bookies were taking too much profit. He thought that there should be a better system, so he began to sell different types of perfume for the different horses. For example, Jasmine might be number 1 and Gardenia number 2. The bettors would get small perfume bottles for their bets and Pierre would hold the money. After the race all the perfume bottles were returned, Pierre kept 5% of the money for his profit and expenses, and he distributed the remaining 95% equally among all those who had perfume bottles corresponding to the winning horse. This was the origin of the parimutuel system as Pierre Oller devised it in 1855. It is still used in the same way today except the perfume bottles have been replaced by electronic totalizator tickets. Notice that the key feature in the parimutuel system is that you are betting against all the other bettors and the house is taking a fixed commission. The house plays a passive role—its profit is always the same. In the fixed betting system you are betting against the house, and the commission is not determined in advance. It can be large or small or even result in a loss for the house.

For example, suppose W_i is the amount bet on horse i to win, Q is the track payback, and there are ten horses. Then the payoff per dollar bet using the parimutuel system if horse number 3 wins is

$$\frac{Q\sum_{i=1}^{10} W_i}{W_3} = \frac{Q(W_1 + W_2 + \cdots + W_{10})}{W_3}.$$

If the track payback is 83%, corresponding to a typical 17% track take, and \$10,000 is bet on all the horses, with \$1,700 bet on horse number 3, the payoff for the typical \$2 bet if number 3 wins will be

$$\frac{0.83(\$10{,}000)(\$2)}{\$1{,}700} = \$9.76.$$

It is awkward to pay \$9.76, so the track takes one more commission, called the breakage. It rounds the \$9.76 down to either \$9.70 or \$9.60. These are the 5¢ and 10¢ breakages we described in Chapter One. Initially most tracks used 5¢ breakage, but because of inflation and rising costs essentially all U.S. tracks now use 10¢ breakage. Most Canadian tracks still use 5¢ breakage, however. Breakage amounts to another 1%–3% on your bets, making the average total commission about 17% + 2%, or 19%. Breakage is more important than is commonly realized. We discuss its impact on Dr. Z system bets in Chapter Nine. Suffice it to say that these small amounts cut deeply into profits.

The parimutuel system works in a similar way for place and show bets as well as for exotic bets. We discuss place and show bets in detail in Chapter Four.

PARI-MUTUEL WAGERING

The only permitted wagering is under the pari-mutuel system, employing an electric totalisator. The only wagering pools at Churchill Downs are for WIN, PLACE, SHOW, DAILY DOUBLE and EXACTA, each with separate and independent calculation and distribution.

Under the pari-mutuel system, the wagering patrons establish the odds and the pay-offs in each pool. From each such pool the commission, provided by Kentucky state law, is deducted with the remainder being the net pool for distribution as pay-offs to ticket holders. Each pool is calculated to the dollar with the pay-off to the dime, the resulting breakage going to the racing association, by law.

The number on your ticket is an interest in the pool involved. All horses coupled in an entry or in the "field" are running for the number on your ticket. Example: Horse No. 1, 1A, 1C and/or 1X are all represented by Ticket No. 1. All horses in a "field" entry are represented by Ticket No. 12.

Purchase your ticket by the number on the program. Please call the number of the horse first, then the quantity of tickets desired: Example: "Number seven, two tickets."

In a Win Pool with a single winner, the amount wagered on the winner is deducted from the net pool to give the profit. This is added to the amount wagered to give the pay-off price, which includes the return of the amount wagered with the profit.

In a Place Pool, with two interests, the amount wagered on both interests is deducted from the net pool with the resulting profit divided equally and added to the amount wagered to give two pay-off prices.

In a Show Pool, with three interests, the profit is divided into three equal parts added to the amount wagered for the three pay-off prices.

Daily Double and Exacta wagers are in separate pools and the pay-off prices are figured by the same calculation process as for Win, Place and Show.

If more than the usual number of interests are involved in any pool, i.e., WIN-one, PLACE-two and SHOW-three, the pools are divided so as to give a proportionate profit to each wagering interest.

APPROXIMATE PAY TO WIN

(FOR $2.00) — IF THE ODDS ARE . . .

Odds	Pays	Odds	Pays	Odds	Pays
1-5	$2.40	6-5	$4.40	5-2	$ 7.00
2-5	2.80	7-5	4.80	3	8.00
1-2	3.00	3-2	5.00	7-2	9.00
3-5	3.20	8-5	5.20	4	10.00
4-5	3.60	9-5	5.60	9-2	11.00
1	4.00	2	6.00	5	12.00

3

Applying Stock Market Efficiency Concepts to Horseracing Betting Markets

THE CROWD IS VERY GOOD AT ESTIMATING THE TRUE PROBABILITY OF WINNING: EFFICIENCY OF THE WIN-BETTING MARKET

We have stated that, on average, the crowd is quite a good predictor of the actual probability of each horse's winning. Let us now look at this more carefully. In Figure 3.1 we have plotted the rate of return for win bets at various odds levels for six different data sets. The same data appear in Table 3.1, and Figure 3.2 summarizes it all. These data include a total of 35,285 races involving over 300,000 horses over the 28-year period 1947–75. The track take has been added back to the amounts the track pays to help you understand more fully what is going on and to permit comparisons among the different track takes. Generally speaking, track takes have risen over the years.

Each investigator found that the odds are a fairly good predictor of the actual probability of winning, but that there are biases for low- and high-odds horses. Low-odds favorites are underbet; their true probability of winning is greater than the crowd believes it is. Thus for horses going off at odds around 0.75–1, the rate of return is 9.1% better than chance. It is 6.4% and 6.1% better than chance for horses going off at odds around 1.25–1 and 2.5–1, respectively. To compensate for this bias, horses that have high odds, the so-called long shots, are overbet. Their actual chances of winning are less than the public thinks. For odds around 6–1 to 12–1, this overbetting amounts to 5.2% more than the track take. However, at 15–1 it is a full 10.2%, and at 33–1 it is a whopping 27.7%. Thus if the track take is 19%, you can expect to lose only about 10% by betting extreme favorites going off at odds from 1–2 to 7–5. You will lose about 13% betting on horses with odds about 8–5 to 4–1 and about 24% with the

Figure 3.1 Rates of return on win bets at various odds levels for six studies involving 35,285 races during 1947–1975—actual returns: dotted lines; track take added back: solid lines

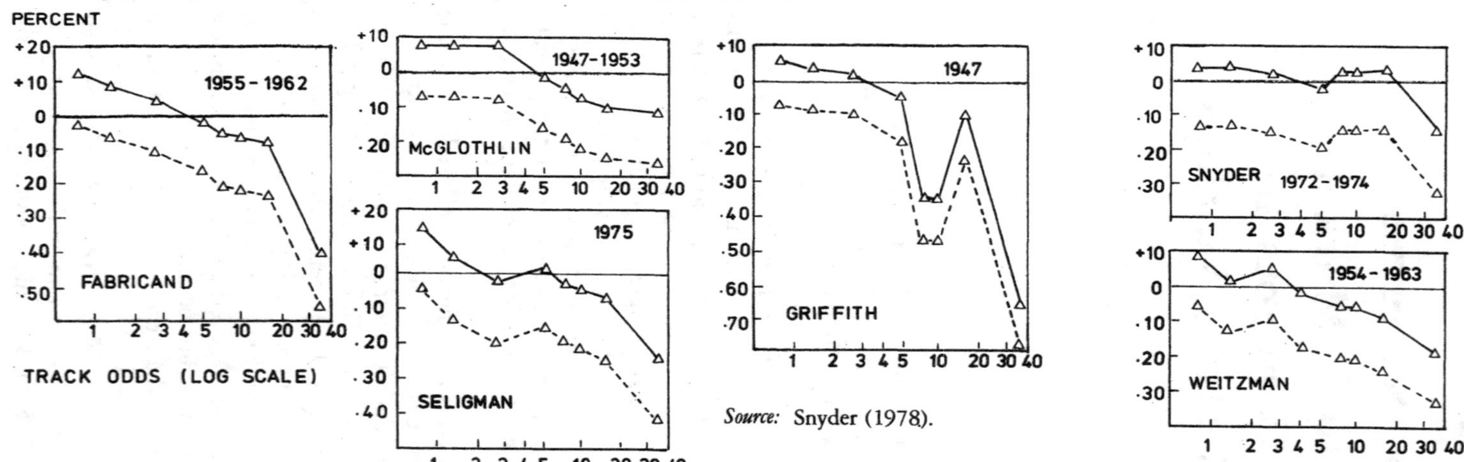

Source: Snyder (1978).

TABLE 3.1 ***Summary of six studies comparing the rate of return on win bets at various odds levels***

Study	Date Published	Racing Dates	No. of Races	Rates of Return by Grouped Odds, Take Added Back (Midpoint of Grouped Odds)							
				0.75	1.25	2.5	5.0	7.5	10.0	15.0	33.0
Griffith	1949	1947	1,124	8.0	4.9	3.1	−3.1	−34.6[a]	−34.1[a]	−10.5	−65.5[a]
McGlothlin	1956	1947–53	9,248	8.0[b]	8.0[a]	8.0[a]	−0.8	−4.6	−7.0[b]	−9.7	−11.0
Weitzman	1965	1954–63	12,000	9.0[a]	3.2	6.8[a]	−1.3	−4.2	−5.1	−8.2[b]	−18.0[a]
Fabricand	1965	1955–62	10,000	11.1[a]	9.0[a]	4.6[a]	−1.4	−3.3	−3.7	−8.1	−39.5[a]
Snyder	1978	1972–74	1,730	5.5	5.5	4.0	−1.2	3.4	2.9	2.4	−15.8
Seligman	1975	1975	1,183	14.0	4.0	−1.0	1.0	−2.0	−4.0	−7.8	−24.2
Combined			35,285	9.1[a]	6.4[a]	6.1[a]	−1.2	−5.2[a]	−5.2[a]	−10.2[a]	−27.7[a]

Source: Adapted from Snyder (1978). [a]Significantly different from zero at 1% level or better. [b]Significantly different from zero at 5% level or better.

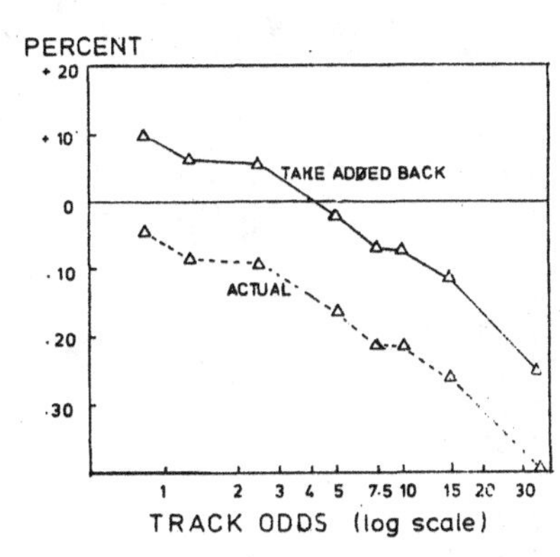

Figure 3.2 Rates of return on win bets at various odds levels: aggregation of six studies involving 35,285 races during 1947–75 *Source:* Snyder (1978).

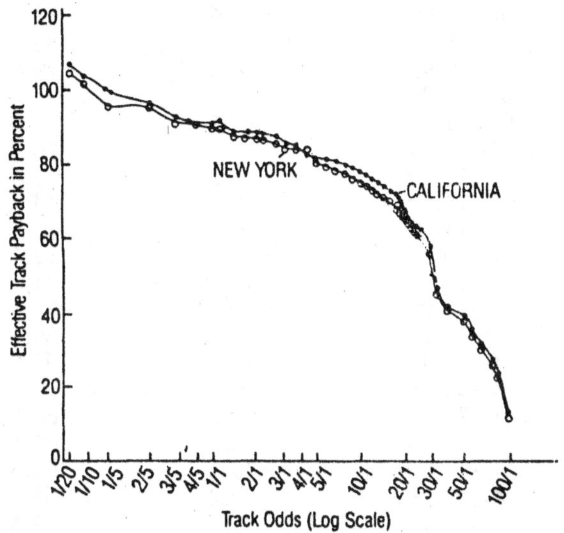

Figure 3.3 The effective track payback less breakage for various odds levels in California and New York

6–1 to 12–1 horses. Betting the long shots yields very large average losses. At 15–1 the average loss is about 29%, and for horses going off at odds around 25–1 to 40–1, it's nearly half the bet, about 47%.

Aggregating the Synder (1978) data and that from Ziemba and Hausch (1985) and adjusting for the current track takes of 15.33% in California and 17.0% in New York gives the following estimates of the effective track

TABLE 3.2 ***Effective track payback less breakage for various odds levels in California and New York***

Quoted Odds	*Odds Range*	*Adjustment (favorite–long-shot bias)*	Effective Track Payback	
			California	*New York*[a]
1–20	0.05– 0.09	20.8	104.5	104.0
1–10	0.10– 0.19	20.3	104.0	102.3
1–5	0.20– 0.39	18.0	101.7	100.0
2–5	0.40– 0.59	14.0	97.7	96.0
3–5	0.60– 0.79	10.0	93.7	92.0
4–5	0.80– 0.99	9.1	92.8	91.1
1–1	1.00– 1.19	8.2	91.9	90.2
6–5	1.20– 1.39	7.3	91.0	89.3
7–5	1.40– 1.49	6.4	90.1	88.4
8–5	1.60– 1.79	6.3	90.0	88.3
9–5	1.80– 1.99	6.2	89.9	88.2
2–1	2.00– 2.49	6.1	89.8	88.1
5–2	2.50– 2.99	6.1	89.8	88.1
3–1	3.00– 3.49	4.5	88.2	86.5
7–2	3.50– 3.99	3.0	86.7	85.0
4–1	4.00– 4.49	1.5	85.2	83.5
9–2	4.50– 4.99	0.0	83.7	82.0
5–1	5.00– 5.99	−1.2	82.5	80.8
6–1	6.00– 6.99	−1.9	81.8	80.1
7–1	7.00– 7.99	−2.6	81.1	79.4
8–1	8.00– 8.99	−3.2	80.5	78.8
9–1	9.00– 9.99	−4.2	79.5	77.8
10–1	10.00–10.99	−5.2	78.5	76.8
11–1	11.00–11.99	−6.2	77.5	75.8
12–1	12.00–12.99	−7.2	76.5	74.8
13–1	13.00–13.99	−8.2	75.5	73.8
14–1	14.00–14.99	−9.2	74.5	72.8
15–1	15.00–15.99	−10.2	73.5	71.8
16–1	16.00–16.99	−11.2	72.5	70.8
17–1	17.00–17.99	−12.2	71.5	69.8
18–1	18.00–18.99	−13.2	70.5	68.8
19–1	19.00–19.99	−14.2	69.5	67.8
20–1	20.00–20.99	−15.2	68.5	66.8
21–1	21.00–21.99	−16.2	67.5	65.8
22–1	22.00–22.99	−17.2	66.5	64.8
23–1	23.00–23.99	−18.2	65.5	63.8
24–1	24.00–24.99	−19.2	64.5	62.8
25–1	25.00–25.99	−20.2	63.5	61.8
30–1	30.00–34.99	−25.2	58.5	56.8
35–1	35.00–39.99	−36.0	47.7	46.0
40–1	40.00–49.99	−39.9	43.8	42.1
50–1	50.00–59.99	−43.7	40.0	38.3
60–1	60.00–69.99	−47.5	36.2	34.5
70–1	70.00–79.99	−51.4	32.3	30.6
80–1	80.00–89.99	−55.2	28.5	26.8
90–1	90.00–99.99	−59.0	24.7	23.0
100–1	100.00– ∞	−70.0	13.7	12.0

[a]The track take in California is 15.33% (it is 17% in New York) for an average payback of 84.67 cents per dollar wagered (83%). Breakage is to the nearest 10 cents below the true computed amount per dollar wagered. At 9–2, the break-even point in the favorite–long-shot bias, breakage amounts to about another 1% commission.

payback in percent for various odd horses. The data are shown in Table 3.2 and Figure 3.3.

Another way to look at the favorite–long-shot bias and the accuracy of the crowd's estimate of the true probability of winning, as reflected in the win odds—is by considering the various levels of favorites. Figure 3.4 shows the relation between the actual probability of winning and the crowd's estimate for the first through the ninth favorites in 729 thoroughbred races involving 5,805 horses in 1978 at Atlantic City. These same data also appear in Table 3.3. The data indicate that the first and third favorites are significantly underbet, while the ninth favorite is significantly overbet. For the other favorites these probabilities are equal in a statistical sense. The crowd's estimate of the probability of winning, however, conforms quite well with the actual probability of winning.

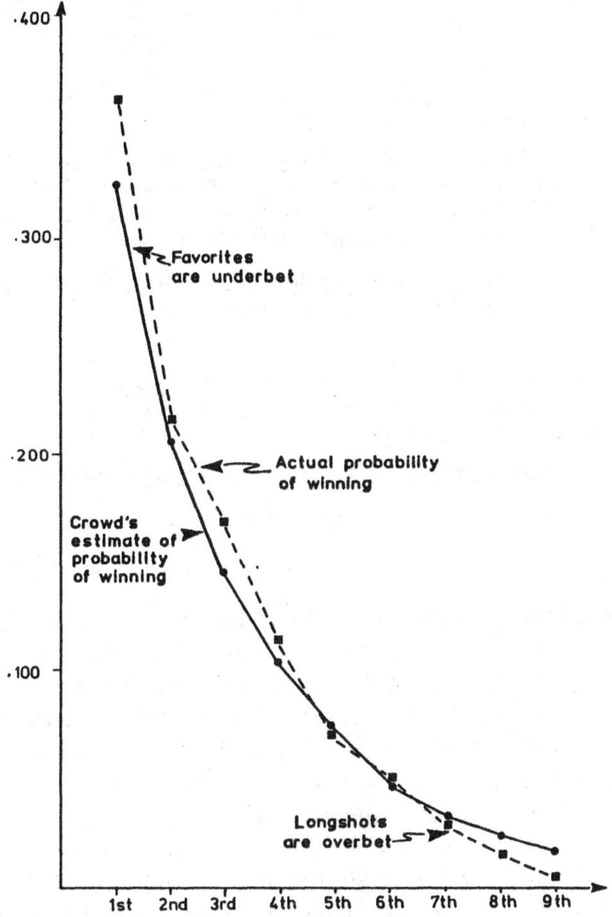

Figure 3.4 Probabilities of the first through the ninth favorites' winning a given race in 729 Atlantic City races involving 5,805 thoroughbred horses in 1978 *Source:* Asch, Malkiel, and Quandt (1982).

TABLE 3.3 ***Comparison of the crowd's estimate of the probability of winning with the actual probability of winning for the first through the ninth favorites in 729 Atlantic City races involving 5,805 horses in 1978***

Favorites in Order of Lowest Odds	Number of Races[a]	Actual Probability of Winning	Crowd's Estimate of Probability of Winning	t Statistic[b]
First	729	0.361	0.325	−2.119[c]
Second	729	0.218	0.205	−0.903
Third	729	0.170	0.145	−1.972[c]
Fourth	724	0.115	0.104	−0.961
Fifth	692	0.071	0.072	0.074
Sixth	598	0.050	0.048	−0.279
Seventh	431	0.030	0.034	0.480
Eighth	289	0.017	0.025	1.096
Ninth	165	0.006	0.018	2.095[c]

Source: Asch, Malkiel, and Quandt (1982).

[a]The number of horses declines because many races have only a small number of horses running. The probabilities adjust for the actual number of horses in each race.

[b]The t statistic is used to determine if the actual probability of winning differs from the crowd's estimate so that there is a true favorite–long-shot bias. The formula for t is

$$\frac{\text{Crowd's estimated probability} - \text{actual probability}}{\text{Standard error of actual probability}},$$

where the standard error is $\sqrt{p(1-p)/n}$, p being the actual probability and n the number of races. For background on these statistical concepts, see a standard statistical text such as Neter, Wasserman, and Whitmore (1978).

[c]Significantly different at the 5% level. That is, we are 95% confident that these probabilities are really different.

In an analogous study involving 20,047 harness races, Ali (1977) found similar results. Once again, as shown in Figure 3.5, the crowd's estimate of the probability of winning tracks the actual probability of winning quite well. The favorite–long-shot bias also occurs in a very consistent fashion. This is shown clearly in Table 1.4. The top favorites are underbet; the second and third choices have equal actual and crowd-generated probabilities of winning. Finally, the fourth to eighth favorites—the long shots—are overbet. Results are not shown for the ninth and tenth favorites because they are based on very few races. This large sample provides further evidence for the efficiency of the win market and the favorite–long-shot bias. It also indicates that this phenomenon is similar in harness as well as thoroughbred races.

Figure 3.5 Probabilities of first, second, third, . . . , tenth favorites' winning a given race in 20,247 harness horse races at various tracks in 1970–74 *Source:* Ali (1977).

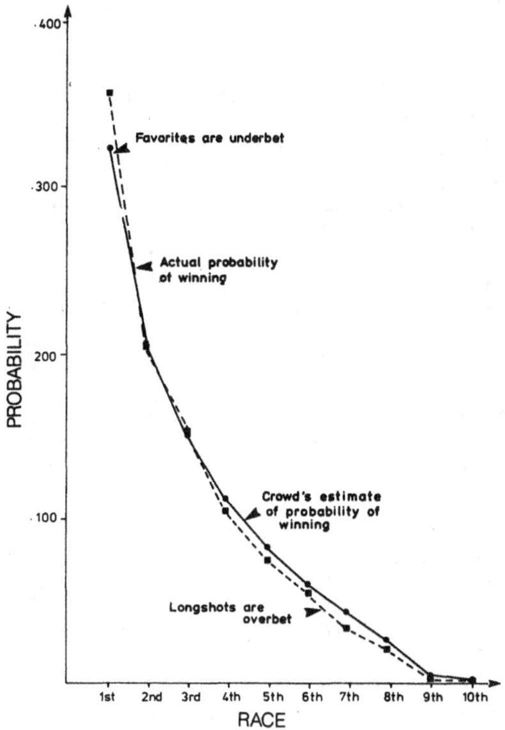

TABLE 3.4 ***Comparison of the crowd's estimate of the probability of winning with the actual probability of winning for the first, second, third, . . . , eighth favorites***

Favorites in Order of Lowest Odds	Number of Races	Actual Probability of Winning	Crowd's Estimate of Probability of Winning	t Statistic[a]
First	20,247	0.3583	0.3237	−10.29[b]
Second	20,247	0.2049	0.2077	0.99
Third	20,247	0.1526	0.1513	−0.52
Fourth	20,247	0.1047	0.1121	3.45[b]
Fifth	20,231	0.0762	0.0827	3.49[b]
Sixth	20,088	0.0552	0.0611	3.01[b]
Seventh	19,281	0.0341	0.0417	5.80[b]
Eighth	15,749	0.0206	0.0276	6.20[b]

Source: Ali (1977).

[a]The t statistic is calculated in the same manner as in Table 3.3.

[b]Significantly different at the 5% level.

Aggregating all the data known provides our best estimate of the probability of winning at various odds levels in California and New York as displayed in Table 3.5 and Figure 3.6. Note, Q is the track payback.

TABLE 3.5 ***Probabilities of winning in percent at various odds levels in California and New York***

Quoted Odds	*Q=84.67% California*	*Q=83% New York*	*Quoted Odds*	*Q=84.67% California*	*Q=83% New York*
1–20	98.0	97.5	12–1	5.7	5.6
1–10	92.0	90.5	13–1	5.3	5.2
1–5	78.9	77.6	14–1	4.9	4.8
2–5	65.7	64.6	15–1	4.5	4.4
3–5	55.6	54.6	16–1	4.2	4.1
4–5	49.3	48.4	17–1	3.9	3.8
1–1	44.2	43.3	18–1	3.7	3.6
6–5	40.0	39.2	19–1	3.4	3.4
7–5	36.4	35.7	20–1	3.2	3.2
8–5	33.6	33.0	21–1	3.0	3.0
9–5	31.3	30.7	22–1	2.9	2.8
2–1	27.9	27.4	23–1	2.7	2.6
5–2	24.2	23.7	24–1	2.6	2.5
3–1	21.0	20.6	25–1	2.3	2.2
7–2	18.4	18.1	30–1	1.8	1.7
4–1	16.4	16.1	35–1	1.4	1.2
9–2	14.7	14.4	40–1	1.0	0.9
5–1	12.8	12.6	50–1	0.7	0.7
6–1	11.0	10.8	60–1	0.6	0.5
7–1	9.6	9.4	70–1	0.4	0.4
8–1	8.6	8.4	80–1	0.3	0.3
9–1	7.6	7.5	90–1	0.3	0.2
10–1	6.9	6.8	100–1	0.1	0.1
11–1	6.3	6.1			

Why do these biases occur? Simple explanations are greed and bragging rights. People simply prefer to bet on horses that will have large payoffs. Not only will they win more, but they can tell their friends about it and reap glory for their cleverness. Bragging rights, a term coined by my colleague Dr. Bruce Fauman, refers to the pleasure one derives from the act of telling one's friends the intricate and clever analysis used to determine a particular winner. Favorites provide little of this ego boosting. There is not much profit or fame derived from betting on a 6–5 favorite who is the best bet of the day in the *Daily Racing Form*'s consensus. Hence, the majority of the crowd simply prefers horses with a low probability of a high payoff if they win to those with a high probability of a lower payoff. Snyder states it well:

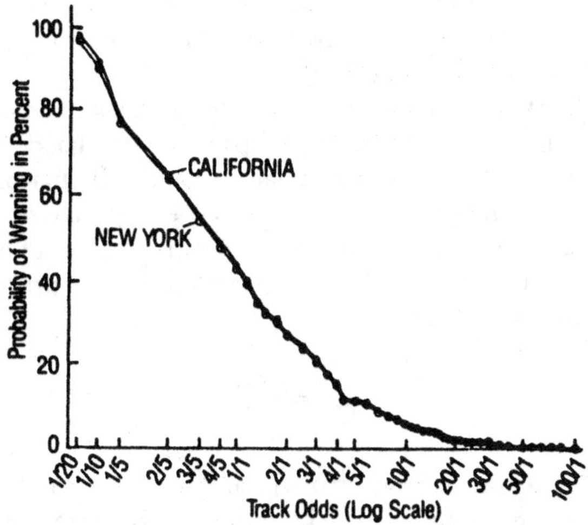

Figure 3.6 Probabilities of winning at various odds levels in California and New York

> There is, of course, no statistical technique which can disentangle the relative importance of "subjective preference for risk" and "increasing marginal utility of money." Every bet also includes, besides a potential monetary gain, the utility derived from all the factors associated with making a bet—analyzing racing forms, pitting one's predictions against others and the elements of luck. These factors are largely absent if one selects a known favorite; there are few players who can skip the challenge of trying to ferret out potential longer-odds winners. Indeed, the main reward of horse betting comes from the thrill of successfully detecting a moderately long-odds winner and thus confirming one's ability to outperform everyone else. Snyder (1978; p. 1,113).

The favorite–long-shot bias seems to occur in all reasonably large data sets.* For win bets the bias is not enough to make positive profits by betting

*Psychologists recognized this phenomenon in the late 1940s. The first seem to have been Preston and Baratta (1948), who investigated subjects in laboratory experiments. This phenomenon is common to many betting and investment situations. Epstein (1977) lists as one of the fallacies of betting behavior that the general public tends to overestimate the probability of infrequent events and underestimate the probability of frequent events. The preference for a big payoff drives down the odds on such wagers, so they are in fact very poor bets. For example, for a $1 bet, gamble A with a 1% chance of receiving $75 might be preferred to gamble B where you receive only $3 but win 40% of the time. Gamble A has an average return of 75¢ per dollar bet, so you lose 25% of your bet on average. However, the attractive gamble B has an expected value of $1.20, for a profitable 20% gain. There is a similar bias in hockey betting (see Ziemba, 1984). Additional discussion of the favorite–long-shot bias appears in Ziemba and Hausch (1985) and Quandt (1986).

on all horses in any odds categories. The best one can do is to bet the favorites and lose about 10% instead of 19%. However, as we shall see, that bias plays an integral role in the winning system for place and show betting that we develop in Chapters Four and Five.

Equally important is the finding that the public's estimate of the probability of winning in various odds groups is a very good estimate of the actual probability of winning. Financial analysts call this phenomenon an *efficient market*. It is similar to conclusions reached by analyses of stock prices indicating that the only way to gain excess returns is to incur additional risk.

Hence, you can use the following estimate of the probability q_3 that horse 3 will win a given race:

$$q_3 = \frac{W_3}{W}, \tag{3.1}$$

where W_3 is the amount bet on 3 to win and W is the total amount bet on all the horses to win. Both W_3 and W appear on the tote board. Of course, W_3/W is related to the odds because the odds, O_3, on horse 3 are simply

$$O_3 = Q\frac{W}{W_3} - 1,$$

where Q is the track payback. The minus one represents the dollar returned per dollar bet if horse 3 actually wins. As an example, suppose \$20,000 is bet on number 3 out of a total win pool of \$80,000. Then the chances that horse 3 wins are about

$$q_3 = \frac{W_3}{W} = \frac{\$20{,}000}{\$80{,}000} = 0.25$$

with odds

$$O_3 = Q\frac{W}{W_3} - 1 = (0.85)\frac{\$80{,}000}{\$20{,}000} - 1 = 2.4,$$

which would be quoted on the totalizator board as 2–1. Equation (3.1) is a good approximation of the true probability of winning. We must always remember, however, that it will overestimate the chance of a long shot's winning and underestimate the chance of a favorite's winning. It is important to notice that just by using equation (3.1) to estimate the probability of each horse's winning, you have a fairly reliable handicapping system. Jeff MacNelly's cartoon Shoe on page 45 makes the same point. Choice of the favorites will put you above the average in Figure 1.1. Indeed, by betting only on horses with final odds of say 3–1 or less, you will do as well or better than Handicapper Hal with no handicapping at all.

CAN YOU WIN BY BETTING ON ONLY THE VERY BEST HORSES?

We have established that the public tends to overbet long shots and underbet favorites. If the track take is 18%, you can expect to lose about 28% by betting horses at 15–1 and about 12% by betting 2–1 favorites. The key is that in all cases the bettors lose. Since they lose 12% at 2–1 and only about 9% at 1–1, the question arises whether you might not actually turn a profit if you bet on the extreme favorites—those going off at odds like 3–5 or 1–5.

One of the largest studies of the relationship between expected value and odds was that by Fabricand (see Figure 3.1). He considered 10,000 races, and his findings were consistent with the summary of the other studies in Figure 3.2. He also considered horses going off at odds like 2–5, 3–5, 4–5, and 1–1. His results are summarized in Table 3.6. As you can see, the loss is small. In the range 3–5 to 1–1 it is less than 5%, and at 2–5 there is even a small profit of 3.4%.

Let's look more fully at some bets in this odds range. The great horses of the twentieth century often ran at odds in this range. It does not take long for the public to recognize a Secretariat or a Man O' War. As soon as these horses won one or two convincing races, their odds plummeted to even money or less. But were the odds even better than they should have been?

TABLE 3.6 ***Fabricand's study of the comparison of the public's perception of the winning probabilities with the true winning probabilities in 10,000 races during 1955–62***

Odds	Number of Horses Entered	Number of Winning Horses	Public's Perception of the Winning Probability (%)	True Probability (%)	Public's Estimate of the Expected Number of Winners plus Two Standard Deviations	Expected Profit per Dollar Wagered (¢)
0.40—0.55	129	92	56.9	71.3	73 ± 11	+3.4
0.60—0.75	295	163	50.2	55.3	148 ± 18	−7.1
0.80—0.95	470	241	44.9	51.3	211 ± 22	−3.8
1.00—1.15	615	289	40.6	47.0	250 ± 25	−2.4
1.20—1.35	789	318	37.1	40.3	293 ± 27	−8.1
1.40—1.55	874	331	34.1	37.9	298 ± 28	−6.1
1.60—1.75	954	339	31.5	35.5	301 ± 29	−4.8
1.80—1.95	1,051	325	29.3	30.9	308 ± 30	−10.5
2.00—2.45	3,223	933	26.3	28.9	848 ± 50	−6.5
2.50—2.95	3,623	835	22.8	23.0	826 ± 50	−13.5
3.00—3.45	3,807	797	20.1	20.9	765 ± 50	−11.0
3.50—3.95	3,652	679	18.0	18.6	657 ± 46	−11.6
4.00—4.45	3,296	532	16.2	16.1	534 ± 42	−15.3
4.50—4.95	3,129	486	14.8	15.5	463 ± 40	−10.6
5.00—5.95	5,586	686	13.2	12.3	737 ± 50	−20.1
6.00—6.95	5,154	565	11.4	11.0	588 ± 46	−18.0
7.00—7.95	4,665	460	10.0	9.9	467 ± 41	−16.4
8.00—8.95	3,990	328	9.0	8.2	359 ± 38	−21.8
9.00—9.95	3,617	295	8.1	8.2	293 ± 33	−14.7
10.00—14.95	12,007	717	6.5	6.0	780 ± 54	−20.7
15.00—19.95	7,041	284	4.7	4.0	331 ± 35	−26.4
20.00—99.95	25,044	340	2.5	1.4	626 ± 50	−54.0
TOTALS	93,011	10,035[a]				

Source: Adapted from Fabricand (1965, 1979).
[a]There were 35 dead heats in the 10,000 races.

Table 3.7 gives the results from bets on fourteen of the greatest horses of the twentieth century.

How would you have done betting on these horses? On average, if you bet them only when they were running at 3–5 or less, the average profit would be 3.8%. Moreover, you would be ahead betting in 10 of the 12 odds categories. In addition, the expected return is higher the lower the odds are. The lowest odds were the three races Man O' War won at 1–100. Unfortunately, even though the sample involves 517 races, statistically it is possible that this entire 3.8% is simply due to chance. One must conclude that even with these great horses you cannot be reasonably sure of making a profit. Further complicating the analysis of these extreme favorites is a phenomenon called a *selection bias*. These horses were selected for the list of greatest horses simply because they won most of their races. Horses that ran several races at low odds, then lost their form, don't appear on this list. Proud Appeal, the 1981 Kentucky Derby favorite, was one such horse. His past performances appear on page 238 in Chapter Ten.

To study the matter more fully, we collected data on all the races run at Aqueduct, Belmont Park, and Saratoga in 1980. These data constitute the major races run in New York that year and include about 3,000 races. In 732 of these races a horse went off at odds of even money or less. The results appear in Table 3.8. On average, the rate of return for odds of even money or less was 0.90, or a 10¢ loss per dollar bet. Again, the highest rate of return was achieved by the lowest-priced horses. For horses going off at 3–10 or less the rate of return was +6%. However, as with the other studies, one cannot conclude that these profits were not due to chance. Indeed, there is no basis to argue that even with these extreme favorites you will do any better than break even.

Readers who are unfamiliar with statistical reasoning, standard deviations, and the like might look at the odds category 9–10. Here the expected return was a meager 0.67, while at 4–5 it was 0.97 and at 1–1 it was 0.96. The statistical analysis shows that, by chance, the returns in this category were quite low. Certainly with a larger sample of races, one would expect the 4–5, 9–10, and 1–1 odds categories to have similar rates of return. Thus, although the sample size of 136 seems quite sizable, it is really too small for definitive conclusions.

Aggregating all the known data provides the following estimates of the probability of winning and the expected value per dollar bet on extreme favorites in California and New York as detailed in Table 3.9 and Figures 3.7 and 3.8.

In summary, the evidence that we have on extreme favorites is as follows: First, the lower the odds on a horse, the higher the expected return seems to be. Second, extreme favorites going off at odds of 3–10 or less do seem to return a modest profit on average. Finally, even in the odds group of less than 3–10, there is no basis for any definitive statement that you can bet on all horses to win at this odds level and make profits. You cannot disprove the hypothesis that you will, at most, simply break even betting these horses to win. To make a definitive statistical statement would require a sample size of at least five years' data in a major racing locality, such as California or New York. At best, even if someone could prove their existence, such profits would be very rare anyway. Your attention is better directed to more profitable place and show bets—which is precisely what we do in the rest of this book.

TABLE 3.7 ***Rate of return on win bets for extreme favorites: fourteen great twentieth-century horses***

Horse	Racing Dates	Wins/ Races	In the Money/ Races	Odds Ranges (wins/races) 1—100 to 1—20	1—15 to 1—7	3—20 to 9—50	1—5 to 2—9
Citation	1947–51	32/45	44/45	1/1	6/6	3/3	5/6
Colin	1907–08	15/15	15/15		3/3		1/1
Count Fleet	1942–43	16/21	21/21	2/2	2/2	1/1	1/2
Equipoise	1930–35	29/51	43/51		4/4	1/2	0/2
Exterminator	1917–24	50/100	84/100	1/1	1/1	1/1	2/2
Forego	1973–78	34/57	50/57	2/2			2/2
Kelso	1959–66	39/63	53/63		1/1	1/1	2/2
Man O' War	1919–20	20/21	21/21	6/6	3/3	1/1	
Nashua	1954–56	22/31	28/31			1/1	3/3
Native Dancer	1952–54	21/22	22/22	3/3	1/1	2/2	3/3
Secretariat	1972–73	16/21	20/21	1/1	4/5		3/3
Swaps	1954–56	19/25	23/25	1/1	1/1	2/2	
Sysonby	1904–05	14/15	15/15	3/3		1/1	
Tom Fool	1951–53	21/30	29/30				
Totals		348/517	468/517	20/20	26/27	14/15	22/26
Percent winners		67.3%	90.5%	100%	96.3%	93.3%	84.6%
Winning payoff				$2.10	$2.20	$2.30	$2.40
Rate of return		1.04 ±0.07[a]		1.05	1.06	1.07	1.02
				1.05 ± 0.06[a] (all odds ranges)			

Note: The data used to construct this table were obtained from the 1982 Edition of the *American Racing Manual.* In calculating the payoffs and rates of return, it is assumed that breakage is to the nearest 5¢ per dollar wagered. For odds less than 1—20, it is assumed that the payoff is $2.10 per $2 wagered, as is standard for a minus pool (see Chapter Fifteen).

HOW ACCURATE IS THE MORNING LINE?

> **THE MORNING LINE**
>
> **. . . is an early estimate of probable odds. In the event of scratches or other material changes after the program is printed, a revised Morning Line will be posted. The actual odds on all races are determined by the bettors.**

Except for the fact that favorites are underbet and long shots are overbet, the public's estimate of the probability of winning is remarkably close to the actual probability of winning. This analysis is based on the final odds of all

TABLE 3.7 ***(continued)***

Odds Ranges (wins/races)							
1—4	3—10 to 1—3	7—20	2—5	9—20	1—2	11—20	3—5
0/2	2/5	1/1	4/5	0/1	0/2		1/1
1/1	1/1	1/1	2/2		1/1		1/1
2/2			1/1		1/2		
2/2	0/1		4/4	0/2	1/2	1/1	3/4
1/1	3/3	1/2		1/3	1/1		3/4
			2/4		1/1		8/12
3/3	6/6		4/7		4/6		1/3
			1/1	1/1	2/2	1/2	1/1
1/1	3/4		2/2		1/1		
2/2	1/1		2/2		1/1		
	2/4		2/2		1/1		
	3/6		1/1				
1/1	1/1		2/2	1/1			1/1
2/2					1/1		
15/17	22/32	3/4	27/33	3/8	15/21	2/3	19/27
88.2%	68.8%	75%	81.8%	37.5%	71.4%	66.7%	70.4%
$2.50	$2.60	$2.70	$2.80	$2.90	$3.00	$3.10	$3.20
1.10	0.89	1.01	1.15	0.54	1.07	1.03	1.13
1.04 ± 0.12[a]				1.02 ± 0.13[a]			

[a]These rates of return and those in Table 3.8 are expected values plus or minus two standard deviations. By Chebychev's inequality such an interval has at least a 75% chance of covering the true rate of return. The standard deviation may be estimated by $\sqrt{\Sigma(X_i - \overline{X})^2/(N - 1)N}$, where X_i is the return in the ith race out of the N races in each category and $\overline{X}$ is the average return.

the bettors at the racetrack. The question arises about the use of the morning-line odds. Are they more or less accurate? Are they any good at all? Are horses whose actual odds are higher than the morning line more likely or less likely to win? How about those horses that go off at lower odds?

The consensus and evidence are that as a predictor of the probability of winning, the morning odds are much less accurate than the actual final odds. Late bettors are those who bet near the end of the betting period. Winning horses are especially favored by these late bettors and losers are not. Horses that go off at odds less than their morning-line odds are more likely to win than those that go off at odds higher than their morning-line odds. Thus if

TABLE 3.8 ***Rate of return on win bets for extreme favorites: 732 races in New York in 1980***

				Odds Ranges (wins/races)		
Track	Racing Dates	Wins/ Races	In the Money/ Races	1—10	1—5	3—10
Aqueduct	Jan. 1–Mar. 17, Mar. 19–May 19, Oct. 15–Dec. 31	208/422 (49.3%)	341/417 (81.8%)	0/0	3/3	1/1
Belmont Park	May 21–July 28, Aug. 27–Oct. 13	154/270 (57%)	231/264 (87.5%)	1/1	1/1	10/13
Saratoga	July 30–Aug. 25	21/40 (52.5%)	39/40 (97.5%)	0/0	0/0	0/0
Totals	313 Days	383/732	611/721	1/1	4/4	11/14
Percent winners		52.3%	84.7%	100%	100%	78.6%
Winning payoff				\$2.20	\$2.40	\$2.60
Rate of return		0.90 ±0.04	0.96 ±0.04	1.10	1.20	1.02
				1.06±0.15		

Notes: The data used to construct this table were obtained from ***Daily Racing Form's Chart Books*** for 1980. Breakage at all three tracks is to the nearest 10¢ per dollar wagered. Thanks are due to Brian Canfield for help in collecting and analyzing this data.

a horse is 3–1 in the morning line and is going off at 6–1, its actual chance of winning is approximately

$$\frac{\text{Track payback}}{6+1} = \frac{0.84}{7} = 14\% \quad \text{and not} \quad \frac{0.84}{3+1} = 21\%.$$

Similarly, an 8–1 shot in the morning line going off at 2–1 has a chance of winning of about

$$\frac{0.84}{2+1} = 28\% \quad \text{and not} \quad \frac{0.84}{8+1} = 9\%.$$

Table 3.10, based on 792 races at Atlantic City in 1978, illustrates the situation.

It indicates that, on average, the horses that win have final odds that are less than the morning line. Horses that do not win and finish second, third, or out of the money have final odds that tend to be larger than their morning-line odds. For example, the second-place finishers have odds 1.16 times the morning-line odds, the third-place finishers 1.22 times the morn-

TABLE 3.8 *(continued)*

Odds Ranges (wins/races)						
2—5	1—2	3—5	7—10	4—5	9—10	1—1
20/31	26/41	19/36	36/70	35/70	29/80	39/90
16/23	17/24	17/28	25/45	29/52	14/44	24/39
1/2	3/5	2/3	4/7	5/6	5/12	1/5
37/56	46/70	38/67	65/122	69/128	48/136	64/134
66.1%	65.7%	56.7%	53.3%	53.9%	35.3%	47.8%
$2.80	$3.00	$3.20	$3.40	$3.60	$3.80	$4.00
0.93	0.99	0.91	0.91	0.97	0.67	0.96
	0.94±0.05			0.87±0.04		

The results of place and show bets on these races are discussed in Chapter Thirteen. See Tables 13.2 and 13.3 and the accompanying discussion.

ing-line odds, and the out-of-the-money finishers a whopping 1.59 times the morning-line odds. Moreover, the last two columns of Table 3.10 indicate that people who bet near the end of the betting period are even more accurate predictors of the actual probability of finish. These data are consistent with the notion of "smart money"—those betting in the last few minutes before a race begins are better informed than the general public. They generally bet at this time so as not to tip their hand regarding their bet. Their predictions of the probability of winning are better than those of the general public.*

*A professional handicapper colleague in Vancouver, Fraser Rawlinson, uses such ideas as an integral part of his betting program. His analysis indicates that the smart money is early as well as late. The early money tends to depress the odds and make the wager on the given horse less attractive. Hence, the final odds may be higher than fair. His research suggests that horses that have early money wagers on the first tote-board reading and late money near the close of betting are sound bets. Since his results are confidential we do not have specific data, but the concept seems sound.

Fraser writes, ". . . betting early also has more disguise value. It makes a horse 'open' as a conspicuous underlay. But then this bet is absorbed as the win pool grows so the odds start to rise, which allays the fears of the public. They think that smart money is only bet late. In fact, smart money is bet early and late. The movements of the odds on the tote board often provide useful information, but they sometimes provide misleading signals. For example, if from 5 minutes to post time a horse's odds are 5–1, 9–2,

An example of how the final odds may differ from the morning-line odds is provided by the first race at Churchill Downs on May 7, 1983. The morning-line favorite, Modicum at 9–5, went off at 8–5 and won the race. In doing so he set a track record of $51\frac{2}{5}$ seconds for the $4\frac{1}{2}$-furlong distance, a full $\frac{2}{5}$ second, or about two lengths, off the previous best. She's Ecstatic, number 9, was second at 3–1 odds, down from 5–1 in the morning line. Number 7, Fern Creek, going off at 4–1, down from 6–1, took third.* The tendency for the final odds for horses finishing in the money to fall from those in the morning line and to rise for those finishing out of the money is borne out in this race.

THE NEED TO LOOK FOR SPECIAL SITUATIONS TO AVOID BETTING ON ALL RACES AND ON INAPPROPRIATE DAYS

The evidence presented in this chapter indicates that the crowd does very well at predicting the actual probability of winning. Late bettors seem to do better than the average, which confirms the notion that their bets really are "smart money." We know from Figure 1.1 and the accompanying discussion that the average bettor is losing about 19% of the money he or she wagers. Just to break even, you must bet on horses that win about 23.5% more often than average. The values in Table 3.10 seem hardly good enough for even these late bettors to win, on average.

We also know that even if you devise a system that will, on average, make a profit, you may still lose by bad luck. A system that, say, wins two out of every five races may still have ten or more straight losses that might bankrupt you. Indeed, in any winning system, you need to add a measure

---

4–1, and then close at 7–2, that is almost always (85% +) the kiss of death. This is a 'snowball' horse, caused by those who only watch the tote board in the last 5 minutes. There are two consecutive drops, rush to bet, which causes a further drop and so on. Such horses may win, but not at a 7–2 rate. Another signal is that of a dead-board favorite. This is the 'public favorite,' whose odds have been in an extremely narrow range with very few odds changes for the entire betting period. For example, the horse may have odds of 5–2 the whole period except for one dip to 2–1 and return to 5–2. These are public favorites that follow the *Daily Racing Form* consensus and not smart-money favorites. My experience is that these favorites that do not have at least five or six odds changes win less than 10% of their races, which is far below what their odds would suggest. Finally, because so many systems are based on favorites—the favorite almost always (about 19 times in 20) will drop a slight notch at about one minute to post time. This is caused by so many people who are "pseudo-smart-money" players—waiting until the last minute or so to bet. A lukewarm favorite at say 9–5 in a five- or six-horse field who only drops to 8–5 may be being 'damned by faint praise.' "

*Fern Creek was actually a Dr. Z system bet; see the discussion at the end of the section on The Kentucky Oaks in Chapter Six.

of safety just to overcome this possibility.* We will do this by confining our Dr. Z system bets to those that make back the 19% and indicate a profit of another 14%–18% or more. This should be enough to account for possible bad luck.

The favorite–long-shot bias also indicates that profits are likely to be made betting on the very best horses in top races. Since these horses are traditionally underbet, they are good possibilities to consider. Tables 3.7 and 3.8, and 3.9 indicate, however, that it is unlikely that betting to win will be profitable. But betting to place or show often is. Indeed, many of our best Dr. Z system bets will be on extreme favorites.

In the next two chapters we develop the Dr. Z system. We advise you when a place or show bet is really good enough to bet and how much you should bet on it. You will not have a good bet in every race. To win you must also be careful to select only bets that really appear promising and wager appropriate amounts. Betting on days when the track conditions are not ideal, such as in the mud or on horses that are not in peak form because they have not run recently, adds to the risk. Poor odds, less than ideal conditions, and the like rule out many races as profitable betting opportunities. Still, there are usually two to four outstanding Dr. Z system bets per day at a typical track.† On average, they make about a 10% profit. We will concentrate on these.

---

*An excellent analysis of this bad-luck phenomenon in the context of trying to devise a winning strategy for the Massachusetts Numbers Game appears in Chernoff (November 1980).

†This book is mainly concerned with thoroughbred racing. However, the Dr. Z option works equally well and in the same way at harness-racing tracks. This is discussed in Chapter Seventeen. However, the number of Dr. Z system bets per day at harness tracks is usually much larger, typically six to eight a day, because there are many more standout favorites. This is caused by the regularity of the top horses, the extreme post-position biases and the extreme ability of the best drivers in comparison with average drivers.

TABLE 3.9 ***Probabilities of winning and rates of return from win bets on extreme favorites in California and New York***

	Probability of Winning		Expected Value per Dollar Bet	
Odds	*CA*	*NY*	*CA*	*NY*
1–10	92.0	90.5	105.0	103.3
1–5	78.7	77.6	101.7	100.0
2–5	65.7	64.6	97.7	96.0
3–5	55.6	54.6	93.7	92.0

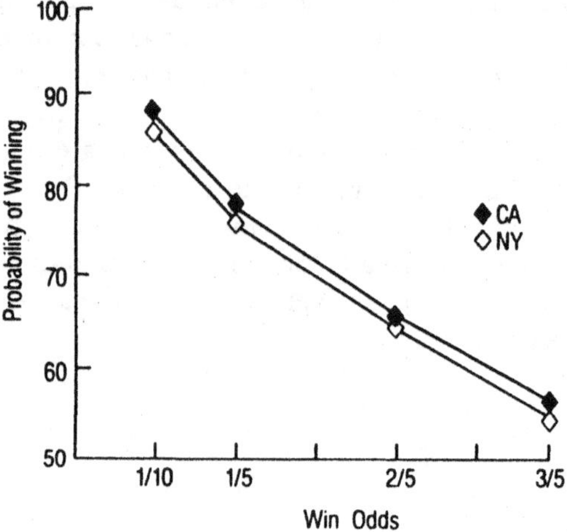

Figure 3.7 Probabilities of winning on extreme favorites in California and New York

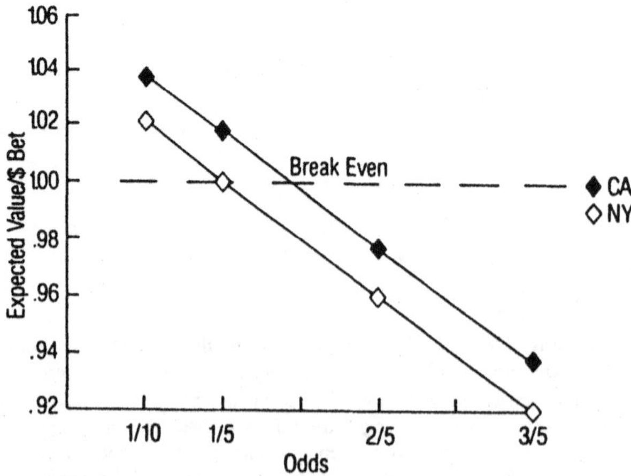

Figure 3.8 Expected value per dollar bet on extreme favorites in California and New York

TABLE 3.10 ***Relationship between the final and morning-line odds for all and late bettors for horses finishing in or out of the money***

Horses Finishing	Final Track Odds as a Percentage of Morning-Line Odds	Odds Produced by Bettors in the Last Eight Minutes of Betting as a Percentage of Morning-Line Odds	Odds Produced by Bettors in the Last Five Minutes of Betting as a Percentage of Morning-Line Odds
First	96	82	79
Second	116	106	101
Third	122	117	107
Out of the money	159	163	149

Source: Asch, Malkiel, and Quandt (1982).

America's Turf Authority Daily Racing Form

Experts' Selections

Consensus Points: 5 for 1st (today's best 7), 2 for 2nd, 1 for 3rd. Today's Best in Bold Type.

Trackman, Graham Ross — **CHURCHILL DOWNS** — Selections Made for Fast Track

	TRACKMAN	HANDICAP	ANALYST	HERMIS	SWEEP	CONSENSUS	
1	WESTWOOD LAKE	MODICUM	MODICUM	MODICUM	PRUNER'S GAL	MODICUM	16
	PRUNER'S GAL	FERN CREEK	SHE'S ECSTATIC	SHE'S ECSTATIC	WESTWOOD LAKE	PRUNER'S GAL	7
	RED'S ABBEY	SHE'S ECSTATIC	FERN CREEK	HAMBURG PLACE	MODICUM	WESTWOOD LAKE	7

FIRST HALF DAILY DOUBLE

WIN PLACE SHOW

4½ FURLONGS

MAIDEN
PURSE $8,000
(Plus $2,000 from the Kentucky Thoroughbred Development Fund)
MAIDEN FILLIES. TWO YEARS OLD. 118 lbs

Track Record—MISS SUMMER TIME (2) 116 lbs.; :51⅘; May 1, 1961
VITE FLYING (2) 117 lbs.; :51⅘; May 6, 1969

MAKE SELECTION BY NUMBER

	Owner / Trainer	Jockey	Morn Line	FINAL ODDS	FINISH
1	PAUL E. DAVIS — MIKE DAVIS; Red, Red "D" on White Diamond Belt, White Diamonds on Sleeves, Red Cap; **HAMBURG PLACE** 118; Ch f (1981), Whitesburg—Bosun Queen	CORBY NIELSEN	12	30	--
2	DONALD JOHNSON — JERRY ROMANS; Red, White Cross Sashes, Red Cap; **RED'S ABBEY** 118; B f (1981), Red Ryder—Satin Abbey	BRENT BARTRAM	15	60	--
3	BERNARD S. FLINT, INC. (Bernard S. Flint) — BERNARD S. FLINT; Gold, Blue and Gold Stars on White Sleeves, White Cap; **SPIEGLER** *113; B f (1981), Clem Pac—Decorative	SCOTT MILLER	6	10	--
4	SARA M. MAHAN — GLENN WISMER; Orange, Black Sash, Black Cap; **PRUNER'S GAL** 118; B f (1981), The Pruner—Gal Sal	CHARLES WOODS, JR.	20	10	--
5	BOB WEST — C. R. McGAUHEY III; Orange, Black Sash, Black Cap; **MODICUM (GB)** 118; Ch f (1981), General Assembly—Sandstream	PAT DAY	9-5	8-5	1
6	CHERRY VALLEY FARM (Seth W. Hancock) — STEVEN PENROD; Red, Gold Hoops, Red Bars on Gold Sleeves, Red Cap; **SINTRA** 118; Ro. f. (1981), Drone—Misty Plum	MARK SELLERS	6	9	--
7	CRIMSON KING FARM (Peter W. Salmen, Jr.) — PETER W. SALMEN, JR.; Crimson, White "CK," White Sleeves, White Cap; **FERN CREEK** 118; B. f. (1981), Crimson Falcon—Crimson Belle	WILLIAM GAVIDIA	6	4	3
8	MURRAY WEST AND BUCK WOODFORD — WILLIAM I. MOTT; Red, Green Sash, Green Sleeves, Red Cap; **WESTWOOD LAKE** 118; Ch. f. (1981), Restivo—Placid Lake	LEROY MOYERS	4	8	--
9	TOM GENTRY — EDUARDO INDA; Yellow, Royal Blue Blocks, Royal Blue Bars on Sleeves, Yellow Cap; **SHE'S ECSTATIC** 118; B. f. (1981), Sauce Boat—She's Armed	EDDIE DELAHOUSSAYE	5	3	2
10	BUCKLAND FARM (Thomas M. Evans) — ROSS R. PEARCE; Dark Blue, White Triangle, Blue Band on White Sleeves, Blue and White Cap; **TRICKY SEA** *113; Ch. f. (1981), Sea Songster—Famous Trick	KEITH ALLEN	12	40	--

Selections 5—8—9—6

★ Fair Mud Runner X Good Mud Runner ⊗ Superior Mud Runner

Past Performances Listed According to Post Position

1st Churchill

4½ FURLONGS. MAIDEN. SPECIAL WEIGHT. Fillies. 2-year-olds.

Hamburg Place 118

Red's Abbey 118

Spiegler 113⁵

Pruner's Gal 118

*Modicum 118

Sintra 118

Fern Creek 118

Westwood Lake 118

She's Ecstatic 118

Tricky Sea 113⁵

4

Finding Profitable Place and Show Bets

UNDERSTANDING THE WIN, PLACE, AND SHOW PAYOFFS

The payoffs to win, as described in Chapter Two, are easy to determine. Consider the 1980 Kentucky Derby, which was run as the ninth race on May 3, 1980, at Churchill Downs in Louisville, Kentucky. The favorite, Rockhill Native, went off at 2.10–1. If he had won, the payoff would have been a $2.10 profit for each dollar bet, for a $3.10 total return. Since payoffs are generally based on $2 bets, the payoff as listed on the tote board would have read $6.20. The second favorite, Rumbo, at 4–1 thus would have paid $2(4 + 1), or $10. The winner was the filly, Genuine Risk, who went off at 13.30–1 and paid $2(13.30 + 1) = $28.60. Five weeks later at the Belmont Stakes these three horses met again.

There are many factors that determine the betting patterns leading to the final odds, but recent performance is one of the most important. Rockhill Native's poor Derby performance moved his odds from 2.10–1 to 12.80–1, a sixfold increase. He would have paid $2(12.80 + 1), or $27.60. Rumbo's strong second-place finish lowered his odds from 4–1 to 1.90–1. Genuine Risk's win moved her odds from 13.30–1 to 5.10–1, so she should have paid $2(5.10 + 1) = $12.20. The invader, Codex, was the favorite at 1.60–1 and finished seventh. Remember that our discussion in Chapter Three indicates that, on average, these odds give a very good estimate of each horse's true chances of winning.

However, long shots often win races in the mud, making these races the most unpredictable. This race was no exception. The 53.40–1 shot, Temperence Hill, was the winner. He paid a whopping $108.80, an amazing payoff in retrospect. Temperence Hill went on to become one of the top thoroughbred money-winners of all time, winning eleven of thirty-one races and $1,567,650.

106th Kentucky Derby, May 3, 1980

$339,300 gross value and $45,000 Gold Cup. Net to winner $250,550; second $50,000; third $25,000; fourth $13,750. 293 nominations.

Horse	Eqt	Wt	PP	¼	½	¾	Mile	Str	Fin	Jockeys	Owners	Odds to $1
Genuine Risk . . .		121	10	7^{1hf}	7^{3}	4^{h}	1^{1hf}	1^{2}	1^{1}	J. Vasquez	Mrs. B. R. Firestone	13.30
Rumbo		126	9	13	12^{1hf}	11^{3}	5^{hf}	3^{3}	2^{1}	L. Pincay Jr.	Gayno Stable and Bell	4.00
Jaklin Klugman .		126	2	8^{hf}	8^{h}	8^{hf}	4^{2hf}	2^{1hf}	3^{4}	D. McHargue	Klugman-Dominguez	7.10
Super Moment . .		126	3	10^{1hf}	9^{1hf}	9^{1hf}	9^{3}	5^{hf}	4no	D. Pierce	Elmendorf	8.60
Rockhill Native . .		126	6	2^{h}	1^{1hf}	2^{h}	2^{hf}	4^{1hf}	5^{nk}	J. Oldham	Harry A. Oak	2.10
Bold 'n Rulling .	b	126	1	6^{1hf}	2^{h}	1^{h}	6^{1hf}	7^{3}	6^{2}	P. Valenzuela	Hughes Brothers	68.70
Plugged Nickle . .		126	11	1^{h}	3^{1hf}	3^{1hf}	3^{1hf}	6^{h}	$7^{3 1/4}$	B. Thornburg	John M. Schiff	2.60
Degenerate Jon .	b	126	4	9^{2hf}	6^{h}	5^{h}	8^{3}	8^{1hf}	$8^{1 1/4}$	R. Hernandez	Barry K. Schwartz	61.70
Withholding		126	12	4^{hf}	10^{1}	10^{1}	11^{2}	9^{2}	9^{2}	M. Morgan	Russell Michael Jr.	64.10
Tonka Wakhan .	b	126	5	12^{h}	13	12^{hf}	12^{3}	10^{2}	$10^{2 1/4}$	M. Holland	Glenn Bromagen	f-58.90
Execution's Reason		126	13	3^{1hf}	5^{hf}	7^{2hf}	10^{1}	11^{3}	11^{3}	R. Romero	Howard B. Noonan	111.80
Gold Stage		126	7	5^{h}	4^{hf}	6^{h}	7^{hf}	12^{1hf}	12no	A. Cordero	Mrs. Philip B. Hofman	41.50
Hazard Duke . .	b	126	8	11^{3}	11^{hf}	13	13	13	13	D. Brumfield	Andrew Adams	f-58.90

Time: :24, :48, 1:12-4/5, 1:37-3/5, 2:02. Track fast. Off at 5:39 EDT. Start good. Won driving.

f-Mutuel field

$2 Mutuels paid — Genuine Risk $28.60 straight, $10.60 place, $4.80 show; Rumbo $5.20 place, $3.40 show; Jaklin Klugman $4.40 show.

Winner—Ch.f. by Exclusive Native—Virtuous, by *Gallant Man; trainer LeRoy Jolley; bred in Kentucky by Mrs. G. Watts Humphrey, Jr.

GENUINE RISK settled nicely as the field came away in good order and was reserved behind PLUGGED NICKLE and inside WITHHOLDING around the first turn and early backstretch. She was eased back slightly and moved to the outside smoothly approaching the half-mile pole, gradually raced to the leaders outside four rivals, and took command entering the stretch; was hit once with the whip right-handed, increased her advantage under six well spaced strokes as Vasquez switched to the left, and continued resolutely to the end. RUMBO dropped back last soon after the start and was kept outside rivals, gradually improving position, swerved under right-handed urging after racing wide into the stretch, and gained steadily under heavy left-hand urging in the final furlong. JAKLIN KLUGMAN saved ground behind the first flight, worked between rivals around the final turn, and moved boldly in pursuit of the winner settling into the homestretch, but could not sustain his bid. SUPER MOMENT stayed close to the rail and closed well from the head of the stretch to outfinish the others. ROCKHILL NATIVE had no difficulty taking a clear lead from between rivals entering thee backstretch, but swerved out and was lightly checked for a stride approaching the six-furlong pole, stayed with the pace to the top of the homestretch, and then weakened. BOLD 'N RULLING raced with the pace along the rail for six furlongs, gave way approaching the stretch and drifted out, then held on fairly well in the straightaway, but pulled up lame. PLUGGED NICKLE rated near the lead outside ROCKHILL NATIVE and BOLD 'N RULLING, bore out slightly on the final turn, then raced true while tiring in the homestretch run. DEGENERATE JON was a factor for six furlongs and tired. WITHHOLDING was very wide outside the first flight and tired. TONKA WAKHAN was outrun. EXECUTION'S REASON was used up early. GOLD STAGE also tired early. HAZARD DUKE was not a factor.

THE WINNER'S PEDIGREE AND CAREER HIGHLIGHTS

GENUINE RISK (Chestnut Filly)	**Exclusive Native**	**Raise a Native**	**Native Dancer**
			Raise You
		Exclusive	**Shut Out**
			Good Example
	Virtuous	***Gallant Man**	***Migoli**
			***Majideh**
		Due Respect II	**Zucchero**
			Auld Alliance

Year	Age	Sts	1st	2nd	3rd	Won
1979	2	4	4	0	0	$100,245
1980	3	8	4	3	1	503,742
1981	4	3	2	0	1	$ 42,600
TOTALS		15	10	3	2	$646,587

At 2 Years	**WON**	**Tempted, Demoiselle**
At 3 Years	**WON**	**Kentucky Derby, Ruffian**
	2ND	**Preakness, Belmont Stakes, Maskette**
	3RD	**Wood**
At 4 Years	**WON**	**2 Allowances**
	3RD	**1 Allowance (No Stakes)**

In each case we know before the race exactly how much each horse will pay to win. It is simply the odds plus one, times two. The situation is quite different for the place and show bets. With these bets you do not know before the race how much the place and show payoffs will be because they depend upon which horses finish in the money. You win your place bet if

Belmont Stakes

EIGHTH RACE
Belmont
JUNE 7, 1980

1 ½ MILES. (2.24) 112th Running THE BELMONT (Grade I). $200,000 Added. 3-year-olds. By subscription of $100 each to accompany the nomination; $1,000 to pass the entry box; $2,000 to start. A supplementary nomination of $5,000 may be made on Wednesday, June 4 with an additional $15,000 to start, with $200,000 added of which 60% to the winner, 22% to second, 12% to third and 6% to fourth. Colts and geldings 126 lbs.; Fillies 121 lbs. Starters to be named at the closing time of entries. The winning owner will be presented with the August Belmont Memorial Cup to be retained for one year, as well as a trophy for permanent possession and trophies will be presented to the winning trainer and jockey and mementoes to the grooms of the first four finishers. Closed Friday, February 15, 1980 with 247 nominations. Supplementary nominees: Pikotazo, Temperence Hill and Ben Fab.
Value of race $293,700, value to winner $176,220, second $64,614, third $35,244, fourth $17,622. Mutuel pool $1,603,057, OTB pool $2,166,811.

Last Raced	Horse	Eqt.A.Wt	PP	¼	½	1	1¼	Str	Fin	Jockey	Odds $1
31May80 ^{7}Bel^{3}	(S)Temperence Hill	b 3 126	3	7^{hd}	$8^{\frac{1}{2}}$	$4^{\frac{1}{2}}$	3^{5}	$2^{\frac{1}{2}}$	1^{2}	Maple E	53.40
17May80 ^{9}Pim^{2}	Genuine Risk	3 121	1	$5^{\frac{1}{2}}$	$5^{\frac{1}{2}}$	$3^{\frac{1}{2}}$	2^{hd}	1^{hd}	$2^{1\frac{1}{2}}$	Vasquez J	5.10
3May80 ^{8}CD^{5}	Rockhill Native	3 126	7	$6^{1\frac{1}{2}}$	$2^{\frac{1}{2}}$	1^{hd}	$1^{\frac{1}{2}}$	3^{5}	3^{2}	Oldham J	12.80
25May80 ^{8}Bel^{1}	Comptroller	3 126	5	$1^{\frac{1}{2}}$	1^{hd}	5^{4}	6^{3}	$5^{\frac{1}{2}}$	4^{hd}	Encinas R I	26.20
24May80 ^{8}Hol^{1}	Rumbo	3 126	8	9^{hd}	$9^{\frac{1}{2}}$	6^{2}	5^{1}	$4^{\frac{1}{2}}$	$5^{2\frac{1}{2}}$	Shoemaker W	1.90
3May80 ^{8}CD^{4}	Super Moment	3 126	9	10	10	9^{1}	7^{2}	7^{6}	$6^{1\frac{1}{2}}$	Pincay L Jr	13.40
17May80 ^{9}Pim^{1}	Codex	3 126	2	$3^{\frac{1}{2}}$	4^{1}	$2^{\frac{1}{2}}$	$4^{\frac{1}{2}}$	6^{3}	7^{9}	Cordero A Jr	1.60
26May80 ^{9}Bel^{6}	Joanie's Chief	3 126	10	$8^{1\frac{1}{2}}$	$7^{\frac{1}{2}}$	$8^{1\frac{1}{2}}$	8^{8}	8^{14}	8^{12}	Santiago A	101.00
17May80 ^{9}Pim^{5}	Bing	3 126	4	4^{hd}	6^{1}	10	10	10	9no	Cruguet J	119.60
1Jun80 ^{10}Mex^{1}	(S)Pikotazo	3 126	6	2^{1}	$3^{1\frac{1}{2}}$	7^{hd}	9^{3}	$9^{\frac{1}{2}}$	10	Hernandez R	8.50

(S) Supplementary nomination.

OFF AT 5:39, EDT. Start good, Won driving. Time, :24$\frac{3}{5}$, :50$\frac{1}{5}$, 1:15$\frac{1}{5}$, 1:39$\frac{3}{5}$, 2:04, 2:29$\frac{4}{5}$, Track muddy.

$2 Mutuel Prices:			
3-(C)-TEMPERENCE HILL	108.80	32.80	15.20
1-(A)-GENUINE RISK		7.80	5.20
7-(G)-ROCKHILL NATIVE			10.40

B. c, by Stop The Music—Sister Shannon, by Etonian. Trainer Cantey Joseph B. Bred by Polk A F Jr (Ky).

TEMPERENCE HILL, unhurried early, moved up outside horses approaching the end of the backstretch, continued his rally into the stretch, caught the leaders with a furlong remaining and proved clearly best under brisk urging. GENUINE RISK, well in hand while saving ground around the first turn, split horses while moving approaching the far turn, gained a brief lead near midstretch but wasn't able to stay with the winner. ROCKHILL NATIVE moved to the leaders from the outside around the first turn, showed speed into the stretch while saving ground and weakened under pressure. COMPTROLLER dueled for the lead into the backstretch, remained prominent to far turn, dropped back while bearing out and lacked a late response. RUMBO, unhurried early, commenced to rally approaching the end of the backstretch, saved ground into the stretch but lacked a further response. SUPER MOMENT was always outrun. CODEX, close up early, made a bid between horses racing into the far turn but was finished after going nine furlongs. JOANIE'S CHIEF failed to be a serious factor. BING gave way soon after going a half. PIKOTAZO stopped badly after racing forwardly into the backstretch. TEMPERENCE HILL raced with mud caulks.

Owners— 1, Loblolly Stable; 2, Firestone Mrs B R; 3, Oak H A; 4, Phipps O; 5, Gayno Stable & Bell Bloodstock Co; 6, Elmendorf; 7, Tartan Stable; 8, Barberino P; 9, Neff B V; 10, Carranza G Z.

Trainers— 1, Cantey Joseph B; 2, Jolley Leroy; 3, Stevens Herbert K; 4, Penna Angel; 5, Bell Thomas R Jr; 6, McAnally Ronald; 7, Lukas D Wayne; 8, Jacobs Eugene; 9, Speck Gordon; 10, Hernandez Claudino.

the horse finishes first or second; it does not matter if the horse is first or second. What matters is the amounts bet to place on the various horses, in particular on the two horses finishing 1-2, relative to the total pool. You win your show bet if the horse you bet on is first, second, or third. The payoff depends upon how much is bet on the three horses finishing in the money in relation to the total pool.

In the 1980 Kentucky Derby, Genuine Risk and Rumbo placed, and $2 bets on each of them paid $10.60 and $5.20, respectively. For show they paid $4.80 and $3.40. The payoff for the third finisher, Jaklin Klugman, was $4.40. In the 1980 Belmont Stakes, Temperence Hill and Genuine Risk paid $32.80 and $7.80, respectively, to place. For show they paid $15.20 and $5.20, and Rockhill Native paid $10.40. Notice that the place payoffs are quite a bit less than the win payoffs would have been, and the show payoffs are lower yet. This is reasonable, since two horses receive place payoffs and three receive show payoffs, while only one horse wins. These are typical payoffs for horses going off at reasonably long odds.

Let's now look at the situation when the top favorites finish in the money. In the 1980 Kentucky Oaks, the Kentucky Derby for fillies, the 3–5 favorite,

Bold 'N Determined, won and paid $2.40 to place and $2.20 to show. With a large amount bet on Bold 'N Determined to place and show, the payoffs on Mitey Lively were $4 and $3, and $3.80 on Honest And True.

This $3.80 show payoff on the 27–1 shot, Honest And True, was less than Genuine Risk's $4.80 at 13.3–1 and Jaklin Klugman's $4.40 at 7.1–1 in the 1980 Kentucky Derby held the next day. This payoff was also smaller than Genuine Risk's $5.20 at 5.1–1 and Rockhill Native's $10.40 at 12.8–1 in the 1980 Belmont Stakes. The payoffs depend upon the amounts bet on the various horses in the place and show pools, not on the win odds.

Kentucky Oaks

EIGHTH RACE
Churchill
MAY 2, 1980

1 1/16 MILES. (1.41⅗) 106th Running KENTUCKY OAKS STAKES (Grade I). Purse $100,000 added, Plus $10,000 KTDF. 3–year–old fillies. By subscription of $100 which covers nomination for both the Kentucky Oaks and the La Troienne. All nomination fees to Kentucky Oaks. $200 to pass entry box, $500 additional to start, $100,000 added, of which with subscription fees and all starting fees to be divided 65% to the winner, 20% to second, 10% to third and 5% to fourth. Weight, 121 lbs. Starters to be named through the entry box Wednesday, April 30, at usual time of closing. If race is divided entries of couplings will be divided. The owner of the winner to receive a silver trophy.

Value of race $129,100, value to winner $83,915, second $25,820, third $12,910, fourth $6,455. Mutuel pool $783,880.

Last Raced	Horse	Eqt.	A.	Wt	PP	St	¼	½	¾	Str	Fin	Jockey	Odds $1
5Apr80 ^{9}OP^{1}	Bold 'N Determined		3	121	2	2	1^{1}	1½	1^{hd}	$1^{1½}$	$1^{1½}$	Delahoussaye E	.60
13Apr80 ^{8}Aqu^{1}	Mitey Lively		3	121	3	4	$3^{3½}$	2½	$2^{1½}$	$2^{2½}$	2½	Velasquez J	6.70
5Apr80 ^{9}OP^{3}	Honest And True	b	3	121	4	1	5^{hd}	5½	5½	3^{2}	3^{3}	Guajardo A	27.00
26Apr80 ^{8}CD^{1}	Ribbon	b	3	121	5	7	7½	7^{2}	$7^{2½}$	4½	4^{3}	Ardoin R	14.00
19Apr80 ^{7}Kee^{3}	Lady Taurian Peace		3	121	7	6	$6^{2½}$	4^{1}	4^{hd}	5^{3}	$5^{3½}$	Day P	64.10
19Apr80 ^{8}Kee^{1}	Sugar And Spice		3	121	6	5	4½	6½	6^{hd}	6^{2}	6¾	Fell J	2.50
19Apr80 ^{7}Kee^{6}	Sweet Audrey		3	121	8	8	8	8	8	7½	7^{6}	Espinoza J C	83.50
19Apr80 ^{8}Kee^{2}	Nice And Sharp		3	121	1	3	2½	$3^{1½}$	3^{hd}	8	8	DePass R	62.20

OFF AT 5:30 EDT. Start good, Won driving. Time, :24⅖, :48⅗, 1:13⅗, 1:38⅕, 1:44⅘ Track fast.

$2 Mutuel Prices:			
2–BOLD 'N DETERMINED	3.20	2.40	2.20
3–MITEY LIVELY		4.00	3.00
4–HONEST AND TRUE			3.80

B. f, by Bold And Brave—Pidi, by Determine. Trainer Drysdale Neil. Bred by Layton G E (Ky).

The first race at Woodbine on June 5, 1980, is a typical payoff, with the top two favorites in the money. Notice that Jah Man has higher win odds than Aftermath, 2.10–1 versus 1.50–1, yet his show payoff is less, $2.30 versus $2.40.

1st Race Woodbine Jun. 5, 1980

6 FURLONGS. (1.08⅗) 3 & 4-Year-Olds, Bred in Can. Maidens Claiming ($16,000). Purse $5,200. —Canada-bred — Value of race $5,200, value to winner $3,120, second $1,040, third $572, fourth $312, fifth $156. Mutuel pool $45,501.

Last Raced	Horse	Wt.	PP.	½	Str	Fin	Odds $1
25May80 ^{10}WO^{5}	Aftermath	114	6	$1^{1½}$	1^{3}	$1^{2½}$	1.50
23May80 ^{4}WO^{5}	Social Expression	117	2	2^{2}	$2^{2½}$	2¾	7.80
28May80 ^{9}WO^{2}	Jah Man	114	5	6^{hd}	4½	3no	2.10
25May80 ^{10}WO^{9}	Kamarian	115	8	$4^{2½}$	3^{2}	4^{2}	9.95
7May80 ^{6}WO^{9}	Irish Taheka	115	7	5½	5^{3}	5^{4}	11.40
28May80 ^{9}WO^{4}	Peterkinooks	114	3	7^{3}	6^{1}	$6^{5½}$	16.00
14May80 ^{6}WO^{11}	Truganini	114	4	3^{1}	7^{6}	$7^{2¾}$	21.80
25Jly79 ^{3}WO^{4}	Lord Treego	114	9	8^{3}	$8^{2½}$	8^{3}	9.85
21May80 ^{1}WO^{9}	Skip's Girl	105	1	9	9	9	100.90

Time, :23⅕, :46⅖, 1:12⅕ Track fast. OFF AT 1:31, EDT.

6-AFTERMATH	5.00	3.10	2.40
3-SOCIAL EXPRESSION		5.80	3.00
5-JAH MAN			2.30

In the fifth race at Pimlico on May 19, 1980, the two top favorites finished second and third. There was, however, a dead heat for third between Mexican Red and Series Six. Since the payoff for show had to be split among four horses rather than three, the returns were minimal. Ashanti Gold paid only $2.20 to show, yet he paid $4.80 to place. The other horses returned only $2.10, the minimum payoff.

5th Race Pimlico May 19, 1980

1 1/16 MILES. (1.41) 3-Year-Olds. Allowance. Purse $10,500. —which have never won two races other than maiden or claiming. — Value of race $10,500, value to winner $6,300, second $2,310, thirds $945 each. Mutuel pool $52,014. Exacta Pool $67,605.

Last Raced		Horse	Wt.	PP.	½	Str	Fin	Odds $1
7Apr80	^{8}Pim^6	Ashanti Gold	112	1	3^1	1^2	1^4	3.90
10May80	^{7}Pim^1	Royal Saim	112	2	6	5^3	2^{nk}	2.30
25Apr80	^{7}Pim^3	Series Six	113	3	1^1	2^4	3	DH-2.50
25Apr80	^{7}Pim^5	Mexican Red	115	4	5^8	3^2	3^7	DH-6.70
19Apr80	^{8}Pim^1	Lambie Boy	117	5	4^4	4^1	5^3	9.20
9May80	^{8}Pim^6	Guns O' Va	112	6	2^6	6	6	4.80

DH—Dead heat.
Time, :23⅗, :46⅘, 1:12, 1:38⅕, 1:45 Track good. OFF AT 2:52 EDT.

1-ASHANTI GOLD	9.80	4.80	2.20
2-ROYAL SAIM		3.40	2.10
3-DH SERIES SIX			2.10
4-DH MEXICAN RED			2.10

$2 EXACTA 1-2 PAID $31.20.

The eighth race at Greenwood on April 21, 1979, featured a nine-horse field. However, three of the horses—Overskate, Sound Reason, and Royal Sparkle—were coupled to form an entry. These horses were all owned by Stafford Farm and were required to run together. Notice that the post positions did not correspond to the numbers of the horses. This is the usual practice with a race containing an entry. It is common practice to couple

8th Race Greenwood Apr. 21, 1979

7 FURLONGS. (1.23) JACQUES CARTER. 4-Year-Olds and Up, Bred In Can. . Purse $20,000 Added. Value of race $23,025, value to winner $13,025, second $5,000, third $3,000, fourth $2,000. Mutuel pool $163,964, Minus show pool $90.67.

Last Raced		Horse	Wt.	PP.	½	Str	Fin	Odds $1
4Nov78	^{8}Lrl^7	Overskate	126	4	$1^{1\frac{1}{2}}$	$1^{1\frac{1}{2}}$	$1^{\frac{3}{4}}$	a-.35
7Apr79	^{7}Grd^3	Maple Grove	120	3	$4^{\frac{1}{2}}$	$2^{1\frac{1}{2}}$	2^{hd}	3.05
14Oct78	^{7}WO^7	Sound Reason	126	6	7^8	3^4	3^7	a-.35
7Apr79	^{7}Grd^8	Royal Sparkle	115	1	5^{hd}	4^2	$4^{2\frac{1}{2}}$	a-.35
25Nov78	^{8}Grd^3	Knight's Turn	123	5	$8^{\frac{1}{2}}$	6^2	$5^{1\frac{1}{2}}$	23.00
10Apr79	^{7}Grd^2	Dancing Relation	120	7	9	7^4	$6^{\frac{1}{2}}$	13.20
5Apr79	^{7}Grd^4	Forzando	116	8	2^{hd}	5^1	7^8	53.40
10Apr79	^{8}Grd^3	Crafty Money	114	2	$3^{\frac{1}{2}}$	$8^{2\frac{1}{2}}$	$8^{1\frac{1}{2}}$	22.15
13Apr79	^{7}Grd^1	Springtide	114	9	6^{hd}	9	9	15.50

a-Coupled: Overskate, Sound Reason and Royal Sparkle.
Time, :23⅘, :47⅗, 1:12⅘, 1:25⅗ Track fast. OFF AT 5:09 EST.

1-OVERSKATE (a-entry)	2.70	2.10	2.10
3-MAPLE GROVE		2.40	2.40
1-SOUND REASON (a-entry)	2.70	2.10	2.10

horses running for the same owner or trainer to prevent possible irregularities. By betting on the entry, you get three horses for the price of one. It is likely at least one of them will finish in the money. Even at 0.35–1 odds to win, the betting on the entry to place and show was greater than usual. When the entry finished 1-3 it paid only the minimum $2.10 to place and show. Maple Grove paid $2.40 to place and also to show.

The payoffs for place and show can vary greatly even on successive races at the same racetrack. Compare the fourth and sixth races at Hialeah Park on April 2, 1979. Notice that Divine Davos at 1.70–1 paid more to place and show than Remnant Wave at 2.30–1. Similarly, Kickapoo Creek at 4.60–1 paid more to show than Princess Naskra at 3.10–1.

4th Race Hialeah Park Apr. 2, 1979

ABOUT 1 ⅛ MILES.(turf). (1.47) 4-Year-Olds, Fillies. Maiden Special weights. Purse $8,500. Value of race $8,500, value to winner $5,100, second $1,530, third $935, fourth $425, balance of starters $85 each. Mutuel pool $39,233. Perfecta Pool $30,087. Trifecta Pool $35,646.

Last Raced	Horse	Wt.	PP.	½	Str	Fin	Odds $1
19Mar79 ^{4}Hia^{3}	Remnant Wave	122	6	$3\frac{1}{2}$	2^{1}	$1\frac{3}{4}$	2.30
19Mar79 ^{4}Hia^{7}	Fuzible	122	5	$6^{1\frac{1}{2}}$	3^{2}	2^{hd}	10.90
7Mar79 ^{1}Hia^{10}	Princess Naskra	117	10	$8^{1\frac{1}{2}}$	6^{hd}	$3^{1\frac{1}{4}}$	3.10
19Mar79 ^{4}Hia^{6}	Proud Lina	122	4	10	$7\frac{1}{2}$	$4\frac{1}{2}$	52.50
20Mar79 ^{4}Hia^{9}	Perhaps Barbara	115	9	4^{4}	$5\frac{1}{2}$	5^{hd}	26.30
21Mar79 ^{5}Hia^{8}	Butter Flower	117	8	$9\frac{1}{2}$	$8^{1\frac{1}{2}}$	6^{1}	25.90
21Mar79 ^{12}Hia^{2}	Our Gallant Lady	122	2	1^{3}	$1\frac{1}{2}$	$7^{1\frac{1}{2}}$	3.70
19Mar79 ^{4}Hia^{8}	Our Prissy	122	7	$5\frac{1}{2}$	9^{4}	8^{hd}	34.60
19Mar79 ^{4}Hia^{4}	Canyon Ride	122	1	7^{1}	$4\frac{1}{2}$	9^{5}	3.00
21Mar79 ^{5}Hia^{7}	Aphaia	122	3	$2^{1\frac{1}{2}}$	10	10	87.20

Time, 1:51 Course firm. OFF AT 1:59 EST.

6-REMNANT WAVE	**6.60**	**3.80**	**2.60**
5-FUZIBLE		**10.00**	**4.80**
10-PRINCESS NASKRA			**3.00**

$2 PERFECTA 6-5 PAID $64.20. $2 TRIFECTA 6-5-10 PAID $184.60.

6th Race Hialeah Park Apr. 2, 1979

7 FURLONGS. (1.20⅗) 4-Year-Olds and Up, Fillies and Mares. Claiming ($7,500 to $6,500). Purse $4,500. Value of race $4,500, value to winner $2,700, second $810, third $450, fourth $180, balance of starters $45 each. Mutuel pool $44,731. Perfecta Pool $33,538. Trifecta Pool $38,892.

Last Raced	Horse	Wt.	PP.	½	Str	Fin	Odds $1
12Mar79 ^{6}Hia^{5}	Divine Davos	116	2	4^{3}	$2\frac{1}{2}$	$1^{1\frac{1}{2}}$	1.70
15Mar79 ^{2}Hia^{6}	Gay Du Nord	116	9	$3^{1\frac{1}{2}}$	$1\frac{1}{2}$	$2\frac{3}{4}$	5.40
12Mar79 ^{6}Hia^{10}	Kickapoo Creek	120	10	2^{hd}	3^{3}	3^{2}	4.60
15Mar79 ^{2}Hia^{4}	Let It Rock	116	11	$6\frac{1}{2}$	5^{3}	$4^{1\frac{1}{2}}$	3.70
5Mar79 ^{10}GP	Step Out Fancy	109	8	1^{hd}	$4\frac{1}{2}$	5^{1}	43.80
23Mar79 ^{3}Hia^{3}	Wouldn't She Tho	107	3	7^{2}	6^{2}	6^{1}	22.20
28Mar79 ^{1}Hia^{6}	True Exchange	114	1	10^{2}	8^{4}	$7^{3\frac{1}{2}}$	129.00
27Mar79 ^{10}Hia^{10}	North WindDancer	111	7	8^{3}	$7\frac{1}{2}$	8^{3}	7.60
9Mar79 ^{8}FD^{4}	Ms. Jackie Blue	114	5	$11^{1\frac{1}{2}}$	$9^{1\frac{1}{2}}$	9^{6}	15.80
2Jan79 ^{6}Crc^{8}	Cap's Cissy	106	6	9^{2}	11^{5}	$10\frac{1}{2}$	83.50
11Dec78 ^{7}Key^{8}	I'm For Triggs'z	116	12	$5\frac{1}{2}$	10^{1}	11^{8}	28.70
20Mar79 ^{7}FD^{5}	Anitas Hat	120	4	12	12	12	54.40

Time, :23⅕, :46⅘, 1:13⅕, 1:26⅘ Track fast. OFF AT 3:00, EST.

2-DIVINE DAVOS	**5.40**	**4.00**	**3.20**
9-GAY DU NORD		**6.60**	**4.20**
10-KICKAPOO CREEK			**3.40**

$2 PERFECTA 2-9 PAID $30.80. $2 TRIFECTA 2-9-10 PAID $147.00.

WHY PLACE AND SHOW BETTING CAN YIELD POSITIVE PROFITS

How can we take advantage of these discrepancies? No such discrepancies occur for win bets, since the win odds are essentially efficient, but they do occur in the place and show pools. A discrepancy or inefficiency occurs when a much lower proportion of the place or show pool is bet on a particular horse than this horse's proportion of the win pool. The Dr. Z system is a method to exploit these inefficiencies in a precise manner. We develop the basic ideas in this and the succeeding chapter. Our focus now is first to get a feel for when these inefficiencies occur so that they can be easily recognized. As an example, suppose the tote board is as follows:

	Horse							
	#1	#2	#3	#4	#5	#6	#7	Totals
Odds	4—5	14—1	6—1	5—2	16—1	11—1	33—1	
Win	8,293	1,009	2,116	4,212	885	1,251	457	18,223
Place	2,560	660	1,386	2,610	696	903	399	9,214
Show	1,570	495	1,860	1,881	543	712	287	6,558

The place pool is about half the win pool, 9,214/18,223, so *you need to find a horse whose place bet is much less than half his win bet*. Less than a third, 2,560/8,293, is bet on horse 1 to place, while for all the other horses, there is more than half as much bet to place as to win. The show pool is about a third the win pool, 6,558/18,223, so you would like to find a horse where relatively much less is bet to show. For horses 2 to 7, the ratio between show bet and win bet is more than a third. For example, horse 2 has

$$\frac{\text{Show bet}}{\text{Win bet}} = \frac{495}{1{,}009} = 0.491.$$

Disregard bets like these. However, horse 1 looks promising. It has

$$\frac{\text{Show bet}}{\text{Win bet}} = \frac{1{,}570}{8{,}293} = 0.185,$$

which is much less than $\frac{1}{3} = 0.333$.

Thus, horse 1 may well be a good bet to place and/or to show. Three key questions must now be answered: (1) How good is the bet? (2) Is the bet really good enough? (3) How much should you bet? We answer question (1) later in this chapter and questions (2) and (3) in Chapter Five.

Let us first look at how the place and show mutuel payoffs are determined. Let Q be the track payback. This is usually about 83%. If P_i is the amount bet on horse i to place, and $P = \sum_{i=1}^{n} P_i$, where P is the place pool and n the number of possible horses, then the payoff per dollar bet on horse i to place is

$$\begin{cases} 1 + \dfrac{PQ - P_i - P_j}{2P_i} & \text{if } \begin{cases} i \text{ is first and } j \text{ is second or} \\ j \text{ is first and } i \text{ is second} \end{cases} \\ 0 & \text{if } i \text{ is not first or second.} \end{cases} \tag{4.1}$$

Thus if horses i and j are first and second, each bettor on i (and also j) to place first receives the amount of his or her bet. The remaining amount in the place pool, after the track take, is then split evenly among the place bettors on i and j. The payoff to horse i to place is independent of whether i finishes first or second, but it is dependent on which horse finished with it. A bettor on horse i to place hopes that a long shot, not a favorite, will finish with it.

Let S_i be the amount bet on horse i to show and $S = \sum_{i=1}^{n} S_i$ be the total show pool. The payoff per dollar bet on show is then

$$\begin{cases} 1 + \dfrac{SQ - S_i - S_j - S_k}{3S_i} & \text{if } \begin{cases} i \text{ is first, second, or third} \\ \text{and finishes with } j \text{ and } k \end{cases} \\ 0 & \text{if } i \text{ is not first, second, or third.} \end{cases} \tag{4.2}$$

To understand equations (4.1) and (4.2), let's suppose horse 1 is in the money with horse 2 for a place bet. The payoff per dollar bet to place on horse 1 is

$$1 + \frac{9{,}214(0.83) - 2{,}560 - 660}{2(2{,}560)} = \$1.86.$$

If horse 4 finishes with horse 1, then 1's payoff for place per dollar bet is

$$1 + \frac{9{,}214(0.83) - 2{,}560 - 2{,}610}{2(2{,}560)} = \$1.48.$$

For show, suppose horse 1 finishes in the money with the long shots 2 and 7. Then the payoff for show per dollar bet on horse 1 is

$$1 + \frac{6{,}558(0.83) - 1{,}570 - 495 - 287}{3(1{,}570)} = \$1.66.$$

If 1 finishes in the money with the other favorites, 3 and 4, then the show payoff drops to

$$1 + \frac{6{,}558(0.83) - 1{,}570 - 1{,}860 - 1{,}881}{3(1{,}570)} = \$1.03.$$

At an actual racetrack, the values would be adjusted for breakage, $2 bets, and $2.10 minimum payout. With 5¢ on the dollar, $1.86 becomes $3.70, $1.48 becomes $2.90, $1.66 becomes $3.30, and $1.03 becomes $2.10. So the payoffs are much larger when relative long shots rather than favorites finish in the money. Notice that as less is bet to place or show on horse 1, the payoff is improved in two ways. For example, with place there is less taken off than $2,560 and likewise less than $2,560 is divided. With proportionally less bet to place or show, the payoff becomes much larger.

Let us now look at some more actual race results to determine the type of situations for which you are looking, so that you can learn to recognize them easily. An extreme case occurs when the place payoff actually exceeds the win payoff, as with Chocolate Lover in the ninth race at Hollywood Park on December 11, 1982. This makes for an outstanding bet.

6207—**NINTH RACE. Mile and one-sixteenth. 3-year-olds & up. Top claiming price $20,000. Purse $10,000.**

6189	Chocolate Lover, Sibille	121	12	4	5^{1}	2^{hd}	$1^{1/2}$	1^{2}	$1^{3\frac{1}{2}}$	1.10
6144	Hanalei Prince, Steiner	x111	1	2	4^{2}	$5^{3\frac{1}{2}}$	3^{4}	3^{2}	2^{hd}	12.00
6135	Royal Earl, Ortega	121	9	10	$10^{1/2}$	9^{5}	$5^{1/2}$	4^{3}	$3^{1\frac{1}{2}}$	5.10
——	Apache Scout, Guzman	116	5	12	12	12	8^{hd}	5^{4}	$4^{1\frac{1}{2}}$	8.30
——	Dancing Casanova, Vinzie	116	11	3	3^{1}	1^{1}	$2^{1\frac{1}{2}}$	2^{1}	5^{3}	19.00
6055	Game Of Spies, Bombek	114	7	6	8^{2}	8^{hd}	4^{hd}	$6^{1/2}$	$6^{2\frac{1}{2}}$	116.80
6144	Mity Busy, Pedroza	114	10	8	11^{5}	$11^{1/2}$	$9^{2\frac{1}{2}}$	7^{hd}	7no	18.10
——	Count By Five, Lipham	114	8	11	9^{hd}	10^{hd}	11^{1}	8^{hd}	8^{1}	43.00
6153	Bold Taste, Cruz	116	6	7	7^{3}	6^{1}	7^{3}	9^{2}	$9^{3\frac{1}{2}}$	111.70
6153	California Fig, Dihssye	116	2	0	6^{hd}	7^{2}	6^{hd}	10^{8}	10^{7}	7.60
6046	Mel's Victory, McHargue	115	3	5	1^{hd}	3^{hd}	10^{2}	11^{3}	11^{3}	33.30
6101	Amazing Career, Frazier	121	4	1	2^{1}	4^{hd}	12	12	12	11:60

Scratched—K's Vindicator, Bidedoon, China Blast.

CHOCOLATE LOVER **4.20 4.40 3.00**
HANALEI PRINCE **8.40 5.20**
ROYAL EARL **3.40**

Time—:23, .46 3/5, 1:11 1/5, 1:37 2/5, 1:44 1/5. Winner—b.g.4 Illustrious—Khal Me Fancy. Trained by s. Morguelan. Mutuel pool $107,821. Exacta Pool $259,467. Attendance—13,801. Total handle $3,175,962.

Claimed—Apache Scount by S. Rahe, trainer G. Lewis, for $10,000. Royal Earl by Lewis Potter, trainer G. Lewis, for $10,000. Chocolate Lover by J. M. Orman, trainer D Vienna, for $10,000.

$5 EXACTA (12-1) PAID $115.00

The extreme inefficiency required to have the place payoff exceed the win payoff is rare, however. It usually occurs when a seemingly unbeatable horse is bet at extremely low odds to win, while the place (and possibly also the show) betting is simply overlooked. The crowd feels that the payoff will be too small to warrant the risk. They could not be more wrong! A typical example of this was the 1983 Florida Derby, where Copelan, a 2–5 shot, paid $3 to place and $2.60 to show. His win payoff had he won would have been $2.80.

Florida Derby

ELEVENTH RACE
Gulfstream
MARCH 5, 1983

1 ⅛ MILES. (1.46⅗) 32nd Running THE FLORIDA DERBY (Grade I). Purse $250,000 guaranteed. 3-year-olds. by subscription of $300 each, which shall accompany the nomination; $1,500 to pass the entry box and $2,500 additional to start, with $250,000 guaranteed. The added money and all fees to be divided 60% to first; 20% to second; 10% to third; 7% to fourth and 3% to fifth. Weight, 122 lbs. Non-winners of a sweepstakes allowed 4 lbs. Horses finishing first, second or third in the Hutcheson Stakes and/or the Fountain of Youth Stakes, will automatically be nominated to the Florida Derby. Supplementary nominations may be made at time of entry., Thursday, March 3 on payment of $5,000 each. This event will not be divided. Preference to winners. Starters to be named through the entry box by the usual time of closing. Florida Derby Trophy to winning owner. Closed Saturday, January 22 with 100 nominations. Supplementary nominee: Croeso

Value of race $250,000, value to winner $150,000, second $50,000, third $25,000, fourth $17,500, fifth $7,500. Mutuel pool $342,939. Perfecta Pool $253,039.

Last Raced	Horse	Eqt.A Wt	PP	St	¼	½	¾	Str	Fin	Jockey	Odds $1
5Feb83 ^{6}BM^{2}	(S)Croeso	b 3 118	12	5	1^{1}	$1^{1\frac{1}{2}}$	$1^{\frac{1}{2}}$	$1^{\frac{1}{2}}$	$1^{1\frac{1}{2}}$	Olivares F	85.00
21Feb83 ^{10}GP^{1}	Copelan	3 122	6	1	$2^{\frac{1}{2}}$	$3^{\frac{1}{2}}$	2^{4}	2^{3}	$2^{3\frac{1}{2}}$	Pincay L Jr	.40
11Feb83 ^{7}GP^{2}	Law Talk	b 3 118	1	2	4^{hd}	6^{1}	$4^{\frac{1}{2}}$	3^{2}	3^{hd}	Hernandez C	17.50
21Feb83 ^{9}GP^{4}	My Mac	b 3 122	13	11	10^{hd}	11^{2}	10^{2}	$5^{\frac{1}{2}}$	$4^{1\frac{1}{2}}$	MacBeth D	13.60
21Feb83 ^{9}GP^{3}	Chumming	3 118	8	6	3^{1}	2^{hd}	3^{hd}	$4^{1\frac{1}{2}}$	5^{3}	Cordero A Jr	5.70
21Feb83 ^{10}GP^{3}	Blink	3 122	2	4	9^{2}	$8^{1\frac{1}{2}}$	8^{hd}	$6^{1\frac{1}{2}}$	6^{1}	St Leon G	35.40
21Feb83 ^{10}GP^{2}	Current Hope	3 122	10	9	8^{hd}	$9^{\frac{1}{2}}$	$7^{\frac{1}{2}}$	7^{3}	7^{3}	Velasquez J	10.20
19Feb83 ^{6}GP^{1}	Princilian	3 118	4	8	$7^{\frac{1}{2}}$	7^{hd}	$9^{1\frac{1}{2}}$	8^{1}	8^{nk}	Patterson G	f-98.10
11Feb83 ^{7}GP^{5}	Pure Grit	3 122	5	13	13	13	13	$10^{1\frac{1}{2}}$	$9^{2\frac{1}{2}}$	Perret C	217.10
21Feb83 ^{10}GP^{5}	Caveat	3 122	11	12	12^{5}	12^{10}	11^{10}	9^{hd}	$10^{2\frac{1}{2}}$	Maple E	21.70
21Feb83 ^{9}GP^{5}	Bet Big	b 3 122	9	7	$5^{\frac{1}{2}}$	$4^{2\frac{1}{2}}$	6^{3}	11^{4}	$11^{5\frac{1}{2}}$	Fell J	86.90
21Feb83 ^{10}GP^{7}	El Cubanaso	b 3 118	7	10	11^{3}	10^{hd}	12^{hd}	13	$12^{2\frac{1}{2}}$	Rivera M A	f-98.10
21Feb83 ^{9}GP^{2}	Thalassocrat	3 122	3	3	6^{1}	$5^{\frac{1}{2}}$	5^{hd}	12^{2}	13	Vasquez J	24.90

f—Mutuel field.
(S) Supplementary nomination.

OFF AT 5:36 Start good, Won driving. Time, :23⅘, :48⅕, 1:11⅘, 1:36⅘, 1:49⅘ Track fast.

$2 Mutuel Prices:

10-CROESO	172.00	35.80	12.40
5-COPELAN		3.00	2.60
1-LAW TALK			5.60

$2 PERFECTA 10-5 PAID $366.20.

Ch. g. by Super Concorde—Melody Tree, by High Tribute. Trainer DiMauro Stephen. Bred by Elmendorf Farm (Ky).

CROESO away alertly from an outside post position took a clear lead going into the first turn, was well-handled while establishing slow fractions, responded when challenged by COPELAN coming to the head of the stretch, shook that one off inside the final eighth and was clear at the finish while under steady left handed pressure in the final eighth. COPELAN broke in front, was unhurried when outrun to first turn, remained prominent from the outside, reached even terms with the winner at the head of the stretch, stayed with him to inside the final eighth, then gave ground grudgingly. LAW TALK raced forwardly, loomed a threat in midstretch, but could not sustain the bid. MY MAC raced along the inside early in hand, was between horses in the stretch run and just failed to catch LAW TALK. CHUMMING had speed from the outset reached the attending position along the backstretch, then steadily gave ground to the finish. BLINK unhurried early, was inside for the stretch turn, but lacked a sufficient response. CURRENT HOPE in hand early, failed to respond to pressure. PRINCILIAN lacked a closing response. PURE GRIT failed to reach contention. CAVEAT showed little. BET BIG was a factor to the second turn, then steadily fell back. EL CUBANASO raced wide on the second turn, then quickly fell back.

This behavior often occurs in the last race or two when many bettors are looking only to the exotics and the win pools for a big payoff to get back to even. This was the case in the eleventh race at Exhibition Park on July 27, 1983. Duffus Castle, at 4.30–1, paid a whopping $15.80 to place and $9.30 to show. If he had won, his payoff would have been only $10.60.

11th One and one-sixteenth miles. Three-year-olds and up. Claiming $4,000. Purse $3,900.

Horse	Jockey	Wt	P	½	¾	Str	Fin	Odds
Dollar Power	Spencer	113	5	1-5	1-3	1-5	1-5	12.60
Duffus Castle	Wrayton	101	8	6-½	4-1	2-h	2-1	4.30
Tagy	Rycroft	115	10	10	9-1	5-½	3-1	17.60
Perfock	Krasner	109	3	8-½	6-½	4-2	4-3½	2.85
Here To Shine	Creighton	113	9	3-1	2-2	3-2	5-no	11.10
Glen Magic	Mena	113	7	4-2	5-2	6-h	6-1	4.30
Individual Boy	L'siere	108	1	9-2½	8-1½	8-5	7-1½	6.05
North Lane	Patzer	117	6	2-2½	2-2½	2-½	3-h	6.75
Concilliator	Adcock	116	4	5-½	10	9-4	9-7	8.90
Silver Ducat	Johnson	113	2	7-2	7-h	10	10	8.00

Time—:47.4, 1:14.1, 1:42, 1:49.1.
Winner: Command Module-Miss Hot Shot.
Trainer: Delores Hehn

DOLLAR POWER	27.20	14.20	9.60
DUFFUS CASTLE		15.80	9.30
TAGY			11.50

Triactor (5,8,10) paid $3,457.50

Many observers consider the greatest performance of all time by a thoroughbred to be Secretariat's win in the 1973 Belmont Stakes by an amazing thirty-one lengths. He broke the track record for the $1\frac{1}{2}$-mile distance by a full two seconds, ten lengths better than any previous horse. Equally impressive is the fact that, at 1–10 win odds, his place payoff profits were double those for win. A $2.40 place payoff in a five-horse field with a 1–10 shot is a truly amazing bet.

Belmont Stakes

EIGHTH RACE Bel June 9, 1973 — **1½ MILES. (2:26⅗). One Hundred-fifth running BELMONT. SCALE WEIGHTS. $125,000 added. 3-year-olds. By subscription of $100 each to accompany the nomination; $250 to pass the entry box; $1,000 to start. A supplementary nomination may be made of $2,500 at the closing time of entries plus an additional $10,000 to start, with $125,000 added, of which 60% to the winner, 22% to second, 12% to third and 6% to fourth. Colts and geldings. Weight, 126 lbs.; fillies, 121 lbs. The winning owner will be presented with the August Belmont Memorial Cup to be retained for one year, as well as a trophy for permanent possession and trophies will be presented to the winning trainer and jockey. Closed Thursday, Feb. 15, 1973, with 187 nominations.**

Value of race $150,200. Value to winner $90,120; second, $33,044; third, $18,024; fourth, $9,012. Mutuel Pool, $519,689. Off-track betting, $688,460.

Last Raced	Horse	EqtAWt	PP	¼	½	1	1¼	Str	Fin	Jockeys	Owners	Odds to $1
5-19-73^{8} Pim^{1}	Secretariat	b3 126	1	1^{h}	1^{h}	1^{7}	1^{20}	1^{28}	1^{31}	RTurcotte	Meadow Stable	.10
6- 2-73^{6} Bel^{4}	Twice a Prince	3 126	4	4^{5}	4^{10}	3^{h}	2^{h}	3^{12}	$2^{\frac{1}{2}}$	BBaeza	Elmendorf	17.30
5-31-73^{6} Bel^{1}	My Gallant	b3 126	3	3^{3}	3^{h}	4^{7}	3^{2}	2^{h}	3^{13}	ACorderoJr	A I Appleton	12.40
5-28-73^{8} GS^{2}	Pvt. Smiles	b3 126	2	5	5	5	5	5	$4^{\frac{3}{4}}$	DGargan	C V Whitney	14.30
5-19-73^{8} Pim^{2}	Sham	b3 126	5	2^{5}	2^{10}	2^{7}	4^{8}	$4^{1\frac{1}{2}}$	5	LPincayJr	S Sommer	5.10

Time, :23⅗, :46⅕, 1:09⅘, 1:34⅕, 1:59, 2:24 (new track record) (against wind in backstretch). Track fast.

$2 Mutuel Prices:			
2-SECRETARIAT	2.20	2.40	...
5-TWICE A PRINCE		4.60	...

(NO SHOW MUTUELS SOLD)

Ch. c, by Bold Ruler—Somethingroyal, by Princequillo. Trainer, L. Laurin. Bred by Meadow Stud, Inc. (Va.). IN GATE—5:38. OFF AT 5:38 EASTERN DAYLIGHT TIME. Start good. Won ridden out.

SECRETARIAT sent up along the inside to vie for the early lead with SHAM to the backstretch, disposed of that one after going three-quarters, drew off at will rounding the far turn and was under a hand ride from Turcotte to establish a record in a tremendous perfomance. TWICE A PRINCE, unable to stay with the leaders early, moved through along the rail approaching the stretch and outfinished MY GALLANT for the place. The latter, void of early foot, moved with TWICE A PRINCE rounding the far turn and fought it out gamely with that one through the drive. PVT. SMILES showed nothing. SHAM alternated for the lead with SECRETARIAT to the backstretch, wasn't able to match stride with that rival after going three-quarters and stopped badly. **Scratched—Knightly Dawn.**

The mighty Kelso, who was horse of the year for an unprecedented five consecutive years from 1960 to 1964, often returned more to place than win as the two following race charts indicate.

Such payoffs occur frequently on the very best horses. John Henry was the horse of the year in 1981, and he is the all-time leading money winner, with earnings of $6,591,860. In the 1983 running of the Arlington Million, he was the favorite of the crowd at 7–5. He lost the race to the 38–1 shot, Tolomeo. His place payoff, however, was $4.80, the same as he would have paid to win had he won.

Place and also show payoffs almost as good as the win payoffs occur frequently with odds-on favorites, such as in the 1977 Kentucky Derby with Seattle Slew, the 1981 Blue Grass Stakes at Keeneland with Proud Appeal, and the E.P. Taylor Stakes at Woodbine with De La Rose. Later in the chapter you will learn how to evaluate how good these payoffs really are.

Some outstanding show bets are on pages 70–77. These include Harry Caray in a claiming race at River Downs; Lamerok in the Bougainvillea

SEVENTH RACE
Aqu 18251
October 19, 1963

2 MILES. (Kelso, Oct. 29, 1960, 3:19⅘, 3, 119.) Forty-fifth running JOCKEY CLUB GOLD CUP. Weight for age. $100,000 added. 3-year-olds and upward. By subscription of $100 each, which shall accompany the nomination; $1,000 additional to start, with $100,000 added. The added money and all fees to be divided 65 per cent to the winner, 20 per cent to second, 10 per cent to third and 5 per cent to fourth. 3-year-olds, 119 lbs.; older, 124 lbs. The Jockey Club will present a Gold Cup to the owner of the winner and trophies will be presented to the winning trainer and jockey. Closed Tuesday, Oct. 1, with 19 nominations.
Value of race $108,900. Value to winner $70,785; second, $21,780; third, $10,890; fourth, $5,445.
Mutuel Pool, $391,933.

Index	Horses	Eq't	A	Wt	PP	¼	½	1	1½	Str	Fin	Jockeys	Owners	Odds to $1
18014Aqu^1	—Kelso		6	124	1	$4^{\frac{1}{2}}$	2^3	1^1	1^2	1^6	1^4	I Vanlez'ela	Bohemia Stable	.15
18170Aqu^5	—Guadalcanal		5	124	2	6^4	5^4	5^8	5^{10}	4^6	2^5	B Sorensen	R L Dotter	17.75
18170Aqu^3	—Garwol		5	124	6	$3^{1\frac{1}{2}}$	3^1	$3^{1\frac{1}{2}}$	$4^{1\frac{1}{2}}$	3^h	$3^{3\frac{1}{2}}$	J Sellers	Harbor View Farm	19.75
18170Aqu^2	—Will I Ruie		3	119	5	2^h	1^h	$2^{1\frac{1}{2}}$	2^2	$2^{1\frac{1}{2}}$	4^{10}	J Ruane	F E Dixon Jr	10.50
18170Aqu^7	—Sensitivo		6	124	3	5^5	4^4	4^3	3^1	5^6	5^8	S Hern'dez	R F Bensinger	30.45
18180Aqu^2	—Left Hook	b	3	119	7	7	6^6	6	6	6	6	W Boland	Hobeau Farm	41.30
18170Aqu^4	—Mr. Consistency	b	5	124	4	1^h	7	Saddle slipped.				J Vasquez	Ann Peppers	9.30

Time, :25, :48⅖, 1:12⅘, 1:39, 2:30, 2:55⅕, 3:22 (with wind in backstretch). Track fast.

$2 Mutuel Prices:

1-KELSO	2.30	2.40	2.10
2-GUADALCANAL		6.20	3.00
6-GARWOL			2.40

Dk. b. or br. g, by Your Host—Maid of Flight, by Count Fleet. Trainer, C. H. Hanford. Bred by Mrs. R. C. duPont. **IN GATE—4:50. OFF AT 4:50 EASTERN DAYLIGHT TIME. Start good. Won easily.**

KELSO, steadied when caught between horses during the initial quarter-mile, took command after three-quarters and, establishing a long lead in the upper stretch, won with speed in reserve. GUADALCANAL saved ground while outrun early and finished determinedly in the middle of the track but was unable to threaten KELSO, although much the best of the others. GARWOL, forwardly placed and in hand to the last half-mile, made a mild challenge entering the stretch and tired. WILL I RULE, forwardly placed until inside the stretch, had nothing left. SENSITIVO moved up boldly near the upper turn but failed to stay. LEFT HOOK, never close, had no mishap. MR. CONSISTENCY was pulled up near the three-quarters mile pole after the rider's saddle had slipped.

SEVENTH RACE
Sar 21296
August 27, 1964

1 1-8 MILES (turf). (Shield Bearer, Aug. 9, 1961, 1:47, 6, 117.) Mechanicville Purse. Allowances. Purse $9,500. 3-year-olds and upward which have not won three races of $2,925 in 1964. 3-year-olds, 116 lbs.; older, 123 lbs. Non-winners of two races of $3,575 at a mile or over since May 30 allowed 3 lbs.; of two such races since April 22, 5 lbs.; of such a race since then, 7 lbs. (Maiden, claiming, optional and starter races not considered.)
Value to winner $6,175; second, $1,900; third, $950; fourth, $475. Mutuel Pool, $106,000.

Index	Horses	Eq't	A	Wt	PP	St	¼	½	¾	Str	Fin	Jockeys	Owners	Odds to $1
20996Aqu^5	—Kelso		7	118	4	3	$2^{1\frac{1}{2}}$	2^1	2^1	$1^{\frac{1}{2}}$	$1^{2\frac{1}{2}}$	I Valenz'ela	Bohemia Stable	.30
21261Sar^2	—Knightsboro	b	5	116	1	1	$1^{2\frac{1}{2}}$	$1^{2\frac{1}{2}}$	1^h	$2^{1\frac{1}{2}}$	$2^{1\frac{1}{2}}$	R Turcotte	N Hellman	15.90
21242Sar^5	—Rocky Thumb	b	4	120	8	8	6^3	6^6	$4^{1\frac{1}{2}}$	$3^{\frac{1}{2}}$	3^5	J Combest	E B Ryan	27.85
21208Sar^1	—Flag		4	118	5	2	3^h	$3^{1\frac{1}{2}}$	3^3	4^3	4^1	R Ussery	R C Kidder	5.15
21157Sar^4	—Jay Dee		5	116	6	7	5^3	5^h	6^3	5^h	5^3	H Gustines	J M Schiff	53.85
21171Sar^2	—Swift Sands	b	6	116	7	4	4^3	4^3	5^3	6^1	6^h	J Ruane	Mrs V Adams	14.85
21242Sar^6	—Dusky Damion	b	7	116	3	5	7^1	7^1	7^3	7^6	7^6	D Pierce	Swiftsure Stable	11.70
21162Ran^5	—Shop		5	116	2	6	8	8	8	8	8	J L Rotz	B Ferrari	75.70

Time, 1:46⅗ (with wind in backstretch). Track hard. NEW COURSE RECORD. EQUALS AMERICAN RECORD.

$2 Mutuel Prices:

4-KELSO	2.60	2.70	2.30
1-KNIGHTSBORO		6.30	4.10
8-ROCKY THUMB			4.90

Dk. b. or br. g, by Your Host—Maid of Flight, by Count Fleet. Trainer, C. Hanford. Bred by Mrs. R.C. duPont, Jr.

IN GATE—5:08. OFF AT 5:08 EASTERN DAYLIGHT TIME. Start good. Won handily.

KELSO, forwardly placed from the start, took command from KNIGHTSBORO after entering the stretch and drew clear while under mild urging. KNIGHTSBORO, away fast, set the pace until inside the stretch but was unable to stay with KELSO. ROCKY THUMB, reserved early, moved to the inside at the final turn but could not better his position when set down in the drive. FLAG, caught between horses and checked slightly approaching the stretch, failed to respond when clear. JAY DEE had no excuse. SWIFT SANDS tired after showing early speed. DUSKY DAMION and SHOP, never close, had no mishaps.

Scratched—21242Sar Grand Applause.

NINTH—1¼ miles, main turf, 3-year-olds up, ARLINGTON MILLION:

Horse and Jockey	PP	¼	¾	1M	Str.	Fin.	$1
Tolomeo [Eddery]	5	2^{hd}	$3^{\frac{1}{2}}$	3^{hd}	$3^{1\frac{1}{2}}$	1^{nk}	38.20
John Henry [McCarron]	13	$3^{\frac{1}{2}}$	$2^{1\frac{1}{2}}$	2^{1}	2^{1}	$2^{\frac{1}{2}}$	1.40
Nijinsky's Secret [Velez]	7	1^{1}	1^{hd}	$1^{\frac{1}{2}}$	$1^{\frac{1}{2}}$	3^{2}	10.30
Thunder Puddles[Cordero]	9	$6^{\frac{1}{2}}$	6^{1}	$6^{1\frac{1}{2}}$	6^{1}	4^{nk}	13.10
a—Erins Isle [Pincay]	2	$8^{1\frac{1}{2}}$	8^{1}	8^{2}	8^{4}	5^{nk}	2.40
Hush Dear [Vasquez]	6	9^{1}	5^{hd}	4^{hd}	4^{1}	6^{2}	19.90
f—Bold Run [Starkey]	8	$4^{\frac{1}{2}}$	4^{hd}	$5^{\frac{1}{2}}$	5^{hd}	7no	36.60
Muscatite [Fires]	3	5^{1}	7^{hd}	7^{hd}	7^{hd}	$8^{\frac{3}{4}}$	24.00
Trevita [Velasquez]	4	7^{hd}	$11^{1\frac{1}{2}}$	11^{1}	10^{5}	$9^{2\frac{1}{2}}$	38.30
Rossi Gold [Day]	1	$11^{\frac{1}{2}}$	13^{4}	13^{2}	13^{1}	10^{1}	21.90
Be My Native [Piggott]	11	12^{hd}	10^{1}	9^{hd}	$9^{\frac{1}{2}}$	$11^{2\frac{1}{4}}$	17.40
Majesty's Prince [Maple]	12	14	14	14	11^{2}	12^{10}	10.40
a—The Wonder [Shoemaker]	14	13^{4}	$9^{\frac{1}{2}}$	$10^{\frac{1}{2}}$	14	13^{nk}	2.40
f—Noble Player [Cauthen]	10	$10^{\frac{1}{2}}$	$12^{1\frac{1}{2}}$	12^{2}	12^{2}	14	36.60

$2 mutuels paid:

Tolomeo	78.40	33.20	17.00
John Henry		4.80	3.40
Nijinsky's Secret			6.00

Time—:24 2/5, :50 3/5, 1:41 3/5, 2:04 2/5. Winner BC 3 by Lypheor-Almagest by Dike. Owned by Carlo d'Alessio. Trained by Luca M. Cumani. Mutuel pool $845,542. Perfecta pool $229,587.

Perfecta [5-11] $439.20

Handicap; Noble Nashua and Maudlin in the Jerome Handicap; Perfect Remedy in the HITS Parade Invitational Futurity; Fearless Miss in a maiden race at Beulah; I'm Smokin in an allowance race at Santa Anita; Foolish Girl in an allowance race at Hollywood Park; Ballysadare in a maiden race at Hialeah; Spectacular Nashua and Sunny And Clear in a claiming race at Woodbine; Honey Fox in the Black Helen Handicap at Hialeah; J. Burns in an allowance race at Arlington;* Glorious Song in the Beldame Stakes at Belmont; Smile and Pine Tree Lane in the 1986 Breeders' Cup Sprint at Santa Anita; Manila, and the entry of Theatrical, and Estrapade in the 1986 Breeders' Cup Turf at Santa Anita; and the 1978 triple crown winner Affirmed in the Charles H. Strub Stakes at Santa Anita in February 1979.

*Perplext's payoff of $8.20 for show at 10.3–1 was good, but not outstanding. Such long shots are typically overbet to win and here to place as well.

103rd Kentucky Derby, May 7, 1977

$267,200 gross value and $15,000 Gold Cup. Net to winner $214,700; second $30,000; third $15,000; fourth $7,500. 297 nominations.

Horse	Eqt	Wt	PP	¼	½	¾	1	Str	Fin	Jockeys	Owners	Odds to $1
Seattle Slew		126	4	2^{1}	2^{4}	2^{4}	1^{h}	1^{3}	$1^{1\frac{3}{4}}$	J. Cruguet	Karen L. Taylor	.50
Run Dusty Run		126	8	$4^{\frac{1}{2}}$	4^{3}	4^{1}	3^{1}	2^{3}	2^{nk}	D. McHargue	Golden Chance Farm	a-5.50
Sanhedrin	b	126	1	$12^{1\frac{1}{2}}$	10^{1}	12^{2}	8^{2}	$4^{1\frac{1}{2}}$	$3^{3\frac{1}{4}}$	J. Velasquez	Darby Dan Farm	14.60
Get the Axe		126	5	9^{2}	$9^{1\frac{1}{2}}$	9^{h}	9^{h}	7^{2}	4no	W. Shoemaker	Bwamazon Farm	27.90
Steve's Friend	b	126	11	$7^{1\frac{1}{2}}$	$7^{1\frac{1}{2}}$	$5^{1\frac{1}{2}}$	4^{2}	$5^{\frac{1}{2}}$	5no	R. Hernandez	Kinship Stable	29.20
Papelote	b	126	14	$5^{1\frac{1}{2}}$	6^{2}	$8^{1\frac{1}{2}}$	$7^{1\frac{1}{2}}$	6^{2}	$6^{2\frac{1}{4}}$	M. A. Rivera	Marvin L. Warner	f-42.80
Giboulee	b	126	13	12^{2}	$8^{\frac{1}{2}}$	10^{h}	$13^{1\frac{1}{2}}$	$9^{1\frac{1}{2}}$	7^{h}	J. Fell	J. L. Levesque	40.20
For the Moment	b	126	10	$1^{\frac{1}{2}}$	1^{h}	1^{1}	2^{3}	$3^{\frac{1}{2}}$	$8^{\frac{3}{4}}$	A. Cordero, Jr.	Gerald Robins	7.00
Affiliate	b	126	7	$10^{\frac{1}{2}}$	12^{2}	11^{h}	$6^{\frac{1}{2}}$	$8^{\frac{1}{2}}$	$9^{1\frac{3}{4}}$	L. Pincay, Jr.	Harbor View Farm	38.20
Flag Officer		126	6	15	$11^{\frac{1}{2}}$	$13^{\frac{1}{2}}$	10^{1}	$10^{1\frac{1}{2}}$	$10^{\frac{1}{2}}$	L. Ahrens	Nasty Stable	46.90
Bob's Dusty		126	3	3^{3}	3^{5}	3^{2}	5^{2}	12^{2}	11^{nk}	J. C. Espinoza	R. N. Lehmann	a-5.50
Sir Sir		126	2	$6^{\frac{1}{2}}$	5^{1}	6^{2}	12^{2}	11^{h}	12^{2}	J. J. Rodriguez	La Luna Stable	f-42.80
Nostalgia	b	126	15	$13^{1\frac{1}{2}}$	$14^{\frac{1}{2}}$	14^{1}	14^{3}	13^{6}	13^{3}	L. Snyder	W. S. Farish III	40.00
Western Wind		126	9	$14^{1\frac{1}{2}}$	15	15	15	14^{7}	14^{10}	R. Turcotte	J. M. Roebling	31.10
Best Person	b	126	12	8^{3}	$13^{\frac{1}{2}}$	7^{1}	11^{1}	15	15	G. Patterson	W. C. Partee	f-42.80

Time: :23, :45-4/5, 1:10-3/5, 1:36, 2:02-1/5. Track fast. Off at 5:41 EDT. Start good. Won ridden out.

Coupled: a-Run Dusty Run and Bob's Dusty. f-Mutuel field.

$2 mutuels paid—Seattle Slew $3.00 straight, $2.80 place, $2.80 show; Run Dusty Run $3.40 place, $3.20 show; Sanhedrin $4.60 show.

Winner—Dk. b. or br. c, by Bold Reasoning—My Charmer, by Poker, trainer William H. Turner, Jr.; bred in Kentucky by Ben S. Castleman.

SEATTLE SLEW swerved sharply to the outside into GET THE AXE, after failing to break smartly, was rushed to the leaders early placing SIR SIR in slightly close quarters, continuing through tight quarters nearing the end of the opening quarter. SEATTLE SLEW forced his way through moving FLAG OFFICER, AFFILIATE and BOB'S DUSTY out. Continuing in full stride, SEATTLE SLEW engaged FOR THE MOMENT at that point to duel for the lead from the outside to the top of the stretch at which stage he disposed of that one when put to extreme pressure, drew off with a rush and prevailed under intermittent urging. RUN DUSTY RUN broke well to gain a forward position, rallied along the outside on the final turn, continued willingly only to lug in through the closing stages and could not reach the winner. RUN DUSTY RUN survived a claim of foul lodged by the rider of SANHEDRIN for alleged interference in the closing stages. The latter, unhurried early while racing along the inner railing, came out for the drive and finished full of run. GET THE AXE closed some ground in his late bid but could not seriously threaten. STEVE'S FRIEND, unhurried early, moved up gradually along the outside on the second turn to loom boldly a furlong away but lacked a further response. PAPELOTE saved ground to no avail. FOR THE MOMENT, away sharply to make the pace, saved ground while dueling with SEATTLE SLEW to the top of the stretch at which point he succumbed suddenly. FLAG OFFICER was outrun. BOB'S DUSTY showed forwardly for three-quarters and retired. SIR SIR was caught in close quarters after the start.

THE WINNER'S PEDIGREE AND CAREER HIGHLIGHTS

SEATTLE SLEW (Dark Bay or Brown Colt)	Bold Reasoning	Boldnesian	Bold Ruler
			Alanesian
		Reason to Earn	Hail to Reason
			Sailing Home
	My Charmer	Poker	Round Table
			Glamour
		Fair Charmer	Jet Action
			Myrtle Charm

Year	Age	Sts	1st	2nd	3rd	Won
1976	2	3	3	0	0	$ 66,669
1977	3	7	6	0	0	641,370
1978	4	7	5	2	0	473,006
Totals		17	14	2	0	$1,208,726

At 2 Years	WON	Champagne
At 3 Years	WON	Kentucky Derby, Flamingo, Wood, Preakness, Belmont Stakes
	UNP	Swaps
At 4 Years	WON	Marlboro Cup, Woodward, Stuyvesant
	2ND	Patterson, Jockey Club Gold Cup

Blue Grass Stakes

SEVENTH RACE
Keeneland
APRIL 23, 1981

1 ⅛ MILES. (1.47⅗) 57th Running THE BLUE GRASS STAKES (Grade I). $150,000 Added. For 3-year-olds. By subscription of $75 each which shall accompany the nomination, $750 to pass the entry box and $750 additional to start, with $150,000 added (plus $15,000 KTDF), of which 65% of all monies to the owner of the winner, 20% to second, 10% to third, and 5% to fourth. Colts and geldings. Weights: colts and geldings, 121 lbs.; fillies, 116 lbs. In the event the number of starters requires the race to be run in more than one division, it will be drawn in accordance with the rules of racing, and not less than 75% of the added purse will be offered in each division. Starters to be named through the entry box by the usual time of closing. The owner of the winner to receive a gold julep cup. No Supplementary Nominations. (In the event the field exceeds twelve and the race is not divided, the race will start at the eighth pole and finish at the sixteenth pole). Closed with 243 nominations.
Value of race $185,975, value to winner $120,558, second $37,095, third $20,047, fourth $9,274. $13,500 Reverts to the KTDF. Mutuel pool $504,894.

Last Raced	Horse	Eqt	A.Wt	PP	St	¼	½	¾	Str	Fin	Jockey	Odds $1
5Apr81 ^{8}Aqu^{1}	Proud Appeal		3 121	6	3	$1^{1\frac{1}{2}}$	$1^{\frac{1}{2}}$	1^{hd}	1^{2}	1^{3}	Fell J	a-.50
29Mar81 ^{9}FG^{11}	Law Me		3 121	5	7	6^{2}	4^{1}	3^{1}	3^{3}	$2^{\frac{1}{2}}$	Day P	85.60
14Apr81 ^{7}Kee^{3}	Golden Derby		3 121	9	4	2^{1}	$2^{1\frac{1}{2}}$	2^{4}	$2^{2\frac{1}{2}}$	3^{hd}	Espinoza J C	a-.50
28Mar81 ^{9}Hia^{3}	Double Sonic		3 121	3	11	11	10^{hd}	$8^{1\frac{1}{2}}$	$5^{1\frac{1}{2}}$	$4^{1\frac{1}{2}}$	Thornburg B	16.60
29Mar81 ^{9}FG^{3}	Beau Rit	b	3 121	10	6	$7^{1\frac{1}{2}}$	6^{1}	6^{hd}	8^{6}	5^{6}	Rubbicco P	12.10
14Apr81 ^{7}Kee^{2}	Sportin' Life		3 121	2	9	9^{3}	7^{hd}	7^{5}	6^{3}	$6^{8\frac{1}{2}}$	Velasquez J	10.30
14Apr81 ^{7}Kee^{4}	Habano		3 121	4	2	3^{2}	3^{1}	$4^{1\frac{1}{2}}$	7^{2}	7^{2}	McHargue D G	48.10
6Apr81 ^{5}Aqu^{1}	Shahnameh		3 121	1	1	5^{hd}	5^{3}	5^{1}	4^{1}	$8^{2\frac{1}{2}}$	Asmussen C B	45.10
18Mar81 ^{9}Hia^{7}	Cinnamon's Choice		3 121	7	10	10^{hd}	11	11	9^{6}	9^{12}	Brumfield D	5.90
14Apr81 ^{7}Kee^{1}	Swinging Light	b	3 121	8	8	8^{hd}	9^{3}	9^{2}	10^{8}	10^{15}	Delahoussaye D J	9.60
16Apr81 ^{8}Kee^{1}	Bysantine	b	3 121	11	5	$4^{\frac{1}{2}}$	$8^{1\frac{1}{2}}$	10^{hd}	11	11	Delahoussaye E	69.00

a-Coupled: Proud Appeal and Golden Derby.
OFF AT 4:48, EST. Start good, Won ridden out. Time, :23⅘, :47⅘, 1:11⅘, 1:38, 1:51⅘ Track sloppy.

$2 Mutuel Prices:

1-PROUD APPEAL (a-entry)	3.00	3.00	2.80
6-LAW ME		30.00	11.20
1-GOLDEN DERBY (a-entry)	3.00	3.00	2.80

Dk. b. or br. c, by Valid Appeal—Proud N' Happy, by Proudest Roman. Trainer Hough Stanley M. Bred by Camp P & Yowell R (Fla).

PROUD APPEAL, away alertly and quickly in command, made all the pace, shook off a challenge by GOLDEN DERBY approaching the lane, responded to intermittent left-handed urging in upper stretch, ducked out slightly just before the furlong marker and again before the sixteenth pole but was straightened away to increase the margin under a hand ride late. LAW ME, allowed to settle early, rallied with left-handed pressure when set down for the drive and was up to gain the place while no threat to the winner. GOLDEN DERBY prompted the early pace, challenged approaching the lane, could not match the winner and weakened in the final strides. DOUBLE SONIC, devoid of early foot, found best stride late. BEAU RIT had no rally. SPORTIN' LIFE had no speed. HABANO had speed for a half and gave way steadily. SHAHNAMEH never launched a serious bid. CINNAMON'S CHOICE was always far back. SWINGING LIGHT never threatened. BYSANTINE flashed brief foot.

Owners— 1, Winfield M H; 2, Whittaker E; 3, Gaines & Lehmann; 4, Elias F & L; 5, Roussel Carol; 6, Farish W S III; 7, Coello M A; 8, Manhasset Stable; 9, Calumet Farm; 10, Zantker E; 11, Saron Stable.

Trainers— 1, Hough Stanley M; 2, McClain Edward T; 3, Adams William E; 4, Krnjaich George; 5, Roussel Louis III; 6, Carroll Del W; 7, Gonzalez Francisco; 8, Picou James E; 9, Veitch John M; 10, Conway James P; 11, Drysdale Neil.

Scratched—Tap Shoes (28Mar81 ^{9}Hia^{1}).

E. P. Taylor Stakes

NINTH RACE
Woodbine
OCTOBER 17, 1981

1 ¼ MILES.(inner-turf). (2.01⅗) *28th Running E P TAYLOR STAKES (Grade III). $100,000 added. Fillies and Mares. 3-year-olds and up. By subscription of $100 each which shall accompany the nomination and an additional $1,000 when making entry; with $100,000 added, plus all fees to be divided 60% to winner, 20% to second, 11% to third, 6% to fourth and 3% to fifth. 3-year-olds. Weight 118 lbs. (53 1/2 kg); older, 124 lbs. (56 kg) (European Scale). (No Canadian-bred allowances). Final entries to be made through the entry box at the closing time then in effect for overnight events. A trophy will be presented to the winning owner. ($35,000 of this purse has been provided through the Province of Ontario's thoroughbred racing and breeding improvement program). Nominations closed Tuesday, September 8, 1981 with 50 nominations). *Formerly run as the Nettie Stakes.
Value of race $115,000, value to winner $69,000, second $23,000, third $12,650, fourth $6,900, fifth $3,450. Mutuel pool $192,125.

Last Raced	Horse	Eqt	A.Wt	PP	¼	½	¾	1	Str	Fin	Jockey	Odds $1
12Oct81 ^{8}Bel^{1}	De La Rose		3 118	4	$8^{3\frac{1}{2}}$	$8^{2\frac{1}{2}}$	$8^{\frac{1}{2}}$	2^{1}	$1^{3\frac{1}{2}}$	$1^{2\frac{1}{2}}$	Maple E	.30
4Oct81 ^{5}Fra^{13}	Sangue		3 118	7	$6^{1\frac{1}{2}}$	$4^{1\frac{1}{2}}$	4^{hd}	$6^{2\frac{1}{2}}$	2^{2}	2^{2}	Lequeux A	a-6.55
30Sep81 ^{5}Fra^{2}	Sajama		3 118	1	$7^{\frac{1}{2}}$	7^{hd}	9	9	4^{hd}	$3^{1\frac{1}{2}}$	Stahlbaum G	a-6.55
3Oct81 ^{9}WO^{2}	Turnablade		4 124	9	9	9	5^{1}	5^{hd}	$5^{1\frac{1}{2}}$	4^{nk}	Hosang G	b-5.90
3Oct81 ^{9}WO^{3}	Lady Face		3 118	2	4^{2}	3^{hd}	6^{hd}	7^{hd}	6^{hd}	$5^{1\frac{1}{2}}$	Penna D	25.55
31Aug81 ^{4}Eng^{2}	Viendra		3 118	6	3^{hd}	5^{hd}	7^{1}	$8^{\frac{1}{2}}$	8^{1}	6^{1}	Swatuk B	24.90
10Oct81 ^{9}WO^{6}	Regent Miss		3 118	8	5^{hd}	6^{1}	2^{hd}	$4^{\frac{1}{2}}$	9	7no	Grubb R	30.65
3Oct81 ^{9}WO^{4}	Suave Princess		3 118	5	1^{hd}	$2^{1\frac{1}{2}}$	3^{1}	$3^{\frac{1}{2}}$	$7^{\frac{1}{2}}$	8^{hd}	Dennie D	b-5.90
2Oct81 ^{6}Med^{2}	Fair Davina		5 124	3	2^{2}	1^{hd}	$1^{\frac{1}{2}}$	1^{hd}	$3^{\frac{1}{2}}$	9	Beckon D	12.80

a-Coupled: Sangue and Sajama; b-Turnablade and Suave Princess.
OFF AT 5:01 EDT. Start good, Won handily. Time, :25⅘, :49⅘, 1:15⅘, 1:41⅕, 2:05⅘ Course firm.

$2 Mutuel Prices:

5-DE LA ROSE	2.60	2.30	2.50
1-SANGUE (a-entry)		3.60	5.80
1-SAJAMA (a-entry)		3.60	5.80

B. f, by Nijinsky II—Rosetta Stone, by Round Table. Trainer Stephens Woodford C. Bred by Miller & West Mr-Mrs R S (Ky).

Owners— 1, DeKwiatkowski H; 2, Nahas N; 3, Nahas N; 4, Sikura J; 5, Hyde E G; 6, Sangster R E; 7, Whispering Hills; 8, Sikura J; 9, Irish Acres Farm.

Trainers— 1, Stephens Woodford C; 2, Zilber Maurice; 3, Zilber Maurice; 4, Mattine T; 5, Merrill Frank H; 6, Hills Barry W; 7, Nemett G S; 8, Allain Emile M; 9, Hickey P Noel.

Scratched—Condessa (4Oct81 ^{4}Fra^{10}).

SECOND RACE
River Downs
APRIL 25, 1983

6 FURLONGS. (1.08⅗) CLAIMING. Purse $2,800. 3-year-olds and upward which have not won three races in 1982–83. Weight, 3-year-olds, 111 lbs.; older, 124 lbs. Non-winners of two races in 1983 allowed 3 lbs.; a race in 1983, 6 lbs. Claiming price $3,000.
Value of race $2,800, value to winner $1,680, second $560, third $280, fourth $140, fifth $84, sixths $28 each. Mutuel pool $17,013. Quinella pool $14,135.

Last Raced	Horse	Eqt	A.Wt	PP	St	¼	½	Str	Fin	Jockey	Cl'g Pr	Odds $1
16Apr83 ^{7}Beu^{7}	Big Hock	b	8 116	7	1	$2^{\frac{1}{2}}$	2^{3}	1^{5}	1^{10}	Neff S	3000	8.30
25Mar83 ^{2}OP^{12}	Harry Caray		7 116	8	5	6^{1}	$7^{\frac{1}{2}}$	$5^{\frac{1}{2}}$	2no	Ouzts P W	3000	1.10
16Mar83 ^{7}Lat^{9}	Market Bagger		9 116	3	9	8^{1}	$8^{\frac{1}{2}}$	6^{1}	3^{1}	Henson J R	3000	5.60
30Dec82 ^{6}Lat^{10}	Joey R. Boy		5 116	1	8	$7^{1\frac{1}{2}}$	5^{1}	$3^{1\frac{1}{2}}$	$4^{1\frac{1}{2}}$	Henry W T	3000	13.40
10Mar83 ^{6}Lat^{9}	Red Mirage	b	9 116	12	4	3^{hd}	3^{1}	7^{2}	$5^{\frac{1}{2}}$	Arnold M W	3000	45.40
7Apr83 ^{2}Beu^{4}	[DH]In My Prime		6 116	5	2	$1^{2\frac{1}{2}}$	1^{1}	2^{1}	6	Matias R R	3000	19.00
9Apr83 ^{1}Beu^{3}	[DH]Bad Billy		9 111	6	12	12	11^{2}	9^{4}	$6^{1\frac{1}{2}}$	Wade R M Jr^{5}	3000	4.70
2Apr83 ^{10}Lat^{6}	Money Layne		5 116	2	7	$4^{1\frac{1}{2}}$	4^{hd}	4^{hd}	8no	Crews W	3000	17.40
29Mar83 ^{4}Lat^{4}	Reconvene		6 116	10	6	9^{5}	9^{5}	$8^{\frac{1}{2}}$	$9^{4\frac{1}{2}}$	Marte I	3000	12.90
31Mar83 ^{2}Lat^{11}	Hurrian's Blizzard		5 116	4	10	10^{hd}	10^{hd}	11^{4}	$10^{\frac{1}{2}}$	Costa A J	3000	41.10
29Mar83 ^{3}Lat^{8}	Edward Norman		5 116	11	3	5^{hd}	6^{hd}	10^{3}	$11^{3\frac{1}{2}}$	Adkins R M	3000	80.80
14Apr83 ^{9}Beu^{7}	Mr. Hurry	b	7 116	9	11	11^{1}	12	12	12	Eyerman M J	3000	68.90

[DH]—Dead heat.
OFF AT 2:29. Start good. Won ridden out. Time, :22⅘, :47⅕, 1:13⅘ Track fast.

$2 Mutuel Prices:

7-BIG HOCK	18.60	7.00	5.60
8-HARRY CARAY		3.00	3.60
3-MARKET BAGGER			5.80

$3 QUINELLA (7–8) PAID $17.40.

B. h, by Caribbean Line—Lotta Rhythm, by Rhymiss. Trainer Arnold Lee C. Bred by Olsen S (Ky).

BIG HOCK raced close up early, came outside of IN MY PRIME to gain a clear lead entering the stretch, then increased his margin through the drive while ridden out. HARRY CARAY outsprinted early rallied along the inside to gain the place but did not menace. MARKET BAGGER improved his position but did not menace. JOEY R. BOY saved ground but did not threaten. IN MY PRIME and BAD BILLY finished in a dead heat for sixth.

Owners— 1, Arnold L C; 2, Danner W J; 3, Dykema C C; 4, Piepmeyer Deborah; 5, Yinger Marti & A; 6, Edwards W H; 7, Neil R; 8, Carr D; 9, Davis Jr & Held; 10, Bauer G; 11, Norman E R Jr; 12, Eyerman L J.

Harry Caray was claimed by Isaacs G; trainer, Isaacs George.

Scratched—Cathy's Good Taste (13Apr83 ^{9}Beu^{7}); Wild and Wooley (6Apr83 ^{3}Lat^{7}); Bo's Brick (6Apr83 ^{9}Beu^{8}); Lil Kicker (18Mar83 ^{4}Tam^{8}).

Bougainvillea Handicap
(2nd Division)

TENTH RACE
Hialeah Park
APRIL 9, 1983

1 ⅛ MILES.(turf). (1.51⅗) 38th Running BOUGAINVILLEA HANDICAP (2nd Div) (Grade II). $40,000 Added. 3–year–olds and upward. By subscription of $150 each, which shall accompany the nomination, $750 to pass the entry box, Starters to pay $750 additional with $40,000 added. The added money and all fees to be divided 60% to the winner, 20% to second, 11% to third, 6% to fourth and 3% to fifth. Weights: Monday, April 4, 1983. Starters to be named through the entry box by the usual time of closing. Trophy to winning owner. Closed with 52 nominations.
Value of race $64,900, value to winner $38,940, second $12,980, third $7,139, fourth $3,894, fifth $1,947. Mutuel pool $105,499. Perfecta Pool $91,448.

Last Raced	Horse	Eqt.	A.	Wt	PP	St	¼	½	¾	Str	Fin	Jockey	Odds $1
30Mar83 ^{7}Hia^{1}	Lamerok	b	4	118	10	5	2½	2½	2^{1}	1^{hd}	1^{1}	Vasquez J	1.50
21Mar83 ^{7}Hia^{2}	Fray Star		5	112	11	9	5½	4^{hd}	4^{hd}	3^{1}	$2^{2½}$	Santiago J A	25.90
7Mar83 ^{9}GP^{2}	Tonzarun		5	110	6	7	4^{2}	$3^{1½}$	3½	$7^{2½}$	3^{hd}	Soto S B	21.40
21Mar83 ^{7}Hia^{10}	Pin Puller	b	4	110	12	14	14	14	13½	9½	4no	Velez J A Jr	11.80
7Mar83 ^{9}GP^{3}	Dhausli		6	114	2	2	6^{3}	5½	$5^{1½}$	5½	5no	St Leon G	20.00
21Mar83 ^{7}Hia^{3}	Gleaming Channel	b	5	113	14	8	1^{2}	1^{4}	1½	$2^{3½}$	6^{hd}	Fann B	19.10
21Mar83 ^{9}Hia^{4}	[DH]Reimbursement	b	4	110	4	1	$13^{1½}$	13^{3}	8½	4^{hd}	7	Smith A Jr	10.30
21Mar83 ^{9}Hia^{8}	[DH]Hail Victorious	b	4	110	1	3	9½	$10^{1½}$	9^{hd}	6^{hd}	7^{2}	Pennisi F A	f-28.10
21Mar83 ^{7}Hia^{7}	Nihoa		4	109	7	4	$8^{1½}$	$7^{1½}$	7^{2}	8½	9½	Samyn J L	20.80
14Mar83 ^{8}Hia^{1}	Unknown Lady		4	113	13	12	$12^{1½}$	11^{hd}	11^{1}	10^{3}	10^{2}	Perret C	3.00
7Mar83 ^{9}GP^{10}	Current Blade	b	5	114	5	13	$11^{1½}$	12^{1}	14	11^{hd}	11½	Bailey J D	16.50
21Mar83 ^{9}Hia^{3}	Sabr Ayoub		4	111	9	11	10½	9^{hd}	12^{3}	12^{6}	12^{6}	Hernandez C	9.20
26Mar83 ^{9}Hia^{3}	Irish Pete		4	112	3	6	3½	6^{5}	$6^{1½}$	13^{3}	13^{2}	Fires E	f-28.10
15Mar83 ^{3}Hia^{5}	Pimpont		6	108	8	10	7^{hd}	8^{2}	10^{hd}	14	14	Shelton R L	f-28.10

[DH]—Dead heat.
f—Mutuel field.

OFF AT 5:52. Start good, Won driving. Time, 1:53 Course firm.

$2 Mutuel Prices:			
7–LAMEROK	5.00	3.80	3.80
8–FRAY STAR		12.40	11.00
4–TONZARUN			10.60

$2 PERFECTA 7–8 PAID $69.60.

B. c, by Round Table—Flying Buttress, by Exclusive Native. Trainer Jolley Leroy. Bred by Brant P M (Ky).

LAMEROK was unhurried when outrun early, joined GLEAMING CHANNEL on the second turn, gained the advantage in midstretch, opened a clear lead and proved best. FRAY STAR raced forwardly between horses and was gaining on the winner at the finish. TONZARUN a factor from the outset, was shuffled back at the head of the stretch, then was gaining slowly at the finish. PIN PULLER was outrun to the head of the stretch, then finished with good energy along the outside. DHAUSLI well-placed continued on well to the finish. GLEAMING CHANNEL quickly sprinted clear, but weakened inside the final eighth. REIMBURSEMENT moved up steadily to reach contention in midstretch, but hung late to finish in a dead-head with HAIL VICTORIOUS. The latter raced along the outside and finished on even terms with REIMBURSEMENT. NIHOA lacked a closing response. UNKNOWN LADY failed to be a serious threat. CURRENT BLADE was outrun. SABR AYOUB was finished after a half. IRISH PETE was a factor for six-furlongs, then gave way. PIMPONT had some early speed.

Owners— 1, Brant P M; 2, Bucare & Stelcar Stables Inc; 3, Everett Don; 4, Heardsdale; 5, Gleis & Grod; 6, Centennial Farms; 7, Glusman Stables; 8, Allen H; 9, Polk A F; 10, Helman O; 11, Buckland Farm; 12, Moubarak A; 13, Drinkhouse M F; 14, Luro Frances W.

Overweight: Fray Star 1 pound; Tonzarun 1; Dhausli 2; Hail Victorious 4; Unknown Lady 4; Irish Pete 5.

Jerome Handicap

EIGHTH RACE
Belmont
AUGUST 29, 1981

1 MILE. (1.33⅘) 112th Running JEROME HANDICAP (Grade II). $100,000 added. To be run Saturday, August 29, 1981. 3–year–olds. By subscription of $200 each which should accompany the nomination; $800 to pass the entry box, with $100,000 added. The added money and all fees to be divided 60% to winner, 22% to second, 12% to third and 6% to fourth. Weights Monday, August 24. Starters to be named at the closing time of entries. Trophies will be presented to the winning owner, trainer and jockey and mementos to the grooms of the first four finishers. Nominations close Wednesday, August 12, 1981. Closed with 27 nominations.
Value of race $115,000, value to winner $69,000, second $25,300, third $13,800, fourth $6,900. OTB pool $364,582.

Last Raced	Horse	Eqt.	A.	Wt	PP	St	¼	½	¾	Str	Fin	Jockey	Odds $1
15Aug81 ^{8}Sar^{4}	Noble Nashua		3	120	3	8	$8^{1½}$	5½	3^{2}	2^{4}	$1^{3½}$	Asmussen C B	3.10
2Aug81 ^{5}Sar^{1}	Maudlin		3	112	7	3	1½	$1^{1½}$	$1^{1½}$	1½	$2^{3½}$	Cordero A Jr	3.90
15Aug81 ^{1}Sar^{4}	Sing Sing	b	3	109	9	11	11	11	7^{hd}	6^{2}	$3^{1½}$	Venezia M	62.10
14Aug81 ^{7}Sar^{1}	Red Wing Prince		3	107	2	6	4½	8^{2}	5^{2}	4^{hd}	$4^{1½}$	Credidio A Jr	24.10
19Jly81 ^{8}Bel^{2}	Proud Appeal		3	126	8	9	5½	3^{hd}	$4^{1½}$	5^{hd}	5^{1}	Fell J	2.20
9Aug81 ^{6}Sar^{2}	Pass The Tab		3	113	10	1	3^{1}	$2^{1½}$	$2^{1½}$	3^{3}	6¾	Vasquez J	13.20
15Aug81 ^{8}Sar^{1}	Willow Hour		3	123	4	4	6½	6^{hd}	6^{hd}	8^{3}	7^{hd}	Maple E	7.10
2Aug81 ^{8}Sar^{3}	Silver Supreme	b	3	114	5	10	10^{4}	9^{1}	8^{4}	7^{hd}	8^{3}	Migliore R	19.60
15Aug81 ^{8}Sar^{7}	Lemhi Gold		3	117	11	2	$9^{1½}$	10^{1}	9^{1}	9^{8}	9^{11}	Velasquez J	11.60
15Aug81 ^{1}Sar^{6}	Swinging Light	b	3	111	6	7	7^{1}	7½	11	11	10^{1}	Martens G	82.90
15Aug81 ^{1}Sar^{1}	Face the Moment		3	112	1	5	2^{1}	4^{1}	10^{3}	10½	11	MacBeth D	27.10

OFF AT 5:04, EDT. Start good, Won ridden out. Time, :22⅗, :44⅘, 1:08⅖, 1:33⅕ Track fast.
New track record.

$2 Mutuel Prices:			
3–(C)–NOBLE NASHUA	8.20	4.20	4.40
7–(G)–MAUDLIN		5.20	5.60
10–(J)–SING SING			13.80

Dk. b. or br. c, by Nashua—Noble Lady, by Vaguely Noble. Trainer Martin Jose. Bred by Grousemont Farm (Ky).

Owners— 1, Flying Zee Stable; 2, Tartan Stable; 3, Sugartown Stable; 4, Daybreak Farm; 5, Meadow Bay Stable; 6, Villareal L; 7, Schott Marcia W; 8, Berry M; 9, Jones Aaron U; 10, Zantker E; 11, Mangurian H T Jr.

Trainers— 1, Martin Jose; 2, Nerud Jan H; 3, Nickerson Victor J; 4, Fernandez Floreano; 5, Hough Stanley M; 6, Barrera Albert S; 7, Picou James E; 8, DeStasio Richard T; 9, Barrera Lazaro S; 10, Conway James P; 11, Root Thomas F Jr.

Overweight: Maudlin 4 pounds; Swinging Light 3.

Scratched—Master Tommy (17Aug81 ^{10}Wat^{2}).

HITS Parade Invitational Futurity

NINTH RACE
Fair Grounds
DECEMBER 26, 1981

6 FURLONGS. (1.09) 2nd Running HITS PARADE INVITATIONAL FUTURITY. $100,000 Guaranteed. For foals of 1979 auctioned off at the Hits Parade Invitational Two-Year Olds In Training Sale of April 26, 1981. Weight, Fillies 117 lbs. Colts and Geldings 120 lbs. Winners of $50,000 or more to carry 3 lbs. additional. Non-winners of a stakes allowed 3 lbs. Non-winners of two races allowed 5 lbs. Maidens allowed 7 lbs. No apprentice allowance. No supplemental nominations. Those Fillies, having paid all nomination, sustaining, qualifying and entry fees to the Hits Parade Invitational Futurity, have the option of paying a $50 nomination fee and running in a $25,000 Added Filly Hits Parade Invitational Futurity.
Value of race $119,020, value to winner $71,412, second $23,804, third $13,092, fourth $7,141, fifth $3,571. Mutuel pool $111,964. Exacta Pool $134,645.

Last Raced	Horse	Eqt.	A.Wt	PP	St	¼	½	Str	Fin	Jockey	Odds $1
17Dec81 ^{8}FG^{4}	Real Dare		2 113	11	6	2^{hd}	$1^{1½}$	1^{6}	1^{13}	Franklin R J	b-4.50
17Dec81 ^{4}FG^{1}	Perfect Remedy	b	2 115	3	4	5^{hd}	$3^{1½}$	3^{4}	2^{5}	Ardoin R	.90
17Dec81 ^{6}FG^{1}	Kin of Kingley	b	2 117	7	7	1^{hd}	2^{3}	2^{hd}	$3^{1½}$	Patin B C	17.70
17Dec81 ^{8}FG^{3}	To Tall Tara		2 114	5	8	$10^{½}$	9^{2}	6^{4}	4^{hd}	Copling D	12.60
17Dec81 ^{4}FG^{5}	Native Ben		2 115	12	11	$9^{1½}$	8^{hd}	$4^{½}$	5no	Frazier R L	33.00
17Dec81 ^{8}FG^{2}	Miss Pro Teen	b	2 114	2	9	6^{hd}	6^{hd}	5^{hd}	6^{4}	Guidry R D	7.90
17Dec81 ^{4}FG^{6}	Positive Dream		2 113	13	14	$12^{½}$	$11^{1½}$	$8^{1½}$	$7^{1½}$	Breen R	b-4.50
17Dec81 ^{4}FG^{4}	Caesar's Conquest		2 113	14	1	13^{6}	13^{4}	9^{3}	8^{2}	Gell V D	a-50.60
17Dec81 ^{4}FG^{2}	Quebec Dancer		2 115	4	5	$7^{½}$	5^{hd}	7^{hd}	$9^{1½}$	Romero R P	11.40
17Dec81 ^{4}FG^{3}	Stiletto		2 115	10	2	3^{hd}	7^{hd}	10^{2}	$10^{2½}$	Herrera C	32.10
17Dec81 ^{6}FG^{4}	Steve Mission	b	2 115	8	10	8^{1}	12^{hd}	11^{1}	11^{1}	Munster L	9.00
17Dec81 ^{6}FG^{2}	Lil Billy Boy	b	2 115	6	12	11^{hd}	10^{hd}	$12^{1½}$	$12^{1½}$	Barbazon D S	54.50
17Dec81 ^{8}FG^{5}	Royce's Pride		2 113	1	3	$4^{1½}$	4^{hd}	13^{hd}	13^{nk}	Barrow T	a-50.60
17Dec81 ^{8}FG^{6}	City Judge		2 115	9	13	14	14	14	14	Guajardo A	133.00

a-Coupled: Caesar's Conquest and Royce's Pride; b-Real Dare and Positive Dream.
OFF AT 4:36 CST. Start good, Won easily. Time, :22⅖, :46, 1:11⅖ Track fast.

$3 Mutuel Prices:				
	2-REAL DARE (b-entry)	16.50	7.80	6.90
	4-PERFECT REMEDY		5.10	5.10
	8-KIN OF KINGLEY			11.10

$3 EXACTA 2-4 PAID $51.90.

B. g, by Beau Groton—Big Dare, by Kentucky Pride. Trainer Dorignac J P III. Bred by Dorignac J P Jr (La).

Owners— 1, Dorignac J P Jr; 2, Franks J; 3, Robert R J; 4, Huffman D; 5, Rollins B; 6, Williams A; 7, Dorignac Margaret; 8, Bader Paula; 9, Trotter W E II; 10, Broussard J E; 11, Faldon M L; 12, Roberts M; 13, Bader Paule; 14, Roberts R F.

Trainers— 1, Dorignac J P III; 2, Marshall Louis G; 3, Calais Ralph; 4, Huffman Don; 5, Gelpi David A; 6, Mabry John C; 7, Dorignac J P III; 8, Fox William I; 9, McKean Clyde Sr; 10, Broussard Joseph E; 11, Dettwiller Dan; 12, Alleman Joe; 13, Fox William I; 14, Alleman Joseph.

Overweight: Stiletto 2 pounds.

Scratched—Knight of Truth (17Dec81 ^{8}FG^{7}).

SECOND RACE
Beulah
APRIL 27, 1983

6 FURLONGS. (1.09⅘) MAIDEN. SPECIAL WEIGHT. Purse $5,400 (includes $2,000 from the OTF). Fillies. 3 and 4-year-olds, Ohio-bred. Weight, 3-year-olds, 112 lbs.; 4-year-olds, 122 lbs.
Value of race $5,400, value to winner $3,240, second $1,080, third $540, fourth $270, fifth $162, sixth $108. Mutuel pool $14,772. Quinella Pool $15.103.

Last Raced	Horse	Eqt.	A.Wt	PP	St	¼	½	Str	Fin	Jockey	Odds $1
	Fearless Miss		4 122	5	5	$2^{2½}$	1^{hd}	1^{1}	$1^{4½}$	Matias R R	2.20
13Dec82 ^{9}Tdn^{8}	Alice Sugar		3 114	9	1	1^{hd}	2^{5}	2^{5}	2^{7}	Gehri D L	6.60
	She's My Partner		3 114	8	9	$6^{1½}$	4^{hd}	3^{2}	3^{4}	Sosa R	17.50
20Apr83 ^{3}Beu^{4}	Papila Fair		3 116	11	8	7^{hd}	6^{1}	6^{1}	$4^{3½}$	Rice D R Jr	12.10
20Apr83 ^{3}Beu^{3}	Victoria Velvet		3 114	2	10	8^{3}	8^{4}	$7^{2½}$	$5^{½}$	Perrotta M	3.10
20Apr83 ^{3}Beu^{6}	Blinda	b	3 114	6	6	4^{1}	5^{3}	4^{2}	6^{4}	Jimenez M A	42.70
	Rullah Mae	b	3 118	4	7	$5^{½}$	$7^{½}$	8^{3}	7^{1}	Lang D D	4.00
13Apr83 ^{2}Beu^{8}	Enthusiastic Lady		3 112	7	4	3^{hd}	3^{hd}	5^{hd}	$8^{2½}$	Delaura K A	6.50
13Apr83 ^{2}Beu^{9}	Bold Nova		3 114	3	12	12	12	10^{5}	$9^{2½}$	Diehl C	96.30
20Apr83 ^{3}Beu^{7}	Mojo Work'n		3 114	12	3	10^{3}	9^{1}	$9^{½}$	10^{5}	Alicea M	64.90
20Apr83 ^{3}Beu^{10}	Evermoor		3 113	1	11	11^{hd}	11^{hd}	$11^{1½}$	11^{2}	Spickard M A	48.50
20Apr83 ^{3}Beu^{11}	Bell Dawn		3 112	10	2	$9^{1½}$	$10^{½}$	12	12	Schwing C	60.70

OFF AT 2:27. Start good. Won ridden out. Time, :22⅖, :46⅘, 1:12⅘ Track fast.

$2 Mutuel Prices:				
	5-FEARLESS MISS	6.40	3.40	3.60
	9-ALICE SUGAR		6.40	5.00
	8-SHE'S MY PARTNER			6.80

$3 QUINELLA (5-9) PAID $40.50.

Ch. f, by Bold Gun—Gala Lege, by Johns Joy. Trainer Cook Robert L. Bred by Green Meadows Farm (Ohio).

FEARLESS MISS was bumped leaving the gate then drove up to prompted the early pacesetter from the outside, took over near the stretch, and drew off in the final furlong under mild urging. ALICE SUGAR sprinted clear from the gate and angled to the rail, continued well into the midstretch, but could not match the winner late. SHE'S MY PARTNER was best of the rest. VICTORIA VELVET was bumped leaving the gate. RULLAH MAE was bumped into the winner leaving the gate. ENTHUSIASTIC LADY was finished early. BOLD NOVA broke out sharply then came in.

Owners— 1, Ryper & Routsong; 2, Sugar J J; 3, Gutheil P A; 4, Miller D L; 5, Sheets M E; 6, Horn, Harmon & McGregor; 7, Slaughter R Jr; 8, Winning Way Farm; 9, Williams J Sr; 10, Wolfe Lavaunne; 11, Group Evermore; 12, McGinnis Esther.

Overweight: Alice Sugar 2 pounds; She's My Partner 2; Papila Fair 4; Victoria Velvet 2; Blinda 2; Rullah Mae 6; Bold Nova 2; Mojo Work'n 2; Evermoor 1.

Scratched—Unruffled Sail (28Oct82 ^{3}Beu^{11}); Anarctic Queen; Gin and Boogie (22Dec82 ^{3}Lat^{5}); Lynda's Babe (17Apr83 ^{2}Beu^{12}).

SANTA ANITA PARK, NOVEMBER 1, 1982

5730—FIFTH RACE. Six furlongs. Classified allowance. 3-year-olds & up. Purse $34,000.

3490	Mr. Prime Minister, Vinzla	117	4	6	$3^{1/2}$	$3^{2 1/2}$	-	$3^{2 1/2}$	1no	5.70
3689	I'm Smokin, Shoemaker	117	3	4	$2^{2 1/2}$	1^{hd}	-	1^{1}	2^{nk}	1.50
5651	Stand Pat, Hansen	114	2	9	9	9	-	$8^{1 1/2}$	$3^{3/4}$	31.90
1133	Murrtheblurr, Harris	115	7	2	1^{hd}	$2^{2 1/2}$	-	$2^{2 1/2}$	$4^{3/4}$	13.60
5651	Double Discount, Castaneda	115	5	5	6^{2}	$6^{1 1/2}$	-	$5^{1/2}$	5no	3.80
1008	Priority, Pincay	117	9	1	4^{hd}	4^{1}	-	4^{hd}	$6^{1 1/2}$	7.30
1689	Kangroo Court, Steiner	x109	1	7	$8^{1 1/2}$	8^{2}	-	$6^{1/2}$	7^{nk}	40.20
3063	Egg Toss, Winland	x109	6	8	$7^{1 1/2}$	7^{1}	-	7^{hd}	$8^{3 1/2}$	5.50
3751	Foyt's Ack, McHargue	116	8	3	$5^{1 1/2}$	$5^{1/2}$	-	9	9	22.50

No scratches

MR. PRIME MINISTER	**13.40**	**6.40**	**5.60**
I'M SMOKIN		**3.20**	**3.60**
STAND PAT			**10.40**

Time—:21 3/5, :43 4/5, :56, 1:08 4/5. Winner—b.g.5. Command Module—Janet Dear. Trained by M. Millerick. Mutuel pool $230,757. Exacta pool $480,359.

$5 EXACTA (4-3) PAID $125.00

HOLLYWOOD PARK, NOVEMBER 21, 1982

6075—THIRD RACE. Mile and one-sixteenth. 3-year-olds & up, fillies & mares. Allowance. Purse $22,000.

Index	Horse and jockey—	Wt.	PP.	ST.	¼	½	¾	Str.	Fin.	To $1
5784	Foolish Girl, Castaneda	114	7	5	4^{2}	3^{hd}	3^{1}	1^{1}	$1^{2 1/2}$	2.00
5784	Dazzlingly, McCarron	116	4	3	2^{hd}	2^{1}	2^{1}	2^{2}	2^{5}	3.60
5784	Joan's Lady, Delahoussaye	116	8	6	6^{1}	6^{1}	4^{hd}	$3^{1/2}$	$3^{2 1/2}$	11.70
5784	Delightedly, Hawley	116	2	7	$5^{1/2}$	5^{2}	$6^{3 1/2}$	5^{3}	4^{1}	1.10
5511	Jewel's Charity, Ortega	113	6	2	$1^{3 1/2}$	1^{3}	$1^{1/2}$	$4^{2 1/2}$	5^{3}	54.70
5608	Petite Maid, Sibille	115	5	8	8	8	7^{2}	$6^{1/2}$	6^{1}	37.30
5707	A Star Attraction, Pierce	115	3	1	3^{2}	$4^{2 1/2}$	$5^{1/2}$	7^{3}	$7^{2 1/2}$	30.70
5773	Ocean Sunset, Campas	115	1	4	7^{1}	7^{hd}	8	8	8	65.50

No scratches.

FOOLISH GIRL	**6.00**	**3.40**	**4.20**
DAZZINGLY		**4.60**	**4.20**
JOAN'S LADY			**5.00**

Time—:23, :46 4/5, 1:12, 1:37, 1:43 2/5. Winner—ch.f. Foolish Pleasure—Millie Ouis. Trained by G. Jones. Mutuel pool $213,470. Exacta pool $339,865.

HIALEAH PARK
TUESDAY, APRIL 26, 1983

WEATHER CLEAR.. TRACK HARD.

10th Hia— About 1 1/16 Miles. Turf. 3 & 4-Year-Olds. Maidens Claiming ($32,000 to $28,000). Purse $8,500. Value to winner $5,100.

2-Ballysadare(Cruguet J 113)	11.40	4.20	5.40
11-Jubilance(Alvarado V 113)		3.20	2.40
10-Marechal Neigh(Fires E 113)			4.40

$2 PERFECTA 2-11 PAID $112.60. $2 TRIFECTA 2-11-10 PAID $865.60.

Time, 1:43. Course Hard. Off at 5:32.

Also ran—Boston Broker, Black And Blue, Proud And Crafty, Utopia Grey, Erd The Third, Friendly Bet, Elton's Song, Charlie's Mercedes and Derby Dream.

4th Race Woodbine Jun. 11, 1980

5 FURLONGS. (.57⅘) 2-Year-Olds, Fillies, Bred in Can. Claiming ($16,000 to $14,000). Purse $5,200. —Canada-bred — Value of race $5,200, value to winner $3,120, second $1,040, third $572, fourth $312, fifth $156. Mutuel pool $39,289. Exactor Pool $71,713.

Last Raced	Horse	Wt.	PP.	⅜	Str	Fin	Odds $1
	SpectacularNashu	117	1	1^{hd}	1^{2}	1^{2}	2.00
29May80 ^{2}WO^{3}	Sunny And Clear	117	2	2^{hd}	2^{hd}	$2\frac{1}{2}$	1.50
29May80 ^{2}WO^{5}	TwentyThreeSouth	114	8	3^{3}	3^{3}	$3\frac{3}{4}$	b-13.40
	Elegant Display	112	4	$6^{2\frac{1}{2}}$	4^{hd}	$4\frac{1}{2}$	a-5.85
4Jun80 ^{1}WO^{3}	Run Sheba	111	6	4^{hd}	5^{4}	5^{3}	10.20
29May80 ^{2}WO^{4}	Suspicious Rose	112	7	7^{hd}	7^{8}	$6^{1\frac{1}{2}}$	a-5.85
4Jun80 ^{1}WO^{2}	Zulu Princess	117	3	5^{hd}	6^{1}	7^{8}	4.70
29May80 ^{2}WO^{6}	Brownie T.	114	5	8	8	8	b-13.40

a-Coupled: Elegant Display and Suspicious Rose; b-Twenty Three South and Brownie T..

Time, :23⅗, :48, 1:01⅗ Track fast. OFF AT 2:48 EDT.

3-SPECTACULAR NASHUA	6.00	2.80	3.40
4-SUNNY AND CLEAR		2.50	2.60
2-TWENTY THREE SOUTH (b-entry)			4.30

$2 EXACTOR 3-4 PAID $20.10.

Black Helen Handicap

NINTH RACE
Hialeah Park
MARCH 5, 1982

1 ⅛ MILES.(turf). (1.45⅗) 40th Running BLACK HELEN HANDICAP (Grade II) $100,000 added. Fillies and Mares. 3-year-olds and up. By subscription of $200 each, which shall accompany the nomination, $1,000 to pass the entry box, starters to pay $1,000 additional with $100,000 added. The added money and all fees to be divided 60% to the winner, 22% to second, 11% to third, 5% to fourth and 2% to fifth. Weights Saturday, Feb. 27, 1982. Starters to be named through the entry box by the usual time of closing. Trophy to winning owner. Nominations closed Fri., Feb. 19, 1982. Closed with 24 nominations.

Value of race $121,800, value to winner $73,080, second $26,796, third $13,398, fourth $6,090, fifth $2,436. Mutuel pool $100.276. Perfecta Pool $120.050.

Last Raced	Horse	Eqt.	A.	Wt	PP	St	¼	½	¾	Str	Fin	Jockey	Odds $1
15Feb82 ^{9}Hia^{1}	Honey Fox		5	123	1	5	$5^{1\frac{1}{2}}$	$4\frac{1}{2}$	$4\frac{1}{2}$	3^{3}	$1\frac{3}{4}$	Samyn J L	1.80
15Feb82 ^{9}Hia^{5}	Endicotta		6	113	4	3	$1^{1\frac{1}{2}}$	$1^{1\frac{1}{2}}$	$1^{1\frac{1}{2}}$	2^{hd}	$2^{1\frac{1}{4}}$	Fires E	40.30
15Feb82 ^{9}Hia^{3}	Shark Song		4	112	2	1	2^{4}	$2^{1\frac{1}{2}}$	2^{3}	$1\frac{1}{2}$	$3\frac{1}{2}$	Migliore R	14.00
15Feb82 ^{9}Hia^{2}	De La Rose		4	124	3	8	7^{3}	7^{6}	6^{3}	$4\frac{1}{2}$	$4^{2\frac{1}{2}}$	Maple E	.60
15Feb82 ^{9}Hia^{4}	Wings of Grace		4	112	6	2	3^{2}	3^{2}	3^{hd}	$5^{1\frac{1}{2}}$	5no	Velasquez J	18.00
16Feb82 ^{8}Hia^{1}	Anti Lib		4	114	5	4	4^{1}	$5\frac{1}{2}$	5^{1}	6^{6}	6^{4}	Vasquez J	11.30
26Feb82 ^{8}Hia^{3}	Friendly Frolic	b	5	109	7	6	8	8	8	8	$7\frac{1}{2}$	Espinoza J C	118.20
15Feb82 ^{9}Hia^{6}	Lady Face	b	4	111	8	7	6^{2}	6^{1}	7^{5}	7^{1}	8	Penna D	73.10

OFF AT 5:12 Start Good, Won driving. Time, 1:47 Course firm.

$2 Mutuel Prices:

1-HONEY FOX	5.60	4.00	7.00
4-ENDICOTTA		14.80	12.60
2-SHARK SONG			15.00

$2 PERFECTA 1–4 PAID $116.80.

B. m, by Minnesota Mac—War Sparkler, by Fort Salonga. Trainer Schulhofer Flint S. Bred by Hartigan J H (Fla).

Owners— 1, Torsney J M; 2, Asbury T; 3, Tikkoo R N; 4, de Kwiatkowski H; 5, Darby Dan Farm; 6, Pen-Y-Bryn Farm; 7, Cashman Mary Lou; 8, Hyde E G.

Trainers— 1, Schulhofer Flint S; 2, Rieser Stanley M; 3, Howe Peter M; 4, Stephens Woodford C; 5, Rondinello Thomas L; 6, Whiteley David A; 7, Vanier Harvey L; 8, Merrill Frank H.

Scratched—Blue Wind (20Feb82^{10}Hia^{7}).

8th Race Arlington Jun. 12, 1980

6 FURLONGS. (1.08⅘) 3-Year-Olds and Up. Allowance. Purse $20,000. —which have not won two races of $9,200 in 1979-80.,— Value of race $20,000, value to winner $12,000, second $4,000, third $2,200, fourth $1,200, fifth $600. Mutuel pool $144,149.

Last Raced	Horse	Wt.	PP.	½	Str	Fin	Odds $1
10Apr80 ^{9}OP^{3}	J. Burns	122	10	$4^{1\frac{1}{2}}$	$1^{\frac{1}{2}}$	1^{1}	1.00
5Jun80 ^{8}AP^{6}	Perplext	115	6	2^{1}	2^{2}	$2^{2\frac{1}{4}}$	10.30
31May80 ^{7}AP^{9}	Sippin Charter	114	1	8^{hd}	$6^{\frac{1}{2}}$	3no	54.50
26May80 ^{7}AP^{4}	Arcadia Type	117	8	$5^{\frac{1}{2}}$	$3^{1\frac{1}{2}}$	4^{hd}	26.90
28Jly79 ^{8}AP^{3}	Liberal	110	9	9^{10}	5^{hd}	$5^{2\frac{3}{4}}$	31.30
5Jun80 ^{8}AP^{4}	Cregan's Cap	119	3	1^{hd}	4^{1}	6^{1}	3.20
2Jun80 ^{5}AP^{3}	Razorback	112	5	$6^{\frac{1}{2}}$	7^{1}	$7^{\frac{3}{4}}$	7.20
26May80 ^{7}AP^{3}	Manifest Victory	115	7	4^{1}	8^{5}	$8^{3\frac{1}{2}}$	24.70
5Jun80 ^{8}AP^{3}	Third And Lex	122	2	10	9^{6}	9^{10}	6.60
22Jly79 ^{3}LaD^{2}	Doc's First Volley	115	4	7^{4}	10	10	74.50

Time, :22⅖, :45, :57⅕, 1:09⅘ Track fast. OFF AT 5:01 1/2 CDT.

10-J. BURNS	4.00	3.40	3.40
6-PERPLEXT		8.00	8.20
1-SIPPIN CHARTER			10.60

Beldame Stakes

EIGHTH RACE
Belmont
OCTOBER 11, 1981

1 ¼ MILES. (2.00) 43rd Running THE BELDAME (Grade I). Purse $200,000 added. Fillies and Mares, 3-year-olds and upward at weight for age. By subscription of $500 each, which should accompany the nomination; $1,500 to pass the entry box, with $200,000 added The added money and all fees to be divided 60% to the winner, 22% to second, 12% to third and 6% to fourth. Weight for age. 3-year-olds, 118 lbs. Older, 123 lbs. Starters to be named at the closing time of entries. Mrs John E. Cowdin has donated a perpetual cup to be held by the owner of the winner for one year. A permanent trophy will be presented to the owner of the winner and trophies to the winning trainer and jockey and mementoes to the grooms of the first four finishers. Closed with 13 nominations Wednesday, September 23, 1981.
Value of race $218,500, value to winner $131,100, seconds $37,145 each, fourth $13,110. Mutuel pool $180,340, OTB pool $154,050.

Last Raced	Horse	Eqt.A.Wt	PP	¼	½	¾	1	Str	Fin	Jockey	Odds $1
27Sep81 ^{8}Bel^{2}	Love Sign	4 123	6	$1^{1\frac{1}{2}}$	$1^{1\frac{1}{2}}$	$1^{\frac{1}{2}}$	$1^{\frac{1}{2}}$	$1^{2\frac{1}{2}}$	1^{7}	Shoemaker W	2.30
27Sep81 ^{8}Bel^{3}	[DH]Jameela	5 123	2	$3^{\frac{1}{2}}$	5^{hd}	$6^{1\frac{1}{2}}$	$3^{\frac{1}{2}}$	3^{4}	2	Fell J	4.10
19Sep81 ^{8}Bel^{7}	[DH]Glorious Song	5 123	4	7	3^{hd}	2^{1}	2^{4}	$2^{1\frac{1}{2}}$	$2^{5\frac{1}{2}}$	Velasquez J	1.70
27Sep81 ^{8}Bel^{4}	Discorama	3 118	3	4^{1}	6^{1}	$5^{\frac{1}{2}}$	$4^{1\frac{1}{2}}$	4^{4}	4^{5}	Hernandez R	15.70
1Oct81 ^{1}Bel^{1}	Anti Lib	3 118	5	$6^{\frac{1}{2}}$	4^{1}	$3^{\frac{1}{2}}$	6^{5}	5^{2}	5^{10}	Vasquez J	17.20
18Sep81 ^{6}Med^{1}	Prismatical	3 118	1	2^{2}	$2^{\frac{1}{2}}$	4^{2}	$5^{\frac{1}{2}}$	6^{6}	$6^{2\frac{1}{2}}$	Cordero A Jr	4.80
26Sep81 ^{8}Key^{7}	Real Prize	3 118	7	$5^{\frac{1}{2}}$	7	7	7	7	7	Maple E	25.10

[DH]—**Dead heat.**

OFF AT 5:14 EDT. Start good, Won ridden out. Time, :24⅘, :48⅘, 1:12⅕, 1:37, 2:01⅘ Track fast.

$2 Mutuel Prices:			
7-(G)-LOVE SIGN	6.60	2.60	2.40
2-(B)-[DH]JAMEELA		2.40	2.80
4-(D)-[DH]GLORIOUS SONG		2.20	3.00

Ch. g, by Exclusive Native—Courtly Dee, by Never Bend. Trainer Watters Sidney Jr. Bred by Eaton Farm Inc & Red Bull Stable (Ky).

Owners— 1, Clark S C Jr; 2, Miron Julie; 3, Dogwood Stable; 4, Gasparri R P; 5, Federico J; 6, Hellston Stable; 7, Wildenstein Stable.

Trainers— 1, Watters Sidney Jr; 2, Fernandez Floreano; 3, Alexander Frank A; 4, Morgan Victor; 5, DeStasio Richard T; 6, Johnson Philip G; 7, Penna Angel.

Scratched—Winter's Tale (1Aug81 ^{8}Sar^{2}).

THIRD RACE
Santa Anita
NOVEMBER 1, 1986

6 FURLONGS. (1.07⅗) 3rd Running BREEDERS' CUP SPRINT (Grade I). Purse $1,000,000. 3-year-olds and upward. Weights, 3-year-olds, 124 lbs. Older, 126 lbs. Fillies and mares allowed 3 lbs. Pre-entry due Monday, October 20.

Total purse $1,000,000. Value of race $913,000; value to winner $450,000; second $225,000; third $108,000; fourth $70,000; fifth $50,000; sixth $10,000. Foal and Nominator Awards $87,000. Mutuel pool $740,896. Exacta Pool $646,507.

Last Raced	Horse	Eqt.	A.	Wt	PP	St	¼	½	Str	Fin	Jockey	Odds $1
27Sep86 8Pha6	Smile		4	126	1	4	2½	1hd	1hd	1¼	Vasquez J	11.00
11Oct86 7Med1	Pine Tree Lane		4	123	8	1	1½	21½	22	21½	Cordero A Jr	13.50
15Oct86 8SA4	Bedside Promise	b	4	126	4	5	71½	71½	52	31½	Pincay L Jr	9.10
15Oct86 8SA1	Groovy		3	124	9	2	32	33½	32½	42½	Santos J A	.40
20Sep86 9LaD1	Taylor's Special		5	126	3	6	61	41	4½	51½	Romero R P	11.80
2Oct86 8SA1	Carload		4	126	6	3	9	8hd	7½	6½	Shoemaker W	32.30
27Sep86 8Pha5	Love That Mac		4	126	7	8	8hd	9	82	73	Day P	17.90
5Oct86 3Fra1	Double Schwartz		5	126	2	7	41½	5½	6hd	82	Eddery P	20.90
5Oct86 3Fra4	Green Desert		3	124	5	9	5hd	6½	9	9	Swinburn W R	32.00

OFF AT 12:22 Start good, Won driving. Time, :21⅕, :43⅗, :55⅘, 1:08⅖ Track fast.

$2 Mutuel Prices:

1-SMILE	24.00	9.80	12.80
8-PINE TREE LANE		10.80	11.00
4-BEDSIDE PROMISE			8.00

$5 EXACTA 1-8 PAID $776.50.

Dk. b. or br. c, by In Reality—Sunny Smile, by Boldnesian. Trainer Schulhofer Flint S. Bred by Genter Frances A Stable (Fla).

SMILE, away in good fashion, vied for the lead while saving ground inside PINE TREE LANE from the beginning, responded readily to right handed pressure in the final furlong and edged away from PINE TREE LANE in deep stretch to prove clearly best in a stiff drive. PINE TREE LANE, off alertly and a pace factor throughout, resisted gamely in the drive but could not stay with the winner in the last sixteenth. BEDSIDE PROMISE, outrun early, was fanned six wide into the stretch and finished willingly for the show. GROOVY, away well and near the early pace outside PINE TREE LANE and SMILE, weakened a bit in the drive. TAYLOR'S SPECIAL, never far back, lacked the needed closing response. DOUBLE SCHWARTZ, in contention early, raced in choppy strides when behind rivals on the backstretch, gave way after a half and was four wide into the stretch. GREEN DESERT was finished after a half, came into the stretch five wide and was not perserved with late when well beaten.

Owners— 1, Frances A Genter Stable; 2, Mathis L D; 3, Jawl Brothers; 4, Ballis & Kruckel; 5, Lucas W F; 6, Glen Hill Farm; 7, Tall Stables; 8, Sangster R E; 9, Maktoum Al Maktoum.

Trainers— 1, Schulhofer Flint S; 2, Lukas D Wayne; 3, Martin R L; 4, Martin Jose; 5, Mott William I; 6, Proctor Willard L; 7, Widmer Wayne; 8, Nelson Charles; 9, Stoute Michael R.

SIXTH RACE
Santa Anita
NOVEMBER 1, 1986

1½ MILES.(Turf). (2.23) 3rd Running BREEDERS' CUP TURF (Grade I). Purse $2,000,000. 3-year-olds and upward. Weights, 3-year-olds, 122 lbs. Older, 126 lbs. Fillies & Mares allowed 3 lbs. Pre-entry due Monday, October 20.

Total purse $2,000,000. Value of race $1,826,000; value to winner $900,000; second $450,000; third $216,000; fourth $140,000; fifth $100,000; sixth $20,000. $174,000 Foal and Nominator Awards. Mutuel pool $1,312,402. Exacta Pool $833,589.

Last Raced	Horse	Eqt.	A.	Wt	PP	¼	½	1	1¼	Str	Fin	Jockey	Odds $1
20Sep86 8Bel1	Manila		3	122	2	41½	4½	52	3½	32½	1nk	Santos J A	8.80
12Oct86 8SA2	Theatrical		4	126	1	21½	21	31	21	1hd	23½	Stevens G L	a-2.70
12Oct86 8SA1	(S)Estrapade		6	123	5	12	12½	11½	11	21½	32½	Toro F	a-2.70
5Oct86 4Fra1	Dancing Brave		3	122	9	5½	81½	4½	42½	46	43½	Eddery P	.50
13Oct86 8SA4	Dahar	b	5	126	3	9	9	9	7hd	51½	52½	Solis A	11.60
19Oct86 3WO1	Ivor's Image		3	119	7	71½	611	61	6½	63	62½	Swinburn W R	135.50
11Oct86 8Bel2	Duty Dance		4	123	8	3½	5hd	82½	9	82	71½	Day P	94.30
5Oct86 4Fra6	Darara		3	119	6	8½	7½	21	51½	71½	86	Saint-Martin Y	19.00
11Oct86 8Bel3	Pillaster		3	122	4	6½	3hd	7hd	83	9	9	Cordero A Jr	131.90

a-Coupled: Theatrical and Estrapade.
(S) Supplementary nomination.

OFF AT 2:01 Start good, Won driving. Time, :24, :47⅗, 1:11⅕, 1:35⅗, 2:25⅖ Course firm.

$2 Mutuel Prices:

2-MANILA	19.60	3.60	5.40
1-THEATRICAL (a-entry)		2.60	3.00
1-ESTRAPADE (a-entry)		2.60	3.00

$5 EXACTA 2-1 PAID $84.50.

B. c, by Lyphard—Dona Ysidra, by Le Fabuleux. Trainer Jolley Leroy. Bred by Cojuangco E M JR (Ky).

MANILA, never far back while under light restraint, moved up along the inside around the far turn, was checked and altered course to the outside of leaders when unable to find room inside ESTRAPADE nearing the final furlong, then finished with good courage to wear down THEATRICAL after his rider lost the whip about 40 yards from the finish. THEATRICAL, prominent from the outset, went after ESTRAPADE approaching the stretch, headed that one with a furlong remaining but wasn't able to withstand the winner while saving ground, held on well to midstretch and weakened. DANCING BRAVE unhurried early, commenced to rally from the outside approaching the end of the backstretch, continued wide into the stretch and tired under pressure. DAHAR failed to be a serious factor. IVOR'S IMAGE between horses much of the way, failed to seriously menace. DUTY DANCE showed some early foot but was finished entering the backstretch. DARARA moved up outside horses approaching the clubhouse turn, raced forwardly until near the end of the backstretch and gave way. PILLASTER tired badly while saving ground much of the way.

Owners— 1, Shannon B M; 2, Firestone & Paulson; 3, Paulson A E; 4, Khaled Abdullah; 5, Summa Stable (Lessee); 6, Fraser S; 7, Phipps O M; 8, H H Aga Khan; 9, Brant P M.

Trainers— 1, Jolley Leroy; 2, Frankel Robert; 3, Whittingham Charles; 4, Harwood Guy; 5, Whittingham Charles; 6, Stoute Michael R; 7, McGaughey Claude III; 8, De Royer-Dupre Alain; 9, Jolley Leroy.

Scratched—Wylfa (5Sep86 4Eng6).

Charles H. Strub Stakes

EIGHTH RACE
Santa Anita
FEBRUARY 4, 1979

1 ¼ MILES. (1.58⅘) 17th Running CHARLES H STRUB STAKES. $200,000 Added. (Grade I). 4–year–olds. (Foals of 1975). By subscription of $100 each, to accompany the nomination; $500 to pass the entry box and $2,000 additional to start; with $200,000 added, of which $40,000 to second, $30,000 to third, $15,000 to fourth and $5,000 to fifth. Supplementary nominations made by Tuesday, January 30, by payment of $7,500. Weight, 114 lbs.; with 1 lb. additional for each total of $40,000 in accumulated first monies won as a three–year–old and four–year–old to $160,000; then 1 lb. additional for each accumulated total of $50,000 in first monies won to $360,000; then 1 lbs. for each additional accumulated total of $60,000 to $600,000. Winners of $300,000 or more as two–year–olds to carry no less than 120 lbs., regardless of later winnings. Starters to be named through the entry box by the closing time of entries. A trophy will be presented to the owner of the winner. CLOSED FRIDAY, DECEMBER 1, 1978 WITH 91 NOMINATIONS. SUPPLEMENTARY NOMINATIONS CLOSE TUESDAY, JANUARY 30, 1979.
TIONS CLOSE TUESDAY, JANUARY 30, 1979. ONE MILE AND ONE–QUARTER.
Value of race $232,500, value to winner $142,500, second $40,000, third $30,000, fourth $15,000, fifth $5,000. Mutuel pool $923,079.

Last Raced	Horse	Eqt.A.Wt	PP	¼	½	¾	1	Str	Fin	Jockey	Odds $1
20Jan79 ^{8}SA^{2}	Affirmed	4 126	8	2^{1}	$3^{1\frac{1}{2}}$	3^{2}	1^{1}	1^{2}	1^{10}	Pincay L Jr	.90
21Jan79 ^{8}SA^{5}	Johnny's Image	4 115	4	3^{hd}	2^{hd}	2½	2^{4}	2^{5}	2^{4}	Hawley S	13.90
20Jan79 ^{8}SA^{5}	Quip	4 115	5	6^{1}	5½	5½	5^{5}	3^{2}	3^{7}	Cordero A Jr	79.80
18Jan79 ^{5}SA^{1}	El Fantastico	b 4 114	2	7^{hd}	8^{4}	8½	7^{2}	5^{2}	4^{3}	Shoemaker W	11.10
20Jan79 ^{8}SA^{1}	Radar Ahead	4 120	7	4^{2}	4^{4}	4^{5}	4^{2}	4^{2}	5^{hd}	McHargue D G	1.50
27Jan79 ^{5}SA^{1}	Thin Slice	4 114	9	9	9	9	8½	7½	6^{1}	Maple E	53.50
20Jan79 ^{8}SA^{4}	Noble Bronze	b 4 116	3	8^{3}	6^{hd}	6^{hd}	6½	6^{2}	7^{5}	Toro F	13.30
20Jan79 ^{8}SA^{6}	Syncopate	4 115	1	5^{2}	$7^{3\frac{1}{2}}$	7^{4}	9	8½	8^{8}	Pierce D	87.40
24Jan79 ^{5}SA^{1}	Quilligan Quail	b 4 114	6	$1^{1\frac{1}{2}}$	1^{1}	1½	3^{hd}	9	9	McCarron C J	56.70

OFF AT 4:38 PST. Start good for all but RADAR AHEAD, Won handily. Time, :23, :47, 1:10⅘, 1:35⅗, 2:01 Track good.

$2 Mutuel Prices:			
10–AFFIRMED	3.80	3.20	3.40
4–JOHNNY'S IMAGE		7.40	4.80
5–QUIP			9.80

Ch. c, by Exclusive Native—Won't Tell You, by Crafty Admiral. Trainer Barrera Lazaro S. Bred by Harbor View Farm (Fla).

AFFIRMED broke alertly then showed his speed nearing the first turn to prompt the pace, raced out in the middle of the track while behind the leader, raced on his own courage to the five sixteenth pole, responded to some left handed urging while disposing of JOHNNY'S IMAGE and drew away in the final furlong. JOHNNY'S IMAGE broke in stride to show speed, forced the pace on the rail, continued inside to battle the winner to the stretch then could not match strides thereafter. QUIP outrun early, kept to his task to improve his position in the drive. EL FANTASTICO had no early speed. RADAR AHEAD broke off balance, moved up behind the winner into the first turn, gave way wide and gradually weakened. NOBLE BRONZE failed to response. SYNCOPATE saved ground for nothing. QUILLIGAN QUAIL set the pace to the half then stopped.

Owners— 1, Harbor View Farm; 2, Tanz Meryl Ann; 3, Tartan Stable; 4, Bradley & Peters; 5, Vail S H; 6, Vanderbilt A G; 7, Breliant W; 8, Elmendorf; 9, Fell & Good & Kessler & Lewis.

Trainers— 1, Barrera Lazaro S; 2, Frankel Robert; 3, Lukas D Wayne; 4, Whittingham Charles; 5, Jones Gary; 6, Burch William; 7, Bucalo John; 8, McAnally Ronald; 9, Alvarez Fernando.

Overweight: Syncopate 1 pound.

Scratched—Little Reb (20Jan79 ^{8}SA^{3}); Wrangle (20Jan79 ^{9}SA^{4}).

EXPECTED RETURN PER DOLLAR BET

You now have good evidence that horses underbet to place and show may be outstanding bets. What you really need to know is how good they really are and how to compare various possible bets. You will learn that the payoffs do not have to be as good as most of those shown previously. Indeed, each day there will be two to four such Dr. Z system bets at a typical track.

Let us now evaluate horses on the basis of their expected return per dollar bet. This is the average return you would expect if this or similar bets were made many times. For example, suppose the dollar bet can return either $2, $1.50, or nothing. If the probabilities of these payoffs are 0.4, 0.3, and 0.3, respectively, then the expected return is

$$0.4(\$2.00) + 0.3(\$1.50) + 0.3(\$0) = \$1.25.$$

So, on average, you would expect to make 25¢ per dollar bet, or a 25% profit. Of course, in any particular race you will receive either \$2, \$1.50, or nothing, so that even though, on average, you make 25% on such bets, you still can lose. However, as you make more and more similar bets, the chance of being behind is less and less. For example, with one race the chance of being behind is 30%—losing the race. With two races it is 27%—losing both races, (0.3)(0.3); plus losing the first race and winning the small prize in the second race, also (0.3)(0.3); and winning the small prize in the first race and losing the second race, also (0.3)(0.3). With three races you have to lose at least two of the three races to be behind, so the probability of being behind drops to 21.6%. With eight races, the probability of being behind is 18.3%; after twenty races it is 9.3%; fifty races, 1.83%; and only 0.15% after one hundred races. Generally, then, if you have a sequence of profitable wagers you will come out ahead as long as the wagers are not too risky and you bet appropriate amounts.

DETERMINING WHEN THERE IS AN INEFFICIENCY IN THE BETTING POOLS AND THUS A GOOD OPPORTUNITY TO BET

To calculate the exact expected value of a dollar bet to place or show on a particular horse requires that we know (1) the probability of all possible in-the-money finishes and (2) the place or show payoff in each case. This we do in our computer model.* For actual use this is too cumbersome, as there can be more than one hundred possible in-the-money finishes. Instead, we utilize simple approximate formulas that require only two sets of figures: the amounts bet to place or show on the horse in question and the total pools. The expected value per dollar bet to place is

$$\text{EX Place} = 0.319 + 0.559\frac{W_i/W}{P_i/P}, \tag{4.3}$$

where P_i and W_i are the amounts bet to place and show, respectively, on horse i, and P and W are the place and win pools. So with the example on page 62, the expected value per dollar bet to place on horse 1 is

$$\text{EX Place} = 0.319 + 0.559\left(\frac{8{,}293/18{,}223}{2{,}560/9{,}214}\right) = 1.20.$$

Thus, on average, you would expect to make a profit of 20% betting horse 1 to place.

*Those interested in these mathematical details may consult Appendix B. This knowledge is not required for a full understanding of the Dr. Z system. The equations presented in this section and the constants, such as 0.319 and 0.559 in equation (4.3), were first derived by Hausch, Ziemba, and Rubinstein (1981) and Hausch and Ziemba (1985).

The expected value per dollar bet to show is

$$\text{EX Show} = 0.543 + 0.369\frac{W_i/W}{S_i/S} \tag{4.4}$$

where S_i is the amount bet on horse i to show out of the total show pool S and W_i and W are as described previously. For the example on page 62, the expected value per dollar bet to show on horse 1 is

$$\text{EX Show} = 0.543 + 0.369\left(\frac{8{,}293/18{,}223}{1{,}570/6{,}558}\right) = 1.24.$$

So, on average, one would expect to make a profit of 24% betting horse 1.

Figures 4.1 and 4.2 graphically display the place and show expected-value-per-dollar-bet equations (4.3) and (4.4), respectively. To use them read W_i/W on the horizontal axis and P_i/P for place or S_i/S for show on the vertical axis, respectively. The line where the two values intersect gives the expected value per dollar bet. For example, for the show bet on horse 1, $W_1/W = 8{,}293/18{,}223 = 0.455$ and $S_1/S = 1{,}570/6{,}558 = 0.239$. These numbers intersect on the 1.24 expected-value line.

FORMULAS FOR DETERMINING THE EXPECTED VALUE PER DOLLAR BET

Equations (4.3) and (4.4) for computing the expected value per dollar bet to place and show, respectively, are based on a track take of 17.1%. This was the track take at Exhibition Park when these equations were developed.

Other tracks will have different takes, and even at the same track the take will vary over time. For example, at Exhibition Park it is now 15.8%. Hence we need to have equations for the expected value per dollar bet to place and show for any track take. They are

$$\text{EX Place} = 0.319 + 0.559\frac{W_i/W}{P_i/P} + \left(2.22 - 1.29\frac{W_i}{W}\right)(Q - 0.829) \tag{4.5}$$

$$\text{EX Show} = 0.543 + 0.369\frac{W_i/W}{S_i/S} + \left(3.60 - 2.13\frac{W_i}{W}\right)(Q - 0.829). \tag{4.6}$$

These equations are just the Exhibition Park equations (4.3) and (4.4) with an adjustment to account for the fact that the track payback Q differs from 0.829.

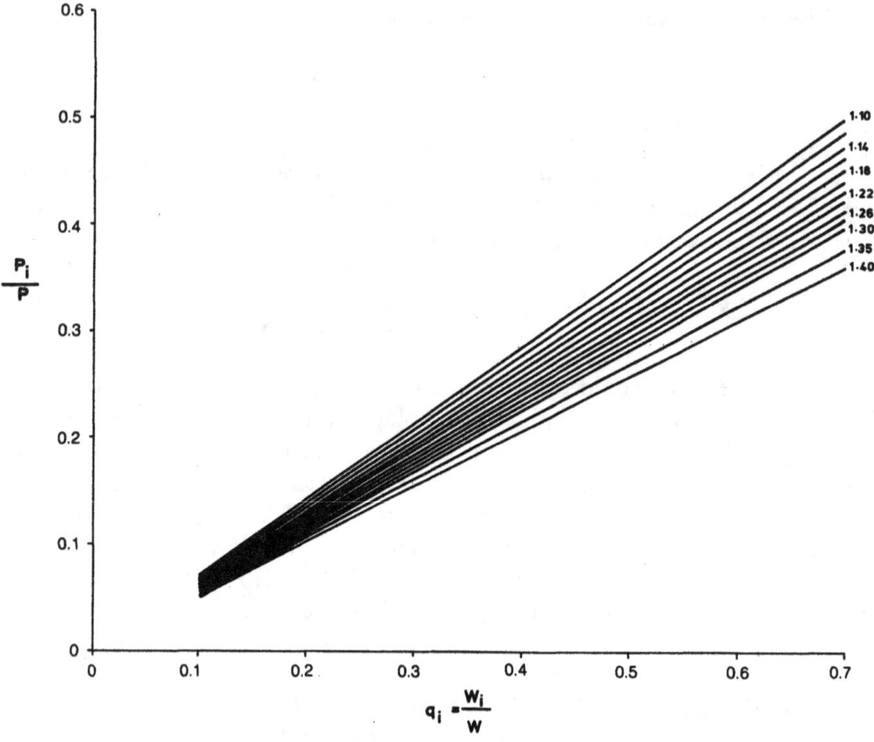

Figure 4.1 The expected return per dollar bet to place when the track take is 17.1%

Let us see how it works on a real race. In the 1979 Kentucky Derby, Spectacular Bid was a 3–5 favorite. At post time the tote board was as follows:

	Totals	#3 Spectacular Bid	Percent of Bet on Spectacular Bid
Odds		3—5	
Win	2,307,288	1,164,220	50.5
Place	949,999	339,277	37.5
Show	749,274	195,419	26.1

Much less was bet on Spectacular Bid to place and show, relative to the total pools, than to win. For show it was only about half as much.

The track take in Kentucky is 15%, so the expected value per dollar bet to place on Spectacular Bid was

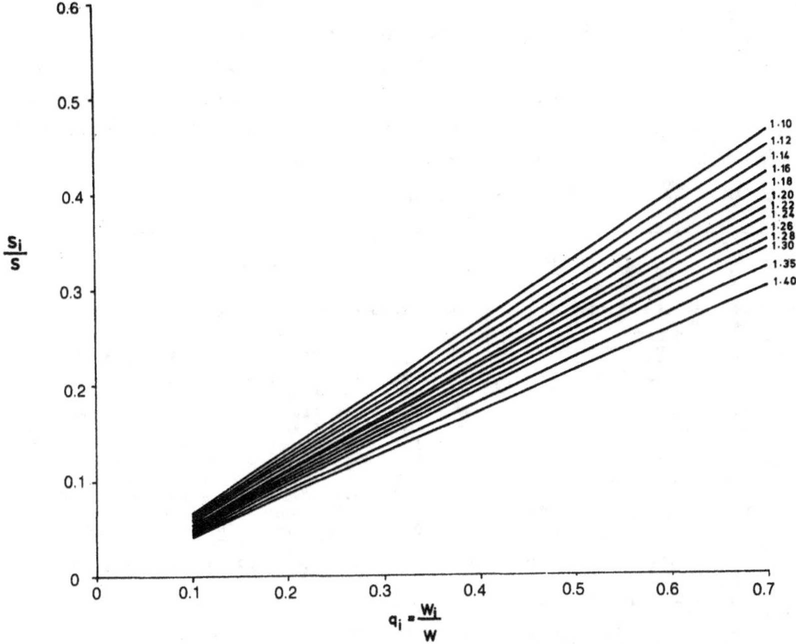

Figure 4.2 The expected return per dollar bet to show when the track is 17.1%

$$
\begin{aligned}
\text{EX Place} &= 0.319 + 0.559\left(\frac{1{,}164{,}220/2{,}307{,}288}{339{,}277/949{,}999}\right) \\
&\quad + \left[2.22 - 1.29\left(\frac{1{,}164{,}220}{2{,}307{,}288}\right)\right](0.85 - 0.829) \\
&\quad + 1.10 + 0.03 \\
&= 1.13.
\end{aligned}
$$

So the expected value was 1.13, or a 13% profit, on average, per dollar bet. The correction amounts to 3%.

For show the expected value per dollar bet was

$$
\begin{aligned}
\text{EX Show} &= 0.543 + 0.369\left(\frac{1{,}164{,}220/2{,}307{,}288}{195{,}419/749{,}274}\right) \\
&\quad + \left[3.60 - 2.13\left(\frac{1{,}164{,}220}{2{,}307{,}288}\right)\right](0.85 - 0.829) \\
&= 1.26 + 0.05 \\
&= 1.31.
\end{aligned}
$$

The expected value of 1.31 to show on Spectacular Bid thus represented an average profit of 31%. The correction amounts to 5%.

Figures similar to Figures 4.1 and 4.2 for the calculation of the expected value per dollar bet to place and show using equations (4.5) and (4.6), respectively, appear in Chapter Five. They are set up there to indicate simply *bet* or *do not bet* in any particular possible betting situation.

The chart of the race was as follows:

105th Kentucky Derby, May 5, 1979

$317,400 gross value and $18,000 Gold Cup. Net to winner $228,650; second $50,000; third $25,000; fourth $13,750. 299 nominations.

Horse	Eqt	Wt	PP	¼	½	¾	1	Str	Fin	Jockeys	Owners	Odds to $1
Spectacular Bid ..		126	3	7^{2}	6^{h}	4½	$2^{1\frac{1}{2}}$	$1^{1\frac{1}{2}}$	$1^{2\frac{3}{4}}$	R. J. Franklin	Hawksworth Farm	.60
General Assembly		126	6	1^{h}	2^{5}	2^{h}	1^{h}	2^{5}	2^{3}	L. Pincay Jr.	B. P. Firestone	a-11.10
Golden Act		126	1	$8^{1\frac{1}{2}}$	9^{h}	8^{h}	7^{4}	3^{h}	$3^{1\frac{3}{4}}$	S. Hawley	W. Oldknow-R. Phipps	19.20
King Celebrity ..	b	125	7	$6^{1\frac{1}{2}}$	7^{4}	5½	5^{3}	4½	$4^{2\frac{1}{2}}$	C. B. Asmussen	Che-Bar Stable	112.40
Flying Paster ..	b	126	9	3^{h}	4^{h}	3^{h}	3^{1}	5^{4}	$5^{3\frac{1}{2}}$	D. Pierce	B. J. Ridder	2.20
Screen King		126	5	10	8^{1}	7^{4}	6^{h}	6½	$6^{3\frac{1}{4}}$	A. Cordero Jr.	Flying Zee Stable	9.80
Sir Ivor Again ..		126	8	9^{h}	10	9^{5}	9^{15}	8^{3}	$7^{1\frac{1}{4}}$	D. MacBeth	Mrs. T. Christopher	a-11.10
Shamgo		126	4	2^{h}	1½	1^{h}	4^{h}	7^{5}	$8^{4\frac{1}{4}}$	F. Olivares	Rogers Red Top Inc.	102.20
Lot o' Gold		126	10	4^{3}	$3^{1\frac{1}{2}}$	6½	8^{h}	9^{20}	9^{25}	D. Brumfield	F. E. Lehmann	50.90
Great Redeemer .	b	126	2	$5^{1\frac{1}{2}}$	5^{3}	10	10	10	10	R. DePass	Mr-Mrs. J. Mohamed	78.70

Time: :24-1/5, :47-2/5, 1:12-2/5, 1:37-3/5, 2:02-2/5. Track fast. Off at 5:39 EDT. Start good. Won driving.

Coupled: a-General Assembly and Sir Ivor Again.

$2 Mutuels paid—Spectacular Bid $3.20 straight, $3.00 place; $2.80 show; General Assembly $5.80 place, $3.40 show; Golden Act $4.20.

Winner—Gr. c. by Bold Bidder-Spectacular, by Promised Land, trainer G. G. (Bud) Delp; bred in Kentucky by Mrs. William Jason and Mrs. William Gilmore.

SPECTACULAR BID ducked in slightly leaving the gate and was settled well off the pace, moved slightly outside on the initial turn, rallied strongly after five-eighths staying well wide to be clear, ranged up outside GENERAL ASSEMBLY with FLYING PASTER inside entering the last turn and was bumped by FLYING PASTER when that one was forced out slightly by GENERAL ASSEMBLY. He responded when roused righthanded leaving the last turn, moved clear nearing the eighth pole but was roused steadily five times left-handed to draw out. GENERAL ASSEMBLY sprinted up on the pace between rivals entering the first turn, shook off SHAMGO and continued gamely when joined by SPECTACULAR BID and FLYING PASTER. He drifted out slightly entering the last turn and gradually gave way. GOLDEN ACT brushed by GREAT REDEEMER leaving the gate, stayed inside to commence his bid after a mile and finished with good courage. KING CELEBRITY moved boldly to the pace inside but was blocked with a half mile left, got clear between rivals entering the stretch and hung. FLYING PASTER broke sharply, rallied inside SPECTACULAR BID and was floated by GENERAL ASSEMBLY entering the last turn and weakened. SCREEN KING pinched back at start, moved widest to launch his bid after 6 furlongs and had nothing left. SIR IVOR AGAIN could only pass tiring rivals. SHAMGO sprinted to the pace inside, maintained a slight advantage for three-quarters of a mile and tired. LOT o' GOLD stayed in striking position for a half, then retired. GREAT REDEEMER stopped badly.

THE WINNER'S PEDIGREE AND CAREER HIGHLIGHTS

SPECTACULAR BID (Gray Colt)	Bold Bidder	Bold Ruler	*Nasrullah
			Miss Disco
		High Bid	To Market
			Stepping Stone
	Spectacular	Promised Land	Palestinian
			Mahmoudess
		Stop On Red	To Market
			Danger Ahead

Year	Age	Sts	1st	2nd	3rd	Won
1978	2	9	7	1	0	$ 384,484
1979	3	12	10	1	1	1,279,183
1980	4	9	9	0	0	1,117,790
TOTAL		30	26	2	1	$2,781,607

At 2 Years	WON	World's Playground, Champagne, Young America, Laurel Futurity, Heritage
	2ND	Dover Stakes
At 3 Years	WON	Kentucky Derby, Preakness Stakes, Flamingo, Blue Grass, Florida Derby, Hutcheson, Fountain of Youth, Marlboro Cup.
	2ND	Jockey Club Gold Cup
	3RD	Belmont Stakes
At 4 Years	WON	Malibu, San Fernando, Charles H. Strub, Santa Anita Handicap, Mervyn Leroy Handicap, California Stakes, Washington Park Stakes, Amory Haskell, *Woodward Stakes. *Walkover.

Only time Spectacular Bid was out of the money was in the 1978 Tyro Stakes when he finished fourth.

Spectacular Bid won the race easily and paid $3.20 to win, $3 to place, and $2.80 to show. The bet to place was excellent. The bet to show was fantastic. To get $2.80 to show with a 3–5 shot when the second favorite is 2.20–1 and the next-best-rated horse is 9.8–1 is a bettor's dream.

With 1.13 as the expected value to place and 1.33 to show, you would expect to receive $2.26 and $2.66 on average, respectively. The actual payoff when you win, of course, must be higher to compensate for the times you lose. In this case the payoffs were even higher because the second favorite, Flying Paster, finished out of the money.

If there is a coupled entry one other correction is needed in the calculation of the expected value per dollar bet to place or show. Occasionally two or three horses are run as a single coupled entry, or simply entry, because an owner or trainer enters these horses in the same race, or there are more horses than the tote board can accommodate. The latter case is usually called a field. In the Kentucky Derby, with up to twenty starters and twelve totalizator positions, the field can contain as many as nine horses. The entry wins, places, or shows if any one of the horses wins, places, or shows. If the horses in the entry come first and second, all the place pool goes to the place tickets on the entry. If two of the three in-the-money horses are the entry then two thirds of the show pool profits goes to the holders of tickets on the entry rather than the usual third.* Finally, the entry gets all the show pool money if the entry has three horses and they finish 1-2-3. Hence you have an advantage betting on an entry. To correct for this, equations (4.5) and (4.6) for expected value per dollar bets to place and show, respectively, are modified as follows:

$$\text{EX Place} = \underbrace{0.319 + 0.559\frac{W_i/W}{P_i/P}}_{\text{Ordinary expected value}} + \underbrace{\left(2.22 - 1.29\frac{W_i}{W}\right)(Q - 0.829)}_{\text{Correction for track-take departures from 17.1\%}}$$

$$+ \underbrace{0.867\frac{W_i}{W} - 0.857\frac{P_i}{P}}_{\text{Correction because the bet is on an entry}} \qquad (4.7)$$

*This is the usual split. However, at some tracks the split is 50-50, so every betting opportunity gets the same portion of the profit.

$$\text{EX Show} = \underbrace{0.543 + 0.369\frac{W_i/W}{S_i/S}}_{\text{Ordinary expected value}} + \left(\underbrace{3.60 - 2.13\frac{W_i}{W}}_{\text{Corrections for track-take departures from 17.1\%}}\right)(Q - 0.829)$$

$$+ \underbrace{0.842\frac{W_i}{W} - 0.810\frac{S_i}{S}}_{\text{Correction because the bet is on an entry}} \tag{4.8}$$

We illustrate the use of these formulas with the following race. Suppose 1 is the entry of horse 1 and horse 1A, that there are six other starters, and that the tote board at post time is as follows:

	Horse							
	#1	#2	#3	#4	#5	#6	#7	Totals
Odds	2–1	10–1	5–2	8–1	4–1	14–1	4–1	
Win	6,772	2,054	6,021	2,521	4,426	1,517	4,222	27,533
Place	2,825	1,274	3,392	1,500	3,123	1,007	3,123	16,426
Show	1,632	744	1,740	835	1,782	600	2,398	9,731

Suppose that the track take is 16%, so $Q = 0.84$, and that we have 10¢ breakage. The expected return per dollar bet to place using equation (4.7) is then

$$\text{EX Place} = \underbrace{0.319 + 0.559\left(\frac{6{,}772/27{,}533}{2{,}825/16{,}335}\right)}_{\text{Ordinary expected value}}$$

$$+ \underbrace{\left[(2.216 - 1.288)\left(\frac{6{,}772}{27{,}533}\right)\right](0.84 - 0.829)}_{\text{Correction for track-take departures from 17.1\%}}$$

$$\underbrace{+ 0.867\left(\frac{6{,}772}{27{,}533}\right) - 0.857\left(\frac{2{,}825}{16{,}335}\right)}_{\text{Coupled-entry correction}}$$

$$= 1.114 + 0.021 + 0.065 = 1.20.$$

Thus the track-take correction is 0.021 and the coupled-entry correction is 0.065. This 0.086 added to the ordinary expected value makes the expected value per dollar bet on the 1-1A entry 1.20, which, as we will see in Chapter Five, would qualify it as a Dr. Z system bet. One would then expect to make 20% profit, on average, by betting on horse 1.

Similarly, the expected return per dollar to show using equation (4.8) is

$$\text{EX Show} = \underbrace{0.543 + 0.369\left(\frac{6{,}772/27{,}533}{1{,}632/9{,}731}\right)}_{\text{Ordinary expected value}}$$

$$+ \underbrace{\left[3.60 - 2.13\left(\frac{6{,}772}{27{,}533}\right)\right](0.84 - 0.829)}_{\text{Track-take correction}}$$

$$+ \underbrace{0.842\left(\frac{6{,}772}{27{,}533}\right) - 0.810\left(\frac{1{,}632}{9{,}731}\right)}_{\text{Coupled-entry correction}}$$

$$= 1.084 + 0.034 + 0.071 = 1.19.$$

Thus the track-take correction is 0.034 and the coupled-entry correction is 0.071. The correction of 0.105 makes the expected value per dollar bet on the entry of horse 1-1A equal to 1.19. This would give an average profit of 19% and qualify it as a Dr. Z system bet to show.

Hence the entry of 1-1A is a good bet to place and to show. The actual payoff depends upon whether or not 1 or 1A, or both, are in the money and the amounts bet on the other horse or horses that also finish in the money.

For example, if the finish is 1-5-3 then the payoff will be

1	6.80	4.60	3.20
	5	4.40	3.00
		3	3.00

In this case, horse 1 at 2–1 receives $4.60 to place and $3.20 to show, which is slightly more than the payoffs on either horse 5 at 4–1 or horse 3 at 5–2. The computation of these payoffs is analogous to those given earlier in this chapter.

If 1 and 1A both finish in the money then the show payoff increases because 1-1A get two-thirds of the show profit rather than one-third. With a finish of 1-5-1A the payoffs will be

1	6.80	4.60	5.80
	5	4.40	3.60
		1A	5.80

The payoff for horse 5 to place remains the same, as does the place payoff for horse 1. However, the show payoff on horse 5 increases to $3.60 and the show payoff on horse 1 now becomes $5.80 instead of $3.20, exceeding the place payoff.

If the finish is 1-1A-5, the payoffs will be

1	6.80	9.60	5.80
	1A	9.60	5.80
		5	3.60

The show profits remain the same on horses 1 and 5, since it is the total amounts bet and not the order of the finish that matters. However, horse 1 now gets the entire place profit and the payoff becomes $9.60, which exceeds the win payoff of $6.80. This is not surprising, because the expected value per dollar bet on horse 1 to win is simply the track payback of 0.84, while the expected return per dollar bet on 1 to place is 1.20. Thus with the favorable outcome of 1 winning and 1A coming in second, the place payoff exceeds the win payoff.

To summarize, equations (4.3) and (4.4) will give you the expected value per dollar bet to place and show, respectively, when the track take is 17.1% or close to this. When the track take differs from 17.1%, equations (4.5) and (4.6) will give you the place and show expected returns, respectively. These equations are the ones you will use most of the time. Figures 5.7–5.10 in Chapter Five provide a shorthand way to determine whether or not a given horse is a Dr. Z system bet or not.

On occasion there will be an entry that is a possible Dr. Z system bet. In this case you need to use equations (4.7) and (4.8) to compute the expected value per dollar bet to place and show, respectively. We have assumed that the entry contains exactly two horses and that there is no other entry. Our calculations indicate that there is generally little change in the expected value when there are three or more horses in the entry or when you are betting on some horse, be it an entry or a single horse, and there is another entry in the race. Generally, the expected value rises slightly when you have an entry of three or more horses rather than just two horses. Similarly, the expected value generally falls slightly when an entry is present and you are not betting on it. Our recommendation is that you keep these matters in mind but simply use equations (4.7) and (4.8). They will give you quite accurate estimates of the true expected value to place and show, respectively.

Now that we have discussed how you can calculate the expected value per dollar bet to place and show on possible Dr. Z system bets, we can turn to the question of how much you should bet and provide further details about the Dr. Z system.

5

How Much Should You Bet?

WHY YOU NEED TO HAVE A GOOD MONEY MANAGEMENT SYSTEM

We know from our discussion in Chapter Four that there are situations where bets can be made to place and show that have expected value in the range 1.15–1.30 or higher. Thus, on average, we expect our profit rates to be 15%–30% or higher. We also know that if we do not bet too much, we can be reasonably sure of being ahead with such bets when they are placed over a fairly long period of time. But how much should we bet?

We can compare various betting systems by seeing how they measure up against several reasonable criteria. Four such criteria are: (1) How much does it gain on average? (2) How fast does it accumulate profits? (3) How long does it take to reach a specified level of profit? (4) How risky is the system—are you taking a big chance of losing most or all of your betting fortune at one blow?

Despite its reasonableness, the first criterion will not help us separate the good systems from the bad ones. The reason is that all betting systems have the same expected profit per dollar wagered—assuming our bets do not influence the odds, which is the case unless our bets get very large. We need to focus on the other three criteria.

To get an idea of what constitutes a good system let's look at some possible betting strategies. In the *Martingale*, or *doubling-up*, system you begin with a bet, say $1, and bet $1 again if the bet is won, but bet $2 if it is lost. If you lose again, you bet $4, then $8, $16, and so on. The idea is to have a good chance of making the $1 profit on each sequence of bets. Let's see how it works.

Win
+1

Total
+1

Loss	Win	Total
−1	+2	+1

Loss	Loss	Loss	Win	Total
−1	−2	−4	+8	+1

So in these cases, $1 is won on each sequence of bets. Trouble arises when you get a sequence like the following:

Loss	Loss	Loss	Loss	Loss	Loss	Loss	Loss	Total
−1	−2	−4	−8	−16	−32	−64	−128	−255

In this case you need to start betting huge sums just to win the $1. You may run out of money first. It may also be difficult to bet so much; suppose your $1's are really $100 bets. Moreover, in the context of horse racing, large bets can greatly influence the odds. With a high bet one simply gets poorer odds. A situation with a good expected value will become less favorable and possibly even unfavorable with a large bet. Betting along the Martingale lines leads to a number of wins of $1 and then a huge loss. Let's put aside this and all other doubling-up strategies. Doubling up after wins is just as bad.

In *pyramid* systems, also known as *d'Alembert* or *progression* systems, you up the bet with a win and decrease it with a loss. For example, you can bet $5 per race and add or subtract $1 with a win or a loss, respectively. The idea is to bet more when you are winning and less when you are losing. The amount of the bet looks like a sequence of pyramids, such as the following:

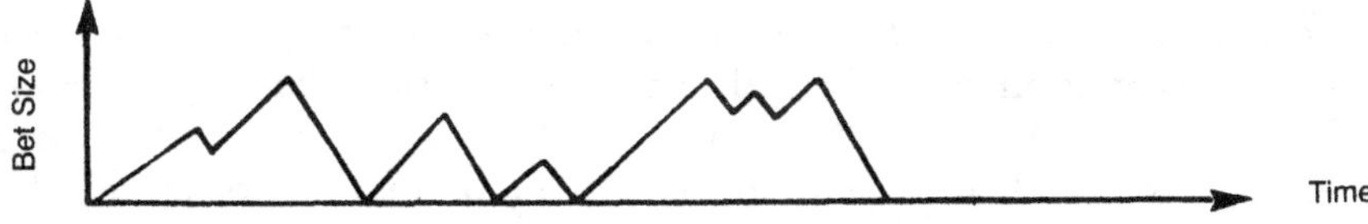

Of course, you can invert this system and bet more when you are losing, so you get a sequence of inverted pyramids or an upside-down image of the preceding graph. Again, these betting systems are arbitrary. They do not consider how good the bet is. We certainly want to bet more when the bet is more attractive. We also want to take into account the fact that as our bet becomes larger, the very act of placing such a bet lowers the worth of the bet, since the odds become less favorable.

None of these systems offers what we want: a good way to make our betting resources grow at a fast rate with low risk, while taking into account the facts that (1) we would like to bet more when the bet, not our previous wins or losses, is more favorable and (2) the size of our bet will influence the odds.

There are several possible systems that we might employ that have such desirable properties.* The basic trade-off is growth versus risk. We can look for the most conservative system, the one with the least risk of losing our betting fortune that still provides modest growth in that fortune. Alternatively, we might strive for a strategy with the largest growth rate. It will be more risky, but in the long run we most likely will have a much higher fortune. We will take the latter route and utilize the Kelly criterion betting system.

USING THE KELLY CRITERION TO MAXIMIZE THE LONG-RUN GROWTH OF YOUR BETTING FORTUNE

John L. Kelly, Jr., was an engineer with the Bell Telephone Company in 1956 when he discovered the betting system that carries his name. His main interest was efficient transmission of electrical signals. Little did he know that his discovery would make him world famous because of its use as the basis of a superb way to invest in securities and to gamble in games like blackjack and horse racing.†

The criterion is simple: Go for the gold! More specifically, the Kelly criterion is to invest so that *the long-run rate of growth of your betting fortune is the highest possible.*

How does it stack up against our three remaining reasonable criteria for evaluating possible betting systems: (1) How fast does it accumulate profits? (2) How long does it take to reach a specified level of profit? and (3) How risky is the system—are you taking a big chance of losing most or all of your betting fortune? Very well, indeed! Since it is based on the first criterion, it accumulates profits faster than any other system. Indeed, it has been proved mathematically that the Kelly criterion has the following property:

> Suppose two people are wagering on the outcome of the same series of favorable betting opportunities; one uses the Kelly criterion and the other uses an essentially different betting strategy. Then the ratio of the Kelly bettor's fortune to that of the other bettor's fortune becomes increasingly large as time goes on, with higher and higher probability. After a long time the Kelly bettor will

---

*Those with mathematical backgrounds who would like to delve deeper into this topic might consult Epstein (1977).

†Those who would like to read more on the Kelly criterion might consult the papers by Breiman, Hakansson, and Thorp in Ziemba and Vickson (1975), as well as those by Bell and Cover (1980), Ethier and Tavare (1983), Finkelstein and Whitley (1981), Friedman (1981), Griffin (1984), and McLean, Ziemba, and Blazenko (1987). Thorp (1975) is especially lucid. These papers are highly mathematical. Although Kelly has received most of the credit, it was Breiman who really showed how attractive the Kelly criterion was around 1960. Thorp and others have used it to develop successful investment strategies. The discussion in this section contains the properties of the Kelly criterion pertinent to the Dr. Z system.

have infinitely more wealth than the other bettor with a probability approaching 1. In fact, if a Kelly bettor at the racetrack also has access to fair casino bets, he is more likely to be ahead even after the first bet.

The Kelly betting system is also the best-possible wagering system in terms of the second criterion of reaching a specified goal as soon as possible. It has the following property:

> Suppose that a bettor is wagering on the outcome of a sequence of favorable betting opportunities and that he or she has a goal of reaching a fortune of $\$M$ as soon as possible. By betting according to the Kelly criterion, the expected time to reach M will be lower than with any other betting system, provided that M is sufficiently large.

Our third criterion is safety. What is the chance of losing all or a major portion of your betting fortune? Since the Kelly criterion is based on growth, it is riskier than some other possible betting systems. However, an adjustment of the Kelly betting amount can be made to make the system as safe as desired. We can make a trade-off and accept less growth in return for more security. We can do this by adopting a fractional Kelly betting system.

Figures 5.1–5.6 illustrate three possible betting situations that mirror what you are likely to encounter with some typical Dr. Z system bets. We suppose that the expected value per dollar bet is 1.20 so that you have a 20% profit on average. Let's consider three possible bets:*

1. You win \$2 with probability 0.4 and lose \$1 with probability 0.6, assuming a place bet on a reasonably long-priced horse. In this case the optimal Kelly criterion bet is to wager 10% of your money on each race.
2. You win \$1 with probability 0.625 and lose \$1 with probability 0.375, assuming a place bet on a favorite or a show bet on a longer-priced horse. In this case the optimal Kelly criterion bet is to wager 25% on each race.
3. You win \$0.594 with probability 0.771 and lose \$1 with probability 0.229, assuming a show bet on a favorite. The optimal bet is to wager 38.6% of your betting fortune on each race.

---

*These examples are merely illustrative. The calculations are made using the methods in MacLean, Ziemba, and Blazenko (1987). However, they typify possible Dr. Z system bets. The betting amounts suggested as a fraction of your betting fortune are accurate for small bets that do not influence the odds too much. For larger fortunes and bets, the optimal wagers are kept down in order to reflect the effect of our bet on the possible payoffs. In actual Dr. Z system bets, the possible payoffs are numerous rather than having just one possible outcome as supposed here. But these simplified cases generate the same conclusions as would the actual bets.

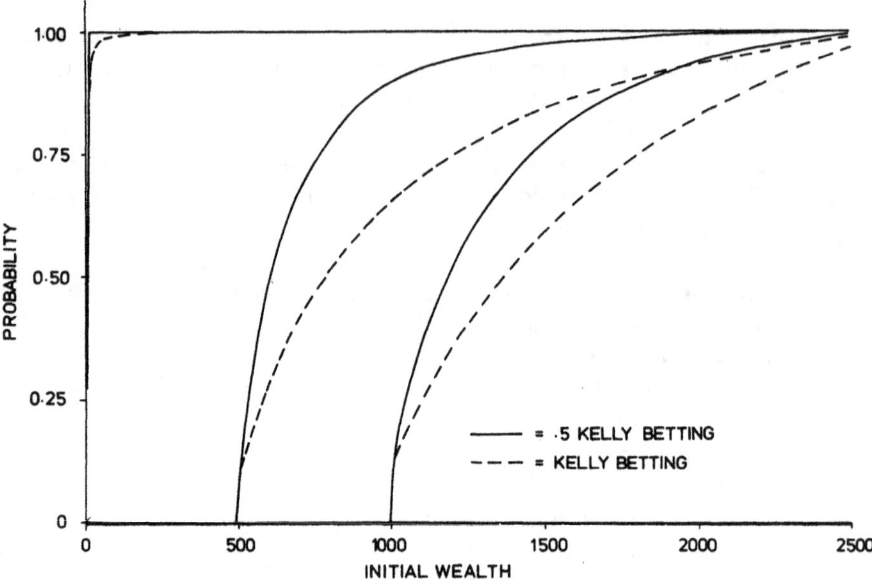

Figure 5.1 Relative growth and probabilities of doubling, tripling, and quadrupling initial wealth for various fractions of wealth bet for the gamble win $2 with probability 0.4 and lose $1 with probability 0.6

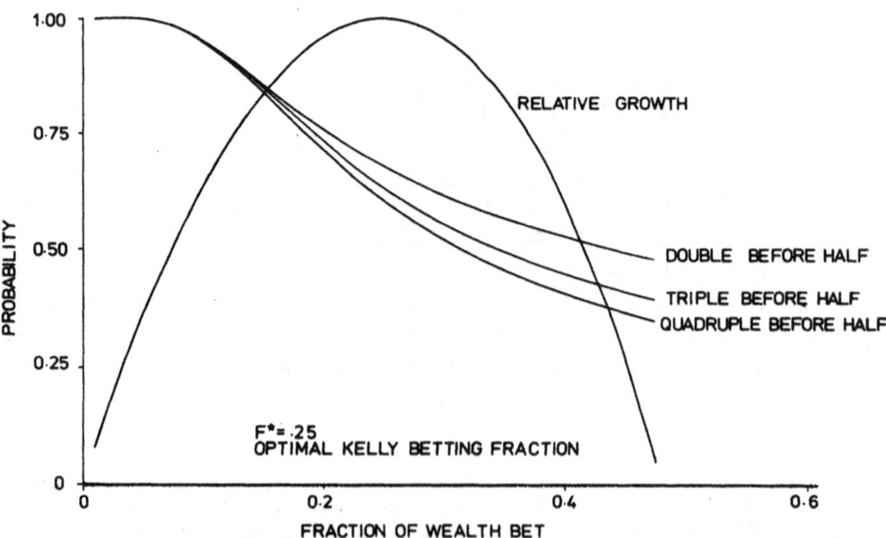

Figure 5.2 Probability of reaching $2,500 before falling to $0, $500, and $1,000 with various initial wealth levels with Kelly and 0.5-Kelly betting strategies for the gamble win $2 with probability 0.4 and lose $1 with probability 0.6

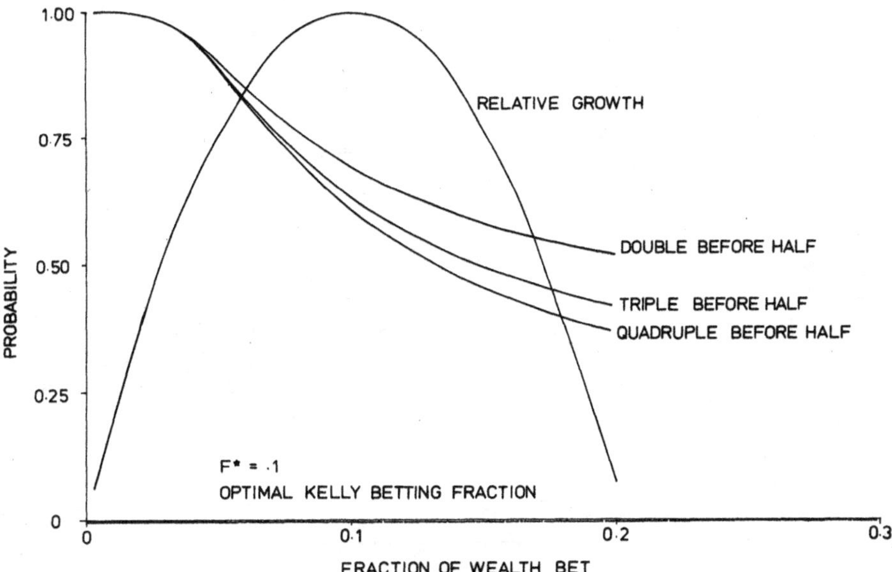

Figure 5.3 Relative growth and probabilities of doubling, tripling, and quadrupling initial wealth for various fractions of wealth bet for the gamble win $1 with probability 0.625 and lose $1 with probability 0.375

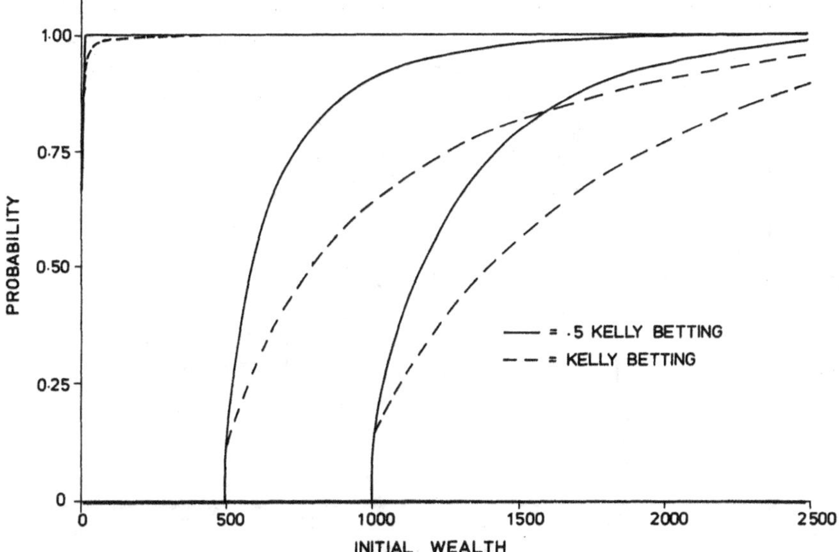

Figure 5.4 Probability of reaching $2,500 before falling to $0, $500, and $1,000 with various initial wealth levels with Kelly and 0.5-Kelly betting strategies for the gamble win $1 with probability 0.625 and lose $1 with probability 0.375

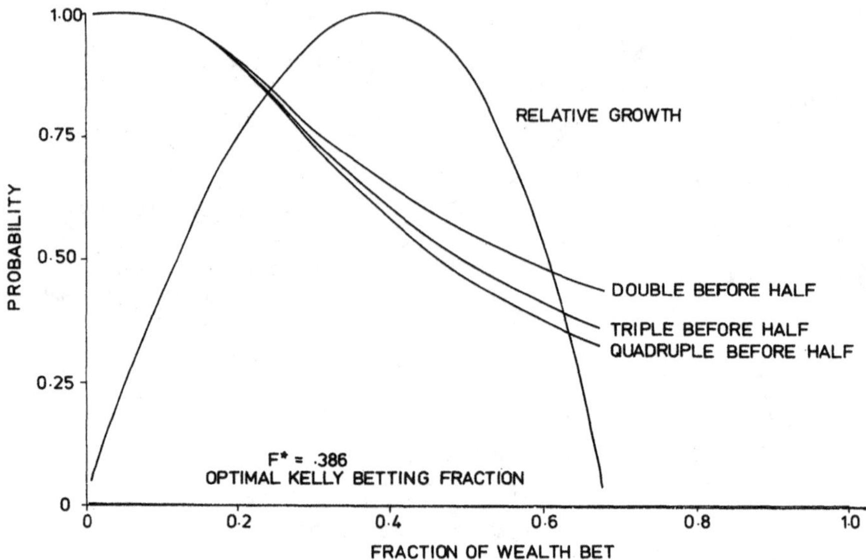

Figure 5.5 Relative growth and probabilities of doubling, tripling, and quadrupling initial wealth for various fractions of wealth bet for the gamble win $0.594 with probability 0.771 and lose $1 with probability 0.229

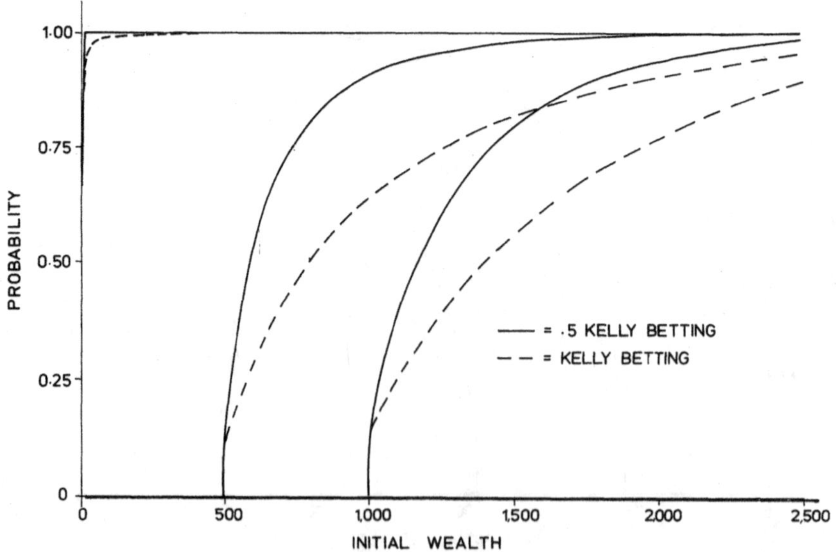

Figure 5.6 Probability of reaching $2,500 before falling to $0, $500, and $1,000 with various initial wealth levels with Kelly and 0.5-Kelly betting strategies for the gamble win $0.594 with probability 0.771 and lose $1 with probability 0.229

Figures 5.1, 5.3, and 5.5 display the relative growth rates for bets 1, 2, and 3, respectively. Notice that as you bet more or less than the optimal Kelly fraction of your initial wealth, the growth rate declines. Eventually, if you bet very small amounts or very large amounts, the growth rate becomes virtually zero. To maintain high growth you need to make bets close to the optimal Kelly betting amounts. These figures also display the probability that you will double, triple, or quadruple your initial betting wealth before it falls to one half. For example, in Figure 5.1, which corresponds to bet 1, the optimal Kelly bet is 10% of your betting wealth. This maximizes the rate of growth of your betting fortune. The chance of doubling before halving is about 70%, tripling before halving about 65%, and quadrupling before halving about 60%.

There is never any reason to bet any more than the optimal Kelly bet, since both the relative growth and the security decrease. By betting less than the Kelly bet, the relative growth decreases but the security improves. For example, if you bet half the optimal Kelly bet, or 5% of your wealth, the growth rate drops to about 78% of the maximum. But the chances of doubling, tripling, and quadrupling are all around 85%. Figures 5.3 and 5.5 show similar results for the safer bets 2 and 3. In these cases the optimal Kelly bets are larger because the risk of losing is much less. The probabilities of doubling, tripling, and quadrupling your fortune before losing half of it when you bet the optimal Kelly amount are similar to those in Figure 5.1. However, these probabilities are much higher if you make bets in the 5%–10% range, as in bet 1.

Figures 5.2, 5.4, and 5.6 give the probabilities that you will reach a goal of $2,500 before dropping to $1,000, $500, or $0 for situations 1, 2, and 3. The graphs give the optimal Kelly-bet values, as well as half the optimal Kelly-bet values, for various levels of initial wealth. For example, in Figure 5.2 the chance of going to $0 is almost negligible if you have a betting fortune of at least $100 or more.* Starting with an initial wealth of $1,500, the chance of reaching $2,500 before falling to $1,000 is about 0.60 and 0.80 with full-Kelly and 0.5-Kelly betting, respectively. Similarly, the chances of reaching $2,500 before falling to $500 are about 0.83 and 0.95, respectively, for full-Kelly and 0.5-Kelly betting strategies. Figures 5.4 and 5.6 provide a similar analysis for the safer cases of 2 and 3.

AN IMPORTANT OBSERVATION: In this book we advocate using the Kelly criterion. It has the property that the long-run rate of growth of your betting fortune is maximized. As we just discussed and as is shown in Figures 5.1–5.6, this entails some risk, since some of the bets made can be quite large. Those who wish to lower this risk (and also the corresponding growth

*In our calculations we have used $1 as the bankruptcy point, as the minimum bet at racetracks is $2.

rate) can simply use a fractional-Kelly betting system. Figures 5.1, 5.3, and 5.5 will give you advice regarding what fraction is appropriate for your particular preference for trade-offs between growth and risk. There will be no change in the way you decide whether to bet or not as described in the following section, "Steps in Applying the Dr. Z System," page 106. However, the amount bet should be decreased. For example, if the Kelly optimal bet is $100 and your preferred fraction is 0.6, then you bet $60. Professional blackjack teams use fractional-Kelly strategies of from 0.2 to 0.8. This is advisable since their edge is about 2%, and the risks of losing are quite high. In our Dr. Z system bets, the edge is considerably higher—at least 10%. It is our opinion that using the ordinary Kelly criterion rather than a fractional-Kelly betting system is preferable.

MORE ON THE KELLY CRITERION: ITS DESIRABLE PROPERTIES AND LIMITATIONS

We believe that the Kelly criterion is the best possible betting system for use on place and show bets and we utilize it in the Dr. Z system. It has many good properties and a few bad properties.

Good Properties

1. The Dr. Z system can be used on a race-by-race basis. For example, you don't need to worry about what races might come up later in the day or what happened in earlier races. All you need to know to make the optimal bet on a particular race is your betting fortune and the characteristics of the bet in question.
2. The more attractive the betting situation, the more the Kelly criterion tells you to bet. For example, in coin-tossing bets where you win $1 with probability p and lose $1 with probability $1 - p$, you simply bet that fraction of your fortune that equals your edge. So if your fortune is $100 and $p = 0.55$ and $1 - p = 0.45$, you bet the fraction $0.55 - 0.45 = 0.10$, or $10.* For more complicated bets, such as those to place and show, the optimal bet is also a fraction of your wealth. However, if the amount of the bet is so large that it influences the odds, the optimal bet is not a fraction of your wealth. In all cases, the amount bet is larger the more preferable the betting situation.

*If the horse has odds of O–1 and wins with probability p and loses with probability $q = 1 - p$, then the optimal fraction becomes $(pO - q)/O$. This is the edge divided by the odds. So for a 3–1 shot who wins with probability 0.4, you bet 20% of the current betting fortune, since $[0.4(3) - 0.6]/3 = 0.2$.

3. The Kelly criterion allows you to take into account the effect of your bets on the odds. The optimal bet is made by considering all bets by the crowd, as well as the track take.
4. You can never really go broke with the Kelly criterion system of betting. Since you are generally wagering an amount proportional to your betting wealth, you simply will bet less when you are losing. So if your betting fortune becomes quite small, your bets will be smaller yet.
5. The Kelly criterion tells you to bet more when you are winning because your betting wealth is higher.

Bad Properties

1. The Kelly-criterion bets tend to be quite high whenever the bets look especially attractive. Thus in an extended losing streak, your betting fortune will drop off considerably. If that happens it will take quite a while to recoup these losses.
2. If you have two identical betting opportunities in successive races and win one of the bets and lose the other, you will wind up behind. For example, suppose you are betting 10% of your fortune of $100. If you win, your fortune becomes $100 + $10 = $110. Then you bet $11, and if you lose your fortune becomes $99. Conversely, if you lose first, your fortune becomes $100 − $10 = $90. Then you bet $9, and if you win you have $99. In either case, you will end up with $99, which is less than your original stake of $100.

BETTING SIMULATION

Despite its properties, few bettors actually use the Kelly strategy. In fact, many bettors seem to feel their money management techniques at the track are far less important than their handicapping. Thinking that way, they then tend to use fairly simple betting strategies like flat betting or proportional betting. To demonstrate that money management really does make a difference and that Kelly betting is the way to go, we present some simulation results that appear in Ziemba and Hausch (1985) for comparing various betting schemes. The betting schemes compared are Kelly, half Kelly, flat, proportional, and base bet plus square-root betting.

In flat betting, you wager the same amount on each race. This scheme is attractive because it is so simple, and it seems to be the most common betting strategy at the track. It suffers, however, from not having the bet size depend on the size of your current bankroll or the characteristics of the horse, the factors in the race, and the public's betting.

In proportional betting, you wager a constant fraction of your bankroll.

So, if your bankroll is increasing or decreasing, then your bets are increasing or decreasing, too. Proportional betting is *not* Kelly betting, and, while the bet size is influenced by the size of your bankroll, the system still suffers from not having the bet size depend on the characteristics of the wager.

Base bet plus square root (BBPSR) advocates flat betting if you are behind. However, if you are ahead, then bet the same flat bet plus the square root of your current profits. With this scheme, the bet size is a function of your bankroll but, like proportional betting, it does not take specific race factors into account.

Hollywood Park's average win pool is on the order of $300,000. The simulation supposes a win pool of this size, plus whatever we bet. It also supposes a track payback proportion of 0.83. The simulation assumes 700 good wagers can be identified each season, and then 1,000 seasons are simulated. For each season, the bets are made sequentially and the bankroll is updated after the outcome of each race. The 700 wagers are chosen at random from the following five wager opportunities:

True Probability of Horse Winning	*Win Pool ($)*	*Win Bet by the Public on our Horse ($)*	*Mutuel $ Payoff on a $2 bet (our bet will lower this)*	*Likelihood of each Wager Being Chosen in Simulation*
0.57	300,000	124,500	4	0.10
0.38	300,000	83,000	6	0.30
0.285	300,000	62,250	8	0.30
0.228	300,000	49,800	10	0.20
0.19	300,000	41,500	12	0.10
Total				Average 1.00

If you bet $1, then the first wager will have a gross return of $2 with probability 0.57 and $0 with probability 0.43. The expected return on the first wager is then

$$0.57(\$2) + 0.43(\$0) = \$1.14.$$

The other four wager opportunities also have an expected return of $1.14. Note that as our wagers increase, however, payoffs will fall somewhat. This is accounted for in the simulation. The simulation assumes an initial wealth of $1,000 and the money management schemes tested are Kelly, half Kelly, proportional betting with proportions of 1%, 2%, 3%, 4%, 5%, and 10%, flat betting of 1%, 2%, 3%, 4%, 5%, and 10% of the initial $1,000 bankroll; and BBPSR with flat bets of 1%, 2%, 3%, 4%, 5%, and 10% of the initial $1,000.

TABLE 5.1 ***Simulation results (1,000 trials of 700 races) (initial bankroll of $1,000): Edge is 14%***

	Final Bankroll					Number of Seasons out of 1000 When the Final Bankroll Was							
System	*Minimum*	*Maximum*	*Mean*	*Median*	*Bankrupt*	*>$2*	*>$250*	*>$500*	*>$1,000*	*>$5,000*	*>$10,000*	*>$50,000*	*>$100,000*
Kelly Bet	18	453883	48135	17269	0	1000	957	916	870	692	598	302	166
Half-Kelly Bet	145	111770	13069	8043	0	1000	999	990	954	654	430	30	1
1% Flat Bet	307	3067	1861	1857	0	1000	1000	999	980	0	0	0	0
2% Flat Bet	0	5377	2824	2822	9	991	990	988	978	9	0	0	0
3% Flat Bet	0	7682	3739	3770	36	964	963	962	957	191	0	0	0
4% Flat Bet	0	9986	4495	4685	94	906	906	906	904	432	0	0	0
5% Flat Bet	0	12282	5213	5526	134	866	866	866	864	584	33	0	0
10% Flat Bet	0	23747	7637	8722	349	651	651	651	651	613	425	0	0
1% BBPSR Bet	291	18795	4612	3855	0	1000	1000	999	916	376	80	0	0
2% BBPSR Bet	0	23943	6443	5617	10	990	988	986	934	557	192	0	0
3% BBPSR Bet	0	28480	7918	7165	52	948	948	947	914	667	314	0	0
4% BBPSR Bet	0	32545	8953	8233	121	879	879	877	859	689	406	0	0
5% BBPSR Bet	0	36462	9868	9333	180	820	820	819	808	704	463	0	0
10% BBPSR Bet	0	54029	11968	9953	417	583	583	583	581	562	498	7	0
1% Proportional Bet	435	8469	2535	2270	0	1000	1000	999	965	43	0	0	0
2% Proportional Bet	173	57087	6628	4360	0	1000	999	991	940	443	180	7	0
3% Proportional Bet	65	243281	15343	6799	0	1000	994	973	919	592	396	65	18
4% Proportional Bet	49	483355	26202	8669	0	1000	979	935	882	627	459	146	61
5% Proportional Bet	38	548382	32415	8907	0	1000	941	899	841	609	475	179	90
10% Proportional Bet	18	364587	13662	602	0	1000	575	515	455	304	221	78	36

The 1,000 trials produced 1,000 different final bankrolls for each system. The mean and the median bankrolls are given in Table 5.1. Also listed are the smallest and largest final bankrolls, the number of trials exceeding certain specified levels, and the number of trials ending in bankruptcy (tapouts).

Table 5.1 shows substantial differences in the means, medians, and the risks of each system. In other words, the choice of betting scheme really matters! The difference in risks can be seen by comparing how many times the final bankrolls of each system exceed the various specified levels and how many times the system taps out. The results seem to overwhelmingly favor the Kelly system. Only a very conservative bettor would prefer the fractional Kelly system—it had a very respectable median and showed a profit 95% of the time. Any other individual, though, would seem to prefer the Kelly scheme—it had, by far, the highest median, showed a profit 87% of the time, and 17% of the time the $1,000 grew to more than $100,000.

*ASSUMPTIONS OF THE DR. Z SYSTEM**

There are three basic assumptions that underlie the Dr. Z system.

First, it is assumed that the market for win bets is efficient. Specifically, we suppose that the probability that a given horse wins the race in question is equal to the fraction of money bet on that horse to win. So if W_i is bet on horse i to win and the total win pool is W, then the probability that horse i wins the race is

$$q_i = \frac{W_i}{W}. \tag{5.1}$$

For example, if the win pool is $10,000 and $2,500 is bet on horse 4, then $q_4 = 0.25$, so horse 4 has a 25% chance of winning.

We know from our discussion in Chapter Three that equation (5.1) is quite accurate except for the favorite–long-shot bias. It serves us well as a working hypothesis. The errors in overestimating long shots' chances of winning and underestimating favorites' chances of winning are not a problem.†

Second, it is assumed that the Harville (1973) formulas can be used to estimate the probability of all possible win, place, and show finishes. They are based on the following reasonable idea: Suppose a race has four horses with probabilities of winning of $\frac{1}{3}$, $\frac{1}{2}$, $\frac{1}{12}$, and $\frac{1}{12}$, respectively. Now if horse 1 wins, then the probability that horse 2 is second is

*This section contains some discussion that is more mathematical than the rest of the text. Understanding it is not required to use the Dr. Z system, the steps of which are explained in detail in the following section.

†Readers with mathematical backgrounds can find more on this in Appendix B.

$$\frac{\frac{1}{2}}{1-\frac{1}{3}}=\frac{3}{4}$$

and the probability that horse 3 is second is

$$\frac{\frac{1}{12}}{1-\frac{1}{3}}=\frac{1}{8}.$$

The probability that horse 4 is second is also $\frac{1}{8}$.

The idea is that the relative chances of winning of the various horses left in the race remain the same. It is as if horse 1 were eliminated from the race and 2 and 3 are vying to win the next position, that is, to come in second.

The Harville formula for place is as follows: Let q_i be the probability that i wins the race as determined by equation (5.1) and q_j be the probability that j wins the race. Then the probability that i wins the race and j is second is

$$q_{ij} = \underbrace{(q_i)}_{\substack{\text{Probability}\\ \text{that } i \text{ is}\\ \text{first}}} \underbrace{\left(\frac{q_j}{1-q_i}\right)}_{\substack{\text{Probability}\\ \text{that } j \text{ is}\\ \text{second once}\\ \text{it is known}\\ \text{that } i \text{ is first}}}. \tag{5.2}$$

So for our example, with $q_1 = \frac{1}{3}$, $q_2 = \frac{1}{2}$, $q_3 = \frac{1}{12}$, and $q_4 = \frac{1}{12}$, the probability that 1 is first and 2 is second is

$$q_{12} = \underbrace{(q_1)}_{\substack{\text{Probability}\\ \text{that 1 wins}}} \underbrace{\left(\frac{q_2}{1-q_1}\right)}_{\substack{\text{Probability}\\ \text{that 2 is}\\ \text{second if 1}\\ \text{wins}}} = \left(\frac{1}{3}\right)\left(\frac{\frac{1}{2}}{1-\frac{1}{3}}\right)=\frac{1}{4}.$$

Similarly, the probability that 4 is first and 1 is second is

$$q_{41} = \underbrace{(q_4)}_{\substack{\text{Probability}\\ \text{that 4 wins}}} \underbrace{\left(\frac{q_1}{1-q_4}\right)}_{\substack{\text{Probability}\\ \text{that 1 is}\\ \text{second if 4}\\ \text{wins}}} = \left(\frac{1}{12}\right)\left(\frac{\frac{1}{3}}{1-\frac{1}{12}}\right) = \frac{1}{33}.$$

The Harville formula for show follows. We now consider the possibility that three horses are in the money and call them i, j, and k. Then the probability that i wins the race, j is second, and k is third is

$$q_{ijk} = \underbrace{(q_i)}_{\substack{\text{Probability}\\ \text{that } i \text{ wins}}} \underbrace{\left(\frac{q_j}{1-q_i}\right)}_{\substack{\text{Probability}\\ \text{that } j \text{ is}\\ \text{second if}\\ i \text{ wins}}} \underbrace{\left(\frac{q_k}{1-q_i-q_j}\right)}_{\substack{\text{Probability}\\ \text{that } k \text{ is}\\ \text{third if } i \text{ wins}\\ \text{and } j \text{ is second}}} \tag{5.3}$$

So for our example, with $q_1 = \frac{1}{3}$, $q_2 = \frac{1}{2}$, $q_3 = \frac{1}{12}$, and $q_4 = \frac{1}{12}$ the probability that 1 is first, 2 is second and 3 is third is

$$q_{123} = \underbrace{(q_1)}_{\substack{\text{Probability}\\ \text{that 1 wins}}} \underbrace{\left(\frac{q_2}{1-q_2}\right)}_{\substack{\text{Probability}\\ \text{that 2 is}\\ \text{second if}\\ \text{1 wins}}} \underbrace{\left(\frac{q_3}{1-q_1-q_2}\right)}_{\substack{\text{Probability}\\ \text{that 3 is}\\ \text{third if 1 wins}\\ \text{and 2 is second}}}$$

$$= \left(\frac{1}{3}\right)\left(\frac{\frac{1}{2}}{1-\frac{1}{3}}\right)\left(\frac{\frac{1}{12}}{1-\frac{1}{3}-\frac{1}{2}}\right) = \frac{1}{8}.$$

Similarly, the probability that 4 is first, 1 is second, and 2 is third is

$$q_{412} = \underbrace{(q_4)}_{\substack{\text{Probability}\\ \text{that 4 wins}}} \underbrace{\left(\frac{q_1}{1 - q_4}\right)}_{\substack{\text{Probability}\\ \text{that 1 is}\\ \text{second if}\\ \text{4 wins}}} \underbrace{\left(\frac{q_2}{1 - q_4 - q_1}\right)}_{\substack{\text{Probability}\\ \text{that 2 is}\\ \text{third if 4 wins}\\ \text{and 1 is second}}}$$

$$= \left(\frac{1}{12}\right)\left(\frac{\frac{1}{3}}{1 - \frac{1}{12}}\right)\left(\frac{\frac{1}{2}}{1 - \frac{1}{12} - \frac{1}{3}}\right) = \frac{2}{77}.$$

The Harville formulas are used in the Dr. Z model to estimate the probabilities of all possible finishes so that we can get an overall worth of any possible bet once we know how much is bet to win, place, and show on the various horses. They are also useful in the analysis of other bets, such as those occurring in minus pools, which we discuss in Chapter Fifteen.*

PARIS ROAD, ch. g. 1975, by Jungle Road-Made In Paris, by Succession
Owner: R. J. McCance. Trainer: Robert McCance. 1980. 5 3 0 0 $5.985 **114**
Breeder: Mr. and Mrs. R. W. Hall (B.C., Canada). **$6,250** 1979 5 2 0 0 $3,204

21Jun80	^{5}EP	$1\frac{1}{16}$	$:49^1$	$1:14^2$	1:48	ft	16	115	$4^{1\frac{3}{4}}$	$2^{\frac{1}{2}}$	1^2	$1^{\frac{1}{2}}$	WlknsnW^2	5000	71	ParisRoad115	Gail'sPunch	10
4Jun80	^{5}EP	$6\frac{1}{2}$ f	:23	$:46^4$	1:20	sy	25	116	$4^{2\frac{1}{2}}$	$3^{2\frac{1}{2}}$	$2^{\frac{1}{2}}$	1^h	WlksonW^1	4000	78	ParisRoad116	TicketCount	9
23May80	^{6}EP	$6\frac{1}{2}$ f	$:22^2$	$:45^4$	1:19	ft	20	114	10^{13}	6^{12}	8^{12}	8^{14}	MelansnG^9	4000	69	Ionion Sea 117	Hacker	10
2May80	^{1}EP	$6\frac{1}{2}$ f	$:22^2$	$:46^3$	$1:20^3$	ft	20	119	$8^{5\frac{3}{4}}$	$5^{2\frac{3}{4}}$	1^2	$1^{2\frac{1}{4}}$	MelansnG^6	3200	75	ParisRoad119	FireBall	10
18Apr80	^{6}EP	6 f	$:23^2$	$:47^3$	$1:13^4$	sy	40	115	8^{12}	8^{10}	6^{10}	7^{11}	WlknsnW^9	4000	72	KakaDeHrt114	Citizen'sAwrd	10
14Jly 79	^{4}EP	$1\frac{1}{16}$	$:47^4$	$1:12^4$	$1:46^4$	ft	31	113	9^{11}	10^{12}	9^{13}	9^{13}	FrazierD^8	3000	64	ElliesBoy113	RoyalTruce	10
30Jun79	^{4}EP	$6\frac{1}{2}$ f	$:22^4$	$:46^3$	$1:19^4$	gd	14	119	$7^{5\frac{1}{2}}$	$6^{7\frac{1}{2}}$	5^{12}	$5^{9\frac{1}{4}}$	BrayR^{10}	3200	70	SuperWin114	BowHunter	10
16Jun79	^{4}EP	$1\frac{1}{16}$	$:48^4$	$1:14^4$	1:49	sy	6	116	8^{12}	8^{10}	7^{14}	7^{19}	BrayR^6	4000	49	Kevin'sAward114	PlmThePea	8
30May79	^{1}EP	$6\frac{1}{2}$ f	$:22^4$	$:46^3$	$1:19^4$	ft	$3\frac{1}{4}$*	122	$5^{3\frac{1}{4}}$	$3^{3\frac{1}{2}}$	$2^{\frac{1}{2}}$	$1^{2\frac{1}{2}}$	BrayR^{10}	2500	79	ParisRoad122	CoolArtic	10
16May79	^{1}EP	$6\frac{1}{2}$ f	$:22^3$	$:46^3$	$1:19^4$	ft	23	115	7^5	$5^{3\frac{1}{2}}$	$1^{\frac{1}{2}}$	1^2	BrayR^1	2500	79	ParisRoad115	LaBelleMichell	10

The Harville formulas are based on the concept that the relative chance that each of several horses will finish first is not changed when one of them is eliminated. However, the acid test is how well they predict real races. As a test, we used them to compute the expected values using races over 110 days at Exhibition Park in 1978 and 75 days at Santa Anita in 1973–74.† The object was to compare the Harville formulas' estimates of the expected values with the observed expected values. Naturally, we were interested primarily in situations where the expected value was greater than one, since

*Although very useful and accurate most of the time, the Harville formulas overestimate the probability of coming in second or third for Silky Sullivan-type horses. Those are late chargers that either have that burst of speed in the stretch to overtake several horses and win the race or they do not and finish quite far back. For these horses the probability of finishing second or third is virtually zero. The record of Paris Road, who had this characteristic while racing at Exhibition Park in 1981, appears above. This overestimation does not cause us any difficulty, for we recommend that in the rare instance when you encounter such a horse you simply do not bet on the horse for place or show.

†The actual formulas used to do this are quite complex and appear in Appendix B. These data are discussed more fully in Chapter Nine.

TABLE 5.2 ***Results of betting $10 to place or show on horses with expected returns of at least* E *at Exhibition Park in 1978 and Santa Anita in 1973–74***

Details of Bets

Expected Return Is at Least *E*	Exhibition Park 1978: Number of Bets to Place	Total Net Profit ($)	Net Rate of Return (%)	Number of Bets to Show	Total Net Profit ($)	Net Rate of Return (%)	Santa Anita 1973–74: Number of Bets to Place	Total Net Profit ($)	Net Rate of Return (%)	Number of Bets to Show	Total Net Profit ($)	Net Rate of Return (%)
1.04	225	51	2.3	612	332	5.4	103	123	11.9	307	−180	−5.9
1.08	126	−101	−8.0	386	535	13.9	52	128	24.6	162	69	4.3
1.12	69	111	16.1	223	408	18.3	22	92	41.8	89	30	3.4
1.16	40	51	12.8	143	263	18.4	7	23	32.9	46	124	27.0
1.20	18	53	29.4	95	217	22.8	3	−13	−43.3	27	62	23.0
1.25	11	−27	−24.5	44	112	25.5	0	0	—	9	60	66.7
1.30	3	−30	−100.0	27	108	40.0	0	0	—	5	51	102.0
1.50	0	0	—	3	60	200.0	0	0	—	0	0	—

Summary

Expected Return Is at Least *E*	Exhibition Park: Number of Bets to Place and Show	Total Net Profit ($)	Net Rate of Return (%)	Santa Anita: Number of Bets to Place and Show	Total Net Profit ($)	Net Rate of Return (%)	Totals: Number of Bets to Place and Show	Total Net Profit ($)	Net Rate of Return ($)
1.04	837	383	4.6	410	−57	−1.4	1247	326	2.6
1.08	512	434	8.5	214	197	9.2	726	631	8.7
1.12	292	519	17.8	111	122	11.0	403	641	15.9
1.16	183	314	17.2	53	147	27.7	236	461	19.5
1.20	113	270	23.9	30	49	16.3	143	319	22.3
1.25	55	85	15.5	9	60	66.7	64	145	22.7
1.30	30	78	26.0	5	51	102.0	35	129	36.9
1.50	3	60	200.0	0	0	—	3	60	200.0

that is when profits are made. We therefore compared the expected values when the Harville formulas indicated that the expected value was at least 1.04 so that we could expect a 4% profit or more.

The results appear in Table 5.2. It is supposed that we bet $10 on every horse whose expected value was at least 1.04, as estimated by using the Harville formulas in conjunction with the efficient-win-market assumption (5.2). The results were quite encouraging because the estimated expected return was reasonably close to the actual average return. Indeed, even wagering such equal bets you would make a nice profit. Of course, we will want to bet more when the odds, as measured by the expected return, are higher and the measured probability of the risk of losing is lower. We do this with the Kelly-criterion betting system, the third key assumption of the Dr. Z system.

The third major assumption underlying the Dr. Z system is that we bet according to the Kelly criterion. As we discussed in the preceding sections of this chapter, this strategy provides the maximum rate of growth of your betting fortune.

The actual mathematical model underlying the Dr. Z system considers the effect of our bets on all the possible payoffs for place and show.* It then calculates the optimal bets for place and show, taking into account the track take and the relative amounts bet to win, place, and show on the various horses. To make the Dr. Z system easy to use at racetracks, we have made approximations of the true optimal solutions, enabling you easily to estimate the expected value per dollar bet to place or show on any given horse and to determine how much you should wager out of your betting fortune.

The expected-value equations appeared in Chapter Four; the equations for the optimal amount to bet for place and show follow. In the following section, we provide you with detailed steps in applying the Dr. Z system, including charts that indicate when a bet is a Dr. Z system bet and how much you should bet. To obtain the maximum accuracy, different equations are necessary for different wealth levels and sizes of the track's betting pools. All these equations appear in Chapter Sixteen; they were used to calculate the charts that appear in the following section.

Equations for place and show betting with a betting wealth of $500 follow. The place-betting equation is appropriate when the place pool is between $10,000 and $150,000 and the show-betting equation is appropriate for a show pool between $6,000 and $100,000. These equations are to be used only if the expected-value equations from Chapter Four indicate that a bet should be made.†

---

*Mathematical details of the model appear in Appendix B.

†These formulas for optimal place and show bets assume a track payback Q of 0.829. For other values of Q we have developed a correction factor for the optimal bet sizes. It is similar to the correction factors for expected value to place and show in equations (4.5) and (4.6). This feature is discussed in Chapter Sixteen.

$$\text{Place bet} = \left[505q_i + 527q_i^2 - \left(\frac{386q_iP_i}{q_iP - 0.60P_i}\right)\right]\left(\frac{P - 10{,}000}{140{,}000}\right) \tag{5.4}$$
$$+ \left[375q_i + 525q_i^2 - \left(\frac{271q_iP_i}{q_iP - 0.70P_i}\right)\right]\left(\frac{150{,}000 - P}{140{,}000}\right)$$

$$\text{Show bet} = \left[131 + 2{,}150q_i^2 - 1{,}778q_i^3 - \left(\frac{150S_i}{q_iS - 0.70S_i}\right)\right]\left(\frac{S - 6{,}000}{94{,}000}\right)$$
$$+ \left[86 + 1{,}516q_i^2 - 968q_i^3 - \left(\frac{90.7S_i}{q_iS - 0.85S_i}\right)\right]\left(\frac{100{,}000 - S}{94{,}000}\right) \tag{5.5}$$

Recall that $q_i = W_i/W$, where W_i is the win bet on i and the win pool is W, P_i is the place bet on i, P is the place pool, S_i is the show bet on i, and S is the show pool.

We illustrate these equations in the examples later in the chapter. Now let's go over the full steps in applying the Dr. Z system.

STEPS IN APPLYING THE DR. Z SYSTEM

Full details on how to apply the Dr. Z system follow. First, there is a set of rules indicating when you should consider not betting. Second, there are some useful hints and cautions that you should keep in mind in selecting your bets. Finally, there are the steps in the evaluation of a possible Dr. Z system bet, including charts to determine whether to bet or not and, if so, how much you should bet. Before starting you should establish your bankroll, determine the track take, buy the program and *Daily Racing Form,* and prepare your betting aids. Detailed examples of three actual races using these procedures are then provided. More examples appear in succeeding chapters.

We recommend that you *do not bet* in any of the following situations:

1. On days when the track is not fast. This especially means heavy, sloppy, or muddy tracks, but also includes tracks listed as in fair or good condition. Horses' performances are extremely variable on such tracks.
2. When there is a minus pool and some horse or horses are bet so heavily to place or show that the payoff on all horses will be $2.10 if this horse or any of the entry horses are in the money. Minus pools are discussed in detail in Chapter Fifteen.*

*All general rules have exceptions. An exception to situation 2 is Louisiana or any other locale where the minimum payoff is $2.20. There the bet is good if the horse is going off at odds of 1–2 or less. The wager on such a $2.20 guaranteed minus pool payoff can be quite large. At 1–2 odds the chance of winning the show wager is about 95.5% (see Figure 6.2) for an edge of about 5%. The odds are

3. When the horse in question is going off at odds of more than 8–1. Since these long shots are traditionally overbet, the possible payoff that you might get is not sufficient to justify the risk involved.*
4. When the horse in question is a Silky Sullivan-type runner. These are horses whose records indicate that they are late chargers who come from far off the pace and either win the race or finish out of the money. You can recognize these horses by consulting the past performances. If a horse has run that kind of race in its last ten outings, don't bet it to place or show.
5. When the expected return per dollar bet is less than 1.14 for the top tracks and 1.18 for other tracks. The tracks with sufficiently large betting pools and superior horses to warrant the 1.14 expected-value cutoff are as follows:

Aqueduct, New York	Hialeah, Florida	Monmouth Park, New Jersey
Arlington Park, Illinois	Hollywood Park, California	Oaklawn Park, Arkansas
Belmont Park, New York	Keeneland, Kentucky	Pimlico, Maryland
Churchill Downs, Kentucky	Longacres, Washington	Santa Anita Park, California
Del Mar, California	Los Alamitos, California	Saratoga, New York
Golden Gate, California	Louisiana Downs, Louisiana	Sportsman's Park, Illinois
Gulfstream Park, Florida	Meadowlands, New Jersey	Woodbine, Ontario
Hawthorne, Illinois		

At all other tracks use an expected value cutoff of 1.18. Figures 5.7–5.10 can be used for this purpose.

6. A cutoff of 1.10 is warranted for the very best races when the conditions are ideal. These include stakes races with purses of more than $50,000. Such a cutoff is suggested even for nontop tracks, but only for these major races.

Figures 5.7–5.10 can be used to determine whether or not a bet is worth making to achieve a cutoff of 1.14 or 1.18. If you are using a 1.10 cutoff for one of the very best races, we suggest that you use the 1.14 charts with the provision that they will be a little on the conservative side—that is, you can be slightly above the line and the bet will still be worth making.

If you want to do the calculations in your head, then you look for a horse whose fraction bet to place out of the total place pool is much less

---

1–10 for a $2.20 payoff. Hence the optimal Kelly wager, namely the edge divided by the odds is a staggering 50% of one's fortune. With such a large risk we recommend a fractional Kelly wager of a quarter to a half this amount. As the odds become lower, the wager becomes even better and the Kelly criterion would suggest an even larger bet.

*An exception to situation 3 can occur in a race in which the horse with odds of more than 8–1 odds is the second or third favorite, as was Smile in the 1986 Breeders' Cup Sprint, see page 76.

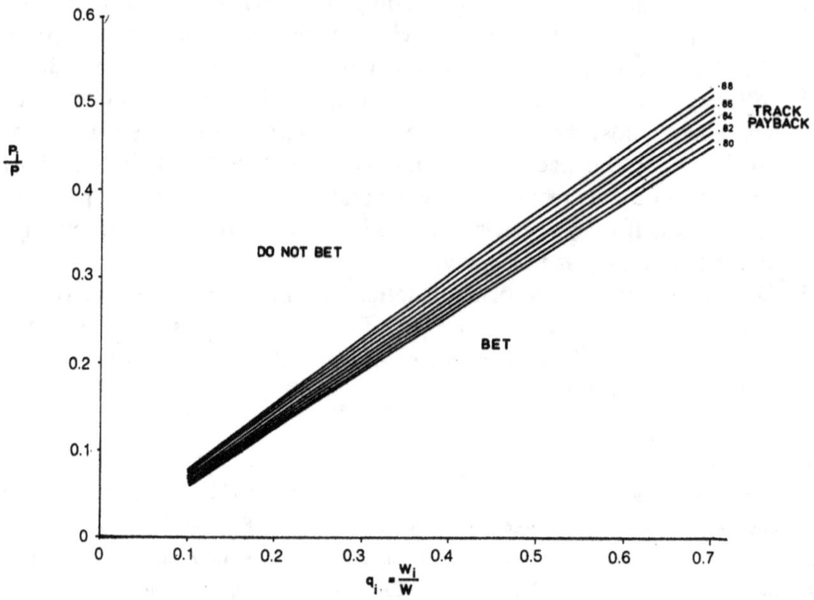

Figure 5.7 Graph indicates whether or not to make a place bet when the expected-value cutoff is 1.14 and the track payback varies from 0.80 to 0.88—*bet* if value is on or below the appropriate line; *do not bet* otherwise

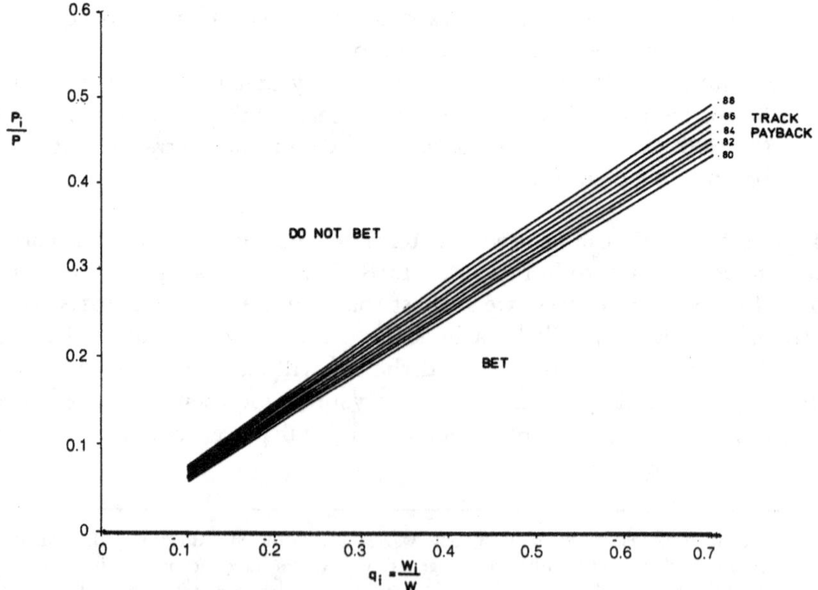

Figure 5.8 Graph indicates whether or not to make a place bet when the expected-value cutoff is 1.18 and the track payback varies from 0.80 to 0.88—*bet* if value is on or below the appropriate line; *do not bet* otherwise

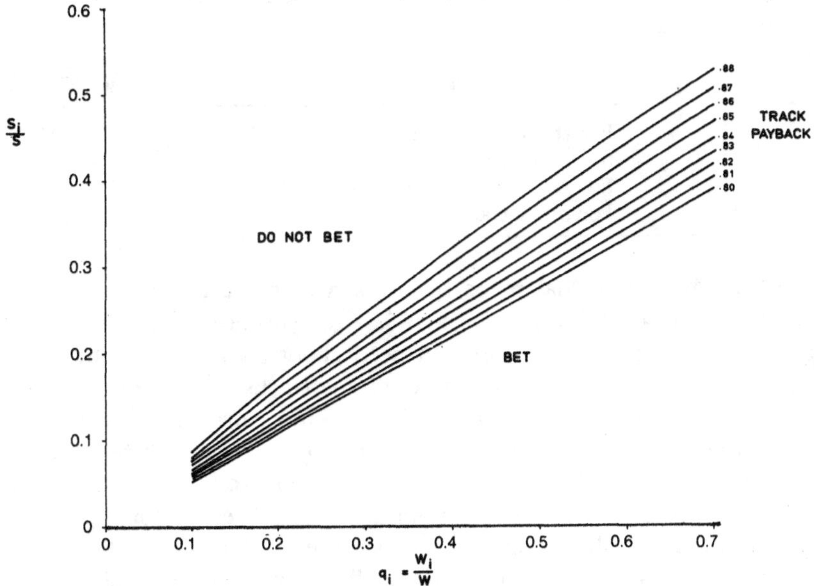

Figure 5.9 Graph indicates whether or not to make a show bet when the expected-value cutoff is 1.14 and the track payback varies from 0.80 to 0.88—*bet* if value is on or below the appropriate line; *do not* bet otherwise

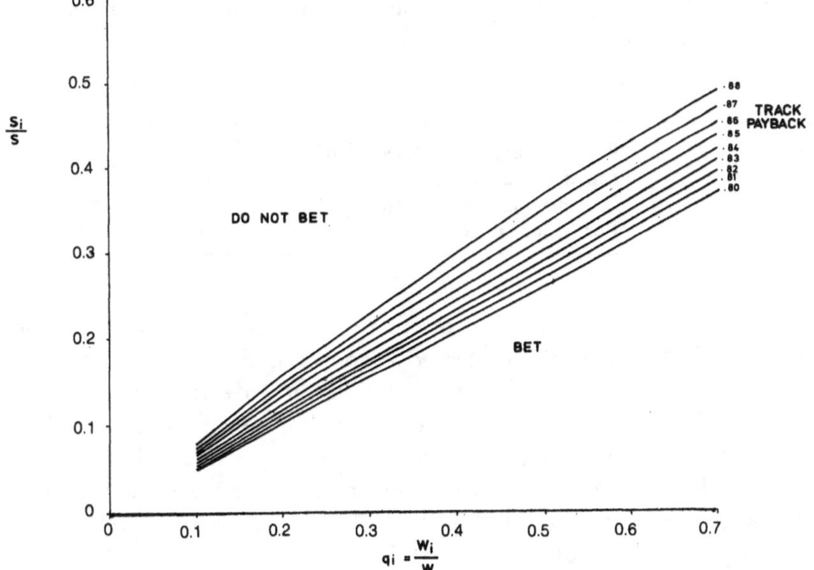

Figure 5.10 Graph indicates whether or not to make a show bet when the expected-value cutoff is 1.18 and the track payback varies from 0.80 to 0.88—*bet* if value is on or below the appropriate line; *do not* bet otherwise

than the fraction bet on this horse to win. Use the following cutoffs, which are based on equation (4.3):

Cutoff	*When to use*	$(W_i/W)/(P_i/P)$
1.10	For the very best races with top dependable horses	1.40
1.14	For races at the top tracks	1.47
1.18	For other tracks	1.54

So about 40% more has to be bet to win to make the expected value such that there is a 10% edge. For a 14% edge you need about 47% more bet to win, and for an 18% edge you need about 54% more to be bet to win. These values do *not* take into account the tracks take correction when the track take is below 17.1%. Roughly speaking equation (4.5) indicates that you gain about 1.5% in expected return to place for each percent that the track take is below 17.1%. So if the edge seems to be about 18% with a track take of 15% the real edge is about 21%. It's easier for a place bet to be worth making than a show bet since the 1.40 is 1.51, the 1.47 is 1.62, and the 1.54 is 1.73; see below. Still you will find that about 85% of the Dr. Z bets are to show. Of the 15% of the bets that are to place many are on odds-on favorites. Always check a 3–5 or 4–5 shot for a possible Dr. Z system bet to place as well as to show.

For show bets you wager when the fraction in the show pool bet on the horse you are considering is sufficiently small. These fractions are for various expected value cutoffs using equation (4.4):

Cutoff	*When to use*	$(W_i/W)/(S_i/S)$
1.10	For the very best races with top dependable horses	1.51
1.14	For races at the top tracks	1.62
1.18	For other tracks	1.73

So about 51% more has to be bet to win to make the expected value such that there is a 10% edge. For a 14% edge you need about 62% more to be bet to win, and for an 18% edge you need about 73% more to be bet to win. These values do *not* put in the edge that you get if the track take is less than 17.1%. Roughly speaking, equation (4.6) indicates that you gain about 3% in expected return for each percent that the track take is below 17.1%. So if the edge seems to be about 14% then with a track take of 15% the real edge is about 20%.

For the size of the wager, remember to bet a bit more as the edge becomes higher and a lot more as the probability of winning increases.

We recommend that you *display caution* in the following circumstances:

1. It may be advisable not to bet on horses coming off a long layoff. A particularly dangerous situation is the standout who, for example, last year won six of eight starts and was second in the other two races. He has not run this year. Now it is August and he is made a prohibitive favorite in a long race, all on the basis of his past record and some excellent recent workouts at short distances. There is a good chance this horse will die in the stretch and finish out of the money. In general you have to use some judgment in these long-layoff situations. If you want to be cautious, do not bet on any horse that has not run in the last three weeks. Top-flight stakes horses often run less frequently and the three-week rule should be made six weeks.
2. You should be cautious betting on first-time starters. Super workouts are no substitute for actual racing experience. Bet on them only if the conditions seem ideal otherwise and the odds are excellent. Quirin (1979) has shown that on average first-time starters return less than 50¢ per dollar wagered.
3. We argued in Chapters Three through Five that the win odds generated by the crowd can be used with the Harville formulas to generate good predictors of a horse's chances of finishing second or third, so we bet when the expected payoff was large in comparison with fair odds. This was done without reference to the horses' and jockeys' actual records. There is no doubt, however, that a person feels more comfortable when the bet is on a horse that is frequently in the money, at today's distance, running against similar-quality horses,

	Expected-Value Cutoff	
Size of Place Pool ($)	1.14	1.18
Small 2,000–9,999	Use Figure 5.11	Use Figure 5.14
Medium 10,000–49,999	Use Figure 5.12	Use Figure 5.15
Large 50,000+	Use Figure 5.13	Use Figure 5.16

Size of Show Pool ($)	1.14	1.18
Small 1,200–5,999	Use Figure 5.17	Use Figure 5.20
Medium 6,000–29,999	Use Figure 5.18	Use Figure 5.21
Large 30,000+	Use Figure 5.19	Use Figure 5.22

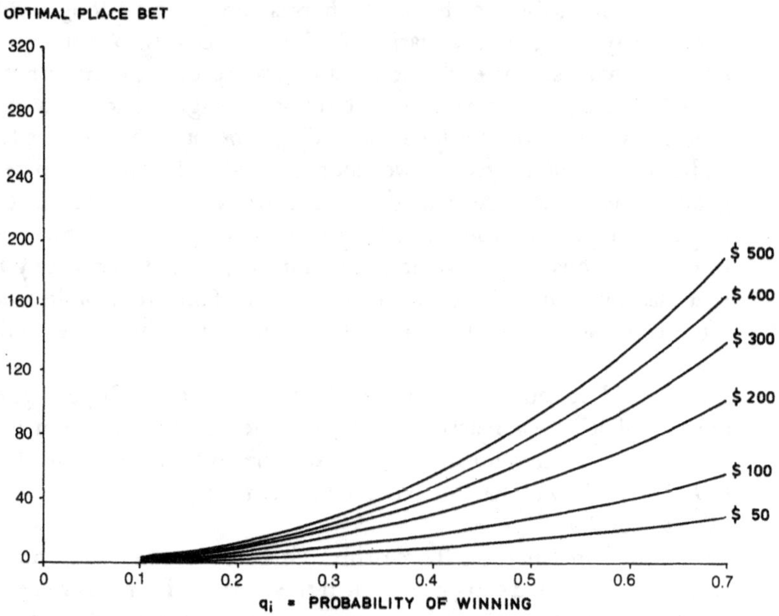

Figure 5.11 Optimal place bet for various q_i and betting-wealth levels when the expected return is 1.14 and the place pool is small ($2,000–$9,999)

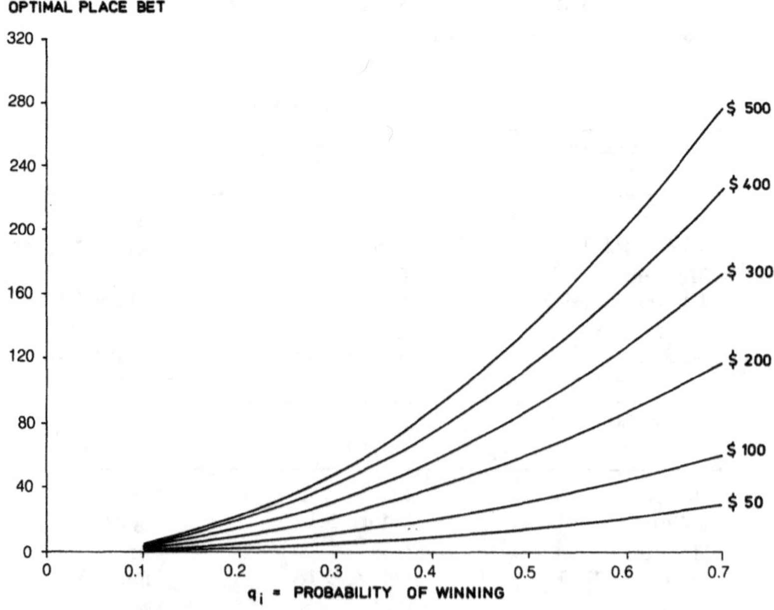

Figure 5.12 Optimal place bet for various q_i and betting-wealth levels when the expected return is 1.14 and the place pool is medium ($10,000–$49,999)

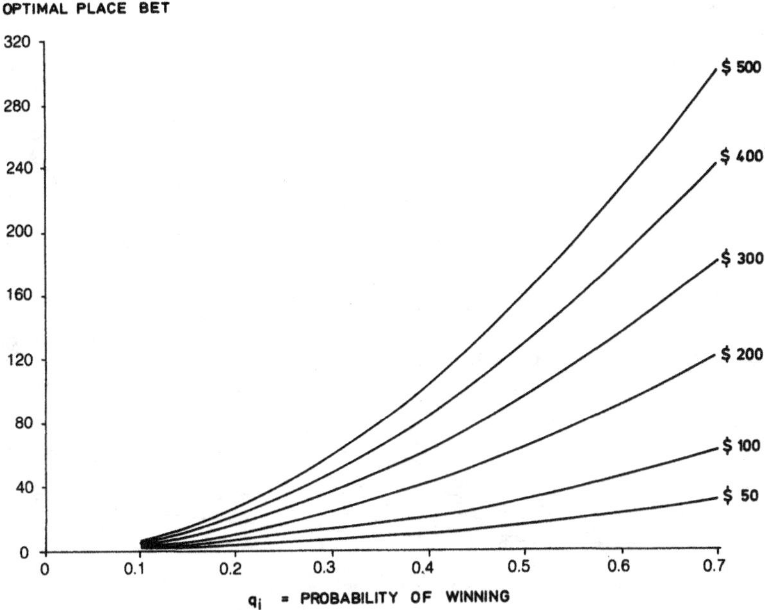

Figure 5.13 Optimal place bet for various q_i and betting-wealth levels when the expected return is 1.14 and the place pool is large ($50,000+)

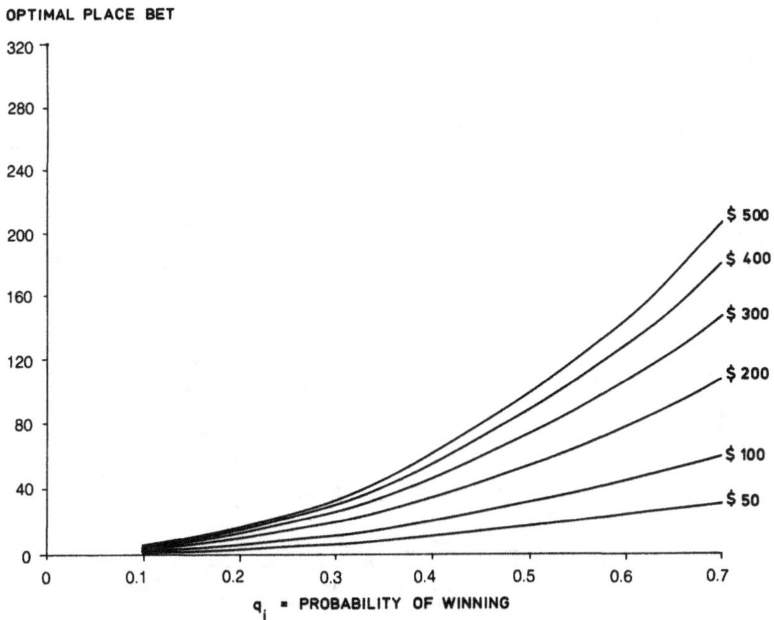

Figure 5.14 Optimal place bet for various q_i and betting-wealth levels when the expected return is 1.18 and the place pool is small ($2,000–$9,999)

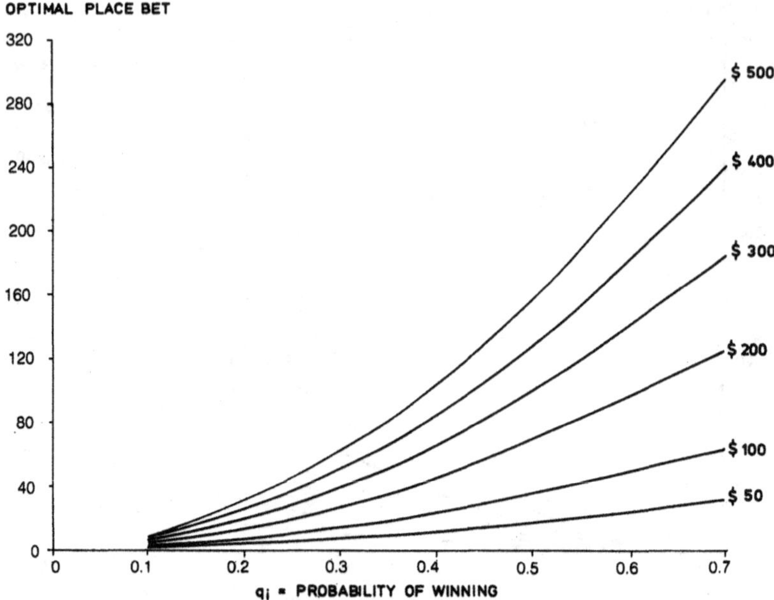

Figure 5.15 Optimal place bet for various q_i and betting-wealth levels when the expected return is 1.18 and the place pool is medium ($10,000–$49,999)

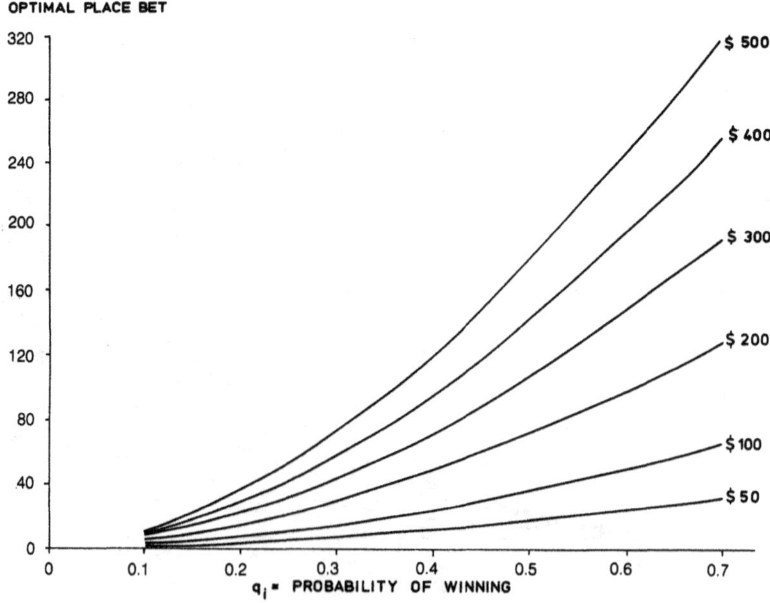

Figure 5.16 Optimal place bet for various q_i and betting-wealth levels when the expected return is 1.18 and the place pool is large ($50,000+)

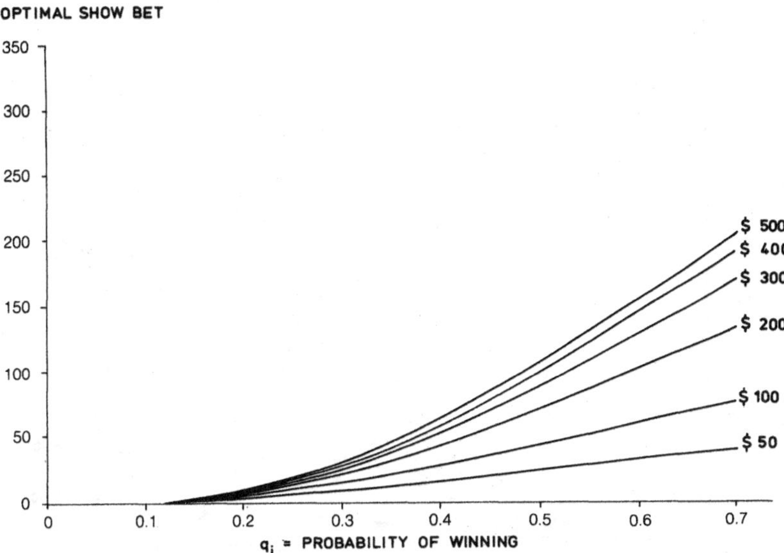

Figure 5.17 Optimal show bet for various q_i and betting-wealth levels when the expected return is 1.14 and the show pool is small ($1,200–$5,999)

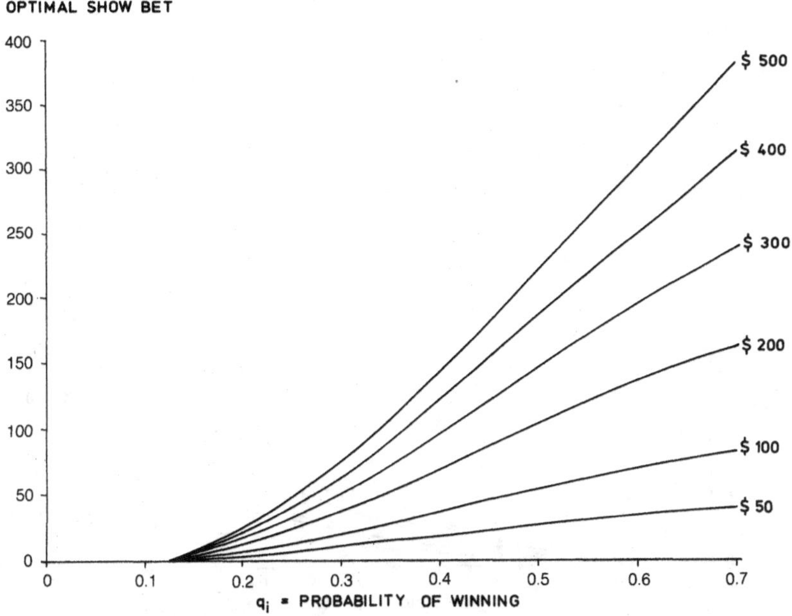

Figure 5.18 Optimal show bet for various q_i and betting-wealth levels when the expected return is 1.14 and the show pool is medium ($6,000–$29,999)

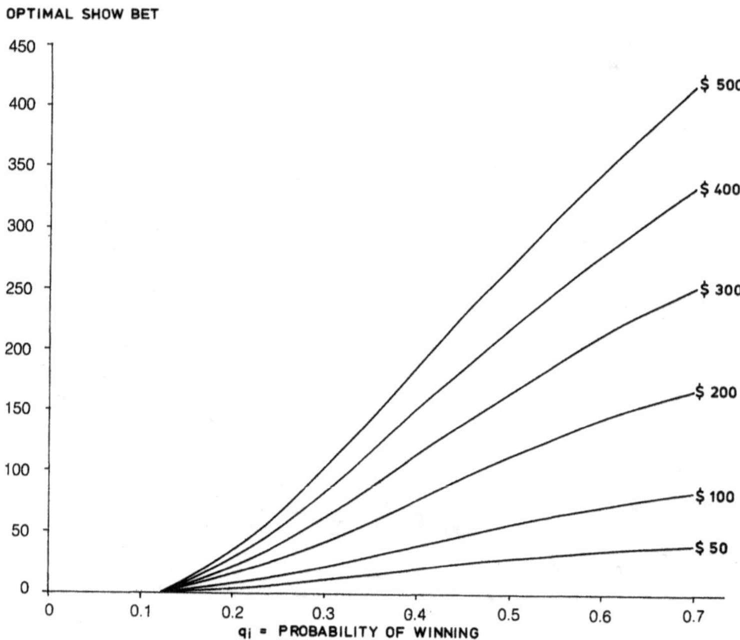

Figure 5.19 Optimal show bet for various q_i and betting-wealth levels when the expected return is 1.14 and the show pool is large ($30,000+)

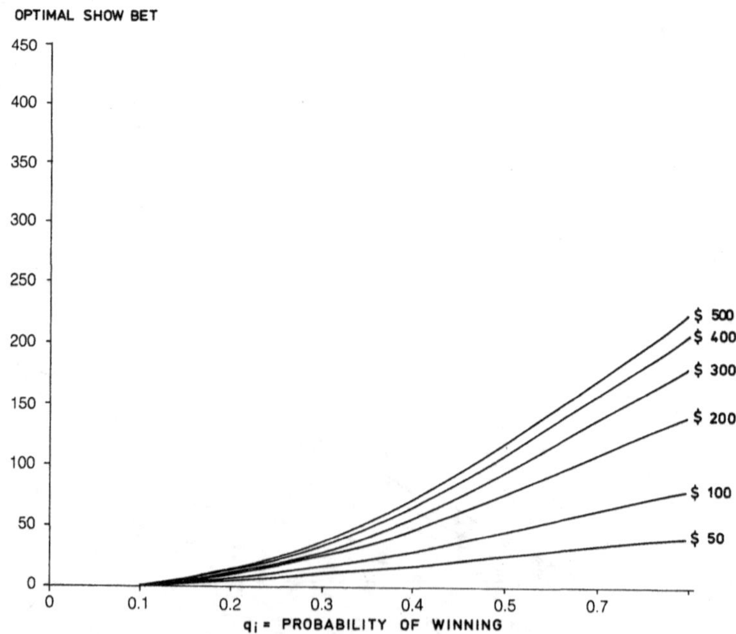

Figure 5.20 Optimal show bet for various q_i and betting-wealth levels when the expected return is 1.18 and the show pool is small ($1,200–$5,999)

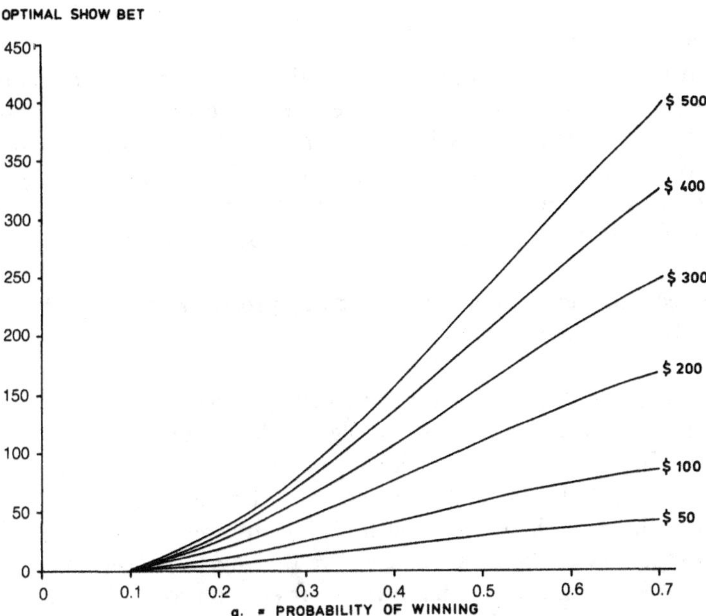

Figure 5.21 Optimal show bet for various q_i and betting-wealth levels when the expected return is 1.18 and the show pool is medium ($6,000–$29,999)

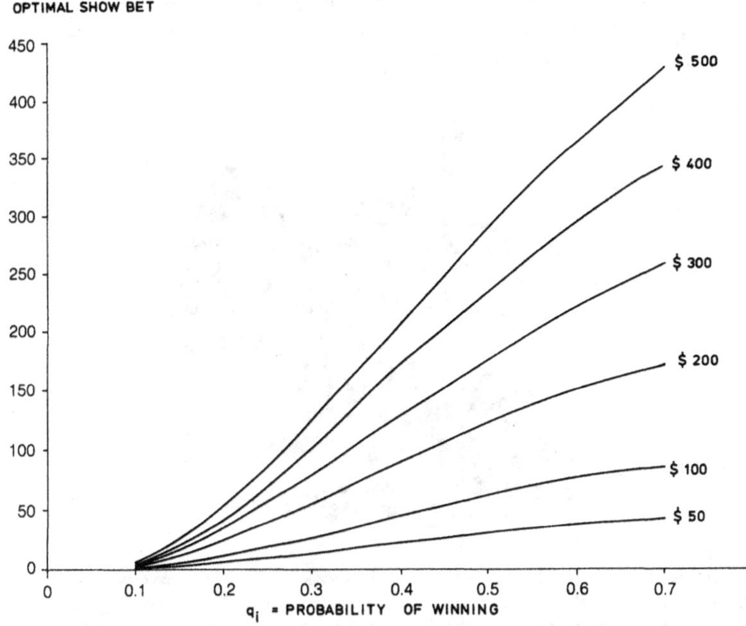

Figure 5.22 Optimal show bet for various q_i and betting-wealth levels when the expected return is 1.18 and the show pool is large ($30,000+)

and with his regular jockey—ideally one of the top jockeys at the current meet. Many of the best Dr. Z wagers to place and show occur in the top races of the day when the best horses are running. Also by then most of the patrons have lost a lot of money and are avoiding the very wagers we will be making. When the situation is not so comfortable as all that, you may wish to lower your bet. On average, this caution should provide you with the greater security you wish and only slightly less growth in your betting fortune.

We recommend the following betting procedure for determining and placing Dr. Z system bets:

1. Situate yourself so that you have a clear view of the tote-board mutuels and are in a position to be able to place a bet near the end of the betting period. Most tracks have two or more tote boards. The one that is best to use is often the one farthest away from the finish line. Check to see how long the lines are in a few races so that you can judge how late you can wait before betting. The lines may be shorter in the clubhouse. If you are with a friend, one of you can be watching the tote board and the other holding a place in the betting-window lineup.
2. Start looking for possible Dr. Z system bets four to six minutes before post time or even earlier. Use the following charts to see how good a promising bet really is before you bet. Recheck it when you are ready to bet. Do not bet any sooner than necessary.*

*Since the publication of the first edition of this book many people have begun to use the Dr. Z system, especially in Southern California. In Chapter 17, we investigate how many people can play the Dr. Z system. Suffice it to say caution should be used not to bet too early especially if you suspect others are making the same bets—sprinting to the window at the buzzer as suggested by the cartoon from *Fortune* magazine is the safest approach.

3. Figures 5.7–5.10 may be used to determine whether or not you should bet. If there is a possible place or show bet, you will need to look at only one figure. If you are considering a place bet and a show bet you will need to look at two figures. If you are at a top track with an expected-value cutoff of 1.14, use Figure 5.7 for place and Figure 5.9 for show. If you are at another track, use Figure 5.8 for place and Figure 5.10 for show.

   To use these figures evaluate W_i/W for the horizontal axis and P_i/P or S_i/S for the vertical axis for place and show, respectively. If the point where the values intersect is *on or below the line* corresponding to the track payback of your track, then *bet*. If it is *above the line, do not bet*.

   For example, consider a hypothetical show bet on horse 3 at a top track such as Churchill Downs. The expected-value cutoff is 1.14, so we use Figure 5.9. The track take is 15%, so the track payback is 0.85. Suppose W_3 = \$50,000 is bet on 3 to win, out of a total win pool of W = \$100,000, and S_3 = \$20,000 is bet on 3 to show, out of a show pool of S = \$50,000. Then $W_3/W = 0.5$ and $S_3/S = 0.4$. Since these numbers cross above the $Q = 0.85$ line, you do not bet. If instead S_3 = \$15,000, the $S_3/S = 0.3$, and you should bet since the numbers now cross below the $Q = 0.85$ line.

   Now consider a hypothetical place bet on horse 5 at a track such as Exhibition Park. The expected-value cutoff is 1.18, so we use Figure 5.8. The track take is 16.3%, so the track payback is about 0.84. Suppose W_5 = \$10,000, W = \$30,000, P_5 = \$2,000, and P = \$12,000. Then $W_5/W = 0.333$ and $P_5/P = 0.167$. Since these numbers cross below the $Q = 0.84$ line, you should bet.
4. Figures 5.11–5.22 may be used to determine how much you should bet. Again, you consult one figure for each possible bet.

   To use these figures, first evaluate $q_i = W_i/W$ for the horizontal axis then read off the optimal Kelly bet on the vertical axis corresponding to the amount of your betting wealth. For example, for the show bet on horse 3 at Churchill Downs with an expected-value cutoff of 1.14 and a large show pool of \$50,000, we use Figure 5.19. Since $q_3 = W_3/W$ = \$50,000/\$100,000 = 0.5, the optimal bet with a betting fortune of \$300 is about \$170; with a fortune of \$500 it is about \$275.

   For the place bet on horse 5 at Exhibition Park, with an expected-value cutoff of 1.18 and a medium-sized place pool of \$12,000, we use Figure 5.15. Since $q_5 = W_5/W$ = \$10,000/\$30,000 = 0.333, the optimal bet with a betting fortune of \$200 is \$36; with a fortune of \$50 it is \$10.

Let's now look at some Dr. Z system bets on real races.

THE FIRST RACE, CHURCHILL DOWNS, LOUISVILLE, KENTUCKY, MAY 6, 1983

The actual payoff that you will receive from a Dr. Z system bet can vary greatly. Our main premise is that you should bet when the odds are favorable for you—that is, when the expected return per dollar bet is sufficiently high, say at least 1.14. In this and the next two sections, we show how the Dr. Z system was used when the payoff was expected to be (1) medium, as on Fern Creek in the first race at Churchill Downs on May 6, 1983; (2) small, as on C'est Moi Cheri in the sixth race at Hollywood Park on June 5, 1982; and (3) relatively large, as on B.C. Place in the King's Favor Purse at Longacres on August 14, 1983. All these were outstanding bets. It is important that you understand that the expected return per dollar bet and not the expected payoff is the crucial concept for selecting good bets.

Fern Creek was a typical Dr. Z system bet. The program, past performances, experts' selections, and chart of this race appear in the section "How Accurate Is the Morning Line?" on page 48 in Chapter Three. The tote boards are shown in the following table.

	Totals	#7 Fern Creek	Expected Value per Dollar Bet on Fern Creek to Show[a]	Optimal Bet to Show on Fern Creek[a]
With six minutes to post time				
Odds		4—1		
Win	96,028	15,563		
Show	37,193	3,549	1.24	
With two minutes to post time				
Odds		4—1		
Win	118,803	19,230		
Show	45,209	4,163	1.26	28

[a]Since the track take in Kentucky is 15% for thoroughbreds, the expected value per dollar bet on Fern Creek to show using equation (4.6) is ►

$$\blacktriangleright \text{EX Show Fern Creek} = \underbrace{0.543 + 0.369\left(\frac{19{,}230/118{,}803}{4{,}163/45{,}209}\right)}_{\text{Ordinary expected value}}$$

$$+ \underbrace{(3.60 - 2.13)\left(\frac{19{,}230}{118{,}803}\right)(0.85 - 0.829)}_{\text{Correction for track-take departure from 17.1\%}}$$

$$= 1.19 + 0.07$$

$$= 1.26.$$

This indicates that we expect to make 26%, on average, by betting on Fern Creek to show.

With our betting fortune of $500 the optimal bet was $28. This bet can be calculated using equation (5.5), as follows:

$$\text{Show bet} = \left[131 + 2{,}150q_i^2 - 1{,}778q_i^3 - \left(\frac{150}{q_iS/S_i - 0.70}\right)\right]\left(\frac{S - 6{,}000}{94{,}000}\right) + \left[86 + 1{,}516q_i^2 - 968q_i^3 - \left(\frac{90.7}{q_iS/S_i - 0.85}\right)\right]\left(\frac{100{,}000 - S}{94{,}000}\right). \tag{5.5}$$

For Fern Creek, $q_i = 19{,}230/118{,}803 = 0.1619$, $S_i = 4{,}163$, and $S = 45{,}209$. Hence

$$\begin{aligned}\text{Show bet} &= \left[131 + 2{,}150(0.1619)^2 - 1{,}778(0.1619)^3 - \left(\frac{150}{(0.1619)(45{,}209)/(4{,}163) - 0.70}\right)\right]\left(\frac{45{,}209 - 6{,}000}{94{,}000}\right)\\ &\quad + \left[86 + 1516(0.1619)^2 - 968(0.1619)^3 - \left(\frac{90.7}{(0.1619)(45{,}209)/(4{,}163) - 0.85}\right)\right]\left(\frac{100{,}000 - 45{,}209}{94{,}000}\right)\\ &= (131 + 56.4 - 7.6 - 141.8)(0.417) + (86 + 39.7 - 4.1 - 99.9)(0.583)\\ &= 15.8 + 12.7\\ &= \$28.50.\end{aligned}$$

A quick check of Figure 5.9 (the track take in Kentucky is 15%) with $q_i = 0.1619$ and $S_i/S = 0.092$ indicates a Dr. Z bet should be made. Figure 5.22 suggests a bet of $24.* The final tote board values were:

	Totals	#7 Fern Creek	Expected Value per Dollar Bet on Fern Creek to Show	Optimal Bet to Show on Fern Creek ($)
Odds		4—1		
Win	133,999	21,397		
Show	50,569	4,677	1.25	24

Obviously, it would be best to do all our calculations on the final tote board figure, since then we would not have to worry about the odds changing after we bet. Unfortunately, the best we can do is base our calculations on the tote board one or two minutes before all betting ends. For this race the "two-minute problem" is no problem at all, since on the basis of the final tote board we have

$$\text{EX Show Fern Creek} = 1.25$$

*The figures give the optimal bet when the expected return to show is 1.14 or 1.18. Fern Creek, however, has an expected return of 1.26. This difference explains why the "true" optimal bet using equation (5.5) is higher than the "conservative" optimal bet from the figures. When one is using a 1.14 cutoff and the expected value greatly exceeds this value, it is better to use the 1.18 figure instead—it will give a more accurate bet. By keeping to the 1.14 figure, your bet will be more conservative and smaller.

and

$$\text{Show bet} = \$24.$$

These two values are very close to those calculated with two minutes to post time. The two-minute problem is discussed in more detail in Chapter Nine.

As mentioned in Chapter Three, the favorite, Modicum, won the race, setting a new track record for $4\frac{1}{2}$ furlongs. She's Ecstatic finished second, and Fern Creek took third. The chart of the race was as follows:*

FIRST RACE **Churchill** MAY 6, 1983 — 4 ½ FURLONGS. (.51⅗) MAIDEN. SPECIAL WEIGHT. Purse $8,000 (plus $2,000 from KTDF). Fillies. 2-year-olds. Weight, 118 lbs. 6TH DAY. WEATHER CLEAR. TEMPERATURE 79 DEGREES.

Total purse $10,000. Value of race $8,700, value to winner $5,200, second $2,000, third $1,000, fourth $500. ($1,300 reverts to the KTDF). Mutuel pool $251,926.

Last Raced	Horse	Eqt.A.Wt	PP	St	¼	Str	Fin	Jockey	Odds $1
20Apr83 ³Kee²	Modicum	2 118	5	5	$1^{1/2}$	1^2	1^4	Day P	1.70
28Apr83 ³Kee³	She's Ecstatic	2 118	9	8	3^{hd}	3^2	2^3	Delahoussaye E	3.40
	Fern Creek	b 2 118	7	6	2^2	$2^{1\frac{1}{2}}$	3^{nk}	Gavidia W	4.20
	Sintra	2 118	6	10	$9^{1\frac{1}{2}}$	6^3	4^3	Sellers M S	9.90
	Spiegler	2 113	3	3	$6^{1/2}$	$4^{1/2}$	$5^{2\frac{1}{2}}$	Miller S E⁵	10.00
28Apr83 ³Kee⁵	Pruner's Gal	2 118	4	4	4^2	$5^{1/2}$	6^4	Woods C R Jr	18.40
	Westwood Lake	2 118	8	7	7^3	7^1	$7^{3/4}$	Moyers L	8.10
	Tricky Sea	2 113	10	9	5^{hd}	8^3	8^3	Allen K K⁵	43.20
	Hamburg Place	2 118	1	1	8^{hd}	9^5	9^6	Neilson C	33.20
	Red's Abbey	2 118	2	2	10	10	10	Bartram B E	60.00

OFF AT 1:52. Start good. Won handily. Time, :22, :45⅕, :51⅘ Track fast.
(New track record.)

Official Program Numbers			
$2 Mutuel Prices: 5-MODICUM	5.40	2.80	2.40
9-SHE'S ECSTATIC		3.40	2.60
7-FERN CREEK			3.40

Ch. f, by General Assembly—Sandstream, by Sandford. Trainer McGaughey C R III. Bred by Coggan J R S (GB).

MODICUM, hustled to the lead just after the start, made all the pace and increased the margin in the lane with a hand ride. SHE'S ECSTATIC, always well placed, was no match for the winner but finished strongly to be easily second best. FERN CREEK prompted the early pace but had no late rally. SINTRA lacked the needed response.

Owners— 1, West B; 2, Gentry T; 3, Crimson King Farm; 4, Cherry Valley Farm; 5, Flint B S Inc; 6, Mahan Sara M; 7, West & Woodford; 8, Buckland Farm; 9, Davis P E; 10, Johnson D.

The $3.40 show payoff on Fern Creek returned $40.80 for the $24 bet, for a profit of $16.80.

THE SIXTH RACE, HOLLYWOOD PARK, INGLEWOOD, CALIFORNIA, JUNE 5, 1982

C'est Moi Cheri was a Dr. Z system bet in the sixth race at Hollywood Park on June 5, 1982. Near post time the tote board was as follows:

	Totals	#7 C'est Moi Cheri	Expected Value per Dollar Bet on C'est Moi Cheri to Show[a]	Optimal Bet to Show on C'est Moi Cheri[a] ($)
Odds		1—1		
Win	335,698	136,125		
Show	56,841	12,284	1.29	213

*We actually bet the $28 value indicated on our calculator for a return of $47.60 and profit of $19.60.

[a]From equation (4.6), the expected value per dollar bet to show on C'est Moi Cheri is

$$\text{EX Show C'est Moi Cheri} = 0.543 + 0.369\left(\frac{136{,}125/335{,}698}{12{,}284/56{,}841}\right) + (3.60 - 2.13)\left(\frac{136{,}125}{335{,}698}\right)(0.85 - 0.829)$$

$$= 1.23 + 0.06$$

$$= 1.29.$$

Thus with California's 15% track take, we expect to make 29%, on average, betting on C'est Moi Cheri. The optimal bet using equation (5.5) is

$$\text{Show bet C'est Moi Cheri} = \left[131 + 2{,}150(0.4055)^2 - 1{,}778(0.4055)^3 - \left(\frac{150}{(0.4055)(56{,}841)/(12{,}284) - 0.70}\right)\right]\left(\frac{12{,}284 - 6{,}000}{94{,}000}\right)$$
$$+ \left[86 + 1516(0.4055)^2 - 968(0.4055)^3 - \left(\frac{90.7}{(0.4055)(56{,}841)/(12{,}284) - 0.85}\right)\right]\left(\frac{100{,}000 - 12{,}284}{94{,}000}\right)$$
$$= \$213,$$

since $q_i = 136{,}125/335{,}698 = 0.4055$, $S = 56{,}841$, and $S_i = 12{,}284$.

Figure 5.9, with $q_i = 136{,}125/335{,}698 = 0.4055$ and $S_i/S = 12{,}284/56{,}841 = 0.2161$, indicates that a Dr. Z bet should be made. Since $q_i = 0.4055$, Figure 5.19 indicates that the optimal bet with a betting wealth of $500 is $184. (Using Figure 5.22 with the 1.18 cutoff, we get an optimal bet of $208.)

C'est Moi Cheri was a wire-to-wire winner, beating the second-place finisher Kiss 'Em Goodbye by 4½ lengths. Visual Emotion took third. The payoff for show for C'est Moi Cheri was a smashing $3.40. She paid $3.60 to place and $4.00 to win. The bet of $208 returned $353.60, for a profit of $145.60.* The chart of the race was as follows:

*Our actual bet of $213 returned $362.10, for a $149.10 profit.

Experts' Selections

Consensus Points: 5 for 1st (today's best 7), 2 for 2nd, 1 for 3rd. Today's Best in Bold Type.

Trackman, Warren Williams **HOLLYWOOD PARK** Selections Made for Fast Track

	TRACKMAN	HANDICAP	ANALYST	HERMIS	SWEEP	CONSENSUS	
6	NAN'S DANCER	NAN'S DANCER	C'EST MOI CHERI	NAN'S DANCER	C'EST MOI CHERI	NAN'S DANCER	19
	C'EST MOI CHERI	C'EST MOI CHERI	NAN'S DANCER	C'EST MOI CHERI	NAN'S DANCER	C'EST MOI CHERI	16
	JUNE THREE	KISS 'EM GOODBYE	JUNE THREE	KISS 'EM GOODBYE	JUNE THREE	JUNE THREE	3

Analyst's Hollywood Comment

SIXTH RACE
1—C'Est Moi Cheri
2—Nan's Dancer
3—June Three

C'EST MOI CHERI is a half sister to the quick Cheri Meri and she seems to have inherited that ability to ramble. She's had 14 works since Jan. 28, the best being 1:00 4/5, :35 3/5b, :59, :58 2/5, :34 1/5, 1:00hg, 1:10 2/5, 1:11 1/5 and 1:00. She'll be tough to catch at first asking. NAN'S DANCER found her running legs last out when she was beaten a neck by the promising Miss Elea in 1:22 3/5 for 7 panels. If the top filly needs the outing she'll be extremely hard to handle. Mandella debuts JUNE THREE, and the trainer has a good percentage of wins with first-timers.

6th Hollywood

6 FURLONGS HOLLYWOOD PARK

6 FURLONGS. (1.07⅗) MAIDEN. Purse $17,000. Fillies and mares. 3-year-olds and upward. Weights, 3-year-olds, 115 lbs.; older, 122 lbs.

Golden Lady Belle — Ch. f. 3, by Golden Eagle II—Baffi's Lady, by Petrone
Own.—Di Baffi Stable 115 Br.—Pernicano G J (Cal) 1982 0 M 0 0
Tr.—Rose Larry 1981 0 M 0 0
Lifetime 0 0 0 0
Jun 4 Hol 3f ft :36² hg May 29 Hol 5f ft 1:02¹ hg May 19 Hol 5f ft 1:04 hg May 11 Hol 5f ft 1:01¹ h

Visual Emotion — Ch. f. 3, by King Emperor—Join the Waves, by Sailer
Own.—Jones B C 115 Br.—Jones B C (Ky) 1982 1 M 0 0
Tr.—Russell John W 1981 0 M 0 0
Lifetime 1 0 0 0
29May82-6Hol 6f :21⁴ :45 1:10²ft 26 114 89¼ 916 910 1012 ShoemakerW10 ⒻMdn 73 RiseDePie,FoxyTmmie,BellePrleus 10
May 25 Hol 5f ft 1:01¹ h May 19 Hol 6f ft 1:18 h May 13 Hol 5f ft 1:01⁴ hg May 7 Hol 6f ft 1:14¹ h

Real Notion — B. f. 3, by Torsion—Bekky's Star, by Dark Star
Own.—Groves F N (Lessee) 115 Br.—McLean-Robbins-Fonzone (Ky) 1982 7 M 1 0 $6,450
Tr.—Sullivan John 1981 3 M 0 0 $800
Lifetime 10 0 1 0 $7,250
22May82-4Hol 7f :22⁴ :45⁴ 1:22³ft 25 114 41¼ 31½ 33 47½ Castaneda M4 ⒻMdn 77 MissElea,Nn'sDncer,LedingAdvocte 7
9May82-4Hol 1 1/16 :46⁴ 1:11³ 1:43²ft 12 114 75 65 67¾ 717 DelahoussyeE6 ⒻMdn 61 Broadtail,Fndngerin,VoodooQueen 10
21Apr82-6SA 1 1/16 :46² 1:11 1:43²ft 47 117 87¼ 75½ 55¼ 46¼ Valenzuela PA4 ⒻMdn 78 Nncy'sBby,BilyKnockn,Comptbilty 12
10Apr82-4SA 1 1/16 :46² 1:11¹ 1:43⁴ft 24 117 2½ 31 52¼ 76¼ Valenzuela PA3 ⒻMdn 75 GreySusan,‡Compatability,Fostoria 9
13Feb82-4SA 1 1/16 :47¹ 1:12¹ 1:44⁴ft 10 117 65¼ 78 611 712 DelahoussyeE2 ⒻMdn 65 Permeability,HastyNijinsky,Celind 12
31Jan82-3SA 6f :21⁴ :44³ 1:09³ft 3½ 117 78¼ 77½ 69½ 57¾ DelahoussyeE4 ⒻMdn 82 SweetMystery,Celinda,HwiinShke 12
17Jan82-3SA 6f :21⁴ :45² 1:11¹ft 8½ 117 85¾ 54¾ 3nk 2nk DelahoussyeE4 ⒻMdn 82 RgingStorm,RelNotion,SlutToLov 12
9Dec81-6Hol 6f :22 :46¹ 1:12 ft 7 117 54¼ 53 56¼ 58¼ Toro F4 ⒻMdn 68 Melinda's Plum, Visto,CitizenKate 11
1Nov81-3SA 6f :22 :44⁴ 1:10¹ft 43 116 65½ 64¾ 63¼ 53¼ DelahoussyeE1 ⒻMdn 84 Vihava,Marie'sFastLass,HwiinShke 8
2Oct81-6SA 6f :22¹ :45⁴ 1:11¹ft 86 115 98 811 811 812 DelahoussyeE7 ⒻMdn 70 EnglishGirl,PyOrPly,GloriousGren 11
May 31 Hol 4f ft :51⁴ h May 19 Hol 4f ft :52¹ h May 7 Hol 4f ft :48⁴ h May 1 Hol 4f ft :47¹ h

My Native Princess — B. f. 3, by Our Native—Marching Melody, by Go Marching
Own.—Littlest Ranch Inc 115 Br.—Backer J W (Ky) 1982 1 M 0 0
Tr.—Brunson Sam 1981 0 M 0 0
Lifetime 1 0 0 0
29May82-6Hol 6f :21⁴ :45 1:10²ft 81 115 55¾ 56¼ 65 75¾ Aragon J4 ⒻMdn 79 RiseDePie,FoxyTmmie,BellePrleus 10
May 22 Hol 5f ft 1:02¹ hg ●May 5 EP 4f ft :48¹ hg ●Apr 27 EP 6f ft 1:16⁴ hg

Kiss 'em Goodbye — B. f. 3, by Annihilate 'em—Free Guess, by Correlation
Own.—Magee Mr or Mrs R W 115 Br.—Greathouse L F (Ky) 1981 1 M 0 0
Tr.—Taliaferro Charles L
Lifetime 1 0 0 0
18Nov81-6Hol 6f :22 :45 1:10³ft 14 117 43¼ 54 713 69 Sibille R9 ⒻMdn 75 FilomenGle,IrishBlld,Melind'sPlum 9
Jun 3 Hol 3f ft :35 hg May 29 Hol 6f ft 1:13⁴ h May 22 Hol 6f ft 1:15¹ h May 18 Hol 5f ft 1:03¹ h

June Three — Dk. b. or br. f. 3, by Ramsinga—June Too, by Fleet Nasrullah
Own.—Sifton J 115 Br.—Stoneacres Farm (Man-C) 1982 0 M 0 0
Tr.—Mandella Richard 1981 0 M 0 0
Lifetime 0 0 0 0
Jun 1 Hol 4f ft :48² h May 26 Hol 7f ft 1:28³ hg May 19 Hol 6f ft 1:16¹ hg ●May 11 GD tr.t 6f ft 1:13⁴ hg

C'Est Moi Cheri — Dk. b. or br. f. 3, by Don B—Oui Oui Cheri, by Bar le Duc
Own.—Kirkorian B & Lynn 115 Br.—Warton J (Fla) 1982 0 M 0 0
Tr.—Cleveland Gene 1981 0 M 0 0
Lifetime 0 0 0 0
May 30 Hol 5f ft 1:00⁴ h May 25 Hol 3f ft :35³ b May 9 Hol 5f ft :59 h ●May 4 Hol 5f ft :58² h

Nan's Dancer — B. f. 3, by Marshua's Dancer—Film Festival, by Spring Double
Own.—Bolas G A 115 Br.—Tackett P (Ky) 1982 2 M 1 0 $3,825
Tr.—Rettele Loren 1981 0 M 0 0
Lifetime 2 0 1 0 $3,825
22May82-4Hol 7f :22⁴ :45⁴ 1:22³ft 3½ 114 2hd 1hd 1hd 2nk McCarron C J1 ⒻMdn 84 MissElea,Nn'sDncer,LedingAdvocte 7
15May82-6Hol 6f :21⁴ :44³ 1:10²ft 27 115 1113 1015 78¾ 53¼ Black K7 ⒻMdn 82 Native Gal, RiseDePie,FallenAngel 12
Jun 3 Hol 3f ft :36³ h May 29 Hol 5f ft :59⁴ h May 11 Hol 6f ft 1:12³ h May 5 Hol 5f ft 1:01⁴ h

SIXTH RACE Hollywood JUNE 5, 1982

6 FURLONGS. (1.07⅗) MAIDEN. Purse $17,000. Fillies and mares. 3-year-olds and upward. Weights, 3-year-olds, 115 lbs.; older, 122 lbs.

Value of race $17,000, value to winner $9,350, second $3,400, third $2,550, fourth $1,275, fifths $212.50 each. Mutuel pool $521,071.

Last Raced	Horse	Eqt.	A.	Wt	PP	St	¼	½	Str	Fin	Jockey	Odds $1
	C'Est Moi Cheri		3	115	7	4	1^{1}	$1^{3\frac{1}{2}}$	$1^{3\frac{1}{2}}$	$1^{4\frac{1}{2}}$	Sibille R	1.00
18Nov81 ^{6}Hol^{6}	Kiss 'em Goodbye		3	116	5	1	4^{2}	$3^{\frac{1}{2}}$	3^{4}	2^{hd}	Black K	10.90
29May82 ^{6}Hol^{10}	Visual Emotion		3	115	2	5	$3^{\frac{1}{2}}$	2^{1}	2^{2}	$3^{4\frac{1}{2}}$	Olivares F	52.60
22May82 ^{4}Hol^{2}	Nan's Dancer		3	115	8	7	7^{6}	$6^{\frac{1}{2}}$	4^{1}	4^{hd}	McCarron C J	1.50
22May82 ^{4}Hol^{4}	[DH] Real Notion	b	3	115	3	3	$6^{\frac{1}{2}}$	7^{3}	7^{2}	5	Castaneda M	18.20
29May82 ^{6}Hol^{7}	[DH] My Native Princess		3	115	4	6	5^{hd}	5^{hd}	5^{hd}	5^{3}	McHargue D G	25.80
	Golden Lady Belle		3	115	1	8	8	8	8	7^{nk}	Ortega L E	59.60
	June Three	b	3	115	6	2	2^{1}	4^{2}	6^{1}	8	Toro F	8.80

[DH]—Dead heat.

OFF AT 4:46. Start good. Won handily. Time, :22, :44⅘, :57, 1:10 Track fast.

$2 Mutuel Prices:			
7-C'EST MOI CHERI	4.00	3.60	3.40
5-KISS 'EM GOODBYE		7.60	5.00
2-VISUAL EMOTION			9.80

Dk. b. or br. f, by Don B—Oui Oui Cheri, by Bar le Duc. Trainer Cleveland Gene. Bred by Warton J (Fla).

C'EST MOI CHERI sprinted clear without need of urging, drew away to a long lead into the stretch, was reminded of her task with one crack of the whip at midstretch, and steadily drew away in hand. KISS 'EM GOODBYE, well-placed throughout, was no match for the winner but closed gamely to edge VISUAL EMOTION for the place. The latter moved nearest the winner at the far turn and flattened out in the final furlong. NAN'S DANCER stayed to the outside around the far turn and showed little punch from the middle of the track. REAL NOTION showed nothing. MY NATIVE PRINCESS lugged in throughout and finished on even terms with REAL NOTION. GOLDEN LADY BELLE was outrun. JUNE THREE tired badly.

Owners— 1, Kirkorian B & Lynn; 2, Magee Mr or Mrs R W; 3, Jones B C; 4, Bolas G A; 5, Groves F N (Lessee); 6, Littlest Ranch Inc; 7, Di Baffi Stable; 8, Sifton J. **Overweight:** Kiss 'em Goodbye 1 pound.

THE KING'S FAVOR PURSE, LONGACRES, RENTON, WASHINGTON, AUGUST 14, 1983

B. C. Place was a Dr. Z system bet in the seventh race, the King's Favor Purse at Longacres on August 14, 1983. One minute before post time the tote board was as follows:

	Totals	#4 B. C. Place	Expected Value per Dollar Bet on B. C. Place[a]	Optimal Bet to Show on B. C. Place[a] ($)
Odds		7—2		
Win	31,422	5,583		
Show	16,101	1,785	1.17	9

[a]From equation (4.6), the expected value per dollar bet on B. C. Place was

$$\begin{aligned}\text{EX Show B. C. Place} &= 0.543 + 0.369\left(\frac{5{,}583/31{,}422}{1{,}785/16{,}101}\right)\\ &\quad + \left[(3.60 - 2.13)\left(\frac{5{,}583}{31{,}422}\right)\right](0.84 - 0.829)\\ &= 1.13 + 0.04\\ &= 1.17.\end{aligned}$$

Thus with Washington's 16% track take we expect to make 17%, on average, betting on B. C. Place. The optimal bet for a betting wealth of $500 calculated using equation (5.5) is $9, since q_i = 5,583/31,422 = 0.1777, S = 16,101, and S_i = 1,785.

7th Lga 1 1-16 MILES. (1:39⅘). CLAIMING. Purse, $7,000. 3-year-olds. Weight, 120 lbs. Non-winners since April 26 allowed 3 lbs.; non-winners in 1983, 6 lbs. (Races for $16,000 or less not considered.) Claiming price, $20,000.

Tusa 120 Ch. c, 1980, by Kentuckian—Shesarunner, by Your Host.
Breeder, Plemmonston Stud (Wash.). 1983. 4 1 1 1 $4,275
Owner, G. M. Stable. Trainer, Eugene Zeren. $20,000 1982. 0 M 0 0 ——
15Jly 83 1Lga 1 1/16 :4731:1311:453ft 2 *120 89½ 54½ 2h 1nk JmsM5 M20000 71 Tusa 120 Think Fresh 9
22Jun83 2Lga 1 1/16 :4631:1211:461sy 8½ 120 1017 812 57½ 21 JmsM9 M16000 67 Military Merit 120 Tusa 10
3Jun83 4Lga 6½f :222 :4541:173ft 19 120 54 56½ 36 38 StvnG7 M20000 73 RipAdhem120 MilitaryMerit 9
25May83 3Lga 6f :221 :4541:113ft 10 1155 1114 1115 919 716 NlsnM8 M16000 62 DetermindFire120 LittleMike 11
July 10 Lga 5f ft 1:04⅘b May 18 Lga 3f ft :36⅗bcg May 4 Lga 5f ft 1:03⅕bgc

Moonshine Way 114 Dk. b. or br. g, 1980, by Noholme Way—She Shine, by Pilot John.
Breeder, Mr.-Mrs. Guy C. Roberts (Wash.). 1983. 7 2 1 2 $9,060
Owner, Larry Schneider. Trainer, Brad Taylor. $20,000 1982. 2 M 0 1 $485
LIFETIME (thru 1982) 2 M 0 1 $485
6Aug83 8Lga 6½f :22 :4511:164ft 5½ 119 78½ 76¼ 63½ 21½ BazeG3 20000 83 ShortSocks120 MoonshneWay 8
30Jly 83 7Lga 1 1/16 :4731:1211:442ft 4¾ *119 64½ 63¾ 44½ 44 BazeG8 20000 73 C. W. Moss 114 John Day 12
20Jly 83 7Lga 6½f :213 :4421:154ft 6½ 122 87¼ 87½ 613 65½ PierceL4 25000 84 Saber Ben 119 Just Cavorting 11
26Jun83 4Lga 6½f :214 :4431:16 ft 4 114 89 78½ 67½ 32 StevnsG3 25000 87 RipAdhem119 FortiethPrince 9
15Jun83 7Lga 6f :22 :4521:103ft 18 114 1113 1011 56½ 11½ StevenG4 16000 83 MoonshneWy114 NoteofHope 12
2Jun83 2Lga 6½f :213 :4441:164ft 2¼ *122 45 78½ 35 15 PiercL2 M12500 75 MoonshinWay122 OuttaCache 12
11May83 2Lga 6f :223 :4621:12 ft 3¾ 121 31½ 32½ 45½ 34 PrcL10 M10000 72 FriendlyAtom115 LittleClinkr 11
21Oct82 4Lga 6½f :213 :45 1:174sy 5 120 610 58½ 46 32 PiercL8 M16000 78 LetsGoDtch120 MornngEagle 12
6Aug82 4Lga 5½f :223 :4621:053ft 20 120 96¾ 99¾ 811 88 CperB3 M20000 76 Deblynton 120 Taiwocondo 9
May 30 Lga 3f ft :36⅗b MAY 8 LGA 3F M :36HG May 4 Lga 4f ft :51⅘b

Satus Way 114 Dk. b. or br. g, 1980, by Noholme Way—Satus Lady, by Happy Trail.
Breeder, Mr.-Mrs. Ben Harris (Wash.). 1983. 5 0 0 0 $755
Owner, Ben Harris. Trainer, Ben Harris. $20,000 1982.10 2 2 2 $17,680
LIFETIME (thru 1982) 10 2 2 2 $17,680
30Jly 83 7Lga 1 1/16 :4731:1211:442ft 14 114 31½ 42½ 1117 1120 FrazirB9 20000 57 C. W. Moss 114 John Day 12
14Jly 83 9Lga 1 1/16 :4641:1221:451m 17 114 1121 1017 915 713 PruittJ11 32000 60 RedBrnRtrns120 Lyon'sShdw 11
11Jun83 9Lga 1 1/16 :46 1:11 1:443ft 5¾ 1105 613 812 820 722 BrnsVJ5 40000 54 Ourteshun117 FlyingBob 8
27May83 9Lga 6½f :22 :4531:18 ft 12 1095 916 913 78¾ 43½ BrnesVJ9 32000 75 ShortSocks119 Lyon'sShadow 9
14May83 7Lga 6f :22 :45 1:094ft 11 114 814 813 712 616 PruittJ4 40000 71 SplndorBoy120 DancgDrctor 8
27Nov82 9YM 1 :50 1:16 1:44 sl 6-5 *121 1011 76 42 1½ PruittJ9 HcpS 56 Satus Way 121 Fleet Spud 10
31Oct82 9YM 1 1/16 :4611:11 1:43 ft 17 114 97½ 73¾ 24 23 PruittJ9 AlwS 97 Table Sean 119 Satus Way 10
10Oct82 7Lga 1 :4811:1441:421sl 5 120 69¾ 64½ 56 42¾ PrittJ4 Aw6500 56 Tubafor 120 Pic O'Morn 6
29Sep82 8Lga 1 :4841:15 1:44 hy 4¼ 116 69 65½ 79¼ 33½ PrittJ1 Aw6500 45 ExclusivBiddr118 DynamoDoc 8
19Sep82 9Lga 1 :46 1:1031:364ft 25 118 32 33 57 510 PruittJ7 HcpS 75 Dave's Reality 122 Tubafor 10
4Sep82 5Lga 6f :213 :45 1:111m 3½ 120 47½ 44½ 21 16½ PruittJ1 Mdn 90 SatusWay120 MilitaryMerit 7
Aug 11 Lga 5f ft 1:02⅕b JULY 24 LGA 5F FT 1:00H July 7 Lga 4f ft :54⅕b

B. C. Place 117 B. c, 1980, by Mark's Place—Sextant, by Ship Leave.
Breeder, McDonald Farms Ltd (B.C.-C.). 1983.12 1 2 2 $12,066
Owner, C. A. Roberts. Trainer, Cy Anderson. $20,000 1982. 1 M 0 0 $1,000
LIFETIME (thru 1982) 1 M 0 0 $1,000
1Aug83 8EP 1 1/16 :24 :4821:472ft 7½ 113 54¾ 4¾ 2½ 2½ MenaJG6 25000 73 Troika111 B.C.Place 8
24Jly 83 9EP 1⅜ :4741:41 2:203ft 46 122 44 41½ 410 49½ MenaJG6 SplW 71 TimelyOne VictoriousLd 7
17Jly 83 7EP 1 1/16 :4731:13 1:452ft 8¼ 114 43 42½ 612 411 LosethC5 23000 73 ScotT.N.Me Maj'sPromise 8
10Jly 83 8EP 6½f :224 :4621:184ft 24 115 42 63¾ 814 912 ZookDJ9 25000 72 SelCove Elit'sCommand 10
10Jly83—Wide
1Jly 83 7EP 1 1/16 :4821:1411:473gd 5 116 72¾ 95 79½ 77½ ZookDJ7 25000 65 Gus'sLittleBuddy CriASmile 10
25Jun83 2EP 1 1/16 :48 1:13 1:462ft 6-5 *114 2h 13 16 16 ZkDJ5 M23000 79 B.C.Place StrChllenger 6

Rushin' In 114 Ch. g, 1980, by Sibirri—Daurna, by Equinaut.
Breeder, Rainier Stables (Wash.). 1983. 7 2 0 0 $5,775
Owner, Corky Van Osten. Trainer, Eugene Stallings. $20,000 1982. 3 1 0 0 $1,200
LIFETIME (thru 1982) 3 1 0 0 $1,200
30Jly 83 7Lga 1 1/16 :4731:1211:442ft 19 114 1110 1111 811 89½ JamesM4 20000 67 C. W. Moss 114 John Day 12
20Jly 83 7Lga 6½f :213 :4421:154ft 43 114 65 77¼ 819 812 JamesM7 25000 78 Saber Ben 119 Just Cavorting 11
3Jly 83 5Lga 1 1/16 :4711:1211:454ft 41 114 68½ 56 22½ 1½ GslvFA10 16000 70 Rushin' In 114 I'm Cricket 12
19Jun83 4Lga 6f :22 :4531:103ft 29 114 1010 1011 1012 99½ GnlvsFA3 20000 74 DerBingo121 FortiethPrince 11
29May83 3Lga 6f :214 :4531:111ft 4¼ 114 44 56½ 69½ 68¾ HnnMA3 c16000 72 Crash Cache 114 Der Bingo 7
6May83 6Lga 6f :22 :4531:114m 9-5 *117 22 22 12½ 1½ AragonJ5 12500 77 Rushin'sIn117 SunDrcThundr 9
30Apr83 2Lga 6f :214 :45 1:111ft 21 117 54¼ 44½ 712 74½ HnnMA9 20000 75 Prime Fire 117 Proxy's Boy 9
7Nov82 1PM 6f :223 1:131ft 8½ 118 2½ 2½ 2h 1h VnsW4 M20000 81 Rushin'In118 BrokersLark 9
14Oct82 4Lga 6f :214 :45 1:10 ft 26 120 3½ 32½ 35 68¾ PrittJ7 M12500 77 Proxy's Boy 120 Teepee Rings 12
1Sep82 4Lga 6f :22 :4611:124ft 9 120 78 919 1120 1017 LsthC9 M12500 55 Whatsup 120 Anahuy 12
Aug 7 Lga 5f ft 1:02⅕b July 28 Lga 3f m :38⅗b July 16 Lga 4f ft :48h

Predication 120 Dk. b. or br. c, 1980, by Pretense—Madame Axe, by The Axe II.
Breeder, Wood River Ranch (Calif.). 1983.10 2 4 1 $10,080
Owner, K-L Stables. Trainer, Craig Roberts. $20,000 1982. 3 M 0 0 ——
LIFETIME (thru 1982) 3 M 0 0 ——
3Aug83 8Lga 6f :22 :4511:094ft 9½ 119 64¾ 67¼ 916 912 BazeMB4 25000 75 ShootngClam114 CouponTycn 9
14Jly 83 9Lga 1 1/16 :4641:1221:451m 7¾ 119 79¾ 1118 1121 1120 BazeG8 32000 53 RedBrnRtrns120 Lyon'sShdw 11
14Jly83—Checked sharply on second turn.
2Jly 83 6Lga 1 1/16 :4841:1321:453ft 3½ 114 2½ 2h 31 23 FrazrB5 c25000 68 RedBaronRtrns117 Predction 8
22Jun83 6Lga 6½f :221 :4531:164sy 9-5 *114 22 21½ 33 1½ FrzierB7 20000 85 Predcatin114 RedBaronRetrn 7
26May83 7Lga 6f :222 :46 1:112ft 4¼ 120 1½ 11 1h 22½ FrazirB7 20000 76 Nativistic 122 Predication 8
13May83 8Lga 6f :22 :4531:103ft 7½ 120 64½ 67 611 412 StevenG4 20000 71 Phil E. B. Jon 117 John Day 12
30Apr83 1Lga 6f :222 :4621:12 ft 2¼ *120 53 42½ 34½ 1h StvnG6 M16000 76 Predication 120 Barb's Boy 12
5Mar83 2PM 6f :223 :4641:13 sy 9-5 120 21 1h 1½ 25 StevensG9 Mdn 77 FlyingBob120 Predication 12
19Feb83 5PM 6f :222 :4621:13 gd 3-4 *120 12½ 12 1h 33 GnslvsFA4 Mdn 79 BridgeTender120 FlyingBob 6
5Feb83 2PM 6f :222 :4611:122ft 2¼ *120 11½ 11½ 22½ 26½ StevensG9 Mdn 78 PrairieBreakr120 Prediction 12
20Dec82 2Hol 6½f :214 :4441:18 ft 9¾ 118 64½ 67½ 69¾ 612 VzlaP7 M32000 68 DarkAce116 Elated 12
Aug 1 Lga 4f ft :51⅕b JULY 12 LGA 4F SY :48⅗H June 12 Lga 5f ft 1:05b

Count On Zu **114** B. g, 1980, by Zulu Tom—Count On Sue, by Eastern Flier.
Breeder, Dr.-Mrs. Wm. W. Lien (Wash.). 1983. 6 2 0 1 $7,095
Owner, Dr.-Mrs. W. W. Lien. Trainer, N. E. Norton. $20,000 1982. 5 M 0 1 $830
LIFETIME (thru 1982) 5 M 0 1 $830
30Jly 83 7Lga 1 1/16 :4731:1211:442ft 10 114 1210 109 3/4 711 69 StevnsG1 20000 68 C. W. Moss 114 John Day 12
17Jly 83 5Lga 6 1/2f :213 :4421:163ft 27 114 129 1213 109 62 1/2 StvnsG10 20000 83 Nuncio 114 Der Bingo 12
8Jun83 6Lga 1 1/16 :4641:1311:47 ft 2 1/2 114 59 1/2 42 1/2 22 1h StevenG3 16000 64 Count On Zu 114 C. W. Moss 7
3Jun83 5Lga 1 1/16 :4731:1331:47 ft 5 114 48 1/2 34 41 3/4 1no StevenG1 12500 64 Count On Zu 114 I'm Cricket 8
3Jun83—Bumped in stretch.
19May83 3Lga 6 1/2f :221 :4531:182ft 3 1/4 *120 1010 710 610 35 1/2 AgnJ12 M12500 71 CatchAFool121 LittleClinker 12
4May83 4Lga 5 1/2f :221 :4641:06 ft 7 120 85 1/4 88 1/4 88 3/4 62 3/4 ArgnJ1 M12500 81 Gulf King 120 Venture Bay 12
4May83—Steadied at 7-16 pole.
21Oct82 4Lga 6 1/2f :213 :45 1:174sy 12 120 1017 819 612 45 KwlsL5 M16000 75 LetsGoDtch120 MornngEagle 12
7Oct82 4Lga 1 :4811:1431:431m 20 120 76 3/4 57 46 33 KnwlL5 M16000 50 WhereWasIt120 ExtraExclsiv 10
29Sep82 4Lga 1 :5011:18 1:464hy 10 120 912 811 66 1/4 63 1/2 KnwlL9 M12500 31 Whirlin Sterlin 120 R. Jesson 10
16Sep82 4Lga 6 1/2f :222 :4541:193ft 14 120 1113 1017 713 64 KnwlL11 M8000 67 Battlestr120 PalouseLautrec 12
Aug 12 Lga 4f m :48 2/5h JULY 7 LGA 5F FT 1:00H June 29 Lga 5f ft 1:02bc

Colonel Jerry **114** Ch. g, 1980, by Big Stir—Feathers Sue, by Feathers.
Breeder, Mr.-Mrs. G. E. Morrison (Wash.). 1983. 9 0 3 2 $4,822
Owner, W. L. Hooper. Trainer, LaDonna Damron. $20,000 1982. 11 1 2 1 $3,672
LIFETIME (thru 1982) 11 1 2 1 $3,672
30Jly 83 7Lga 1 1/16 :4731:1211:442ft 7 1/4 114 96 1/4 74 3/4 54 3/4 32 1/2 PruittJ2 20000 74 C. W. Moss 114 John Day 12
24Jly 83 3Lga 1 1/16 :4731:1211:441ft 5 1/2 114 33 1/2 3nk 11 2 1/2 PruittJ5 16000 77 C.W. Moss 120 Colonel Jerry 9
24Jly83—Steadied at start.
10Jly 83 7Lga 6 1/2f :213 :4431:16 ft 14 114 89 107 3/4 815 77 WalesH2 25000 82 Hot Drums 120 Cookie Shoes 12
2Jly 83 8Lga 6f :222 :4531:102ft 33 117 52 41 3/4 76 1/4 76 3/4 PrttJ9 Aw8000 77 More Action 120 Vitez 9
3Jun83 6Lga 6 1/2f :22 :4511:171ft 7 114 68 57 1/2 56 56 1/2 PruittJ2 25000 76 DncngDirctr120 HoHoCharlie 7
19May83 9Lga 6f :213 :4441:101ft 50 117 1012 1112 1117 1115 PrittJ2 Aw8500 70 Steel Prince 117 Dr. Sea 12
29Apr83 9Lga 6f :22 :4521:111ft 5 1/4 117 57 49 38 32 1/4 PrittJ4 Aw8000 78 Just For Bill 118 Dr. Sea 9
24Apr83 9YM 6f :234 :4831:17 hy 3 1/4 117 32 3 1/2 32 21 1/2 HngwhR6 HcpS 56 Pic O'Morn 117 Colonel Jerry 7
17Apr83 8YM 5 1/2f :221 :4531:04 ft 13 117 42 1/2 21 1/2 22 23 1/2 HlwtR2 Aw1600 91 Muckledeedun120 ColonlJerry 6
27Nov82 9YM 1 :50 1:16 1:44 sl 30 123 75 1/4 42 1/2 53 814 Dahlqst1 HcpS 42 Satus Way 121 Fleet Spud 10
20Nov82 9YM 6f :22 :47 1:153m 9-5 *122 75 1/4 45 65 612 DlqtT4 Aw1200 55 JudgesLast117 ImaBallofFire 9
Aug 10 Lga 5f ft 1:01 3/5b July 22 Lga 3f ft :35 2/5hc June 29 Lga 5f ft 1:01 3/5b

Figure 5.9, with $q_i = 0.1777$ and $S_i/S = 1{,}785/16{,}101 = 0.1109$, indicates that a show bet should be made. Since $q_i = 0.1777$, Figure 5.18 indicates that the optimal bet with a betting wealth of $500 is $15.

At post time the tote board was as follows:

	Totals	#4 B. C. Place	Expected Value per Dollar Bet on B. C. Place
Odds			7—2
Win	38,816	6,886	
Show	19,172	2,286	1.13

Colonel Jerry grabbed the early lead and was a wire-to-wire winner. Rushin' In took second, and B. C. Place was third. The show payoff of $4.40 on B. C. Place resulted in a return of $33 for the $15 bet, or an $18 profit.* The chart of the race was

*Our $9 returned $19.80, for a $10.80 profit. In most cases the charts give conservative betting values slightly less than the true optimal value. However, for some small bets the charts indicate a slightly larger bet.

SEVENTH RACE
Lga
Aug. 14, 1983

1 1-16 MILES. (1:39⅗). CLAIMING. Purse, $7,000. 3-year-olds. Weight, 120 lbs. Non-winners since April 26 allowed 3 lbs.; non-winners in 1983, 6 lbs. (Races for $16,000 or less not considered.) Claiming price, $20,000.

Value to winner, $3,850; second, $1,330; third, $1,015; fourth, $630; fifth, $175. Mutuel Pool, $82,525. Exacta Pool, $143,738.

Last Raced	Horses	EqtAWt	PP	St	¼	½	¾	Str	Fin	Jockeys	Owners	Odds to $1
30Jly 83 ^{7}Lga^{3}	Colonel Jerry	b3 114	8	4	$4^{3\frac{1}{2}}$	2^{3}	1^{2}	1^{5}	1^{4}	PruittJ	W L Hooper	3.60
30Jly 83 ^{7}Lga^{8}	Rushin' In	3 114	5	2	2^{2}	$3^{1\frac{1}{2}}$	3^{1}	2^{4}	$2^{6\frac{1}{2}}$	MillsJW	C Vanosten	24.80
1Aug83 ^{8}EP^{2}	B. C. Place	3 117	4	3	3^{h}	$4^{1\frac{1}{2}}$	4^{3}	$4^{1\frac{1}{2}}$	$3^{2\frac{1}{2}}$	NicoloP	C A Roberts	3.70
15Jly 83 ^{1}Lga^{1}	Tusa	3 120	1	8	8	8	7^{h}	7^{5}	4^{1}	JamesM	G M Stable	6.20
30Jly 83 ^{7}Lga^{6}	Count On Zu	3 114	7	6	$6^{1\frac{1}{2}}$	6^{5}	6^{4}	$6^{\frac{1}{2}}$	$5^{\frac{1}{2}}$	StevensG	Dr-Mrs W W Lien	14.75
6Aug83 ^{8}Lga^{2}	Moonshine Way	3 119	2	5	5^{4}	$5^{1\frac{1}{2}}$	$5^{\frac{1}{2}}$	3^{1}	6^{4}	BazeG	L Schneider	2.55
3Aug83 ^{8}Lga^{9}	Predication	3 120	6	1	$1^{2\frac{1}{2}}$	1^{h}	$2^{1\frac{1}{2}}$	5^{h}	$7^{\frac{3}{4}}$	PedrozaMA	K-L Stables	4.10
30Jly 83 ^{7}Lga^{11}	Satus Way	b3 116	3	7	7^{2}	7^{1}	8	8	8	BazeD	B Harris	20.25

OFF AT 4:54. START GOOD. WON EASILY. Time, :23⅗, :47⅗, 1:12, 1:38⅕, 1:44⅘. Track fast.

$2 Mutuel Prices			
8—COLONEL JERRY	9.20	4.10	3.20
5—RUSHIN' IN		16.60	8.10
4—B.C. PLACE			4.40

$5 EXACTA (8-5) PAID $326.50.

Ch. g, by Big Stir Feathers Sue, by Feathers. Trainer, Ladonna Damron. Bred by Mr.-Mrs. G. E. Morrison (Wash.).

THE BEAT THE RACETRACK CALCULATOR™

At the racetrack, Figures 5.7 to 5.10 can be used to determine whether or not a given bet to place or show has an expected value of at least 1.14 or 1.18 and thus qualifies as a Dr. Z system bet. For a place bet one simply computes the ratios W_i/W and P_i/P for the horse in question and determines if the intersection of these numbers is above (do not bet) or on or below (bet) the appropriate track-take line. For a show bet you use W_i/W and S_i/S. Similarly, Figures 5.11 to 5.22 can be used to determine how much to bet to place or show with 1.14 or 1.18 the expected-value cutoffs. From the horizontal axis you read off the optimal bet corresponding to a given probability of winning $q_i = W_i/W$ and your betting-wealth level, using the figure corresponding to the mutuel pool size where the race is being run. These values are approximate, but quite usable. When they err, it is usually on the conservative side, suggesting slightly lower bets than is optimal.

The Beat the Racetrack Calculator™ automatically takes into account factors such as your betting wealth, the track take, the size of the mutuel pools, and whether an entry is present. The aim of the Beat the Racetrack Calculator™ is to enable you to perform the calculations you need to evaluate a possible bet as quickly, accurately, and simply as possible. You are then free to watch the tote board and evaluate possible bets as post time nears. Your evaluation of a particular bet should take less than a minute.

The BTR Calculator is a plug-in ROM, for use with the Hewlett Packard 41CV or 41CX calculator. An HP41CV calculator, the ROM, an overlay, and an instruction book are available for $325 from Dr. Z Investments, Inc., Box 35334, Los Angeles, California 90035. For those who already have a HP41 series calculator, the ROM, overlay, and instruction booklet are available for $140. California residents please add sales tax. Write to the address for information on additional products, updates, and Canadian prices. (The publisher makes no warranties concerning this offer. Please refer all inquiries to the address noted above.)

6

Using the Dr. Z System at the Racetrack

Now that you have a basic understanding of our approach to winning at the racetrack using Dr. Z system bets, we can show you how it is used in typical betting situations. We describe eight races at six different tracks in California, British Columbia, New York, Kentucky, and Washington.

I was at the track when these races were run. This is the usual application of the Dr. Z system. However, betting on races being run in other locales is becoming more and more popular. We discuss this type of betting in Chapter Seven.

Most of the Dr. Z system bets are on horses to show. There are occasional place bets. In some situations you make bets to show on two different horses or to place and show on the same horse. A race at Exhibition Park and the Santa Ynez Stakes at Santa Anita described here provide examples of the latter situations. (Chapter Nine provides details on the relative distribution of the various types of Dr. Z system bets.)

THE SIXTH RACE AND THE TRIPLE BEND HANDICAP, HOLLYWOOD PARK, INGLEWOOD, CALIFORNIA, MAY 8, 1982

Southern California boasts three of the nation's top tracks: Santa Anita Park in Arcadia near the Pasadena Rose Bowl, Del Mar near San Diego, and Hollywood Park in Inglewood near the Forum sports arena just south of the city. These tracks alternate their seasons, so top-quality racing is available all year to the millions of racing fans in the area. Top jockeys, such as Chris McCarron, Sandy Hawley, Eddie Delahoussaye, Bill Shoemaker, Walter Guerra, Darrell McHargue, and Laffit Pincay, Jr., ride there regularly for the nation's highest purses on extraordinary, high-quality thoroughbreds. The fair weather brings huge crowds to the tracks and the relative wealth of the area results in extremely high betting pools. For example, typically 30,000 people bet over $5 million daily at Santa Anita Park. On opening day and occasions with major stakes races, the crowd can swell to well over 50,000 and the handle to nearly $10 million.

Such conditions are very good for Dr. Z system bettors. The track is usually fast. The quality of horses and jockeys is such that there is a large percentage of races that are run true-to-form—that is, more or less as expected. The large pools mean that Dr. Z system bets placed near the end of the betting period can be made in substantial amounts without depressing the place or show odds too much.

In May 1982, I was a visiting professor at UCLA. Since Hollywood Park was only a scant half-hour drive on the San Diego freeway from our home in West Los Angeles, it was easy to visit. Most Saturdays and Sundays have major races with purses of $50,000 or more. These draw the top horses, and both the spectacle and the investment possibilities make for a very enjoyable afternoon.

Saturday, May 8, 1982, was clear and warm and featured the $50,000 added Triple Bend Handicap. It was a good day to visit Hollywood Park. On that day there were two Dr. Z system bets, and they both won. As we have previously stated, two to four Dr. Z system bets per day is about typical. On average, Dr. Z system bets win about 60% of the time. Chapter Nine provides a more detailed discussion of these win rates.

The sixth race was a maiden race for three-year-olds and upward for a purse of $18,000. Maiden races are for horses that have never won a race in their career and hence are largely unproven. One must use extreme caution in betting on such races. Swing Till Dawn was making his first start, a situation that calls for even more caution. However, his pedigree and workouts were outstanding. This colt had the promise to be something special. The rest of the field was quite weak except for the second and third choices of the crowd: The Hague and Colonialism. Chris McCarron, the meet's leading jockey, was in the irons of Swing Till Dawn. Chris's consistency and winning ways added a measure of confidence to the information provided by the consensus group of experts and the outstanding workouts.

Swing Till Dawn did look like a top prospect, but I would bet only if the odds were good enough! They were. With one minute to post time the tote board was as follows:

	Totals	#4 Swing Till Dawn	Expected Value per Dollar Bet on Swing Till Dawn
Odds		7—5	
Win	339,272	116,637	
Place	131,740	33,380	1.11
Show	69,682	15,621	1.17

The expected value per dollar wagered on Swing Till Dawn was 1.11 to place and 1.17 to show. My betting fortune that day was $1,000, so I did not bet to place, but wagered $222 to show.*

At post time the situation was similar, and the final tote board was

	Totals	#4 Swing Till Dawn	Expected Value per Dollar Bet on Swing Till Dawn
Odds		7—5	
Win	350,246	119,896	
Place	137,398	34,816	1.11
Show	73,113	16,543	1.16

These values gave expected values to place and show of 1.11 and 1.16, respectively.

As expected, Swing Till Dawn won the race, followed by the long shot Beau Glacier. This provided a handsome $4 place payoff on the 7–5 favorite, Swing Till Dawn. However, it was still not quite good enough to qualify as a Dr. Z system bet. The betting public's second choice, The Hague, finished third. The fairly heavy betting to show on The Hague dropped Swing Till Dawn's show payoff to $2.80, which was still better than a typical show payoff for a 7–5 favorite. My bet of $222 to show returned $310.80, for a profit of $88.80. The payoffs were

4–	Swing Till Dawn...........	4.80	4.00	2.80
10–	Beau Glacier..............		14.40	6.40
7–	The Hague			2.80

The feature race of the day was the 7-furlong $50,000 added Triple Bend Handicap. It featured such top horses as Shanekite, Remember John, Never Tabled, Fingal, Laughing Boy, Rock Softly, Gifted Dancer, and Pompeii Court. Never Tabled had two wins and a second in three recent local starts. He had not run until he was a five-year-old, but his brief record was quite impressive. Fingal was a strong horse who had won nearly $350,000 in the fifty races of his career. He came into the Triple Bend off three consecutive impressive victories at Santa Anita. As the favorite in four previous races, however, he had failed to win and twice had been out of the money.

*You may determine these expected values and optimal bet sizes in several ways. The equations given in Chapters Four, Five, and Sixteen or the calculator discussed on page 128 will calculate them exactly. The charts provided in Chapters Four and Five may be used to determine fairly accurate expected values and betting amounts.

8th Hollywood

7 FURLONGS. (1.19⅘) 4th Running of THE TRIPLE BEND HANDICAP. $50,000 added. 3-year-olds and upward. By subscription of $50 each, which shall accompany the nomination, $500 additional to start, with $50,000 added, of which $10,000 to second, $7,500 to third, $3,750 to fourth and $1,250 to fifth. Weights, Monday, May 3. Starters to be named through the entry box by closing time of entries. A trophy will be presented to the owner of the winner. Closed Wednesday, April 28, 1982, with 15 nominations.

Never Tabled — Dk. b. or br. h. 5, by Never Bend—Table Flirt, by Round Table
Br.—Wygod M J (Ky) 1982 3 2 1 0 $24,200
Own.—Wygod M J 112 Tr.—Mandella Richard 1980 0 M 0 0
Lifetime 3 2 1 0 $24,200
2May82-3Hol 6f :223 :444 1:084ft *2-5 120 31½ 22 22½ 2no McCarronCJ2 Aw22000 93 Jenny'sDvid,NeverTbled,StrikItBig 5
15Apr82-7SA 6f :214 :444 1:09 ft *1 120 2½ 2hd 12 15½ McCarronCJ7 Aw19000 93 Never Tabled, Santir,TonysLanding 9
2Apr82-6SA 6f :214 :45 1:101ft 2¾ 118 32 31 12½ 16 Pincay L Jr2 Mdn 87 NeverTbled,Hwkire,SpnishNugget 10
●Apr 26 SA 6f ft 1:112 h Apr 11 SA 5f ft 1:021 h Mar 31 SA 4f ft :502 b Mar 25 SA 7f ft 1:25 h

Fingal ✻ — B. g. 8, by Gaelic Dancer—Meog, by Noor
Br.—Claiborne Farm (Cal) 1982 6 3 1 0 $56,500
Own.—Meverach & Vallone 113 Tr.—Frankel Robert 1981 14 6 2 1 $144,250
Lifetime 50 20 8 5 $344,513 Turf 10 4 1 1 $70,200
21Apr82-5SA a6½f Ⓣ:211 :4331:13 fm 3 115 31½ 32½ 33 1no DelahoussayeE4 75000 94 Fingal, Tellaround, Gray Dandy 12
4Apr82-2SA 6½f :214 :443 1:152ft *4-5 115 54 42½ 1hd 12½ DelahoussayeE5 60000 93 Fingal, Amen Brother, Tellaround 8
21Mar82-1SA 6f :214 :444 1:091ft *1 116 55½ 43 32 11 DelahoussayeE5 50000 92 Fingal, Incorporator, Beach Walk 8
21Feb82-5SA a6½f Ⓣ:212 :4311:13 fm*1-2 116 2hd 21 34 46 DelahoussayeE4 62500 88 FrndlyUncAln,Incorprtr,AmnBrthr 11
6Feb82-5SA a6½f Ⓣ:21 :4311:123fm*4-5 115 63½ 67 34½ 23½ DelahoussayeE4 70000 92 Gray Dandy, Fingal, Steelinctive 10
30Jan82-4SA 6f :212 :434 1:082ft *4-5e 118 98 910 66 42¾ DelahoussayeE2 62500 93 MinstrelGrey,MrbleCourt,Tellround 9
25Oct81-5SA a6½f Ⓣ:211 :4331:14 fm*4-5 120 34 35 31 54½ McCarron C J4 70000 85 Tellaround, Dandy Wit, Gray Dandy 8
11Oct81-7SA 6f :22 :451 1:10 ft *1 121 21 21½ 21½ 1nk McCrronCJ10 Aw32000 88 Fingal, Marble Court, Sham'sFool 10
2Oct81-5SA 6½f :22 :443 1:154ft *3-2 117 32½ 32 2hd 12 McCarronCJ3 Aw34000 91 Fingal, Double Discount, Parsec 5
22Aug81-7Dmr 1 1/16 Ⓣ:4631:11 1:421fm *3 116 1hd 1hd 23 77 DelahoussayeE1 80000 91 Sosegado, Me Good Man, Partout 10
May 6 Hol 3f ft :371 b Apr 30 Hol 4f ft :471 h Apr 15 SA 4f ft :491 h Mar 29 SA 4f gd :484 h

Remember John — B. g. 3, by The Irish Lord—Yoweee, by Crezier
Br.—Valenti P (Cal) 1982 4 3 1 0 $92,750
Own.—Sheridan Mr-Mrs J 110 Tr.—Vienna Darrell 1981 6 1 2 1 $52,900
Lifetime 10 4 3 1 $145,650
1May82-7Hol 6f :22 :442 1:083ft *3-5 122 2hd 1hd 11 1½ McCrronCJ4 Debonair 94 RemmbrJohn,ArtDirctor,RingProud 5
31Mar82-8SA 6½f :213 :441 1:151ft 3 117 1½ 1hd 1½ 1¾ DelhoussyeE1 Baldwin 94 RmmbrJohn,TmToExplod,CrystlStr 7
21Mar82-4SA 6½f :212 :44 1:152ft *2-3 115 1½ 11 13 15 DelhoussyeE1 Aw20000 93 RemembrJohn,CltlcSbr,EstrSrmon 6
17Feb82-8SA 6f :212 :434 1:083ft 20 117 1hd 21 22½ 23 DlhoussyE6 Blsa Chca 92 TmToExplod,RmmbrJohn,JornytS 10
9Sep81-8Dmr 1 :453 1:111 1:372ft 10 117 1hd 1hd 51½ 97½ McCarronCJ8 Dmr Fut 73 GatoDelSol,TheCaptain,RingProud 10
26Aug81-8Dmr 1 :454 1:103 1:364ft 6½ 117 1½ 11½ 2hd 55½ Toro F6 Balboa 78 TheCaptain,DistantHeart,GtoDelSol 9
12Aug81-8Dmr 6f :22 :45 1:11 ft *4-5 120 1hd 1½ 1hd 31 McCarronCJ5 De Anza 82 King'sFinder,Heln'sBu,RmmbrJohn 5
29Jly81-8Dmr 6f :221 :452 1:104ft *4-5 114 1½ 1½ 12½ 11¾ McCrrCJ5 ⓈGradution 84 RemmbrJohn,King'sFindr,DistntHrt 9
18Jly81-8Hol 6f :213 :444 1:102ft 19 115 2hd 2hd 1½ 2hd Toro F10 Hol Juv 85 TheCptin,RememberJohn,Hln'sBu 12
5Jly81-6Hol 6f :22 :453 1:112ft *6-5e 116 69 57½ 34 22¾ Toro F7 ⓈMdn 77 SwetndNturl,RmmbrJohn,Wicklow 11
Apr 29 Hol 3f ft :363 h Apr 27 Hol 5f ft 1:012 h Apr 24 SA 6f ft 1:133 h Apr 19 SA 5f ft :58 h

Rock Softly — B. g. 4, by Rock Talk—Softly, by Solo Landing
Br.—Retler Mr-Mrs R H (Md) 1982 9 1 2 3 $107,250
Own.—Byrn-Dvis-Glsn-Nvk-Rsnbrg 115 Tr.—Newsom Jesse C 1981 21 4 5 1 $138,625
Lifetime 35 5 7 6 $251,675 Turf 13 1 3 1 $66,725
18Apr82-7SA 1 :453 1:10 1:343ft 3½ 120 33 2½ 2½ 1no McCarronCJ5 Aw40000 96 Rock Softly, Sir Dancer, Tell Again 8
28Mar82-7SA 1 1/16 :451 1:084 1:411ft *8-5 117 37½ 59½ 47½ 34½ DelhoussyeE4 Aw35000 90 Sunshine Swag, A Run, RockSoftly 8
20Mar82-8GG 1 Ⓣ:48 1:1221:364yl 9½ 117 31½ 86½ 1014 1021 LamanceC9 S F Mle H 62 Silveyville, Visible Pole, ASureHit 10
6Mar82-7SA 1⅛ Ⓣ:4521:0941:463fm 4½ 119 57 54 42½ 22 DelhoussyeE4 Aw45000 92 Lake City, Rock Softly, Braughing 7
28Feb82-6SA 1 1/16 :47 1:104 1:412ft *2½ 117 2hd 2hd 31½ 2nk DelhoussyeE6 Aw40000 94 Egg Toss, Rock Softly, Western 6
21Feb82-8SA 1¼ Ⓣ:4341:34 1:591fm 18 116 68 44 46½ 67¾ Black K10 Sra Nvda H 83 HighCounsel,HndsomeOn,IrishHrt 11
7Feb82-8SA 1¼ :451 1:344 2:002ft 51 115 56½ 54 47 37 Black K8 C H Strub 80 It's the One, Dorcaro, Rock Softly 8
17Jan82-8SA 1⅛ :452 1:092 1:473ft 36 114 66½ 54½ 32 35¾ Black K5 Sn Frndo 85 It's the One, Princelet, Rock Softly 9
3Jan82-8SA 7f :221 :454 1:26 hy 13 114 89½ 813 716 416 Black K2 Malibu 54 Island Whirl, Shanekite, It'stheOne 8
20Dec81-7Hol 7f :22 :444 1:22 ft 3½ 121 62¾ 3½ 11 1¾ Black K3 Aw32000 87 RockSoftly,LaughingBoy,DustyHul 8
May 5 Hol 4f ft :493 hg Apr 25 Hol 5f ft 1:054 h Apr 16 Hol tr.t 4f ft :523 h Apr 10 Hol tr.t 4f ft :52 h

Laughing Boy B. c. 4, by Shecky Greene—Pomade, by Prince John

Br.—Elmendorf Farm (Ky) 1982 6 1 3 0 $31,100

Own.—Elmendorf 112 Tr.—Stidham Michael 1981 12 2 2 0 $37,975

Lifetime 21 4 5 0 $76,150 Turf 3 0 1 0 $7,100

29Apr82-8Hol 6f :22 :443 1:082ft *3-2 114 31½ 2½ 1½ 12½ McCarronCJ2 Aw26000 95 LaughingBoy,BeachWalk,Redoutble 7

17Apr82-5SA a6½f ⓣ:212 :44 1:132fm 19 114 34½ 32½ 2½ 22½ Hansen R D1 Aw32000 90 Captain Nick,LaughingBoy,Isopach 9

11Apr82-5SA 6½f :22 :451 1:17 sy *9-5 115 65½ 65½ 64¼ 73½ Toro F6 Aw26000 82 Tellround,Redoutble,He'sSomthing 7

26Feb82-7SA 6f :22 :444 1:084ft 9½ 115 74½ 52½ 11½ 2no Toro F1 Aw26000 94 MisterWilder,LughingBoy,Tllround 7

13Feb82-5SA 6½f :213 :442 1:161ft 7 115 88½ 79½ 55½ 2nk Toro F4 Aw26000 89 Kearney,LaughingBoy,Mari'sBook 10

28Jan82-7SA 6½f :212 :434 1:153ft 6 113 55½ 45 42½ 65½ Guerra W A1 Aw26000 86 Tooovrprim,MistrWildr,Cloonwillin 7

20Dec81-7Hol 7f :22 :444 1:22 ft 4¾ 114 52¾ 41½ 41½ 2¾ McCarronCJ1 Aw32000 86 RockSoftly,LaughingBoy,DustyHul 8

9Dec81-7Hol 6½f :221 :45 1:154ft 17 114 54½ 32½ 42½ 42½ McCarronCJ8 Aw25000 88 PompeiiCourt,KngrooCourt,Dorcro 8

13Nov81-7Hol 6f :22 :443 1:084ft 26 115 65½ 53 52 54½ Rivera M A4 Aw26000 88 Hcwind,KngrooCourt,PompiiCourt 8

29Oct81-7SA 6f :22 :443 1:09 ft 16 114 42¾ 45½ 66¾ 68¼ ValenzuelPA4 Aw34000 85 Shnekite,ImportntMemo,NtivFishr 7

Apr 25 Hol 4f ft :482 h Apr 7 SA 4f ft :474 h Apr 3 SA 5f ft 1:02 h Mar 29 SA 4f gd :481 h

Gifted Dancer Ch. c. 4, by L'Enjoleur—Second Coming, by Sir Gaylord

Br.— C T Chenery Estate (Va) 1982 4 3 1 0 $47,700

Own.—Roden W F 117 Tr.—Russell John W 1981 8 1 5 1 $34,950

Lifetime 15 5 7 1 $84,620 Turf 5 2 2 0 $39,450

23Apr82-7Hol 6f :221 :444 1:092ft *9-5 118 41½ 2hd 1hd 2nk Pincay L Jr5 Aw35000 90 PirateLw,GiftedDncer,MisterWilder 7

26Mar82-5SA a6½f ⓣ:213 :44 1:141fm *2½ 117 22½ 1hd 1½ 11 Pincay L Jr6 Aw32000 88 GftdDncr,AnswrtoMusc,SRullhRn 12

7Mar82-5SA a6½f ⓣ:211 :4331:14 fm*7-5 120 63¾ 42½ 2½ 1¾ Pincay L Jr6 Aw23000 89 GftdDncr,RnOfDmonds,Hostd'Oro 11

24Feb82-6SA 6f :213 :441 1:09 ft *2 117 44½ 41¾ 3nk 12¾ Pincay L Jr7 Aw19000 93 GiftedDncer,RglFlcon,VikingHustlr 7

31Dec81-5SA 6½f :224 :462 1:192hy *2¾ 113 2hd 32½ 21½ 22½ ShoemkerW3 Aw18000 70 Tuff to Beat, Gifted Dancer, Mufti 7

16Dec81-3Hol 6f :222 :452 1:101ft 3½ 117 32½ 22½ 22½ 1½ Pincay L Jr2 50000 86 GiftedDncer,MsterJono,Logrhythm 6

13Jun81-9Hol 1 1/16 ⓣ:4611:1031:414fm 3¾ 115 34½ 31 42 75½ McHrgueDG6 Aw22000 84 MasterThatch,RegalSport,Enhnce 12

29May81-8Hol 1 1/16 ⓣ:4731:12 1:424fm 3 115 1hd 1hd 1hd 2nk McHrgueDG6 Aw24000 85 MsterJono,GiftedDncer,MsterThtch 9

15May81-9Hol 6f :214 :443 1:094ft 3¼ 115 52¾ 54½ 33 34½ McHrgueDG3 Aw22000 83 Menswer,Jeff'sEncore,GiftedDncer 7

8May81-7Hol 6½f :222 :45 1:162ft 3 115 2hd 2hd 2hd 2hd Toro F1 Aw22000 88 Fair Hint, Gifted Dancer, Breached 6

May 6 Hol 5f ft 1:033 h May 1 Hol 5f ft 1:012 h Apr 17 SA 6f ft 1:144 h Apr 11 SA 6f ft 1:181 h

Pompeii Court B. h. 5, by Tell—Port Damascus, by Damascus

Br.—Keck H B (Ky) 1982 4 2 0 1 $46,800

Own.—Lewyk & Crowe 116 Tr.—Anderson Laurie N 1981 16 5 5 3 $45,954

Lifetime 24 9 7 4 $97,634

7Mar82-3SA 1 :443 1:083 1:342ft *2½ 116 2½ 1½ 1½ 1hd Hawley S1 Aw40000 97 PompCort,KngrooCort,SonofDodo 7

18Feb82-7SA 1 :451 1:09 1:333ft 11 114 1½ 11 13 14½ Hawley S2 Aw32000 101 PompeiiCourt,QuntumLep,Western 8

5Feb82-7SA 6½f :212 :433 1:15 ft 11 115 42½ 42½ 43 33¾ Sibille R5 Aw32000 91 VictorySmpl,BondRullh,PompCourt 8

20Jan82-5SA 7f :214 :45 1:244sy 4¾ 115 2hd 1hd 1hd 42 Sibille R1 Aw32000 74 Gristle,QuntumLep,AnswertoMusic 5

18Dec81-7Hol 6f :214 :443 1:093ft 9 115 3nk 3nk 32 55 Sibille R6 Aw30000 84 Hacwind,BennyBob,CrestoftheWve 7

9Dec81-7Hol 6½f :221 :45 1:154ft 5½ 116 1hd 1½ 12 11¼ Sibille R2 Aw25000 91 PompeiiCourt,KngrooCourt,Dorcro 8

27Nov81-7Hol 6½f :223 :453 1:183sy *3 115 1hd 11½ 21½ 2¾ Sibille R4 Aw25000 76 DndyWit,PompiiCourt,Sli'sRoylDrm 8

13Nov81-7Hol 6f :22 :443 1:084ft 15 115 1hd 2½ 2½ 34½ Sibille R1 Aw26000 89 Hcwind,KngrooCourt,PompiiCourt 8

17Oct81-8StP 6f :222 :451 1:101ft *9-5 118 55½ 54¼ 35 44 Garcia C1 Aw6500 94 Kinlin, Flashys Champ,ThreeforYou 7

30May81-9NP 1 1/16 :472 1:113 1:43 ft 2¾ 119 11 1hd 2hd 3nk Hedge R2 Cont'ntal H 100 MisterCountry,Ky.Alt,PompiiCourt 7

May 3 Hol 6f ft 1:131 h Apr 23 SA 6f ft 1:121 h Apr 16 SA 4f ft :483 h Mar 31 SA 5f ft 1:012 h

Shanekite B. c. 4, by Hoist Bar—Win Shane, by Anyoldtime

Br.—Udko Selma (Cal) 1982 4 0 2 0 $30,000

Own.—Uoko Selma 117 Tr.—Landers Dale 1981 10 6 0 0 $161,000

Lifetime 20 8 4 0 $213,125 Turf 1 0 1 0 $12,000

17Apr82-8SA a6½f ⓣ:21 :4311:13 fm 7½ 118 65½ 62¾ 3½ 21½ Hawley S1 Sn Simn H 92 Shagbark, Shanekite, Belfort 8

24Mar82-8SA 5½f :213 :442 1:021ft 4½ 118 — — — — HawleyS6 El Conejo H — ToB.OrNot,Belfort,Terresto'sSinger 8

24Mar82—Lost rider

9Jan82-8SA 7f :213 :434 1:204ft 3½ 119 43½ 41½ 89 812 Hawley S6 Sn Crlos H 84 Solo Guy, ‡King Go Go, Smokite 8

3Jan82-8SA 7f :221 :454 1:26 hy *8-5 120 51½ 1½ 2½ 26 Hawley S6 Malibu 64 Island Whirl, Shanekite, It'stheOne 8

19Dec81-8Hol 7f :212 :434 1:218ft *4-5 117 41½ 41½ 11 12½ Hawley S4 Yuletide H 89 Shanekite, FlyingChick,IslandWhirl 5

28Nov81-8Hol 1 :48 1:13 1:384m 3½ 113 1hd 1½ 3½ 42½ Hawley S4 Ntv Dvr.H 69 Syncopate, King Go Go, Wickerr 6

11Nov81-8Hol 6f :213 :441 1:081ft 2¾ 114 52½ 11 14 12½ HawleyS8 Sprnt Chmp 96 Shanekite,Syncopte,BigPresenttion 8

11Nov81—Run in two divisions, 8th & 9th races.

29Oct81-7SA 6f :22 :443 1:09 ft *4-5 118 22½ 22½ 2hd 15 Hawley S1 Aw34000 93 Shnekite,ImportntMemo,NtivFishr 7

4Sep81-8Dmr 1 1/16 :453 1:092 1:41 ft 8 117 34 45½ 46 511 Hawley S6 El Cajon 84 Island Whirl, Rock Softly, Damas 9

24Aug81-8Dmr 1 :452 1:101 1:363ft *3-2 117 31½ 22 22 43½ Pincay L Jr4 Aw30000 81 AtYourPlesure,Sli'sRoylDrem,Dscro 6

Apr 30 Hol 6f ft 1:142 h Apr 24 SA 4f ft :494 h Apr 13 SA ⓣ 5f yl 1:04 h (d) Apr 5 SA HC 5f gd 1:041 h (d)

Remember John was the only three-year-old scheduled to be in the race. His record of three victories and one second in four 1982 races was quite impressive. He was consistently running under 1:09 for 6 furlongs. Despite this blinding speed, fear of the older horses or some other reason caused his owner to scratch Remember John. Rock Softly was moving up in class. His 96 speed rating in a recent 1-mile victory at Santa Anita made him a definite threat. Laughing Boy was similar. He appeared to be outclassed, but a convincing 6-furlong victory at Hollywood the previous week in $1{:}08^2$ meant that he could not be ruled out. Gifted Dancer had four wins and two seconds in his last six races. However, today's competition was much stronger than he had previously faced. Pompeii Court had just run two smashing mile-race victories at Santa Anita. In one of them as an 11–1 shot, he had broken the track record by running a $1{:}33^3$ mile, a sizzling time. The final horse in the race was Shanekite, who had a brilliant but erratic record. In 1981, he had six wins in ten outings and finished out of the money in the remaining four races. He had not won in 1982 and had even lost his rider, Sandy Hawley, in a recent race. However, if sharp, he could run 6 furlongs in 1:08 flat and could handle this competition. This was a classic match.

The noted handicapper and Harvard dropout Andy Beyer believes thoroughbred handicapping is the supremely challenging intellectual activity. This race presented such a challenge for talented handicappers. We, of course, have argued in this book that you should leave such handicapping to these experts. You have to be very good to beat them, but you can rely on their skills to establish fair win odds and then use this information to select a place or show bet if one is good enough.

Shanekite was made an even-money favorite of the crowd. The tote board 1 minute before post time was as follows:

	Totals	#8 Shanekite	Expected Value per Dollar Bet on Shanekite
Odds		1—1	
Win	398,851	155,321	
Place	131,018	40,952	1.05
Show	59,163	14,585	1.18

These values provided an expected value per dollar bet of 1.05 to place and 1.18 to show. Thus Shanekite was a Dr. Z system bet to show but not good enough to bet to place. My betting fortune was $1,088, reflecting my earlier win in the sixth race. The optimal Dr. Z system bet was $310 to show on Shanekite. The totals at post time were similar:

	Totals	#8 Shanekite	Expected Value per Dollar Bet on Shanekite
Odds		1—1	
Win	407,589	158,523	
Place	139,217	42,739	1.06
Show	60,030	15,108	1.17

Never Tabled won the race, followed by Shanekite and Pompeii Court. The chart of the race was as follows:

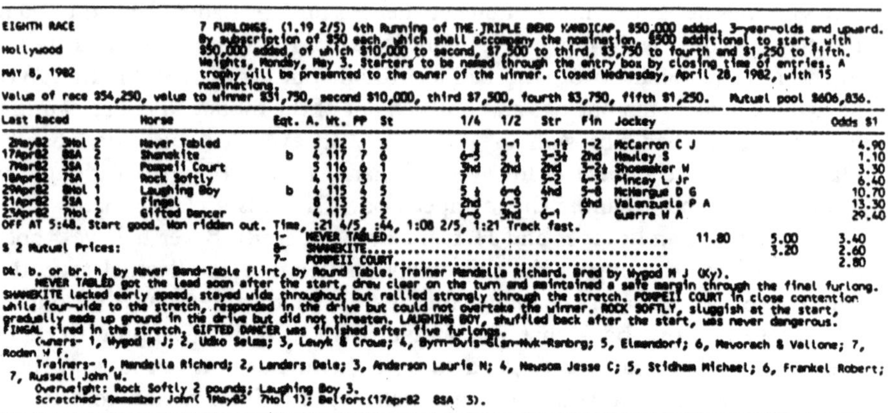

EIGHTH RACE
Hollywood
MAY 8, 1982

7 FURLONGS. (1.19 2/5) 4th Running of THE TRIPLE BEND HANDICAP. $50,000 added. 3-year-olds and upward. By subscription of $50 each, which shall accompany the nomination, $500 additional to start, with $50,000 added, of which $10,000 to second, $7,500 to third, $3,750 to fourth and $1,250 to fifth. Weights, Monday, May 3. Starters to be named through the entry box by closing time of entries. A trophy will be presented to the owner of the winner. Closed Wednesday, April 28, 1982, with 15 nominations.

Value of race $54,250, value to winner $31,750, second $10,000, third $7,500, fourth $3,750, fifth $1,250. Mutuel pool $606,836.

Last Raced			Horse	Eqt.	A.	Wt.	PP	St	1/4	1/2	Str	Fin	Jockey	Odds $1
2May82	3Hol	2	Never Tabled		5	112	1	3	1 ½	1-1	1-1½	1-2	McCarron C J	4.90
17Apr82	8SA	2	Shanekite	b	4	117	7	6	6-5	5 ½	3-3½	2hd	Hawley S	1.10
7Mar82	3SA	1	Pompeii Court		5	116	6	1	3hd	2hd	2hd	3-2½	Shoemaker W	3.30
18Apr82	7SA	1	Rock Softly		4	117	3	7	7	7	5-2	4-3	Pincay L Jr	6.40
29Apr82	8Hol	1	Laughing Boy	b	4	115	4	5	5 ½	6-6	4hd	5-8	McHargue D G	10.70
21Apr82	5SA	1	Fingal		8	113	2	4	2hd	4-3	7	6hd	Valenzuela P A	13.30
25Apr82	7Hol	2	Gifted Dancer		4	117	5	2	4-6	3hd	6-1	7	Guerra W A	29.40

OFF AT 5:48. Start good. Won ridden out. Time, :21 4/5, :44, 1:08 2/5, 1:21 Track fast.

$ 2 Mutuel Prices:				
1-	NEVER TABLED	11.80	5.00	3.40
8-	SHANEKITE		3.20	2.60
7-	POMPEII COURT			2.80

Dk. b. or br. h, by Never Bend-Table Flirt, by Round Table. Trainer Mandella Richard. Bred by Wygod M J (Ky).

NEVER TABLED got the lead soon after the start, drew clear on the turn and maintained a safe margin through the final furlong. SHANEKITE lacked early speed, stayed wide throughout but rallied strongly through the stretch. POMPEII COURT in close contention while four-wide to the stretch, responded in the drive but could not overtake the winner. ROCK SOFTLY, sluggish at the start, gradually made up ground in the drive but did not threaten. LAUGHING BOY, shuffled back after the start, was never dangerous. FINGAL tired in the stretch, GIFTED DANCER was finished after five furlongs.

Owners- 1, Wygod M J; 2, Udko Selma; 3, Lewyk & Crowe; 4, Bymn-Dvis-Glsn-Mvk-Rsnbrg; 5, Elmendorf; 6, Mevorach & Vallone; 7, Roden W F.

Trainers- 1, Mandella Richard; 2, Landers Dale; 3, Anderson Laurie N; 4, Newsom Jesse C; 5, Stidham Michael; 6, Frankel Robert; 7, Russell John W.

Overweight: Rock Softly 2 pounds; Laughing Boy 3.

Scratched- Remember John(1May82 7Hol 1); Belfort(17Apr82 8SA 3).

The payoff for show for Shanekite was $2.60. This was a little poorer than expected for an even-money favorite with an expected value of 1.17. One might hope to get at least $2.80 or possibly $3. However, because the top three choices out of the small seven-horse field had finished in the money, Shanekite's payoff was lowered, so with breakage it became $2.60. Despite the fact that the place payoff of $3.20 on Shanekite seems quite high, it was still not a Dr. Z system bet. My show bet of $310 returned $403, for a profit of $93—a 30% return on investment.

THE WHITNEY HANDICAP, SARATOGA RACETRACK, SARATOGA, NEW YORK, AUGUST 1, 1981

The fifty-sixth running of the Whitney Handicap at Saratoga featured a strong card of horses vying for their share of the $150,000 added purse. Amber Pass was the consensus favorite, followed by Winter's Tale and Glorious Song. The race was also to include such strong horses as The Liberal Member, Ring of Light, Temperence Hill, and Noble Nashua. A series of minor colds and other ailments as well as strategy for upcoming races led to the scratching of four horses: Amber Pass, Glorious Song, Temperence Hill, and Classic Trail. This left eight starters. Winter's Tale was established as a 3–2 favorite of the betting public. He had his regular jockey, Jeffrey Fell, in the irons and the number 1 post position. In twelve starts he had finished first or second on ten occassions and as a favorite was always in the money. An upset possibility was Fio Rito, who had performed brilliantly at low odds against much weaker competition.

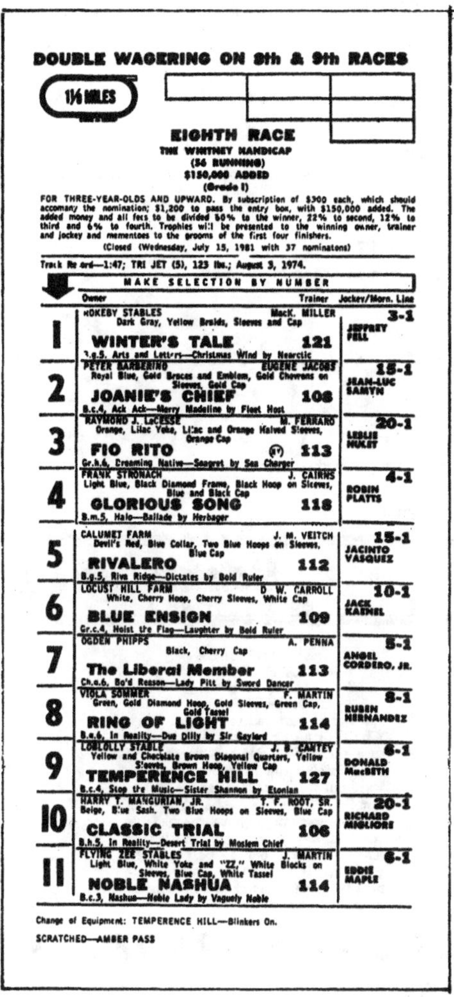

DOUBLE WAGERING ON 8th & 9th RACES

1⅛ MILES

EIGHTH RACE
THE WHITNEY HANDICAP
(54 RUNNING)
$150,000 ADDED
(Grade I)

FOR THREE-YEAR-OLDS AND UPWARD. By subscription of $300 each, which should accomany the nomination; $1,200 to pass the entry box, with $150,000 added. The added money and all fees to be divided 60% to the winner, 22% to second, 12% to third and 6% to fourth. Trophies will be presented to the winning owner, trainer and jockey and mementoes to the grooms of the first four finishers.

(Closed (Wednesday, July 15, 1981 with 37 nominatons)

Track Record—1:47; TRI JET (5), 123 lbs.; August 3, 1974.

MAKE SELECTION BY NUMBER

No.	Owner / Colors / Horse / Breeding	Trainer	Weight	Jockey	Morn. Line
1	ROKEBY STABLES — Dark Gray, Yellow Braids, Sleeves and Cap — **WINTER'S TALE** — B.g.5, Arts and Letters—Christmas Wind by Nearctic	MacK. MILLER	121	JEFFREY FELL	3-1
2	PETER BARBERINO — Royal Blue, Gold Braces and Emblem, Gold Chevrons on Sleeves, Gold Cap — **JOANIE'S CHIEF** — B.c.4, Ack Ack—Merry Madeline by Fleet Host	EUGENE JACOBS	108	JEAN-LUC SAMYN	15-1
3	RAYMOND J. LaCESSE — Orange, Lilac Yoke, Lilac and Orange Halved Sleeves, Orange Cap — **FIO RITO** — Gr.h.6, Dreaming Native—Seagret by Sea Charger	M. FERRARO	113	LESLIE HULET	20-1
4	FRANK STRONACH — Light Blue, Black Diamond Frame, Black Hoop on Sleeves, Blue and Black Cap — **GLORIOUS SONG** — B.m.5, Halo—Ballade by Herbager	J. CAIRNS	118	ROBIN PLATTS	4-1
5	CALUMET FARM — Devil's Red, Blue Collar, Two Blue Hoops on Sleeves, Blue Cap — **RIVALERO** — B.g.5, Riva Ridge—Dictates by Bold Ruler	J. M. VEITCH	112	JACINTO VASQUEZ	15-1
6	LOCUST HILL FARM — White, Cherry Hoop, Cherry Sleeves, White Cap — **BLUE ENSIGN** — Gr.c.4, Hoist the Flag—Laughter by Bold Ruler	D. W. CARROLL	109	JACK KAENEL	10-1
7	OGDEN PHIPPS — Black, Cherry Cap — **The Liberal Member** — Ch.a.6, Bold Reason—Lady Pitt by Sword Dancer	A. PENNA	113	ANGEL CORDERO, JR.	5-1
8	VIOLA SOMMER — Green, Gold Diamond Hoop, Gold Sleeves, Green Cap, Gold Tassel — **RING OF LIGHT** — B.a.6, In Reality—Due Dilly by Sir Gaylord	F. MARTIN	114	RUBEN HERNANDEZ	8-1
9	LOBLOLLY STABLE — Yellow and Chocolate Brown Diagonal Quarters, Yellow Sleeves, Brown Hoop, Yellow Cap — **TEMPERENCE HILL** — B.c.4, Stop the Music—Sister Shannon by Etonian	J. B. CANTEY	127	DONALD MacBETH	6-1
10	HARRY T. MANGURIAN, JR. — Beige, Blue Sash, Two Blue Hoops on Sleeves, Blue Cap — **CLASSIC TRIAL** — B.h.5, In Reality—Desert Trial by Moslem Chief	T. F. ROOT, SR.	106	RICHARD MIGLIORE	20-1
11	FLYING ZEE STABLES — Light Blue, White Yoke and "ZZ," White Blocks on Sleeves, Blue Cap, White Tassel — **NOBLE NASHUA** — B.c.3, Nashua—Noble Lady by Vaguely Noble	J. MARTIN	114	EDDIE MAPLE	6-1

Change of Equipment: TEMPERENCE HILL—Blinkers On.

SCRATCHED—AMBER PASS

The odds on Winter's Tale were reasonably good throughout the betting period. An expected value of 1.15 just two minutes before post time qualified Winter's Tale as a Dr. Z system bet. The tote board was as follows:

	Totals	#1 Winter's Tale	Expected Value per Dollar Bet to Show on Winter's Tale
Odds		3—2	
Win	424,370	131,021	
Show	52,609	11,011	1.15

With an initial wealth of $2,500, the optimal bet to show on Winter's Tale was $270. At post time the odds to show had dropped slightly.

	Totals	#1 Winter's Tale	Expected Value per Dollar Bet to Show on Winter's Tale
Odds		3—2	
Win	486,875	159,273	
Show	57,957	14,313	1.09

The expected value per dollar bet to show on Winter's Tale was now 1.09.

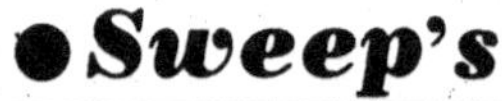

Saratoga Analysis

EIGHTH RACE
1—Amber Pass
2—Winter's Tale
3—Glorious Song

Recently restored to his best form, AMBER PASS gets a slight nod to capture the nine-furlong Whitney. The Pass Catcher colt impressed in Delaware but will have to be at his best to handle WINTER'S TALE. This veteran also seems to have reached his form of last year, a possibility that makes him the one to beat. GLORIOUS SONG is at her best and her best makes her eligible to handle the males in this event.

SELECTIONS • GRADED ENTRIES

Saratoga

Consensus Totals Based on 5 points for First (7 for Best Bet), 2 for 2nd, 1 for 3rd. Best Bet in **Bold Type.** **Clocker Selections not included in Consensus.**

	TRACKMAN	HANDICAP	ANALYST	HERMIS	SWEEP	CLOCKER	CONSENSUS	
8	Amber Pass Winter's Tale Glorious Song	Glorious Song Amber Pass Winter's Tale	Amber Pass The Liberal Member Temperence Hill	Winter's Tale Amber Pass Temperence Hill	Amber Pass Winter's Tale Glorious Song	Winter's Tale Amber Pass The Liberal Memoer	Amber Pass Winter's Tale Glorious Song	21 15 7

8 SARATOGA 1⅛ MILES (SARATOGA — Start & Finish)

1 ⅛ MILES. (1.47) 54th Running THE WHITNEY HANDICAP (Grade I). $150,000 Added. 3-year-olds and upward. By subscription of $300 each, which should accompany the nomination; $1,200 to pass the entry box, with $150,000 added. The added money and all fees to be divided 60% to the winner, 22% to second, 12% to third and 5% to fourth. Weights Monday, July 27. Starters to be named at the closing time of entries. Trophies will be presented to the winning owner, trainer and jockey and mementoes to the grooms of the first four finishers. Closed with 37 nominations.

Winter's Tale

B. g. 5, by Arts And Letters—Christmas Wind, by Nearctic
Br.—Mellon P (Va)
Own.—Rokeby Stable **Tr.—Miller Mack** **121**

	St.	1st	2nd	3rd	Amt.
1981	5	1	3	0	$48,170
1980	7	5	1	0	$462,800

Date-Race	Cond	Dist	Fractions	Race	Running line	Jockey	Wt	Odds	Chart
19Jly81- 7Bel	fst	1 1/16	:46⅕ 1:10 1:40⅘	3↑Allowance	3 5 55 51½ 1½ 12½	Fell J	b 115	*.60	98-12 Winter's Tale 1152½ Niteange 115¾ Far Out East 1152¾ Handily 6
4Jly81- 8Bel	sly	1¼	:47⅗ 1:36 2:02	3↑Suburban H	7 2 21 67½ 711 711	Fell J	123	3.80	79-20 TemperenceHill127hdRingofLight115¾HighlandBlde113nk Faltered 8
13Jun81- 8Bel	fst	1⅛	:46⅗ 1:10 1:46⅗	3↑Nassau Cty H	3 3 2½ 2½ 24 24	Fell J	125	*.50	90-14 Fool'sPrayer1124Winter'sTale1252½HerbWter1123½ Best of others 5
6Jun81- 1Bel	fst	1	:46⅖ 1:10⅖ 1:34⅘	3↑Allowance	5 3 33 21½ 21½ 21½	Fell J	122	*.60	92-14 Amber Pass 1151½ Winter's Tale 1225½King'sWish1156 Stmbld st. 5
15May81- 8Bel	fst	7f	:23⅕ :46⅖ 1:23⅗	Allowance	2 4 32 21 25 2¾	Fell J	122	*.60	83-19 Rivalero 122¾ Winter's Tale 122hd Tax Holiday 1053 Gamely 6
6Sep80- 7Bel	fst	1⅛	:45 1:09⅖ 1:47	3↑Marlboro H	8 3 32 3nk 12 14½	Fell J	123	3.30	92-15 Winter'sTle1234½GloriousSong117nkJklinKlugmn1183½ Ridden out 8
2Aug80- 8Sar	fst	1⅛	:46 1:09⅗ 1:48⅕	3↑Whitney	7 7 79 88 711 714	Fell J	126	3.70	80-10 State Dinner 120½ Dr. Patches 114½ Czaravich 1232½ Outrun 8
19Jly80- 8Bel	fst	1½	:51⅗ 2:05 2:28⅘	3↑Brooklyn H	4 3 21 11½ 13 15	Fell J	120	3.40	77-20 Winter's Tale 1205 State Dinner1213½RingofLight1142 Ridden out 5
4Jly80- 8Bel	fst	1¼	:47⅗ 1:36 2:00⅘	3↑Suburban H	1 2 1½ 2½ 11 1hd	Fell J	114	2.70	97-14 Winter's Tale 114hd State Dinner 117hd Czaravich 1271½ Driving 7
15Jun80- 8Bel	fst	1⅛	:46⅗ 1:10⅖ 1:47⅕	3↑Nassau Cty H	8 1 1½ 11 14 17¾	Venezia M	111	3.90e	91-17 Winter's Tale 1117¾ Crow's Nest1095DewanKeys114nk Ridden out 8

LATEST WORKOUTS Jly 25 Bel 4f fst :47 h Jly 16 Bel (T) 6f fm 1:13⅗ h (d) Jly 14 Bel 4f fst :49⅗ b Jly 10 Bel 4f fst :47⅗ b

Joanie's Chief *

B. c. 4, by Ack Ack—Merry Madeline, by Fleet Host
Br.—Hillbrook Farm (Ky)
Own.—Barberino P **Tr.—Jacobs Eugene** **108**

Turf Record	St.	1st	2nd	3rd
	6	1	0	0

	St.	1st	2nd	3rd	Amt.
1981	12	2	3	4	$96,081
1980	16	1	2	2	$38,780

Date-Race	Cond	Dist	Fractions	Race	Running line	Jockey	Wt	Odds	Chart
19Jly81- 9Del	fst	1 1/16	:46 1:10 1:41⅘	3↑Wm Dupont Jr	7 9 816 86¾ 710 44¾	Samyn J L	111	14.40	94-12 Amber Pass 119nk Phleming 118hd Herb Water 1084½ Mild rally 10
3Jly81- 8Bel	my	6f	:22⅕ :45 1:09	3↑True North H	4 6 78 75 52½ 11½	Samyn J L	109	23.70	97-16 Jonie'sChief1091½ProudAppel117nkGuiltyConscience1133½ Driving 7
27Jun81- 6Bel	fst	6f	:22⅖ :45 1:09⅖	3↑Allowance	6 5 33 47½ 46½ 35	Cordero A Jr	119	4.40	90-16 Engine One 1131½ Pikotazo 1193½ Joanie's Chief 119no Wide 6
6Jun81- 7Bel	fst	1	:46⅕ 1:10⅖ 1:35⅗	3↑Allowance	6 5 33 34½ 25 25	Cordero A Jr	117	2.10	85-14 GuiltyConscienc1155Joni'sChif1171½PrincCrimson115½ Lugged in 10
1May81- 8Aqu	fst	6f	:23⅕ :46 1:10⅕	Allowance	7 4 54 34 32½ 21½	Cordero A Jr	119	*.80	88-26 IrishSwords1191½Joanie'sChief1192½SpartnEmperor1153½ Gamely 7
20Apr81- 8Aqu	fst	6f	:23 :46⅖ 1:11⅕	Allowance	5 3 34 33½ 21 12½	Cordero A Jr	116	2.60	85-30 Joanie's Chief 1162½Miroman119hdTrafficBreaker115¾ Ridden out 7
21Mar81-10Hia	fst	1⅛	:46⅘ 1:10⅕ 1:48⅗	3↑Seminole H	3 5 66½ 68½ 711 68¾	Velez R I	106	23.50	80-19 Boyne Valley 1101¾ Land of Eire 1111 Poor Dad115no No menace 9
14Mar81- 8Hia	fst	1⅛	:48 1:12⅕ 1:48⅘	Allowance	4 3 21 2hd 11½ 2½	Velez R I	115	*1.30	89-09 Sailor Talk 119½ Joanie's Chief 1158½ Bing 115no Game try 7
28Feb81- 9GP	fst	1¼	:48 1:36⅘ 2:03⅕	3↑Gulf Park H	3 6 55½ 88½ 811 87½	Velez R I	105	19.20	73-18 Hurry Up Blue 1191 YosiBoy1111ImperialDilemma113¾ No excuse 9
14Feb81- 9GP	fst	1⅛	:48⅗ 1:12 1:49	3↑Donn H	2 4 43 47 33 35	Velez R I	107	8.80	82-20 Hurry Up Blue 1162½ Tunerup 1262½Joanie'sChief1072 Bid, evenly 5

LATEST WORKOUTS Jly 29 Sar 5f sly 1:03⅗ b Jly 18 Bel tr.t 3f fst :37⅖ b Jly 11 Bel tr.t 5f fst 1:02 b Jly 2 Bel tr.t 3f gd :37⅕ b

Amber Pass

B. c. 4, by Pass Catcher—Amberina, by Somerset
Br.—DiLibero E M (Fla)
Own.—Entremont **Tr.—Hine Hubert** **116**

	St.	1st	2nd	3rd	Amt.
1981	5	3	1	1	$130,490
1980	10	3	2	4	$199,097

Date-Race	Cond	Dist	Fractions	Race	Running line	Jockey	Wt	Odds	Chart
19Jly81- 9Del	fst	1 1/16	:46 1:10 1:41⅘	3↑Wm Dupont Jr	3 7 59 55 22 1nk	Asmussen C B	b 119	*.80	99-12 Amber Pass 119nk Phleming 118hd Herb Water 1084½ Driving 10
6Jun81- 1Bel	fst	1	:46⅖ 1:10⅖ 1:34⅘	3↑Allowance	2 2 1hd 11½ 11½ 11½	Asmussen C B	b 115	1.60	94-14 Amber Pass 1151½ Winter's Tale 1225½ King's Wish 1156 Driving 5
25May81- 8Bel	fst	1	:44⅕ 1:08⅗ 1:33⅘	3↑Metropol'n H	1 2 11 1½ 31½ 33½	Hernandez R	b 115	5.10	95-22 Fappiano 1152¾ Irish Tower 127¾ Amber Pass 1157½ Weakened 7
2May81- 8Aqu	gd	7f	:22⅖ :45⅕ 1:23	3↑Carter H	6 1 31½ 2hd 22 1½	Maple E	b 114	5.60e	86-19 Amber Pass 114½ GuiltyConscience1111Dunham'sGift1161 Driving 7
18Apr81- 6Pim	fst	6f	:23 :45⅗ 1:10⅗	Allowance	4 4 2hd 1hd 2hd 2nk	McCauley W H	b 114	*.90	93-18 Rex Imperator 119nkAmberPass11410FoolsDance1124 Drifted out 5
6Sep80- 7Bel	fst	1⅛	:45 1:09⅖ 1:47	3↑Marlboro H	5 2 2hd 1hd 69 716	MacBeth D	b 116	11.00	76-15 Winter'sTl1234½GloriousSong117nkJklinKlugmn1183½ Speed 6 fur. 8
16Aug80- 8Sar	fst	1¼	:45⅘ 1:36⅕ 2:02⅘	Travers	9 2 2hd 13 1hd 31½	MacBeth D	b 126	12.50	84-13 TmprncHll1261½FrstAlbrt126noAmbrPss1266¾ Drifted out,bumped 9
2Aug80- 9Mth	fst	1⅛	:46⅘ 1:10⅘ 1:49⅖	Mth Invit H	1 3 42½ 41¾ 43 32¾	MacBeth D	b 121	2.10e	85-18 Thanks to Tony 111½ Superbity 1242½ Amber Pass 121nk Mild bid 8
20Jly80- 8Hol	fst	1¼	:45⅖ 1:35 2:00⅘	Swaps	8 2 22 12½ 14 2hd	MacBeth D	b 123	4.70	87-14 First Albert 123hd Amber Pass 1234 Mr. Mud 1142½ Sharp 11
5Jly80- 8Bel	fst	1⅛	:45⅕ 1:09⅕ 1:49	Dwyer	3 2 22 21½ 13 11	MacBeth D	b 114	4.00	82-17 Amber Pass 1141 Temperence Hill 129hd Comptroller1193 Driving 8

LATEST WORKOUTS ●Jly 17 Pim 3f fst :34 h Jly 12 Pim 7f fst 1:28 h ●Jly 7 Pim 7f gd 1:28⅖ h ●Jly 1 Pim 5f fst :59 h

Fio Rito * Gr. h. 6, by Dreaming Native—Seagret, by Sea Charger
Br.—LeCesse R (NY)
Own.—LeCesse R Tr.—Ferraro Michael
113 Turf Record St. 1st 2nd 3rd 2 0 0 0 | 1981 St. 5 1st 4 2nd 1 3rd 0 Amt. $58,772 | 1980 12 9 2 0 $192,309

20Jly81- 8Bel sly 1 :45⅘ 1:09⅘ 1:35 3↑[S]EvanShipman 4 4 1hd 2hd 1½ 12½ Hulet L b 117 *.30 93-15 Fio Rito 1172½ Sir Ack 121½ Naskra's Breeze 117nk Drew Clear 7
4Jly81- 9FL fst 170 :47⅕ 1:11 1:40⅗ 3↑[S]Gen.sullivan 2 3 2hd 16 16 18½ Hulet L b 120 *.10e 98-17 Fio Rito 1208½ Sea Bourne 1172 D. J.'s Nitecap 1144 Easily 5
13Jun81- 8FL fst 170 :47⅗ 1:11 1:40⅕ 3↑[S]Allowance 3 2 11 18 18 111 Hulet L b 118 *.20 114-10 FioRito 11811 Holiday Chip 118nk Publisher 1101 Ridden out 7
7Jun81- 6FL fst 6f :22 :45 1:09⅘ 3↑Allowance 5 2 43½ 33½ 2hd 17 Hulet L b 114 *.20 105-08 Fio Rito 1147 Mari Juno 1041½ Lake Placid 1145 Drew clear 5
25May81- 9FL fst 6f :23⅕ :46⅕ 1:10⅘ 3↑[S]Williamson 1 5 51½ 33 33 31½ Hulet L b 115 *.10e 99-12 [D]Sea Bourne 119½ Al's Sky Lab 119½ Fio Rito 1157 Rallied 5
25May81-Placed second through disqualification
28Dec80- 8Aqu fst 1⅛ [•]:48⅘ 1:13⅘ 1:46⅖ 3↑[S]Alex M. Robb 6 3 1hd 2hd 32 22 Saumell L b 126 *.50 80-18 Sir Ack 1192 Fio Rito 126nk Quintessential 123hd Gamely 8
10Dec80- 8Aqu fst 6f [•]:22⅘ :45⅘ 1:10⅕ 3↑[S]Joe Palmer 5 2 43½ 42½ 42 1nk Saumell L b 126 *1.00 93-11 Fio Rito 126nk Kim's Chance 122no Sir Ack 1193½ Wide, just up 5
27Nov80- 8Aqu fst 1⅛ :48⅘ 1:12⅘ 1:56 3↑Queens Cty H 4 1 11½ 1hd 35½ 58½ Hulet L b 120 *2.60 73-24 Fool'sPryer1121½RingofLight1155½Pictursqu1141½ Unruly, slow st. 7
9Nov80- 8FL sly 1¼ :48⅗ 1:39⅗ 2:07⅗ 3↑[S]Wadsworth H 6 1 12 11½ 13 15½ Hulet L b 138 *.20e 93-17 Fio Rito 1385½ Green Parade 1144½ Captain Pat 126nk Easily 7
6Oct80- 8Bel fst 1⅛ :46 1:11 1:51⅗ 3↑[S]Bongard H 5 2 11 11 11 11½ Hulet L b 126 *.70 70-26 Fio Rito 1261½ Kim's Chance 1243 Sir Ack 117no Driving 5

Glorious Song B. m. 5, by Halo—Ballade, by Herbager
Br.—Taylor E P (Can)
Own.—Stronach F Tr.—Cairns John
118 Turf Record St. 1st 2nd 3rd 5 3 1 0 | 1981 St. 6 1st 2 2nd 2 3rd 0 Amt. $180,485 | 1980 11 6 4 1 $525,617

1Jly81- 9WO fst 1⅛ :46⅘ 1:10⅘ 1:48 3↑Dom Day H 2 3 31½ 2½ 14½ 15½ Platts R 125 *.35 102-14 Glorious Song 1255½ DrivingHome1262½ByeByeTony112hd Handily 8
26Apr81- 8Hol fst 1 :46⅕ 1:11⅕ 1:36⅖ 3↑M'vy Leroy H 6 4 53½ 32 1hd 2nk Toro F 121 *1.70 84-21 ElvnStitchs115nkGloriousSong1212½SummrTmGuy1145½ Sharp try 8
8Mar81- 8SA fst 1¼ :45⅘ 1:34⅕ 1:59⅗ S Anita H 11 8 89½ 66½ 57 55½ McHargue D G 119 10.30 86-11 John Henry 1281 King Go Go 1171½ Exploded 115no Wide 11
22Feb81- 8SA fst 1⅛ :44⅘ 1:08⅘ 1:47⅕ ⒻS Margar'a H 6 4 47 44½ 31 2nk McCarron C J 130 *1.10 93-12 Princess Karenda 118nkGloriousSong1301½Ack'sSecret1222 Sharp 10
31Jan81- 8SA gd 1⅛ :46⅗ 1:10⅘ 1:43⅕ ⒻS Maria H 1 3 32 2hd 12½ 12 McCarron C J 127 *.50 85-23 GlorosSong1272TrckRbbry1175MssHntngtn11310 Eased final yds. 4
10Jan81- 8SA fst 7f :21⅘ :43⅘ 1:20⅕ San Carlos H 1 7 75½ 63 46 46½ Hawley S 120 4.50 92-10 FlyingPstr1243½ToB.OrNot1232DoublDiscount1151½ Flattened out 8
6Sep80- 7Bel fst 1⅛ :45 1:09⅘ 1:47 3↑Marlboro H 4 7 710 63½ 22 24½ Velasquez J 117 *1.70 87-15 Winter'sTale1234½GloriousSong117nkJklinKlugmn1183½ Went well 8
16Aug80- 9Mth fst 1⅛ :46⅘ 1:11⅕ 1:48 3↑A Haskell H 2 5 75½ 4nk 2½ 21½ Velasquez J 117 6.70 93-15 SpctclrBd1321½GlorsSng1171½ThClVrgnn1124 DriftedOut,brushed 8
12Jly80- 9WO fm 1¼ Ⓣ:45⅘ 1:37⅕ 2:01⅗ [S]Maturity 2 4 35½ 11½ 13 13½ Leblanc J B 121 *.25 99-09 Glorious Song 1213½ Great State 1261 Nice Idea 1211 Handily 6
1Jly80- 7WO fst 1⅛ :48 1:11⅘ 1:50⅘ 3↑Dom Day H 2 5 54½ 3nk 11½ 11 Leblanc J B 123 *.30 91-13 Glorious Song 1231 Maple Grove 1184 Knight'sTurn1181½ Handily 8
LATEST WORKOUTS Jly 25 Sar 5f fst 1:00⅘ b Jly 18 WO 1 fst 1:40⅕ b Jly 13 WO 5f fst :58⅗ b Jun 28 WO 4f fst :48⅘ b

Rivalero * B. g. 5, by Riva Ridge—Dictates, by Bold Ruler
Br.—Stokes R G (Va)
Own.—Calumet Farm Tr.—Veitch John M
112 Turf Record St. 1st 2nd 3rd 1 0 0 0 | 1981 St. 6 1st 2 2nd 0 3rd 1 Amt. $50,904 | 1980 14 4 1 3 $140,149

19Jly81- 8Bel fst 7f :22⅘ :45 1:21⅘ 3↑Tom Fool 5 5 69 66½ 34½ 34½ Vasquez J 119 12.00 91-12 Rise Jim 1191½ ProudAppeal1212½Rivalero119hd Lckd Lt.response 6
4Jly81- 5Bel sly 1⅛ :47 1:11 1:42⅕ 3↑Allowance 1 4 42 2½ 2hd 11½ Vasquez J 119 3.40 91-20 Rivalero 1191½ Dr. Tipton 1152½ Voodoo Rhythm 1171 Ridden out 6
6Jun81- 1Bel fst 1 :46⅗ 1:10⅗ 1:34⅘ 3↑Allowance 4 5 45 46 49½ 413 Vasquez J 115 9.10 81-14 Amber Pass 1151½ Winter's Tale 1225½ King's Wish 1156 Evenly 5
25May81- 8Bel fst 1 :44⅕ 1:08⅘ 1:33⅗ 3↑Metropol'n H 3 6 610 611 614 619 Saumell L 115 26.00 80-22 Fappiano 1152½ Irish Tower 127½ Amber Pass 1157½ Outrun 7
15May81- 8Bel fst 7f :23⅕ :46⅖ 1:23⅘ Allowance 6 6 54½ 43 35½ 1½ Vasquez J 122 9.80 84-19 Rivalero 122½ Winter's Tale 122hd Tax Holiday 1053 Driving 6
7May81- 8Bel fst 7f :23⅕ :46⅖ 1:22⅘ Allowance 7 7 63½ 53 48 412 Fell J b 122 4.20 77-21 Fappiano 1224 Miroman 119no Dynamite Cap 1157½ Off slowly 7
16Oct80- 5Med fst 1¼ :47⅕ 1:35⅖ 2:00⅖ 3↑Med Cup H 11 7 98½ — — — Fell J b 116 14.10 — — Tunerup 1176 Dr. Patches 1168 Dewan Keys 115no Bled 12
4Oct80- 6Bel yl 1⅛ [T]:47⅕ 1:11 1:44⅘ 3↑Handicap 5 3 35 47½ 511 511 Fell J b 115 1.60 67-22 Not Tomorrow 1103½ No Neck 1131½ [DH]T. V. Series 112 Tired 5
6Sep80- 6Med fst 1⅛ :45⅗ 1:10⅗ 1:44 3↑Jrsy Blues H 6 4 38 62½ 43 41½ Fell J b 119 *1.20 88-21 Tunerup 112no Dewan Keys 1141 Foretake 114nk Brushed 8
16Aug80- 5Sar fst 1⅛ :46⅗ 1:10⅗ 1:56⅕ 3↑Allowance 4 4 412 37½ 1hd 1hd Fell J b 119 *.70 96-13 Rivalero 119hd Pianist 1154½ Picturesque 115hd Driving 6
LATEST WORKOUTS Jly 27 Sar 4f sly :47⅗ h Jly 17 Bel 3f fst :36⅕ b Jly 13 Bel 4f fst :47⅗ h Jly 3 Bel 3f sly :36 b

The Liberal Member Ch. g. 6, by Bold Reason—Lady Pitt, by Sword Dancer
Br.—Phipps O (Ky)
Own.—Phipps O Tr.—Penna Angel
113 Turf Record St. 1st 2nd 3rd 8 1 1 1 | 1981 St. 2 1st 0 2nd 1 3rd 1 Amt. $54,910 | 1979 9 3 1 1 $166,149

18Jly81- 8Bel fst 1½ :49⅗ 2:01⅗ 2:26 3↑Brooklyn H 2 7 67 2½ 21½ 24 Cordero A Jr 113 5.40 86-15 Hechizado 1164 The Liberal Member113½PeatMoss1113½ 2nd best 10
11Jly81- 7Bel fst 1 :45⅗ 1:09⅗ 1:35⅗ 3↑Allowance 1 6 42 31 3½ 3½ Cordero A Jr 115 8.00 90-16 NearEast115½DiplomaticNote115hdTheLiberalMember1153 Evenly 8
15Dec79- 8Aqu fst 1⅝ [•]:48⅕ 2:04⅗ 2:43⅗ 3↑Gallant Fx H 3 10 710 56½ 69 611 Encinas R I 126 *2.30 97-15 Identical 1106 Ethnarch 1182½ Land of Eire 114½ Outrun 12
1Sep79- 8AP fm 1½ Ⓣ:48 2:06⅕ 2:32⅕ 3↑Arlington H 10 8 822 78½ 36½ 413 Encinas R I 117 2.70 65-28 Bowl Game 1244½ Young Bob1108Liveinthesunshine105½ Bid,tired 14
12Aug79- 8Sar my 1⅛ :47⅗ 1:12⅘ 1:51⅘ 3↑B Baruch H 4 6 610 610 516 522 Encinas R I 117 *2.10 54-25 Overskate 128½ Timbo 108½ Native Courier 1153½ Outrun 7
4Aug79- 8Sar fst 1⅛ :48⅕ 1:10⅘ 1:47⅗ 3↑Whitney 6 6 41 41 3nk 31½ Encinas R I 120 7.00 96-12 Star DeNaskra120½Cox'sRidge117½TheLiberalMember120½ Rallied 6
21Jly79- 8Bel fst 1½ :50⅗ 2:03⅗ 2:28⅘ 3↑Brooklyn H 4 4 32½ 13 11½ 1½ Encinas R I 114 6.10 76-24 The LiberalMember114½BowlGame119hdStateDinner1232½ Driving 5
11Jly79- 6Bel fst 1½ :48⅗ 2:02⅘ 2:28⅗ 3↑Handicap 4 6 57½ 18 114 115 Encinas R I 114 *.80 77-17 The LiberalMember11415Framarco1092½Yamasaki1126 Ridden out 7
30Jun79- 6Bel fm 1⅜ [T]:49⅕ 1:36⅖ 2:14 3↑Allowance 4 5 42½ 2hd 12 12½ Encinas R I 115 2.20 99-07 TheLiberlMember1152½IvoryHunter1155½Metphor115½ Ridden out 5
17Jun79- 4Bel fm 1¼ [T]:49⅕ 1:38⅖ 2:01⅗ 3↑Allowance 8 7 67½ 31 42 31½ Encinas R I 117 4.30 83-15 NonCommercil1131½[D]SndroTsc112hdThLibrlMmbr1171½ Impeded 11
17Jun79-Placed second through disqualification
LATEST WORKOUTS Jly 31 Sar 4f fst :50 b Jly 17 Bel 4f fst :47⅗ b Jly 7 Bel 4f fst :47⅗ h Jun 30 Bel 5f fst 1:01 b

Ring of Light * B. g. 6, by In Reality—Due Dilly, by Sir Gaylord
Br.—Chenery C T Estate of (Va)
Own.—Sommer Viola Tr.—Martin Frank **114**
St. 1st 2nd 3rd Amt.
1981 12 4 4 1 $221,074
1980 21 7 2 5 $340,959

4Jly81- 8Bel sly 1¼ :47⅗ 1:36 2:02 3↑Suburban H 2 1 11 12 13 2hd Asmussen C B 115 16.80 90-20 TemperenceHill127hdRingofLight115½HighlndBld113nk Just failed 8
21Jun81-10Suf fst 1⅛ :47 1:11⅕ 1:49⅖ 3↑Mass H 8 7 85½ 43 55½ 48½ Maple E 119 *1.20e 85-15 Soldier Boy 1142½ Niteange 1082 Driving Home 1144 Rallied 9
7Jun81- 9Suf fst 6f :22⅖ :45⅗ 1:10⅗ 3↑Suf Downs H 3 10 1011 86¾ 53½ 1no Maple E 116 3.30e 88-29 Ring of Light 116no Dave's Friend 1281½ Triocala 1121½ Driving 10
30May81- 6Bel fst 7f :23⅖ :46 1:22⅖ 3↑Handicap 2 6 56 55½ 21½ 22½ Maple E 120 *1.30 87-17 Rise Jim 1222½ Ring of Light 1201½ Dr. Patches 118nk 2nd best 6
17May81- 8Bel fst 6f :22⅖ :45⅗ 1:09⅘ 3↑Roseben H 5 8 811 88 41½ 1¾ Maple E 113 7.00e 93-22 Ring of Light 113¾ Guilty Conscience1121Convenient114½ Driving 8
11Apr81- 8Aqu fst 1¼ :47⅖ 1:35⅗ 2:00⅘ 3↑Excelsior H 3 2 21½ 24 25 24¾ Asmussen C B 113 9.60 87-22 Irish Tower 1274¾ Ring of Light 113½ Relaxing 1251 Held place 6
4Apr81- 7Aqu fst 1⅛ :47⅕ 1:11 1:49⅗ Allowance 5 4 33½ 1hd 16 15 Cordero A Jr 122 *.40 86-25 RingofLight1225CreativePlan1143DegenerateJon1173½ Ridden out 6
28Mar81- 8Aqu fst 1 :45 1:09⅕ 1:35 3↑Westchster H 4 6 44½ 32½ 2½ 2no Fell J 114 6.70 91-20 Dunham's Gift 115no Ring ofLight114nkDr.Blum124½ Sharp effort 6
14Mar81- 8Aqu fst 6f ⊡:23⅕ :46⅖ 1:11⅕ 3↑Toboggan H 4 4 44½ 43½ 45 45½ Lovato F Jr 114 3.50 83-18 Dr.Blum1232¼GuiltyConscience115noDunham'sGift1182¾ No factor 4
6Mar81- 8Aqu sly 1⅟₁₆ ⊡:48⅕ 1:14⅕ 1:47⅗ Allowance 6 3 32 1½ 13 12½ McCarron G 117 *1.80 76-37 Ring of Light 1172½ Contare 1083¾ Hasty Tam 1157¾ Easily 8
LATEST WORKOUTS ●Jly 30 Sar 4f sly :45⅗ h ●Jly 25 Bel tr.t 6f fst 1:14 b ●Jly 12 Bel tr.t 5f fst :59 h ●Jun 30 Bel tr.t 6f fst 1:12 h

Temperence Hill * B. c. 4, by Stop The Music—Sister Shannon, by Etonian
Br.—Polk A F Jr (Ky)
Own.—Loblolly Stable Tr.—Cantey Joseph B **127**
Turf Record St. 1st 2nd 3rd: 3 0 0 1
St. 1st 2nd 3rd Amt.
1981 6 3 1 0 $368,090
1980 17 8 3 1 $1,130,452

18Jly81- 8Bel fst 1½ :49⅖ 2:01⅗ 2:26 3↑Brooklyn H 5 6 77 810 713 817 Maple E 128 2.30 73-15 Hechizado 1164 TheLiberalMember113¾PeatMoss1113½ No factor 10
4Jly81- 8Bel sly 1¼ :47⅗ 1:36 2:02 3↑Suburban H 1 4 49 45 33½ 1hd MacBeth D 127 3.20 90-20 TmprncHill127hdRingofLght115¾HghlndBld113nk Brushed, driving 8
14Jun81- 8Hol fst 1¼ :45⅗ 1:34⅘ 2:00⅖ 3↑Gold Cup H 2 4 55½ 75¾ 56½ 56 Maple E 129 3.20 83-16 DCtermn120hdElevenStitchs1222½SuprMomnt117nk Lacked room 10
25May81- 8Hol fst 1⅛ :45⅗ 1:10⅕ 1:48⅖ 3↑Californian 3 4 411 52½ 32½ 2hd Maple E 130 *1.60 87-15 Eleven Stitches 122hd Temperence Hill 130nk Kilijaro1233¾ Sharp 12
10Apr81- 9OP fst 1⅟₁₆ :46⅘ 1:11⅖ 1:43⅖ Oaklawn H 4 5 43 1hd 1½ 12 Maple E 126 *.60 91-18 Temperence Hill1262SunCatcher1231½Uncool1142½ Brushed, clear 5
28Mar81- 9OP fst 1⅟₁₆ :49 1:13 1:44⅕ Razorback H 1 5 56½ 31 2hd 1nk Maple E 124 *.40 87-21 Temperence Hill 124nk Blue Ensign1133Belle'sRuler1124½ Driving 6
25Oct80- 8Aqu sf 1½ Ⓣ:51⅘ 2:13 2:39⅗ 3↑Turf Classic 5 4 33 68 711 716 Maple E 121 2.40 27-57 Anifa 1233 Golden Act 1265 John Henry 126nk Tired 8
18Oct80-10LaD gd 1¼ :49⅕ 1:39⅗ 2:06⅗ Super Derby 3 4 25 1½ 13 15½ Maple E 126 *.50 92-19 Temperence Hill 1265½ First Albert 126½CactusRoad126no Driving 8
4Oct80- 8Bel fst 1½ :49⅘ 2:05⅕ 2:30⅕ 3↑J C Gold Cup 1 3 43 1½ 13 15½ Maple E 121 2.30 69-19 TemperenceHill1215½JohnHenry1262IvoryHunter1263½ Ridden out 7
6Sep80- 7Bel fst 1⅛ :45 1:09⅖ 1:47 3↑Marlboro H 6 8 811 74½ 55 512 Maple E 119 6.20 80-15 Winter'sTale1234¾GloriousSong117nkJklinKlugmn1183½ No factor 8
LATEST WORKOUTS Jly 31 Sar 3f fst :26⅕ b Jly 17 Bel 3f fst :36⅗ h Jly 13 Bel 6f fst 1:15 b Jly 3 Bel 3f sly :38⅘ b

Classic Trial B. h. 5, by In Reality—Desert Trial, by Moslem Chief
Br.—Mangurian H T Jr (Fla)
Own.—Mangurian H T Jr Tr.—Root Thomas F Sr **106**
Turf Record St. 1st 2nd 3rd: 6 1 0 1
St. 1st 2nd 3rd Amt.
1981 15 2 0 2 $27,559
1980 4 1 0 1 $7,430

29Jly81- 4Sar sly 1⅛ :47⅗ 1:12⅕ 1:50 3↑Allowance 1 1 13 13 15 17 Hernandez R b 119 10.20 85-18 ClassicTril1197NephewScott1173½OurCptinWillie1162½ Ridden out 8
23Jly81- 9Crc fst 1 :47⅗ 1:13⅗ 1:41⅘ 3↑Allowance 7 7 613 58½ 46½ 42½ Puckett H5 b 114 *1.40 76-25 Cherokee Sky 1001½ End of Lent 110½ Four Lane 117½ Rallied 7
11Jly81- 8Crc fm 1⅟₁₆ Ⓣ:47⅗ 1:12 1:43⅗ 3↑Allowance 3 6 53¾ 810 56½ 44½ Cardone E b 121 *2.60 81-14 Tax Haven 1102½ Nataniel 1172 Golden Jackpot 117hd Blocked 10
4Jly81- 9Crc fst 1⅛ :47⅖ 1:13 1:52⅘ 3↑American H 9 9 814 88½ 610 47½ Cardone E b 110 25.50 78-19 Poking 1154 Noble Warrior 1193 Roogh Lord 114½ Rallied 10
27Jun81- 7Crc fst 170 :47⅗ 1:12⅘ 1:43⅖ 3↑Allowance 7 6 65 47½ 47 38 Cardone E b 122 6.90 85-16 Court Of Flags 1183GleamingChannel1135ClassicTrial1224 Rallied 7
13Jun81- 8Crc fm *1⅟₁₆ Ⓣ 1:45⅖ 3↑Allowance 3 8 86½ 55½ 31 13 Cardone E b 119 5.30 88-12 ClssicTril1193BrodwyHys1192½BrveYoungMench1153½ Drew clear 9
30May81- 8Crc fst 7f :22⅗ :45⅗ 1:26⅘ 3↑Allowance 6 10 1117 1115 97¼ 82½ Cardone E b 120 28.30 80-11 NocturnlPhntom109¾ChiefMgistrte114nkTrilAppel109hd No factor 12
18May81- 7Hia fst 1⅟₁₆ :47 1:12⅘ 1:47⅖ 3↑Allowance 1 4 411 48 65½ 42½ Cardone E b 118 8.50 64-30 Fast Summer 110hdEndofLent1112OverDeposited104nk Weakened 6
9May81- 6Hia gd *1⅟₁₆ Ⓣ 1:44⅕ 3↑Allowance 2 7 75 44 43½ 35½ Cardone E b 118 18.80 72-21 Gleaming Channel 1094½ Mini Pie 1181 Classic Trial 1183 Rallied 8
11Mar81-10Hia fm 1⅛ Ⓣ 1:49 Allowance 5 4 48½ 87½ 912 810 Cardone E b 116 25.40 79-10 Ransom Ozzie 1161½Roustabout1161½MortalFriends116½ Fell back 10
LATEST WORKOUTS Jun 25 Crc 3f sly :36⅗ b Jun 21 Crc 4f fst :50 b

Noble Nashua Dk. b. or br. c. 3, by Nashua—Noble Lady, by Vaguely Noble
Br.—Grousemont Farm (Ky)
Own.—Flying Zee Stable Tr.—Martin Jose **114**
St. 1st 2nd 3rd Amt.
1981 9 5 0 1 $269,755
1980 4 2 1 0 $62,007

19Jly81- 8Hol fst 1¼ :45 1:35⅗ 2:01⅕ Swaps 6 6 611 22½ 1½ 12½ Pincay L Jr 123 *2.30 85-20 Noble Nashua 1232½ Dorcaro 1157 Stancharry 123¾ Handily 7
5Jly81- 8Bel fst 1⅛ :46⅗ 1:11⅗ 1:49⅕ Dwyer 3 4 31½ 41½ 11½ 12¾ Asmussen C B 119 4.70 81-23 Noble Nashua 1192¾ TapShoes1264SilverExpress1141¾ Drew clear 10
18Jun81- 7Bel fst 7f :22⅗ :44⅘ 1:21⅘ 3↑Allowance 1 3 1hd 2hd 2hd 1hd Maple E 112 2.20 93-17 NobleNashua112hdFiveStarFlight1144½DHWestOnBrod111 Driving 6
25May81- 9Key fst 1⅛ :46⅗ 1:10⅖ 1:49 Penn Derby 4 1 12½ 1½ 3nk 55¾ Asmussen C B b 122 3.90 84-16 Summing1221½Sportin'Lif1221½ClssicGoGo1221¾ Brushed, bore in 9
2May81- 8CD fst 1¼ :45⅕ 1:36 2:02 Ky Derby 9 14 1311 1311 108¼ 911 Asmussen C B 126 71.70 76-12 Pleasant Colony 126¾ Woodchopper 1263 Partez 1262½ No threat 21
18Apr81- 9Aqu fst 1⅛ :45⅗ 1:10⅖ 1:49⅗ Wood Mem'l 6 2 2½ 22 49 414 Cordero A Jr 126 5.50 73-23 Pleasant Colony 1263 Highland Blade1265CuretheBlues1266 Tired 6
5Apr81- 8Aqu fst 1 :45 1:08⅘ 1:33⅗ Gotham 1 3 32 34½ 36 38½ Cordero A Jr 123 3.40 89-19 ProudAppeal123noCuretheBlues1268½NobleNashua1235½ Steadied 6
25Feb81- 8Aqu gd 1⅟₁₆ ⊡:47 1:12⅕ 1:43 Whirlaway 4 1 12 11 14 19½ Cordero A Jr 119 *.40 99-20 Noble Nashua 1199½ Royal Pavilion 1194½ Summing 1196 Easily 5
6Feb81- 9Tam fst 6f :22⅖ :46⅖ 1:12⅗ Allowance 5 3 43 32½ 2½ 15½ Cordero A Jr 116 *.10 82-24 Noble Nashua 1165½ Rit Cat 113no Sible Sue 11410 Drew out 7
25Oct80- 9Lrl sly 1⅟₁₆ :46⅕ 1:11⅗ 1:44⅖ Lrl Futurity 2 2 23 22½ 310 414 Cordero A Jr 122 3.50 72-19 Cure the Blues 1226½ Matching Gift 1226KanReason1221 Bumped 7
LATEST WORKOUTS Jly 29 Sar 5f sly 1:00⅖ h Jly 2 Bel tr.t 5f gd :59⅘ h ●Jun 26 Bel tr.t 6f fst 1:14⅗ b Jun 15 Bel tr.t 4f my :48⅖ h (d)

Fio Rito took to the lead and held off Winter's Tale's late charge to steal the race. The payoff to show on Winter's Tale was $2.80, a reasonable payoff for a 3–2 shot, most of whose main opposition was scratched. My $270 bet returned $378, for a profit of $108. The chart of the race was as follows:

Whitney Handicap

EIGHTH RACE
Saratoga
AUGUST 1, 1981

1 ⅛ MILES. (1.47) 54th Running THE WHITNEY HANDICAP (Grade I). $150,000 Added. 3-year-olds and upward. By subscription of $300 each, which should accompany the nomination; $1,200 to pass the entry box, with $150,000 added. The added money and all fees to be divided 60% to the winner, 22% to second, 12% to third and 5% to fourth. Weights Monday, July 27. Starters to be named at the closing time of entries. Trophies will be presented to the winning owner, trainer and jockey and mementoes to the grooms of the first four finishers. Closed with 37 nominations.

Value of race $175,500, value to winner $105,300, second $38,610, third $21,060, fourth $10,530. Mutuel pool $265,447, OTB pool $414,227.

Last Raced	Horse	Eqt.A.Wt	PP	St	¼	½	¾	Str	Fin	Jockey	Odds $1
20Jly81 8Bel1	Fio Rito	b 6 113	3	4	1hd	1½	1½	11	1nk	Hulet L	10.20
19Jly81 7Bel1	Winter's Tale	b 5 121	1	8	41½	5½	5hd	3hd	21	Fell J	1.50
4Jly81 8Bel2	Ring of Light	6 114	7	5	31½	31	21	2½	3hd	Hernandez R	6.80
18Jly81 8Bel2	The Liberal Member	6 114	6	3	5hd	4hd	62	41	4½	Cordero A Jr	3.00
19Jly81 9Del4	Joanie's Chief	4 108	2	2	7½	71	8	61½	5½	Samyn J L	19.50
19Jly81 8Hol1	Noble Nashua	3 114	8	6	6½	6hd	41	51½	61¼	Maple E	4.20
19Jly81 8Bel3	Rivalero	5 114	4	7	8	8	7½	71½	72	Vasquez J	12.70
19Jly81 9Del8	Blue Ensign	b 4 109	5	1	21½	21	3½	8	8	Kaenel J L	51.00

OFF AT 5:45 EDT. Start good, Won driving. Time, :23⅗, :46⅗, 1:10, 1:34⅘, 1:48 Track fast.

$2 Mutuel Prices:			
3-(D)-FIO RITO	22.40	6.20	3.80
1-(A)-WINTER'S TALE		4.00	2.80
8-(I)-RING OF LIGHT			4.20

Gr. h, by Dreaming Native—Seagret, by Sea Charger. Trainer Ferraro Michael. Bred by LeCesse R (NY).

FIO RITO broke through before the start, went right after the leaders, raced well out from the rail while making the pace, responded readily when challenged by RING OF LIGHT approaching the stretch and, after gaining a clear advantage with a furlong remaining, was all out to turn back WINTER'S TALE. The latter, never far back, moved up along the inside approaching the far turn, continued to save ground into the stretch and finished with good courage. RING OF LIGHT, reserved behind the early leaders into the backstretch, made a run from the outside at the far turn, remained prominent into the stretch but wasn't good enough. THE LIBERAL MEMBER, reserved early, rallied between horses after entering the stretch but failed to sustain his bid. JOANIE'S CHIEF, outrun early while saving ground, angled out entering the stretch and finished with good energy. NOBLE NASHUA, taken back early, commenced to rally while racing wide approaching the end of the backstretch, loomed a threat leaving the far turn but lacked a late response. RIVALERO was always outrun. BLUE ENSIGN, a forward factor to the far turn, drifted out while weakening.

Owners— 1, LeCesse R; 2, Rokeby Stable; 3, Sommer Viola; 4, Phipps O; 5, Barberino P; 6, Flying Zee Stable; 7, Calumet Farm; 8, Locust Hill Farm.

Trainers— 1, Ferraro Michael; 2, Miller Mack; 3, Martin Frank; 4, Penna Angel; 5, Jacobs Eugene; 6, Martin Jose; 7, Veitch John M; 8, Carroll Del W.

Overweight: The Liberal Member 1 pound; Rivalero 2.

Scratched—Amber Pass (19Jly81 9Del1); Glorious Song (1Jly81 9WO1); Temperence Hill (18Jly81 8Bel8); Classic Trial (29Jly81 4Sar1).

THE SANTA YNEZ STAKES, SANTA ANITA, FEBRUARY 2, 1983

The first national conference on thoroughbred handicapping was held in Los Angeles, February 1–3, 1983. It was a great opportunity for us to hear the latest theories and experiences of many of America's top handicappers.* Also, we could combine the trip with a visit to Santa Anita on February 2.

Set at the foot of the San Gabriel mountains in Arcadia, California, Santa Anita is one of America's most beautiful tracks. The warm southern California climate and the enormous Los Angeles population base contribute to the huge betting crowds. With its average daily handle of over $5 million and

*For those interested in the latest in handicapping, see our guide to this literature in Chapter Sixteen.

large purses, Santa Anita draws an unusually high standard of jockeys, trainers, and thoroughbreds. Saturday and Sunday cards often contain races with purses worth several hundred thousand dollars. During the weekdays the purses and crowds are smaller but still considerable. For example, on Wednesday, February 2, the purses ranged from $12,000–$75,000 (added) with most races in the $15,000–$30,000 range.

It was a cold, wet day; the track condition was listed as muddy. Such offtracks are usually a signal that the bettor should be cautious or not bet at all. The poor track condition can yield races that are not run true to form. In such cases long shots often replace favorites in the winner's circle, and the races are run in slow times. The grounds crew at Santa Anita, however, is famed for its handling of the track. The members of the crew knew that they needed to seal the track before the rain came. It was sealed by rolling the dirt track hard so that there would be a firm backing, even though the topsoil was muddy. The success of their work was apparent all day long when fractional and winning times were just about typical for a fast track. The muddy track gave a slight edge to strong front-runners, which, because of the efficiency in the win pool, was presumably reflected in the odds.* Dr. Z system bettors should be cautious on such days unless they have confidence that the horses are more or less running true to form.

Although we felt that the track would be all right for our Dr. Z system bets, we carefully monitored the situation throughout the day. In your own betting we recommend that you exercise caution or even stay home on offtrack days until and unless you feel confident about your analysis of the situation. For your first few visits, try to select days when conditions are ideal: beautiful, sunny weekend days with the best horses and large pools.

The feature race of the day was the Santa Ynez Stakes with a $75,000 added purse ($83,550 total) for three-year-old fillies. The race was run over 7 furlongs and featured some top sprinters. The standout in the race, Fabulous Notion, had a perfect record with five strong wins in five outings. Her speed ratings were in the 90s for the sprint races and 83 in her only route race, which she won by six lengths.† All her wins were convincing. Today she

*There is very little published evidence that the bettors adjust their wagers to reflect track biases. The question is whether the market for win bets remains efficient. Many handicappers believe that it does not remain efficient and that track biases are one of the key places to look for so-called overlays. One of the major track biases is that of post position. The advantage varies from track to track and by the length of the race. For example, Pimlico is reputed typically to have a tremendous inside bias for speed horses particularly in the route races. For some data on this see Quirin (1979). The effect of these biases on win and exotic bets at Exhibition Park in 1982, 1983, and 1984 has been studied by Canfield, Fauman, and Ziemba (1986). They found that the biases exist and are strong but that the public typically picks upon the bias and bets it down to negate the edge. Some profitable bets exist in exotic wagers on off-tracks when the biases are not as well understood by the public. The shrewd observer of biases and their changes can use this information to great advantage.

†A speed rating of 100 equals the track record at this distance. For every 1/5 second off the track record, one point is deducted. Hence a rating of 83 indicates that the race was run $3\frac{2}{5}$ seconds slower than the track record. Speed ratings above 80 are good; those above 90 are outstanding.

had her steady jockey, Donald Pierce, a good post position, and strong recent workouts. Minor drawbacks were the additional weight assignment to 124 pounds and a month's layoff since her convincing win in the California Breeder's Championship Stakes on December 30, 1982. Fabulous Notion was the top choice of all the Santa Anita handicappers and the *Daily Racing Form*'s consensus best bet of the day. The second choice was A Lucky Sign, who had a strong record of three wins in five starts. Her speed ratings were outstanding and very consistent. She would be guided in the irons by the great Chris McCarron, who had led her to two consecutive wins at Santa Anita recently.* Today she was picking up weight to start at 121 and was assigned the outside post position in the number 9 slot. Other strong horses were the undefeated Autumn Magic and Sophisticated Girl.

Experts' Selections

Consensus Points: 5 for 1st (today's best 7), 2 for 2nd, 1 for 3rd. Today's Best in Bold Type.

Trackman, Warren Williams **SANTA ANITA PARK** Selections Made for Fast Track

	TRACKMAN	HANDICAP	ANALYST	HERMIS	SWEEP	CONSENSUS	
8	FABULOUS NOTION	**FABULOUS NOTION**	FABULOUS NOTION	**FABULOUS NOTION**	FABULOUS NOTION	**FABULOUS NOTION**	29
	A LUCKY SIGN	A LUCKY SIGN	SOPHISTICATED GIRL	A LUCKY SIGN	A LUCKY SIGN	A LUCKY SIGN	9
	SOPHISTICATED GIRL	TIME OF SALE	A LUCKY SIGN	SOPHISTICATED GIRL	SOPHISTICATED GIRL	SOPHISTICATED GIRL	5

ANALYST'S *Santa Anita Comment*

EIGHTH RACE

1—Fabulous Notion
2—Sophisticated Lady
3—A Lucky Sign

FABULOUS NOTION has yet to taste defeat and appears headed for her sixth straight win today despite giving away chunks of weight to her rivals. She must give 10 pounds to SOPHISTICATED GIRL, who won her last gamely and ran champion Landaluce to two lengths in the Oak Leaf here last fall. The weight factor could easily tell in this spot. A LUCKY SIGN has won two stakes here at the meet, but will be stretching out an extra furlong today off strictly speed breeding. AUTUMN MAGIC has won her lone two starts but gets the acid test today. She can't be overlooked.

*As usual, Chris McCarron and Laffit Pincay, Jr., were locked in a duel for top jockey of the meet. As indicated by the following table, Pincay and McCarron were running 1-2 considerably above the other jockeys.

8th Santa Anita

7 FURLONGS. (1.20) 32nd Running of THE SANTA YNEZ STAKES (Grade II). $75,000 added. Fillies. 3-year-olds. (Allowance). By subscription of $50 each to accompany the nomination, $100 to pass the entry box and $750 additional to start, with $75,000 added, of which $15,000 to second, $11,250 to third, $5,625 to fourth and $1,875 to fifth. Weight, 121 lbs. Winners of $50,000 twice in 1982–83, 3 lbs. additional; of $50,000 three times in 1982–83, 5 lbs. Non-winners of two races of $25,000 since December 25 or two of $25,000 or one of $50,000 at any time allowed 2 lbs.; of a race of $25,000 since December 25 or two of $15,000 or one of $25,000 at any time, 4 lbs.; of a race of $12,000, 7 lbs. Starters to be named through the entry box by the closing time of entries. A trophy will be presented to the owner of the winner. Closed Wednesday, January 26, 1983 with 18 nominations.

Autumn Magic

B. f. 3, by Proud Clarion—Autumn Ember, by Gallant Man

Br.—Jones B & Humphrey Louise (Ky) 1983 1 1 0 0 $11,000

Own.—Mirkin Claudia H & M **114** **Tr.—Jones Gary** 1982 1 1 0 0 $9,350

Lifetime 2 2 0 0 $20,350

14Jan83-7SA 1 1/16 :46 1:103 1:424ft *8-5 115 43 31½ 1hd 1½ Toro F2 ⒻAw20000 87 AutumnMgic,‡ChicNtiv,OrintlChmp 9

26Dec82-3SA 6f :214 :444 1:092ft 11 117 86¼ 64 22½ 12 Toro F5 ⒻMdn 91 Autumn Magic, Toga, SpruceSong 10

Jan 25 SA 4f m :484 h Dec 16 SA 4f ft :473 h Dec 9 SA 6f ft 1:13 h Dec 2 SA 6f ft 1:141 h

Sophisticated Girl

Dk. b. or br. f. 3, by Stop the Music—Close Control, by Dunce

Br.—Meredith Dr-Mrs C G (Md) 1982 5 2 1 0 $86,391

Own.—Golden Eagle Farm **114** **Tr.—Jones Gary**

Lifetime 5 2 1 0 $86,391

30Dec82-5SA 1 1/16 :454 1:11 1:441ft *2-5 117 712 57 2hd 11½ DlhoussyE3 ⒻAw20000 80 SophstctdGrl,HcklbrryHony,Mrznrs 9

28Nov82-8Hol 1 1/16 :46 1:104 1:422ft *6-5e 120 87¼ 74¼ 77½ 59¾ DlhossyE6 ⒻHol Strlt 73 FbulosNoton,O'HppyDy,StphnBryn 9

23Oct82-8SA 1 1/16 :454 1:094 1:414ft 18 115 46¼ 35 24 22 DlhossyE1 ⒻOak Leaf 90 Landluce,SophistictedGirl,GrnjRein 7

11Oct82-6SA 1 :461 1:113 1:383ft 3 117 67¼ 52¾ 31½ 12½ DelahoussyeE4 ⒻMdn 75 SophisticatedGirl,Mnznres,MuyJup 8

1Oct82-4SA 6f :211 :442 1:10 ft 10 117 1111 911 912 43½ DelahoussyeE5 ⒻMdn 84 Osage Lady, Tiptopper, Loan 12

Jan 25 SA 5f m 1:03 h Jan 19 SA 4f gd :474 h Jan 12 SA 5f ft 1:002 h Jan 7 SA 4f ft :50 h

Fabulous Notion

B. f. 3, by Somethingfabulous—Careless Notion, by Jester

Br.—Stark R (Cal) 1982 5 5 0 0 $378,368

Own.—PineMeadowsThoroughbreds **124** **Tr.—Jordan James**

Lifetime 5 5 0 0 $378,368

30Dec82-8SA 7f :211 :442 1:22 ft *2-3 122 32½ 21 12 14 PiercD9 ⒻⓈCal Brdrs 90 FblosNoton,EstrnBttor,I'mPrstgs 10

28Nov82-8Hol 1 1/16 :46 1:104 1:422ft 8¾ 120 2hd 1hd 14 16 Pierce D3 ⒻHol Strlt 83 FbulosNoton,O'HppyDy,StphnBryn 9

5Nov82-10LA 6f :22 :452 1:102ft *1-2 120 1½ 11 11 1½ PncLJr1 ⒻSaddleback 93 FbulosNoton,EstrnBttor,LonForgnr 7

13Oct82-6SA 6f :214 :45 1:093ft *3-5 118 22 2½ 1½ 12½ Pincay LJr6 ⒻAw20000 90 FabulousNotion,Infantes,OsageLdy 6

3Oct82-3SA 6f :211 :442 1:091ft *3-5 117 1½ 12 14 16½ Pincay L Jr4 ⒻⓈMdn 92 FabulousNotion,Castleind,Ally'sLdy 7

Jan 31 SA 4f ft :47 h ● Jan 25 SA 6f m 1:143 h Jan 20 SA 5f ft 1:002 h ● Jan 15 SA 5f ft :58 h

Eastern Bettor

Dk. b. or br. f. 3, by Out of the East—Happy Bettor, by Crazy Kid

Br.—Hanson Stock Farm (Cal) 1983 1 0 0 0 $4,500

Own.—Hanson Stock Farm **119** **Tr.—Rettele Loren** 1982 8 3 3 0 $75,108

Lifetime 9 3 3 0 $79,608

12Jan83-8SA 6f :211 :44 1:093ft 5½ 119 96¼ 89 56¼ 46½ McHrDG4 ⒻPasadena 83 ALuckySign,LotusDncer,PstryCun 12

30Dec82-8SA 7f :211 :442 1:22 ft 7 120 53½ 54½ 45½ 24 SibillR6 ⒻⓈCal Brdrs 86 FblosNoton,EstrnBttor,I'mPrstgs 10

26Nov82-8BM 6f :224 :462 1:124gd 2½ 116 33½ 22 2hd 13 Hall D C2 ⒻⓈCrtshp 76 EstrnBttor,LuckyLksd,MkThSnshn 7

17Nov82-8Hol 6½f :213 :442 1:161ft 4 115 74¾ 65 714 610 VlenzulPA8 ⒻTrlingua 79 LuckyLkesid,I'mPrstigious,Cstllnd 10

5Nov82-10LA 6f :22 :452 1:102ft 5 120 33½ 31½ 31 2½ VlnlPA7 ⒻSaddleback 92 FbulosNoton,EstrnBttor,LonForgnr 7

24Oct82-4SA 6f :213 :442 1:094ft 26 114 31½ 2½ 1hd 11¼ VlenzulPA5 ⒻAw20000 89 EstrnBttor,ALuckySign,LonForignr 7

15Oct82-3SA 6f :22 :451 1:11 ft 4¼ 117 42 53¾ 42¾ 12 Sibille R7 ⒻM32000 83 EsternBettor,KnitTwo,HonyDon't 12

11Jun82-4Hol 5f :214 :443 :572ft 13 116 1011 918 918 812 McHargue DG4 ⒻMdn 80 Barzell, Lituya Bay, Body Talk 10

16May82-4AC 2f :223ft 4¼ 115 5 32 21½ Vilches A4 Mdn — ArticultdProof,EstrnBttor,FbldImg 9

Jan 26 SA 5f sl 1:013 h Jan 20 SA 5f ft 1:01 h Jan 6 SA 5f ft 1:02 h Dec 25 SA 5f ft :584 h

O'Happy Day

Dk. b. or br. f. 3, by Cojak—Holiday Greetings, by Best Turn

Br.—Linton R M (Md) 1982 8 2 2 0 $132,345

Own.—Poyer & Steinmann **114** **Tr.—Rettele Loren** Turf 1 0 0 0 $2,250

Lifetime 8 2 2 0 $132,345

18Dec82-8BM 1 1/16 :47 1:122 1:462ft *1 115 65¼ 2½ 21½ 2½ BazeRA4 ⒻB M Lassie 66 BabyDoon,O'HppyDy,AmbitiousGl 14

8Dec82-8Hol 1 1/16 Ⓣ:462 1:114 1:43 fm 3½ 117 2½ 2hd 21½ 45 HwleyS9 ⒻTrksh Trsrs 79 LituyaBay,GoldSpruce,GranjaReina 9

28Nov82-8Hol 1 1/16 :46 1:104 1:422ft 28 120 65½ 64¼ 45 26 Hawley S9 ⒻHol Strlt 77 FbulosNoton,O'HppyDy,StphnBryn 9

5Nov82-7Hol 1 :464 1:113 1:381ft 9½ 118 1hd 2hd 1hd 1no Hawley S4 ⒻAw20000 75 O'HappyDy,GrnjRein,DoubleSmoke 7

21Oct82-6SA 1 1/16 :462 1:112 1:443ft 3½ 117 21 2hd 1½ 1¾ Sibille R8 ⒻMdn 78 O'HppyDy,CsSh'sALdy,ContnntlGrl 8

1Oct82-4SA 6f :211 :442 1:10 ft 54 117 43½ 55¾ 56¾ 63¾ Sibille R3 ⒻMdn 84 Osage Lady, Tiptopper, Loan 12

4Sep82-6Dmr 6f :214 :45 1:102ft 23 117 65½ 511 57¼ 412 Sibille R3 ⒻMdn 74 OlympicSkis,NtliB.Frindly,RdEmbr 12

25Aug82-6Dmr 6f :222 :452 1:102ft 12 117 74¾ 812 813 512 Sibille R12 ⒻMdn 74 MissBigWig,DncingGust,IsbllD'Est 12

Jan 31 SA 4f ft :473 h Jan 26 SA 5f sl 1:013 h Jan 17 SA 6f ft 1:123 h Jan 12 SA 5f ft :593 h

D'Arques — Dk. b. or br. f. 3, by Crystal Water—Real Effort, by Sailor
Br.—Stolich R & Aebi Fran (Cal) 1983 1 1 0 0 $9,350
Own.—Demeter & Oatlands Stable **114** Tr.—Canty John 1982 8 M 3 0 $13,025
Lifetime 9 1 3 0 $22,375

12Jan83-4SA 6f :21^2 :44^3 1:10^{3}ft *6-5 117 6^3 6^5 3^{nk} 1½ ShoemkrW^{10} Ⓕ[S]Mdn 85 D'Arques, Agigael, Shesqueennow 11
29Dec82-4SA 6f :21^4 :45 1:10 ft *6-5 117 2^{hd} 1½ 1^{1}½ 2^2 ShoemkerW^3 Ⓕ[S]Mdn 86 PstryQueen,D'Arques,Shesquennow 9
18Nov82-6Hol 6f :22^1 :45^1 1:10^{2}ft *6-5 117 3^1 3½ 2^{hd} 2no Sibille R^2 Ⓕ[S]Mdn 85 BlueJetSet,D'Arques,Casey'sPoona 9
28Oct82-6SA 6f :21^3 :44^2 1:09^{3}ft 11 117 5^{1}½ 4^{6}½ 3^2 2^{1}½ ShoemkerW^3 Ⓕ[S]Mdn 89 I'mPrstigious,D'Arqus,StphniBryn 10
16Oct82-3SA 6f :21^2 :44^3 1:08^{4}ft 11 117 3^{4}½ 3^5 3^6 4^{9}½ ShoemkerW^6 Ⓕ[S]Mdn 84 ALuckySign,Vivaciously,ChiquitGt 12
27Aug82-4Dmr 6f :22 :45^1 1:11 ft 15 117 2^{hd} 6^{5}½ 8^{11}10^{15} Diaz A L^9 Ⓕ[S]Mdn 68 WickedFall,KookieKper,LdeirG'nd 11
11Aug82-4Dmr 6f :22 :45^4 1:11^{3}ft 6¾ 117 1^{2}½ 1^{2}½ 2^{3}½ 4^{9}½ Diaz A L^8 Ⓕ[S]Mdn 70 GrnjRein,OlympicBronze,NtlieN'Me 9
1Aug82-4Dmr 6f :22^1 :45^4 1:12^{2}ft 4¼ 117 1^{hd} 5^6 5^{4}½ 4^{5}½ Diaz A L^4 Ⓕ[S]Mdn 70 ShowMeDeer,NtliN'M,Ms.Spllbindr 6
27May82-4Hol 5f :22 :45^1 :57^{3}ft 15 116 4^{2}½ 4^{5}½ 5^{13} 6^{14} Olivares F^{10} ⒻMdn 77 JustLikeHelen,SlewMnet,LdirG'nd 10
Jan 28 SA 6f sl 1:17^3 h Jan 6 SA 5f ft 1:00^4 h Dec 20 SA 6f ft 1:13^3 h

Time Of Sale — Dk. b. or br. f. 3, by Drum Fire—Run Tara Run, by Run for Nurse
Br.—Northwest Farms (Wash) 1983 1 1 0 0 $12,100
Own.—Northwest Farms **119** Tr.—Knight Chay R 1982 6 2 1 1 $66,949
Lifetime 7 3 1 1 $79,049

21Jan83-7SA 6½f :21^3 :44^3 1:16^{3}ft 2¼ 121 2^{1}½ 2^{1}½ 1^{1}½ 1^{nk} McCrrnCJ^6 ⒻAw22000 87 TimeOfSle,LonForignr,ShriliBrown 6
23Oct82-8SA 1$\frac{1}{16}$:45^4 1:09^4 1:41^{4}ft 27 115 2^{hd} 4^{5}½ 6^{17} 7^{23} CstnedM^3 ⒻOak Leaf 69 Landluce,SophisticatedGirl,GrnjRein 7
11Oct82-8SA 7f :22^2 :45 1:21^{4}ft 14 120 1^{hd} 2^2 2^8 3^{11} McCrrnCJ^1 ⒻAnoakia 80 Landaluce, Rare Thrill, TimeOfSale 8
18Sep82-9Lga 1 :46^1 1:12^1 1:38^{1}ft *1 121 2^1 3^1 6^{10} 7^{16} LiphmT^9 ⒻMrcr Grl H 62 Pretencia, Theonia First, Aunt Iva 10
5Sep82-9Lga 6½f :22 :45 1:18^{1}ft *2¾ 118 4^{1}¼ 4^{2}½ 4^4 2½ LiphamT^7 [S]Gtstn Fut 77 Big Flyer, Time Of Sale, Thurman 12
16Aug82-8Dmr 1 :46 1:11 1:38^{2}ft 16 113 5^{2}¼ 4^{2}¾ 5^{2}¾ 1½ ShomkrW^8 ⒻSorrento 76 Time Of Sale,ShariliBrown,Infantes 8
30Jly82-6Dmr 6f :22^1 :45^4 1:11^{4}ft 22 110^5 3^{1}½ 2^{2}½ 2^{2}½ 1½ CapitineNM^3 ⒻM35000 79 TimeOfSale,Blanquit,Nvonod'sStr 12
Jan 30 SA 4f gd :49^3 h Jan 20 SA 3f ft :35 h Jan 16 SA 5f ft :59^2 h Jan 5 SA 6f ft 1:13^3 hg

A Lucky Sign — B. f. 3, by Lucky Mike—Zealous Sally, by In Zeal
Br.—Old English Rancho (Cal) 1983 1 1 0 0 $42,250
Own.—Hdly-Jhnstn-ElzJhnstn(Trst) **121** Tr.—Headley Bruce 1982 4 2 1 0 $54,825
Lifetime 5 3 1 0 $97,075

12Jan83-8SA 6f :21^1 :44 1:09^{3}ft *2¼ 119 4^2 2^{2}½ 2^{hd} 1^2 McCrrCJ^2 ⒻPasadena 90 ALuckySign,LotusDncer,PstryCun 12
29Dec82-8SA 6f :21^1 :43^4 1:09^{4}ft *9-5 118 2^{hd} 2½ 1½ 1½ McCrrCJ^5 ⒻLa Cntnla 89 ALuckySign,LotusDncr,OrintlChmp 8
24Oct82-4SA 6f :21^3 :44^2 1:09^{4}ft *2-3 118 1^{1}½ 1½ 2^{hd} 2^{1}¼ Pincay LJr^6 ⒻAw20000 88 EstrnBttor,ALuckySign,LonForignr 7
16Oct82-3SA 6f :21^2 :44^3 1:08^{4}ft *6-5 117 1½ 1^{2}½ 1^6 1^7 McCarronCJ^5 Ⓕ[S]Mdn 94 ALuckySign,Vivaciously,ChiquitGt 12
3Oct82-3SA 6f :21^1 :44^2 1:09^{1}ft 6¼ 117 2½ 3^2 4^{6}½ 4^{12} McCarronCJ^6 Ⓕ[S]Mdn 80 FabulousNotion,Castlelnd,Ally'sLdy 7
Jan 7 SA 5f ft 1:00 h Dec 23 SA 5f sl 1:00 h ●Dec 17 SA 5f ft :58^3 h ●Dec 9 SA 6f ft 1:10^2 hg

TABLE 6.1 *Leading jockeys at Santa Anita Park from December 26, 1982–January 30, 1983*

Jockey	Mounts	First	Second	Third	Winning Percentage	In-the-Money Percentage
McCarron, C. J.	166	41	27	19	25	52
Pincay, L. Jr.	141	37	26	12	26	53
Delahoussaye, E.	173	24	27	19	14	41
Shoemaker, W.	96	15	12	11	16	40
Black, K.	110	14	10	8	13	29
Valenzuela, P. A.	159	13	16	20	08	31
Hawley, S.	130	12	16	15	09	33
Steiner, J. J.[a]	120	12	11	13	10	30
Romero, R. P.	126	11	13	18	09	33
Toro, F.	119	10	11	20	08	35

[a]Apprentice.

Both Fabulous Notion and A Lucky Sign looked like outstanding horses, with Fabulous Notion the top choice. Either one seemed like a good bet if the odds to place or show were good enough. A Lucky Sign was about a 3–1 shot to win throughout the betting period, and her place and show odds were never favorable. However, Fabulous Notion was an outstanding show bet and a good place bet. The evolution of the odds, betting pools, and optimal betting amounts was as follows:

		#3 Fabulous Notion	*Expected Return per Dollar Bet on Fabulous Notion*	*Optimal Bet on Fabulous Notion*	*Totals ($)*
	Odds	4—5			
	Win bet	21,010			49,084
12 min	Place bet	7,502	0.99	0	19,955
to post	Show bet	1,048	1.60	334	6,617
	Odds	1—1			
	Win bet	24,315			57,123
9 min	Place bet	8,842	0.99	0	23,518
to post	Show bet	1,166	1.70	335	8,142
	Odds	4—5			
	Win bet	28,713			67,145
7 min	Place bet	11,032	0.98	0	28,825
to post	Show bet	1,485	1.67	343	10,080
	Odds	4—5			
	Win bet	42,157			97,510
5 min	Place bet	13,397	1.08	0	40,261
to post	Show bet	2,357	1.67	366	15,892
	Odds	1—1			
	Win bet	46,491			110,022
4 min	Place bet	14,550	1.10	0	46,040
to post	Show bet	3,142	1.48	358	17,762
	Odds	1—1			
	Win bet	70,673			166,666
1 min	Place bet	19,631	1.17	99	67,792
to post	Show bet	5,763	1.31	282	26,155
	Odds	4—5			
	Win bet	95,726			209,713
	Place bet	23,415	1.21	187	79,062
Final	Show bet	8,387	1.25	303	32,493

With one minute to post time, the expected value to place was 1.17 and to show 1.31. Our betting fortune was $1,000. The optimal betting equations programmed into our calculator indicated a place bet of $99 and a show bet of $282 on Fabulous Notion. As the following chart of the race indicates, A Lucky Sign won the race, followed by Sophisticated Girl, and Fabulous Notion. Thus we won our show bet and lost our place bet. Our profit was (282)(0.4) − 99 = 112.80 − 99 = 13.80.

EIGHTH RACE
Santa Anita
FEBRUARY 2, 1983

7 FURLONGS. (1.20) 32nd Running of THE SANTA YNEZ STAKES (Grade II). $75,000 added. Fillies. 3-year-olds. (Allowance). By subscription of $50 each to accompany the nomination, $100 to pass the entry box and $750 additional to start, with $75,000 added, of which $15,000 to second, $11,250 to third, $5,625 to fourth and $1,875 to fifth. Weight, 121 lbs. Winners of $50,000 twice in 1982–83, 3 lbs. additional; of $50,000 three times in 1982–83, 5 lbs. Non-winners of two races of $25,000 since December 25 or two of $25,000 or one of $50,000 at any time allowed 2 lbs.; of a race of $25,000 since December 25 or two of $15,000 or one of $25,000 at any time, 4 lbs.; of a race of $12,000, 7 lbs. Starters to be named through the entry box by the closing time of entries. A trophy will be presented to the owner of the winner. Closed Wednesday, January 26, 1983 with 18 nominations.

Value of race $82,800, value to winner $49,050, second $15,000, third $11,250, fourth $5,625, fifth $1,875. Mutuel pool $321,268.

Last Raced	Horse	Eqt.	A.	Wt	PP	St	¼	½	Str	Fin	Jockey	Odds $1
12Jan83 ^{8}SA^{1}	A Lucky Sign	b	3	121	8	4	2^{1}	$1^{\frac{1}{2}}$	$1^{1\frac{1}{2}}$	$1^{\frac{3}{4}}$	McCarron C J	3.00
30Dec82 ^{5}SA^{1}	Sophisticated Girl	b	3	116	2	7	7^{1}	7^{3}	$3^{\frac{1}{2}}$	$2^{\frac{3}{4}}$	Delahoussaye E	10.10
30Dec82 ^{8}SA^{1}	Fabulous Notion	b	3	124	3	8	$6^{\frac{1}{2}}$	4^{2}	$2^{2\frac{1}{2}}$	$3^{4\frac{1}{2}}$	Pierce D	.80
12Jan83 ^{8}SA^{4}	Eastern Bettor		3	119	4	5	$3^{1\frac{1}{2}}$	$3^{1\frac{1}{2}}$	4^{3}	$4^{2\frac{1}{2}}$	Valenzuela P A	14.60
18Dec82 ^{8}BM^{2}	O'Happy Day	b	3	114	5	2	5^{3}	$5^{\frac{1}{2}}$	$5^{1\frac{1}{2}}$	$5^{\frac{1}{2}}$	Hawley S	28.90
14Jan83 ^{7}SA^{1}	Autumn Magic		3	115	1	6	8	8	7^{2}	6^{6}	Toro F	6.10
21Jan83 ^{7}SA^{1}	Time Of Sale	b	3	119	7	1	1^{hd}	$2^{1\frac{1}{2}}$	6^{2}	$7^{8\frac{1}{2}}$	Pincay L Jr	22.50
12Jan83 ^{4}SA^{1}	D'Arques		3	114	6	3	$4^{\frac{1}{2}}$	6^{1}	8	8	Shoemaker W	38.30

OFF AT 4:00. Start good for all but FABULOUS NOTION. Won driving. Time, :22⅕, :44⅘, 1:10, 1:23⅘ Track sloppy.

$2 Mutuel Prices:			
9–A LUCKY SIGN	8.00	3.60	3.40
2–SOPHISTICATED GIRL		7.00	3.80
3–FABULOUS NOTION			2.80

B. f, by Lucky Mike—Zealous Sally, by In Zeal. Trainer Headley Bruce. Bred by Old English Rancho (Cal).

A LUCKY SIGN, engaged for the lead at once, disposed of TIME OF SALE in the upper stretch and held SOPHISTICATED GIRL safe. The latter lacked early speed, rallied strongly on the outside around the turn and was gaining on the winner at the end. FABULOUS NOTION broke in the air and was off behind her field, rallied on the outside around the turn, then weakened slightly in the final sixteenth. EASTERN BETTOR went evenly. AUTUMN MAGIC was never a factor. TIME OF SALE vied for the early lead inside the winner and tired in the stretch. D'ARQUES had brief early speed and also tired badly in the stretch. All starters except O'HAPPY DAY wore mud calks.

Owners— 1, Hdly-Jhnstn-Eliz Jhnstn(Trstee); 2, Golden Eagle Farm; 3, Pine Meadows Thoroughbreds; 4, Hanson Stock Farm; 5, Poyer & Steinmann; 6, Mirkin Claudia H & M; 7, Northwest Farms; 8, Demeter & Oatlands Stable.

Overweight: Sophisticated Girl 2 pounds; Autumn Magic 1.

Scratched—Flying Lassie (12Jan83 ^{8}SA^{6}).

THE SEVENTH RACE, EXHIBITION PARK, VANCOUVER, BRITISH COLUMBIA, APRIL 13, 1983

The seventh race on the card Wednesday, April 13, 1983, was an allowance race for three-year-olds with a purse of $6,400. The 6-furlong race featured two standouts, Intoxicator and Highly Rumored, running against four considerably weaker horses. It was the second day of the 1983 meet and this race was the first of the year for all six starters. They all had spent their racing careers at Exhibition Park and had not run since the late summer of 1982.

It was a beautiful, clear night with Vancouver's springtime view of the mountains and ocean coast at its best. The track was fast. I was anxious to see what changes the new season had brought and to get organized for the summer betting. I knew, as well, that the early part of any new meet is a time to be cautious; it is wise to wait until the horses' forms become well established. Hence I kept my betting fortune to a modest $300.

Both Intoxicator and Highly Rumored looked quite promising. They were ridden by two top local jockeys, Kenny Skinner and Chris Loseth, respectively. Both Skinner and Loseth were former Exhibition Park jockey champions who were returning from riding stints in the United States to be in Vancouver for the summer meet.

Intoxicator was purchased for $105,000, a handsome sum for a Vancouver-based thoroughbred, and had been lightly raced. The *Daily Racing Form*'s consensus of experts thought that he was ready for a big race and installed Intoxicator as an overwhelming favorite. The impressive rating of 33 out of 35 in the consensus made him the best bet for the day. Highly Rumored was expected to give Intoxicator a good run for the money but to be outclassed. Since both Intoxicator and Highly Rumored had not run much during 1982, had failed at low odds, and would be starting for the first time this season, I was cautious. I liked them both but would bet only if the odds were good.

SEVENTH RACE

INTOXICATOR came up a touch short in that stakes attempt last July but is again prepping well for his seasonal bow and will take some beating. HIGHLY RUMORED showed much promise last year and has also been lively in the mornings. PRIVATIZATION showed nothing after that impressive debut but may be ready for better things now.

EXPERTS' SELECTIONS

Consensus Points: 5 for 1st (best 7), 2 for 2d, 1 for 3d. Best in CAPITALS.

Trackman, Tim Toon **EXHIBITION PARK** **Selections Made for Fast Track**

RACE	TRACKMAN	HERMIS	HANDICAP	ANALYST	SWEEP	CONSENSUS	
7	INTOXICATOR	Intoxicator	INTOXICATOR	INTOXICATOR	INTOXICATOR	INTOXICATOR	33
	Highly Rumored	Highly Rumored	Sargeant Boots	Highly Rumoured	Highly Rumored	Highly Rumored	9
	Sargeant Boots	Sargeant Boots	Highly Rumored	Privatization	Privatization	Sargeant Boot	4

Throughout the betting period the odds on both Intoxicator and Highly Rumored were good and both looked like Dr. Z system bets.

With one minute to post time the tote board was as follows:

	Totals	#1 Intoxicator	#5 Highly Rumored
Odds		3—5	7—5
Win	22,814	11,006	7,850
Show	4,564	1,408	950

The optimal bets were $90 on Intoxicator and $50 on Highly Rumored.* The expected values per dollar bet were 1.14 and 1.18, respectively. The last-minute betting was concentrated on Highly Rumored to win and Intoxicator to show. This reinforced the Highly Rumored show bet and made the Intoxicator show bet not quite so good. The tote board at post time was

	Totals	#1 Intoxicator	#5 Highly Rumored
Odds		4—5	6—7
Win	28,486.00	13,044.00	10,170.00
Show	6,637.00	2,016.00	1,358.00
Expected value		1.12	1.21
Optimal bet		$90	$50

The race was run true to form. Intoxicator was a wire-to-wire winner by 9 lengths over Highly Rumored. The 40–1 long shot, Cari A Smile, finished third. The chart of the race and mutuel payoffs were as follows:

7th Six furlongs. Three-year-olds. Claiming Allowance. Purse $6.400.

Horse	Jockey	Wt	P	¼	½	Str	Fin	Odds
Intoxicator	Skinner	120	1	1-2	1-3	1-5	1-9	.80
Highly Rumored	Luseth	120	5	3-4	2-3	2-5	2-3½	1.35
Cari A Smile	Mills	110	2	4-4	4-2	4-2	3-2	41.20
Sargeant Boots	Johnson	115	3	6	5-4	5-4	4-nk	19.95
Dave's Man	Creighton	115	6	2-h	3-4	3-1	5-2	9.45
Privatization	Krasner	120	4	5-1½	6	6	6	17.80

Time—:22.4, :45.4, 1:11.

Winner: Drum Fire-Must Dream.

Trainer: W. MacDonald.

INTOXICATOR	**3.60**	**2.50**	**2.50**
HIGHLY RUMORED		**2.60**	**2.80**
CARI A SMILE			**4.40**

Intoxicator paid as much to show as to place, and Highly Rumored paid more. This happens often with Dr. Z system bets. My bets of $90 on Intoxicator and $50 on Highly Rumored returned $112.50 and $70, respectively, for a $42.50 profit.

THE KENTUCKY OAKS, CHURCHILL DOWNS, LOUISVILLE, KENTUCKY, FRIDAY, MAY 6, 1983

The Kentucky Oaks is the Kentucky Derby for fillies. It is run each year the Friday before the first Saturday in May, which is the day the Derby is run, and features the top three-year-old fillies. The $1\frac{1}{8}$-mile race is for a $150,000 added purse. In the 1940s and 1950s, the Kentucky Oaks, the

*The calculation of the optimal wagers when there are two different bets is discussed in Chapter Sixteen.

Pimlico Oaks, and the Coaching Club American Oaks at Belmont were referred to as the triple crown for fillies. In recent years the triple crown usually refers to three races all run at Belmont: the Acorn Mile, the Mother Goose, and the Coaching Club American Oaks. Davona Dale won the Kentucky Oaks, the Black Eyed Susan Stakes at Pimlico (formerly the Pimlico Oaks), and the triple crown in 1979, an impressive record over the brief two-month period in May and June when these five races were held.

We had been in Chicago for a Management Science Conference, where I participated in sessions on options pricing, efficient markets, and the mathematics of gambling. During the week preceding the race, while I was doing research at the Keeneland racetrack library in Lexington for this book, the spring rains had been continual and extremely heavy.* Fortunately, the rain ended on Wednesday, and by the end of the day on Thursday, the track even had to be watered. On Friday the weather was sunny, and the track was blazing fast. In the first race, Modicum, running in his second career start, broke the $4\frac{1}{2}$-furlong track record by $\frac{2}{5}$ second to win the race in $51\frac{2}{5}$ seconds. A description of this race appeared in Chapter Five.

Princess Rooney was an overwhelming favorite to win the 1983 Kentucky Oaks. She had nine previous races and had won them all by margins of 3, 4, 8, 10, 12, and even 18 lengths. In only one race was the outcome in doubt. She held on for a half-length victory in a $30,000 allowance race. She had run recently, winning her two races at the Keeneland meet by a total of $19\frac{1}{2}$ lengths.

Many observers had hopes that her owner, Paula Tucker, and trainer, Frank Gomez, could be persuaded to enter Princess Rooney in the 1983 Kentucky Derby. No doubt she would have been one of the favorites, along with Sunny's Halo and Marfa. Since a filly had won the Kentucky Derby only twice in 108 runnings, the chance of such a victory was appealing to many observers ever since Genuine Risk won in 1980. It is well known that the Derby, with its 20 starters and intense competition, is a very demanding and difficult race. Many horses never recover from a Derby race. For a stallion whose value might escalate by $10 million as a result of a Derby victory, such a risk is well worth taking. But for a filly there is not much money to be gained in breeding. The risks of the race may well dominate the possible added prestige and breeding value. As Princess Rooney's trainer summed it up, ". . . you would not have Chris Evert play Jimmy Connors at Wimbledon."

So Princess Rooney was in the Oaks. The rest of the field was reasonably strong and would give Princess Rooney her toughest test to date. The main competition was from the Tom Gentry filly, Rosy Spectre, who had finished

*The Keeneland library on the grounds of the Keeneland Racetrack has a wonderful collection of books and materials on all aspects of thoroughbred racing. Their materials date to the eighteenth century. It is open to the public and has a very courteous and helpful staff.

Last Race Exacta Wagering Now Available

WIN	PLACE	SHOW

1⅛ MILES

START FINISH

STAKE

Purse $150,000-Added

8

THE KENTUCKY OAKS
(One Hundred and Ninth Running)

FILLIES, THREE YEARS OLD. By subscription of $100 each: $750 to pass the entry box; $750 additional to start with $150,000 added of which 65% of all monies to the owner of the winner, 20% to second, 10% to third and 5% to fourth. Weight, 121 lbs. Closed Tuesday, February 15, 1983 with 187 Nominations. A silver trophy to the winning owner.

Track Record—AEROFLINT (3) 116 lbs.; 1:48⅖; Nov. 18, 1961
LAS OLAS (4) 111 lbs.; 1:48⅖; Nov. 21, 1959

MAKE SELECTION BY NUMBER

	Owner / Trainer	Jockey/Morn. Line
1	PAULA TUCKER — FRANK GOMEZ Light Blue, White Dots, White Chevrons on Sleeves, Light Blue Cap **PRINCESS ROONEY** 121 Gr.f.(1980), Verbatim—Parrish Princess by Drone Bred in Kentucky by Ben and Tom Roach	1-5 JACINTO VASQUEZ
2	MRS. V. LEVAN, MRS. B. WALTERS AND L. WESTON — ADRIAN J. MAXWELL Pink, Grey Blocks, Pink Cap **BRIGHT CROCUS** 121 Ch.f.(1980), Clev er Tell—Bold Saffron by Bold Hour Bred in Kentucky by T. I. Harkins	8 SANDY HAWLEY
3	EVERETT LOWRANCE — JAMES ECKROSH Orange, Green "L," Green Bars on Sleeves, Orange Cap **FIFTH QUESTION** 121 Gr.f.(1980), Fifth Marine—Little Divy by Royal Cap Bred in Oklahoma by Everett Lowrance	10 PAT DAY
4	WHITE FOX FARM (Dewey White) — ELWOOD McCANN Maroon, Silver Hoops, Mar. Chev. on Silver Slvs., Silv. Cap **SHAMIVOR** 121 Dk.b. or br.f.(1980), Sham—Ivorie II by Sir Ivor Bred in Florida by Waldemar Farms, Inc. & Gerald R Robins	15 DON BRUMFIELD
5	TOM GENTY — EDUARDO INDA Yellow, Royal Blue Blocks, Royal Blue Bars on Sleeves, Yellow Cap **ROSY SPECTRE** 121 Ch.f.(1980), Nijinsky II—Like a Charm by Pied d'or Bred in Kentucky by Tom Gentry	15 EDDIE DELAHOUSSAYE
6	W. S. KILROY AND W. S. FARISH — DEL W. CARROLL II Green, Yellow Chevrons, Green Cap **Weekend Surprise** 121 B.f.(1980), Secretariat—Lassie Dear by Buckpasser Bred in Kentucky by W. S. Farish III & W. S. Kilroy	20 CHRIS McCARRON
7	RYEHILL FARM (James P. Ryan) — WOODFORD C. STEPHENS Navy, Gold Belt, Gold Blocks on Sleeves, Gold Cap **BEMISSED** 121 Ch.f.(1980), Nijinsky II—Bemis Heights by Herbager Bred in Maryland by Ryehill Farm	20 FRANK LOVATO, JR.
8	WANAJA FARM & B. T. ENERGY (Janie Martin and Don Ball) — JACK VAN BERG Gold, Purple "V," Purple Sleeves, Purple Cap **BRINDY BRINDY** 121 Ch.f.(1980), Grand Revival—Belle Of Caledon by Bull Vic Bred in Kentucky by John McGarrah	12 KENNETH JONES

(horse symbol) Indicates Foaled In Kentucky

Selections 1—2—3—8

Experts' Selections

Consensus Points: 5 for 1st (today's best 7), 2 for 2nd, 1 for 3rd. Today's Best in Bold Type.

Trackman, Graham Ross **CHURCHILL DOWNS** Selections Made for Fast Track

8	PRINCESS ROONEY	PRINCESS ROONEY	PRINCESS ROONEY	PRINCESS ROONEY	PRINCESS ROONEY	PRINCESS ROONEY	35
	WEEKEND SURPRISE	SHAMIVOR	ROSY SPECTRE	BRIGHT CROCUS	ROSY SPECTRE	ROSY SPECTRE	4
	FIFTH QUESTION	BRINDY BRINDY	FIFTH QUESTION	WEEKEND SURPRISE	BRIGHT CROCUS	WEEKEND SURPRISE	3

8th Churchill

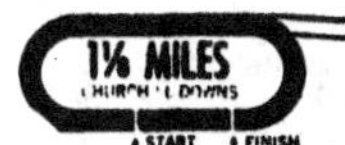

1 $\frac{1}{8}$ MILES. (1.48$\frac{4}{5}$) 109th Running KENTUCKY OAKS (Grade I). $150,000 added. Fillies. 3-year-olds. By subscription of $100 each; $750 to pass the entry box; $750 additional to start with $150,000 added of which $65% of all monies to the owner of the winner, 40% to second, 10% to third and 5% to fourth. Weight, 121 lbs. Starters to be named through the entry box Wednesday, May 4, by the usual time of closing. If the race is divided entries or couplings will be divided. A silver trophy to the winning owner. Closed with 187 nominations.

Princess Rooney

Gr. f. 3, by Verbatim—Parrish Princess, by Drone
Own.—Tucker Paula 121 **Br.—Roach B & T (Ky)** 1983 3 3 0 0 $110,333
Tr.—Gomez Frank 1982 6 6 0 0 $223,815
Lifetime 9 9 0 0 $334,148

23Apr83-7Kee 1$\frac{1}{16}$:46^3 1:11^3 1:45^{2}sy *1-5 121 1^{hd} 1^{hd} $1^{2\frac{1}{2}}$ $1^{9\frac{1}{2}}$ Vasquez J^4 ⒻAshland 79-24 PrincessRooney,Shamivor,Decision 6
13Apr83-7Kee a7f 1:27^{2}ft *1-3 123 2^1 2^{hd} 1^3 1^{10} Vasquez J^8 ⒻAw28000 86-21 PrincessRooney,FiestyBll,SilvrdSilk 8
5Mar83-7GP 7f :22^1 :45 1:23^{4}ft *1-5 114 $3^{1\frac{1}{2}}$ $3^{\frac{1}{2}}$ $1^{\frac{1}{2}}$ $1^{\frac{1}{2}}$ Vasquez J^2 Aw30000 85-19 PrncssRoony,Mrgnmrgnmrgn,Alchs 8
23Oct82-6Med 1$\frac{1}{16}$:47^1 1:11 1:43 ft *1-3 121 $1^{\frac{1}{2}}$ 1^2 1^7 1^{11} Vasquez J^6 ⒻGardenia 94-11 PrncssRoony,FrOnc'nMyLf,GldSprc 7
10Oct82-8Bel 1 :46^1 1:11^3 1:39 ft *6-5 119 1^{hd} $1^{1\frac{1}{2}}$ 1^6 1^8 Fell J^2 ⒻFrizette 70-29 PrncssRny,WnnngTck,WkndSrprs 13
11Sep82-9Crc 7f :22^2 :45^4 1:23^{4}ft *1-5 116 1^1 $1^{2\frac{1}{2}}$ 1^8 1^{12} PnnisFA^7 ⒻMelaleuca 97-14 PrincssRoony,Hiusonso,Rin'sMissy 8
1Sep82-9Crc 7f :22^2 :46 1:25^{1}ft *4-5 116 $1^{\frac{1}{2}}$ $1^{1\frac{1}{2}}$ 1^{10} 1^{18} Pennisi FA^1 ⒻAw10000 90-18 PrncssRoony,CortUnn,FlwlssDmnd 5
7Jun82-7Crc 5f :22^3 :46^3 :59^{3}ft *6-5 114 $1^{\frac{1}{2}}$ $1^{1\frac{1}{2}}$ 1^3 1^4 Pennisi F A^1 ⒻAw9500 94-15 PrncssRoony,Ishudhdtht,RoyltyMss 6
22May82-3Crc 5f :22^4 :47 1:00^{2}ft *2 115 3^{nk} 1^{hd} 1^2 1^3 Pennisi F A^9 ⒻMdn 90-14 Princess Rooney, Rilia, Marie V. 9
May 2 CD 6f gd 1:16 b Apr 21 Kee 5f ft 1:00^2 b Apr 12 Kee 3f gd :36 b ●Apr 8 Kee 5f sy 1:02^3 b (d)

Bright Crocus

B. f. 3, by Clev Er Tell—Bold Saffron, by Bold Hour
Own.—Levan-Waters-Weston 121 **Br.—Harkins T I (Ky)** 1983 4 1 1 0 $87,809
Tr.—Maxwell Adrian J 1982 8 3 1 1 $48,764
Lifetime 12 4 2 1 $136,573 Turf 8 3 1 1 $48,764

16Apr83-10Hia 1$\frac{1}{8}$:47^1 1:12 1:49^{4}ft *1 121 $5^{2\frac{1}{2}}$ $6^{3\frac{1}{2}}$ $4^{8\frac{1}{2}}$ 5^{11} Hawley S^1 ⒻPoinsetta 72-23 Thinghatab,Overreaction,BuffloGl 15
16Apr83—Crowded, st'd
26Mar83-10FG 1$\frac{1}{16}$:47^2 1:12^4 1:45^{4}gd 6 121 5^5 $5^{3\frac{1}{2}}$ 2^{hd} $1^{5\frac{1}{2}}$ Hawley S^2 ⒻFg Oaks 83-24 Bright Crocus, MissMolly,Shamivor 6
28Feb83-9GP 1$\frac{1}{16}$ 1:45^{2}ft 31 114 $8^{5\frac{3}{4}}$ 2^3 2^5 $3^{6\frac{1}{4}}$ VsqzJ^7 ⒻBonnie Miss 68-24 Unccompnd,‡MssMolly,BrghtCrcs 12
28Feb83—Placed second through disqualification
7Feb83-9GP 7f :22^1 :45^1 1:23^{2}gd 14 114 $8^{2\frac{1}{2}}$ $6^{3\frac{1}{2}}$ 9^{10} 9^{12} McBtD^8 ⒻForwardGal 75-21 Unccompnid,Lis'sCpitl,QuxotcLdy 15
23Sep82♦3Ascot(Eng) 1 1:47^{1}gd *2 128 Ⓣ 8 PgttL ⒻHooverFilliesMile(Gr.3) Acclimatise, DancingMeg,Alligatrix 8
9Sep82♦6Doncaster(Eng) 1 1:39^{1}gd 6 119 Ⓣ 1^5 PiggottL ⒻMay Hill Stks BrghtCrocs,SlkPyjms,GoodbyShlly 8
7Aug82♦4Newmarket(Eng) 7f 1:29^{3}gd 3$\frac{1}{2}$ 128 4^2 PggttL ⒻSweet Solera Stks Flamenco, Acclimatise, Montervie 8
24Jly82♦2Ascot(Eng) 6f 1:15^{2}gd 3$\frac{1}{2}$ 127 Ⓣ $3^{2\frac{1}{2}}$ PgttL ⒻPrincessMargaretStk RoylHroin,HnrysScrt,BrightCrocus 6
6Jly82♦4Newmarket(Eng) 6f 1:12^{1}gd 2 125 Ⓣ $4^{3\frac{1}{4}}$ PttL ⒻCherryHintonStks(Gr.3) CrimeofPassion,Crolside,SilkPyjms 8
26Jun82♦1Newmarket(Eng) 6f 1:15^{4}gd *1-2 125 Ⓣ 1^1 PgttL ⒻDance In Time Stk BrghtCrocs,KyTThMnstrl,HntrsGrv 5
May 4 CD 4f m :50 b ●May 1 CD 5f sy 1:01^4 h Apr 13 Hia 4f ft :50^2 b Apr 8 Hia 4f ft :50 b

Fifth Question

Gr. f. 3, by Fifth Marine—Little Divy, by Royal Cap
Own.—Lowrance E 121 **Br.—Lowrance Everett (Okla)** 1983 6 2 1 2 $101,635
Tr.—Eckrosh James 1982 2 2 0 0 $21,003
Lifetime 8 4 1 2 $122,638

23Apr83-7Kee 1$\frac{1}{16}$:46^3 1:11^3 1:45^{2}sy 4$\frac{1}{4}$ 116 $4^{8\frac{1}{2}}$ 6^{13} 5^{12} 5^{32} Day P^5 ⒻAshland 47-24 PrincessRooney,Shamivor,Decision 6
9Apr83-9OP 1$\frac{1}{16}$:47^3 1:12^3 1:44^{3}ft 3$\frac{1}{4}$ 115 $7^{5\frac{1}{2}}$ 6^4 $2^{3\frac{1}{2}}$ $2^{\frac{1}{2}}$ Day P^9 ⒻFantasy 84-21 BrndyBrndy,FfthQston,ChsAPrtnr 11
9Apr83—Bothered
30Mar83-9OP 170:46^2 1:12^2 1:43 ft 3 118 $6^{8\frac{1}{2}}$ $4^{7\frac{1}{2}}$ 2^1 1^6 Day P^1 ⒻAw30000 81-23 FfthQstn,BrndyBrndy,FrOnc'nMyLf 7
18Mar83-9OP 6f :22^4 :46^2 1:13 ft 4$\frac{1}{4}$ 118 12^{11} $10^{6\frac{3}{4}}$ $7^{5\frac{1}{2}}$ $3^{\frac{1}{2}}$ Day P^{11} ⒻMagnolia 79-22 Lt.Prl,ForOnc'nMyLif,FifthQuston 12
21Feb83-9OP 6f :22^1 :46^3 1:13^{1}sy *1 118 $6^{4\frac{1}{2}}$ $5^{5\frac{1}{2}}$ $4^{6\frac{1}{2}}$ $3^{5\frac{1}{2}}$ Day P^3 ⒻM Wash 73-27 Lt.Perle,ElgntExprinc,FifthQustion 7
11Feb83-7OP 5$\frac{1}{2}$f :22^4 :48 1:08^{2}gd 8$\frac{1}{4}$ 116 $8^{9\frac{1}{2}}$ 6^8 $5^{5\frac{3}{4}}$ $1^{\frac{1}{2}}$ HghtwrTW^3 ⒻAw25000 76-28 FifthQuestion,Lt.Perl,BrindyBrindy 9
26Dec82-8Haw 1$\frac{1}{16}$:48 1:12^2 1:45^{2}ft 3 114 2^{hd} $1^{1\frac{1}{2}}$ $1^{1\frac{1}{2}}$ 1^2 HghtwrTW^3 ⒻDurazna 71-23 Fifth Question, O Yoko,SheWillTell 5
8Dec82-2Haw 6$\frac{1}{2}$f :22^2 :45^4 1:19 ft 16 119 11^{15} 8^{12} 3^1 1^{hd} HightowerTW^7 ⒻMdn 78-22 FifthQuestion,SuprDot,SrtogRvlry 11
May 3 CD 5f sy 1:05^2 b Apr 21 Kee 4f ft :52 b Apr 7 OP 5f ft 1:05^3 b Mar 28 OP 4f sl :54 b

Shamivor — Dk. b. or br. f. 3, by Sham—Ivoire II, by Sir Ivor

Own.—White Fox Farm **121** Br.—Waldomar Fms Inc&RobinsG (Fla) 1983 6 2 3 1 $60,410

Tr.—McCann Elwood Sr 1982 4 2 0 0 $10,300

Lifetime 10 4 3 1 $70,710

23Apr83-7Kee 1$\frac{1}{16}$:46^3 1:11^3 1:45^{2}sy 12 114 2^{hd} 2^{hd} $2^{2\frac{1}{2}}$ $2^{9\frac{1}{2}}$ BrumfildD^3 ⒻAshland 69-24 PrincessRooney,Shamivor,Decision 6

26Mar83-10FG 1$\frac{1}{16}$:47^2 1:12^4 1:45^{4}gd 3$\frac{3}{4}$ 115 1^3 1^2 1^{hd} $3^{7\frac{1}{2}}$ RomeroRP^3 ⒻFg Oaks 75-24 Bright Crocus, MissMolly,Shamivor 6

5Mar83-9FG 1^{40} :49^1 1:14^3 1:43 ft 3-2 117 1^2 $1^{1\frac{1}{2}}$ $1^{1\frac{1}{2}}$ 2^{hd} Ardoin R^1 ⒻDava Dale 78-21 Duped, Shamivor, Juliet's Pet 5

20Feb83-9FG 1^{40} :46^4 1:12^4 1:42^{3}ft *4-5 120 1^{hd} 1^3 $1^{2\frac{1}{2}}$ $1^{4\frac{1}{2}}$ EspinozJC^7 ⒻAw11000 80-25 Shamivor,MadamNorm,YellowBow 8

13Feb83-9FG 6f :22 :46 1:12^{1}ft 4$\frac{3}{4}$ 117 3^2 $3^{1\frac{1}{2}}$ 4^1 2^3 EspinozaJC^7 ⒻThelma 81-20 Duped, Shamivor, Sally Stride 8

14Jan83-7FG 1^{40} :47 1:13^3 1:43^{2}ft *8-5 119 $1^{1\frac{1}{2}}$ 1^6 1^5 $1^{4\frac{1}{2}}$ EspinozJC^2 ⒻAw10000 76-19 Shamivor,Tani'sNuPearl,Kristy'sFir 9

23Dec82-8FG 6f :22^1 :46^3 1:13 ft 3 119 $11^{7\frac{1}{2}}$ $6^{2\frac{3}{4}}$ 3^1 1^1 McKnight J^7 ⒻAw9000 80-21 Shmivor,WinterWitch,CityPrincss 11

16Dec82-6FG 6f :22^3 :47 1:13^{3}ft *9-5 119 1^2 1^3 1^3 1^7 McKnight J^{10} ⒻMdn 77-22 Shmivor,RobbngAround,LdyBrtrm 11

27Nov82-9FG 6f :22^2 :47^2 1:13^{3}m 65 112 3^{nk} 2^{hd} 6^6 8^{16} McKhtJ^{10} ⒻPontalba 61-25 Duped, How Clever, Distant Mom 11

17Nov82-2CD 6f :22^2 :46^2 1:11^{4}ft 27 120 4^2 $2^{1\frac{1}{2}}$ 4^2 $4^{7\frac{1}{2}}$ Maple S^{10} ⒻMdn 79-23 Shea Lee,I'mDriven,JamacianSpell 12

Apr 22 Kee 3f ft :35 b ●Apr 18 Kee 5f ft 1:00 h Apr 12 Kee 6f ft 1:12^2 h Mar 25 FG 4f ft :52 b

Rosy Spectre — Ch. f. 3, by Nijinsky II—Like A Charm, by Pied d'Or

Own.—Gentry T E **121** Br.—Gentry T E (Ky) 1983 4 2 2 0 $22,920

Tr.—Inda Eduardo 1982 1 M 1 0 $2,400

Lifetime 5 2 3 0 $25,320

27Apr83-5Kee 1$\frac{1}{16}$:49 1:13^3 1:47^{2}ft *6-5 115 $8^{3\frac{3}{4}}$ $6^{3\frac{3}{4}}$ $3^{1\frac{1}{2}}$ $1^{\frac{1}{2}}$ Day P^9 ⒻAw15700 69-18 RosySpectre,BroadwayDolcie,Exult 9

19Apr83-2Kee a7f 1:29^{2}ft *2-3 118 4^1 5^3 3^{nk} 2no Day P^8 ⒻAw14600 76-18 Plchee,RosySpectre,BrodwyDolcie 11

8Apr83-4Kee a7f 1:28^{3}sy *4-5 118 $4^{5\frac{1}{2}}$ 3^2 1^3 1^5 Romero R P^6 ⒻMdn 80-14 RosySpectr,Mrdith'sMomnt,ClvrRn 8

26Mar83-5Hia 7f :22^4 :46 1:26 ft *3-2 119 $6^{4\frac{3}{4}}$ $4^{4\frac{1}{2}}$ $2^{2\frac{1}{2}}$ $2^{2\frac{1}{2}}$ Vasquez J^{10} ⒻMdn 70-17 YoWon'tBSorry,RsySpctr,PcktLnr 12

15Aug82-4Dmr 6f :22 :45 1:10^{3}ft 17 117 8^9 7^{13} 5^9 $2^{3\frac{1}{2}}$ McHargue DG^9 ⒻMdn 81-12 BrillintMove,RosySpctr,AdriticGirl 10

May 4 CD 4f m :49^3 b Apr 25 Kee 4f gd :51 b Apr 16 Kee 4f gd :50 b Apr 3 Kee 5f ft 1:00^1 b

Weekend Surprise — B. f. 3, by Secretariat—Lassie Dear, by Buckpasser

Own.—Kilroy & Farish III **121** Br.—Farish III & Kilroy (Ky) 1983 2 0 0 1 $3,730

Tr.—Carroll Del W II 1982 9 5 1 2 $190,588

Lifetime 11 5 1 3 $194,318

2May83-8CD 7f :23^3 :47 1:25^{2}sy *9-5 121 8^7 $7^{5\frac{3}{4}}$ 6^5 $3^{1\frac{1}{2}}$ Day P^8 ⒻLa Troien 79-18 HowClever,SuperBell,WkndSurpris 8

13Apr83-7Kee a7f 1:27^{2}ft 5 123 $6^{4\frac{1}{2}}$ $6^{5\frac{1}{4}}$ 7^9 7^{16} BrumfildD^3 ⒻAw28000 70-21 PrincessRooney,FiestyBll,SilvrdSilk 8

25Nov82-8CD 1$\frac{1}{16}$:49^2 1:14^1 1:47 gd *2-5e119 3^1 4^2 3^1 $1^{\frac{1}{2}}$ Day P^1 ⒻGold Rod 73-23 WekndSurpris,NtionlBnnr,QurrlOvr 6

11Nov82-8CD 1 :47^1 1:12 1:37^{4}ft *1 122 $4^{1\frac{1}{2}}$ 4^1 $1^{\frac{1}{2}}$ $1^{3\frac{1}{4}}$ BrumfldD^6 ⒻPcahonts 80-20 WeekendSurprise,Dcision,QurrlOvr 9

11Nov82—Run in two divisions, 6th and 8th races

4Nov82-7CD 7f :23^2 :46^3 1:25 ft *1-2 121 5^7 $5^{4\frac{1}{2}}$ 1^{hd} $1^{1\frac{1}{2}}$ Day P^1 ⒻAw13700 82-24 WkndSrprs,PrttyPrfct,YKy'sLdyKt 6

10Oct82-8Bel 1 :46^1 1:11^3 1:39 ft 9$\frac{1}{4}$ 119 $7^{6\frac{1}{4}}$ 6^9 4^9 3^{12} VelasquezJ^4 ⒻFrizette 58-29 PrncssRny,WnnngTck,WkndSrprs 13

18Sep82-7Bel 7f :23 :46^1 1:24 ft 5$\frac{1}{2}$ 119 5^{13} 5^{12} $4^{8\frac{1}{2}}$ $3^{4\frac{1}{2}}$ Velasquez J^2 Matron 77-17 WngsofJov,ShrThFntsy,WkndSrprs 5

29Aug82-8Sar 6f :22^1 :45^3 1:09^{4}ft 2$\frac{1}{4}$ 119 $5^{9\frac{1}{2}}$ $5^{4\frac{3}{4}}$ $3^{3\frac{1}{2}}$ $5^{6\frac{1}{4}}$ VelsquzJ^1 ⒻSpinaway 85-15 ShrThFntsy,SngngSsn,MdnghtRptr 6

4Aug82-8Sar 6f :22^1 :45^2 1:11 ft 3-2e114 7^{10} 6^{11} $4^{5\frac{1}{2}}$ 1^1 VlsqzJ^7 ⒻSchuylervile 85-13 WkndSurpris,ShrThFntsy,FlyingLss 7

2Jun82-8Bel 5$\frac{1}{2}$f :22^3 :45^4 1:04^{1}ft 2$\frac{3}{4}$ 116 6^5 $5^{3\frac{1}{2}}$ $5^{4\frac{1}{4}}$ 2^2 VelsquezJ^7 ⒻRosedale 92-11 GlJubil,WkndSurpris,SubvrsivChick 7

May 1 CD 3f sy :38^4 b Apr 25 Kee 5f gd 1:01^2 b Apr 19 Kee 4f ft :50^3 b Apr 12 Kee 3f gd :36^2 b

Bemissed — Ch. f. 3, by Nijinsky II—Bemis Heights, by Herbager

Own.—Ryehill Farm **121** Br.—Ryehill Farm (Md) 1983 4 0 0 1 $27,423

Tr.—Stephens Woodford C 1982 9 4 1 2 $254,432

Lifetime 13 4 1 3 $281,855 Turf 5 3 0 2 $111,969

23Apr83-8Pim 1$\frac{1}{16}$Ⓣ:50 1:16^{1}1:50 yl 3$\frac{1}{2}$ 110 5^5 4^3 $3^{2\frac{1}{2}}$ 3^1 LtFJr^5 ⒻGallorette H 60-39 WeddingPrty,SunnySprkler,Bmissd 8

9Apr83-9OP 1$\frac{1}{16}$:47^3 1:12^3 1:44^{3}ft 17 121 $5^{4\frac{1}{2}}$ $3^{1\frac{1}{2}}$ 4^4 4^5 Lovato FJr^4 ⒻFantasy 80-21 BrndyBrndy,FfthQston,ChsAPrtnr 11

30Mar83-9OP 1^{70} :46^2 1:12^2 1:43 ft *1 115 7^{11} 6^{12} 5^{12} 4^{17} Maple E^7 ⒻAw30000 64-23 FfthQstn,BrndyBrndy,FrOnc'nMyLf 7

14Feb83-9GP 7f :23^1 :46^2 1:23^{4}ft 8 117 4^3 $5^{2\frac{1}{4}}$ $6^{7\frac{1}{2}}$ 6^{11} MapleE^7 Golden Grass 74-21 Cast Party, Smart Style, Reap 9

14Feb83—Run in two divisions 7th & 9th races

14Nov82-8Aqu 1$\frac{1}{8}$:49^1 1:14 1:52 ft *1-2e121 2^4 4^2 4^5 4^6 LovtFJr^3 ⒻDemoiselle 69-23 OnlyQueens,GoldSpruce,NtionlBnnr 7

30Oct82-8Lrl 1$\frac{1}{16}$:47^1 1:12^1 1:44 ft 2e122 $3^{3\frac{1}{2}}$ 2^{hd} $1^{2\frac{1}{2}}$ $1^{3\frac{1}{4}}$ Lovato F Jr^7 ⒻSelima 88-15 Bemissed, Icy Time, No BodyElse's 9

21Oct82-8Aqu 1$\frac{1}{8}$Ⓣ:48^{2}1:13 1:51^{4}fm 2e121 $3^{6\frac{1}{2}}$ $3^{2\frac{1}{2}}$ 1^{hd} 1no LovtFJr^5 ⒻMiss Grillo 85-15 Bemissed, Cryptic, Magnifique 8

16Oct82-8Bow 7f :22^2 :44^3 1:24^{3}ft 6$\frac{1}{4}$ 119 $5^{5\frac{1}{2}}$ $4^{6\frac{1}{2}}$ 4^3 $4^{2\frac{3}{4}}$ LtFJr^3 ⒻⓈKindergrtn 79-25 SngngSsn,NorthrnStng,NoBdyEls's 8

19Sep82-9WO 1 [T]:48^{1}1:14 1:40^{3}yl *1 112 $6^{5\frac{1}{4}}$ 3^{nk} 1^{hd} $1^{1\frac{3}{4}}$ LovatoFJr^6 ⒻNatalma 75-25 Bemissed,HoldMClosr,DonnsFncy 13

3Sep82-8Bel 1 Ⓣ:47^{4}1:12^{2}1:38^{1}yl *4-5e112 $3^{2\frac{1}{2}}$ $2^{\frac{1}{2}}$ 2^2 $3^{3\frac{1}{2}}$ MpleE^9 ⒻEvening Out 70-26 Cryptic, NationalBanner,Bemissed 11

May 2 CD 5f gd 1:04 b Apr 7 OP 4f ft :49 b Mar 27 OP 5f ft 1:02^4 b Mar 20 Hia 3f ft :35 h

Brindy Brindy — Ch. f. 3, by Grand Revival—Belle of Caledon, by Bull Vic

Own.—Wanaja Fm & Energy B T **121** Br.—McGarrah John (Ky) 1983 5 1 1 1 $179,880

Tr.—Van Berg Jack C 1982 6 4 0 1 $40,998

Lifetime 11 5 1 2 $220,878

9Apr83-9OP 1$\frac{1}{16}$:47^3 1:12^3 1:44^{3}ft 59 115 1^1 $1^{1\frac{1}{2}}$ $1^{3\frac{1}{2}}$ $1^{\frac{1}{2}}$ Jones K^3 ⒻFantasy 85-21 BrndyBrndy,FfthQston,ChsAPrtnr 11

30Mar83-9OP 1^{70} :46^2 1:12^2 1:43 ft 30 112 1^2 1^5 1^1 2^6 Jones K^2 ⒻAw30000 75-23 FfthQstn,BrndyBrndy,FrOnc'nMyLf 7

18Mar83-9OP 6f :22^4 :46^2 1:13 ft 14e118 3^{nk} $3^{\frac{1}{2}}$ 6^4 8^8 Jones K^1 ⒻMagnolia 72-22 Lt.Prl,ForOnc'nMyLif,FifthQuston 12

21Feb83-9OP 6f :22^1 :46^3 1:13^{1}sy 5$\frac{1}{2}$ 115 2^1 4^4 5^{12} 5^{15} EspinozJC^5 ⒻM Wash 64-27 Lt.Perle,ElgntExprinc,FifthQustion 7

11Feb83-7OP 5$\frac{1}{2}$f :22^4 :48 1:08^{2}gd *2 116 $3^{1\frac{1}{2}}$ 2^2 2^3 $3^{1\frac{1}{2}}$ Day P^9 ⒻAw25000 74-28 FifthQuestion,Lt.Perl,BrindyBrindy 9

11Nov82-6CD 1 :46 1:10^4 1:38^{1}ft 6 117 1^{hd} $1^{\frac{1}{2}}$ $1^{1\frac{1}{2}}$ $1^{2\frac{1}{2}}$ EspnzJC^3 ⒻPcahonts 78-20 BrndyBrndy,Rbrt'sDll,IsssN'Answrs 7

11Nov82—Run in two divisions, 6th and 8th races

27Oct82-5Kee 6$\frac{1}{2}$f :23^1 :46^2 1:17^{2}ft 8$\frac{1}{2}$ 115 $1^{\frac{1}{2}}$ $1^{\frac{1}{2}}$ 1^5 1^5 EspinozJC^4 ⒻAw14600 90-18 BrindyBrindy,SwziGirl,Don'tTellDd 6

19Oct82-4Kee 6f :22^2 :45^4 1:10^{4}ft 8 112 $1^{1\frac{1}{2}}$ $2^{\frac{1}{2}}$ $3^{1\frac{1}{2}}$ $3^{2\frac{1}{4}}$ EspinozJC^7 ⒻAw14600 86-18 DoblThCont,PrttyPrfct,BrndyBrndy 7

22Aug82-6EIP 5$\frac{1}{2}$f :22^2 :45^4 1:05^{1}ft 7$\frac{1}{2}$ 119 $1^{\frac{1}{2}}$ $1^{\frac{1}{2}}$ $1^{\frac{1}{2}}$ 1^{hd} EspinozaJC^8 ⒻAw8400 94-11 BrindyBrindy,CongnilJni,HilltopSis 8

14Aug82-6FP 5$\frac{1}{2}$f :22^2 :47^2 1:06^{4}ft 6 116 $2^{\frac{1}{2}}$ $2^{1\frac{1}{2}}$ 2^{hd} 4^6 Evans RD^{10} ⒻJuvenile 77-26 SilveredSilk,SusieCircle,Arlecchin 10

14Aug82—Run in two divisions, 6th and 8th races

●Apr 26 Kee 5f ft 1:01^2 b Apr 6 OP 5f sl 1:06 b Mar 26 OP 5f ft 1:04^3 b Mar 14 OP 4f ft :49^4 b first or second in each of her five career starts. The *Daily Racing Form*'s consensus gave Princess Rooney a perfect 35/35 rating, since she was rated the best bet of the day by all five of their expert selectors. She had the advantageous post position, number 1, and was ridden by the veteran jockey Jacinto Vasquez. The 1–5 morning-line odds in the program and the *Daily Racing Form*'s expert selection's best bet of the day seemed justified. Weekend Surprise, number 6, was scratched, so the field had seven starters.

I expected that Princess Rooney would be heavily bet to win and that there likely would be a Dr. Z bet to place or to show or both. To my amazement, the first reading of the tote board with about twenty-three minutes to post time was as follows:

	Totals	#1 Princess Rooney
Odds		1—9
Win	61,214	44,920
Place	27,930	14,808
Show	268,441	257,150

The 1–9 win odds did not surprise me. I figured the win odds would rise to about 1–5 at post time. When I looked at the show pools it was clear to me that someone or some group of individuals had bet about $250,000 to show on Princess Rooney.* Out of the show pool of $268,441, the bet on Princess Rooney was $257,150. Since the show bet is usually less than the place bet, $18,441 seemed like the bet of the early bettors. The quarter-million-dollar bet dominated the show pool and made it six times as large as the win pool—quite a reversal from the usual situation where the show pool is a half or a third or even less of the win pool.

Why would someone make such a large bet? Presumably they figured that Princess Rooney was virtually unbeatable and it was extremely unlikely that she would not be in the money and finish at least third. Such huge bets on one or more horses cause what is known as a *minus pool*. The minus means that if the horse or horses come in, then the track actually loses money.

Let us see how it would work in this case. With a 15% track take for expenses, taxes, and the like, there would be only

$$(0.85)(\$268,441) = \$228,175$$

*Ty Perry of Louisville, Kentucky, wrote to tell us . . . "I had to laugh at [a page] of your book, first reading of the toteboard. Friday, May 6, 1983 was a very long, long day for me. I work at a $50 minimum window at Churchill Downs in the small row of ticket windows near the paddock. The bettors were lined up all day long betting on Princess Rooney to show. They came with paper sacks, brief cases, overnight bags—it seemed to me like everybody in the racetrack was betting $10,000 to show. Then, of course, I had to cash them all! A real fun day."

to pay back to bettors who have wagered \$257,150 to show on Princess Rooney. So even if nothing was bet on the other two horses finishing in the money with Princess Rooney, the payoff per \$2 bet would be

$$\$2\left(\frac{\$228{,}175}{\$257{,}150}\right) = \$1.77.$$

Now you cannot pay someone \$1.77 when they bet \$2 and the horse wins. So instead, a minimum payment is made, which is usually \$2.10. In Chapter Fifteen, where minus pools are discussed, we argue that when this is the case you should generally not bet on any horses. There are possible exceptions but they are rare. However, according to Kentucky state law the minimum payoff is \$2.20, not \$2.10. This changed the situation considerably, since the possible payoff was doubled from a 5% profit to one of 10%. In fact, as we show later, this was a good bet.

Let us now look at the evolution of the betting pools and the odds and observe what happened here so that we can determine whether or not there was a Dr. Z system bet to place or show on Princess Rooney or on some other horse.

With nineteen minutes to post time the show pool was as follows:

	Totals	#1	#2	#3	#4	#5	#6	#7	#8
Show	349,530	328,730	2,778	4,725	1,557	2,820	—	1,893	7,027

The minus pool on Princess Rooney was still very strong. The show betting on all the other horses was 2% or less of that bet on the favorite.

The tote board was as follows:

	Totals	#1 Princess Rooney
With eleven minutes to post time		
Odds		1—5
Win	145,041	99,919
Place	85,618	40,263
Show	450,401	408,145
With seven minutes to post time		
Odds		3—10
Win	212,365	138,700
Place	136,645	59,579
Show	574,561	501,401
With three minutes to post time		
Odds		3—10
Win	286,185	184,515
Place	211,798	104,052
Show	661,941	561,447

With one minute to post time		
Odds		3—10
Win	316,312	205,230
Place	233,221	112,657
Show	687,849	580,667

I hope by now that you have noticed that the best bet on Princess Rooney was to place, not show, and that it was good enough to qualify as a Dr. Z system bet. Only about half the place pool was bet on Princess Rooney, while about two thirds was bet on Princess Rooney to win. At one minute to post time, the expected value of a place bet on Princess Rooney dipped to 1.10, which made it a Dr. Z system bet, although just barely.* Since our betting wealth was $1,500, the optimal bet to place was $665.

What about betting on Princess Rooney to show as well? The payoff would be $2.20 if she finished in the money, so in order to analyze the situation we needed the probability of her finishing in the money. The probability that Princess Rooney would win the race was about 0.692 and 0.224 that she would finish second.† Hence she would place in the race with a probability of 0.916. The probability that Princess Rooney would be third was 0.061. Thus the chance that she would show was 0.977. Hence the expected value per dollar bet to show on Princess Rooney was

$$\text{EX Show} = \underbrace{0.977(\$1.10)}_{\text{Win}} + \underbrace{0.023(0)}_{\text{Loss}} = \$1.075.$$

The quarter-million-dollar bet thus looked quite good. About 98% of the time the big bettor would win $25,000. Two percent of the time he or she

*An expected value of 1.10 is justified here because of the very high quality of horses, the size of the mutuel pool, and the strong favorite bias discussed in Chapter Four.

†With one minute to post time, Princess Rooney was a 3–10 shot. According to the discussion concerning the underbetting of extreme favorites in Chapter Three her chance of winning was about $p = 0.692$, see Table 3.5. There were six other horses in the race, each with a chance of winning of about 0.051. From the Harville formulas, equations (5.2) and (5.3), the probability that Princess Rooney would come in second was about

$$\frac{nq_jq_1}{1-q_j} = \frac{6(0.051)(0.692)}{1-0.051} = 0.224,$$

and third, about

$$\frac{n(n-1)q_jq_kq_1}{1-q_j-q_k} = \frac{6(5)(0.051)^2(0.692)}{1-2(0.051)} = 0.061.$$

Thus the probability of placing was 0.692 + 0.224 = 0.916, and the probability of showing was 0.916 + 0.061 = 0.977. Approximate values of these probabilities can be read directly from Tables 6.12 and 6.32, respectively.

would lose the $250,000. So, on average, he or she would make a profit of 7.5%, or $18,750, with very little risk. Hence this was one case where it was a good idea to bet in a minus pool. The $2.20 minimum payoff made the expected return of 1.075 a handsome figure, considering the risk. With a $2.10 minimum payoff, the expected return would drop to about 1.025, and the return would not be high enough to jusify the risk. In conclusion, the show bet was a good one and similar bets are to be encouraged as long as the conditions are ideal: fast track, proper weighting of horse, post position, recent races, and so forth. However the place bet with an expected value of 1.10 was still the preferred bet.*

Princess Rooney took the lead and won wire to wire. In the stretch several horses challenged her, but she was able to pull away from them to a comfortable win. Bright Crocus took second, and Bemissed was third. Rosy Spectre was never a factor. Our bet of $665 returned $798 for a profit of $133.

At post time the tote board was as follows:

	Totals	#1 Princess Rooney	#2 Bright Crocus	#7 Bemissed
Odds		1—5	13—1	24—1
Win	361,955	238,957	20,401	11,842
Place	258,807	130,649	17,640	10,780
Show	718,936	601,892	11,682	10,320

The chart of the race was as follows:

EIGHTH RACE
Churchill
MAY 6, 1983

1 ⅛ MILES. (1.48⅗) 109th Running KENTUCKY OAKS (Grade I). $150,000 added. Fillies. 3-year-olds. By subscription of $100 each; $750 to pass the entry box; $750 additional to start with $150,000 added of which $65% of all monies to the owner of the winner, 40% to second, 10% to third and 5% to fourth. Weight, 121 lbs. Starters to be named through the entry box Wednesday, May 4, by the usual time of closing. If the race is divided entries or couplings will be divided. A silver trophy to the winning owner. Closed with 187 nominations.
Value of race $179,950, value to winner $116,968, second $35,990, third $17,995, fourth $8,997. Mutuel pool $1,339,698, Minus show pool $82,377.16.

Last Raced	Horse	Eqt.A.Wt	PP	St	¼	½	¾	Str	Fin	Jockey	Odds $1
23Apr83 ^{7}Kee^{1}	Princess Rooney	3 121	1	2	1^{hd}	1^{1}	1^{1}	$1^{1\frac{1}{2}}$	$1^{1\frac{1}{4}}$	Vasquez J	-.20
16Apr83 ^{10}Hia^{5}	Bright Crocus	3 121	2	5	7	7	$6^{\frac{1}{2}}$	4^{5}	2^{2}	Hawley S	13.90
23Apr83 ^{8}Pim^{3}	Bemissed	3 121	6	7	4^{1}	4^{1}	3^{hd}	$2^{\frac{1}{2}}$	$3^{\frac{1}{2}}$	Lovato F Jr	24.60
27Apr83 ^{5}Kee	Rosy Spectre	3 121	5	4	5^{2}	6^{2}	5^{1}	3^{hd}	$4^{6\frac{1}{2}}$	Delahoussaye E	16.50
23Apr83 ^{7}Kee^{5}	Fifth Question	3 121	3	6	6^{hd}	5^{hd}	7	5^{3}	$5^{5\frac{1}{2}}$	Day P	8.50
9Apr83 ^{9}OP^{1}	Brindy Brindy	3 121	7	1	2^{1}	$3^{3\frac{1}{2}}$	$4^{1\frac{1}{2}}$	6^{hd}	6^{nk}	Jones K	8.10
23Apr83 ^{7}Kee^{2}	Shamivor	3 121	4	3	3^{4}	$2^{\frac{1}{2}}$	2^{3}	7	7	Brumfield D	34.50

OFF AT 5:37. Start good. Won driving. Time, :23⅘, :47, 1:12, 1:37⅘, 1:50⅘ Track fast.

$2 Mutuel Prices:			
1-PRINCESS ROONEY	2.40	2.40	2.20
2-BRIGHT CROCUS		5.80	2.20
7-BEMISSED			2.20

Gr. f, by Verbatim—Parrish Princess, by Drone. Trainer Gomez Frank. Bred by Roach B & T (Ky).

PRINCESS ROONEY, racing in unchareteristic uneven fashion, broke alertly and smoothly came around BRINDY BRINDY to secure the lead completing the opening quarter-mile, but raced with head turned toward the inside while apparently trying to bear out after settling into the backstretch, and bobbled at the three-eights pole and again approaching the quarter-pole. The drived slightly into the stretch, responded to intermittent right hand urging, and held BRIGHT CROCUS clear while swerving slightly near the wire. BRIGHT CROCUS brushed several times with FIFTH QUESTION while being taken under restraint in the run to the clubhouse turn, was eased to the outside completing six furlongs, willingly raced to the leaders and appeared briefly threatening inside the last sixteenth, but was not gaining at the end. BEMISSED, rated forwardly, moved outside PRINCESS ROONEY for the stretch drive and responded gamely, although no match for the top two. ROSY SPECTRE had room along the rail to loom a threat in the drive and then hung. FIFTH QUESTION brushed with BRIGHT CROCUS early and was outrun. BRINDY BRINDY was lightly raced after she was displaced by PRINCESS ROONEY and tired after six furlongs. SHAMIVOR was used up racing outside the first flight. Equipment: No blinkers.

Owners— 1, Tucker Paula; 2, Levan-Waters-Weston; 3, Ryehill Farm; 4, Gentry T E; 5, Lowrance E; 6, Wanaja Fm & Energy B T; 7, White Fox Farm.

Scratched—Weekend Surprise (2May83 ^{8}CD^{3}).

*Regrettably Kentucky State law has recently lowered the minimum payoff to $2.10 so, at least at present, such bets are not worth making. Louisania still has a $2.20 minimum payoff.

As a check on our regression estimate of the expected value to place on Princess Rooney, we found that if Princess Rooney were to pay exactly $2.40 then

$$\text{EX Place} = \$2.40(0.916)/\$2 = 1.10,$$

which agreed with our 1.10 estimate from equation (4.6) and our calculator. It was likely that Princess Rooney would pay $2.40 to place if she finished first or second, although it was possible, depending on the pools, for the payoff to be $2.20 or $2.60. The estimates here are a little on the conservative side, since the expected value of a win bet might exceed 0.90. With a higher win probability, the placing and showing probabilities, and expected values, would be slightly higher. The analysis and conclusion remain the same.

THE CHANCE OF COLLECTING PLACE AND SHOW WAGERS ON VARIOUS ODDS HORSES

Tables 6.2 and 6.3 and Figures 6.1 and 6.2 give our best estimate of the chance of various odds horses placing and showing. These estimates are based on the Harville (1973) formulas based on a prototypical race.* These estimates seem to be reasonably accurate. The values for very low odds horses tend to overstate the true probability, since the Harville formulas break down when the probability of winning is very high. However, these values provide us with a reasonably accurate forecast of the success probabilities.

THE MATINEE HANDICAP, HOLLYWOOD PARK, INGLEWOOD, CALIFORNIA, APRIL 24, 1982

The late races of each day's card often contain Dr. Z system bets. They generally feature better, more consistent horses running for larger purses. Even more importantly, by then most of the crowd have lost a lot of money

*Let q be the probability of the horse winning. To determine the place probability it is necessary to know about the other horses in the race. The assumption made was that there were seven other horses, one with probability .3(1-q), two with probability .2(1-q), two with probability .1(1-q), and two with probability .05(1-q). These seven probabilities plus q add up to 1. As long as the real race being considered is not drastically different than the assumed race, these place probabilities are quite accurate. Using the Harville's (1973) formulas, when a horse's probability of winning is q, then its probability of placing is

$$q + \frac{.3(1\text{-}q)q}{1\text{-}.3(1\text{-}q)} + 2\left\{\frac{.2(1\text{-}q)q}{1\text{-}.2(1\text{-}q)}\right\} + 2\left\{\frac{.1(1\text{-}q)q}{1\text{-}.1(1\text{-}q)}\right\} + 2\left\{\frac{.05(1\text{-}q)q}{1\text{-}.05(1\text{-}q)}\right\}$$
$$= q + (1\text{-}q)q\left[\frac{3}{7+3q} + \frac{4}{8+2q} + \frac{2}{9+q} + \frac{1}{9.5+.5q}\right].$$

The show probabilities are computed using the same assumptions.

Figure 6.1 The probability of placing at various odds levels in California and New York

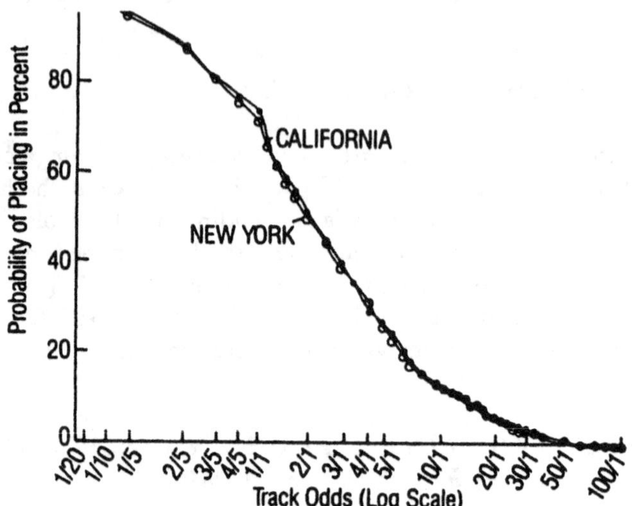

TABLE 6.2 ***Probabilities of placing in percent at various odds levels in California and New York***

Quoted Win Odds	*California*	*New York*	*Quoted Win Odds*	*California*	*New York*
1–20	99.0	98.5	11–1	13.6	13.2
1–10	98.5	98.0	12–1	12.3	12.1
1–5	96.3	95.8	13–1	11.5	11.3
2–5	89.9	89.2	14–1	10.7	10.5
1–2	86.3	85.4	15–1	9.8	9.6
3–5	82.7	81.8	16–1	9.2	9.0
4–5	77.1	76.2	17–1	8.6	8.3
1–1	72.0	71.0	18–1	8.1	7.9
6–5	67.3	66.3	19–1	7.5	7.5
7–5	62.9	62.0	20–1	7.1	7.1
3–2	61.1	60.2	21–1	6.6	6.6
8–5	59.3	58.5	22–1	6.4	6.2
9–5	56.2	55.4	23–1	6.0	5.8
2–1	51.4	50.7	24–1	5.8	5.5
5–2	45.8	45.1	25–1	5.1	4.9
3–1	40.7	40.1	30–1	4.0	3.8
7–2	36.4	35.9	35–1	3.1	2.7
4–1	32.9	32.4	40–1	2.2	2.0
9–2	29.9	29.3	50–1	1.6	1.6
5–1	26.4	26.0	60–1	1.3	1.1
6–1	22.9	22.6	70–1	0.9	0.9
7–1	20.2	19.8	80–1	0.7	0.7
8–1	18.3	17.9	90–1	0.6	0.5
9–1	16.2	16.0	100–1	0.3	0.3
10–1	14.8	14.6			

Figure 6.2 The probability of showing at various odds levels in California and New York

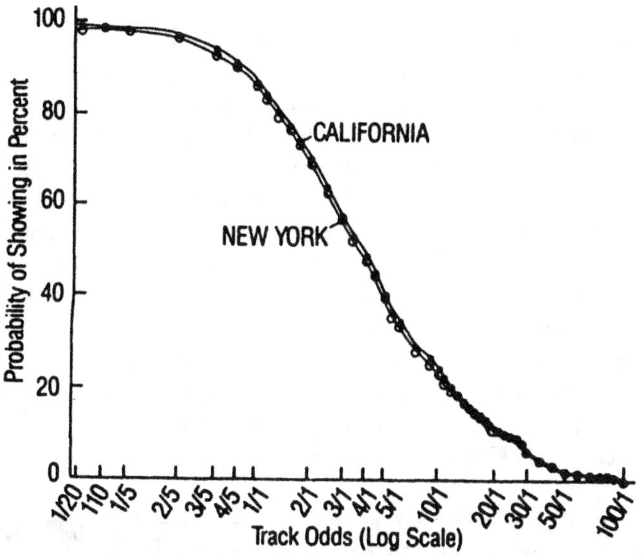

TABLE 6.3 ***Probabilities of showing in percent at various odds levels in California and New York***

Quoted Win Odds	*California*	*New York*	*Quoted Win Odds*	*California*	*New York*
1–20	99.5	99.0	11–1	22.2	21.6
1–10	99.0	98.5	12–1	20.3	20.0
1–5	98.5	98.0	13–1	19.0	18.7
2–5	97.5	97.3	14–1	17.7	17.3
1–2	95.9	95.5	15–1	16.3	16.0
3–5	94.3	93.8	16–1	15.3	15.0
4–5	91.1	90.6	17–1	14.3	14.0
1–1	87.7	87.0	18–1	13.6	13.3
6–5	84.3	83.6	19–1	12.6	12.6
7–5	80.8	80.1	20–1	11.9	11.9
3–2	79.3	78.5	21–1	11.2	11.2
8–5	77.7	77.0	22–1	10.8	10.5
9–5	74.9	74.1	23–1	10.1	9.7
2–1	70.2	69.5	24–1	9.7	9.4
5–2	64.4	63.6	25–1	8.7	8.3
3–1	58.7	57.9	30–1	6.8	6.5
7–2	53.5	52.9	35–1	4.9	4.6
4–1	49.2	48.6	40–1	3.8	3.5
9–2	45.3	44.6	50–1	2.7	2.7
5–1	40.7	40.2	60–1	2.3	1.9
6–1	36.0	35.4	70–1	1.6	1.6
7–1	32.1	31.5	80–1	1.2	1.2
8–1	29.2	28.6	90–1	1.0	0.8
9–1	26.2	25.9	100–1	0.4	0.4
10–1	24.1	23.8			

and want to find some bets that will allow them to recoup their losses. Betting to place or show, especially on low-priced horses, does not interest them much. Indeed, they are more interested in wagering on longer-priced win bets and in the exotic pools. Thus from the seventh race on, there is a good chance of locating one or more outstanding Dr. Z system bet.

The ninth, and final, race at Hollywood Park on April 24, 1982, provided an outstanding Dr. Z system bet. The $1\frac{1}{16}$-mile race on the turf was the $40,000 added second division of the Matinee Handicap. Whenever the number of entries exceeds about twelve, many handicaps are run in two divisions. The two divisions can be thought of simply as different races. They are usually run on different days.

The favorite in the race was Tacora, a Chilean horse, who was to be ridden by the great jockey Chris McCarron. Tacora had a strong and consistent record and deserved his favorite position. Other strong horses in the race were Sweet Maid, Granja Deseo, and Viendra.

Experts' Selections

Consensus Points: 5 for 1st (today's best 7), 2 for 2nd, 1 for 3rd. Today's Best in Bold Type.

Trackman, Warren Williams — **HOLLYWOOD PARK** — Selections Made for Fast Track

	TRACKMAN	HANDICAP	ANALYST	HERMIS	SWEEP	CONSENSUS	
9	TACORA	COAX ME HOME	VIENDRA	TACORA	GRANJA DESEO	TACORA	14
	SWIFT BIRD	TACORA	CHATEAU DANCER	CHATEAU DANCER	SWEET MAID	GRANJA DESEO	6
	GRANJA DESEO	CHATEAU DANCER	TACORA	VIENDRA	TACORA	VIENDRA	6

ANALYST'S *Hollywood Comment*

NINTH RACE

1—Viendra
2—Chateau Dancer
3—Tacora

VIENDRA was fourth to Star Pastures in a Group III event in England and was a forward contender in other highly regarded events in Britain. She connected in her third start in the U.S. over a fine field. Lipham handles her nicely and looks well placed to continue her winning ways. CHATEAU DANCER seems to be improving with each race and Russell appears to have her razor sharp right now. Guerra takes over the controls. TACORA has won three of seven turf starts and was second to Manzanera Feb. 26. McCarron got acquainted with her last start. COAX ME HOME seems to enjoy the turf and usually gives a good account of herself. With Pat V. aboard she may be sent to the lead along with I FELL IN LOVE.

9th Hollywood

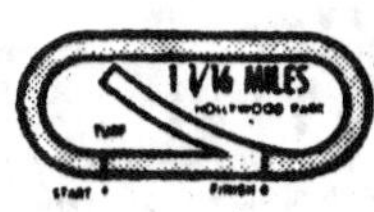

1 1/16 MILES. (TURF). (1.39⅘) 4th Running of THE MATINEE HANDICAP (2nd Division). $40,000 added. Fillies and mares, 3-year-olds and upward, which have not won $24,000* other than claiming or starter since December 25, 1981. By subscription of $50 each, which shall accompany the nomination, $500 additional to start, with $40,000 added, of which $8,000 to second, $6,000 to third, $3,000 to fourth and $1,000 to fifth. Weights, Monday, April 19. Starters to be named through the entry box by closing time of entries. A trophy will be presented to the owner of the winner. *A race worth $24,000 to the winner. Closed Wednesday, April 14, 1982 with 36 nominations.

Swift Bird

B. m. 5, by Northern Dancer—Flood Light, by Bold Lad
Br.—Belair Farm Ltd (Ky) 1982 6 0 0 2 $15,250
Own.—Nakamura K **114** **Tr.—Doyle A T** 1981 16 3 2 3 $110,500
Lifetime 39 6 4 10 $191,450 Turf 10 2 0 3 $46,825

17Apr82-7SA 1 :451 1:094 1:35 ft 3½ 115 2½ 31 45½ 67 DlhossyE7 ⒻB Thghtfl 87 Contrefaire, Aduana, Track Jester 11
10Apr82-8SA 1 1/16 :454 1:094 1:42 ft 18 115 54½ 54½ 52 5½ CastnedM1 ⒻSt Lca H 90 Si, Coax Me Home, Sweet Maid 8
17Mar82-9SA 1 1/16 :471 1:122 1:47 sy 5 114 43 31½ 3½ 33¼ ShmrW2 ⒻLa Merced 62 Miss Huntington, Si, Swift Bird 7
19Feb82-8SA a6½f Ⓣ:212 :4341:142fm 9 114 62¾ 54½ 63¾ 53¼ VlenzulPA2 ⒻAw35000 84 ExcitableLady,PlentyO'Toole,Sison 6
24Jan82-9SA 1 1/16 :471 1:11 1:422ft 17 114 2½ 2hd 11 31 GuerraWA3 ⒻAw40000 88 Balletomane, Tangaroa, Swift Bird 7
14Jan82-8SA 6½f :213 :441 1:152ft 28 116 65½ 77½ 911 87 ShoemkrW9 ⒻAw40000 86 Mtching,PstForgtting,StopDncing 10
25Nov81-8Hol 1 1/16 :453 1:093 1:413ft 6 117 26 44½ 69½ 611 PincyLJr3 ⒻPrncsnsn 76 BScout,ImptintLss,MissHuntington 8
4Nov81-8SA 1 1/16 :454 1:094 1:411ft 4 117 32 32½ 33 66 PincayLJr1 ⒻManta H 89 HppyGuess,MissHuntington,BScout 7
30Sep81-8SA a6½f Ⓣ:213 :44 1:134fm 13 113 75¾ 69 712 59¼ DlhssE6 ⒻAtmn Dys H 81 Kilijro,Ack'sSecret,MissHuntington 9
30Sep81—Run in two divisions, 8th & 9th races.
8Aug81-8Dmr 1 Ⓣ:4721:1111:352fm 13 115 31 31 64¼ 75¾ ShmrW2 ⒻPalomar H 91 Kilijaro, Lisawan, Satin Ribera 9
Apr 4 SA 1 ft 1:412 h Mar 29 SA tr.t 6f gd 1:161 h Mar 24 SA 6f ft 1:122 h Mar 13 SA 6f sl 1:162 h

Sweet Maid

B. m. 5, by Proud Clarion—Honor Maid, by Prince John
Br.—Elmendorf Farm (Ky) 1982 1 0 0 1 $9,750
Own.—Elmendorf **114** **Tr.—McAnally Ronald** 1981 11 2 2 1 $72,026
Lifetime 31 6 6 3 $154,191 Turf 8 0 1 1 $10,000

10Apr82-8SA 1 1/16 :454 1:094 1:42 ft 34 114 67½ 86½ 73 3nk AsssnCB5 ⒻSt Lca H 91 Si, Coax Me Home, Sweet Maid 8
10Oct81-6Bel 1 :47 1:104 1:36 ft 27 115 77½ 77½ 56 58¼ SantiagoA2 ⒻAw35000 80 ExprssivDnc,DmMystrius,TinTnToo 7
20Sep81-1Bel 1 1/16 :48 1:131 1:454gd 6½ 119 43½ 44 39 313 Venezia M2 ⒻHcp0 60 WaywardLass,Nora'sLss,SweetMid 4
16Aug81-8Sar 1⅛Ⓣ:4741:1241:503yl 51 111 716 77¼ 57 513 Venezia M7 ⒻDiana H 61 DeLaRose,RokebyRose,Euphrosyne 8
29Jly81-6Sar 7f :231 :463 1:242sy 4½ 119 69¼ 69 36 27¼ Venezia M5 ⒻAw35000 73 Love You Dear,SweetMaid,Avenare 6
3Jly81-7Bel 1 1/16 Ⓣ:4721:1111:433yl 8¼ 117 67½ 68¾ 56½ 47¾ Venezia M3 ⒻAw35000 70 StephniLigh,MovItNow,Mrs.Robrts 7
22Jun81-8Bel 1 :461 1:111 1:354ft 23 118 69 65 46 56 VnzM6 ⒻTw'light Tear 83 Jameela,ChainBracelet,IslandChrm 6
22Mar81-7Aqu 1⅛ :484 1:133 1:532ft 2 120 66½ 64½ 21 1nk Venezia M3 ⒻHcp0 68 SweetMaid,Skagerrak,Nalee'sFntsy 6
11Mar81-8Aqu 170⊡:4911:1431:461sy *6-5 122 54½ 52¾ 67½ 611 Venezia M6 ⒻHcp0 60 Cinto Tora, General J., Ms. Balding 6
8Feb81-8Aqu 1⅛⊡:47 1:1141:513sy 6¼ 113 715 710 48 411 VnzM5 ⒻRare Treat H 77 Pinkton,EnglishTrifle,I'llBeAround 9
Apr 20 SA 4f ft :504 h Apr 4 SA 1 ft 1:434 h ●Mar 29 SA 6f gd 1:132 h ●Mar 24 SA 1 ft 1:38 h

Coax Me Home *

Ch. m. 5, by Windy Sands—Carry Me Home, by Coursing
Br.—Old English Rancho (Cal) 1982 5 1 1 1 $27,240
Own.—Johnston-Johnston Est et al **115** **Tr.—Warren Donald** 1981 9 4 1 2 $75,750
Lifetime 19 6 4 3 $116,590 Turf 5 2 0 1 $28,540

10Apr82-8SA 1 1/16 :454 1:094 1:42 ft 16 115 33 33 31 2nk Sibille R3 ⒻSt Lca H 91 Si, Coax Me Home, Sweet Maid 8
25Mar82-8SA 1⅛Ⓣ:4741:1211:481fm 2½ 114 11 1½ 11½ 5nk Hawley S5 ⒻAw40000 86 BScout,MssHuntngton,PlntyO'Tool 6
26Feb82-8SA 1⅛Ⓣ:4531:10 1:473fm 6½ 117 22 2hd 2½ 43¾ Pincay LJr5 ⒻAw40000 85 Manzanera,Tacor,MissHuntington 10
14Feb82-10TuP 1 1/16 Ⓣ:4821:1341:461fm 3¼ 123 31½ 1hd 1hd 32 PowllJP6 ⒻSns Grl H 86 Bttlewind,ElevenPlicns,CoxMHom 11
3Jan82-10TuP 1 Ⓣ:48 1:1411:41 fm *1 122 32 31½ 3½ 1½ PowllJP7 Chrs Evrt H 86 CoaxMeHome,DeRuci,SunsetStrip 11
3Jan82—Run in two divisions, 8th & 10th races.
25Sep81-11Pom 1 1/16 :473 1:12 1:442ft *1-2e 117 55 45½ 46½ 35 MenaF8 ⒻLs Mdrns H 85 ConkyJohnston,LRegl,CoxMeHome 9
3Sep81-9Dmr 1 1/16 :453 1:103 1:44 ft *4-5 117 22½ 21½ 2hd 2nk PincyLJr3 ⒻJun Drlng 80 Bishop Again, CoaxMeHome,Nuera 5
3Sep81—Run in two division, 8th & 9th races.
7Aug81-7Dmr 7½f Ⓣ:224 :46 1:292fm 10 117 1½ 2hd 1½ 1nk Pincay LJr5 ⒻAw26000 94 CoaxMeHome,MiQuimer,BerryBush 9
11Apr81-8SA 1 1/16 :452 1:10 1:414ft 18 116 42 43 45 410 VlnzulPA1 ⒻSt Lca H 82 Finance Charge, Si, Swift Bird 10
26Mar81-9SA 1 1/16 :461 1:112 1:43 ft 14 119 27 21 1½ 1nk Hawley S9 ⒻAw32000 86 CoaxMeHome,Flordelisada,Tangaro 9
Apr 19 SA Ⓣ 5f fm 1:023 h (d) Apr 4 SA 5f ft :592 h Mar 21 SA 5f ft 1:002 h Mar 13 SA 5f sl 1:041 h

Granja Deseo

B. m. 5, by Astray—Marimacho, by Lake Erie
Br.—Granja Vista del Rio (Cal) 1982 7 1 0 1 $33,875
Own.—Granja Vista del Rio Stable **116** **Tr.—Palma Hector O** 1981 19 2 5 4 $76,150
Lifetime 38 4 7 6 $126,450 Turf 19 3 3 3 $93,075

3Apr82-8SA 1¼ :461 1:353 2:003ft 16 115 710 711 713 612 Pierce D7 ⒻSta Brb H 74 Ack'sSecret,Lndresse,PlentyO'Tool 8
25Mar82-8SA 1⅛Ⓣ:4741:1211:481fm 6½ 119 68½ 65½ 32½ 4hd ShoemkrW4 ⒻAw40000 86 BScout,MssHuntngton,PlntyO'Tool 6
13Mar82-8SA 1½Ⓣ:4842:0222:272gd 12 112 713 713 715 411 ShomkrW7 Sn Mrno H 67 LemhiGold,Exploded,ChnceyBidder 8
13Mar82—Run in two divisions, 8th & 9th races.
26Feb82-8SA 1⅛Ⓣ:4531:10 1:473fm 11 121 921 916 98¼ 76 Sibille R2 ⒻAw40000 83 Manzanera,Tacor,MissHuntington 10
18Feb82-8SA 1⅛Ⓣ:4641:1121:483fm 16 115 712 75 43½ 33½ Sibille R2 ⒻAw40000 80 BerryBush,SatinRibera,GranjDeseo 7
5Feb82-8SA 1⅛Ⓣ:4531:0941:47 fm 14 115 718 714 54¼ 53¼ Sibille R7 ⒻAw45000 89 Daeltown, Lisawan, Berry Bush 7
15Jan82-8SA 1⅛Ⓣ:4821:1231:494fm 5 115 87½ 84¼ 2½ 1½ Sibille R1 ⒻAw35000 78 Granja Deseo, Balletomane,Gracias 8
4Dec81-8Hol 1 1/16 Ⓣ:4721:1121:42 fm 7¾ 118 912 97½ 54¾ 31 Sibille R2 ⒻAw27000 88 Saharet, Tap DancerII,GranjaDeseo 9
5Nov81-8SA 1⅛Ⓣ:4611:1021:48 fm 5½ 1155 514 612 47½ 42½ WnlndWM1 ⒻAw34000 84 Battlewind, Syria, Forseek 9
28Oct81-7SA 1⅛Ⓣ:4721:1241:503fm 2½ 1135 65½ 64½ 31½ 1hd WnlndWM2 ⒻAw28000 74 Granja Deseo, Colacka, Grasiosa 6
Apr 21 SA 4f ft :472 h Apr 15 SA 5f ft 1:001 h Mar 21 SA 5f ft 1:014 h Mar 6 SA 6f ft 1:131 h

I Fell in Love — **B. f. 4, by Somethingfabulous—Selection, by T V Lark**
Br.—Ring Connie M (Cal) 1982 3 1 0 0 $20,750
Own.—Ring Mrs Connie M **114** **Tr.—Clapp Roger E** 1981 11 3 1 2 $52,725
Lifetime 17 5 1 2 $82,075 Turf 6 2 0 0 $28,600
1Apr82-8SA 1 :47 1:11 2 1:36 4sy 3¾ 109 5 11½ 13 15 16½ Steiner J J3 ⒻAw35000 85 I Fell in Love, Viga,WesternStarlet 6
3Mar82-8SA 6½f :21 3 :44 1:14 2ft 28 114 54 59½ 57½ 610 SteinrJJ3 ⒻLs Cngs H 88 ExctblLdy,‡QnfCrnll,Pppy'sLckyGrl 7
3Mar82—Placed fifth through disqualification
13Jan82-5SA a6½f Ⓣ:21 3 :44 3 1:15 4fm *2¾ 114 85 56 35 107¼ AsmssnCB4 ⒻAw32000 73 Chuck O Luck, Que Appeal, Larla 11
29Dec81-7SA 1 1/16 :46 3 1:10 4 1:42 1ft 6¼ 109 5 31½ 32½ 33 33¼ Steiner J J4 ⒻAw35000 87 ImptintLss,MssHuntngton,IFllnLov 6
25Nov81-4Hol 1 :45 3 1:10 3 1:36 2ft *1 117 22½ 2½ 21½ 23½ Pincay LJr3 ⒻAw26000 80 TrckJester,IFellinLove,Spokswomn 5
18Oct81-7SA 6½f :22 1 :45 1 1:15 3ft 7¼ 117 54 66 46 32¼ Pincay LJr6 ⒻAw32000 89 Rosy Cloud, La Pistola, IFellinLove 7
30Sep81-9SA a6½f Ⓣ:21 3 :43 3 1:14 1fm 16 117 1012 1011 99 77¼ PcLJr2 ⒻAtmn Dys H 81 Save WildLife,Disconiz,IGotSpeed 11
30Sep81—Run in two divisions, 8th & 9th races.
29Aug81-8Dmr 1 1/16 :46 1:10 2 1:42 1ft 9 116 49½ 45 36 58¾ Hawley S4 ⒻTory Pns 80 NorthernFble,GlittrHittr,Rj'sDlight 6
9Aug81-5Dmr 1 Ⓣ:46 3 1:11 1 1:36 3fm 9 112 11½ 11½ 12 1nk McCrrCJ10 ⒻAw24000 91 I Fell in Love,Nuera,Movin'Money 10
29Jly81-7Dmr 1 1/16 Ⓣ:46 4 1:12 1:44 4fm 40 107 5 12 12 45½ 1114 WnlndWM9 ⒻAw24000 71 Reinstate, Rihuana, Jetssean 12
●Apr 21 SA 3f ft :33 h Apr 11 SA 5f ft 1:00 3 h Mar 28 SA 1 ft 1:40 2 h Mar 22 SA 3f ft :34 3 h

Viendra — **Ch. f. 4, by Raise a Native—Friendly Relations, by Nearctic**
Br.—Harcourt H (Fla) 1982 2 1 0 0 $13,750
Own.—Sangster R E **113** **Tr.—Gosden John H M** 1981 8 1 2 0 $25,247
Lifetime 10 2 2 0 $38,997 Turf 10 2 2 0 $38,997
15Apr82-5SA 1⅛ Ⓣ:48 1:12 4 1:49 1fm 11 114 65½ 31 1½ 1¾ Lipham T3 ⒻAw25000 81 Viendra, Sangue, Coral Dance 11
4Mar82-5SA 1¼ Ⓣ:47 1 1:37 2:01 1fm 8¾ 113 78¼ 34 38½ 612 Lipham T10 Aw21000 69 Rostropovich, Garibi, Latrone 10
17Oct81-9WO 1¼ [T]:49 2 1:41 1 2:05 2fm 25 118 53¼ 84¾ 88¼ 67½ SwtukB6 ⒻE P Taylor 72 De La Rose, Sangue, Sajama 9
31Aug81♦4Newcastle(Eng) 1¼ 2:09 fm 2¼ 119 Ⓣ 23 Hide E ⒻVirginia Vielle, Viendra, Docklands 4
18Aug81♦4York(Eng) 1½ 2:35 1gd 11 126 Ⓣ 9 CthnS ⒻYorkshire Oaks(Gr1) Condessa, Leap Lively, Fiesta Fun 11
1Aug81♦2Goodwood(Eng) 1¼ 2:09 3gd 7 117 Ⓣ 42¾ CuthenS ⒻNassau(Gr2) Go Leasing, Vielle, Strigida 11
8Jly81♦3Newmarket(Eng) 1 1:40 3gd 20 115 Ⓣ 43¾ CauthenS ⒻChild(Gr3) Star Pastures, Tolmi, Seasurf 10
24May81♦4Longchamp(Fra) a1¼ 2:15 gd 10 128 Ⓣ 715 CuthnS ⒻPrix St Alary(Gr1) Tootens, Tropicaro, Last Love 10
15May81♦3Newbury(Eng) 1¼ 2:11 gd 4 119 Ⓣ 2hd CuthenS ⒻSr Chas Clre Strigida, Viendra, Leah 8
6May81♦1Chester(Eng) a7½f 1:37 4sf 3½ 123 Ⓣ 12½ CuthnS ⒻSefton(Mdn) Viendr,WhtHeven,CoptHllPrincess 10
Apr 10 SA Ⓣ 1 fm 1:41 4 h (d) Apr 5 SA Ⓣ 5f gd 1:02 1 h (d) Mar 31 SA 4f ft :51 h Mar 25 SA Ⓣ 7f fm 1:29 h

Chateau Dancer — **Ch. f. 4, by Giacometti—Delray Dancer, by Chateaugay**
Br.—Smth-Stvns-Mhlstn-Mfrd (Ky) 1982 2 0 1 1 $14,200
Own.—Pegasus Stud & St George **115** **Tr.—Russell John W** 1981 6 0 0 3 $15,328
Lifetime 14 2 3 5 $55,775 Turf 13 2 3 5 $55,250
27Mar82-8SA a6½f Ⓣ:21 3 :44 1 1:14 3fm 12 117 3½ 32½ 2½ 31 PncLJr2 ⒻMonrovia H 85 CatGirl,ExcitableLady,ChteuDncer 10
28Feb82-7SA a6½f Ⓣ:21 4 :44 3 1:14 2fm 2¾ 117 73¾ 32½ 2hd 21½ Pincay LJr3 ⒻAw26000 85 Vocalist,ChateauDancer,BrightLdy 10
9Dec81-8Hol 1 1/16 Ⓣ:48 3 1:12 3 1:42 4fm 11 112 2hd 2hd 2½ 32¼ ShmkrW7 ⒻMorgaise 83 Saison, Kell MyPet,ChateauDancer 9
4Dec81-8Hol 1 1/16 Ⓣ:47 2 1:11 2 1:42 fm *2½ 113 54½ 53¾ 65¼ 65½ ShoemkrW9 ⒻAw27000 83 Saharet, Tap DancerII,GranjaDeseo 9
20Nov81-8Hol 1 Ⓣ:48 1:12 1:36 fm 4¾ 114 76½ 95¾ 53¾ 31 CastnedM6 ⒻAw28000 88 Syria,VelvetChieftain,ChteuDncer 10
7Sep81-5Dmr 6f :21 4 :44 3 1:09 3ft 5¾ 115 44½ 45 58 59 McHrgDG3 ⒻAw21000 81 La Pistola, Matching, Track Jester 5
21Aug81-8Dmr 7½f Ⓣ:22 3 :45 4 1:29 4fm *3 109 66¼ 11 2hd 32¾ ShoemkrW4 ⒻAw24000 89 ElevenPelicans,Rihun,ChteuDncer 10
10Apr81♦4Newbury(Eng) a7¼f 1:32 4sf 3½ 126 Ⓣ 47½ PiggottL ⒻFred Darling Marwell, Star Pastures, FastFriend 4
13Sep80♦5Doncaster(Eng) 1 1:42 2gd 4½ 124 Ⓣ 35½ Eddery P ⒻMay Hills ExclusivlyRisd,SilknKnot,ChtuDncr 8
12Jly80♦2York(Eng) 6f 1:15 gd *6-5 129 Ⓣ 13 PggttL ⒻJohn Courage ChtuDncr,MrstonMgn,DiscoDncing 7
Apr 20 SA 6f ft 1:14 h Apr 14 SA 5f ft 1:01 2 h Apr 6 SA 5f ft 1:00 h ●Mar 9 SA 5f ft :58 2 h

***Tacora** — **B. m. 5, by Mr Long—Temuquita, by Nipigon**
Br.—Alamos P B (Chile) 1982 3 1 1 0 $32,000
Own.—Maggio C J **116** **Tr.—Rossi Lee J** 1981 7 0 3 0 $23,200
Lifetime 13 4 4 0 $70,432 Turf 7 3 1 0 $25,632
20Mar82-8SA 1⅛ :45 4 1:09 4 1:47 1ft 11 114 64 64 45½ 47¾ McCrrCJ3 ⒻSta AnaH 85 TrackRobbery,Mnzner,Ack'sSecret 8
26Feb82-8SA 1⅛ Ⓣ:45 3 1:10 1:47 3fm 14 118 45½ 41¼ 31 21¾ GuerraWA8 ⒻAw40000 87 Manzanera,Tacor,MissHuntington 10
5Feb82-4SA 1 1/16 :45 2 1:10 3 1:43 1ft 9-5 115 59½ 42 21 11½ McHrgDG2 ⒻAw30000 85 Tacora, Astrious, Katsura 6
21Oct81-9SA 1 :45 1:09 1 1:36 ft *1 115 47 23 22½ 2¾ CastnedM6 ⒻAw34000 88 Impatient Lass, Tacora, Forseek 9
1Oct81-8SA 1 1/16 :47 2 1:11 2 1:42 3ft 3¼ 117 53½ 54½ 33 2½ Pincay LJr4 ⒻAw40000 87 Tangaroa, Tacora, Happy Guess 6
13Sep81-11Dmf 1 1/16 :46 2 1:11 1:43 ft 33 112 53½ 41½ 11½ 11¾† OrtgLE4 ⒻEncinitas H 85 ‡Tacora, Satin Ribera, Battlewind 7
†13Sep81—Disqualified and placed second
17Jun81-9Hol 1 1/16 Ⓣ:46 4 1:12 1 1:41 4fm 3¾ 117 1019 1016 98¾ 86¾ Pincay LJr2 ⒻAw30000 83 RomnProspct,BshpAgn,Glc'sFntsy 10
25May81-8GG 1⅜ Ⓣ:49 3 1:38 4 2:15 4fm 16 110 77½ 65½ 710 88¾ LmnceC7 ⒻYba Bna H 80 MrzyDots,PrncssKrnd,PrncssToby 10
29Apr81-9Hol 1 1/16 Ⓣ:46 4 1:12 1 1:42 fm 7 115 811 87½ 53¾ 43 McHrgDG3 ⒻAw32000 86 Soft Reply, Spiffy Laree, Jetssean 9
26Mar81-9SA 1 1/16 :46 1 1:11 2 1:43 ft 12 115 — — — — DlhoussyE7 ⒻAw32000 — CoaxMeHome,Flordelisada,Tangaro 9
26Mar81—Lost rider
Apr 18 SA 1 ft 1:39 2 h. Apr 13 SA 4f ft :48 3 h Apr 5 SA 1 ft 1:41 3 h Mar 13 SA 5f sl 1:04 4 h

Throughout the betting period, Viendra was an outstanding Dr. Z system bet. At 5–1 he was going off at odds less than his morning line, which as we argued in Chapter Three is a good sign. Viendra's rider, Terry Lipham, was not one of Hollywood's top jockey's. However, he had guided Viendra to a victory on the turf in his last start, recently run at neighboring Santa Anita. Viendra was tied for the second pick in the *Daily Racing Form*'s consensus and was the Analyst's top choice. The day was a typical clear southern California day and the track was fast. In short, there was nothing to rule him out as a possible Dr. Z system bet if the odds were good.

At the end of the betting period the tote board was as follows:

	Totals	#6 Viendra
Odds		5—1
Win	129,233	16,353
Show	27,488	1,149

About one eighth of the money in the win pool was bet on Viendra, (16,353/129,233 = 1/7.9), but only about one twenty-fourth of the show pool was bet on Viendra, (1,149/27,488 = 1/23.9). Thus three times more money, relatively, was bet on Viendra to win than to show. Viendra looked like an outstanding Dr. Z system bet. But how good was the bet?

Since the track take in California is 15%, the expected value per dollar bet to show on Viendra using equation (4.6) is

$$\begin{aligned}\text{EX Show Viendra} &= 0.543 + 0.369\left(\frac{16{,}353/129{,}233}{1{,}149/27{,}488}\right)\\ &\quad + \left[3.60 - (2.13)\left(\frac{16{,}353}{129{,}233}\right)\right](0.85 - 0.829)\\ &= 1.66 + 0.07\\ &= 1.73.\end{aligned}$$

The expected value of 1.73 meant that, on average, we should expect to make a profit of 73% by betting on Viendra to show. The optimal bet was \$52.* Alternatively, with an expected-value cutoff of 1.14 at Hollywood

*The expected value of 1.73 was so high that there were problems using equation (5.5) to indicate the optimal bet. This was because equation (5.5) is the result of a statistical regression using data that had a maximum expected return to place or show of 1.40 plus the adjustment for track takes that differ from 17.1%. This was a reasonable methodology, since occurrences of expected returns greater than 1.40 are rare. What should be done when one of those outstanding occurrences, like Viendra, occurs? The approach we suggest is to pretend that the expected return is not really 1.73, but rather to determine the optimal bet with equation (5.5) on the premise that the expected return is 1.40. This is done by pretending that the public's show bet on Viendra is not really \$1,149, but a larger value that will yield an expected return of 1.40. From equation (4.4) we can calculate this larger value, for adjusted S_i, as $\bar{S}_i = q_i\, S/2.32 = (0.1265)(27{,}488)/2.32 =$ \$1,498 for Viendra. Using $q_i = 0.1265$, S = 27,488,

Park, Figure 5.9 indicated that a bet should be made. From Figure 5.21 a bet of about $15 was suggested. Again, because the expected value was so much higher than 1.18 the bet was quite conservative.

Viendra ran a strong race but was beaten by the favorite, Tacora. I Fell in Love took third. Because the Dr. Z system bet was so good, Viendra at 5–1 paid $8.80 to place and a whopping $9.40 to show. What a bet! My $52 bet to show returned $244.40, for a profit of $192.40. The chart of the race was as follows:

NINTH RACE
Hollywood
APRIL 24, 1982

1 1/16 MILES. (TURF) (1.39 4/5) 4th Running of THE MATINEE HANDICAP (2nd Division). $40,000 added. Fillies and mares. 3-year-olds and upward, which have not won $24,000* other than claiming or starter since December 25, 1981. By subscription of $50 each, which shall accompany the nomination, $500 additional to start, with $40,000 added, of which $8,000 to second, $6,000 to third, $3,000 to fourth and $1,000 to fifth. Weights, Monday, April 19.
Starters to be named through the entry box by closing time of entries. A trophy will be presented to the owner of the winner. *A race worth $24,000 to the winner. Closed Wednesday, April 14, 1982 with 36 nominations.

Value of race $44,900, value to winner $26,900, second $8,000, third $6,000, fourth $3,000, fifth $1,000. Mutuel pool $206,780.
Exacta Pool $428,516.

Last Raced			Horse	Eqt.	A.	Wt.	PP	St	1/4	1/2	3/4	Str	Fin	Jockey	Odds $1
20Mar82	8SA	4	Tacora	b	5	116	8	5	3 ½	3hd	5-1	4-2½	1 ¾	McCarron C J	2.40
15Apr82	5SA	1	Viendra		4	113	6	7	6 ½	7-3	6-1	3hd	2hd	Lipham T	5.70
1Apr82	8SA	1	I Fell in Love	b	4	114	5	3	1-1	1 ½	1hd	1-1	3-2½	Steiner J J	10.60
3Apr82	8SA	6	Granja Deseo		5	116	4	8	8	8	8	6-2	4hd	Shoemaker W	4.70
10Apr82	8SA	2	Coax Me Home		5	115	3	1	2hd	4 ½	3hd	2 ½	5-1½	Valenzuela P A	4.50
10Apr82	8SA	3	Sweet Maid		5	114	2	4	5hd	6hd	7-2	7 ½	6 ½	Asmussen C B	8.30
17Apr82	7SA	6	Swift Bird	b	5	115	1	2	4 ½	2-1½	2-1	5 ½	7-4	McHargue D G	12.80
27Mar82	8SA	3	Chateau Dancer		4	115	7	6	7-3	5-1½	4 ½	8	8	Guerra W A	7.50

OFF AT 6:07. Start good. Won driving. Time, :23 1/5, :47 3/5, 1:11 3/5, 1:35 2/5, 1:41 2/5 Course firm.

$ 2 Mutuel Prices:				
8-	TACORA	6.80	3.80	3.00
6-	VIENDRA		8.80	9.40
5-	I FELL IN LOVE			7.80

$5 EXACTA 8-6 PAID $169.00.

B. m, by Mr Long-Temuquita, by Nipigon. Trainer Rossi Lee J. Bred by Alamos P B (Chile).

TACORA, in contention from the outset, responded for the final drive, found room between horses in the upper stretch and outfinished VIENDRA. The latter, unhurried for six furlongs, went outside to rally entering the stretch and finished strongly. I FELL IN LOVE, used up making the early pace, weakened in the final furlong. GRANJA DESEO, devoid of early speed, rallied wide and did not threaten. COAX ME HOME lodged a bid near the rail entering the stretch but weakened in the final furlong. SWIFT BIRD forced the early pace outside of I FELL IN LOVE and tired in the stretch. CHATEAU DANCER, in good position between horses for six furlongs, tired in the stretch.

Owners- 1, Maggio C J; 2, Sangster R E; 3, Ring Mrs Connie M; 4, Granja Vista del Rio Stable; 5, Johnston-Johnston Est et al; 6, Elmendorf; 7, Nakamura K; 8, Pegasus Stud & St George.

Trainers- 1, Rossi Lee J; 2, Gosden John H M; 3, Clapp Roger E; 4, Palma Hector O; 5, Warren Donald; 6, McAnally Ronald; 7, Doyle A T; 8, Russell John W.

Overweight: Swift Bird 1 pound .

Scratched- Vocalist(23Apr82 8GG 1).

Attendance 30,386. Total Mutuel Pool $4,784,784.

---

and $\bar{S}_i = 1{,}498$ in equation (5.5) yields the suggested bet of $52. This approach indicates a lower bet than is optimal, but usually it is close. The use of equations (5.4) and (5.5) in such situations is discussed further in Chapter Sixteen. For Viendra, $q_i = 16{,}353/129{,}233 = 0.1265$, $S = 27{,}488$, and the adjusted $\bar{S}_i = 1{,}498$. From equation (4.6), EX Show Viendra = 1.40 + 0.07 = 1.47, and from equation (5.5),

$$\text{Show bet Viendra} = \left[131 + 2{,}150(0.1265)^2 - 1{,}780(0.1265)^3 - \left(\frac{150}{(0.1265)(27{,}488)/1{,}498 - 0.70}\right)\right]\left(\frac{27{,}488 - 6{,}000}{94{,}000}\right)$$

$$+ \left[86 + 1{,}516(0.1265)^2 - 968(0.1265)^3 - \left(\frac{90.7}{(0.1265)(27{,}488)/1{,}498 - 0.85}\right)\right]\left(\frac{100{,}000 - 27{,}488}{94{,}000}\right) = \$52.$$

1-3/16 MILES

WIN	PLACE	SHOW

NINTH

LONGACRES DERBY (46th Running)

PURSE $100,000 ADDED. FOR THREE-YEAR-OLDS. By subscription of $150, which shall accompany the nomination, $500 to pass the entry box, $1,000 additional to start with $100,000 added, of which $20,000 to second, $15,000 to third and $10,000 to fourth and $3,000 to fifth. All nominations, entry and starting fees to the winner. Closed with 44 nominations.

Track Record—REGALBERTO (3) 122—1:54 ONE MILE AND THREE-SIXTEENTH

	OWNER	TRAINER	JOCKEY
1	Tri Star Stable, R. Tsang & W. Bowie Chinese red, gold stars on back, red cap **JUNCTION ROAD** Br. c. 3 Junction—Cycool (KY)	Dave Forster 115	6 Kenneth Skinner
2	Osborne Farm Yellow, brown cross sashes, brown stripe on sleeves, yellow cap **ALLOWANCE** Ch. c. 3 Champagne Supper—Fund (WA)	Howard Belvoir 106	50 Gallyn Mitchell
3	Marvin Pietila & Estate of Waino Pietila Blue, white band, blue cap **PRAIRIE BREAKER** B. g. 3 Sir Paulus—Addie O Lea (WA)	Dick Wilkinson 124	4/5 Gary Stevens
4	Mr. & Mrs. Peter J. Whiting Yellow, brown sash, yellow cap **MYTHICALLY** B. c. 3 Run of Luck—Never Vain (CA)	L. Shoemaker 118	9/2 Paul Nicolo
5	Loto Can, Inc. Red & black stripes, red & black cap **COUNTRY BORN** B. g. 3 Native Born—Runnun Tell (WA)	Gary Vickery 110	30 Mike James
6	Selvin, Siegel, Wellman et al Beige, bulldog on back, matching cap **LIFAREGAL** B. c. 3 President—Regal Key (FRA)	Jim Penney 117	5 Martin Pedroza
7	Poor Four Stable White, red flame & yellow emblem on back, red & yellow cap **SABER BEN** Ch. c. 3 Champagne Supper—Saber Deb (WA)	Howard Belvoir 108	50 Basil Frazier
8	Rimrock Stable & Edwards Bloodstock Dark blue, blue & gray checks on sleeves, gray E on back, matching cap **DYNAMO DOC** Br. c. 3 Bold Commander—Little Girl Lost (KY)	Ed Walsh 115	10 Danny Sorenson
9	Heather Dedomenico Yellow, brown cross sashes, brown stripe on sleeves, D on back, yellow cap **HEATHER ALA RONI** Br. f. 3 Theologist—Scarlet Heather (WA)	Dan Kenney 110	15 Jerry Taketa
10	Vaughan Stable Orange, blue sleeves & sash, orange cap **RED BARON RETURNS** Ch. c. 3 Mateor—T. V. Return (WA)	Kay Vaughan 110	50 J. W. Mills

CLOCKER'S SELECTION: 3-4-6

9th Lga

1 3-16 MILES. (1:54). 46TH RUNNING OF THE LONGACRES DERBY. Purse, $100,000-added. 3-year-olds. By subscription of $150, which shall accompany the nomination, $500 to pass the entry box, $1,000 additional to start with $100,000-added, of which $20,000 to second, $15,000 to third, $10,000 to fourth and $3,000 to fifth. All nominations, entry and starting fees to the winner. High weights preferred. Closed Friday, July 15 with 44 nominations.

Junction Road **115** Dk. b. or br. c, 1980, by Junction—Cycool, by Cyane.
Breeder, Morris-O'Brien (Ky.). 1983. 8 3 2 2 $31,062
Owner, Tri Star Stable-R. Tsang-W. Bowie. Trainer, Dave Forster. 1982. 0 M 0 0 ——
31Jly 83 9Lga 1⅛ :4541:0941:494ft 9 117 515 49½ 44½ 32¼ SkinnrK8 HcpS 82 PrairieBreaker124 Mythically 8
16Jly 83 9EP 1 1/16 :4731:1241:444ft 9-5 ^116 41¾ 1h 12½ 13 SkinnrK3 HcpS 87 JunctionRoad116 PhylThBses 8
3Jly 83 8Lga 6½f :222 :45 1:144ft 5½ 117 42½ 21½ 33 28 SkrK5 Aw10000 87 ExclusivBiddr119 JnctinRoad 9
25Jun83 9Lga 1 1/16 :4631:1121:424ft 2½ 122 76¾ 43 44½ 58¾ PircL4 Aw10000 76 Dynamo Doc 117 Ourteshun 8
25Jun83—Wide.
15Jun83 9Lga 6½f :221 :4431:16 ft 2½ ^120 42½ 43 44½ 31¾ RycftC8 Aw9400 87 PicO'Morn120 ExclusiveBddr 8
18May83 9EP 6½f :214 :4521:182ft 6-5 ^120 69½ 75¾ 51¼ 1½ RyctD7 Aw6400 86 JnctionRoad120 MoneySprgs 9
30Apr83 6EP 6½f :22 :4521:18 ft 1-2 ^120 35 24 13 15 RycrftD6 Mdn 88 JunctionRoad VictoriousLd 9
16Apr83 7EP 6f :23 :4631:114ft 2-3 ^120 21 2h 1½ 2¾ RycrftD3 Mdn 92 ThroghAndClr JunctionRoad 9
16Apr83—Jumped gate trks st
Aug 11 EP 5f ft 1:03⅗b June 13 Lga 4f ft :47⅕h June 8 EP 5f ft 1:03h

Allowance **106** Ch. c, 1980, by Champagne Supper—Fund, by Speak John.
Breeder, Osborne Farm (Wash.). 1983. 6 0 1 1 $4,116
Owner, Osborne Farm. Trainer, Howard Belvoir. 1982. 11 2 0 3 $10,210
LIFETIME (thru 1982) 11 2 0 3 $10,210
7Aug83 9Pla 1 :46 1:11 1:364ft 3¾ 118 34 34½ 45½ 45¾ ColtonR4 HcpS 87 MissMackee121 Wnd'emHgh 7
27Jly 83 6Lga 1 1/16 :4611:11 1:432sy 4¼ 119 36½ 1½ 2h 2½ BazeMB4 25000 81 Bold Treaty 116 Allowance 7
7Jly 83 9Lga 6f :222 :4441:082ft 39 117 63¾ 79 1020 918 MhGV6 Aw8500 76 DncingDirctr119 FortithPrnc 11
30Jun83 8Lga 6f :214 :4421:09 ft 34 111 712 712 614 79¾ MtchlGV6 40000 81 DancngDirectr120 TudrRmmr 10
28Jan83 1SA 1 :4711:1331:421sl 9 116 716 819 pulled up ToroF8 32000 BranBey DarkAce 8
14Jan83 9SA 1 1/16 :4741:12 1:434ft 5 116 52 32½ 33½ 32 ToroF1 32000 80 Bick'sAKick DarkAce 9
29Dec82 2SA 1 :4521:1031:372ft 3¼ ^116 810 86¼ 64½ 75 SmkrW5 32000 76 DarkAce MoorsMountain 10
23Dec82 5Hol 1 1/16 :4721:1321:471sl 4¾ 115 57 66 611 64 ShkrW7 50000 55 SterlingSilva Brazenesian 8
19Nov82 1Hol 6f :22 :4521:111gd 21 115 94½ 54 58 31 BlackK8 40000 80 AllTheBest FuzzyFreeze 9
10Oct82 9Lga 1 1/16 :4721:1341:482sl 26 122 915 1015 1023 1021 LosthC12 SpwS 36 Dave's Reality 122 Chirp 13
19Sep82 9Lga 1 :46 1:1031:364ft 6¾ 120 79½ 89½ 610 613 BazMB10 HcpS 72 Dave's Reality 122 Tubafor 10
5Sep82 7Lga 6½f :22 :45 1:173ft 25 120 55 44½ 36 12 BzMB1 Aw7500 81 Allowance 120 Sailalong 9
JULY 19 LGA 3F FT :35⅖B June 22 Lga 5f ft 1:02⅖bc June 14 Lga 5f ft 1:01⅘bc

Prairie Breaker **124** B. g, 1980, by Sir Paulus—Addie O. Lea, by Orazio.
Breeder, Waino-Marvin Pietila (Wash.). 1983. 11 8 1 1 $85,793
Owner, Marvin Pietila-Estate of Waino Pietila. Tr., D. Wilkinson. 1982. 0 M 0 0 ——
31Jly 83 9Lga 1⅛ :4541.0941:494ft 3-5 ^124 615 510 34 12 StevenG7 HcpS 84 PrairieBreaker124 Mythically 8
17Jly 83 9Lga 1 1/16 :4531:1011:431ft 4-5 ^122 512 38½ 2h 15½ StevenG7 HcpS 83 PrairiBreakr122 SonofSibirri 7
3Jly 83 9Lga 1 :4541:1041:362ft 4¾ 119 88¼ 32½ 11 11½ StevenG8 HcpS 87 PrairiBreakr119 DynamoDoc 8
18Jun83 9Lga 6½f :214 :4411:142ft 2¾ 120 77 78½ 67 45 StvnsG10 HcpS 92 King Alphonse 124 Sailalong 11
29May83 9Lga 6f :212 :4411:094ft 3 116 78¼ 79¼ 48 11½ StevnsG4 HcpS 87 Prairie Breaker116 Sailalong 8
8May83 9Lga 5½f :213 :45 1:04 m 7¾ 122 98¼ 711 714 32 StvnsG11 AlwS 90 NoTheologian120 Intoxicator 11
24Apr83 9PM 1 1/16 :4811:1241:442ft 1-2 ^123 54 2h 12 13 StevnsG5 HcpS 94 PrairiBreakr123 RahRahRah 5
14Apr83 9PM 6f :223 :46 1:103ft 1-5 ^121 21½ 3½ 2h 1½ StvnsG5 Aw3000 94 PrairieBreaker121 JustFrBill 5
20Mar83 9PM 1 :4741:1321:384ft 3-5 ^117 36½ 2h 15 112 StvsG1 Aw3100 87 PrairieBreakr117 ScappsBay 7
20Feb83 9PM 1 1/16 :4631:1241:474gd 6-5 ^120 26 26 22 22½ BazeG3 HcpS 74 Boss C. 121 Prairie Breaker 12
5Feb83 2PM 6f :222 :4611:122ft 8 120 21½ 21½ 12½ 16½ BazeG12 Mdn 85 PrairieBreakr120 Prediction 12
AUG 11 LGA 5F FT 1:00⅕B JULY 14 LGA 5F M 1:00⅗H June 16 Lga 4f ft :50b

Mythically **118** B. c, 1980, by Run of Luck—Never Vain, by Prince Tenderfoot.
Breeder, Mr.-Mrs. P. J. Whiting (Calif.). 1983. 8 2 5 0 $36,490
Owner, Mr.-Mrs. P. J. Whiting. Trainer, Leonard Shoemaker.
31Jly 83 9Lga 1⅛ :4541:0941:494ft 3¾ 120 38½ 36½ 23 22 NicoloP2 HcpS 82 PrairieBreaker124 Mythically 8
9Jly 83 11Pln 1 1/16 :47 1:1131:44 ft 1 ^119 31 2h 1h 21½ NicoloP5 HcpS 83 IdealMoment114 Mythically 8
19Jun83 8GG Ⓣ1 1/16 :4621:1121:45 fm 4½ 114 11 11 11 2nk NicoloP2 HcpS 77 BrianKe Mythically 11
10Jun83 6GG 1 1/16 :46 1:1041:432ft 3½ 120 21½ 1h 13 16 NclP2 Aw13000 86 Mythically HundrdollrJo 8
21May83 6GG 1 1/16 :47 1:1111:44 ft 2½ ^112 12 13 16 17 NicoloP9 Mdn 83 Mythically Exhibit 10
7May83 1GG 1 1/16 :4611:11 1:45 ft 8-5 ^118 2½ 2½ 3½ 2¾ NicoloP4 Mdn 77 HonoredOne Mythically 9
7May83—Lugged out, bumped stretch.
23Apr83 2GG 6f :223 :4631:13 sy 7-5 ^118 43½ 52½ 41 21 †NicoloP6 Mdn 73 BlckShrrod Mythically 10
†Disqualified and placed fifth.
8Apr83 7GG 6f :223 :4641:113ft 3 118 83¾ 74¾ 33½ 2nk NcloP5 M25000 81 Interim Mythically 10
8Apr83—Bumped hard break, lacked room 3 1-2.
Aug 11 Lga 5f ft 1:02⅖b JULY 23 GG 7F FT 1:27⅘H JULY 2 GG 7F FT 1:25⅖h

Country Born ✱ **110** B. g, 1980, by Native Born—Runnun Tell, by Tell.
Breeder, L & M Farms, Inc (Wash.). 1983. 6 1 2 1 $9,965
Owner, Loto Can, Inc. Trainer, Gary Vickery. 1982. 5 2 1 0 $30,656
LIFETIME (thru 1982) 5 2 1 0 $30,656
10Aug83 8Lga 1 1/16 :4671:11 1:434ft 5½ 118 11 13 13 15½ BzMB8 Aw8500 80 CountryBorn118 Lyon'sShadw 12
27Jly 83 7Lga 1 1/16 :4721:12 1:443sy 3½ 119 11 11½ 13 2½ BzMB4 Aw8500 75 Lyon'sShadow117 CountryBrn 7
14Jly 83 9Lga 1 1/16 :4641:1221:451m 3½ ^119 15 14 11½ 31¾ BazeMB7 32000 71 RedBrnRtrns120 Lyon'sShdw 11
15Jun83 9Lga 6½f :221 :4431:16 ft 5½ 120 2½ 3½ 32½ 44¾ BzMB6 Aw9400 84 PicO'Morn120 ExclusiveBddr 8
15Jun83—Wide.
25May83 9Lga 6f :222 :4541:103ft 3 ^119 42 32½ 31 22½ BzMB1 Aw8500 80 PhilE.B.Jon122 CountryBorn 11
8May83 9Lga 5½f :213 :45 1:04 m 4¾ 120 53½ 55 57½ 66 BazeMB9 AlwS 86 NoTheologian120 Intoxicator 11
8May83—Wide on turn.
10Oct82 9Lga 1 1/16 :4721:1341:482sl 7¾ 122 31½ 33 1229 1340 BazeMB3 SpwS Dave's Reality 122 Chirp 13
26Sep82 9Pla 6½f :222 :4611:191m 4¾ 121 11½ 15 15 112 BazMB6 SpwS 89 CountryBorn121 PicO'Morn 12
5Sep82 9Lga 6½f :22 :45 1:181ft 3½ 121 31 31½ 913 129½ HowgR8 SpwS 68 Big Flyer 121 Time of Sale 12
21Aug82 4Lga 6f :221 :46 1:113ft 8-5 ^120 1h 1h 12 16 HowgR9 Mdn 78 CountryBorn120 ShotABid 11
July 8 Lga 7f ft 1:24h June 9 Lga 7f ft 1:28b MAY 21 LGA 6F FT 1:13⅗H

***Lifaregal 117** B. c, 1980, by President—Regal Key, by Royal and Regal.
Breeder, M. Desandre (Fra.). 1983. 5 1 0 0 $15,700
Owner, Selvin-Siegel-Wellman et al. Trainer, Edwin Gregson. 1982. 8 2 4 1 $23,714
LIFETIME (thru 1982) 8 2 4 1 $23,714
24Jly 83 8Hol 1¼ :4631:3512:01 ft 35 114 77½ 66 611 68½ MezaRQ6 AlwS 77 Hyperborean115 MyHabitony 9
19Jun83 8GG Ⓣ1 1/16 :4621:1121:45 fm 4 118 88½ 87½ 54½ 74 MenaF7 HcpS 73 BrianKe Mythically 11
11Jun83 8Hol Ⓣ1 1/16 :49 1:1331:43 fm 18 115 96½ 94½ 51½ 53 PierceD9 HcpS 81 BaronO'Dublin TanksBridge 9
21May83 8Hol Ⓣ1 1/16 :4611:1021:412fm 4¼ 118 914128 1210129¾ ShkrW13 HcpS 82 Barberstown LovrBoy 13
30Apr83 9Hol 1 1/16 :4821:1321:463gd 4¼ 115 35½ 34 31½ 1nk TroF2 Aw24000 62 Lifaregal O'HappyDay 6
13Nov82 3Marseill(Fra) Ⓣa1¼ sf 122 15 GoudotB Px Dlahnte Lifaregal HatTrick MyWinter 10
13Nov82—No time taken; no wagering.
16Oct82 1Lyon(Fra) Ⓣa1 1/16 sf 128 42¼ GoudotB Px D Rouvrs RoyaldeLuze OretDiamant MisWn 11
16Oct82—No time taken; no wagering.
29Sep82 1Marseill(Fra) Ⓣa1⅛ gd 121 11 BlscG PxMsAndn(Mdn) Lifaregal Royal deLuze Cargy 9
29Sep82—No time taken; no wagering.
AUG 8 DMR 1M FT 1:37⅘H Aug 1 Dmr 5f ft 1:00b July 19 Hol 5f ft :59⅘h

Saber Ben 108 Ch. c, 1980, by Champagne Supper—Saber Deb, by Saber Charge.
Breeder, Osborne Farms (Wash.). 1983. 4 1 0 0 $4,235
Owner, Poor Four Stable. Trainer, Howard Belvoir. 1982. 6 1 3 0 $8,655
LIFETIME (thru 1982) 6 1 3 0 $8,655
31Jly 83 9Lga 1⅛ :4541:0941:494ft 37 111 821 815 713 512 FrazierB1 HcpS 72 PrairieBreaker124 Mythically 8
20Jly 83 7Lga 6½f :213 :4421:154ft 26 119 10101011 46 1¾ BazeMB8 25000 90 Saber Ben 119 Just Cavorting 11
7Jly 83 9Lga 6f :222 :4441:082ft 64 122 106¾1015 918 815 PiercL8 Aw8500 79 DncingDirctr119 FortithPrnc 11
30Jun83 8Lga 6f :214 :4421:09 ft 27 113 10151016 924 917 StevenG2 40000 74 DancngDirectr120 TudrRmmr 10
14Dec82 6BM 6f :223 :4541:104ft 9 114 97 108½ 79¼ 88½ LncC1 Aw12000 77 SportingBlood NIN'Shn 10
14Dec82—Lacked racing room in backstretch.
30Nov82 6BM 6f :24 :49 1:15 sy8-5 *113 42 31 22 22½ LmcC5 Aw12000 62 DistantMan SaberBen 5
19Nov82 8BM 6f :222 :4531:113sy 3½ 113 69½ 48 37 24 LmcC4 Aw12000 78 NoTheologian SaberBen 6
31Oct82 9PM 6f :214 :45 1:114ft 11 120 812 918 48½ 24½ BazeMB6 HcpS 83 Kim Como 117 Saber Ben 12
24Oct82 9Lga 1⅛ :47 1:1141:513m 21 116 1214121514271429 MrcVV11 HcpS 46 Yuma Queen 114 Tubafor 14
8Oct82 5Lga 6f :223 :4641:13 m 14 120 65¾ 67¼ 41½ 15 BzMB2 M25000 71 Saber Ben 120 Noodle Roni 8
Aug 10 Lga 5f ft 1:01⅕b June 22 Lga 5f ft 1:02⅗bc June 14 Lga 5f ft 1:00⅗h

Dynamo Doc 115 Dk. b. or br. c, 1980, by Bold Commander—Little Girl Lost, by Tudor
Grey. Breeder, Jim Eagle (Ky.). 1983. 7 2 1 0 $17,220
Owner, Rimrock Stable-Edwards Bloodstock. Tr., Ed Walsh. 1982. 10 1 3 3 $21,460
LIFETIME (thru 1982) 10 1 3 3 $21,460
3Jly 83 9Lga 1 :4541:1041.362ft 8½ 119 78¼ 54½ 53½ 21½ SornsnD4 HcpS 85 PrairiBreakr119 DynamoDoc 8
3Jly83—Wide on second turn.
25Jun83 9Lga 1 1/16 :4631:1121:424ft 2¼*117 89¾ 53¼ 2h 16 SrnD5 Aw10000 85 Dynamo Doc 117 Ourteshun 8
19Jun83 9Lga 6½f :214 :4411:142ft 32 120 108¾109¼ 77 56½ PierceL7 HcpS 90 King Alphonse 124 Sailalong 11
29May83 9Lga 6f :212 :4411:094ft 12 120 810 810 612 67¼ PierceL3 HcpS 80 Prairie Breaker116 Saiialong 8
23Apr83 7GG 1 1/16 :4711:1141:511ft 56 112 fell SornsnD4 AlwS ParisPrince119 TanksBrigade 12
14Apr83 8GG 1 :5011:1441:392ft 6 113 67½ 610 58 46 SrnD5 Aw13000 65 TanksBrigade Thurman 6
14Apr83—Broke in tangle
22Mar83 6GG 6f :231 :4641:123m 4½ 113 66½ 66¾ 55¾ 1no SrnD5 Aw11000 76 DynamoDoc AuntieRose 6
22Mar83—Bobbled at break
24Oct82 9Lga 1⅛ :47 1:1141:513m 4¾ 119 812 78¼ 34 511 PierceL1 HcpS 64 Yuma Queen 114 Tubafor 14
10Oct82 9Lga 1 1/16 :4721:1341:482sl 7½ 122 1117 813 47 36¾ PiercL11 SpwS 50 Dave's Reality 122 Chirp 13
29Sep82 8Lga 1 :4841:15 1:44 hy 5¾ 120 818 712 66¼ 21 PiercL5 Aw6500 48 ExclusivBiddr118 DynamoDoc 8
19Sep82 9Lga 1 :46 1:1031:364ft 8¼ 120 69 57 47 46½ PierceL2 HcpS 78 Dave's Reality 122 Tubafor 10
AUG 11 LGA 4F FT :47⅗H Aug 7 Lga 7f ft 1:28⅘b Aug 1 Lga 5f ft 1:01⅖b

Heather Ala Roni × 110 Dk. b. or br. f, 1980, by Theologist—Scarlet Heather, by Cold
Command. Br., Paskey Dedomenico (Wash.). 1983. 3 2 0 0 $20,750
Owner, Heather Dedomenico. Trainer, Dan Kenney. 1982. 4 1 1 0 $22,467
LIFETIME (thru 1982) 4 1 1 0 $22,467
30Jly 83 9Lga 1 1/16 :4531:11 1:434ft 2¼*116 23 1h 34½ 513 FrazirB3 HcpS 67 ⒻStllrPrfrmr118 WindyJnny 9
9Jly 83 9Lga 1 :4631:1111:363gd 3¾ 113 21 1h 1h 11 FrazirB5 HcpS 86 ⒻHthrAlaRni113 StlrPrfrmr 11
9Jly83—Bumped at 1-2 pole.
23Jun83 8Lga 6f :22 :4531:103m 4 117 21½ 21 13 19 FrzirB5 Aw8000 83 ⒻHeathrAlaRni117 LttlGngr 7
23Jun83—Carried wide on turn.
24Oct82 9Lga 1⅛ :47 1:1141:513m 9½f119 23½ 2h 9131222 FrazirB13 HcpS 53 Yuma Queen 114 Tubafor 14
3Oct82 9Lga 1 1/16 :4741:1321:471m 16 119 12 11 2h 23½ FrazerB2 SpwS 59 ⒻFlagDeLune119 HthrAlaRni 14
17Sep82 3Lga 6½f :214 :4511:174ft 6¾ 118 1h 12 13 18 BazG11 M20000 80 ⒻHeatherAlaRoni118 Garvin 11
28Aug82 3Lga 6f :214 :4541:111ft 12 118 65½ 45 56 414 SorensnD2 Mdn 66 ⒻThoniaFrst118 UnitdFeatre 7
JULY 25 LGA 4F FT :46⅗H July 19 Lga 1m ft 1:37⅖h July 4 Lga 5f ft 1:02⅘b

Red Baron Returns 110 Ch. c, 1980, by Mateor—T.V. Return, by Flying Lark.
Breeder, O'Harrow-Vaughan (Wash.). 1383.10 3 1 1 $15,185
Owner, Vaughan Stable. Trainer, Kay Vaughan. 1982. 7 2 0 2 $6,510
LIFETIME (thru 1982) 7 2 0 2 $6,510
10Aug83 8Lga 1 1/16 :4621:11 1:434ft 5¼ 120 12181014 612 57¾ MJW10 Aw8500 72 CountryBcrn118 Lyon'sShadw 12
27Jly 83 7Lga 1 1/16 :4721:12 1:443sy 2¼*120 79 76¾ 57½ 33½ MlIJW2 Aw8500 72 Lyon'sShadow117 CountryBrn 7
14Jly 83 9Lga 1 1/16 :4641:1221:451m 5¼ 120 1015 711 47½ 11½ MillsJW6 32000 73 RedBrnRtrns120 Lyon'sShdw 11
2Jly 83 6Lga 1 1/16 :4841:1321:453ft 6¾ 117 42 31 2h 13 MillsJW4 25000 71 RedBaronRtrns117 Predction 8
22Jun83 6Lga 6½f :221 :4531:164sy 2½ 117 34 31½ 2h 2½ MillsJW2 20000 84 Predcatin114 RedBaronRetrn 7
15Jun83 6Lga 6½f :221 :4441:154ft 6¼ 117 67 613 79¾ 69¼ SornsnD1 25000 81 Candy Patch 120 Hot Drums 8
3Jun83 6Lga 6½f :22 :4511:171ft 16 117 711 714 610 43½ SornsnD5 25000 79 DncngDirctr120 HoHoCharlie 7
3Jun83—Veered in, steadied at start.
14May83 7Lga 6f :22 :45 1:094ft 9½ 114 712 710 610 515 StevnsG8 40000 72 SplndorBoy120 DancgDrctor 8
24Apr83 9YM 6f :234 :4831:17 hy3-2e*124 64 65¼ 711 721 MlgrinT1 HcpS 37 Pic O'Morn 117 Colonel Jerry 7
2Apr83 9YM 5f :222 :4531:013gd 5¾ 117 59 59½ 53¾ 13 MgmTM7 HcpS 72 RedBarnRetrns117 ShotABid 9
22Sep82 8Lga 6½f :223 :4621:183ft 3-2 *120 74¼ 31 1h 12 BazeG1 20000 76 RedBaronRetrns120 C.W.Mss 8
Aug 3 Lga 5f ft 1:00⅖h July 21 Lga 5f ft 1:00⅖h JULY 9 LGA 5F SY 1:00H

THE LONGACRES DERBY, LONGACRES, RENTON, WASHINGTON, AUGUST 14, 1983

Longacres is one of America's top tracks, serving the metropolitan Seattle area. A top race brings out a huge crowd. One of the major races of the year was the forty-sixth running of the Longacres Derby. It was a $100,000 added race over $1\frac{3}{16}$ miles for three-year-olds. The $73,000 winner's share of the purse drew a number of strong horses, including Junction Road, Mythically, Lifaregal, and Dynamic Doc. The overwhelming favorite, however, was Prairie Breaker. With eight wins, a second, and a third in eleven starts against tough competition in 1983, Prairie Breaker certainly was the horse to beat.

The crowd established Prairie Breaker as a 4–5 favorite. In the best stakes races, top horses going off at less than even money are often Dr. Z system bets. An especially appealing situation, often leading to outstanding payoffs, arises when there are no other top choices and the betting is spread fairly evenly among the rest of the field. That seemed to be the case in this race. With one minute to post time, the tote board was as follows:

	Totals	#3 Prairie Breaker	Expected Value per Dollar Bet to Place and Show on Prairie Breaker
Odds		4—5	
Win	104,409	47,510	
Place	59,752	16,655	1.25
Show	43,936	11,950	1.19

The expected values to place and show with Longacres 16% track take, using equations (4.5) and (4.6), were then

$$\begin{aligned}\text{EX Place Prairie Breaker} &= 0.319 + 0.559\left(\frac{47{,}510/104{,}409}{16{,}655/59{,}752}\right)\\ &\quad + \left[2.22 - 1.29\left(\frac{47{,}510}{104{,}409}\right)\right](0.84 - 0.829)\\ &= 1.23 + 0.02\\ &= 1.25.\end{aligned}$$

$$\begin{aligned}\text{EX Show Prairie Breaker} &= 0.543 + 0.369\left(\frac{47{,}510/104{,}409}{11{,}950/43{,}936}\right)\\ &\quad + \left[3.60 - 2.13\left(\frac{47{,}510}{104{,}409}\right)\right](0.84 - 0.829)\\ &= 1.16 + 0.03\\ &= 1.19.\end{aligned}$$

Hence Prairie Breaker was a Dr. Z system bet to place, as well as to show.

Equations (5.4) and (5.5) suggested bets of \$155 to place and \$221 to show on Prairie Breaker:

$$\begin{aligned}\text{Place bet Prairie Breaker} &= \Bigg[505(0.4550) + 527(0.4550)^2 \\ &\quad - \left(\frac{386(0.4550)(16{,}655)}{(0.4550)(59{,}752) - (0.60)(16{,}655)}\right)\Bigg]\left(\frac{59{,}752 - 10{,}000}{140{,}000}\right) \\ &\quad + \Bigg[375(0.4550) + 525(0.4550)^2 \\ &\quad - \left(\frac{271(0.4550)(16{,}665)}{(0.4550)(59{,}752) - (0.70)(16{,}665)}\right)\Bigg]\left(\frac{150{,}000 - 59{,}752}{140{,}000}\right) \\ &= \$155.\end{aligned}$$

$$\begin{aligned}\text{Show bet Prairie Breaker} &= \Bigg[131 + 2{,}150(0.4550)^2 - 1{,}778(0.4550)^3 \\ &\quad - \left(\frac{150(11{,}950)}{(0.4550)(43{,}936) - (0.70)(11{,}950)}\right)\Bigg]\left(\frac{43{,}936 - 6{,}000}{94{,}000}\right) \\ &\quad + \Bigg[86 + 1{,}516(0.4550)^2 - 968(0.4550)^3 \\ &\quad - \left(\frac{90.7(11{,}950)}{(0.4550)(43{,}936) - (0.85)(11{,}950)}\right)\Bigg]\left(\frac{100{,}000 - 43{,}936}{94{,}000}\right) \\ &= \$221.\end{aligned}$$

However, these equations were developed assuming that there was only one bet to be made to place or show, but not both. When the two bets are on the same horse, the total amount recommended to be bet is too large and needs to be scaled down according to the following formulas:

$$\text{Optimal place bet} = \text{minimum}\left[\begin{array}{l}\text{place bet from equation (5.4)'} \\ 1.59\begin{pmatrix}\text{Place bet from} \\ \text{equation (5.4)}\end{pmatrix} - 0.639\begin{pmatrix}\text{show bet from} \\ \text{equation (5.5)}\end{pmatrix}\end{array}\right] \tag{6.1}$$

$$\text{Optimal show bet} = 0.907\begin{pmatrix}\text{show bet from} \\ \text{equation (5.5)}\end{pmatrix} - 0.134\begin{pmatrix}\text{place bet from} \\ \text{equation (5.4)}\end{pmatrix}$$

Hence

Optimal place bet
Prairie Breaker = minimum{\$155, 1.59(\$155) − 0.639(\$221)}

= minimum{\$155, \$105}

= \$105 and

Optimal show bet

Prairie Breaker = 0.907(\$221) − 0.134(\$155)

= \$179.

We made these bets on Prairie Breaker. When the horses were going into the starting gate, however, Junction Road acted up and it was decided to scratch him. The odds on Prairie Breaker then dropped to 3–5, and further betting was allowed for a few minutes. Track management likes to have refunded money due to a scratch bet on other horses so their take is not diminished. Fortunately for us, the expected value per dollar bet to place and show on Prairie Breaker remained high enough to qualify it as a Dr. Z system bet. When the race began, the final tote board was as follows:

	Totals	#3 Prairie Breaker	Expected Value per Dollar Bet on Prairie Breaker
Odds		3—5	
Win	134,897	63,997	
Place	77,600	25,622	1.14
Show	57,805	18,208	1.13

As Charlie Brown might have predicted, the 53–1 long shot, Red Baron Returns, stole the race from Prairie Breaker. Mythically took third. Our payoffs were outstanding, since Prairie Breaker paid a whopping \$3.40 to place and a substantial \$2.50 to show. The \$3.40 was more than the \$3.20 Prairie Breaker would have paid to win had he won. Since he was a Dr. Z system bet, the payoff was likely to be large. When the extreme long shot, Red Baron Returns, finished in place money, Prairie Breaker's return skyrocketed to the \$3.40. Mythically was reasonably heavily bet to show, so the show payoff on Prairie Breaker was lowered to the \$2.50. Our bets of \$105 to place and \$179 to show returned \$178.50 and \$223.75, respectively, for a profit of \$118.25. The chart of the race was as follows:

NINTH RACE
Lga
Aug. 14, 1983

1 3-16 MILES. (1:54). 46TH RUNNING OF THE LONGACRES DERBY. Purse, $100,000-added. 3-year-olds. By subscription of $150, which shall accompany the nomination, $500 to pass the entry box, $1,000 additional to start with $100,000-added, of which $20,000 to second, $15,000 to third, $10,000 to fourth and $3,000 to fifth. All nominations, entry and starting fees to the winner. High weights preferred. Closed Friday, July 15 with 44 nominations.

Value of race, $120,600. Value to winner, $72,600; second, $20,000; third, $15,000; fourth, $10.000; fifth, $3,000. Mutuel Pool, $270,302.

Last Raced	Horses	EqtAWt	PP	St	¼	½	¾	Str	Fin	Jockeys	Owners	Odds to $1
10Aug83 ^{8}Lga^{5}	Red Baron Returns	3 113	9	8	$8^{1\frac{1}{2}}$	$8^{1\frac{1}{2}}$	8^{h}	$5^{3\frac{1}{2}}$	$1^{2\frac{1}{2}}$	MillsJW	Vaughan Stable	53.10
31Jly 83 ^{9}Lga^{1}	Prairie Breaker	3 124	2	6	$4^{\frac{1}{2}}$	6^{4}	5^{2}	3^{h}	2^{4}	StevensG	Pietila-Estat ofWPtila	.75
31Jly 83 ^{9}Lga^{2}	Mythically	3 118	3	2	3^{1}	$3^{1\frac{1}{2}}$	3^{3}	1^{1}	3^{nk}	NicoloP	Mr-Mrs P J Whiting	3.95
7Aug83 ^{9}Pla^{4}	Allowance	3 106	1	3	5^{h}	$5^{\frac{1}{2}}$	7^{4}	7^{1}	$4^{1\frac{1}{2}}$	MitchellGV	Osborne Farms	45.45
31Jly 83 ^{9}Lga^{5}	Saber Ben	3 109	6	7	$7^{2\frac{1}{2}}$	7^{4}	6^{h}	8^{2}	5^{2}	FrazierB	Poor Four Stable	57.75
24Jly 83 ^{8}Hol^{6}	Lifaregal	3 117	5	5	6^{5}	4^{1}	4^{h}	4^{h}	6^{nk}	PedrozaMA	Selvin-Siegel-Wellmn	7.40
10Aug83 ^{8}Lga^{1}	Country Born	b3 111	4	1	$2^{1\frac{1}{2}}$	2^{3}	$2^{1\frac{1}{2}}$	6^{2}	7^{1}	JamesM	Loto Can, Inc	15.35
30Jly 83 ^{9}Lga^{5}	Heather Ala Roni	3 112	8	4	$1^{\frac{1}{2}}$	$1^{1\frac{1}{2}}$	1^{1}	2^{h}	$8^{2\frac{1}{2}}$	TaketaJ	H Dedomenico	47.85
3Jly 83 ^{9}Lga^{2}	Dynamo Doc	b3 115	7	9	9	9	9	9	9	SorensonD	RmrckStabl-E Bldsck	4.95

OFF AT 6:08. START GOOD. WON DRIVING. Time, :22⅘, :46⅗, 1:11, 1:37⅘, 1:47⅘. Track fast.

$2 Mutuel Prices				
	10—RED BARON RETURNS	108.20	20.60	6.00
	3—PRAIRIE BREAKER		3.40	2.50
	4—MYTHICALLY			2.90

Ch. c, by Mateor—T. V. Return, by Flying Lark. Trainer, Kay Vaughan. Bred by O'Harrow-Vaughan (Wash.).

RED BARON RETURNS, permitted to settle in stride early, gradually worked his way forward on the final turn, drove between horses in the upper stretch to run down the leaders with a rush and won going away. PRAIRIE BREAKER raced within striking distance early, was sent up along the outside going into the far turn, raced wide into the stretch and closed strongly in the final furlong. MYTHICALLY was forwardly placed from the beginning, ran down the leaders to take command briefly in the upper stretch but lacked the needed closing kick. ALLOWANCE saved ground while being outrun early, responded when settled for the drive and finished willingly. LIFAREGAL raced within striking distance early, but could not sustain his bid in the drive. COUNTRY BORN prompted the pace for six furlongs and gave way. HEATHER ALA RONI went to the front at once, saved ground while setting the pace and gave way in the drive. DYNAMO DOC was always outrun. **JUNCTION ROAD FLIPPED IN THE GATE AND WAS ORDERED SCRATCHED WITH ALL WAGERS ON HIM BEING REFUNDED.**

Overweight—Country Born, 1 pound; Heather Ala Roni, 2; Red Baron Returns, 3; Saber Ben, 1.
Scratched—Junction Road.

7

Using the Dr. Z System in Other Situations

We now turn to using the Dr. Z system when you are not at the track where the race is run. Usually the race is shown on closed-circuit TV monitors and there is local betting. However, as long as you have access to the win, place, and show mutuel pools, you can apply the Dr. Z system. We describe two such instances: piping in an important national race, such as the Kentucky Derby or the Belmont Stakes, which may go to fifty or more different racetracks; and viewing a whole card from a nearby racetrack in a theaterlike atmosphere, such as is done with New York State racing cards at the Teletrack facility in New Haven, Connecticut and at Inside Track in Manhattan.

THE BELMONT STAKES, JUNE 5, 1982: OTHER-TRACK BETTING AT GOLDEN GATE FIELDS, ALBANY, CALIFORNIA

The Belmont Stakes is the third and final jewel in the Triple Crown. In 1982, for the first time, betting on both the Preakness and the Belmont Stakes was allowed at several other tracks, including Golden Gate Fields in Albany, California, and Los Alamitos Race Course in Los Alamitos, California. Each of these tracks had separate betting pools and betting closed just before the actual race at the home track. The race was then viewed on closed-circuit television or on the infield screen if there was one. With separate betting pools, all the tracks paid different amounts to win, place, and show for the horses in the money. The idea of other-track betting is gaining popularity, and in the future we will probably see more and more such races.

The Belmont field included the highly touted Linkage, as well as the

Kentucky Derby and Preakness winners, Gato Del Sol and Aloma's Ruler. These three horses were all ridden by their regular jockeys, Bill Shoemaker, Eddie Delahoussaye, and Jack Kaenel, respectively. The other leading contender was Conquistador Cielo, who had impressive Eastern wins but was running on only four days' rest. His regular jockey, Eddie Maple, was unable to ride because of an injury and had been replaced by Laffit Pincay, Jr. Delahoussaye, Pincay, and Shoemaker flew in from California to ride the race. It is common for top jockeys such as these to fly across the country to ride in an important race. They usually return immediately to their home track so they miss only one day's races there.

The final tote board betting amounts at Golden Gate were:

	#1	#2	#3	#4	#5	#6
Odds	4—1	80—1	60—1	9—1	30—1	10—1
Win	28,027	1,717	2,371	13,755	4,234	13,303
Place	9,311	721	1,040	6,851	2,529	7,185
Show	5,034	703	962	2,931	1,729	3,356

	#7	#8	#9	#10	#11	Totals
Odds	8—5	20—1	40—1	8—1	7—2	
Win	56,629	5,917	3,565	15,759	30,301	175,578
Place	24,353	2,598	2,035	6,512	8,653	71,788
Show	11,491	1,639	1,339	3,051	3,658	35,893

A quick scan of the tote board pointed to a possible show bet on number 11, Conquistador Cielo. From equation (4.6), the expected return on a dollar bet to show was 1.24. For different wealth levels, the optimal bets were*

Wealth level	100	500	1,000	2,500	5,000	10,000
Optimal bet	5	25	38	76	99	145

Conquistador Cielo won the race by an impressive 14 lengths, breaking the track record at Belmont for $1\frac{1}{2}$ miles on an off track. He was followed by Gato Del Sol and Illuminate, who finished third.

The mutuel payoffs at Golden Gate were as follows:

*These bets were computed using the equations in Tables 16.3 and 16.4.

11	9.80	6.80	5.60
	1	6.60	4.60
		8	10.20

Compare these mutuel payoffs with those in the chart of the race at Belmont that follows:

Belmont Stakes

EIGHTH RACE
Belmont
JUNE 5, 1982

1 ½ MILES. (2.24) 114th Running THE BELMONT STAKES (Grade I). Purse $200,000 added. 3-year-olds. By subscription of $100 each to accompany the nomination; $1,000 to pass the entry box; $2,000 to start. A supplementary nomination of $5,000 may be made on Wednesday, June 2 with an additional $15,000 to start, with $200,000 added of which 60% to the winner, 22% to second, 12% to third and 6% to fourth. Colts and Geldings, 126 lbs. Fillies, 121 lbs. Starters to be named at the closing time of entries. The winning owner will be presented with the August Belmont Memorial Cup to be retained for one year, as well as a trophy for permanent possession and trophies will be presented to the winning trainer and jockey and mementoes to the grooms of the first four finishers. Closed Tuesday, February 16, 1982 with 332 nominations.
Value of race $266,200, value to winner $159,720, second $58,564, third $31,944, fourth $15,972. Mutuel pool $1,201,491, OTB pool $2,248,366.

Last Raced	Horse	Eqt.	A.	Wt	PP	¼	½	1	1¼	Str	Fin	Jockey	Odds $1
31May82 ^{8}Bel^{1}	Conquistador Cielo		3	126	11	$2^{\frac{1}{2}}$	$1^{1\frac{1}{2}}$	1^{hd}	1^{4}	1^{10}	1^{14}	Pincay L Jr	4.10
1May82 ^{8}CD^{1}	Gato Del Sol		3	126	1	$9^{1\frac{1}{2}}$	8^{3}	5^{1}	4^{2}	2^{1}	2^{4}	Delahoussaye E	6.40
23May82 ^{8}Bel^{3}	Illuminate		3	126	8	8^{hd}	11	8^{1}	$6^{1\frac{1}{2}}$	5^{4}	$3^{3\frac{3}{4}}$	Velasquez J	11.20
15May82 ^{8}Pim^{2}	Linkage		3	126	7	5^{2}	3^{1}	3^{5}	2^{hd}	$3^{\frac{1}{2}}$	$4^{\frac{1}{2}}$	Shoemaker W	2.20
15May82 ^{8}Key^{3}	High Ascent		3	126	3	$4^{1\frac{1}{2}}$	5^{4}	$2^{2\frac{1}{2}}$	3^{3}	4^{hd}	$5^{5\frac{3}{4}}$	Lovato F Jr	40.90
24May82 ^{7}Bel^{2}	Lejoli		3	126	9	11	9^{hd}	9^{4}	5^{hd}	6^{2}	$6^{1\frac{3}{4}}$	Samyn J L	23.80
24May82 ^{7}Bel^{1}	Estoril	b	3	126	6	$6^{\frac{1}{2}}$	$6^{1\frac{1}{2}}$	6^{3}	7^{3}	7^{8}	7^{13}	Fell J	9.20
28May82 ^{7}Bel^{1}	Royal Roberto	b	3	126	4	$10^{\frac{1}{2}}$	$10^{\frac{1}{2}}$	7^{2}	9^{10}	9^{12}	$8^{1\frac{1}{4}}$	Cordero A Jr	7.20
15May82 ^{8}Pim^{1}	Aioma's Ruler		3	126	10	$3^{1\frac{1}{2}}$	$4^{\frac{1}{2}}$	4^{hd}	8^{4}	8^{hd}	9^{13}	Kaenel J L	7.30
22May82 ^{1}Bel^{4}	Anemal		3	126	2	1^{1}	2^{3}	10^{10}	10^{16}	10	10	Martens G	44.10
15May82 ^{8}Pim^{3}	Cut Away	b	3	126	5	7^{3}	7^{3}	11	11	—	—	Bailey J D	25.70

Cut Away, Eased.

OFF AT 5:39, Start good, Won ridden out. Time, :23⅘, :47⅕, 1:12, 1:37⅘, 2:03⅕, 2:28⅕, Track sloppy.

$2 Mutuel Prices:				
	11–(K)–CONQUISTADOR CIELO	10.20	7.40	6.80
	1–(A)–GATO DEL SOL		8.00	6.40
	8–(H)–ILLUMINATE			6.40

B. c, by Mr Prospector—K D Princess, by Bold Commander. Trainer Stephens Woodford C. Bred by Iandoli L E (Fla).

CONQUISTADOR CIELO, very wide into the first turn, opened a clear advantage while racing well out in the track nearing the backstretch, continued wide while making the pace, responded readily when challenged by HIGH ASCENT, shook off that rival before going nine furlongs and drew off steadily under a hand ride. GATO DEL SOL, reserved early, moved up outside horses midway of the far turn, continued very wide into the stretch but was no match for the winner while besting the others. ILLUMINATE, badly outrun for a mile, saved ground into the stretch while rallying but lacked a further response. LINKAGE, never far back while under light restraint, rallied while racing well out in the track racing into the far turn, remained a factor to the stretch and gave way. HIGH ASCENT, well placed into the backstretch, made a run along the inside to engage CONQUISTADOR CIELO approaching the end of the backstretch, remained a factor until near the stretch but had nothing left. LEJOLI, badly outrun early, made up some ground approaching the stretch but lacked a further response. ESTORIL had no apparent excuse. ROYAL ROBERTO saved ground to no avail. ALOMA'S RULER, away alertly, was allowed to follow the leader into the backstretch and was finished at the far turn. ANEMAL, hustled to the front along the inside at the first turn, stopped badly. CUT AWAY wasn't able to keep up through the run down the backstretch and was eased during the late stages. LEJOLI raced with mud caulks.

Owners— 1, deKwiatkowski H; 2, Peters L J; 3, Humphrey G W Jr; 4, Christiana Stable; 5, Buckland Farm; 6, Peskoff S D; 7, Seeligson A A Jr; 8, Key West Stable; 9, Scherr N; 10, Pappas D J; 11, Allen H.

Trainers— 1, Stephens Woodford C; 2, Gregson Edwin; 3, Kay Michael; 4, Clark Henry S; 5, Campo John P; 6, Blusiewicz Leon; 7, Doyle A T; 8, Iselin James H; 9, Lenzini John J Jr; 10, Gullo Thomas J; 11, Jacobs Eugene.

Los Alamitos Race Course also had other-track betting on the Belmont Stakes. Their final tote board figures and payoffs help show the large differences in the public opinions in different locations.

At Los Alamitos they were as follows:

	#1	#2	#3	#4	#5	#6
Odds	5—2	99—1	99—1	11—1	40—1	8—1
Win	10,877	217	342	3,350	955	4,565
Place	4,340	116	140	1,701	438	2,507
Show	1,725	108	103	702	323	1,493

	#7	#8	#9	#10	#11	Totals
Odds	1—1	40—1	99—1	12—1	6—1	
Win	19,388	862	394	3,197	5,428	49,575
Place	7,238	263	221	1,362	1,986	20,312
Show	3,222	234	194	653	877	9,634

11	15.40	7.40	6.00
	1	4.40	4.00
		8	17.20

There was no Dr. Z system bet at Los Alamitos.

The efficient win-market hypothesis discussed in Chapter Three suggests that the win odds should have been approximately the same across all the tracks. The bettors at Belmont, however, had considerably more information than the bettors at the other tracks. They knew how the horses had been running, how the jockeys were doing, what the track conditions were, how the horses looked in the paddock and the parade to post, and so on. Therefore, we would expect (1) different odds at the different tracks and (2) the odds at Belmont to be the most accurate odds. Since the Belmont odds are the best estimate of each horse's winning probability, Dr. Z system bettors away from Belmont would actually prefer to use the Belmont Park win figures against their own track's place and show figures when looking for possible bets. This would be possible if Belmont's tote-board figures were displayed over the closed-circuit televisions. For example, if you were at Los Alamitos, the following Belmont Park win figures were displayed (these are the actual final tote-board figures for the on-track betting at Belmont Park, page 178.):

	#1	#2	#3	#4	#5	#6
Odds	6—1	70—1	60—1	12—1	40—1	10—1
Win	94,915	8,829	9,825	51,938	15,127	60,191
	#7	**#8**	**#9**	**#10**	**#11**	**Totals**
Odds	9—5	18—1	25—1	7—1	5—2	
Win	231,728	35,788	22,656	86,085	189,160	806,242

These figures indicate that the Belmont Park bettors had a higher opinion of Conquistador Cielo than the bettors at the other tracks. At Los Alamitos, you could scan these win figures and the place and show pools shown at your track. These would indicate a possible place and show bet on number 11, Conquistador Cielo. The values to isolate would then be:

	#11 Conquistador Cielo	Totals	
Win	189,160	806,242	from Belmont
Place	1,986	20,312	from Los Alamitos
Show	877	9,634	from Los Alamitos

The expected return on a place bet was then 1.70 and 1.56 on a show bet.

For different wealth levels the optimal bets were then

Wealth level	100	500	1,000	2,500	5,000
Optimal place bet	9	47	94	229	294
Optimal show bet	18	84	102	154	177

Note that Belmont had Conquistador Cielo at 5–2 odds, while Los Alamitos had him at 6–1, so it would seem there existed an overlay in the win pool, as well as for place and show, at Los Alamitos. Whether to make a win bet and how much to bet are beyond the scope of this book, but the attractiveness of the betting possibility should be apparent to the reader.*

*We have analyzed this problem. Readers with technical backgrounds might wish to refer to Hausch and Ziemba (1987).

THE CLOUT HANDICAP, AQUEDUCT, NOVEMBER 12, 1981: A VISIT TO TELETRACK, NEW HAVEN, CONNECTICUT

The Teletrack facility in New Haven, Connecticut, provides a new concept in horse-race observation and wagering. Since there are no racetracks in Connecticut and many in neighboring New York, it is natural for the races in New York to be used for Connecticut betting. The facility resembles a movie theater where the races are shown live. During the year, thoroughbred races from Aqueduct, Belmont, and Saratoga, and harness races from Roosevelt and Yonkers are featured. The odds, win, place, and show pools, as well as the projected features payoffs, are flashed on the screen as the betting proceeds. Although the Teletrack pools are separate from the track's pools, they also include the bets from about 180 off-track betting shops in Con-

START
1⅜ MILES
FINISH
Turf Course

SEVENTH RACE

PURSE $18,000

THE CLOUT

FOR THREE-YEAR-OLDS AND UPWARD WHICH HAVE NEVER WON TWO RACES OTHER THAN MAIDEN, CLAIMING OR STARTER. Three-year-olds, 120 lbs.; older, 122 lbs. Non-winners of a race other than maiden or claiming over a mile and a furlong since October 15 allowed 3 lbs.; of such a race since October 1, 5 lbs.

If the Stewards consider it inadvisable to run this race on the turf course it will be run on the main track at one mile and three furlongs.

ONE MILE AND THREE FURLONGS (Turf Course)
Track Record—2:14 1/5: FLUORESCENT LIGHT (4), 115 lbs.; November 7, 1978.

MAKE SELECTION BY NUMBER

	Owner / Trainer	Jockey/Morn. Line
1	WALTER HAEFNER — V. J. NICKERSON Blue and White Stripes, Blue Sleeves, White Chevrons, Blue Cap **IVANOFF (Ire.) 117** Ch.c.4, Connaught—True Rocket by Roan Rocket	**6-1** JEAN-LUC SAMYN
2	BROWN BADGETT — WAYNE MURTY Brown and Green Diamonds, Green Sleeves, Brown Hoop, Green Cap, Brown Visor **NATOMAS BREEZE *112** Ch.c.4, Secretariat—Spanish Breeze by Windy City 2nd	**4-1** RICHARD MIGLIORE
3	CALUMET FARM — J. M. VEITCH Devil's Red, Blue Collar, Two Blue Hoops on Sleeves, Blue Cap **COME RAIN OR SHINE 117** Ch.c.4, Nijinsky 2nd—Sign Of The Times by Francis S.	**3-1** ANGEL CORDERO, JR.
4	ARCHIE R. DONALDSON — K. E. JENSEN Maroon, Light Blue Ball, Blue Sleeves, Two Maroon Hoops, Maroon and Blue Cap **THE MESSANGER 117** Dk b or br c.4, Big Soruce—Taratan by Summer Tan	**6-1** LARRY SAUMELL
5	AUGUSTIN STABLES — J. E. SHEPPARD White and Green Halves, White Sleeves, Green Cap **STATE OF SIEGE 115** Ch.g.3, Damascus—Herbalesian by Herbager	**20-1** DARYL MONTOYA
6	CAESAR P. KIMMEL — J. J. TONER Orange, Black Cross Sashes, Black Diamonds on Sleeves, Orange and Black Cap **ON THE GRASS *112** Ch.c.4, Vaguely Noble—Bellevarde by Herbager	**15-1** Constantino Hernandez
7	SANTO LUCA — OWNER Red, Blue Diamond Hoop, Blue Diamonds on Sleeves, Red Cap, Blue Tassel **SANTO'S JOE 119** Gr.c.4, Northern Jove—Maria L. by Mystic 2nd	**5-1** EDDIE MAPLE
8	ARCADY STABLE — F. I. WRIGHT Kelly Green, Light Green Sash and "A," Kelly Green and Light Green Halved Sleeves, Light Green Cap **ICEBOX CAKE 112** Gr.f.3, Irecapade—Ore to Grow On by Lucky Debonair	**15-1** JEFFREY FELL
9	STEPHEN C. CLARK, JR. — S. WATTERS, JR. Yellow, Blue Braid, Sleeves and Cap **COUNTRY CORNER *112** B.g.4, One For All—Dance by Native Dancer	**10-1** VICTOR MOLINA
10	MRS. DION K. KERR — R. NIEMINSKI Light Blue, Green Sash, Green Hoop on Sleeves, Blue Cap **ERIN'S TIGER 115** Ch.c.3, Terrible Tiger—Irish Exchange by Swaps	**6-1** CASH ASMUSSEN

Change of Equipment: ICEBOX CAKE—Blinkers On.

SCRATCHED—DANGEROUS MISSION, LOTHIAN, KITCHEN COMMANDER, BEYOND RECALL, AIRBUS necticut. The total handle is small, averaging about $400,000 per day and reaching as high as $650,000 on Saturdays. The take at Teletrack was 17% plus 10¢ breakage, for a total commission of about 20%. The track take in New York was 14%. Except for the small pools and relatively high commission, the facility allows for easy adaptation of the Dr. Z system. The flashing pools let you stand near or even in a betting line, so a bet can be made very close to post time.

I was in the East giving lectures in the finance seminars at New York and Yale universities on efficient market ideas in horse-racing betting markets. I took the opportunity to visit Teletrack, which like Yale is in New Haven. That afternoon, November 12, 1981, races from Aqueduct were being featured.

Come Rain or Shine, number 3 in the seventh race, was a 3–1 morning-line favorite ridden by Angel Cordero, Jr., the leading jockey at Aqueduct, with an in-the-money percentage of 57%. He was a Dr. Z system bet throughout the betting period. With two minutes to post time the betting pools were

	Totals	#3 Come Rain or Shine
Odds		5—2
Win	10,463	2,313
Show	837	115

The expected value per dollar bet to show on Come Rain or Shine was thus 1.14, as may be calculated using equation (4.4). Since the show pools were so small, I decided to be cautious and make a flat bet of $20. The show pools of $115 and $837 were so small that one or two sizable bets would greatly affect the show odds. During the final betting, the win odds on Come Rain or Shine rose to 3–1. My bet and the others had lowered the expected value per dollar bet to show on Come Rain or Shine to 1.12. The final mutuels at Teletrack were:

	Totals	#3 Come Rain or Shine
Odds		3—1
Win	12,032	2,471
Show	1,312	174

3	8.00	3.80	3.40
2		3.20	2.60
4			7.00

Come Rain or Shine easily won the race and paid $3.40 to show. The final mutuels at Aqueduct were:

3–	Come Rain Or Shine.......	6.20	3.00	2.40
2–	Natomas Breeze		2.80	2.20
4–	The Messanger			5.80
$2 EXACTA	3–2 Paid $14.40			

Hence my $20 bet produced a profit of $14. Notice that these payoffs were different and that Come Rain or Shine was not a Dr. Z system bet to show at Aqueduct.

THE GROWTH OF INTERTRACK WAGERING

Teletrack opened in 1981 and intertrack wagering on the classic races began in 1982. These were the start of a tremendous growth in off-track and other-track wagering. Besides Teletrack, there is Inside Track, located in Manhattan on Second Avenue between Fifty-third and Fifty-fourth streets and numerous Nevada Sports books, including posh Caesar's Palace, on the strip in Las Vegas. The Palace Station in Las Vegas and other race books now routinely offer future book odds on the classic races, including the Breeders' Cup. Some bargains appear in these future book odds because the odds change daily and differ across race books. One must be careful though, as the average takes are very high.

An important advantage for players of the Dr. Z place and show system at Caesar's Palace and many of the other Las Vegas books is that the on-track place and show pools are shown on the TV monitors at least once just prior to some of the races from California. Normally these pools are not shown; however, for these races you not only have the pools flashed in front of you very near the end but your wagers do not influence the odds. Hence, you can wager larger amounts than the equations and tables in Chapters Five and Sixteen would indicate.

To determine the optimal Kelly wager in the simplest way, multiply the place or show pool values by 100. So for a show bet on horse i, multiply the show pool S and the show bet S_i by 100. (You do not need to multiply the win pool information.) Then the optimal bet formulas in Chapter Fifteen or the Beat the Racetrack calculator™ will give you the correct Kelly wager. For example, Is She Coming was the consensus best bet of the day at Golden Gate Fields on Tuesday, April 27, 1986. I was at Caesar's with a bankroll of $1,000. Is She Coming had been first or second in all three of her 1986 races, the last of which was at Golden Gate two weeks earlier. She had post position 1, a good rider in Russell Baze, and a fast track. At post time the mutuels were:

Odds	*Totals*	*#1 Is She Coming 4–5*	*Expected Value Per Dollar Bet*	*Optimal Wager If You Influence the Odds: One Bet at a Time*	*Optimal Wager If You Do Not Influence the Odds: One Bet at a Time*	*Optimal Wagers*
Win	49,313	21,820				
Place	35,350	10,740	1.16	190	262	170
Show	14,450	4,482	1.12	207	386	315

A cutoff of 1.10 meant Dr. Z bets to place and show on Is She Coming. Determining the suggested Kelly bet is complicated because there are bets to place and show and the wagers do not influence the odds. The values given for the optimal wagers were computed with the Beat the Racetrack calculator,(TM) which is very handy for such situations. Taken by themselves, the suggested wagers to place and show, if you were to influence the odds, are $190 and $207, respectively. When you do not influence the odds, the calculator suggests $262 and $386, respectively. These values are easily obtained with the formulas in Chapter Sixteen or with the calculator by multiplying the place and show mutuel values by 100; then your bet is small compared with these values. So you use 3,535,000 instead of 35,350 for the place pool.

When there are place and show bets on the same horse, equations (16.5) and (16.6) in Chapter Sixteen indicate what the optimal Kelly bets should be. In this case the suggested bets are: $170 to place and $315 to show for a total wager of $485. This is a further reminder of the huge wagers the Kelly criterion suggests for odds-on favorites with acceptable edges. I cut the actual bets to $100 to place and $200 to show because for such a large wager I preferred a fractional Kelly wager, especially with such a complicated betting situation.

Is She Coming won the race and paid $3.80 to win, $2.60 to place, and $2.60 to show. I made $90 on my wager. The mutuels were:

3.80	2.60	2.60
	4.00	2.80
		4.80

The scope of intertrack wagering is impressive. The 116 Off-Track Betting shops in New York City have per capita wagering of about $30 per day. On Belmont Stakes day in 1986, Inside Track had 195 paid admissions who wagered $135,976, or $697 per person, on the Belmont Stakes alone. The major appeal of Inside Track over the OTB shops is the absence of the additional 5% betting surcharge taken off all winning wagers. We strongly recommend that you never submit to such additional taxes. The usual track takes are high enough already. An additional 5% makes them prohibitive.

MULTIPLE TRACK BETTING ON THE CLASSIC RACES

The 43,157 spectators who watched the 1986 Belmont Stakes at Belmont Park wagered $7,049,282, or $163 per person. The classic was simulcast to 48 racetracks in the United States and Canada for an additional handle of $5,869,281. Because each racetrack had a separate pool, the payoffs were different at each track. In fact, they varied considerably: A $2 win wager on Danzig Connection paid $18 at Belmont Park, $4.80 at Prescott Downs in Arizona, and $32.60 at the Meadows Standardbred complex in Pennsylvania. Details for the 1986 Kentucky Derby are similar. A $2 win wager on Ferdinand paid as low as $13.20 and as high as $90; see the details in the chart on page 184.

In Hausch and Ziemba (February 1987), we have studied the problem of optimal wagering on these classic events. Our interest centers on how one might best exploit the differences in payoffs, both across pools and across tracks. We developed two models to solve this problem. Both are difficult to implement at the tracks because they require agents at the host track and each of the cross tracks who can relay odds information to a central decision-maker who, after analyzing all the information, relays back the amounts they should wager. We do, however, suggest a simpler scheme for one bettor at one track. More will be said about implementing the systems later.

The first model developed is based on the Kelly criterion. This model is more complicated than the model discussed in Chapter 5 since now we have possible place and show bets at all the tracks in addition to possible win bets at all the cross tracks. A second complication is determining the win probabilities. The efficiency studies of the win market have indicated that the public's win odds, adjusted for the favorite/long-shot bias, provide good estimates of these probabilities. However, when we consider cross-track wagering we not only have a different set of win odds for each participating track, but, as demonstrated by the Ferdinand example above, these odds can vary considerably. Rather than take a weighted average of all the tracks' odds to arrive at a set of win probabilities, it was decided to only use the home track's odds. This seemed reasonable since the public at the home track has an informational advantage over the bettors at the cross tracks. This advantage results from several factors:

1. Since stakes races are usually run near the end of the day's racing, the home track public has watched the jockeys in, perhaps, several races already; they have been able to observe the condition of the

Summary and Comparison of 1986 Kentucky Derby Simulcast

Organization	1986 Total Handle	1985 Total Handle	Increase (Decrease)	Percent	Win Price
Aqueduct	$1,946,146	*	–	–	$37.40
Arizona Downs		$205,948	–	–	
Arlington Park		(2)			
Assiniboia Downs	39,260	*	–	–	48.10
Atlantic City	(1)				
Balmoral	(2)				
Bay Meadows	(3)				
Blue Bonnets	(4)				
Blue Ribbon Downs	264,459	169,674	$94,785	55.9	40.60
Calder Race Course		562,453	–	–	
Canterbury Downs	402,494	*	–	–	34.60
Charles Town	136,551	136,290	261	0.2	47.60
Connaught Park	(4)				
Connecticut OTB	712,955	574,238	138,717	24.2	33.20
Darby Downs		143,589	–	–	
Delaware Park	168,416	235,821	(67,405)	(-28.6)	55.20
Edmonton	78,590	*	–	–	52.90
Elmira Raceway	13,105	*	–	–	53.10
Evangeline Downs	48,182	*	–	–	90.00
Exhibition Park	151,379	*	–	–	53.40
Fairmount Park	227,756	231,356	(3,600)	(-1.6)	39.80
Fairplex	93,106	*	–	–	13.20
Finger Lakes	41,507	*	–	–	37.40
Fort Erie	(4)				
Fresno (Valley Racing)	(3)	55,466	–		
Garden State	1,179,008	*	–	–	40.40
Golden Gate Fields	841,681	512,563	329,118	64.2	33.20
Hialeah Park	631,431	*		–	63.20
Hollywood Park	1,533,286	1,192,408	340,878	28.6	16.80
Jefferson Downs	144,700	112,378	32,322	28.8	57.20
La Mesa Park	23,244	22,354	890	4.0	38.20
Les Bois	41,815	*	–	–	45.20
Longacres	293,873	398,850	(104,977)	(-26.3)	41.20
Louisiana Downs	600,221	549,234	50,987	9.3	50.40
Maywood Park	(2)	(2)			
Monmouth Park	(1)				
New York OTB	6,158,475	6,569,478	(411,003)	(-6.3)	26.20
Penn National	154,011	127,553	26,458	20.7	39.60
Pimlico	602,475	478,184	124,291	26.0	34.60
Playfair	58,802	65,962	(7,160)	(-10.9)	52.80
Regina Exhibition	14,383	*	–	–	31.50
River Downs	377,461	251,980	125,481	49.8	36.80
Rockingham Park		153,856	–	–	
Sacramento	(3)				
San Juan Downs	16,959	16,584	375	2.3	45.60
Santa Cruz	21,122	19,878	1,244	6.3	17.80
Santa Fe Downs	58,073	77,186	(19,113)	(-24.8)	40.20
Santa Rosa	(3)				
Saratoga Raceway	(5)				
Sportsman's Park	1,098,798	975,176	123,622	12.7	34.60
Stampede Park	83,832	*	–	–	56.80
Stockton	(3)				
Suffolk Downs	348,305	212,363	135,942	64.0	31.20
Sunland Park	73,834	71,461	2,373	3.3	34.80

The Meadowlands	(1)				
Thistledown	343,435	266,184	77,251	29.0	58.80
Turf Paradise	260,960	•	–	–	43.60
Waterford Park	58,644	51,215	7,429	14.5	54.20
Woodbine	399,614	•	–	–	79.60
Yakima Valley	33,990	34,873	(883)	(-2.5)	45.20
Yonkers Raceway	(5)				
Total Off-Track	$19,776,332	$14,474,555	$5,301,777	36.6%	
Total Wagered On Track	$ 6,165,119	$ 5,770,074	$ 395,045	6.8%	
Total Wagered On Derby	$25,941,451	$20,244,629	$5,696,822	28.1%	
Number Of Off-Track Participants	56	32			

(1) Included in Garden State's handle (intertrack wagering).
(2) Included in Sportsman's Park handle (intertrack wagering).
(3) Included in Golden Gate's handle (intertrack wagering).
(4) Included in Woodbine's handle (intertrack wagering).
(5) Included in Aqueduct's handle (intertrack wagering).
• Did not participate in 198[illegible].

track and possibly note any track biases, and they have seen the horses in the paddock and in the parade-to-post.

2. The home crowd also has a better sense of whether or not their track tends to favor front-runners, late chargers, those on the rail, etc.
3. Since the home track is usually a larger track that has many major races, the home public may have had first-hand experience watching some of these horses race earlier in the season.

Thus, the hope is that the efficiency of the win market is maintained at the home track despite that not necessarily being the case at the cross tracks.

Table 5.2 showed that it was not necessary to correct for the favorite/long-shot bias when using the Harville formulas to calculate expected return to place and to show. This was because there was a reverse favorite/long-shot bias for the probability a horse will finish second or third. These two biases cancel when calculating the probability of placing or showing. If we take the home track's win market as efficient, then our models can include possible win betting at the cross tracks. This possibility of betting to win means we need unbiased win probabilities and, therefore, we must now use Table 3.5 to correct for the favorite/long-shot bias. Despite these complications, this first model has all of the advantages of the Kelly criterion. For example, it maximizes the long-run rate of growth of the investor's profit.

Our second model is a *risk-free* hedging or *arbitrage* model. The idea is to make the bets so that no matter which horses finish in the money you cannot lose. One cannot really guarantee this in any real betting application because the bets would have to be placed prior to post time and payoffs might subsequently change. However, it can be close to a perfect hedge. This approach is very similar to so-called programmed trading on futures and cash values in stock market indices such as the S&P 500. When the futures prices get high, one sells the futures and buys the stocks and vice versa when the futures prices are too low. One can, more or less, lock in "guaranteed profits." Although the percentage gain is small, big players make millions from these trades.

To see the results of these models on an example, let's look at the 1982 Preakness Stakes. The card had seven horses:

Horse	*Finish*
1. Reinvested	
2. Cut Away	3rd
3. Water Bank	
4. Bold Style	
5. Laser Light	
6. Linkage	2nd
7. Aloma's Ruler	1st

The 3–5 favorite, Linkage, failed to win, but he was a dynamite Dr. Z system bet to show at Pimlico in Maryland, paying $2.60. The place bet was also good and paid $2.60, as shown in the following chart:

EIGHTH RACE
Pimlico
MAY 15, 1982

1 $\frac{3}{16}$ MILES. (1.54) 107th Running PREAKNESS STAKES (Grade I). $200,000 Added. 3-year-olds. By subscription of $100 each this fee to accompany the nomination, $2,500 to pass the entry box, starters to pay $2,500 additional. All eligiblity, entrance and starting fees to the winner, with $200,000 added of which $40,000 to second, $20,000 to third and $10,000 to fourth. Weight, 126 lbs. Starters to be named through the entry box Thursday, May 13, two days before the race by the usual time of closing. The Preakness field will be limited to fourteen entries. A replica of the Woodlawn Vase will be presented to the winning owner to remain his or her personal property. Closed Tuesday, February 16, 1982 with 324 nominations. One supplemental Nominee: Reinvested. Value of race $279,900, value to winner $209,900, second $40,000, third $20,000, fourth $10,000. Mutuel pool $864,360. Exacta Pool $392,864.

Last Raced	Horse	Eqt	A.	Wt	PP	St	¼	½	¾	Str	Fin	Jockey	Odds $1
8May82 8Aqu1	Aloma's Ruler		3	126	7	1	1^1	1^1	1^1	$1^{1½}$	$1^{½}$	Kaenel J L	6.90
22Apr82 7Kee1	Linkage		3	126	6	2	4^1	$3^{½}$	3^{hd}	2^6	$2^{6¾}$	Shoemaker W	.50
1May82 7CD1	Cut Away	b	3	126	2	3	$3^{½}$	$4^{1½}$	$4^{½}$	6^5	3^2	Bailey J D	41.60
1May82 8CD16	Bold Style	b	3	126	4	5	$2^{½}$	$2^{½}$	2^1	$3^{½}$	4^2	Moyers L	26.20
1May82 8CD2	Laser Light		3	126	5	7	7	7	$5^{1½}$	5^{hd}	5no	Maple E	5.30
1May82 8CD3	(S)Reinvested		3	126	1	4	$5^{½}$	$5^{½}$	7	4^{hd}	6^4	MacBeth D	7.60
1May82 8CD4	Water Bank		3	126	3	6	6^4	6^2	$6^{½}$	7	7	Castaneda M	12.00

(S) Supplementary nomination. OFF AT 5:41. Start good, Won driving. Time, :23⅘, :48, 1:12, 1:36⅘, 1:55⅖ Track fast.

$2 Mutuel Prices:			
7-(G)-ALOMA'S RULER	15.80	4.60	3.60
6-(F)-LINKAGE		2.60	2.60
2-(B)-CUT AWAY			6.00

$2 EXACTA 7-6 PAID $30.40.

Dk. b. or br. c, by Iron Ruler—Aloma, by Native Charger. Trainer Lenzini John J Jr. Bred by Silk Willoughby Farm (Fla).

ALOMA'S RULER broke in stride and was quickly angled to the rail, taken in hand and relaxed nicely while setting the pace. He turned back BOLD STYLE entering the far turn and accelerated to increase his advantage under light rousing approaching the stretch. ALOMA'S RULER then continued resolutely in response to alternate right and left handed whipping to determinedly hold off LINKAGE. LINKAGE, reserved snugly outside, was always within striking distance. He responded willingly when set down entering the stretch and closed steadily in a game effort. CUT AWAY, rated along the rail, eased out between horses at the top of the stretch, split foes near the eighth pole and finished willingly. BOLD STYLE broke sluggishly and slightly in the air was rushed to prompt the early pace outside ALOMA'S RULER, was sent up to challenge entering the far turn and fell back. LASER LIGHT circled wide to reach contention midway around the far turn and weakened in the drive while bumping repeatedly with REINVESTED. REINVESTED, in hand behind horses to the far turn, swung outside entering the stretch and bumped with LASER LIGHT the final sixteenth. WATER BANK was not a factor.

Owners— 1, Scherr N; 2, Christiana Stable; 3, Allen H; 4, Mayer L; 5, Live Oak Plantation; 6, Harbor View Farm; 7, Elmendorf.

Trainers— 1, Lenzini John J Jr; 2, Clark Henry S; 3, Jacobs Eugene; 4, Van Berg Jack C; 5, Kelly Patrick J; 6, Hough Stanley M; 7, McAnally Ronald.

Scratched—Cupecoy's Joy (1May82 8CD10).

These bets were even better at Los Alamitos in California. There, Linkage paid $3.20 to place and $2.80 to show. The win, place, and show payoffs at Pimlico and Los Alamitos, as well as at Centennial in Colorado, Golden Gate in California, and Penn National in Pennsylvania, were (the best payoffs to win, place, and show are circled and were at different tracks):

Centennial

	W	P	S
7	23.60	(7.00)	(5.40)
	6	2.60	2.20
		2	6.60

Los Alamitos

	W	P	S
7	(24.40)	6.00	3.80
	6	(3.20)	(2.80)
		2	6.00

Pimlico

	W	P	S
7	15.80	4.60	3.60
	6	2.60	2.60
		2	6.00

Penn National

	W	P	S
7	15.40	4.60	3.80
	6	2.60	2.40
		2	(7.40)

Golden Gate

	W	P	S
7	20.40	5.60	4.60
	6	2.80	2.60
		2	6.00

Using Pimlico's win odds, adjusted for the favorite/long-shot bias, to determine win probabilities, together with the Harville formulas, we can calculate the chance that each horse will win and the expected return per dollar bet to win, place, and show. For Golden Gate, Centennial, Los Alamitos, and Penn National we have:

		Cut Away				*Linkage*	*Aloma's Ruler*
Number	1	2	3	4	5	6	7
Finish		3				2	1
Win Probability	.090	0.11	.056	.023	.125	.597	.098

Expected Return on a $1 Bet to Win

Golden Gate	.837	.246	.437	.708	.788	.955	1.000
Centennial	.900	.389	.370	.570	.825	.836	(1.147)
Los Alamitos	.666	.391	.347	.777	.713	1.015	(1.196)
Penn National	.954	.484	.588	(1.109)	.650	.896	.755

Expected Return on a $1 Bet to Place

Golden Gate	.749	.193	.349	.582	.669	(1.149)	.880
Centennial	.769	.238	.260	.329	.719	1.084	(1.120)
Los Alamitos	.794	.233	.277	.556	.778	(1.336)	.888
Penn National	.673	.399	.391	.737	.586	(1.101)	.731

Expected Return on a $1 Bet to Show

Golden Gate	.837	.181	.405	.413	.817	(1.153)	.996
Centennial	.747	.197	.340	.252	.803	1.008	(1.138)
Los Alamitos	.890	.200	.392	.341	(1.180)	(1.293)	.873
Penn National	.710	.235	.451	.388	.769	1.099	.793

The circled bets look most promising and satisfy our minimum edge of 10%. When you run the Kelly criterion optimal model on a computer with a $2,500 bankroll, you wind up with eight suggested bets totaling $2,437. Five of these bets won and returned $3,716.90 for a profit of $1,279.90:

Horse	*Bet*	*Track*	*Exp. Return*	*Bet*	*Payoff*	*Return*
4	Win	P.N.	1.109	$14	—	—
7	Win	L.A.	1.196	40	24.00	480.00
6	Place	L.A.	1.336	855	3.00	1,282.50
7	Place	Cen.	1.120	46	6.60	151.80
5	Show	L.A.	1.180	172	—	—
6	Show	G.G.	1.153	571	2.60	742.30
6	Show	L.A.	1.293	656	2.60	852.80
7	Show	Cen.	1.138	83	5.00	207.50
				$2,437		$3,716.90
					Profit =	$1,279.90

The returns calculated above include our bettor's effect on the odds. For instance, Aloma's Ruler paid $24.40 to win at Los Alamitos. Were our bettor to have wagered the suggested $40, the payoff would have dropped to $24.00. Notice that the expected return to win on #7 exceeded 1.10 at both Centennial and Los Alamitos but the only bet was at Los Alamitos. This was because the bet at Los Alamitos was better, 1.196 versus 1.147 at Centennial. The $40 bet at Los Alamitos lowered the expected return below 1.196, but, presumably, it did not fall below 1.147. This also happened with the place bets on #6; a wager of $855 was made at Los Alamitos with its expected return of 1.336, while zero was wagered at Golden Gate with its expected return of 1.149. However, there are show bets at two tracks on #6 even though the 1.293 expected return at Los Alamitos exceeds the 1.153 expected return at Golden Gate. This is because these quoted expected returns are on the first dollar wagered. When one wagers $656 to show on #6 at Los Alamitos, the expected return on further dollars is below 1.153. Therefore the optimal strategy was to not wager more at Los Alamitos but to make a wager at Golden Gate.

So the Kelly criterion model did very well. We also did similar calculations on the 1983–1985 Preakness, the 1982–1985 Belmont, and the 1984–1985 Kentucky Derby, having been able to collect the final mutuel figures for from two to nine cross tracks on each race. Assuming an initial wealth of $2,500 for each race, the Kelly criterion model had the following results:

Race	*Horses in Race*	*Tracks*	*Wagers*	*Total Wagers*	*Wagers Won*	*Return*	*Profit*
Preakness 82	7	4	8	$ 2,437	6	$ 3,716.90	$1,279.90
Preakness 83	11	8	13	1,949	1	1,647.30	−301.70
Preakness 84	10	3	8	2,282	0	0.00	−2,282.00
Preakness 85	11	6	11	1,817	4	2,014.40	197.40
Belmont 82	11	4	20	942	5	1,880.40	938.40
Belmont 83	12	7	20	2,452	6	2,578.80	126.80
Belmont 84	11	2	3	1,371	1	2,331.00	960.00
Belmont 85	9	9	15	471	1	78.30	−392.70
K. Derby 84	12	6	13	2,027	5	3,027.20	1,000.20
K. Derby 85	12	6	7	1,973	3	3,094.50	1,121.50
Totals			118	$17,721	32	$20,368.80	$2,647.80

Although there were losses on three races (including a huge loss on the 1984 Preakness when Swale finished out of the money) the experiment had a total profit of $2,647.80. This is an 14.9% return on money wagered and an average return per race of $265. While the average profit is positive, the results are based on only ten races and there is considerable variation in the races' profits. The standard error of the mean is $342 and, therefore, no statistically significant statements can be made about positive profits on the basis of these results. While more evidence is clearly needed, the results do certainly suggest that the scheme has potential.

There are many difficulties associated with implementing the capital-growth model, not the least of them being communicating all the tote-board information from each track to a central decision-maker. Even then, the optimization problem must be solved, the bets must be reported to the agents, and the agents must make the wagers. All of this takes time, and the odds may change in the last few minutes of betting. Chapter 9 studies the odds changes in the last two minutes of betting and finds that expected returns change somewhat but profitable bets two minutes from the end tend to remain profitable based on final odds. However, that study was for the case of one track. The cross-track scheme requires more than two minutes to execute and, therefore, our results are likely an overestimate of the possible profits. There are, however, simpler versions of this scheme possible for one bettor at one track. If the stakes race is televised, then our bettor, with a portable television at a cross track, can view the home odds when they are shown on television. With these odds giving "true" win probabilities, our bettor can search for overlays at the cross track.* Our bettor could simply bet a flat amount to win on horses going off at longer odds than at the home track or he could be as sophisticated as to bring a portable computer to the track as well as the TV and run the capital-growth model for one track. This latter scheme will be tested here with the Triple Crown race data.

As an example, consider the 1984 Kentucky Derby simulcast at Golden Gate Fields in Albany, California. Golden Gate had six wagers with expected returns exceeding 1.10. Assuming an initial wealth of $2,500, the capital-growth model gives the following optimal wagers:

Wager Type	*Horse*	*Expected Return*	*Optimal Bet*	*Payoff on a $2 Bet*	*Realized Return*
Win	2	1.236	$ 15	—	—
Win	10	1.159	—	$11.20	—
Place	2	1.153	—	—	—
Place	10	1.410	249	7.40	$ 921.30
Show	2	1.353	261	—	—
Show	10	1.275	295	5.00	737.50
Totals			$820		$1,658.80
				Profit =	$838.80

This portfolio has four wagers totaling $820. Note that the win bet on #10 and the place bet on #2 are zero even though they have expected returns exceeding 1.10. This is because the possibility of #2, the entry of Vanlan-

*We wish to thank Victor Lespinasse for suggesting this one-track model. It is a scheme he currently employs.

dingham and Pine Circle, doing well in the race is better accounted for with the higher returning win and show bets on them. Also, the possibility of #10, Swale, doing well is better accounted for with the higher returning place and show bets on him. Swale did win the 1984 Derby, followed by Coax Me Chad and At The Threshold for a 10-12-9 finish. Therefore the only bets that could be cashed were the place and show bets on Swale for a return of $1,658.80 and a profit of $838.80.

This one-track capital-growth model was applied to all the tracks with the following results.

Race	*Number of Cross Tracks*	*Average Wager at Each Cross Track*	*Average Realized Return at Each Cross Track*	*Average Profit at Each Cross Track*
Preakness 82	4	$1,173.25	$1,724.80	$551.55
Preakness 83	8	909.25	353.79	−555.46
Preakness 84	3	868.67	0.00	−868.67
Preakness 85	6	799.67	789.37	−10.30
Belmont 82	4	407.25	639.02	231.78
Belmont 83	7	532.71	488.63	−44.08
Belmont 84	2	1,158.00	1,982.10	824.10
Belmont 85	9	78.33	7.80	−70.53
Kentucky Derby 84	6	520.67	884.92	364.25
Kentucky Derby 85	6	1,161.33	1,438.42	277.08
Average	5.5	$ 760.91	$ 830.88	$ 69.97

The average wagers on a race varied from $78.33 to $1,173.25, and the average profits varied from −$868.67 to $824.10. The average of these ten average wagers was $760.91, and the average of these ten average profits was $69.97, or 9.2% on the money wagered. Again, there is such variability in the profits that no statistically significant statements can be made about positive profits on average.

While the results of the capital-growth model look promising, there is not enough evidence to claim that the cross-track market is inefficient, i.e., expected profits are positive. However, it turns out another procedure can very simply demonstrate that it is inefficient. If we can develop risk-free hedges, then, clearly, there are inefficiencies that can be exploited. Our risk-free-hedging model asks, what is the minimum amount that can be wagered to win to assure a return of $1? If this amount is less than $1, then we have found a risk-free hedge. With the opportunity of betting at only one track, the answer to this question is 1/Q dollars, where Q is the track's payback proportion. Since Q is less than one, then 1/Q is an amount greater than $1. With the opportunity of betting at several tracks, each with a different set of odds, we may be able to lower this minimum amount to below $1. Clearly, we will bet on each horse at the track that gives it the longest odds.

To see how this system works, consider the 1983 Preakness. The final win odds were collected from eleven tracks that allowed wagering on this race. The highest of the eleven win payoffs on horse 1, the entry of Deputed Testamony and Parfait, was $58.80 at Louisiana Downs. Thus, a win bet of $0.0340 there would have returned $1 when, in fact, Deputed Testamony won the race. This bet and the bets on the remainder of the horses are:

Horse	*Highest Payoff on a $2 Win Bet*	*Track*	*Wager That Will Return $1*
1	$ 58.80	Louisiana Downs	$0.0340
2	25.40	Louisiana Downs	0.0787
3	69.20	Los Alamitos	0.0289
4	339.80	Hollywood	0.0059
5	113.80	Louisiana Downs	0.0176
6	11.40	Louisiana Downs	0.1754
7	21.20	Pimlico	0.0943
8	153.20	Louisiana Downs	0.0131
9	232.20	Hollywood	0.0086
10	4.40	Los Alamitos	0.4545
11	81.20	Los Alamitos	0.0246
		Total =	$0.9356

Thus, by wagering $0.9356, our bettor is guaranteed $1 regardless of who wins the race. This is a certain profit of $0.0646 per $0.9356 wagered, or a guaranteed 6.9% rate of return in a two-minute race.

Obviously, risk-free hedging is, in practice, not possible. Like the capital-growth system, track odds need to be sent to a central decision-maker several minutes before the end of betting, and during that time the odds can change. The system does, however, demonstrate the large discrepancies in betting across the tracks and shows how simple it can be to take advantage of them. The system was applied to the data from other Triple Crown races with the following results:

Race	*# Horses in Race*	*# Tracks*	*Profit*	
Preakness 82	7	5	− 3.3%	(0%)
Preakness 83	11	11	6.9%	
Preakness 84	10	4	− 4.8%	(0%)
Preakness 85	11	7	2.5%	
Belmont 82	11	5	13.6%	
Belmont 83	12	9	8.5%	
Belmont 84	11	2	−11.3%	(0%)
Belmont 85	9	11	5.0%	
Kentucky Derby 84	12	7	0.1%	
Kentucky Derby 85	12	6	10.1%	
		Average =	4.7%	

Three of the races did not have enough variance in the win odds across the tracks to allow a risk-free profit. This is not surprising for the 1984 Belmont because we had data from only two tracks. Also, the results for the 1982 and 1984 Preakness are based on only five and four tracks, respectively. In these three races, our bettor would obviously make no wagers with this system, for a 0% return. In the other seven races, risk-free profits were attainable, for an average risk-free profit of 4.7% over the ten races. Since this approach involves little risk, it has less profit potential than the Kelly model approach. The 4.7% profit rate may seem slight, but it is guaranteed (except for changes in the odds in the final few minutes) and is really quite impressive for a two-minute investment! Also, it does demonstrate that the win market with cross-track wagering is not efficient. With place and show bets, the risk-free hedging results might be improved. Among other things, one would not have to bet every horse to win. However, each horse must have some money on it to win, place, or show.

Our exercise indicates that cross-track betting provides one more possible edge for the horse player. Doing calculations like those we did to get optimal wagers is cumbersome, and the data necessary to implement it may involve possible legal problems. Still we find that optimizing over four to nine tracks yields nice profits. With the growth in cross-track betting, as many as fifty or more tracks allow such wagering on major events such as the Triple Crown races. And this includes a large number of tracks geographically very close, such as in California. Obviously, one thing to watch for is high prices on horses not popular or familiar in your betting locale. A good example was the 1983 Arlington Million. See the chart on page 68. It offered an excellent Dr. Z bet on John Henry, paying $4.80 for a 7–5 shot. The invader Tolomeo, at 38–1, won and combined with John Henry for a $439 exacta. In England, Tolomeo was 4–1 to win. At Louisiana Downs the $3 exacta paid more than $6,000. Obviously, there were some cross-track betting possibilities there.

8

A Great Race: John Henry versus Lemhi Gold in the Oak Tree Invitational at Santa Anita, October 31, 1982

THE FIELD

It was a classic matchup: John Henry versus Lemhi Gold. John Henry had won the Oak Tree the previous two years enroute to garnering horse-of-the-year honors in 1981. The future of the seven-year-old gelding was clouded because a minor ankle injury had kept him on the sidelines for most of the 1982 season. Running recently at Santa Anita in the Burke Handicap as a warmup, he had managed a credible race, but finished fourth, out of the money. He was the sentimental favorite of the record 55,031 fans, yet the fact that he had won only one of his last four races, and that on a disqualification, tempered their enthusiasm. He had his usual jockey, the great Bill Shoemaker. Was he ready? Lemhi Gold, on the other hand, was coming extraordinarily sharp after demolishing the best horses on the East Coast in the Marlboro Cup and the Jockey Cup Gold Cup at Belmont. He was also returning to the scene of one of his greatest triumphs, his victory over Perrault in the San Juan Capistrano Invitational in April (see pages xxx–xxx for a discussion of this race). Chris McCarron, who rode Lemhi Gold in the Capistrano, was in the irons again for the Oak Tree. A convincing win would likely give the four-year-old horse-of-the-year honors for 1982.

As was to be expected, the betting was heavy, especially on the two top choices but also on other strong horses in the field, such as Pelerin and Craelius. There were outstanding Dr. Z system bets to place and show on John Henry. The discussion of these bets focuses on the evolution of the odds, betting pools, and the expected value of various bets as post time approached. It is in this fashion that we suggest you approach the Dr. Z system, always watching the board from about six minutes to post time until you actually bet with about a minute or two to go. Your task is to watch the board and let the expert handicappers establish the win odds.

As we discussed in Chapter Three, on average, these odds closely represent the true probability of each horse's winning. So you need not worry whether Lemhi Gold or John Henry is the better horse. You are simply looking for a good bet. The discussion of this race also gives us a good opportunity to consider three important aspects of the mutuel payoffs: (1) how the payoffs are calculated, (2) the effect on these payoffs of which horses finish in the money, and (3) the effect on these payoffs of breakage.

TURF COURSE 1½ MILES

EXACTA RACE

EIGHTH RACE

THE OAK TREE
$300,000

For three-year-olds and upward. By Invitation, with no nomination or starting fees. The winner to receive $180,000, with $60,000 to second, $36,000 to third, 18,000 to fourth and $6,000 to fifth. Three-year-olds, 122 lbs.; older, 126 lbs. A trophy will be presented to the owner of the winner.

OAK TREE RECORD—CZAR ALEXANDER (Cordero) 1969 2:23⅗

Course Record—FIDDLE ISLE (5) 124 March 21, 1970 2:23

MAKE SELECTIONS BY NUMBER — OWNER — TRAINER — PROBABLE ODDS — JOCKEY

1 Doherty & Snowden — Charles Whittingham — 4
Black, green sash, sleeves and cap
PELERIN (Fr) 126 — Laffit Pincay, Jr.
B.h. '77, Sir Gaylord—Padrona, by St. Paddy
Breeder—Sir Philip Oppenheimer (France)

2 Mrs. Howard B. Keck — Charles Whittingham — 8
Blue, coral pink hoop, sleeves and cap
CRAELIUS 122 — Ray Sibille
B.c. '79, Avatar—Nas-Mahal, by Nasrullah
Breeder—Howard B. Keck (Kentucky)

3 Naji Nahas — Jean-Pierre Dupuis — 30
Red, royal blue sleeves, red and blue cap
BUCHANETTE 119 — Alain Lequeux
B.f. '79, Youth—Duke's Little Gal
Breeder—Nelson B. Hunt (Kentucky)

4 Aaron U. Jones — L. S. Barrera — 6/5
White, red cross sashes, red bar on sleeves, white and red cap
LEMHI GOLD 126 — Chris McCarron
Ch.c. '78, Vaguely Noble—Belle Marie
Breeder—Owner (Kentucky)

5 Walter Harris — Eldon Hall — 30
Yellow, black stripes, yellow and black "HHH" on white ball on back, yelow cap
REGALBERTO 126 — Fernando Toro
B.c. '78, Roberto—Every Evening, by Roi Dagobert
Breeder—Red Oak Farm (Florida)

6 Dotsam Stable — Ronald McAnally — 7/5
Brown, blue hoop, blue bar on sleeves, brown and blue cap
JOHN HENRY 126 — William Shoemaker
B.g. '75, Ole Bob Bowers—Once Double
Breeder—Golden Chance Farm, Inc. (Kentucky)

7 C. L. Hirsch — Warren Stute — 30
Black, gold diamonds on sleeves, gold cap
MAIPON (Chi) 126 — Marco Castaneda
Ch.h. '77, Tantoul—Doninda, by Cardinal 2nd
Breeder—Haras Dadinco (Chile)

JOCKEY STANDINGS
(Through Saturday, October 30, 1982)

Jockey	Mts.	1st	2nd	3rd	Win Pct.	In Money Pct.
Laffit Pincay, Jr.	156	31	21	22	19.8	47.4
Patrick Valenzuela	147	26	22	15	17.7	42.9
Sandy Hawley	130	22	22	14	16.9	44.6
Ray Sibille	160	21	12	20	13.1	33.1
Chris McCarron	116	20	16	17	17.2	45.7
Eddie Delahoussaye	126	17	14	20	13.5	40.5
Kenny Black	102	17	7	14	16.7	37.3
Terry Lipham	95	12	6	7	12.6	26.3
Darrel McHargue	89	10	11	3	11.2	27.0
Marco Castaneda	128	6	15	12	4.7	25.8
William Shoemaker	75	6	12	12	8.0	40.0
Donald Pierce	53	6	6	4	11.3	30.2

Experts' Selections

Consensus Points: 5 for 1st (today's best 7), 2 for 2nd, 1 for 3rd. Today's Best in Bold Type.

Trackman, Warren Williams **SANTA ANITA PARK** Selections Made for Fast Track

	TRACKMAN	HANDICAP	ANALYST	HERMIS	SWEEP	CONSENSUS	
8	JOHN HENRY	JOHN HENRY	LEMHI GOLD	JOHN HENRY	LEMHI GOLD	JOHN HENRY	19
	LEMHI GOLD	LEMHI GOLD	JOHN HENRY	LEMHI GOLD	JOHN HENRY	LEMHI GOLD	16
	CRAELIUS	CRAELIUS	CRAELIUS	MAIPON	PELERIN	CRAELIUS	3

ANALYST'S *Santa Anita Comment*

EIGHTH RACE

1—Lemhi Gold
2—John Henry
3—Craelius

LEMHI GOLD returns home after a very successful Eastern invasion where he accounted for several prestigious races in New York and is in line for Horse of the Year honors, but not until he gets past last year's top horse, JOHN HENRY. These two warriors engage in their first meeting and it could result in one of the best features of the season. LEMHI GOLD has developed by leaps and bounds during the fall and must be given the edge over the comebacking JOHN HENRY. The latter had his outing in the Burke, a race he obviously needed and, had to give chunks of weight away to his rivals. He's much better prepared today. CRAELIUS is coming to around very nicely now, running second in the Burke, and had a :59 2/5 work Thursday. PELERIN can't be discounted off one dull effort.

8th Santa Anita

1½ MILES. (TURF). (2.23) 14th Running of THE OAK TREE INVITATIONAL (Grade I). Purse $300,000. (Weight for age). 3-year-olds and upward. By invitation, with no nomination or starter fees. The winner to receive $180,000, with $60,000 to second, $36,000 to third, $18,000 to fourth and $6,000 to fifth. Weights, 3-year-olds, 122 lbs.; older, 126 lbs. The Oak Tree Racing Association will invite a representative field of horses to compete. The field will be drawn by the closing time of entries. A trophy will be presented to the owner of the winner. Invitations Thursday, October 21, 1982.

***Pelerin** — B. h. 5, by Sir Gaylord—Padrona, by St Paddy
Br.—Oppenheimer Sir P (Fra) — 1982 3 0 1 0 $8,000
Own.—Doherty & Snowden — 126 — Tr.—Whittingham Charles — 1981 6 4 0 0 $172,007
Lifetime 19 5 2 0 $229,996 — Turf 19 5 2 0 $229,996

17Oct82-8SA 1¼ⓣ:47^{1}1:34^{3}1:58^{3}fm 2½ 122 6$^{6\frac{3}{4}}$ 6^{6} 6$^{6\frac{1}{4}}$ 6$^{5\frac{1}{4}}$ PincayLJr^{3} C F Brk H 89 Mehmet, Craelius, It's the One 7
8Oct82-8SA 1⅛ⓣ:46^{1}1:10 1:46^{2}fm*6-5 117 8^{7} 6$^{5\frac{1}{2}}$ 5$^{3\frac{1}{2}}$ 2^{nk} Pincay L Jr^{3} Aw40000 95 Tell Again, Pelerin, Dare You II 8
6Sep82-7Dmr $1\frac{1}{16}$ⓣ:47^{4}1:11^{3}1:42^{2}fm 4 120 8^{10} 8^{11} 8^{12} 7$^{4\frac{3}{4}}$ Pincay L Jr^{2} Aw32000 92 DareYouII,GoldenFlak,RustyCnyon 8
4Oct81♦4Longchamp(Fra) a1½ 2:35^{1}sf 33 130 ⓣ 17^{21} HideE Arc de Triomphe (Gr1) Gold River, Bikala, April Run 24
6Sep81♦5BadenBaden(Ger) a1½2:27^{3}gd*7-5 130 ⓣ 1^{2} StrkG GrssrPr vn Bdn (Gr1) Pelerin, Hohritt, Maivogel 8
25Jly81♦4Ascot(Eng) 1½ 2:35^{2}gd 7½ 133 ⓣ 5^{11} TylrB Kng Geo VI-Q Elz (Gr1) Shergar, Madam Gay, Fingals Cave 7
19Jun81♦2Ascot(Eng) 1½ 2:38^{1}fm 7 124 ⓣ 1^{3} TaylorB Hardwick (Gr2) Pelerin, Light Cavalry, Lancastrian 9
7May81♦2Chester(Eng) a1⅝ 2:58^{4}gd*7-5 130 ⓣ 1$^{1\frac{1}{2}}$ TaylorB Ormonde (Gr3) Pelerin, Billbroker, Shaftsbury 5
11Apr81♦4Newbury(Eng) 1½ 2:44^{1}sf 16 120 ⓣ 1^{hd} TaylorB John Porter (Gr2) Pelerin, Cracaval, Shining Finish 9
20Aug80♦4York(Eng) 1½ 2:34^{4}gd 11 119 ⓣ 4^{13} Reid J Grt Voltgeur (Gr2) Prince Bee, Light Cavalry, Saviour 5
Oct 28 SA ⓣ5f fm 1:00 h (d) Oct 23 SA ⓣ3f fm :36 h (d) Oct 15 SA ⓣ4f fm :48^{1} h (d) Oct 4 SA ⓣ6f fm 1:15^{3} h (d)

Craelius B. c. 3, by Avatar—Nas-Mahal, by Nasrullah
Br.—Keck H B (Ky) 1982 11 4 5 0 $142,525
Own.—Keck Mrs H B 122 Tr.—Whittingham Charles 1981 2 M 0 0 $425
Lifetime 13 4 5 0 $142,950 Turf 7 2 4 0 $95,775
17Oct82-8SA 1¼Ⓣ:4711:3431:583fm 13 114 41¾ 31½ 2hd 2hd McCrrnCJ4 C F Brk H 94 Mehmet, Craelius, It's the One 7
3Oct82-8SA 1⅛Ⓣ:46 1:1011:461fm*9-5e118 88½ 85¾ 33 22½ ShomkrW5 Volante H 93 Lamerok, Craelius, Sari's Dreamer 9
3Sep82-8Dmr 1 1/16:461 1:101 1:414ft *3-2e117 86 62¾ 42½ 1nk ShoemkerW4 El Cajon 91 Craelius, Poley, Kerlan 10
22Aug82-8Dmr 1⅛Ⓣ:4631:1111:49 fm 5½e116 119 82¾ 43½ 73¾ ShmkrW9 Dmr Dby H 89 GiveMStrngth,WtrBnk,TkThFloor 13
8Aug82-9Dmr 1 Ⓣ:4641:1111:353fm *1 116 53½ 31½ 2hd 2½ ShmrW7 La Jla Mle H 94 TakeTheFloor,Craelius,SwordBlade 8
8Aug82—Run in two divisions, 8th & 9th races.
21Jly82-9Dmr 7½fⓉ:223 :4621:304fm *1 114 88 85¼ 5¾ 12½ ShomkrW6 Oceanside 85 Crelius,TkeTheFloor,SwingTillDwn 8
21Jly82—Run in two divisions, 8th & 9th races.
8Jly82-8Hol 1 1/16Ⓣ:4621:1021:403fm 3½e114 64½ 52½ 1½ 21 Shoemaker W7 Wstwd 95 Sun Worship, Craelius, Ask Me 11
26Jun82-8Hol 1⅛:463 1:102 1:464ft 6 113 99 89 826 828 HawleyS1 Silvr Scrn H 67 Journey at Sea, Cassaleria,Guachan 9
26May82-9Hol 1 1/16Ⓣ:4621:1111:421fm*3-5 120 42½ 1½ 1½ 12 McCarronCJ8 Aw22000 88 Craelius, SwingTillDawn,Reconfirm 8
16May82-4Hol 1 1/16:472 1:114 1:421ft *1 114 1hd 1hd 12 15 McCarron C J3 Mdn 84 Crelius,Pleztobefirst,SlickNSneky 10
●Oct 28 SA Ⓣ5f fm :592 h (d) Oct 23 SA Ⓣ3f fm :36 h (d) Oct 14 SA Ⓣ5f fm 1:013 h (d) Sep 21 SA 6f ft 1:13 h

***Buchanette** B. f. 3, by Youth—Duke's Little Gal, by Duke of Dublin
Br.—Hunt N B (Ky) 1982 9 2 1 1 $47,944
Own.—Nahas N 119 Tr.—Dupuis Jean-Pierre Turf 9 2 1 1 $47,944
Lifetime 9 2 1 1 $47,944
18Oct82◆5StCloud(Fra) a1 5/16 2:274sf 7½ 121 Ⓣ 1hd DbrcqG ⒻPx de Flore (Gr 3) Buchntt,DoublingTm,UnknownLdy 13
12Oct82◆4Longchamp(Fra) a1¼ 2:192sf 2½ 120 Ⓣ 44¾ DbrcqG Px du Ranelagh WelshTerm,AlfredsChoic,Tompkins 7
27Sep82◆5MLaffitte(Fra) a1¼ 2:091gd 15 113 Ⓣ 4nk KsssJL La Cpe d'Mlfftte(Gr3) Coquelin,ByllytheKid,BeMyNative 13
13Sep82◆5Evry(Fra) a1½ 2:392gd*6-5 120 Ⓣ 2nk DbrcqG Px Mrice de Nexn Rubino, Buchanette, Blau 7
21Aug82◆5Deauville(Fra) a1 11/16 3:011gd 9 120 Ⓣ 12 DbrcG ⒻPx de Pomone(Gr2) Zalataia, Akiyda, April Run 13
2Aug82◆5Vichy(Fra) a1½ 2:35 gd 5 111 Ⓣ 45½ KsssJL Gr Px de Vchy(Gr3) Karkour, No Attention, Palikaraki 12
27Jun82◆2Longchamp(Fra) a1¼ 2:102gd 4½ ·123 Ⓣ 33½ SmniH ⒻPx de Mlleret(Gr2) Grease, Parannda, Buchanette 7
13Jun82◆4Chantilly(Fra) a1 5/16 2:164sf 21 128 Ⓣ 68½ SmniH ⒻPx de Diane(Gr1) Harbour, Akiyda, Paradise 14
16May82◆1Longchamp(Fra) a1 5/16 2:191gd 4 123 Ⓣ 12 DbrcG ⒻPx La Ce(Mdn) Buchnette,LuckyProspctor,Shnnky 9

Lemhi Gold Ch. c. 4, by Vaguely Noble—Belle Marie, by Candy Spots
Br.—Jones A U (Ky) 1982 11 6 2 1 $1,060,375
Own.—Jones A U 126 Tr.—Barrera Lazaro S 1981 7 2 1 0 $50,070
Lifetime 18 8 3 1 $1,110,445 Turf 7 5 1 0 $480,305
9Oct82-8Bel 1½:473 2:04 2:311ft 2½ 126 28 14 15 14½ McCrrCJ2 J C Gld Cp 64 LmhiGold,SilvrSuprm,ChristmsPst 10
18Sep82-8Bel 1¼:473 1:36 2:01 ft 7½e115 31 11 15 18¾ VsquzJ2 Mrlbro Cup H 93 LemhiGold,SilverSuprem,PirofDucs 8
29Aug82-8AP 1¼Ⓣ:4621:35 1:584fm 3½ 126 85¾ 52¼ 44½ 45¼ McCrrCJ5 Bud Million 120 Perrault, Be My Native, Motavato 14
7Aug82-8Sar 1⅛:472 1:11 1:474ft 5¾ 117 47 45 56¼ 45¾ McCrrnCJ1 Whitney H 90 Silver Buck,Winter'sTale,TapShoes 6
10Jly82-8Bel 1½Ⓣ:4912:0142:26 fm *1 126 13 1½ 1hd 1nk McCrrCJ2 SwordDncr 94 Lemhi Gold, Erins Isle, Field Cat 5
31May82-8Hol 1½Ⓣ:4922:0132:251fm*3-5 123 32 3½ 1hd 22½ Guerra WA6 Hol Inv H 91 Exploded, Lemhi Gold, The Bart 6
18Apr82-8SA a1¾ Ⓣ:46 2:453fm 3 121 43½ 1hd 12½ 17 GurrWA4 S J Cp Iv H 99 Lemhi Gold, Exploded, Perrault 9
13Mar82-8SA 1½Ⓣ:4842:0222:272gd 2½ 119 12½ 12½ 15 15 GuerrWA4 Sn Mrno H 78 LemhiGold,Exploded,ChnceyBidder 9
13Mar82—Run in two divisions, 8th & 9th races.
25Feb82-8SA 1⅛Ⓣ:4641:1111:48 fm*8-5 113 42 41½ 1½ 11½ Guerra W A8 Aw35000 87 LemhiGold,Fingal'sCave,Essenbee 10
15Feb82-8SA 1 1/16:462 1:10 1:41 ft 3½ 114 43 31½ 33½ 31½ Guerra WA1 El Monte 95 WoodlandLad,SirDncer,LemhiGold 10
Oct 28 SA Ⓣ5f fm 1:013 b (d) ●Oct 23 SA Ⓣ5f fm :593 h (d) Oct 6 Bel 5f ft 1:022 b Sep 29 Bel 5f ft :591 h

Regalberto B. c. 4, by Roberto—Every Evening, by Roi Dagobert
Br.—Red Oak Farm (Fla) 1982 9 3 2 3 $128,070
Own.—Harris W 126 Tr.—Hall Eldon 1981 13 6 2 1 $163,200
Lifetime 30 10 9 5 $346,400 Turf 9 2 2 2 $76,625
10Oct82-8BM 1 Ⓣ:4621:1031:36 fm*8-5 123 32 45 66 87½ Toro F9 Mrks Plce H 92 Silveyville,MountainMrine,Cinnpo 10
6Sep82-8Dmr a1¼:463 1:344 1:57 ft 14 119 11½ 11 2hd 22 Toro F9 Dmr Inv H 90 Muttering, Regalberto, Exploded 9
26Aug82-8Dmr 1 1/16Ⓣ:4921:13 1:432fm 14 119 21 2½ 2hd 12 Toro F2 Aw30000 92 Regalberto, Island Whirl, Monarch 6
11Jly82-11Pln 1⅛:47 1:11 1:51 ft *3-5 125 42 43¼ 2½ 24½ AndrsJR1 Alamedan H 76 Sir Optimist, Regalberto, Kilty 9
27Jun82-8GG 1⅛:461 1:10 1:502ft *6-5 123 47 46 31½ 32½ SrnsD2 [S]Citatn Inv H 78 SenstionlGuy,HllowdEnvoy,Rglbrto 8
6Jun82-8GG 1⅜Ⓣ:4831:3822:163fm 6¼ 117 2hd 11 3½ 3¾ SornsonD6 Rlng Grn H 84 DonRoberto,CptinGenerl,Reglbrto 11
31May82-8GG 1 1/16Ⓣ:4841:1221:441fm*4-5 123 32 32 31 31¾ SorensonD5 Nor Iva H 79 SensationalGuy,JunBrrer,Reglberto 5
17Mar82-8GG 1 1/16:472 1:114 1:432sy 2¼ 123 43 42 1hd 14½ SrnsnD4 [S]Sky Sl Iv H 86 Reglbrto,ExcutivCounsl,PlsntPowr 6
6Mar82-6GG 1 :463 1:103 1:352ft *1-2 117 69¾ 43½ 3½ 11¼ Sorenson D3 Aw17000 91 Reglberto,KobukCountry,Foyt'sAck 7
18Sep81-11Bmf 1 1/16:452 1:093 1:412ft *2-3 124 32½ 1hd 11½ 14 Baze R A1 Sn Mteo H 92 Regalberto, Chiaroscuro,Silveyville 6
Oct 29 SA 5f ft 1:00 h ●Oct 23 BM 1 ft 1:37 h ●Oct 16 BM 5f ft :584 h Oct 9 BM 3f ft :36 h

John Henry B. g. 7, by Ole Bob Bowers—Once Double, by Double Jay
Br.—Golden Chance Farm Inc (Ky) 1982 3 1 0 1 $356,300
Own.—Dotsam Stable 126 Tr.—McAnally Ronald 1981 10 8 0 0 $1,798,030
Lifetime 66 30 12 7 $3,379,110 Turf 37 21 8 4 $2,212,962
17Oct82-8SA 1¼Ⓣ:4711:3431:583fm*4-5 129 31½ 42 42¾ 41¾ ShomkrW6 C F Brk H 92 Mehmet, Craelius, It's the One 7
28Mar82-8SA 1½Ⓣ:4622:00 2:24 fm*1-2 126 33 33 43½ 34¾ ShoemkrW3 Sn Ls Ry 90 Perrault, Exploded, John Henry 5
7Mar82-8SA 1¼:45 1:342 1:59 ft *6-5 130 913 51¾ 2½ 2no Shoemaker W9 S A H 94 ‡Perrault, John Henry, It'stheOne 11
7Mar82—Placed first through disqualification
6Dec81-8Hol 1½Ⓣ:49 2:03 2:264fm*2-5 126 12 11 3½ 42 ShomkrW5 Hol Trf Cp 84 ProvidntilII,QuntoConqur,Goldiko 10
8Nov81-8SA 1½Ⓣ:4721:5932:232fm*2-5 126 1½ 1½ 2hd 1nk ShoemkrW4 Oak Tree 98 John Henry, Spence Bay, The Bart 7
10Oct81-8Bel 1½:48 2:021 2:282ft *3 126 42½ 21 11½ 1hd ShomkrW8 J C Gld Cp 78 John Henry, Peat Moss, Relaxing 11
30Aug81-6AP 1¼Ⓣ:5011:4222:073sf *1e126 86½ 56 31 1no ShmkrW12 Arl Million — John Henry, The Bart, MadamGay 12
11Jly81-8Bel 1½Ⓣ:4942:03 2:264fm*1-3 126 31½ 11 11½ 13½ ShmkrW3 Swd Dancer 90 John Henry,PassingZone,PeatMoss 5
14Jun81-8Hol 1¼:453 1:344 2:002ft *6-5 130 66¼ 65¾ 46½ 42¾ PcLJr7 Hol Gd Cup H 86 ‡Ctermn,ElevnStitchs,SuprMomnt 10
17May81-8Hol 1½Ⓣ:5112:04 2:274fm*2-5 130 2½ 2½ 1½ 1¾ Pincay LJr5 Hol Inv H 81 John Henry, Caterman,GalaxyLibra 7
Oct 26 SA 6f ft 1:141 b ●Oct 16 SA 3f ft :342 b Oct 10 SA Ⓣ1⅛ fm 1:47 h Oct 5 SA 1⅛ ft 1:522 h

```
*Maipon                                   Ch. h. 5, by Tantoul—Doninda, by Cardanil II
                                          Br.—Haras Dadinco (Chile)              1982 11 2 4 1   $128,900
Own.—Hirsch C L                      126  Tr.—Stute Warren                       1981  5 1 2 0   $10,778
                                      Lifetime   23 6 6 4   $173,854             Turf 19 6 5 4   $171,680
22Oct82-8SA   1⅛ T:46^1 1:10 1:46^1fm  3¾ 120  2^2 2^2½ 2½ 1¾   McHrgueDG^6 Aw40000 96 Maipon,Ptti'sTriumph,RustyCnyon 7
10Oct82-8SA   a6½f T:22 :44^3 1:13^4fm 7¼ 122  4^4½ 3^2 4^2¼ 2^2½ McHrgueDG^6 Aw40000 87 Shagbark, Maipon, J. D. Quill  8
26Aug82-8Dmr  1 1/16 T:49^2 1:13 1:43^2fm 3½ 119 4^6 5^4 4^2¾ 4^4½ ShoemkerW^1 Aw30000 87 Regalberto, Island Whirl, Monarch 6
15Aug82-8Dmr  1⅛ T:48^4 1:12^1 1:48^2fm 20 117  1½ 3^2 5^3 6^5¼   McHrguDG^7 E Read H 91 Wickerr, Spence Bay, Perrault 7
6Aug82-8Dmr   1 1/16 T:49^1 1:13 1:43 fm*8-5 118 4^1¾ 3^1½ 3^2 2^1¼ McHargue D G^1 HcpO 93 Wild Surf, Maipon, Buen Chico 6
20Jun82-8Hol  1 1/16 T:46^1 1:09^4 1:40^1fm 58 115 5^3½ 5^3¼ 3^1½ 1^no McHrguDG^5 Inglwd H 98 Maipon, Spence Bay, Wickerr 11
12Jun82-5Hol  1⅛ T:48 1:11^4 1:47^1fm 4¼ 115  4^5 4^2 2½ 2¾      Toro F^1   Aw35000 93 Tell Again, Maipon, Le Duc de Bar 6
22May82-5Hol  1 1/16 T:47^2 1:11^1 1:40^4fm 15 115 5^3½ 5^3¼ 6^2¼ 4^2¼ Toro F^2 Aw40000 93 CaptainNick,PirteLw,Ptti'sTriumph 8
7May82-8Hol   1 1/16 :46 1:10^2 1:41^3ft 7 115 2½ 2^hd 3^5½ 6^9¾ McHrgueDG^4 Aw35000 77 Haughty But Nice, A Run, Baltanas 6
25Apr82-7Hol  1 1/16 T:47^1 1:10^3 1:40^4fm 4¼ 115 3^1½ 4^2¼ 3^1½ 3^3¾ McHrgueDG^5 Aw35000 91 Captain Nick, Bold East, Maipon 9
   Oct 28 SA 5f ft :59^2 h     Oct 19 SA 5f ft 1:01^3 h     Oct 14 SA T 1⅛ fm 1:56^3 h (d)     ●Oct 8 SA 1 ft 1:38^3 h
```

THE EVOLUTION OF THE ODDS

The tote board was as follows:

	#4 Lemhi Gold	Expected Return per Dollar Bet on Lemhi Gold	#6 John Henry	Expected Return per Dollar Bet on John Henry	Totals
With thirteen minutes to post time					
Odds	1—1		6—5		
Win pool	65,479		55,997		158,188
Place pool	31,689	Less than 1	11,471	1.42	61,500
Show pool	9,590	1.04	3,589	1.61	27,681
With six minutes to post time					
Odds	1—1		3—2		
Win pool	107,579		84,224		253,450
Place pool	38,062	Less than 1	17,086	1.30	87,180
Show pool	12,576	1.15	5,327	1.61	43,988
With two minutes to post time					
Odds	1—1		6—5		
Win pool	134,946		116,897		327,850
Place pool	41,809	Less than 1	22,037	1.29	103,162
Show pool	18,943	1.08	8,667	1.51	59,641
With one minute to post time					
Odds	1—1		6—5		
Win pool	155,771		134,642		374,383
Place pool	43,616	0.95	25,381	1.24	112,130
Show pool	24,618	1.03	10,917	1.45	69,772

Throughout the betting period, John Henry, horse number 6, remained an outstanding place and show bet with expected values way above the 1.14 cutoff for Dr. Z system bets that we suggested for top tracks in Chapter Five. There never was a possible bet on Lemhi Gold to place, since the expected value stayed under 1 throughout the betting period. The show betting indicated a possible bet, although not high enough to warrant a bet near the end of the betting period. The optimal betting amounts on John Henry for various wealth levels were*

Initial wealth	50	250	500	1,000	5,000	10,000
Place bet	3	17	33	73	374	739
Show bet	18	95	192	335	1,224	2,147
Total bet	21	112	225	408	1,598	2,886
Place profit	3.30	18.70	36.30	80.30	374.00	739.00
Show profit	16.20	85.50	153.60	268.00	979.20	1,502.90
Total profit	19.50	104.20	189.90	348.30	1,353.20	2,241.90

The tote board at post time was as follows:

	#2 Craelius	#4 Lemhi Gold	Expected Return per Dollar Bet on Lemhi Gold	#5 Regalberto
Odds	13—1	4—5		35—1
Win pool	24,785	183,551		9,082
Place	14,673	48,446	0.96	6,469
Show	9,040	29,009	1.04	6,205

	#6 John Henry	Expected Return per Dollar Bet on John Henry	Totals
Odds	7—5		
Win pool	149,879		425,976
Place	27,894	1.22	122,847
Show	14,007	1.34	79,645

*The expected returns given here were computed using equations (4.5) and (4.6). The betting amounts were calculated using the equations in Chapter Sixteen. You can estimate these values using the charts in Chapter 5.

The chart of the race was as follows:

Oak Tree Invitational

EIGHTH RACE
Santa Anita
OCTOBER 31, 1982

1 ½ MILES.(turf). (2.23) 14th Running THE OAK TREE. $300,000 Added. (Grade I). 3-year-olds and upward. By invitation, with no nomination or starting fees. The winner to receive $180,000, with $60,000 to second, $36,000 to third, $18,000 to fourth and $6,000 to fifth. Weight, 3-year-olds, 122 lbs. Older, 126 lbs. The Oak Tree Racing Association will invite a representative field of horses to compete. The field will be drawn by the closing time of entries. A trophy will be presented to the owner of the winner. Invitations Thursday, October 21.
Value of race $300,000, value to winner $180,000, second $60,000, third $36,000, fourth $18,000, fifth $6,000. Mutuel pool $628,468. Exacta Pool $477,157.

Last Raced	Horse	Eqt.	A.	Wt	PP	¼	½	1	1¼	Str	Fin	Jockey	Odds $1
17Oct82 ^{8}SA^{4}	John Henry		7	126	6	$4^{1\frac{1}{2}}$	4^{1}	4^{1}	2^{2}	$2^{2\frac{1}{2}}$	$1^{2\frac{1}{2}}$	Shoemaker W	1.40
17Oct82 ^{8}SA^{2}	Craelius	b	3	122	2	3^{1}	$3^{1\frac{1}{2}}$	1^{hd}	$1^{1\frac{1}{2}}$	$1^{\frac{1}{2}}$	$2^{1\frac{1}{2}}$	Sibille R	13.60
10Oct82 ^{8}BM^{8}	Regalberto		4	126	5	$2^{1\frac{1}{2}}$	$2^{2\frac{1}{2}}$	3^{hd}	$4^{2\frac{1}{2}}$	$3^{\frac{1}{2}}$	3^{2}	Toro F	38.80
17Oct82 ^{8}SA^{6}	Pelerin		5	126	1	$5^{\frac{1}{2}}$	7	7	$6^{\frac{1}{2}}$	6^{4}	$4^{1\frac{1}{4}}$	Pincay L Jr	8.10
9Oct82 ^{8}Bel^{1}	Lemhi Gold		4	126	4	$1^{\frac{1}{2}}$	1^{hd}	2^{hd}	3^{hd}	4^{3}	5^{4}	McCarron C J	.90
18Oct82 ^{5}Fra^{1}	Buchanette		3	119	3	7	5^{1}	$5^{4\frac{1}{2}}$	5^{3}	$5^{\frac{1}{2}}$	6^{10}	Lequeux A	55.60
22Oct82 ^{8}SA^{1}	Maipon		5	126	7	$6^{\frac{1}{2}}$	$6^{\frac{1}{2}}$	6^{hd}	7	7	7	Castaneda M	27.50

OFF AT 4:24 Start good, Won driving. Time, :24⅖, :47⅖, 1:10⅗, 1:35⅕, 1:59⅗, 2:24, Course firm.

$2 Mutuel Prices:			
6-JOHN HENRY	4.80	4.20	3.80
2-CRAELIUS		6.20	4.80
5-REGALBERTO			6.00

$5 EXACTA 6-2 PAID $102.00.

B. g, by Ole Bob Bowers—Once Double, by Double Jay. Trainer McAnally Ronald. Bred by Golden Chance Farm Inc (Ky).

JOHN HENRY, taken in hand after the start, remained unhurried outside horses for seven furlongs, moved up to challenge outside of CRAELIUS at the far turn, wore down that one under strong handling in the final furlong and drew clear near the end. CRAELIUS, reserved in good position along the rail for a mile, moved suddenly inside of LEMHI GOLD to take the lead nearing the far turn, resisted gamely when challenged by JOHN HENRY but weakened in the closing yards. REGALBERTO forced the early pace outside of LEMHI GOLD, dropped back a bit on the final turn but rallied gamely outside the leaders through the stretch drive. PELERIN failed to seriously threaten. LEMHI GOLD darted to the lead at once, maintained a short advantage for a mile and gradually tired thereafter. BUCHANETTE brushed with PELERIN entering the front stretch the first time, raced within easy striking distance of the leaders for a mile, took up inside of LEMHI GOLD at the far turn and did not threaten in the drive. Lequeux, aboard BUCHANETTE, lodged a claim of foul against LEMHI GOLD but, after reviewing the videotapes, the stewards alowed the order of finish to stand.

Owners— 1, Dotsam Stable; 2, Keck Mrs H B; 3, Harris Walt; 4, Doherty & Snowden; 5, Jones Aaron U; 6, Nahas N; 7, Hirsch C L.

Trainers— 1, McAnally Ronald; 2, Whittingham Charles; 3, Hall Eldon; 4, Whittingham Charles; 5, Barrera Lazaro S; 6, Dupuis Jean-Pierre; 7, Stute Warren.

The bets on John Henry were extremely good ones. With a final expected value of 1.22 to place and 1.34 to show, you would expect a reasonably good payoff. However, with Lemhi Gold finishing out of the money, the payoff was outstanding.

The payoffs were computed as follows. For place, total profit to be shared by backers of John Henry and Craelius equals total place pool minus track take minus dollar bets returned to John Henry and Craelius backers

$$= 122{,}847 - \underbrace{0.15(\$122{,}847)}_{\substack{\text{15\% take in} \\ \text{California,} \\ \text{or \$18,427.05}}} - \$27{,}894 - \$14{,}673$$

$$= \$61{,}852.95.$$

$$\text{Share to John Henry's backers} = \frac{\$61{,}852.95}{2} = \$30{,}926.48.$$

$$\text{Payoff per dollar bet} = \underbrace{\$1}_{\text{Return of bet}} + \underbrace{\frac{\$30{,}926.48}{\$27{,}894}}_{\text{Profit}} = \$2.1087.$$

$$\text{Payoff per \$2 ticket} = 2(\$2.1087) \text{ less breakage} = \$4.20.$$

In this case breakage, or rounding down to the nearest 20¢ on a $2 ticket, amounted to 1.74¢, about 1% of the amount bet. The share to Craelius backers was also $30,926.48, but since there were fewer of them, the payoff was higher.

$$\text{Payoff per dollar bet} = \$1 + \frac{\$30{,}926.48}{\$14{,}673} = \$3.1077.$$

$$\text{Payoff per \$2 ticket} = 2(\$3.1077) \text{ less breakage} = \$6.20.$$

The breakage was 1.54¢, about 1% of the amount bet.

The payoffs to place were $4.20 on John Henry and $6.20 on Craelius, the latter reflecting the fact that more money was bet on John Henry. Throughout the betting period, John Henry was a system bet to place, with an expected value of over 1.20, which ended up at 1.22, so you would have expected, on average, to make a profit of 22¢ for each dollar wagered. Since it was certainly possible for John Henry to finish out of the money, to make a real profit you have to receive more when he is in the money. In this case, the actual profit was $2.20 per $2 ticket, or 110%. The payoff was this high on the 7–5 shot John Henry because the relative long shot Craelius, who went off at 13–1, came in second.

WHAT IF LEMHI GOLD HAD BEEN IN THE MONEY?

Clearly, if Lemhi Gold had come in second, the payoff on John Henry would have been lower. But how much less?

The total profit to be shared would have been

$$\underbrace{\$122{,}847}_{\text{Total place pool}} - \underbrace{\$18{,}427.05}_{\text{Track take}} - \underbrace{\$27{,}894}_{\text{Dollar bets on John Henry}} - \underbrace{\$48{,}446}_{\text{Dollar bets on Lemhi Gold}} = \$28{,}079.05,$$

which is considerably less than the \$61,852.95 with Craelius. John Henry's share would be \$28,079.95/2 = \$14,039.98.

The payoff per \$2 ticket on John Henry would have been

$$2\left(\frac{\$14{,}039.98}{\$27{,}894.00} + \$1\right) \text{less breakage} = \$3.00$$

and on Lemhi Gold,

$$2\left(\frac{\$14{,}039.98}{\$48{,}446} + \$1\right) \text{less breakage} = \$2.40.$$

The breakage on Lemhi Gold would have been 17.96¢, or about 9% of the amount bet, which, added to the 15%, would have made a startling 24% commission! The results show that the payoff to John Henry would still have been quite good, while Lemhi Gold would have paid only \$2.40.

Thus with the Dr. Z system bet on John Henry, the payoff would be good if the other favorite came in and outstanding if he did not. Over the long run, with many bets of this kind, on average you should make about the 10% plus indicated for Dr. Z system bets in Chapter Nine. The key is to get good payoffs when the horse actually comes in that more than compensate for when he finishes out of the money.

The situation with show betting is much the same. Let us now go through the analysis both to be sure that the message is clear and to discover any important differences.

Total profit to be shared by backers of John Henry, Craelius, and Regalberto = **total show pool minus track take minus dollar bets returned to John Henry, Craelius, and Regalberto backers**

$$= \$79{,}645 - \underbrace{0.15(\$79{,}645)}_{\$11{,}946.75} - \$14{,}007 - \$9{,}040 - \$6{,}205$$

$$= \$38{,}446.25.$$

Thus each of the three horses' backers would have received \$38,446.25/3 = \$12,815.42 profit.

The payoffs on John Henry per \$2 ticket were

$$2\left(\frac{\$12{,}815.42}{\$14{,}007} + \$1\right) \text{less breakage} = \$3.80;$$

on Craelius,

$$2\left(\frac{\$12{,}815.42}{\$9{,}040} + \$1\right) \text{ less breakage} = \$4.80;$$

and on Regalberto,

$$2\left(\frac{\$12{,}815.42}{\$6{,}205} + \$1\right) \text{ less breakage} = \$6.00.$$

Breakage amounted to 2.99¢ for John Henry, 3.53¢ for Craelius, and 13.1¢ for Regalberto on each $2 ticket.

Now how would these payoffs have been affected if Lemhi Gold had finished in the money? Let us suppose that John Henry, Lemhi Gold, and Craelius were in the money. As we know, the order of their finish does not matter. What counts is how much is bet on each of the horses finishing in the money.

The total profit to be shared would have been

$$\underbrace{\$79{,}645}_{\text{Total show pool}} - \underbrace{\$11{,}946.75}_{\text{Track take}} - \underbrace{\$14{,}007}_{\text{Dollar bets on John Henry}} - \underbrace{\$9{,}040}_{\text{Dollar bets on Craelius}} - \underbrace{\$29{,}009}_{\text{Dollar bets on Lemhi Gold}} = \$15{,}642.25.$$

Each horse's share would have been $15,642.25/3 = $5,214.08; thus the payoffs on John Henry per $2 ticket would have been

$$2\left(\frac{\$5{,}214.08}{\$14{,}007} + \$1\right) \text{ less breakage} = \$2.60;$$

on Craelius,

$$2\left(\frac{\$5{,}214.08}{\$9{,}040} + \$1\right) \text{ less breakage} = \$3.00;$$

and on Lemhi Gold,

$$2\left(\frac{\$5{,}214.08}{\$29{,}009} + \$1\right) \text{ less breakage} = \$2.20.$$

Breakage would have amounted to 14.4¢ for John Henry, 15.4¢ for Craelius, and 15.9¢ for Lemhi Gold for each $2 bet. Thus $2.744 was rounded to $2.60, $3.154 to $3.00, and $2.359 to $2.20. As you can see, breakage mounts up! It is a considerable additional cost. Adding it to the track take often makes the total track commission over 20% of the amount bet. It is an even higher percentage of the profits. In this case it would have been

$$\frac{15.4¢}{60¢ + 15.4¢}(100) = 20.4\%$$

just for breakage on John Henry. On Lemhi Gold it would have been

$$\frac{15.9¢}{20¢ + 15.9¢}(100) = 44.3\%.$$

Breakage is such an important aspect of betting that we discuss it more thoroughly, indicating its effect on Dr. Z system bets, in Chapter Nine. However, it is clear that (1) breakage is more important for show betting than place betting, since the payoffs are generally lower; and (2) it is a very significant cost, especially when the payoffs are low and the exact payoff is just below the next breakage level—for example, a $2.59 payoff becomes $2.40 rather than $2.60.

The exercise of assuming that Lemhi Gold was in the money taught us that (1) the payoff amounts on all the horses become much smaller when a favorite with a heavy amount bet to place or show on it finishes in the money; (2) the payoff on the Dr. Z system bet horse becomes lower but still can be reasonably good; and (3) the effect is usually greater on show bets than place bets, since less is generally bet to show than place, with the result that a large amount bet on the favorite has more of an impact on the payoffs. In conclusion, John Henry was a great bet to place and show. When the favorite finished out of the money, the payoffs were very high. Even if Lemhi Gold had come in the money, the payoffs to John Henry would have been quite reasonable considering he was a 7–5 shot.

9

Results of Computer Studies Using the Dr. Z System over Long Periods

In this chapter we show you how the Dr. Z system performs over long periods. To do this we collected data for entire meetings at three different major tracks during different years. These include the 1978 summer meeting at Exhibition Park involving 9,037 horses, running in 1,065 races over 110 days; the 1973–74 winter meeting at Santa Anita involving 5,895 horses, running in 627 races over 75 days; and the 1981–82 winter meeting at Aqueduct involving 3,470 horses, running in 380 races over 43 days. We also show our own results using the Dr. Z system on Kentucky Derby day for 1981–86. In all these cases, use of the Dr. Z system resulted in substantial profits.

We also investigate three crucial issues: the importance of the track take and breakage and the fact that you must make bets a minute or two before the race is run. The combined effect of the track take and breakage is very large indeed, which means you should be aware of how much these commissions are at your local track; they have a considerable effect on profits. The evidence shows that the last-minute betting can reduce the attractiveness of some Dr. Z system bets. In most such cases, however, the bets remain good ones. Bets placed two minutes before the horses run usually do lead to substantial profits. We also look at some other characteristics of Dr. Z system bets, such as How large are they? How often do you make them? What happens on non-fast-track days?

EXHIBITION PARK: THE 1978 SUMMER SEASON

Exhibition Park has one long racing season each year. It runs from early April through October. There are usually four racing cards per week, each of about ten races. The horses running at Exhibition Park are of good quality and the betting in this wealthy seaport city is quite high, averaging about $1 million per day. Much of this money is bet on such features as the daily double, quinella, exactor, sweep six, and triactor. The win, place, and show pools remain quite high as well.

The 1978 season ran for 110 days and involved 9,037 horses running in the 1,065 races. We collected data on the win, place, and show pools for every one of these horses in all these races. The track take was 18.1% (it is now 15.8%), and Exhibition Park has 5¢ breakage. We calculated the expected value per dollar bet for place and show for all 9,037 horses using equations similar to (4.3) and (4.4). Whenever the expected value was 1.20 or better, we would place a Dr. Z system bet. The amount of the bet was determined by equations similar to (5.5) and (5.6).* Using an initial wealth of $2,500, our wealth over the season, if we bet on every Dr. Z system bet,

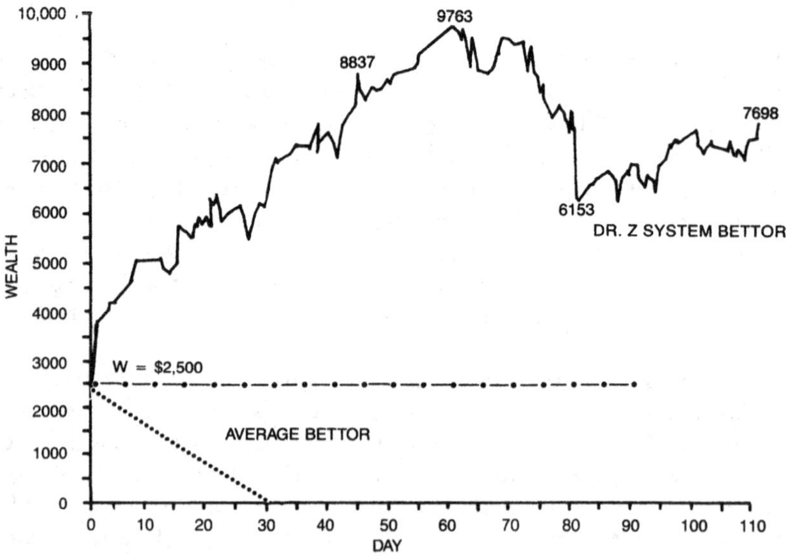

Figure 9.1 Betting-wealth-level history for Dr. Z system bets at the 1978 summer meeting at Exhibition Park using an expected-value cutoff of 1.20

regardless of weather, grew to $7,698, yielding a profit of $5,198. The history of our betting fortune over the season appears in Figure 9.1. The average bettor starting with a $2,500 fortune would have lost it all by the

*This study was done by Hausch, Ziemba, and Rubinstein (1981). Since that time we have developed even more exact equations to calculate both the expected returns and the amount to bet. These differences are minor, however, although the results from the new equations would most likely lead to slightly higher profits.

32nd day. Our fortune generally moved up along the typical jagged line that represents actual wins and losses. It peaked once at $8,837 on the 44th day, then at $9,763 on the 62nd day. From about the 70th to the 80th day, there was a substantial losing streak.

The data in Figure 9.1 include every Dr. Z system bet regardless of track condition. As we discussed in Chapter Five, we recommend that you do not bet when the track is not fast. Of the 87 days on which we placed Dr. Z system bets, using the conservative 1.20 expected-value cutoff,* the track was fast on 57 days, and it was slow, muddy, heavy, wet, or sloppy on 30 days. The results reveal that on the 57 fast-track days, we bet $32,501 and received $38,364, a profit of $5,863, or 18%. However, on the other 30 days we bet $17,180 and received $16,515, a loss of $665, or −3.9%. If we had eliminated these non-fast-track days, our profit for the year would have been $5,863 on our $2,500 investment.

SANTA ANITA: THE 1973–74 WINTER MEETING

Southern California has three major thoroughbred racetracks: Del Mar, where the "turf meets the surf" 25 miles north of San Diego; Hollywood Park, in Inglewood, situated near the Los Angeles International Airport and adjacent to the Forum, home of the Lakers and Kings; and Santa Anita in Arcadia, near the foot of the San Gabriel mountains and not far from the Rose Bowl in Pasadena. Thoroughbred racing is very active in southern California and the three tracks alternate seasons, resulting in year-round quality racing. Santa Anita has two seasons: The Oak Tree meeting usually runs from early October to early November, and the winter meeting typically begins the day after Christmas and runs until early April. Mark Rubinstein, with the aid of Michael Alhadeff of Longacres Racetrack, collected data on the win, place, and show mutuels for the 5,895 horses running in 627 races over 75 days in the 1973–74 winter meeting at Santa Anita.

The horses running at Santa Anita are of unusually high quality and include some of America's finest bloodstock. The betting pools are large, averaging over $5 million per day. The win, place, and show pools are very large. It takes a large bet to have much influence on the odds. The track take was 17.5% (it is now 15.33%), and Santa Anita has 10¢ breakage.

As with our Exhibition Park bets, we calculated the expected value per dollar bet using equations similar to (4.3) and (4.4). Because of the higher-

---

*Recall from Chapter Five that we now recommend 1.18 as the preferred expected-value cutoff for tracks like Exhibition Park.

quality horses and larger betting pools, we utilized a 1.16 expected-value cutoff for our Dr. Z system bets. Using an initial wealth of $2,500, our wealth over the season—if we bet on every Dr. Z system bet whose expected value to place or show was at least 1.16*—grew to $5,337, for a profit of $2,837. The history of our betting fortune over the season appears in Figure 9.2. The average bettor starting with $2,500 is bankrupt by the 24th day. The Dr. Z system bets at Santa Anita were large, which led to considerable swings in our betting fortune. We peaked out at $4,635 on the 35th day, then at $6,559 on the 71st day. Although there were several losing streaks, the overall trend was a substantial increase in wealth over time. The calculations of the optimal place and show bets were calculated using the equations in Chapter Sixteen.

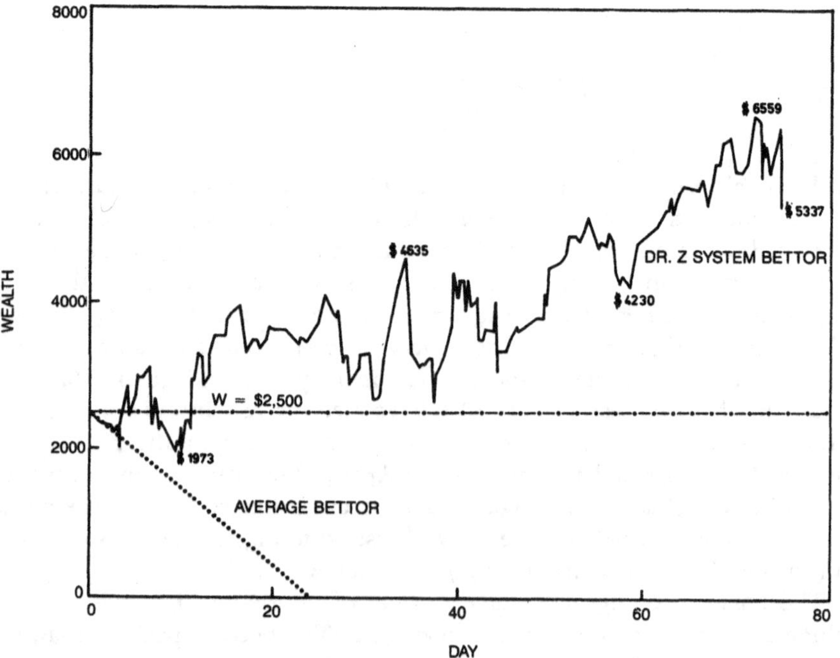

Figure 9.2 Betting-wealth-level history for Dr. Z system bets at the 1973–74 winter meeting at Santa Anita using an expected-value cutoff of 1.16

*Since it rarely rains in Arcadia, we did not worry about eliminating non-fast-track days, since there would be so few. We recommend, however, that you do not bet at Santa Anita on non-fast-track days. We now recommend an expected-value cutoff of 1.14 for top-quality tracks such as Santa Anita.

AQUEDUCT: THE 1981–82 WINTER SEASON

Aqueduct is one of the three major thoroughbred racing tracks in New York State. The others are Belmont and Saratoga. Between them and the Meadowlands in New Jersey, they provide top-quality racing for the millions in the New York metropolitan area throughout the year. Aqueduct's racing season typically runs from mid-October to mid-May and Belmont's in the summer except for August, which is reserved for beautiful Saratoga near Albany.

Richard van Slyke collected the win, place, and show mutuels for us for the 43-day period December 27, 1981–March 27, 1982. During this period, 3,470 horses ran in 380 races. In New York the betting occurs off-track as well as at the racetrack. The off-track betting mutuels are then combined with the on-track values a few minutes before post time. The off-track bettors do not know the actual mutuel pools and their bets amount to about half of the total pools. When this money enters the tote board of the track in

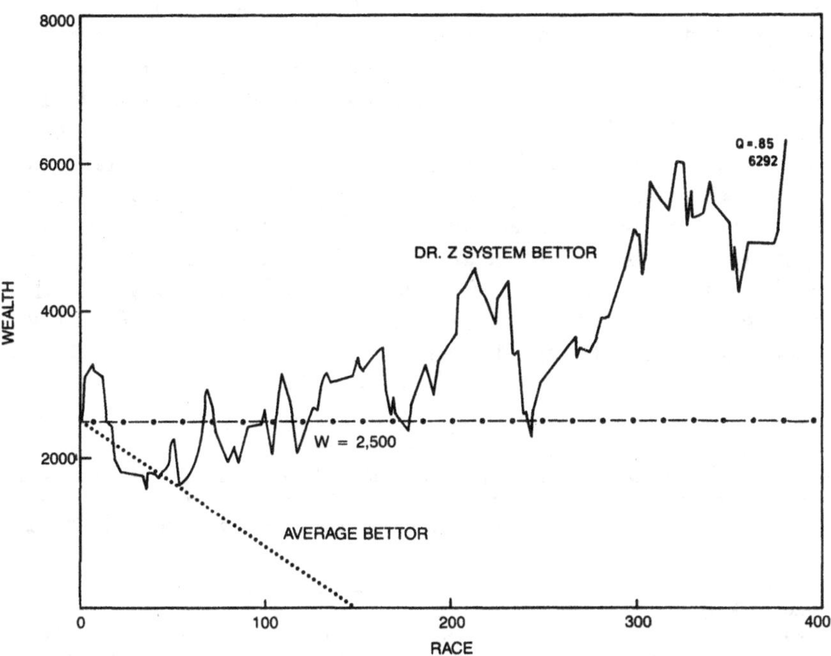

Figure 9.3 Betting-wealth-level history for Dr. Z system bets at the 1981–82 Aqueduct winter meeting using an expected-value cutoff of 1.14

one fell swoop, many Dr. Z system bets occur. The track take in New York was 15%. Aqueduct has 10¢ breakage. We calculated the expected value per dollar bet to place and show for all 3,470 horses using equations (4.5) and (4.6). Whenever the expected value per dollar bet was at least 1.14, we would make a Dr. Z system bet, whose amount was determined using equations in Chapter Sixteen. From an initial wealth of $2,500, our wealth over the season grew to $6,292, for a profit of $3,792. The history of our betting fortune over the season appears in Figure 9.3. The average bettor would have lost his fortune by the 148th race. As with the Exhibition Park and Santa Anita data, there is a jagged look to the line tracing our wealth level that reflects both individual wins and losses and winning and losing streaks.

HOW IMPORTANT IS THE TRACK TAKE?

The track take amounts to a commission of 14%–22% on every dollar wagered. It pays for purses, taxes, and expenses, and it also provides profits for the racetrack owners. An additional 1% or 2% makes a large difference in the payoffs and especially in the profits you make with a winning system. This effect is illustrated in Table 9.1, which provides payoff figures for track takes of 14% to 18%. On a bet that would return $9.83 without track take (and breakage), $1.38 is lost to a track that has a 14% track take. After that, about 10¢ is lost for each percentage increase in the track take. At 17%, that means 29¢. With a payoff of $6.51, 92¢, or nearly a dollar, is lost—even with a low track take of 14%. Another $6\frac{1}{2}$¢ is lost for each percentage increase in the track take. For a 17% track take, that means another 19¢, or $1.11 in total. For a small payoff, such as $3.85, the percentage effect is the same, but the actual dollar costs are less. A 14% track take amounts to 54¢, and 17% to 65¢.

TABLE 9.1 ***Effect on payoffs of 14%, 15%, 16%, 17%, and 18% track takes***

Payoff of a $2 Bet before Track Take ($)	Payoff after Track Take But before Breakage with Varying Track Takes ($)				
	14%	15%	16%	17%	18%
9.83	8.45	8.35	8.26	8.16	8.06
6.51	5.59	5.53	5.46	5.40	5.34
3.85	3.31	3.27	3.23	3.20	3.16

The effect on profits is even more dramatic. You lose not only because there are additional costs in each race, but also because your betting wealth is less, which means the actual bets you make are smaller. During the 1981–82 season, Aqueduct had a 15% track take. Dr. Z system bets yielded a final wealth of $6,292, for a profit of $3,792. Aqueduct recently increased the track take to 17%, while prior to 1981–82 it was 14%. Figure 9.4 shows what the effect would have been on both our betting wealth and profits if this higher track take had been operative in 1981–82, and it also shows how much better we would have done with a 14% track take. With a 17% track take, our final betting wealth would have fallen to $5,058. Our profit of $3,792 would have dropped by $1,234 to $2,558—nearly a third of the profits—due to a 2% increase in the track take. With a track take of 14%, the final betting wealth would have grown to $7,090, for a profit of $4,590, or $798 more than with the 15% track take. As a rule of thumb, you may assume that each 1% increase in the track take eats up about a sixth of the profits. At a track take of 20% or more, there simply would not be many Dr. Z system bets, and total profits would likely be quite small.

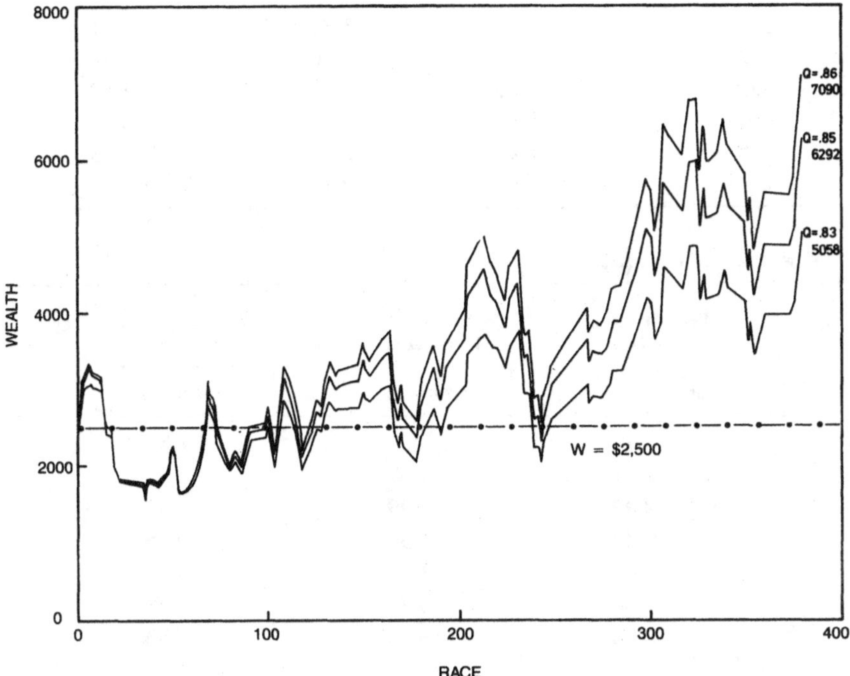

Figure 9.4 Betting-wealth-level histories for Dr. Z system bets at the 1981–82 Aqueduct winter meeting using an expected-value cutoff of 1.14 for track takes of 14%, 15%, and 17%

HOW IMPORTANT IS BREAKAGE?

In addition to the track take of 14%–22%, bettors must also pay an additional commission, called breakage. As we have indicated, this commission refers to the funds not returned to the betting public because the payoffs are rounded down to the nearest 10¢ or 20¢ on a $2 bet. For example, a payoff net of the track take of $6.39 would pay $6.30 or $6.20, respectively. Breakage occurs in the win, place, and show as well as in the exotic pools.

TABLE 9.2 ***Effect of 5¢ and 10¢ breakage on payoff and profit***

Payoff on a $2 Bet after Track Take But before Breakage ($)	Payoff after 5¢ Breakage ($)	Payoff after 10¢ Breakage ($)	Percentage of Payoff Lost to 5¢ Breakage
10.35	10.30	10.20	0.48
8.57	8.50	8.40	0.82
6.39	5.30	6.20	1.41
4.61	4.60	4.60	0.22
3.87	3.80	3.80	1.81
2.95	2.90	2.80	1.69
2.68	2.60	2.60	2.99
2.39	2.30	2.20	3.91
2.26	2.20	2.20	2.65
2.08	2.10	2.10	−0.96

TABLE 9.2 ***(Continued)***

Percentage of Payoff Lost to 10¢ Breakage	Percentage of Profit Lost to 5¢ Breakage	Percentage of Profit Lost to 10¢ Breakage
1.45	0.60	1.80
1.75	1.07	2.59
2.97	2.09	4.32
0.22	0.38	0.38
1.81	3.74	3.74
5.08	5.26	15.79
2.99	13.33	13.33
7.94	23.08	48.72
2.65	23.08	23.08
−0.96	−25.00	−25.00

We refer to rounding down to the nearest 10¢ on a $2 bet as 5¢ breakage, that is, 5¢ per dollar, and rounding down to the nearest 20¢ on a $2 bet as 10¢ breakage. Initially, most tracks utilized a 5¢ breakage. In recent years, however, more and more tracks have switched to 10¢ breakage. It amounts to a substantial additional commission and more profits for the track. Table 9.2 illustrates the difference between these two types of breakage and their effect on total payoff and total profits.

As Table 9.2 shows, the 10¢ breakage is never less than 5¢ breakage and usually is considerably more. As a percentage of the payoff, breakage usually increases as the payoff becomes smaller, unless the payoff is close to the breakage round-off amount. An exception is the minus pool; in that case $2.10 must be paid even if the payoff before breakage is only $2.08. In Louisiana, the minimum payoff is $2.20. Minus pools are discussed in Chapter Fifteen.

Our calculations indicate that, on average, bettors using the Dr. Z system lose about 1.6% of the total payoff on their bets to 5¢ breakage and 2.8% to 10¢ breakage. Adding these amounts to the track take gives the total commission. For example, at Churchill Downs in Louisville, Kentucky, the 15% track take becomes about 18% with their 10¢ breakage, and at Exhibition Park in Vancouver, British Columbia, the 15.8% track take also becomes about 17.4% with their 5¢ breakage. To determine the true commission at a given racetrack, you must take into account both the breakage and the track take. A table of track takes for various U.S. states, Mexico, and Canadian provinces appears in Appendix A.

The full extent of the effect of breakage is shown in what it does to profits. Using the 1978 Dr. Z system bets for Exhibition Park without breakage, an initial wealth of $2,500 would leave you with $8,319 at the end of the year. With 5¢ breakage you would have $7,521,* and with 10¢ breakage, $6,918. The effect of breakage throughout the 1978 season is shown in Figure 9.5. In addition to taking money away from total wealth, breakage has the effect of lowering the bet size, since a lower betting wealth means smaller bets and lower future profits. These calculations indicate that 5¢ breakage averages 13.7% of profits, and 10¢ breakage averages 24.1% of profits on Dr. Z system bets.

To summarize, breakage, especially the very common 10¢ variety, is a very substantial cost. The costs are highest when you are making bets on short-odds horses. Unfortunately, this is an unavoidable aspect of the Dr. Z system.

---

*This $7,521 final wealth is different from the $7,698 in Figure 9.1, because Figure 9.5 uses a 1.18 expected-value cutoff and Figure 9.1 uses a 1.20 expected-value cutoff.

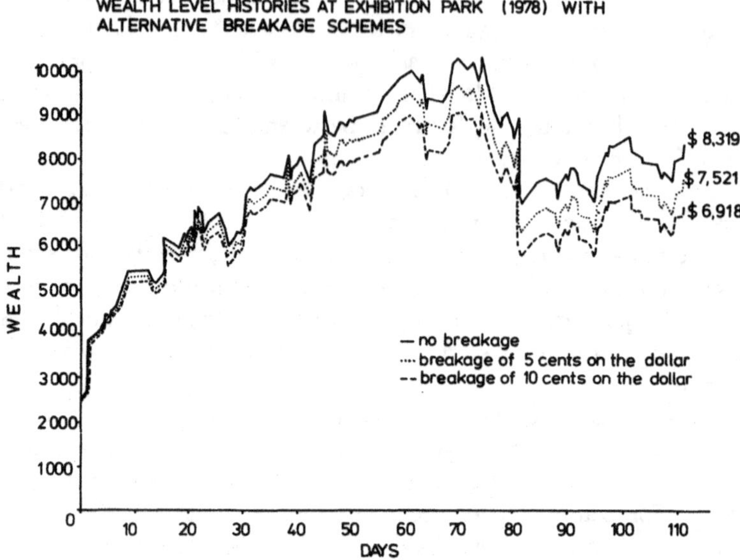

Figure 9.5 Wealth-level histories of Dr. Z system bets at Exhibition Park in 1978 with alternative breakage schemes

THE TWO-MINUTE PROBLEM: BETS AT EXHIBITION PARK IN 1980

The computer studies described in this chapter for the races at Exhibition Park in 1978, Santa Anita in 1973–74, and Aqueduct in 1981–82 give convincing evidence of the validity of using the Dr. Z system over extended periods. These studies were based on the win, place, and show mutuel pools at the end of the betting period. In practice, it takes thirty seconds or so to determine your optimal bet and a minute or so actually to make the bet. Even with the charts in Chapter Five or with some appropriate way of determining the optimal bet size, you need to utilize the betting information one to two minutes before the end of the betting period.

You need to find out just when the betting stops at any particular racetrack you are attending. This may be exactly at the listed post time or possibly a few minutes later. The key is to watch where the horses are. When they get close to the starting gate, you know that the totalizer machines will be closed soon. An exception occurs when there is a late scratch or an incident among the horses. Then the betting can go on for several more minutes. In a recent race at Exhibition Park, the final one on the card, which features the heavily bet triactor, there were three late scratches. Management, wanting to make sure that their commission would not be lost, held up the race for over thirty minutes so that the refunded money could be rebet.

In the rest of this book, the betting described used the tote values as they stood one or two minutes before the end of the betting period, that is, when we made our actual bets. On occasion, a bet is a Dr. Z system bet with two minutes to go, but as a result of the late betting, it is no longer a good bet at post time. This difficulty does not seem to happen very often, and has not proved to be a serious problem for us.

To study the possible effects of the two-minute problem, we did a computer analysis of this phenomenon.* On nine days during July and August 1980, during which ninety races were run, we went to Exhibition Park and recorded data at two minutes before post time and then at thirty-second intervals until the race was run. We utilized a betting fortune of $2,500 and made our Dr. Z system bets using the win, place, and show pools two minutes before the race. We then based our results on the final win, place, and show pools. There were twenty-two Dr. Z system bets at the two-minute mark, using our conservative cutoff of 1.20 expected value. The results appear in Table 9.3 and Figure 9.6.

Our $2,500 grew to $3,716, for a profit of $1,216, or 48.6%, on our initial investment. The twenty-two bets were for a total of $5,304, so our rate of return was 22.9%. Since we were choosing only bets with an expected value of at least 1.20 with two minutes to the race, we expected an average rate of return in this range. The expected value at post time was often less than it was with two minutes to go. However, it never fell to less than 1.00, breaking even, and only three times to less than 1.10. It increased five times in the twenty-two races. On most of the days, there were two Dr. Z system bets. One day had three, another four. Nineteen of the bets were to show and only three to place. In one race we bet to place and show on the same horse. *We won sixteen of the twenty-two bets, or 72.7%. Weighting by the amount bet, we won 77.1% of the time.* We made bets ranging from $7 to $688. Two of the largest bets were lost: $511 and $591. In one of these cases, the bet was on a horse that had not run recently; of course, we do not recommend such a bet in the Dr. Z system. Figure 9.6 shows that the general trend of our betting wealth was up, at the 22.9% average growth rate per dollar bet, but our fortune went up and down significantly when there were several big wins or a large loss. With random betting, a $2,500 betting fortune would have dwindled to about $1,500, so we were about $2,200 ahead of the typical bettor. In Appendix B we have calculated that the probability that we could have done this much better than the average bettor simply by chance is negligible: three chances in one hundred thousand. Similarly, given this is typical betting, the probability of being ahead in

*See also the additional results in Chapters Thirteen, Fourteen, and Seventeen that users of the Dr. Z system have supplied to us.

TABLE 9.3 ***Results from summer 1980 Exhibition Park betting: Twenty-two Dr. Z system bets during ninety races over ten days***

Date	Race	Regression Estimate of Expected Return per Dollar, Two Minutes before End of Betting	Regression Estimate of Expected Return per Dollar, at the End of Betting	Regression Estimate of Optimal Bet Two Minutes before End of Betting ($)	Finish	Net Return Based on Final Data with Consideration of Our Bets Affecting Odds		Final Wealth ($)
								$2,500
July 2	9	120	122	19,SHOW ON 4	5-6-7	− $19		2,481
"	10	120	123	72,SHOW ON 8	8-1-2	72		2,553
July 9	7	121	110	292,SHOW ON 1	2-7-1	131		2,684
"	10	135	122	248,PLACE ON 1	1-6-2	260		2,944
July 16	6	131	122	487,PLACE ON 9	9-8-6	536	682	3,626
		139	117	292,SHOW ON 9		146		
"	7	125	127	7,SHOW ON 1	5-2-8	−7		3,619
July 23	3	149	149	30,SHOW ON 2	2-10-7	92		3,711
"	4	139	134	573,SHOW ON 10	6-10-4	201		3,912
July 30	8	121	111	215,PLACE ON 4	4-1-5	129		4,041
"	9	123	125	591,SHOW ON 6	8-1-5	−591		3,450
Aug 6	6	128	112	39,SHOW ON 4	4-3-1	59		3,509
"	9	124	103	51,SHOW ON 2	4-1-3	−51		3,458
Aug 8	1	121	132	87,SHOW ON 1	1-10-4	139		3,597
"	3	127	111	635,SHOW ON 3	3-4-7	127		3,724
"	4	126	113	126,SHOW ON 2	2-7-1	82		3,806
Aug 11	8	121	112	94,SHOW ON 8	8-6-2	113		3,919
"	9	131	130	688,SHOW ON 5	5-3-4	138		4,057
Aug 13	3	128	106	33,SHOW ON 2	1-6-7	−33		4,024
"	6	131	122	205,SHOW ON 5	5-8-4	144		4,168
"	7	134	133	511,SHOW ON 6	8-5-9	−511		3,657
"	10	123	109	108,SHOW ON 5	3-5-1	59		3,716

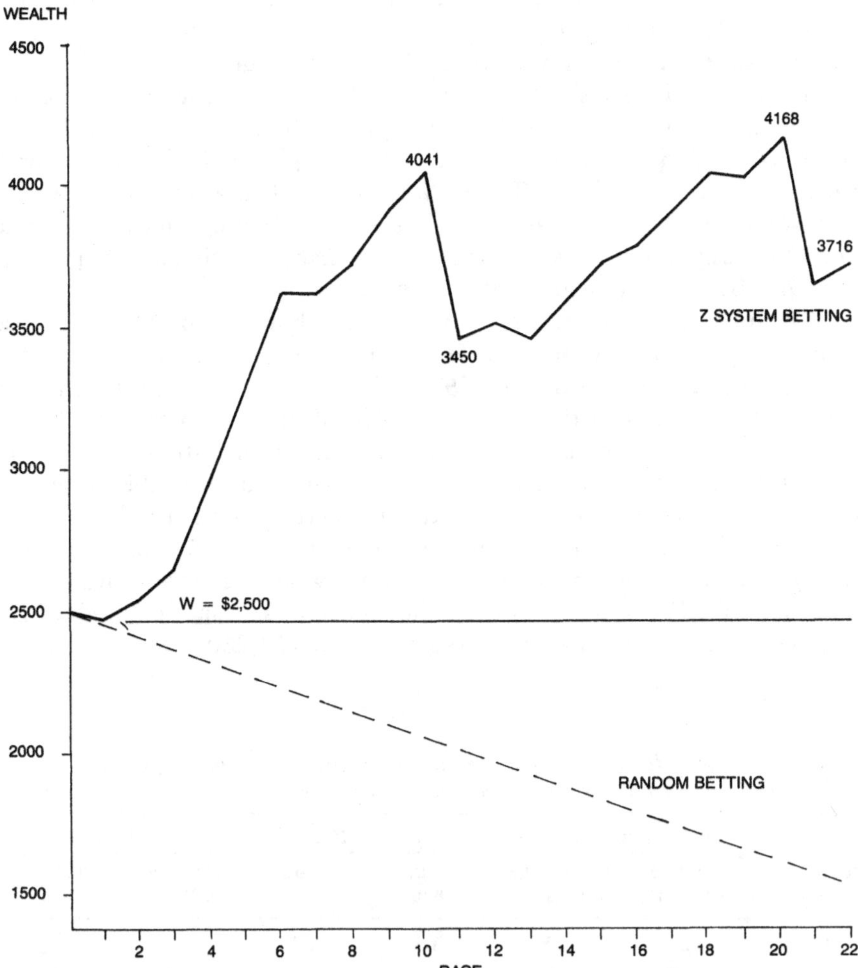

Figure 9.6 Results from summer 1980 Exhibition Park betting: Twenty-two Dr. Z system bets during ninety races over ten days

our bets after twenty-two Dr. Z system bets is 94.6%. The results, then, do seem to represent true exploitation of a market inefficiency.

CHARACTERISTICS OF DR. Z SYSTEM BETS

Table 9.5 summarizes results of the Dr. Z system bets made at Aqueduct in 1981–82, Santa Anita in 1973–74, Exhibition Park in 1978 and 1980, and at Churchill Downs on the 1981 to 1986 Kentucky Derby Days. The data sets for Aqueduct, Santa Anita, and 1978 Exhibition Park were collected after each racing season was completed. The 1980 Exhibition Park and Kentucky Derby Days data sets were collected race by race at the track. In all cases an initial betting wealth of $2,500 was assumed.*

The expected-value cutoffs used were 1.10 on the Derby Days, reflecting the superior quality of horses; 1.14 at Aqueduct and Santa Anita, reflecting the overall high quality of horses; and 1.20 at Exhibition Park.† These cutoff values were determined from Table 5.2 and from other calculations we made. We worked on the basis of an expected 20% rate of return on the first dollar bet. Obviously this 20% would drop when we started betting larger amounts, since our bets would begin to affect the odds.

The most common Dr. Z system wager is a show bet on a favorite. Good show and place bets occur about 85% and 15% of the time, respectively. The percent of bets won is about 59%, while the percent of bets won when weighted by the size of the bet is 72%. This difference arises from the fact that the large bets are on favorites which often finish in-the-money, while small bets are placed on longer-odds horses, which finish in the money less often. At a track like Santa Anita with large betting pools, our bets did not affect the odds very much, and our average bet was about 7% of our wealth. The average bet dropped to about 5% of our wealth at tracks with smaller betting pools. In the course of these thousands of races and hundreds of Dr. Z system bets, the total amount wagered was $172,260.

TABLE 9.4 ***Distribution of bet sizes with initial wealth of $2,500 at Exhibition Park in 1978 and Aqueduct in 1981–82***

Bet Size ($)	Exhibition Park 1978		Aqueduct 1981/82		Totals	
	Number of Bets	Percentage of Bets	Number of Bets	Percentage of Bets	Number of Bets	Percentage of Bets
0–50	22	13	18	14	40	13
51–100	37	21	10	8	47	16
101–200	35	20	20	16	55	19
201–400	39	22	42	34	81	27
401–600	16	9	12	10	28	9
601–1,000	19	11	17	14	37	12
1,001 +	6	4	5	3	10	3
Totals	174	100	124	100	298	100

*Additional results by other players of the Dr. Z system appear in Chapters Thirteen, Fourteen, and Seventeen.

†We recommend 1.18 as the best cutoff at tracks like Exhibition Park.

TABLE 9.5 ***Summary statistics on Dr. Z system bets made at Aqueduct in 1981–82; Santa Anita in 1973–74; Exhibition Park in 1978 and 1980; and at the 1981–1986 Kentucky Derby days with an initial betting wealth of $2,500***

Track and Season	*Number of Races*	*Track Take (%)*	*Expected Value Cutoff*	*Number of Dr. Z System Bets*	*Number of Bets Won*	*Percentage of Bets Won*
Aqueduct 1981–82	380	15	1.14	124	68	55
Santa Anita 1973–74	627	15	1.14	192	114	59
Exhibition Park 1978	1,065	18.1	1.20	174	97	56
Exhibition Park 1980	90	17.1	1.20	22	16	73
Kentucky Derby Days[a] 1981–86	60	15 and 16	1.10	40	32	80
Totals and weighted averages	2,222	—	—	552	327	59

TABLE 9.5 ***(Continued)***

Track and Season	*Percentage of Bets Won Weighted by Size of Bet*	*Total Money Wagered ($)*	*Track Take ($)*	*Total Profits ($)*	*Average Payout per $2 Bet ($)*	*Rate of Return on Bets Made (%)*
Aqueduct 1981–82	65	42,686	6,403	3,792	3.33	8.9
Santa Anita 1973–74	69	51,631	7,745	2,837	3.16	5.5
Exhibition Park 1978	72	49,991	9,048	5,198	3.08	10.4
Exhibition Park 1980	77	5,403	924	1,216	3.18	22.5
Kentucky Derby Days[a] 1981–86	91	22,549	3,463	6,555	2.84	29.1
Totals and weighted averages	72	172,260	27,583	19,598	3.10	11.4

[a]The size of the Derby Day bets here are different from those in Chapters Ten, Eleven, and Twelve, because these optimal bets were calculated on the basis of an initial betting wealth of $2,500.

The size distribution of our bets at Exhibition Park in 1978 and Aqueduct in 1981–82 appears in Table 9.4.* The track take amounted to $27,583. Our profit was $19,598, an 11.4% rate of return on dollars wagered. Higher rates of return were achieved for races where we were actually at the track, when we were able to skip rainy days and avoid horses that did not meet the simple handicapping qualifications mentioned in Chapter Five. The lower rates of return, as expected, were at the tracks where we had no information other than the win, place, and show mutuel pools.

Finally, the average payout per $2 bet ranged from $2.97 to $3.33 at the various tracks, with an average value of $3.10. This value was actually a relatively high show return, considering that the Dr. Z system often picks heavy favorites.

TABLE 9.6 ***Size distribution of Dr. Z system bets with $10,000 initial betting wealth at Santa Anita in 1973–74 and Exhibition Park in 1978***

	Santa Anita				Exhibition Park			
	Place		Show		Place		Show	
Size ($)	% of Bets	% of $Bet	% of Bets	% of $Bet	% of Bets	% of $Bet	% of Bets	% of $Bet
0–50	7.1	0.3	2.6	0.1	29.4	3.6	17.0	1.0
51–100	0	0	1.3	0.1	23.5	6.7	13.8	2.8
101–200	0	0	3.9	0.4	5.9	2.9	22.3	9.3
201–300	21.4	6.1	5.2	1.0	5.9	4.4	14.9	10.3
301–500	7.1	3.2	9.1	2.6	23.5	30.6	8.5	9.1
501–700	14.3	10.3	13.0	5.7	0	0	6.4	10.5
701–1,000	14.3	14.4	7.8	4.8	0	0	7.4	17.5
1,001+	35.8	65.7	57.1	85.3	11.8	51.8	9.7	39.5
	n = 14	$11,932	n = 77	$104,142	n = 17	$4,954	n = 94[a]	$33,507

Total place bets — Total show bets — Total Santa Anita betting = $116,074

Total place bets — Total show bets — Total Exhibition Park betting = $38,461

[a]Two of these bets had $EX_s^i \geqslant 1.20$ and $s_i^{\cdot} = 0$.

*For comparison with higher betting wealths, see Table 9.6, which shows an initial betting wealth of $10,000 at Exhibition Park in 1978 and Santa Anita in 1973–74.

10

The Kentucky Derby: The Most Exciting Two Minutes in Sports

THE PAGEANTRY

The Kentucky Derby is the world's most famous horse race. It is called the most exciting two minutes in sports. Since 1875, the country's best three-year-old thoroughbreds "run for the roses" at Churchill Downs in Louisville, Kentucky, on the first Saturday in May. The Derby is the first jewel of the Triple Crown of horse racing; it is followed by the Preakness and the Belmont Stakes. The winner receives a rose garland of some five hundred dark red roses, which, since 1932, has been hand sewn by Mrs. Kingsley Walker. The winning horse, jockey, trainer, and owner also share the substantial purse and racing immortality. The tradition and prestige of the race are immense, although hard to grasp fully without a visit to the Derby. The intensity of excitement builds as the prospects of the favorites for the Derby are evaluated in the early months of the year and culminates during Derby Week. For a full week, Louisville is alive with activities and enthusiasm much like those of football bowl games. There are parties, parades, Ohio river cruises, awards, and hundreds of reporters jostling amid the more than one hundred thousand visitors enjoying the atmosphere of mint juleps, fine weather, and lush surroundings, while they discuss the pros and cons of the various Derby hopefuls.

As many as twenty horses enter the $1\frac{1}{4}$-mile race. Many more would like to enter. The field is kept down by limiting it to the horses with the highest earnings from previous races. The legendary Secretariat in 1973 ran the fastest Derby and set the Churchill Downs track record of $1{:}59^2$ for $1\frac{1}{4}$ miles. In fact, Secretariat is the only horse ever to have won the Derby in less than two minutes. Northern Dancer ran the course in two minutes flat in 1964. Figure 10.1 shows the eleven fastest Derby winners and how the horses might have finished. Remember that one fifth of a second roughly equals one length. The times of different races are not really comparable, since track conditions are so variable. However, the Secretariat time is still a most remarkable feat.*

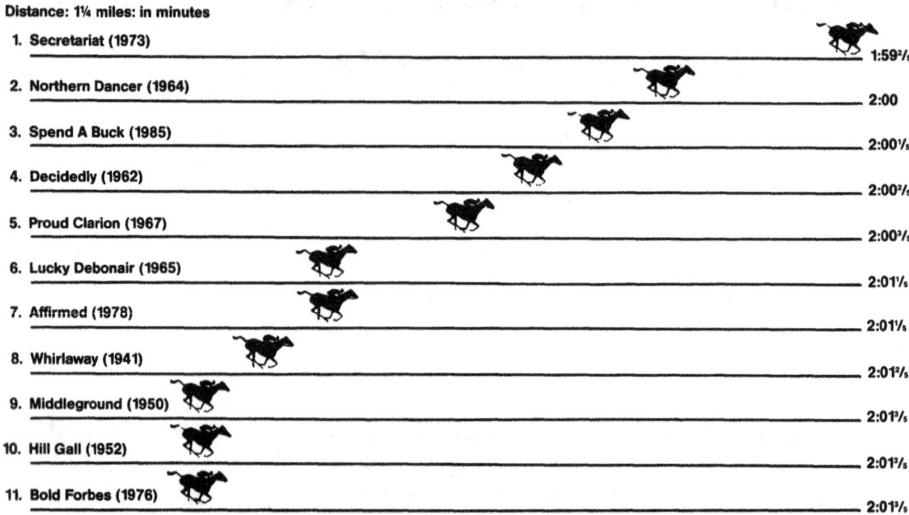

Figure 10.1 The eleven fastest winners of the Kentucky Derby

The usual starting gate with stalls for twelve horses is supplemented with a second gate to accommodate all twenty starters. This mass of horseflesh thundering in front of the stands for the first time is quite a sight. The huge number of starters means hard work for the jockeys, who try to angle for good positions. As a result of the difficulty of achieving good position and the intense competition, many prerace favorites falter badly in the Derby. For many of them, their careers never regain their prerace promise.

Despite this hazardous aspect, owners, trainers, and jockeys are willing year after year to try their best to have a Derby winner. In addition to the prestige and the more than half-million-dollar purse, the owner can expect to see the value of his or her Derby-winning horse increase by millions. Inflation and rising expectations have pushed the value of the best bloodstock to astronomical heights. Although the breeding performance of a stallion may be influenced significantly by his racing performance, his price reacts dramatically to this record, often quite out of proportion to its true importance.

*Secretariat's performance in the Derby was the start of perhaps the greatest sequence of outstanding stakes victories in the history of thoroughbred racing. He broke the track record in the Preakness and Belmont Stakes, the latter by a full two seconds. He then broke two other track records. In all, he set records at five different distances at five different tracks. The chart of his Belmont Stakes victory appears in Chapter Four on page 66. Charts of the other races in 1973 appear in Quinn (1984).

Kentucky Derby Winners

Year	*Winner*	*Owner*
1875	Aristides, ch. c.	H. P. McGrath
1876	Vagrant, br. g.	William Astor
1877	Baden-Baden, ch. c.	Daniel Swigert
1878	Day Star, ch. c.	T. J. Nichols
1879	Lord Murphy, b. c.	Geo. W. Darden & Co.
1880	Fonso, ch. c.	J. S. Shawhan
1881	Hindoo, b. c.	Dwyer Bros.
1882	Apollo, ch. g.	Morris & Patton
1883	Leonatus, b. c.	Chinn & Morgan
1884	Buchanan, ch. c.	W. Cottrill
1885	Joe Cotton, ch. c.	J. T. Williams
1886	Ben Ali, br. c.	J. B. Haggin
1887	Montrose, b. c.	Labold Bros.
1888	Macbeth II, b. g.	Chicago Stable
1889	Spokane, ch. c.	Noah Armstrong
1890	Riley, b. c.	Edward Corrigan
1891	Kingman, b. c.	Jacobin Stable
1892	Azra, b. c.	Bashford Manor
1893	Lookout, b. c.	Cushing & Orth
1894	Chant, b. c.	Leigh & Rose
1895	Halma, blk. c.	Byron McClelland
1896	Ben Brush, b. c.	M. F. Dwyer
1897	Typhoon II, ch. c.	J. C. Cahn
1898	Plaudit, br. c.	J. E. Madden
1899	Manuel, b. c.	A. H. & D. H. Morris
1900	Lieut. Gibson, b. c.	Charles H. Smith
1901	His Eminence, b. c.	F. B. VanMeter
1902	Alan-a-Dale, ch. c.	T. C. McDowell
1903	Judge Himes, b. c.	C. R. Ellison
1904	Elwood, b. c.	Mrs. C. E. Durnell
1905	Agile, b. c.	S. S. Brown
1906	Sir Huon, b. c.	George J. Long
1907	Pink Star, b. c.	J. Hal Woodford
1908	Stone Street, b. c.	C. E. Hamilton
1909	Wintergreen, b. c.	J. B. Respess
1910	Donau, b. c.	William Gerst
1911	Meridian, b. c.	R. F. Carman
1912	Worth, br. c.	H. C. Hallenbeck
1913	Donerail, b. c.	T. P. Hayes
1914	Old Rosebud, b. g.	H. C. Applegate
1915	Regret, ch. f.	H. P. Whitney
1916	George Smith, blk. c.	John Sanford
1917	Omar Khayyam, ch. c.	Billings & Johnson
1918	Exterminator, ch. g.	W. S. Kilmer
1919	Sir Barton, ch. c.	J. K. L. Ross
1920	Paul Jones, br. g.	Ral Parr
1921	Behave Yourself, b. c.	E. R. Bradley
1922	Morvich, br. c.	B. Block
1923	Zev, br. c.	Rancocas Stable

Kentucky Derby Winners (continued)

Year	*Winner*	*Owner*
1924	Black Gold, blk. c.	Mrs. R. M. Hoots
1925	Flying Ebony, blk. c.	G. A. Cochran
1926	Bubbling Over, ch. c.	Idle Hour Stock Farm
1927	Whiskey, b. c.	H. P. Whitney
1928	Reigh Count, ch. c.	Mrs. J. D. Hertz
1929	Clyde Van Dusen, ch. g.	H. P. Gardner
1930	Gallant Fox, b. c.	Belair Stud
1931	Twenty Grand, b. c.	Greentree Stable
1932	Burgoo King, ch. c.	E. R. Bradley
1933	Brokers Tip, br. c.	E. R. Bradley
1934	Cavalcade, br. c.	Mrs. Dodge Sloane
1935	Omaha, ch. c.	Belair Stud
1936	Bold Venture, ch. c.	M. L. Schwartz
1937	War Admiral, br. c.	Glen Riddle Farm
1938	Lawrin, b. c.	Woolford Farm
1939	Johnstown, b. c.	Belair Stud
1940	Gallahadion, b. c.	Milky Way Farm
1941	Whirlaway, ch. c.	Calumet Farm
1942	Shut Out, ch. c.	Greentree Farm
1943	Count Fleet, br. c.	Mrs. John D. Hertz
1944	Pensive, ch. c.	Calumet Farm
1945	Hoop, Jr., b. c.	F. W. Hooper
1946	Assault, ch. c.	King Ranch
1947	Jet Pilot, ch. c.	Maine Chance Farm
1948	Citation, ch. c.	Calumet Farm
1949	Ponder, dk. b. c.	Calumet Farm
1950	Middleground, ch. c.	King Ranch
1951	Count Turf, b.c.	J. J. Amiel
1952	Hill Gail, b. c.	Calumet Farm
1953	Dark Star, br. c.	Cain Hoy Stable
1954	Determine, gr. c.	A. J. Crevolin
1955	Swaps, ch. c.	R. C. Ellsworth
1956	Needles, b. c.	D. & H. Stable
1957	Iron Liege, b. c.	Calumet Farm
1958	Tim Tam, dk. b. c.	Calumet Farm,
1959	[a] Tomy Lee, b. c.	Fred Turner, Jr.
1960	Venetian Way, ch. c.	Sunny Blue Farm
1961	Carry Back, br. c.	Mrs. Katherine Price
1962	Decidedly, gr. c.	El Peco Ranch
1963	Chateaugay, ch. c.	Darby Dan Farm
1964	[a] Northern Dancer, b. c.	Windfields Farms
1965	Lucky Debonair, b. c.	Mrs. Ada L. Rice
1966	Kauai King, dk. b. c.	Michael J. Ford
1967	Proud Clarion, b. c.	Darby Dan Farm
1968	[b] Forward Pass	Calumet Farm
1969	Majestic Prince, ch. c.	Frank McMahon
1970	Dust Commander, ch. c.	Robert Lehmann
1971	Canonero II, b. c.	Edgar Calbett
1972	Riva Ridge, b. c.	Meadow Stable
1973	Secretariat, ch. c.	Meadow Stable

Kentucky Derby Winners (continued)

Year	Winner	Owner
1974	Cannonade, b. c.	John M. Olin
1975	Foolish Pleasure, b. c.	John L. Greer
1976	Bold Forbes, dk. b. c.	E. R. Tizol
1977	Seattle Slew, dk. b. c.	Karen L. Taylor
1978	Affirmed, ch. c.	Harbor View Farm
1979	Spectacular Bid, gr. c.	Hawksworth Farm
1980	Genuine Risk, ch. f.	Mrs. Bertram Firestone
1981	Pleasant Colony, dk. b. c.	Buckland Farm
1982	Gato Del Sol, gr. c.	Hancock & Peters
1983	[a] Sunny's Halo, ch. c.	D. J. Foster Stable
1984	Swale, dk. b. or. br. c.	Claiborne Farms
1985	Spend A Buck, b. c.	Hunter Farm
1986	Ferdinand, ch. c.	Mrs. Elisabeth A. Keck
1987	Alysheba, b. c.	D. & P. Scharbauer

[a]Indicates an imported horse [b]Awarded first place after disqualification of winner.

Derby Details

1875—Aristides' time of 2:37¾ was the fastest 1½ miles ever run in the United States by a three-year-old carrying 100 pounds.

1877—The official measurement of the track was 1 mile and 17 inches around.

1886—Bookmakers did not operate at the track because of failure to reach a license agreement with the management.

1892 and 1905—The smallest fields that ever started a Derby went to the post —3.

1895—On the west side of the track, the new grandstand with its twin spires was completed.

1896—The first Derby at 1¼ miles was run.

1904—Mrs. Charles Elwood Durnell of Missouri was the first woman to own a Derby winner.

1913—Donerail, the longest-priced winner of a Derby, paid $184.90 straight. Thomas P. Hayes of Lexington, Kentucky, was the last man to breed, own, and train a Derby winner.

1915—Regret won and is the first filly to have this distinction. She carried 112 pounds.

1917—Omar Khayyam (England) was the first imported horse to win a Derby. Tomy Lee (England) won in 1959. Northern Dancer (1964) was foaled in Canada but is not considered an imported horse.

1919—Sir Barton won the Derby and became the first of America's Triple Crown winners.

1920—This is the first year that all colts and geldings carried 126 pounds and fillies, 121.

1924—The Golden Jubilee Derby. The 14-karat gold cup, valued at $5,000, was presented for the first time. Lemon & Son, jewelers, designed the cup.

1926—Radio Station WHAS broadcast the Derby locally for the first time.

1929—1.19 inches of rain fell making this the wettest Derby on record. Clyde Van Dusen was the first son of Man o' War to win a Derby. In 1937, War Admiral was the second and last. The first coast-to-coast broadcast of the Derby was heard over the National Broadcasting Company network.

1932—Since the use of the starting gate, the field was at the post for the longest time—15½ minutes.
1933—Colonel E. R. Bradley won his fourth Derby with Brokers Tip. The trainer of the four winners was H. J. "Dick" Thompson. The names of all Bradley horses began with a "B".
1941—Whirlaway ran the Derby distance in 2:01⅖, a record that stood for twenty-one years.
1945—Due to wartime restrictions, all racing was banned in the United States on January 3. With victory in Europe on VE Day, May 8, racing was resumed. The Derby was held on June 9. Only once before, April 29, 1901, was the Derby not run in May.
1948—Citation became the eighth Triple Crown winner and the first thoroughbred to win over a million dollars in purses.
1952—The Derby was televised, live, nationally for the first time.
Eddie Arcaro won his fifth Derby on Hill Gail, a record for one jockey and since tied by Bill Hartack.
Ben A. Jones trained his sixth winner, also a record.
1964—Northern Dancer set a new track record for a 1¼-mile Derby—2:00.
1969—Richard M. Nixon, 37th President, was first man in this office to attend the Derby.
1973—Secretariat, enroute to the first Triple Crown Championship in 25 years, wins the Derby in track record time of 1:59⅖.
1974—100th Derby won by Cannonade, who earned $274,000, the largest Derby purse in history.
1976—Bold Forbes defeats Honest Pleasure, the first horse ever to have more than $1 million bet on him to win.
1977—Seattle Slew, at $.50 to the dollar, wins the Derby and later a Triple Crown Championship.
1978—Steve Cauthen rides his first Derby and wins on Harbor View Farm's Affirmed, the second Triple Crown winner in as many years.
1979—Spectacular Bid, second horse to pass $2 million in winnings (March 1980), wins Derby at $.60 to the dollar.
1980—Genuine Risk, paying $28.60, became the first filly in 65 years to win the Derby.
1983—The Canadian bred Sunny's Halo won the Derby.
1984—Swale won the Derby and later the Belmont and then tragically died.
1985—Spend A Buck led wire to wire in the third-fastest Derby.
1986—Ferdinand, ridden by 54-year-old Bill Shoemaker, won the Derby at 17–1.
1987—Alysheba, ridden by Chris McCarron, with only one win in ten starts, won the Derby at 8–1.

Derby Facts

RECORD GROSS PURSE—$793,600 in 1987.
RECORD WINNER'S SHARE—$618,600 to Alysheba in 1987.
LARGEST FIELD—23 in 1974.
SMALLEST FIELD—Three in 1892 and 1905.
FASTEST RUNNING—Secretariat, 1:59⅖ in 1973.
SLOWEST RUNNING—Stone Street, 2:15⅕ in 1908.
SHORTEST-PRICED WINNERS—Count Fleet (1943) and Citation (1948, coupled with Coaltown), $2.80.
LONGEST-PRICED WINNER—Donerail (1913), $184.90.

MOST WINS, OWNER—Calumet Farm with eight (Whirlaway, 1941; Pensive, 1944; Citation, 1948; Ponder, 1949; Hill Gail, 1952; Iron Liege, 1957; Tim Tam, 1958; Forward Pass, 1968).
MOST WINS, TRAINER—Ben A. Jones with six (Lawrin, 1938; Whirlaway, 1941; Pensive, 1944; Citation, 1948; Ponder, 1949; Hill Gail, 1952).
MOST WINS, JOCKEY—Five apiece by Eddie Arcaro (Lawrin, 1938; Whirlaway, 1941; Hoop Jr., 1945; Citation, 1948; Hill Gail, 1952) and Bill Hartack (Iron Liege, 1957; Venetian Way, 1960; Decidedly, 1962; Northern Dancer, 1964; Majestic Prince, 1969).
FOREIGN-BRED WINNERS—English-bred Omar Khayyam (1917) and Tomy Lee (1959), Canadian-bred Northern Dancer (1964), and Sunny's Halo (1983).
WINNERS—104 colts, seven geldings, two fillies (Regret, 1915, and Genuine Risk, 1980).

The Kentucky Derby Trophy

The gold cup presented to the winner of the Kentucky Derby was first designed for Churchill Downs president Matt Winn to commemorate the 50th anniversary of the race in 1924. Designed and produced by Lemon & Son, a prominent Louisville jeweller, the trophy has been given to every Derby winner's owner ever since.

The trophy is manufactured in New England from Lemon & Sons molds. The cup is 14k gold on a marble base. It is housed in a silk-lined mahogany case especially built to display the trophy.

To commemorate the 100th Kentucky Derby in 1974, a special version of the Derby cup was created. The horseshoe on the front face of the cup was studded with diamonds and emeralds, bringing the trophy's value to over $16,000. Today with rising gold prices, the trophy without jewels is valued at nearly $45,000.

At the Derby, the trophy, along with smaller silver replicas for the winning jockey and trainer, stands on the infield presentation stand above the winners circle. At the conclusion of the race the trophies are presented by the Governor of Kentucky and Churchill Downs president Lynn Stone.

The cups are left in Louisville for engraving and then are presented permanently to the winning owner, trainer and jockey. Prior to 1924, other types of trophies were given at the Kentucky Derby, generally pieces of antique silver. Today the Kentucky Derby trophy has become a familiar symbol of the greatest two minutes in sports.

Secretariat was syndicated in 1972 as a two-year-old for what was then* a record $6.08 million into 32 shares. The performances of this Triple Crown winner's sons have not yet measured up to their sire's brilliance. Still he is the fifteenth leading all-time sire according to the average earnings index of his offspring published in the *Blood-Horse*. However, his daughters have been more outstanding. Lady's Secret has won more than $2 million, including the 1986 Breeder's Cup Distaff and an amazing seven other Grade I stakes. She also won horse-of-the-year honors for 1986. Secretariat is the leading all-time broodmare sire. His daughter Six Crowns bred Chief's Crown, who won over $2 million and was the favorite in all three Triple Crown races in 1985. Secretariat's stud fee in 1986 was about $100,000 for each of the approximately fifty-three mares he services each year. Each share entitles the owner to one breeding privilege to an approved mare of his or her choice. Breeding receipts to mares above the first thirty-two are often shared in lot fashion. For example, if there are twenty additional breeds these fees go to the twenty share owners who are successful in the draw. Half of this fee is paid in advance, and half is paid when a live foal is delivered. In the past ten years, he has averaged thirty-eight live foals, three of which are the customary fee to Claiborne Farms in Paris, Kentucky, where he lives and breeds. Secretariat's annual gross income is in effect then about $100,000 times 35, or about $3.5 million. Although expenses such as insurance, a whopping 4%–5% or more of his value each year, are high and taxes and depreciation complicated, it is clear that the return is impressive. The stud fee is kept up by the bidding for the yearlings as they are sold at auction. Secretariat's yearlings averaged $202,023 for his first ten crops. Still, these prices may well justify the fee, especially if there is a glimmer of hope of producing a new Secretariat.†

---

*The current highest syndications are in the $35 plus million range, including Conquistador Cielo and Devil's Bag.

†The 1982 horse of the year, Conquistador Cielo, was syndicated for $36.4 million and commands a stud fee in the $150,000 range. At the height of the market in 1983–85, the top stud fees were about $500,000 for Seattle Slew and a whopping $1 million for Northern Dancer; Northern Dancer's yearlings were selling for an average of $2 million plus, which justified the fee. One sold for $10.2 million. That "colt" and the other nine top-priced fillies and colts have had rather mediocre records so far; see Appendix A. Indeed, not one of the 167 yearlings sold at auction in North America for $1 million or more has earned $1 million! The price of a share of Seattle Slew peaked at $3.5 million, putting his value at $140 million. Northern Dancer's son Dantzig had only three starts. He won them all convincingly, winning $30,000. However, in 1986, as the leading lifetime active sire, the eighty of his yearlings sold so far have fetched an average of $370,906. The famous thoroughbred breeding farms, such as Calumet, Claiborne, Elmendorf, Gainesway, Spendthrift, Tom Gentry, and others, are located in the Lexington, Kentucky, area, a scant two-hour drive away from Churchill Downs. Except for Calumet, these farms are generally open to the public by appointment. You can see most of the top stallions. Nearly all of the best stallions are in Kentucky, although Northern Dancer is at Windfield Farms in Maryland. A good information guide is *The Complete Guide to Kentucky Horse Country*, Classic Publishers, Prospect, Kentucky 40059. A good guide for information on all aspects of the 112 runnings of the Derby up to 1986 is *The Kentucky Derby: Churchill Downs 1875–1986*, available at no cost from the Kentucky Thoroughbred Owners and Breeders Association, Box 4158, Lexington, Kentucky 40544.

THE SPECTACLE

Our first visit to Kentucky for the Derby was in 1981 for the 107th running of this classic race. The city of Louisville was a massive jam of cars and people. All the hotels within 70 miles were full, even at two to five times their normal rates. Churchill Downs begins to fill up early in the morning, and racing begins at 11:30. About 46,000 people have the cherished reserved seats. Such seats are difficult to come by for newcomers, since most seats are reserved from year to year. The rest of the fans are allowed to roam the grounds and congregate in the field. They come by the thousands from all over the United States and Canada.

The Kentucky Derby Statistics for 1983 give you an idea of the scope of the spectacle.

DERBY DAY STATISTICS 1983

Derby souvenir glasses sold — 100,000
Mint juleps sold — 80,000
Bourbon for juleps — 8,000 quarts
Ice for juleps — 60 tons
Mint for juleps — 150 bushels
Soft drinks sold — 4,000 gallons
Shrimp sold in clubhouse — 1,000 pounds
Price for a platter of shrimp on Millionaires' Row — $80
Hot dogs sold — 7 miles (73,920 dogs at 6 inches each)
Price for a hot dog — $1.50
Beer sold — 1,500 16-gallon kegs (two-thirds in the infield)
Total commodes and urinals — 890:
In the grandstand — 230
In the clubhouse — 300
On Millionaires' Row — 60
In the infield — 250
Portable units — 50 (half in the infield)
Trash cans — 500
Trash — 21.6 truckloads (975 cubic yards)
Post-Derby clean-up workers — 300
Tulip blossoms — 14,000
Daily Racing Forms sold — 20,000
Spires — 1 pair
Men wearing hats with twin spires — 1
Betting windows — 1,000
Betting windows for wagers of at least $50 — 50
Average total betting per person for Derby Day — $41.25
Average winnings per person — $6.19
Anti-gambling evangelists outside the Downs — 2
Length of ABC-TV broadcast — 90 minutes
ABC-TV cameras covering the race — 24
Passes for "working" press — 1,625
Band members playing "My Old Kentucky Home" — 130
Time to play "My Old Kentucky Home" — 2:30
Millionaires on Millionaires' Row — 2,336
Total Downs seating — 45,094
Former presidents, Republican — 1
Former presidents, Democrat — 1
Vice presidents — 1
Democratic governors from out of state — 6
Democratic governors from Kentucky — 1
Republican governors — 0
Members of Congress — 6
Famous sports figures (not linked to horse racing) — 7
Members of royalty — 2
Actors — 11
Ex-Yippies — 1

On May 2, 1981, despite rather cool weather in the 50s, 144,000 were in attendance. It was a great event for us. But could we apply the Dr. Z system? We knew the pools would be astronomical, so last-minute betting would not affect the odds much. But could we get near the windows to place a bet just before each race was run? We were quite pleased and surprised to find that despite the huge crowd, conditions were amazingly good for the Dr. Z system. There were the usual infield tote boards, which people from

Churchill Downs

Sweep's Graded Handicap

FIRST RACE–5 Furlongs. 11:30 EDT
2-Year-Olds, Colts and Geldings. Maiden Special weights. Purse $8,400.

P.P.	Horse	Jockey	Wgt	Odds
1	Good n' Dusty	No Rider	122	
3	Big Sandy Magnet	Gonzlaez R Jr	122	
8	Don's First Bid	Tauzin L	122	
2	Rash Investment	Sayler B	122	
4	Richwood Lad	Breen R	122	
5	The Great Upheave	Bullard B A	5117	
6	Big J B	Wirth B	7115	
7	Bronze N' Bold	Romero R P	122	
9	Shilling	Melancon L	122	
10	The Big E.	Espinoza J C	122	
11	Sunset Mark	Sayler B	122	

COUPLED–Rash Investment and Sunset Mark; Big Sandy Magnet and The Great Upheave; Richwood Lad and Shilling.

SECOND RACE–6 Furlongs. 12:15 EDT
3-Year-Olds: Claiming ($15,000 to $13,000). Purse $8,900.

P.P.	Horse	Jockey	Wgt	Odds
1	English Squire	No Rider	117	1-1
7	Bloomer Ridge	Tauzin L	113	4-1
4	Good Grip	Sipus E J	113	6-1
5	Pleasure Man	Romero R P	117	8-1
8	Tru Touch	McKnight J	117	8-1
2	Grandpa's Jamie	Bullard B A	5108	15-1
9	Lid	Morgan M R	113	15-1
3	Captain J. J.	Ramos A	113	30-1
6	Twibil	Nicolo P	117	30-1

COUPLED–Grandpa's Jamie and Lid.

THIRD RACE–6 Furlongs. 1:00 EDT
4-Year-Olds and Up. Claiming ($10,000 to $9,000). Purse $7,800.

P.P.	Horse	Jockey	Wgt	Odds
1	Lavalier	Delahoussaye E	118	3-1
3	Jeffervescent	Lively J	117	4-1
9	Cosmic Jove	No Rider	117	6-1
13	Bridgets Boy	Foster D E	117	5-1
6	Navajo Warrior	Bullard B A	5112	8-1
12	Revised	Whited D E	117	8-1
14	Play Havoc	Breen R	117	8-1
5	Barrister Sib	No Rider	117	10-1
8	Seven Diplomats	Wirth K	117	15-1
10	Big Hock	Day P	117	15-1
11	Jimminey Crockett	Melancon L	117	15-1
4	Master Smart	No Rider	117	20-1
2	Rapid Trace	Beech J Jr	113	30-1
7	Another Ali	Burns C W	117	30-1
15	Breezy Jester	Whited D E	117	8-1

COUPLED–Revised and Breezy Jester.

FOURTH RACE–1$\frac{1}{16}$ Miles. 1:50 EDT
4-Year-Olds and Up. Claiming ($18,000 to $16,000). Purse $10,500.

P.P.	Horse	Jockey	Wgt	Odds
9	Bag of Fish	Romero R P	117	4-1
12	Bordeaux Native	Sipus E J	113	5-1
11	Most Decidedly	Ledezma C	117	6-1
4	Mister Guy	No Rider	117	6-1
1	Easy Diggin	Melancon L	117	8-1
3	Bright Desi	Whited D E	117	10-1
6	Marileo	Espinoza J C	117	10-1
8	Snow Seed	Whited D E	117	10-1
10	Torsions Lad	Snyder L	113	10-1
2	Judy's Joker	No Rider	113	15-1
5	Peremptory	Cordero A Jr	110	20-1
7	Mark Him Great	Warner T	117	30-1

COUPLED–Bright Desi and Snow Seed.

FIFTH RACE–6 Furlongs. 2:40 EDT
3 & 4-Year-Olds. Allowance. Purse $9,900.

P.P.	Horse	Jockey	Wgt	Odds
1	Illhandleit	Romero R P	110	3-1
2	Ixtapan	Melancon L	110	4-1
4	Manny T.	Whited D E	113	4-1
7	Super Ridge	Delahoussaye E	120	5-1
6	Greek Minstrel	No Rider	113	8-1
5	A Toast to Harry	Wirth K B	110	10-1
3	Shot N' Missed	Foster D E	120	12-1
9	Big Bragger	No Rider	110	20-1
8	Lagnaf	Bowlds M A	110	30-1

SIXTH RACE–5 Furlongs. 3:30 EDT
81st Running DEBUTANTE STAKES ALLOWANCE. 2-Year-Olds, Fillies. . Purse $25,000 Added.

P.P.	Horse	Jockey	Wgt	Odds
3	Cypress Bay	Dellie D	119	5-2
4	Mystical Mood	Velasquez J C	119	3-1
10	Miss Preakness	Espinoza J C	119	5-1
1	Shoo Fly Shecky	Romero R P	114	6-1
9	Priceless Hero	McKnight J	119	8-1
12	Top Canary	Cordero A Jr	119	8-1
11	Pure Platinum	Day P	119	15-1
2	Ali's Oolah	Sayler B	114	20-1
5	Trunk Line	Martinez L J	114	15-1
6	Amazing Love	No Rider	114	6-1
7	Betty Money	Sayler B	114	20-1
8	Kirby	Melancon L	114	20-1

COUPLED–Shoo Fly Shecky and Amazing Love; Ali's Oolah and Betty Money; Trunk Line and Pure Platinum.

SEVENTH RACE–1$\frac{1}{16}$ Miles. 4:20 EDT
3-Year-Olds. Allowance. Purse $50,000.

P.P.	Horse	Jockey	Wgt	Odds
4	Mythical Ruler	Wirth K B	122	4-5
2	Master Tommy	Lively J	117	2-1
5	What It Is	Espinoza J C	119	10-1
3	Marion Frances	Breen R	113	12-1
7	Cornish Music	No Rider	113	12-1
6	Poona's Stage	No Rider	113	15-1
1	Fast Earl	No Rider	113	20-1

EIGHTH RACE–1¼ Miles. 5:38 EDT
107th Running KENTUCKY DERBY SCALE WEIGHT (Grade I). 3-Year-Olds. . Purse $200,000 Added.

P.P.	Horse	Jockey	Wgt	Odds
5	Proud Appeal	Fell J	126	2-1
7	Pleasant Colony	Velasquez J	126	4-1
16	Cure the Blues	Shoemaker W	126	4-1
19	Tap Shoes	Hernandez R	126	6-1
15	Bold Ego	Lively J	126	8-1
1	Splendid Spruce	McHargue D M	126	15-1
11	Woodchopper	Delahoussaye E	126	20-1
13	Classic Go Go	Black A S	126	12-1
2	Golden Derby	Espinoza J C	126	2-1
12	Well Decorated	MacBeth D	126	30-1
4	Double Sonic	Thornburg B	126	12-1
9	Noble Nashua	Asmussen C B	126	30-1
10	Hoedown's Day	Chapman T M	126	12-1
3	Partez	Hawley S	126	12-1
17	Beau Rit	Rubbicco P	126	12-1
18	Television Studio	Whited D E	126	12-1
8	Pass the Tab	Pincay L Jr	126	30-1
6	Habano	Feliciano B R	126	12-1
14	Top Avenger	Snyder L	126	50-1
20	Wayward Lass	Asmussen C B	121	30-1

COUPLED–Golden Derby and Proud Appeal; Noble Nashua and Wayward Lass.

NINTH RACE–6 Furlongs. 6:50 EDT
4-Year-Olds and Up. Allowance. Purse $13,500.

P.P.	Horse	Jockey	Wgt	Odds
4	Rossi Gold	Day P	119	8-5
6	Samoyed	Shoemaker W	119	3-1
5	Conge	Romero R P	122	4-1
3	Sun Czar	Whited D E	117	8-1
2	Mountain Native	Melancon L	115	8-1
1	Iron Pegasus	No Rider	119	15-1
7	Phillip J. C.	Marino A G	115	15-1
8	Straight and Smart	White R D	7112	20-1

TENTH RACE–1$\frac{1}{16}$ Miles. 7:35 EDT
3 & 4-Year-Olds. Allowance. Purse $10,500.

P.P.	Horse	Jockey	Wgt	Odds
12	Lothian	Hernandez R	120	2-1
5	Sorroto	No Rider	120	4-1
6	Hard Silver	Pincay L Jr	123	6-1
9	Tan U Tell	No Rider	110	8-1
2	Wolfgang Grr	Martinez L J	110	10-1
4	D. J. Road	Delahoussaye E	113	10-1
3	Mr. Bobeva	Delahoussaye E	110	10-1
8	Goat Burchett	Feliciano B R	120	15-1
11	Clearly Proud	Melancon L	110	15-1
1	Crimson Spruce	Day P	110	20-1
7	Salad King	Sayler B	110	20-1
10	Right J. G.	Whited D E	110	20-1

COUPLED–Mr. Bobeva and D. J. Road.

the stands use to follow the betting activities. There also is a convenient tote board in the back of the grandstand. It is near the paddock area where the horses are saddled and the jockeys, trainers, and owners discuss last-minute strategy prior to each race. Opposite the tote board and paddock is a small row of ticket windows. Since this area is far away from the track, it clears out prior to each race when the patrons scramble to get a good view of the race on nearby closed-circuit TV sets. With such a huge crowd the area did not completely clear out, but we had the enviable opportunity to stand in short, two- to five-deep lines and watch the tote board. Thus we could easily make bets well within one minute of post time, and we were routinely making them with fifteen to thirty seconds to go.

Jockey Standings

Jockey	Starts	1st	2nd	3d
Pincay, L. Jr.	503	119	105	61
Gall, D.	540	106	93	93
Sibille, R.	515	105	82	70
Baze, R. A.	511	99	93	79
Delahoussaye, E.	506	90	84	74
Pettinger, D. R.	485	89	72	67
Migliore, R.	517	88	79	57
Vigliotti, M. J.	487	87	75	60
Fell, J.	451	85	67	59
Cooksey, P. J.	506	84	70	53

(January 1 through April 28, inclusive.)

America's Turf Authority Racing Form

Experts' Selections

Consensus Points: 5 for 1st (today's best 7), 2 for 2nd, 1 for 3rd. Today's Best in Bold Type.

Trackman, Graham Ross

CHURCHILL DOWNS

Selections Made for Fast Track

	TRACKMAN	HANDICAP	ANALYST	HERMIS	SWEEP	CONSENSUS	
1	BIG SANDY MAGNET GOOD N' DUSTY BRONZE N' BOLD	GOOD N' DUSTY BRONZE N' BOLD RASH INVESTMENT	GOOD N' DUSTY BRONZE N' BOLD THE BIG E.	GOOD N' DUSTY BIG SANDY MAGNET DON'S FIRST BID	GOOD N' DUSTY BIG SANDY MAGNET DON'S FIRST BID	GOOD N' DUSTY BIG SANDY MAGNET BRONZE N' BOLD	22 9 5
2	TRU TOUCH BLOOMER RIDGE LID	ENGLISH SQUIRE GOOD GRIP TRU TOUCH	ENGLISH SQUIRE TRU TOUCH PLEASURE MAN	**ENGLISH SQUIRE** TRU TOUCH GOOD GRIP	ENGLISH SQUIRE BLOOMER RIDGE GOOD GRIP	ENGLISH SQUIRE TRU TOUCH BLOOMER RIDGE	22 10 4
3	COSMIC JOVE LAVALIER JEFFERVESCENT	LAVALIER BIG HOCK BARRISTER SIB	BIG HOCK LAVALIER BARRISTER SIB	BARRISTER SIB COSMIC JOVE REVISED	LAVALIER JEFFERVESCENT COSMIC JOVE	LAVALIER COSMIC JOVE BIG HOCK	14 8 7
4	PEREMPTORY JUDY'S JOKER BAG OF FISH	JUDY'S JOKER MISTER GUY BAG OF FISH	BAG OF FISH EASY DIGGIN BORDEAUX NATIVE	JUDY'S JOKER MISTER GUY BAG OF FISH	BAG OF FISH BORDEAUX NATIVE MOST DECIDEDLY	BAG OF FISH JUDY'S JOKER PEREMPTORY	13 12 5
5	GREEK MINSTREL ILLHANDLEIT MANNY T.	GREEK MINSTREL ILLHANDLEIT SUPER RIDGE	MANNY T. SUPER RIDGE GREEK MINSTREL	MANNY T. GREEK MINSTREL IXTAPAN	ILLHANDLEIT IXTAPAN MANNY T.	GREEK MINSTREL MANNY T. ILLHANDLEIT	13 12 9
6	MYSTICAL MOOD MISS PREAKNESS PRICELESS HERO	CYPRESS BAY MISS PREAKNESS BETTY MONEY	CYPRESS BAY MYSTICAL MOOD MISS PREAKNESS	CYPRESS BAY MISS PREAKNESS MYSTICAL MOOD	CYPRESS BAY MYSTICAL MOOD MISS PREAKNESS	CYPRESS BAY MYSTICAL MOOD MISS PREAKNESS	20 10 8
7	**MYTHICAL RULER** WHAT IT IS POONA'S STAGE	**MYTHICAL RULER** MASTER TOMMY WHAT IT IS	**MYTHICAL RULER** MASTER TOMMY WHAT IT IS	MYTHICAL RULER WHAT IT IS MASTER TOMMY	**MYTHICAL RULER** MASTER TOMMY WHAT IT IS	**MYTHICAL RULER** WHAT IT IS MASTER TOMMY	33 7 7
8	PLEASANT COLONY PROUD APPEAL DOUBLE SONIC	PROUD APPEAL SPLENDID SPRUCE BOLD EGO	PROUD APPEAL CURE THE BLUES PLEASANT COLONY	PROUD APPEAL CURE THE BLUES TAP SHOES	PROUD APPEAL PLEASANT COLONY CURE THE BLUES	PROUD APPEAL PLEASANT COLONY CURE THE BLUES	22 8 5
9	SUN CZAR IRON PEGASUS ROSSI GOLD	ROSSI GOLD CONGE IRON PEGASUS	CONGE ROSSI GOLD IRON PEGASUS	ROSSI GOLD SUN CZAR CONGE	ROSSI GOLD SAMOYED CONGE	ROSSI GOLD CONGE SUN CZAR	18 9 7
10	LOTHIAN WOLFGANG GRR MR. BOBEVA	LOTHIAN CRIMSON SPRUCE D. J. ROAD	SORROTO LOTHIAN MR. BOBEVA	LOTHIAN WOLFGANG GRR MR. BOBEVA	LOTHIAN SORROTO HARD SILVER	LOTHIAN SORROTO WOLFGANG GRR	22 7 4

THE DR. Z SYSTEM BETS

The first Dr. Z system bet occurred in the third race on Jeffervescent. He was a California horse with a reasonably good record, having finished in the money in eleven of his twenty-two starts. He was dropping in class and coming off a layoff, with this his first start of 1981.

Betting a horse that is coming off a substantial layoff is always a great risk, so we were cautious regarding Jeffervescent and would not make a large bet. At the end of the betting, the tote board stood as follows:

	Totals	#4 Jeffervescent
Odds		7—2
Win	317,312	58,621
Show	139,742	15,825

The track take is 15% in Kentucky. Using equation (4.4), we calculated the expected value per dollar bet at 1.21. Our betting fortune was $1,000, which indicated a bet of $62. Jeffervescent won the race and paid a handsome $5.20 to show. This provided a $99.20 profit for our $62 bet. The payoffs were:

4–	Jeffervescent.............	9.00	5.80	5.20
11–	Play Havoc...............		10.60	7.20
5–	Master Smart.............			6.00

The fifth race was an allowance race for three-year-olds who had never won a race other than a maiden or a claiming. Hence it was filled both with horses with mediocre records and those who were upcoming horses. Shot N' Missed had finished second in his only race and was awarded first place through a disqualification. His speed rating of 90 in the short $4\frac{1}{2}$-furlong race was reasonably good for this group.

Near post time the expected value on Shot N' Missed was 1.31, which indicated a bet of $197. The tote board at post time was

	Totals	#3 Shot N' Missed
Odds		5—2
Win	474,181	108,367
Show	206,585	25,760

Ixtapan won the race, followed by Lagnaf, and Shot N' Missed took third. The payoffs were:

2–	Ixtapan..................	12.20	5.80	4.00
9–	Big Bragger..............		14.20	5.20
3–	Shot N' Missed...........			4.40

The show payoff on Shot N' Missed was a substantial $4.40 for a 5–2 shot. The 1.28 expected value, plus the fact that the favorite in the race, Manny T., finished out of the money, while two longer-priced horses were in the money, caused the high payoff. Our bet of $197 returned $433.40, for a profit of $236.40.

The sixth race was the eighty-first running of the $25,000 added Debutante Stakes for two-year-old fillies. It featured a two-horse entry and eight other starters after Ali's Oolah and Trunk Line were scratched. The ten starters all had brief racing careers. Most of them were running only their second race. Six of them had won their only race. The favorites were Cypress Bay, Top Canary, Mystical Mood, and Miss Preakness. Cypress Bay looked the best, winning her only start as a 3–2 favorite by 7 lengths, with a 94 speed rating. She seemed like a reasonable bet if the odds were good—and they were.

One minute before post time the tote board was as follows:

	Totals	#4 Cypress Bay
Odds		1—1
Win	522,550	204,439
Show	213,710	51,883

This gave an expected value of 1.19. With our betting fortune of $1,335.60, a bet of $510 to show on Cypress Bay was suggested.

At post time the odds were similar:

	Totals	#4 Cypress Bay	Expected Value per Dollar Bet on Cypress Bay	Optimal Bet on Cypress Bay ($)
Odds		1—1		
Win	535,218	209,225		
Show	219,930	53,287	1.20	510

Pure Platinum, part of the number 2 entry, won the race, followed by Miss Preakness. Cypress Bay held on for third and paid $3. Our $510 bet returned $765, for a $255 profit. The payoffs were:

3–	Pure Platinum.............	77.80	24.00	8.40
8–	Miss Preakness...........		9.00	4.60
4–	Cypress Bay..............			3.00

The seventh race—the Twin Spires, a $50,000 allowance for three-year-olds—was to feature the standout Mythical Ruler. Mythical Ruler won all his races during 1981 and three of five in 1980, always finishing in the money. When he was scratched and so could run in the Derby, the top choices became Master Tommy and What It Is. Master Tommy was a Dr. Z system bet throughout the betting period.

The final tote board was:

	Totals	#2 Master Tommy
Odds		4—5
Win	548,084	245,308
Show	186,601	50,924

This gave an expected value of 1.20 and an optimal bet of $781 with our fortune of $1,590.60.

What It Is won the race, beating Master Tommy. Cornish Music took third. The payoffs were:

4–	What It Is.................	7.80	3.20	2.20
2–	Master Tommy............		2.80	2.20
6–	Cormish Music............			2.20

Despite the 1.20 expected value per dollar bet to show on Master Tommy, which qualified it as a Dr. Z system bet, the payoff was only $2.20. Given the fact that there were only six starters, when the other favorite, What It Is, finished in the money with a substantial show bet, the show pool yielded a $2.20 payoff for all in-the-money finishers. This is one of the difficulties of playing a Dr. Z system bet with few starters and two or more major favorites. If all the favorites are in the money, the payoff will be small. If the horse you have bet is the only favorite in the money, then the show payoff will be more substantial.

Our bet of $781 returned $859.10 for a profit of $78.10. Our betting fortune was now $1,668.70.

PROUD APPEAL VERSUS JOHNNY CAMPO IN THE 107TH KENTUCKY DERBY

The eighth race was the 107th running of the Kentucky Derby. The favorite was Proud Appeal. He had won nine of his ten starts and was to be ridden by his steady jockey, Jeffrey Fell. Races like his recent $1{:}33^3$ with a 98 speed rating in the Gotham Stakes at Aqueduct made him look exceptionally strong. The other top horses were Pleasant Colony, Cure the Blues, Bold Ego, and Tap Shoes. Pleasant Colony had a mediocre record, but he was coming off a convincing win in the recent Wood Memorial at Aqueduct. Moreover, his colorful trainer, Johnny Campo, had gone on record that Pleasant Colony was the best horse and would win the race. Cure the Blues had been soundly beaten by 8 lengths by Pleasant Colony in the Wood Memorial. The rest of his record was impeccable—a loss by a nose to Proud Appeal in the Gotham and six straight convincing victories. Bold Ego had won ten of his thirteen starts and was coming off three straight victories, including the Arkansas Derby. He was ridden by his regular jockey, John Lively. Tap Shoes had just won the Flamingo Stakes and had won five of his nine starts. He had had only one bad race and was being ridden as usual by Ruben Hernandez.

It is romantic to win the Kentucky Derby, so I bet $50 on my favorite horse, Proud Appeal, to win. Pleasant Colony turned out to be a Dr. Z system bet. At post time the tote board was as follows:

	Total	#4 Pleasant Colony
Odds		7—2
Win	2,614,993	480,510
Show	950,079	132,845

The expected value per dollar bet on Pleasant Colony to show had dropped to 1.09, but with our fortune of $1,668.70, we had bet $342.

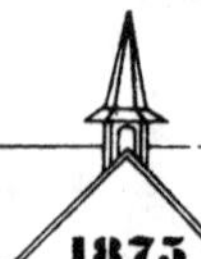

107th Running
KENTUCKY DERBY
EIGHTH RACE

1875 — 1981

$200,000 ADDED — ONE MILE and ONE-QUARTER — TRACK RECORD—SECRETARIAT (3), 126 lbs., 5-5-73, 1:59-2/5
(Plus $20,000 from the Kentucky Thoroughbred Development Fund)

For three-year-olds. By subscription of $100 each which covers nomination for both The Kentucky Derby and Derby Trial. All nomination fees to Derby winner. $4,000 to pass entry box, $3,500, additional to start. $200,000 added, of which $50,000 to second, $25,000 to third, $12,500 to fourth. $100,000 guaranteed to winner (to be divided equally in the event of a dead heat). Weight 126 lbs. The owner of the winner to receive a gold trophy. Closed Tuesday, February 17, 1981, with 432 nominations.

USE THESE NUMBERS FOR BUYING PARI MUTUEL TICKETS

No.	Owner	Trainer	Colors	Horse	Wt.	Breeding	Jockey	Morning Line
1	FREDERICK E. LEHMANN & GAINESWAY (John R. Gaines)	W. E. ADAMS	Blue, Green Pine Tree, Blue Cap	GOLDEN DERBY	126	Ro c, 1978, Master Derby—Old Goldie by Young Emperor BRED IN KENTUCKY BY FREDERICK E. LEHMANN	JULIO ESPINOZA (P. P. 2)	2
1a	M. H. WINFIELD, ROBERT ENTENMANN, JOHN R. GAINES & STANLEY M. HOUGH	STANLEY M. HOUGH	Black, Tan "W" and Braces, Tan Chevrons on Sleeves, Tan Cap	PROUD APPEAL	126	Dk b or br c, 1978, Valid Appeal—Proud N' Happy by Proudest Roman BRED IN FLORIDA BY R. YOWELL & P. CAMP	JEFF FELL (P. P. 5)	2
2	FLYING ZEE STABLE (Carl Lizza, Jr. & Herbert Hockreiter)	JOSE MARTIN	Light Blue, White "ZZ" and Yoke, White Cap	NOBLE NASHUA	126	Dk b or br c, 1978, Nashua—Noble Lady by Vaguely Noble BRED IN KENTUCKY BY GROUSEMONT FARM	CASH ASMUSSEN (P. P. 9)	30
2b	FLYING ZEE STABLE (Carl Lizza, Jr. & Herbert Hockreiter)	JOSE MARTIN	Light Blue, White "ZZ" and Yoke, White Cap	WAYWARD LASS	121	Dk b or br f, 1978, Hail The Pirates—Young Mistress by Third Martini BRED IN FLORIDA BY H. A. LURO	CASH ASMUSSEN (P. P. 20)	30
3	SURF & TURF STABLE (Earl Shultz & Alan Yasukochi)	C. R. KNIGHT	Yellow, Yellow Seahorse on Green Ball, Yellow Bars on Green Sleeves, Yellow and Green Cap	SPLENDID SPRUCE	126	B c, 1978, Big Spruce—Splendid Spree by Damascus BRED IN KENTUCKY BY LILLIE F. WEBB	DARREL McHARGUE (P. P. 1)	15
4	BUCKLAND FARM (Thomas M. Evans)	JOHN P. CAMPO	Dark Blue, White Triangle, Dark Blue Bars on White Sleeves, Blue and White Cap	PLEASANT COLONY	126	Dk b or br c, 1978, His Majesty—Sun Colony by Sunrise Flight BRED IN VIRGINIA BY T. M. EVANS	JORGE VELASQUEZ (P. P. 7)	4
5	LEOPOLDO VILLAREAL	ALBERT BARRERA	Royal Blue, Royal Blue "V" on Light Blue Ball, Light Blue Stripes on Royal Blue Sleeves, Royal Blue Cap	PASS THE TAB	126	Gr c, 1978, Al Hattab—Dantina by Gray Phantom BRED IN CALIFORNIA BY LEOPOLDO VILLAREAL	LAFFIT PINCAY, JR. (P. P. 8)	30
6	GREENTREE STABLE (John Hay Whitney)	J. M. GAVER, JR.	Pink, Black Stripes on Sleeves, Pink Cap	WOODCHOPPER	126	Gr c, 1978, Hatchet Man—Musical Chairs by Swaps BRED IN KENTUCKY BY GREENTREE STUD INC.	EDDIE DELAHOUSSAYE (P. P. 11)	30
7	HERBERT ALLEN	EUGENE JACOBS	White, Red Cross Sashes, Red Blocks on Sleeves, White Cap	WELL DECORATED	126	Dk b or br c, 1978, Raja Baba—Paris Breeze by Majestic Prince BRED IN FLORIDA BY HERBERT ALLEN	DON MacBETH (P. P. 12)	30
8	DOUBLE B RANCH (J. D. Barton) & JOSEPH KIDD	JACK VAN BERG	Light Blue, White "B" in Horseshoe, Light Blue Cap	BOLD EGO	126	Dk b or br c, 1978, Bold Tactics—Coya's Ego by Bullin BRED IN NEW MEXICO BY J. D. BARTON	JOHN LIVELY (P. P. 15)	8
9	BERTRAM R. FIRESTONE	LE ROY JOLLEY	Green, White Diamond Frame, White Diamonds on Sleeves, Green Cap	CURE THE BLUES	126	B c, 1978, Stop the Music—Quick Cure by Dr. Fager BRED IN VIRGINIA BY MR. & MRS. BERTRAM R. FIRESTONE	WILLIAM SHOEMAKER (P. P. 16)	9-2
10	ARTHUR B. HANCOCK III & LEONE J. PETERS, et al	HORATIO A. LURO	White, Purple Star, Purple Band on Sleeves, White Cap	TAP SHOES	126	Ch c, 1978, Riva Ridge—Bold Ballet by Bold Bidder BRED IN KENTUCKY BY LEONE J. PETERS & ARTHUR HANCOCK III	RUBEN HERNANDEZ (P. P. 19)	6
11	ULF JENSEN, KARL HOLMAN, RAYMOND RONCARI & EDMUND DiGIULIO	LARRY S. BARRERA	White, Red Heart, White Bars on Red Sleeves, Red Cap	FLYING NASHUA	126	B c, 1978, Nashua—Joys Will by Yes You Will BRED IN KENTUCKY BY FREEMAN & PERKINS	ANGEL CORDERO, JR. (P. P. 22)	30
12 FIELD	MR. & MRS. HENRY GREENE & ELIZABETH DAVIS	D. WAYNE LUKAS	Lavender, Purple Chevrons, Purple Circled "DG," Purple Sleeves, Lavender Cap	PARTEZ	126	B c, 1978, Quack—Lady Marguery by Tim Tam BRED IN KENTUCKY BY H. B. NOONAN & RUNNYMEDE FARM INC.	SANDY HAWLEY (P. P. 3)	8
13 FIELD	FRED & LOU ELIAS	GEORGE P. KRNJAICH	Orange, Black "EB" in Black Diamond Frame, Orange Cap	DOUBLE SONIC	126	Ro c, 1978, Nodouble—Eloquent Es by Palestinian BRED IN FLORIDA BY ELIAS BROTHERS FARM	BUCK THORNBURG (P. P. 4)	8
14 FIELD	MARCO A. COELLO	FRANCISCO GONZALEZ	Grey, Red Panel, Blue Sleeves, Grey Cap	HABANO	126	Dk b or br c, 1978, Ferrol—Miss Tepeji by Breezy Lane BRED IN MEXICO BY ESTEVEZ M. GUILLERMO	BENNY FELICIANO (P. P. 6)	8
15 FIELD	JO ANN DOMINGUEZ, MARIE FREIDEL & CHRIS THATCHER	ROGER DOMINGUEZ	Blue, Gold "R&R" in Gold Diamond Frame, Blue Bars on Gold Sleeves, Blue Cap	HOEDOWN'S DAY	126	B c, 1978, Bargain Day—Miss Hoedown by Dance Lesson BRED IN CALIFORNIA BY MR. & MRS. ROGER DOMINGUEZ	TOMMY CHAPMAN (P. P. 10)	8
16 FIELD	V. W. WINCHELL	J. C. MEYER	Maroon, White Circled "VHW," White Stripes on Sleeves, White Cap	CLASSIC GO GO	126	Dk b or br c, 1978, Pago Pago—Classic Perfection by Never Bend BRED IN KENTUCKY BY V. W. WINCHELL	ANTHONY BLACK (P. P. 13)	8
17 FIELD	W. P. BISHOP	DWIGHT VIATOR	Blue, White "B," Blue Stars on White Sleeves, Blue Cap	TOP AVENGER	126	B c, 1978, Staunch Avenger—Atop by Dunce BRED IN TEXAS BY W. P. BISHOP	LARRY SNYDER (P. P. 14)	8
18 FIELD	CAROLE R. ROUSSEL	LOUIE ROUSSEL III	Light Blue, Cerise Dots, Light Blue Cap	BEAU RIT	126	B g, 1978, Lord Rebeau—Rit N Rough by Rough 'N Tumble BRED IN FLORIDA BY EARLY BIRD STUD	PHIL RUBBICCO (P. P. 17)	8
19 FIELD	BWAMAZON FARM (M. A. Waldheim)	ANTHONY BASILE	White, Blue Hoops, Blue Stripes on Sleeves, Blue Cap	TELEVISION STUDIO	126	B g, 1978, Within Hail—Put On T.V. by T.V. Lark BRED IN KENTUCKY BY BWAMAZON FARM	DAVID WHITED (P. P. 18)	8
20 FIELD	AL RISEN, JR. & PAXTON PRICE	FRED WIRTH	Gold, Red Cross Sashes, Red Bars on Sleeves, Red Cap	MYTHICAL RULER	126	Ro c, 1978, Ruritania—Our Nanny by Victorian Era BRED IN KENTUCKY BY OSCAR PENN	KEVIN WIRTH (P. P. 21)	8

Indicates Foaled in Kentucky.

1-1a—Frederick E. Lehmann & John R. Gaines—M. H. Winfield, Robert Entenmann, John R. Gaines & Stanley M. Hough Entry

2-2b—Flying Zee Stable Entry

FIELD—12-13-14-15-16-17-18-19-20

Selections—1a-4-9-10

107th-Kentucky Derby

Route the Field Will Travel

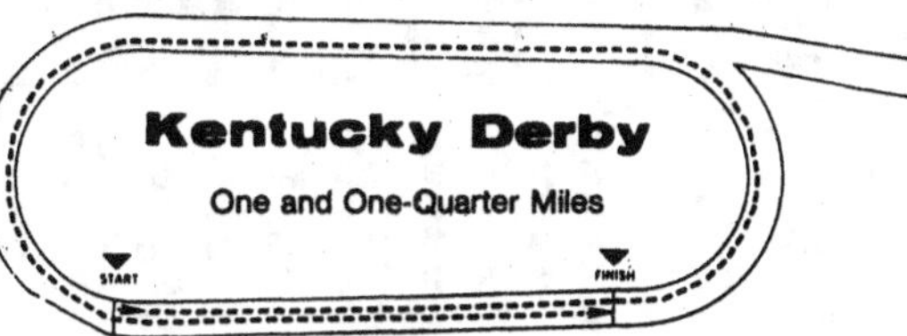

8th Churchill

1 ¼ MILES. (1.59⅖) 107th Running KENTUCKY DERBY SCALE WEIGHT (Grade I). $200,000 Added (plus $20,000 from KTDF). 3-year-olds. By subscription of $100 which covers nomination for both the Kentucky Derby and Derby Trial. All nomination fees to Derby winner. $4,000 to pass entry box Thursday, April 30, $3,500 additional to start. $200,000 added, of which: $50,000 to second, $25,000 to third, $12,500 to fourth. $100,000 guaranteed to the winner (to be divided equally in the event of a dead heat.) Weight, 126 lbs. Starters to be named through the entry box Thursday, April 30, at the time of closing. The maximum number of starters for the Kentucky Derby will be limited to twenty. In the event more than twenty entries pass through the entry box at the usual time of closing, the twenty starters will be determined at that time with preference given to those that have accumulated the highest earnings. For those that enter and are eliminated under this condition, the nomination fee and the fee to pass through the entry box, will be refunded. The owner of the winner to receive a gold trophy. (Closed with 432 nominations.)

Coupled—Golden Derby and Proud Appeal; Noble Nashua and Wayward Lass.

Splendid Spruce — B. c. 3, by Big Spruce—Splendid Spree, by Damascus

Own.—Surf and Turf Stable — **126** — Br.—Webb Lillie F (Ky) — Tr.—Knight Chay R

1981	6	2	1	0	$219,100
1980	5	2	1	0	$23,500

Date-Race	Dist	Fractions	Odds	Wt	Calls	Jockey	Race	Speed	Company	Field
12Apr81-8SA	1⅛	:453 1:101 1:49 ft	15	120	65¾ 52¾ 2½ 1¾	McHrguDG2	S A Dby	84	SplnddSprc,JhnlN'Hrld,Hdwn'sDy	13
28Mar81-8SA	1 1/16	:46 1:10 1:42 ft	48	116	21 21 2½ 2nk	McHrDG3	SanFelipeH	91	Stnchrry,SplndidSpruc,FlyingNshu	12
1Mar81-7SA	1 1/16	:462 1:13 1:474sy	2¾	117	27 11½ 18 120	Pincay L Jr6	Alw	62	SplendidSpruce,Prtez,GelicNvonod	6
12Feb81-8SA	1 1/16	:47 1:111 1:422ft	6¾	117	46½ 58½ 67½ 64¾	Pincay L Jr6	Alw	84	Litigator, Gaelic Navonod, Seafood	6
31Jan81-7SA	1 1/16	:471 1:114 1:444gd	8¼	116	31 3½ 4½ 54¼	Shoemaker W1	Alw	72	Jetzier, Heavy Hand, Tell Again	7
17Jan81-7SA	1	:462 1:103 1:351ft	5¾	117	54 76½ 54½ 47¾	Shoemaker W3	Alw	85	Stnchrry,InvincibleDooley,TellAgin	7
10Sep80-8Dmr	1	:462 1:11 1:361ft	*2¾	114	119 910 610 78¾	ShmrW3	Del Mar Fut	78	BoldAndGold,LooksLikRin,SrDncr	12
27Aug80-8Dmr	1	:46 1:111 1:372ft	3½	115	54½ 43½ 43½ 21¾	ShoemakerW5	Balboa	79	BoldAndGold,SplndidSpruc,SirDncr	7
18Aug80-7Dmr	1	:461 1:12 1:382ft	*8-5	117	42 1hd 1½ 11¾	Shoemaker W6	Alw	76	SplendidSpruc,Dgn,LongLivThKing	8
19Jly80-8Hol	6f	:212 :442 1:10 ft	11	122	95½ 118 118 107¾	LphT6	Hol Juv Chmp	79	Loma Malad, Motivity, Bold Ego	13
3Jly80-1Hol	6f	:221 :451 1:102ft	*9-5	116	64 57½ 2hd 1¾	Shoemaker W9	Mdn	85	Splendid Spruce, Thriver, Partez	11

●Apr 29 CD 5f ft :592 h   Apr 24 CD 7f gd 1:292 h   ●Apr 18 SA 4f ft :462 h   Apr 9 SA 5f ft :592 h

Golden Derby — Ro. c. 3, by Master Derby—Old Goldie, by Young Emperor

Own.—Lehmann F E & Gaines J R — **126** — Br.—Lehmann Frederick E (Ky) — Tr.—Adams William E

1981	3	0	0	2	$23,067
1980	7	3	0	2	$78,292

Date-Race	Dist	Fractions	Odds	Wt	Calls	Jockey	Race	Speed	Company	Field
23Apr81-7Kee	1⅛	:472 1:113 1:512sy	*1-2e	121	2½ 2hd 22 33¾	EspnzJC8	Blue Grass	76	ProudAppeal,LawMe,GoldenDerby	11
14Apr81-7Kee	1 1/16	:464 1:103 1:441ft	16	113	11½ 11½ 1hd 33½	Espinoza J C1	Alw	81	SwingingLght,Sportn'Lf,GoldnDrby	8
28Mar81-8Lat	1	:46 1:11 1:38 ft	2½	122	33½ 511 828 836	Hawley S3	Spiral	53	MythiclRuler,ClssicGoGo,IronGem	10
6Sep80-8AP	7f	:221 :444 1:234ft	3½e	122	64¾ 35 68½ 814	HwleyS8	Arl Was Fut	69	WellDcortd,LordAvi,FirwyPhntom	15
20Aug80-8AP	6f	:222 :46 1:13 gd	*2-3e	124	1½ 1hd 2½ 31½	EspnzJC1	Arch Ward	75	FirwyPhntom,Linnleur,GoldenDrby	9
21Jly80-8Bel	6f	:222 :46 1:112ft	3½	122	21 1hd 11½ 1hd	McHrguDG1	Tremont	85	GoldenDerby,GrtProspctor,LordAvi	9
28Jun80-8CD	5½f	:22 :444 1:041ft	4¾	125	2½ 2½ 12½ 1½	EspinozaJC3	Jeff Cup	102	GoldenDerby,PlinSpking,BoldTyson	7
31May80-8CD	5f	:221 :454 :58 ft	5½	117	2½ 2½ 11½ 1no	EspnJC5	Bshfrd Man	94	GoldnDrby,WrongImprssion,Stublm	9
7May80-7Spt	4f	:212 :453ft	7½	112	5 2½ 33 34	SpencrSA3	Spt Jvnle	92	FullofDrive,BoldTyson,GoldenDrby	7
23Apr80-7Kee	4½f	:222 :462 :53 ft	7½	116	6 1hd 3½ 56¾	EspinozJC6	Lafayette	83	FirmBoss,BndthTims,SilvrDollrBoy	7

Apr 29 CD 4f ft :51 b   Apr 22 Kee 3f ft :384 b   Apr 20 Kee 4f sy :492 b   Apr 13 Kee 3f ft :38 b

Partez B. c. 3, by Quack—Lady Marguery, by Tim Tam
Br.—Noonan-Runnymede Farm (Ky) 1981 5 1 2 0 $27,900
Own.—Davis E & Greene Mr-Mrs H 126 Tr.—Lukas D Wayne 1980 8 2 1 2 $77,821
Turf 1 1 0 0 $16,500
12Apr81-8SA 1⅛ :453 1:101 1:49 ft 9½ 120 53½ 62¾ 55½ 67 McCrronCJ1 S A Dby 77 SplnddSprc,JhnlN'Hrld,Hdwn'sDy 13
5Apr81-4SA 1⅛ Ⓣ:4511:09 1:471fm*7-5 114 13½ 13½ 13 10 Hawley S2 Alw 91 Partez, Tell Again, Quantum Leap 6
21Mar81-6SA 1 1/16 :461 1:111 1:433gd 3½ 114 43 3nk 3nk 21 Hawley S2 Alw 82 Seafood, Partez, Table Torch 8
15Mar81-8SA 1 :453 1:103 1:36 ft 16 116 99½ 813 812 714 LiphamT9 San Rafael 75 JohnleN'Hrold,MingsotChif,ARun 10
1Mar81-7SA 1 1/16 :462 1:13 1:474sy 3½ 120 313 36½ 28 220 Lipham T1 Alw 42 SplendidSpruce,Prtez,GelicNvonod 6
15Nov80-8SA 1 1/16 :463 1:11 1:434ft *2½ 118 42 31½ 43½ 31½ Lipham T7 Norfolk 81 Sir Dancer, Chiaroscuro, Partez 8
15Nov80—Run in two divisions 8th & 9th races.
29Oct80-8SA 7f :214 :444 1:23 ft 6½ 117 54½ 55 52½ 1½ LiphmT2 Sunny Slope 85 Partez, Chiaroscuro, Loma Malad 7
17Oct80-7SA 1 :454 1:112 1:38 ft *9-5 120 23 2½ 1½ 2hd McHargue D G1 Alw 79 Dialect, Partez, Table Torch 9
10Sep80-8Dmr 1 :462 1:11 1:361ft 22 114 87 64½ 42½ 44 LiphmT4 Del Mar Fut 83 BoldAndGold,LooksLikRin,SrDncr 12
27Aug80-8Dmr 1 :46 1:111 1:372ft 6½ 115 3½ 54 58½ 911 Lipham T6 Balboa 79 BoldAndGold,SplndidSpruc,SirDncr 7
3Aug80-1Dmr 1 :474 1:121 1:374ft 8-5 118 32 44½ 2½ 11 Lipham T6 Mdn 79 Partez,SprkOfBlue,SportingBrother 9
3Jly80-1Hol 6f :221 :451 1:102ft 15 116 1hd 1½ 1hd 31¾ Valenzuela P A1 Mdn 83 Splendid Spruce, Thriver, Partez 11
24May80-1Hol 5f :221 :453 :573ft 5 115 42½ 41 58 57 Lipham T8 Mdn 85 Fair Hint, GreatGame,FAbulousToo 7
Apr 20 Kee 5f sy 1:011 b ●Apr 10 SA 3f ft :342 h Apr 3 SA 3f ft :353 hg Mar 31 SA Ⓣ 5f fm 1:011 h (d)

Double Sonic Ro. c. 3, by Nodouble—Eloquent Es, by Palestinian
Br.—Elias Brothers Farm (Fla) 1981 5 1 0 1 $114,907
Own.—Elias F & L 126 Tr.—Krnjaich George 1980 12 4 2 1 $53,001
23Apr81-7Kee 1⅛ :472 1:113 1:512sy 17 121 1013 813 58½ 43¾ ThrnbrgB3 Blue Grass 76 ProudAppeal,LawMe,GoldenDerby 11
28Mar81-9Hia 1⅛ :47 1:104 1:491ft 6½ 122 67 67½ 68 35 ThornbrgB3 Flamingo 81 TpShoes,WellDecorted,DoublSonic 7
6Mar81-9GP 1⅛ :47 1:111 1:502ft 12 122 1017 1011 45½ 411 SmithAJr11 Fla Derby 69 Lord Avie, Akureyri, Linnleur 11
4Feb81-9GP 7f :223 :452 1:232ft 14 122 312 416 59½ 44 SmithAJr5 Hutcheson 83 Lord Avie, Spirited Boy, Linnleur 7
3Jan81-9Crc 1 1/16 :472 1:121 1:462ft 14 121 1321 914 51½ 11 SthAJr11 TrpParkDby 87 DoubleSonic,Akureyrt,MightBHom 14
20Dec80-9Crc 1 1/16 :47 1:123 1:462ft 14 117 914 75 53½ 32 SthAJr7 Whtaplesure 85 Akureyri, ‡Linnleur, Double Sonic 9
20Dec80—Placed second through disqualification
6Dec80-9Crc 1 1/16 :484 1:133 1:464ft 3½ 117 108½ 714 612 58½ CrdnE5 Cty Of Miami 76 CatchThatPass,BearCt,RoylPruner 12
15Nov80-9Crc 1 70 :472 1:132 1:462ft *3-5 119 68½ 58½ 48 22½ CrdonE5 [S]J H Bright 75 Bear Cat, Double Sonic,MalcolmW. 6
1Nov80-9Crc 1 70 :464 1:133 1:453ft 4½ 116 717 77½ 45½ 37½ CrdnE6 Ponce Deleon 74 RooghLord,MlcolmW.,DoubleSonic 7
11Oct80-7Crc 1 :48 1:134 1:414ft *3-2 114 510 47 31½ 1½ CrdoneE3 F Pleasure 79 DoblSonc,StotHrtdMn,GovrnorBob 7
11Oct80—Run in Two Divisions: 7th & 9th Races.
1Oct80-7Crc 1 :482 1:14 1:42 ft 3½ 114 44½ 411 43½ 12 Cardone E4 Alw 78 DoblSonc,Mry'sKngdom,IncrdblJhn 5
8Sep80-9Crc 1 70 :491 1:153 1:471ft 6 116 52¾ 63½ 1hd 13½ Cardone E4 Alw 74 DoublSonic,RinBouRunnr,ZmbziWy 6
29Aug80-8Crc 6f :224 :461 1:12 ft 7½ 118 87 69 516 514 Jimenez I J5 Alw 78 StoutHertedMn,Hrry'sHze,ErlyBob 8
20Aug80-8Crc 6f :222 :461 1:131ft 20 118 88¾ 711 613 49¾ Jimenez I J6 Alw 76 Spirited Boy,CraftyEd,MalcolmW. 11
2Aug80-3Crc 6f :223 :47 1:133ft 22 117 98½ 98½ 32 2nk Jimenez I J5 Mdn 84 ‡StoutHrtdMn,DoublSonc,VldDncr 12
2Aug80—Place first through disqualification.
23Jly80-5Crc 5f :23 :464 :593sy 17 116 1011 915 815 817 Cardone E10 Mdn 80 SpiritdBoy,‡GovrnorBob,GlicPnny 12
12Jly80-6Crc 5f :231 :473 1:012ft 28 116 911 811 66 64¾ Jimenez I J7 Mdn 83 MlcolmW.,Tigirish,PickersDelight 11
Apr 22 Kee 3f ft :364 b Apr 16 Kee 1 ft 1:42 b Mar 27 Crc 3f ft :373 b Mar 21 Crc 1 ft 1:43 b

Proud Appeal × B. c. 3, by Valid Appeal—Proud N Happy, by Proudest Roman
Br.—Camp & Yowell (Fla) 1981 5 5 0 0 $269,230
Own.—Winfield M H et al 126 Tr.—Hough Stanley M 1980 4 3 0 0 $72,737
23Apr81-7Kee 1⅛ :472 1:113 1:512sy *1-2e 121 1½ 1hd 12 13 Fell J6 Blue Grass 80 ProudAppeal,LawMe,GoldenDerby 11
5Apr81-8Aqu 1 :45 1:084 1:333ft 9-5 123 1½ 1½ 1hd 1no Fell J3 Gotham 98 ProudAppel,CuretheBlus,NoblNshu 6
22Mar81-8Aqu 7f :22 :443 1:221ft *1-3 121 1hd 1½ 15 14½ Fell J1 Bay Shore 90 ProudAppl,WillowHour,RoylPvilion 4
7Mar81-8Aqu 6f ⊡:224 :4641:112sy *4-5 126 2hd 2hd 1hd 13 Fell J5 Swift 87 Proud Appeal,Triocala,BuffaloLuck 5
22Feb81-8Aqu 6f ⊡:22 :4511:094sy 1e 117 3½ 2hd 1hd 1½ Fell J1 Woodhaven 95 Proud Appeal,Triocala,BuffaloLuck 5
29Jly80-9Mth 5½f :222 :461 1:051sy *4-5 122 77½ 68¾ 49½ 410 Fell J1 Tyro 79 Khrtoum,TrvellingMusic,JohnnyKs 8
30Jun80-8Bel 5½f :232 :463 1:042ft *3-5 122 2½ 2hd 1½ 11½ Fell J6 Great Amer 93 ProudAppeal,IncredibleLuck,KidKs 7
16Jun80-8Bel 5½f :222 :461 1:051ft 4 117 32½ 32 11½ 16 Fell J4 Youthful 89 Proud Appeal, Kid Kas, Lockjaw 9
17May80-3Crc 5f :23 :47 :594ft 9-5 115 12 11½ 14 16½ Guerra W A8 Mdn 96 Proud Appeal,Hypnotized,CraftyEd 8
●Apr 19 Kee 5f ft :594 h Apr 1 Bel tr.t 4f ft :463 h Mar 18 Bel tr.t 4f ft :483 h ●Mar 3 Bel tr.t 4f ft :473 h

***Habano** Dk. b. or br. c. 3, by Ferrol—Miss Tepeji, by Breezy Lane
Br.—Gillermo Estevez M (Mex) 1981 3 1 0 0 $33,479
Own.—Coello M A 126 Tr.—Gonzalez Francisco 1980 9 8 1 0 $167,645
23Apr81-7Kee 1⅛ :472 1:113 1:512sy 48 121 32 45 713 718 McHrDG4 Blue Grass 62 ProudAppeal,LawMe,GoldenDerby 11
14Apr81-7Kee 1 1/16 :464 1:103 1:441ft 6½ 118 21½ 63½ 811 826 Cordero A Jr2 Alw 59 SwingingLght,Sportn'Lf,GoldnDrby 8
6Mar81-8Mex 7f :231 :463 1:272ft *1-9e 117 32½ 33 21 1½ CordroAJr4 Qutzlcotl 79 Habano, Distinct Lover, Offset 11
14Dec80-10Mex 1 :483 1:152 1:441ft *1-3e 117 32½ 2hd 2½ 1½ Soto S B2 Fut 62 Habano, Consolapa, Linea Maginot 8
29Nov80-10Mex 7f :232 :471 1:262ft *1-9e 117 21 2½ 11½ 18 Soto S B5 Cudad 84 Habano, Linea Maginot,SenorRicky 6
16Nov80-10Mex 6½f :232 :461 1:192ft *1-2e 117 41 31½ 2hd 13½ Mercado F3 Alw 86 Habano, Senor Ricky, Henares 7
30Aug80-10Mex 7f :23 :471 1:254gd *4-5 117 75 62½ 12 110 Soto S B15 Anhuac 87 Habano, Alvertido, Jereba 15
19Aug80-9Mex 6½f :224 :463 1:203ft *1-2 117 31½ 2hd 1hd 2hd Cervantes J G2 Alw 80 Jereba, Habano, Don Nicho 6
2Aug80-10Mex 6½f :222 :461 1:202m *2-3e 117 42½ 42 1hd 1nk CrvntsJG9 Cuhtemoc 81 Habano, Definido, Linea Maginot 12
19Jly80-10Mex 6f :222 :461 1:123ft *6-5e 117 52 31½ 2½ 14 CervantesJG7 Cridors 88 Habano, Definado, Senor Ricky 14
10Jun80-7Mex 5f :23 :462 :584ft 8-5 117 1½ 1hd 11 13 Cervantes J G5 Alw 95 Habano, Senor Ricky, Fly Victory 8
27May80-1Mex 5f :224 :462 :592ft 36 117 1hd 1hd 15 14½ Cervantes J G5 Mdn 92 Habano, Impresor, Cascabelillo 10
Apr 20 Kee 1 1/16 sy 1:50 b Apr 12 Kee 1 1/16 ft 1:50 b

Pleasant Colony

```
Pleasant Colony                Dk. b. or br. c. 3, by His Majesty—Sun Colony, by Sunrise Flight
                               Br.—Evans T M (Va)                          1981  3 1 1 0  $114,179
Own.—Buckland Farm        126  Tr.—Campo John P                            1980  5 2 1 0   $87,968
                                                                           Turf  1 0 1 0   $12,848
18Apr81-9Aqu  1⅛:454 1:102 1:493ft   13 126  413 37 13 13    Fell J5      Wood Mem'l 87 PlsntColony,HighlndBld,CurthBlus 6
6Mar81-9GP    1⅛:47  1:111 1:502ft    4 122  1118 911 57 513 BrccileVJr6  Fla Derby 67 Lord Avie, Akureyri, Linnleur  11
16Feb81-9GP   1 1/16:48 1:121 1:442ft 17 122 813 86 3nk 2no  BrcclVJr8    YouthStks 79 Akureyri, PleasantColony,LordAvie 9
9Nov80-8Aqu   1⅛:474 1:123 1:501ft   5½ 116  710 64¾ 32 2½   BraccileVJr6 Remsen    83 ‡Akureyri,PlsntColony,FoolishTnnr 8
     9Nov80—Placed first through disqualification
27Oct80-8Aqu  1⅛(T):4841:1441:544sf  43 115  13141213 57½ 2¾ BraccileVJr12 Pilgrim 69 Akureyri, Pleasant Colony, Jetzier 14
13Oct80-8Bow  7f :224 :453 1:25 ft   6½ 113  78 76½ 74 52½   BrfldD10   Mar Nursery 78 John'sRoll,PintdShild,MtchingGift 11
     13Oct80—Run in Two Divisions 8th & 9th Races.
22Sep80-2Med  170:471 1:132 1:443ft   4½ 118  711 49 13 18½  Asmussen C B8   Mdn  78 PlsntColony,CmmntyIntrst,SldCrdt 8
1Sep80-4Bel   7f :223 :461 1:243ft   28 118  3½ 42 613 618   Brumfield D7    Mdn  63 Summing, Academy H., Bay Ridge 7
  Apr 29 CD 4f ft :491 b    Apr 15 Bel tr.t 4f gd :484 b    ●Apr 11 Bel tr.t 1 ft 1:383 h    Apr 6 Bel tr.t 1 gd 1:40 h (d)
```

Pass the Tab

```
Pass the Tab                   Gr. c. 3, by Al Hattab—Dantina, by Gray Phantom
                               Br.—Villareal L (Cal)                       1981  3 0 2 0   $38,800
Own.—Villareal L          126  Tr.—Barrera Albert S                        1980  6 6 0 0  $129,287
18Apr81-8Spt  1⅛:462 1:122 1:493ft   *3½ 126  22 3½ 3nk 2½   Rivera M A11   Ill Dby 97 Paristo, Pass the Tab, Bitterrook 13
9Apr81-8Aqu   1 :444 1:09 1:351ft    *4-5 119 1½ 2½ 1½ 23    Cordero A Jr3     Alw 87 Cdt High, Pass The Tab,Mr.Wilford 7
7Mar81-8Aqu   6f [•]:224 :4641:112sy  2 126   32 32 47 515   Nicolo P3       Swift 72 Proud Appeal,Triocala,BuffaloLuck 5
31Aug80-11SFe 6½f:221 :442 1:161ft   *1-5 118 2hd 13 18 113  KillnM7   S Fe Futur'y 99 PssTheTb,Shlli'sDnsr,DrconicSpok 10
22Aug80-6SFe  6½f:221 :44 1:161ft    *1-5 118 2hd 13 16 113  Killen M9         SplW 99 PassTheTb,DrconicSpoke,FirstAwy 9
17Jly80-7Aks  6f :223 :454 1:123m    *2½ 122  98½ 99½ 32½ 14 Killen M5      Aks Juv 74 Pass The Tab, Louis S.,CrossFlags 12
22Jun80-10LaM 4½f:223 :451 :511ft    *1-3 119 2 32½ 1nk 19½  KllnM4   Switch Frsom 100 Pass The Tab, Sir L. J., Little Art 10
14Jun80-9LaM  4½f:232 :464 :523ft    *1-3 119 4 1½ 11 16½   Killen M3          Alw 93 PssThTb,BouncngArond,KngHoopr 9
10May80-3SFe  4½f:222 :45 :513ft     *3-2 118 1 1½ 13 115   Killen M4          Mdn 98 PassTheTab,MgicPrter,TheRipper 10
  Apr 28 CD 7f ft 1:26 h    Apr 3 Bel tr.t 4f ft :474 h    Mar 28 Bel tr.t 5f ft 1:00 h    ●Mar 15 Aqu 5f ft 1:00 h
```

Noble Nashua

```
Noble Nashua                   Dk. b. or br. c. 3, by Nashua—Noble Lady, by Vaguely Noble
                               Br.—Grousement Farm (Ky)                    1981  4 2 0 1   $54,576
Own.—Flying Zee Stable    126  Tr.—Martin Jose                             1980  4 2 1 0   $62,007
18Apr81-9Aqu  1⅛:454 1:102 1:493ft   5½ 126  2½ 22 49 414    CrdrAJr6    WoodMem'l 73 PlsntColony,HighlndBld,CurthBlus 6
5Apr81-8Aqu   1 :45 1:084 1:333ft    3½ 123  32 34½ 38 38½   Cordero AJr1   Gotham 89 ProudAppel,CuretheBlus,NoblNshu 6
25Feb81-8Aqu  1 1/16[•]:47 1:1211:43 gd*2-5 119 12 11 14 19½ CordrAJr4  Whirlaway 99 NobleNashua,RoylPvilion,Summing 5
6Feb81-9Tam   6f :222 :462 1:123ft   *1-9 116 43 32½ 2½ 15½  Cordero A Jr5     Alw 82 Noble Nashua, Rit Cat, Sible Sue 7
25Oct80-9Lrl  1 1/16:461 1:113 1:442sy 3½ 122 23 22½ 310 414 Cordero A Jr2 Lrl Fut 72 CuretheBlues,MtchingGift,KnRson 7
12Oct80-8Bel  1 :461 1:113 1:371ft   4½ 122  32 1hd 11 22½   CrdrAJr8   Champagne 80 Lord Avie, Noble Nashua, Sezyou 9
29Sep80-7Bel  6½f:224 :454 1:164ft   *2-3 122 31 32 2½ 1nk   Pincay L Jr1      Alw 92 NobleNashua,ReallySmrt,JiggsAlrm 6
18Sep80-6Bel  6f :223 :462 1:103ft    3 118   67 42½ 1hd 15  Pincay L Jr8      Mdn 89 Noble Nashua,SambaBoy,HaveOne 10
  Apr 14 Bel tr.t 6f ft 1:161 b    Apr 1 Bel tr.t 4f ft :461 h    ●Mar 25 Bel tr.t 5f ft :583 h    ●Mar 18 Bel tr.t 5f ft :593 b
```

Hoedown's Day

```
Hoedown's Day                  B. c. 3, by Bargain Day—Miss Hoedown, by Dance Lesson
                               Br.—Dominguez Mr-Mrs Roger (Cal)            1981  3 1 1 1  $100,200
Own.—Dominguez-Freidel-Thatcher 126 Tr.—Dominguez Roger                    1980  8 4 2 0   $64,525
12Apr81-8SA   1⅛:453 1:101 1:49 ft   39e120  41¾ 32½ 32 32¾  ChapmnTM5    S A Dby 81 SplnddSprc,JhnlN'Hrld,Hdwn'sDy 13
7Mar81-8GG    1 1/16:474 1:131 1:474sl 3 122 23 24 36 212    ChpnTM5   Calif Derby 52 AlwaysACinch,Hoedown'sDy,Okubo 6
21Feb81-8GG   1 :452 1:094 1:352ft   6½e119  1hd 11 13 11½   ChpnTM8     Gold Rush 91 Hdwn'sDy,AlysACnch,SnppyBrgn 13
1Nov80-8BM    1 1/16:45 1:094 1:421ft 6 117  22 23 11½ 2¾    ChpTM4   Elcam'oReal 87 ChrgngStr,Hodown'sDy,SnshnSwg 13
17Oct80-8BM   1 :452 1:094 1:36 ft   3½e115  11½ 11½ 1hd 2hd Munoz E8    San Mateo 89 AlysACnch,Hdn'sDy,LngLvThKng 10
30Oct80-8BM   6f :222 :45 1:094ft    3-2 119  31½ 43 45½ 46½ MnozE7  Francis Drak 84 MkeHimFmous,LomMld,DressyNtiv 7
29Aug80-11Sac 1 :461 1:104 1:363ft   *2-3 119 11½ 12 12½ 16  MnozE5   S Fjuvchamp 93 Hoedown'sDy,JdRing,AndrwThoms 8
30Jly80-11Bmf 6f :222 :453 1:112ft    6-5 122 41½ 32 1½ 12   Munoz E4      Mid Pen 83 Hoedown'sDay,Reglberto,Soderling 5
3Jun80-8GG    5½f:221 :454 1:043ft    5 117   1½ 12 13 13½   Munoz E5     Tanforan 88 Hodown'sDy,Rglbrto,BlowngSnow 11
29Apr80-8GG   5f :22 :453 :583ft      3½ 118  32 54¾ 68 67   Winick D1    Juvenile 84 D. Aminoil, Hematite,BlowingSnow 8
16Apr80-4GG   5f :221 :453 :573ft    *8-5 118 1hd 11½ 12 15  Winick D10        Mdn 96 Hoedown'sDy,SirEchelon,Hemtite 12
  Apr 25 CD 7f ft 1:30 h    ●Apr 21 CD 4f ft :483 h    ●Apr 10 SA 4f ft :453 h    Apr 4 GG 5f ft :593 hg
```

Woodchopper

```
Woodchopper                    Gr. c. 3, by Hatchet Man—Musical Chairs, by Swaps
                               Br.—Greentree Stud Inc (Ky)                 1981  5 3 0 2  $160,105
Own.—Greentree Stable     126  Tr.—Gaver John M Jr                         1980  1 M 0 0
11Apr81-9OP   1⅛:471 1:112 1:502ft   2½ 123  98½ 85½ 67 33¾  ShomkrW6   Aks Derby 87 BoldEgo,TopAvenger,Woodchopper 9
29Mar81-9FG   1⅛:462 1:113 1:504ft    6 113  1012 97½ 45 11 VelasquezJ4 La Derby 90 Woodchopper, A Run, Beau Rit 13
13Mar81-9FG   140:48 1:133 1:42 ft   *8-5 119 811 58 3½ 12½ McKnight J7       Alw 83 Woodchopper,ExctlyE.,MotorCop 10
5Mar81-5FG    1 1/16:473 1:134 1:463ft *8-5 119 613 54½ 12½ 13 McKnight J8    Mdn 79 Woodchopper,LitningInBottle,Rust 8
19Feb81-4FG   6f :221 :471 1:121ft   17 119  109½ 1110½ 710 37½ McKnight J7   Mdn 76 LiutnntCorly,LssSon,Woodchoppr 12
23Aug80-4Sar  6f :224 :462 1:112ft   12 118  11121113 10131014 Gonzalez M A4   Mdn 69 JungleJove,Summing,CountrAttck 12
  Apr 28 CD 1 ft 1:38 h    Apr 10 OP 3f ft :37 b    Apr 7 OP 6f ft 1:144 h    Mar 27 FG 4f ft :49 h
```

Well Decorated
Dk. b. or br. c. 3, by Raja Baba—Paris Breeze, by Majestic Prince
Br.—Allen H (Fla) 1981 3 1 1 0 $61,835
Own.—Allen Herbert 126 Tr.—Jacobs Eugene 1980 6 3 0 1 $306,607
14Apr81-7Kee 1 1/16 :464 1:103 1:441ft *1-2 113 43 53½ 42 43½ MacBeth D6 Alw 81 SwingingLght,Sportn'Lf,GoldnDrby 8
28Mar81-9Hia 1⅛ :47 1:104 1:491ft 3½ 122 1½ 1hd 12 21 MacBethD5 Flamingo 85 TpShoes,WellDecorted,DoublSonic 7
9Mar81-9Hia 7f :222 :444 1:221ft 5½ 119 32½ 34 2hd 1no MacBeth D1 Bahamas 92 WellDecorted,DshO'Plesure,TpShos 8
25Oct80-9Lrl 1 1/16 :461 1:113 1:442sy 6 122 45½ 36½ 413 516 AsmussenCB3 Lrl Fut 70 CuretheBlues,MtchingGift,KnRson 7
12Oct80-8Bel 1 :461 1:113 1:371ft 2½ 122 21 2hd 32 48 ♦PncyLJr6 Champagne 74 Lord Avie, Noble Nashua, Sezyou 9
♦12Oct80—Dead heat
6Sep80-8AP 7f :221 :444 1:234ft 6 122 77¾ 57½ 3nk 12 PncLJr4 Arl Was Fut 83 WellDcortd,LordAvi,FirwyPhntom 15
23Aug80-8Sar 6½f :222 :453 1:17 ft 4½ 122 1hd 1hd 22 38 Venezia M3 Hopeful 79 Tap Shoes,LordAvie,WellDecorated 9
4Aug80-8Sar 6f :22 :45 1:101ft 4½ 117 11 12 14 14½ VeneziaM5 Sar Spec'l 89 WellDecorated,TapShoes,Motivity 10
24Jly80-5Bel 6f :222 :46 1:111ft 1¾ 118 11 1hd 11 1nk Venezia M4 Mdn 86 WellDecorated,JungleJove,CutHigh 9
Apr 21 Kee 4f ft :48 bg ●Apr 11 Kee 4f sy :47 b ●Mar 25 GP 5f ft :592 h Mar 21 GP 1 ft 1:39 h

Classic Go Go
B. c. 3, by Page Pago—Classic Perfection, by Never Bend
Br.—Winchell V H (Ky) 1981 10 7 2 0 $207,383
Own.—Winchell V H 126 Tr.—Meyer Jerome C 1980 5 1 1 1 $10,360
25Apr81-7CD 1 :472 1:114 1:374ft *1 122 22 21 21 24 Delahoussaye E1 Alw 76 MythclRulr,ClsscGoGo,TlvsonStudo 4
16Apr81-7Kee 7f :23 :454 1:24 ft *2-5 121 3½ 1hd 12 11½ Black A S1 Alw 86 ClssicGoGo,WthCuton,Contorsonst 6
28Mar81-8Lat 1 :46 1:11 1:38 ft *3-5 122 48½ 33 24 26½ Black A S2 Spiral 82 MythiclRuler,ClssicGoGo,IronGem 10
16Mar81-8Pim 6f :224 :454 1:101gd *3-5 122 44½ 45 46½ 49 Black A S4 H Jacobs 86 Century Prince, J. D.Quill,IrishKing 5
28Feb81-9Bow 1 1/16 :471 1:122 1:464ft *1-3 122 68½ 34 12½ 15 Black A S9 Bowie 72 ClssicGoGo,HonorbleMn,BostonTe 10
16Feb81-9Bow 7f :23 :46 1:231ft 8-5 122 64¾ 53½ 2hd 13 Fann B6 Gen. George 89 ClsscGoGo,ThrtyEghtPcs,AztcCrwn 9
7Feb81-8Aqu 1⅛ [⊡]:473 1:12 1:503ft 5¾ 117 56¾ 45 2hd 11½ Fann B1 Lucky Draw 93 ClassicGoGo,RoyalPavilion,Triocala 7
1Feb81-8Key 6f :222 :454 1:112ft 3½ 122 68 42½ 2hd 11½ Black A S2 Alw 85 ClssicGoGo,HoldOnPto,Rock'NRdy 6
14Jan81-7Aqu 1 1/16 [⊡]:483 1:14 1:451ft 4½ 109 43½ 2hd 1hd 1nk Migliore R3 HcpO 88 ClssicGoGo,SwpforPowr,MornngHz 9
10Jan81-5Aqu 1 1/16 [⊡]:472 1:134 1:463ft 23 1157 22 2hd 14 17 Migliore R5 Alw 81 ClssicGoGo,RoylPvilion,EverNoble 10
29Dec80-3Med 1 1/16 :502 1:161 1:484ft *7-5 1135 53½ 31 1hd 1¾ Kaenel J L4 Mdn 65 ClassicGoGo,TurnAngle,HastyScott 7
19Dec80-4Med 6f :23 :472 1:142ft 2¾ 118 43 44½ 42½ 32½ Lovato F Jr7 Mdn 68 JeffreyH.,Standpoint,ClassicGoGo 12
11Dec80-4Med 6f :23 :464 1:13 ft 3½ 120 85¼ 42½ 21½ 2½ Fann B10 Mdn 77 Bitterrook,ClssicGoGo,PssingAge 11
3Dec80-3Med 170 :481 1:133 1:433ft 8¾ 118 21 2½ 33 43½ MacBeth D3 Mdn 80 Main Stem,GreyTiger,MorningHaze 8
6Nov80-4Med 6f :223 :46 1:12 ft 67 118 108½ 1017 915 811 Chatman H G8 Mdn 72 GreekMinstrel,Simbari,SuperHawk 10
Apr 12 Kee 5f ft 1:012 b ●Mar 27 Lat 3f sy :363 h Mar 18 Bow 6f ft 1:121 h

Top Avenger
B. c. 3, by Staunch Avenger—Atop, by Dunce
Br.—Bishop W P (Tex) 1981 3 1 1 0 $75,720
Own.—Bishop W P 126 Tr.—Viator Dwight 1980 5 5 0 0 $93,620
11Apr81-9OP 1⅛ :471 1:112 1:502ft 20 120 2½ 2½ 21½ 21½ Snyder L5 Aks Derby 90 BoldEgo,TopAvenger,Woodchopper 9
29Mar81-9FG 1⅛ :462 1:113 1:504ft 5 123 46 41½ 58 713 TrosclirAJ5 La Derby 77 Woodchopper, A Run, Beau Rit 13
13Feb81-8OP 6f :22 :461 1:12 ft *1 121 41¾ 4¾ 2hd 11¾ Trosclair A J6 HcpO 85 Top Avenger, Lockjaw, KanofSpots 9
31Dec80-9FG 6f :221 :461 1:111ft *2-5 124 11½ 1hd 1hd 1no TrosclairAJ7 Sugar Bl 89 TopAvenger,Contorsionist,GlassStr 9
30Nov80-9FG 6f :214 :454 1:11 ft *1 122 46½ 3½ 12 14½ TrsclrAJ12 OldHckory 90 Top Avenger,GlassStar,SilentBasis 14
1Sep80-10EvD 6f :224 :46 1:13 ft *3-5 120 21 21 11 15 TrosclrAJ11 Lfyte Fty 83 TopAvenger,CjunMoccsin,Lt.Stev 12
21Aug80-6EvD 6f :232 :47 1:131ft *1-2 120 4nk 2hd 11 14½ Trosclair A J6 Trials 82 Top Avenger, Rust, Honey Pro 9
25Jly80-5LaD 5f :224 :473 1:00 ft 3 120 2½ 1½ 11 14 Trosclair A J2 Mdn 95 Top Avenger, Dr. No, Dr. Spanky 12
Apr 29 CD 4f ft :513 b ●Apr 25 CD 6f ft 1:132 h Apr 21 CD 5f ft 1:032 b ●Mar 24 FG 1 ft 1:394 h

Bold Ego
Dk. b. or br. c. 3, by Bold Tactics—Coya's Ego, by Buffin
Br.—Barton J D (NM) 1981 5 3 0 0 $205,990
Own.—Double B Ranch & Kidd J 126 Tr.—Van Berg Jack 1980 8 7 0 1 $176,686
11Apr81-9OP 1⅛ :471 1:112 1:502ft *2-3 123 1½ 1½ 11½ 11½ Lively J9 Aks Derby 91 BoldEgo,TopAvenger,Woodchopper 9
14Mar81-9OP 170 :462 1:114 1:412ft 3 122 11 11 15 15½ Lively J4 Rebel H 89 BoldEgo,CatchThtPss,ChpelCreek 10
28Feb81-9OP 6f :214 :46 1:114sy 3½ 117 11 1½ 14 16½ Lively J4 HcpO 86 Bold Ego, Lockjaw, Vodika Collins 8
13Feb81-8OP 6f :22 :461 1:12 ft 4 120 2hd 2hd 42½ 56¼ Lively J5 HcpO 79 Top Avenger, Lockjaw, KanofSpots 9
21Jan81-8SA 6f :213 :441 1:094ft 5½ 122 11 1hd 2½ 59 Jones K1 San Miguel 81 Motivity, Royal Forbes, Torso 6
14Sep80-10Alb 6f :214 :451 1:112ft *2-5 118 2hd 1½ 13 15¼ CshnJL9 N. Mex Futy 86 Bold Ego, Bin ABattle,ColonelDay 10
6Sep80-18Alb 6f :221 :454 1:131m *1-3 118 31 3nk 31 11 Cushing J L6 SplW 77 BoldEgo,Draconic'sLdy,IrishEye's 10
19Jly80-8Hol 6f :212 :442 1:10 ft 8½ 122 1hd 1hd 1½ 33½ CshJL2 Hol JuvChmp 83 Loma Malad, Motivity, Bold Ego 13
8Jun80-10Rui 4f :23 :47 ft *2-3 120 1 2hd 1hd 12¾ CshJL3 [S]R Gr' DeFut 88 Bold Ego, Dr. Me Up, First Away 10
30May80-?Rui 4f :223 :473ft *1-5 120 1 11 12 14¾ Cushing J L1 SplW 85 BoldEgo,CowboyLoving,AlaskanStr 8
4May80-11Sun 5f :22 :451 :572ft *6-5 120 1hd 1hd 11 12¾ CushingJL1 R Allison 96 BoldEgo,ElegantLaura,SquawBred 11
25Apr80-12Sun 5f :22 :452 :573ft *6-5 120 1hd 1hd 12 14 Cushing J L8 SplW 95 BoldEgo,ElegntLur,CcheInvestmnt 8
29Mar80-5Sun 4f :223 :453ft 15 118 3 1hd 12 14½ Cushing J L6 Mdn 96 BoldEgo,JohnnyDark,Casey'sImge 10
Apr 25 CD 1⅛ ft 1:56 b ●Apr 19 CD 7f ft 1:29 h ●Apr 4 OP 1 sy 1:42 b Mar 29 OP 7f sy 1:263 h

Cure the Blues ✕

B. c. 3, by Stop the Music—Quick Cure, by Dr Fager
Br.—Firestone B R Mr–Mrs (Va) 1981 3 1 1 1 $47,004
Own.—Firestone B R 126 **Tr.—Jolley Leroy** 1980 5 5 0 0 $131,102

18Apr81-9Aqu 1⅛ :454 1:102 1:493ft *1-5 126 1½ 12 23 38 VsquzJ1 Wood Mem'l 79 PlsntColony,HighlndBld,CurthBlus 6
5Apr81-8Aqu 1 :45 1:084 1:333ft *2-3 126 2½ 2½ 2hd 2no Vasquez J6 Gotham 98 ProudAppel,CuretheBlus,NoblNshu 6
26Mar81-9Hia 7f :23 :453 1:23 sy *1-9 122 22½ 1hd 14 15 Vasquez J1 Alw 88 CurethBlus,GovrnorBob,LPromnur 6
25Oct80-9Lrl 1 1/16 :461 1:113 1:442sy *1-2 122 13 12½ 16 16½ Turcotte R L1 Lrl Fut 86 CuretheBlues,MtchingGift,KnRson 7
13Oct80-9Bow 7f :223 :442 1:232ft *1-3 116 2hd 13 16 15 TrcttRL1 MarNursery 88 CuretheBlus,CnturyPrinc,JunglJov 6
13Oct80—Run in Two Divisions 8th & 9th Races.
6Oct80-8Bow 6f :223 :452 1:10 ft *1-5 113 13 13 15 17 Passmore W J3 Alw 90 CuretheBlues,SilentBsis,Viky'sChrg 6
20Sep80-7Bow 7f :231 :462 1:244ft *2-5 115 2½ 1hd 18 110 Turcotte R L3 Alw 81 CurthBlus,DoublWhmmy,HighJump 7
16Apr80-3Pim 5f :24 :472 :584ft *3-5 120 11½ 12 15 110 Turcotte R L1 Mdn 91 CurthBlus,PlyfulChstr,RunBoldRun 6
Apr 15 Aqu 5f gd :593 h ●Apr 2 Aqu 4f m :47 b Mar 25 Hia 2f ft :243 b ●Mar 19 Hia 6f ft 1:093 h

Beau Rit

B. g. 3, by Lord Rebeau—Rit-n-Rough, by Rough'n Tumble
Br.—Early Bird Stud (Fla) 1981 6 3 1 1 $96,100
Own.—Roussel Carole 126 **Tr.—Roussel Louie III** 1980 2 1 1 0 $6,000

23Apr81-7Kee 1⅛ :472 1:113 1:512sy 12 121 67 67½ 815 55½ RbbccP10 Blue Grass 75 ProudAppeal,LawMe,GoldenDerby 11
29Mar81-9FG 1⅛ :462 1:113 1:504ft 11 126 810 63½ 33 33 RubbiccoP6 La Derby 87 Woodchopper, A Run, Beau Rit 13
14Mar81-9FG 1 1/16 :472 1:124 1:45 ft *8-5 122 44 32 21½ 2no RbbccoP6 La Dby Trl 87 SenateChairmn,BeuRit,Andy'sWish 9
8Feb81-9FG 1 1/16 :471 1:124 1:461ft *8-5 119 58½ 35½ 11½ 1hd RbbccP10 HPradeDby 81 BeuRit,BoysNiteOut,CircleofSteel 13
25Jan81-8FG 1 1/16 :47 1:131 1:463ft 8-5 119 39 2½ 11½ 11 RbbccP9 H P DbyTrls 79 Beau Rit, Nobubble, Contorsionist 9
9Jan81-5FG 140 :48 1:14 1:424ft *1-2 119 21 2½ 1hd 11 Rubbicco P7 Alw 79 Beau Rit, Nobubble, Hurricane Bay 7
24Dec80-4FG 6f :224 :471 1:124m *2-5 119 1hd 1hd 15 15 Rubbicco P2 Mdn 81 Beau Rit, Rust, Effy Says 11
4Dec80-4FG 6f :224 :481 1:112ft 23 119 2½ 2hd 2½ 21 Rubbicco P8 Mdn 87 Bold Ivor, Beau Rit, Captense 12
Apr 22 Kee 3f ft :36 b ●Apr 16 Kee 5f ft 1:001 h Mar 21 FG 5f ft 1:023 b Mar 13 FG 3f ft :38 b

Television Studio

B. g. 3, by Within Hail—Put on T V, by T V Lark
Br.—Bwamazon Farm (Ky) 1981 2 0 0 1 $2,560
Own.—Bwamazon Farm 126 **Tr.—Basile Anthony** 1980 11 3 2 3 $101,106

25Apr81-7CD 1 :472 1:114 1:374ft 11 122 310 46 45½ 37 Day P3 Alw 73 MythclRulr,ClsscGoGo,TlvsonStudo 4
3Apr81-6Kee a7f 1:26 ft 2½ 123 74½ 77½ 69½ 621 Brumfield D8 Alw 72 Sportin'Lif,MronFrncs,CrwfordSpcl 8
22Nov80-8CD 1 1/16 :49 1:14 1:47 ft 6½ 119 56 52½ 23 1nk BrumfldD2 Ky Jky Cb 73 TelevisionStudio,Linnleur,BrCrkDm 8
1Nov80-7CD 1 1/16 :49 1:143 1:483ft 8-5 117 43½ 31 11 14 Brumfield D4 Alw 65 TlvisionStudio,TwstnAlong,Skyclon 6
21Oct80-4Kee 1 1/16 :483 1:144 1:481ft *6-5 117 58 51½ 3nk 2hd Brumfield D4 Mdn 65 ‡BcksGlor,TlvsonStdo,RmnSttsmn 12
21Oct80—Placed first through disqualification
11Oct80-3Kee 1 1/16 :483 1:144 1:493ft 3 117 1012 74½ 3½ 2½ Haire D8 Mdn 57 MrinEist,TlvsonStudo,RlodndChrg 12
15Sep80-3AP 7f :233 :474 1:291sl 2½ 122 62¾ 63½ 34½ 24¾ Patterson A6 Mdn 51 FllLine,TlvisionStudio,WstrnBufflo 8
18Aug80-5AP 6f :224 :464 1:141sl 16 122 87¾ 79½ 56 55½ Patterson A7 Mdn 66 Corsicana, King Pali, Global Jet 8
8Aug80-4AP 5½f :222 :462 1:051ft 17 122 85¾ 67½ 54½ 47¾ Patterson A4 Mdn 81 IntrpdHttr,MsssppRbl,RldndChrg 11
21Jly80-3AP 5½f :224 :472 1:07 sy 3¾ 122 87½ 89¾ 412 414 Patterson A9 Mdn 66 Broadway Raider, MannyT.,FallLine 9
27May80-3AP 5f :224 :454 :574ft 4½ 122 78 77 611 314 Patterson A2 Mdn 83 ThRzzul,Buck'sLstDrm,TlvsonStdo 8
16May80-3AP 5f :223 :454 :58 ft *7-5e 122 57 44½ 46 39¾ Patterson A5 Mdn 86 MontryGift,ThRizzuli,TlvisionStudo 9
15Apr80-3Kee 4½f :223 :46 :52 gd 4-5 121 7 812 611 318 Morgan M R7 Mdn 77 RodgrRnhrt,Prnr'sEdg,TlvsonStdo 10
●Apr 20 Kee 6f sy 1:15 h Apr 10 Kee 5f ft 1:053 b Apr 2 Kee 3f ft :363 b Mar 29 Kee 7f ft 1:30 b

Tap Shoes

Ch. c. 3, by Riva Ridge—Bold Ballet, by Bold Bidder
Br.—Hancock A III & Peters L J (Ky) 1981 2 1 0 1 $110,592
Own.—Peters L. & Hancock III et al 126 **Tr.—Luro Horatio A** 1980 7 4 1 1 $197,084

28Mar81-9Hia 1⅛ :47 1:104 1:491ft *3-5 122 43 31 22 11 HernndezR6 Flamingo 86 TpShoes,WellDecorted,DoublSonic 7
9Mar81-9Hia 7f :222 :444 1:221ft *9-5 122 78¾ 711 43 3nk HernndezR6 Bahamas 92 WellDecorted,DshO'Plesure,TpShos 8
12Oct80-8Bel 1 :461 1:113 1:371ft *3-2 122 54 53¾ 65½ 611 HrnndR1 Champagne 71 Lord Avie, Noble Nashua, Sezyou 9
13Sep80-8Bel 7f :223 :452 1:234ft *1-2 122 2hd 1hd 11 11¾ HernandezR1 Futurity 83 TapShoes,DashO'Plesure,McCrcken 6
23Aug80-8Sar 6½f :222 :453 1:17 ft 2½ 122 62¾ 42 12 12 HernandezR5 Hopeful 87 Tap Shoes,LordAvie,WellDecorated 9
13Aug80-8Sar 6f :213 :443 1:10 ft 5½ 115 89½ 88 45 11¾ HernandezR3 Sanford 90 Tap Shoes, Triocala,PaintedShield 10
4Aug80-8Sar 6f :22 :45 1:101ft 21 117 61½ 32 34½ 24½ HernndzR9 Sar Spec'l 84 WellDecorated,TapShoes,Motivity 10
4Jly80-8Suf 5½f :222 :463 1:053ft *8-5 114 56 54½ 42 34½ O'DrscllJ4 Mayflower 91 And More, Lockjaw, Tap Shoes 12
18Jun80-6Bel 5½f :231 :473 1:062ft 4½ 118 52½ 41½ 11½ 16½ Hernandez R10 Mdn 83 Tap Shoes, Chapel Creek, Behold 10
Apr 22 Kee 3f ft :394 b Apr 18 Kee 1 1/16 ft 1:453 h Apr 11 Hia 5f ft 1:01 b Apr 6 Hia 5f ft 1:00 h

Mythical Ruler — Ro. c. 3, by Ruritania—Our Nanny, by Victorian Era
Br.—Penn O (Ky) — 1981 3 3 0 0 $53,660
Own.—Risen Al Jr & Price Paxton — **122** — Tr.—Wirth Fred — 1980 5 3 1 1 $17,520

25Apr81-7CD	1	:472	1:114	1:374ft	2½	122	12	11	11	14	Wirth K B4	Alw	80	MythclRulr,ClsscGoGo,TlvsonStudo	4
28Mar81-8Lat	1	:46	1:11	1:38 ft	10	114	13	13	14	16½	Wirth K1	Spiral	89	MythiclRuler,ClssicGoGo,IronGem	10
20Mar81-8Lat	1	:464	1:121	1:401ft	3	115	2hd	12	12½	14	Wirth K4	Alw	78	MythiclRulr,MgicDust,RgingBufflo	7
13Sep80-5Lat	6f	:221	:461	1:122ft	*2-5	1157	36½	31½	31½	2hd	Wirth B2	Alw	86	Magic Dust,MythicalRuler,GiGiBear	6
16Aug80-9EIP	6f	:224	:46	1:112ft	7-5	116	15	12	12	11¾	WrthB7	J C Elp Mem	93	Mythical Ruler, Iron Gem,GiGiBear	7
8Aug80-8EIP	5½f	:222	:46	1:062ft	*1-2	1137	2hd	2hd	11	12	Wirth B5	Alw	88	MythicalRuler,GiGiBear,I'mforNavy	6
26Jly80-3EIP	5f	:224	:46	:583ft	3	10910	1½	14	15	19½	Wirth B10	Mdn	98	Mythical Ruler, Mr.D.H.S.,SeaCzar	11

●Apr 18 CD 6f ft 1:14 h

EIGHTH RACE
Churchill
MAY 2, 1981

1 ¼ MILES. (1.59⅖) 107th Running KENTUCKY DERBY SCALE WEIGHT (Grade I). $200,000 Added (plus $20,000 from KTDF). 3-year-olds. By subscription of $100 which covers nomination for both the Kentucky Derby and Derby Trial. All nomination fees to Derby winner. $4,000 to pass entry box Thursday, April 30, $3,500 additional to start. $200,000 added, of which: $50,000 to second, $25,000 to third, $12,500 to fourth. $100,000 guaranteed to the winner (to be divided equally in the event of a dead heat.) Weight, 126 lbs. Starters to be named through the entry box Thursday, April 30, at the time of closing. (This provision waived, by court order, permitting Flying Nashua and Mythical Ruler to start). The maximum number of starters for the Kentucky Derby will be limited to twenty. In the event more than twenty entries pass through the entry box at the usual time of closing, the twenty starters will be determined at that time with preference given to those that have accumulated the highest earnings. For those that enter and are eliminated under this condition, the nomination fee and the fee to pass through the entry box, will be refunded. The owner of the winner to receive a gold trophy. (Closed with 432 nominations.)
Total purse $424,700. Value of race $413,450, value to winner $317,200, second $55,000, third $27,500, fourth $13,750. ($11,250 reverts to KTDF.) Mutuel pool $4,566,179.

Last Raced		Horse	Eqt.	A.	Wt	PP	¼	½	¾	1	Str	Fin	Jockey	Odds $1
18Apr81	9Aqu1	Pleasant Colony		3	126	7	171	16hd	15½	4½	11½	1¾	Velasquez J	3.50
11Apr81	9OP3	Woodchopper		3	126	11	20½	192	191½	11½	5hd	23	Delahoussaye E	34.20
12Apr81	8SA6	Partez	b	3	126	3	121	121	101	22	21	32¼	Hawley S	f-7.90
25Apr81	7CD2	Classic Go Go		3	126	13	19½	182½	17hd	92	7hd	4no	Black A S	f-7.90
25Apr81	7CD3	Television Studio	b	3	126	18	21	20hd	20½	102	81	51½	Whited D E	f-7.90
18Apr81	8Spt2	Pass the Tab		3	126	8	111	101	7½	31	6½	6nk	Pincay L Jr	31.10
12Apr81	8SA1	Splendid Spruce	b	3	126	1	101	9½	9½	5½	4hd	7nk	McHargue D G	13.60
12Apr81	8SA4	Flying Nashua	b	3	126	21	18hd	153	16hd	15hd	93	82¾	Cordero A Jr	48.00
18Apr81	9Aqu4	Noble Nashua		3	126	9	142	13hd	131½	131	102½	9no	Asmussen C B	71.70
11Apr81	9OP1	Bold Ego		3	126	15	21	2hd	2hd	1hd	31	102¾	Lively J	9.90
23Apr81	7Kee4	Double Sonic		3	126	4	161	21	21	171	111	112¾	Thornburg B	f-7.90
12Apr81	8SA3	Hoedown's Day		3	126	10	61½	71	111½	121½	12½	12nk	Chapman T M	f-7.90
23Apr81	7Kee5	Beau Rit	b	3	126	17	15hd	171½	181	18½	13hd	13nk	Rubbicco P	f-7.90
28Mar81	9Hia1	Tap Shoes		3	126	19	131	143	141½	14½	146	147	Hernandez R	7.60
18Apr81	9Aqu3	Cure the Blues	b	3	126	16	81½	6hd	8hd	16½	152	152	Shoemaker W	4.70
14Apr81	7Kee4	Well Decorated		3	126	12	4½	4hd	4hd	6½	16½	16½	MacBeth D	65.10
25Apr81	7CD1	Mythical Ruler	b	3	126	20	51	51½	5hd	7½	172	172½	Wirth K B	f-7.90
23Apr81	7Kee1	Proud Appeal		3	126	5	3½	31½	32	8hd	183	182	Fell J	a-2.30
11Apr81	9OP2	Top Avenger		3	126	14	1hd	11	1hd	191	193	194½	Snyder L	f-7.90
23Apr81	7Kee7	Habano		3	126	6	9hd	111	122	201½	204	205	Feliciano B R	f-7.90
23Apr81	7Kee3	Golden Derby		3	126	2	7½	82½	62½	21	21	21	Espinoza J C	a-2.30

a–Coupled: Proud Appeal and Golden Derby.
f—Mutuel field.

OFF AT 5:41 EDT. Start good. Won ridden out. Time, :21⅘, :45⅘, 1:10⅘, 1:36, 2:02 Track fast.

$2 Mutuel Prices:

4-PLEASANT COLONY	9.00	5.60	4.40
6-WOODCHOPPER		23.40	13.00
12-PARTEZ (f-field)			4.00

Dk. b. or br. c, by His Majesty—Sun Colony, by Sunrise Flight. Trainer Campo John P. Bred by Evans T M (Va).

PLEASANT COLONY, taken in reserve leaving the gate and then patiently and well ridden, was under good control by the jockey while rapidly working into contention through the field on the final turn and settled outside the leaders for the drive at the head of the stretch. He raced past PARTEZ with authority and Velasquez using the whip four times left-handed and once on the right, and was ridden out by hand to hold WOODCHOPPER safe. WOODCHOPPER, also held in reserve the first half-mile, threaded between horses and closed resolutely from the top of the top of the stretch to be gradually increasing his advantage over the others. PARTEZ, reserved just off of the first flight for a half-mile, reached the front between calls in the early stretch but offered no resistance to the winner, relaxed when Hawley mis-judged the finish line and rose in the irons at the sixteenth pole as he was relinquishing second to WOODCHOPPER, then finished evenly with the jockey riding him out the final yards. CLASSIC GO GO, another reserved off of the fast early pace, advanced steadily on the final turn and into the last furlong, then was hanging at the end. TELEVISION STUDIO, last from the gate and well back into the far turn, lost ground circling horses and finished determinedly near the center of the track. PASS THE TAB briefly appeared threatening on the stretch turn and tired. SPLENDID SPRUCE raced on the inside and lacked a closing response. FLYING NASHUA was in traffic most of the race and lacked a rally. NOBLE NASHUA did not threaten. BOLD EGO was lightly rated with a fast early pace, responded to take command on the stretch turn but had little left the final quarter-mile. DOUBLE SONIC made up ground the last half-mile without threatening. HOEDOWN'S DAY tired. BEAU RIT saved ground. TAP SHOES was in close traffic at the first turn. CURE THE BLUES was kept wide and tired. WELL DECORATED was a factor for a mile and faltered. MYTHICAL RULER was extremely wide. PROUD APPEAL bid for the lead along the rail in the backstretch and stopped. TOP AVENGER was used up with the fast early pace. HABANO was used up early. GOLDEN DERBY was shuffled back along the rail at the first turn, recovered to race forwardly placed but stopped in the drive.

Owners— 1, Buckland Farm; 2, Greentree Stable; 3, Davis E & Greene Mr-Mrs H; 4, Winchell V H; 5, Bwamazon Farm; 6, Villareal L; 7, Surf and Turf Stable; 8, Digiulio & Holman & Jensen & Ronca; 9, Flying Zee Stable; 10, Double B Ranch & Kidd J; 11, Elias F & L; 12, Dominguez-Freidel-Thatcher; 13, Roussel Carole; 14, Peters L & Hancock III et al; 15, Firestone B R; 16, Allen Herbert; 17, Risen Al Jr & Price Paxton; 18, Winfield M H et al; 19, Bishop W P; 20, Coello M A; 21, Lehmann F E & Gaines J R.

Scratched—Wayward Lass (1May81 [8]CD[3]).

THE WINNER'S PEDIGREE AND CAREER HIGHLIGHTS

PLEASANT COLONY (Dark Bay or Brown Colt)	His Majesty	*Ribot	Tenerani
			Romanella
		Flower Bowl	*Alibhai
			Flower Bed
	Sun Colony	Sunrise Flight	Double Jay
			Misty Morn
		*Colonia	Cockrullah
			Naiga

Year	Age	Sts	1st	2nd	3rd	Won
1980	2	5	2	1	0	$87,968
1981	3	9	4	2	1	877,415
TOTALS		14	6	3	1	$965,383

At 2 Years	WON	*Remsen
	2nd	Pilgrim
	UNP	Maryland Nursery
		*Placed first through disqualification.
At 3 Years	WON	Kentucky Derby, Wood, Preakness, Woodward
	2nd	Fountain of Youth, Travers
	3rd	Belmont Stakes
	UNP	Florida Derby, Marlboro Cup

Pleasant Colony did indeed win the race, followed by Woodchopper and Partez. Proud Appeal was in the race until the mile pole, then faltered badly and finished eighteenth. He also became one of the horses whose career was essentially destroyed by the Derby. Never regaining his earlier form, he was quickly retired to stud, where he now stands for Gainesway Farms.

Pleasant Colony paid $4.40 to show, so our bet of $342 returned $752.40, for a profit of $410.40.

It was a great day for us. In addition to the fun we had had, all five of our Dr. Z system bets had been winners. Our only loss was the win bet on Proud Appeal. Our $1,000 stake grew to $2,079.10. We vowed to come back to try it again the following May.

11

A Great Day for Canada: Sunny's Halo Wins the 1983 Kentucky Derby

THE KENTUCKY MOOD

We had been in Chicago in May 1983 for the semiannual joint meetings of the Operations Research Society of America and the Institute of Management Sciences. I had organized several sessions dealing with the latest theory and practice of trading stock options and with the mathematics of gambling. We had also read some research papers and I had a number of meetings involved with my activities as finance editor of the journal *Management Science*.

One of my UBC students, Brian Canfield, who was keen to learn more about stock market activities and horse-race betting, came along as well. When Don went back to Northwestern, Brian and I drove to Kentucky. Don flew down later for Derby Day. It takes about six hours to reach the Kentucky border, and the mood suddenly changes from industrial towns and rolling farm country to beautifully kept bluegrass horse farms with their white board fences. It had been two years since my last visit, and we had a whole week before the Derby to explore the farms in the Lexington area and do research for this book at the Keeneland and Churchill Downs racetracks and at the Keeneland racing library. The first few days brought an unbelievable amount of heavy spring rain. Finally, at midweek, the weather cleared and remained pleasant throughout our stay. It took the track at Churchill Downs only about a day to dry out, and the sun was so strong that the track had to be watered only two days after the torrential drenching it took.

This area of Kentucky has the greatest assembly of horse farms in the world and much of the finest bloodstock. As I mentioned in Chapter Ten, most of the farms allow visitors with appointments, and I highly recommend that you visit them. The highlight for us was a visit to Claiborne farms in

Paris, Kentucky. This 3,200-acre farm supports twenty-eight major stallions and about five hundred mares, yearlings, and other horses. It was a rare treat to see such great horses as Secretariat, Spectacular Bid, Nijinski II, Riva Ridge, Conquistador Cielo, Coastal, Drone, Damascus, and Mr. Prospector close up. The investment side of racing involves a fantastic set of investment gambles. Horses' values can vary by millions of dollars as the result of a single event—for instance, a convincing victory in an important race or a minor injury. The price of the best bloodstock has reached astronomical levels. The twenty-eight stallions at Claiborne include some of the world's best. Their total value is several hundred million dollars.

The most important auction of yearlings takes place at Keeneland. At the July 1983 sale, 301 yearlings sold for an average price of $501,495, or over $150 million in total. These are amazing sums for horses that have never run a race. The competitive bidding among racing's elite millionaires, each hoping to obtain the best bloodstock, drives the prices to these unheard-of sums. Prices are dependent on the horse's pedigree, the fame and performance of his sire and dam and their heritage, and on the physical appearance of the young animal.

Northern Dancer, the 1964 Derby winner in what was then the record time of two minutes flat, has been the star of the show of late. His offspring have proved to be outstanding runners and even better sires. His stud fee of as much as $700,000 with no guarantee of a live foal may sound outrageously expensive. However, it has certainly paid off, and if the chemistry is right, the returns can be smashing. At this sale, one filly yearling of his sold for $2.5 million and a yearling colt for $10.2 million. These prices were paid by Sheikh Mohammed bin Rashid al Maktoum of the oil-rich United Arab Emirate state of Dubai, who outbid Robert Sangster, the British sports pool magnate. Their personal grudge match, spurred on because Sangster had won the auction in the previous two years, is money in the bank for consigners of Northern Dancer's offspring. It is hard to imagine that at such prices these yearlings are wise investments. Indeed, the $10.2 million colt, Snaffi Dancer, was never raced. In fact, most of the high-priced yearlings have been financial flops. See Appendix A for some details. The purchases are a bit like giving the good-looking son of a top baseball star married to a former Olympic-medal-winning daughter of a famous distance runner a contract for $2 million per year when he turns eighteen. In total, thirteen Northern Dancer yearlings were sold at the 1983 Keeneland and Saratoga sales for a total of $26,110,000, or $2,008,462 each. All told, his offspring have sold at auction for over $87 million. Not bad for a twenty-two-year-old horse who as a colt drew no interest when offered for sale for $25,000. He was still serving about thirty-five mares each year until his retirement in 1987.

The breeding of top thoroughbreds has become a giant pyramid, with prices dependent on how much the offspring might be sold for after a brief racing career, rather than on a horse's real earnings potential. Despite the current recession and lower track attendance and despite modest prices for medium- and lower-quality thoroughbreds, the best are flying high for now at least.*

Derby Day brought good weather, although there was a threat of showers late in the day that might have affected the Derby. We situated ourselves near the paddock area behind the grandstands, where we could watch the tote board and make bets near post time. There was no trouble making bets within one minute of post time. And we knew that with the size of the pools, the conditions were good for application of the Dr. Z system.

AMERICA'S TURF AUTHORITY Racing Form

Experts' Selections

Consensus Points: 5 for 1st (today's best 7), 2 for 2nd, 1 for 3rd. Today's Best in Bold Type.

Trackman, Graham Ross — **CHURCHILL DOWNS** — Selections Made for Fast Track

	TRACKMAN	HANDICAP	ANALYST	HERMIS	SWEEP	CONSENSUS	
1	ERUDITE ROAD STREET URCHIN HIS KNOCKERS	HUSTLIN BARB ERUDITE ROAD BEAUTIFUL BAY	BEAUTIFUL BAY HUSTLIN BARB LUMINARIA G.	**HUSTLIN BARB** LUMINARIA G. BEAU VOU	HUSTLIN BARB BEAU VOU BEAUTIFUL BAY	HUSTLIN BARB ERUDITE ROAD BEAUTIFUL BAY	19 7 7
2	FOXFIRE COVE ATENSHEIS IRON SKILLET	MY DAY DREAM IRON SKILLET APPLE JENNIE	RAJ UT TULLE'S FOOLY IRON SKILLET	BAIL ME OUT TULLE'S FOOLY RAJ UT	TULLE'S FOOLY IRON SKILLET RARE PICTURE	TULLE'S FOOLY RAJ UT IRON SKILLET	9 6 6
3	**BIRDBRAIN** SAME SEA TRADERS JET	GREAT BALANCE BIRDBRAIN LOOKS LIKE DAD	LOOKS LIKE DAD GREAT BALANCE DOLFINAIR	DOLFINAIR GREAT BALANCE LOOKS LIKE DAD	**GREAT BALANCE** LOOKS LIKE DAD DOLFINAIR	GREAT BALANCE BIRDBRAIN LOOKS LIKE DAD	16 9 9
4	FLAG ADMIRAL SLASH AND CUT CLUB SHOOTER	FLAG ADMIRAL GRINDSTONE TURN CLEVER ENCOUNTER	FLAG ADMIRAL SOUTHERN BOY CLEVER ENCOUNTER	SOUTHERN BOY FLAG ADMIRAL GRINDSTONE TURN	FLAG ADMIRAL SOUTHERN BOY GRINDSTONE TURN	FLAG ADMIRAL SOUTHERN BOY GRINDSTONE TURN	22 9 4
5	HEAD GAMES FOLLOW DUSTY JACK SLADE	FIGHTIN HILL HEAD GAMES STRAIGHT SHOT	HEAD GAMES CHIDESTER GREAT POSSIBILITY	CHIDESTER JACK SLADE HEAD GAMES	HEAD GAMES CHIDESTER JACK SLADE	HEAD GAMES CHIDESTER FIGHTIN HILL	18 9 5
6	CAN'THOLDMEBACK LIBERTY LANE OIL CITY	BACKSTABBER LIBERTY LANE OIL CITY	**LIBERTY LANE** BAYOU BLACK CELTIC SABER	BAYOU BLACK LIBERTY LANE CELTIC SABER	LIBERTY LANE BAYOU BLACK CELTIC SABER	LIBERTY LANE BAYOU BLACK BACKSTABBER	18 9 5
7	LE COU COU HIGH HONORS SAVERTON	HIGH HONORS LE COU COU THALASSOCRAT	HIGH HONORS CUCKOLD LE COU COU	CUCKOLD HIGH HONORS COMMON SENSE	CUCKOLD HIGH HONORS COMMON SENSE	HIGH HONORS CUCKOLD LE COU COU	16 12 8
8	SUNNY'S HALO SLEW O' GOLD HIGHLAND PARK	**SUNNY'S HALO** MARFA PLAY FELLOW	SUNNY'S HALO MARFA PAX IN BELLO	MARFA SUNNY'S HALO CAVEAT	SUNNY'S HALO MARFA CAVEAT	**SUNNY'S HALO** MARFA SLEW O' GOLD	24 11 2
9	MAJOR RUN BROADWAY REVIEW DUST OFF THE MAT	BROADWAY REVIEW BAL BAY DAVRICK	SORROTO SWAY BAL BAY	SWAY MAJOR RUN SORROTO	SWAY SORROTO MAJOR RUN	SWAY SORROTO MAJOR RUN	12 8 8
10	OLD HUNDRED MATTI BABES TOM LIGHTFOOT	MATTI BABES CAPTAIN PHIL TO THE PENNY	TO THE PENNY CAPTAIN PHIL HARD UP	CAPTAIN PHIL TO THE PENNY TOM LIGHTFOOT	CAPTAIN PHIL TO THE PENNY TOM LIGHTFOOT	CAPTAIN PHIL TO THE PENNY MATTI BABES	14 10 7

A MEXICAN FILLY IS THE FIRST DR. Z SYSTEM BET

The first Dr. Z system bet occurred in the first race, a $6\frac{1}{2}$-furlong race for four-year-old and older fillies and mares. The morning-line favorites were Hustlin Barb, Luminaria G., and Beautiful Bay. None of the horses had outstanding records, but each had shown flashes of brilliance. Hustlin Barb was dropping sharply in class to the $7,500 claiming level, which installed

*Readers who would like to learn more about the breeding industry and keep up with the latest events in racing might consult the *Blood-Horse*. It is a beautifully produced weekly magazine that is also a very useful source of information (Box 4038, Lexington, Kentucky 40544, $2 per issue). The inevitable slump in stud fees for the top prospects did not materialize until 1986, when prices dropped about 20%–30%. Currently the best investments are thought to be in fillies of racing age.

her as the favorite despite a poor 1983 season with only one in-the-money finish in five starts. Beautiful Bay did not show much except for a win and a second in February against weaker competition. Luminaria G. was a Mexican horse who was claimed in her first race in the United States. She was moving back to the $7,500 claiming level, where she had won convincingly, after a disappointing fourth-place finish as the favorite in her last start. The crowd made Luminaria G. the favorite.

Luminaria G. looked like a possible Dr. Z system bet to show. The tote board was as follows:

	Totals	#5 Luminaria G.	Expected Value per Dollar Bet on Luminaria G.
With four minutes to post time			
Odds		8—5	
Win	105,272	31,967	
Show	50,087	9,852	1.17

	Totals	#5 Luminaria G.	Expected Value per Dollar Bet on Luminaria G.
With two minutes to post time			
Odds		8—5	
Win	119,144	37,003	
Show	53,218	10,699	1.17
With one minute to post time			
Odds		8—5	
Win	130,255	41,577	
Show	57,643	12,210	1.16

With our betting fortune of $1,000 we bet $159 to show on Luminaria G. At post time the tote board stood as follows:

	Totals	#5 Luminaria G.	Expected Value per Dollar Bet on Luminaria G.
Odds		7—5	
Win	147,291	50,374	
Show	62,113	13,728	1.17

Luminaria G. won the race, followed by Beautiful Bay and Beau Vou. Hustlin Barb finished out of the money. The chart of the race was as follows:

FIRST RACE
Churchill
MAY 7, 1983

6 ½ FURLONGS. (1.16) CLAIMING. Purse $5,500. Fillies and mares. 4-year-olds and upward. Weight, 121 lbs. Non-winners of two races since March 15 allowed 3 lbs.; two races since February 11, 6 lbs.; a race since April 8, 9 lbs. Claiming price, $7,500. (Races where entered for $6,000 or less not considered.) 7TH DAY. WEATHER CLEAR. TEMPERATURE 77 DEGREES.

Value of race $5,500, value to winner $3,575, second $1,100, third $550, fourth $275. Mutuel pool $279,336.

Last Raced	Horse	Eqt.A.Wt	PP	St	¼	½	Str	Fin	Jockey	Cl'g Pr	Odds $1
30Mar83 ^{9}Lat^{4}	Luminaria G.	4 114	5	5	$1^{1\frac{1}{2}}$	1^{2}	$1^{3\frac{1}{2}}$	$1^{6\frac{1}{2}}$	Solomon G	7500	1.40
5Apr83 ^{4}OP^{4}	Beautiful Bay	6 107	1	4	$3^{\frac{1}{2}}$	3^{1}	$2^{1\frac{1}{2}}$	2^{nk}	Allen K K^{5}	7500	4.40
28Apr83 ^{1}Kee^{3}	Beau Vou	b 6 112	4	7	7^{2}	$6^{1\frac{1}{2}}$	3^{3}	3^{2}	Johnson P A	7500	8.20
9Dec82 ^{8}Lat^{4}	His Knockers	4 112	8	1	2^{1}	$2^{1\frac{1}{2}}$	$4^{\frac{1}{2}}$	4^{1}	Sellers M S	7500	16.20
28Apr83 ^{1}Kee^{8}	Street Urchin	b 6 112	6	3	$5^{\frac{1}{2}}$	5^{1}	5^{2}	$5^{2\frac{1}{2}}$	Woods C R Jr	7500	27.80
30Mar83 ^{5}OP^{6}	Hustlin Barb	b 4 107	7	2	6^{1}	$4^{\frac{1}{2}}$	6^{3}	6^{5}	Troilo W D^{5}	7500	2.40
28Apr83 ^{1}Kee^{4}	Quasarita	4 115	3	8	8	8	7^{2}	$7^{6\frac{1}{2}}$	Moran M T	7500	22.20
28Apr83 ^{1}Kee^{7}	Erudite Road	b 4 112	2	6	4^{1}	7^{2}	8	8	Moyers L	7500	14.10

OFF AT 11:33. Start good. Won driving. Time, :23⅕, :46⅖, 1:11⅕, 1:18⅕ Track fast.

Official Program Numbers↘

$2 Mutuel Prices:				
5–LUMINARIA G.		4.80	3.40	2.80
1–BEAUTIFUL BAY			4.60	3.20
4–BEAU VOU				3.60

Ch. f, by Going Around—Permisa, by Bal Musette. Trainer Ashabraner Billy G. Bred by Mora B Cardenas (Mex).

LUMINAIRIA G., hustled to the lead just after the start, made all the pace but was kept to pressure when drawing off in the lane. BEAUTIFUL BAY, well placed early, could not stay with the winner but continued willingly to gain the place. BEAU VOU made a mild bid to clearly best the others. HIS KNOCKERS prompted the early pace and gave way. HUSTLIN BARB never menaced.

Owners— 1, Ashabraner B G; 2, Ford L; 3, Lang T L; 4, Niemann Sara; 5, Big Ten Stable; 6, Sefa F; 7, Dykema C C; 8, Sundance Stable.

Overweight: Luminaria G. 2 pounds; Quasarita 3.

Luminaria G. was claimed by Sutton H E; trainer, Fires William H.

Scratched—Irish Breeze (22Apr83 ^{2}Kee^{8}).

Luminaria G.'s $2.80 payoff gave us a profit of $63.60 on our $159 bet.

CHRIS McCARRON STEALS THE RACE

The third race was a claiming race for four-year-old horses and older horses who had not won two recent races. Nine horses were competing in the 6-furlong race. The consensus favorite was Great Balance. Dolfinar, Superstep, Traders Jet, Steel Britches, Birdbrain, and Looks Like Dad were the competition. Dolfinar and Traders Jet had strong records with numerous wins. Traders Jet was also lightweighted at 112 pounds and was ridden by the great Chris McCarron, who had flown in from California to ride Desert Wine in the Derby. As usual, Chris was in a head-to-head competition with Laffit Pincay, Jr., as the nation's top-money-winning jockey. Table 11.1 shows the earnings of the top jockeys and trainers in 1983. Going into Derby Day, Pincay and McCarron had a considerable edge both in earnings and place percentage over their California colleague Eddie Delahoussaye and two New York-based jockeys, Angel Cordero, Jr., and Jorge Velasquez. The colorful Californian Laz Barrera was comfortably in first place among the trainers.

Traders Jet's recent races showed little, and he was dropping sharply in class. Great Balance had the best lifetime earnings and an impressive $2,000-plus winnings per start. Twice he had been claimed while winning at claim-

TABLE 11.1 *The 1983 money-leading jockeys and trainers going into Derby Day*

	Money Leaders				
Jockey	Mounts	Winners	Seconds	Place Percentage	Purses Won ($)
Pincay	474	112	81	40.7	2,847,202
C. McCarron	508	124	82	40.6	2,838,763
Delahoussaye	455	61	80	31.0	2,220,685
Cordero	426	86	65	35.4	1,977,782
Velasquez	373	73	46	31.9	1,930,844
Day	483	96	85	37.5	1,700,726
Davis	516	88	62	29.1	1,440,435
Alvarado	498	66	75	28.3	1,423,979
Valenzuela	428	53	55	25.2	1,333,447
Hawley	372	51	44	25.5	1,301,919

Trainers	Starts	Winners	Seconds	Place Percentage	Purses Won ($)
Barrera	109	39	17	51.3	1,431,305
Lukas	167	21	21	25.2	1,209,207
Van Berg	505	55	56	22.0	1,163,514
Whittingham	127	29	12	32.3	1,149,980
Gosden	97	20	12	33.0	887,660
Palma	191	29	31	31.4	670,370

ing prices in the $18,000–$20,000 range. After little success running against $25,000 claimers, he was returning to run against these cheaper horses again.

The tote board pointed to Great Balance as a possible Dr. Z system bet to show:

	Totals	#4 Great Balance	Expected Value per Dollar Bet on Great Balance
With one minute to post time			
Odds		5—2	
Win	292,291	63,973	
Show	135,425	19,178	1.18

Our betting fortune of $1,063.60 suggested a bet of $78. At post time the tote board stood as follows:

	Totals	#4 Great Balance	Expected Value per Dollar Bet on Great Balance
Odds		5—2	
Win	314,811	68,376	
Show	141,625	22,799	1.11

Chris McCarron stole the race and led Traders Jet for a victory and an $18.80 win payoff. Great Balance held on for second, and Superstep took third. With Dolfinar and Looks Like Dad out of the money and Traders Jet and Superstep relative long shots, the show payoff on Great Balance was a smashing $4. Our $78 bet was doubled. The chart of the race was as follows:

THIRD RACE
Churchill
MAY 7, 1983

6 FURLONGS. (1.09⅕) CLAIMING. Purse $7,500. 4–year–olds and upward. Weight, 122 lbs. Non–winners of two races since March 7 allowed 2 lbs.; a race since then, 4 lbs.; two races since January 7, 6 lbs. Claiming price, $18,000; for each $500 to $16,000 allowed 1 lb.(Races where entered for $14,000 or less not considered.)

Value of race $7,500, value to winner $4,875, second $1,500, third $750, fourth $375. Mutuel pool $621,311.

Last Raced	Horse	Eqt.A.Wt	PP	St	¼	½	Str	Fin	Jockey	Cl'g Pr	Odds $1
11Mar83 ^{10}FG^{9}	Traders Jet	4 112	3	1	1^{hd}	2^{hd}	$1^{\frac{1}{2}}$	1no	McCarron C J†	16000	8.40
15Apr83 ^{4}OP^{5}	Great Balance	b 6 120	4	4	4^{hd}	3^{hd}	$2^{1\frac{1}{2}}$	2^{4}	Moyers L	18000	2.80
16Apr83 ^{10}FP^{4}	Superstep	b 5 116	2	3	$3^{1\frac{1}{2}}$	5^{hd}	3^{2}	$3^{2\frac{1}{2}}$	Diaz J L	18000	10.20
16Mar83 ^{8}OP^{7}	Portuguese Picnic	6 116	7	5	$8^{1\frac{1}{2}}$	$6^{1\frac{1}{2}}$	5^{hd}	$4^{1\frac{1}{2}}$	Woods C R Jr	18000	41.50
8Apr83 ^{8}OP^{5}	Looks Like Dad	b 4 116	8	7	$5^{1\frac{1}{2}}$	4^{hd}	$4^{1\frac{1}{2}}$	5^{nk}	Brumfield D	18000	2.60
4Mar83 ^{10}OP^{11}	Birdbrain	4 111	6	6	7^{3}	8^{2}	$6^{1\frac{1}{2}}$	6^{4}	Allen K K^{5}	18000	7.80
9Apr83 ^{5}OP^{1}	Dolfinair	9 116	1	9	9	9	7^{2}	7^{3}	Barrow T	18000	4.80
20Apr83 ^{5}Kee^{9}	Steel Britches	4 116	5	2	2^{hd}	$1^{\frac{1}{2}}$	8^{2}	8^{nk}	Sellers M S	18000	6.70
17Dec82 ^{7}FG^{11}	Same Sea	b 4 116	9	8	$6^{\frac{1}{2}}$	$7^{1\frac{1}{2}}$	9	9	Foster D E	18000	32.80

OFF AT 1:01. Start good. Won driving. Time, :22, :45, :57⅖, 1:10⅘ Track fast.

$2 Mutuel Prices:			
3-TRADERS JET	18.80	7.60	5.40
4-GREAT BALANCE		4.80	4.00
2-SUPERSTEP			6.20

B. g, by Trader Ed—Daisy Jet, by Bronze Jet. Trainer Kirk James C. Bred by Mills P D (Pa).

TRADERS JET broke in stride to make or force the pace throughout and narrowly outgamed GREAT BALANCE in the final furlong. The latter was always well placed, challenged the winner throughout the lane, could not catch that one but was easily second best. SUPERSTEP vied for the lead most of the way but had no late rally. PORTUGESE PICNIC had no speed. LOOKS LIKE DAD was shuffled back shortly after the start, recovered to launch a bid entering the lane but could not sustain it. STEEL BRITCHES dueled for the early lead and stopped.

Owners— 1, Kirk J C; 2, Marrocco A; 3, Reavis M L et al; 4, Stinson R W el al; 5, Craig J C; 6, Mjaka Stable; 7, Ketchum W; 8, Bachelor E; 9, Link F.

† **Apprentice allowance waived:** Traders Jet 7 pounds. **Corrected weight:** Great Balance 120 pounds.

Great Balance was claimed by Hyman Carol; trainer, Kirk James C.

TWO DR. Z SYSTEM BETS IN THE BOLD FORBES

The fourth race was a 1-mile allowance race for three-year-olds. The favorites were Southern Boy and Flag Admiral, and they were to be ridden by California's two top jockeys, Chris McCarron and Laffit Pincay, Jr. Like McCarron, Pincay had flown in for the Derby and was to ride Caveat. Southern Boy had just run in the Arkansas Derby and was completely outclassed by the likes of Sunny's Halo and Caveat. He had had some good races early in the year, but his recent record was mediocre. Flag Admiral was coming off a convincing win in the mud at Keeneland. His previous three starts were disasters. Despite their undistinguished records, Southern Boy and Flag Admiral did seem to be the legitimate favorites. They had proved themselves much faster, at least whenever they ran a strong race. Fellow Californian jockeys Terry Lipham and Eddie Delahoussaye were riding Bill Hicks and Clever Encounter, respectively, to warm up for their mounts on Paris Prince and Sunny's Halo, respectively, in the Derby. Both Bill Hicks and Clever Encounter had had good recent races, but they appeared to be outclassed by the favorites.

Both Southern Boy and Flag Admiral were favorites of the betting public and relatively overlooked to show. The tote board read as follows:

	Totals	#6 Southern Boy	Expected Value per Dollar Bet on Southern Boy	#7 Flag Admiral	Expected Value per Dollar Bet on Flag Admiral
With four minutes to post time					
Odds		6—5		2—1	
Win	312,797	116,195		87,134	
Show	150,399	36,980	1.16	26,753	1.18
With one minute to post time					
Odds		6—5		9—5	
Win	358,410	134,508		100,908	
Show	167,613	42,721	1.14	30,011	1.19

We bet $300 on Southern Boy to show and $200 on Flag Admiral to show. At post time the tote board was as follows:

	Totals	#6 Southern Boy	Expected Value per Dollar Bet on Southern Boy	#7 Flag Admiral	Expected Value per Dollar Bet on Flag Admiral
Odds		1—1		9—5	
Win	403,104	155,710		113,712	
Show	180,904	48,779	1.13	32,047	1.19

Flag Admiral won the race, followed by Clever Encounter, and Southern Boy took third. With the two top choices finishing in the money, the show payoffs were slightly depressed, but not as much as usual, since they both were Dr. Z system bets. Flag Admiral paid $2.80 and Southern Boy $2.40. Our bets of $300 and $200 on Southern Boy and Flag Admiral, respectively, paid $360 and $280 for a profit of $140. The chart of the race was as follows:

FOURTH RACE
Churchill
MAY 7, 1983

1 MILE. (1.33$\frac{3}{5}$) ALLOWANCE. Purse \$10,000 (plus \$2,500 from KTDF). 3-year-olds, which have not won a race other than maiden or claiming. Weight, 120 lbs. Non-winners of \$9,750 allowed 3 lbs.; \$7,150, 5 lbs.; \$4,550. (Races where entered for \$15,000 or less not considered in allowances.)

Total purse \$12,500. Value of race \$12,375, value to winner \$8,125, second \$2,500, third \$1,250, fourth \$500. (\$125 reverts to the KTDF). Mutuel pool \$790,782.

Last Raced	Horse	Eqt.	A.	Wt	PP	St	¼	½	¾	Str	Fin	Jockey	Odds $1
23Apr83 ^{4}Kee^{1}	Flag Admiral		3	117	7	5	$6^{1\frac{1}{2}}$	$2^{1\frac{1}{2}}$	$1^{1\frac{1}{2}}$	1^{3}	$1^{7\frac{1}{2}}$	Velasquez J	1.90
16Apr83 ^{8}Kee^{3}	Clever Encounter		3	115	11	1	$10^{1\frac{1}{2}}$	11	8^{3}	3^{5}	2^{2}	Delahoussaye E	5.00
16Apr83 ^{9}OP^{9}	Southern Boy		3	115	6	7	3^{hd}	$5^{1\frac{1}{2}}$	$2^{1\frac{1}{2}}$	2^{2}	3^{7}	McCarron C J	1.10
22Apr83 ^{6}Kee^{3}	Grindstone Turn	b	3	112	8	3	5^{1}	$6^{1\frac{1}{2}}$	$4^{\frac{1}{2}}$	4^{1}	$4^{\frac{3}{4}}$	Melancon L	23.50
30Apr83 ^{4}Det^{2}	Gastgeber	b	3	112	9	4	$7^{\frac{1}{2}}$	7^{hd}	6^{1}	$5^{\frac{1}{2}}$	5^{4}	Bartram B	49.90
28Apr83 ^{8}Kee^{4}	My Z. Bomb	b	3	114	3	9	$2^{1\frac{1}{2}}$	3^{hd}	$3^{1\frac{1}{2}}$	$7^{1\frac{1}{2}}$	$6^{\frac{1}{2}}$	Gavidia W	27.10
2May83 ^{2}CD^{8}	Club Shooter		3	112	2	10	8^{hd}	$9^{\frac{1}{2}}$	10^{2}	9^{4}	$7^{\frac{3}{4}}$	Moyers L	a-30.10
30Apr83 ^{3}RD^{1}	Bill Hicks		3	112	1	6	$1^{1\frac{1}{2}}$	1^{1}	$5^{1\frac{1}{2}}$	$6^{1\frac{1}{2}}$	8^{2}	McKnight J	50.60
15Apr83 ^{2}Kee^{8}	Sly Russell C.	b	3	114	5	11	$9^{1\frac{1}{2}}$	$8^{1\frac{1}{2}}$	7^{hd}	8^{hd}	9^{7}	Solomon G	45.40
30Apr83 ^{6}CD^{4}	Slash And Cut	b	3	112	4	8	4^{hd}	$4^{\frac{1}{2}}$	9^{hd}	10^{2}	10^{3}	Woods C R Jr	15.80
24Mar83 ^{6}OP^{9}	Ranjac	b	3	115	10	2	11	10^{3}	11	11	11	Barrow T	a-30.10

a-Coupled: Club Shooter and Ranjac.

OFF AT 1:51. Start good. Won ridden out. Time, :22$\frac{4}{5}$, :46, 1:10$\frac{4}{5}$, 1:35$\frac{3}{5}$ Track fast.

$2 Mutuel Prices:			
7-FLAG ADMIRAL	5.80	3.60	2.80
10-CLEVER ENCOUNTER		4.40	2.80
6-SOUTHERN BOY			2.40

B. c, by Hoist The Flag—Lord's Lady, by Sir Gaylord. Trainer Inda Eduardo. Bred by Gentry T (Ky).

FLAG ADMIRAL, just behind the early leaders, came up to challenge leaving the backstretch, took clear command approaching the lane and increased the margin steadily while ridden out to the wire. CLEVER ENCOUNTER, void of early foot, commenced a rally approaching the lane, continued willingly when set down for the drive and was up to gain the place. SOUTHERN BOY, well placed early, had no rally. GRINDSTONE TURN lacked the needed response. MY Z. BOMB prompted the early pace and gave way. BILL HICKS made the early pace and stopped. SLASH AND CUT had speed for a half.

Owners— 1, Gentry T; 2, Proler I; 3, Ackel & Garber; 4, Wolfman Mr-Mrs J C; 5, Jones F Jr; 6, Zimmerman G A; 7, Collins M B; 8, Lacoco & Rogers; 9, McMakin N; 10, Hunter C; 11, Meyer Deborah.

Overweight: Clever Encounter 3 pounds; My Z. Bomb 2; Sly Russell C. 2; Ranjac 3.

JUST CALL ME GEORGE

The fifth race was the Pleasant Colony, an allowance race for three-year-olds. Head Games, Chidester, and Fightin Hill were the top choices. Jorge Velasquez, the great Panamanian jockey (who likes to be called "George" rather than "Horgay"), Eddie Maple, Jean Cruguet, and Don Brumfield were using the race as a warmup before their Derby mounts on Marfa, Chumming, Play Fellow, and Highland Park, respectively. The top three choices along with Great Possibility, Straight Shot, and Jack Slade all looked like possible winners. The odds on Head Games were the best. He had also finished first or second in five of his six career starts.

With one minute to post time, the tote board was as follows:

	Totals	#1 Head Games	Expected Value per Dollar Bet on Head Games
Odds		2—1	
Win	415,685	103,216	
Show	182,613	32,715	1.12

With our betting fortune of $1,281.60, a bet of $33 to show on Head Games was suggested. At post time the tote board was:

	Totals	#1 Head Games	Expected Value per Dollar Bet on Head Games
Odds		2—1	
Win	447,119	112,623	
Show	195,902	39,257	1.07

Unfortunately, Head Games finished out of the money, so we lost our $33 bet, leaving our betting fortune as $1,248.60. The chart of the race was as follows:

FIFTH RACE
Churchill
MAY 7, 1983

1 1/16 MILES. (1.41⅗) ALLOWANCE. Purse $12,000 (plus $3,000 from KTDF). 3-year-olds, which have not won two races other than maiden or claiming. Weight, 121 lbs. Non-winners of $9,750 twice allowed 3 lbs.; $7,800 twice, 6 lbs.; $5,850 twice, 9 lbs. (Races where entered for $20,000 or less not considered in allowances.)

Total purse $15,000. Value of race $12,450, value to winner $7,800, second $2,400, third $1,500, fourth $750. ($2,550 reverts to the KTDF.) Mutuel pool $878,344.

Last Raced	Horse	Eqt.	A.	Wt	PP	St	¼	½	¾	Str	Fin	Jockey	Odds $1
6Apr83 ^{9}Hia^{2}	Straight Shot		3	112	6	2	1½	1½	1½	1^{1}	1^{nk}	Cruguet J	6.60
30Apr83 ^{6}CD^{1}	Fightin Hill	b	3	114	2	7	7^{1}	$6^{2½}$	$3^{1½}$	2½	2^{2}	Maple E	5.50
16Apr83 ^{8}OP^{3}	Chidester		3	112	7	3	$2^{1½}$	$2^{3½}$	2^{3}	3^{3}	$3^{2½}$	Patterson G	3.20
27Apr83 ^{8}Kee^{2}	Follow Dusty	b	3	115	3	5	$5^{2½}$	4^{hd}	4^{2}	4^{3}	4^{1}	Moran M T	18.10
16Apr83 ^{2}OP^{1}	Head Games	b	3	118	1	4	3^{2}	3^{2}	$5^{1½}$	$5^{2½}$	5^{4}	Velasquez J	2.30
27Apr83 ^{8}Kee^{5}	Fancy Friend		3	112	9	6	6^{1}	$8^{1½}$	7^{3}	6^{hd}	6^{nk}	Moyers L	30.50
28Apr83 ^{8}Kee^{1}	Jack Slade		3	114	8	8	$8^{1½}$	9	8^{4}	8^{8}	7½	Brumfield D	5.00
27Apr83 ^{8}Kee^{6}	Twist The Goods		3	114	4	9	9	7^{2}	$6^{1½}$	$7^{1½}$	8^{11}	Gavidia W	59.60
22Apr83 ^{6}Kee^{1}	Great Possibility		3	112	5	1	4^{hd}	5½	9	9	9	Espinoza J C	8.70

OFF AT 2:41. Start good. Won driving. Time, :24⅘, :48⅕, 1:12⅕, 1:37⅗, 1:44⅕ Track fast.

$2 Mutuel Prices:			
6-STRAIGHT SHOT	15.20	7.80	4.80
2-FIGHTIN HILL		7.00	5.00
7-CHIDESTER			3.80

Dk. b. or br. c, by Norcliffe—Princess Jamie, by Prince John. Trainer Evans John D III. Bred by Davis W R (Fla).

STRAIGHT SHOT, taken under a rating hold after quickly taking the lead, saved ground into the final turn, gradually came out to meet the challenge of FIGHTIN HILL and held that one safe. FIGHTIN HILL, in close and taken in hand leaving the gate, advanced between horses after a half-mile, loomed boldly on the outside in the stretch drive and was not quite good enough. CHIDESTER raced lapped outside the winner into the early stretch, was carried out just slightly and weakened. FOLLOW DUSTY saved ground to no avail. HEAD GAMES raced wide throughout. JACK SLADE was not a serious factor. GREAT POSSIBLITY raced wide.

Owners— 1, Gartin R; 2, Lasater D; 3, Craig J C; 4, Lehmann R N; 5, Blass Patricia; 6, Zimmerman Mary M; 7, Adams A; 8, Lang T L; 9, Strapro Stable.

Overweight: Fightin Hill 2 pounds; Follow Dusty 3; Jack Slade 2; Twist The Goods 2.

THE DREADNOUGHT

The sixth race was the Dreadnought, a 7-furlong allowance race with a purse of $14,000. The top choices were Bayou Black, Liberty Lane, the entry of Backstabber and Can'tholdmeback, and Oil City. Bayou Black looked very sharp, with five consecutive in-the-money finishes, all but one with speed ratings in the 90s. He also had the services of jockey Eddie Delahoussaye. Liberty Lane was also a very consistent horse with nearly as good a record. The bet was on Bayou Black.

The tote board was as follows:

	Totals	#3 Bayou Black	Expected Value per Dollar Bet on Bayou Black
With three minutes to post time			
Odds		8—5	
Win	407,823	131,439	
Show	165,867	30,306	1.25
With one minute to post time			
Odds		8—5	
Win	469,967	149,753	
Show	188,358	37,275	1.20

With our betting fortune of $1,248.60, a bet of $317 to show on Bayou Black was suggested.

At post time the tote board was as follows:

	Totals	#3 Bayou Black	Expected Value per Dollar Bet on Bayou Black
At post time			
Odds		8—5	
Win	482,830	154,423	
Show	191,848	38,018	1.20

Bayou Black won the race, followed by Noted and Liberty Lane. The show payoff on Bayou Black was $3, so we made a profit of $158.50 on our $317 bet. The chart of the race was as follows:

SIXTH RACE
Churchill
MAY 7, 1983

7 FURLONGS. (1.21⅗) ALLOWANCE. Purse $14,000 (plus $3,500 from KTDF). 4-year-olds and upward, which have not won $4,875 twice since June 26 other than maiden, claiming or starter. Weight, 121 lbs. Non-winners of $10,400 since April 8 allowed 3 lbs.; $9,750 since January 7, 6 lbs.; $8,450 since October 8, 9 lbs. (Maiden, claiming and starter races not considered in allowance.)

Total purse $17,500. Value of race $16,625, value to winner $11,375, second $2,800, third $1,750, fourth $700. ($875 reverts to the KTDF). Mutuel pool $909,035.

Last Raced	Horse	Eqt.A.Wt	PP	St	¼	½	Str	Fin	Jockey	Odds $1
30Mar83 ^{9}FG^{2}	Bayou Black	7 115	2	1	$2^{3\frac{1}{2}}$	1^{1}	$1^{2\frac{1}{2}}$	$1^{2\frac{1}{4}}$	Delahoussaye E	1.60
26Apr83 ^{7}Kee^{2}	Noted	4 112	1	5	$6^{2\frac{1}{2}}$	6^{7}	3^{2}	2^{4}	Sellers M S	13.20
28Apr83 ^{6}Kee^{3}	Liberty Lane	5 114	6	6	$4^{\frac{1}{2}}$	3^{1}	2^{1}	3^{1}	Brumfield D	2.30
16Apr83 ^{6}OP^{6}	Oil City	6 118	3	3	5^{1}	5^{2}	$4^{1\frac{1}{2}}$	$4^{2\frac{1}{2}}$	Velasquez J	7.30
16Apr83 ^{8}Kee^{2}	Can'tholdmeback	b 7 115	4	4	3^{hd}	$4^{3\frac{1}{2}}$	5^{2}	5^{5}	Moyers L	4.90
16Apr83 ^{8}FP^{1}	Deuces Are Loose	4 115	5	2	1^{hd}	$2^{2\frac{1}{2}}$	6^{6}	6^{2}	Woods C R Jr	20.40
20Apr83 ^{5}Kee^{2}	Celtic Saber	b 4 117	7	7	7	7	7	7	Pincay L Jr	8.10

OFF AT 3:30. Start good. Won handily. Time, :23⅗, :45⅗, 1:09⅘, 1:23 Track fast.

$2 Mutuel Prices:			
3-BAYOU BLACK	5.20	4.00	3.00
2-NOTED		9.20	5.20
6-LIBERTY LANE			2.80

Dk. b. or br. h, by Droll Role—Dymond Island, by Drone. Trainer Brothers Frank L. Bred by Stall A M (Ky).

BAYOU BLACK was rated confidently from the beginning, saved ground disposing of DEUCES ARE LOOSE on the turn and finished out handily. NOTED came outside horses for the stretch drive, was no match for the winner but clearly bested the rest. LIBERTY LANE responded when called upon to loom briefly menacing outside the winner in the early stretch and weakened. OIL CITY gave an even eoofrt. CAN'THOLDMEBACK tired. DEUCES ARE LOOSE was used up after a half mile.

Owners— 1, Stall & Burke; 2, Rogers Red Top Farm & Madden; 3, Foley D; 4, Partee W C; 5, Rutter J H; 6, Watson & Higgs; 7, Gentry T E.

Corrected weight: Bayou Black 112 pounds. **Overweight:** Bayou Black 3 pounds; Liberty Lane 2; Celtic Saber 5.

Scratched—Backstabber (19Apr83 ^{8}Kee^{4}); Third and Lex (28Apr83 ^{6}Kee^{8}).

THE TWIN SPIRES: ALMOST DERBY HORSES

The Twin Spires was a $50,000 added-stakes race for three-year-olds over a $1\frac{1}{8}$-mile distance. The top choices were High Honors, Le Cou Cou, Common Sense, and Daring Diabolo. These horses and the rest of the field had run against the likes of Derby horses Caveat, Total Departure, Pax In Bello, Sunny's Halo, Slew O' Gold, Parfaitement, Current Hope, Chumming, Marfa, Desert Wine, Highland Park, and Freezing Rain. These were the horses not quite good enough to be in the Derby. By convention, the top twenty nominated horses rated in terms of earnings are allowed in the race. As horses are scratched, more places become available, but at twenty-fourth and twenty-ninth on the earnings list, Le Cou Cou and High Honors did not make the final twenty. The top thirty earners of 1983 appear in Table 11.2 on page 258.

High Honors had had six strong races out of seven, including a third-place finish in the Wood Memorial behind Slew O' Gold and Parfaitement. Le Cou Cou had a history of finishing close whenever he had started at astronomical odds. He was a scant 3 lengths off the pace at 102–1 in the Derby Trial, beaten only by Caveat, Total Departure, and Pax In Bello. The crowd made High Honors, who was ridden by Jorge Velasquez, an odds-on favorite. He was also a Dr. Z system bet for show.

The tote board was as follows:

	Totals	#3 High Honors	Expected Value per Dollar Bet on High Honors
With two minutes to post time			
Odds		4—5	
Win	463,915	217,972	
Show	222,910	70,409	1.15
With one minute to post time			
Odds		3—5	
Win	495,324	237,351	
Show	231,893	74,281	1.15

We bet $688 to show on High Honors. At post time the tote board was:

	Totals	#3 High Honors	Expected Value per Dollar Bet on High Honors
Odds		3—5	
Win	520,042	250,319	
Show	240,612	78,267	1.14

High Honors crossed the finish line first. Then Donald Howard, the jockey of the second horse, Le Cou Cou, lodged a claim of foul against Jorge Velasquez, who rode High Honors. A flashing INQUIRY sign is not good for one's blood pressure, but since, at worst, High Honors would be knocked down to second, we calmly waited for the decision of the stewards. The claim was allowed, and High Honors was taken down. So the official order of finish was Le Cou Cou first, High Honors second, and Common Sense third. Our show bet on High Honors paid \$2.40, so we made a profit of \$137.60 on our \$688 bet. Of course, High Honors' show payoff would be the same whether he finished first or second. The payoff would have changed only if one or more horses had been disqualified out of the money. The chart of the race was as follows:

SEVENTH RACE
Churchill
MAY 7, 1983

$1\frac{1}{8}$ MILES. (1.48$\frac{4}{5}$) 1st Running TWIN SPIRES STAKES. SPECIAL WEIGHT. \$50,000 Added. 3-year-olds. Weight, 121 lbs. \$250 to pass the entry box with \$50,000-added of which 65% goes to the winner, 20% to second, 10% to third, and 5% to fourth.

Value of race \$52,500, value to winner \$34,125, second \$10,500, third \$5,250, fourth \$2,625. Mutuel pool \$1,035,392.

Last Raced	Horse	Eqt.	A.	Wt	PP	St	¼	½	¾	Str	Fin	Jockey	Odds \$1
23Apr83 ^{8}Aqu^{3}	[D]High Honors	b	3	121	2	5	3^{hd}	$3^{\frac{1}{2}}$	2^{hd}	1^{hd}	1^{nk}	Velasquez J	.70
30Apr83 ^{9}CD^{4}	Le Cou Cou	b	3	121	1	1	1^{hd}	1^{1}	1^{1}	$2^{\frac{1}{2}}$	$2^{1\frac{1}{2}}$	Howard D L	4.70
23Apr83 ^{7}Aqu^{4}	Common Sense	b	3	121	7	3	$6^{1\frac{1}{2}}$	$4^{1\frac{1}{2}}$	$4^{1\frac{1}{2}}$	3^{3}	3^{3}	Penney J C	8.20
28Apr83 ^{7}Kee^{11}	Thalassocrat		3	121	4	6	$7^{1\frac{1}{2}}$	$7^{1\frac{1}{2}}$	$7^{1\frac{1}{2}}$	4^{5}	4^{9}	MacBeth D	15.90
27Apr83 ^{8}Kee^{1}	Cuckold	b	3	121	3	8	$8^{1\frac{1}{2}}$	$8^{1\frac{1}{2}}$	8^{2}	7^{hd}	5^{5}	Delahoussaye E	16.50
30Apr83 ^{9}CD^{12}	Saverton		3	121	8	4	4^{1}	$5^{\frac{1}{2}}$	5^{hd}	5^{hd}	6^{hd}	Woods C R Jr	9.80
30Apr83 ^{9}CD^{11}	Derby Double	b	3	121	10	7	5^{hd}	6^{hd}	6^{hd}	6^{hd}	7^{hd}	Moran M T	a-18.30
16Apr83 ^{9}OP^{11}	Daring Diabolo		3	121	9	9	10	10	9^{hd}	9^{2}	8^{2}	Brumfield D	16.50
30Apr83 ^{9}CD^{14}	Asked To Run	b	3	121	6	2	$2^{1\frac{1}{2}}$	2^{1}	3^{hd}	$8^{1\frac{1}{2}}$	9^{2}	Rubbicco P	a-18.30
30Apr83 ^{6}CD^{8}	Weed Eater	b	3	121	5	10	9^{1}	9^{hd}	10	10	10	Moyers L	53.10

[D]–High Honors Disqualified and placed second.
a–Coupled: Derby Double and Asked To Run.

OFF AT 4:21. Start good. Won driving. Time, :23$\frac{3}{5}$, :47$\frac{3}{5}$, 1:11$\frac{4}{5}$, 1:36$\frac{4}{5}$, 1:49$\frac{4}{5}$ Track fast.

\$2 Mutuel Prices:			
2–LE COU COU	11.40	3.60	3.00
3–HIGH HONORS		2.80	2.40
7–COMMON SENSE			3.20

Le Cou Cou—Gr. c, by Zen—Bold Summer, by Ballydonnell. Trainer Arnett James G. Bred by Clark Duane B (Ill).

HIGH HONORS, always well placed, drifted in with right handed pressure in midstretch brushed with LE COU COU before taking command at the furlong marker and proved best. Following a stewards' inquiry and an objection by the rider of LE COU COU for interference in the stretch run, HIGH HONORS was disqualified an placed second. LE COU COU broke in stride to make the early pace, began to drift out after the three-sixteenths pole, brushed with the winner just before the eighth pole and could not match that one late. COMMON SENSE, never far back, lacked the needed response against the top two. THALASSACRAT improved position in upper stretch. SAVERTON had brief speed. ASKED TO RUN prompted the early pace and gave way.

Owners— 1, Galbreath D M; 2, Clark D B; 3, J & L Stable; 4, Wilson H P; 5, Combs B II; 6, Zimmerman Mary M; 7, Golden Chance Farm Inc; 8, Diabolo Stable; 9, Golden Chance Farm Inc; 10, Clement F B & Linda.

THE 109TH KENTUCKY DERBY

The eighth race of the day was the Kentucky Derby. The full field of twenty horses contained no superhorses. It was a wide-open race. The writers' choices for the winner, as displayed in Table 11.2, included Marfa, Slew O'Gold, Caveat, Play Fellow, Sunny's Halo, and Explosive Wagon. In addition, Chumming, Highland Park, Desert Wine, Current Hope, Parfaitement, Pax In Bello, and Paris Prince each had a genuine chance to win. But the center of attention was Marfa. You can see why by consulting his past-performance chart. He had a tendency to lug, that is, to move laterally without reason during a race. Hence he was in constant trouble. So far this behavior had only led to one disqualification, which had occurred in his last race, the Blue Grass Stakes at Keeneland. Copelan, the leading money earner among Derby hopefuls (see Table 11.2) had been injured in that race and was out of Derby contention. It was not clear if Marfa had been involved. Marfa's running style also hampered him and possibly other horses in at least four other races. He was also a controversial starter in the Spiral Stakes because of some irregularities in his earnings record. A day before the race, it was

TABLE 11.2 *1983 Kentucky Derby prospects' earnings and the racing writers' picks*

Here's the way racing writers pick the finish

Billy Reed, Courier-Journal: 1. Marfa. 2. Sunny's Halo. 3. Current Hope. 4. Chumming. Time 2:01⅕.

Bob Adair, Courier-Journal: 1. Slew O' Gold. 2. Caveat. 3. My Mac. 4. Parfaitement. Time 2:02⅘.

Richard Sowers, Courier-Journal: 1. Caveat. 2. Marfa. 3. Highland Park. 4. Play Fellow. Time 2:03⅗.

Dale Austin, Baltimore Sun: 1. Play Fellow. 2. Parfaitement. 3. Caveat. 4. Marfa. Time: 2:00.

Bill Christine, Los Angeles Times: 1. Sunny's Halo. 2. Caveat. 3. Balboa Native. 4. Marfa. Time 2:02⅖.

Russ Harris, New York Daily News: 1. Sunny's Halo. 2. Caveat. 3. Marfa. 4. Pax In Bello. Time 2:02⅖.

Mike Barry, Louisville Times: 1. Play Fellow. 2. Marfa. 3. Current Hope. 4. Sunny's Halo. Time 2:02⅖.

Jim Bolus, Louisville Times: 1. Play Fellow. 2. Sunny's Halo. 3. Slew O' Gold. 4. Caveat. Time 2:02.

Rich Bozich, Louisville Times: 1. Sunny's Halo. 2. Play Fellow. 3. Desert Wine. 4. Marfa. Time 2:02⅘.

Dave Koerner, Louisville Times: 1. Slew O' Gold. 2. Play Fellow. 3. Pax In Bello. 4. Parfaitement. Time 2:01⅕.

Graham Ross, Daily Racing Form: 1. Sunny's Halo. 2. Slew O' Gold. 3. Play Fellow. 4. Highland Park. Time 2:01⅗.

Bob Roesler, New Orleans Times-Picayune/States Item: 1. Sunny's Halo. 2. Caveat. 3. Play Fellow. 4. Desert Wine. Time 2:01⅕.

Ed Schuyler, Associated Press: 1. Caveat. 2. Sunny's Halo. 3. Marfa. 4. Highland Park. Time 2:02⅗.

Steven Crist, New York Times: 1. Explosive Wagon. 2. Pax In Bello. 3. Marfa. 4. Balboa Native. Time 2:01⅗.

Andrew Beyer, Washington Post: 1. Marfa. 2. Play Fellow. 3. Caveat. 4. Sunny's Halo. Time 2:03.

Derby prospects' unofficial earnings

1.	Copelan	$569,090
2.	Desert Wine	527,315
3.	Sunny's Halo	481,019
4.	Marfa	386,943
5.	Highland Park	382,858
6.	Total Departure	378,868
7.	Current Hope	263,537
8.	Pax in Bello	256,473
9.	Caveat	238,337
10.	Luv a Libra	232,818
11.	Paris Prince	231,940
12.	My Mac	207,197
13.	Bounding Basque	201,322
14.	Balboa Native	177,625
15.	Play Fellow	166,787
16.	Slew o' Gold	158,940
17.	Parfaitement	157,088
18.	Chumming	151,826
19.	Explosive Wagon	151,110
20.	Elegant Life	148,854
21.	Coax Me Matt	137,053
22.	* Noble Home	132,500
23.	* Hail to Rome	119,660
24.	Le Cou Cou	107,793
25.	Dixieland Band	96,867
26.	Freezing Rain	89,325
27.	Country Pine	74,158
28.	Law Talk	68,107
29.	High Honors	46,940
30.	Saverton	29,123

* Includes only original purse awards for Spiral Stakes.

TABLE 11.3 ***Previous day's preliminary wagering on the 1983 Kentucky Derby***

	Horse	Odds	Win ($)	Place ($)	Show ($)
1.	Balboa Native, Total Departure, and Marfa	5—2	68,469	18,760	13,171
2.	Chumming and Caveat	5—1	36,245	14,994	9,424
3.	Freezing Rain and Highland Park	17—1	13,189	4,854	4,497
4.	Slew O' Gold	10—1	21,341	8,181	4,953
5.	Play Fellow	12—1	17,720	7,757	4,035
6.	Desert Wine	18—1	12,766	4,567	3,165
7.	Country Pine	50—1	4,286	1,368	938
8.	Sunny's Halo	5—2	63,329	20,783	12,106
9.	Current Hope	13—1	17,562	6,528	3,282
10.	Parfaitement	60—1	3,570	1,323	1,063
11.	Pax In Bello	25—1	8,171	3,232	2,054
12–16.	Law Talk, Paris Price, My Mac, Explosive Wagon, and Luv A Libra	8—1	25,877	13,382	13,817
			293,525	105,729	72,505

discovered that he was about $2,000 short to qualify. Since he was the top horse in the race, so the story goes, he was allowed to run. He ran a smashing 98 to win by 8 lengths. The gray colt was a brilliant but erratic and possibly dangerous runner. He was to be ridden by Jorge Velasquez, who had just been disqualified in the previous race. Win or lose, he seemed to be the horse to determine the outcome of the race. The entry of Marfa, Balboa Native, and Total Departure was installed as the race favorite at 5–2.

The second choice, listed at 5–1 in the morning line, but the consensus choice and best bet of the day, was the Canadian horse, Sunny's Halo. In the preliminary betting (see Table 11.3) he was also going off at 5–2. Sunny's Halo had a strong record as a two-year-old at Woodbine in Toronto. He had done poorly in two summer races in New York. His trainer, David Cross, eliminated thirty-two of his stable of thirty-five horses to concentrate on Sunny's Halo, who he thought was possibly the horse of a lifetime. Sunny's Halo responded with a win in the Rebel Handicap at Oaklawn Park in Arkansas. Cross was then looking to the Derby. His wife had bet $200 at 100–1 odds in the Las Vegas winter book that the colt would take the Derby. With 405 nominations, the odds on any nonprominent horse are quite large. Cross wanted a rider with proven Derby experience. Who could be better than the 1982 winner, Eddie Delahoussaye? Eddie had been scheduled earlier in the year to ride Roving Boy, the 1982 Eclipse award champion for a juvenile colt or gelding, and a possible superhorse. Unfortunately, he had been injured in January at Santa Anita. Delahoussaye was glad to ride for Cross. He had led Sunny's Halo to a 4-length victory in the Arkansas Derby with a 96 speed rating. He looked strong; however, tradition was not on his side. No Arkansas Derby winner had ever won the Kentucky Derby, and no horse since Jet Pilot in 1947 had won the Derby with only two starts as a three-year-old.

I liked quite a few horses in the race as possible long-shot winners. Marfa and Sunny's Halo certainly were the class, but Marfa was risky and Sunny's Halo lightly raced. I would bet on them, especially Sunny's Halo, if they were Dr. Z system bets. I was still hoping to bet on a winner in the Derby. Since there were so many strong horses, I diversified my bet of $50 over seven top contenders going off at relatively long odds. I bet $10 to win on number 2, the entry of Chumming and Caveat; on number 3, the entry of Freezing Rain and Highland Park; on number 4, Slew O' Gold; on number 5, Play Fellow; and on number 6, Desert Wine.

The Dr. Z system bet, if there was to be one, seemed to be on Sunny's Halo. The tote board was as follows:

	Totals	#8 Sunny's Halo	Expected Value per Dollar Bet on Sunny's Halo
With fifty-four minutes to post time			
Odds		5—2	
Win	2,155,976	482,703	
Show	768,057	119,245	1.14
With thirty-four minutes to post time			
Odds		5—2	
Win	2,564,483	592,960	
Show	930,971	142,078	1.16
With twenty minutes to post time			
Odds		5—2	
Win	2,879,256	668,880	
Show	1,026,474	160,470	1.15
With eight minutes to post time			
Odds		5—2	
Win	3,041,257	711,776	
Show	1,077,595	170,164	1.15
With one minute to post time			
Odds		5—2	
Win	3,099,808	729,747	
Show	1,098,076	175,643	1.14

With our betting fortune of $1,494.70 reflecting my $50 win bet, we bet $87 to show on Sunny's Halo.

At post time the tote board read:

	Totals	#8 Sunny's Halo	Expected Value per Dollar Bet on Sunny's Halo
Odds		5—2	
Win	3,143,669	745,524	
Show	1,099,990	179,758	1.14

109th Running

KENTUCKY DERBY

EIGHTH RACE

1875 — 1983

$250,000 ADDED — **ONE MILE and ONE-QUARTER**

TRACK RECORD—SECRETARIAT (3), 126 lbs., 5-5-73, 1:59-2/5

For three-year-olds. By subscription of $200 each. All nomination fees to the winner. $5,000 to pass entry box, $5,000 additional to start. $250,000 added, of which $60,000 to second, $30,000 to third, $15,000 to fourth, (to be divided equally in the event of a dead heat). Weight 126 lbs. The owner of the winner to receive a gold trophy.

Closed Tuesday, February 15, 1983, with 405 nominations.

USE THESE NUMBERS FOR BUYING PARI MUTUEL TICKETS

	OWNER	TRAINER	JOCKEY and Morning Line
1	ROBERT H. SPREEN Yellow, Brown "RS," Brown Bars on Sleeves, Yellow Cap **BALBOA NATIVE** 126 Ch c, 1980, Native Royalty—Diamond Till by Model Fool BRED IN KENTUCKY BY R. E. OWENS	D. WAYNE LUKAS	5-2 SANDY HAWLEY (P. P. 3)
1a	REBALOT STABLE (Stephen V. Lyons & Jay Templeman) Copper and Yellow Diamond Quarters, Yellow Bars on Copper Sleeves, Copper Cap **TOTAL DEPARTURE** 126 B c, 1980, Greek Answer—Life Style by Manifesto BRED IN FLORIDA BY JOHN H. HARTIGAN	D. WAYNE LUKAS	5-2 PAT VALENZUELA (P. P. 9)
1x	L. ROBERT FRENCH, JR., BARRY BEAL & D. WAYNE LUKAS Forest Green, White Dots, Forest Green Cap **MARFA** 126 Gr c, 1980, Foolish Pleasure—Gray Matter by Stratmat BRED IN KENTUCKY BY TOM GENTRY	D. WAYNE LUKAS	5-2 JORGE VELASQUEZ (P. P. 18)
2	HICKORY TREE STABLE (James P. Mills) Green, Yellow Sash, Yellow Blocks on Sleeves, Green Cap **CHUMMING** 126 Dk b or br c, 1980, Alleged—Gulls Cry by Sea-Bird BRED IN VIRG.NIA BY NEWSTEAD FARM	WOODFORD C. STEPHENS	5 EDDIE MAPLE (P. P. 4)
2b	AUGUST BELMONT IV, et al Scarlet, Maroon Sleeves, Black Cap **CAVEAT** 126 Dk b or br c, 1980, Cannonade—Cold Hearted by The Axe II BRED IN MARYLAND BY RYEHILL FARM	WOODFORD C. STEPHENS	5 LAFFIT PINCAY, JR. (P. P. 20)
3	BWAMAZON FARM (Millard A. Waldheim) White, Royal Blue Hoops, Royal Blue Stripes on Sleeves, Royal Blue Cap **FREEZING RAIN** 126 Ch c, 1980, It's Freezing—All's Well by Well Mannered BRED IN KENTUCKY BY BWAMAZON FARM	ANTHONY BASILE	15 WILLIAM GAVIDIA (P. P. 8)
3c	BWAMAZON FARM (Millard A. Waldheim) & BRERETON C. JONES White, Royal Blue Hoops, Royal Blue Stripes on Sleeves, Royal Blue Cap **HIGHLAND PARK** 126 Ch c, 1980, Raise a Native—Old Goat by Olden Times BRED IN KENTUCKY BY BWAMAZON FARM	ANTHONY BASILE	15 DON BRUMFIELD (P. P. 19)
4	EQUUS EQUITY STABLE (Delmar L. Pearson, Jr. Lessee) Black, Silver Yoke, Silver Bars on Sleeves, Silver Cap **SLEW O' GOLD** 126 B c, 1980, Seattle Slew—Alluvial by Buckpasser BRED IN KENTUCKY BY CLAIBORNE FARM	SIDNEY WATTERS, JR.	6 ANGEL CORDERO, JR. (P. P. 1)
5	NANCY VANIER, CARL LAUER & ROBERT VICTOR Yellow, Blue Sash, Yellow Cap **PLAY FELLOW** 126 B c, 1980, On The Sly—Play For Keeps by Run For Nurse BRED IN KENTUCKY BY MR. & MRS. PAUL BAKEWELL III	HARVEY L. VANIER	4 JEAN CRUGUET (P. P. 2)
6	T90 RANCH (Dan J. Agnew) & CARDIFF STUD (Fred Sahadi) Red, Red "T90" on White Ball, White Cap **DESERT WINE** 126 B c, 1980, Damascus—Anne Campbell by Never Bend BRED IN KENTUCKY BY BRERETON C. JONES & WARNERTON FARMS	JERRY FANNING	15 CHRIS McCARRON (P. P. 5)
7	DANIEL M. GALBREATH Brown and White Diamonds, White Sleeves, Brown Cap **COUNTRY PINE** 126 B c, 1980, His Majesty—Mountain Sunshine by Vaguely Noble BRED IN KENTUCKY BY DANIEL M. GALBREATH	THOMAS L. RONDINELLO	20 MICHAEL VENEZIA (P. P. 7)
8	DAVID J. FOSTER RACING STABLE (David J. Foster, et al) Orange, White Stripes, Orange Cap **SUNNY'S HALO** 126 Ch c, 1980, Halo—Mostly Sunny by Sunny BRED IN CANADA BY DAVID J. FOSTER	DAVID C. CROSS, JR.	5 EDDIE DELAHOUSSAYE (P. P. 10)
9	ROBERT BAKER & HOWARD KASKEL Orange, White Sash, White Stripes on Sleeves, Orange Cap **CURRENT HOPE** 126 Ro c, 1980, Little Current—Kahoolawe by Warfare BRED IN KENTUCKY BY MR. & MRS. J. C. MABEE	ROGER LAURIN	12 ALEXIS SOLIS (P. P. 12)
10	MRS. BERNARD DANEY Red, Black Cross Sashes, Black Band on White Sleeves, White Cap **PARFAITEMENT** 126 Ch c, 1980, Halo—Double Axle by The Axe II BRED IN PENNSYLVANIA BY BLACK GATE NURSERY TRUST	J. WILLIAM BONIFACE	20 HERBERT McCAULEY (P. P. 13)
11	MR. & MRS. ARNOLD A. WILLCOX Crimson, Black Collar and Cuffs, Gold Sleeves, Crimson Cap **PAX IN BELLO** 126 B c, 1980, Hold Your Peace—Chicanery by Pretense BRED IN FLORIDA BY MR. & MRS. ARNOLD A. WILLCOX	STEVEN T. JERKENS	15 JEFFREY FELL (P. P. 14)
12 FIELD	BUCKRAM OAK FARM (Mahmoud Fustok) Green, Red Sash, Red Band on Sleeves, Red Cap **LAW TALK** 126 B c, 1980, Wardlaw—Tellinoid by Captain's Gig BRED IN FLORIDA BY S. L. HAYMAN & ELLIOTT FUENTES	LEONARD IMPERIO	30 CARLOS MARQUEZ (P. P. 6)
13 FIELD	PEGGY McREYNOLDS Green, Pink Stripes, Pink Sleeves, Green Cap **EXPLOSIVE WAGON** 126 Ch c, 1980, Explodent—Gypsy Wagon by Conestoga BRED IN FLORIDA BY WINDY CITY STABLE	GENE C. NORMAN	30 CHARLES MUELLER (P. P. 11)
14 FIELD	ARONOW STABLE (Donald J. Aronow) Red, White "A," White Braces, White Bars on Sleeves, Red Cap **MY MAC** 126 Dk b or br g, 1980, Minnesota Mac—My Mom Nullah by My Dad George BRED IN FLORIDA BY ROYAL WAY FARM	NEWCOMB GREEN	30 DONALD MacBETH (P. P. 15)
15 FIELD	DOLLY GREEN Red, Gold Yoke, Gold Bars on Sleeves, Red Cap **PARIS PRINCE** 126 Ch c, 1980, Exclusive Native—Dancers Countess by Northern Dancer BRED IN KENTUCKY BY HOLTSINGER, INC.	LAZARO S. BARRERA	30 TERRY LIPHAM (P. P. 16)
16 FIELD	VIVIANNE DeCOSTA & STANLEY YAGODA Gold, Purple Triangular Panel, Gold and Purple Diagonal Quartered Sleeves, Gold and Purple Cap **LUV A LIBRA** 126 B c, 1980, Diplomat Way—Lip Talk by Assegai BRED IN FLORIDA BY FARNSWORTH FARM	HELIODORO GUSTINES	30 JULIO ESPINOZA (P. P. 17)

Indicates Foaled in Kentucky.

1-1a-1x—Robert H. Spreen—Rebalot Stable—L. Robert French, Jr., Barry Beal & D. Wayne Lukas Entry

2-2b—Hickory Tree Stable—August Belmont IV, et al Entry

3-3c—Bwamazon Farm—Bwamazon Farm & Brereton C. Jones Entry

FIELD—12-13-14-15-16

Selections—1x-5-8-2b

109th-Kentucky Derby-109th

8th Churchill

1 ¼ MILES. (1.59⅘) 109th Running KENTUCKY DERBY (Grade I). $250,000 added. 3-year-olds. By subscription of $200 each. All nomination fees to the winner. $5,000 to pass the entry box, $5,000 additional to start, with $250,000 added of which $60,000 to second, $30,000 to third and $15,000 to fourth (to be divided equally in the event of a dead heat). Weight 126 lbs. Starters to be named through the entry box Thursday, May 5, at usual time of closing. The maximum number of starters for the Kentucky Derby will be limited to twenty. In the event more than twenty entries pass through the entry box at the time of closing, the twenty starters and up to eight also eligibles will be determined at that time with preference given to those horses that have accumulated the highest earnings. Should any entry(ies) be withdrawn from the starting field prior to 4 P.M. scratch time, Friday, May 6, vacancies will be filled from the also eligible list and placed in the outside post positions in order of preference. For those that pass the entry box and are eliminated under this condition the entry fee will be refunded. Gold trophy to the winning owner. Closed with 405 nominations Tuesday, February 15, 1983.

Coupled—Balboa Native, Total Departure and Marfa; Chumming and Caveat; Freezing Rain and Highland Park.

Mutuel Field—Law Talk, Luv A Libra, Paris Prince, Explosive Wagon, My Mac.

Slew O' Gold

B. c. 3, by Seattle Slew—Alluvial, by Buckpasser
Br.—Claiborne Farm (Ky) 1983 4 2 1 1 $136,740
Own.—Equusequity Stable 126 Tr.—Watters Sidney Jr 1982 3 2 0 0 $22,200
Lifetime 7 4 1 1 $158,940

23Apr83-8Aqu 1⅛ :48¹ 1:12¹ 1:51 ft *6-5 126 5² 41¾ 1hd 1nk Maple E1 Wood Mem 80-24 SlewO'Gold,Prfitement,HighHonors 7
23Apr83—Run in two divisions 7th & 8th races
13Apr83-1Aqu 1⅛ :48³ 1:12³ 1:50⁴ft *1 117 1hd 1¹ 16 17¾ Cordero AJr4 Aw23000 81-19 Slew O' Gold, Law Talk, El Cubano 6
19Mar83-10Tam 1 1/16 :48 1:13 1:47¹ft 2¼ 118 42½ 43½ 2³ 2¾ RiverHJr2 Tampa Bay 82-21 Morgnmrgnmrgn,SlwO'Gld,QckDp 14
19Mar83—Steadied, checked
5Mar83-10Tam 1 1/16 :47⁴ 1:13⁷ 1:47²ft *2-5 118 86¾ 43 32½ 33¾ MolnVH4 Sam F Davis 78-23 Sverton,TwoTurnsHome,SlwO'Gold 8
13Nov82-8Aqu 1⅛ :48² 1:12⁴ 1:50¹gd *9-5e 115 52½ 5³ 6¹⁰ 6¹² Lovato F Jr11 Remsen 72-20 PxInBllo,Chumming,PrimitivPlsur 11
23Oct82-9Aqu 1 :47 1:12¹ 1:37²ft 3¾ 117 2½ 1hd 11½ 11¾ Lovato F Jr8 Aw20000 79-21 Slew O' Gold, Last Turn,Chumming 9
15Oct82-3Aqu 6½f :23² :47 1:18⁴ft *3-5 118 2½ 2½ 1½ 1nk Cordero A Jr8 Mdn 81-26 SlewO'Gold,Countertrde,MjestyCov 8
May 5 CD 4f ft :48 h Apr 30 CD 6f sy 1:14 h ●Apr 20 Bel tr.t 5f sy :59² b ●Apr 10 Bel tr.t 6f sy 1:13¹ h (d)

Play Fellow *

B. c. 3, by On the Sly—Play for Keeps, by Run for Nurse
Br.—Bakewell Mr–Mrs P III (Ky) 1983 6 3 1 1 $153,568
Own.—Vanier Nancy&Lauer&Victor 126 Tr.—Vanier Harvey L 1982 4 1 3 0 $13,220
Lifetime 10 4 4 1 $166,788

28Apr83-7Kee 1⅛ :46⁴ 1:11 1:49²sy 19 121 8¹² 45½ 1hd 1no Cruguet J3 Blue Grass 90-16 Play Fellow, ‡Marfa, Desert Wine 12
2Apr83-10Hia 1⅛ :47¹ 1:11¹ 1:49²ft 4¾ 118 139½128½117 103¾ Cruguet J1 Flamingo 81-18 CurrntHop,Chmmng,Gn'lPrcttonr 14
2Apr83—Wide, brushed
19Mar83-10Hia 1⅛ :45³ 1:09³ 1:48⁴ft *6-5 112 108¾ 6⁸ 5⁵ 3½ Cruguet J9 Everglades 87-18 Gn'lPrcttnr,OhMyWndlnd,PlyFllw 12
28Feb83-7GP 7f :22² :45 1:23²ft *1 122 6⁷ 6⁷ 31½ 15½ Cruguet J5 Aw21000 87-24 PlayFellow,SmartStyle,GunCarrige 8
9Feb83-8GP 7f :22 :44⁴ 1:23³ft *8-5 119 10⁹ 99¾ 3nk 1² Cruguet J9 Aw14000 86-24 Play Fellow, Tarmoud,HighHonors 12
26Jan83-8GP 6f :22 :45 1:09⁴ft 6¼ 119 95½ 6⁶ 2⁴ 22½ Cruguet J2 Aw14000 87-20 JusticeSnders,PlyFellow,ElPerico 10
23Nov82-3CD 7½f :23¹ :46³ 1:34 m *9-5 118 2hd 1² 1¹ 22¾ Gallitano G3 Aw11200 72-35 Jenkins Ferry, PlayFellow,Ida'sSon 6
13Nov82-4CD 7f :23³ :47² 1:26³ft *8-5 118 3½ 2½ 2½ 2½ Gallitano G8 Aw11200 73-22 DarkSuce,PlyFellow,NibbleOnDrrell 8
3Nov82-5CD 6f :22³ :46³ 1:12⁴gd *1e 121 41½ 32½ 1½ 13¼ Gallitano G11 Mdn 82-26 Play Fellow, Great Boy, Lazaro 12
22Oct82-3Kee 6½f :22² :45⁴ 1:19 ft 3 120 55½ 11½ 1² 21¼ Haire D1 Mdn 81-18 NturllyBlu,PlyFllow,GrndstonTurn 12
●Apr 20 Kee 7f ft 1:25² h Apr 16 Kee 5f gd 1:01 b Mar 31 Hia 4f sy :48 b Mar 26 Hia 5f ft 1:03 b

Route the Field Will Travel

Kentucky Derby

One and One-Quarter Miles

START

FINISH

Country Pine

B. c. 3, by His Majesty—Mountain Sunshine, by Vaguely Noble
Br.—Galbreath D M (Ky) 1983 7 2 1 1 $63,958
Own.—Galbreath D M 126 Tr.—Rondinello Thomas L 1982 2 1 0 0 $10,200
Lifetime 9 3 1 1 $74,158

23Apr83-7Aqu 1⅛ :48¹ 1:12² 1:51²ft 3¾ 126 5⁵ 3½ 2hd 2no Bailey JD8 Wood Mem 78-24 BoundingBsque,CountryPin,AztcRd 8
23Apr83—Run in two divisions 7th & 8th races; Wide
2Apr83-10Hia 1⅛ :47¹ 1:11¹ 1:49²ft 13e 118 9⁵ 4³ 73¼ 82¾ Bailey J D2 Flamingo 83-18 CurrntHop,Chmmng,Gn'lPrcttonr 14
2Apr83—Steadied
23Mar83-5Hia 7f :23 :45³ 1:22 ft *4-5 118 3² 2hd 1½ 1² Bailey J D6 Aw11000 93-16 Country Pine, Luv ALibra,Tarmoud 7
21Feb83-10GP 1 1/16 :47⁴ 1:12 1:43³ft 3½ 113 67¼ 4⁵ 6⁸ 47¼ Fell J2 Ftn Youth 76-24 Copelan, Current Hope, Blink 8
21Feb83—Run in two divisions 9th & 10th races
9Feb83-9GP 7f :22¹ :45 1:22⁴ft 3½ 112 10⁵ 84¾ 53¼ 3¾ VelsquezJ8 Hutcheson 89-24 CurrntHop,HighlndPrk,CountryPn 13
18Jan83-5GP 6f :22² :45⁴ 1:10¹ft *1 122 2² 1³ 1⁵ 1⁹ Velasquez J8 Aw14000 88-18 CountryPine,Stn'sChrger,SlickRulr 9
8Jan83-6GP 6f :21⁴ :44³ 1:10⁴sy 3½ 122 106¾1014 69½ 54½ Velasquez J2 Aw14000 81-17 Sligh Jet, Unreal Zeal, Pure Grit 12
28Nov82-4Aqu 7f :22⁴ :46¹ 1:25 ft *6-5 118 2½ 2¹ 1² 12½ Velasquez J4 Mdn 76-28 CountryPine,ThWholTickt,QutiGold 9
11Nov82-4Aqu 6f :22² :46 1:10⁴ft 6¼ 118 3¹ 95¾ 76¾ 57¼ Velasquez J1 Mdn 80-19 Jeff'sCompnion,JungleDust,Nevdo 13
May 5 Bel 4f ft :49 b May 1 Bel 4f ft :48² b Apr 22 Bel 3f ft :38 b Apr 17 Bel tr.t 6f gd 1:13² h

Freezing Rain *
Ch. c. 3, by It's Freezing—All's Well, by Well Mannered
Br.—Bwamazon Farm (Ky) 1983 5 2 1 0 $64,640
Own.—Bwamazon Farm 126 Tr.—Basile Anthony 1982 5 3 0 2 $24,685
Lifetime 10 5 1 2 $89,325
28Apr83-7Kee 1⅛ :464 1:11 1:492sy 2½e121 1012 69 55½ 59½ Gavidia W1 Blue Grass 80-16 Play Fellow, ‡Marfa, Desert Wine 12
21Apr83-7Kee 7f :224 :451 1:234ft *2-3 120 89¼ 89½ 33½ 21 Solomone M2 Aw28000 86-15 DerbyDouble,FrezingRin,Hrry'NBill 9
9Apr83-7Kee 6f :221 :451 1:111sy *4-5 118 96 75½ 33½ 1½ BrumfieldD4 Lafayette 86-25 Freezing Rain, Harry'NBill,Hamlet 11
5Mar83-9GP 7f :222 :452 1:233ft *4-5 119 66½ 73½ 52½ 53½ Brumfield D9 Aw30000 82-19 Slewpy,Victorious,Gen'lPrctitioner 9
8Jan83-9GP 6f :22 :443 1:10 sy 4½e114 77½ 56½ 33 1¾ BrmfldD7 Spect'ul Bid 89-17 FreezingRin,WriteOff,TotlDeprture 9
27Nov82-4CD 7f :24 :48 1:254m *1 115 32 41½ 2hd 1nk Brumfield D6 Aw15700 78-29 FreezingRain,BrshBrother,DrkSuce 8
10Nov82-6CD 6f :22 :453 1:111ft *6-5 115 62½ 31½ 1½ 14 Brumfield D3 Aw11200 90-22 FreezingRin,ShrpTimes,SlyRussllC. 9
22Oct82-4Kee 6½f :223 :46 1:181ft *4-5 115 93½ 65 53½ 32 Day P10 Aw13500 84-18 Admirl'sGin,SoringTims,FrzingRin 12
13Oct82-4Kee 6f :221 :46 1:112ft *2-3 115 96½ 75½ 44 31 Day P3 Aw13500 84-16 DerbyDouble,HndStnd,FrezingRin 12
20May82-5AP 5f :231 :464 :584ft *3-5 122 22 2½ 2½ 1nk Day P4 Mdn 92-29 Freezing Rain, Spare Card, Dakota 9
May 5 CD 4f ft :48 h Apr 16 Kee 5f gd 1:032 b Apr 7 Kee 4f ft :492 b Apr 2 Kee 7f ft 1:284 b

Balboa Native *
Ch. c. 3, by Native Royalty—Diamond Till, by Model Fool
Br.—Owens R E (Ky) 1983 5 2 0 2 $141,000
Own.—Spreen R H 126 Tr.—Lukas D Wayne 1982 7 1 1 2 $36,625
Lifetime 12 3 1 4 $177,625
16Apr83-9OP 1⅛ :462 1:113 1:492ft *3 123 1425 1418 1016 711 Velasquez J1 Ark Dby 85-19 Sunny's Halo, Caveat, Exile King 14
27Mar83-11FG 1⅛ :474 1:123 1:503ft 3½ 118 711 77 44 1½ Velasquez J7 La Dby 91-19 BalboNtive,FoundPerlHrbor,Slewpy 8
27Mar83—Wide.
5Mar83-8SA 1 :46 1:103 1:353ft 16 116 713 79½ 58 36½ DlhossyE1 San Rafael 83-16 Desert Wine, Naevus, BalboaNative 7
5Mar83—Fanned wide into stretch
6Feb83-5SA 1 1/16 :47 1:121 1:444m 4 118 916 816 57 11½ Pincay L Jr9 Aw20000 77-19 BlboNtive,FletScrmmr,BrodwyHrry 9
9Jan83-2SA 1 1/16 :453 1:101 1:413ft *2½ 118 88½ 89½ 47½ 36½ Toro F4 Aw20000 86-10 Debt, Fleet Naskra, Balboa Native 8
3Dec82-5Hol 1 1/16 :451 1:101 1:424ft 4½ 117 1013 75½ 4¾ 32 Pincay L Jr4 Aw19000 79-20 SprDmond,DomntngDooly,BlbNtv 10
30Oct82-3SA 1 :452 1:094 1:352ft 4 117 411 48 46½ 45½ Romero R P2 Aw23000 85-10 RollANaturl,GlemMchine,SweetMn 5
16Oct82-7Kee 1 1/16 :471 1:112 1:433ft 23 121 98½ 913 1012 925 Meza R Q5 Brdrs' Fut 63-17 HighlandPark,Caveat,BrightBaron 12
8Sep82-8Dmr 1 :461 1:122 1:384sl 12 114 913 711 510 312 VlnlPA9 Dmr Futurity 62-30 RovingBoy,DesertWine,BalboNtive 9
28Aug82-6Dmr 1 :461 1:112 1:37 ft 3½ 117 3½ 31½ 37 12 Valenzuela P A9 Mdn 83-13 Balboa Native, Brian Ke, Adolfo 10
21Aug82-6Dmr 6f :223 :46 1:111ft 13 118 52½ 53½ 63 21 Valenzuela P A11 Mdn 81-12 MonsiurExcitmnt,BlboNtiv,Subsdz 12
1Aug82-6Dmr 1 :473 1:131 1:382ft 2½ 116 21 78½ 710 718 Lipham T4 Mdn 58-14 TnksBrigd,Morry'sChmp,DbonirHrc 8
Apr 23 Kee 4f ft :49 b Apr 19 SA 5f m 1:04 h (d) Apr 10 SA 4f ft :481 h

Chumming
Dk. b. or br. c. 3, by Alleged—Gulls Cry, by Sea-Bird
Br.—Newstead Farm (Va) 1983 6 1 1 1 $166,316
Own.—Hickory Tree Stable 126 Tr.—Stephens Woodford C 1982 4 2 1 1 $361,000
Lifetime 10 3 2 2 $527,316 Turf 1 0 0 0 $160
30Apr83-9CD 1 :462 1:11 1:374m *3-2e116 128½ 116½ 67½ 59½ Maple E12 Dby Trl 71-28 Caveat,TotalDeparture,PaxInBello 14
2Apr83-10Hia 1⅛ :471 1:111 1:492ft 9½ 118 64½ 75 62½ 2nk Maple E9 Flamingo 85-18 CurrntHop,Chmmng,Gn'lPrcttonr 14
2Apr83—Altered course
5Mar83-11GP 1⅛ :481 1:113 1:494ft 5½ 118 21½ 34½ 45½ 56½ CordrAJr8 Flordia Dby 77-19 Croeso, Copelan, Law Talk 13
21Feb83-9GP 1 1/16 :481 1:12 1:443ft 3½ 114 43½ 63 52½ 3½ Maple E8 Ftn Youth 77-24 HighlandPark,Thlssocrt,Chumming 9
21Feb83—Brushed; Run in two divisions 9th & 10th races
11Feb83-7GP 1 1/16 :481 1:122 1:433ft *6-5 119 31 1hd 11 1½ Maple E7 Aw16000 83-21 Chumming, Law Talk, GameDancer 7
19Jan83-5GP a1 ① 1:372fm 6-5 119 911 76½ 66½ 68¼ Maple E2 Aw16000 84-13 Reap, Cancun, Smart Style 10
13Nov82-8Aqu 1⅛ :482 1:124 1:501gd 2½ 115 1½ 1½ 2½ 21¾ Maple E1 Remsen 82-20 PxInBllo,Chumming,PrimitivPlsur 11
2Nov82-7Aqu 1 :454 1:104 1:36 ft *4-5 122 42½ 1½ 11½ 12¾ Maple E8 Aw20000 86-16 Chumming,RisingRaj,Nshu'sHidewy 8
23Oct82-9Aqu 1 :47 1:121 1:372ft *2½ 122 63 65 55½ 34½ Bailey J D2 Aw20000 74-21 Slew O' Gold, Last Turn,Chumming 9
8Oct82-4Bel 1 :47 1:13 1:394ft 6 118 33½ 3nk 2hd 1½ Maple E7 Mdn 66-25 Chumming,MomentofJoy,Tnyosho 11
May 5 CD 4f ft :481 b Apr 28 CD 4f ft :484 b Apr 23 Bel 1 ft 1:41 h Apr 12 OP 5f ft 1:033 b

Desert Wine *
B. c. 3, by Damascus—Anne Campbell, by Never Bend
Br.—Jones B-Warnerton Farms (Ky) 1983 4 2 1 0 $166,315
Own.—Cardiff StudFarm&T90Ranch 126 Tr.—Fanning Jerry 1982 8 3 3 1 $361,000
Lifetime 12 5 4 1 $527,315
28Apr83-7Kee 1⅛ :464 1:11 1:492sy 4 121 2½ 21½ 43½ 37½ McCrrnCJ5 Blue Grass 82-16 Play Fellow, ‡Marfa, Desert Wine 12
28Apr83—Placed second through disqualification, steadied near 3/16 pole
10Apr83-4SA 1⅛ :46 1:102 1:492ft *4-5 120 63½ 42½ 77½ 69½ McCrrCJ10 S A Derby 73-19 Marfa, My Habitony, Naevus 10
10Apr83—Wide 7/8 turn
27Mar83-8SA 1 1/16 :454 1:094 1:413ft *2-3 124 1½ 1hd 2hd 2hd McCrrCJ6 SanFelipeH 93-13 ‡Naevus, Desert Wine,FifthDivision 5
27Mar83—Placed first through disqualification; Bumped in stretch
5Mar83-8SA 1 :46 1:103 1:353ft *6-5 119 1½ 11½ 12 12½ McCrrnCJ3 San Rafael 90-16 Desert Wine, Naevus, BalboaNative 7
12Dec82-8Hol 1 1/16 :454 1:101 1:414ft 6½e121 2hd 3nk 2hd 2nk McCrronCJ3 Hol Fut'y 86-20 RovingBoy,DesertWin,FifthDivision 9
27Nov82-8Hol 7f :214 :434 1:212ft 3 122 43 42½ 34 33 OlivaresF2 Hol Prevue 87-14 Copelan, R. Awacs, Desert Wine 8
30Oct82-8SA 1 1/16 :45 1:091 1:413ft 3e118 2hd 1hd 21½ 24½ Lipham T2 Norfolk 88-10 Roving Boy, Desert Wine, Aguila 9
6Oct82-8SA 7f :214 :442 1:223ft *3-5 124 21½ 21 1hd 1½ ShmrW4 Sunny Slope 87-15 Desert Wine, Aguila, Crispen 4
8Sep82-8Dmr 1 :461 1:122 1:384sl 9-5e120 13 1½ 1½ 2½ ShmrW5 Dmr Futurity 73-30 RovingBoy,DesertWine,BalboNtive 9
25Aug82-8Dmr 1 :454 1:094 1:352ft *4-5 117 21½ 32 45 — Olivares F5 Balboa — — Roving Boy, Encourager,FullChoke 5
25Aug82—Lost rider
17Jly82-8Hol 6f :212 :441 1:093ft 2½ 116 31½ 32 1hd 16½ OlvrsF4 Hol Juv Chmp 89-10 Desert Wine, Ft. Davis, Full Choke 6
27Jun82-4Hol 5½f :221 :451 1:04 ft *4-5 116 21½ 22½ 2½ 11½ Olivares F7 Mdn 91-12 Desert Wine,SonOfSong,BlueSeas 11
●Apr 22 Kee 5f ft :594 h Apr 5 SA 6f ft 1:123 h Mar 24 SA 5f ft :592 b Mar 19 SA 6f ft 1:124 h (d)

Law Talk
B. c. 3, by Wardlaw—Tellinoid, by Captain's Gig
Br.—Hayman & Fuentes (Fla) 1983 5 1 2 2 $52,207
Own.—Buckram Oak Farm 126 Tr.—Imperio Leonard 1982 5 1 0 2 $15,900
Lifetime 10 2 2 4 $68,107
13Apr83-1Aqu 1⅛ :483 1:123 1:504ft 2 117 67 33½ 26 27¾ Smith A Jr3 Aw23000 73-19 Slew O' Gold, Law Talk, El Cubano 6
2Apr83-8Aqu 1 :463 1:11 1:363ft *4-5 114 42 32 32½ 35¾ Samyn J L3 Gotham 77-23 Chas Conerly, ElegantLife,LawTalk 6
2Apr83—Run in Two Divisions: 7th & 8th Races; Lacked room, std
5Mar83-11GP 1⅛ :481 1:113 1:494ft 18 118 65 44½ 33½ 34¾ HrnndzC1 Flordia Dby 78-19 Croeso, Copelan, Law Talk 13
11Feb83-7GP 1 1/16 :481 1:122 1:433ft 3 122 65½ 32½ 21 2½ Samyn J L5 Aw16000 82-21 Chumming, Law Talk, GameDancer 7

Parfaitement
Ch. c. 3, by Halo—Double Axle, by The Axe II
Br.—Black Gates Nursery Trust (Pa) 1983 3 2 1 0 $86,058
Own.—Daney Mrs Bernard 126 Tr.—Boniface J William 1982 6 5 1 0 $71,030
Lifetime 9 7 2 0 $157,088
23Apr83-8Aqu 1⅛ :481 1:121 1:51 ft 3 126 2½ 1hd 2hd 2nk McClWH7 Wood Mem 80-24 SlewO'Gold,Prfitement,HighHonors 7
23Apr83—Run in two divisions 7th & 8th races
15Apr83-8Aqu 1 :462 1:103 1:37 ft 2½ 107 2hd 1½ 11½ 12¾ Davis R G2 HcpO 81-29 Parfaitement,MouseCorps,Tumrshu 5
2Apr83-9Grd 6½f :234 :48 1:201ft *6-5 119 1hd 1hd 14 15¾ McClWH4 Woodstock 85-18 Parfitement,BgO'Bucks,NleesPoint 6
26Dec82-8Key 1 1/16 :482 1:133 1:471ft *2-3 119 21½ 2½ 12½ 1½ McClyWH1 Allegheny 68-30 Parfaitement, BalaGala,Jane'sPoise 6
4Dec82-8Key 6f :22 :452 1:104ft *4-5 121 34 31½ 2½ 2² Agnello A5 Dragoon 85-22 TwoDavids,Parfitement,OnionJuice 8
20Nov82-8Key 7f :222 :451 1:24 ft *2-3 122 31½ 2½ 11 18 Wilson R8 ⓈPa Futy 87-21 Parfaitement,Jne'sPoise,RoylDuel 10
7Nov82-8Key 7f :224 :453 1:241ft 2½ 117 2½ 21 12 11½ Agnello A6 Freetex 86-23 Parfaitement, Jane'sPoise,BalaGala 6
23Oct82-7Key 6f :223 :462 1:13 ft *6-5 120 2hd 2hd 13 11½ Agnello A8 Aw10000 76-29 Prfitement,ChocolteDncer,GoosGrs 8
12Oct82-3Key 6f :224 :463 1:122ft 11 120 43½ 2½ 13 110 Terry J5 ⓈMdn 79-29 Prfitement,JzzMster,ChckbookBrkr 7
●Mar 26 Pim 6f ft 1:14 h

Pax In Bello
B. c. 3, by Hold Your Peace—Chicanery, by Pretense
Br.—Willcox Mr-Mrs A A (Fla) 1983 3 1 1 1 $18,635
Own.—Willcox Mrs A A 126 Tr.—Jerkens Steven T 1982 9 3 3 1 $243,923
Lifetime 12 4 4 2 $262,558
30Apr83-9CD 1 :462 1:11 1:374m 2½ 122 31½ 32 2½ 3nk Fell J13 Dby Trl 80-28 Caveat,TotalDeparture,PaxInBello 14
11Apr83-9Hia 1 1/16 :471 1:111 1:424ft *1-9 125 12½ 14 1½ 21¾ Fell J5 ⓈD. Chappel H 87-22 Saverton, Pax InBello,FancyFriend 6
11Apr83—Wide
21Mar83-5Hia 7f :224 :451 1:224ft *2-5 118 22 2hd 12½ 12¾ Fell J5 Aw13000 89-20 PxInBello,SuperRolfe,MyBestChoic 6
13Nov82-8Aqu 1⅛ :482 1:124 1:501gd 5 113 84 42½ 1½ 11¾ Fell J9 Remsen 84-20 PxInBllo,Chumming,PrimitivPlsur 11
23Oct82-8Lrl 1 1/16 :463 1:123 1:45 ft 18 122 45 73¼ 44½ 21 Perret C5 Lrl Futurity 82-21 CstPrty,PxInBello,PrimitivePlesur 11
23Oct82—Blocked
16Oct82-7Med 6f :221 :453 1:103ft *4-5 116 41½ 33 22 22¾ Miranda J4 Comet 87-15 Bet Big,PaxInBello,GeminiDreamer 7
12Sep82-8Bel 7f :23 :461 1:241ft 7½ 122 53½ 64½ 33½ 35½ Miranda J4 Bel Fut 76-19 Copelan,Satan'sCharger,PaxInBello 6
12Sep82—Very wide
28Aug82-8Sar 6½f :221 :444 1:163ft 4½ 122 3½ 65½ 67 44½ Miranda J4 Hopeful 85-13 Copelan, Victorious, Aloha Hawaii 9
28Aug82—Jumped a shadow
14Aug82-6Sar 6f :222 :46 1:10 ft 4½ 119 41¾ 1½ 13 12¾ Miranda J5 Aw19000 90-11 Pax In Bello, Thalassocrat, Savour 7
30Jly82-4Bel 5½f :223 :462 1:051ft 2½ 118 41¾ 31½ 12 11½ Miranda J8 Mdn 89-16 PaxInBello,RisingRaja,TimelyHitter 9
11Jun82-3Mth 5f :221 :453 :58 ft 2½e 118 1hd 1½ 1hd 2no Lopez C5 Mdn 96-18 Truby, Pax In Bello, Dashing Duke 9
1Jun82-5Mth 5f :222 :453 :581ft 8 118 41¾ 44½ 48 59¾ Perret C8 Mdn 85-15 Pappa Riccio, Dashing Duke, Truby 8
Apr 28 CD 5f ft :594 h Apr 24 Bel 1 gd 1:46 b Apr 21 Bel tr.t 5f ft :59 h Apr 17 Bel tr.t 6f gd 1:16 b

My Mac
Dk. b. or br. g. 3, by Minnesota Mac—My Mom Nullah, by My Dad George
Br.—Royal Way Farm (Fla) 1983 5 1 0 0 $134,895
Own.—Aronow Stable 126 Tr.—Green Newcomb 1982 15 5 5 2 $72,302
Lifetime 20 6 5 2 $207,197 Turf 1 0 0 0 $2,052
16Apr83-9OP 1⅛ :462 1:113 1:492ft 5½ 123 710 46½ 67½ 58¾ MacBeth D14 Ark Dby 87-19 Sunny's Halo, Caveat, Exile King 14
2Apr83-10Hia 1⅛ :471 1:111 1:492ft 16 122 116 85½ 52¾ 72½ MacBeth D6 Flamingo 83-18 CurrntHop,Chmmng,Gn'lPrcttonr 14
2Apr83—Steadied, blocked
5Mar83-11GP 1⅛ :481 1:113 1:494ft 14 122 118½1010 57 44¾ McBthD13 Flordia Dby 78-19 Croeso, Copelan, Law Talk 13
21Feb83-9GP 1 1/16 :481 1:12 1:443ft 8½ 122 85 32½ 42 4¾ MacBethD6 Ftn Youth 77-24 HighlandPark,Thlssocrt,Chumming 9
21Feb83—Run in two divisions 9th & 10th races. Wide
5Jan83-9Crc 1 1/16 :474 1:13 1:463ft 8½ 121 76 53½ 11 1½ McBethD8 Trp Pk Dby 86-19 My Mac, Caveat, Blink 11
18Dec82-9Crc 170 :472 1:122 1:422ft 6½ 117 79½ 410 33 22¾ MrqzC6 What A Pleas 95-13 WorldAppel,MyMc,SunnyLooking 11
30Nov82-9Crc 170 :49 1:14 1:441ft *6-5 119 33½ 21½ 21 21½ Marquez C3 Aw14000 88-14 Sunny Looking, My Mac, Blink 5
11Nov82-9Crc a1 1/16 Ⓣ 1:474fm*3-2 119 55 43 32½ 51¾ MarquezC9 Cty Miami 74-24 Blink,Disstistction,‡JudgMyBudgt 11
11Nov82—Placed fourth through disqualification
3Nov82-9Crc 1 :463 1:131 1:402ft *9-5 119 35 31½ 2hd 1nk Marquez C5 Aw20000 86-21 MyMc,Bobbi'sPlesure,FleetL'Hurux 8
16Oct82-10Crc 1 1/16 :474 1:134 1:473ft 15 115 65½ 41¾ 12½ 1½ MrquezC4 Fool'sh Plsr 81-20 My Mac, Blink, Judge My Budget 11
23Sep82-7Crc 6f :222 :453 1:114ft *6-5 116 2½ 1hd 12½ 11¾ Marquez C4 Aw11000 93-16 My Mac, Royality Miss,Devil'sPawn 5
13Sep82-9Crc 1 :484 1:133 1:401ft 2½ 112 32½ 31 42½ 44 Velez J A Jr6 Aw13000 83-20 Bobbi's Pleasure, Luv ALibra,Blink 6
18Aug82-9Crc 6f :221 :462 1:123ft 9-5 1077 43½ 32 33¾ 32¾ Feriole M F1 Aw10000 86-18 HelloHndsome,Bobbi'sPlsur,MyMc 5
30Jly82-8Crc 6f :22 :454 1:124ft 4¾ 1057 61½ 33 11 14½ Feriole M F3 Aw9500 88-17 My Mac, Gloversville, High Tracy 12
21Jly82-7Crc 5½f :222 :463 1:063ft 8½ 112 51¾ 41½ 31½ 2½ Velez J A Jr4 Aw9500 91-17 Dr. Butcher, My Mac, Top Case 7
2Jly82-5Crc 5½f :23 :471 1:064ft *8-5 114 1hd 1hd 1hd 2no Velez J A Jr1 40000 91-15 High Tracy, My Mac, Here's toPaul 6
14Jun82-5Crc 5f :224 :471 1:003ft *8-5 118 12 13 12 2½ Rocco J1 30000 88-16 What What,MyMac,FleetL'Heureux 7
7Jun82-2Crc 5f :224 :473 1:01 ft 5¾ 115 42¾ 2½ 1½ 1¾ Rocco J4 M25000 87-15 MyMac,MarkJilyne,StrikingPrince 11
28May82-4Crc 5f :233 :484 1:022sy 7 115 43½ 32 31½ 42 Baltazar C6 M25000 78-22 KeenBluffer,FncyFrind,‡TudorGnrl 9
28May82—Placed third through disqualification
20May82-3Crc 5f :232 :481 1:02 ft *6-5 115 34 34 35 46 Rocco J1 M30000 76-17 Sailor's Lad, Tudor General, Fort 7
May 2 CD 6f gd 1:132 h Mar 26 Hia 7f ft 1:282 h Mar 21 Hia 5f ft 1:032 b Mar 17 Crc 4f sy :494 h (d)

```
Paris Prince *                              Ch. c. 3, by Exclusive Native—Dancers Countess, by Northern Dancer
                                            Br.—Holtsinger Inc (Ky)                      1983  5  1  1  0     $145,925
Own.—Green Dolly                       126  Tr.—Barrera Lazaro S                         1982  7  3  1  0      $86,015
                                       Lifetime   12  4  2  0   $231,940                 Turf  1  0  0  0       $3,324
23Apr83-7GG   1⅛ :471 1:114 1:511sl     6 119   65¾ 32  11  1¾   Lipham T7  Cal Derby 77-27 ParisPrince,TanksBrigade,BillyBll 12
10Apr83-4SA   1⅛ :46  1:102 1:492ft   18e 120   88½ 75¾ 55  58¾  Lipham T3  S A Derby 73-19 Marfa, My Habitony, Naevus 10
23Mar83-8SA   6½f :22  :442 1:151ft    11 117   4nk 34  33  26   DelhoussyeE4 Baldwin 88-19 TotlDprtur,PrisPrinc,Morry'sChmp 9
23Feb83-8SA   6f :214  :442 1:093ft     4 120   62¼ 44  41¾ 58¼  DlhossyE2 Bolsa Chica 82-19 Dedicata, Maariv, Hyperborean 6
12Feb83-8SA   7f :223  :452 1:222ft    12 119   63¼ 63¼ 47½ 45¼  DlhssyE7 San Vicente 83-14 Shecky Blue, Full Choke, Naevus 7
      12Feb83—Wide throughout
27Nov82-8Hol  7f :214  :434 1:212ft    3½ 119   53½ 64¼ 57½ 67½  PincyLJr1 Hol Prevue 82-14 Copelan, R. Awacs, Desert Wine 8
17Nov82-3Hol  6f :222  :451 1:091ft  *3-2 120   2½  2hd 11½ 14   Pincay L Jr5 Aw21000 91-17 PrisPrince,RollANturl,‡SterlingSilv 7
30Oct82-8SA   1 1/16 :45 1:091 1:413ft  4 118   811 912 710 49¼  Pincay L Jr6 Norfolk 84-10 Roving Boy, Desert Wine, Aguila 9
20Oct82-8SA   1 1/16 :464 1:113 1:433ft *7-5 117  1½ 1hd 1½ 12¼  PincayLJr5 El Rio Rey 83-16 ParisPrince,WildAgin,Morry'sChmp 8
7Oct82-8Bel   1 1/16 Ⓣ:4741:1131:42 fm 3½ 113   2hd 54  55½ 46   VelsquzJ3 Prince John 80-14 Caveat, Fortnightly, Nivernay 7
16Sep82-8Bel  6½f :223 :461 1:181ft    13 122   21  32  31  2½   Graell A5  Aw19000 84-19 Cast Party, ParisPrince,SmartStyle 9
28Aug82-5Sar  6f :22   :453 1:113ft  *8-5 118   1hd 1hd 1½  11   Graell A2  Mdn 82-13 ParisPrince,StopCrd,ClssicMoment 8
    May 5 CD 4f ft :483 b       Apr 17 SA Ⓣ 4f fm :494 h       Apr 3 SA 4f ft :474 h       Mar 18 SA 5f ft 1:00 h
```

```
Total Departure                             B. c. 3, by Greek Answer—Life Style, by Manifesto
                                            Br.—Hartigan J H (Fla)                       1983  5  1  1  1      $75,569
Own.—Rebalot Stable                    126  Tr.—Lukas D Wayne                            1982  8  4  0  0     $315,469
                                       Lifetime   13  5  1  1   $391,038
30Apr83-9CD   1 :462 1:11  1:374m      3¾ 122   51½ 21  1½  2hd  Velasquez J11 Dby Trl 80-28 Caveat,TotalDeparture,PaxInBello 14
10Apr83-4SA   1⅛ :46  1:102 1:492ft   3½e 120   1hd 11½ 11  46¾  Pincay LJr2 S A Derby 75-20 Marfa, My Habitony, Naevus 10
23Mar83-8SA   6½f :22  :442 1:151ft    *2 117   2hd 1½  13  16   Pincay L Jr9 Baldwin 94-19 TotlDprtur,PrisPrinc,Morry'sChmp 9
19Jan83-9GP   7f :22   :443 1:232ft    *2 123   11  11½ 21½ 69   Fires E1 ⓈFloridian H 78-20 Pure Grit, Sunny Looking, Bet Big 9
8Jan83-9GP    6f :22   :443 1:10 sy  *2-3 122   12  2hd 21  32   Fires E1 Spect'ul Bid 87-17 FreezingRin,WriteOff,TotlDeprture 9
30Oct82-8SA   1 1/16 :45 1:091 1:413ft  7 118   1hd 2hd 47½ 716  McCarron CJ8 Norfolk 77-10 Roving Boy, Desert Wine, Aguila 9
9Oct82-7Bel   1 :452 1:102 1:374ft      8 122   1hd 21½ 36  59¾  Fell J8 Champagne 66-25 Copelan, PappaRiccio,ElCubanaso 13
29Sep82-8Bel  7f :223  :451 1:242ft  *8-5 122   2½  2½  33½ 72½  Fires E10 Cowdin 77-18 What'sDat,PappaRiccio,CastParty 11
28Aug82-8AP   7f :22   :45  1:233ft  *7-5 122   11½ 12½ 13½ 16   Fires E3 Arlwashfut 84-21 TotlDeprture,CoxMMtt,HighIndPrk 8
11Aug82-8AP   6f :223  :46  1:111ft   7-5 124   12½ 13½ 13  13¾  Fires E6 Arch Ward 86-17 TotlDeprture,HighIndPrk,PssingBs 8
28Jly82-8AP   5½f :22  :454 1:044ft  *4-5 115   2½  2hd 12½ 13   Fires E8 Joliet 91-24 TotalDeparture,SpreCrd,PrePlnned 9
5Jly82-8AP    5½f :214 :452 1:042ft  *3-5 115   31½ 31  43½ 47¾  Fires E5 Primer 85-14 GreatHunter,PssingBse,HighIndPrk 6
21Apr82-3GP   5f :223  :46   :581ft   8-5 122   13  15  17  111  Fires E12 Mdn 95-20 TotlDprtr,ProspctvFlsh,NtTwTms 12
    Apr 6 SA 5f ft 1:012 h       Mar 31 SA 6f ft 1:124 h
```

```
Sunny's Halo *                              Ch. c. 3, by Halo—Mostly Sunny, by Sunny
                                            Br.—Foster D J (Ont-C)                       1983  2  2  0  0     $245,190
Own.—D J Foster Stable                 126  Tr.—Cross David C Jr                         1982 11  5  2  1     $235,829
                                       Lifetime   13  7  2  1   $481,019
16Apr83-9OP   1⅛ :462 1:113 1:492ft    *3 126   15  15  14  14   DelhoussyE13 Ark Dby 96-19 Sunny's Halo, Caveat, Exile King 14
26Mar83-9OP   170 :462 1:121 1:421gd   2½ 121   41¾ 51¼ 1hd 13   Snyder L2 Rebel H 85-15 Sunny's Halo, Sligh Jet,LeCouCou 11
      26Mar83—Boxed in stretch turn
4Nov82-6Med   1 1/16 :454 1:093 1:432ft 30 122  31  34½ 47½ 69   PennaD10 Yng Amer'a 83-14 Slewpy, Bet Big, El Cubanaso 11
23Oct82-8Lrl  1 1/16 :463 1:123 1:45 ft *2½ 122 1hd 42  811 916  BrcclVJr9 Lrl Futurity 67-21 CstPrty,PxInBello,PrimitivePlesur 11
11Oct82-9WO   1⅛ :472 1:122 1:533sy  *1-4 122   14  16  16  17½  PnnD3 ⓈCoro'n Fut'y 72-29 Snny'sHlo,RsngYongStr,HlbrtnHsk 8
25Sep82-9WO   1 1/16 :472 1:124 1:452sy *1-3 123 11½ 13 15  16½  Penna D1 Grey 82-28 Snny'sHlo,RsngYngStr,HrdScrmblr 9
12Sep82-9WO   7f :233  :462 1:234ft  *4-5 122   1½  11½ 13½ 17¾  Penna D4 Swynford 90-20 Sunny'sHlo,ScrtWrd,RsngYoungStr 6
18Aug82-8Sar  6f :22   :443 1:102ft    2½ 122   42½ 42  55  57½  Fell J5 Sanford 80-15 Copelan, Smart Style, Safe Ground 5
21Jly82-8Bel  6f :224  :453 1:101ft  *8-5 122   33½ 33½ 33  32   Fell J3 Tremont 89-17 Laus'Cause,RulingGold,Sunny'sHlo 6
4Jly82-9WO    6f :221  :453 1:102ft  *6-5 114   43  3½  15  110  Penna D3 Colin 91-12 Snny'sHlo,SqrCornwll,‡MyrnsRssn 10
19Jun82-7WO   5½f :22  :454 1:053sy    2¾ 115   31½ 34  34½ 21¾  Penna D1 ⓈClarendon 87-19 SvnStons,Sunny'sHlo,SqurCornwll 10
24May82-9WO   5f :22   :452  :581ft    2¾ 117   57  411 26  28½  Penna D5 Victoria 86-18 Flying Pocket, Sunny'sHalo,Snazee 7
9May82-4WO    5f :231  :483 1:014ft    4½ 120   76¼ 68  44  1hd  Penna D7 ⓈMdn 77-25 Sunny'sHalo,TugO'Nr,RiseARegent 9
    May 1 CD 1 sy 1:413 h       ●Apr 26 CD 1 ft 1:433 b       Apr 10 OP 1 ft 1:40 h       Apr 5 OP 6f sy 1:183 b
```

Explosive Wagon *
Ch. c. 3, by Explodent—Gypsy Wagon, by Conestoga
Br.—Windy City Stable (Fla) 1983 6 3 0 1 $68,460
Own.—McReynolds Peggy 126 Tr.—Norman Gene 1982 9 6 2 1 $82,650
Lifetime 15 9 2 2 $151,110
23Apr83-9LaD 1 1/16 :484 1:134 1:452sl *2-5 124 4nk 1hd 14 14 MuellrC2 Hldy In Dxie 85-22 ExplosvWgon,Empr'sClths,Hrrwgt 7
27Mar83-11FG 1⅛ :474 1:123 1:503ft *6-5 123 64½ 64 54 55½ Mueller C8 La Dby 85-19 BalboNtive,FoundPerlHrbor,Slewpy 8
27Mar83—Rank early, carried out first turn
12Mar83-10FG 1 1/16 :482 1:13 1:434ft *4-5 119 51¾ 31½ 11½ 15½ Mueller C2 Dby Trl 93-14 ExplosvWgon,HlToRom,TmrtyPrnc 7
19Feb83-10FG 1 1/16 :472 1:114 1:45 ft 13 116 76¾ 55½ 2hd 13 MuellrC8 Le Comte H 87-19 ExplosvWgon,FndPrlHrbr,PrntFrl 11
5Feb83-9FG 6f :214 :453 1:11 ft 9-5 120 13 12 31 56¾ Mueller C6 Blk Gold H 83-17 ProntoForli,OnForAunti,WillowDriv 7
15Jan83-9FG 6f :22 :454 1:111ft *1-3 122 2½ 1½ 2hd 34 Mueller C5 HcpO 85-18 ProntoForl,WllowDrv,ExplosvWgon 9
31Dec82-9FG 6f :213 :454 1:112ft 2½ 119 64½ 52¾ 11½ 14 MullrC3 Sugar Bowl H 88-22 ExplosvWgn,ErnstLck,Mndbgglng 10
12Dec82-5FG 6f :222 :46 1:122gd *4-5 116 1hd 1½ 1hd 1½ Mueller C2 Aw11000 83-22 ExplosiveWagon,Hmlet,ChnceALot 9
17Oct82-4LaD 6½f :221 :443 1:161ft *8-5 122 2½ 2hd 1hd 18 Mueller C6 Aw17000 101-07 ExplosvWgon,ChncALot,HlToRom 12
2Oct82-9LaD 6½f :223 :453 1:17 ft 9½ 122 2½ 11 13½ 13 Mueller C4 Aw18000 97-09 ExplosiveWagon,WildAgin,JoeJoe 12
24Sep82-6LaD 6f :23 :462 1:12 ft *9-5 122 41½ 3nk 2½ 1nk Mueller C5 Aw14000 89-15 ExplosvWgon,MomntOfRlty,DblLn 12
3Sep82-9LaD 6f :23 :461 1:12 ft 2½ 120 2½ 22 22½ 21 Mueller C2 Aw14000 88-12 ChncALot,ExplosvWgon,ChrlyKrk 10
27Aug82-7LaD 6f :222 :453 1:12 ft 4½ 122 41½ 2hd 11½ 32 Perrodin E J4 Aw15000 87-10 Mr.Stormn,Soy'sHop,ExplosvWgn 10
6Aug82-6LaD 6f :223 :454 1:111ft *8-5 120 41¾ 33 34 24 Mueller C4 Aw12500 89-10 TmrtyPrnc,ExplsvWgn,SnbrndBby 11
22Jly82-5LaD 6f :222 :454 1:131ft 4 120 14 16 16 14½ Mueller C7 Mdn 83-16 ExplosvWgn,OcnKngdm,LndngChf 12
●May 5 CD 5f ft 1:001 h Apr 21 LaD 4f ft :473 b Apr 16 LaD 5f ft :58 b Mar 25 FG 4f ft :492 b

Current Hope
Ro. c. 3, by Little Current—Kahoolawe, by Warfare
Br.—Mabee Mr-Mrs J C (Ky) 1983 5 3 1 0 $213,293
Own.—Baker & Kaskel 126 Tr.—Laurin Roger 1982 8 2 0 2 $50,244
Lifetime 13 5 1 2 $263,537
2Apr83-10Hia 1⅛ :471 1:111 1:492ft 37 122 149½ 64 1½ 1nk Solis A11 Flamingo 85-18 CurrntHop,Chmmng,Gn'lPrcttonr 14
2Apr83—Wide, driving
5Mar83-11GP 1⅛ :481 1:113 1:494ft 10 122 97¾ 78½ 79 710 VlsquzJ10 Flordia Dby 73-19 Croeso, Copelan, Law Talk 13
21Feb83-10GP 1 1/16 :474 1:12 1:433ft 4½ 117 45½ 23 2½ 22½ MacBethD7 Ftn Youth 81-24 Copelan, Current Hope, Blink 8
21Feb83—Run in two divisions 9th & 10th races
9Feb83-9GP 7f :221 :45 1:224ft 9½ 114 1311 94¾ 1hd 1no Solis A11 Hutcheson 90-24 CurrntHop,HighlndPrk,CountryPn 13
9Feb83—Lost whip
15Jan83-7GP 7f :222 :45 1:233ft 3½ 1145 77½ 77½ 13 16 Solis A2 Aw15000 86-20 CurrentHope,ElCubno,DerbyDouble 9
27Nov82-8Aqu 1 :461 1:12 1:373ft 13 114 89¾ 44 54 69½ Fell J8 Nashua 69-29 IEnclose,LoosCnnon,MomntofJoy 11
4Nov82-6Med 1 1/16 :454 1:093 1:432ft 33 119 916 811 68½ 58¾ Fell J1 Yng Amer'a 83-14 Slewpy, Bet Big, El Cubanaso 11
23Oct82-8Lrl 1 1/16 :463 1:123 1:45 ft 31 122 107¾ 2hd 12 46¾ Fell J8 Lrl Futurity 76-21 CstPrty,PxInBello,PrimitivePlesur 11
16Oct82-3Aqu 7f :231 :47 1:244ft *6-5 117 11½ 11½ 15 13 Cordero AJr1 Aw19000 77-26 CurrentHope,ProudCapitl,Ski'sHert 7
29Sep82-6Bel 7f :224 :453 1:233ft 2½ 117 55 52¾ 32 35½ Russ M L3 Aw19000 78-18 WhiteBirch,GlxyGuide,CurrentHope 8
29Sep82—Forced wide
7Jly82-7Bel 5½f :221 :46 1:053ft 7 115 35 34½ 42½ 53½ Russ M L1 Juvenile 84-18 Victorious,NorthernIce,Laus'Cause 7
24Jun82-4Bel 6f :23 :461 1:103ft 11 118 11½ 11 12 14 Russ M L9 Mdn 89-12 CrrntHop,LgndryWlth,FlonosFllw 10
3Jun82-4Bel 5f :222 :453 :574ft 3½ 117 22 22 24 38½ Russ M L3 Mdn 97-12 What's Dat, Sluggard,CurrentHope 8
May 5 CD 4f ft :48 h Apr 30 CD 1 sy 1:464 b Apr 25 Kee 6f gd 1:163 b Apr 18 Bel tr.t 5f ft :594 h

Luv A Libra
B. c. 3, by Diplomat Way—Lip Talk, by Assagai
Br.—Farnsworth Farm (Fla) 1983 5 0 2 0 $19,180
Own.—DeCosta Viviann & Yagoda 126 Tr.—Gustines Heliodoro 1982 15 2 5 3 $213,638
Lifetime 20 2 7 3 $232,818
30Apr83-9CD 1 :462 1:11 1:374m 15 122 108 74½ 77¾ 712 Fires E6 Dby Trl 68-28 Caveat,TotalDeparture,PaxInBello 14
2Apr83-10Hia 1⅛ :471 1:111 1:492ft 69 122 84¾ 96 83½ 42 Fires E4 Flamingo 83-18 CurrntHop,Chmmng,Gn'lPrcttonr 14
2Apr83—Shuffled back
23Mar83-5Hia 7f :23 :453 1:22 ft 2½ 115 42 1hd 2½ 22 Vasquez J4 Aw11000 91-16 Country Pine, Luv ALibra,Tarmoud 7
12Mar83-6Hia 6f :222 :454 1:111ft 4¾ 115 4¾ 44½ 41¾ 2hd Alvarado V1 Aw11000 87-14 Sylvia's Time, Luv A Libra, Truby 8
12Mar83—Taken up
5Jan83-9Crc 1 1/16 :474 1:13 1:463ft 54 121 87 119½ 1010 1012 Lee M A2 Trp Pk Dby 74-19 My Mac, Caveat, Blink 11
18Dec82-9Crc 1 70 :472 1:122 1:422ft 10 120 46½ 615 819 924 RssML2 What A Pleas 74-13 WorldAppel,MyMc,SunnyLooking 11
13Nov82-8Aqu 1⅛ :482 1:124 1:501gd 33 122 31 2½ 47 49¾ Vergara O5 Remsen 74-20 PxInBllo,Chumming,PrimitivPlsur 11
4Nov82-6Med 1 1/16 :454 1:093 1:432ft 75 122 711 711 816 815 Maple E3 Yng Amer'a 77-14 Slewpy, Bet Big, El Cubanaso 11
9Oct82-7Bel 1 :452 1:102 1:374ft 26 122 1012 918 917 817 Lee M A6 Champagne 59-25 Copelan, PappaRiccio,ElCubanaso 13
25Sep82-9Crc 1 1/16 :481 1:134 1:474ft 7 120 63¾ 53½ 21½ 1nk LeeMA1 [S]Fla Stallion 80-15 Luv A Libra, Blink, El Kaiser 14
13Sep82-9Crc 1 :484 1:133 1:401ft *1 112 2½ 2½ 2hd 2no Aviles O B4 Aw13000 87-20 Bobbi's Pleasure, Luv ALibra,Blink 6
28Aug82-9Crc 6f :212 :452 1:12 ft 21 118 87½ 59 54¾ 23½ LeeMA2 [S]Fla Stallion 88-10 El Kaiser, Luv A Libra, Blink 11
20Aug82-9Crc 6f :221 :461 1:124ft *6-5 114 54½ 44½ 41¾ 21 Lee M A4 Aw9500 87-19 King Billy, Luv A Libra, Top Case 7
31Jly82-9Crc 5½f :221 :461 1:053ft 46 116 86¾ 97¾ 66¾ 56½ LeeMA6 [S]Fla Stallion 90-15 ElKiser,NightMover,HelloHndsom 13
10Jly82-9Crc 5½f :22 :454 1:05 ft 24 113 57½ 57½ 53½ 35½ Lee M A2 Criterium 95-11 El Kaiser, Night Mover, LuvALibra 6
28Jun82-5Crc 5½f :224 :473 1:073ft 2½e115 54 32½ 12 14½ Lee M A2 Mdn 87-20 LuvALibr,MonsieurNsty,‡DrvishHro 9
9Jun82-4Crc 5f :224 :46 1:00 ft 10 115 53 46 45½ 26½ Danjean R7 Mdn 85-24 NightMover,LuvALibr,Gloversville 10
27May82-2Crc 5f :224 :471 1:011sy *3-5 115 34½ 36 35 2½ Aviles O B6 M40000 85-20 CrowningWish,LuvALibr,Km'sDlvry 7
17May82-6Crc 5f :224 :473 1:011ft *2½ 115 33 45½ 42 31½ Danjean R1 Mdn 84-17 Bobbi'sPlesur,Glovrsvill,LuvALibr 12
30Apr82-3GP 5f :23 :47 :592gd 6 122 2½ 2hd 21½ 33½ Londono O J3 Mdn 85-18 Cordon, Gun Carriage, Luv A Libra 8
May 5 CD 4f ft :502 b Apr 29 CD 3f sy :381 b Apr 24 Hia 5f sy :592 b Apr 20 Hia 6f ft 1:133 h

Marfa ✻
Own.—French Jr, Beal & Lukas 126
Gr. c. 3, by Foolish Pleasure—Gray Matter, by Stratmat
Br.—Gentry T (Ky) 1983 9 3 3 0 $384,544
Tr.—Lukas D Wayne 1982 2 M 0 1 $2,400
Lifetime 11 3 3 1 $386,944
28Apr83-7Kee 1⅛ :464 1:11 1:492sy *3-2 121 69½ 56 2hd 2no† VelsquezJ7 Blue Grass 90-16 Play Fellow, ‡Marfa, Desert Wine 12
†28Apr83—Disqualified and placed fourth, bore in upper stretch
10Apr83-4SA 1⅛ :46 1:102 1:492ft 3½e 120 78¼ 65½ 31½ 13 VelsquezJ7 S A Derby 82-19 Marfa, My Habitony, Naevus 10
26Mar83-9Lat 1 1/16 :461 1:103 1:422ft *3½ 120 46 31½ 1hd 18 Velasquez J10 Spiral 98-24 Marfa, Noble Home, Hail ToRome 12
26Mar83—Daily Racing Form Time 1:44 1/5; Lugged in
16Mar83-8SA 1 1/16 :461 1:104 1:423ft *2 117 84¾ 84½ 56½ 45½ PincayLJr7 S Catalina 82-17 FastPassge,Hyperboren,MyHbitony 8
16Mar83—Forced wide 7/8 turn, lugged in through stretch
6Mar83-5SA 1 1/16 :46 1:104 1:433ft 5½ 120 76¾ 54½ 2hd 2nk Toro F7 Aw20000 83-17 Silent Fox, Marfa,LouisvilleSummit 9
6Mar83—Wide 3/8 turn lugged in through stretch; Broke slowly
13Feb83-6SA 1 1/16 :463 1:112 1:432ft 4 118 43 11 15 13½ Toro F10 Mdn 84-12 Marfa, Blue Seas, Gato Montes 12
13Feb83—Off poorly wide
30Jan83-4SA 7f :221 :451 1:244gd 2¼ 118 35 31½ 2½ 2no Toro F4 Mdn 76-22 Added Feature, Marfa, Flint Fire 7
9Jan83-6SA 1 1/16 :461 1:104 1:414ft 3½ 118 66½ 53½ 55½ 56 Toro F6 Mdn 86-09 Major Henry, Fast Screen,BlueSeas 8
1Jan83-4SA 6f :213 :444 1:094ft 7½ 118 912 911 75¼ 22 Pincay L Jr3 Mdn 87-11 Fast Passage, Marfa, Viron 10
7Nov82-6Hol 1 1/16 :471 1:114 1:44 ft 7½ 118 52¼ 31½ 32 34½ Pincay L Jr2 Mdn 70-20 EminentLad,RightOnCenter,Marfa 10
17Oct82-6SA 1 1/16 :461 1:104 1:422ft 4¼ 117 51¾ 53¾ 710 825 Pincay L Jr7 Mdn 64-09 FfthDvson,SomthngByond,Estpnd 10
Apr 22 Kee 5f ft 1:001 b Apr 4 SA 5f ft 1:013 h

Highland Park ✻
Own.—Bwamazon Farm & Jones 126
Ch. c. 3, by Raise a Native—Old Goat, by Olden Times
Br.—Bwamazon Farm (Ky) 1983 4 2 1 0 $76,648
Tr.—Basile Anthony 1982 11 6 2 3 $306,210
Lifetime 15 8 3 3 $382,858
28Apr83-7Kee 1⅛ :464 1:11 1:492sy 2½e 121 33½ 34½ 68¼ 715 BrumfldD6 Blue Grass 75-16 Play Fellow, ‡Marfa, Desert Wine 12
19Apr83-7Kee 1 1/16 :471 1:112 1:444ft *1-3 123 32 2hd 1hd 1no Vasquez J3 Aw28000 82-18 HighlandPrk,PssingBse,RomnForce 8
21Feb83-9GP 1 1/16 :481 1:12 1:443ft *2-3 122 2hd 2hd 1½ 1nk BrumfildD9 Ftn Youth 78-24 HighlandPark,Thlssocrt,Chumming 9
21Feb83—Run in two divisions 9th & 10th races
9Feb83-9GP 7f :221 :45 1:224ft *9-5 122 61 31½ 2hd 2no BrumfildD9 Hutcheson 90-24 CurrntHop,HighlndPrk,CountryPn 13
20Nov82-8CD 1 1/16 :50 1:143 1:47 sy *3-5 122 22 22 21½ 13¼ BrumfildD2 Jcky Club 73-26 Highland Park,CoaxMeMatt,Caveat 5
6Nov82-8CD 1 :464 1:112 1:381ft *2-5 122 31 2½ 11½ 16 Brumfield D7 Iroquois 78-24 HighlandPark,CoxMeMtt,WhiteFig 8
16Oct82-7Kee 1 1/16 :471 1:112 1:433ft 2¾ 121 3½ 2hd 2hd 1no Lively J10 Brdrs' Fut 88-17 HighlandPark,Caveat,BrightBaron 12
9Oct82-6Kee a7f 1:283sy *6-5 123 1hd 11 12 14½ Brumfield D2 Aw28200 80-22 HighlndPrk,WillowDrv,RunForGrco 6
28Aug82-8AP 7f :22 :45 1:233ft 9½ 122 52¼ 43½ 35½ 36½ RomrRP8 Ap Wsh Fut 77-21 TotlDeprture,CoxMMtt,HighlndPrk 8
11Aug82-8AP 6f :223 :46 1:111ft 3 124 33 35 23 23¾ RomroRP3 Arch Ward 82-17 TotlDeprture,HighlndPrk,PssingBs 8
23Jly82-8Aks 6f :22 :45 1:11 ft *7-5 113 42 2½ 1½ 12½ Romero R P6 Juvenile 82-20 HighlandPark,HandStand,TriSwps 10
5Jly82-8AP 5½f :214 :452 1:042ft 2½e 115 52¼ 52½ 22 3¾ Romero R P3 Primer 92-14 GreatHunter,PssingBse,HighlndPrk 6
30May82-3AP 5f :223 :463 :591ft 9-5 122 11 11½ 12½ 17 Fires E3 Mdn 90-23 HighlandPark,SpareCard,FinalFight 7
20Apr82-3Kee 4½f :223 :454 :52 ft 2 118 4 2hd 21 23 Brumfield D2 Mdn 92-05 BoldUprsng,HghlndPrk,KntnLndng 8
3Apr82-3Kee 4½f :222 :464 :531gd *6-5 119 4 52¼ 32 31¾ Brumfield D5 Mdn 87-11 It'sDewn,HppinessRod,HighlndPrk 11
May 5 CD 4f ft :48 h Apr 25 Kee 5f gd 1:013 b ●Apr 18 Kee 3f ft :35 h ●Apr 14 Kee 1 ft 1:422 h

Caveat ✻
Own.—Belmont A et al 126
Dk. b. or br. c. 3, by Cannonade—Cold Hearted, by The Axe II
Br.—Ryehill Farm (MD) 1983 7 1 3 0 $144,458
Tr.—Stephens Woodford C 1982 11 3 3 3 $133,432
Lifetime 18 4 6 3 $277,890 Turf 5 3 2 0 $78,656
30Apr83-9CD 1 :462 1:11 1:374m *3-2e 122 138¾137 43½ 1hd Pincay L Jr9 Dby Trl 80-28 Caveat,TotalDeparture,PaxInBello 14
16Apr83-9OP 1⅛ :462 1:113 1:492ft 8¾ 120 1319 1012 35½ 24 Maple E11 Ark Dby 92-19 Sunny's Halo, Caveat, Exile King 14
16Apr83—Bumped soundly at 3/8 pole
6Apr83-9OP 1 1/16 :482 1:141 1:45 ft 8-5 116 44 43 2hd 2hd Maple S3 Aw30000 83-26 Exile King, Caveat, Sligh Jet 5
19Mar83-10Hia 1⅛ :453 1:093 1:484ft 4¾ 114 64½ 43½ 42 41 Maple E1 Everglades 87-18 Gn'lPrcttnr,OhMyWndlnd,PlyFllw 12
19Mar83—Hit by whip
5Mar83-11GP 1⅛ :481 1:113 1:494ft 22 122 1210 1112 913 1016 Maple E11 Flordia Dby 67-19 Croeso, Copelan, Law Talk 13
21Feb83-10GP 1 1/16 :474 1:12 1:433ft 3½ 117 57 65¼ 46 58½ Maple E6 Ftn Youth 74-24 Copelan, Current Hope, Blink 8
21Feb83—Bumped; Run in two divisions 9th & 10th races
5Jan83-9Crc 1 1/16 :474 1:13 1:463ft 4 121 1010 96¾ 43 2½ Maple E9 Trp Pk Dby 85-19 My Mac, Caveat, Blink 11
29Dec82-9Crc 7f :222 :453 1:253ft *2-5 119 65 57½ 37½ 35¼ Brumfield D2 Aw20000 83-17 Gn'lPrcttonr,Morgnmorgnmrgn,Cvt 7
27Nov82-8Lrl 1 1/16 :474 1:134 1:451ft *1 122 86 64½ 21 31½ MplE4 [S]Maryland Juv 81-26 DixieIndBnd,DeputedTestmony,Cvt 9
20Nov82-8CD 1 1/16 :50 1:143 1:47 sy 7-5 122 43 33 32 36 Maple E3 Jcky Club 67-26 Highland Park,CoaxMeMatt,Caveat 5
25Oct82-8Aqu 1⅛ Ⓣ:502 1:162 1:573sf *3-2 122 87 62 2hd 2hd Maple E1 Pilgrim 56-56 Fortnightly,Cavet,DomintingDooley 8
16Oct82-7Kee 1 1/16 :471 1:112 1:433ft 2 121 84¾ 63¼ 1hd 2no Maple E2 Brdrs' Fut 88-17 HighlandPark,Caveat,BrightBaron 12
7Oct82-8Bel 1 1/16 Ⓣ:474 1:113 1:42 fm 2¾ 117 53 31½ 1½ 12 Maple E1 Prince John 86-14 Caveat, Fortnightly, Nivernay 7
10Sep82-9Bel 1 Ⓣ:461 1:111 1:35 fm *9-5 119 64 41 2½ 1no Maple E7 Aw20000 90-12 Caveat,LoverBoyLeslie,ElCubanso 11
10Aug82-9Sar 1 [T]:502 1:152 1:404yl *2 118 85½ 2hd 14 19 Maple E4 Mdn 72-28 Caveat, Sobieski, So Intent 10
16Jly82-4Bel 7f Ⓣ:231 :462 1:252fm 3½e 118 41½ 43½ 2½ 2nk Bailey J D6 Mdn 77-18 Bartow, Caveat, Upper Court 12
9Jly82-4Bel 6f :224 :463 1:113ft 4e 118 1½ 41½ 68½ 614 Maple E1 Mdn 70-22 CthdrlAsl,DomntngDly,NghtTmBg 11
18Jun82-4Bel 5f :223 :462 :591ft 2¼ 118 54½ 53¾ 53 56 Cordero A Jr7 Mdn 92-15 PrimitivePlesure,CthdrlAisl,Lutyns 8
May 5 CD 4f ft :493 b Apr 28 CD 4f ft :51 b Apr 23 Bel 6f ft 1:114 h ●Apr 13 OP 4f sy :474 h

The chart of the race was as follows:

109th Kentucky Derby

EIGHTH RACE
Churchill
MAY 7, 1983

1 ¼ MILES. (1.59⅖) 109th Running KENTUCKY DERBY (Grade I). Purse $250,000 added. 3-year-olds. By subscription of $200 each. All nomination fees to the winner, $5,000 to pass the entry box, $5,000 additional to start, with $250,000 added of which $60,000 to second, $30,000 to third and $15,000 to fourth (to be divided equally in the event of a dead heat). Weight 126 lbs. Starters to be named through the entry box Thursday, May 5, at usual time of closing. The maximum number of starters for the Kentucky Derby will be limited to twenty. In the event more than twenty entries pass through the entry box at the time of closing, the twenty starters and up to eight also eligibles will be determined at that time with preference given to those horses that have accumulated the highest earnings. Should any entry be withdrawn from the starting field prior to 4 p.m. scratch time, Friday, May 6, vacancies will be filled from the also eligible list and placed in the outside post positions in order of preference. For those that pass the entry box and are eliminated under this condition the entry fee will be refunded. Gold trophy to the winning owner. Closed with 405 nominations Tuesday, February 15, 1983.
Value of race $531,000, value to winner $426,000, second $60,000, third $30,000, fourth $15,000. Mutuel pool $5,546,977.

Last Raced	Horse	Eqt.	A.	Wt	PP	¼	½	¾	1	Str	Fin	Jockey	Odds $1
16Apr83 ^{9}OP^{1}	Sunny's Halo		3	126	10	2^{hd}	$2^{\frac{1}{2}}$	$1^{\frac{1}{2}}$	1^{hd}	$1^{\frac{1}{2}}$	1^{2}	Delahoussaye E	2.50
28Apr83 ^{7}Kee^{2}	Desert Wine		3	126	5	$3^{1\frac{1}{2}}$	3^{3}	3^{hd}	$2^{1\frac{1}{2}}$	$2^{2\frac{1}{2}}$	2^{nk}	McCarron C J	15.90
30Apr83 ^{9}CD^{1}	Caveat	b	3	126	20	$16^{2\frac{1}{2}}$	$17^{1\frac{1}{2}}$	15^{1}	11^{hd}	$7^{1\frac{1}{2}}$	3^{1}	Pincay L Jr	b-6.70
23Apr83 ^{8}Aqu^{1}	Slew O' Gold		3	126	1	$7^{\frac{1}{2}}$	7^{2}	6^{2}	7^{hd}	3^{hd}	4^{nk}	Cordero A Jr	10.10
28Apr83 ^{7}Kee^{4}	Marfa	b	3	126	18	$13^{\frac{1}{2}}$	14^{2}	$14^{1\frac{1}{2}}$	8^{1}	$4^{1\frac{1}{2}}$	5^{1}	Velasquez J	a-2.40
28Apr83 ^{7}Kee^{1}	Play Fellow	b	3	126	2	11^{2}	10^{hd}	$10^{\frac{1}{2}}$	6^{1}	$5^{\frac{1}{2}}$	6^{2}	Cruguet J	10.90
30Apr83 ^{9}CD^{3}	Pax In Bello		3	126	14	8^{hd}	$9^{1\frac{1}{2}}$	$8^{\frac{1}{2}}$	$9^{1\frac{1}{2}}$	6^{hd}	7^{hd}	Fell J	24.40
23Apr83 ^{7}Aqu^{2}	Country Pine		3	126	7	12^{1}	$12^{1\frac{1}{2}}$	$11^{1\frac{1}{2}}$	$10^{\frac{1}{2}}$	$9^{2\frac{1}{2}}$	$8^{2\frac{1}{2}}$	Venezia M	47.40
16Apr83 ^{9}OP^{7}	Balboa Native	b	3	126	3	$19^{\frac{1}{2}}$	16^{hd}	18^{1}	$18^{1\frac{1}{2}}$	14^{hd}	9^{nk}	Hawley S	a-2.40
23Apr83 ^{7}GG^{1}	Paris Prince	b	3	126	16	$9^{1\frac{1}{2}}$	8^{hd}	7^{1}	5^{1}	$8^{1\frac{1}{2}}$	10^{2}	Lipham T	f-10.90
2Apr83 ^{10}Hia^{1}	Current Hope		3	126	12	$18^{\frac{1}{2}}$	20	19^{hd}	17^{1}	$10^{1\frac{1}{2}}$	11^{nk}	Solis A	18.30
30Apr83 ^{9}CD^{5}	Chumming		3	126	4	20	18^{1}	20	19^{1}	13^{2}	12^{nk}	Maple E	b-6.70
28Apr83 ^{7}Kee^{5}	Freezing Rain		3	126	8	17^{2}	$19^{\frac{1}{2}}$	17^{1}	$16^{1\frac{1}{2}}$	$16^{2\frac{1}{2}}$	13^{hd}	Gavidia W	c-23.50
16Apr83 ^{9}OP^{5}	My Mac	b	3	126	15	14^{hd}	15^{3}	16^{1}	15^{hd}	$11^{\frac{1}{2}}$	14^{4}	MacBeth D	f-10.90
23Apr83 ^{9}LaD^{1}	Explosive Wagon		3	126	11	10^{hd}	$11^{1\frac{1}{2}}$	12^{1}	14^{2}	15^{2}	15^{1}	Mueller C	f-10.90
23Apr83 ^{8}Aqu^{2}	Parfaitement		3	126	13	$6^{1\frac{1}{2}}$	6^{1}	$5^{\frac{1}{2}}$	$4^{\frac{1}{2}}$	$12^{\frac{1}{2}}$	16^{2}	McCauley W H	41.20
28Apr83 ^{7}Kee^{7}	Highland Park	b	3	126	19	5^{hd}	5^{2}	$4^{1\frac{1}{2}}$	$3^{1\frac{1}{2}}$	17^{1}	17^{hd}	Brumfield D	c-23.50
30Apr83 ^{9}CD^{7}	Luv A Libra		3	126	17	4^{hd}	4^{hd}	9^{1}	12^{1}	19^{6}	18^{2}	Espinoza J C	f-10.90
13Apr83 ^{1}Aqu^{2}	Law Talk		3	126	6	15^{2}	13^{hd}	13^{1}	13^{1}	$18^{1\frac{1}{2}}$	19^{15}	Marquez C	f-10.90
30Apr83 ^{9}CD^{2}	Total Departure		3	126	9	$1^{\frac{1}{2}}$	$1^{1\frac{1}{2}}$	2^{1}	20	20	20	Valenzuela P A	a-2.40

a–Coupled: Marfa, Balboa Native and Total Departure; b–Caveat and Chumming; c–Freezing Rain and Highland Park. f—Mutuel field.

OFF AT 5:40. Start good, Won driving. Time, :23⅘, :47⅕, 1:11⅘, 1:36⅘, 2:02⅕ Track fast.

$2 Mutuel Prices:			
8–SUNNY'S HALO	7.00	4.80	4.00
6–DESERT WINE		12.20	9.80
2–CAVEAT (b–entry)			5.20

Ch. c, by Halo—Mostly Sunny, by Sunny. Trainer Cross David C Jr. Bred by Foster D J (Ont–C).

SUNNY'S HALO, rating kindly from the beginning, assumed command on his own courage in the backstretch, drew away from DESERT WINE under a hand ride in the upper stretch and maintained his margin under steady right-hand urging the final furlong. DESERT WINE stalked SUNNY'S HALO from the outside, could not stay with SUNNY'S HALO after drawing on even terms with him just before the quarter-pole, but continued resolutely under left-hand urging and held off CAVEAT's late bid for the place. CAVEAT, taken in hand and eased toward the inside for a saving of ground after the start, was forced extremely wide rallying around CURRENT HOPE into the stretch and closed steadily in a very good effort. SLEW O' GOLD, bothered slightly by PLAY FELLOW at the start, saved ground most of the way and bested MARFA in a duel with that rival through the homestretch. MARFA relaxed outside horses off of the pace, maintained a straight course under a left-hand whip in the stretch drive and lacked a sufficient response. PLAY FELLOW, in good position behind the first flight, was hanging when jockey Cruguet misjudged the finish line and rose for a stride at the sixteenth marker, and finished out evenly. PAX IN BELLO had a clear run at the leaders along the rail for the drive and failed to respond. COUNTRY PINE gave an even effort. BALBOA NATIVE made up some ground belatedly. PARIS PRINCE stayed outside rivals and tired. CURRENT HOPE was steered very wide for the stretch run. CHUMMING gave a dull effort. FREEZING RAIN was not a serious factor. MY MAC was outrun. EXPLOSIVE WAGON tired. PARFAITEMENT lost ground outside the first flight and faltered. HIGHLAND PARK stayed outside SUNNY'S HALO and DESERT WINE into the final turn before giving way. LUV A LIBRA was used up early. LAW TALK showed nothing. TOTAL DEPARTURE, brushed by SUNNY'S HALO at the start, stopped after going three-quarters in a race remarkably free of trouble for the size of the field.

Owners— 1, D J Foster Racing Stable; 2, Cardiff Stud & T 90 Ranch; 3, Belmont A et al; 4, Equusequity Stable; 5, Beal & French Jr & Lukas; 6, Vanier Nancy & Lauer & Victor; 7, Willcox Mrs A A; 8, Galbreath D M; 9, Spreen R H; 10, Green Dolly; 11, Baker & Kaskel; 12, Hickory Tree Stable; 13, Bwamazon Farm; 14, Aronow Stable; 15, McReynolds Peggy; 16, Daney Mrs Bernard; 17, Bwamazon Farm & Jones; 18, DeCosta Viviann & Yagoda; 19, Buckram Oak Farm; 20, Rebalot Stable.

Delahoussaye ran a perfect race with Sunny's Halo and beat the fading Desert Wine by 2 lengths. Sunny's Halo won the $426,000 first prize and racing immortality. It was a great day for trainer Cross and the owner, Toronto stockbroker Pud Foster. Mrs. Cross won $20,000 on her bet. Desert Wine held on for second, just edging out the late-charging Caveat and Slew O' Gold. Marfa had a charge at the mile pole but was unable to challenge the leaders. He was never a factor in the race. It is interesting that the top five finishers were ridden by the top five jockeys listed in Table 11.1. The three California leaders, Pincay, McCarron, and Delahoussaye, finished 3-2-1. Delahoussaye had turned in a rare double, complementing his win in 1982 with Gato Del Sol. He also had a second on the 34–1 shot Woodhopper in 1981. Sunny's Halo paid a handsome $4 to show, so our bet of $87 was doubled. With my $50 win bet subtracted, our profit was $37.

IT WAS NEVER LIKE THIS IN LOUISIANA

The ninth race was a $1\frac{1}{16}$-mile claiming race for four-year-olds and upward for a purse of $10,000. The field of eight horses included the entry of Dust Off the Mat and Broadway Review. Although Sway, Sorroto, and Major Run were the top choices, the field was wide open. The remaining starters, Bal Bay, Davrick, and Bell Swinger, as well as the entry, looked like tough competition. The extent of the competition and the evenness of the field were borne out by the fact that the morning-line odds varied only within the narrow range of 5–2 to 8–1.

Sway appealed to me. He had won the most money per career start; was recently claimed twice; had finished second in his last start at this distance, running against $50,000 claimers who were superior to today's $35,000 claimers; and he was a very consistent horse, having finished in the money in his last eleven starts and twenty-seven times out of thirty-two career starts. Although consistent, his speed ratings were not really superior to his competition. For example, at Keeneland both Broadway Review and Sorroto had recently run 85s at today's distance, while Sway's second at Oaklawn Park was an 82. It is, of course, difficult to compare speed ratings across days and tracks, but the message was clear: Sway looked good and he liked to be in there close, but I would bet only if the odds were good. They were.

Sway was made an 8–5 favorite, and the tote board read as follows:

	Totals	#5 Sway	Expected Value per Dollar Bet on Sway
With five minutes to post time			
Odds		8—5	
Win	263,172	82,933	
Show	78,790	18,477	1.10
With one minute to post time			
Odds		8—5	
Win	309,244	87,900	
Show	96,649	20,194	1.11

With our betting fortune of $1,531.70, we bet $91 on Sway to show. At post time the tote board read:

	Totals	#5 Sway	Expected Value per Dollar Bet on Sway
Odds		8—5	
Win	328,700	94,398	
Show	102,009	22,468	1.09

Derby Day brings out individuals of many types searching for a day of excitement, some fun, and (hopefully) some winnings. Many want to make a big killing. Close to where we were standing, a fellow from Louisiana was talking about his troubles that day. Going into the ninth race he was about $5,000 behind in his bets. The entry of Dust Off the Mat and Broadway Review at 5–2 looked like it would get him even with a $2,000 win bet. With two good horses, it seemed to be a good bet, so he made it. Things looked good for him when Broadway Review, number 1A, crossed the finish line first. Unfortunately for the man from Louisiana, Don Brumfield, the jockey on the second-place finisher, Bal Bay, claimed foul, and the claim was allowed. It was the second time that day a winner had been disqualified, and he complained that he had had both of them. This reversal did not sit well with the man from Louisiana, who saw his big gain back to even go up in smoke. He rushed out of the track quite angry over his $7,000 loss on the day, yelling that the races were fixed in Kentucky and vowing to never return.

Sway did manage to take third and pay $2.80 for show, so we won our Dr. Z system bet. The chart of the race was as follows:

NINTH RACE
Churchill
MAY 7, 1983

1 1/16 MILES. (1.41⅗) CLAIMING. Purse $10,000. 4-year-olds and upward. Weight, 123 lbs. Non-winners of two races at a mile or over since March 7 allowed 2 lbs.; one such race since April 7, 4 lbs.; two such races since January 7, 6 lbs. Claiming price, $35,000; for each $1,000 to $30,000 allowed 1 lbs. (Races where entered for $27,500 or less no considered.)

Value of race $10,000, value to winner $6,500, second $2,000, third $1,000, fourth $500. Mutuel pool $563,224.

Last Raced	Horse	Eqt.	A.	Wt	PP	St	¼	½	¾	Str	Fin	Jockey	Cl'g Pr	Odds $1
28Apr83 ^{4}Kee^1	[D]Broadway Review		5	121	8	8	8	8	8	3^{hd}	1^{hd}	Gavidia W	35000	a-2.90
19Mar83 ^{10}OP^7	Bal Bay		8	117	1	6	5^4	5^3	$4^{1/2}$	5^2	2^{hd}	Brumfield D	35000	7.70
16Apr83 ^{5}OP^2	Sway		6	117	5	3	2^{hd}	$2^{1/2}$	$1^{1\frac{1}{2}}$	1^{hd}	$3^{3/4}$	Patterson G	35000	1.70
19Apr83 ^{8}Kee^2	Sorroto	b	6	117	4	4	$3^{1/2}$	3^2	$2^{1\frac{1}{2}}$	$2^{1\frac{1}{2}}$	4^1	Espinoza J C	35000	3.60
15Apr83 ^{7}Kee^3	Bell Swinger		5	117	7	7	7^3	7^3	$6^{1\frac{1}{2}}$	$4^{1\frac{1}{2}}$	5^3	Melancon L	35000	8.10
19Apr83 ^{8}Kee^6	Davrick	b	4	117	6	5	4^4	4^2	$5^{1/2}$	7^6	$6^{2\frac{1}{2}}$	Moyers L	35000	18.20
28Apr83 ^{4}Kee^2	Major Run	b	6	117	3	2	1^{hd}	1^{hd}	$3^{1/2}$	6^{hd}	7^{13}	Gallitano G	35000	12.00
19Apr83 ^{8}Kee^4	Dust Off the Mat		4	121	2	1	$6^{1\frac{1}{2}}$	$6^{1\frac{1}{2}}$	$7^{1\frac{1}{2}}$	8	8	McKnight J	35000	a-2.90

[D]-Broadway Review Disqualified and placed second.
a-Coupled: Broadway Review and Dust Off the Mat.
OFF AT 6:50. Start good. Won driving. Time, :25⅕, :49, 1:13⅗, 1:39⅘, 1:46⅗ Track sloppy.

$2 Mutuel Prices:				
	2-BAL BAY	17.40	6.40	3.60
	1-BROADWAY REVIEW (a-entry)		4.20	2.80
	5-SWAY			2.80

Bal Bay—B. g, by Vertex—Marsh Harbour, by First Landing. Trainer Edwards Larry D. Bred by Red Oak Farm Inc (Fla).

BROADWAY REVIEW, void of early foot, commenced a rally when set down for the drive, cut over on BAL BAY near the eighth pole, drew clear briefly but was all out to withstand BAL BAY at the wire. Following an objection by the rider of BAL BAY for interference in the stretch run, BROADWAY REVIEW was disqualified and placed second. BAL BAY, allowed to settle, challenged when set down for the drive, was bothered by BROADWAY REVIEW in midstretch but recovered to come again and just missed. SWAY pressed the early pace, took clear command approaching the lane but could not withstand the top two. SORROTO, well placed early, had no late rally. DAVRICK had brief speed. MAJOR RUN made the early pace and gave way. DUST OFF THE MAT tired after a half.

Owners— 1, Brown Mrs W L Lyons; 2, Sefa F; 3, Partee W C; 4, Donamire Farm; 5, Foyt A J Jr; 6, Racevitch H; 7, Golden Chance Farm; 8, Zimmerman G A.

Corrected weight: Broadway Review 121 pounds; Dust Off the Mat 121.

Derby Day again was an excellent day for us. We made nine Dr. Z system bets, all to show, in eight races, and all but one finished in the money to win for us. Taking into account the $50 loss on our win bets on the Derby, our $1,000 initial stake grew to $1,568. Typically, on an average day at the track, there are two to four Dr. Z system bets. In some cases, there are as few as one or even none. Over the three years on Derby Day we had five, five, and now nine Dr. Z system bets. The reason for the large number of Dr. Z system bets was likely due to the massive crowd and the many rich visitors who were, as usual, looking for the big killing and felt it to be in the win pools. Their betting behavior led to a substantial opportunity for good profits by Dr. Z system bettors. We were also using a fairly risky cutoff of 1.10 to reflect the very high quality of horses running on Derby Day. Over the day $11,851,527 was bet, as detailed below, and with the track take and breakage total losses by the bettors were close to $2 million. We were glad to be winners.

DETAILED BETS ON ALL RACES DERBY DAY

	Win	Place	Show	Total
First Race	$ 147,291	$69,932	$62,113	$279,336
Second Race	213,562	117,077	104,080	434,719
Third Race	314,811	164,875	141,625	621,311
Fourth Race	403,105	206,773	180,904	790,782
Fifth Race	447,119	235,323	195,902	878,344
Sixth Race	482,830	234,357	191,848	909,035
Seventh Race	520,042	274,738	240,612	1,035,392
Eighth Race (Derby)	3,143,669	1,293,318	1,109,990	5,546,977
Ninth Race	328,700	140,126	94,398	563,224
Tenth Race	332,499	116,186	74,033	522,718
Totals	$ 6,333,628	$2,852,705	$2,395,505	$11,581,838
Daily Double				269,689
Grand Total				$11,851,527

12

Derby Day 1982, 1984, 1985, and 1986

KENTUCKY DERBY DAY 1982

Bill was busy with his classes at UCLA so I made the Derby trip alone this year. Normal life in Louisville stops several days around the "Run for the Roses," and the race generates tremendous revenues for the city. But, the horse-racing industry has long been very important to the whole state of Kentucky. Its benefits include the employment of thousands and an investment that has been estimated at about $2 billion. It also generates about $140 million annually in revenues for the state and has significant positive effects on tourism. Other states have caught on to this industry's many benefits (New York, for instance, currently spends about $14 million annually on programs for horse owners who keep and race their horses in-state) but, at least for the time being, Kentucky is the focal point of the nation's horse industry.

The 1982 Kentucky Derby had been nicknamed the "Demolition Derby" because of the many outstanding three-year-olds sidelined from the race due to injuries. In fact, the list of no-shows was more impressive than the race's entrants. Timely Writer had impressive victories in the Flamingo Stakes and the Florida Derby, but had required emergency abdominal surgery in late April. Deputy Minister, the 1981 two-year-old champion, had been injured in Florida. Conquistador Cielo, later to win the Belmont Stakes and horse-of-the-year honors, and Aloma's Ruler, later to win the Preakness Stakes, were both recovering from minor ailments. Stalwart had been retired and Let's Don't Fight had died. Hostage, the Arkansas Derby winner, had been injured in a workout at Churchill Downs. Linkage was also missing. He was fit, but after three hard races in five weeks—winning the Blue Grass Stakes by 5 lengths only nine days before, also winning the Forerunner

Purse, and placing in the Louisiana Derby—he needed a rest and was skipping the Derby for the Preakness.

Despite the missing horses there were some impressive starters. The crowd's favorite was Air Forbes Won. His jockey, Angel Cordero, Jr., won the 1976 Derby aboard Air Forbes Won's sire, Bold Forbes. Air Forbes Won was undefeated in four starts this year, including two at Aqueduct, the Wood Memorial and the Gotham Stakes. The second favorite was Don Brumfield's mount, El Baba. In ten starts the only horses to have beaten El Baba were Linkage and Hostage, both no-shows in the Derby. Laffit Pincay, Jr., trying for his first Derby victory in nine attempts, was aboard Muttering, the Santa Anita Derby winner. Other contenders included Star Gallant with the great Bill Shoemaker, Royal Roberto, Laser Light, the one-eyed Cassaleria, Water Bank, Rockwall, and Gato Del Sol. Rock Steady had been scratched, leaving nineteen starters.

Saturday morning I joined the tens of thousands entering the twin-spired Churchill Downs. To pass the time before the first race, I perused the racing form and observed the crowd. The diversity of the crowd made it even more interesting than the racing form. At one extreme there were the celebrities and wealthy horse owners who arrived in chauffeur-driven limousines. At the other extreme there were the party-loving people milling around the infield, many of whom never see a horse all day. I positioned myself at the tote board in the back of the grandstand. It was, as we had learned at Kentucky '81, the most convenient location to watch the mutuels and bet.

The experts' selections for the day's races show that they gave the nod to El Baba:

America's Turf Authority Daily Racing Form **Experts' Selections**

Consensus Points: 5 for 1st (today's best 7), 2 for 2nd, 1 for 3rd. Today's Best in Bold Type.

Trackman, Graham Ross — **CHURCHILL DOWNS** — Selections Made for Fast Track

	TRACKMAN	HANDICAP	ANALYST	HERMIS	SWEEP	CONSENSUS	
1	DOOR KING NATIVE NASHUA A TOAST TO HARRY	TONIMAROW BARRISTER SIB VERACITY	TONIMAROW BARRISTER SIB VERACITY	TONIMAROW VERACITY M. J.'S GLORY	TONIMAROW BARRISTER SIB VERACITY	TONIMAROW BARRISTER SIB DOOR KING	20 6 5
2	PRETTY MA AMI LOVE WAY COME ON CAMILLA	ALZABELLA COME ON CAMILLA ARTANIA	LIBRELLA ALZABELLA LOVE WAY	LOVE WAY ALZABELLA COME ON CAMILLA	LOVE WAY JAY'S PROMISE ALZABELLA	LOVE WAY ALZABELLA PRETTY MA AMI	13 10 5
3	FOUR CHAMP'S LE BON MAN BIRDBRAIN	STAR DRONE BIRDBRAIN LADYS SAMSON	STAR DRONE FOUR CHAMP'S BIRDBRAIN	STAR DRONE ALIAS JAKE BIRDBRAIN	STAR DRONE BIRDBRAIN FOUR CHAMP'S	STAR DRONE FOUR CHAMP'S BIRDBRAIN	20 8 7
4	SUPER RIDGE EXCLUSIVE ROMEO GI GI BEAR	ROSSI GOLD EXCLUSIVE ROMEO BACKSTABBER	**ROSSI GOLD** NO BAY BACKSTABBER	**ROSSI GOLD** NO BAY SUPER RIDGE	**ROSSI GOLD** SUPER RIDGE BACKSTABBER	ROSSI GOLD SUPER RIDGE EXCLUSIVE ROMEO	26 8 4
5	AM JOY DUST OFF THE MAT POP'S LITTLE MAN	STOLEN GOODS ORANGEVILLE BARACO	DUST OFF THE MAT AM JOY STOLEN GOODS	BARACO ORANGEVILLE STOLEN GOODS	STOLEN GOODS BARACO ORANGEVILLE	STOLEN GOODS BARACO AM JOY	12 8 7
6	WHAT IT IS OIL CITY TIM'S MARKFIVE	WHAT IT IS D. J. ROAD MIROMAN	WHAT IT IS D. J. ROAD OIL CITY	MIROMAN TIM'S MARKFIVE EXECUTION'S REASON	OIL CITY D. J. ROAD WHAT IT IS	WHAT IT IS OIL CITY D. J. ROAD	16 8 6
7	**LISTCAPADE** SOY EMPEROR JOHNNY CAN HOP	LISTCAPADE CUT AWAY NOTED	LISTCAPADE NOTED SOY EMPEROR	LISTCAPADE SOY EMPEROR NOTED	LISTCAPADE SOY EMPEROR NOTED	**LISTCAPADE** SOY EMPEROR NOTED	27 7 5
8	MUTTERING EL BABA ROYAL ROBERTO	**EL BABA** MUTTERING AIR FORBES WON	EL BABA AIR FORBES WON MUTTERING	EL BABA AIR FORBES WON MUTTERING	EL BABA AIR FORBES WON MUTTERING	EL BABA MUTTERING AIR FORBES WON	24 10 7
9	DOUBLE THREES ENDEMONIADO LUDICROUS	AVATOIL DUAL TRACKS ARGONAFTIS	ARGONAFTIS GENUINE MAGIC AVATOIL	AVATOIL ARGONAFTIS DOUBLE THREES	ARGONAFTIS GENUINE MAGIC DUAL TRACKS	ARGONAFTIS AVATOIL DOUBLE THREES	13 11 6
10	AVIONIC OLD HUNDRED ROYAL NIN	AVIONIC BRAD SHY OMAR	AVIONIC NO SAD NEWS DASH AND C.	AVIONIC NO SAD NEWS NATIVE DIGGER	AVIONIC OLD HUNDRED NO SAD NEWS	AVIONIC NO SAD NEWS OLD HUNDRED	25 5 4

ALZABELLA IS THE FIRST DR. Z SYSTEM BET

The first Dr. Z bet was in the second race for three-year-old maiden fillies. Two minutes before post time the mutuels on the lightly raced Alzabella were:

	Totals	#8 Alzabella	Expected Value per Dollar Bet on Alzabella
Odds		2—1	
Win	220,845	60,820	
Show	96,105	15,716	1.23

With Kentucky's track take of 15%, equation (4.4) indicated that the expected value per dollar bet to show was 1.23. With my betting fortune of $400, the optimal bet was $88. Alzabella and her jockey, Jorge Velasquez, ran an excellent race and won by 5 lengths. When she paid $3.80 to show, my $88 bet returned $167.20, for a profit of $79.20.

The mutuel payoffs were:

8–	Alzabella	5.80	4.00	3.80
5–	Librella		8.00	5.80
6–	Sans Pareil			5.60

A LATE SCRATCH

The fourth race was an allowance race for horses at least four years old. It was the first outing of 1982 for three of the seven runners. The class of the field was Rossi Gold. In his twenty-six races he finished in the money twenty times and had lifetime earnings of $500,608. He was the "best pick of the day" by three of the five *Daily Racing Form* experts and was the favorite of the crowd. One minute to post, the mutuels were:

	Totals	#5 Rossi Gold	Expected Value per Dollar Bet on Rossi Gold
Odds		3—5	
Win	388,375	184,016	
Show	163,553	43,207	1.26

A 1.26 expected return to show on a heavy favorite such as Rossi Gold means a large Dr. Z system bet. The optimal bet was $294 out of my bankroll of $479.20. I bet just as the horses were entering the starting gate. However, at that moment, Exclusive Romeo injured himself at the gate and was scratched. This meant a delay of the race for five minutes while the public was allowed to collect refunds on Exclusive Romeo and rebet. This also meant the Dr. Z bet on Rossi Gold could turn sour if, during the delay, there was heavy betting on him to show. As the final mutuels indicate, this was, fortunately, not the case:

	Totals	#5 Rossi Gold	Expected Value per Dollar Bet on Rossi Gold
Odds		3—5	
Win	387,974	193,574	
Show	155,275	46,062	1.22

Rossi Gold won with a strong finish and paid $2.40 to show. This was a good payoff considering he was a 3–5 favorite in a six-horse field. My $294 bet returned $352.80, for a profit of $58.80 and a final bankroll of $538. The mutual payoffs were:

5–	Rossi Gold................	3.20	2.40	2.40
2–	Backstabber		3.00	2.60
7–	Billboard..................			4.20

BARACO IN THE FIFTH

The fifth race, for three-year-olds, also had a small field of only seven horses. The consensus of the *Daily Racing Form*'s experts gave the nod to Stolen Goods, but the public preferred the front-running Baraco. The public, however, overlooked the show bet on Baraco. With two minutes to post, the mutuels were:

	Totals	#1 Baraco	Expected Value per Dollar Bet on Baraco
Odds		7—5	
Win	432,641	152,413	
Show	179,553	40,439	1.18

I made the optimal bet of $167. The final mutuels were similar:

	Totals	#1 Baraco	Expected Value per Dollar Bet on Baraco
Odds		6—5	
Win	441,870	157,536	
Show	182,503	41,956	1.17

Baraco took the lead out of the gate but could not outrun Am Joy in the stretch. He did hang on for second, beating Orangeville by a neck. The $3 show payoff meant a profit of $83.50 and a bankroll of $621.50. The mutuel payoffs were:

4–	AM Jof	24.00	7.20	4.60
1–	Baraco		3.60	3.00
5–	Orangeville			4.20

THE DEMOLITION DERBY: THE 108TH RUN FOR THE ROSES

The next bet was not until the eighth race, the Derby. The program and the past performances of the horses follow.

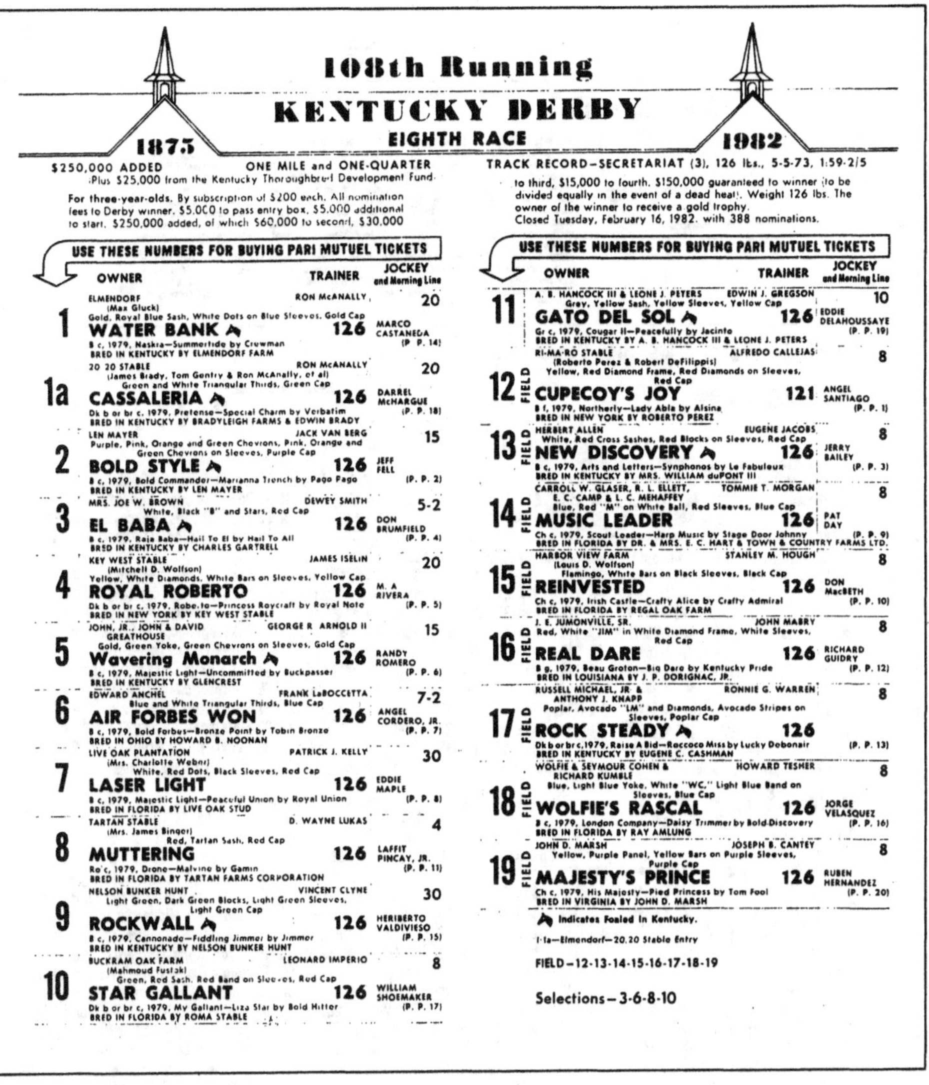

108th Running

KENTUCKY DERBY

1875 — EIGHTH RACE — 1982

$250,000 ADDED — ONE MILE and ONE-QUARTER — TRACK RECORD—SECRETARIAT (3), 126 lbs., 5-5-73, 1:59-2/5

(Plus $25,000 from the Kentucky Thoroughbred Development Fund)

For three-year-olds. By subscription of $200 each. All nomination fees to Derby winner. $5,000 to pass entry box, $5,000 additional to start. $250,000 added, of which $60,000 to second, $30,000 to third, $15,000 to fourth. $150,000 guaranteed to winner (to be divided equally in the event of a dead heat). Weight 126 lbs. The owner of the winner to receive a gold trophy.
Closed Tuesday, February 16, 1982, with 388 nominations.

USE THESE NUMBERS FOR BUYING PARI MUTUEL TICKETS

No.	Owner / Colors	Trainer	Horse	Wt.	Jockey	Morning Line	P.P.	Breeding
1	ELMENDORF (Max Gluck); Gold, Royal Blue Sash, White Dots on Blue Sleeves, Gold Cap	RON McANALLY	WATER BANK ♞	126	MARCO CASTANEDA	20	14	B c, 1979, Naskra—Summertide by Crewman. BRED IN KENTUCKY BY ELMENDORF FARM
1a	20 20 STABLE (James Brady, Tom Gentry & Ron McAnally, et al); Green and White Triangular Thirds, Green Cap	RON McANALLY	CASSALERIA ♞	126	DARREL McHARGUE	20	18	Dk b or br c, 1979, Pretense—Special Charm by Verbatim. BRED IN KENTUCKY BY BRADYLEIGH FARMS & EDWIN BRADY
2	LEN MAYER; Purple, Pink, Orange and Green Chevrons, Pink, Orange and Green Chevrons on Sleeves, Purple Cap	JACK VAN BERG	BOLD STYLE ♞	126	JEFF FELL	15	2	B c, 1979, Bold Commander—Marianna Trench by Pago Pago. BRED IN KENTUCKY BY LEN MAYER
3	MRS. JOE W. BROWN; White, Black "B" and Stars, Red Cap	DEWEY SMITH	EL BABA ♞	126	DON BRUMFIELD	5-2	4	B c, 1979, Raja Baba—Hail To El by Hail To All. BRED IN KENTUCKY BY CHARLES GARTRELL
4	KEY WEST STABLE (Mitchell D. Wolfson); Yellow, White Diamonds, White Bars on Sleeves, Yellow Cap	JAMES ISELIN	ROYAL ROBERTO	126	M. A RIVERA	20	5	Dk b or br c, 1979, Robe.to—Princess Roycraft by Royal Note. BRED IN NEW YORK BY KEY WEST STABLE
5	JOHN, JR., JOHN & DAVID GREATHOUSE; Gold, Green Yoke, Green Chevrons on Sleeves, Gold Cap	GEORGE R ARNOLD II	Wavering Monarch ♞	126	RANDY ROMERO	15	6	B c, 1979, Majestic Light—Uncommitted by Buckpasser. BRED IN KENTUCKY BY GLENCREST
6	EDWARD ANCHEL; Blue and White Triangular Thirds, Blue Cap	FRANK LaBOCCETTA	AIR FORBES WON	126	ANGEL CORDERO, JR.	7-2	7	B c, 1979, Bold Forbes—Bronze Point by Tobin Bronze. BRED IN OHIO BY HOWARD B. NOONAN
7	LIVE OAK PLANTATION (Mrs. Charlotte Weber); White, Red Dots, Black Sleeves, Red Cap	PATRICK J. KELLY	LASER LIGHT	126	EDDIE MAPLE	30	8	B c, 1979, Majestic Light—Peaceful Union by Royal Union. BRED IN FLORIDA BY LIVE OAK STUD
8	TARTAN STABLE (Mrs. James Binger); Red, Tartan Sash, Red Cap	D. WAYNE LUKAS	MUTTERING	126	LAFFIT PINCAY, JR.	4	11	Ro c, 1979, Drone—Malvine by Gamin. BRED IN FLORIDA BY TARTAN FARMS CORPORATION
9	NELSON BUNKER HUNT; Light Green, Dark Green Blocks, Light Green Sleeves, Light Green Cap	VINCENT CLYNE	ROCKWALL ♞	126	HERIBERTO VALDIVIESO	30	15	B c, 1979, Cannonade—Fiddling Jimmer by Jimmer. BRED IN KENTUCKY BY NELSON BUNKER HUNT
10	BUCKRAM OAK FARM (Mahmoud Fustok); Green, Red Sash, Red Band on Sleeves, Red Cap	LEONARD IMPERIO	STAR GALLANT	126	WILLIAM SHOEMAKER	8	17	Dk b or br c, 1979, My Gallant—Liza Star by Bold Hitter. BRED IN FLORIDA BY ROMA STABLE
11	A. B. HANCOCK III & LEONE J. PETERS; Grey, Yellow Sash, Yellow Sleeves, Yellow Cap	EDWIN J. GREGSON	GATO DEL SOL ♞	126	EDDIE DELAHOUSSAYE	10	19	Gr c, 1979, Cougar II—Peacefully by Jacinto. BRED IN KENTUCKY BY A. B. HANCOCK III & LEONE J. PETERS
12 FIELD	RI-MA-RO STABLE (Roberto Perez & Robert DeFilippis); Yellow, Red Diamond Frame, Red Diamonds on Sleeves, Red Cap	ALFREDO CALLEJAS	CUPECOY'S JOY	121	ANGEL SANTIAGO	8	1	B f, 1979, Northerly—Lady Abla by Alsina. BRED IN NEW YORK BY ROBERTO PEREZ
13 FIELD	HERBERT ALLEN; White, Red Cross Sashes, Red Blocks on Sleeves, Red Cap	EUGENE JACOBS	NEW DISCOVERY ♞	126	JERRY BAILEY	8	3	B c, 1979, Arts and Letters—Synphonos by Le Fabuleux. BRED IN KENTUCKY BY MRS. WILLIAM duPONT III
14 FIELD	CARROLL W. GLASER, R. L. ELLETT, E. C. CAMP & L. C. MEHAFFEY; Blue, Red "M" on White Ball, Red Sleeves, Blue Cap	TOMMIE T. MORGAN	MUSIC LEADER	126	PAT DAY	8	9	Ch c, 1979, Scout Leader—Harp Music by Stage Door Johnny. BRED IN FLORIDA BY DR. & MRS. E. C. HART & TOWN & COUNTRY FARMS LTD.
15 FIELD	HARBOR VIEW FARM (Louis D. Wolfson); Flamingo, White Bars on Black Sleeves, Black Cap	STANLEY M. HOUGH	REINVESTED	126	DON MacBETH	8	10	Ch c, 1979, Irish Castle—Crafty Alice by Crafty Admiral. BRED IN FLORIDA BY REGAL OAK FARM
16 FIELD	J. E. JUMONVILLE, SR.; Red, White "JIM" in White Diamond Frame, White Sleeves, Red Cap	JOHN MABRY	REAL DARE	126	RICHARD GUIDRY	8	12	B g, 1979, Beau Groton—Big Dare by Kentucky Pride. BRED IN LOUISIANA BY J. P. DORIGNAC, JR.
17 FIELD	RUSSELL MICHAEL, JR & ANTHONY J. KNAPP; Poplar, Avocado "LM" and Diamonds, Avocado Stripes on Sleeves, Poplar Cap	RONNIE G. WARREN	ROCK STEADY ♞	126		8	13	Dk b or br c, 1979, Raise A Bid—Roccoco Miss by Lucky Debonair. BRED IN KENTUCKY BY EUGENE C. CASHMAN
18 FIELD	WOLFIE & SEYMOUR COHEN & RICHARD KUMBLE; Blue, Light Blue Yoke, White "WC," Light Blue Band on Sleeves, Blue Cap	HOWARD TESHER	WOLFIE'S RASCAL	126	JORGE VELASQUEZ	8	16	B c, 1979, London Company—Daisy Trimmer by Bold Discovery. BRED IN FLORIDA BY RAY AMLUNG
19 FIELD	JOHN D. MARSH; Yellow, Purple Panel, Yellow Bars on Purple Sleeves, Purple Cap	JOSEPH B. CANTEY	MAJESTY'S PRINCE	126	RUBEN HERNANDEZ	8	20	Ch c, 1979, His Majesty—Pied Princess by Tom Fool. BRED IN VIRGINIA BY JOHN D. MARSH

♞ Indicates Foaled in Kentucky.

1-1a—Elmendorf—20.20 Stable Entry

FIELD—12-13-14-15-16-17-18-19

Selections—3-6-8-10

108th-Kentucky Derby

Route the Field Will Travel

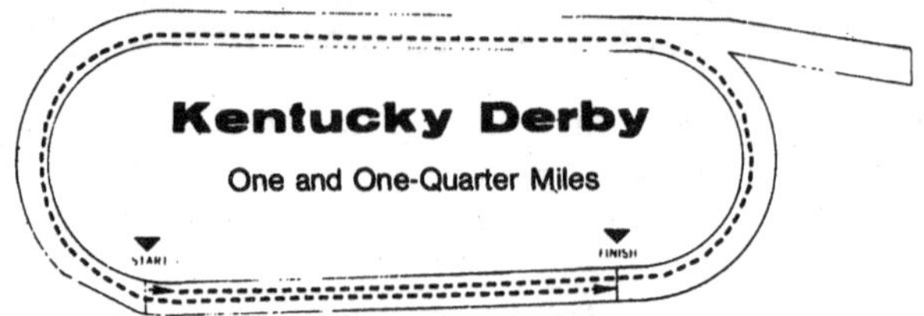

8th Churchill

1 ¼ MILES. (1.59⅗) 108th Running KENTUCKY DERBY Scale Weight (Grade I) $250,000 added (plus $25,000 from the KTDF). 3-year-olds. By subscription of $200. All nomination fees to winner. $5,000 to pass entry box Thursday, April 29, $5,000 additional to start. $250,000 added, of which $60,000 to second, $30,000 to third, $15,000 to fourth. $150,000 guaranteed to winner (to be divided equally in the event of a dead heat). Weight, 126 lbs. Fillies 121, lbs. Starters to be named through the entry box Thursday, April 29, at time of closing. The maximum number of starters for The Kentucky Derby will be limited to twenty. In the event more than twenty entries pass through the entry box at the usual time of closing, the twenty starters and up to eight also-eligibles will be determined at that time with preference given to those that accumulated the highest earnings. Should any entry(ies) be withdrawn from the starting field prior to 4 P.M. scratch time, Friday, April 30, vacancies will be filled from the also-eligible list and placed in the outside post position(s) in order of preference. For those that pass the entry box and are eliminated under this condition, the entry fee will be refunded. The owner of the winner to receive a gold trophy. Nominations close Tuesday, February 16. (Closed with 388 nominations.)

Coupled—Water Bank and Cassaleria.

Cupecoy's Joy

B. f. 3, by Northerly—Lady Abla, by Alsina
Br.—Perez R (NY) 1982 6 2 3 1 $121,606
Own.—Ri-Ma-Ro Stables 121 Tr.—Callejas Alfredo L 1981 8 2 2 3 $91,814
Lifetime 14 4 5 4 $213,420

Entered 30Apr82- 8 CD
27Mar82-9Lat 1 1/16 :463 1:113 1:443ft 9¼ 115 2hd 23 25 35 SntgoA10 Jim B Spiral 82 Goodn'Dusty,FstGold,Cupcoy'sJoy 12
17Mar82-8Aqu 6f :224 :46 1:11 gd 8-5 115 31 31½ 32 2nk Santiago A5 [S]Catskill 86 PayorPly,Cupecoy'sJoy,FdedPoster 7
20Feb82-8Aqu 6f ⊡:223 :4541:11 ft *2 121 2hd 1hd 14 2hd Santiago A4 ⒻCicada 89 Bold Ribbons,Cupecoy'sJoy,Adept 11
3Feb82-8Aqu 6f ⊡:221 :4641:144sy *2-3 121 — — 13 1nk SntA2 Ⓕ[S]Sag Harbor 70 Cupecoy'sJoy,HstyDmscn,LdyHoot 7
3Feb82—Running positions omitted because of weather conditions.
6Jan82-8Aqu 6f ⊡:221 :4511:101ft 3¼ 114 1hd 1½ 2hd 1no SantigoA8 [S]Montauk 93 Cpcoy'sJoy,AskMhmmd,Jn'sKnsmn 8
1Jan82-8Aqu 6f ⊡:23 :4731:133sy 5¼ 115 32½ 31½ 21 21¼ SantigoA4 ⒻRosetown 75 NncyHung,Cupcoy'sJoy,ScrltBgoni 8
6Dec81-8Aqu 6f ⊡:224 :47 1:13 ft 13 122 2hd 3½ 21½ 32 Santiago A3 ⒻTreetop 77 Trove, Larida, Cupecoy's Joy 6
29Nov81-8Aqu 7f :231 :464 1:253ft 19 119 51¾ 41½ 55½ 711 SantigoA14 [S]A T Cole 62 AskMuhmmd,ScrltBgon,GlfordLd 15
18Nov81-8Aqu 7f :223 :46 1:251m 6¼ 115 13 11½ 12 12¼ SntgA1 Ⓕ[S]East View 75 Cupecoy'sJoy,DamLittle,KeyStark 12
28Oct81-1Aqu 7f :231 :463 1:244m 2 116 11 1hd 35½ 38¾ SntigoA1 Ⓕ[S]Aw22000 68 ScrletBegoni,FreePss,Cupcoy'sJoy 6
18Oct81-8Aqu 7f :23 :46 1:243ft 5 114 11½ 11 2hd 31½ SantigoA3 [S]D Runyon 76 GuilfordLd,MjesticKt,Cupecoy'sJoy 7
2Sep81-8Bel 6f :222 :454 1:112ft *3-2 114 1hd 1½ 2hd 22¼ SntigoA6 Ⓕ[S]Mohawk 83 PetiuMurill,Cupcoy'sJoy,PrmirWho 7
14Aug81-8Sar 6f :223 :454 1:112ft 5¼ 116 11½ 14 14 21 Santiago A5 [S]Empire 82 SluteMeSir,Cupecoy'sJoy,BrightRx 9
13Jly81-4Bel 6f :23 :464 1:122ft 3½ 117 14 15 16 18 Santiago A10 Ⓕ[S]Mdn 80 Cupecoy'sJoy,GrndOldFlg,DmLittl 13
●Apr 25 CD 5f ft :59 h ●Mar 25 Lat 4f ft :464 b ●Mar 12 Bel tr.t 4f ft :464 h Mar 6 Bel tr.t 1 ft 1:46 b

Bold Style

B. c. 3, by Bold Commander—Marianna Trench, by Pago Pago
Br.—Mayer Len (Ky) 1982 4 3 0 1 $98,870
Own.—Mayer L 126 Tr.—Van Berg Jack C 1981 7 1 2 2 $21,331
Lifetime 11 4 2 3 $120,201 Turf 1 1 0 0 $10,020

10Apr82-9OP 1⅛ :474 1:123 1:513ft 12 123 11 21 33½ 33 SnyderL1 Arknsas Dby 82 Hostage, El Baba, Bold Style 10
20Mar82-9OP 170 :46 1:122 1:434ft 3 116 34½ 2½ 1hd 1no Snyder L2 Rebel H 77 BoldStyle,Mjesty'sPrince,LostCrek 8
12Mar82-8OP 170 :471 1:123 1:434ft *3-2 114 1hd 12½ 14 14½ Snyder L2 Aw15000 77 Bold Style, Hidden Image, Railin 12
23Jan82-10TuP a7½f Ⓣ:231 :48 1:35 fm*3-2 118 63¾ 73¾ 41½ 12 MrtinzFIII1 Phoenix H — Bold Style, Many More, Briskoric 12
27Dec81-10TuP 6½f :213 :433 1:151ft 13 120 86¾ 710 58½ 58½ WhtdDE6 Ariz Para Ft 86 Tropic Ruler,JungleBlade,Intrigue 12
16Dec81-8TuP 6½f :224 :444 1:16 ft 3 120 32 42½ 21½ 24 Snyder L4 Fut Trl 87 Jungle Blade, Bold Style, Big Sam 10
28Nov81-3CD 6f :221 :453 1:12 ft 9 118 73½ 22 21 1hd Snyder L9 Mdn 86 BoldStyl,ForbiddnPlsur,ShsRchOn 12
9May81-11TuP 5f :212 :442 :563ft 21 119 66½ 1014 37 36 StllsWE11 PhoenixFut 88 ClassyCraft,Orphan'sArt,BoldStyle 12
29Apr81-9TuP 4½f :222 :452 :512ft 7½ 119 6 31½ 2hd 22½ Stallings W E2 SplW 92 Gusto Gal, Bold Style,PepperSpeed 9
13Apr81-3TuP 4½f :223 :46 :523ft 5¼ 118 8 67 47 44¾ Stallings W E10 Mdn 84 KhalitDusty,GentilPersoon,JoJulie 10
1Apr81-4TuP 4½f :222 :454 :521ft 5 118 3 47½ 57 33 Stallings W E3 Mdn 88 Cintolove, A Jolla Wind,BoldStyle 10
Apr 27 CD 1 gd 1:422 h Apr 19 CD 7f ft 1:29 h ●Mar 30 OP 6f ft 1:15 b Mar 18 OP 5f ft 1:013 h

New Discovery

B. c. 3, by Arts and Letters—Synphonos, by Le Fabuleux

Own.—Allen H **126** **Br.—DuPont Mrs W III (Ky)** 1982 6 1 2 1 $85,398

Tr.—Jacobs Eugene 1981 11 M 1 4 $49,156

Lifetime 17 1 3 5 $134,554

22Apr82-7Kee 1⅛ :46^3 1:10 1:48 ft 14 121 7^{10} 8^{14} 7^{20} 7^{25} VelsquezJ^7 Blue Grass 72 Linkage,GtoDelSol,WveringMonrch 9

3Apr82-9GP 1⅛ :47^1 1:11^1 1:49^{3}ft 12 118 5^{10} 5^{10} 6^{12} 5^{13} Vasquez J^6 Fla Derby 71 TimelyWriter,StarGallnt,OurEscpde 7

6Mar82-10Hia 1⅛ :46^2 1:10^4 1:49^{3}sy 14 122 10^{7½} 6^{3¼} 3^{4½} 2^{3½} VelsquezJ^{12} Flamingo 80 TimelyWriter,NewDiscovry,LDnsur 16

13Feb82-10Hia 1⅛ :46^1 1:10^2 1:48^{4}ft 7¼ 112 4^{8½} 4^{4½} 2^{hd} 2^{1½} VlsquzJ^3 Everglades H 86 RoylRobrto,NwDiscovry,VictorinLn 8

30Jan82-10Hia 6f :22^2 :45^4 1:11^{2}ft 5¼ 120 8^{8½} 8^{10} 4^1 1^{2½} Velasquez J^6 Mdn 86 NwDscovry,PrncWstport,TThPnny 12

16Jan82-6Hia 6f :22^2 :46^1 1:11^{3}ft 2¾ 120 10^{12} 9^{11} 9^{9¾} 3^{7½} Velasquez J^4 Mdn 77 GllntWind,TnciousLdr,NwDiscovry 12

14Nov81-8Aqu 1⅛ :48^1 1:13^1 1:50^{4}ft 24 114 11^9 10^9 10^{15} 8^{16} Fell J^9 Remsen 65 LserLight,RelTwister,Wolfie'sRscl 11

5Nov81-6Med 1 1/16 :47^1 1:11^3 1:44^{3}ft 16 119 9^{6¼} 8^{8¾} 11^{12} 10^{12} CrdrAJr^8 Yng America 74 DeputyMinister,LsrLight,RlTwistr 14

24Oct81-8Lrl 1 1/16 :47 1:12^2 1:44^{3}gd 7¾ 116 1^2 2^{hd} 5^7 5^{13} Lovato F Jr^7 Lrl Fut'y 72 DeputyMinistr,LsrLight,‡CgyCougr 8

10Oct81-7Bel 1 :46^4 1:11^1 1:36^{2}ft 35e 122 8^{4¼} 5^{3¾} 5^{4½} 3^{7¾} SamynJL^5 Champagne 78 TimelyWritr,BforDwn,NwDiscovry 13

26Sep81-8Bel 7f :22^2 :45^2 1:23^{4}ft 43 115 9^{11} 8^6 5^{4¾} 3^6 McHargueDG^4 Cowdin 77 NtiveRj,TimelyWriter,NewDiscovry 9

17Sep81-6Bel 7f :22^4 :46^1 1:24^{3}m 8-5 118 2½ 1^1 2½ 4^{4½} Vasquez J^4 Mdn 74 Bid'sMjestic,TidsOfChng,Bmbolino 8

22Jly81-8Bel 6f :22^2 :45^2 1:10^{2}ft 31 113 9^{5¼} 6^{4¼} 7^{3¾} 7^3 AsmssnCB^{10} Tremont 87 ReglSton,MincdWords,RingProud 11

10Jly81-4Bel 5½f :23 :46^2 1:05^{3}ft *1 118 1^{hd} 1½ 1^3 3^{nk} Fell J^9 Mdn 87 Pavrotti,NewDiscovery,BronzeCup 10

21Jun81-8Bel 5½f :22 :45^2 1:04^{3}ft 9 113 5^8 5^6 5^5 4^{4½} Fell J^4 Gr. American 87 FullVntur,Hrschlwlkr,ShippngMgnt 8

8Jun81-8Bel 5½f :22 :45^3 1:04^{4}ft 17 115 6^{10} 6^7 5^{5½} 3^{5¼} Fell J^2 Youthful 86 DeputyMinister,Ringro,NwDiscovry 6

18May81-4Bel 5f :23^1 :46^4 :59^{1}ft 4¼ 118 3^3 4^3 5^{4¾} 3^{8¾} Fell J^7 Mdn — Hrschlwlkr,PrncWstport,NwDscvry 8

Apr 27 CD 1 gd 1:41^3 b Apr 17 GP 5f ft 1:01 b ●Mar 31 GP 6f ft 1:13^3 b ●Mar 24 GP 1 ft 1:42 b

El Baba

B. c. 3, by Raja Baba—Hail to El, by Hail to All

Own.—Brown Mrs J W **126** **Br.—Gartrell C & Farish W S III (Ky)** 1982 5 3 2 0 $233,860

Tr.—Smith Dewey 1981 5 5 0 0 $151,003

Lifetime 10 8 2 0 $384,863

10Apr82-9OP 1⅛ :47^4 1:12^3 1:51^{3}ft *1 126 3^1 4^{1¼} 2^3 2^2 BrmfldD^8 Arknsas Dby 83 Hostage, El Baba, Bold Style 10

28Mar82-10FG 1⅛ :46^4 1:11^2 1:50^{3}ft 2¼ 123 3^4 2^{1½} 1^{hd} 1¾ Brumfield D^1 La Dby 91 El Baba, Linkage,SpoonfulofHoney 8

13Mar82-9FG 1 1/16 :47^2 1:12 1:44^{2}ft *2-3 125 2^{2½} 2^{1½} 2^{2½} 2^4 Brumfield D^6 Dby Trl 86 Linkage, El Baba,SpoonfulofHoney 8

27Feb82-9OP 6f :22^2 :47 1:12^{3}m *1-3 124 2^{2½} 2^{hd} 1^2 1^3 Brumfield D^7 HcpO 82 El Baba, Moro, Johnny B. Fast 7

12Feb82-8OP 6f :22^3 :46^3 1:12^{1}gd *4-5 123 6^{1¾} 2^{1½} 1½ 1½ Brumfield D^5 HcpO 84 ElBaba,LostCreek,DropYourDrwers 8

31Dec81-9FG 6f :22^2 :45^4 1:11^{3}ft *1-2 122 2^{1½} 1^{hd} 2^{hd} 1^{hd} BrmfldD^1 Sgr Bowl H 87 El Baba, Talk oftheTimes,TuninIn 13

21Nov81-8CD 1 1/16 :47^3 1:12^3 1:45^{1}ft *6-5 119 1½ 1^{1½} 1^{1½} 1^{3½} RomroRP^4 Ky Jky Clb 82 El Baba,CrowntheKing,TalentTown 9

11Nov81-7CD 7f :23^2 :47 1:24^{4}ft *2-5 114 2^{1½} 4^{1½} 2^{hd} 1^2 Brumfield D^2 Aw18500 83 El Baba, Am Joy, Broad Minded 6

31Oct81-2Kee 6f :22^2 :46^2 1:11^{2}ft *1 121 2^{hd} 1½ 1^5 1^9 Brumfield D^8 Aw14500 85 El Baba, Dreamtide, Kings Dusty 12

24Oct81-2Kee 6f :22^4 :46^3 1:11^{4}gd *2 118 1½ 1^3 1^6 1^{16} Brumfield D^{10} Mdn 83 El Baba, Birdbrain, Stiletto 12

Apr 29 CD 4f ft :48^3 b ●Apr 24 CD 1 ft 1:39^1 h Apr 6 OP 5f ft 1:02^4 b ●Mar 26 FG 4f ft :48 h

Royal Roberto

Dk. b. or br. c. 3, by Roberto—Princess Roycraft, by Royal Note

Own.—Key West Stable **126** **Br.—Key West Stable (NY)** 1982 7 1 2 1 $71,085

Tr.—Iselin James H 1981 2 2 0 0 $18,600

Lifetime 9 3 2 1 $89,685 Turf 1 1 0 0 $7,800

24Apr82-8CD 1 :45 1:09^3 1:36^{1}ft 3¼ 122 8^{13} 5^{8½} 4^{4½} 3^{1½} RiverMA^9 Derby Trial 86 Listcapade,StarGllnt,RoylRoberto 10

15Apr82-7Kee 7f :22^2 :45^1 1:22^{4}ft 8¾ 120 9^{8¾} 8^{9½} 3^{2½} 2½ Rivera M A^7 Aw30200 91 Linkage, Royal Roberto, CenterCut 9

3Apr82-9GP 1⅛ :47^1 1:11^1 1:49^{3}ft 11 122 6^{13} 6^{12} 4^7 4^{11} Samyn J L^4 Fla Derby 73 TimelyWriter,StarGallnt,OurEscpde 7

6Mar82-10Hia 1⅛ :46^2 1:10^4 1:49^{3}sy 4¼ 122 15^{12} 12^{11} 7^7 6^{5¾} Samyn J L^{16} Flamingo 78 TimelyWriter,NewDiscovry,LDnsur 16

13Feb82-10Hia 1⅛ :46^1 1:10^2 1:48^{4}ft 4¼ 114 6^{13} 5^{9½} 3^{nk} 1^{1½} Fell J^7 Everglades H 88 RoylRobrto,NwDiscovry,VictorinLn 8

5Feb82-8Hia 1 1/16 :48 1:12^1 1:44 ft *1 116 8^{5¼} 6^7 3^{4½} 2^{1½} Fell J^3 Aw15000 82 Bold'nCold,RoyalRoberto,OurBoss 10

12Jan82-8Hia 7f :23 :45^3 1:23^{4}ft 4¼ 116 11^{13} 8^{17} 7^6 4^{1¾} Fell J^{11} Aw14000 82 ShootngDuck,H'sAnAngl,ShrpFutr 12

14Nov81-5Med 1^{70} Ⓣ:48^1 1:13 1:42^{1}gd *8-5 117 8^{10} 6^8 4^3 1no Perret C^8 Aw13000 79 RoylRoberto,RedBrigde,JsonThRcr 8

15Oct81-4Aqu 6f :23 :46^4 1:12^{3}ft 4 118 10^{6¼} 7^{3¾} 5^{1¼} 1^{1¼} Fell J^{12} [S]Mdn 78 RoylRoberto,CtchMe,QuitOldFrind 12

Mar 31 GP 4f ft :51 b Mar 18 GP 4f ft :50^3 b Mar 4 GP 4f ft :51 b

Wavering Monarch

c. 3, by Majestic Light—Uncommitted, by Buckpasser

Own.—Greathouse Family **126** **r.—Glencrest Farm (Ky)** 1982 3 2 0 1 $36,948

Tr.—Arnold George R II 1981 0 M 0 0

Lifetime 3 2 0 1 $36,948

22Apr82-7Kee 1⅛ :46^3 1:10 1:48 ft 5¼ 121 3^2 2^1 2^{2½} 3^6 RomroRP^9 Blue Grass 91 Linkage,GtoDelSol,WveringMonrch 9

14Apr82-8Kee a7f 1:26^{1}ft *3-5 117 1^{hd} 1½ 1^2 1^{10} Romero R P^2 Aw14500 92 WvrngMonrch,PopcrnCssrl,Frl'sJt 10

2Apr82-4Kee a7f 1:28 ft *1 116 5^{2½} 3^{nk} 1^2 1^{7½} Romero R P^6 Mdn 83 WvrngMonrch,PocktflfHp,BtthTms 8

Apr 29 CD 4f ft :48^4 b Apr 21 Kee 3f ft :35^4 b ●Apr 11 Kee 4f ft :48 b Apr 8 Kee 5f ft :59 h

Air Forbes Won

B. c. 3, by Bold Forbes—Brönze Point, by Tobin Bronze

Own.—Anchel E **126** **Br.—Noonan H B (Ohio)** 1982 4 4 0 0 $173,880

Tr.—LaBoccetta Frank 1981 0 M 0 0

Lifetime 4 4 0 0 $173,880

17Apr82-8Aqu 1⅛ :47^2 1:11^2 1:51 ft *3-5 126 2½ 2^{1½} 2½ 1^{nk} CordrAJr^2 Wood Mem 80 AirForbesWon,Shimtoree,LsrLight 10

3Apr82-8Aqu 1 :44^2 1:08^3 1:35^{3}gd 2¼ 114 5^{4½} 2^{hd} 1½ 1^{3¼} Venezia M^7 Gotham 88 AirForbesWon,Shimtor,BigBrvRock 8

20Mar82-5Aqu 7f :23^2 :46^2 1:23^{4}ft *1-5 122 3^{2½} 3^{2½} 1^{hd} 1^3 Cordero AJr^4 Aw16000 82 AirForbesWon,Illuminate,MjorFrnk 7

4Mar82-4Aqu 6f ⊡:23 :46^4 1:11^{1}ft *3-5 122 2^{1½} 2^{hd} 1^3 1^{7½} Cordero A Jr^{12} Mdn 88 AirForbsWon,SilvrPik,ElvtorShos 12

●Apr 26 CD 7f sy 1:29^2 h ●Apr 12 Aqu 7f ft 1:26 b ●Mar 29 Aqu 6f ft 1:12^3 h ●Mar 18 Aqu 4f gd :46^1 h (d)

```
Laser Light                             B. c. 3, by Majestic Light—Peaceful Union, by Royal Union
                                        Br.—Live Oak Stud (Fla)                1982  3  0  0  2    $22,844
Own.—Live Oak Plantation          126   Tr.—Kelly Patrick J                    1981  5  2  2  0   $207,580
                              Lifetime   8  2  2  2   $230,424
17Apr82-8Aqu  1⅛:472 1:112 1:51 ft   6½ 126   89¾ 56 33 32½  Maple E8 Wood Mem  77 AirForbesWon,Shimtoree,LsrLight 10
 3Apr82-9GP   1⅛:471 1:111 1:493ft   16 122   32 46 715 720  Maple E7 Fla Derby 64 TimelyWriter,StarGallnt,OurEscpde 7
18Mar82-9GP   1 1/16:47 1:114 1:434ft  *6-5 119  712 55 35 34¾  Maple E5 Aw14000  77 Hostage, Nor Bee, Laser Light  7
29Nov81-8Hol  1 1/16:481 1:141 1:474sl  3¼ 121  1011 109 916 920  Maple E3 Hol Fut'y  36 Stalwart, Cassaleria, Header Card 12
14Nov81-8Aqu  1⅛:481 1:131 1:504ft  *2-3e 113  54½ 11½ 15 15  Maple E8 Remsen  81 LserLight,RelTwister,Wolfie'sRscl 11
 5Nov81-6Med  1 1/16:471 1:113 1:443ft  *9-5 119  1212 98¾ 45½ 23  MapleE9 Yng America  83 DeputyMinister,LsrLight,RITwistr 14
24Oct81-8Lrl  1 1/16:47 1:122 1:443gd  6¾ 122  56 4¾ 21½ 2no  Montoya D5 Lrl Fut'y  85 DeputyMinistr,LsrLight,‡CgyCougr 8
12Oct81-4Bel  1 :48 1:124 1:372ft  9¼ 118  76½ 51¾ 11½ 12½  Maple E3 Mdn  81 LsrLight,LWshingtonin,TidsOfChnc 7
    Apr 26 CD 6f sy 1:153 h      Apr 14 Bel 5f ft 1:001 b      Apr 10 Hia 3f ft :37 b      ●Mar 30 Hia 5f sy 1:00 hg

Music Leader                            Ch. c. 3, by Scout Leader—Harp Music, by Stage Door Johnny
                                        Br.—Hart E C & Town&CntryFm (Fla)      1982  5  1  0  1    $10,942
Own.—Glaser C W                   126   Tr.—Morgan T T                         1981 14  4  2  4   $116,957
                              Lifetime  19  5  2  5   $127,899                 Turf  1  1  0  0    $20,430
10Apr82-7OP   170:47 1:131 1:431ft  6 116  43½ 41¼ 44 66¾  Whited D E6 Aw35000  73 DropYourDrawers,HiPi,Listcapade 10
29Mar82-9OP   170:474 1:132 1:454ft  *2 115  3½ 4nk 31½ 35¼  Whited D E6 Aw25000  61 UnoRoberto,JudoJima,MusicLeader 8
20Mar82-9OP   170:46 1:122 1:434ft  32 113  48½ 33 34 41¾  Whited D E4 Rebel H  75 BoldStyle,Mjesty'sPrince,LostCrek 8
13Mar82-9FG   1 1/16:472 1:12 1:442ft  46 114  714 714 616 628  Poyadou B E8 Dby Trl  62 Linkage, El Baba,SpoonfulofHoney 8
 7Feb82-8DeD  6½f:241 :492 1:233ft  *2-5 117  1hd 1½ 13 12½  Cahanin J T3 Aw5500  80 MusicLeder,JukboxCindrll,NtivSbr 10
31Dec81-9FG   6f :222 :454 1:113ft  12 118  97¾ 105¼ 89¾ 810  Ardoin R8 Sgr Bowl H  77 El Baba, Talk oftheTimes,TuninIn 13
19Dec81-5FG   6f :222 :462 1:124ft  *3-5e 115  65½ 46 56½ 52¼  Ardoin R2 Aw11500  79 ToughImp,GrayJohn,InevitbleLeder 8
29Aug81-9AP   7f :222 :461 1:291sy  18e 122  65½ 56 34½ 31¼  ArdonR7 Ap Wash Fty  55 LtsDontFight,TropicRulr,MuscLdr 15
21Aug81-8LaD  6½f:224 :454 1:18 ft  8-5 122  3nk 3nk 1½ 12  Ardoin R6 Aw16000  92 MusicLeder,InevitbleLdr,SwordDvil 8
 1Aug81-7LaD  a7½f Ⓣ:232 :472 1:313fm *8-5 114  53½ 31 1hd 13½  Ardoin R3 Grady Mad  89 MusicLedr,JustinScott,MissMolki 11
23Jly81-8Aks  6f :221 :441 1:09 ft  30 116  84¼ 53¼ 33 23  Howard D L5 Juvenile  89 CruznDud,MusicLdr,LtsDontFight 11
11Jly81-5LaD  6f :222 :454 1:122ft  17 114  65¾ 68¾ 54½ 31¾  Poyadou B E6 Envoy  85 CruzenDude,CherokCircl,MusicLdr 8
13Jun81-9LaD  5f :221 :462 :592ft  11 114  1111 1113 85 59  Ardoin R2 Carousel  85 CruzenDud,HommdLovin,RosJudg 13
 3May81-11Sun 5f :221 :461 :583gd  5 118  97 98½ 88½ 68½  BrossetteAD6 R A Fut  80 PluckyHussy,RISpculton,InvtblLdr 12
24Apr81-6Sun  5f :223 :47 :591m  2½ 118  21½ 22 12 13¼  Brossette A D6 SplW  86 Music Leader, T. Dykes,Johu'sMary 9
29Mar81-10DeD 4f :222 :48 ft  6½e 118  8 89¼ 79¼ 34  BrssttAD1 JeanLafFut  89 UminAreDens,RglAvngr,MusicLdr 10
20Mar81-7DeD  4f :231 :484ft  5¼ 118  4 4nk 32½ 22  BrossetteAD9 Fut Trls  87 GryJohn,MusicLeder,HommdLovin 9
27Feb81-3DeD  4f :24 :492ft  4½ 122  2 11½ 12 1hd  Brossette A D2 Mdn  86 MusicLeader,GrayJohn,BuzzinBebe 9
15Feb81-3DeD  2½f :281ft  3½ 116  4 53¾ 34½  Lyda R4 Mdn  — CcheKing,Tmle'sBndit,MusicLedr 10
    Apr 27 CD 1 gd 1:422 h      Apr 6 OP 5f ft 1:02 b

Reinvested                              Ch. c. 3, by Irish Castle—Crafty Alice, by Crafty Admiral
                                        Br.—Regal Oak Farm (Fla)               1982  8  3  2  0    $61,180
Own.—Harbor View Farm             126   Tr.—Hough Stanley M                    Turf  1  1  0  0     $7,800
                              Lifetime   8  3  2  0   $61,180
17Apr82-8Aqu  1⅛:472 1:112 1:51 ft  20 126  79 710 67½ 55  MiglorR10 Wood Mem  75 AirForbesWon,Shimtoree,LsrLight 10
20Mar82-10Tam 1 1/16:47 1:113 1:451ft  11 114  86½ 3½ 1hd 11¼  Luhr RD10 Tampa Dby  93 Reinvested,StgeReviewer,RITwistr 12
11Mar82-7GP   1 1/16:474 1:12 1:44 ft  *6-5 122  1hd 1½ 1hd 1no  Brumfield D7 Aw13000  81 Rinvstd,DoYourDncing,SldConqust 8
22Feb82-3Hia  1 1/16:482 1:131 1:444ft  *1 118  2hd 1½ 2½ 21  Brumfield D2 Aw14000  78 Star Choice, Reinvested, Pavarotti 7
13Feb82-10Hia 1⅛:461 1:102 1:484ft  6¾e 114  2½ 21 67¼ 616  BrfldD6 Everglades H  72 RoylRobrto,NwDiscovry,VictorinLn 8
 3Feb82-7Hia  1⅛:47 1:11 1:514ft  *8-5 120  43 33 1½ 2no  Fell J3 Aw14000  73 Moore Dusty,Reinvested,CatchVilla 8
22Jan82-6Hia  1⅛Ⓣ 1:51 fm  4 120  67½ 45 2½ 1½  Fell J12 Mdn  79 Reinvested, Phaedra, GuidingRule 12
 9Jan82-4Hia  7f :232 :463 1:251ft  *1 120  105¾ 86¾ 65¾ 79¾  Vasquez J2 Mdn  67 Limrick,I'mPurGold,PrvtEncountr 12
    ●Apr 29 CD 4f ft :48 h      Apr 15 Bel tr.t 4f ft :481 b      ●Apr 9 Bel tr.t 1 gd 1:39 h      Mar 31 Hia 4f ft :482 h

Muttering                               Ro. c. 3, by Drone—Malvine, by Gamin
                                        Br.—Tartan Farms Corp (Fla)            1982  2  1  1  0   $208,800
Own.—Tartan Stable                126   Tr.—Lukas D Wayne                      1981  7  3  1  0   $108,429
                              Lifetime   9  4  2  0   $317,229
 4Apr82-4SA   1⅛:453 1:094 1:473ft  5 120  33 31½ 1½ 1no  Pincay L Jr6 Sa Derby  91 Muttring,PrncSpllbound,JournyAtS 9
 6Mar82-8SA   1 :443 1:091 1:342ft  9¼ 121  610 43 42 2½  McCrrnCJ9 San Rafael  96 PrincSpllbound,Muttring,Unprdctbl 9
23Dec81-8Hol  1 1/16:471 1:113 1:431ft  5½ 117  31 1hd 11 13  PncLJr7 Auld Lg Syne  79 Muttering, King's Finder,Cassaleria 9
31Oct81-8SA   1 1/16:461 1:103 1:421ft  8¼ 118  75¼ 75½ 65½ 43¼  Pincay L Jr2 Norfolk  87 Stalwart, Racing Is Fun,GatoDelSol 9
14Oct81-8SA   1 1/16:462 1:113 1:433ft  3 120  41 52½ 1hd 23½  PincayLJr6 El Rio Rey  79 PrincSpllbound,Muttrng,SpdBrokr 10
 4Oct81-4SA   1 :463 1:113 1:373ft  3 117  3½ 2½ 2½ 1½  Pincay L Jr5 Aw21000  81 Muttering,MillStrm,Smugglr'sGold 6
15Aug81-4Dmr  1 :462 1:12 1:391ft  2¼ 117  1hd — — —  McHrgueDG3 Aw18000  — Spiritino, Carrie's Ten, Far Niente 6
    15Aug81—Eased
18Jly81-8Hol  6f :213 :444 1:102ft  14 117  84¾ 1112 1114 1015  Lipham T6 Juv Champ  70 TheCptin,RememberJohn,Hln'sBu 12
10Jly81-6Hol  6f :22 :452 1:111ft  5½ 116  43 31½ 2½ 1½  Delahoussaye E1 Mdn  81 Muttering,LuckyLegnd,Mggi'sBst 12
    ●Apr 23 Kee 6f ft 1:13 b      ●Apr 15 Kee 5f ft :591 h      Mar 31 SA 3f ft :354 b      ●Mar 23 SA 6f ft 1:103 h
```

Real Dare

B. g. 3, by Beau Groton—Big Dare, by Kentucky Pride
Br.—Dorignac J P Jr (La) 1982 8 6 0 1 $108,069
Own.—Jumonville J E Sr 126 Tr.—Mabry John C 1981 2 1 0 0 $72,012
Lifetime 10 7 0 1 $180,081

24Apr82-6JnD 7f :24 - :483 1:292sy *1-3 123 65¾ 25 1hd 12½ Guidry RD6 [S]Aw10000 73 RelDre,AnothrDoctor,ElctronicDvic 6
28Mar82-10FG 1⅛ :464 1:112 1:503ft 6 126 76 64 814 828 Cauthen S7 La Dby 63 El Baba, Linkage,SpoonfulofHoney 8
6Mar82-9FG 1 1/16 :483 1:14 1:473sy *1-3 119 52¼ 41½ 3½ 31¼ FrlRJ4 [S]Cres Cty Dby 73 Gnilrew, Long Traffic, Real Dare 9
27Feb82-9FG 1 1/16 :483 1:14 1:463gd *1-9 123 12 13 18 113 FrnlRJ9 [S]Hit Par Inv 79 RelDre,PmsProvOut,KnightofTruth 9
18Feb82-9FG 1 1/16 :48 1:134 1:461ft *1-9 123 15 16 18 117 FrnlnRJ1 [S]Hit Par Trl 81 RelDre,Cesr'sConqust,PmsProvOut 7
31Jan82-9FG 6f :23 :464 1:11 ft *2-5 120 22 2½ 11½ 19 FrnlnRJ6 [S]Gentilly H 90 RelDre,FirstCowboy,ExclusiveMstr 8
16Jan82-7FG 6f :223 :463 1:113ft *1-2 112 22 2hd 13 110 FranklinRJ4 [S]Aw16000 87 Real Dare,FirstCowboy,TommyBolo 7
6Jan82-8FG 6f :223 :463 1:123ft *1-3 116 31 13 15 15 Franklin R J7 Aw9500 82 RealDre,TwiceBurned,LeedsCreek 10
26Dec81-9FG 6f :222 :46 1:112ft .4½e 113 2hd 11½ 16 113 FrnlRJ11 Hts Prde Fty 88 RelDre,PerfectRemdy,KinofKingly 14
17Dec81-8FG 6f :223 :471 1:141sy 7 113 1211 1211 87 43¼ Walker B J Jr7 Fut Trl 71 DesertMirge,MissProTeen,ToTllTr 12
Apr 14 JnD 4f ft :46 b Mar 20 FG 1 ft 1:424 h

Rock Steady

Dk. b. or br. c. 3, by Raise a Bid—Roccoco Miss, by Lucky Debonair
Br.—Cashman E C (Ky) 1982 5 1 0 0 $5,883
Own.—Knapp & Michael Jr 126 Tr.—Warren Ronnie 1981 7 2 1 1 $14,428
Lifetime 12 3 1 1 $20,311

24Apr82-8CD 1 :45 1:093 1:361ft 29e 113 35½ 46½ 33 41½ RomroRP5 Derby Trial 86 Listcapade,StarGllnt,RoylRoberto 10
16Apr82-8Kee 7f :224 :46 1:231ft 32 112 84¼ 87¾ 86¼ 511 Melancon L4 Aw18100 79 Deep Freeze, LeadAstray,JudoJima 8
26Mar82-8Lat 6f :231 :471 1:121sl *4-5 114 41¼ 3½ 15 16 Solomon G2 Aw6600 83 RockStdy,Micky'sBnns,BloomrRidg 7
6Feb82-9FG 6f :223 :451 1:103ft 15e 111 -82½ 87 712 717 NemtiW8 Black Gld H 75 Linkage, Cagey Cougar,TalentTown 8
16Jan82-5FG 170 :474 1:131 1:422ft 2¾ 116 43 53¼ 65½ 56½ Elmer D2 Aw9700 74 Mid Yell, Enlightenment,BostonZip 8
31Dec81-9FG 6f :222 :454 1:113ft 9¾e 114 86¼ 94¾ 912 910 ImprtoJ10 Sgr Bowl H 77 El Baba, Talk oftheTimes,TuninIn 13
16Dec81-5FG 6f :223 :471 1:132gd *3-2 119 33 32 1hd 14 Melancon L5 Aw9500 78 RockStedy,Orngeville,TwiceBurnd 10
18Nov81-6CD 6f :221 :453 1:11 ft 3 115 51¾ 52¾ 36½ 23¾ Melancon L4 Aw12300 87 Tunin In, RockSteady,DeepFreeze 12
2Nov81-5CD 7f :24 :48 1:263ft 6¼ 120 1hd 11 13 14 Melancon L2 Mdn 74 RockStdy,RunJohnnyRun,TopBrick 9
3Sep81-4Bel 7f :231 :463 1:251ft 5 118 31 62¾ 44 45¾ Maple E3 M60000 70 Wolfie'sRascal,ClearMn,ChpterOne 9
3Aug81-9FE 4½f :224 :462 :524ft 5 120 5 66 33½ 33¼ Sayler B3 Mdn 93 PublicImage,NearWillie,RockStedy 9
13Jun81-2CD 5f :223 :462 1:001ft 14 122 109½ 1011 1011 1013 Sayler B8 Mdn 75 Bronzn'Bold,EnglishCoin,MistyBid 12

Water Bank

B. c. 3, by Naskra—Summertide, by Crewman
Br.—Elmendorf Farm (Fla) 1982 6 3 2 0 $120,800
Own.—Elmendorf 126 Tr.—McAnally Ronald 1981 3 M 0 2 $7,450
Lifetime 9 3 2 2 $128,250

17Apr82-8GG 1⅛ :471 1:103 1:483ft 9-5e 119 68½ 68¼ 43½ 2½ CstnedM7 Calif Derby 89 Rockwall, Water Bank, Cassaleria 7
6Apr82-8GG 1 :48 1:13 1:383gd *8-5 120 63¾ 31½ 2hd 1hd CastnedM3 Gold Rush 75 WaterBank,LordAdvocate,GalaArry 7
21Mar82-8SA 1 1/16 :472 1:113 1:421ft 3-2e 116 2hd 2hd 78¼ 712 ShmrW1 San Felipe H 78 AdvanceMan,GatoDelSol,Cassaleria 7
20Feb82-8SA 1 1/16 :46 1:102 1:422ft 14 115 84 32 31½ 1½ McHrgDG8 S Catalina 89 WaterBank,BarginBlcony,CrystlStr 8
7Feb82-3SA 1 1/16 :47 1:113 1:433ft *6-5 118 31½ 42 31 1¾ Castaneda M5 Mdn 83 WterBnk,ConsciousEffort,NtivBllo 9
9Jan82-6SA 1 1/16 :471 1:113 1:432ft *1 118 55 43½ 23 24¾ Castaneda M6 Mdn 79 Linda's Brother,WaterBank,Exhibit 9
23Dec81-8Hol 1 1/16 :471 1:113 1:431ft *2-3e 114 96¼ 83 66½ 56 CstdM9 Auld Lg Syne 73 Muttering, King's Finder,Cassaleria 9
21Nov81-6Hol 6f :214 :444 1:103ft 3 118 64¼ 55½ 43½ 31¾ Castaneda M7 Mdn 82 World Ruler,Menderes,WaterBank 12
7Nov81-3SA 6½f :221 :452 1:163ft 7 118 64½ 55½ 45½ 31¾ DelahoussyeE2 [S]Mdn 85 Bunnell,ProspectiveStar,WterBnk 11
●Apr 27 CD 6f gd 1:152 h Apr 15 GG 4f ft :50 h Apr 3 SA 5f ft 1:002 h Mar 29 SA 6f gd 1:154 h

Rockwall

B. c. 3, by Cannonade—Fiddling Jimmer, by Jimmer
Br.—Hunt N B (Ky) 1982 2 1 1 0 $133,400
Own.—Hunt N B 126 Tr.—Clyne Vincent 1981 4 1 0 1 $13,125
Lifetime 6 2 1 1 $146,525

17Apr82-8GG 1⅛ :471 1:103 1:483ft 41 112 3½ 1hd 11½ 1½ VldvsHA2 Calif Derby 90 Rockwall, Water Bank, Cassaleria 7
4Apr82-6SA 1 1/16 :453 1:103 1:424ft 12 117 79¼ 41½ 32 22½ Sibille R7 Aw21000 84 Tell Don, Rockwall, Penngrove 9
27Dec81-4SA 1 :471 1:12 1:362ft 8 120 77½ 76 55 46¼ Sibille R8 Aw20000 81 BargainBlcony,Botrell,AlmoStrnger 8
20Dec81-6Hol 1 :463 1:123 1:39 ft 3 117 811 76¼ 52¼ 11¼ Sibille R5 Mdn 71 Rockwall,FirstLarry,Linda'sBrother 9
12Dec81-6Hol 1 1/16 :46 1:12 1:452ft *2¼ 117 89¾ 2hd 21 32 Sibille R4 Mdn 66 LimoJohn,ChrgeBetween,Rockwll 10
29Nov81-6Hol 1 :494 1:16 1:422sl 21 117 614 66 45 42½ Ramirez O3 Mdn 52 Botrell, Native Bello, Hell's Island 6
●Apr 29 CD 5f ft 1:01 h Apr 25 CD 1 ft 1:464 b Apr 15 SA 3f ft :352 h Apr 10 SA 1 ft 1:374 h

Wolfie's Rascal

B. c. 3, by London Company—Daisy Trimmer, by Bold Discovery
Br.—Amlung R (Fla) 1982 6 2 1 0 $72,662
Own.—Cohen, Cohen, Kumble 126 Tr.—Tesher Howard M 1981 6 2 0 1 $39,395
Lifetime 12 4 1 1 $112,057

17Apr82-8Aqu 1⅛ :472 1:112 1:51 ft 21 126 55½ 46 43 42½ VelsquzJ5 Wood Mem 77 AirForbesWon,Shimtoree,LsrLight 10
27Mar82-9Lat 1 1/16 :463 1:113 1:443ft *8-5 120 85¾ 814 614 612 BrcclVJr8 Jim BSpiral 75 Goodn'Dusty,FstGold,Cupcoy'sJoy 12
6Mar82-10Hia 1⅛ :462 1:104 1:493sy 14 122 119 85 66 55½ BrccileVJr11 Flamingo 78 TimelyWriter,NewDiscovry,LDnsur 16
24Feb82-8Aqu 1⅛ [•]:472 1:122 1:511ft 2¼ 117 31½ 1hd 1hd 11¾ BrcclVJr6 Lucky Draw 90 Wolfi'sRscl,AskMuhmmd,FstGold 11
12Feb82-8Aqu 1 1/16 [•]:474 1:123 1:441ft *2 119 2hd 1hd 2½ 21 SantiagoA3 Whirlaway 91 AskMuhmmd,Wolfie'sRscl,FstGold 7
13Jan82-8Aqu 170 [•]:481 1:132 1:424ft *9-5 119 42½ — 11½ 12¼ Santiago A2 Aw18000 88 Wolfie'sRscl,SkinDncr,Shy'sRbllion 6
13Jan82—Running positions omitted because of weather conditions.
7Dec81-7Aqu 1 1/16 [•]:474 1:123 1:462ft 3 117 2½ 2hd 1½ 13¼ Santiago A7 Aw17000 82 Wolfie'sRscl,ClssHero,MortggeMn 12
22Nov81-8Aqu 1 :46 1:11 1:364ft 5½e 114 84¼ 77 68 68¼ Santiago A6 Nashua 74 Our Escapade,John'sGold,Hostage 10
14Nov81-8Aqu 1⅛ :481 1:131 1:504ft 54 113 33 43½ 38 39¾ Santiago A3 Remsen 71 LserLight,RelTwister,Wolfie'sRscl 11
26Oct81-5Aqu 1 :464 1:122 1:383sy 7½ 117 32½ 64¾ 77½ 79¼ Velasquez J6 Aw17000 63 LiftOneA.,SealedConquest,RedRng 8
3Sep81-4Bel 7f :231 :463 1:251ft 8¾ 114 41½ 1hd 12½ 14¾ Velasquez J7 M55000 76 Wolfie'sRascal,ClearMn,ChpterOne 9
13Aug81-5Crc 6f :231 :47 1:134ft 11 116 62¾ 55½ 56½ 56¾ Guerra W A4 M50000 76 Drakus Here, Fitz's Night,IrishPete 6
Apr 13 Aqu 6f ft 1:15 h Apr 5 Kee 6f ft 1:142 h ●Mar 23 Lat 6f ft 1:132 h Mar 13 Hia 7f ft 1:292 b

Star Gallant
Dk. b. or br. c. 3, by My Gallant—Liza Star, by Bold Hitter
Br.—Roma Stable (Fla) 1982 4 2 2 0 $124,600
Own.—Buckram Oak Farm 126 Tr.—Imperio Leonard 1981 2 2 0 6 $41,760
Lifetime 6 4 2 0 $166,360
24Apr82-8CD 1 :45 1:093 1:361ft *1-3 122 1½ 15 1½ 2¼ Hawley S4 Derby Trial 87 Listcapade,StarGllnt,RoylRoberto 10
3Apr82-9GP 1⅛ :471 1:111 1:493ft 6-5 122 11½ 12 1hd 22 Hawley S1 Fla Derby 82 TimelyWriter,StarGallnt,OurEscpde 7
22Mar82-9GP 1 1/16 :471 1:111 1:431ft 2¼ 117 11½ 11 11 14 Hawley S5 Ftn Youth 85 StarGallant,DistinctivePro,CutAwy 9
16Feb82-9Hia 7f :223 :443 1:23 ft *1-3 116 22 1hd 11 14 Hawley S7 Aw14000 88 Star Gallant, CutAway,Rex'sProfile 7
23Dec81-8Aqu 6f [□]:214 :4531:111gd*2-3 113 53¾ 2hd 13 12¼ Hernandez C3 Alsab 88 StrGllnt,FoxmorFlght,WndFrmThS 7
10Dec81-4Aqu 6f [□]:224 :47 1:11 ft *9-5 1117 42½ 2hd 12 16 Hernandez C10 Mdn 89 Star Gallant,Shimatoree,Joy'sMac 14
●Apr 22 CD 3f ft :343 h ●Mar 30 GP 4f gd :47 b ●Mar 15 Hia 6f ft 1:102 h ●Mar 7 Hia 4f ft :453 h

Cassaleria
Dk. b. or br. c. 3, by Pretense—Special Charm, by Verbatim
Br.—Bradyleigh FarmsInc&Brady (Ky) 1982 4 1 0 2 $121,600
Own.—20/20 Stable 126 Tr.—McAnally Ronald 1981 8 2 2 4 $234,070
Lifetime 12 3 2 6 $355,670
17Apr82-8GG 1⅛ :471 1:103 1:483ft 9-5e 122 56½ 47½ 33½ 3½ McHrDG3 Calif Derby 89 Rockwall, Water Bank, Cassaleria 7
4Apr82-4SA 1⅛ :453 1:094 1:473ft 8 120 912 85 54½ 65¼ ShoemkrW7 Sa Derby 86 Muttring,PrncSpllbound,JournyAtS 9
21Mar82-8SA 1 1/16 :472 1:113 1:421ft 3-2e 123 3½ 4¾ 2½ 3¾ McHrDG5 San FelipeH 89 AdvanceMan,GatoDelSol,Cassaleria 7
6Feb82-8BM 1 1/16 :461 1:102 1:424ft *2-3 120 711 78¾ 45 1½ McHrDG3 El CamReal 85 Cassaleria, CrystalStar,TropicRuler 9
23Dec81-8Hol 1 1/16 :471 1:113 1:431ft *2-3e 120 63½ 41¾ 32 33 McHrDG5 AuldLgSyne 76 Muttering, King's Finder,Cassaleria 9
29Nov81-8Hol 1 1/16 :481 1:141 1:474sl 4¼ 121 79¼ 57 2½ 2½ McHrguDG8 Hol Fut'y 55 Stalwart, Cassaleria, Header Card 12
14Nov81-8BM 1 1/16 :451 1:101 1:413gd *8-5 115 610 31½ 11 13½ McHrDG2 ElCamoReal 91 Cassaleria, Songhay, Lucky Ship 9
18Oct81-2SA 1 1/16 :464 1:114 1:424ft *7-5 118 43½ 31 13 110 Castaneda M3 Mdn 87 Cassaleria,ChargeBetween,BisonBy 7
7Oct81-4SA 1 :463 1:113 1:37 ft 3¾ 118 47 33 31½ 3nk Ortega L E2 Mdn 84 Stalwart,CompanyChairman,Cssleri 9
23Aug81-6Dmr 1 :463 1:113 1:374ft 4½ 117 52½ 42 33½ 35½ Ortega L E3 Mdn 73 OkieCityLd,StndupComedin,Cssleri 9
1Aug81-6Dmr 6f :224 :454 1:104ft 4 118 79 47 35½ 37 Ortega L E5 Mdn 77 ExplosiveTwist,SpeedBroker,Csslri 8
26Jun81-6Hol 5½f :223 :464 1:054ft 21 116 97 78¼ 46 22 Castaneda M6 M50000 80 Spiritino, Cassaleria, Convince Me 12
●Apr 27 CD 6f gd 1:152 b Apr 13 SA 5f ft 1:001 h

Gato Del Sol
Gr. c. 3, by Cougar II—Peacefully, by Jacinto
Br.—Hancock III & Peters (Ky) 1982 4 0 2 1 $86,365
Own.—Hancock III & Peters 126 Tr.—Gregson Edwin 1981 8 2 1 3 $220,828
Lifetime 12 2 3 4 $307,193
22Apr82-7Kee 1⅛ :463 1:10 1:48 ft 3¾ 121 46 46 34½ 25½ DlhossyE3 Blue Grass 91 Linkage,GtoDelSol,WveringMonrch 9
4Apr82-4SA 1⅛ :453 1:094 1:473ft 7½ 120 812 98 67 43¼ DelhoussyE4 Sa Derby 88 Muttring,PrncSpllbound,JournyAtS 9
21Mar82-8SA 1 1/16 :472 1:113 1:421ft 4¼ 118 76½ 75¼ 43 2nk DlhssyE6 San Felipe H 90 AdvanceMan,GatoDelSol,Cassaleria 7
25Feb82-7SA 6½f :221 :45 1:152ft 9-5 115 67¾ 66½ 65½ 33¼ DelhoussyeE5 Aw22000 90 LuckyLegend,RcingIsFun,GtoDlSol 6
29Nov81-8Hol 1 1/16 :481 1:141 1:474sl 5¾ 121 89¼ 77¼ 711 714 DelhoussyE6 Hol Fut'y 42 Stalwart, Cassaleria, Header Card 12
14Nov81-8Hol 7f :211 :432 1:22 ft 3½ 122 511 59½ 33½ 2½ DlhossyE5 Hol Prevue 86 Sepulveda,GatoDelSol,DesertEnvoy 6
31Oct81-8SA 1 1/16 :461 1:103 1:421ft 3¾ 118 911 86½ 55½ 32½ DelhoussyeE3 Norfolk 87 Stalwart, Racing Is Fun,GatoDelSol 9
9Sep81-8Dmr 1 :453 1:111 1:372ft 3¾ 114 1012 105½ 73¼ 1hd DelhoussyE2 Dmr Fut 81 GatoDelSol,TheCaptain,RingProud 10
26Aug81-8Dmr 1 :454 1:103 1:364ft 5¼ 115 79 46 54½ 33½ DelahoussyeE7 Blaboa 80 TheCaptain,DistantHeart,GtoDelSol 9
14Aug81-6Dmr 1 :47 1:124 1:39 ft *8-5 117 3nk 11½ 13 17 McCarron C J5 Mdn 73 Gato Del Sol, Kell's Boy, ClubFlush 8
10Jly81-6Hol 6f :22 :452 1:111ft *2½e 116 66 67¼ 67 77 Vaienzuela P A2 Mdn 74 Muttering,LuckyLegnd,Mggi'sBst 12
28Jun81-6Hol 5½f :221 :461 1:051ft 5¼e 116 79¾ 69 55¾ 33½ Delahoussaye E5 Mdn 81 Irisher, Zanyo, Gato Del Sol 12
Apr 29 CD 4f ft :483 b Apr 18 Kee 4f sy :504 b ●Apr 12 Kee 6f ft 1:133 b ●Apr 3 SA 3f ft :342 h

Majesty's Prince
Ch. c. 3, by His Majesty—Pied Princess, by Tom Fool
Br.—Marsh J D (Va) 1982 3 1 1 0 $37,512
Own.—Marsh J D 126 Tr.—Cantey Joseph B 1981 8 2 3 2 $71,849
Lifetime 11 3 4 2 $109,361 Turf 4 2 2 0 $47,264
10Apr82-9OP 1⅛ :474 1:123 1:513ft 5e 117 1016 109¾ 811 56¼ KenelJL2 Arknsas Dby 79 Hostage, El Baba, Bold Style 10
20Mar82-9OP 170 :46 1:122 1:434ft 4½e 115 718 59 46 2no Kaenel J L6 Rebel H 77 BoldStyle,Mjesty'sPrince,LostCrek 8
5Mar82-7OP 6f :222 :471 1:13 ft 6 114 77½ 65 3½ 1½ Kaenel J L11 Aw15000 80 Mjesty'sPrince,Hvgrtdt,HrfordMn 12
14Nov81-8Aqu 1⅛ :481 1:131 1:504ft 5½ 115 65 1113 1117 917 MacBeth D1 Remsen 64 LserLight,RelTwister,Wolfie'sRscl 11
24Oct81-8Lrl 1 1/16 :47 1:122 1:443gd 9-5 122 67½ 65¾ 47 49 Maple E1 Lrl Fut'y 76 DeputyMinistr,LsrLight,‡CgyCougr 8
24Oct81—Placed third through disqualification
1Oct81-8Bel 1 1/16 (T):4741:1111:43 fm*9-5 117 31 3nk 2hd 2hd Maple E5 Prince John 81 Gnom'sGld,Mjsty'sPrnc,DncngSchl 7
14Sep81-8Bel 1 (T):4531:1021:351fm*2-5 115 2½ 2hd 21½ 24¾ Maple E4 Cascade H 84 DncngSchool,Mjsty'sPrnc,BbyDuck 8
4Sep81-3Bel 1 (T):48 1:1231:384gd*2-3 119 12½ 13½ 13½ 15¾ Maple E3 Aw20000 71 Mjsty'sPrnc,DncngSchool,OrEscpd 6
20Aug81-2Sar 6f :23 :462 1:104ft 4e 122 31½ 51½ 3½ 2nk Maple E4 Aw19000 86 TalcPlot,Mjesty'sPrince,IrishMrtini 8
6Aug81-4Sar 1 [T]:4831:1431:39 gd 2¼ 118 11 11 11½ 13¾ Maple E4 Mdn 81 Mjsty'sPrnc,ClssHro,Who'sFrDnnr 10
20Jly81-6Bel 6f :224 :461 1:123sy 14 118 1023 1021 616 36 Maple E6 Mdn 73 JttingPlsur,BronzCup,Mjsty'sPrnc 10
Mar 31 OP 6f gd 1:152 b Mar 1 OP 5f gd 1:034 h

Throughout the eighty minutes between the seventh race and the Derby, the best bet was Air Forbes Won to show. The final mutuels suggested an optimal bet of $99:

	Totals	#1 Air Forbes Won	Expected Value per Dollar Bet on Air Forbes Won
Odds		5—2	
Win	2,853,976	641,476	
Show	1,006,969	129,486	1.25

Gato Del Sol, ridden by Eddie Delahoussaye, ran an impressive race to win the Churchill classic by $2\frac{1}{2}$ lengths over Laser Light and Reinvested. Gato Del Sol, a 21–1 shot, was the last horse away from the gate, and he stayed near the rear until the backstretch. Then he picked up ground outside on the final turn and ran strongly until the finish. Delahoussaye had planned this late charge on the outside since coming in second on Woodchopper in the 1981 Kentucky Derby. Woodchopper had been trapped inside, which had probably cost him the race, and Delahoussaye was determined not to repeat that strategy. El Baba and Air Forbes Won ran second and third for most of the race, but both weakened in the final stretch to finish eleventh and seventh, respectively. The $99 loss dropped my betting fortune to $522.50.

The chart of the race was as follows:

108th Kentucky Derby, May 1, 1982

$550,100 gross value and $40,000 Gold Cup. Net to winner $428,850; second $60,000; third $30,000; fourth $15,000. 388 nominations.

Horse	Eqt	Wt	PP	¼	½	¾	Mile	Str	Fin	Jockeys	Owners	Odds to $1
Gato Del Sol		126	18	19	19	10½	5½	1½	$1^{2\frac{1}{2}}$	E. Delahoussaye	Hancock & Peters	21.20
Laser Light		126	8	18^{hd}	17^{hd}	18½	10^{1}	9^{hd}	2^{nk}	E. Maple	Live Oak Plantation	18.20
Reinvested		126	10	$16^{1\frac{1}{2}}$	16½	14^{1}	7^{1}	2½	$3^{2\frac{1}{2}}$	D. MacBeth	Harbor View Farm	f-8.90
Water Bank		126	13	$14^{1\frac{1}{2}}$	$12^{1\frac{1}{2}}$	$16^{1\frac{1}{2}}$	8^{2}	5^{hd}	4¾	M. Castaneda	Elmendorf	a-12.60
Muttering		126	11	4^{hd}	5½	4½	4^{hd}	4^{hd}	5^{3}	L. Pincay	Tartan Stable	4.20
Rockwall	b	126	14	12^{1}	9^{1}	$5^{1\frac{1}{2}}$	6^{1}	$7^{1\frac{1}{2}}$	6¾	H. Valdivieso	Nelson B. Hunt	47.80
Air Forbes Won		126	7	3^{hd}	3^{3}	3^{2}	3^{3}	3^{hd}	$7^{1\frac{1}{4}}$	A. Cordero	Edward Anchel	2.70
Star Gallant		126	16	6^{1}	7½	9^{hd}	9^{1}	10^{1}	8no	W. Shoemaker	Buckram Oak Farm	15.70
Majesty's Prince		126	19	13^{hd}	13½	17^{1}	14^{2}	11½	9^{hd}	R. Hernandez	John D. Marsh	f-8.90
Cupecoy's Joy		121	1	$1^{1\frac{1}{2}}$	$1^{3\frac{1}{2}}$	1^{4}	1½	8^{hd}	10½	A. Santiago	Ri-Ma-Ro Stable	f-8.90
El Baba		126	4	2½	2^{3}	2^{2}	2^{hd}	6^{hd}	11^{1}	D. Brumfield	Mrs. Joe W. Brown	3.30
Wavering Monarch		126	6	11^{2}	10^{hd}	11^{hd}	11½	12^{2}	$12^{1\frac{1}{4}}$	R. Romero	Greathouse family	39.50
Cassaleria		126	17	15^{hd}	15^{hd}	15^{hd}	13½	13½	13^{nk}	D. McHargue	20/20 Stable	a-12.60
Royal Roberto		126	5	17^{1}	18½	19	17½	14½	14½	M. Rivera	Key West Stable	9.30
Music Leader	b	126	9	$8^{1\frac{1}{2}}$	8½	8^{hd}	$12^{1\frac{1}{2}}$	15^{hd}	$15^{2\frac{1}{2}}$	P. Day	Glaser-Ellett, et al	f-8.90
Bold Style	b	126	2	7^{2}	4^{hd}	7^{hd}	15½	16½	16^{nk}	J. Fell	Len Mayer	29.30
Wolfie's Rascal		126	15	5½	6^{hd}	6½	16^{2}	17^{3}	$17^{1\frac{1}{2}}$	J. Velasquez	Cohen-Cohen-Kumble	f-8.90
New Discovery		126	3	10½	11^{hd}	13^{hd}	$18^{1\frac{1}{2}}$	18^{4}	18^{6}	J. Bailey	Herbert Allen	f-8.90
Real Dare		126	12	9^{1}	14^{1}	$12^{1\frac{1}{2}}$	19	19	19	R. Guidry	J. E. Jumonville, Sr.	f-8.90

Time: :23, :46-1/5, 1:10-4/5, 1:37-1/5, 2:02-2/5. Track fast. Off at 5:40 EDT. Start good. Won driving.

f-mutuel field. A-coupled Water Bank and Cassaleria.

$2 mutuels paid — Gato Del Sol $44.40 straight; $19.00 place; $9.40 show, Laser Light $17.00 place; $9.20 show; Reinvested (field) $4.40 show.

Winner — Gr. c, by *Cougar II — Peacefully, by Jacinto. Trainer Edwin Gregson. Bred in Kentucky by Hancock III & Peters.

GATO DEL SOL came away relaxed in last position and clear of horses, advanced on the outside under his own courage in the backstretch, picked up the field with a strong run completing the turn to take command before the furlong pole, was unaffected by REINVESTED leaning on him briefly and drew clear under strong right hand use of the whip into the final yards. LASER LIGHT also relaxed in the early running, followed GATO DEL SOL around horses leaving the backstretch and was wide straightening away for the final stretch drive, loomed boldly but could not sustain his bid while gamely besting REINVESTED for the place. REINVESTED, intimidated by WATER BANK leaving the half-mile marker and bothering CASSALERIA, swung slightly out on that rival getting room on the outside to follow GATO DEL SOL approaching mid-stretch, leaned in briefly under right hand urging and hung. WATER BANK saved ground early, found room between rivals with a stretch bid and hung. MUTTERING, well placed from the beginning, made a bid between horses entering the stretch and weakened slightly. ROCKWALL finished well without being a threat. AIR FORBES WON responded with a strong run to reach the leaders completing the final turn and weakened late. STAR GALLANT was never a serious factor. MAJESTY'S PRINCE bore out slightly while tiring. CUPECOY'S JOY set the pace in comfortable fashion into the stretch turn before giving way. EL BABA, well situated closest to the pace, drew on even terms for the lead entering the stretch and weakened suddenly. CASSALERIA was being outrun when bothered by REINVESTED in the backstretch and never became a factor. ROYAL ROBERTO was outrun at all stages. BOLD STYLE saved ground racing forwardly placed for six furlongs and tired. WOLFIE'S RASCAL lost ground and dropped back early. NEW DISCOVERY gave a dull effort. REAL DARE tired badly.

Scratched: Rock Steady

THE WINNER'S PEDIGREE AND CAREER HIGHLIGHTS

GATO DEL SOL Grey Colt	*Cougar II	Tale of Two Cities	Tehran
			Menda II
		Cindy Lou II	Madaro
			Maria Bonita
	Peacefully	Jacinto	Bold Ruler
			Cascade II
		Morning Calm	Hail to Reason
			Yellow Mist

Year	Age	Sts	1st	2nd	3rd	Won
1981	2	8	2	1	3	$220,828
1982	3	9	2	3	1	$588,779
TOTALS		17	4	4	4	$809,607

At 2 Years	WON	Del Mar Futurity
	2nd	Hollywood Revue
	3rd	Balboa Stakes
At 3 Years	WON	Kentucky Derby
	2nd	San Felipe, Blue Grass Stakes
	3rd	
	UNP	Santa Anita Derby

DUAL TRACKS IN THE NINTH

The final Dr. Z bet of the day was on Dual Tracks in the ninth race. With two minutes to post time the mutuels suggested an optimal bet of $67:

	Totals	#3 Dual Tracks	Expected Value per Dollar Bet on Dual Tracks
Odds		3—1	
Win	397,004	75,441	
Show	110,222	11,621	1.28

Dual Tracks made his move in the stretch, but could only grab third behind Avatoil and Genuine Magic. But with a show bet, a third is as good as a win! His $3.80 show payoff meant a return of $127.30 and a profit of $60.30. The mutuel payoffs were:

4–	Avatoil	7.80	4.40	3.60
8–	Genuine Magic...........		4.20	3.20
3–	Dual Tracks..............			3.80

The Dr. Z system had won four races out of five for the day. My bankroll had increased 46%, from $400 to $582.80. I was already looking forward to Derby '83 (which was discussed in Chapter 11).

KENTUCKY DERBY DAY 1984

The Kentucky Derby is often called "the most exciting two minutes in sports." With scalpers' prices that can be greater than those for the Super Bowl or the Olympics, the spectators can find it is also "the most expensive two minutes in sports!" An extreme example is a six-seat box on the Derby finish line—it officially sells for $510 but may go for as much as $10,000 on the black market! The majority of the spectators are not the box-seat crowd, though. They are the general-admission crowd who pay $10 and head for the infield. Together they composed the 126,453 spectators of the 1984 Derby.

Fillies in the Derby have been relatively rare. The first to win the Run for the Roses was Regret in 1915, who went off as the favorite and led wire to wire. The second and last filly to win was Genuine Risk in 1980. She was third against colts in the Wood Memorial, but was only made the sixth choice by the public in the thirteen-horse field. She paid $28.60 for her 1-length win and later ran second to Codex in the Preakness and second to Temperance Hill in the Belmont. In the first 109 Derbies there have been, including these two, only 32 Derby fillies. The latest was Cupecoy's Joy, who finished tenth in 1982. The 1984 Derby, however, had two fillies that were running as an entry and were sent off as the favorite. The two were Althea and Life's Magic, both trained by D. Wayne Lukas. The highly touted Althea, a daughter of Alydar, had earnings of $1,275,255 and was being ridden by Chris McCarron. She ran away from the Arkansas Derby field, winning by 7 lengths with a 107 speed rating, and was now trying to duplicate the feat of Sunny's Halo—winning the Kentucky Derby after an Arkansas Derby victory. Life's Magic was from the first crop of Cox's Ridge (he had two other Derby starters: Vanlandingham and Pine Circle) and had earned $577,509. Fillies receive a five-pound advantage in the Derby, so both Althea and Life's Magic would be carrying 121 pounds.

Missing from the Derby was the previous year's two-year-old champion, Devil's Bag, who had been scratched the Tuesday before the race. Many felt that this decision was made with his investors' interest in mind. He had been syndicated the previous fall for $36 million (then the second highest after Shareef Dancer's $40 million syndication) and now was not running well. He was undefeated as a two-year-old but in February finished fourth in the Florida Stakes. And at the Derby Trial Stakes, a week before the Derby, he had an unimpressive victory over a weak field. Now it was felt that his stud value would drop considerably more if he raced poorly in the Derby than if he didn't run at all. When he was scratched it was announced that he would be pointed toward the Preakness. But that was not to be. The Monday after the Derby, Devil's Bag was retired from racing when a veterinarian's examination found a small fracture in his knee. He stands at Claiborne Farms in Paris, Kentucky.

The crowd's second choice, after the filly entry, was Swale, a son of Triple Crown winner Seattle Slew. He was trained by Woody Stephens (who was also the trainer of Devil's Bag) and had been ranked second on the Experimental Free Handicap (five pounds below Devil's Bag). His record had been somewhat inconsistent: winning the Gulfstream Hutcheson but finishing third in the Fountain of Youth, beating Dr. Carter in the Florida Derby but then being upset, on an off track, in the Lexington at Keeneland. His jockey was the great Laffit Pincay, Jr., who was trying for his first Derby win in eleven mounts. He had come close with three seconds: Sham in 1973, General Assembly in 1979, and Rumbo in 1980.

The crowd's third choice was Silent King, who had been second in the Louisiana Derby and the Blue Grass Stakes. He would be ridden by Willie Shoemaker, always both a threat and a sentimental favorite. Silent King was a late charger, with almost as dramatic a style as the famous Silky Sullivan. It was not uncommon for him to be 20 or more lengths behind the leader before he made his move. Harry, Teresa, and Tom Meyerhoff, his owners, had bought Spectacular Bid for $37,000 and won the Derby with him in 1979. They had bought Silent King for $22,000 and were hoping to repeat their earlier Derby success.

Other strong contenders were Vanlandingham (winner of four of his last five races) and Pine Circle (second in the Arkansas Derby). Both were owned by Loblolly Stable and trained by Claude McGaughey III. Gate Dancer had been second in the San Felipe and third in the Arkansas Derby. He could be easily spotted with his big purple ear muffs and extension blinkers. They were an attempt to stop him from lugging in on other horses. His rider, Eddie Delahoussaye, was trying for his third consecutive Derby victory. He had won with Gato del Sol and Sunny's Halo the previous two years. Taylor's Special had won the Blue Grass Stakes and the Louisiana Derby and was trained by the thirty-year-old Billy Mott. Fali Time had won the San Felipe and was fourth in the Santa Anita Derby. At The Threshold had won Latonia's Jim Beam Stakes and was fourth in the Arkansas Derby. Also running were Raja's Shark, Bear Hunt, Fight Over, and the field consisting of So Vague, Bedouin, Rexson's Hope, Secret Prince, Majestic Shore, Biloxi Indian, and Coax Me Chad.

The experts' selections showed they were all picking Swale:

Experts' Selections

Consensus Points: 5 for 1st (today's best 7), 2 for 2nd, 1 for 3rd. Today's Best in Bold Type.

Trackman, Charles Scaravilli **CHURCHILL DOWNS** Selections Made for Fast Track

	TRACKMAN	HANDICAP	ANALYST	HERMIS	SWEEP	CONSENSUS	
1	DUSTY CUP TRUCKING FEES LUCKY SMEAD	DUSTY CUP MICKEY LOBE TIMARATA	JUNGLE DUKE SOLAR JUNCTION TIMARATA	DUSTY CUP JUNGLE DUKE TIMARATA	SOLAR JUNCTION JUNGLE DUKE RHONSBORO	DUSTY CUP JUNGLE DUKE SOLAR JUNCTION	15 9 7
2	WARNING FLAG SOLDIER II COURT PROCEDURE	MOUNTAIN HARBOR WARNING FLAG ATLANTIS	COURT PROCEDURE WARNING FLAG ATLANTIS	ATLANTIS WARNING FLAG POPCORN CASSEROLE	WARNING FLAG COURT PROCEDURE POPCORN CASSEROLE	WARNING FLAG COURT PROCEDURE ATLANTIS	16 8 7
3	HOUR OF REASON PRINCESS MONTAGUE KLASHY KERRI	VEGA FURY HOUR OF REASON STRIKING QUICK	**KLASHY KERRI** FAIREST TUMBLER STRIKING QUICK	**KLASHY KERRI** FAIREST TUMBLER STRIKING QUICK	**KLASHY KERRI** STRIKING QUICK FAIREST TUMBLER	KLASHY KERRI HOUR OF REASON VEGA FURY	22 7 5
4	SUN CELLAR JEAN FELIOU LITTLE WAY	ERUDITE SUN CELLAR BRAZENLY BOLD	ERUDITE THUNDER CHICK SUN CELLAR	SUN CELLAR ERUDITE THUNDER CHICK	ERUDITE SUN CELLAR THUNDER CHICK	ERUDITE SUN CELLAR THUNDER CHICK	17 15 4
5	GYPSY PRAYER BITTER COLD SEA SHAM	FLYING WEST GYPSY PRAYER BITTER COLD	GYPSY PRAYER SEA SHAM FAMILY AFFAIR	SEA SHAM GYPSY PRAYER BITTER COLD	GYPSY PRAYER SEA SHAM BITTER COLD	GYPSY PRAYER SEA SHAM BITTER COLD	19 10 5
6	DERBY DOUBLE MY Z. BOMB RONNY TURCOTTE	STEEL ROBBING POLICE PURSUIT MY Z. BOMB	DUST OFF THE MAT DERBY DOUBLE STEEL ROBBING	STEEL ROBBING DERBY DOUBLE DUST OFF THE MAT	DERBY DOUBLE STEEL ROBBING DUST OFF THE MAT	DERBY DOUBLE STEEL ROBBING DUST OFF THE MAT	14 13 7
7	**WORKIN GIRL** LONELY GREEK NEVER REASON	WORKIN GIRL RUN TULLE RUN DUPED	RUN TULLE RUN WORKIN GIRL RAIN SHOWER	RAIN SHOWER RUN TULLE RUN FIRST HONEY	RUN TULLE RUN RAIN SHOWER WORKIN GIRL	WORKIN GIRL RUN TULLE RUN RAIN SHOWER	15 14 8
8	SWALE ALTHEA VANLANDINGHAM	**SWALE** ALTHEA TAYLOR'S SPECIAL	SWALE ALTHEA VANLANDINGHAM	SWALE ALTHEA TAYLOR'S SPECIAL	SWALE TAYLOR'S SPECIAL ALTHEA	**SWALE** ALTHEA TAYLOR'S SPECIAL	27 9 4
9	APPEAL JUDGE CHOCOLATE POP REKAL	REALLY SILVER THE GOOCH BOND JUMPER	CHOCOLATE POP TALK ABOUT SPADE APPEAL JUDGE	TALK ABOUT SPADE REALLY SILVER THE GOOCH	TALK ABOUT SPADE REALLY SILVER THE GOOCH	TALK ABOUT SPADE REALLY SILVER CHOCOLATE POP	12 9 7
10	GOODBODY BOLD DAMON SEE I GONE	GOODBODY BUFFALO HART BOLD DAMON	CAPTAIN J. J. GOODBODY BOLD DAMON	BOLD DAMON GOODBODY IVANOVO	GOODBODY BOLD DAMON SILENCE REIGNS	GOODBODY BOLD DAMON CAPTAIN J. J.	19 11 5

A LOSER AFTER A FOUR-RACE WAIT

We arrived at Churchill Downs in time for the first race and were looking forward to a successful day of wagering. Unfortunately we had to display remarkable restraint because the first Dr. Z bet was in the fifth race, a 6-furlong allowance race for fillies. The horses were not impressive but they were being ridden by many of the premier jockeys. Using this race as a warmup for the big one were Pat Day, Laffit Pincay, Jr., Willie Shoemaker, Eddie Delahoussaye, Herbert McCauley, and Don Brumfield. Brumfield was on Gypsy Prayer, our first Dr. Z system bet of the day. At one minute to post time the mutuels were:

	Totals	*#5 Gypsy Prayer*	*Expected Value per Dollar Bet on Gypsy Prayer*
Odds		2–1	
Win	484,352	130,506	
Show	197,009	38,837	1.11

With our betting wealth of $1,500 the optimal wager was $64 to show. Unfortunately, Gypsy Prayer finished well out of the money leaving us with $1,436, the first time we had been behind at the Derby. The mutuel payoffs were:

3–	Sea Sham	6.40	3.20	2.00
1–	Bitter Cold		3.30	2.00
4–	Persuadable			3.40

THE BAY PHANTOM ALLOWANCE

We did better in the next race, the 7-furlong Bay Phantom Allowance. There were Dr. Z bets to place and show on the favorite, Steel Robbing. Making two bets is more involved so we did our calculations with two minutes to post. The mutuels were:

	Totals	#5 *Steel Robbing*	*Expected Value per Dollar Bet on Steel Robbing*
Odds		1–1	
Win	438,931	173,349	
Place	197,017	56,586	1.12
Show	150,831	39,529	1.16

The suggested wagers were $250 to place and $492 to show. The Beat the Racetrack Calculator(TM) indicates optimal wagers for one bet at a time. With two bets we must revise the calculator's output using equations (16.5) and (16.6) from Chapter 16. This revision indicated an $83 place bet and a $413 show bet. The final tote board gave an expected return on the place bet slightly below our cutoff of 1.10 but the show bet remained good:

	Totals	#5 *Steel Robbing*	*Expected Value per Dollar Bet on Steel Robbing*
Odds		1–1	
Win	528,049	210,937	
Place	232,918	71,442	1.08
Show	175,074	47,667	1.14

When Steel Robbing won he paid $4.20 to win, $3 to place, and $2.60 to show. The $83 place bet and the $413 show bet returned $124.50 and $536.90, respectively, for a profit of $165.40 and a final wealth of $1601.40. The mutuel payoffs were:

5–	Steel Robbin..............	4.30	3.00	2.00
1–	Dust off the Mat..........		3.00	2.00
2–	Police Pursuit.............			3.00

DUPED IN THE SEVENTH

Duped appeared to be underbet to show in the seventh race, a 1-mile allowance race. Two minutes before post time the mutuels were:

	Total	*#3 Duped*	*Expected Value per Dollar Bet on Duped*
Odds		9–5	
Win	448,284	129,405	
Show	184,681	38,255	1.12

The optimal wager was $148. The final mutuels were similar:

	Total	*#3 Duped*	*Expected Value per Dollar Bet on Duped*
Odds		9–5	
Win	535,707	155,812	
Show	213,538	45,700	1.11

Duped was third and paid $3.00. The profit of $74 brought our bankroll to $1675.40. The mutuel payoffs were:

8–	Never Reason.............	17.00	8.40	4.00
4–	Workin Girl		3.20	3.20
3–	Duped....................			3.00

ALTHEA DIES IN THE STRETCH: A LESSON IN DOSAGE ANALYSIS

The eighth race was the Kentucky Derby. As expected, this race received far more betting interest than any of the other races of the day. Total wagering was $5,420,787 at Churchill Downs. There was also $13,521,146 of "other-track" wagering; twenty-two other tracks and the New York and Connecticut OTB systems had made arrangements with Churchill Downs to simulcast the Derby and allow wagering for their public. This enabled bettors around the country to not only watch the Derby but to bet on it as well. The New York OTB had been accepting wagering on the Derby since 1971. They did this without any agreements with Churchill Downs until 1978. Then legislation was passed that disallowed other-track wagering when approval of the home track, racing commissions, and horsemen representatives had not been given. Disagreements among these parties and New York led to minimal other-track betting in 1981 and no other-track betting in 1982 and 1983. Churchill Downs's share from the agreement that was finally made in 1984 was approximately $650,000, 51% of which goes to the horsemen as increases in purses.

The program for the Derby and its entrants' impressive past performances follow:

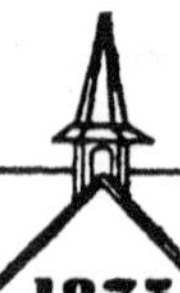

PRELIMINARY BETTING

110th RUNNING—KENTUCKY DERBY

1875 1984

$250,000 ADDED ONE MILE and ONE-QUARTER TRACK RECORD—SECRETARIAT (3), 126 lbs., 5-5-73, 1:59-2/5

For three-year-olds. By subscription of $200 each. All nomination fees to the winner. $10,000 to pass entry box, $10,000 additional to start. $250,000 added, of which $100,000 to second, $50,000 to third, $25,000 to fourth, (to be divided equally in the event of a dead heat). Weight 126 lbs. The owner of the winner to receive a gold trophy.

Closed Wednesday, February 15, 1984, with 312 nominations.

USE THESE NUMBERS FOR BUYING PARI MUTUEL TICKETS

No.	Owner	Trainer	Horse	Wt.	Jockey	Odds
1	David Aykroyd, Helen Alexander & Helen Groves	D. Wayne Lukas	ALTHEA	121	Chris McCarron	5-2
1a	Hal Hatley Racing Stables	D. Wayne Lukas	LIFE'S MAGIC	121	Don MacBeth	5-2
2	Loblolly Stable	Claude R. McGaughey III	VANLANDINGHAM	126	Pat Day	10
2b	Loblolly Stable	Claude R. McGaughey III	PINE CIRCLE	126	Mike Smith	10
3	Erwin Heiman	Salvatore Campo	RAJA'S SHARK	126	Rick Wilson	20
4	Taylor's Purchase Farm	Roger Laurin	BEAR HUNT	126	Jerry Bailey	20
5	Swamazon Farm	John Parisella	FIGHT OVER	126	Octavio Vergara	20
6	Jim Mamakos & Mark Stuehm	Gary Jones	FALI TIME	126	Sandy Hawley	12
7	William F. Lucas	William I. Mott	TAYLOR'S SPECIAL	126	Sam Maple	7-2
8	Hawksworth Farm Associates	Grover G. Delp	SILENT KING	126	Bill Shoemaker	15
9	W. Cal Partee	Lynn Whiting	AT THE THRESHOLD	126	Eddie Maple	20
10	Claiborne Farm	Woodford C. Stephens	SWALE	126	Laffit Pincay, Jr.	3
11	Kenneth Opstein	Jack C. Van Berg	GATE DANCER	126	Eddie Delahoussaye	15
12 FIELD	Hyperion Thoroughbreds, Ltd.	G. M. Russell	SO VAGUE	126	P. A. Cooksey	12
13 FIELD	Elmendorf Farm	Richard Mandella	BEDOUIN	126	Ray Sibille	12
14 FIELD	Elsie A. Rose Stable Inc.	Harold J. Rose	REXSON'S HOPE	126	Robert Gaffglione	12
15 FIELD	Elaine M. Brodsky	William V. Terrill	SECRET PRINCE	126	Craig Perret	12
16 FIELD	Oldknow & Phipps	Loren Rettele	MAJESTIC SHORE	126	John Lively	12
17 FIELD	Sundance Stable	Dianne Carpenter	BILOXI INDIAN	126	Garth Patterson	12
18 FIELD	Elmer Miller	Ronnie G. Warren	COAX ME CHAD	126	Herbert McCauley	12

FIELD—12-13-14-15-16-17-18

Selections—1-10-7-2

110th – KENTUCKY DERBY

8th Churchill

1 ¼ MILES. (1.59⅗) 110th Running KENTUCKY DERBY (Grade I) Scale weight Stakes. $250,000 Added. 3-year-olds. With a subscription fee of $200 each, an entry fee of $10,000 each and a starting fee of $10,000 each. All fees to be paid to the winner. $250,000 shall be paid by Churchill Downs Incorporated (the "Association") as the Added Purse. Second place shall receive $100,000, third place shall receive $50,000 and fourth place shall receive $25,000 from the Added Purse. (The Added Purse and fees to be divided equally in the event of a dead heat.) Starters shall be named through the entry box on Thursday, May 3, 1984, at the usual time of closing. The maximum number of starters shall be limited to twenty and each shall carry a weight of 126 lbs., fillies, 121 lbs. In the event that more than twenty entries pass through the entry box at the time of closing, the starters shall be determined at that time with preference given to those horses that have accumulated the highest earnings, excluding earnings won in a restricted race. For purposes of this preference, a "restricted race" shall mean a state-bred restricted race (a race where entries are restricted to horses qualifying under state breeding programs), a sales restricted race (a race where entries are restricted by the origin of purchase), and a money restricted sweepstake (a race where entries are restricted by the amount of money previously earned). The owner of the winner shall receive a gold trophy. No supplementary nominations shall be accepted. (Closed with 312 nominations.)

Route the Field Will Travel

Kentucky Derby

One and One-Quarter Miles

START FINISH

Coupled—Althea and Life's Magic; Vanlandingham and Pine Circle.

Mutuel Field—So Vague, Bedouin, Rexson's Hope, Secret Prince, Majestic Shore, Biloxi Indian, Coax Me Chad.

Althea

Ch. f. 3, by Alydar—Courtly Dee, by Never Bend
Br.—Alexander-Aykroyd-Groves (Ky) 1984 4 3 1 0 $582,630
Own.—Alexander-Aykroyd-Groves **121** Tr.—Lukas D Wayne 1983 9 5 3 0 $692,625
Lifetime 13 8 4 0 $1,275,255

21Apr84-9OP 1⅛ :463 1:101 1:464ft 3 121 11 1½ 16 17 VlenzuelPA10 Ark Dby 109-04 Althea, Pine Circle, Gate Dancer 11
14Apr84-9OP 1 1/16 :463 1:104 1:411ft *3-5 121 52 31½ 1hd 2¾ Pincay LJr1 ⒻFantasy 101-11 MyDarlingOne,Althea,PersonbleLdy 6
14Apr84—Lost her footing at the start
11Mar84-8SA 1 1/16 :472 1:113 1:433ft *3-5 117 32 1½ 11 1¾ PncLJr2 ⒻSnta Susna 83-18 Althea,PersonableLady,Life'sMagic 5
25Feb84-8SA 1 :462 1:11 1:37 ft *1 124 51¾ 42 42½ 1no PcLJr1 ⒻLas Virgenes 83-18 Althea,VagabondGal,MyDarlingOne 6
18Dec83-8Hol 1 1/16 :454 1:101 1:413ft 2¾ 118 2½ 1hd 34 611 Pincay L Jr4 Hol Fut'y 76-14 Fali Time, Bold T. Jay,Life'sMagic 12
18Dec83—Rough trip bumped
27Nov83-8Hol 1 1/16 :464 1:112 1:43 ft *6-5 120 11 11 11½ 11½ PncLJr6 ⒻHol Starlet 80-20 Althea, Life's Magic, Spring Loose 6
12Nov83-8SA 1 1/16 :463 1:113 1:442sy *4-5 117 11 11½ 1½ 2½ PincyLJr1 ⒻOak Leaf 78-23 Life's Magic, Althea, Percipient 9
26Oct83-8SA 7f :222 :451 1:231ft *1-9 123 2hd 2hd 2½ 21½ Pincay LJr2 ⒻAnoakia 83-20 Percipient, Althea, PersonableLady 4
14Sep83-8Dmr 1 :454 1:102 1:344ft *1-3 117 11 12½ 16 16½ Pincay LJr4 Dmr Fut'y 94-14 Althea, Juliet's Pride, Gumboy 5
4Sep83-8Dmr 1 :453 1:102 1:36 ft *1-3 119 110 114 114 118 PncyLJr4 ⒻDebutante 88-17 Althea, Diachrony, Victorious Joy 6
23Jly83-8Hol 6f :214 :441 1:092ft 2½ 117 2hd 13 17 110 PncyLJr3 Jvnl Cham'p 90-21 Althe,RejectdSuitor,AutoCommndr 9
9Jly83-8Hol 6f :22 :444 1:103ft *2-5e117 2hd 2hd 1hd 22 PncLJr11 ⒻLandaluce 82-23 Simple Magic, Althea,Reb'sGateau 11
22Jun83-6Hol 5f :214 :443 :57 ft *4-5 117 2hd 1½ 12½ 16½ Pincay L Jr10 ⒻMdn 92-19 Althea,MissCamouflge,BigPotentil 10
●Apr 7 SA 5f ft :581 h ●Apr 4 SA 5f ft :594 h Mar 30 SA 5f ft :592 h Mar 23 SA 5f ft 1:004 h

Raja's Shark

Dk. b. or br. g. 3, by Raja Baba—Shark's Jaws, by Mitey Prince
Br.—Brittingham B C (Ky) 1984 3 0 1 1 $82,070
Own.—Feiner I **126** Tr.—Campo Salvatore 1983 4 3 0 1 $29,940
Lifetime 7 3 1 2 $112,010

21Apr84-8Aqu 1⅛ :463 1:114 1:512ft 5½ 126 34 31 2hd 2½ Wilson R2 Wood 77-30 Leroy S., Raja's Shark, Bear Hunt 7
1Apr84-9Lat 1 1/16 :46 1:101 1:424ft 29 121 44 44 44 42¾ Wilson R5 Jim Beam 93-18 AtThThrshld,BldSthrnr,ThWddGst 12
25Mar84-8Lat 1 :462 1:104 1:38 sy 2½ 112 2hd 14 1½ 31 Wilson R6 Aw10700 80-26 So Vague, A Gift, Raja's Shark 9
26Nov83-8Aqu 1 :444 1:11 1:382gd *2 114 31½ 31½ 22 34 Nied J Jr4 Nashua 70-24 DonRickles,ArabianGift,Raja'sShrk 9
20Nov83-8Key 6f :22 :452 1:111ft *1-5 117 23½ 22 13 13½ Nied J Jr1 Believe It 85-22 Rj'sShrk,BoldFlunky,ChristophrRyn 6
20Nov83—Drifted in,clear
16Oct83-6Key 7f :222 :451 1:231ft *4-5 117 21 21 14 19¾ Nied J Jr1 Aw10500 91-19 Raja'sShark,BoldFlunky,Moqnglade 9
16Oct83—Bore out, handily
27Sep83-5Key 6f :223 :462 1:12 ft 3½ 120 1hd 11½ 12½ 18 Nied J Jr6 Mdn 81-22 Raj'sShrk,Jimboel,MyWhiteKnight 8
May 1 CD 6f ft 1:163 b ●Apr 18 Key 5f gd :594 h ●Apr 10 Key 1 ft 1:41 b Mar 30 Lat 4f ft :573 b

Bear Hunt

B. c. 3, by Naskra—Ashwood Bow, by Gun Bow
Br.—Little W P (Ky) 1984 5 2 0 2 $192,060
Own.—Taylors' Purchase Farm **126** Tr.—Laurin Roger 1983 3 2 0 1 $28,800
Lifetime 8 4 0 3 $220,860 Turf 1 0 0 0 0

21Apr84-8Aqu 1⅛ :463 1:114 1:512ft 9-5 126 2hd 1½ 1hd 31 MacBeth D5 Wood 77-30 Leroy S., Raja's Shark, Bear Hunt 7
7Apr84-8Aqu 170⊡:47 1:1121:402ft 4½ 114 12 11½ 14 14¾ MacBeth D1 Gotham 98-16 Bear Hunt, Lt. Flag, On The Sauce 5
18Mar84-3Aqu 170⊡:48 1:1331:431ft 3½ 117 14½ 11 12½ 13½ MacBeth D2 Aw22000 84-24 BerHunt,Dixie'sIslnd,Groom'sImge 7
18Feb84-8Hia 1 1/16 Ⓣ 1:413fm 6½ 112 1314 1415 1423 1417½ MapleE5 Dade County 73-11 Dr.Schwartzman,Klytone,Clejucm 14
18Feb84—Wide 1st turn
17Jan84-9Hia 1 1/16 :462 1:103 1:433ft 2½ 121 2hd 22½ 32 35½ Maple E1 Aw16000 79-19 Turnberry,TimeforaChnge,BerHunt 8
9Dec83-7Aqu 1 1/16 ⊡:4931:1431:462ft 2½ 117 1hd 11½ 11½ 12¾ Maple E7 Aw24000 79-19 BerHunt,IsYourPlesur,Cindy'sFrind 7
30Oct83-6Aqu 6f :223 :463 1:122ft 6½ 118 21 2½ 22 11 Cruguet J3 Mdn 78-22 Bear Hunt, Romanoletti, Treanor 12
30Oct83—Lugged in, driv.
18Sep83-4Bel 6f :23 :462 1:113ft 8 118 75½ 33 35 39 Cruguet J9 Mdn 76-28 BsketWeve,ChimesKeeper,BrHunt 10
18Sep83—Off Slow
May 2 CD 4f ft :484 b Apr 27 Bel 5f ft :592 h Apr 18 Bel tr.t 5f ft 1:031 b Apr 14 Bel tr.t 4f ft :50 b

So Vague *
B. c. 3, by Empery—Merry Says So, by Advocator
Br.—Cashman E C (Ky) 1984 5 1 2 0 $14,565
Own.—Hyperion Thoroughbreds 126 Tr.—Russell Gerry M 1983 17 3 2 1 $85,300
Lifetime 22 4 4 1 $100,964
26Apr84-7Kee 1⅛ :473 1:122 1:521ft 74 121 817 919 819 722¾ CookseyPJ9 Bluegrass 53-31 Tylor'sSpecil,SilntKing,ChrmdRook 9
19Apr84-7Kee 7f :231 :46 1:233gd 22 120 58¼ 511 48½ 215 Cooksey P J5 Aw29300 73-27 Devil's Bag, So Vague, Triple Sec 5
1Apr84-9Lat 1 1/16 :46 1:101 1:424ft 10 121 1214 911 1016 1017½ CookseyPJ9 Jim Beam 78-18 AtThThrshld,BldSthrnr,ThWddGst 12
25Mar84-8Lat 1 :462 1:104 1:38 sy 3½ 115 69½ 44½ 2½ 11 Cooksey P J2 Aw10700 89-26 So Vague, A Gift, Raja's Shark 9
8Mar84-9Lat 6f :223 :462 1:14 fr *1-2 119 57 34½ 35½ 24 Cooksey P J1 Aw10600 78-30 AncntHombr,SoVgu,KntuckyRnmkr 7
18Dec83-8Hol 1 1/16 :454 1:101 1:413ft 31 121 1213 1213 1211 911½ CookseyPJ1 Hol Fut'y 76-14 Fali Time, Bold T. Jay,Life'sMagic 12
7Dec83-8Hol 7f :212 :44 1:221ft 17f 115 1614 1110½ 58½ 1¾ CoksyPJ2 Hol Prevue 86-18 SoVgu,CountryMnor,FrnchLgionir 16
29Nov83-6Lat 6f :231 :472 1:141ft *1-2 122 64¾ 64½ 35 1¾ Cooksey P J8 Aw7000 73-28 So Vague, Running Monk,C.R.Ryan 7
23Nov83-6CD 6f :223 :462 1:133sy 22 117 77½ 77 42½ 22½ Cooksey P J6 Aw11200 75-31 FairlyStraight,SoVgue,CountryHick 7
23Nov83—Wide stretch
11Nov83-4CD 7f :23 :464 1:264m 14 118 54½ 66½ 34 39 Cooksey P J8 Aw11200 64-31 LocustBayou,TruckingFees,SoVgue 6
2Nov83-7CD 6½f :23 :464 1:20 sy 40 110 1012 96½ 67½ 48½ Cooksey P J8 Aw11200 72-27 Whitebrush,BigPistol,SeamnTeelo 11
2Nov83—Wide
28Oct83-5Kee 1 1/16 :483 1:142 1:481sy 2½ 114 65½ 52½ 49½ 410 Cooksey P J8 Aw16000 55-26 Halogen, Bookmark, Coffer Dam 8
12Oct83-3Kee 1 1/16 :472 1:123 1:452ft 2½ 117 64 53½ 57½ 510 Cooksey P J5 Aw15000 69-15 LoadedDeck,IdelMtch,Wyne'sPride 8
21Aug83-8Sar 6½f :214 :451 1:172ft 31f 122 1212 1111 98½ 68½ ♦ Cooksey P J1 Hopeful 78-23 Capitol South, Don Rickles, Swale 13
♦21Aug83—Dead heat
12Aug83-2CD 6f :224 :463 1:131ft 3½ 117 51½ 2hd 1½ 12½ Day P7 Mdn 95-20 So Vague, East St. Clair, Karabein 7
5Aug83-1CD 6f :222 :461 1:121gd 9½ 119 77½ 44 58 411 Melancon L7 Mdn 74-19 FlyingFinish,Whitbrush,BlushOfFm 8
29Jly83-3CD 6f :221 :46 1:122ft 9 118 54 53 2½ 2½ Cooksey P J3 Mdn 83-12 Big Pistol, So Vague, Dolcie's Boy 7
22Jly83-2CD 6f :214 :454 1:123ft 5½ 117 64½ 96½ 98 68½ Day P1 Mdn 77-18 TransE.T.,PublicMenace,EstSt.Clir 10
26Jun83-8RD 6f :222 :461 1:133ft 4½ 112 814 712 67¾ 41½ Cooksey P J4 Rascal 74-33 TllMedows,SilverShooter,DndyRidn 8
26Jun83—Run in two divisions, 8th and 9th races
10Jun83-1CD 5f :224 :46 :594ft 91 117 94 95 64 54½ Tauzin L0 Mdn 86-16 BlndSpt,OrMchlSth,BlndMnsBlff 10
11May83-3CD 5f :231 :47 :593ft 50 118 32 42½ 53½ 57½ Wedlake D3 Mdn 83-15 ‡LaPwn,TrickyNick,CounterAction 7
4May83-1CD 4½f :23 :472 :534gd 22 117 8 74½ 64¾ 610 Wedlake D5 Mdn 80-08 GreyPocket,J'sNtive,ShkeRttlnkick 8
Apr 24 Kee 3f sy :363 b ●Apr 13 Kee 6f sy 1:132 b ●Apr 10 Kee 3f sy :35 b ●Mar 30 Kee 3f gd :361 b

Life's Magic *
B. f. 3, by Cox's Ridge—Fire Water, by Tom Rolfe
Br.—Parrish Mr-Mr D & D C III (Ky) 1984 3 0 1 1 $40,250
Own.—Hatley & Klein 121 Tr.—Lukas D Wayne 1983 7 2 4 1 $537,250
Lifetime 10 2 5 2 $577,500
8Apr84-8SA 1⅛ :452 1:10 1:49 ft 9½e 115 714 611 69½ 59 CrdrAJr1 S. Anita Dby 75-16 MightyAdvrsry,Prcisionist,PrincTru 8
8Apr84—Checked
11Mar84-8SA 1 1/16 :472 1:113 1:433ft 2¾ 115 43 42 42 3¾ CrdrAJr1 ⒻSntaSusna 82-18 Althea,PersonableLady,Life'sMagic 5
16Feb84-7SA 1 :463 1:114 1:38 ft *1-3 119 53 42½ 22½ 21½ Pincay LJr6 ⒻAw35000 76-23 VagabondGal,Life'sMagic,Dichrony 6
16Feb84—Wide, bumped
18Dec83-8Hol 1 1/16 :454 1:101 1:413ft 11 118 88½ 74¾ 44½ 34 CordroAJr10 Hol Fut'y 83-14 Fali Time, Bold T. Jay,Life'sMagic 12
27Nov83-8Hol 1 1/16 :464 1:112 1:43 ft 2 120 41½ 21 32 21½ McCrrCJ5 ⒻHolStrlet 78-20 Althea, Life's Magic, Spring Loose 6
12Nov83-8SA 1 1/16 :463 1:113 1:442sy 9-5 115 44½ 21½ 2½ 1½ McCrrCJ6 ⒻOak Leaf 79-23 Life's Magic, Althea, Percipient 9
5Nov83-8SA 1 1/16 :464 1:113 1:441ft 2 117 51½ 42 31 2no Pincay L Jr8 Norfolk 80-20 Fali Time, Life's Magic, Artichoke 10
10Oct83-8Bel 1 :454 1:101 1:363ft *3-2e 119 74½ 32½ 32½ 2no CordrAJr10 ⒻFrizette 82-15 MssOcn,Lf'sMgc,LuckyLuckyLcky 10
4Sep83-8AP 7f :22 :442 1:232ft 3½ 119 910 812 38 23¾ ShrW5 ⒻArl Wsh Lass 81-22 MissOceana,Life'sMgic,BottleTop 11
4Sep83—Circled rivals leaving three-eighths pole.
25Aug83-3Dmr 6f :221 :454 1:121ft 4 117 714 611 44 12 Pincay LJr3 ⒻAw17000 77-22 Life's Magic, Diachrony,EarlyQuest 7
May 1 CD 4f ft :48 b Apr 26 CD 5f ft 1:003 b Apr 4 SA 5f ft :583 b Mar 28 SA 5f ft 1:00 b

Fight Over
Gr. c. 3, by Grey Dawn II—Quarrel, by Raise a Native
Br.—Swamazon Farm (Ky) 1984 5 2 1 1 $40,572
Own.—Swamazon Farm-Saharese 126 Tr.—Parisella John 1983 5 1 0 0 $40,464
Lifetime 10 3 1 1 $80,036
26Apr84-7Kee 1⅛ :473 1:122 1:521ft 2½ 121 45 46 47½ 410¾ CordroAJr6 Bluegrass 65-31 Tylor'sSpecil,SilntKing,ChrmdRook 9
25Mar84-11FG 1⅛ :463 1:104 1:493ft 9½ 123 58½ 32½ 21½ 32 Migliore R6 La Dby 94-10 Tylor'sSpecil,SilentKing,FightOver 7
25Mar84—Stumbled coming out of gate
10Mar84-10FG 1 1/16 :47 1:11 1:43 ft 6½ 116 2hd 32½ 22 23½ Walker B JJr1 Dby Trl 93-16 Tylor'sSpecil,FightOver,SilentKing 5
10Mar84—Steadied and came out on second turn
22Feb84-9FG 1 40 :48 1:14 1:411ft *1-2 119 34½ 1½ 1½ 1no Romero R P4 Aw10000 87-25 Fight Over, Tellicherry, Con Artist 7
8Feb84-9FG 6f :22 :46 1:114ft *2-3 119 32 21½ 11½ 13½ Romero R P1 Aw5200 86-25 Fight Over, W. T. Door, Little Fleet 8
27Aug83-8AP 7f :222 :46 1:27 sy 7 122 96 1015 1015 1118¾ Day P8 Arl Was Fut 48-36 AllFirdUp,HolmOnTop,SmrtNSlick 17
10Aug83-8Sar 6f :221 :454 1:11 ft 9½ 119 64½ 45 46½ 57¾ MacBeth D1 Sanford 77-16 Big Walt,FillRon'sPockets,AgileJet 8
1Aug83-8Sar 6f :221 :46 1:123m 6½ 122 35 36 24 45 McBethD6 Sar Special 72-24 Swale, Shuttle Jet, Big Walt 7
1Aug83—Wide stretch
22Jun83-8Bel 5½f :223 :462 1:053ft 25 113 66 53 11 13½ MacBeth D6 Juvenile 87-22 Fight Over,I'mHoppy,RestlessChris 8
8Jun83-8Bel 5½f :222 :462 1:062ft 7 115 2½ 3½ 33 45½ MacBeth D5 Youthful 77-22 AttawyToGo,I'mHoppy,BrodwyBrry 5
May 3 CD 4f sy :49 b ●Apr 21 Bel tr.t 5f ft :581 b Apr 15 Bel tr.t 7f sy 1:253 b ●Apr 9 Bel tr.t 5f ft :592 b

Fali Time
B. c. 3, by Faliraki—First Time Out, by First Landing
Br.—Mamakos & Stubrin (Cal) 1984 4 2 1 0 $222,600
Own.—Mamakos & Stubrin 126 Tr.—Jones Gary 1983 7 3 2 1 $748,829
Lifetime 11 5 3 1 $971,429 Turf 1 0 1 0 $15,000
8Apr84-8SA 1⅛ :452 1:10 1:49 ft 2¾ 120 23 22 33½ 44 HwleyS7 S. Anita Dby 80-16 MightyAdvrsry,Prcisionist,PrincTru 8
25Mar84-8SA 1 1/16 :462 1:103 1:423ft *3-2 122 42¾ 41½ 1½ 1hd HwleyS1 San Felipe H 88-17 FaliTime,GateDancer,Commemorte 6
25Mar84—Wide, stretch
3Mar84-8SA 1 :444 1:091 1:35 ft *9-5 122 38 33½ 22½ 25 Hawley S6 San Rafael 88-14 Precisionist,FaliTime,Commemorte 6
8Jan84-8SA 7f :222 :452 1:231ft *2-5 124 2½ 2hd 1hd 1nk HwlyS3 ⓈBrds Champ 84-20 FliTime,Fortune'sKingdom,BuenJef 6
18Dec83-8Hol 1 1/16 :454 1:101 1:413ft 11 121 43½ 31 2hd 1½ Hawley S9 Hol Fut'y 87-14 Fali Time, Bold T. Jay,Life'sMagic 12
25Nov83-8Hol 1 Ⓣ:473 1:122 1:373gd 5½ 120 22 22½ 21 2½ Hawley S3 Hoist Flag 79-22 Precisionist, Fali Time, Tights 8
25Nov83—Run in two divisions 6th and 8th races
5Nov83-8SA 1 1/16 :464 1:113 1:441ft 18 118 3nk 2hd 1½ 1no Hawley S8 Norfolk 80-20 Fali Time, Life's Magic, Artichoke 10
21Oct83-6SA 6f :221 :453 1:103ft 3½ 117 2½ 31 1½ 13½ DelahoussyeE7 ⓈMdn 85-20 FaliTime,QuieroDinero,CrystlCourt 7
15Aug83-6Dmr 6f :223 :454 1:12 ft 11 117 21 21½ 21 32 Baltazar C0 ⓈMdn 76-24 Donner Party, ‡EasyEasy,FaliTime 10
15Aug83—Placed second through disqualification; Impeded
4Aug83-6Dmr 6f :23 :462 1:112ft 3¾ 116 52½ 68¾ 50 59 Baltazar C2 ⓈMdn 72-24 BoldT.Jy,Corontd,OnO'ClockJump 10
13Jly83-6Hol 6f :221 :45 1:101ft 11 116 23 36 28 37½ Baltazar C6 Mdn 78-19 Precisionist,TriumphntBnnr,FliTim 8
Apr 30 CD 1 gd 1:394 h Apr 25 CD 6f ft 1:17 b ●Apr 20 SA Ⓣ5f fm 1:004 h (d) Apr 16 SA 4f ft :473 b

Bedouin *

Ro. c. 3, by Al Hattab—Lady in Red, by Prince John
Own.—Elmendorf 126 Br.—Elmendorf Farm (Ky) 1984 6 1 2 1 $35,850
Tr.—Mandella Richard 1983 6 2 0 0 $101,029
Lifetime 12 3 2 1 $136,879 Turf 3 1 1 0 $27,075

26Apr84-8Hol 1 1/16 Ⓣ:483 1:123 1:424fm *4-5 114 4½ 42 42 1½ Hawley S4 Aw24000 85-17 Bedouin, Armin, Known For Style 5
18Apr84-8SA 1⅛ Ⓣ:463 1:113 1:492fm 6 118 76½ 54 62½ 2¾ HawleyS6 ⓈLa Puente 75-21 Loft, Bedouin, Bean Bag 9
16Apr84—Wide
7Apr84-4SA 1 1/16 :454 1:104 1:432ft 4½ 114 47½ 32 3½ 21 Hawley S1 Aw33000 83-18 Swivel, Bedouin, Barcelona 6
7Apr84—Wide
29Mar84-7SA 1 1/16 :471 1:113 1:424ft 6½ 117 74 65½ 612 610½ DelhoussyeE5 Aw30000 77-18 Distant Ryder, Lotsa Honey, Bozina 8
29Mar84—Bumped at start
5Feb84-8BM 1 1/16 :461 1:103 1:422ft 5 120 1013 99 812 811 LamnceC11 El Camino 76-17 FrenchLegionire,GtDncr,HwnlyPlin 11
5Feb84—Broke in a tangle
22Jan84-7SA 1 1/16 :463 1:104 1:434ft *6-5 117 611 59 46½ 34½ DelhoussyeE3 Aw27000 78-21 Tights, Bold Batter Up, Bedouin 6
18Dec83-8Hol 1 1/16 :454 1:101 1:413ft 31 121 1112 99½ 88½ 47 DelhoussyE8 Hol Fut'y 88-14 Fali Time, Bold T. Jay,Life'sMagic 12
25Nov83-8Hol 1 Ⓣ:473 1:122 1:373gd 2½ 118 810 713 611 58½ PincayLJr2 Hoist Flag 73-22 Precisionist, Fali Time, Tights 8
25Nov83—Run in two divisions 6th and 8th races
13Nov83-6SA 1 :473 1:13 1:392m *9-5 116 63½ 43 1hd 15½ Hawley S3 Aw24000 71-26 Bedouin,PenutsTurn,ForeignLegion 7
28Aug83-4Dmr 1 :461 1:12 1:38 ft 3 116 76½ 510 32½ 13½ Hawley S2 Mdn 78-16 Bedouin,Intimidtion,OverlndJourny 8
7Aug83-4Dmr 1 :47 1:121 1:383ft 5½ 116 812 813 513 416½ McCarron C J7 Mdn 65-18 Accontbly,PlntyCnscs,SpclKndGy 10
27Jly83-6Dmr 5½f :224 :461 1:044ft *9-5 117 68½ 711 513 418 McCarron C J2 Mdn 72-20 Bozina, UsuallyReliable,EndDisplay 8

●Apr 16 SA Ⓣ4f fm :483 h (d) Apr 4 SA 4f ft :483 h Mar 29 SA 1 ft 1:391 h Mar 22 SA 5f ft 1:01 h

Rexson's Hope

Dk. b. or br. c. 3, by Rexson—Abe's Miss, by Abe's Hope
Own.—Rose Elsie A Stable Inc 126 Br.—Hawkesworth J A Jr (Fla) 1984 6 0 1 2 $101,725
Tr.—Rose Harold J 1983 16 4 1 2 $118,403
Lifetime 22 4 2 4 $220,128 Turf 1 0 0 1 $4,293

26Apr84-7Kee 1⅛ :473 1:122 1:521ft 8½ 121 712 611 613 512¾ GffglioneR6 Bluegrass 63-31 Tylor'sSpecl,SilntKing,ChrmdRook 9
26Apr84—Broke through the gate prior to the start
31Mar84-10GP 1⅛ :463 1:101 1:473ft 10 122 915 812 611 48¾ Gaffglione R2 Fla Dby 85-14 Swale, Dr. Carter, Darn That Alarm 9
17Mar84-10Tam 1 1/16 :464 1:114 1:443ft 4½ 122 1313 78¾ 46 2no GfflnR8 Budtmpa Dby 96-19 BoldSouthernr,Rxson'sHop,Sticklr 13
3Mar84-11Hia 1⅛ :462 1:093 1:47 ft 47 122 813 718 47½ 36½ GffglioneR4 Flamingo 91-13 TimeforChnge,Dr.Crter,Rxson'sHop 8
11Feb84-10Hia 1⅛ :463 1:10 1:47 ft 22 119 918 811 36½ 35½ GffglionR9 Everglades 91-09 TimeforChnge,Bello,Rexson'sHop 11
7Jan84-9Crc 1 1/16 :472 1:124 1:46 ft 28 121 1414 106¾ 2hd 21½ † GffglonR6 Trp Pk Dby 87-14 MornngBob,‡Rxson'sHop,DnRckls 15
† 7Jan84—Disqualified and placed fifth; Impeded horses
24Dec83-9Crc 170 :474 1:134 1:432ft 8½ 120 98½ 73½ 46½ 45½ GfflnR8 What A Plesr 87-16 MorningBob,D.White,Plentyofsense 9
24Dec83—Run in two divisions 7th & 9th races
26Nov83-7Crc a1 1/16 Ⓣ 1:414fm 3½ 119 1022 810 45 38½ GffglionR3 City Miami 92-05 Dr.Schwrtzmn,D.Whit,Rxson'sHop 10
26Nov83—Run in two divisions: 7th & 9th Races
29Oct83-9Crc 1 1/16 :473 1:14 1:481ft 4½ 120 1018 65 11½ 15½ GfflnR4 ⓈFla Stallion 78-18 Rexson'sHope,UpperStr,MelTicket 11
29Oct83—Run in two divisions, 7th and 9th races
22Oct83-3Crc 1 1/16 :484 1:14 1:464ft 9½ 114 32½ 21½ 12½ 15 Gaffelione R2 Aw13000 80-17 Rxson'sHop,FlordDsgn,CmmtlOfOn 8
8Oct83-8Crc 170 :471 1:13 1:451ft 8 118 3nk 2½ 55½ 612½ St. Leon G.8 Aw12000 72-16 Plentyofsense,MajorBaron,PapKoo 9
24Sep83-9Crc 7f :223 :462 1:261sy 15 118 118½ 1013 77¾ 66¾ Mrqzc14 ⓈFla Stallion 78-17 ALndnFg,Plntyfsns,BwmnsExprss 14
14Sep83-6Crc 6f :223 :471 1:132ft 25 114 42 41½ 1hd 14½ Bain G W5 35000 85-20 Rxsn'sHp,‡Pt'sGllnt,MyPpSysTHp 11
5Sep83-8Crc 6½f :221 :453 1:194ft 22 113 65½ 811 811 810½ Bain G W4 Aw11500 73-17 RoylRemilu,PrivteLndr,AlbrtGlimor 8
25Aug83-8Crc 6f :224 :464 1:141ft 15 118 42½ 44½ 43 34½ Bain G W7 Aw11500 77-22 ThRghtWrong,RoylRml,Rxson'sHop 8
18Aug83-9Crc 6f :223 :463 1:121ft 31 113 41½ 44 610 611 Bain G W2 Aw13000 80-16 BouRllh,BowmnsExprss,Glmor'sRn 7
8Aug83-8Crc 6f :224 :471 1:132ft 12 112 88 87 77¾ 65¾ Russ M L10 Aw11500 79-17 FntstcPrspct,ThRghtWrn,NhlmsB 11
28Jly83-7Crc 6f :223 :462 1:132sy 5 1077 47½ 58½ 57½ 55½ Neider D A4 Aw11500 79-21 Glimore'sRun,I'mHoppy,RoylRmilu 6
28May83-3Hia 5f :224 :47 1:003ft *9-5 118 31½ 32½ 33 1¾ Bain G W1 M40000 83-28 Rexson'sHope,PrivteSecretry,NitBt 9
20Apr83-6Hia 5f :223 :47 1:001ft 4½ 118 45½ 410 46 44½ † Bain G W8 Mdn 80-24 ExubrntDvl,PrncO'Rulh,I'mHoppy 11
†20Apr83—Disqualified and placed last
12Apr83-1Hia 5f :224 :471 1:001ft 12 118 33 31½ 2½ 22 Bain G W11 Mdn 83-20 WildExubrnc,Rxson'sHop,Dr.Prppi 11
1Apr83-3Hia 3f :233 :344ft 5 118 2 32 54½ Bain G W2 Mdn 83-12 HolmOnTop,WildExubrnc,Dr.Prppi 14

Apr 24 Kee 4f sy :52 b Apr 14 Crc 5f sy 1:032 b Mar 29 Crc 4f ft :48 h Mar 15 Tam 4f ft :50 b

Taylor's Special *

B. c. 3, by Hawkin's Special—Bette's Gold, by Espea
Own.—Lucas W F 126 Br.—Foley Dravo G (Ky) 1984 6 5 1 0 $307,233
Tr.—Mott William I 1983 7 4 1 1 $62,707
Lifetime 13 9 2 1 $369,940

26Apr84-7Kee 1⅛ :473 1:122 1:521ft *9-5 121 11 14 12½ 13½ Day P5 Bluegrass 76-31 Tylor'sSpecil,SilntKing,ChrmdRook 9
25Mar84-11FG 1⅛ :463 1:104 1:493ft *2 118 1hd 11 11½ 11 Maple S1 La Dby 96-18 Tylor'sSpecil,SilentKing,FightOver 7
10Mar84-10FG 1 1/16 :47 1:11 1:43 ft *4-5 121 1hd 12 12 13½ Romero R P3 Dby Trl 97-16 Tylor'sSpecil,FightOver,SilentKing 5
18Feb84-10FG 1 1/16 :461 1:112 1:451ft *2-3 122 2hd 11½ 13 21 RomroRP7 Lecomte H 85-21 SilentKing,Tylor'sSpcil,FirlyStright 8
4Feb84-10FG 6f :223 :462 1:113gd *3-5 121 54½ 31½ 2hd 13½ RomrRP3 Blck Gold H 87-24 Tylr'sSpcl,FlyngFnsh,BtwxtN'Btwn 8
14Jan84-10FG 6f :213 :453 1:114ft *2-3 120 64½ 33 2½ 1hd Romero R P7 HcpO 86-23 Tylr'sSpcl,FlyngFnsh,BtwxtN'Btwn 8
19Nov83-8CD 1 1/16 :482 1:124 1:461ft *2 119 12 13 1hd 33½ BrmfldD5 Ky Jcky Cb 74-22 BiloxIndn,CountryMnor,Tylor'sSpcl 7
31Oct83-8CD 1 :462 1:104 1:371ft *6-5 117 12 12 13 12 Brumfield D3 Iroquois 83-16 Tylor'sSpecil,Bello,AtTheThreshold 9
21Oct83-5Kee 6½f :224 :454 1:172sy 2¾ 115 1hd 12 15 16½ Brumfield D3 Aw16000 90-19 Tylor'sSpecil,Bello,ConfidentilKelly 8
3Sep83-9CD 7f :231 :461 1:244ft 3¾ 116 2½ 2½ 11 2nk McKnightJ4 Perryville 83-15 BiloxiIndin,Tylor'sSpecil,Whitbrush 8
13Aug83-7CD 6f :221 :453 1:121ft *8-5 118 2hd 11½ 12½ 1¾ McKnight J4 Aw11300 85-17 Tylor'sSpecil,TrickyNick,DirtyBirdi 7
8Jly83-8CD 5½f :222 :46 1:05 ft *8-5 115 74½ 76 98 1113 MyrsL6 Bashford Mnr 83-20 BtwxtN'Btwn,RlShrpDncr,BlxIndn 13
24Jun83-3CD 5½f :231 :46 1:054ft *3-5 119 31 11½ 12 12 Moyers L8 Mdn 92-12 Tylor'sSpecil,LouN'Mur,FirwyTrvlr 8

●Apr 23 CD 4f gd :46 h Apr 16 CD 1 ft 1:391 h ●Apr 8 FG 5f ft :583 h ●Mar 21 FG 4f ft :464 h

Silent King *

Ch. c. 3, by Screen King—[illegible], by Jet Action
Own.—Hawksworth Farm 126 Br.—Gaines-Johnson-Sturgill (Ky) 1984 4 1 2 1 $106,110
Tr.—Delp Grover G 1983 3 3 0 0 $15,120
Lifetime 7 4 2 1 $121,230

26Apr84-7Kee 1⅛ :473 1:122 1:521ft 2¾ 121 921 814 35½ 23½ ShoemkrW2 Bluegrass 73-31 Tylor'sSpecil,SilntKing,ChrmdRook 9
25Mar84-11FG 1⅛ :463 1:104 1:493ft 2½ 120 719 715 45½ 21 Solis A2 La Dby 95-18 Tylor'sSpecil,SilentKing,FightOver 7
10Mar84-10FG 1 1/16 :47 1:11 1:43 ft 9-5 118 518 519 39 35 Mueller C2 Dby Trl 92-16 Tylor'sSpecil,FightOver,SilentKing 5
18Feb84-10FG 1 1/16 :461 1:112 1:451ft 6-5e 115 824 817 33½ 11 Mueller C1 Lecomte H 86-21 SilentKing,Tylor'sSpcil,FirlyStright 8
14Dec83-9FG 140 :472 1:14 1:413ft *2-5 119 611 55½ 11 15 Franklin R J2 Aw10200 85-23 SilentKing,DewnForUs,HomByTwlv 8
7Dec83-10FG 140 :463 1:132 1:413ft *4-5 115 811 43 11 15½ Franklin R J5 Aw10200 85-19 SilntKing,HomByTwlv,MsssspplMn 10
27Nov83-2FG 1 1/16 :48 1:152 1:48 sy 4½ 119 710 54½ 12 19 Franklin R J10 M30000 72-25 SilentKing,RbornofWtr,Ol'BluEys 12

May 3 CD 4f sy :502 b Apr 24 Kee 4f sy :483 b ●Apr 20 Kee 6f gd 1:12 h Apr 13 Kee 1 sy 1:433 b

Vanlandingham *
B. c. 3, by Cox's Ridge—Populi, by Star Envoy
Br.—Loblolly Farm (Ky) 1984 4 3 1 0 $99,280
Own.—Loblolly Stable 126 Tr.—McGaughey Claude III 1983 1 1 0 0 $7,200
Lifetime 5 4 1 0 $106,560
31Mar84-9OP 1 1/16 :444 1:094 1:41 ft *6-5 115 34 2½ 1½ 11½ Day P7 Rebel 103-05 Vnlndinghm,WindFlyr,Lvsumdoubl 10
2Mar84-8OP 1 :45 1:093 1:351ft *2-3 121 1hd 11 15 110 Day P4 Aw17500 — — Vnlndinghm,DirtyBirdie,ShrperThn 7
26Jan84-7Aqu 1 1/16 ⊡:48 1:1231:441m 3 117 1½ 1hd 11½ 13 Lovato F Jr7 Aw22000 91-10 Vanlndinghm,ChrmedRook,LeroyS. 9
7Jan84-5Aqu 1 1/16 ⊡:49 1:15 1:48 ft *1 117 31½ 2½ 22 26 Lovato F Jr3 Aw22000 66-24 Lt.Flag,Vanlndinghm,Cooper'sHwk 7
26Nov83-1CD 1 :473 1:132 1:382ft *4-5 117 12 11 1½ 11½ Day P8 Mdn 77-21 Vnlndinghm,Pemcor,ThundrChick 11
Apr 30 CD 7f gd 1:271 h Apr 27 CD 4f ft :492 b Apr 16 OP 6f ft 1:15 b Apr 10 OP 4f ft :49 b

Secret Prince
Dk. b. or br. c. 3, by Cornish Prince—Secret Lanvin, by Lanvin
Br.—Mereworth Farm (Ky) 1984 4 2 0 1 $123,974
Own.—Brodsky Elaine M 126 Tr.—Terrill William V 1983 6 2 2 0 $92,720
Lifetime 10 4 2 1 $216,694
28Apr84-8CD 1 :46 1:101 1:353ft 10 122 44 36 35 37½ Perret C5 Dby Trl 84-16 Devil'sBag,BiloxiIndin,SecretPrince 5
7Apr84-8Aqu 170⊡:47 1:1121:402ft *2-3 126 33 49½ 421 424½ Bailey J D4 Gotham 73-16 Bear Hunt, Lt. Flag, On The Sauce 5
17Mar84-8Aqu 6f ⊡:223 :4641:111ft *6-5 114 72½ 52½ 1hd 12½ Perret C6 Bay Shore 88-22 ScrtPrnc,ThWddngGust,I'mARondr 9
17Mar84—Wide, easily
1Mar84-7Hia 7f :224 :453 1:223ft 9-5 115 35½ 22½ 1½ 12½ Perret C1 Aw20000 90-20 SecretPrince,Vision,CountrfitMony 7
18Dec83-8Hol 1 1/16 :454 1:101 1:413ft 33 121 66½ 63½ 67½ 711¼ Vasquez J7 Hol Fut'y 76-14 Fali Time, Bold T. Jay,Life'sMagic 12
18Dec83—Stumbled, checked
7Dec83-8Hol 7f :212 :44 1:221ft *7-5 119 85½ 85½ 78½ 85½ VasquezJ6 Hol Prevue 80-18 SoVgu,CountryMnor,FrnchLgionir 16
12Nov83-8Aqu 1⅛ :474 1:12 1:49 gd *1 117 21½ 2½ 2½ 25½ Vasquez J3 Remsen 84-20 Dr.Carter,SecretPrince,HilBoldKing 8
29Oct83-6Aqu 1 :48 1:132 1:381ft 2 115 1hd 11 14 14½ VsquezJ1 Excl. Native 75-28 SecretPrince,HomcomingGm,Spndr 8
14Oct83-4Bel 1 1/16 :472 1:122 1:434gd *1-2 118 2½ 13 15 12½ Vasquez J5 Mdn 83-23 ScrtPrinc,DncingCrown,Rj'sAccord 7
26Sep83-4Bel 1 :46 1:11 1:364ft 5 118 32½ 3nk 21 22½ Vasquez J6 Mdn 78-18 Legatee, Secret Prince,MightyJoe 12
Apr 24 Bel 1 sy 1:401 b (d) Apr 2 Aqu ⊡ 6f ft 1:121 h Mar 24 Aqu ⊡ 1 ft 1:413 h ●Mar 10 Hia 6f ft 1:12 h

At The Threshold *
Ch. c. 3, by Norcliffe—Winver, by Vertex
Br.—Karunsky-Levien (NY) 1984 4 2 0 1 $266,015
Own.—Partee W C 126 Tr.—Whiting Lynn 1983 9 4 1 3 $97,635
Lifetime 13 6 1 4 $363,650
21Apr84-9OP 1⅛ :463 1:101 1:464ft 3½ 126 64½ 63½ 47½ 47 McCrronCJ11 Ark Dby 102-04 Althea, Pine Circle, Gate Dancer 11
1Apr84-9Lat 1 1/16 :46 1:101 1:424ft 3½ 121 65½ 55 33 11 Day P2 Jim Beam 96-18 AtThThrshld,BldSthrnr,ThWddGst 12
1Apr84—Altered course
10Mar84-9OP 1 :461 1:102 1:342m *4-5 123 49½ 48 34½ 33½ Allen K K1 HcpO — — Whitbrush,LuckyLrry,AtThThrshold 5
25Feb84-9OP 6f :211 :44 1:092ft *2-3e 120 79½ 68 43½ 1½ Patterson G1 HcpO 98-03 AtThThrshld,WdrdPrspct,StJEprss 7
27Nov83-8Aqu 1⅛ :463 1:121 1:521ft 3½ 119 1110 65½ 31½ 11½ Day P8 SA T Cole 74-23 AtThThrshold,RstlssFt,Grom'sImg 14
27Nov83—Bushed, clear
16Nov83-7CD 6f :222 :46 1:124sy 5½ 115 1½ 11 12 1½ Espinoza JC1 Aw12500 82-34 AtTheThreshold,Whitebrush,Textile 7
31Oct83-8CD 1 :462 1:104 1:371ft 84 114 53½ 42½ 33 32 Espinoza JC6 Iroquois 81-16 Tylor'sSpecil,Bello,AtTheThreshold 9
21Oct83-5Kee 6½f :224 :454 1:172sy 4 115 64½ 56 48½ 513½ Moyers L4 Aw16000 77-19 Tylor'sSpecil,Bello,ConfidentilKelly 8
11Oct83-7Kee 6f :224 :461 1:103ft 5½ 115 2½ 3½ 2hd 21 Moyers L1 Aw15700 88-14 BetwixtN'Betwn,AtThThrshold,Bllo 5
24Sep83-8Lat 6½f :232 :464 1:201ft *7-5e 116 65 68½ 65½ 34½ Foster DE7 Ky Special 72-34 TllGrssWlkr,MchoDvl,AtThThrshld 12
27Aug83-7CD 6½f :233 :473 1:192ft 4 117 31 31 21 1nk Rubbicco P5 Aw10400 83-11 AtTheThreshold,SemnTeelo,NicTry 6
4Jun83-7CD 5f :23 :452 :581ft 7½ 117 31 43½ 37 37½ Espinoza JC3 Aw11200 90-17 DltTrc,SupportngCst,AtThThrshold 6
23Apr83-3Kee 4½f :233 :472 :533sy *6-5 117 4 2½ 11½ 11½ Espinoza J C5 Mdn 87-13 AtTheThreshold,Monywtchr,NicTry 6
●Apr 30 CD 5f gd 1:011 b Apr 26 OP 3f ft :36 b ●Apr 15 OP 6f ft 1:134 b Apr 10 OP 4f ft :492 b

Swale *
Dk. b. or br. c. 3, by Seattle Slew—Tuerta, by Forli
Br.—Claiborne Farm (Ky) 1984 4 2 1 1 $244,290
Own.—Claiborne Farm 126 Tr.—Stephens Woodford C 1983 7 5 1 1 $491,951
Lifetime 11 7 2 2 $736,241
17Apr84-7Kee 1 1/16 :471 1:112 1:452sy *1-9 123 32½ 25½ 25 26 Pincay LJr2 Lexington 71-23 HelsAGretDel,Swle,TimelyAdvocte 5
31Mar84-10GP 1⅛ :463 1:101 1:473ft 2½ 122 2½ 2hd 1½ 1½ Pincay L Jr7 Fla Dby 94-14 Swale, Dr. Carter, Darn That Alarm 9
17Mar84-9GP 1 1/16 :473 1:111 1:43 ft *2-5 122 2½ 2hd 32 31½ MapleE7 Ftn Of Youth 84-17 DrnThtAlrm,CounterfeitMoney,Swl 8
7Mar84-9GP 7f :223 :452 1:221ft *1 122 3nk 2hd 1hd 10 Maple E10 Hutcheson 93-21 Swale, For Halo, Darn That Alarm 12
7Mar84—Wide, ridden out
5Nov83-8Med 1 1/16 :461 1:112 1:451ft 2½ 122 47½ 33 22 1no MapleE7 Yng America 83-20 Swale, Disastrous Night, Dr.Carter 16
8Oct83-7Kee 1 1/16 :471 1:112 1:44 ft *1 121 2hd 1hd 1hd 1hd Maple E3 Brdrs' Fut 86-14 Swale, Spender, Back BayBarrister 8
10Sep83-8Bel 7f :223 :452 1:24 ft *8-5 122 1½ 1hd 2½ 1no Maple E4 Futurity 82-15 Swale, Shuttle Jet, Hail Bold King 5
21Aug83-8Sar 6½f :214 :451 1:172ft 3½ 122 32 21½ 1hd 33½ Maple E3 Hopeful 82-23 Capitol South, Don Rickles, Swale 13
1Aug83-8Sar 6f :221 :46 1:123m 2½ 117 2hd 12 14 1½ Maple E4 Sar Special 77-24 Swale, Shuttle Jet, Big Walt 7
21Jly83-4Bel 6f :223 :454 1:112ft *3-5 118 12 16 14 11½ Maple E7 Mdn 85-20 Swale, Capitol South, Legatee 7
7Jly83-4Bel 5f :223 :454 :58 ft *2-3 118 1½ 11½ 1½ 22½ Maple E2 Mdn 96-19 Shuttle Jet, Swale, Rowdy Yates 8
7Jly83—Lugged in
May 3 CD 4f sy :50 b Apr 29 CD 7f ft 1:291 h ●Apr 25 CD 5f ft :591 h ●Apr 15 Kee 4f ft :48 b

Majestic Shore
Ch. c. 3, by Majestic Prince—Golden Shore, by Windy Sands
Br.—Oldknow & Phipps (Ky) 1984 4 1 2 1 $61,900
Own.—Oldknow & Phipps 126 Tr.—Rettele Loren 1983 0 M 0 0
Lifetime 4 1 2 1 $61,900
21Apr84-8GG 1⅛ :452 1:09 1:472ft 10 112 33 33 32 2½ Hawley S5 Calif Dby 95-11 DistntRyder,MjsticShor,TsunmiSlw 8
21Apr84—Wide
1Apr84-6SA 1 1/16 :47 1:113 1:434ft *2-3 118 52 43 32½ 1½ Delahoussaye E4 Mdn 82-16 MjesticShore,Bronzed,You'rMyLov 6
25Mar84-6SA 1 1/16 :463 1:121 1:442ft 8-5 118 2hd 2hd 1½ 2nk Delahoussaye E6 Mdn 79-17 Ocean View,MajesticShore,Koshare 7
10Mar84-4SA 6½f :214 :45 1:171ft 4 118 916 611 58 34½ Delahoussaye E6 Mdn 88-18 ImpSociety,UsullyRelibl,MjsticShor 9
Apr 30 Hol 7f ft 1:27 h Apr 14 SA 5f ft 1:004 h Apr 8 SA 5f ft 1:001 h

Biloxi Indian B. c. 3, by George Navonod—Three Quarter Girl, by Cohoes
Br.—Brewer Mark & Linda (Ky) 1984 4 2 1 0 $79,300
Own.—Sundance Stable 126 Tr.—Carpenter Diane 1983 12 6 1 1 $174,904
Lifetime 16 8 2 1 $254,204
28Apr84-8CD 1 :46 1:101 1:353ft 5½ 122 21½ 22 21½ 22½ Patterson G4 Dby Trl 89-16 Devil'sBag,BiloxiIndin,SecretPrince 5
25Mar84-11FG 1⅛:463 1:104 1:493ft 2¾ 123 31 44½ 720 — Patterson G5 La Dby — — Tylor'sSpecil,SilentKing,FightOver 7
25Mar84—Eased
17Mar84-10FG 1$\frac{1}{16}$:474 1:13 1:443ft *1-9 123 12½ 12 11½ 16 PttersonG6 [R]Hits Dby 89-17 BiloxiIndin,ARoylBid,Beu'sExpress 7
8Mar84-10FG 1$\frac{1}{16}$:463 1:121 1:461ft *1-5 123 11 12½ 15 15 MunsterL7 [R]Dby Prep 81-22 BiloxiIndin,Beu'sExprss,Mr.Mvrick 8
17Dec83-10FG 6f :213 :452 1:103ft *7-5 123 63¾ 43 1hd 12 PttrsG2 [R]Hit PrdeFut 92-14 BiloxiIndin,Beu'sExpress,FullCourt 9
8Dec83-11FG 6f :214 :452 1:11 ft *2-5 123 43 21 2hd 1no Day P11 [R]Fut Trls 90-17 BloxIndn,Bu'sExprss,WhrlngShttl 13
19Nov83-8CD 1$\frac{1}{16}$:482 1:124 1:461ft 19 119 22 23 2hd 13 PttrsonG2 Ky Jcky Cb 77-22 BiloxIndn,CountryMnor,Tylor'sSpcl 7
31Oct83-8CD 1 :462 1:104 1:371ft 2¾ 119 42½ 32 23 45 Moyers L5 Iroquois 78-16 Tylor'sSpecil,Bello,AtTheThreshold 9
15Oct83-6Bel 1 :461 1:094 1:341ft 77 122 98½ 815 817 718 MoyrsL10 Champagne 76-14 Devil'sBag,Dr.Crter,OurCsey'sBoy 12
28Sep83-8Bel 7f :223 :451 1:212ft 81 119 64½ 68½ 512 49 Moyers L2 Cowdin 86-19 Devil's Bag, Dr. Carter, Exit Five B. 9
3Sep83-9CD 7f :231 :461 1:244ft *7-5 116 75½ 54½ 43 1nk Moyers L7 Perryville 83-15 BiloxiIndin,Tylor'sSpecil,Whitbrush 8
27Aug83-8AP 7f :222 :46 1:27 sy 17 122 107 1316 79¾ 610 MoyrsL17 Arl Was Fut 57-36 AllFirdUp,HolmOnTop,SmrtNSlick 17
14Aug83-8AP 6f :22 :453 1:121ft 5½ 114 31½ 22 22 21½ Moyers L6 Arch Ward 80-26 Bello, Biloxi Indian, Delta Trace 11
8Jly83-8CD 5½f :222 :46 1:05 ft 3½ 118 95½ 65½ 64 33½ BrfldD7 Bashford Mnr 92-20 BtwxtN'Btwn,RlShrpDncr,BlxIndn 13
28Jun83-7CD 5½f :222 :46 1:053gd 5½ 117 23 22½ 2hd 13 Brumfield D2 Aw12000 93-19 BiloxiIndin,BtwxtN'Btwn,TrckyNck 8
3Jun83-3CD 5f :23 :463 1:00 sy *8-5 119 42½ 21½ 1hd 11½ Moyers L5 Mdn 89-22 BiloxiIndin,NiceTry,FrnksFulloBens 7
May 3 CD 3f sy :38 b Apr 26 CD 4f ft :494 b Apr 22 CD 1 sy 1:38 b Apr 18 CD 1 sl 1:411 b

Pine Circle Dk. b. or br. c. 3, by Cox's Ridge—Gaebale, by Gallant Man
Br.—Loblolly Stable (Ky) 1984 3 0 1 0 $120,725
Own.—Loblolly Stable 126 Tr.—McGaughey Claude III 1983 7 1 2 2 $26,210
Lifetime 10 1 3 2 $146,935
21Apr84-9OP 1⅛:463 1:101 1:464ft 24 118 117 105½ 69½ 27 Day P7 Ark Dby 102-04 Althea, Pine Circle, Gate Dancer 11
16Mar84-3SA 1$\frac{1}{16}$:461 1:101 1:43 ft 10 118 69½ 613 617 615 Toro F1 Aw32000 71-20 FftySxInRow,M.DoblM.,BoldBttrUp 6
22Jan84-7SA 1$\frac{1}{16}$:463 1:104 1:434ft 8½ 120 48 612 616 516 McCarronCJ1 Aw27000 67-21 Tights, Bold Batter Up, Bedouin 6
10Dec83-8Haw 1$\frac{1}{16}$:474 1:132 1:462gd *3 112 109¾ 46 31½ 12½ † Smith M E5 Haw Jvle 66-30 ‡PineCircle,DoublClvr,BlushOffFm 11
10Dec83—Bore out in stretch; †Disqualified and placed second
5Nov83-2CD 1 :471 1:124 1:392ft *4-5 117 55 52½ 2hd 12½ Day P2 Mdn 72-18 PineCircle,Bookmrk,WellWhtElse 12
19Oct83-4Kee 1$\frac{1}{16}$:481 1:132 1:48 gd *7-5 116 67 54½ 32½ 2¾ Allen K K3 Mdn 65-24 TelegrphKey,PineCircle,QuickLrnr 12
26Aug83-2CD 6½f :23 :463 1:184ft 5¾ 119 611 67½ 48 47 Allen K K4 Mdn 79-13 Dolcie'sBoy,CoaxMeAgin,Grundoon 6
19Aug83-1CD 6f :22 :461 1:114ft 2¾ 118 67 33½ 36½ 35 Allen K K6 Mdn 82-13 ScornedLad,CoxMeAgin,PineCircle 8
16Jly83-1CD 5½f :234 :46 1:043ft 11 119 69¾ 57½ 34 37¾ Allen K K4 Mdn 90-14 BlindMn'sBluff,FlyingFinish,PnCrcl 8
16Jly83—Ducked in and had to steady
24Jun83-3CD 5½f :231 :46 1:054ft 8 119 64½ 56 58 54½ Day P5 Mdn 88-12 Tylor'sSpecil,LouN'Mur,FirwyTrvlr 8

Coax Me Chad B. c. 3, by L'Enjoleur—Platterland, by First Landing
Br.—Brooks Louis Sr (Ky) 1984 3 0 0 0
Own.—Miller E E 126 Tr.—Warren Ronnie G 1983 12 2 1 2 $155,886
Lifetime 15 2 1 2 $155,886
1Apr84-9Lat 1$\frac{1}{16}$:46 1:101 1:424ft 57 121 99 68½ 68½ 63½ McClyWH8 Jim Beam 92-10 AtThThrshld,BldSthrnr,ThWddGst 12
11Feb84-10Hia 1⅛:463 1:10 1:47 ft 85 119 1121 1123 1020 1020¾ St LeonG1 Everglades 76-09 TimeforChnge,Bello,Rexson'sHop 11
7Jan84-9Crc 1$\frac{1}{16}$:472 1:124 1:46 ft 20 121 1112 1117½ 911 810 DePass R8 Trp Pk Dby 79-14 MornngBob,‡Rxson'sHop,DnRckls 15
24Dec83-7Crc 1$\frac{1}{16}$:483 1:14 1:442ft *6-5 120 89½ 710 67½ 35½ DePssR4 What A Plesr 82-16 PpKoo,CounterfeitMony,CoxMChd 9
24Dec83—Run in two divisions 7th & 9th races
13Dec83-7Crc 7f :224 :463 1:26 ft 4 116 68½ 64½ 41¾ 2½ DePass R2 Aw12000 85-22 D. White, CoaxMeChad,JimBracken 6
19Nov83-8CD 1$\frac{1}{16}$:482 1:124 1:461ft 8 122 712 611 45½ 44½ EspnzJC4 Ky Jcky Cb 69-22 BiloxIndn,CountryMnor,Tylor'sSpcl 7
19Nov83—Bore out
5Nov83-8Med 1$\frac{1}{16}$:461 1:112 1:451ft 23 122 813 712 412 58½ MoyrsL9 Yng America 73-20 Swale, Disastrous Night, Dr.Carter 16
8Oct83-7Kee 1$\frac{1}{16}$:471 1:112 1:44 ft 3¾e 121 65¾ 65¾ 53¾ 43 EspinozJC6 Brdrs' Fut 83-14 Swale, Spender, Back BayBarrister 8
8Oct83—Wide
4Sep83-10RD 1$\frac{1}{16}$:472 1:121 1:463ft 2½ 120 611 44½ 1hd 13½ EspnJC9 Ml Hglf Crdl 76-23 CoaxMeChad,TallGrssWlker,ThDh 12
27Aug83-8AP 7f :222 :46 1:27 sy 5½f 122 1714 1516 65¾ 42½ EspnJC11 Arl Was Fut 64-36 AllFirdUp,HolmOnTop,SmrtNSlick 17
27Aug83—Circled horses
14Aug83-8AP 6f :22 :453 1:121ft 54 114 117¾ 99½ 89½ 52½ Cuffari S4 Arch Ward 79-26 Bello, Biloxi Indian, Delta Trace 11
14Aug83—Drifted in drive
30Jly83-6CD 6f :223 :46 1:114ft 4½ 1177 67 68½ 44 37 Cuffari S3 Aw11300 88-15 Textile, Trans E. T., Coax Me Chad 6
8Jly83-8CD 5½f :222 :46 1:05 ft 11e 115 129 1313 119 89½ CffrS13 Bashford Mnr 86-20 BtwxtN'Btwn,RlShrpDncr,BlxIndn 13
28Jun83-7CD 5½f :222 :46 1:053gd 19 1107 79 612 56 44 Cuffari S4 Aw12000 89-19 BiloxiIndin,BtwxtN'Btwn,TrckyNck 8
28Jun83—Drifted out in the final furlong
1Jun83-3CD 5f :23 :464 1:00 ft 3½ 10810 64½ 68 43 12½ Cuffari S5 Mdn 89-15 CoxMChd,OurMichlSmith,StrtKing 6
Apr 25 CD 7f ft 1:294 b Apr 15 CD 6f ft 1:142 b

Gate Dancer B. c. 3, by Sovereign Dancer—Sun Gate, by Bull Lea
Br.—Davis W R (Fla) 1984 5 1 2 2 $168,125
Own.—Opstein K 126 Tr.—Van Berg Jack C 1983 4 2 2 0 $32,700
Lifetime 9 3 4 2 $200,825
21Apr84-9OP 1⅛:463 1:101 1:464ft *6-5 118 74¾ 53½ 26 37 DelhoussyeE6 Ark Dby 102-04 Althea, Pine Circle, Gate Dancer 11
21Apr84—Forced out a bit first turn
25Mar84-8SA 1$\frac{1}{16}$:462 1:103 1:423ft 4½ 117 67¾ 54¾ 41½ 2hd DlhssyE2 San Felipe H 88-17 FaliTime,GateDancer,Commemorte 6
25Mar84—Lugged in late
14Mar84-8SA 1$\frac{1}{16}$:471 1:111 1:433gd 4 120 97½ 78½ 34½ 33½ DlhssyE5 [S]S Catalina 79-26 Tights, Prince True, Gate Dancer 10
20Feb84-4SA 1$\frac{1}{16}$:461 1:111 1:432ft *6-5 115 511 46 1½ 11¾ DelhoussyeE6 Aw30000 84-16 GateDncer,PrinceTrue,HevenlyPlin 7
20Feb84—Lugged in stretch
5Feb84-8BM 1$\frac{1}{16}$:461 1:103 1:422ft 4 120 912 67½ 56 22 Cauthen S1 El Camino 85-17 FrenchLegionire,GtDncr,HvnlyPlin 11
5Feb84—Lacked room
29Dec83-8SA 6f :214 :441 1:09 ft 11 120 68½ 58½ 45 25 DlgdilloC1 [S]Los Feliz 88-24 Commemort,GtDncr,MightyAdvrsry 8
29Dec83—Lugged in
16Dec83-6Hol 6f :22 :45 1:10 ft *1 114 41¾ 2½ 1hd 1¾ McCarronCJ5 Aw25000 87-22 GteDncer,LuckyBuccner,PrincBowr 6
16Dec83—Bore in, driving
16Jly83-5Aks 5½f :221 :452 1:062ft *2-3 117 41½ 31 2hd 2½ Jones K2 Aw12000 77-25 Izapappa,GateDancer,MedianPrince 8
25Jun83-4Aks 5½f :23 :472 1:071m 6½ 118 31¾ 1½ 15 18 Jones K11 Mdn 74-33 Gate Dancer, Wind Flyer, Dr. Log 12
●May 2 CD 4f ft :48 h Apr 16 OP 7f ft 1:232 hg Apr 8 SA 5f ft 1:001 b ●Mar 21 SA 6f ft 1:111 hg

The only Dr. Z bet on the Derby was a show bet on the favorite, the Althea-Life's Magic entry, and it remained a good choice throughout the betting. The mutuels at one minute to post and the final mutuels were:

	Totals	*#1 Althea-Life's Magic*	*Expected Value per Dollar Bet on Althea-Life's Magic*
Odds (With one minute to post time)		5–2	
Win	2,948,148	644,258	
Show	1,171,951	175,516	1.21
Odds (At post time)		5–2	
Win	2,964,252	646,965	
Show	1,177,438	176,024	1.21

Unfortunately for us, the 1984 Kentucky Derby was not won by Althea or Life's Magic. Instead it was won very impressively by Swale. He had a good start and in the first turn was third following Althea and Bear Hunt. On the backstretch he moved outside of Althea to take the lead. Althea at this point quickly slipped to the back and by the finish line was only ahead of Majestic Shore, who had eased up at the mile pole. Coax Me Chad and At The Threshold picked up ground on the other horses in the stretch but could not match Swale who won by $3\frac{1}{4}$ lengths.

At one minute to post the optimal wager was $121 to show on the Althea-Life's Magic entry. Thus our bankroll was reduced to $1554.40. Although there were two races remaining, we decided to join the mass exodus from Churchill Downs. Our profit of $54.40 was disappointing relative to our other Derbies, and it certainly would not have paid for box seats on the finish line, but any profit at the end of the day puts you ahead of the majority of the bettors.

Swale ran in the Preakness two weeks later but faded to a disappointing seventh. He rebounded to win the Belmont to become the tenth all-time leading earner with $1,583,660. Sadly and very unexpectedly, however, Swale died shortly after being exercised eight days after the Belmont. He is buried at Claiborne Farms.

This Kentucky Derby turned out to be further evidence of the power of *dosage theory*. Dosage theory is an attempt to evaluate the influence of a horse's pedigree on his or her running style, and it has been nothing short of spectacular in its success at narrowing down the horses that can possibly win the Derby. The notion is based on a group of horses called the *chefs de race*. They are a relatively small number of sires whose effect on the running style of their offspring has been determined. This is only possible if they do in fact tend to pass a particular running style on to their offspring and, because

EIGHTH RACE
Churchill
MAY 5, 1984

1 ¼ MILES. (1:59⅖) 110th Running KENTUCKY DERBY (Grade I) Scale weight Stakes. $250,000 Added. 3-year-olds. With a subscription fee of $200 each, an entry fee of $10,000 each and a starting fee of $10,000 each. All fees to be paid to the winner. $250,000 shall be paid by Churchill Downs Incorporated (the "Association") as the Added Purse. Second place shall receive $100,000, third place shall receive $50,000 and fourth place shall receive $25,000 from the Added Purse. (The Added Purse and fees to be divided equally in the event of a dead heat.) Starters shall be named through the entry box on Thursday, May 3, 1984, at the usual time of closing. The maximum number of starters shall be limited to twenty and each shall carry a weight of 126 lbs., fillies, 121 lbs. In the event that more than twenty entries pass through the entry box at the time of closing, the starters shall be determined at that time with preference given to those horses that have accumulated the highest earnings, excluding earnings won in a restricted race. For purposes of this preference, a "restricted race" shall mean a state-bred restricted race (a race where entries are restricted to horses qualifying under state breeding programs), a sales restricted race (a race where entries are restricted by the origin of purchase), and a money restricted sweepstake (a race where entries are restricted by the amount of money previously earned). The owner of the winner shall receive a gold trophy. No supplementary nominations shall be accepted. (Closed with 312 nominations.)

Value of race $712,400, value to winner $537,400, second $100,000, third $50,000, fourth $25,000. Mutuel pool $5,420,787.

Last Raced	Horse	Eqt.	A.	Wt	PP	¼	½	¾	1	Str	Fin	Jockey	Odds $1
17Apr84 ^{7}Kee^2	Swale		3	126	15	$3^{1\frac12}$	3^1	2^1	1^2	1^5	$1^{3\frac14}$	Pincay L Jr	3.40
1Apr84 ^{9}Lat^6	Coax Me Chad		3	126	19	17^3	$17^{1\frac12}$	$14^{1\frac12}$	7^{hd}	2^{hd}	2^2	McCauley W H	f-9.90
21Apr84 ^{9}OP^4	At The Threshold		3	126	14	$11^{\frac12}$	$9^{1\frac12}$	$6^{\frac12}$	$4^{1\frac12}$	$3^{\frac12}$	3^{nk}	Maple E	37.70
21Apr84 ^{9}OP^3	[D]Gate Dancer	b	3	126	20	$19^{\frac12}$	18^3	15^1	$9^{1\frac12}$	6^1	$4^{\frac34}$	Delahoussaye E	18.90
8Apr84 ^{8}SA^4	Fali Time	b	3	126	7	$7^{\frac12}$	$7^{\frac12}$	$7^{1\frac12}$	$6^{\frac12}$	5^{hd}	5^1	Hawley S	18.70
21Apr84 ^{9}OP^2	Pine Circle		3	126	18	$14^{\frac12}$	14^4	$11^{\frac12}$	$12^{\frac12}$	$7^{\frac12}$	$6^{\frac34}$	Smith M E	b-6.00
26Apr84 ^{7}Kee^4	Fight Over		3	126	6	6^{hd}	5^1	3^1	$2^{1\frac12}$	4^1	7^{hd}	Vergara O	78.90
8Apr84 ^{8}SA^5	Life's Magic		3	121	5	$13^{1\frac12}$	13^1	$9^{\frac12}$	8^1	8^3	8^1	Brumfield D	a-2.80
26Apr84 ^{7}Kee^2	Silent King		3	126	11	20	20	20	19	11^2	9^3	Shoemaker W	4.80
26Apr84 ^{7}Kee^5	Rexson's Hope	b	3	126	9	$18^{1\frac12}$	19^4	19^3	$18^{\frac12}$	$10^{\frac12}$	10^{nk}	Gaffglione R	f-9.90
26Apr84 ^{7}Kee^7	So Vague		3	126	4	$15^{\frac12}$	$15^{1\frac12}$	18^3	$16^{\frac12}$	$12^{\frac12}$	11^2	Cooksey P J	f-9.90
28Apr84 ^{8}CD^2	Biloxi Indian	b	3	126	17	$5^{1\frac12}$	4^{hd}	4^{hd}	3^{hd}	$9^{1\frac12}$	$12^{1\frac14}$	Patterson G	f-9.90
26Apr84 ^{7}Kee^1	Taylor's Special		3	126	10	9^1	8^{hd}	8^{hd}	10^2	13^2	13^3	Maple S	6.80
21Apr84 ^{8}Aqu^2	Raja's Shark	b	3	126	2	$8^{2\frac12}$	$11^{1\frac12}$	12^1	14^{hd}	14^{hd}	14^{hd}	Wilson R	59.10
26Apr84 ^{8}Hol^1	Bedouin		3	126	8	$16^{1\frac12}$	16^1	$17^{\frac12}$	$17^{\frac12}$	16^2	15^{nk}	Sibille R	f-9.90
31Mar84 ^{9}OP^1	Vanlandingham		3	126	12	$4^{\frac12}$	6^{hd}	$10^{1\frac12}$	$11^{\frac12}$	$15^{\frac12}$	16^2	Day P	b-6.00
28Apr84 ^{8}CD^3	Secret Prince		3	126	13	$10^{\frac12}$	$12^{\frac12}$	$13^{\frac12}$	$13^{\frac12}$	$17^{\frac12}$	$17^{2\frac14}$	Perret C	f-9.90
21Apr84 ^{8}Aqu^3	Bear Hunt	b	3	126	3	$2^{\frac12}$	$2^{\frac12}$	5^1	$15^{1\frac12}$	$18^{1\frac12}$	$18^{7\frac12}$	MacBeth D	57.40
21Apr84 ^{9}OP^1	Althea		3	121	1	$1^{\frac12}$	1^1	1^{hd}	$5^{\frac12}$	19	19	McCarron C J	a-2.80
21Apr84 ^{8}GG^2	Majestic Shore		3	126	16	12^5	10^{hd}	$16^{\frac12}$	—	—	—	Lively J	f-9.90

Majestic Shore, Eased.
[D]-Gate Dancer Disqualified and placed fifth.
a-Coupled: Life's Magic and Althea; b-Pine Circle and Vanlandingham.
f—Mutuel field.

OFF AT 5:40. Start good for all but GATE DANCER. Won driving. Time, :23⅘, :47⅘, 1:11⅘, 1:36⅘, 2:02⅖ Track fast.

$2 Mutuel Prices:				
	10-SWALE	8.80	4.80	3.40
	12-COAX ME CHAD (f-field)		8.00	4.00
	9-AT THE THRESHOLD			13.80

Dk. b. or br. c, by Seattle Slew—Tuerta, by Forli. Trainer Stephens Woodford C. Bred by Claiborne Farm (Ky).

SWALE, away in good order, went after ALTHEA from the outside approaching the end of the backstretch, took over soon after starting the turn, drew off quickly entering the stretch and was under pressure to hold sway. COAX ME CHAD, outrun to the far turn, moved through along the inside leaving the far turn, came out slightly during the drive and finished well to best the others. AT THE THRESHOLD rallied racing into the far turn, remained a factor into the stretch while racing between horses but wasn't good enough, and leaned in slightly brushing with FIGHT OVER. GATE DANCER broke poorly from his outside post positon, raced wide into the stretch while advancing but failed to sustain his bid while lugging in and bumping FALI TIME several times. GATE DANCER WAS DISQUALIFIED AND PLACED FIFTH FOLLOWING A STEWARDS INQUIRY AND A FOUL CLAIMED BY THE RIDER OF FALI TIME. FALI TIME, never far back, remained a factor into the stretch while racing between horses and was bothered by GATE DANCER during the drive. PINE CIRCLE made up some ground approaching the final furlong but lacked a late response. FIGHT OVER, well placed into the backstretch, moved through along the inside nearing the far turn, raced forwardly into the stretch, then brushed with AT THE THRESHOLD while tiring. A CLAIM OF FOUL AGAINST COAX ME CHAD BY THE RIDER OF FIGHT OVER, FOR ALLEGED INTERFERENCE THROUGH THE STRETCH, WAS NOT ALLOWED. LIFE'S MAGIC moved up along the inside nearing the end of the backstretch but was finished soon after going seven furlongs. SILENT KING, badly outrun for a mile, passed tired horses while racing very wide. REXSON'S HOPE was without speed. SO VAGUE failed to be a serious factor. BILOXI INDIAN gave way after racing forwardly for a mile. TAYLOR'S SPECIAL, wide throughout, raced within striking distance to the far turn but lacked a further response. RAJA'S SHARK saved ground to no avail. BEDOUIN raced extremely wide. VANLANDINGHAM was finished racing into the far turn and came back sore. SECRET PRINCE tired. BEAR HUNT prompted the pace into the backstretch, held on well until near the end of the backstretch and had nothing left. ALTHEA had speed from the outset, made the pace to the far turn while saving ground but was finished after going seven furlongs. MAJESTIC SHORE dropped back steadily while racing wide approaching the end of the backstretch and was eased when unable to keep up.

Owners— 1, Claiborne Farm; 2, Miller E E; 3, Partee W C; 4, Opstein K; 5, Mamakos & Stubrin; 6, Loblolly Stable; 7, Bwamazon Farm-Sabarese; 8, Mel Hatley Racing Stable; 9, Hawksworth Farm; 10, Rose Elsie A Stable Inc; 11, Hyperion Thoroughbreds; 12, Sundance Stable; 13, Lucas W F; 14, Feiner I; 15, Elmendorf; 16, Loblolly Stable; 17, Brodsky Elaine M; 18, Taylors' Purchase Farm; 19, Alexander-Aykroyd-Groves; 20, Oldknow & Phipps.

Trainers— 1, Stephens Woodford C; 2, Warren Ronnie G; 3, Whiting Lynn; 4, Van Berg Jack C; 5, Jones Gary; 6, McGaughey Claude III; 7, Parisella John; 8, Lukas D Wayne; 9, Delp Grover G; 10, Rose Harold J; 11, Russell Gerry M; 12, Carpenter Diane; 13, Mott William I; 14, Campo Salvatore; 15, Mandella Richard; 16, McGaughey Claude III; 17, Terrill William V; 18, Laurin Roger; 19, Lukas D Wayne; 20, Rettele Loren.

they appear frequently enough in pedigrees, it has been statistically possible to determine this influence. Using this information and a particular horse's pedigree, two measures have been developed to help predict whether the horse will have great speed and early maturity but little endurance, great endurance but late maturity and little speed, or will be more suited to a race of the classic distance like the Derby by being somewhere in the middle. The first measure, the *dosage index* (DI), is a ratio of the number of "speed" chefs de race in a horse's pedigree to the number of "stamina" chefs de race. The second measure, the *center of distribution* (CD), calculates an average level between speed and stamina in the pedigree. (Appendix C gives a more complete discussion of dosage theory.) No Derby winner since 1940 has had a DI greater than 4 or a CD above 1.25. And except for three Belmont winners (Damascus, Conquistador Cielo, and Creme Fraiche), the same is true for the Belmont Stakes. The evidence is thus fairly strong: Horses with high DIs and CDs cannot be expected to win the three-year-old classic races, and this is regardless of whether they are heavy favorites or not. In this 1984 Derby, seven out of the twenty horses had DIs greater than 4.00 and/or CDs greater than 1.25. Not one of these horses finished better than tenth! Included in these seven horses was nineteenth place Althea with a DI of 5.55. Swale had a DI of 1.93 and a CD of 0.68, both well within the limits.

KENTUCKY DERBY DAY 1985

About 44,000 thoroughbreds were foaled in 1982, and each had a chance to win the 1985 Kentucky Derby three years later. By the time of the eighth race on May 4, 1985, these 44,000 potential winners had been whittled down to an exclusive group of thirteen horses, the smallest Derby field since Genuine Risk beat twelve other contenders in 1980. There were all the ingredients for a great race: two pacesetters considered to have stamina, a favorite who had had convincing wins from in front and from behind, and several strong stretch runners.

The infield crowd was somewhat less congested this year than earlier years. This was a result of Churchill Downs' decision to recoup some of its losses through the racing season by doubling Derby Day admission prices. The infield admission increased from $10 to $20, grandstand boxes went from $190 to $380, boxes on the finish line went for $1,020, and the sixteen-seat boxes on Millionaire's Row were $5,000 this year. Given the existence of a black market that charges prices far exceeding Churchill Downs' previous prices, the track did not have to worry about selling their grandstand seats. The infield crowd was somewhat more price sensitive though, and total attendance fell to 108,573, the lowest in 25 years. This reduced attendance did seem to affect the ticket scalpers; with fewer people at the track, they were unable to maintain their high prices. For instance, reserved seats that the scalpers were trying to sell for $250 early in the morning were going for $45 by the time of the first race. For Churchill Downs, though, even with the reduced attendance, the doubled prices led to a dramatic increase in gate receipts and, perhaps surprisingly, total wagering increased as well. The latter was partly due to Churchill Downs finally satisfying the crowd's love of exotic wagering; for the first time, Derby Day had a daily double on the first two races and exacta wagering on the other eight races, including the Derby.

The big Derby favorite this year was the versatile Chief's Crown. His brilliant record seemed to suggest that the winner of the race was a given and that the more challenging handicapping task was to determine the second-place finisher. He was a champion two-year-old, had won the Breeder's Cup Juvenile race at Hollywood Park the previous November, had nine wins and two seconds in twelve career starts, and had earnings of $1,229,422. He had won his last six races, including the Swale Stakes, the Flamingo Stakes, and the Blue Grass Stakes, and could run in front or from behind. All of his ability had not gone unnoticed; he had been syndicated for $20 million even before the Breeders' Cup. There was an element of uncertainty, though—like all the horses in the race, Chief's Crown had never raced $1\frac{1}{4}$ miles, and his DI of 5.00 pointed toward his stamina being suspect. A victory would make him the first Derby winner in many years to do so with a DI greater than 4.00.

Chief's Crown was partly owned by Star Crown Stable and Three Chimneys Farm. The former is the estate of Carl Rosen, who had bred Chief's Crown. Rosen's first great success had been with the filly Chris Evert. He had decided to name a horse after the tennis star, Chris Evert, when his sportswear firm signed her to promote some of its sportswear. Chris Evert, the horse, won the filly Triple Crown and had a 50-length victory over Miss Musket in their famous match race. She was bred to Secretariat, the 1973 Triple Crown winner, and their filly was appropriately named Six Crowns. Six Crowns and Danzig, a son of Northern Dancer, then produced Chief's Crown. An impressive pedigree!

This grandson of Secretariat was being trained by Roger Laurin, the son of Secretariat's trainer, Lucien Laurin. And he would be ridden by Don MacBeth, trying for his first Derby win in eight starts. His best finish had been third on Reinvested in 1982. Interestingly, Chief's Crown was the first Juvenile champion to make it to the Derby since Rockhill Native in 1980—an indication of the high levels of training skill and out-and-out luck needed to keep a horse injury free and at the peak of fitness!

Despite his remarkable record, Chief's Crown went off as only a 6–5 favorite. Many of the bettors were impressed by the other horses and decided they had a serious shot at the "Chief." Among them was Spend A Buck, one of the expected pacesetters, who got the crowd's nod as second favorite at 4–1 odds. This son of Buckaroo had earnings of $991,709 and, with his seven wins, two seconds, and two thirds, had never been out of the money in his eleven career races. The previous year he had been third in the Breeders' Cup Juvenile to Chief's Crown and Tank's Prospect, and this year he had a $10\frac{1}{2}$-length victory in the Cherry Hill Mile and a $9\frac{1}{2}$-length victory in the Garden State Stakes. In the reins, Angel Cordero, Jr., was looking for his third Derby victory, having won with Cannonade in 1974 and Bold Forbes in 1976. Unlike his jockey, Spend A Buck's trainer and owner were relative newcomers to this arena. Trainer Cam Gambolati had been in the business for many years but he had just received his head-trainer license in November 1983. And owner Dennis Diaz had entered racing only two years earlier. In fact, Spend A Buck was one of the very first horses he had ever purchased! And he paid only $12,500 for him as a yearling! Spend A Buck had a DI of 1.40 and CD of 0.25, which indicated that, despite his speed, he had sufficient stamina for the classic races.

Sent off as third favorite at 9–2 odds was the classy Proud Truth, running in the colors of John W. Galbreath's Darby Dan Farm. His sire, Graustark, would undoubtedly have been favored in the 1966 Derby, but he fractured a coffin bone in the Blue Grass Stakes and was retired from racing. Proud Truth had only started racing five months earlier, winning twice in December as a two-year-old. In his six starts as a three-year-old he won three, including the Fountain of Youth Stakes and the Florida Derby, and finished second in the Wood Invitational and the Flamingo Stakes. His earnings in these races were $453,927. His trainer was John Veitch, who had trained Alydar during his 1978 Triple Crown duel with Affirmed. His jockey was the veteran Jorge Velasquez. In his six previous Derby mounts, he won aboard Pleasant Colony in 1981, came second on Alydar, and finished third on Dike in 1969 and Sanhedrin in 1977. At 87, Galbreath was looking for his third Derby, having won with Chateaugay in 1963 and Proud Clarion in 1967. His first racing win was in 1935, fifty years before! Proud Truth, a stretch runner, had a DI of 0.74 and a CD of 0.07, both indicative of stamina.

The race's anticipated speed duel involved Spend a Buck and the other pacesetter, Eternal Prince. A much-asked question was whether they would burn each other out or would they be able to conserve enough for a strong finish? Two months earlier, Eternal Prince seemed an very unlikely Derby starter, having, at that point, never won a race. But in March and April he proved himself to be a legitimate starter by winning four of his last five races, including the Gotham Stakes and the Wood Invitational. George Steinbrenner III, the owner of the New York Yankees, bred the colt and then sold him for $17,000 to Brian Hurst. After the Gotham, Steinbrenner bought back a 37.5% interest in the horse for a reported $1 million. This transaction raised the value of the Majestic Prince colt to $2.6 million. On the Wednesday before the Derby, 12.5% interests were sold to both Spendthrift Farm and John and Pauletta Post. This deal reportedly totaled $1.7 million, raising his value to $6.8 million. A Derby victory would probably raise Eternal Prince's value, as it would any other horse's, on the order of another $10-plus million. His jockey was Richard Migliore, the 1981 Apprentice Eclipse Award winner, and his trainer was Butch Lenzini, a previous classic winner with Aloma's Ruler in the 1984 Preakness. Eternal Prince was another horse with a DI greater than 4. His DI of 7 made his endurance very suspect. John Galbreath had the distinction of being the only individual to have bred a Kentucky Derby winner and have owned a World Series baseball champion team. A Derby win for Eternal Prince would allow George Steinbrenner to share this distinction.

Spendthrift's purchase of a 12.5% interest in Eternal Prince meant that he and Rhoman Rule had to race as a coupled entry. This entry allowed bettors to wager simultaneously on a pacesetter and a late closer, and they sent them off as the fourth favorite at odds of 7–1. Rhoman Rule had won the Everglades Stakes and was third behind Eternal Prince and Proud Truth in the Wood Memorial. He was trained by Angel Penna, Jr., and ridden by Jacinto Vasquez. The latter had previously won the Derby on Genuine Risk in 1980 and Foolish Pleasure in 1975. Rhoman Rule's DI of 3.57 and CD of 0.87 were indicative of stamina.

Another late charger was the Danzig colt, Stephan's Odyssey. His only victory as a three-year-old had been in the Lexington Stakes, but he was second in the Fountain of Youth and third in the Flamingo. This was the first Derby start for his owner, Henryk deKwiatkowski, despite having been involved with such formidable runners as Conquistador Cielo, Danzig, De La Rose, and Sabin. Woody Stephens, his trainer, had already won Derbies with Cannonade in 1974 and Swale the previous year. His jockey was again Laffit Pincay, Jr. A DI of 2.53 and CD of 0.67 put Stephan's Odyssey well within the stamina guidelines.

Trainer D. Wayne Lukas had Tank's Prospect as his eighth Derby starter in five years. His first seven were Partez (third in 1981); Muttering (fifth in 1982); Marfa, Balboa Native, and Total Departure (fifth, ninth, and twentieth in 1983); and Life's Magic and Althea (eighth and nineteenth in 1984). Tank's Prospect won two races early in 1985 but really only had two preps for this race, a poor finish in the Santa Anita Derby and an impressive $6\frac{1}{2}$-length victory in the Arkansas Derby. The son of Mr. Prospector was bought for $625,000 at the Keeneland sale by Eugene Klein, once owner of the San Diego Chargers. His jockey was the first-time Derby starter, Gary Stevens. On the negative side, the dosage theory would say that both of his dosage figures, a DI of 9.40 and a CD of 1.31, were too high for the classic distance.

Eddie Delahoussaye, a winner of derbies on Gato Del Sol in 1982 and Sunny's Halo in 1983, would be aboard Skywalker. The Santa Anita Derby winner was trained by Mike Whittingham, son of the Hall of Famer trainer Charles Whittingham. His 7.80 DI suggested low stamina and the public sent him off at odds of 17–1.

The five other Derby starters were sent off at odds of 40–1 or longer. They included Chris McCarron's mount, Fast Account. He had been second in the Santa Anita Derby and the Derby Trial and was trained by Patricia Johnson, the fifth female trainer of a Derby entrant. Darryl McHargue's mount was I Am The Game, second finisher to Spend A Buck in both the Cherry Hill Mile and Garden State Stakes. The Riva Ridge colt, Encolure, was being ridden by Ronald Ardoin and was trained by Tommy Morgan. He had finished second in his prep race, the Arkansas Derby. Trainer Joe Manzi had won the Kentucky Oaks with Fran's Valentine the day before and was hoping for back-to-back victories with Floating Reserve. This colt had finished second to Chief's Crown in the Blue Grass Stakes and was ridden by Sandy Hawley. The final starter was the lightly raced Irish Fighter. He had thirds in the Arkansas and Louisiana derbies and was ridden by Pat Day.

The experts' picks for the day's races follow. Two experts selected Chief's Crown as the best bet of the day, and he was a strong consensus favorite.

Experts' Selections

Consensus Points: 5 for 1st (today's best 7), 2 for 2nd, 1 for 3rd. Today's Best in Bold Type.

Trackman, Charles Scaravilli **CHURCHILL DOWNS** Selections Made for Fast Track

	TRACKMAN	HANDICAP	ANALYST	HERMIS	SWEEP	CONSENSUS	
1	WAR EAGLE II STRIPIT NORTHERN TRIP	TESTY TOM VADERS FORCE GRIGRI	TESTY TOM GOODTIMES TWO GRIGRI	TESTY TOM GRIGRI YOUNG NASKRA	TESTY TOM EXACTLY E. GOODTIMES TWO	TESTY TOM WAR EAGLE II GRIGRI	20 5 4
2	DANG RIGHT NORTHERN FALLS HONEY JADE	DANG RIGHT TOP MAN STREAKING JACK	DANCEMAN DANG RIGHT NORTHERN FALLS	DANG RIGHT DANCEMAN NORTHERN FALLS	DANG RIGHT DANCEMAN TOP MAN	DANG RIGHT DANCEMAN NORTHERN FALLS	22 9 4
3	SMOKEY SHERRY EXECUTIVE POSITION K. J. MA KATE	SMOKEY SHERRY ICE SCULPTURE AM TUNED UP	SMOKEY SHERRY K. J. MA KATE ICE SCULPTURE	K. J. MA KATE SMOKEY SHERRY SHE'S A SLEEPER	K. J. MA KATE SMOKEY SHERRY ICE SCULPTURE	SMOKEY SHERRY K. J. MA KATE ICE SCULPTURE	19 13 4
4	DISCO QUICKER CLOUHALO I'LL BE TICKLED	CLOUHALO I'LL BE TICKLED DISCO QUICKER	HERE COMES LOVE CLOUHALO I'LL BE TICKLED	I'LL BE TICKLED CLOUHALO HERE COMES LOVE	CLOUHALO I'LL BE TICKLED HERE COMES LOVE	CLOUHALO I'LL BE TICKLED HERE COMES LOVE	16 11 7
5	BITTY BITTY BERTA NATTY ROSE I'M NO NO	FLYING RUMOR GLORIOUS VIEW REACH FOR IT	BITTY BITTY BERTA FLYING RUMOR REAL TIME	BITTY BITTY BERTA GOING FOR GOLD FLYING RUMOR	BITTY BITTY BERTA FLYING RUMOR GOING FOR GOLD	BITTY BITTY BERTA FLYING RUMOR GOING FOR GOLD	20 10 3
6	STILL CRAZY RIVO SINGLE BID	SINGLE BID BOLD AND VIBRANT ANO DE RABLER	**SINGLE BID** BOLD AND VIBRANT RIVO	**SINGLE BID** HELEN'S BIRDIE BOLD AND VIBRANT	**SINGLE BID** BOLD AND VIBRANT HELEN'S BIRDIE	**SINGLE BID** BOLD AND VIBRANT STILL CRAZY	27 7 5
7	HI PI BOPPING ROBBINS DIRTY BIRDIE	SOVEREIGN EXCHANGE DIRTY BIRDIE HI PI	DIRTY BIRDIE HI PI BOPPING ROBBINS	BOPPING ROBBINS DIRTY BIRDIE HI PI	HI PI SOVEREIGN EXCHANGE BOPPING ROBBINS	HI PI DIRTY BIRDIE BOPPING ROBBINS	14 10 9
8	**CHIEF'S CROWN** PROUD TRUTH STEPHAN'S ODYSSEY	**CHIEF'S CROWN** STEPHAN'S ODYSSEY RHOMAN RULE	CHIEF'S CROWN SPEND A BUCK PROUD TRUTH	CHIEF'S CROWN ETERNAL PRINCE PROUD TRUTH	SPEND A BUCK CHIEF'S CROWN STEPHAN'S ODYSSEY	CHIEF'S CROWN SPEND A BUCK STEPHAN'S ODYSSEY	26 7 4
9	TURN HERE STEEL EXPLOSION CHANGE OF DREAMS	SILVER WRAITH EXCLUSIVE ARTS TURN HERE	SILVER WRAITH EXCLUSIVE ARTS STEEL EXPLOSION	EXCLUSIVE ARTS STEEL EXPLOSION INCENSE	EXCLUSIVE ARTS SILVER WRAITH INCENSE	EXCLUSIVE ARTS SILVER WRAITH TURN HERE	14 12 6
10	SWAY ZEN KING PAVAROTTI	ZEN KING SWAY JOHN LAW	SWAY ZEN KING MISSISSIPPI MAN	SWAY MISSISSIPPI MAN SENSE OF REALITY	SWAY MISSISSIPPI MAN ZEN KING	SWAY ZEN KING MISSISSIPPI MAN	22 10 5

THE FIRST BET WAS ON DANCEMAN

By the time of the first race we were already situated in our traditional Derby Day spot, at the tote board near the paddock. The first race, for $4,000 claimers, had a 1.08 expected return to place on Testy Tom. We were holding to a 1.10 cutoff so we passed up the bet and watched Testy Tom drive for second, a half length behind the winner. We knew that passing him up was the proper long-term strategy but that did not seem to be much of a consolation at the time. In the second race, a 6 furlong, $16,000 claimer, a Dr. Z bet did develop on Chris McCarron's mount, Danceman. The final mutuels were:

	Totals	#10 *Danceman*	*Expected Value per Dollar Bet on Danceman*
Odds		9–5	
Win	253,717	74,152	
Show	119,182	23,104	1.13

With an initial wealth of $1,500 the suggested bet was $239. Prior to the race this large bet was justified by the odds on the horse and the high expected return. Danceman's finish made it difficult to justify any bet, however, and we were left with a wealth of $1,261. The mutuel payoffs were:

9–	Aston Pillar	64.20	23.80	17.40
8–	Northern Falls.		9.40	6.00
4–	Gary N			17.40

SMOKEY SHERRY GETS US GOING

Matters improved in the third race, a $4\frac{1}{2}$-furlong maiden race for two-year-old fillies. Smokey Sherry's mutuels one minute before post were:

	Totals	#7 *Smokey Sherry*	*Expected Value per Dollar Bet on Smokey Sherry*
Odds		4–5	
Win	185,180	81,558	
Show	73,240	19,232	1.19

The suggested bet was $515. The final mutuels, which included our bet, showed a considerable drop in the expected return on a show bet:

	Totals	*#7 Smokey Sherry*	*Expected Value per Dollar Bet on Smokey Sherry*
Odds		4–5	
Win	214,125	92,227	
Show	81,609	23,711	1.12

These mutuels recommended a lower bet of $432, but the $515 wager returned a profit of $154.50 when Smokey Sherry came third in a close finish and paid $2.60. This left our wealth at $1,415.50. The mutuel payoffs were:

5–	Executive Position.........	6.60	4.00	2.00
2–	AM Tuned Up.............		5.00	3.20
7–	Smokey Sherry............			2.00
$2 EXACTA	(5–2) Paid $34.00			

The final mutuels for races two and three demonstrate the crowd's love of exotic wagering. Race 2, with no exotic wagering (except for the daily double coupled and bet with race 1), had $253,717 bet to win. Race 3 had a much larger betting public but, due to exacta wagering, had only $214,125 bet to win!

CLOUHALO CHARGES TO WIN THE FOURTH

The fourth race, 7 furlongs for three-year-old fillies, also had a Dr. Z bet. The mutuels one minute from the end of betting were:

	Totals	*#1 Clouhalo*	*Expected Value per Dollar Bet on Clouhalo*
Odds		2–1	
Win	290,754	76,555	
Show	126,217	22,758	1.12

The suggested wager was $129 and the final mutuels were similar:

	Totals	*#1 Clouhalo*	*Expected Value per Dollar Bet on Clouhalo*
Odds		2–1	
Win	316,616	82,166	
Show	131,800	24,773	1.09

Clouhalo, a late charger, was fourth going into the stretch and then finished strongly to win by a head. She paid $3.20 to show for a profit of $77.40. This raised our wealth to $1,492.90. The mutuel payoffs were:

1–	Clouhalo..................	6.40	3.40	3.20
6–	Here Comes Love		3.20	3.00
3–	Shagpoke			5.20
$2 EXACTA	(1–6) Paid $17.00			

FLYING RUMOR GETS US BACK IN THE BLACK

Flying Rumor, the favorite in the fifth race, developed into a Dr. Z bet early on and remained so throughout the betting. The crowd steadily increased as Derby time approached but, perhaps surprisingly, it became easier to bet close to the end of betting as the day wore on. This occurs on Derby Day because the crowd flocks around closed-circuit televisions to watch the races. As the crowd increases everyone tries to bet early to allow time to situate themselves with a good view of a television. A result of this is that one can bet with mutuels very close to the final figures. For Flying Rumor we were able to work with the mutuels thirty seconds from the end of betting:

	Totals	*#8 Flying Rumor*	*Expected Value per Dollar Bet on Flying Rumor*
Odds		4–5	
Win	296,858	136,139	
Show	144,947	33,329	1.31

With the low odds and terrific edge the Kelly bet was a whopping $867! The final mutuels were similar:

	Totals	*#8 Flying Rumor*	*Expected Value per Dollar Bet on Flying Rumor*
Odds		3–5	
Win	328,095	153,695	
Show	154,309	37,013	1.29

Flying Rumor assumed the lead early on in the race and dominated other horses convincingly by widening her lead at the finish. She only paid $3.40 for win but paid $2.40 for both place and show. Thus our profit was $173.40 for a bankroll of $1666.30. We were finally back in the black! The mutuel payoffs were:

8–	Flying Rumor	3.40	2.40	2.40
1–	Bitty Bitty Berta............		2.40	2.40
4–	Woodford County..........			2.40
$2 EXACTA	(9–1) Paid $5.00			

BOLD AND VIBRANT WINS THE SIXTH AND WE PASS THE SEVENTH

Bold and Vibrant was a good bet in the sixth race. The final mutuels were:

	Totals	*#4 Bold and Vibrant*	*Expected Value per Dollar Bet on Bold and Vibrant*
Odds		7–5	
Win	373,675	128,074	
Show	160,886	35,581	1.15

Bold and Vibrant gained the early lead, was pressured strongly but prevailed with a $\frac{3}{4}$-length victory. The show payoff was $2.60, so our Kelly bet of $433 returned a profit of $129.90 for a new wealth of $1796.20. The mutuel payoffs were:

4–	Bold and Vibrant	5.00	3.00	2.60
1–	Single Bid		3.00	2.00
3–	Rivo			3.00
$2 EXACTA	(4–1) Paid $9.00			

In the seventh race, Hi Pi looked like a strong contender but the expected return on a show bet was only 1.07. We passed up the bet and watched our horse never be a factor in the race. Thus, unlike race 1, we were rewarded for complying with our 1.10 cutoff.

THE 111TH KENTUCKY DERBY

The Derby was next. Its program and the past performances of its entrants follows:

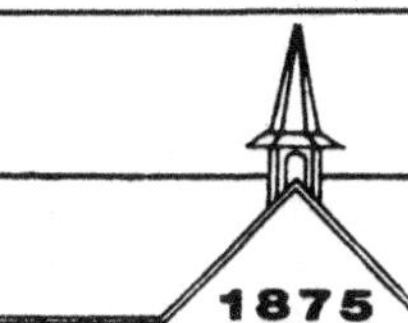

EIGHTH RACE

111th RUNNING OF THE KENTUCKY DERBY

EXACTA WAGERING ON THIS RACE

1875 **1985**

$250,000 ADDED **ONE MILE and ONE-QUARTER** **TRACK RECORD—SECRETARIAT (3), 126 lbs., 5-5-73, 1:59-2/5**

The race to be run FOR THREE-YEAR-OLDS with a subscription fee of $200 each, an entry fee of $10,000 each and a starting fee of $10,000 each. All fees to be paid to the winner. $250,000 shall be paid by Churchill Downs Incorporated (the "Association") as the Added Purse. Second place shall receive $100,000, third place shall receive $50,000 and fourth place shall receive $25,000 from the Added Purse. (The Added Purse and fees to be divided equally in the event of a dead heat.) Weight of 126 lbs. The owner of the winner shall receive a gold trophy. NO SUPPLEMENTARY NOMINATIONS SHALL BE ACCEPTED.

CLOSED FRIDAY, FEBRUARY 5, 1985 WITH 359 NOMINATIONS.

USE THESE NUMBERS FOR BUYING PARI MUTUEL TICKETS

No.	PP	Owner	Trainer	Colors	Horse	Weight	Breeding	Jockey	Morning Line
1	PP3	BROWNELL COMBS II, LESSEE	ANGEL PENNA, JR.	Blue, orange bars on sleeves, orange cap	**RHOMAN RULE**	126	B c, 1982, Stop the Music—Morning Bird by Swaps. BRED IN PENNSYLVANIA BY MRS. LEWIS C. LEDYARD	JACINTO VASQUEZ	5
1a	PP5	BRIAN J. HURST, GEORGE M. STEINBRENNER III, PAULETTA & JOHN A. POST & SPENDTHRIFT FARM, INC. (Brownell Combs II, et al)	J. J. LENZINI, JR.	Black, silver star, silver chevrons on sleeves, silver cap	**ETERNAL PRINCE**	126	B c, 1982, Majestic Prince—Eternal Queen by Fleet Nasrullah. BRED IN FLORIDA BY KINSMAN STUD FARM	RICHARD MIGLIORE	5
2	PP1	IZZIE PROLER	BILLY S. BORDERS	Royal blue, green triangle, blue band on green sleeves, green cap	**IRISH FIGHTER** ^	126	Ch c, 1982, Irish River (Fr)—Go On Dreaming by Dewan. BRED IN KENTUCKY BY SEVEN HILLS CORPORATION	PAT DAY	30
3	PP2	STAR CROWN STABLE (Estate of Carl Rosen) AND THREE CHIMNEYS FARM (Robert Clay), ET AL	ROGER LAURIN	Green and pink diagonal quarters, green and pink stripes on sleeves, pink cap	**CHIEF'S CROWN** ^	126	B c, 1982, Danzig—Six Crowns by Secretariat. BRED IN KENTUCKY BY CARL ROSEN	DON MacBETH	9-5
4	PP4	MR. & MRS. EUGENE V. KLEIN	D. WAYNE LUKAS	Blue, gold triangular panel, gold band on sleeves, blue cap	**TANK'S PROSPECT** ^	126	B c, 1982, Mr. Prospector—Midnight Pumpkin by Pretense. BRED IN KENTUCKY BY E. A. SELTZER	GARY STEVENS	8
5	PP6	HENRYK deKWIATKOWSKI	WOODFORD C. STEPHENS	White, red cross sashes, red dots on sleeves, white cap	**STEPHAN'S ODYSSEY** ^	126	Dk b or br c, 1982, Danzig—Kennelot by Gallant Man. BRED IN KENTUCKY BY KENNELOT STABLES, LTD.	LAFFIT PINCAY, JR.	8
6	PP7	ESTATE OF FRED PORTER	TOMMY T. MORGAN	Blue, gold "P", gold sleeves, blue cap	**ENCOLURE** ^	126	B c, 1982, Riva Ridge—Jabot by Bold Ruler. BRED IN KENTUCKY BY CLAIBORNE FARM	RONALD ARDOIN	30
7	PP8	KING T. LEATHERBURY AND ANDREW MANDJURIS	KING T. LEATHERBURY	Pink, green diamond frame, pink band on green sleeves, pink cap	**I AM THE GAME**	126	B c, 1982, Lord Gaylord—Kitchen Window by Dead Ahead. BRED IN MARYLAND BY WARNER L. JONES, JR.	DARREL McHARGUE	30
8	PP9	ROBERT E. HIBBERT	JOSEPH MANZI	Black, rust hoops, rust cap	**FLOATING RESERVE** ^	126	B c, 1982, Olden Times—Tick Tock by Quack. BRED IN KENTUCKY BY ROBERT E. HIBBERT	SANDY HAWLEY	20
9	PP 10	HUNTER FARM (Dennis W. Diaz)	CAM GAMBOLATI	Electric blue, blue "HF" on silver ball, silver band on sleeves, blue and silver cap	**SPEND A BUCK** ^	126	B c, 1982, Buckaroo—Belle De Jour by Speak John. BRED IN KENTUCKY BY HARPER IRISH HILL FARM	ANGEL CORDERO, JR.	6
10	PP 11	DARBY DAN FARM (John W. Galbreath)	JOHN M. VEITCH	Fawn, brown sleeves, fawn cap	**PROUD TRUTH** ^	126	Ch c, 1982, Graustark—Wake Robin by Summer Tan. BRED IN KENTUCKY BY MRS. JOHN W. GALBREATH	JORGE VELASQUEZ	9-2
11	PP 12	OAK CLIFF STABLE (Tom Tatham, Lessee)	MIKE WHITTINGHAM	Green and tan blocks, green band and cuffs on tan sleeves, green cap	**SKYWALKER** ^	126	Dk b or br c, 1982, Relaunch—Bold Captive by Boldnesian. BRED IN KENTUCKY BY OAK CLIFF THOROUGHBREDS, LTD.	EDDIE DELAHOUSSAYE	12
12	PP 13	WILLIAM R. HAWN	PATTI L. JOHNSON	White, blue cross sashes, white and blue halved sleeves, white cap	**FAST ACCOUNT** ^	126	DK b or b c, 1982, Private Account—Fast Beauty by Fleet Nasrullah. BRED IN KENTUCKY BY WILLIAM R. HAWN	CHRIS McCARRON	20

^ INDICATES FOALED IN KENTUCKY

1 & 1a—BROWNELL COMBS II LESSEE—BRIAN J. HURST, GEORGE M. STEINBRENNER III, PAULETTA AND JOHN A. POST AND SPENDTHRIFT FARM, INC. (Brownell Combs II, et al) Entry

SELECTIONS—3-10-1a-9

111th — KENTUCKY DERBY

8th Churchill

1¼ MILES. (1.59⅘) 111th Running KENTUCKY DERBY STAKES SCALE WEIGHT (Grade I). $250,000 Added. 3-year-olds. With a subscription fee of $200 each, an entry fee of $10,000 each and a starting fee of $10,000 each. All fees to be paid to the winner. $250,000 shall be paid by Churchill Downs Incorporated (the "Association") as the added purse. Second place shall receive $100,000, third place shall receive $50,000 and fourth place shall receive $25,000 from the added purse. (The added purse and fees to be divided equally in the event of a dead heat.) Starters shall be named through the entry box on Thursday, May 2, 1985, at the usual time of closing. The maximum number of starters shall be limited to twenty and each shall carry a weight of 126 lbs. In the event that more than twenty entries pass through the entry box at the time of closing, the starters shall be determined at that time with preference given to those horses that have accumulated the highest earnings, excluding earnings won in a restricted race. For purposes of this preference, a "restricted race" shall mean a state bred restricted race (a race where entries are restricted to horses qualifying under state breeding programs), a sales restricted race (a race where entries are restricted by the origin of purchase), and a restricted sweepstakes (a race where entries are restricted by money previously earned, sweepstakes previously won, sweepstakes won at varying distances or sweepstakes won within periods of time preceding race.) The owner of the winner shall receive a gold trophy. No supplementary nominations shall be accepted. (Closed with 360 nominations.)

Route the Field Will Travel

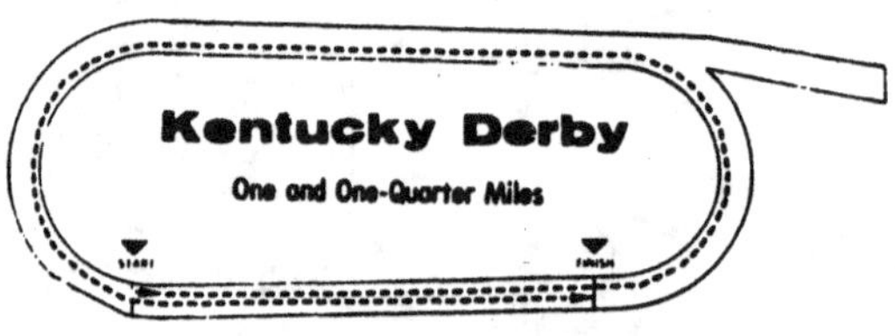

Irish Fighter

Own.—Proler I **126**
Ch. c. 3, by Irish River—Go On Dreaming, by Dewan
Br.—Seven Hills Corp (Ky) 1985 6 2 0 3 $94,625
Tr.—Borders Billy S 1984 0 M 0 0
Lifetime 6 2 0 3 $94,625

20Apr85-9OP 1⅛ :46^{3} 1:11 1:48^{2}ft 37 115 5^{5}¾ 5^{1}¼ 3^{4}½ 3^{7}½ HernndzC^{6} Ark Dby 84-18 Tnk'sProspect,Encolure,IrishFightr 9
20Apr85—Grade I; Steadied and had to wait for room second turn
31Mar85-11FG 1⅛ :47 1:12 1:50^{1}ft 40 113 3^{2}½ 3^{2} 2^{2} 3^{2} HrnndzR^{1} Lou Dby 91-21 Violado,CremeFriche,IrishFighter 11
31Mar85—Grade III
16Mar85-10FG 1$\frac{1}{16}$:47^{4} 1:13^{1} 1:45^{4}sl 3 116 3^{4}½ 2^{1} 2^{hd} 3^{2} Hernandez C^{4} Dby Trl 81-20 Mischifnmnd,NordcScndl,IrshFghtr 6
23Feb85-10FG 1$\frac{1}{16}$:47^{2} 1:12^{4} 1:45^{4}ft 7½ 115 8^{6}¾ 9^{7}¼ 6^{9} 6^{9}¾ WlkrBJJr^{6} Lecomte H 74-24 Encolure,NorthernBid,TenTimsTn 11
30Jan85-9FG 6f :22^{2} :46^{4} 1:12 gd *2-3 119 4^{1}¾ 3^{1} 1^{3} 1^{3} Walker B J Jr^{5} Aw9000 85-18 Irish Fighter, Single Bid, Delierio 8
10Jan85-4FG 6f :22^{3} :46^{3} 1:12 ft *4-5 119 1^{hd} 1^{2}½ 1^{4} 1^{5} Walker B J Jr^{9} Mdn 85-20 IrshFghtr,PocktofMrcls,Sllm'sJwl 12
Apr 14 Kee 7f ft 1:28 b Apr 9 Kee 5f ft 1:01^{2} b Mar 25 FG 7f ft 1:26^{2} h Mar 10 FG 7f ft 1:26^{1} b

Chief's Crown *

Own.—Star Crown Stable **126**
B. c. 3, by Danzig—Six Crowns, by Secretariat
Br.—Rosen C (Ky) 1985 3 3 0 0 $308,532
Tr.—Laurin Roger 1984 9 6 2 0 $920,890
Lifetime 12 9 2 0 $1,229,422

25Apr85-7Kee 1⅛ :48^{2} 1:12 1:47^{3}ft *1-3 121 1^{1}½ 1^{1} 1^{3} 1^{5}½ McBethD^{2} Bluegrass 99-16 Chief'sCrown,FlotingRsrv,BnnrBob 4
25Apr85—Grade I
30Mar85-11Hia 1⅛ :48^{4} 1:12^{2} 1:48^{2}ft 6-5 122 1^{hd} 1^{1} 1^{2}½ 1^{1} † McBethD^{5} Flamingo 90-12 ‡Chf'sCrwn,PrdTrth,Stphn'sOdyssy 8
30Mar85—Grade I; Disq. placed 2nd; reversed by Fla board Apr 9, awarded 1st money
2Mar85-10GP 7f :22^{3} :45^{1} 1:22^{2}ft *1-3 122 2^{hd} 2^{hd} 1^{1} 1^{3}½ MacBeth D^{9} Swale 92-15 Chief'sCrown,CremeFrich,ChrokFst 9
10Nov84-1Hol 1 :45 1:10 1:36^{1}ft *2-3 122 6^{4}¾ 3^{2}½ 2^{1} 1¾ McBethD^{5} Br Cp Jv — — Chf'sCrwn,Tnk'sPrspct,SpndABck 10
10Nov84—Grade I
27Oct84-8SA 1$\frac{1}{16}$:46^{3} 1:10^{4} 1:42^{2}ft *1-3 118 2½ 1^{hd} 1^{hd} 1^{1}½ McBethD^{6} Norfolk 89-13 Chief'sCrown,MtthewT.Prkr,VivMxi 6
27Oct84—Grade I
6Oct84-8Bel 1 :45^{2} 1:10^{3} 1:36^{3}ft *1-2 122 2^{1} 1^{2} 1^{3} 1^{6} McBethD^{4} Cowdin 82-17 Chif'sCrown,BionicLight,ScriptOho 8
6Oct84—Grade I
15Sep84-5Bel 7f :22^{4} :46 1:23^{1}sy *2-3 122 6^{8} 6^{4} 3^{4} 2^{1} MacBethD^{5} Futurity 85-18 SpctclrLov,Chf'sCrown,Mgzy'sRllh 8
15Sep84—Grade I
26Aug84-8Sar 6½f :21^{4} :44^{4} 1:16 ft *1 122 3^{3}½ 3½ 1½ 1^{3}¾ McBethD^{3} Hopeful 92-15 Chif'sCrown,TiffnyIc,Mugzy'sRullh 9
26Aug84—Grade I
3Aug84-8Sar 6f :22^{3} :46 1:10^{1}ft *2 117 3^{3} 2^{hd} 1^{hd} 1^{2}¾ McBethD^{4} Sar Spec'l 89-19 Chf'sCrown,DoItAgnDn,SkyCmmnd 6
3Aug84—Grade II
5Jly84-6Bel 5½f :22^{2} :45^{4} 1:04^{2}ft *1 118 1^{hd} 2^{hd} 1^{1} 1^{5} MacBeth D^{5} Mdn 93-15 Chief'sCrown,DesertWr,TigerBiddr 9
22Jun84-4Bel 5½f :22^{1} :46^{1} 1:05^{3}ft 5½ 118 4^{3}½ 4^{6}½ 3^{4}½ 2^{1} MacBeth D^{1} Mdn 86-21 SecretryGnrl,Chif'sCrown,TiffnyIc 10
13Jun84-4Bel 5f :22^{4} :46^{2} :58^{4}ft 3 118 4^{6}½ 6^{13} 5^{13} 4^{1}½ Cordero A Jr^{8} Mdn 81-18 Don'tFoolWthM,Attrbut,MountRlty 8
May 1 CD 4f sy :47^{3} b Apr 22 Kee 4f ft :49^{3} b ●Apr 17 Kee 5f ft :58^{4} h ●Apr 6 GP 4f ft :48^{1} b

Rhoman Rule

B. c. 3, by Stop The Music—Morning Bird, by Swaps

Br.—Ledyard Mrs L C (Pa) 1985 3 2 0 1 $120,480

Own.—Combs B Lessee 126 Tr.—Penna Angel Jr 1984 5 1 1 1 $73,448

Lifetime 8 3 1 2 $193,928

20Apr85-8Aqu 1⅛:48 1:11^3 1:48^{4}gd 3 126 3^5 3^4 2^4 3^5 VsquezJ^1 Wood Inv 86-10 EternlPrinc,ProudTruth,RhomnRul 6

20Apr85—Grade I

16Mar85-10Hia 1⅛:48^4 1:12 1:47^{4}ft 6-5 112 1^2 1^{2½} 1^5 1^8 VasquezJ^8 Everglades 93-13 RhomanRule,CremeFriche,IrishSur 8

16Mar85—Grade II

2Mar85-1GP 7f :22^1 :44^4 1:22 ft *3-2 117 4^2 2^{hd} 1^3 1^{10} Vasquez J^1 Aw16000 94-15 Rhoman Rule, J. O.'s Best,Magloire 9

18Oct84-8Med 1$\frac{1}{16}$:46 1:11^1 1:45 ft 7½ 119 6^{11} 4^4 4^{4½} 4^3 HrnndR^8 Yng America 81-22 ScrptOho,SpndABck,Tnk'sProspct 11

18Oct84—Grade I; Drifted out

6Oct84-8Lrl 1$\frac{1}{16}$:46^4 1:12^2 1:43 ft 33 122 8^{4¾} 5^3 2½ 3^{2½} HrnndzR^{12} Laurel Fty 90-15 MghtyAppling,CutlssRlty,RhomnRl 12

6Oct84—Grade I

8Sep84-5Bel 7f :22^2 :45^3 1:24 ft 13 119 7^{5½} 5^4 3^{5½} 2^4 Hernandez R^8 Aw20000 78-17 Herat, Rhoman Rule, Stonewhite 8

8Aug84-4Sar 7f :22^4 :46^2 1:25 ft 4f 118 3^1 2½ 1^3 1^{3½} Hernandez R^{11} Mdn 77-16 RhomnRul,CoyotDncr,FbulousMov 13

26Jly84-6Bel 6f :22^3 :46^1 1:11^{3}ft 13 118 8^{5½} 6^{6½} 9^{13} 8^{17½} Samyn J L^9 Mdn 66-17 SalemDrive,Anconeus,Haberdsher 10

26Jly84—Broke slowly

●Apr 29 CD 6f ft 1:14^2 h Apr 19 Bel 3f ft :36 b Apr 15 Bel 6f ft 1:14 b ●Apr 7 Hia 6f ft 1:12 b

Tank's Prospect

B. c. 3, by Mr Prospector—Midnight Pumpkin, by Pretense

Br.—Seltzer E A (Ky) 1985 4 3 0 0 $513,850

Own.—Klein Mr–Mrs E V 126 Tr.—Lukas D Wayne 1984 7 1 2 2 $418,595

Lifetime 11 4 2 2 $932,445

20Apr85-9OP 1⅛:46^3 1:11 1:48^{2}ft 3 123 4^{5½} 4¾ 1^1 1^{6½} StevnsGL^9 Ark Dby 92-18 Tnk'sProspect,Encolure,IrishFightr 9

20Apr85—Grade I

6Apr85-8SA 1⅛:46^3 1:10^3 1:48^{2}ft 3½ 122 4^2 8^{3¾} 8^{12} 9^{11½} VelsquzJ^7 S A Dby 76-10 Skywalker,FstAccount,Nostlgi'sStr 9

6Apr85—Grade I

3Feb85-8BM 1$\frac{1}{16}$:45^3 1:09^3 1:41 ft 2½ 120 3^{1½} 4¾ 1^{hd} 1½ VlsquzJ^4 Camino Real 87-13 Tnk'sProspect,RightCon,‡Skywlker 9

3Feb85—Grade III

6Jan85-4SA 1 :45^2 1:10^1 1:36 ft *1-3 115 1½ 1^3 1^{2½} 1¾ DelhoussyeE^1 Aw24000 88-06 Tnk'sProspct,ProtctYourslf,FtrFbl 6

16Dec84-8Hol 1$\frac{1}{16}$:45^3 1:10^3 1:43^{2}gd 3½ 121 9^{6½} 8^5 4^{2½} 4^{2½} VelsquezJ^4 Hol Futy — — Stphn'sOdyssy,FrstNormn,RghtCn 13

16Dec84—Grade I

10Nov84-1Hol 1 :45 1:10 1:36^{1}ft 26 122 7^{6½} 4^5 3^{2½} 2¾ VelsquezJ^4 Br Cp Jv — — Chf'sCrwn,Tnk'sPrspct,SpndABck 10

10Nov84—Grade I

27Oct84-8Aqu 1⅛:48^1 1:12^1 1:49^{1}m 3 122 4^{5½} 4^{3½} 4^{5½} 3^4 VlsquzJ^2 Champagne 85-16 FrCrtnDc,MghtAppling,Tnk'sPrspct 6

27Oct84—Grade I; Came over

18Oct84-8Med 1$\frac{1}{16}$:46 1:11^1 1:45 ft 16 119 7^{14} 7^{7½} 5^6 3^1 McBtD^9 Yng America 83-22 ScrptOho,SpndABck,Tnk'sProspct 11

18Oct84—Grade I; Drifted in

5Oct84-6SA 6f :22^2 :45^3 1:10^{3}ft 4¾ 117 6^{7¾} 6^{6½} 3^2 1^{3½} Delahoussaye E^6 Mdn 85-16 Tnk'sProspct,Chiftin'sClss,QulityJt 9

11Jly84-4Hol 6f :22^3 :46 1:11^{1}ft 8½ 116 6^{3½} 4^{3½} 4^3 2^{2½} Valenzuela P A^6 Mdn 78-16 Mtronomc,Tnk'sProspct,RylOlymp 9

1Jly84-6Hol 5½f:22^4 :45^1 1:04^{3}ft 14 116 7^{6½} 6^{8½} 6^{8½} 5^{6¾} Valenzuela P A^3 Mdn 81-16 Lomax, Royal Olympia, Michadilla 8

Apr 14 SA 5f ft 1:01^4 h Apr 1 SA 6f ft 1:13^3 h ●Mar 27 Hol 1 sy 1:44^2 h Mar 22 SA 7f ft 1:27 h

Eternal Prince

B. c. 3, by Majestic Prince—Eternal Queen, by Fleet Nasrullah

Br.—Kinsman Stud Farm (Fla) 1985 5 4 0 0 $379,740

Own.—Combs B III et al 126 Tr.—Lenzini John J Jr 1984 3 M 2 0 $9,622

Lifetime 8 4 2 0 $389,362

20Apr85-8Aqu 1⅛:48 1:11^3 1:48^{4}gd 2½ 126 1^1 1^{2½} 1^4 1^{2¾} MigliorR^5 Wood Inv 91-10 EternlPrinc,ProudTruth,RhomnRul 6

20Apr85—Grade I

6Apr85-8Aqu 1 :44^1 1:08^2 1:34^{2}ft 18 114 1^{1½} 1^{1½} 1^2 1^5 MigliorR^7 Gotham 94-21 EternalPrince,PanchoVilla,ElBasco 7

6Apr85—Grade II

23Mar85-8Aqu 7f :22^4 :45^3 1:22^{1}ft 3¾ 114 2^1 3^{nk} 5^{5½} 6^{8½} MigliorR^6 Bay Shore 81-23 Pancho Villa, ElBasco,SpendABuck 9

23Mar85—Grade II

13Mar85-7Aqu 7f :23^1 :46^4 1:25^{1}ft *4-5 122 1½ 1^1 1^4 1^{6¾} Migliore R^6 Aw25000 75-28 EternlPrince,SuperScope,Vrbscum 7

4Mar85-6Aqu 6f ⊡:23 :46^2 1:11^{2}ft *1 122 1^{1½} 1^2 1^6 1^8 Migliore R^5 Mdn 87-22 EternlPrinc,ChngThLock,Alx'sGm 10

31Jly84-9Mth 5½f:22^1 :45 1:04 ft 30 113 10^8 7^{10} 7^9 4^{13} Delgado A^8 Tyro 82-15 DoublyClr,Zggy'sBoy,Whtvr'sRght 11

16Jly84-6Bel 6f :22^3 :46 1:11^{2}ft 14 118 2^{hd} 2^{hd} 2^{hd} 2^4 Cordero A Jr^1 Mdn 81-24 NickelBck,EternlPrince,Anconeus 13

27Jun84-4Bel 5½f:23 :47^1 1:06^{3}ft 2½ 118 1^{hd} 1½ 1^{1½} 2^{1½} Migliore R^5 M40000 81-17 BernCgney,EternlPrinc,WstrnChmp 9

●Apr 29 CD 5f ft 1:00^3 h Apr 15 Aqu 5f ft 1:02 b Apr 2 GS 5f ft :57^2 b ●Mar 20 Aqu 4f ft :46^2 h

Stephan's Odyssey

Dk. b. or br. c. 3, by Danzig—Kennelot, by Gallant Man

Br.—Kennelot Stables Ltd (Ky) 1985 4 1 1 1 $88,535

Own.—deKwiatkowski H 126 Tr.—Stephens Woodford C 1984 4 3 0 0 $651,100

Lifetime 8 4 1 1 $739,635

16Apr85-7Kee 1$\frac{1}{16}$:47^3 1:11^1 1:42^{3}ft *1-2 118 4^6 5^{4½} 3^{1½} 1^{1½} Pincay LJr^4 Lexington 93-16 Stephan'sOdyssey,Tjw,NorthernBid 7

30Mar85-11Hia 1⅛:48^4 1:12^2 1:48^{2}ft 3½ 122 4^2 4^{2½} 3^{2½} 3^{1½} Maple E^4 Flamingo 89-12 ‡Chf'sCrwn,PrdTrth,Stphn'sOdyssy 8

30Mar85—Grade I

2Mar85-11GP 1⅛:47^3 1:11^3 1:50 ft *1 122 5^{3½} 4^2 5^5 6^{4½} Maple E^1 Florida Dby 78-15 ProudTruth,IrishSur,DoItAgainDn 11

2Mar85—Grade I

18Feb85-10GP 1$\frac{1}{16}$:46^3 1:11^1 1:43^{3}ft 2¾ 122 11^{12} 9^{6½} 5½ 2^{nk} Maple E^{11} Fntain Yth 83-22 PrdTrth,Stphn'sOdyssy,DItAgnDn 14

18Feb85—Grade II

16Dec84-8Hol 1$\frac{1}{16}$:45^3 1:10^3 1:43^{2}gd 11 121 10^9 4^{2½} 1^{1½} 1^1 Maple E^8 Hol Futy — — Stphn'sOdyssy,FrstNormn,RghtCn 13

16Dec84—Grade I

2Dec84-3Hol 6f :22 :45^2 1:09^{3}ft 4 118 6^{5½} 3^{1½} 2^{hd} 1no Pincay L Jr^1 Aw22000 101-05 Stphn'sOdyssy,ImgofGrtnss,PrBwlr 6

28Oct84-6Aqu 7f :22^1 :45 1:22^{3}gd *9-5 122 5^{3½} 3^{1½} 3^2 4^{3½} McCarron G^3 Aw20000 84-14 AnotherReef,SecretryGnrl,SkipTril 7

28Oct84—Drifted

21Oct84-6Bel 6f :22^4 :46^2 1:12 ft *2-3 118 4^3 3^{2½} 2½ 1^{1½} Day P^4 Mdn 82-21 StphnsOdss,RllngMnstrl,DmscsSm 11

21Oct84—Bumped,clear

●May 2 CD 4f m :48 h Apr 28 CD 1 m 1:46^2 b Apr 24 Kee 5f ft 1:01^4 b ●Apr 11 Hia 6f ft 1:13^1 b

Encolure — B. c. 3, by Riva Ridge—Jabot, by Bold Ruler
Own.—Porter F Est of — 126 — Br.—Claiborne Farm (Ky) — Tr.—Morgan Tom T
1985 6 2 2 0 $213,600
1984 5 2 2 0 $68,224
Lifetime 11 4 4 0 $281,824

20Apr85-9OP 1⅛ :463 1:11 1:482ft 50 126 2hd 2hd 21 26½ Ardoin R5 Ark Dby 85-18 Tnk'sProspect,Encolure,IrishFightr 9
20Apr85—Grade I
31Mar85-11FG 1⅛ :47 1:12 1:501ft 10 123 86¾ 74¾ 814 812¾ Ardoin R8 Lou Dby 80-21 Violado,CremeFriche,IrishFighter 11
31Mar85—Grade III
23Mar85-10FG 1 1/16 :464 1:124 1:452ft *6-5 123 38 35½ 14 11 ArdonR9 [R]Hits P Dby 85-19 Encolur,UndrOrdrs,Dusty'sDynmit 10
14Mar85-10FG 1 1/16 :474 1:131 1:462sy *4-5 123 3½ 1hd 12½ 22 Ardoin R8 [R]Dry Trl 78-21 UnderOrdrs,Encolur,FlshyDimond 10
23Feb85-10FG 1 1/16 :472 1:124 1:454ft 41 114 22 21 11½ 11 Ardoin R3 Lecomte H 83-24 Encolure,NorthernBid,TenTimsTn 11
13Jan85-10FG 6f :221 :461 1:11 ft 5 116 53 84¾ 35 47 Faul J H7 Mstr Dby 83-19 Mrshu'sEchelon,TnTimsTn,MstrCll 8
15Dec84-10FG 6f :22 :461 1:112ft 9 115 63¾ 21½ 11½ 14½ ArdR10 [R]Hits Prd Fut 88-17 Encolure,UnderOrders,KamaSutra 13
6Dec84-11FG 6f :223 :472 1:142gd 3 115 64¾ 57 25 24 Ardoin R9 [R]Fut Trl 69-32 KamaSutra,Encolure,BshfulAngel 11
6Dec84—Run in three divisions, 7th, 9th and 11th races
15Nov84-10LaD 6f :223 :461 1:114ft *4-5 122 43½ 42½ 33 48¾ Ardoin R8 Aw7400 75-26 MsterCll,JunglePilgrim,NtivCrwmn 9
8Nov84-4LaD 7f :23 :463 1:252ft *6-5 120 2hd 2hd 13 15 Ardoin R9 Mdn 97-21 Encolure, Oceail's Pride, Rivaten 12
8Jun84-4LaD 5f :23 :472 1:002gd 2 120 44 46 38 210 Frazier R L7 Mdn 79-23 Politariat, Encolure, Two Cheers 10
Apr 30 CD 5f ft 1:013 b ●Apr 16 OP 5f ft :594 b Mar 28 FG 5f sy 1:054 b Mar 20 FG 5f ft 1:023 b

I Am The Game * — B. c. 3, by Lord Gaylord—Kitchen Window, by Dead Ahead
Own.—Leatherbury & Mandjeris — 126 — Br.—Jones W L Jr (Md) — Tr.—Leatherbury King T
1985 7 3 2 1 $200,183
1984 1 1 0 0 $12,000
Lifetime 8 4 2 1 $212,183

20Apr85-8GS 1⅛ :453 1:092 1:454ft 17 117 48 44½ 26 29½ AtlCW1 Garden State — — SpndABuck,IAmThGm,DoItAginDn 9
6Apr85-8GS 1 :452 1:10 1:352ft 12 115 1421 1316 712 210½ AntlCW3 Chryhill M H — — SpendABuck,IAmTheGm,KingBbr 14
23Mar85-8Aqu 7f :224 :453 1:221ft 5½ 117 53 51¾ 78½ 79½ VsquezJ9 Bay Shore 81-23 Pancho Villa, ElBasco,SpendABuck 9
23Mar85—Grade II
9Mar85-8Lrl 1 :461 1:113 1:38 ft *2-5 112 2hd 1½ 13½ 13½ DldA2 [S]St De Naskra 82-27 IAmThGm,JoyfllJohn,LttlBoldJohn 5
18Feb85-8Lrl 1 :461 1:114 1:373ft *2-5 119 3½ 2hd 2½ 36 DelgdoA6 Gen George 78-20 Roo Art, JoyfullJohn,IAmTheGame 8
3Feb85-8Lrl 7f :231 :463 1:241sy *6-5 122 11 12 11½ 15½ DlgdoA2 F. Scott Key 90-28 IAmThGm,Sprrowvon,JoyfullJohn 10
23Jan85-8Lrl 6f :222 :454 1:104ft *1-3 113 21½ 2hd 1hd 11 DelgadoA1 W P Burch 89-14 IAmTheGme,JyBryn,AlongCmeJons 6
30Dec84-7Aqu 6f [•]:23 :464 1:112ft 2½ 118 1½ 1½ 14 14 Cordero A Jr6 Mdn 87-15 IAmThGm,FrstCnqst,HstryRspnds 11
Apr 30 CD 5f ft 1:013 b ●Apr 17 Lrl 4f ft :471 b ●Apr 3 Lrl 3f ft :35 bg Mar 29 Lrl 3f ft :363 b

Floating Reserve — B. c. 3, by Olden Times—Tick Tock, by Quack
Own.—Hibbert R E — 126 — Br.—Hibbert R E (Ky) — Tr.—Manzi Joseph
1985 6 1 1 0 $110,295
1984 1 1 0 0 $11,000
Lifetime 7 2 1 0 $121,295

25Apr85-7Kee 1⅛ :482 1:12 1:473ft 13 121 31½ 32 34 25½ Hawley S1 Bluegrass 93-16 Chief'sCrown,FlotingRsrv,BnnrBob 4
25Apr85—Grade I
6Apr85-8SA 1⅛ :463 1:103 1:482ft 11 122 73¾ 53 52¾ 43½ Hawley S4 S A Dby 84-18 Skywalker,FstAccount,Nostlgi'sStr 9
6Apr85—Grade I
17Mar85-8SA 1 1/16 :444 1:10 1:431ft 6½ 120 814 86½ 65½ 54 Maple E3 Sn Felipe H 81-15 ImgeofGrtnss,Skywlkr,Nostlgi'sStr 9
17Mar85—Grade I
23Feb85-8SA 1 :454 1:101 1:361ft 2¼ 122 75 58 44½ 63½ PincyLJr5 San Rafael 84-13 SmartenUp,FstAccount,Stn'sBower 9
23Feb85—Grade II; Drifted out; took up sharply at 5/16; crowded late
6Feb85-8SA 1 1/16 :463 1:104 1:423ft 3¼ 117 54 63¾ 32½ 1¾ PncLJr9 [R]S. Catalina 88-15 FlotngRsrv,BrcnsChrg,BldrThnBld 11
6Feb85—Bumped, driving
19Jan85-4SA 6½f :214 :442 1:154ft *4-5 120 54½ 54½ 44½ 45½ DelhoussyeE4 Aw24000 85-16 LuckyNGreen,PerfecTrvl,Infntrymn 6
19Jan85—Broke slowly, bumped; wide into stretch, lugged in, bumped late; Lugged in
26Dec84-6SA 6f :221 :452 1:103ft 10 118 3½ 31 1½ 14 Hawley S1 Mdn 85-15 FlotingRsrv,‡EvrBrillint,CptinVgors 8
26Dec84—Veered out sharply, bumped hard start
●Apr 22 Kee 4f ft :464 h Apr 17 Kee 1 ft 1:404 h ●Mar 31 SA 6f ft 1:101 h Mar 13 SA 5f ft :594 h

Spend A Buck — B. c. 3, by Buckaroo—Belle De Jour, by Speak John
Own.—Hunter Farm — 126 — Br.—Harper Roe (Ky) — Tr.—Gambolati Cam
1985 3 2 0 1 $323,724
1984 8 5 2 1 $667,985
Lifetime 11 7 2 2 $991,709

20Apr85-8GS 1⅛ :453 1:092 1:454ft *2-5 122 13½ 13 16 19½ CrdrAJr2 GardenState — — SpndABuck,IAmThGm,DoItAginDn 9
6Apr85-8GS 1 :452 1:10 1:352ft 8-5 122 12½ 12 16 110½ CrdrAJr7 Chryhill M H — — SpendABuck,IAmTheGm,KingBbr 14
23Mar85-8Aqu 7f :224 :453 1:221ft *7-5 123 31 41½ 34½ 35½ CordrAJr1 Bay Shore 84-23 Pancho Villa, ElBasco,SpendABuck 9
23Mar85—Grade II
10Nov84-1Hol 1 :45 1:10 1:361ft 6½ 122 1hd 12½ 11 31½ CordrAJr3 Br Cp Jv — — Chf'sCrwn,Tnk'sPrspct,SpndABck 10
10Nov84—Grade I
18Oct84-8Med 1 1/16 :46 1:111 1:45 ft *1 122 11½ 11 1½ 2¾ CrdrAJr4 Yng America 83-22 ScrptOho,SpndABck,Tnk'sProspct 11
18Oct84—Grade I
22Sep84-9AP 1 :444 1:10 1:38 ft 3 122 21 2hd 1½ 1½ HusseyC6 Arl Was Fut 71-24 SpendABuck,Dusty'sDarby,VivaMxi 7
22Sep84—Grade I
2Sep84-11RD 1 1/16 :473 1:12 1:451ft *6-5 120 11 14 18 115 Hussey C6 M H Cradle 83-18 SpendABuck,GrndNtive,Alex'sGm 13
16Aug84-7Crc 6f :223 :461 1:124ft *1-2 112 11½ 14 18 19½ Hussey C1 Aw15000 87-23 SpendABuck,SecretGol,Mr.Introinn 5
4Aug84-9Crc 5½f :223 :47 1:07 ft *3-5 116 23 22 22½ 22½ Hussey C4 Criterium 87-21 Smile, Spend A Buck,CherokeeFast 7
4Aug84—Run In Divisions
25Jly84-8Crc 5½f :224 :463 1:06 ft 2½ 113 1½ 11½ 13 14 Hussey C3 Aw11000 95-20 SpndABck,Mr.Intronn,PlyngPoltcs 8
14Jly84-2Crc 5½f :23 :47 1:071ft 5½ 116 11½ 1hd 12 1nk Hussey C6 Mdn 89-19 SpndABck,HckryHllFlyr,SprbAnsr 12
●May 1 CD 4f sy :47 h ●Apr 17 GS 4f ft :452 h ●Apr 3 GS 4f ft :452 h ●Mar 22 Aqu 3f ft :352 h

Proud Truth
Ch. c. 3, by Graustark—Wake Robin, by Summer Tan
Br.—Galbreath Mrs J W (Ky) 1985 6 3 2 0 $435,927
Own.—Darby Dan Farm 126 Tr.—Veitch John M 1984 2 2 0 0 $18,000
Lifetime 8 5 2 0 $453,927
20Apr85-8Aqu 1⅛ :48 1:113 1:484gd *8-5 126 47 46 36 22¾ VelsquzJ4 Wood Inv 88-10 EternlPrinc,ProudTruth,RhomnRul 6
20Apr85—Grade I
30Mar85-11Hia 1⅛ :484 1:122 1:482ft *6-5 122 2hd 31 22½ 21 VelsquzJ7 Flamingo 89-12 ‡Chf'sCrwn,PrdTrth,Stphn'sOdyssy 8
30Mar85—Grade I; Placed 1st thru disq.; reversed by Fla. board Apr 9, awarded 2nd money
2Mar85-11GP 1⅛ :473 1:113 1:50 ft 2 122 66½ 65¼ 33½ 1nk VelsquzJ7 Florida Dby 82-15 ProudTruth,IrishSur,DoItAgainDn 11
2Mar85—Grade I; Steadied, driving
18Feb85-10GP 1 1/16 :463 1:111 1:433ft *9-5 112 910 86¼ 3nk 1nk VelsquzJ9 Fntain Yth 83-22 PrdTrth,Stphn'sOdyssy,DItAgnDn 14
18Feb85—Grade II
4Feb85-8GP 1 1/16 :463 1:113 1:442ft *4-5 117 63½ 41¾ 11 16 Velasquez J2 Aw16000 79-18 ProdTrth,CrownngHnrs,ScrtryGnrl 10
5Jan85-9Crc 1 1/16 :481 1:13 1:463ft *8-5 121 1316 915 68 42¾ VlsqzJ15 Trop Pk Dby 83-14 Irish Sur, Artillerist, Banner Bob 16
5Jan85—Grade II
26Dec84-8Crc 7f :222 :454 1:251ft *1 119 77¼ 58 52¼ 13 Velasquez J1 Aw10000 90-22 ProudTruth,Bowladrome,ReglBrek 12
26Dec84—BrkeInTangle,Clr
2Dec84-6Aqu 6f :224 :47 1:122ft 2e118 84½ 76¾ 31 12¾ Velasquez J2 Mdn 79-24 Proud Truth,TakeControl,Buckner 10
Apr 28 CD 5f m 1:024 b Apr 19 Bel 3f ft :353 b ●Apr 14 Bel 6f ft 1:131 h ●Apr 9 Hia 3f sy :361 b

Skywalker *
Dk. b. or br. c. 3, by Relaunch—Bold Captive, by Boldnesian
Br.—Oak Cliff Thds Ltd (Ky) 1985 4 2 1 0 $291,200
Own.—Oak Cliff Stable 126 Tr.—Whittingham Michael 1984 2 1 0 0 $39,500
Lifetime 6 3 1 0 $330,700
6Apr85-8SA 1⅛ :463 1:103 1:482ft *6-5 122 3½ 3½ 2hd 1no PincyLJr9 S A Dby 87-10 Skywalker,FstAccount,Nostlgi'sStr 9
6Apr85—Grade I
17Mar85-8SA 1 1/16 :444 1:10 1:431ft *2¼ 120 611 32 2½ 2no Day P5 Sn Felipe H 85-15 ImgeofGrtnss,Skywlkr,Nostlgi'sStr 9
17Mar85—Grade I
3Feb85-8BM 1 1/16 :453 1:093 1:41 ft *6-5 120 64½ 52¾ 41 31 † Day P6 Camino Real 86-13 Tnk'sProspect,RightCon,‡Skywlker 9
3Feb85—Grade III; †Disqualified and placed fourth
13Jan85-4SA 1 1/16 :462 1:112 1:42 ft *6-5 118 2½ 2hd 1½ 12½ Day P2 Aw24000 91-13 Skywalker,Turkoman,RoyalOlympia 7
16Dec84-8Hol 1 1/16 :453 1:103 1:432gd 9¾ 121 1311 63¾ 67 54 Day P6 Hol Futy — — Stphn'sOdyssy,FrstNormn,RghtCn 13
16Dec84—Grade I
24Nov84-6Hol 1 :461 1:111 1:361sy 6¾ 118 710 53½ 22 1no Delahoussaye E4 Mdn 94-07 Skywlkr,FstAccount,ExclusivDrling 8
●Apr 30 CD 5f ft 1:002 h ●Apr 24 CD 1 ft 1:372 h Apr 18 CD 1 ft 1:39 h Apr 14 CD 3f ft :353 b

Fast Account *
Dk. b. or br. c. 3, by Private Account—Fast Beauty, by Fleet Nasrullah
Br.—Hawn W R (Ky) 1985 4 0 3 0 $91,780
Own.—Hawn W R 126 Tr.—Johnson Patricia L 1984 8 2 3 1 $52,550
Lifetime 12 2 6 1 $144,330
27Apr85-9CD 1 :452 1:112 1:373sy 2½ 122 53½ 1½ 1hd 2½ McCrrnCJ6 Dby Trl 80-26 CrmFrich,FstAccount,NordicScndl 11
27Apr85—Grade III
6Apr85-8SA 1⅛ :463 1:103 1:482ft 25 122 52½ 41½ 1hd 2no StevnsGL3 S A Dby 87-10 Skywalker,FstAccount,Nostlgi'sStr 9
6Apr85—Grade I
17Mar85-8SA 1 1/16 :444 1:10 1:431ft 6 119 714 98 87½ 64 StvnsGL9 Sn Felipe H 81-15 ImgeofGrtnss,Skywlkr,Nostlgi'sStr 9
17Mar85—Grade I; Broke slowly, wide final 3/8
23Feb85-8SA 1 :454 1:101 1:361ft 3e122 63½ 66¼ 54¾ 21½ StvnsGL2 San Rafael 86-13 SmartenUp,FstAccount,Stn'sBower 9
23Feb85—Grade II; Brushed
24Dec84-7Hol 1 :46 1:103 1:362ft 4½ 115 51½ 45 12½ 13½ McCrrCJ7 [R]KnndyRd 93-13 FstAccount,AirAlert,ProtectYourslf 9
9Dec84-6Hol 1 :463 1:114 1:374ft *4-5 118 2hd 1hd 1hd 11 McCarron C J7 Mdn 86-10 FastAccount,Bonham,BeAHawaiin 12
24Nov84-6Hol 1 :461 1:111 1:361sy *2 118 3nk 1hd 12 2no McCarron C J7 Mdn 94-07 Skywlkr,FstAccount,ExclusivDrling 8
7Nov84-6Hol 1 :46 1:114 1:373ft *1-2e118 41½ 32 4¾ 31 McCarron C J5 Mdn — — ProtctYorslf,ByShorDrv,FstAccont 8
17Oct84-8SA 7f :224 :453 1:234ft 15 114 105½ 107 97½ 65 McCrrCJ1 SunnySlope 76-18 MtthwT.Prkr,PrivtJungl,Dn'sDiblo 11
17Oct84—Grade III; Extremely wide into stretch
3Oct84-6SA 6f :22 :453 1:113ft 3 117 68 57 45 2no Valenzuela P A1 Mdn 80-18 Dr.Riva,FastAccount,JusttheFacts 12
8Sep84-6Dmr 6f :222 :452 1:101ft 10 117 42 32½ 22½ 22 McCracken C J7 Mdn 85-12 Carlod,FstAccount,SouthernShow 12
27Aug84-6Dmr 6f :223 :454 1:104ft 37 117 74½ 69½ 511 56¾ Lipham T4 Mdn 77-19 Proudest Doon, Carload,ProBowler 8
Apr 26 CD 3f ft :36 b Apr 21 SA 5f ft 1:022 h Apr 16 SA 4f ft :513 b Apr 5 SA 3f ft :36 b

As expected, the crowd sent Chief's Crown off as the favorite in the eighth race. And, as often happens with favorites, the crowd underbet him to place and show relative to the win betting. Thus, there were good Dr. Z bets to place and show. One minute before the end of betting the mutuels were:

	Totals	*#3 Chief's Crown*	*Expected Value per Dollar Bet on Chief's Crown*
Odds		6–5	
Win	2,920,516	1,100,759	
Place	1,116,332	300,980	1.12
Show	1,049,757	260,940	1.13

Individually, the Kelly bets were $294 to place and $544 to show. Chapter Sixteen's equations (16.5 and 16.6) deal with multiple wagers on the same horse and show that the correct wagers are $120 to place and $454 to show. The final mutuels were very similar:

	Totals	*#3 Chief's Crown*	*Expected Value per Dollar Bet on Chief's Crown*
Odds		6–5	
Win	2,930,042	1,104,743	
Place	1,120,258	302,859	1.12
Show	1,055,394	264,522	1.13

The speed duel between Spend A Buck and Eternal Prince, despite being much anticipated, never developed. Eternal Prince broke poorly, was boxed in going into the first turn, faded in the backstretch, and finally finished next to last. Spend A Buck, however, burst from his gate, gained the lead, held a 5- or 6-length lead throughout the race, and made it look easy winning wire to wire. This made him the nineteenth wire-to-wire winner in Derby history. The most recent had been Bold Forbes in 1976 who, interestingly, had also been ridden by Cordero. Spend A Buck's victory and, particularly, Chief's Crown's loss were further evidence in support of dosage theory. Spend A Buck's time of 2:00$\frac{1}{5}$ was the third-fastest Derby win after Secretariat and Northern Dancer. Chief's Crown found himself 6 lengths behind the leader in the backstretch and could never make up the distance. In the final turn, Stephan's Odyssey began his charge through horses, but Spend A Buck never faded. Stephan's Odyssey did, however, catch a tiring Chief's Crown for second. A game 92–1 Fast Account and Proud Truth began their drives in the final turn and finished fourth and fifth, respectively. The chart of the race follows:

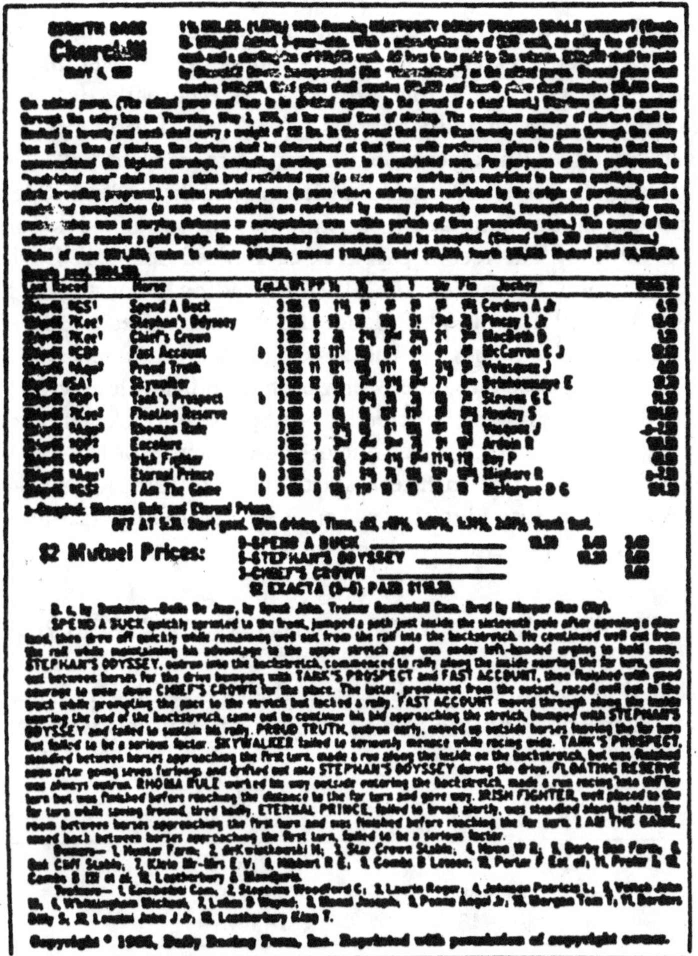

Churchill

Horse	Jockey
Spend A Buck	Cordero A Jr
Stephan's Odyssey	Pincay L Jr
Chief's Crown	MacBeth D
Fast Account	McCarron C J
Proud Truth	Velasquez J
Skywalker	Delahoussaye E
Tank's Prospect	Stevens G L
Floating Reserve	Hawley S
Rhoman Rule	Vasquez J
Encolure	Ardoin R
Irish Fighter	Day P
Eternal Prince	Migliore R
I Am The Game	McHargue D G

$2 Mutuel Prices:

SPEND A BUCK

STEPHAN'S ODYSSEY

CHIEF'S CROWN

Chief's Crown's third-place finish paid $2.80 to show, so our $454 show bet netted us $181.60. This covered the lost place bet for a net profit of $61.60 and a bankroll of $1,857.80.

Having won the Derby, Spend A Buck's owner, Dennis Diaz, faced a tough choice, albeit an enviable one. He could try for the Triple Crown by taking his colt to the $350,000-added Preakness or he could run him in the Jersey Derby. The lure of the latter was the biggest payoff in the history of racing—were Spend A Buck to win, he would earn the $600,000 winner's purse plus a $2 million bonus for a sweep of the Cherry Hill Mile, the Garden State Stakes, the Kentucky Derby, and the Jersey Derby. Beyond the prize money, there were at least three other considerations. First, an extra nine days rest with the Jersey Derby might be in the best interest of the horse. Second, the chance of winning the Jersey Derby seemed greater than winning the Triple Crown since the former did not figure to have the likes of Chief's Crown, Proud Truth, and a clean-starting Eternal Prince. Third, how much greater could syndication value and eventual stud fees be expected to be with the Triple Crown? Diaz eventually decided not to go the traditional route of the Preakness. The Jersey Derby was no walkover, however; Spend A Buck never had a lead of more than half a length and, heading into the stretch, Creme Fraiche even took the lead. Spend A Buck fought back, though, and at the finish it was the son of Buckaroo by a neck for $2.6 million. The record paycheck catapulted Spend A Buck to second place, after John Henry, on the all-time leading earners list. In his next race, the Haskell Invitational Handicap, he was upset by the 35–1 Skip Trial. Facing older horses for the first time, he ran a repeat of the Jersey Derby to win his last race, the Monmouth Handicap; four-year-old Carr de Naskra edged by him in the stretch, but Spend A Buck gamely came back to win by a nose. With a never-out-of-the-money record of ten wins, three seconds, and two thirds in fifteen starts and total earnings of $4,220,689, Spend A Buck was retired to stud at Lane's End Farm in Versailles, Kentucky, with his first foals due to arrive in 1987.

TURN HERE IS THE FINAL DR. Z SYSTEM BET

We decided to remain for the ninth race when a possible Dr. Z bet developed early on Turn Here. At one minute to post the mutuels were:

	Totals	#6 *Turn Here*	*Expected Value per Dollar Bet on Turn Here*
Odds		8–5	
Win	274,369	86,338	
Show	90,413	18,746	1.14

The Kelly bet was $343. The final mutuels show considerable win betting on Turn Here in the last minute:

	Totals	#6 *Turn Here*	*Expected Value per Dollar Bet on Turn Here*
Odds		7–5	
Win	311,357	104,979	
Show	92,959	20,091	1.15

The late-win betting on Turn Here appeared to not be completely smart money because, while Turn Here was never far back and he had strong finish, he could not catch Silver Wraith. He held second-place by 7 lengths, though, and paid $2.60 for a profit of $102.90 and a final wealth of $1960.70. The mutuel payoffs were:

1–	Silver Wraith	7.60	3.00	2.00
6–	Turn Here		3.40	2.00
9–	Exclusive Arts.............			2.00
$2 EXACTA	(1–6) Paid $19.00			

Derby Day had again been profitable. The $460.70 winnings were less than the previous years but, considering our bad start for the day, we felt very successful.

A nice comparison of this year's Derby wagering with those since 1927 follows. It shows an impressive increase in wagering over the years; obviously this is a trend that Churchill Downs is hoping will continue. We plan to be there next year to do our part!

HOW THE BETTING WENT

COMPARATIVE DERBY TABLE

Year	Totals	Year	Totals
1985...	$5,770,074	1955....	1,677,178
1984....	5,420,787	1954....	1,543,097
1983....	5,546,977	1953....	1,532,731
1982....	5,011,575	1952....	1,565,901
1981....	4,566,179	1951....	1,294,474
1980....	4,163,063	1950....	1,248,026
1979....	4,006,511	1949....	1,032,582
1978....	4,425,828	1948......	670,833
1977....	3,655,225	1947....	1,253,042
1976....	3,449,065	1946....	1,202,474
1975....	3,365,130	1945......	776,408
1974....	3,444,649	1944......	651,444
1973....	3,284,962	1943......	587,392
1972....	2,885,325	1942......	631,198
1971....	2,648,139	1941......	654,353
1970....	2,383,972	1940......	456,149
1969....	2,625,524	1939......	584,977
1968....	2,350,470	1938......	528,742
1967....	1,933,028	1937......	585,606
1966....	2,133,378	1936......	472,750
1965....	2,227,484	1935......	412,846
1964....	2,144,079	1934......	382,584
1963....	1,818,087	1933......	229,312
1962....	1,553,916	1932......	277,105
1961....	1,483,164	1931......	495,886
1960....	1,490,199	1930......	584,894
1959....	1,502,151	1929......	675,106
1958....	1,635,000	1928......	620,643
1957....	1,401,017	1927......	676,443
1956....	1,666,550		

COMPARATIVE TABLE ALL RACES

Year	Totals	Year	Totals
1985..	$12,330,650	1955....	4,280,278
1984...	11,717,499	1954....	4,234,231
1983...	11,851,527	1953....	4,306,065
1982...	11,348,720	1952....	4,064,420
1981...	10,957,614	1951....	3,675,542
1980...	10,122,067	1950....	3,558,382
1979....	9,937,563	1949....	3,168,733
1978...	10,336,443	1948....	3,051,779
1977....	8,811,486	1947....	3,636,403
1976....	8,435,463	1946....	3,608,208
1975....	7,736,500	1945....	2,380,796
1974....	7,868,734	1944....	3,139,982
1973....	7,627,965	1943....	1,801,889
1972....	7,164,717	1942....	1,963,011
1971....	6,389,567	1941....	1,935,651
1970....	5,811,127	1940....	1,503,983
1969....	6,106,346	1939....	1,674,599
1968....	5,506,069	1938....	1,511,689
1967....	4,625,222	1937....	1,535,604
1966....	5,308,285	1936....	1,269,183
1965....	5,285,382	1935....	1,031,972
1964....	5,173,018	1934......	999,140
1963....	4,677,594	1933......	745,603
1962....	4,150,312	1932......	850,809
1961....	3,915,567	1931....	1,374,822
1960....	4,008,078	1930....	1,664,409
1959....	4,019,824	1929....	1,709,670
1958....	4,227,033	1928....	1,890,050
1957....	3,800,250	1927....	1,934,232
1956....	4,360,232		

DETAILED BETS ON THE DERBY

	Win	Place	Show	Total
Irish Fighter	58,623	29,511	54,107	142,241
Chief's Crown	1,104,743	302,859	264,522	1,672,124
e-Rhoman Rule, ...				
Eternal Prince	287,218	128,190	114,602	530,010
Tank's Prospect ...	198,834	99,818	80,217	378,869
Stephan's Odyssey	170,463	81,213	81,287	333,463
Encolure	23,548	11,643	22,312	57,503
I Am the Game	24,054	10,864	20,411	55,329
Floating Reserve .	18,111	7,766	14,727	40,604
Spend a Buck	476,731	187,155	160,353	824,239
Proud Truth	410,563	187,845	146,928	745,336
Skywalker	130,938	60,506	73,458	264,902
Fast Account	26,216	12,888	21,970	61,074
Totals	$ 2,930,042	$1,120,258	$1,055,394	$5,105,694

Exacta: $664,380.
Grand Total: $5,770,074.

DETAILED BETS ON ALL RACES DAY

	Win	Place	Show	Total
First Race	$ 122,278	$62,221	$59,806	$244,305
Second Race ...	253,717	132,510	119,182	505,409
Third Race	214,175	99,854	92,227	406,256
Fourth Race	316,616	149,860	131,800	598,276
Fifth Race	328,095	144,769	154,309	627,173
Sixth Race	373,675	159,580	160,886	694,141
Seventh Race ...	395,617	165,356	150,902	711,875
Eighth Race (Derby)	2,930,042	1,120,258	1,055,394	5,105,694
Ninth Race	311,357	116,970	92,959	521,286
Tenth Race	266,946	98,334	88,970	454,250
Totals	$ 5,512,518	$2,249,712	$2,106,435	$9,868,665

Daily Double: $290,493.
Exacta: $2,171,492.
Grand Total: $12,330,650.

KENTUCKY DERBY DAY 1986

This was the first year that the Triple Crown races were being officially promoted as a package. That task was the responsibility of the newly formed Triple Crown Productions. Certainly, the major impetus for its formation in 1985 was that year's Kentucky Derby winner, Spend A Buck, having passed up the Preakness and the Belmont for the more lucrative Jersey Derby. Triple Crown Productions brings together Churchill Downs, Pimlico Race Course, and Belmont Park to market their series of races. It also requires that horses be nominated for all three races. In 1986, the nomination fee was $600 by January 15 or $3,000 by March 17. The fees generated $343,200 and, split three ways, gave each race an additional $114,400 to be added to its gross purse. The organization's future plans include a bonus package for the Triple Crown and the development of corporate sponsorship.

Attendance increased from 108,573 in 1985, when the higher admission prices were instituted, to 123,819 in 1986. However, this was still far behind the 163,628 that attended in 1974. The addition of a turf course (scheduled for racing in 1987) and changes in the winner's circle have reduced the fans' available space in the infield, so it is unlikely that the 1974 attendance record will ever be broken. Despite the decreased general attendance, 1986 had the usual number of celebrities. Former President Gerald Ford was there and is beginning to be considered a regular Derby attendee. Other politicians in attendance were two Democratic senators, Bill Bradley and Gary Hart. The vast spectrum of the television industry was well represented by the extremes of Walter Cronkite and Miami Vice's Don Johnson. Among other spectators were dancer Ginger Rogers, singer Ricky Skaggs, former Green Bay Packer Paul Hornung, and the president of Toyota Motor Corporation, Shoichiro Toyoda.

By the end of the ten races at Churchill Downs, a record $13,114,331 had been wagered, and a record $6,165,119 was wagered on the Derby itself. The fifty-six sites that received Derby simulcasts and allowed betting on the race also did well with $19,776,332 in wagers. This other-track betting added to the on-track wagering meant that $25,941,451 was bet on the Derby!

The crowd's favorite was the impressive Snow Chief. His owners, Carl Grinstead and Ben Rochelle, had become favorites of the media, and because of Rochelle's years in vaudeville they had been dubbed "the Sunshine Boys." Coming into the Derby, Snow Chief had proved his versatility by winning over all kinds of tracks and from on or off the pace. He also had demonstrated his consistency by winning all four of his races that year and having seven wins in his last eight races. All of this added up to a remarkable $1,719,040 in earnings! Alex Solis would be in the irons—something he had done on all but the first three of Snow Chief's races. Solis would be competing with his uncle, Jacinto Vasquez, the jockey of Mogambo. Despite strong finishes at $1\frac{1}{8}$ miles in the Santa Anita and Florida derbies, the big concern about Snow Chief was his stamina. Like all the other horses in the Derby, he had never run the classic distance of $1\frac{1}{4}$ miles. Could he handle it? The concern was due to his DI. His DI of 5 indicated a speed horse perhaps lacking the stamina to finish strongly in a $1\frac{1}{4}$-mile race. If he did win, he would be the first horse with a DI greater than 4 to do so since 1929! There was considerable debate, however, about the significance of Snow Chief's DI since, because he had much Argentine blood, he had only two chefs de race in his pedigree (Tom Fool three generations back and Eight Thirty four generations back). In other words, because of this limited dosage information, one could be very suspicious of any conclusions drawn on the basis of Snow Chief's DI. It seemed that only actually racing the $1\frac{1}{4}$ miles would indicate his stamina.

Badger Land, son of Preakness winner Codex, was the crowd's second choice. This year he had won the Los Feliz, the Everglades, and the Flamingo Stakes, and was second (both times to Snow Chief) in his other two races. He was trained and partly owned by D. Wayne Lukas, still looking for his first Derby win, and would be ridden by Jorge Velasquez, winner of the 1981 Kentucky Derby aboard Pleasant Colony. Badger Land's dosage figures indicated sufficient stamina for the Derby (a DI of 1 and a CD of −0.33) but, like Snow Chief, they were on the basis of only two chefs de race in his pedigree and so were somewhat suspect.

Mogambo was another horse trying to beat the dosage theory. His CD of 1.13 was on the right side of the historical 1.25 cutoff but his DI was high at 4.64. Despite this, the crowd sent him off as third choice at 8–1 odds. This year he had finished third behind Snow Chief and Badger Land in the Florida Derby but later won the Gotham Mile over Groovy and Tasso. And two weeks earlier he rallied to a second place finish behind Broad Brush. His trainer, Leroy Jolley, and his jockey, Jacinto Vasquez, were hoping to combine for a third Derby victory, having won with Foolish Pleasure in 1975 and the filly Genuine Risk in 1980.

Rampage was the first Derby starter for his owners, Nancy and John Reed. Purchased for $18,000 as a yearling, his earnings stood at $340,086 for eight races. His last race had been his best; on a sloppy track he posted the second-fastest time ever for the $1\frac{1}{8}$ mile Arkansas Derby. His dosage figures were a DI of 1.11 and a CD of 0.18, neither excluding him from Derby contention.

Bold Arrangement, third topweight on the English Free Handicap, was making history as the first important European-trained horse to cross the Atlantic specifically for the Derby. Omar Khayyam and Tomy Lee, both bred in England, had won earlier Derbies, but they had spent considerable time training and racing in the United States. Bold Arrangement's owners,

Anthony and Ray Richards, and trainer, Clive Brittain, had been given much applause for their Derby challenge because the difficulty of keeping a horse in top form after travelling as far as across the Atlantic is well recognized. Also, Bold Arrangement would be racing on dirt, something he had done for the first time only nine days earlier in the Blue Grass Stakes at Keeneland. This earlier race would normally make this Derby challenge doubly difficult since, even if a long trip is properly handled and the horse races well the first time out, the change finally takes its toll and the horse often weakens the next time out. Brittain had anticipated these difficulties and brought Bold Arrangement over a few pounds above normal weight to reduce the adverse effects of any weight loss. Also, Brittain felt that running the Blue Grass first had not been a liability, but rather had been an important prep for the Derby and gave his horse some experience racing on dirt. Keeping Bold Arrangement in top form was not the only problem, however. There was also considerable red tape: Bold Arrangement had been subject to a quarantine period upon entering the United States and had been housed in special facilities at both Keeneland and Churchill Downs. In light of all of this involved preparation the reports that Bold Arrangement "was here to win!" seemed to be more than just idle rumors. Another factor in his favor had to be his jockey, the great Chris McCarron. McCarron, despite his remarkable racing career, was still looking for his first Derby win. In six starts, his best finish had been Desert Wine's second to Sunny's Halo in 1983.

Willie Shoemaker, the most experienced Derby jockey, was making his latest of 24 Derby appearances on the Nijinsky II colt, Ferdinand. His three victories had been on Swaps in 1955, Tomy Lee in 1959, and Lucky Debonair in 1965. His 1957 run on Gallant Man would have been an easy win, too, but Shoemaker misjudged the finish line and stood up too early. Although he quickly realized his mistake, it was too late, and Iron Leige beat his horse by a nose. Unlike Ferdinand's jockey, however, owner Elizabeth Keck and trainer Charles Whittingham have had little Derby experience; this was her first Derby starter, despite thirty years in racing, and this was only his third starter, despite half a century of training, two Eclipse awards, induction into the racing's Hall of Fame, and seven national earning-leader titles. The reason they rarely made this trip to Churchill Downs was a common dislike of racing two-year-olds. Consequently, the Derby comes up too early in most of their horses' campaigns. Ferdinand was an exception, however. Because he matured quite early, they raced him five times in 1985. In 1986, he won the Santa Catalina, finished second in the Los Feliz and the San Rafael, and was third in the Santa Anita Derby. As a late charger, Ferdinand would face one of the difficulties of the Derby: the need to get safely through the large field of horses which requires skill and a certain amount of luck. His dosage figures (DI of 1.50 and CD of 0.55) pointed toward sufficient stamina for the classic races.

Many handicappers revised their opinions of Broad Brush after his win in the Wood Memorial Invitational at Aqueduct. In that race he upset Mogambo, Groovy, and Tasso and was even able to ease up somewhat in the final eighth, as is his style when he has the lead. Broad Brush, son of Ack Ack, had displayed remarkable consistency by winning his previous four races and having had seven wins in his last eight races. Vince Bracciale, Jr., was his jockey and his trainer was Richard Small. Owner Bob Meyerhoff's brother Harry was the owner of Spectacular Bid, the 1979 Derby winner.

This race was felt by many to be one of the most competitive Derbies in years. The wagering public sent half of the sixteen horses off at odds shorter than 20–1. These were the seven horses discussed above and Vernon Castle, a lightly raced son of Seattle Slew. Vernon Castle finished second in his only race as a two-year-old and had been impressive in winning a maiden race and the California Derby this year.

The speed horse Groovy was being sent off at long odds despite winning the Spectacular Bid Stakes and finishing second in the Bay Shore and the Gotham and third in the Wood Memorial. The Blue Grass winner, Bachelor Beau, and the second-place horse in the Arkansas Derby, Wheatly Hall, were also considered to be long shots. The field consisted of Wise Times, Icy Groom, Southern Appeal, Zabaleta, and Fobby Forbes.

The following selections of the experts shows a preference, although not an overwhelming one, for Snow Chief:

Experts' Selections

Consensus Points: 5 for 1st (today's best 7), 2 for 2nd, 1 for 3rd. Today's Best in Bold Type.

Trackman, Charles Scaravilli

CHURCHILL DOWNS

Selections Made for Fast Track

	TRACKMAN	HANDICAP	ANALYST	HERMIS	SWEEP	CONSENSUS	
1	BUFFALO BEAU SUPER LEADER RIVERMANS PLEASURE	MORROTO POWER POZ RIVERMANS PLEASURE	BUFFALO BEAU POWER POZ MORROTO	FOOLISH WAN BUFFALO BEAU MORROTO	BUFFALO BEAU FOOLISH WAN POWER POZ	BUFFALO BEAU MORROTO FOOLISH WAN	17 7 7
2	MARSHESSEAUX TRICKY FINGERS JET SET PEG	TRICKY FINGERS MARSHESSEAUX PUT HER ON ICE	MARSHESSEAUX DROSERA JOY TO RAISE	MARSHESSEAUX DROSERA TRICKY FINGERS	MARSHESSEAUX DROSERA JOY TO RAISE	MARSHESSEAUX TRICKY FINGERS DROSERA	22 8 6
3	COLONEL RANIER BOLD SIGNATURE RENTED CONDO	BOLD SIGNATURE COLONEL RANIER RENTED CONDO	BOLD SIGNATURE COLONEL RANIER WHISTLING BURG	COLONEL RANIER BOLD SIGNATURE WHISTLING BURG	COLONEL RANIER BOLD SIGNATURE WHISTLING BURG	COLONEL RANIER BOLD SIGNATURE WHISTLING BURG	19 16 3
4	**BURNISHED BRIGHT** HIGH SHOALS TOUGH IT OUT	BURNISHED BRIGHT MR. ZIPPITY DO DAH HIGH SHOALS	BURNISHED BRIGHT HIGH SHOALS ADMIT	BURNISHED BRIGHT BOLD FAGER ROYALTY HILL	BURNISHED BRIGHT HIGH SHOALS ROYALTY HILL	BURNISHED BRIGHT HIGH SHOALS MR. ZIPPITY DO DAH	27 7 2
5	SON OF THE DESERT ROMMEL'S CHOICE SURFER X.	SURFER X. SON OF THE DESERT DESE DAYS	SURFER X. ROMMEL'S CHOICE DESE DAYS	SURFER X. BUCK REAPER ROMMEL'S CHOICE	SURFER X. ROMMEL'S CHOICE BUCK REAPER	SURFER X. ROMMEL'S CHOICE SON OF THE DESERT	21 7 7
6	CLEVER WAKE SOVEREIGN'S ACE ARTICHOKE	SOVEREIGN'S ACE ARTICHOKE DIAPASON	ARTICHOKE CLEVER WAKE SOVEREIGN'S ACE	SOVEREIGN'S ACE ARTICHOKE CHEYENNE CHEREE	ARTICHOKE SOVEREIGN'S ACE CLEVER WAKE	SOVEREIGN'S ACE ARTICHOKE CLEVER WAKE	15 15 8
7	HOPEFUL WORD RED ATTACK CZAR NIJINSKY	**CZAR NIJINSKY** HOPEFUL WORD RED ATTACK	CZAR NIJINSKY HOPEFUL WORD LITTLE MISSOURI	HOPEFUL WORD RED ATTACK CZAR NIJINSKY	HOPEFUL WORD CZAR NIJINSKY RED ATTACK	HOPEFUL WORD CZAR NIJINSKY RED ATTACK	19 16 6
8	BROAD BRUSH BADGER LAND SNOW CHIEF	SNOW CHIEF MOGAMBO WISE TIMES	MOGAMBO SNOW CHIEF RAMPAGE	SNOW CHIEF BADGER LAND MOGAMBO	SNOW CHIEF MOGAMBO BADGER LAND	SNOW CHIEF MOGAMBO BROAD BRUSH	18 10 5
9	HABITONIA GEMINI DREAMER ANTON PILLAR	HABITONIA PICK 'N WIN J. R.'S PLEASURE	**HABITONIA** GEMINI DREAMER ANTON PILLAR	**HABITONIA** INCENSE ANTON PILLAR	**HABITONIA** INCENSE GEMINI DREAMER	**HABITONIA** GEMINI DREAMER INCENSE	31 5 4
10	IN ONE PIECE REALLY COOL BROADWAY SHOWGIRL	PERFECTLY PRETTY REALLY COOL IN ONE PIECE	ME N' AMANDA REALLY COOL PERFECTLY PRETTY	REALLY COOL ME N' AMANDA JUST ABOUT ENOUGH	REALLY COOL BROADWAY SHOWGIRL ME N' AMANDA	REALLY COOL ME N' AMANDA PERFECTLY PRETTY	16 8 6

OTHERS ARE PLAYING THE DR. Z SYSTEM

In 1986, it appeared that our ideas on betting were finally being employed by others at the Derby. Several people were keeping track of place and show overlays and were calculating ratios of win bets to place and show bets. Also, more than one individual at the track was using the Beat the Racetrack Calculator.(TM) While this was all very flattering, it also meant that it would likely be tougher to realize a profit this year. This was because if too many people bet on the same place and show overlays, then their returns had to drop. In Chapter Seventeen, we analyze this problem of many Dr. Z bettors at the same track. Our findings are that when the place and show pools are as large as those on the Derby, then having many Dr. Z bettors is no problem, there's plenty of action for everyone. The other nine races on the day's card had considerably smaller mutuels, though, and, consequently, several other bettors could have a noticeable effect. In fact, this was what was observed during the course of the day; expected returns that were somewhat above our 1.10 cutoff one or two minutes before post usually had final expected returns below 1.10. They never dropped below 1.05, but it was clear there were several of us using the same strategy. Despite this, we still made a profit for the day. That made it easier to decide that, overall, it was a delight to see others employing our system.

The first race was a mile for maiden three-year-olds and upward. Buffalo Beau went off as a 3–5 favorite and was a good Dr. Z bet throughout the betting. With his low odds and a 1.12 expected return to show, the optimal bet was a large one, $470 out of a $1,500 bankroll! Buffalo Beau showed he deserved the public's backing when he quickly gained the lead and even widened it to 7 lengths at the finish. He paid $3.40 to win, $2.60 to place and a good $2.40 to show. This meant a profit of $94 and a bankroll of $1,594. The chart of the race was as follows:

FIRST RACE
Churchill
MAY 3, 1986

1 MILE. (1.33$\frac{3}{5}$) MAIDEN. SPECIAL WEIGHT. Purse $9,000 (plus $3,100 from KTDF). 3-year-olds and upward. Weight, 3-year-olds, 110 lbs.; older, 122 lbs. 8TH DAY. WEATHER CLEAR. TEMPERATURE 57 DEGREES.

Total purse $12,100. Value of race $10,085; value to winner $5,850; second $2,420; third $1,210; fourth $605. ($2,015 reverts to KTDF.) Mutuel pool $263,395.

Last Raced	Horse	Eqt.	A.	Wt	PP	St	¼	½	¾	Str	Fin	Jockey	Odds $1
19Apr86 ^{2}OP^{2}	Buffalo Beau	b	3	113	2	4	$1^{\frac{1}{2}}$	1^{1}	1^{2}	1^{6}	$1^{7\frac{1}{2}}$	Stevens G L	.70
22Apr86 ^{1}Kee^{5}	Rivermans Pleasure		4	122	6	3	$4^{\frac{1}{2}}$	6^{hd}	$6^{2\frac{1}{2}}$	4^{hd}	2^{nk}	Fires E	11.10
	Foolish Wan		3	122	7	1	7	7	5^{1}	$3^{\frac{1}{2}}$	3^{nk}	Melancon L	11.80
24Apr86 ^{2}Kee^{4}	Morroto	b	4	122	4	6	2^{hd}	2^{2}	$2^{2\frac{1}{2}}$	2^{2}	4^{2}	Woods C R Jr	17.00
4Jan86 ^{3}Crc^{9}	Power Poz		3	110	1	5	5^{1}	$4^{1\frac{1}{2}}$	3^{hd}	5^{3}	5^{5}	Day P	2.60
	Super Leader		3	112	5	2	$3^{\frac{1}{2}}$	5^{hd}	7	7	$6^{4\frac{1}{2}}$	Solis A	8.50
9Apr86 ^{7}Kee^{6}	Resilience		3	112	3	7	6^{1}	3^{hd}	$4^{\frac{1}{2}}$	6^{hd}	7	Foster D E	28.60

OFF AT 11:36. Start good. Won ridden out. Time, :23$\frac{1}{5}$, :46$\frac{4}{5}$, 1:12$\frac{2}{5}$, 1:37$\frac{3}{5}$ Track fast.

Official Program Numbers

$2 Mutuel Prices:			
2-BUFFALO BEAU	3.40	2.60	2.40
6-RIVERMANS PLEASURE		5.80	3.80
7-FOOLISH WAN			3.60

TRICKY FINGERS IN THE SECOND

The second race was a 6-furlong allowance race for three-year-old fillies. Tricky Fingers was a 7–5 favorite and was ridden by Pat Day (who would later ride Rampage in the Derby). Her odds and a 1.12 expected return suggested a bet of $360. Tricky Fingers caught second in the stretch but paid only $2.40 to show when the second and third favorites in the race finished in the money as well. Thus, the profit was $72 for a bankroll of $1,666. The chart of the race was as follows:

SECOND RACE
Churchill
MAY 3, 1986

6 FURLONGS. (1.09) ALLOWANCE. Purse $11,000 (plus $3,800 from KTDF). Fillies. 3-year-olds which have not won two races other than maiden, claiming or starter. Weight, 121 lbs. Non-winners of $7,475 twice allowed 3 lbs.; $5,525 twice, 6 lbs.; $4,225 twice, 9 lbs. (Races where entered for $25,000 or less not considered in allowances.)

Total purse $14,800. Value of race $14,610; value to winner $9,620; second $2,960; third $1,480; fourth $550. ($190 reverts to the KTDF). Mutuel pool $434,364.

Last Raced	Horse	Eqt.	A.	Wt	PP	St	¼	½	Str	Fin	Jockey	Odds $1
18Apr86 4Kee2	Marshesseaux		3	121	8	1	21½	12	12½	12½	Solomone M	1.70
23Jly85 9Mth4	Tricky Fingers		3	118	6	5	5½	52½	42	22¼	Day P	1.40
15Dec85 3Hol5	Joy To Raise		3	121	2	4	3½	3½	21	31	Velasquez J	5.60
18Apr86 4Kee6	Int'l. Affair	b	3	115	1	2	41½	41½	3hd	44	Woods C R Jr	28.70
18Apr86 4Kee4	Jet Set Peg	b	3	118	3	8	6½	62	64	56	Fires E	22.40
22Mar86 11Lat9	Put Her On Ice	b	3	121	4	7	72½	73	72½	61¼	Miller S E	31.70
22Mar86 4Lat1	She's Native		3	115	5	3	1½	21	51	72½	Foster D E	16.20
17Apr86 3Kee2	Drosera		3	118	7	6	8	8	8	8	Delahoussaye E	8.50

OFF AT 12:15. Start good. Won ridden out. Time, :22, :45⅘, :57⅘, 1:10⅘ Track fast.

$2 Mutuel Prices:				
	1-MARSHESSEAUX	5.40	2.80	2.40
	7-TRICKY FINGERS		2.80	2.40
	3-JOY TO RAISE			3.00

EDDIE DELAHOUSSAYE COMES THROUGH IN THE THIRD

Race 3 was another six-furlong test. Eddie Delahoussaye's mount, Rented Condo, was the public's favorite. He was a good Dr. Z bet just prior to post, and his 8–5 odds suggested a $328 wager. He had the lead for much of the race but was strongly pressured throughout. He bore up under the pressure until Colonel Ranier overtook him in the stretch. He paid $3 to both place and show, so the profit was $164 for a wealth of $1,830. The chart was as follows:

THIRD RACE
Churchill
MAY 3, 1986

6 FURLONGS. (1.09) ALLOWANCE. Purse $11,000 (plus $3,800 from KTDF). 4-year-olds and upward which have not won two races other than maiden, claiming or starter. Weight, 121 lbs. Non-winners of $7,800 twice since July 4 allowed 3 lbs.; $6,500 twice in 1985–86, 6 lbs.; $3,900 twice since September 30, 9 lbs. (Races where entered for $25,000 or less not considered in allowances.)

Total purse $14,800. Value of race $14,420; value to winner $9,620; second $2,960; third $1,100; fourth $740. ($380 reverts to KTDF.) Mutuel pool $545,563. Exacta pool, $214,108.

Last Raced	Horse	Eqt.	A.	Wt	PP	St	¼	½	Str	Fin	Jockey	Odds $1
11Apr86 4Kee1	Colonel Ranier		4	121	2	3	4½	41	44	1¾	Lovato F Jr	2.20
29Jun85 9EIP2	Rented Condo		4	118	6	4	31½	1hd	1hd	23½	Delahoussaye E	1.60
10Apr86 1Kee4	Groshawker		4	112	3	2	2hd	2hd	2½	31¼	McDowell M	46.50
14Apr86 8OP2	Bold Signature		4	118	1	1	1hd	32½	3½	42½	Day P	1.90
10Jan86 7Aqu8	Great Reef		4	112	5	7	7	7	7	52½	Espinoza J C	32.70
14Apr86 8OP6	Easterly	b	4	112	7	5	5½	5hd	5hd	61½	Snyder L	50.80
14Apr86 8OP7	Whistling Burg	b	4	113	4	6	68	64	6½	7	Vasquez J	10.50

OFF AT 1:01. Start good. Won driving. Time, :22⅕, :46, :58⅖, 1:10⅗ Track fast.

$2 Mutuel Prices:				
	2-COLONEL RANIER	6.40	3.00	3.20
	6-RENTED CONDO		3.00	3.00
	3-GROSHAWKER			6.20

$2 EXACTA (2–6) PAID $19.80.

THE WHAS STAKES

The fourth race was the inaugural running of the WHAS Stakes, a five-furlong race for two-year-olds. One of the horses was a first-time starter, and the others had been only lightly raced. This was not surprising given they were young horses and it was early in the season. The 3–2 favorite was Burnished Bright, a $9\frac{1}{2}$-lengths winner in her only race. Shortly before post she had had a 1.12 expected return to show, which suggested a bet of $375. Her final mutuels reflected others betting on her to show:

	Totals	*#10 Burnished Bright*	*Expected Value per Dollar Bet on Burnished Bright*
Odds		3–2	
Win	354,555	118,244	
Show	168,938	40,118	1.09

Burnished Bright had a late charge but it was only good enough for third. The first two horses were the two favorites after Burnished Bright, so her show payoff was only $2.80. With a profit of $150, my bankroll was now at $1,980. The chart follows:

FOURTH RACE
Churchill
MAY 3, 1986

5 FURLONGS. (.57⅘) 1st Running WHAS STAKES ALLOWANCE. $30,000 Added (plus $5,000 from KTDF). 2-year-olds. By subscription of $50 each, $150 to pass the entry box, $150 additional to start, with $30,000 added, of which 65% of all monies to the owner of the winner, 20% to second, 10% to third and 5% to fourth. Weight, colts and geldings, 121 lbs.; fillies, 118 lbs. Non-winners of $7,800 allowed 3 lbs.; $7,800, 5 lbs.; $5,850, 7 lbs. The field will be limited to fourteen (14) starters with as many as four (4) horses placed on the also eligible list. If more than fourteen (14) entries pass the entry box, preference will be given to high weights with consideration to the sex allowance, however, a same owner entry cannot start to the exclusion of a single interest. Any horse excluded from running because of the aforementioned preference shall be refunded the entry fee. Starters to be named through the entry box at the usual time of closing. A trophy to the winning owner given by WHAS. (Closed with 45 nominations.)
Total purse $40,100. Value of race $35,600; value to winner $22,815; second $7,020; third $4,010; fourth $1,755. ($4,500 reverts to KTDF). Mutuel pool $692,414. Exacta Pool $267,421.

Last Raced	Horse	Eqt.	A.	Wt	PP	St	$\frac{3}{16}$	$\frac{3}{8}$	Str	Fin	Jockey	Odds $1
31Mar86 ^{10}Tam^{1}	Z. Plasty		2	121	2	1	$4^{1\frac{1}{2}}$	$3^{1\frac{1}{2}}$	$2^{1\frac{1}{2}}$	$1^{1\frac{1}{4}}$	Martin C W	4.20
4Apr86 ^{3}Kee^{1}	Mr. Zippity Do Dah		2	121	7	5	2^{2}	$1^{\frac{1}{2}}$	1^{2}	2^{nk}	Espinoza J C	2.70
8Apr86 ^{3}Kee^{1}	Burnished Bright		2	118	10	7	$5^{1\frac{1}{2}}$	5^{2}	$3^{\frac{1}{2}}$	$3^{\frac{1}{2}}$	Day P	1.50
23Apr86 ^{3}Kee^{1}	High Shoals		2	121	1	2	3^{hd}	4^{1}	4^{2}	4^{3}	Lovato F Jr	6.10
	Templar Hill	b	2	114	5	12	12	$9^{\frac{1}{2}}$	6^{hd}	$5^{2\frac{1}{2}}$	Imparato J	61.70
29Mar86 ^{9}Tam^{3}	La Mama Cosa		2	113	11	10	$8^{\frac{1}{2}}$	7^{1}	7^{2}	$6^{2\frac{1}{2}}$	Gehri D L	96.50
26Apr86 ^{3}CD^{1}	Jinnys Tap Shoes	b	2	114	9	8	11^{hd}	12	9^{3}	7^{hd}	Miller S E	45.70
11Apr86 ^{3}Kee^{1}	Tough It Out		2	121	4	4	$1^{\frac{1}{2}}$	2^{2}	5^{2}	$8^{\frac{3}{4}}$	Brumfield D	19.30
18Apr86 ^{3}Kee^{1}	Royalty Hill		2	121	3	3	6^{1}	$6^{1\frac{1}{2}}$	$8^{2\frac{1}{2}}$	9^{5}	Allen K K	24.90
18Apr86 ^{3}Kee^{2}	Admit		2	115	6	9	10^{1}	11^{hd}	$10^{\frac{1}{2}}$	10^{3}	Delahoussaye E	20.30
4Apr86 ^{3}Kee^{4}	Coaxing Chad		2	114	12	11	9^{hd}	10^{2}	11^{2}	11^{8}	McCauley W H	132.10
21Mar86 ^{2}DeD^{5}	Logan Burch	b	2	114	8	6	7^{2}	8^{hd}	12	12	Solomone M	136.00

OFF AT 1:52. Start good. Won driving. Time, :22⅕, :45⅗, :58⅘ Track fast.

$2 Mutuel Prices:				
	2–Z. PLASTY	**10.40**	**5.20**	**3.60**
	7–MR. ZIPPITY DO DAH		**4.00**	**3.00**
	10–BURNISHED BRIGHT			**2.80**

$2 EXACTA (2–7) PAID $29.80.

SON OF THE DESERT IN THE FIFTH

The next race's best bet was on Son Of The Desert. At 3–1 odds with a 1.12 expected return, the optimal bet was just $33. This small bet was because of the horse's long odds, at least relative to most of the Dr. Z bet situations. The expected return dropped significantly by post time:

	Totals	*#4 Son Of The Desert*	*Expected Return per Dollar Bet on Son Of The Desert*
Odds		3–1	
Win	345,542	72,160	
Show	151,119	24,625	1.05

Son Of The Desert finished the race strongly but could not catch the winner, Dese Days. Son Of The Desert paid $3.60 for a $26.40 profit and a new wealth of $2,006.40. The chart follows:

FIFTH RACE Churchill MAY 3, 1986 — **1 1/16 MILES. (1.41 3/5) ALLOWANCE. Purse $14,000 (plus $4,900 from KTDF). 3-year-olds which have not won three races other than maiden, claiming or starter. Weight, 121 lbs. Non-winners of $10,400 at one mile or over allowed 3 lbs.; $8,450 twice, 6 lbs.; $7,800 twice, 9 lbs. (Races where entered for $25,000 or less not considered in allowances.)**

Total purse $18,900. Value of race $18,410; value to winner $12,285; second $3,780; third $1,400; fourth $945. ($490 reverts to the KTDF.) Mutuel pool $652,803. Exacta pool, $225,142.

Last Raced	Horse	Eqt.	A.	Wt	PP	St	1/4	1/2	3/4	Str	Fin	Jockey	Odds $1
19Apr86 9OP13	Dese Days	b	3	115	5	3	1^{hd}	$1^{1\frac{1}{2}}$	$1^{2\frac{1}{2}}$	1^{1}	$1^{\frac{1}{2}}$	Delahoussaye E	4.30
26Apr86 9CD5	Son Of The Desert		3	121	4	6	6	6	3^{4}	2^{4}	$2^{6\frac{1}{2}}$	Woods C R Jr	3.00
26Apr86 9CD10	Buck Reaper		3	112	1	2	$5^{2\frac{1}{2}}$	$5^{\frac{1}{2}}$	$5^{\frac{1}{2}}$	4^{3}	$3^{3\frac{1}{2}}$	Rubbicco P	22.10
25Apr86 7RD8	Conscious Aim		3	108	2	5	3^{hd}	3^{2}	$2^{\frac{1}{2}}$	3^{1}	$4^{4\frac{1}{4}}$	Godoy C R5	42.60
17Apr86 7Kee5	Rommel's Choice	b	3	109	6	4	4^{2}	4^{1}	6	6	$5^{\frac{3}{4}}$	Day P	2.20
23Apr86 5Kee1	Surfer X.	b	3	121	3	1	$2^{1\frac{1}{2}}$	$2^{\frac{1}{2}}$	4^{1}	5^{hd}	6	Fires E	1.60

OFF AT 2:40. Start good. Won driving. Time, :23 3/5, :47, 1:12, 1:38, 1:44 3/5 Track fast.

$2 Mutuel Prices:			
5–DESE DAYS	10.60	4.80	3.80
4–SON OF THE DESERT		4.20	3.80
1–BUCK REAPER			6.00

$2 EXACTA (5–4) PAID $51.40.

SIX WINNERS IN A ROW FOR THE DR. Z SYSTEM

The winning streak continued in the sixth race when Artichoke ended up being the good bet a minute before post. He had an expected return of 1.11, and the suggested bet was $57. Again, his expected return suffered from others wagering on him to show just before post time:

	Totals	*#3 Artichoke*	*Expected Return per Dollar Bet on Artichoke*
Odds		5–2	
Win	418,114	94,988	
Show	187,573	30,563	1.09

Artichoke, second by a nose to the 13–1 Sovereign's Ace, paid $3.60 to show. A $45.60 profit increased my wealth to $2,052. The chart follows:

SIXTH RACE
Churchill
MAY 3, 1986

7 FURLONGS. (1.21⅕) 52nd Running CHURCHILL DOWNS STAKES ALLOWANCE. $30,000 Added (plus $5,000 from KTDF). 4-year-olds and upward. By subscription of $30 each, $150 to pass the entry box, $150 additional to start, with $30,000 added, of which 65% of all monies to the owner of the winner, 20% to second, 10% to third and 5% to fourth. Weight, 123 lbs. Non-winners of $30,000 twice in 1986 allowed 3 lbs.; $15,000 twice in 1985–86, 6 lbs.; $12,025 twice since July 4, 9 lbs.; $9,750 in 1986, 12 lbs. If the race is divided, it will be drawn in accordance with the rules of racing. In the event that this race is not divided, the field will be limited to fourteen (14) starters with as many as four (4) horses placed on the also eligible list. If more than fourteen (14) entries pass the entry box, preference will be given to high weights, however a same owner entry cannot start to the exclusion of a single interest. Any horse excluded from running because of the aforementioned preference shall be refunded the entry fee. Starters to be named through the entry box at usual time of closing. A trophy to the winning owner. High weights preferred. (Closed with 31 nominations.)
Total purse $38,780. Value of race $35,280; value to winner $21,957; second $7,756; third $3,878; fourth $1,689. ($3,500 reverts to KTDF.) Mutuel pool $802,223. Ecacta pool $314,866.

Last Raced	Horse	Eqt.	A.	Wt	PP	St	¼	½	Str	Fin	Jockey	Odds $1
13Apr86 ^{11}FG^{3}	Sovereign's Ace		4	117	8	1	1^{2}	1^{2}	1^{2½}	1no	Rubbicco P	13.50
5Apr86 ^{5}Kee^{6}	Artichoke		5	120	3	9	9	8^{½}	3^{1½}	2^{¾}	Velasquez J	2.60
22Apr86 ^{7}Kee^{2}	Clever Wake		4	116	7	2	3^{2}	2^{½}	2^{1½}	3^{1½}	Pincay L Jr	3.10
17Apr86 ^{9}OP^{5}	Diapason	b	6	114	9	5	7^{½}	7^{hd}	6^{1}	4^{¾}	Johnson P A	4.90
26Apr86 ^{9}LaD^{2}	Head Games	b	6	115	1	7	4^{½}	3^{1½}	4^{1}	5^{2}	Delahoussaye E	8.60
5Apr86 ^{8}OP^{1}	Cheyenne Cheree		6	114	5	4	8^{½}	9	5^{hd}	6^{2½}	Day P	3.60
23Apr86 ^{6}Kee^{4}	Silver Wraith	b	5	112	2	8	6^{2}	5^{1}	7^{1½}	7^{4}	Fires E	a-20.80
28Mar86 ^{9}OP^{6}	Double Ready		6	114	6	3	2^{hd}	4^{hd}	8^{2½}	8^{nk}	Snyder L	11.40
15Apr86 ^{6}Kee^{4}	Katzenjammer		4	114	4	6	5^{2}	6^{½}	9	9	Woods C R Jr	a-20.80

a-Coupled: Silver Wraith and Katzenjammer.

OFF AT 3:30. Start good. Won driving. Time, :22⅖, :45⅗, 1:10⅕, 1:22⅗ Track fast.

$2 Mutuel Prices:

7-SOVEREIGN'S ACE	29.00	11.40	5.80
3-ARTICHOKE		5.20	3.60
6-CLEVER WAKE			3.40

$2 EXACTA (7–3) PAID $128.00.

The seventh race had only four horses so the track decided not to allow show betting. With no good place bets I waited for the eighth race, the 112th running of the Kentucky Derby. That race's program and the past performances of its entrants follows:

112th Running of the Kentucky Derby

Kentucky Derby 112

EIGHTH RACE
EXACTA WAGERING ON THIS RACE
TRACK RECORD–SECRETARIAT (3), 126 lbs., 5/5/73, 1:59⅖
ONE MILE and ONE-QUARTER

1 PP1 — MRS. ELIZABETH A. KECK — CHARLES WHITTINGHAM — 20
Blue, pink hoops, pink sleeves, pink cap
FERDINAND ♘ 126
Ch c, 1983, Nijinsky II—Banja Luka by Double Jay
BRED IN KENTUCKY BY HOWARD B. KECK
WILLIAM SHOEMAKER

2 PP2 — PETER M. BRANT — LEROY JOLLEY — 10
Kelly green, light green yoke, light green band on sleeves, kelly green cap
MOGAMBO ♘ B 126
Ch c, 1983, Mr. Prospector—Lakeville Miss by Rainy Lake
BRED IN KENTUCKY BY PETER M. BRANT
JACINTO VASQUEZ

3 PP4 — ANTHONY and RAY RICHARDS — CLIVE BRITTAIN — 12
White and black halves, yellow sleeves, white and black cap
BOLD ARRANGEMENT 126
Ch c, 1983, Persian Gold—Arrangement by Floribunda
BRED IN GREAT BRITTAIN BY MRS. R. D. PEACOCK
CHRIS McCARRON

4 PP7 — NORTH RIDGE FARM RACING PARTNERSHIP (Allen E. Paulson, lessee) — JOHN L. SULLIVAN — 30
Red, blue diamond frame, blue blocks on sleeves, red cap
VERNON CASTLE ♘ B 126
Dk b or br c, 1983, Seattle Slew—Rullian's Princess by Prince John
BRED IN KENTUCKY BY NORTH RIDGE FARM
EDDIE DELAHOUSSAYE

5 PP8 — NANCY and H. JOHN REED — GARY A. THOMAS — 20
Red, white panel, white band on sleeves, red cap
RAMPAGE B-L 126
B c, 1983, Southern Baby—Noble Betheney by Vaguely Noble
BRED IN FLORIDA BY DUE PROCESS STABLE
PAT DAY

6 PP9 — ROBERT E. MEYERHOFF — RICHARD W. SMALL — 10
Blue, yellow diamonds, yellow and blue halved sleeves, yellow cap
BROAD BRUSH B 126
B c, 1983, Ack Ack—Hay Patcher by Hoist The Flag
BRED IN MARYLAND BY ROBERT E. MEYERHOFF
VINCE BRACCIALE, JR.

7 PP10 — JEFF LUKAS, MEL HATLEY, AND D. WAYNE LUKAS — D. WAYNE LUKAS — 3
White, Orange Framed "MH", Brown and Orange Bars on Sleeves, White Cap
BADGER LAND ♘ B 126
B c, 1983, Codex—Gimleroom by Racing Room
BRED IN KENTUCKY BY JEFF LUKAS AND MEL HATLEY
JORGE VELASQUEZ

8 PP11 — JOHN McKINNON — JACK VAN BERG — 30
Green plaid, red "M", red sleeves, red cap
WHEATLY HALL B-L 126
B c, 1983, Norcliffe—Bonzo La by Miracle Hill
BRED IN FLORIDA BY JOHN McKINNON
GARY L. STEVENS

9 PP12 — CARL E. GRINSTEAD AND BEN ROCHELLE — MELVIN F. STUTE — 6-5
Cerise, blue "G" in diamond frame, blue bars on sleeves, cerise and blue cap
SNOW CHIEF B 126
Dk b or br c, 1983, Reflected Glory—Miss Snowflake by Snow Sporting
BRED IN CALIFORNIA BY BLUE DIAMOND RANCH
ALEX SOLIS

10 PP13 — RICHARD A. WATERFIELD AND JACK A. TAFEL — PHILIP M. HAUSWALD — 15
Grey, red cross sashes, red cap
BACHELOR BEAU ♘ B 126
Ch g, 1983, Raised Socially—Matriculation by Arts and Letters
BRED IN KENTUCKY BY MJAKA I. STABLE
LARRY MELANCON

11 PP14 — J. A. BALLIS AND TED KRUCKEL — HOWARD CROWELL — 30
Black, silver diamond frame, silver "B", silver chevrons on sleeves, cherry red cap
GROOVY B-L 126
Ch c, 1983, Norcliffe—Tinnitus by Restless Wind
BRED IN TEXAS BY MARSHALL T. ROBINSON
LAFFIT PINCAY, JR.

FIELD **12** PP3 — RUSSELL L. REINEMAN STABLE, INC. (Russell L. Reineman, et. al.) — PHIL GLEAVES — 12
Red, white "R", black and white stripes on sleeves, white cap
WISE TIMES ♘ B-L 126
B c, 1983, Mr. Leader—Trying Times by He's a Pistol
BRED IN KENTUCKY BY NUCKOLS BROS.
KEITH ALLEN

FIELD **13** PP5 — WILLIAM J. FLEMING — SAM T. RAMER — 12
Green, navy blue cross sashes, blue bars on sleeves, green cap
ICY GROOM ♘ B 126
Ch c, 1983, Blushing Groom (Fr.)—Hey Babe by Roberto
BRED IN KENTUCKY BY ROBERT G. KLUENER
EDDIE MAPLE

FIELD **14** PP6 — HOWARD M. BENDER — MARVIN L. MONCRIEF — 12
Light blue, dark blue "B", dark blue stripes on sleeves, light blue cap
SOUTHERN APPEAL L 126
B c, 1983, Valid Appeal—Southern Gem by Tropical Breeze
BRED IN MARYLAND BY GLADE VALLEY FARMS, INC.
JESSE DAVIDSON

FIELD **15** PP15 — MICHAEL RIORDAN, lessee — JOHN GOSDEN — 12
Royal blue, silver diamond hoop, blue cap
ZABALETA ♘ B 126
B c, 1983, Shecky Greene—Winver by Vertex
BRED IN KENTUCKY BY EUGENE Q. PARR
DARREL McHARGUE

FIELD **16** PP16 — DUE PROCESS STABLE (Robert Brennan) — CARLOS A. GARCIA — 12
Green, green shamrock on white ball, orange bars on sleeves, green cap
FOBBY FORBES B 126
B c, 1983, Bold Forbes—Plum Happy by Round Table
BRED IN FLORIDA BY DUE PROCESS STABLE
RANDY ROMERO

First Time On Bute—WHEATLY HALL, GROOVY, FOBBY FORBES
First Time On Lasix—WHEATLY HALL, GROOVY, WISE TIMES

♘ INDICATES FOALED IN KENTUCKY

FIELD — 12, 13, 14, 15 & 16

SELECTIONS—9-7-2-6

Past Performances for Derby Field

Route the Field Will Travel

One and One-Quarter Miles

START

FINISH

8th Churchill

1 ¼ MILES. (1.59⅖) 112th Running THE KENTUCKY DERBY Grade I. $350,000 Added. 3-year-olds with an entry fee of $10,000 each and a starting fee of $10,000 each. All fees will be paid to the winner. $350,000 added shall be paid by Churchill Downs Incorporated as the Added Purse. Second place shall receive $100,000, third place shall receive $50,000 and fourth place shall receive $25,000 from the Added Purse (the Added Purse and fees to be divided equally in the event of a dead heat). Starters shall be named through the entry box on Thursday, May 1, 1986, at the usual time of closing (the "Closing"). The maximum number of starters shall be limited to twenty (20) and each shall carry a weight of 126 pounds. In the event that more than twenty entries pass through the entry box at the Closing, the starters shall be determined at the Closing with preference given to those horses that have accumulated the highest earnings in graded sweepstakes, including all money paid for performance in such Graded Stakes. Should additional starters be needed to bring the field to 20, the remaining starters shall be determined at the Closing with preference given to those horses that have accumulated the highest earnings in Non-Restricted Sweepstakes. For purposes of this preference, a "Non-Restricted Sweepstakes" shall mean those Sweepstakes whose conditions contain no other restrictions other than that of age or sex. In the case of ties resulting from preference or otherwise, the additional starter(s) shall be determined by lot. An "also eligible" list will not be maintained and in no event will starters be added or allowed to run in the race which are not determined to be starters at the Closing. The owner of the winner for the race shall receive a gold trophy. Nominations to each and all of the Triple Crown races, The Kentucky Derby, The Preakness and The Belmont (the "Races"), may be made only by payment of a single subscription fee to Triple Crown Productions, Inc., as agent for Churchill Downs Incorporated. The Maryland Jockey Club, and the New York Racing Association Inc. (The Associations"). The subscription fee for 422 nominations received by January 15, 1986, is $600 and for 30 nominations received by March 17, 1986 is $3,000. (These fees are to be apportioned equally among the three Associations to be part of the total purse for each of the three races.) No supplementary nominations for any of the races will be accepted.

Mutuel Field — Wise Times, Icy Groom, Southern Appeal, Zabaleta, Fobby Forbes.

Ferdinand — **Ch. c. 3, by Nijinsky II—Banja Luka, by Double Jay**
Br.—Keck H B (Ky) 1986 4 1 2 1 $162,250
Own.—Keck Mrs H B **126** **Tr.—Whittingham Charles** 1985 5 1 1 2 $178,650
Lifetime 9 2 3 3 $340,900

6Apr86-5SA 1⅛ :47^1 1:11 1:48^{3}ft 5½ 122 5^5 5^4 5^{4}½ 3^7 ShmkrW^2 S A Dby 79-15 Snow Chief, Icy Groom, Ferdinand 7
6Apr86—Grade I
22Feb86-8SA 1 :45^3 1:10^2 1:35^{3}ft *9-5 116 7^{7}½ 4^{1}½ 1^2 2½ ShmkrW^9 Sn Rafael 89-16 VarietyRoad,Ferdinnd,JettingHome 9
22Feb86—Grade II
29Jan86-8SA 1 1/16 :46^2 1:11 1:43 ft 2¼ 114 6^{4}¾ 6^{4}½ 3^2 1½ ShmkrW^6 ⓇSta Ctlna 86-15 Ferdinand,VrietyRod,GrndAllegince 8
29Jan86—Lacked room, steadied at intervals 5/16 to 1/8
4Jan86-8SA 1 :45^3 1:10^3 1:36^{1}ft *4-5 114 3^{2}½ 3½ 1^{1}½ 2^{hd} ShoemkrW^3 ⓇLs Feliz 87-13 Badger Land,Ferdinand,CutByGlass 7
4Jan86—3-wide into stretch
15Dec85-8Hol 1 :44^3 1:09 1:34^{1}ft 34 121 9^{5}¾ 3^{5}½ 3^{5}½ 3^{6}½ ShomkrW^2 Hol Fut 85-09 SnowChief,ElectricBlue,Ferdinand 10
15Dec85—Grade I
3Nov85-1SA 1 :47^1 1:12 1:37^{2}ft *2-5 117 3^{2}½ 1^1 1^1 1^{2}½ Ward W A^1 Mdn 81-15 Ferdinand,StrRibot,ImperiousSpirit 6
20Oct85-6SA 1 :46^3 1:12 1:37^{3}ft *2½ 117 5^{3}¾ 2½ 2^{hd} 2no Toro F^7 Mdn 80-17 AcksLikRuler,Frdinnd,Frnkinstrlli 10
20Oct85—Lugged in stretch, bumped late
6Oct85-6SA 6f :21^4 :45^1 1:10^{1}ft 19 117 9^6 5^{6}¾ 4^8 3^{11} Shoemaker W^3 Mdn 76-16 JudgeSmells,OurGreyFox,Frdinnd 12
8Sep85-6Dmr 6f :22^3 :46 1:10^{2}ft 4½ 118 10^{12}10^{12} 8^{9}½ 8^{11}½ Shoemaker W^5 Mdn 74-08 DonB.Blue,ElCorzon,AuBonMrche 11
●Apr 29 CD 5f ft :58^3 h Apr 24 CD 1 ft 1:38^4 h Apr 17 SA 7f ft 1:24^3 h Apr 13 SA 4f ft :52 b

Mogambo — **Ch. c. 3, by Mr Prospector—Lakeville Miss, by Rainy Lake**
Br.—Brant P M (Ky) 1986 4 2 1 1 $358,150
Own.—Brant P M **126** **Tr.—Jolley Leroy** 1985 7 2 1 3 $300,096
Lifetime 11 4 2 4 $658,246

19Apr86-8Aqu 1⅛ :47^2 1:11^1 1:50^{3}ft 2¾ 126 3^2 3^{2}½ 3^4 2½ VsquezJ^7 Wood Inv 81-18 Broad Brush, Mogambo, Groovy 7
19Apr86—Grade I; Ducked in st
5Apr86-8Aqu 1 :44^4 1:08^3 1:34^{3}ft 3¾ 121 5^4 3^{4}½ 3^4 1¾ VasquezJ^9 Gotham 93-18 Mogambo, ‡Groovy, Tasso 9
5Apr86—Grade II; Bore in, driving
1Mar86-9GP 1⅛ :46^4 1:12 1:51^{4}ft 8-5e 122 6^{10} 5^8 4^8 3^{6}¾ CordrAJr^1 Fla Derby 66-29 SnowChief,BadgerLand,Mogambo 16
1Mar86—Grade I
17Feb86-3GP 7f :22^3 :45^3 1:23^{3}ft *1-5 119 4^{5}½ 4^3 2^3 1^1 Cordero AJr^1 Aw25000 86-27 Mogambo, Bill 'NHarry,DomDancer 5
2Nov85-1Aqu 1 :45^2 1:10^4 1:36^{1}ft *1 122 9^{5}¾ 4^3 6^4 6^{2}½ CordrAJr^5 Br Cp Juv 83-10 Tasso, Storm Cat, Scat Dancer 13
2Nov85—Grade I; Tkn up after st
19Oct85-8Bel 1 :46^2 1:12 1:37^{1}ft 2 122 4^7 3^{2}½ 1^3 1^{9}¾ CrdrAJr^4 Champagne 79-17 Mogambo, Groovy, Mr. Classic 5
19Oct85—Grade I
10Oct85-8Med 1 1/16 :46 1:10^2 1:43^{3}ft 5 119 6^6 4^{4}½ 3^{1}½ 3^{nk} CrdrAJr^{12} YoungAmr. 85-15 StormCt,DnzigConnction,Mogmbo 12
10Oct85—Grade I
28Sep85-8Bel 7f :22^1 :45^4 1:23^{4}ft 5 122 6^{6}½ 6^{5}½ 4^6 3^{5}½ CordrAJr^1 Cowdin 77-18 Ketoh, Mr. Classic, Mogambo 11
28Sep85—Grade I
15Sep85-5Bel 6f :22^4 :46^2 1:11^{3}ft *1-3 117 3^2 2^{hd} 3½ 3^1 Cordero AJr^1 Aw24000 83-16 Real Courage,Rambulara,Mogambo 6
10Jly85-6Bel 5½f :22^4 :46^2 1:05 ft *1-3 118 2^{hd} 1^{hd} 1^{hd} 1^{3}½ Cordero A Jr^6 Mdn 90-23 Mogambo, Mr.Classic,ProudWorld 10
13Jun85-6Bel 5½f :23^1 :46^4 1:04^{3}ft *1-2 118 1^{1}½ 1^2 2^{hd} 2^{2}¾ Cordero A Jr^4 Mdn 89-23 Ogygian, Mogambo, Gallant Chief 10
●Apr 27 CD 6f ft 1:11^2 h Apr 17 Bel 3f sy :36^3 b ●Apr 13 Bel 6f ft 1:11^1 h ●Apr 3 Bel tr.t 3f ft :34^4 b

Wise Times — **B. c. 3, by Mr. Leader—Trying Times, by He's a Pistol**
Br.—Nuckols Bros (Ky) 1986 5 2 0 1 $98,138
Own.—R L Reineman Stable Inc **126** **Tr.—Gleaves Philip** 1985 4 1 1 0 $13,520
Lifetime 9 3 1 1 $111,658

12Apr86-7Kee 1 1/16 :47^2 1:12 1:44^{4}ft 4e 112 4^{4}½ 4^{1}½ 1½ 1^2 Allen KK^5 Lexington 82-20 WisTims,CountryLight,BluBuckroo 9
12Apr86—Grade III
23Mar86-11FG 1⅛ :48 1:12^2 1:50^{2}ft 8 118 10^{9}½ 10^{11} 8^{8}½ 5^{4}½ BileyJD^{12} Lou Dby 87-17 ContryLght,BolshoBy,LghtnngTch 13
23Mar86—Grade III
3Mar86-6GP 1 1/16 :49 1:14 1:46^{2}ft *3-5 117 3^{1}½ 3^2 1^{hd} 1^4 Bailey J D^1 Aw18000 69-36 WiseTimes,ExpditionMoon,OnRtinr 8
17Feb86-10GP 1 1/16 :47^2 1:12 1:45 ft 18 112 8^{12} 8^{12} 5^{10} 4^{7}½ BaileyJD^9 Fountin Yth 69-27 MyPrinceChrming,Mykw,PplPowr 10
17Feb86—Grade II; Run in divisions
20Jan86-5GP 7f :23^1 :46^1 1:25 ft 9½ 117 8^{4}½ 5^6 4^7 3½ Bailey J D^9 Aw15000 78-24 MyPrincChrming,Accipitt,WisTims 9
31Aug85-8Haw 6½f :23^1 :47 1:17^{2}ft 7 112 5^2 2^{2}½ 2^{1}½ 2^{1}¾ BrumfldD^3 Arch Ward 84-23 Bar Tender, Wise Times, Im Artie 10
6Aug85-3Haw 5½f :23 :47 1:06^{2}ft 5 122 4^{4}½ 6^{11} 5^3 1½ Brumfield D^1 Mdn 80-24 WiseTimes,NoblMjsty,FirwyDoctor 7
3Jly85-4AP 5f :22^2 :46^1 :59 ft 8½ 122 7^{4}¾ 8^{6}¾ 6^{5}¾ 6^{5}¾ Fires E^3 Mdn 85-16 KennyLne,KeepItEsy,CelebritySlr 11
5Jun85-3AP 5f :22^4 :46^3 :59^{4}ft 11 122 9^{5}½ 8^{7}½ 5^{5}¾ 4^{4}½ Fires E^4 Mdn 82-20 TigrBright,TournmntPlyr,Quckcpd 10
May 1 CD 4f gd :52^2 b Apr 26 CD 1⅛ ft 1:55^2 h Apr 21 Kee 5f sy 1:03^1 b Apr 11 Kee 3f ft :36^3 b

***Bold Arrangement**
Ch. c. 3, by Persian Bold—Arrangement, by Floribunda
Br.—Peacock R D Mrs (Eng) 1986 2 0 0 2 $28,943
Own.—Richards A & R 126 Tr.—Brittain Clive E 1985 9 4 2 1 $77,326
Lifetime 11 4 2 3 $106,269 Turf 10 4 2 2 $79,709
24Apr86-7Kee 1⅛ :483 1:131 1:511ft 5¾ 121 94¾ 84¼ 72¾ 3¾ EdderyP10 Blue Grass 80-20 BchlorB,BolshoBoy,BoldArrngmnt 11
24Apr86—Grade I
20Mar86◆3Doncaster(Eng) 1 1:481gd 2¼ 112 Ⓣ 31½ RobnsnP RaPtMiStk Mc'sReef,Tremblnt,BoldArrngemnt 4
26Oct85◆4Doncaster(Eng) 1 1:411gd 5 126 Ⓣ 21½ †Eddery P W Hill Fut St Bkhroff,BoldArrngement,Normrood 9
†26Oct85—Disqualified and placed fourth
13Oct85◆5Longchamp(Fra) 1 1:40 gd 5½ 123 Ⓣ 2hd Piggott L Gd Crit Gr I FemmElit,BoldArrngmnt,NoKfrou 11
22Sep85◆4Longchamp(Fra) 7f 1:22 gd 10 123 Ⓣ 31¼ Piggott L Prix Sala Gr I BiserVole,ReglStte,BoldArrgemnt 10
30Aug85◆4Sandown(Eng) 7f 1:291gd 5 126 Ⓣ 11 Eddery P Solario Stakes BldArrngmnt,BrghtAsNght,KlnHhts 5
13Aug85◆4Newcastle(Eng) 7f 1:302gd 16 123 Ⓣ 22 RbnsP SeatonDelvStks(Gr.3) MoorgtMn,BoldArrngmnt,Rckstrw 10
31Jly85◆3Goodwood(Eng) 6f 1:133gd 25 123 Ⓣ 46¾ StrkG Richmond Stks(Gr.2) Nomination, Green Desert,Stalker 10
16Jly85◆4Leicester(Eng) 6f 1:14 gd*4-5 125 Ⓣ 1½ RbnsP Work Man Stks BoldArrngmnt,MtThGrk,DrkPromis 3
6Jly85◆4Nottingham(Eng) 6f 1:14 fm 2 127 Ⓣ 13 RobnsonP DSI Stks BldArrngmnt,BlEydBy,MrphysWhls 5
11Jun85◆5Goodwood(Eng) 6f 1:153gd 14 126 Ⓣ 11 MrrA East Dean Stks(Mdn) BoldArrngemnt,AlDiwn,JumboHirt 16
May 1 CD 3f gd :37 b ●Apr 22 Kee 5f m :594 h

Icy Groom *
Ch. c. 3, by Blushing Groom—Hey Babe, by Roberto
Br.—Kluener Robert G (Ky) 1986 6 2 2 0 $166,380
Own.—Fleming W 126 Tr.—Ramer Sam T 1985 1 M 1 0 $2,855
Lifetime 7 2 3 0 $169,235
24Apr86-7Kee 1⅛ :483 1:131 1:511ft *2¼ 121 32 63 41¾ 43¼ DlhossyE9 Blue Grass 78-20 BchlorB,BolshoBoy,BoldArrngmnt 11
24Apr86—Grade I
6Apr86-5SA 1⅛ :471 1:11 1:483ft 12 122 44 44 22½ 26 DlhossyE6 S A Dby 80-15 Snow Chief, Icy Groom, Ferdinand 7
6Apr86—Grade I
19Mar86-8SA 1⅛ :462 1:11 1:492ft 2½ 116 54 52½ 1½ 12½ DelhoussyE3 Ⓡ Brdbry 82-20 IcyGroom,ImperiousSpirit,Bugarian 7
2Mar86-6SA 1 1/16 :454 1:104 1:43 ft 4 116 34 32½ 1½ 21 DelhoussyeE7 Aw30000 85-13 ImpriousSpirt,IcyGroom,Scrpbook 11
1Feb86-6SA 6f :22 :461 1:113m 3½ 118 68½ 42½ 2hd 12 Delahoussaye E6 Mdn 80-24 IcyGroom,GoodCommnd,NtivePriss 8
1Feb86—Broke in air; wide into stretch
19Jan86-4SA 6f :212 :44 1:091ft *2 118 52½ 46½ 39½ 613½ Delahoussaye E3 Mdn 78-12 FollowThDncr,JdgAnglcc,SrTyson 12
22Jun85-3CD 5½f :224 :464 1:062gd 2½ 119 42½ 32 31½ 2¾ Gavidia W3 Mdn 88-15 StellarRivl,IcyGroom,TimelyAlbert 11
Apr 29 CD 5f ft 1:041 b Apr 1 SA 5f ft 1:013 h Mar 27 SA 4f ft :483 h Mar 15 SA tr.t 5f sl 1:032 h

Southern Appeal
B. c. 3, by Valid Appeal—Southern Gem, by Tropical Breeze
Br.—Glade Valley Farms Inc (Md) 1986 4 1 0 0 $16,000
Own.—Bender H M 126 Tr.—Moncrief Marvin L 1985 10 2 1 1 $178,292
Lifetime 14 3 1 1 $194,292
12Apr86-8Pim 1 1/16 :47 1:121 1:461ft *2-5 122 25 35½ 47½ 511¼ DdsJ5 Ⓢ Deputed Test 62-26 Pilgrim Prince, WarmAsToast,Kalli 5
12Apr86—Stumbled st.
5Apr86-4Pim 1 1/16 :484 1:14 1:452ft *1-2e 114 1½ 11½ 14 18 Davidson J1 Aw15000 77-18 Southern Appeal, Ken's Hat,SoSam 6
22Mar86-9Lat 1 1/16 :464 1:102 1:441ft 21 121 75 88½ 68¼ 69½ DvdsonJ6 Jim Beam 79-19 BrodBrush,MircleWood,BchelorBu 12
22Mar86—Grade III
17Feb86-9GP 1 1/16 :482 1:124 1:453ft 20 122 55½ 710 913 910½ BrmfldD8 Fountin Yth 62-27 EnsignRhythm,Jig'sHven,RglDrmr 10
17Feb86—Grade II; In tight; Run in divisions
30Nov85-8Lrl 1 1/16 :4721:1331:461+sy 3 122 4¾ 31 56¼ 614 DdsnJ6 Ⓢ Mdjuvchamp 63-23 MircleWood,BugEyedBetty,LilTylr 10
16Nov85-9Pha 1 1/16 :472 1:124 1:47 sy 7½ 122 55½ 49 45½ 411 Saumell L2 Heritage 58-22 Admirl'sImge,BuckieBoy,DoublFint 9
19Oct85-9Crc 1 1/16 :482 1:134 1:484gd *2½ 120 107¾ 1013 1017 1517¾ DPssR2 Ⓡ Fla Stallion 58-24 SctDncr,SnnyProspctr,SnwyMntn 19
19Oct85—In Reality Division; Steadied
5Oct85-8Lrl 1 1/16 :4711:1211:441+ft 13 122 51¾ 32 21 11 DavidsonJ1 Lrl Fut'y 87-17 SouthernAppl,PplPowr,MirclWood 6
5Oct85—Grade I
1Sep85-10RD 1 1/16 :474 1:121 1:444ft 4½ 120 21 2½ 22 26 Davidson J1 Cradle 79-18 GoForItMtt,SothrnAppl,StdyEffrt 10
19Aug85-7Pim 6f :233 :471 1:123ft *6-5 114 41½ 33½ 34 32½ Davidson J7 Aw10000 80-22 MircleWood,BigPlop,SouthernAppl 7
30Jly85-7Mth 5½f :223 :461 1:044ft 31 116 86½ 97¼ 74 44½ Thornburg B4 Tyro 86-11 CntryLght,Mnlghtdlght,Brnt'sDng 11
30Jly85—Run in divisions
10Jly85-9Suf 6f :222 :46 1:131ft 5½ 114 86¾ 1214 1111 99 Day P6 Mayflower 66-17 AvngngStorm,MdDocsFolly,HlyBy 15
29Jun85-7Bow 5½f :223 :46 1:041ft 4½ 113 2½ 43½ 57¾ 48½ Saumell L4 Ⓢ Playpen 89-21 Air Miracle, Bridge Out, Carnmore 8
3Jun85-3Bow 5f :23 :471 :594ft *4-5 120 11 11 12 11½ Dimitropoulos D1 Mdn 91-20 SouthernAppeal,NastyMn,Tentsive 8
May 1 CD 4f gd :522 b Apr 27 Lrl 6f ft 1:123 h Apr 11 Lrl 3f ft :391 b Apr 4 Lrl 3f ft :393 b

Vernon Castle
Dk. b. or br. c. 3, by Seattle Slew—Rullian's Princess, by Prince John
Br.—North Ridge Farm (Ky) 1986 2 2 0 0 $160,475
Own.—Paulson A E (Lessee) 126 Tr.—Sullivan John 1985 1 M 1 0 $4,840
Lifetime 3 2 1 0 $165,315
19Apr86-8GG 1⅛:452 1:094 1:48 ft *7-5 116 32½ 32 1hd 14 DlhossyE6 Cal Dby 93-12 VrnonCstl,ImprosSprt,PrncBbbyB. 10
19Apr86—Grade II
29Mar86-6SA 1 1/16:463 1:122 1:441ft *6-5 117 31 12 14½ 18½ Delahoussaye E5 Mdn 80-20 VernonCstl,RidgRviw,PlumbStright 9
29Mar86—Broke slowly, bumped start
28Sep85-6Bel 6f :222 :46 1:111ft *6-5 118 77½ 76½ 44 2nk Cruguet J10 Mdn 86-18 Post Star, VernonCastle,I'mAhead 10
28Sep85—Lugged in
May 1 CD 4f gd :493 b Apr 14 SA 6f ft 1:124 h Apr 8 SA 5f ft 1:022 h Mar 23 SA 1 ft 1:404 h

Rampage *
B. c. 3, by Northern Baby—Noble Bethenny, by Vaguely Noble
Br.—Due Process Stable (Fla) 1986 4 3 0 0 $330,576
Own.—Reed Mr-Mrs H J 126 Tr.—Thomas Gary A 1985 4 1 2 0 $9,510
Lifetime 8 4 2 0 $340,086
19Apr86-9OP 1⅛:454 1:101 1:481sy 4½ 118 74¾ 63¾ 22 11½ Day P8 Ark Dby 93-07 Rampage,WheatlyHall,FamilyStyle 14
19Apr86—Grade I
29Mar86-9OP 1 1/16:454 1:10 1:431ft 7½ 114 79½ 69½ 58½ 41¾ Allen J L8 Rebel 83-16 Rare Brick, Clear Choice, The Flats 8
18Mar86-8OP 1 1/16:461 1:12 1:433ft *1 122 44 54½ 21½ 1½ Day P1 Aw25000 83-22 Rampage, Trobio, Peripat 7
19Feb86-7OP 1 1/16:472 1:13 1:46 ft 3½ 116 911 76¾ 2½ 12¾ Day P10 Aw14500 71-26 Rampage, Cowboy Bill, Peripat 10
7Dec85-8Haw 1 1/16:47 1:123 1:454ft 3½ 112 10111215 713 611 Day P1 Haw Juv 58-26 Ice Over,RegalDreamer,Jay'sTiger 14
22Nov85-6CD 1 :471 1:123 1:374ft 2½ 112 42½ 41¾ 4nk 2½ Allen K K3 Aw11965 79-18 Betrayer, Rampage, Proctoring 6
8Nov85-7CD 1 1/16:491 1:133 1:453ft 2½ 115 53½ 41½ 21½ 21 Day P4 Aw15575 79-18 OaklandBoy,Rampage,NobleMjesty 6
11Oct85-5Cby 1 :491 1:142 1:401ft 4½ 117 42 1½ 12 13½ Pettinger D R4 Mdn 80-15 Rampge,TulsHurricne,GlidingClyde 6
May 1 CD 4f gd :49 b Apr 17 OP 4f ft :492 b

Broad Brush ×
B. c. 3, by Ack Ack—Hay Patcher, by Hoist the Flag
Br.—Meyerhoff R E (Md) 1986 5 4 1 0 $523,108
Own.—Meyerhoff Robert E 126 Tr.—Small Richard W 1985 4 3 0 0 $42,335
Lifetime 9 7 1 0 $565,443
19Apr86-8Aqu 1⅛:472 1:111 1:503ft 7 126 21 21 11 1½ BrcclVJr3 Wood Inv 82-18 Broad Brush, Mogambo, Groovy 7
19Apr86—Grade I; Ducked out, drvng
22Mar86-9Lat 1 1/16:464 1:102 1:441ft *1 121 1hd 1hd 11 12 BrcclVJr2 Jim Beam 89-19 BrodBrush,MircleWood,BchelorBu 12
22Mar86—Grade III; Ducked out late stretch
1Mar86-8Pim 1 1/16:464 1:112 1:441ft *6-5 122 1hd 11 13½ 1no BrccilVJr1 Fred Tesio 83-20 BrodBrush,FobbyForbes,DoublFint 7
20Feb86-7Pim 1 1/16:471 1:131 1:441m *2-3 122 2hd 1hd 12½ 11½ BrcclVJr6 Gen George 83-25 Broad Brush, Fast Step, Swallow 7
20Feb86—Run in divisions; Drifted,driving
5Jan86-6Lrl 7f :223 :461 1:253ft *1-2 119 43 1hd 2hd 2no WrtDR3 [S]StrDeNskra 83-22 LilTyler,BrodBrush,AnotherShelter 5
5Jan86—Broke whip
21Dec85-8Lrl 1 :453 1:10 1:35 ft 2½ 110 3½ 1hd 13½ 17½ WrtDR5 Inner Harbor 97-10 BrodBrush,GoldenOlden,TkeTheStg 6
27Nov85-7Pha 1 1/16:48 1:134 1:47 m 2½ 120 1½ 11 13 1hd Black A S4 Aw12000 69-24 Broad Brush, April Cat, Lil GlennL. 5
8Nov85-6Pha 1 1/16:474 1:14 1:464ft 5 118 1hd 11½ 12½ 13 Black A S2 Mdn 70-28 BrodBrush,HomlyHomr,HddonHour 6
13Oct85-3Lrl 1 :472 1:131 1:391ft 2e 120 63½ 76½ 67½ 64½ Jenkins J P3 Mdn 72-17 The Lone Ranger,Cupola,Vak[illegible] 9
●Apr 29 Pim 5f ft 1:00 h ●Apr 18 Pim 3f sy :343 h Apr 11 Pim 1 ft 1:40 h Apr 10 Pim 3f ft :37 h

Badger Land
B. c. 3, by Codex—Gimlieroom, by Racing Room
Br.—Mel Hatley Stable & Lukas (Ky) 1986 5 3 2 0 $450,650
Own.—Lukas-Lukas & Hatley 126 Tr.—Lukas D Wayne 1985 7 2 0 0 $51,475
Lifetime 12 5 2 0 $502,125
5Apr86-10Hia 1⅛:462 1:10 1:47 ft *1-3 122 2½ 1½ 13 14 VelsquzJ6 Flamingo 97-13 BdgrLnd,BolshoiBoy,AnnpolsJohn 10
5Apr86—Grade I
22Mar86-11Hia 1⅛:454 1:094 1:461ft *1-2 114 55½ 42 12 14 VelsquzJ4 Everglades 101-15 BadgerLand,OneMgicMoment,Glow 8
22Mar86—Grade II; Drifted out clear
1Mar86-9GP 1⅛:464 1:12 1:514ft 17 122 21½ 2½ 22½ 21¾ VelsquzJ13 Fla Derby 71-29 SnowChief,BadgerLand,Mogambo 16
1Mar86—Grade I
2Feb86-8BM 1 1/16:452 1:093 1:423sy 11 120 56½ 54¾ 32 22½ MigliorR1 Cm Rl Dby 78-28 Snow Chief, BadgerLand,DarbyFair 6
2Feb86—Grade III
4Jan86-8SA 1 :453 1:103 1:361ft 5½ 117 57 42 21½ 1hd Pincay LJr1 [R]Ls Feliz 87-13 Badger Land,Ferdinand,CutByGlass 7
4Jan86—Broke slowly, bumped start
22Dec85-7Hol 7f :223 :453 1:231ft 4 117 62¾ 73¾ 65½ 66¾ PincyLJr5 [R]Rvng Boy 81-17 HyKing,DncingPirte,TimeToSmoke 9
28Nov85-9CD 1 1/16:484 1:141 1:464m 6½ 116 88¾ 95½ 64¾ 43¾ VelsquzJ8 Ky Jky Clb 70-27 MustinLke,BchelorBeu,ReglDremr 10
28Nov85—Grade III
23Oct85-7SA 1 :47 1:121 1:393ft 9-5 117 53½ 31½ 32½ 11½ Pincay L Jr2 Aw26000 70-25 BdgerLnd,SmokeyOrbit,RisdOnStg 7
13Oct85-8SA 1 1/16:454 1:103 1:443ft 5½ 118 78½ 79¾ 69 68¾ PincayLJr9 Norfolk 69-17 Snow Chief, Lord Allison,DarbyFair 9
13Oct85—Grade I; Fanned wide 7/8 turn
11Sep85-8Dmr 1 :471 1:113 1:36 ft 18 114 68½ 65½ 56½ 45¾ StevnsGL1 Dmr Fut 82-15 Tsso,Arewehvingfunyet,SnowChief 6
11Sep85—Grade I
22Aug85-7Sar 7f :223 :452 1:232ft 3-2 122 65½ 68½ 66½ 59 Velasquez J6 Aw24000 76-13 HyNowHrry,DnzgConncton,BckBoy 8
29Jly85-3Bel 6f :222 :461 1:114ft 3½ 118 54 33 12 14 Velasquez J2 Mdn 83-18 Badger Land, J. O. Cross,LordPacal 8
●Apr 28 CD 5f ft :592 h ●Apr 23 CD 6f ft 1:132 b Apr 16 CD 6f ft 1:164 b Mar 14 GP 5f ft 1:031 b

Wheatly Hall
Ch. c. 3, by Norcliffe—La Bonze, by Miracle Hill
Br.—McKinnon John (Fla) 1986 4 2 2 0 $118,300
Own.—McKinnon J 126 Tr.—Van Berg Jack C 1985 0 M 0 0
Lifetime 4 2 2 0 $118,300
19Apr86-9OP 1⅛ :45^4 1:10^1 1:48^1sy *2½ 115 2^{hd} 1^{hd} 1^2 $2^{1\frac{1}{2}}$ Snyder L^2 Ark Dby 91-07 Rampage,WheatlyHall,FamilyStyle 14
19Apr86—Grade I
9Apr86-9OP 1$\frac{1}{16}$:46^1 1:11 1:42^3ft *1-3 120 $2^{1\frac{1}{2}}$ 2^1 1^2 1^6 Snyder L^2 Aw14500 88-20 Wheatly Hall, Sir Bubby, Sum ItUp 8
28Mar86-7OP 1$\frac{1}{16}$:46^3 1:11^3 1:43^3ft *2-3 122 $5^{5\frac{1}{2}}$ $3^{1\frac{1}{2}}$ $2^{\frac{1}{2}}$ $1^{1\frac{1}{2}}$ Snyder L^6 Mdn 83-18 Wheatly Hall, Mole, Dr. Cho Cho 8
7Mar86-6OP 1 :47^1 1:12 1:38^1ft 2¾ 122 3^2 $3^{\frac{1}{2}}$ 2^{hd} 2no Snyder L^5 Mdn 81-24 WllyByGolly,WhetlyHll,Dr.ChoCho 10
Apr 28 CD 1 ft 1:39 h ●Apr 16 OP 1 ft 1:42 b Mar 18 OP 7f ft 1:28^3 b ●Mar 4 OP 5f ft :59 bg

Snow Chief *
Dk. b. or br. c. 3, by Reflected Glory—Miss Snowflake, by Snow Sporting
Br.—Blue Diamond Ranch (Cal) 1986 4 4 0 0 $783,300
Own.—Grinstead & Rochelle 126 Tr.—Stute Melvin F 1985 9 5 2 1 $935,740
Lifetime 13 9 2 1 $1,719,040
6Apr86-5SA 1⅛ :47^1 1:11 1:48^3ft *1-3 122 $1^{1\frac{1}{2}}$ 1^2 $1^{2\frac{1}{2}}$ 1^6 Solis A^3 S A Dby 86-15 Snow Chief, Icy Groom, Ferdinand 7
6Apr86—Grade I
1Mar86-9GP 1⅛ :46^4 1:12 1:51^4ft *3-2 122 $1^{1\frac{1}{2}}$ $1^{\frac{1}{2}}$ $1^{2\frac{1}{2}}$ $1^{1\frac{3}{4}}$ Solis A^{12} Fla Derby 73-29 SnowChief,BadgerLand,Mogambo 16
1Mar86—Grade I
2Feb86-8BM 1$\frac{1}{16}$:45^2 1:09^3 1:42^3sy *2-3 120 $2^{1\frac{1}{2}}$ 2^{hd} 1^{hd} $1^{2\frac{1}{2}}$ Solis A^2 Cm Rl Dby 79-28 Snow Chief, BadgerLand,DarbyFair 6
2Feb86—Grade III
12Jan86-8SA 7f :22^1 :44^4 1:21^3ft *2-5 126 $5^{2\frac{1}{2}}$ $6^{1\frac{3}{4}}$ 1^1 1^4 Solis A^7 [S]Ca Br Chp 92-11 Snow Chief, Variety Road,AirPirate 8
15Dec85-8Hol 1 :44^3 1:09 1:34^1ft 3 121 2^{hd} $1^{3\frac{1}{2}}$ 1^5 $1^{6\frac{1}{2}}$ Solis A^9 Hol Fut 92-09 SnowChief,ElectricBlue,Ferdinand 10
15Dec85—Grade I
29Nov85-8Hol 1 :45^1 1:11 1:37 sy *1 120 $6^{6\frac{1}{2}}$ 2^4 2^4 2^5 Solis A^5 Hoist T Flg 73-20 DarbyFair,SnowChief,AcksLikRuler 6
2Nov85-14SA 1 :47^3 1:12^1 1:36^2ft *2-5 122 $5^{3\frac{1}{2}}$ 3^2 3^2 1^{hd} Solis A^4 [S]B J Ridder 86-13 SnowChief,VrietyRod,RisedOnStge 7
13Oct85-8SA 1$\frac{1}{16}$:45^4 1:10^3 1:44^3ft *3-2 118 $5^{5\frac{1}{2}}$ 5^6 $3^{2\frac{1}{2}}$ 1^3 Solis A^2 Norfolk 78-17 Snow Chief, Lord Allison,DarbyFair 9
13Oct85—Grade I
2Oct85-8SA 7f :22^1 :45^1 1:23^3ft *2½ 119 $7^{6\frac{3}{4}}$ $5^{4\frac{3}{4}}$ 4^4 2^{nk} Solis A^5 Sny Slp 82-17 LouisianSlew,SnowChief,DonB.Blue 8
11Sep85-8Dmr 1 :47^1 1:11^3 1:36 ft 7¾ 117 $5^{2\frac{1}{2}}$ 4^1 $3^{4\frac{1}{2}}$ $3^{2\frac{1}{2}}$ Solis A^5 Dmr Fut 85-15 Tsso,Arewehvingfunyet,SnowChief 6
11Sep85—Grade I
4Sep85-8Dmr 6f :22^1 :45^1 1:10 ft 7½ 117 $5^{2\frac{3}{4}}$ 2^5 $2^{1\frac{1}{2}}$ $1^{1\frac{3}{4}}$ Meza R Q^7 [R]Rcho Sfe 88-17 SnowChif,LittlRdCloud,QuickTwist 7
30Jun85-5Hol 5½f :21^2 :43^3 1:02^4ft 8½ 115 6^{14} 6^{17} 6^{14} $6^{9\frac{1}{2}}$ Meza R Q^4 Dsrt Wine — — HlcoScmpr,LttlRdCloud,SrMhmoud 9
19Jun85-5Hol 5f :22^4 :45^2 :57^3ft 2½ 118 $2^{\frac{1}{2}}$ 1^{hd} 1^{hd} $1^{2\frac{1}{2}}$ Meza M G^4 [S]Mdn — — SnowChif,GloryPth,WindAtHisBck 10
●Apr 25 SA 5f ft :58^2 h Apr 20 SA 1 ft 1:38^2 h ●Apr 14 SA 6f ft 1:11^1 h ●Apr 3 SA 4f ft :45^2 h

Bachelor Beau *
Ch. g. 3, by Raised Socially—Matriculation, by Arts and Letters
Br.—Mjaka I Stable (Ky) 1986 4 1 2 1 $231,310
Own.—Waterfield & Tafel 126 Tr.—Hauswald Philip 1985 5 2 2 0 $62,077
Lifetime 9 3 4 1 $293,387
24Apr86-7Kee 1⅛ :48^3 1:13^1 1:51^1ft 20 121 1^1 1^1 1^{hd} $1^{\frac{3}{4}}$ MinconL^1 Blue Grass 81-20 BchlorB,BolshoBoy,BoldArrngmnt 11
24Apr86—Grade I
22Mar86-9Lat 1$\frac{1}{16}$:46^4 1:10^2 1:44^1ft 5¾ 121 2^{hd} 2^{hd} 2^1 3^2 MinconL^7 Jim Beam 87-19 BrodBrush,MircleWood,BchelorBu 12
22Mar86—Grade III
8Mar86-9OP 1 :45^4 1:10^1 1:36^1ft 6½ 115 $2^{1\frac{1}{2}}$ $2^{2\frac{1}{2}}$ 2^6 2^{11} MinconL^{12} Southwest 80-20 RreBrick,BchelorBeu,SwinginSwy 14
21Feb86-9OP 6f :21^4 :45^1 1:10^2ft 6½ 114 4^3 $3^{3\frac{1}{2}}$ $2^{3\frac{1}{2}}$ $2^{2\frac{3}{4}}$ MelanconL^3 Mt Valley 85-24 RareBrick,BchelorBeu,SwinginSwy 7
7Dec85-8Haw 1$\frac{1}{16}$:47 1:12^3 1:45^4ft 2½ 112 $4^{2\frac{1}{2}}$ 3^3 5^7 $5^{10\frac{3}{4}}$ Allen K K^8 Haw Juv 58-26 Ice Over,RegalDreamer,Jay'sTiger 14
28Nov85-9CD 1$\frac{1}{16}$:48^4 1:14^1 1:46^4m *8-5e 116 3^1 $3^{1\frac{1}{2}}$ 2^1 2^2 Allen KK^2 Ky Jky Clb 72-27 MustinLke,BchelorBeu,ReglDremr 10
28Nov85—Grade III
9Nov85-8CD 1 :45^1 1:10^1 1:37^1ft 8 117 3^1 1^{hd} 1^1 2^{hd} Allen K K^3 Iroquois 83-23 Tile,BachelorBeau,DncetotheWire 11
24Oct85-5Kee 6f :23 :46^3 1:13^3m 9-5 118 3^{nk} $1^{\frac{1}{2}}$ 1^2 1^3 Melancon L^6 Aw15800 74-32 BachelorBeau,HotCircuit,MjorBold 6
9Oct85-2Kee 6f :23 :46^2 1:12 ft 7¾ 120 $1^{1\frac{1}{2}}$ 1^2 1^6 1^7 Melancon L^{11} Mdn 82-18 BchelorBu,BluBuckroo,Thor'sDncr 12
●Apr 21 Kee 5f sy 1:03^3 h Apr 16 Kee 4f gd :51^2 bg Mar 17 OP 3f ft :36^4 b Mar 7 OP 3f ft :37 b

Groovy ✻

Ch. c. 3, by Norcliffe—Tinnitus, by Restless Wind

Br.—Robinson M T (Tex) 1986 4 1 1 1 $109,667

wn.—Ballis J A 126 Tr.—Crowell Howard 1985 5 1 2 0 $136,800

Lifetime 9 2 3 1 $246,467

Apr86-8Aqu 1⅛ :472 1:111 1:503ft 3¾ 126 11 11 21 3¾ Perret C2 Wood Inv 81-18 Broad Brush, Mogambo, Groovy 7

19Apr86—Grade I

Apr86-8Aqu 1 :444 1:083 1:343ft 8¾ 114 11½ 13 13½ 2¾ † SantosJA8 Gotham 92-18 Mogambo, ‡Groovy, Tasso 9

5Apr86—Grade II; Bore in; †Disqualified and placed fifth

Mar86-7Aqu 7f :223 :451 1:22 ft 5 117 21 1hd 2hd 24½ SntosJA6 Bay Shore 86-25 Zabaleta, Groovy, Belocolus 8

22Mar86—Grade II; Run in Divisions

3Jan86-9GP 6f :213 :444 1:114sy *4-5 113 1½ 12 12½ 1¾ Perret C1 Spec Bid 80-21 Groovy,KennyLane,LimitedPractice 6

2Nov85-1Aqu 1 :452 1:104 1:361ft 23 122 11½ 31½ 1014 1016 MrphDJ11 Br Cp Juv 69-10 Tasso, Storm Cat, Scat Dancer 13

2Nov85—Grade I; Stumbled after st

9Oct85-8Bel 1 :462 1:12 1:371ft 11 122 12 12 23 29¾ McBtD1 Champagne 69-17 Mogambo, Groovy, Mr. Classic 5

19Oct85—Grade I

0Oct85-8Med 1 1/16 :46 1:102 1:433ft *2 119 12 1½ 43½ 57½ McBtD10 Young Amer. 77-15 StormCt,DnzigConnction,Mogmbo 12

10Oct85—Grade I

4Sep85-6Bel 7f :222 :453 1:222ft 4¾ 122 1½ 1½ 22½ 29½ MurphyDJ6 Bel Fut 80-09 Ogygian, Groovy, Mr. Classic 6

14Sep85—Grade I

2Sep85-8Med 6f :222 :45 1:103ft 8 112 31½ 1hd 12½ 12½ MrphyDJ9 Frevr Cstng 89-10 Groovy, Hey Now Harry, Kruckel 11

Apr 29 CD 7f ft 1:244 h ●Apr 16 Bel 5f sy 1:014 b Apr 4 Bel 3f ft :36 b Mar 30 Bel tr.t 7f ft 1:242 h

Zabaleta

B. c. 3, by Shecky Greene—Winver, by Vertex

Br.—Parr E O (Ky) 1986 5 2 2 1 $196,450

Own.—Riordan M D 126 Tr.—Gosden John 1985 0 M 0 0

Lifetime 5 2 2 1 $196,450

19Apr86-9GS 1⅛ :462 1:113 1:51 ft *6-5 117 1hd 2hd 2hd 2½ McHrgDG8 Garden St 73-21 FobbyForbes,Zabalet,MircleWood 10

19Apr86—Ducked out,brshd

5Apr86-8Aqu 1 :444 1:083 1:343ft *6-5 121 21½ 23 23½ 43 McHrDG5 Gotham 90-18 Mogambo, ‡Groovy, Tasso 9

5Apr86—Grade II; Placed third through disqualification

22Mar86-7Aqu 7f :223 :451 1:22 ft 3½ 114 32 31 1hd 14½ McHrDG4 Bay Shore 91-25 Zabaleta, Groovy, Belocolus 8

22Mar86—Grade II; Run in Divisions

26Feb86-8SA 6f :213 :441 1:09 ft 9½ 116 31 3½ 1½ 2½ McHrDG6 Ⓢ BlsaChica 92-16 Ketoh, Zabaleta, Bold And Greene 11

9Feb86-6SA 6f :211 :44 1:10 ft 4½ 117 32 2hd 11½ 1hd McHargue D G1 Mdn 88-16 Zabalet,AckAckHeir,Intuitiveness 12

Apr 26 GS 5f ft 1:01 h Apr 14 Aqu 6f ft 1:16 b ●Mar 31 Aqu 6f ft 1:132 b Mar 8 Hol 4f ft :483 h

Fobby Forbes ✻

B. c. 3, by Bold Forbes—Plum Happy, by Round Table

Br.—Due Process Stable (Fla) 1986 6 2 4 0 $249,070

Own.—Due Process Stable 126 Tr.—Garcia Carlos A 1985 2 2 0 0 $14,400

Lifetime 8 4 4 0 $263,470

19Apr86-9GS 1⅛ :462 1:113 1:51 ft 2½ 115 611 43 3½ 1½ RomroRP10 Garden St 74-21 FobbyForbes,Zabalet,MircleWood 10

5Apr86-9GS 1 :462 1:114 1:384ft *8-5 116 44½ 52½ 3½ 2½ RomrRP9 Chrry Hill H 80-22 BordxBob,FobbyForbs,MrclWood 12

19Mar86-6GS 1 :47 1:123 1:392ft *2-5 115 55 21 12 14½ Romero R P2 Aw12500 78-28 FobbyForbs,Dnny'sKys,NorthForst 7

19Mar86—Changed reins,clr

1Mar86-8Pim 1 1/16 :464 1:112 1:441ft 5½ 116 64¾ 53½ 23½ 2no HunterMT5 Fred Tesio 83-20 BrodBrush,FobbyForbes,DoublFint 7

20Feb86-8Pim 1 1/16 :472 1:124 1:453m 8-5 116 32½ 31½ 1hd 1¾ † HuntrMT6 Gen George 76-25 ‡FobbyForbs,LilTylr,ForkUnionCdt 6

†20Feb86—Disqualified and placed second; Bore in; Run in divisions

1Feb86-8Lrl 7f :231 :464 1:241ft 2 112 65½ 75 53½ 21 HntrMT2 F. Scott Key 89-12 Big Plop, Fobby Forbes,Spiderman 7

31Dec85-8Lrl 1 1/16 :482 1:14 1:464ft *7-5 114 3½ 11 12½ 13½ Hunter M T9 Aw13000 79-21 FobbyForbes,BelivItAll,CrckdWht 10

15Dec85-5Lrl 7f :23 :47 1:243ft 7½ 120 86 63¾ 22 1no Hunter M T12 Mdn 88-17 FobbyForbes,ClicoJk,Alden'sIgloo 12

Apr 28 CD 5f ft 1:00 h ●Apr 13 Lrl 5f ft 1:00 h Apr 3 Lrl 3f ft :363 b ●Mar 28 Lrl 5f ft 1:003 h

The public sent Snow Chief off as the favorite, but at 2–1 odds it was clear he was not considered to be a sure winner. Badger Land was next at 5–2 odds, and, after him, no other horse was better than 8–1. Our experience at the Derby has been that the favorite is a good Dr. Z bet to place and/or to show. This year was different only in that there were Dr. Z bets to show on both favorites, Snow Chief and Badger Land. It seemed like a great opportunity for some financial diversification! The final Derby mutuels for the two horses were:

	Totals	#7 Badger Land	#9 Snow Chief	Expected Value per Dollar Bet on Badger Land	Expected Value per Dollar Bet on Snow Chief
Win	2,981,734	679,529	785,434		
Show	1,176,247	185,640	184,032	1.11	1.20

The Beat the Racetrack Calculator™ gave optimal bets of $60 and $368 for Badger Land and Snow Chief, respectively. The calculator supposes only one bet is made at a time, not two as in this case. So I had to make an ad-hoc adjustment to these amounts. The proper adjustment seemed to be to lower each bet somewhat. I also decided to let dosage theory play a part in this adjustment and lowered Snow Chief's bet a greater percentage than Badger Land's. Therefore, $50 on Badger Land and $300 on Snow Chief seemed reasonable.

Badger Land's chances of winning dissolved immediately after the gates opened. Squeezed at the start, he began the race trailing the fifteen other horses. Badger Land's early speed was not to be a factor in the race. He began his long rally back and, by the mile mark, had courageously worked his way from the outside to third, but it had cost him too dearly, and he fell to fifth at the finish.

Snow Chief, on the other hand, did not seem to have any excuses. Nor, to his credit, were any offered by his trainer, Mel Stute. Well positioned early in the race, Snow Chief even gained the lead as the horses were turning for home. But shortly thereafter he faded and finished a distant eleventh. Rampage's fate was sealed when he found himself boxed in by a fading Snow Chief ahead and Wheatly Hall at his right. Checking himself, working to the outside, and then finishing very strongly was only good enough for fourth.

The 17–1 long shot, Ferdinand, was the eventual winner, but required a brilliant ride by Bill Shoemaker. Ferdinand and Mogambo, in the first two post positions, both had to check themselves at the start when Icy Groom and Wise Times dropped in. Ferdinand, unlike Badger Land, had closing speed, so Shoemaker kept him on the rail and let him fall back until,

EIGHTH RACE
Churchill
MAY 3, 1986

1 ¼ MILES. (1.59⅖) 112th Running THE KENTUCKY DERBY Grade I. $350,000 Added. 3-year-olds with an entry fee of $10,000 each and a starting fee of $10,000 each. All fees will be paid to the winner. $350,000 added shall be paid by Churchill Downs Incorporated as the Added Purse. Second place shall receive $100,000, third place shall receive $50,000 and fourth place shall receive $25,000 from the Added Purse (the Added Purse and fees to be divided equally in the event of a dead heat). Starters shall be named through the entry box on Thursday, May 1, 1986, at the usual time of closing (the "Closing"). The maximum number of starters shall be limited to twenty (20) and each shall carry a weight of 126 pounds. In the event that more than twenty entries pass through the entry box at the Closing, the starters shall be determined at the Closing with preference given to those horses that have accumulated the highest earnings in graded sweepstakes, including all money paid for performance in such Graded Stakes. Should additional starters be needed to bring the field to 20, the remaining starters shall be determined at the Closing with preference given to those horses that have accumulated the highest earnings in Non-Restricted Sweepstakes. For purposes of this preference, a "Non-Restricted Sweepstakes" shall mean those Sweepstakes whose conditions contain no other restrictions other than that of age or sex. In the case of ties resulting from preference or otherwise, the additional starter(s) shall be determined by lot. An "also eligible" list will not be maintained and in no event will starters be added or allowed to run in the race which are not determined to be starters at the Closing. The owner of the winner for the race shall receive a gold trophy. Nominations to each and all of the Triple Crown races, The Kentucky Derby, The Preakness and The Belmont (the "Races"), may be made only by payment of a single subscription fee to Triple Crown Productions, Inc., as agent for Churchill Downs Incorporated. The Maryland Jockey Club, and the New York Racing Association Inc. (The Associations"). The subscription fee for 422 nominations received by January 15, 1986, is $600 and for 30 nominations received by March 17, 1986 is $3,000. (These fees are to be apportioned equally among the three Associations to be part of the total purse for each of the three races.) No supplementary nominations for any of the races will be accepted.
Value of race $784,400; value to winner $609,400; second $100,000; third $50,000; fourth $25,000. Mutuel pool $5,350,857. Exacta Pool $814,262.

Last Raced	Horse	Eqt.	A.	Wt	PP	¼	½	¾	1	Str	Fin	Jockey	Odds $1
6Apr86 5SA3	Ferdinand		3	126	1	15hd	16	11½	5½	11	12¼	Shoemaker W	17.70
24Apr86 7Kee3	Bold Arrangement		3	126	4	14hd	11½	7½	2½	3½	2¾	McCarron C J	9.10
19Apr86 8Aqu1	Broad Brush		3	126	9	71½	6½	61½	1hd	2hd	3nk	Bracciale V Jr	14.40
19Apr86 9OP1	Rampage		3	126	8	111½	101½	91	72	63	41½	Day P	9.00
5Apr86 10Hia1	Badger Land	b	3	126	10	9½	9½	81	3½	43	54	Velasquez J	2.60
19Apr86 9OP2	Wheatly Hall		3	126	11	8½	7½	51½	61	5hd	61½	Stevens G L	47.70
19Apr86 9GS1	Fobby Forbes		3	126	16	12hd	12½	14hd	101½	7½	73¼	Romero R P	f-16.00
24Apr86 7Kee4	Icy Groom		3	126	5	10hd	131½	121	9½	83	82	Maple E	f-16.00
12Apr86 7Kee1	Wise Times	b	3	126	3	13½	15½	151½	111½	10hd	9nk	Allen K K	f-16.60
19Apr86 8Aqu2	Mogambo		3	126	2	16	14½	16	145	112½	103¾	Vasquez J	8.80
6Apr86 5SA1	Snow Chief	b	3	126	12	45	46	3hd	41	9hd	11nk	Solis A	2.10
19Apr86 9GS2	Zabaleta	b	3	126	15	21	21½	21½	8½	123½	123	McHargue D G	f-16.00
12Apr86 8Pim5	Southern Appeal	b	3	126	6	6½	51½	10hd	13½	132	138½	Davidson J	f-16.00
24Apr86 7Kee1	Bachelor Beau	b	3	126	13	31	3½	42	12hd	146	1411	Melancon L	60.00
19Apr86 8GG1	Vernon Castle		3	126	7	5hd	83	13hd	16	152	157½	Delahoussaye E	12.20
19Apr86 8Aqu3	Groovy		3	126	14	11	11	1hd	152	16	16	Pincay L Jr	57.30

f—Mutuel field.

OFF AT 5:40. Start good. Won driving. Time, :22⅕, :45⅕, 1:10⅕, 1:37, 2:02⅘ Track fast.

$2 Mutuel Prices:				
	1-FERDINAND	**37.40**	**16.20**	**8.60**
	3-BOLD ARRANGEMENT		**9.40**	**6.80**
	6-BROAD BRUSH			**9.20**
	$2 EXACTA (1-3) PAID $385.00.			

Ch. c, by Nijinsky II—Banja Luka, by Double Jay. Trainer Whittingham Charles. Bred by Keck H B (Ky).

FERDINAND bothered following the start, dropped well back while lacking room along the inside racing to the first turn, came out while beginning to advance after entering the backstretch, moved through inside the leaders after splitting horses through the upper stretch and drew away under lefthanded pressure. BOLD ARRANGEMENT, outrun early, rallied while racing well out in the track approaching the end of the backstretch, loomed boldly between horses leaving the far turn and continued on with good courage to gain the place. BROAD BRUSH, reserved into the backstretch, made a bold bid between horses nearing the stretch but wasn't good enough in a long drive. RAMPAGE, steadied along early, was moving well when blocked behind a wall of horses nearing the stretch, was checked again when unable to find room inside SNOW CHIEF approaching the final furlong, then finished well after angling out for room. BADGER LAND lacked room after the start, moved boldly around horses approaching the stretch but weakened during the drive. WHEATLY HALL moved up approaching the far turn, remained a factor to the stretch and tired. FOBBY FORBES failed to be a serious factor while racing very wide during the late stages. ICY GROOM angled over shortly after the start tightening it up on FERDINAND, MOGAMBO and WISE TIMES, then failed to be a serious factor. WISE TIMES, forced to steady soon after the start, was always outrun. MOGAMBO lacked room after the start and was never close. SNOW CHIEF, allowed to follow the early leaders, gained a brief advantage approaching the five-sixteenth pole, moved to the inside leaving the far turn and gave way readily under pressure. ZABALETA prompted the pace into the backstretch, reached the front briefly when GROOVY gave way suddenly at the far turn, then was bothered along the inside while tiring after entering the stretch. SOUTHERN APPEAL tired. BACHELOR BEAU raced forwardly to the far turn and had nothing left. VERNON CASTLE was finished early while saving ground. GROOVY saved ground while showing speed to the far turn and stopped suddenly.

Owners— 1, Keck Mrs H B; 2, Richards A & R; 3, Meyerhoff Robert E; 4, Reed Mr-Mrs H J; 5, Lukas-Lukas & Hatley; 6, McKinnon J; 7, Due Process Stable; 8, Fleming W; 9, R L Reineman Stable Inc; 10, Brant & Calumet Farm; 11, Grinstead & Rochelle; 12, Riordan M D; 13, Bender H M; 14, Waterfield & Tafel; 15, Paulson A E (Lessee); 16, Ballis J A.

Trainers— 1, Whittingham Charles; 2, Brittain Clive E; 3, Small Richard W; 4, Thomas Gary A; 5, Lukas D Wayne; 6, Van Berg Jack C; 7, Garcia Carlos A; 8, Ramer Sam T; 9, Gleaves Philip; 10, Jolley Leroy; 11, Stute Melvin F; 12, Gosden John; 13, Moncrief Marvin L; 14, Hauswald Philip; 15, Sullivan John; 16, Crowell Howard.

by the first turn, he was in last place. He began to pick up horses on the backstretch and, coming out of the final turn, he was near the lead but behind a wall of horses. Rather than lose ground by going to the outside, Shoemaker's experienced eye discerned the makings of an opening. From the outside of Wheatly Hall, Ferdinand darted ahead and inside to gain the rail, and then from there, he squeezed by Broad Brush to gain the lead. A pretty daring move for any jockey, let alone a fifty-four-year-old one! Ferdinand then drew away to win by more than 2 lengths over Bold Arrangement and Broad Brush. Twenty-one years after winning his third Derby, Shoemaker had finally captured number four! The chart of the race is on page 333.

Dosage theory once again demonstrated its power when Ferdinand, a low-dosage horse, prevailed, while the favored Snow Chief, a high-dosage horse, finished far back at eleventh. Perhaps the race also said something about the use of medications. Of the sixteen horses, the only two not on Butazolidin and/or Lasix were the top two horses, Ferdinand and Bold Arrangement!

Ferdinand paid $37.40 to win at Churchill Downs. Each of the fifty-six sites that allowed wagering on the Derby had separate pools and, thus, each paid a different amount to win on Ferdinand. The disparity among the payoffs was astonishing. For instance, Ferdinand paid $16.80 at Hollywood Park and $90 at Evangeline Downs. A Ferdinand bettor at Hollywood must have wished he or she had been at Evangeline that day. (More details on these payoffs appear in Appendix C.)

I was also wishing that the $350 worth of wagers on Snow Chief and Badger Land had been on Ferdinand at Evangeline. However, there was still a profit of $202 for the day. It was clear there were others using our system and it was also clear that this reduced the profit possible, but positive profits still seemed to be the order of Derby Day.

The 1987 Derby took place after we completed this book so we were unable to describe here our results there. However we were able to add the dosage aspects to Appendix C.

BETTING THE FAVORITE TO SHOW IN THE KENTUCKY DERBY

The favorite in the Kentucky Derby is usually a good bet to show. People want to pick the Derby winner, not the show horse. Hence the show odds are usually very good on these top horses and provide a substantial edge. Let's look at some of them and keep track of their dosage indices as well (consult Appendix C for details on dosage):

		Totals	#9 Snow Chief	% of Pool	Edge (%)
1986	Odds		2–1		
	Win	2,981,734	785,434	26	
	Show	1,176,247	184,032	16	16

Result: Snow Chief was 11th, so the bet was lost. DI = 5.00 > 4.00 (the suggested largest DI for a horse to be a classic contender and thus to have a good chance of doing well in the Derby).

		Totals	#3 Chief's Crown	% of Pool	Edge (%)
1985	Odds		6–5		
	Win	2,908,203	1,096,756	38	
	Show	1,047,040	259,971	25	16

Result: Chief's Crown was third and paid $2.80 to show. DI = 5.00 > 4.00.

		Totals	#1 Althea	% of Pool	Edge (%)
1984	Odds		1–1		
	Win	2,964,252	1,777,438	40	
	Show	646,965	176,024	27	21

Result: Althea finished nineteenth, and Life's Magic coupled with Althea finished eighth, so the bet was lost. DI = 5.55 > 4.00 for Althea, DI = 1.89 < 4.00 for Life's Magic.

		Totals	#8 Sunny's Halo	% of Pool	Edge (%)
1983	Odds		5–2		
	Win	3,143,669	745,529	24	
	Show	1,099,990	179,758	16	14

Result: Sunny's Halo won the race and paid $4 to show. DI = 1.82 < 4.00.

		Totals	#1 Air Forbes Won	% of Pool	Edge (%)
1982	Odds		5–2		
	Win	2,853,976	641,476	22	
	Show	1,006,969	129,486	13	25

Result: Air Forbes Won finished seventh, so the bet was lost. DI > 4.00.

		Totals	*#4 Pleasant Colony*	*% of Pool*	*Edge (%)*
1981	Odds		7–2		
	Win	2,614,993	480,510	18	
	Show	950,079	132,845	14	9

Result: Pleasant Colony won the race and paid $4.40 to show. DI = 1.32 < 4.00.

We have been going to the Derby each year since 1981 and bet on these six horses. The result was three winners out of six bets with a flat bet loss of 7%:

$$\frac{0+2.80+0+4.00+0+4.40}{6\ \$2} = 7\%\ \text{loss.}$$

There was a small loss on the six bets but over the years such bets have usually been well worth making. If you made equal flat bets on all of the Kentucky Derby favorites from 1960 to 1980, as shown in Table 12.1, you would have collected a show payoff in eighteen of the twenty-one years that varied from $2.20 to $3.60 for a rate of profit of 25.7%. For the period from 1960 to 1986 you would have collected in twenty-one of the twenty-six years for a rate of profit of 16.3%. We, of course, recommend that you bet only when you have a sufficient edge to make back the track take and breakage plus an average edge of 10% or more. For place and show bets we recommend using an edge of about 10% as the cutoff on the very best races, about 14% for general races at the top tracks (see page 106 for a list of them) and 18% on the remaining tracks. Except for 1979, we do not have access to the exact pool values but, as detailed in Table 12.1, it is clear that at least eleven of the bets had an edge of 10% or more.

Combining the Dr. Z system with dosage provides an even more powerful system. The idea is to wager on the Dr. Z horses only when they are classic contenders. With this filter rule, the winning bet on Chief's Crown would have not been made, but the losses on Snow Chief, Althea, Air Forbes Won, and Rockhill Native would have been avoided. From 1972–86, years for which we have the data, such a system would have made at least eight or as many as twelve bets, all of which were winners.

The necessary modification to really bet in the most advantageous fashion is to combine the dosage theory with the Dr. Z method using probabilities that combine the track odds with the dosage index. Such an approach is explored in Hausch, Winkler, and Ziemba (1987).

TABLE 12.1 ***Results of betting the favorite in the Kentucky Derby to show 1960–1980***

Year	*Name of Favorite*	*Odds*	*Finish*	*Payoff to Show ($)*	*Dr. Z System Bet with an Edge of 10% or more?*	*Dosage Index ≤ 4.00*
1980	Rockhill Native	2–1	5th	0	Can't Tell	No
1979	Spectacular Bid	3–5	1st	2.80	For Sure[a]	Yes
1978	Alydar	6–5	2nd	2.40	Can't Tell	Yes
1977	Seattle Slew	1–2	1st	2.80	For Sure	Yes
1976	Honest Pleasure	2–5	2nd	2.20	Probably	Yes
1975	Foolish Pleasure	9–5	1st	3.60	For Sure	Yes
1974	Cannonade (entry with Judger who finished eighth)	3–2	1st	2.40	Can't Tell	Yes
1973	Secretariat	3–2	1st	3	For Sure	Yes
1972	Riva Ridge	3–2	1st	3	For Sure	Yes
1971	Unconscious	5–2	5th	0	Can't Tell	DNA[b]
1970	My Dad George	5–2	2nd	3.20	Probably	DNA
1969	Majestic Prince	7–5	1st	2.60	Probably	Yes
1968	Forward Pass	2–1	2nd	3.20	Probably	DNA
1967	Damascus	8–5	3rd	3.40	For Sure	DNA
1966	Kauai King	2–1	1st	3.60	For Sure	Yes
1965	Bold Lad	2–1	10th	0	Can't Tell	DNA
1964	Hill Rise	7–5	2nd	2.60	Probably	DNA
1963	Candy Spots	3–2	3rd	2.80	For Sure	DNA
1962	Ridan	1–1	3rd	3	For Sure	DNA
1961	Carry Back	5–2	1st	3.20	Probably	Yes
1960	Bally Ache	8–5	2nd	3	For Sure	DNA

[a]The edge on Spectacular Bid was 31% with the following tote board values:

	Totals	#3 Spectacular Bid	% of Pool	Edge
Win	2,307,288	1,164,220	51	
Show	749,274	195,419	26	31%

[b]Data not available to us

13

Betting on Favorites

BETTING TO WIN MAY BE PROFITABLE WITH GOOD HANDICAPPING

In Chapter Three we presented considerable evidence that favorites are underbet to win by about 7% (see Tables 3.1 and 3.5 and Figures 3.1 and 3.2). Thus if the track take is 15%, as it is at Churchill Downs, then the strategy of betting all favorites to win would likely lose about 8%, plus breakage of about 3% (with Churchill Downs's 10¢ breakage), for a total loss of about 11%. Presumably, good handicapping would eliminate some of the losers and also horses that are poor bets (that is, those going off at lower odds than their chance of winning), so a modified system would actually achieve profits. Since it is not our intention in this book to discuss handicapping methods in detail (although some hints appear in Chapters Fourteen and Sixteen), we will not pursue this possibility here either. But we mention it here for those readers who are skilled in handicapping and who wish to develop such procedures. We now turn our attention to place and show betting on the favorite.

BETTING THE FAVORITE TO PLACE OR SHOW

An interesting and easy strategy to follow is always to bet the favorite of the crowd to place or show. Generally, this will be a *losing* strategy. As with win bets, the favorites are underbet, so the actual average loss will generally be about 5%–10% less than the track take plus breakage. However, if you restrict your bets to horses that have good *odds* for place or show, then it can be a winning strategy.

Table 13.1 provides details on such bets over 1,080 races, on 120 days

TABLE 13.1 ***Rate of return versus expected value for favored horses in 1,080 races on 120 days in 1981–82 at Keystone Race Track, Bensalem, Pennsylvania***

	Place			Show					
Expected Value of a $1 Bet[a]	Number of Bets[b]	Total Profit ($)	Rate of Return (%)	Number[b] of Bets	Total Profit ($)	Rate of Return (%)	Total Number of Bets	Total Profit ($)	Rate of Return (%)
0.85 or less	104	−39.60	−38.1	9	−3.40	−37.8	113	−43.00	−38.1
0.86–0.90	175	−30.70	−17.5	44	−14.20	−32.3	219	−44.90	−20.5
0.91–0.95	264	−59.90	−22.7	131	−23.70	−18.8	395	−83.60	−21.2
0.96–1.00	219	1.50	+0.7	252	−28.05	−11.1	471	−26.55	−5.6
1.01–1.05	151	−15.70	−10.4	214	−17.70	−8.3	365	−33.40	−9.2
1.06–1.10	80	−4.40	−5.5	188	−30.80	−11.1	268	−25.20	−9.4
1.11–1.17	44	−1.50	−3.4	129	−5.30	−4.1	173	−6.80	−3.9
1.18–1.20	15	7.50	+50.5	33	3.50	+10.6	48	+11.00	+22.9
1.21–1.25	16	−2.40	−15.0	35	7.60	+21.7	51	+5.20	+10.2
1.26–1.30	8	3.70	+46.3	20	10.80	+54.0	28	+14.50	+51.9
1.31–1.35	—	—	—	9	−3.00	−33.3	9	−3.00	−33.3
1.36–1.40	1	1.40	+140.4	5	3.60	+72.0	6	+5.00	+83.3
1.41–1.45	—	—	—	3	3.80	+126.7	3	+3.80	+126.7
1.46 or more	1	−1.00	−100.0	3	2.90	+36.7	4	+1.90	+47.5
Totals	1,078	−141.1	−13.1	1,075	−83.95	−7.8	2,153	−225.05	−10.5
				Summary					
1.00 or less	762	−128.7	−16.9	436	−69.35	−15.9	1,198	−198.05	−16.5
1.01–1.17	275	−21.60	−7.9	531	−43.80	−8.3	806	−65.40	−8.1
1.18 or more	41	9.20	22.4	108	29.20	27.0	149	38.40	25.8

[a]Computed using the Exhibition Park regression equations (4.3) and (4.4).

[b]Data were unavailable for a few races, so the total number of races is slightly less than 1,080.

from September 13 to December 13, 1981, and February 8 to March 27, 1982, at Keystone Race Track in Bensalem, Pennsylvania. These data were generously supplied to us by Jerry Rosenwald of Havertown, Pennsylvania. The favorite to win is determined for each race. Then using the Exhibition Park regression equations (4.3) and (4.4), the expected value of a $1 bet to place and show is estimated, based on the final tote-board values. These are categorized as 0.85 or less, 0.86–0.9, and so on, all the way to 1.40–1.45, and 1.46 or more. Recall that 1.40 means that one expects to receive $1.40, or 40¢ profit for each dollar wagered according to these formulas.

The table shows that if you make place or show bets on horses with an expected value of 1.00 or less, you will have losses of about 16.5%. Since Keystone is in Pennsylvania, its track take is 17%. Keystone's 5¢ breakage—that is, their rounding down to the nearest 10¢ on each $2 bet—amounts to about another 1.5% for favorites. Thus bets on favored horses with an expected value of 1.00 or less gain about 2% (18.5% − 16.5%) above the average bet made by the crowd. Bets on horses with an expected value between 1.01 and 1.17 lose about 8%, or are about 10.5% (18.5% − 8%) better than chance. Betting on every favorite results in losses of 13.1% to place and 7.8% to show, or an average of 10.5%. This is an improvement of about 8% (18.5% − 10.5%) over chance. Thus the underbetting-of-favorites bias for place and show betting is similar to that for win bets.

If, however, you stick to place and show bets where the expected value is 1.18 or more, then you can make substantial *profits*. Indeed, over this 120-day racing period, there were forty-one such place bets that returned an average profit of 22.4% and 107 show bets that returned an average profit of 27%. In total, the 149 bets returned an average profit of 25.8%. The value of 1.18 for the cutoff maximizes total profits; this value is typical for a "medium-quality" track such as Keystone.

Notice that bets are not placed on each race. In fact, only one or two bets of this type are made on a typical day. The horses bet on are all favorites; thus they will be coming in the money about 60%–70% of the time. This strategy is a very safe, conservative approach, and you do not need a large fortune to make relatively sizable bets. Of course, these extra bets would depress the odds to place and show slightly, so actual winnings would be a little less than the 25.8% profit rate. For example, starting with a bankroll of $1,500 and making bets of $250 on each of these horses would result in a profit of about ($250)(149)(0.258) = $9,610. This is a handsome profit, considering that you are taking very little risk. In fact, the chance of ever losing the $1,500 during an entire season of betting is only about 4% if we assume that favorites are in the money about 65% of the time.* That 4%

*As experts in probability theory will note, this value is obtained by summing the binomial probabilities that consider all the possible sequences of wins and losses that lead to ruin.

represents a chance of about 1 in 25. This compares very favorably with random betting, where you almost certainly will lose the entire $1,500. If you bet $25 per race with a bankroll of $150, then your expected profit will be $961 and the chance of losing the entire $150 will still be 4%.

The $250 we just cited is a typical betting amount for a serious application of such a system. Individuals might wish to bet more or less in each race. The more you bet, the larger your total profits will tend to be. However, because large bets will reduce the payoff in a parimutuel system, the individual payoffs per dollar bet will decrease and the risk of losing your bankroll will increase.

In the basic Dr. Z system advocated in this book, you make bets on horses other than the favorite using charts that have been provided to indicate the size of the optimal bet. Nevertheless, as the data in Table 13.1 indicate, a flat bet on the favorite to place or show when the place or show odds are favorable is a very good strategy.

BETTING EXTREME FAVORITES: THE BALLERINA, EXHIBITION PARK, OCTOBER 11, 1982

Horses that go off at odds of about 1–2 or less may be classified as extreme favorites. Betting on such horses to win may seem quite risky, since they must win at least two of every three races to break even. However, they often are outstanding place or show bets.

The eighth running of The Ballerina, a $50,000 added feature race at Exhibition Park on October 11, 1982, provides such an example. The field of eleven contained two long-shot entries and a large group of strong horses. Davette was a late scratch. The invader from Longacres in Renton, Washington, Belle of Rainier, completely outclassed the field. Belle of Rainier had twelve wins and fifteen in-the-money finishes in eighteen career races against very high caliber competition. Her advantageous post position, number 1, and the reliability of her steady jockey, D. Sorensen, seemed to overcome her high weight assignment of 126 pounds. Belle of Rainier was the top pick of all the *Daily Racing Form*'s experts. She was the day's best bet of four of the five experts and the consensus best bet with a rating of 33 out of a possible 35.

EXPERTS' SELECTIONS

Consensus Points: 5 for 1st (best 7), 2 for 2d, 1 for 3d. Best in CAPITALS.

Trackman, Tim Toon | **EXHIBITION PARK** | **Selections Made for Fast Track**

RACE	TRACKMAN	HERMIS	HANDICAP	ANALYST	SWEEP	CONSENSUS	
9	BELLE OF RAINIER Okan Dee Select Brief Grief	BELLE OF RAINIER Okan Dee Select Miss Zulu Gold	BELLE OF RAINIER Au Printemps Okan Dee Select	BELLE OF RAINIER Okan Dee Select Au Printemps	Belle of Rainier Indellare Miss Zulu Gold	BELLE OF RAINIER Okan Dee Select Au Printemps	33 7 3

9

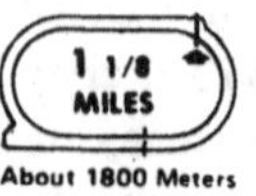

About 1800 Meters

EXACTOR FEATURE

THE 8th RUNNING OF "THE BALLERINA" — $50,000-added. A handicap for fillies and mares three-year-olds and upward. by subscription of $100 each, $300 to pass the entry wicket and $100 to start. With $50,000 added of which $31,500 to the winner, $10,000 to second, $5,000 to third, $2,500 to fourth and $1,000 to fifth. All nomination, entry and starting fees to be divided: 70% to the winner, 20% to second and 10% to third. Weights to be announced Monday, October 4th. Starters to be named through the entry wicket Friday, October 8th by 8:30 a.m. Closed with 11 nominations.

SELECTIONS: 3—9—6

ASK FOR HORSE BY THIS NUMBER	OWNER	TRAINER	Post Position Jockey Morning Line
1	Irene Reed Blue, gold trim, "MIR" on back **DREAM DISTURBER** 112 Ch m 6. Winning Shot—Seldom Dreams	Pat Jarvis	P.P. 2 Joel Mena 30
1A	Mr. & Mrs. A. Jarvis Lilac, green trim, "J" on back **DAVETTE** 113 Roan f 4. No Back Talk—Yukon Belle	A. Jarvis	P.P. 4 D. J. Zook 30
2	M. & W. Bowes & F. Reichelt Green, gold trim, gold sash front & back **CHEMAINUS BELLE** 113 Roan f 4. Keep Your Promise—Satin Sue	W. Bowes	P.P. 3 Danny Williams 30
2B	Norland Stable Green, yellow & orange hoops **BLUSHING MINSTREL** 112 Dk b/br f 4. Borrower—Taos Trail	E. Sams	P.P. 12 Ray Creighton 30
3	Al Benton Royal blue, white V front and back **BELLE OF RAINIER** 126 Ro f 3. Windy Tide—Lap Wing	William Findlay	P.P. 1 Danny Sorenson 8/5
4	Tri Star Stable, Bowie & D. Bowman Red, gold trim, 3 stars on back **AU PRINTEMPS** 116 B f 3. Dancing Champ—*Lorgnette II	D. Forster	P.P. 5 Brian Johnson 8
5	Mrs. B. Dahl Light & dark blue vertical stripes **OKAN DEE SELECT** 120 Dk b/br f 3. Docile Boy—Marnie Dee	B. Dahl	P.P. 6 Mark Patzer 6
6	B.C. Interior Stock Farm Yellow, black diamonds, "BCI" on back & sleeves **CINDERS SHADOW** 116 Dk b/br m 6. Ship Leave—Shy Shadow	Frank Barroby	P.P. 7 Joan Phipps 6
7	J. Diamond Blue, white diamonds on back & sleeves **SALT TREATY** 112 B f 4. Bold Reason—Gay Gusher	H. Johnson	P.P. 8 Chad Hoverson 20
8	Elmbrook Stables Yellow, green trim, emblem on back **INDELLARE** 119 B f 4. Indefatigable—Emellare	A. May	P.P. 9 Chris Loseth 12
9	Pour Four Stable White, red flames, emblem on back **MISS ZULU GOLD** 117 Ch f 3. Zulu Tom—Norm's Choice	H. Belvoir	P.P. 10 Sam Krasner 6
10	Connie Guindon All red **BRIEF GRIEF** 120 Ch m 5. Sandy Fleet—Good Grief Mama	T. Taylor	P.P. 11 Victor Mercado 8

No. 1 & 1A—Dream Disturber and Davette, coupled

No. 2 & 2B—Chemainus Belle and Blushing Minstrel, coupled

DECLARED — Lady Of York

9th Exhibition

1⅛ MILES. (1.48⅖) 8th Running THE BALLERINA HANDICAP. $50,000 Added. Fillies and Mares, 3-year-olds and upward. By subscription of $100 each, $300 to pass the entry wicket and $100 to start. With $50,000 added of which $31,500 to the winner, $10,000 to second, $5,000 to third, $2,500 to fourth and $1,000 to fifth. All nomination entry and starting fees to be divided 70% to the winner, 20% to second and 10% to third.

Belle of Rainier *

Ro. f. 3, by Windy Tide—Lap Wing, by Donut King
Br.—Benton A (Wash) 1982 9 6 0 0 $132,615
Own.—Benton A 126 **Tr.—Findlay William A** 1981 9 6 2 1 $142,066
Lifetime 18 12 2 1 $274,681

26Sep82-9Lga	1 3/16	:48	1:14^{1}	2:01^{4}sl	*1	121	$1^{3½}$	1^{2}	$1^{3½}$	1^{2}	SrnsD^{6}	ⒻB Roberts H	61	Belle of Rainier, Gi Gi, Latrone	14
4Sep82-9EP	1 1/16	:47^{4}	1:13	1:46^{2}m	*3-4	127	1^{1}	$1^{1½}$	$1^{1½}$	1^{3}	SrnsnD^{1}	ⒻSenorita H	79	BllofRnr,APrntmps,Chftn'sCmmnd	9
29Aug82-9Lga	1⅛	:46^{4}	1:10^{4}	1:49^{2}ft	*3-4	124	$1^{1½}$	2^{hd}	1^{3}	1^{4}	SrnsD^{1}	ⒻSacajawea H	86	BellofRinir,OknDSlct,MissZuluGold	6
15Aug82-9Lga	1 3/16	:46^{3}	1:11^{3}	1:58^{1}ft	4	118	2^{hd}	$1^{½}$	$4^{5½}$	5^{11}	SrnsnD^{6}	Lga Derby H	68	Cassaleria,FlyingJudgement,GlArry	9
31Jly82-9Lga	1 1/16	:46^{1}	1:11	1:43^{4}ft	*2-3	123	$1^{3½}$	1^{3}	1^{2}	$1^{2½}$	SrnsnD^{8}	ⒻM Donohoe	80	BellofRinir,OknDSlct,NoMorLmons	9
10Jly82-9Lga	1	:45^{3}	1:10	1:34^{4}ft	*2-3	120	$1^{1½}$	1^{2}	1^{3}	$1^{5½}$	SornsnD^{2}	ⒻB. Ross H	95	BllofRnr,NoMorLmons,MssZulGold	9
19Jun82-9Lga	6½f	:21^{3}	:44^{3}	1:16^{4}ft	*3-5	123	$5^{4¾}$	5^{5}	$6^{6½}$	$4^{2½}$	SornsnD^{8}	ⒻMs Stakes	82	NoMorLmons,EsyTrmph,SddnWnds	8
22May82-9Lga	6f	:22	:45	1:09^{2}ft	*4-5	120	2^{2}	$2^{1½}$	$1^{½}$	1^{5}	SornsnD^{1}	ⒻIngenue H	89	BellofRinir,NoMorLmons,RoylTurn	6
28Apr82-9Lga	5½f	:21^{3}	:45^{2}	1:05 gd	*3-5	118	2^{hd}	$1^{½}$	2^{hd}	$6^{6¾}$	SornsonD^{8}	Ⓕ[S]Seafair	80	MssZuluGold,HYuLulu,BrroomBby	12
30Oct81-8BM	6f	:22	:47^{4}	1:10^{3}ft	*4-5	120	2^{3}	$2^{1½}$	2^{hd}	1^{3}	SrnsnD^{3}	ⒻBurlingame	87	BellofRinir,GoldnPlum,AuPrintmps	9

Dream Disturber *

Ch. m. 6, by Winning Shot—Seldom Dreams, by Mr Mustard
Br.—O'Connor H R (BC-C) 1982 11 2 0 0 $11,853
Own.—Reed Mrs I 112 **Tr.—Jarvis Pat** 1981 13 2 4 2 $20,271
Lifetime 45 11 5 5 $50,890

2Oct82-8EP	1 1/16	:47^{4}	1:14^{3}	1:48 m	2½	114	3^{4}	4^{5}	$3^{6½}$	$4^{6¼}$	JohnsnBG^{5}	ⒻAw10000	65	LdyofYork,BlushingMinstrel,Indellr	8
17Sep82-9EP	1 1/16	:47	1:12	1:45^{2}ft	*3-2	113	1^{hd}	$1^{2½}$	$1^{2½}$	$1^{2½}$	Johnson B G^{1}	Ⓕ 40000	84	DrmDisturbr,DncingProud,BonnLos	7
27Aug82-7EP	6½f	:22^{1}	:45^{3}	1:16^{3}ft	6½	113	$6^{7¾}$	$6^{3¼}$	1^{2}	1^{8}	Johnson B G^{2}	Ⓕ 32000	95	DrmDsturbr,Ldd'sLss,MdmSplndor	7
13Aug82-9EP	6½f	:22^{3}	:46	1:19^{4}m	21	110^{5}	7^{12}	7^{15}	5^{12}	$4^{5½}$	Adcock T^{7}	Ⓕ 32000	73	CrftyMdm,MdmSplndor,WdmntClr	7
23Jly82-9EP	1 1/16	:48	1:13	1:45^{3}ft	17	109^{5}	$3^{1½}$	$6^{2¼}$	$7^{5¾}$	$5^{7¾}$	Adcock T^{4}	Ⓕ 32000	75	Bonnie Lois, Tru Talk, Struckup	9
18Jun82-9Lga	1 1/16	:47	1:12^{4}	1:44^{4}ft	16	117	4^{7}	$8^{6¼}$	7^{9}	6^{17}	Loseth C^{1}	ⒻAw8800	58	ThreeMisses,TniMoro,EsterFredom	8
12Jun82-9Lga	1 1/16	:47	1:12^{1}	1:45^{1}ft	34	116	4^{9}	$6^{5¾}$	4^{5}	$5^{6¼}$	Loseth C^{2}	ⒻAw11000	67	LovelyWine,PrunePickr,ConniCoco	8
31May82-7Lga	1 1/16	:48^{1}	1:13^{1}	1:44^{3}ft	16	113	$4^{5½}$	4^{2}	5^{7}	7^{12}	Frazier B^{6}	ⒻAw11200	64	Bbe'sJoy,ConnieCoco,PrunePicker	7
26May82-9Lga	6½f	:22	:45^{3}	1:17^{1}ft	32	117	7^{6}	$8^{8½}$	$7^{8¾}$	7^{13}	Frazier B^{1}	ⒻAw7200	70	Shoot It Out, Serageous, TaniMoro	8
5May82-9Lga	6f	:22	:45^{3}	1:09^{3}ft	14	117	$8^{5¾}$	6^{7}	$6^{7¾}$	6^{10}	Baze M B^{9}	ⒻAw9000	78	Mondolu,GoldRunLdy,Blw'sLittlSis	9

Sep 28 EP 4f ft :49 h   Sep 16 EP 3f ft :36^{2} b   Sep 7 EP 4f ft :48^{1} h

Chemainus Belle

Ro. f. 4, by Keep Your Promise—Satin Sue, by Roman Note
Br.—Reichelt Faye L (BC-C) 1982 9 1 0 2 $13,465
Own.—Bowes M & W & Reichelt 113 **Tr.—Bowes Wilf A** 1981 13 2 2 2 $12,306
Lifetime 31 3 4 5 $29,205

19Sep82-8Lga	1	:45^{3}	1:10^{3}	1:36^{4}ft	75	120	5^{7}	5^{4}	5^{7}	$3^{5½}$	HoversonC^{9}	ⒻAw12000	79	Flmme,ExpressSuccss,ChminusBll	10
12Sep82-9Lga	1⅛	:47^{1}	1:12^{3}	1:52^{4}sy	44	116	6^{8}	11^{16}	12^{33}	12^{21}	Hoverson C^{5}	ⒻAlki H	48	BriefGrief,ExprssSuccss,Mondolu	12
28Aug82-8EP	1 1/16	:47	1:12^{1}	1:45^{1}ft	25	115	6^{8}	$6^{6½}$	7^{11}	7^{14}	Adcock T^{2}	ⒻAw12000	71	HomeRunGl,Struckup,CindrsShdow	9
31Jly82-9EP	1 1/16	:47	1:11^{3}	1:44^{2}ft	24	113	6^{10}	$6^{7½}$	7^{10}	6^{11}	KplG^{3}	Ⓕ[S]WVncouver	78	HomRunGl,CindrsShdow,BonniLois	8
21Jly82-9EP	1 1/16	:47^{3}	1:12^{2}	1:45^{1}ft	14	115	8^{7}	$8^{6¾}$	$6^{9¾}$	6^{13}	Kipling G^{2}	ⒻAw12000	72	CindersShadow,Dvette,HomeRunGl	8
3Jly82-9EP	1 1/16	:48^{1}	1:13^{3}	1:47^{3}sy	6½	118	$8^{8¾}$	$9^{9½}$	8^{14}	7^{14}	Kipling G^{4}	ⒻVanity H	59	ThreeLeders,Dvette,CindersShdow	10
18Jun82-9EP	1 1/16	:46^{2}	1:12	1:46^{1}ft	27	115	7^{12}	$6^{4½}$	1^{2}	1^{3}	KplnG^{8}	ⒻCover Girl H	80	ChmnusBll,MdmoslIB,CndrsShdow	9
9Jun82-8EP	1 1/16	:47	1:12^{1}	1:46 ft	14	115	6^{12}	$6^{9½}$	$5^{8½}$	$3^{5½}$	Kipling G^{6}	ⒻAw8000	75	Davette,BonnieLois,CheminusBelle	7
26May82-9EP	6½f	:22^{3}	:46^{2}	1:18^{3}ft	40	115	$4^{4½}$	5^{4}	$4^{4½}$	4^{3}	Kipling G^{3}	ⒻAw8500	82	JmmedFlight,TrctbleTrdrop,SltTrty	7
26Sep81-7EP	1⅛	:46^{4}	1:12^{3}	1:52^{3}ft	80	115	12^{10}	$10^{8¾}$	9^{17}	9^{14}	Carter G^{4}	ⒻB. C. Oaks	65	Dvette,JmmedFlight,Michel'sBest	12

●Oct 5 EP 6f gd 1:15^{2} h   Sep 3 EP 5f ft 1:00^{3} h   Aug 27 EP 2f ft :23^{4} h   Aug 23 EP 5f ft 1:03 h

Davette

Ro. f. 4, by No Back Talk—Yukon Belle, by Akimbo
Br.—Jarvis Mr-Mrs A (BC-C) 1982 13 1 4 1 $20,585
Own.—Jarvis Mr-Mrs A 113 **Tr.—Jarvis Albert** 1981 15 3 0 1 $46,910
Lifetime 37 6 8 3 $100,076

2Oct82-8EP	1 1/16	:47^{4}	1:14^{3}	1:48 m	3	115	2^{hd}	2^{4}	$5^{8½}$	8^{13}	Zook D J^{1}	ⒻAw10000	58	LdyofYork,BlushingMinstrel,Indellr	8
11Sep82-8EP	1 1/16	:47^{2}	1:12^{4}	1:46^{3}m	9½	114	2^{hd}	2^{2}	$5^{6½}$	8^{10}	Zook DJ^{3}	ⒻB Belles H	68	HomeRunGl,CindersShdow,SltTrty	10
28Aug82-8EP	1 1/16	:47	1:12^{1}	1:45^{1}ft	8½	115	1^{2}	2^{hd}	3^{6}	5^{12}	Zook D J^{8}	ⒻAw12000	73	HomeRunGl,Struckup,CindrsShdow	9
14Aug82-9EP	6½f	:22^{3}	:46^{3}	1:19^{4}m	8¼	116	1^{hd}	1^{hd}	$3^{1½}$	2^{6}	Zook D J^{1}	ⒻMilady	73	OknDeeSelect,Dvette,MdmoisllBu	10
31Jly82-9EP	1 1/16	:47	1:11^{3}	1:44^{2}ft	4½	116	$1^{½}$	2^{hd}	4^{7}	7^{11}	ZDJ^{8}	Ⓕ[S]WVancouver	78	HomRunGl,CindrsShdow,BonniLois	8
21Jly82-9EP	1 1/16	:47^{3}	1:12^{2}	1:45^{1}ft	9½	115	1^{1}	1^{2}	$2^{½}$	2^{6}	Zook D J^{6}	ⒻAw12000	79	CindersShadow,Dvette,HomeRunGl	8
3Jly82-9EP	1 1/16	:48^{1}	1:13^{3}	1:47^{3}sy	4	114	1^{3}	$1^{1½}$	$2^{2½}$	2^{6}	Zook D J^{8}	ⒻVanity H	67	ThreeLeders,Dvette,CindersShdow	10
18Jun82-9EP	1 1/16	:46^{2}	1:12	1:46^{1}ft	3½	115	1^{3}	1^{2}	2^{2}	$5^{5½}$	ZkDJ^{5}	ⒻCover Girl H	74	ChmnusBll,MdmoslIB,CndrsShdow	9
9Jun82-8EP	1 1/16	:47	1:12^{1}	1:46 ft	*2¾	114	1^{2}	1^{4}	1^{6}	$1^{4½}$	Zook D J^{7}	ⒻAw8000	81	Davette,BonnieLois,CheminusBelle	7
29May82-9EP	1 1/16	:47^{2}	1:13^{2}	1:47^{2}ft	7¾	115	$3^{1½}$	$4^{1½}$	6^{12}	6^{16}	ZkDJ^{7}	ⒻVancouver H	58	MdemoiselleBeu,SernLdyB,ThrLdrs	7

Sep 30 EP 3f ft :36^{2} h   Sep 20 EP 4f ft :51^{1} b   Sep 10 EP 2f gd :26^{1} b   ●Sep 6 EP 4f ft :49 h

Au Printemps B. f. 3, by Dancing Champ—Lorgnette II, by High Hat
Br.—Livestock Consultants Inc (Md) 1982 8 3 1 1 $47,555
Own.—Bowie&Bowman&TriStrStble 116 Tr.—Forster Dave 1981 8 2 4 1 $26,108
Lifetime 16 5 5 2 $73,663
24Sep82-9EP 1⅛ :471 1:122 1:52 gd 3¾ 115 31½ 31½ 2hd 2hd JhsBG1 ⒻB C oaks H 82 ‡MssZlGld,APrntmps,ChftnsCmnd 8
24Sep82—Placed first through disqualification
11Sep82-8EP 1 1/16 :472 1:124 1:463m 3¼ 113 32½ 43½ 915 915 JhnsBG1 ⒻB Belles H 63 HomeRunGl,CindersShdow,SltTrty 10
4Sep82-9EP 1 1/16 :474 1:13 1:462m 6¾ 115 53 32½ 21½ 23 JhnsBG9 ⒻSenorita H 76 BllofRnr,APrntmps,Chftn'sCmmnd 9
20Aug82-9EP 1 1/16 :474 1:13 1:452ft *2-3e 116 53¾ 32 1hd 11 WillimsDR7 ⒻAw12000 84 AuPrintmps,MiniChillo,EsyTriumph 7
4Aug82-9EP 6½f :223 :461 1:174ft *7-5 116 96½ 65 44¼ 37¼ WllsDR8 ⒻQueenChrlo 82 MissZuluGold,LdyCeJy,AuPrintmps 9
24Jly82-3EP 6½f :23 :461 1:171ft 4¾ 116 43 31 1hd 12½ WilliamsDR5 ⒻAw8000 92 AuPrintemps,LdyCeJy,EsyTriumph 7
23Jun82-8EP 1 1/16 :471 1:122 1:451ft 2½e 116 53 44½ 49 512 WilliamsDR4 ⒻAw7000 73 OkanDeeSelect,HeavyHeart,Cedarly 8
4Jun82-8EP 6½f :224 :464 1:193ft 2¼ 120 43 42 42¾ 45¼ WilliamsDR2 ⒻAw6500 75 D.W.'sDrm,RockinHwk,AutumSpirit 9
26Dec81-8BM 1 1/16 :471 1:124 1:462ft *2¼ 112 84½ 34½ 11 2nk JhnsBG2 ⒻBm Lassie 67 BlmyDys,AuPrintmps,CountrftCon 14
4Dec81-6BM 1 :463 1:122 1:391ft *2 114 79 31 12 1¾ JohnsnBG9 ⒻAw11000 73 Au Printemps, Hazel Too, Dini K. 10
Sep 22 EP 4f ft :473 h Sep 1 EP 5f ft :594 h ●Aug 17 EP 5f ft :594 h

Okan Dee Select Dk. b. or br. f. 3, by Docile Boy—Marni Dee, by Cecil County
Br.—Hochsteiner Gail (BC-C) 1982 12 6 3 0 $83,285
Own.—Dahl Beatrice E 120 Tr.—Dahl Beatrice 1981 6 2 2 0 $11,072
Lifetime 18 8 5 0 $94,357
24Sep82-9EP 1⅛ :471 1:122 1:52 gd *2¼ 125 42½ 43 43 52¾ PtzrM8 ⒻB C oaks H 79 ‡MssZlGld,APrntmps,ChftnsCmnd 8
11Sep82-8EP 1 1/16 :472 1:124 1:463m *7-5 120 66½ 53½ 35½ 66¾ PatzerM9 ⒻB Belles H 71 HomeRunGl,CindersShdow,SltTrty 10
29Aug82-9Lga 1⅛ :464 1:104 1:492ft 9-5 120 31½ 1hd 23 24 PtzrM5 ⒻSacajawea H 82 BellofRinir,OknDSlct,MissZuluGold 6
14Aug82-9EP 6½f :223 :463 1:194m 5¼ 118 75¾ 43¼ 11½ 16 Patzer M8 ⒻMilady 79 OknDeeSelect,Dvette,MdmoisllBu 10
31Jly82-9Lga 1 1/16 :461 1:11 1:434ft 3½ 121 57½ 23 22 22½ BzeMB2 ⒻM Donohoe 77 BellofRinir,OknDSlct,NoMorLmons 9
17Jly82-8EP 1 1/16 :473 1:123 1:461ft 2 122 1hd 1hd 1hd 11 PtrM8 Ⓕ[S]LibertionH 80 OknDeeSelect,Cdrly,BoldUndrwritr 8
1Jly82-7EP 1 1/16 :473 1:122 1:444ft *7-5 119 86¾ 32 2hd 1nk PtzerM2 ⒻNanaimo H 87 OknDeeSelect,BoldUndrwritr,Cdrly 9
23Jun82-8EP 1 1/16 :471 1:122 1:451ft *6-5 1115 43 11½ 12 11¾ Patzer M6 ⒻAw7000 85 OkanDeeSelect,HeavyHeart,Cedarly 8
9Jun82-9EP 1 1/16 :473 1:132 1:454ft 17 1115 49½ 1hd 14 16 Patzer M2 ⒻAw12000 82 OknDeeSlct,CollnCrig,EsyTriumph 10
24May82-8EP 1 1/16 :48 1:14 1:473ft 6½ 117 43 31½ 69 716 PtrM7 ⒻButn &BowH 57 BorrowdMid,Rgl'sFncy,EsyTriumph 9
●Sep 19 EP 5f ft 1:013 h ●Aug 25 EP 5f ft :592 h

Cinders Shadow * Dk. b. or br. m. 6, by Ship Leave—Shy Shadow, by Merger
Br.—Hall R M (BC-C) 1982 14 3 2 3 $37,259
Own.—Hall R M 116 Tr.—Barroby Frank 1981 5 1 0 1 $5,950
Lifetime 48 11 6 7 $73,930
2Oct82-8EP 1 1/16 :474 1:143 1:48 m *2½e 117 66¾ 57 69 58 Phipps J8 ⒻAw10000 63 LdyofYork,BlushingMinstrel,Indellr 8
26Sep82-9Lga 1 1/16 :48 1:141 2:014sl 52 119 913 1091½ 1119 913 PppsJ11 ⒻB RobertsH 48 Belle of Rainier, Gi Gi, Latrone 14
11Sep82-8EP 1 1/16 :472 1:124 1:463m 30 115 42¾ 32½ 21½ 21 PhippsJ4 ⒻB Belles H 77 HomeRunGl,CindersShdow,SltTrty 10
28Aug82-8EP 1 1/16 :47 1:121 1:451ft 3¾ 115 34½ 43¾ 26 38½ HoversonC3 ⒻAw12000 76 HomeRunGl,Struckup,CindrsShdow 9
14Aug82-9EP 6½f :223 :463 1:194m 8½ 116 65¾ 78¾ 77¼ 57¼ Hoverson C5 ⒻMilady 72 OknDeeSelect,Dvette,MdmoisllBu 10
31Jly82-9EP 1 1/16 :47 1:113 1:442ft *1 118 34½ 34 25 25 HrsC1 Ⓕ[S]WVncouver 84 HomRunGl,CindrsShdow,BonniLois 8
21Jly82-9EP 1 1/16 :473 1:122 1:451ft 8½ 113 21 22 1½ 16 HoversonC1 ⒻAw12000 85 CindersShadow,Dvette,HomeRunGl 8
9Jly82-9EP 6½f :222 :46 1:182ft 3 117 44½ 42½ 11½ 12½ Hoverson C1 ⒻAw8000 86 CindersShdow,SltTrety,BonnieLois 7
3Jly82-9EP 1 1/16 :481 1:133 1:473sy 13 112 55½ 57½ 39½ 37¾ HovrsonC7 ⒻVanity H 65 ThreeLeders,Dvette,CindersShdow 10
18Jun82-9EP 1 1/16 :462 1:12 1:461ft 6 112 36 53½ 73¼ 33¾ HrsnC1 ⒻCover Girl H 76 ChmnusBll,MdmosllB,CndrsShdow 9
Sep 24 EP 3f ft :36 h Sep 18 EP 4f ft :483 h Sep 8 EP 4f ft :49 h Sep 3 EP 4f ft :484 h

Salt Treaty B. f. 4, by Bold Reason—Gay Gusher, by Tom Rolfe
Br.—Aitken E T & L F (Ky) 1982 10 0 1 2 $7,725
Own.—Diamond J 112 Tr.—Johnson Harry 1981 17 4 5 3 $38,747
Lifetime 32 6 7 5 $53,177
2Oct82-8EP 1 1/16 :474 1:143 1:48 m 5½ 113 56¾ 67½ 79¼ 68½ HoversonC6 ⒻAw10000 62 LdyofYork,BlushingMinstrel,Indellr 8
11Sep82-8EP 1 1/16 :472 1:124 1:463m 10e 111 711 75½ 46½ 36 HvrsnC10 ⒻB Belles H 72 HomeRunGl,CindersShdow,SltTrty 10
28Aug82-8EP 1 1/16 :47 1:121 1:451ft 14 114 911 86¾ 56¾ 49½ Krasner S7 ⒻAw12000 75 HomeRunGl,Struckup,CindrsShdow 9
14Aug82-9EP 6½f :223 :463 1:194m 23 113 916 916 912 914 Krasner S9 ⒻMilady 65 OknDeeSelect,Dvette,MdmoisllBu 10
2Aug82-4EP 6½f :231 :47 1:173m *2 113 43 52½ 411 516 Krasner S4 ⒻAw9000 74 BlshngMnstrl,WodmntClr,SrnLdyB 5
21Jly82-9EP 1 1/16 :473 1:122 1:451ft 5½ 114 75½ 65¼ 54¾ 47 Krasner S7 ⒻAw12000 78 CindersShadow,Dvette,HomeRunGl 8
9Jly82-9EP 6½f :222 :46 1:182ft 4¼ 114 612 66¾ 31½ 22½ Krasner S2 ⒻAw8000 83 CindersShdow,SltTrety,BonnieLois 7
26May82-9EP 6½f :223 :462 1:183ft 3¾ 1125 714 69 54½ 33 Patzer M5 ⒻAw8500 82 JmmedFlight,TrctbleTrdrop,SltTrty 7
5May82-9EP 6½f :224 :46 1:181ft 4½ 1115 78¼ 78¼ 45 44¼ Patzer M7 ⒻAw10000 83 CindersShdow,Dvette,Michel'sBst 10
23Apr82-9EP 6½f :224 :464 1:191ft 5 1205 99 65½ 46 46 Patzer M1 ⒻAw12000 76 ThreeLdrs,MdmoisllBu,Michl'sBst 10
Oct 1 EP 2f ft :241 b Sep 25 EP 7f gd 1:321 h Sep 18 EP 5f ft 1:00 h Sep 10 EP 2f gd :241 h

```
Indellare                           B. f. 4, by Indefatigable—Emellare, by Czar Alexander
                                    Br.—Elmbrook Stable (Alb-C)        1982 13 3 1 2   $56,613
Own.—Elmbrook Stables          119  Tr.—May Alan                       1981 15 4 7 3   $39,030
                              Lifetime 35 9 8 7 $101,483
20ct82-8EP   1 1/16:474 1:143 1:48 m    7½ 117  79¾ 811 48½ 36    Skinner K3 (F)Aw10000 65 LdyofYork,BlushingMinstrel,Indellr 8
26Sep82-9Lga 1 3/16:48 1:141 2:014sl    32 121  1013 1414 1327 1321 LsthC8 (F)B Roberts H 40 Belle of Rainier, Gi Gi, Latrone 14
11Sep82-8EP  1 1/16:472 1:124 1:463m    6¼ 120  1023 1018 813 78¾ RycrftD2 (F)B Belles H 69 HomeRunGl,CindersShdow,SltTrty 10
29Aug82-9StP 6f :23 :462 1:111ft        4¼ 118  78½ 76¾ 76¾ 78½   Hedge R6 (F)Lilac H 82 Tyrosong, Fair Tania, Lil 'Ol Gal 7
15Aug82-9StP 1 1/16:463 1:113 1:45 ft   8½ 116  79½ 57¾ 43 1½     HedgR4 [S]Cal Mat'y H 91 Indellare, Regimen, Atlas Wonder 7
9Aug82-9NP   1 3/8:473 1:38 2:164ft     28 121  914 914 913 49¾   HedgR6 Spd To Spare 90 Rgimn,BlckIsButiful,MirclMmoris 10
2Aug82-9NP   1 1/16:463 1:123 1:462ft   *1e 122 911 98½ 74 21     Hedge R8 (F)Distaff H 82 TwilightTresure,Indellre,OnThRoll 10
13Jly82-9NP  1 1/16:47 1:124 1:46 ft    3½e 121 1112 910 73 11    HdR9 (F)Madamoiselle 85 Indellre,MissJoBy,TwilightTresure 11
22Jun82-9NP  6½f :224 :464 1:19 gd      6¼ 115  68½ 77¾ 85 53¾   MrccMJ1 (F)CelebrityH 83 SlightlyShdy,TlghtTrsr,AvlnchEprss 9
11Jun82-7NP  1 1/16:483 1:134 1:461ft   *2-3 118 66½ 66¼ 67 56    MerciecMJ4 (F)Aw9000 78 SlightlyShady,WilliesLdy,AdVlorem 6
   Sep 25 EP 2f gd :261 h

Miss Zulu Gold                      Ch. f. 3, by Zulu Tom—Norm's Choice, by Bold Combatant
                                    Br.—Owens G (Wash)                 1982 12 3 1 2   $50,140
Own.—Poor Four Stable          117  Tr.—Belvoir Howard                 1981 6 2 0 0    $8,800
                              Lifetime 18 5 1 2 $58,940
24Sep82-9EP  1 1/8:471 1:122 1:52 gd    9 118   2½ 2½ 1hd 1hd†    LsthC6 (F)B C oaks H 82 ‡MssZlGld,APrntmps,ChftnsCmnd 8
   †24Sep82—Disqualified and placed second
4Sep82-9EP   1 1/16:474 1:13 1:462m     11 119  21 21½ 35½ 49     KrsnerS3 (F)Senorita H 70 BllofRnr,APrntmps,Chftn'sCmmnd 9
29Aug82-9Lga 1 1/8:464 1:104 1:492ft    20 117  21½ 33½ 35 34½   BzeG2 (F)Sacajawea H 81 BellofRinir,OknDSlct,MissZuluGold 6
4Aug82-9EP   6½f :223 :461 1:174ft      12 118  32 21 2hd 1nk     KrsrS6 (F)QueenCharlo 89 MissZuluGold,LdyCeJy,AuPrintmps 9
31Jly82-9Lga 1 1/16:461 1:11 1:434ft    28 114  34½ 58 716 725    Baze G7 (F)M Donohoe 55 BellofRinir,OknDSlct,NoMorLmons 9
24Jly82-9Lga 1 :452 1:104 1:364ft       22 113  34½ 44 1120 1219  SrnsnD5 (F)Luella G. H 66 Flamme, Prune Picker, Tani Moro 12
10Jly82-9Lga 1 :453 1:10 1:344ft        21 116  21½ 22 35 312     Baze G7 (F)B. Ross H 83 BllofRnr,NoMorLmons,MssZulGold 9
30Jun82-9Lga 1 :46 1:113 1:394sy        4¼ 118  56½ 47 49½ 817   DvidsonJR9 (F)Aw11000 53 VitaLark,GreyPaulus,SwitchinBer 10
19Jun82-9Lga 6½f :213 :443 1:164ft      7½ 118  33½ 42½ 87¼ 76¾  DdsnJR1 (F)Ms Stakes 78 NoMorLmons,EsyTrmph,SddnWnds 8
22May82-9Lga 6f :22 :45 1:092ft         2 121   34½ 43 47 513     DdsnJR4 (F)Ingenue H 76 BellofRinir,NoMorLmons,RoylTurn 6

Brief Grief *                       Ch. m. 5, by Sandy Fleet—Good Grief Mama, by Jax Up
                                    Br.—Guindon R R (Wash)             1982 9 2 2 1    $29,190
Own.—Guindon Bonnie            120  Tr.—Taylor Roy                     1981 12 3 1 0   $35,244
                              Lifetime 31 7 7 2 $71,743            Turf 1 0 0 0     $729
26Sep82-9Lga 1 3/16:48 1:141 2:014sl    11 121  23½ 22 614 1016   BazeG1 (F)B Roberts H 45 Belle of Rainier, Gi Gi, Latrone 14
12Sep82-9Lga 1 1/8:471 1:123 1:524sy    15 120  23 2hd 1hd 1¾     Baze M B10 (F)Alki H 69 BriefGrief,ExprssSuccss,Mondolu 12
21Aug82-8Lga 6½f :22 :451 1:17 ft       5¾ 119  77½ 55½ 45½ 48   Baze M B2 (F)Aw10000 76 Ms.DocShdow,Sergous,DimondVill 12
14Aug82-9Lga 1 1/16:482 1:14 1:48 sl    9½ 117  45¼ 54¼ 49 413    BMB2 (F)PrimadonnaH 46 Tani Moro, Flamme, Mondolu 9
6Aug82-8Pla  1 :471 1:122 1:381ft       *3-4 120 11½ 1½ 11½ 2      Wright D7 (F)Aw2300 86 JustLikMm,BrfGrf,CountryLovsong 7
17Jly82-9Pla 6½f :23 :463 1:18 ft       3¼ 120  21 22 11 11¼     WrhtD6 (F)Lilac City H 95 Brief Grief, Shoot It Out, Misti O. 9
26Jun82-9Pla 6f :224 :463 1:124ft       9-5 118  2hd 2½ 2hd 31½   Wright D1 Aw2200 84 RecklessPlesure,ChifYkim,BrifGrif 7
12Jun82-9Pla 6f :221 :45 1:103ft        3½ 118  21 22 2½ 2hd      Wright D5 Aw2200 97 Seakist Charley, Brief Grief,BiPago 7
21May82-9Pla 6f :232 :464 1:122ft       5 118   33 33½ 65 84      WrightD7 Inaugural H 84 MrvinsMoving,HyMount,RibotAgn 10

Blushing Minstrel *                 Dk. b. or br. f. 4, by Borrower—Taos Trail, by Black Mountain
                                    Br.—Ca-Ro-Li Farms Ltd (BC-C)      1982 10 2 2 1   $16,020
Own.—Norland Stables           112  Tr.—Sams Edward                    1981 13 1 5 3   $18,543
                              Lifetime 30 4 7 7 $42,461
20ct82-8EP   1 1/16:474 1:143 1:48 m    9e 114  1hd 14 12½ 2hd    Patzer M2 (F)Aw10000 71 LdyofYork,BlushingMinstrel,Indellr 8
17Sep82-8Lga 6½f :213 :443 1:162ft      3½ 117  65¼ 83¾ 97¾ 76¼  DavidsonJR3 (F)Aw8000 81 Fancy Mink,SailOnRoni,Serageous 10
28Aug82-8EP  1 1/16:47 1:121 1:451ft    6¾ 113  45 76¼ 813 816    JohnsnBG4 (F)Aw12000 69 HomeRunGl,Struckup,CindrsShdow 9
14Aug82-9EP  6½f :223 :463 1:194m       2 115   31½ 2hd 41¾ 47    Johnson BG2 (F)Milady 72 OknDeeSelect,Dvette,MdmoisllBu 10
2Aug82-4EP   6½f :231 :47 1:173m        2¾ 113  21½ 1hd 16 19     Patzer M3 (F)Aw9000 90 BlshngMnstrl,WodmntClr,SrnLdyB 5
23Jly82-9Lga 6½f :22 :451 1:162ft       18 114  98¼ 73¾ 1hd 12    Sorenson D9 (F) 40000 87 BlushingMinstrl,Bdnot,FrnchJwlls 10
18Jun82-9EP  1 1/16:462 1:12 1:461ft    29 114  68 86¼ 86¼ 86¾    CrtRL4 (F)Cover Girl H 73 ChmnusBll,MdmoslIB,CndrsShdow 9
9Jun82-8EP   1 1/16:47 1:121 1:46 ft    5½ 110  46½ 56½ 614 613   Krasner S3 (F)Aw8000 68 Davette,BonnieLois,CheminusBelle 7
24May82-7EP  6½f :224 :462 1:183ft      2¾ 1115 22 32½ 22½ 21¾   Patzer M2 (F) 32000 83 Lddi'sLss,BlushngMnstrl,ToscMgc 10
10May82-9EP  6½f :222 :461 1:19 ft      7¾ 1125 67¾ 68 46½ 32½   Patzer M3 (F)Aw8000 80 LddsLss,TrctblTrdrp,BlshngMnstrl 10
   ●Sep 28 EP 5f ft 1:003 h     ●Aug 26 EP 4f ft :464 b     ●Aug 13 EP tr.t 2f sl :243 b
```

A comparison of Belle of Rainier's record with the rest of the field, including the second and third consensus picks, Okan Dee Select and Au Printemps, reveals why the favorite was bet down to 2–5. The mutuel pools were:

	Totals	Belle of Rainier
Win	34,414	20,005
Place	19,347	8,105
Show	14,763	5,485

These values yielded expected returns per dollar bet on Belle of Rainier of*

$$\text{EX Show} = 0.543 + 0.369\left(\frac{W_3/W}{S_3/S}\right)$$

$$= 0.543 + 0.369\left(\frac{20{,}005/34{,}414}{5{,}485/14{,}763}\right) = 1.12,$$

and

$$\text{EX Place} = 0.319 + 0.559\left(\frac{W_3/W}{P_3/P}\right)$$

$$= 0.319 + 0.559\left(\frac{20{,}005/34{,}414}{8{,}108/19{,}347}\right) = 1.09.$$

Both the EX Show and the EX Place are low for Dr. Z system bets, but in light of the extreme favorite bias, the show bet is still interesting, while the place bet is marginal.

Belle of Rainier won the race easily, followed by the 90–1 shot Brief Grief and Au Printemps, who went off at 10–1 (as the third favorite of the crowd). The crowd's second pick, Okan Dee Select, went off at nearly 7–1 and finished out of the money.

The chart of the race and the mutuel payoffs were as follows:

9th One and one-eighth miles. Three-year-olds and up, fillies and mares. Handicap. Purse $50,000-added.

Horse	Jockey	Wt	P	1	1¼	Str	Fin	Odds
Belle Of Rainier	Srnsn	126	1	1-1	1-h	2-1	1-1¼	.45
Brief Grief	Mercado	120	10	4-½	3-h	1-h	2-1¼	90.90
Au Printemps	Johnson	116	4	9-1	8-1	3-2½	3-¾	10.20
Indellare	Loseth	119	8	11	11	10-1	4-nk	15.75
Okan Dee Select	Patzer	120	5	10-2	9-3	4-1	5-3	6.60
Dream Disturber	Mena	113	2	3-1	4-4	6-3	6-2	37.15
Salt Treaty	Hverson	113	7	7-1	7-h	7-2	7-3	20.35
Cinders Shadow	Phipps	116	6	6-2½	6-h	9-3	8-nk	18.20
Miss Zulu Gold	Zook	117	9	2-2	2-2	8-1	9-6	18.85
Chemainus Belle	Williams	117	3	8-½	11	10-6	10-7	3.25
Blushing Minstrel	Cghtn	114	11	5-½	5-h	11	11	32.50

Time — :23, :47, 1:12.1, 1:38.1, 1:51.3.

BELLE OF RAINIER	2.90	3.20	2.60
BRIEF GRIEF		35.80	10.80
AU PRINTEMPS			4.60

*The equations for EX Show and EX Place are those for Exhibition Park discussed in Chapter Four. These equations, (4.3) and (4.4), are quite accurate for other tracks as long as their track take is close to Exhibition Park's 17.1%. More accurate regression equations based on differing track takes also appear in Chapter Four, as equations (4.5) and (4.6).

Thus even though EX Show was greater than EX Place, the place bet appeared to be the preferable one when Brief Grief came in second. In fact, the place payoff exceeded the win payoff.

More insight into the relative merits of the win, place, and show bets on Belle of Rainier results from a consideration of the probability of possible finishes. Belle of Rainier's probability of winning was about

$$q_3 = \frac{W_3}{W} = \frac{20{,}005}{34{,}415} = 0.581.$$

Thus with a \$2.90 payoff to win, the expected return per dollar bet was about 84¢, or an average loss of 16¢, which is close to the track take. The probability of finishing second was about 0.257; therefore, the probability of placing was 0.581 plus 0.257, or 0.834.* The \$3 place payoff yielded an expected return per dollar bet of \$1.25, or 25¢ profit. Finally, the probability of finishing third was about 0.107, and showing 0.945. Hence with a \$2.60 payoff, the expected return per dollar bet was \$1.23, or 23% profit. Thus even with a 90–1 shot finishing second, the show return was nearly as good as the place payoff. These values indicate that the place and show bets were both quite good. But just how unusual were the \$3 and \$2.60 payoffs? With expected values of 1.09 and 1.12 and probabilities of placing and showing of 0.838 and 0.945, you would expect payoffs for \$2 bets of \$2.46 and \$2.66, respectively, or \$2.40 and \$2.60 with breakage.

To summarize: Bets on extreme favorites to place or show when the expected values qualify as Dr. Z system bets should be treated as such—good bets. Nearly always, such horses will finish in the money and provide modest returns. If one or more long shots come in, the payoffs will be quite substantial, given the low risk. In fact, if the bets on the remaining horses are relatively evenly divided and there are quite a few horses, say eight or more—as there were in The Ballerina—the payoffs on Dr. Z system bets

---

*The probability of winning is $q_3 = W_3/W = 20{,}005/34{,}415 = 0.581$. Since Belle of Rainier was an extreme favorite, assume each of the other nine horses had equal chances of winning of $(1 - 0.581)/9 = 0.047$. Then the probability of finishing second was

$$\frac{9q_iq_3}{1 - q_i} = \frac{9(0.581)(0.047)}{0.953} = 0.257,$$

and the probability of finishing third was

$$\frac{(9)8q_iq_jq_3}{(1 - q_i)(1 - q_i - q_j)} = 0.107.$$

Therefore, the probabilities of placing and showing were 0.838 and 0.945, respectively. These estimates are on the conservative side, since, given the favorite-longshot bias, the probability of winning for such an extreme favorite is higher than 0.581.

will invariably be quite good. A very high percentage of extreme favorites do turn out to be Dr. Z system bets to place or show, simply because the crowd finds such bets distasteful. You hear all around you, "I do not want to bet on that favorite and get only $2.20." Bettors should not be discouraged by the apparent low odds; such odds represent an excellent investment opportunity with a good return and low risk. Of course, since breakage is so important with extreme favorites you will do better at tracks with 5¢ rather than 10¢ breakage. Generally, Canadian tracks have 5¢ breakage and U.S. tracks have 10¢ breakage. Although there may be exceptions, we do not know of any.

BETTING ALL EXTREME FAVORITES TO PLACE AND SHOW

We now provide you with an idea of how you might expect to do betting on nothing but extreme favorites to place or show. The results from a full season of betting at the major New York State racetracks at Aqueduct, Belmont, and Saratoga in 1980 are summarized in Tables 13.2 and 13.3. By betting all favorites that are even money or less, you lose about 2% to place and 4% to show. For win, using Table 3.1, you lose about 10% (14% track take plus 3% breakage minus 7% bias). As with the win bets, the rate of return rises the lower the odds. Thus favorites are increasingly underbet the more they become certain of finishing in the money. According to the data in Tables 13.2 and 13.3, at odds of 3–10 or less, you actually make 13% to place and 5% to show. The place payoff is larger because of the possibility of payoffs greater than the $2.10 show bets generally provide. Even at 1–5, the place payoff can be $2.40. Both the place and show payoffs are statistically significantly greater than breaking even. Thus it appears that you can make profits by making place or show bets on all favorites going off at 3–10 or less. Of course, we recommend that you sift from these extreme favorites those that actually are Dr. Z system bets. Most of these extreme favorites will be Dr. Z system bets, and you will do better by eliminating the few that are not. The minimum payoff in Louisiana is $2.20, so that there your bets on extreme favorites to place and especially to show have an added advantage.

BETTING OVERWHELMING FAVORITES IN MAJOR STAKES AND FUTURITY RACES

McCleary (1981) studied the results of betting on favorites to win, place, and show in major stakes and futurity races during 1977, 1978, and 1979. These are top races in North America with a gross purse of $100,000 or more, and all horses carry equal weights. The futurities are races in which

TABLE 13.2 ***Rate of return on place bets for extreme favorites: 732 races in New York in 1980***

Tracks	Total in-the-Money Places/ Total Races	Odds Ranges (in-the-money places/races) 1—10	1—5	3—10	2—5	1—2	3—5	7—10	4—5	9—10	1—1
Aqueduct, Belmont Park, and Saratoga[a]	543/732	1/1	4/4	14/14	47/56	60/70	55/67	86/128	98/128	80/136	98/134
Percent in-the-money places	74.2	100	100	100	83.9	85.7	82.1	70.5	76.6	58.8	73.1
Payoff range	2.10–5.00	2.10	2.10–2.40	2.10–2.40	2.10–3.00	2.10–3.00	2.20–3.00	2.20–3.00	2.20–3.40	2.20–5.00	2.20–3.80
Average payoff	2.64	2.10	2.28	2.25	2.38	2.51	2.54	2.54	2.67	2.84	2.86
Rate of return	0.98	1.05	1.14	1.13	1.00	1.08	1.04	0.90	1.02	0.84	1.05
	±0.07[b]	1.13 ± 0.06[b]			1.04 ± 0.04[b]			0.95 ± 0.10[b]			

Note: The data used to construct this table and Table 13.3 were obtained from the *Daily Racing Form's Chart Books* for 1980. Breakage at all three tracks is to the nearest 10¢ per dollar wagered. Thanks are due to Brian Canfield for help in collecting and analyzing the data.

[a]The racing dates for both tables were over 311 days: January 1–March 17, March 19–May 19, and October 15–December 31 at Aqueduct; May 21–July 28 and August 27–October 13 at Belmont; and July 30–August 25 at Saratoga.

[b]The rates of return in both Tables 13.2 and 13.3 are expected values ± two standard deviations. The standard deviation may be estimated by $\sqrt{\Sigma(X_i - \overline{X})^2/(N-1)N}$, where X_i is the return in the ith race out of the N races in each category, and $\overline{X}$ is the average return.

TABLE 13.3 ***Rate of return on show bets for extreme favorites:*** *721* ***races in New York in 1980***

Tracks	Total in-the-Money Shows/ Total Races	Odds Ranges (in-the-money shows/races)									
		1—10	1—5	3—10	2—5	1—2	3—5	7—10	4—5	9—10	1—1
Aqueduct, Belmont Park, and Saratoga	611/721	1/1	3/3	13/13	50/55	64/69	56/65	102/121	108/126	105/134	109/134
Percent in-the-money shows	84.7	100	100	100	90.9	92.8	86.2	84.3	85.7	78.4	81.3
Payoff range	2.10–3.20	2.10	2.10	2.10	2.10–2.60	2.10–2.40	2.10–2.60	2.10–2.80	2.10–3.20	2.10–3.20	2.10–3.00
Average payoff	2.27	2.10	2.10	2.10	2.12	2.18	2.24	2.23	2.29	2.35	2.39
Rate of return	0.96	1.05	1.05	1.05	0.96	1.01.	0.97	0.94	0.98	0.92	0.97
	±0.04	1.05 ± 0.00			0.98 ± 0.03			0.95 ± 0.13			

Note: See footnote [b] on Table 13.2.

the horses are nominated at or before birth. Since such fees accumulate and many horses drop out, the value of such races is very high. McCleary's theory is that if the horse was an overwhelming favorite, the owners, the trainers, and the jockeys would be trying their utmost to win, and these horses would be good bets. By "overwhelming," he meant the horse was the *Daily Racing Form*'s consensus for the race, the horse was the betting public's favorite, and there are no rival horses, that is, no other logical contenders with odds at 3–1 or less. McCleary's results indicated profits to win, place, and show that were statistically significant in each of these three years. To extend his analysis, we added the data* for the years 1968, 1976, 1981–82, and 1984–85.† For 1968 we used races with grosses of $50,000 or more since allowing for inflation, this amount corresponds to approximately $100,000 races run at present. Table 13.4 summarizes the results of all these races and in Table 13.5 we restricted these results to situations where the favorite was extreme—even money or less.

The results for the years 1976, 1981–82, and 1984–85 are not as encouraging as those found by McCleary. The yearly average rate of return is the mean return one can expect in a particular year plus or minus some deviations. Thus, according to Table 13.4, a horse player who bets on overwhelming favorites to place will receive an average return of 4% each year with a standard deviation of 22%. In mathematical terms, there is a 65% probability that the horse player will receive between 82¢ and $1.26 per dollar bet. Hence, Tables 13.4 and 13.5 indicate that betting on overwhelming favorites to place or show often results in a positive return. The returns, however, are significantly lower than that of Dr. Z bets.

In Table 13.6, we compare our results—on fast/firm tracks only—to races where rival horses are present. The results indicate that the mean returns on win, place, and show are better when rival horses are allowed. This is a result of better payoffs on favorites, especially in the place and show pools when rival horses are present. Moreover, the percentage of winnings in the place and show pools, though not statistically significant, is slightly higher.

In conclusion, our analyses indicate that betting on overwhelming favorites to place and show will lead to a small positive return. In particular, the higher average rate of return and the lower standard-deviation values in Table 13.5 (compare Table 13.4) indicate that we should restrict the place and show bets to overwhelming favorites who are at even money or less. We can, of course, further increase the profits by restricting wagers to Dr. Z bets.

*The data were obtained from various issues of the *American Racing Manual*. Thanks are due to Brain Canfield for assistance in collecting and analyzing the data in the previous edition of this book.

†Thanks are due to Robert Cheung for assistance in updating this section. The data for the year 1983 were unavailable when this book went to press.

TABLE 13.4 ***Results from bets to win, place, and show on overwhelming favorites in $100,000-plus stakes and futurity races in North America during the 1968, 1976–79, 1981–82, and 1984–85 racing seasons***

Year	# of Races for Win	# of Winners	Profit from $20 Bets to Win ($)	# of Races for Place	# of Placers	Profit from $20 Bets to Place ($)	# of Races for Show	# of Showers	Profit from $20 Bets to Show ($)
1968	58	27	−8	56	43	208	54	45	140
1976	19	9	−84	18	11	−61	18	13	−47
1977	26	17	232	26	21	168	25	23	151
1978	38	29	126	37	35	207	35	33	74
1979	46	34	105	44	42	228	43	42	108
1981	79	25	−490	68	36	−261	68	38	−197
1982	58	27	−38	58	38	66	58	47	84
1984	78	32	−381	78	46	−221	78	56	−148
1985	73	29	−350	72	38	−308	72	46	−219
Totals	475	229	−888	457	310	26	451	343	−54
% of Winnings		48.2			67.8			76.1	
Yearly Average Rate of Return			0.96 ± 0.25			1.04 ± 0.22			1.02 ± 0.16

TABLE 13.5 ***Results from bets to win, place, and show on overwhelming, even-money or better favorites in $100,000-plus stakes and futurity races in North America during the 1968, 1976–79, 1981–82, and 1984–85 racing seasons***

Year	*# of Races for Win*	*# of Winners*	*Profit from $20 Bets to Win ($)*	*# of Races for Place*	*# of Placers*	*Profit from $20 Bets to Place ($)*	*# of Races for Show*	*# of Showers*	*Profit from $20 Bets to Show ($)*
1968	18	9	−128	16	15	44	14	14	46
1976	13	9	8	12	10	28	12	11	18
1977	11	8	18	11	11	72	10	10	41
1978	34	27	86	33	31	137	31	29	36
1979	40	30	39	38	36	148	37	36	65
1981	48	18	−220	37	23	−117	37	29	−27
1982	29	15	−148	29	21	−50	29	28	76
1984	45	23	−184	45	34	5	45	36	−30
1985	41	21	−135	40	25	−150	40	27	−179
Totals	279	160	−664	261	206	117	255	220	46
% of Winnings		57.3			78.9			86.3	
Yearly Average Rate of Return			0.90 ± 0.17			1.06 ± 0.18			1.05 ± 0.13

TABLE 13.6 ***Results from bets to win, place, and show on overwhelming and nonoverwhelming, even-money or better favorites on a fast firm track in $100,00-plus stakes and futurity races in North America during the 1968, 1976, 1981–82, and 1984–85 racing seasons***

Year	# of Races for Win	# of Winners	Profit from $20 Bets to Win ($)	# of Races for Place	# of Placers	Profit from $20 Bets to Place ($)	# of Races for Show	# of Showers	Profit from $20 Bets to Show ($)
			Rival Horses Allowed (nonoverwhelming favorites)						
1968	22	12	−114	20	19	62	18	18	45
1976	20	11	−40	19	14	−13	19	15	−42
1981	39	18	−214	38	25	−89	38	31	−7
1982	42	20	−212	42	29	−88	41	37	64
1984	64	33	−206	62	48	14	58	49	−2
1985	57	31	−133	56	41	−78	53	39	−186
Totals	244	125	−919	237	176	−192	227	189	−128
% of Winnings		51.2			74.3			83.3	
Yearly Average Rate of Return			0.80 ± 0.07			0.99 ± 0.11			1.01 ± 0.12
			Rival Horses Not Allowed (overwhelming favorites)						
1968	15	9	−68	14	13	34	12	12	35
1976	10	6	−22	9	7	1	9	8	5
1981	31	14	−202	30	18	−109	30	24	−9
1982	27	13	−162	27	19	−54	27	26	72
1984	37	19	−144	37	27	−20	37	29	−31
1985	35	19	−91	34	22	−118	34	23	−156
Totals	155	80	−689	151	106	−266	149	122	−84
% of Winnings		51.6			70.2			81.9	
Yearly Average Rate of Return			0.77 ± 0.10			0.90 ± 0.08			0.97 ± 0.13

THE LONGACRES MILE, LONGACRES, RENTON, WASHINGTON, AUGUST 21, 1983

A typical overwhelming favorite was Chinook Pass in the Longacres Mile. He was 8–5 in the morning line, with the next-highest-rated horse, Moonlately, at 5–1. He was also the consensus best bet of the day and the favorite of the crowd at 6–5. Chinook Pass broke the world's record at $5\frac{1}{2}$ furlongs and is a dynamite sprinter. The only question in this race was, Could he last for a mile?

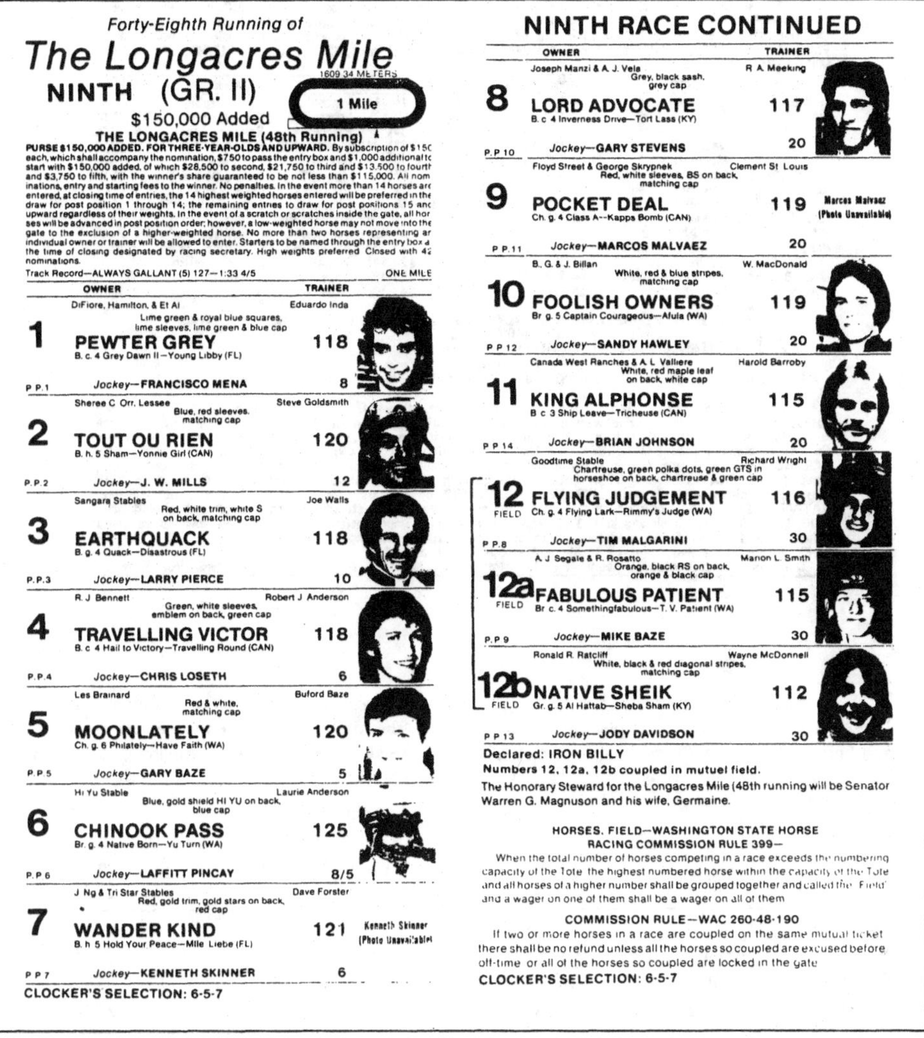

Forty-Eighth Running of

The Longacres Mile

NINTH (GR. II)

$150,000 Added

1609 34 METERS — 1 Mile

THE LONGACRES MILE (48th Running)

PURSE $150,000 ADDED. FOR THREE-YEAR-OLDS AND UPWARD. By subscription of $150 each, which shall accompany the nomination, $750 to pass the entry box and $1,000 additional to start with $150,000 added, of which $28,500 to second, $21,750 to third and $13,500 to fourth and $3,750 to fifth, with the winner's share guaranteed to be not less than $115,000. All nominations, entry and starting fees to the winner. No penalties. In the event more than 14 horses are entered, at closing time of entries, the 14 highest weighted horses entered will be preferred in the draw for post position 1 through 14; the remaining entries to draw for post positions 15 and upward regardless of their weights. In the event of a scratch or scratches inside the gate, all horses will be advanced in post position order; however, a low-weighted horse may not move into the gate to the exclusion of a higher-weighted horse. No more than two horses representing an individual owner or trainer will be allowed to enter. Starters to be named through the entry box at the time of closing designated by racing secretary. High weights preferred. Closed with 42 nominations.

Track Record—ALWAYS GALLANT (5) 127—1:33 4/5 — ONE MILE

NINTH RACE CONTINUED

No.	Horse	Owner	Trainer	Colors	Breeding	Weight	P.P.	Jockey	Odds
1	**PEWTER GREY**	DiFiore, Hamilton, & Et Al	Eduardo Inda	Lime green & royal blue squares, lime sleeves, lime green & blue cap	B. c. 4 Grey Dawn II—Young Libby (FL)	118	P.P.1	Jockey—FRANCISCO MENA	8
2	**TOUT OU RIEN**	Sheree C Orr, Lessee	Steve Goldsmith	Blue, red sleeves, matching cap	B. h. 5 Sham—Yonnie Girl (CAN)	120	P.P.2	Jockey—J. W. MILLS	12
3	**EARTHQUACK**	Sangara Stables	Joe Walls	Red, white trim, white S on back, matching cap	B. g. 4 Quack—Disastrous (FL)	118	P.P.3	Jockey—LARRY PIERCE	10
4	**TRAVELLING VICTOR**	R. J Bennett	Robert J Anderson	Green, white sleeves, emblem on back, green cap	B. c 4 Hail to Victory—Travelling Round (CAN)	118	P.P.4	Jockey—CHRIS LOSETH	6
5	**MOONLATELY**	Les Brainard	Buford Baze	Red & white, matching cap	Ch. g. 6 Philately—Have Faith (WA)	120	P.P.5	Jockey—GARY BAZE	5
6	**CHINOOK PASS**	Hi Yu Stable	Laurie Anderson	Blue, gold shield HI YU on back, blue cap	Br. g. 4 Native Born—Yu Turn (WA)	125	P.P.6	Jockey—LAFFITT PINCAY	8/5
7	**WANDER KIND**	J Ng & Tri Star Stables	Dave Forster	Red, gold trim, gold stars on back, red cap	B. h 5 Hold Your Peace—Mlle Liebe (FL)	121	P.P.7	Jockey—KENNETH SKINNER (Kenneth Skinner (Photo Unavailable))	6
8	**LORD ADVOCATE**	Joseph Manzi & A. J. Vela	R A Meeking	Grey, black sash, grey cap	B. c 4 Inverness Drive—Tort Lass (KY)	117	P.P.10	Jockey—GARY STEVENS	20
9	**POCKET DEAL**	Floyd Street & George Skrypnek	Clement St Louis	Red, white sleeves, BS on back, matching cap	Ch. g. 4 Class A—Kapps Bomb (CAN)	119	P.P.11	Jockey—MARCOS MALVAEZ (Marcos Malvaez (Photo Unavailable))	20
10	**FOOLISH OWNERS**	B. G. & J. Billan	W. MacDonald	White, red & blue stripes, matching cap	Br g. 5 Captain Courageous—Afula (WA)	119	P.P.12	Jockey—SANDY HAWLEY	20
11	**KING ALPHONSE**	Canada West Ranches & A. L. Valliere	Harold Barroby	White, red maple leaf on back, white cap	B c 3 Ship Leave—Tricheuse (CAN)	115	P.P.14	Jockey—BRIAN JOHNSON	20
12 FIELD	**FLYING JUDGEMENT**	Goodtime Stable	Richard Wright	Chartreuse, green polka dots, green GTS in horseshoe on back, chartreuse & green cap	Ch. g. 4 Flying Lark—Rimmy's Judge (WA)	116	P.P.8	Jockey—TIM MALGARINI	30
12a FIELD	**FABULOUS PATIENT**	A J Segale & R. Rosatto	Marion L. Smith	Orange, black RS on back, orange & black cap	Br c. 4 Somethingfabulous—T. V. Patient (WA)	115	P.P.9	Jockey—MIKE BAZE	30
12b FIELD	**NATIVE SHEIK**	Ronald R. Ratcliff	Wayne McDonnell	White, black & red diagonal stripes, matching cap	Gr. g. 5 Al Hattab—Sheba Sham (KY)	112	P.P.13	Jockey—JODY DAVIDSON	30

CLOCKER'S SELECTION: 6-5-7

Declared: IRON BILLY

Numbers 12, 12a, 12b coupled in mutuel field.

The Honorary Steward for the Longacres Mile (48th running will be Senator Warren G. Magnuson and his wife, Germaine.

HORSES. FIELD—WASHINGTON STATE HORSE RACING COMMISSION RULE 399—

When the total number of horses competing in a race exceeds the numbering capacity of the Tote the highest numbered horse within the capacity of the Tote and all horses of a higher number shall be grouped together and called the "Field" and a wager on one of them shall be a wager on all of them

COMMISSION RULE—WAC 260-48-190

If two or more horses in a race are coupled on the same mutual ticket there shall be no refund unless all the horses so coupled are excused before off-time or all of the horses so coupled are locked in the gate

CLOCKER'S SELECTION: 6-5-7

He could; he won the race by 6 lengths and paid $4.30 to win, $3.60 to place, and $3.10 to show. Since the second- and third-place finishers, Travelling Victor and Earthquack, were leading contenders, it is clear that Chinook Pass was also an excellent Dr. Z system bet.* The chart of the race was as follows:

NINTH RACE
Lga
Aug. 21, 1983

1 MILE. (1:33⅘). FORTY-EIGHTH RUNNING OF THE LONGACRES MILE. Purse, $150,000-added for three-year-olds and up. By subscription of $150 each, which shall accompany the nomination, $750 to pass the entry box and $1,000 additional to start with $150,000-added, of which $28,500 to second, $21,750 to third, $13,500 to fourth and $3,750 to fifth, with the winner's share guaranteed to be not less than $115,000. All nominations, entry and starting fees to the winner. In the event more than 14 horses are entered, at closing time of entries, the 14 highest weighted horses entered will be preferred in the draw for post position 1 through 14; the remaining entries to draw for post positions 15 and upward regardless of their weights. In the event of a scratch or scratches inside the gate, all horses will be advanced in post position order; however, a low-weighted horse may not move into the gate to the exclusion of a higher-weighted horse. No more than two horses representing an individual owned or trainer will be allowed to enter. Closed with 42 nominations. Value of race, $182,500. Value to winner, $115,000; second, $28,500; third, $21,750; fourth, $13,500; fifth, $3,750. Mutuel Pool, $462,260.

Last Raced	Horse	EqtA	Wt	PP	St	¼	½	¾	Str	Fin	Jockeys	Owners	Odds to $1
31Jly 83 ^{8}Dmr^{1}	Chinook Pass	4	125	6	1	$1^{2\frac{1}{2}}$	1^{6}	1^{5}	1^{4}	1^{6}	PincayLJr	Hi Yu Stable	1.15
7Aug83 ^{9}Lga^{2}	Travelling Victor	4	118	4	2	4^{3}	3^{h}	3^{2}	2^{h}	2no	LosethC	R J Bennett	11.05
4Aug83 ^{9}Lga^{2}	Earthquack	4	119	3	11	7^{h}	7^{2}	2^{h}	$3^{3\frac{1}{2}}$	3^{nk}	PierceL	Sangara Stables	6.80
7Aug83 ^{8}Lga^{2}	Native Sheik	5	114	13	14	14	14	12^{3}	$6^{2\frac{1}{2}}$	4no	DavidsonJR	R R Ratcliff	f-22.35
7Aug83 ^{9}Lga^{6}	Moonlately	6	120	5	8	5^{h}	6^{h}	$4^{1\frac{1}{2}}$	4^{3}	5^{3}	BazeG	L Brainard	5.85
7Aug83 ^{9}Lga^{4}	Foolish Owners	5	119	12	9	10^{1}	$8^{1\frac{1}{2}}$	6^{2}	5^{3}	6^{3}	HawleyS	B-G-J Billan	16.80
10Jly 83 ^{9}Lga^{4}	Lord Advocate	b4	117	10	13	13^{6}	$12^{\frac{1}{2}}$	9^{1}	7^{5}	$7^{4\frac{1}{2}}$	StevensG	Manzi-Vela	47.70
7Aug83 ^{9}EP^{1}	Wander Kind	b5	121	7	5	$6^{\frac{1}{2}}$	9^{1}	$10^{\frac{1}{2}}$	10^{h}	$8^{1\frac{1}{2}}$	SkinnerK	J Ng-Tri Star Stable	9.40
16Jly 83 ^{9}NP^{6}	Pocket Deal	4	119	11	6	$8^{\frac{1}{2}}$	4^{1}	5^{1}	11^{2}	9no	MalvaezMG	Street-Skrypnek	43.70
6Aug83 ^{8}EP^{1}	King Alphonse	b3	115	14	10	11^{4}	$11^{2\frac{1}{2}}$	$8^{1\frac{1}{2}}$	9^{h}	10no	JohnsonBG	CndaWstRchs-Vallre	21.85
29Jly 83 ^{8}Lga^{8}	Flying Judgement	b4	116	8	12	12^{2}	13^{6}	11^{2}	8^{h}	11^{4}	MalgariniT	Goodtime Stable	f-22.35
5Aug83 ^{8}Dmr^{6}	Pewter Grey	4	118	1	3	$2^{\frac{1}{2}}$	$2^{1\frac{1}{2}}$	7^{1}	12^{2}	12^{1}	MenaF	Difiore-Hmiltn-Et Al	35.45
7Aug83 ^{9}Lga^{3}	Fabulous Patient	b4	118	9	7	9^{1}	$10^{\frac{1}{2}}$	13^{3}	$13^{3\frac{1}{2}}$	$13^{3\frac{1}{2}}$	BazeMB	Segale-Rosatto	f-22.35
7Aug83 ^{9}Lga^{1}	Tout Ou Rien	b5	120	2	4	3^{1}	5^{h}	14	14	14	MillsJW	S C Orr	13.60

f-Mutuel field.

OFF AT 6:30. START GOOD. WON EASILY. Time, :22, :44⅘, 1:09⅗, 1:22⅕, 1:35⅘. Track fast.

$2 Mutuel Prices			
6—CHINOOK PASS	4.30	3.60	3.10
4—TRAVELLING VICTOR		8.10	6.10
3—EARTHQUACK			4.30

Dk. b. or br. g, by Native Born—Yu Turn, by Turn-To. Trainer, Laurie N. Anderson. Bred by Hi Yu Stable (Wash.).

CHINOOK PASS, away alertly, sprinted clear at once, drew off to a commanding advantage on the backstretch, settled for the drive with a good lead and pulled away in the late stages to win with complete authority. TRAVELLING VICTOR raced within striking distance early, was sent up to offer a bid on the final turn, bumped with EARTHQUACK in the upper stretch and narrowly edged that rival in a stiff drive. EARTHQUACK saved ground while being outrun early, moved through along the rail on the second turn, bumped with TRAVELLING VICTOR entering the stretch and just missed for the place while under brisk pressure. A claim of foul against TRAVELLING VICTOR by the rider of EARTHQUACK was not allowed. NATIVE SHEIK, outrun for six furlongs, moved to the outside for the stretch run and closed with a bold rush. MOONLATELY lacked a closing kick. WANDER KIND raced in good position early, but gave way before going a half mile. POCKET DEAL was sent up to offer his best bid nearing the far turn and faltered. PEWTER GREY was hard hustled from the inside and stopped after a half.

Overweight—Earthquack, 1 pound; Fabulous Patient, 3; Native Sheik, 2. Scratched—Iron Billy.

*I did not attend this race, but my colleague Henry Pollacco did and recognized Chinook Pass as a Dr. Z system bet, much to his pleasure. Near post time, the tote board expected values per dollar bets and optimal bets with a betting fortune of $1,000 to place and show were (approximately) as follows:

	Totals	#6 Chinook Pass	Expected Value per Dollar Bet on Chinook Pass ($)	Optimal Bet on Chinook Pass ($)
Odds		6—5		
Win	236,812	91,000		
Place	123,000	35,000	1.13	75
Show	93,000	27,000	1.12	204

Such bets would have returned $135 to place and $316.20 to show, for a profit of $172.20.

14

A Typical Day at the Races: Making the Best Bet in Each Race, Hollywood Park, May 30, 1982

BETTING ON ALL THE RACES

Many, in fact most, visitors to the racetrack and readers of this book will not wish to play only Dr. Z system bets, since these occur only about two to four times each day. To maintain the excitement of the sporting event, they would rather bet on most or all of the races. Our thesis in this book is that if you keep seriously to the Dr. Z system (and do not bet otherwise) it should win for you. What should you do in the races other than those that have Dr. Z system bets?

There are several possibilities. First, we claim no monopoly on winning systems at the racetrack. While we have no specific suggestions other than those made elsewhere in this book, there may well be systems that you could use to make positive profits in these other races. Second, you could make small bets in these other races, on the assumption that the fun will be worth your small losses, at the same time that you reserve bigger bets for the Dr. Z system bets. Finally, you could bet on that horse or horses in each race that are either Dr. Z system bets or have positive expected value. By *positive expected value*, we mean that for each dollar bet you will receive at least a dollar back, *on average*. As we argued in Chapter Nine, positive expected value using our formulas and methods will *not* lead to the maximum profits. In fact, it is probably not good enough for you to be fairly confident of achieving any profits at all. With the approximations and uncertainties involved, you need a higher expected-value cutoff than 1.00. For example, the break-even point for the data in Table 5.2 was 1.02. To make the maximum profits, we recommend 1.14 at tracks such as Santa Anita and Belmont, where there are very large betting pools and superior horses, and 1.18 at other tracks. Recall that an expected value of 1.14 means that, *on average,* you will receive $1.14 for each dollar wagered. Table A.1 in Appendix A indicates the relative sizes of the betting pools at most of the tracks in North America. Those that warrant cutoffs of 1.14 are listed on page 106 in Chapter Five. Nevertheless, if you pick horses with positive expected value you should at least, more or less, break even and do much better than the average bettor. See Table 13.1 in Chapter Thirteen for some values that indicate how you might do if you simply pick the favorite of the crowd to place or show in each race.

USEFUL BETTING RULES

To investigate how such a system might work and to provide you with guidance on what to expect, I went to Hollywood Park in Inglewood, California, on Sunday, May 30, 1982, to try it out.

I used the following rules:

1. Bet $50 on the horse in each race that seems the best bet to place or show.
2. Bet only if the expected value is at least 1.00
3. Do not bet on horses that have not run recently, namely in the last four weeks or six weeks for stakes horses.
4. Concentrate on the top horses, namely, those favored by the crowd and the *Daily Racing Form*'s consensus and those horses that consistently finish in the money in similar-quality races.
5. Stick to the top jockeys, especially when the horse has never been ridden by today's jockey (this consideration is not important for horses that have consistently finished in the money with nontop jockeys riding them again today). See jockey and trainer standings in the following tabulations.
6. Bet to place for Dr. Z system bets only. This is because I also decided to concentrate on show bets. By betting each race, the strategy would be risky and show bets would minimize this risk. Since only about 15% of the Dr. Z system bets are to place, you are unlikely to get good enough place bets in each race to warrant the attention they would need unless they were outstanding bets.
7. For Dr. Z system bets for place and show, I would increase my $50 bet to the optimal Kelly criterion amount using my calculator with an expected-value cutoff of 1.14.

TABLE 14.1 *Jockey standings through Saturday, May 29, 1982*

Jockey	Mounts	Firsts	Seconds	Thirds	Win (%)	In the Money (%)	Ranking
McCarron, C.	182	52	33	14	28.5	54.4	1
Guerra, W.	164	22	25	25	13.4	43.9	5
Pincay, L., Jr.	135	21	23	27	15.5	52.6	2
Hawley, S.	109	19	19	13	17.4	46.8	4
Delahoussaye, E.	125	18	21	14	14.4	42.4	6
Valenzuela, P.	114	14	13	13	12.3	35.1	8
McHargue, D.	113	13	14	13	11.5	35.4	7
Shoemaker, W.	55	13	9	6	23.6	50.9	3
Castaneda, M.	130	12	12	20	9.2	33.8	10
Olivares, F.	112	12	12	15	10.7	34.8	9

TABLE 14.2 *Trainer standings through Saturday, May 29, 1982*

Trainer	Starts	Firsts	Seconds	Thirds	Win (%)	In the Money (%)	Ranking
Frankel, R.	74	9	18	10	12.1	50.0	3
Palma, H.	59	9	7	6	15.2	37.2	13
Vienna, D.	44	9	7	4	20.4	45.4	7
Bernstein, D.	51	8	7	9	15.7	47.1	5
Stute, M.	40	8	7	3	20.0	45.0	8
Whittingham, C.	34	7	4	3	20.6	41.2	11
Gosden, J.	23	7	2	1	30.4	43.5	10
Mitchell, M.	29	7	1	5	24.1	44.8	9
Truman, E.	34	6	9	2	17.6	50.0	3
Russell, J.	33	6	8	3	18.1	51.5	2
Lukas, D. W.	44	6	6	8	13.6	45.5	6
Jones, G.	25	6	4	3	24.0	52.0	1
Mandella, R.	35	6	3	5	17.1	40.0	12

Note: You can find these jockey and trainer standings in your racing program. If you wish to use this information, you need to calculate separately the in-the-money percentages, as we have done here. The program usually gives only the win percentages. Ranking jockeys and trainers by ***numbers*** of winners, as is done in these program listings, is misleading. The best measure for our purposes is ***in-the-money percentage***. The top jockeys of this meeting were Chris McCarron, Laffit Pincay, Jr., and Bill Shoemaker, followed by Sandy Hawley, Walter Guerra, and Eddie Delahoussaye. The trainers were quite evenly matched. It is better not to try to get to the level of detail involved in evaluating trainers in your betting. Leave that to the experts who are establishing fair win odds.

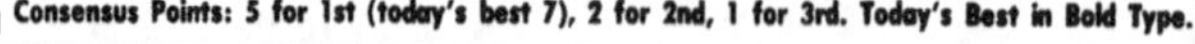

Experts' Selections

Consensus Points: 5 for 1st (today's best 7), 2 for 2nd, 1 for 3rd. Today's Best in Bold Type.

Trackman, Warren Williams

HOLLYWOOD PARK

Selections Made for Fast Track

	TRACKMAN	HANDICAP	ANALYST	HERMIS	SWEEP	CONSENSUS	
1	SO CALLED MY MASTERPIECE TRIPLANE	MY MASTERPIECE SO CALLED TRIPLANE	TRIPLANE QUALIFICATION SO CALLED	TRIPLANE SO CALLED THE METHOD	TRIPLANE THE BIG T. QUALIFICATION	TRIPLANE SO CALLED MY MASTERPIECE	17 10 7
2	CITA SOMBRITA MY DUTCHESS OTRA PROMESA	CITA SOMBRITA MY DUTCHESS BAD BAD LUCY	ROLLING GIRL MY DUTCHESS NATIVE ITCH	MY DUTCHESS ROLLING GIRL BAD BAD LUCY	CITA SOMBRITA MY DUTCHESS ROLLING GIRL	CITA SOMBRITA MY DUTCHESS ROLLING GIRL	15 13 8
3	COLONEL STU DOON'S BAY SHANTIN	MESSAGE TO GARCIA COLONEL STU SHANTIN	COLONEL STU SHANTIN DOON'S BAY	SHANTIN COLONEL STU DOON'S BAY	COLONEL STU SHANTIN DOON'S BAY	COLONEL STU SHANTIN DOON'S BAY	19 11 5
4	B. RICH GEORGE PERRY CABIN MASTER WARRIOR	**MASTER WARRIOR** CHAPEL CREEK PERRY CABIN	B. RICH GEORGE CHAPEL CREEK PERRY CABIN	PERRY CABIN B. RICH GEORGE SALI'S ROYAL DREAM	SALI'S ROYAL DREAM PERRY CABIN MASTER WARRIOR	B. RICH GEORGE PERRY CABIN MASTER WARRIOR	12 11 9
5	INSEARCHOF JET PIRATE EXTRA QUICK	JET PIRATE INSEARCHOF CHECKER'S ORPHAN	INSEARCHOF JET PIRATE FAMILIAR TUNE	JET PIRATE INSEARCHOF MURTAZZ	DISTANT GEM JET PIRATE NAT'S PENNY	JET PIRATE INSEARCHOF DISTANT GEM	16 14 5
6	SPARKLE CRYSTAL LEADING ADVOCATE ASTORIAN	DYNAMIC GIRL LEADING ADVOCATE SPARKLE CRYSTAL	LEADING ADVOCATE SPARKLE CRYSTAL ASTORIAN	ASTORIAN LEADING ADVOCATE SPARKLE CRYSTAL	LEADING ADVOCATE ASTORIAN SPARKLE CRYSTAL	LEADING ADVOCATE SPARKLE CRYSTAL ASTORIAN	16 10 9
7	PIRATE LAW PATTI'S TRIUMPH MOON BALL	PIRATE LAW CONFETTI FAST	MOON BALL CONFETTI FAST	ANOTHER REALM MOON BALL FAST	FAST PIRATE LAW MOON BALL	PIRATE LAW MOON BALL FAST	12 9 8
8	REMEMBER JOHN NEVER TABLED PETRO D. JAY	REMEMBER JOHN NEVER TABLED POMPEII COURT	**NEVER TABLED** REMEMBER JOHN POMPEII COURT	NEVER TABLED REMEMBER JOHN SHANEKITE	**NEVER TABLED** REMEMBER JOHN POMPEII COURT	NEVER TABLED REMEMBER JOHN POMPEII COURT	23 16 3
9	**HEART BEAT** EL PANCHO ANGEL KUNDALINI	HEART BEAT PIERRE LA MONT KUNDALINI	HEART BEAT KUNDALINI PIERRE LA MONT	**HEART BEAT** PIERRE LA MONT EL PANCHO ANGEL	HEART BEAT EL PANCHO ANGEL KUNDALINI	**HEART BEAT** EL PANCHO ANGEL KUNDALINI	29 5 5

SWEEP'S Hollywood Park Graded Handicaps

FIRST RACE — *Probable Post, 1:31*

1 $\frac{1}{16}$ MILES. 4-Year-Olds and Up. Claiming ($16,000 to $14,000). Purse $13,000.

P.P.	Horse.	Prob. Jockey.	Wt.	Comment.	Prob. Odds.
6	TRIPLANE	Delahoussaye E	118	Back where belongs	5-2
3	THE BIG T.	Ortega L E	115	Threat to tag speed	8-1
10	QUALIFICATION	Hawley S	115	Try runaway tactics	5-1
2	SO CALLED	Hansen R D	115	Question of condition	4-1
4	MY MASTERPIECE	Lipham T	118	Held on real gamely	6-1
9	THE METHOD	Steiner J J	5108	Comes off good sprint	8-1
1	DR. STORK	Pierce D	115	Claimed in comeback	12-1
8	FLEET RULER	Olivares F	115	Eliminated at start	12-1
7	ON EL PASEO	Diaz A L	115	$12,500 Sinne claim	15-1
5	MAGIC STAR	Valenzuela P A	115	Probably needed last	20-1

SECOND RACE — *Probable Post, 2:02*

6 ½ FURLONGS. 4-Year-Olds and Up, Fillies and Mares. Claiming ($20,000 to $18,000). Purse $14,000.

P.P.	Horse.	Prob. Jockey.	Wt.	Comment.	Prob. Odds.
8	CITA SOMBRITA	Castaneda M	115	Sharp gal right now	5-2
7	MY DUTCHESS	McCarron C J	113	Chris stays with her	3-1
5	ROLLING GIRL	Steiner J J	5110	Ran well over oval	9-2
3	ALLARRONES COMET	McHrDG	115	Failed as favorite	6-1
2	NATIVE ITCH	Valenzuela P A	115	Sharpened in north	8-1
1	BAD BAD LUCY	Sibille R	118	Overmatched in last	8-1
6	KATHINKA	Hansen R D	115	Improvement needed	15-1
4	GOLDEN POLICY	Diaz A L	113	Lacked late kick	15-1
9	OTRA PROMESA	Black K	115	Hard to boost	20-1

THIRD RACE — *Probable Post, 2:33*

6 FURLONGS. 3-Year-Olds and Up, Bred in Cal. Allowance. Purse $20,000.

P.P.	Horse.	Prob. Jockey.	Wt.	Comment.	Prob. Odds.
6	COLONEL STU	Delahoussaye E	116	Ready for a smasher	2-1
3	SHANTIN	Valenzuela P A	111	Drilled in :58 3/5	7-2
4	DOON'S BAY	McCarron C J	122	Back with leading man	5-2
1	CROFTED	Pincay L Jr	122	Slow starter on rail	8-1
8	MESSAGE TO GARCIA	CstndM	111	Can't be dismissed	8-1
2	READY REB	Olivares F	114	Last far from best	15-1
5	SEAVOY	Diaz A L	116	Found where wire is	15-1
7	WAR HOUSE	Wellington H K	116	Third in Fresno stakes	30-1
9	WINDY SCOTT	Steiner J J	5109	Figures to weaken	30-1

FOURTH RACE — *Probable Post, 3:04*

7 FURLONGS. 3-Year-Olds and Up. Allowance. Purse $26,000.

P.P.	Horse.	Prob. Jockey.	Wt.	Comment.	Prob. Odds.
5	SALI'S ROYAL DREAM	McCrrCJ	116	Edge in tight fit	4-1
6	PERRY CABIN	Olivares F	116	Bobbled at break	5-2
7	MASTER WARRIOR	Sibille R	116	Comes off game try	7-2
1	B. RICH GEORGE	Pincay L Jr	111	Look who takes over	3-1
3	CHAPEL CREEK	McHargue D G	116	Last more like it	6-1
4	SURPRISE GEORGE	DlhoussyE	116	Prepping for router?	10-1
2	SOME LUTE	Valenzuela P A	116	Made lead on grass	20-1

FIFTH RACE — *Probable Post, 3:35*

6 FURLONGS. 3-Year-Olds. Claiming ($40,000 to $35,000). Purse $18,000.

P.P.	Horse.	Prob. Jockey.	Wt.	Comment.	Prob. Odds.
6	DISTANT GEM	Valenzuela P A	116	Fast works, likes track	5-2
4	JET PIRATE	Sibille R	116	Dropping for this	3-1
8	NAT'S PENNY	Delahoussaye E	114	Tough with these	6-1
3	INSEARCHOF	McHargue D G	116	Must be considered	9-2
11	SPECTACULAR BEE	McCrrnCJ	116	Fits better here	8-1
10	CHECKER'S ORPHAN	Pierce D	116	Faltered in router	12-1
9	GRINGO JIM	Pincay L Jr	116	Steps into claimer	12-1
5	EXTRA QUICK	Castaneda M	116	Back at best distance	15-1
2	FAMILIAR TUNE	Ortega L E	112	Good race to easier	15-1
7	MURTAZZ	Lipham T	116	Well backed in north	30-1
1	RAMBLE ON JOHN	Ramirez O	116	Little to endorse	30-1

Blinkers On: Insearchof.

SIXTH RACE — *Probable Post, 4:07*

1 MILE. 3-Year-Olds and Up, Fillies and Mares. Maiden Special weights. Purse $18,000.

P.P.	Horse.	Prob. Jockey.	Wt.	Comment.	Prob. Odds.
7	LEADING ADVOCATE	PincyLJr	114	Soft graduation spot	2-1
9	ASTORIAN	McHargue D G	114	Promise in New York	3-1
3	SPARKLE CRYSTAL	McCrrnCJ	114	McCarron-Gosden team	5-2
4	DYNAMIC GIRL	Hawley S	114	Puts on blinkers	8-1
6	TELL'S TREASURE	Hansen R D	122	Speed for partways	10-1
2	DELICATE GRACE	ValenzuelPA	114	Caved in early	15-1
8	LOST LOOT	Ortega L E	114	Dull dash return	15-1
5	QUIZZICAL	Steiner J J	5117	Didn't beat a soul	30-1
1	JENNIE'S IMAGE	Lipham T	114	Must do much better	30-1

Blinkers On: Dynamic Girl, Tell's Treasure.

SEVENTH RACE — *Probable Post, 4:40*

1 $\frac{1}{16}$ MILES.(turf) 4-Year-Olds and Up. Allowance. Purse $40,000.

P.P.	Horse.	Prob. Jockey.	Wt.	Comment.	Prob. Odds.
5	FAST	McCarron C J	114	Winner if ready	5-2
3	PIRATE LAW	Valenzuela P A	114	Ran well over course	3-1
7	MOON BALL	Castaneda M	114	Staged 48-1 surprise	9-2
6	PATTI'S TRIUMPH	Hawley S	118	No excuses last trip	5-1
9	CONFETTI	Pincay L Jr	114	Wide throughout	6-1
1	HAUGHTY BUT NICE	McHrgDG	114	Gave way on lead	10-1
4	SUNNY WINTERS	DelhoussyeE	116	Didn't belong in last	12-1
2	ANOTHER REALM	Gilligan L	114	Surprise package	12-1
8	GOLDEN FLAK	Hansen R D	114	Back from Golden Gate	3-1

Coupled—Pirate Law and Golden Flak.

EIGHTH RACE — *Probable Post, 5:12*

6 FURLONGS. 30th Running of THE LOS ANGELES HANDICAP (Grade III). 3-Year-Olds and Up. . Purse $75,000 Added.

P.P.	Horse.	Prob. Jockey.	Wt.	Comment.	Prob. Odds.
7	NEVER TABLED	McCarron C J	116	Conditions to order	2-1
1	REMEMBER JOHN	DelhoussyeE	115	Just won from rail	5-2
3	POMPEII COURT	Sibille R	116	Always gives his best	9-2
2	SHANEKITE	Hawley S	117	Doesn't look right	6-1
4	PETRO D. JAY	Castaneda M	116	Equalled world mark	6-1
6	BEACH WALK	Steiner J J	113	Game but in tough	12-1
5	COOL FRENCHY	Aragon J	112	Longshot pilot aboard	20-1
8	TERRESTO'S SINGER	VlnzulPA	113	Rider fits him well	20-1

Blinkers Off: Terresto's Singer.

NINTH RACE — *Probable Post, 5:45*

1 ⅛ MILES.(turf) 4-Year-Olds and Up. Claiming ($50,000). Purse $28,000.

P.P.	Horse.	Prob. Jockey.	Wt.	Comment.	Prob. Odds.
5	HEART BEAT	Pincay L Jr	116	Spotted for top try	8-5
4	EL PANCHO ANGEL	Lipham T	116	Nosedive in class	3-1
2	KUNDALINI	Valenzuela P A	116	Finished fairly well	6-1
7	WANTAZEE	Delahoussaye E	119	May take to turf	4-1
8	PIERRE LA MONT	Hawley S	116	Weakened in marathon	6-1
6	INGRES	Sibille R	116	Passed tiring horses	12-1
3	BUFFALO HART	Pierce D	116	Outrun by better	20-1
1	FABULOUS REASON	CastnedM	116	View from Century	30-1

ANALYST'S *Hollywood Comment*

THIRD RACE

1—Colonel Stu
2—Shantin
3—Doon's Bay

COLONEL STU, a lightly raced colt, showed grit last trip when runner-up to Rawbone in 1:09 flat. He was 1 1/2 lengths ahead of strong rival DOON'S BAY and will be getting six pounds from that foe. He also gets off the rail and Eddie D. SHANTIN ran gamely behind the swift L'Cap last trip and the sophomore will be dropping eight pounds. He has a bullet work of :58 3/5 on the 23rd and seems strictly on the improve. DOON'S BAY is usally in the thick of contention and will be reunited with McCarron today. Despite his 122 pounds he has enough heart to be a strong factor. WINDY SCOTT should give them all something to run at.

FOURTH RACE

1—B. Rich George
2—Chapel Creek
3—Perry Cabin

B. RICH GEORGE is the likely speed of this contest, and although he couldn't hold off Jet Travel and Dena Jo last trip, he doesn't find that type of competition in this line-up. He should be extremely tough to catch from the rail with Pincay aloft. CHAPEL CREEK moved up dramatically last time at 27-1 and seems to be coming around for Cleveland and may start running to some of his spectacular works. He drilled a bullet 1:25 since his improved race. PERRY CABIN was flying at the finish last trip, being lapped on stakes caliber No No. If the speed falters, he could be along in time. SALI'S ROYAL DREAM usually moves up with McCarron aboard, while MASTER WARRIOR may be able to push the top choice.

FIFTH RACE

1—Insearchof
2—Jet Pirate
3—Familiar Tune

INSEARCHOF ran a fine race last trip when he closed willingly and was beaten a neck by the vastly improved Michelle's Dream. The colt has come around this season for Warren Stute and McHargue was aboard for his maiden win April 20 at Santa Anita. He may be able to rate him a bit better now and blinkers should help. JET PIRATE is back in a league where he might utilize his speed. FAMILIAR TUNE was third to Michelle's Dream last out, beaten a length. It was a fine try for only his fifth lifetime start and the slightest improvement could find him right in the hunt. MURTAZZ has every right to move up here, while DISTANT GEM could flash speed in his return off good a.m. works.

SIXTH RACE

1—Leading Advocate
2—Sparkle Crystal
3—Astorian

LEADING ADVOCATE was bumped at the start last time and didn't duplicate her fine effort behind Trust Us May 1, although she finished a creditable third behind the impressive Miss Elea. Pincay takes over the controls today and they should find the charmed circle. SPARKLE CRYSTAL has some nice works for her debut (:14 3/5, 1:41 4/5 and 1:26 4/5). Look for McCarron to get some run from this Sir Gaylord filly. ASTORIAN, a full sister to Agitate, the 1974 Hollywood Derby and Swaps winner, showed some promise in New York last September and Laz Barrera may have her ready to ramble, although her workout times have been moderate. TELL'S TREASURE, a half sister to Ack's Secret, may like a mile and gets off the rail. She came back to work well and gets blinkers.

SEVENTH RACE

1—Moon Ball
2—Confetti
3—Fast

MOON BALL appears to have found his winning stride off a stunning 48-1 tally last journey over a fine group of turf specialists. There is enough speed here for him to stalk again and looks perfectly placed for a repeat. CONFETTI was fourth to the top horse last out and seems to be acclimating nicely now after racing well in Group races in France in 1981. Pincay will be aboard this Hofmans trainee. FAST makes his comeback today after being on the shelf since 1980. He has been working exceptionally well for Whittingham and McCarron will be aboard. The 5-year-old could be right on edge. ANOTHER REALM has every right to improve, while SUNNY WINTERS is working well at Santa Anita and may enjoy the turf.

EIGHTH RACE

1—NEVER TABLED
2—Remember John
3—Pompeii Court

NEVER TABLED showed he was made of stakes timber last out when he pulled away in the stretch to win the Triple Bend 'Cap in 1:21. He is certainly favorably weighted at 116 and off a :35 blowout Friday he looks fit and ready to continue his winning ways. REMEMBER JOHN, a 3-year-old beat his elders last time, stepping 5 panels in :56, a tick off the track mark. He has the rail here and will likely have to battle PETRO D. JAY, who equalled the world mark of 1:07 1/5 last out at Turf Paradise. These two speedsters could easily kill each other off. POMPEII COURT is very sharp, while SHANEKITE may be tailing off.

NINTH RACE

1—Heart Beat
2—Kundalini
3—Pierre La Mont

HEART BEAT has the difficult task of dropping back off a 1 3/8 miles nose defeat on the turf to 1 1/8 miles, but the Frankel trainee seems to be reaching a higher plateau these days and the 5-year-old may have the class advantage. Pincay gave him a top ride last out and they combine again in this nightcap. KUNDALINI ran third at 21-1 last trip and has enjoyed this turf course in the past. He should be a stronger contender. PIERRE LA MONTE hasn't been showing his flair for speed in recent races, but should clear this field if WANTAZEE, who has never been on the turf, can't keep him company. Hawley could steal the race with PIERRE. EL PANCHO ANGEL drops into a league where he can be dangerous. Lipham has given him some fine rides in the past.

THE RESULTS

I arrived for the third race; the first two races featured only cheap claiming horses—that is, those that can be claimed for a small amount of money. The third race was a $20,000 allowance race. Shantin, the second choice in the consensus, had expected values to show in the 1.05–1.10 range and had finished in the money in seven of his ten career starts, mostly against similar-quality opposition. He was also dropping eight pounds from his last race, when he ran a creditable second with an 89 speed rating. Colonel Stu, the favorite, also ran an 89 in his last race, but he was picking up weight and had only one race in 1982 and two in 1981. Even if the odds were good, which they were not, I would be quite nervous about placing a bet on such a horse. The choice was Shantin. The chart of the race follows:

3rd Hollywood

6 FURLONGS. (1.07⅘) ALLOWANCE. Purse $20,000. 3-year-olds and upward bred in California which have not won a race other than maiden or claiming. Weights, 3-year-olds, 114 lbs.; older, 122 lbs. Non-winners of a race other than claiming since March 15 allowed 3 lbs.; such a race since February 15, 6 lbs.

Crofted — Dk. b. or br. g. 4, by Reflected Glory—Shadycroft Gal, by Bupers
Own.—Sorenson Heather D — **122** — Br.—Sorenson Heather D (Cal) — 1982 4 1 1 1 $15,300
Tr.—Gregson Edwin — 1981 5 M 1 0 $3,000
Lifetime 9 1 2 1 $18,300

8May82-7Hol	1 1/16	:46	1:103	1:43 ft	5	114	31½	42	713	717	ShoemkerW6	Aw22000	63	†LittleShah,Wantazee,RomnMjesty	8
20Mar82-4SA	6½f	:214	:443	1:164ft	4	118	63¾	63¾	43½	1½	Shoemaker W9	Mdn	86	Crofted,QuackAttack,RivetsFctor	12
5Mar82-6SA	6½f	:214	:444	1:162ft	8¾	118	42	43¼	33	32	Black K11	Mdn	86	Santir, Rivets Factor, Crofted	12
11Feb82-6SA	6½f	:221	:454	1:182gd	25	117	52½	53½	21	22½	Black K7	Mdn	75	RegalFalcon,Crofted,RivetsFactor	12
29Dec81-6SA	1 1/16	:46	1:111	1:434ft	11	117	78¾	1216	1220	1224	Sibille R8	Mdn	58	‡Poor John, Garibi, Durban Deep	12
20Nov81-6Hol	6f	:22	:452	1:11 ft	5	120	2hd	1hd	2hd	2no	Sibille R5	Mdn	82	Royal Name, Crofted, Arnold	12
18Apr81-1GG	6f	:214	:45	1:111ft	22	118	42½	53¾	88¾	87½	Diaz A5	[S]Mdn	75	Inffbl,AristocrticClown,SnowWrror	8
21Feb81-1GG	1 1/16	:464	1:111	1:434ft	14	118	53¾	811	921	932	Diaz A4	Mdn	52	Truxton'sDoubl,NoPcnc,OurGlmour	9
7Feb81-6GG	6f	:221	:452	1:101ft	15	118	79½	811	711	69¾	Hall D C2	Mdn	78	BoldDrum,VisiblPol,CutiousRobrt	12

●May 23 Hol 6f ft 1:121 h — May 17 Hol 4f ft :47 h — May 6 Hol 4f ft :502 b — ●Apr 26 SA 1 ft 1:41 h

Ready Reb — Gr. c. 3, by Reb's Policy—Tulita, by Tumollo
Own.—Fanning & Harrison — **114** — Br.—Fanning & Harrison (Cal) — 1982 6 1 0 0 $11,900
Tr.—Fanning Jerry — 1981 0 M 0 0
Lifetime 6 1 0 0 $11,900

14May82-3Hol	7f	:214	:441	1:221ft	12	120	52¼	52¼	711	612	Olivares F5	[S]Aw20000	74	L'Ntly,EnvoysIntrigue,MssgToGrci	7
24Apr82-6Hol	6f	:221	:45	1:093ft	2½	118	21	21	2½	1hd	Olivares F5	Mdn	89	ReadyReb,ElderwoodSpecial,Crlyon	5
31Mar82-4SA	6f	:221	:444	1:094ft	12	118	82½	67½	66½	66¼	Lipham T5	[S]Mdn	83	Sobrehombr,PrincChnnon,LottFlt	10
17Mar82-2SA	6f	:214	:453	1:113sy	2½	118	35	32½	35	46¾	Lipham T3	[S]Mdn	73	WindyScott,LottFleet,ThQuiltdKid	7
17Feb82-6SA	6½f	:214	:443	1:16 ft	4	118	52½	33½	57½	411	Olivares F7	[S]Mdn	79	MssgToGrci,Polly'sRulr,Mrni'sDncr	9
3Feb82-4SA	6f	:214	:451	1:101ft	6½	118	3½	2hd	23	711	Olivares F4	[S]Mdn	76	Shantin, Buckohoy,ForgottenMan	11

May 23 Hol 4f ft :502 h — May 9 Hol 5f ft :593 h — May 2 Hol 4f ft :52 b — Apr 21 SA 5f ft 1:00 h

Shantin * — B. g. 3, by Exalted Rullah—Career, by Poona II
Own.—Kelly & Christianson — **111** — Br.—Christianson C T (Cal) — 1982 7 2 2 1 $31,000
Tr.—King Hal — 1981 3 M 1 1 $5,350
Lifetime 10 2 3 2 $36,350

9May82-5Hol	6f	:22	:444	1:09 ft	2½	119	42½	43	23½	22½	McCarron C J4	50000	89	L'Cap, Shantin, Can't Be Beat	6
14Apr82-3SA	6f	:214	:443	1:094ft	5	120	41½	32½	31	42½	Asmussen C B3	62500	86	SkiRacer,Smuggler'sGold,ImSizzler	6
18Mar82-9SA	6f	:214	:452	1:12 m	2½	120	45½	42½	2hd	1½	Guerra W A4	50000	78	Shantin, Daily Report, Il Paladino	7
7Mar82-2SA	6½f	:212	:44	1:144ft	7	120	811	914	911	812	CastanedaM5	Aw20000	84	AdvanceMan,GeneralJimmy,L'Ntty	9
21Feb82-2SA	7f	:214	:44	1:22 ft	12	120	2½	2½	2½	33¼	CastanedaM9	Aw20000	87	Prestigious Lad, Le Smirk, Shantin	9
3Feb82-4SA	6f	:214	:451	1:101ft	*2½	118	1hd	1hd	13	1¾	Asmussen C B8	[S]Mdn	87	Shantin, Buckohoy,ForgottenMan	11
22Jan82-6SA	7f	:221	:452	1:234gd	3	118	2hd	3½	25	212	AsmussenCB11	[S]Mdn	69	DeLaGuerra,Shantin,ForgottenMn	12
26Dec81-3SA	6f	:22	:443	1:092ft	*2¼	118	22½	—	—	—	McCarron C J1	[S]Mdn	—	B.RchGorg,OlympcGol,CrystlDrps	11
26Dec81—Lame															
30Sep81-3SA	6f	:214	:451	1:10 ft	4	118	1hd	1½	1hd	2nk	McCarron C J2	[S]Mdn	88	Gaelic'sSport,Shntin,DesertEnvoy	12
4Sep81-6Dmr	6f	:221	:453	1:11 ft	6½	118	63¾	42	2½	32¾	McCarron CJ12	[S]Mdn	80	PrinceSpellbound,CrystlStr,Shntin	12

●May 23 Hol 5f ft :583 h — May 17 Hol 3f ft :36 h — May 4 Hol 5f ft :584 h — Apr 27 Hol 4f ft :481 h

Doon's Bay
B. g. 4, by Matsadoon—Sinbay, by Bay Ribbon
Br.—Eklund R L (Cal) 1982 3 1 1 1 $16,350
Own.—Eklund R L 122 Tr.—Harte M G 1981 11 M 6 0 $13,470
Lifetime 14 1 7 1 $29,820

14May82-5Hol 6f :221 :444 1:09 ft *2¾ 120 2½ 2½ 34½ 34½ Hawley S5 Aw20000 87 Rawbone, Colonel Stu, Doon's Bay 7
5May82-7Hol 6f :214 :443 1:091ft 6 120 41¾ 53½ 33½ 22½ McCarronCJ4 Aw20000 88 TonysLndng,Doon'sBy,ChrgAccont 6
17Apr82-6SA 6½f :22 :444 1:162ft 5½ 118 31 2½ 11½ 1¾ McCarron C J9 Mdn 88 Doon'sBy,TruceMker,BruinCounty 12
4Dec81-5BM 6f :23 :463 1:12 ft *6-5 118 85½ 74 54½ 74¾ Diaz A L10 AlwM 75 CldBTff,BrvCmmndr,QckrEnCndy 12
14Nov81-1BM 1 :462 1:111 1:371gd *1 118 21 2hd 1hd 2hd Diaz A L4 Mdn 83 Penns Friends, Doon's Bay, StatsU. 9
30Oct81-3BM 1 1/16 :47 1:123 1:451ft *8-5 116 2½ 2hd 33 27 Diaz A L6 Mdn 66 FbulousRson,Doon'sBy,PrciousTim 7
16Oct81-4BM 1 1/16 :461 1:103 1:424ft *9-5 116 21 11 12 2nk Diaz A L4 Mdn 85 ArroyoSeco,Doon'sBy,FbulousRson 9
2Oct81-4BM 1 1/16 :453 1:10 1:424ft *2½ 116 47½ 24 22 21½ Diaz A L6 Mdn 83 Cinnpo, Doon's Bay, Stats U. 8
23Sep81-6BM 6f :223 :452 1:103ft *6-5 116 1hd 2hd 3nk 2no Diaz A L2 Mdn 87 BoldTatt,Doon'sBy,BrveCommnder 7
10Sep81-7Bmf 6f :223 :46 1:112ft 15 116 54 31½ 21½ 2no Diaz A L11 Mdn 83 Rhythmus, Doon's Bay, HighAgain 12
Apr 29 Hol 5f ft 1:033 h Apr 10 SA 7f ft 1:27 h Apr 3 SA 6f ft 1:122 hg

Seavoy
Dk. b. or br. g. 4, by Envoy—Come Sea Me Honey, by Windy Sea
Br.—Pascoe W T III (Cal) 1982 9 1 2 0 $17,350
Own.—Cmpnlli-Myr-Murphy-Thoms 116 Tr.—Stute Melvin F 1981 1 M 0 1 $2,100
Lifetime 10 1 2 1 $19,450

6May82-6Hol 6f :214 :452 1:104ft 3½ 123 31½ 32 1½ 12 Pincay L Jr5 M40000 83 Seavoy, Sales Goal, Blow Taps 12
23Apr82-6Hol 6½f :222 :451 1:17 ft *2 121 1½ 2hd 23 45½ ValenzuelaPA8 M45000 79 DeltaGambler,JsminePrince,Dilville 8
2Apr82-6SA 6f :214 :45 1:101ft *2½ 118 2hd 2½ 45 79¾ Delahoussaye E4 Mdn 77 NeverTbled,Hwkire,SpnishNugget 10
20Mar82-4SA 6½f :214 :443 1:164ft *2½ 118 31½ 21 32½ 52½ Delahoussaye E2 Mdn 83 Crofted,QuackAttack,RivetsFctor 12
5Mar82-6SA 6½f :214 :444 1:162ft *9-5 118 3½ 3nk 1hd 42½ Valenzuela P A4 Mdn 86 Santir, Rivets Factor, Crofted 12
20Feb82-3SA 6f :214 :443 1:091ft 5 117 11½ 12½ 13 2nk Valenzuela P A3 Mdn 92 Cad, Seavoy, Exclusive Session 12
11Feb82-6SA 6½f :221 :454 1:182gd 10 117 1hd 2½ 54½ 613 Valenzuela P A10 Mdn 65 RegalFalcon,Crofted,RivetsFactor 12
29Jan82-6SA 6f :212 :442 1:103ft 2½ 117 11½ 14 1½ 2nk Valenzuela P A7 Mdn 85 Ergo, Seavoy, Peter Jones 12
16Jan82-4SA 6f :214 :45 1:10 ft *2 117 43½ 33 45½ 47¾ Valenzuela P A11 Mdn 80 DrumDrum,RivetsFctor,Cumplnos 12
20Dec81-2Hol 6½f :223 :45 1:182ft 4 118 1½ 1hd 2hd 3nk Valenzuela P A6 Mdn 78 Jensen'sPrince,Marc'sGleem,Sevoy 8
May 27 Hol 5f ft :592 h May 21 Hol 4f ft :51 h May 16 Hol 4f ft :474 h May 1 Hol 5f ft 1:001 h

Colonel Stu
B. c. 4, by Orbit Ruler—Sarasvati, by Oceanus II
Br.—Williams & Cofer (Cal) 1982 1 0 1 0 $4,000
Own.—Cofer R S 116 Tr.—Cofer Riley S 1981 2 0 0 0
Lifetime 4 1 1 0 $12,250

14May82-5Hol 6f :221 :444 1:09 ft 6½ 114 52½ 31½ 22½ 23 Guerra W A1 Aw20000 89 Rawbone, Colonel Stu, Doon's Bay 7
29Mar81-2SA 6½f :213 :443 1:164ft *3¾ 120 42 64¾ 78¾ 712 EstradaJJr5 Ⓢ Aw21000 74 Airroling,Jeff'sEncore,WickdHittr 11
17Jan81-2SA 6½f :214 :443 1:163ft 3½ 120 2½ 1hd 2½ 64¾ McCrrnCJ8 Ⓢ Aw20000 82 HeavyHand,TomMack,BeuVitesse 10
26Dec80-3SA 6f :214 :45 1:102ft *1 118 61½ 42½ 1hd 12½ McCarron C J4 Ⓢ Mdn 87 ColonelStu,FoxieDon,HighlndStyl 12
May 24 Hol 5f ft 1:012 h ● May 10 Hol 5f ft :59 h May 5 Hol 6f ft 1:133 hg Apr 28 Hol 5f ft 1:011 h

War House
B. g. 4, by House Committee—Camera Shy, by Dumpty Humpty
Br.—Santoro M D (Cal) 1982 6 1 0 2 $9,800
Own.—Santoro M 116 Tr.—Finelli Charles 1981 6 1 0 0 $10,725
Lifetime 13 3 0 2 $22,065

8May82-9Fno 6f :213 :441 1:091ft 15 118 31½ 33 34½ 36½ WllingtonHK2 Bulldog 87 AmnBrothr,AnswrtoMusic,WrHous 6
14Apr82-1SA 6f :22 :444 1:10 ft 22 117 107½ 97½ 63¼ 1hd Wellington HK9 12500 88 WarHouse,TragicBell,AnotherTost 11
19Feb82-1SA 6½f :213 :441 1:144ft 20 115 42½ 57 810 1219 Torres R2 16000 77 RoughRidr,SummrSlor,Goff'sDncr 12
31Jan82-1SA 6f :213 :441 1:093ft 14 115 1214 1217 1213 86½ Olivares F6 20000 83 BoldBatim,Predilection,HeavyHnd 12
14Jan82-1SA 6f :214 :45 1:094ft 12 115 52½ 54½ 32½ 34¼ Winland W M4 16000 84 Devon, Qualification, War House 10
3Jan82-1SA 6f :221 :462 1:124hy 12 115 42 31½ 38 618 Winland W M2 16000 56 SuprStrVncnt,OmhMk,EmprorJohn 7
17Aug81-2Dmr 6f :221 :452 1:112ft 13 115 76½ 88 119½ 107½ Valdivieso H A5 25000 73 PasstheBll,ImmnentIssue,Rosewlk 12
7Aug81-9Dmr 6f :223 :453 1:102ft 9½ 116 11 1hd 21 47¾ Mena F6 25000 78 Garfield County,BubbasKid,Geraldo 6
27Jly81-7Dmr 6f :221 :444 1:101ft 11 114 44 68½ 77½ 89¾ Lipham T6 40000 77 GrfldConty,ImportntMmo,MjorDcn 8
12Apr81-6SA 6½f :214 :45 1:162ft 15 116 1hd 64 811 716 ConnollyR7 Ⓢ Aw22000 72 Sunshine Swag, Rawbone, Iona 8

Message To Garcia
Ch. c. 3, by Messenger of Song—Sisal, by Hillsdale
Br.—Ridder B J (Cal) 1982 6 1 0 1 $12,350
Own.—Ridder B J 111 Tr.—Campbell Gordon C 1981 0 M 0 0
Lifetime 6 1 0 1 $12,350

14May82-3Hol 7f :214 :441 1:221ft 17 117 3½ 2hd 2½ 32 CastnedM3 Ⓢ Aw20000 84 L'Ntty,EnvoysIntrigue,MssgToGrci 7
17Apr82-2SA 6f :212 :444 1:10 ft 17 120 53¾ 32 43¾ 64 Lipham T5 Aw19000 84 Polly's Ruler, L'Natty,WindyScott 12
17Mar82-7SA 6f :213 :444 1:11 sy 7 120 42½ 55½ 69½ 615 McCrrnCJ6 Ⓢ Aw20000 68 GnrlJimmy,Polly'sRulr,EbonyBronz 6
28Feb82-5SA 1 1/16 :454 1:094 1:411ft 16 115 33 49 817 923 Sibille R1 Aw20000 72 JourneyatSea,RoyalCptive,AskMe 12
17Feb82-6SA 6½f :214 :443 1:16 ft 4 118 21 21 2½ 1hd McCarron C J9 Ⓢ Mdn 90 MssgToGrci,Polly'sRulr,Mrni'sDncr 3
3Feb82-4SA 6f :214 :451 1:101ft 12 118 76¾ 87½ 77¾ 69¾ McHargue DG2 Ⓢ Mdn 77 Shantin, Buckohoy,ForgottenMan 11
May 26 Hol 5f ft 1:002 h May 10 Hol 5f ft 1:002 h ● Apr 30 Hol 5f ft :591 h Apr 14 SA 4f ft :482 hg

Windy Scott ✻ | B. g. 3, by Doc Scott J—Windy Poppy, by Windy Sea
Own.—J K Houssels Sr Estate | 109^5 | Br.—Houssels J K Jr (Cal) | 1982 6 1 1 2 $16,400
Tr.—Adams George D | 1981 1 M 0 0
Lifetime 7 1 1 2 $16,400

14May82-3Hol	7f	:21^4	:44^1	1:22^{1}ft	22	120	1½	3^1	5^{4}½	5^{5}½	Black K^7	[S]Aw20000	80	L'Ntty,EnvoysIntrigue,MssgToGrci	7
17Apr82-2SA	6f	:21^2	:44^4	1:10 ft	41	120	1hd	1hd	2hd	3^3	Black K^1	Aw19000	85	Polly's Ruler, L'Natty,WindyScott	12
3Apr82-5SA	6f	:22	:45^2	1:09^{3}ft	20	120	2hd	3½	3^5	6^{12}	VldiviesoHA^6	Aw20000	78	B.RichGeorg,Polly'sRulr,Accousticl	9
17Mar82-2SA	6f	:21^4	:45^3	1:11^{3}sy	*2	118	1^1	1½	1^{3}½	1^5	McCarron C J^7	[S]Mdn	80	WindyScott,LottFleet,ThQuiltdKid	7
26Feb82-4SA	6f	:21^4	:45	1:09^{4}ft	5½	118	1½	1^{2}½	1^1	2^{1}½	Carrasco R L^9	M32000	87	Can'tBeBet,WindyScott,ChiefZero	11
5Feb82-3SA	6½f	:21^3	:44^2	1:16^{3}ft	29	118	1½	2hd	4^4	3^8	CarrascoRL^7	[S]M25000	79	FrnchCmndr,HllljhBrthr,WndSctt	12
29Dec81-3SA	6½f	:21^4	:45	1:17^{2}ft	25	115	—	—	—	—	VlenzuelPA^2	[S]M28000	—	Agitto,SuchGentlemn,DistntChrm	12

29Dec81—Bolted

May 26 SA 6f ft 1:15^1 h **May 12 SA 4f sl :52^4 h** **May 6 SA 6f ft 1:18^1 h** **Apr 27 SA 5f ft 1:02^4 h**

At post time the tote board read as follows:

	Totals	#3 Shantin
Odds		2—1
Win	169,900	42,181
Show	55,074	11,784

The expected value was 1.04. Not surprisingly, Shantin won the race and Colonel Stu was out of the money. The payoff to show on Shantin was $3.60, which was a handsome sum for a 2–1 shot going off with an expected value of 1.04. The payoff was high because 24–1 and 18–1 long shots finished second and third. My $50 bet returned $90, for a $40 profit.

The chart of the race was as follows:

THIRD RACE Hollywood MAY 30, 1982

6 FURLONGS. (1.07⅘) ALLOWANCE. Purse $20,000. 3-year-olds and upward bred in California which have not won a race other than maiden or claiming. Weights, 3-year-olds, 114 lbs.; older, 122 lbs. Non-winners of a race other than claiming since March 15 allowed 3 lbs.; such a race since February 15, 6 lbs.

Value of race $20,000, value to winner $11,000, second $4,000, third $3,000, fourth $1,500, fifth $500. Mutuel pool $309,240. Exacta Pool $473,323.

Last Raced	Horse	Eqt.A.Wt	PP	St	¼	½	Str	Fin	Jockey	Odds $1
9May82 ^{5}Hol^2	Shantin	b 3 112	3	8	8½	5^{1}½	4^{2}½	1^{1}½	Valenzuela P A	2.40
14May82 ^{3}Hol^5	Windy Scott	3 109	9	1	1^{1}½	1^3	1^3	2¾	Steiner J J^5	24.20
8May82 ^{9}Fno^3	War House	b 4 117	7	3	5^1	2½	2^1	3½	Wellington H K	18.30
14May82 ^{3}Hol^3	Message To Garcia	b 3 115	8	2	6½	4^1	3½	4nk	Castaneda M	7.00
14May82 ^{5}Hol^2	Colonel Stu	4 116	6	6	7^{1}½	8^3	6^{2}½	5^4	Delahoussaye E	1.40
8May82 ^{7}Hol^7	Crofted	b 4 122	1	9	9	9	8^1	6^{1}½	Pincay L Jr	18.60
14May82 ^{5}Hol^3	Doon's Bay	b 4 122	4	4	4½	7½	7½	7^1	McCarron C J	5.80
14May82 ^{3}Hol^6	Ready Reb	b 3 114	2	7	2hd	3^2	5^1	8^{3}½	Olivares F	22.60
6May82 ^{6}Hol^1	Seavoy	b 4 116	5	5	3hd	6hd	9	9	Diaz A L	35.50

OFF AT 2:40. Start good. Won driving. Time, :22, :44⅗, :57⅕, 1:10⅗ Track fast.

$2 Mutuel Prices:			
3-SHANTIN	6.80	4.80	3.60
9-WINDY SCOTT		17.80	9.60
7-WAR HOUSE			6.60

$5 EXACTA 3-9 PAID $271.00.

B. g, by Exalted Rullah—Career, by Poona II. Trainer King Hal. Bred by Christianson C T (Cal).

SHANTIN, slow to find his best stride after the start, rallied strongly on the outside entering the stretch, wore down WINDY SCOTT and was up in the closing yards. The latter darted to the lead at once, opened up a long lead on the turn but gradually weakened in the final furlong. WAR HOUSE, in contention between horses in the second flight to the stretch, lugged out under left-handed pressure in the deep stretch. MESSAGE TO GARCIA, a bit wide to the stretch, rallied between horses in the upper stretch, was floated out a bit by WAR HOUSE, lodged a claim of foul against SHANTIN, alleging interference in the stretch, but it was dismissed. COLONEL STU lacked early speed and did not reach contention with a mild closing rally while drifting in through the final furlong. DOON'S BAY weakened before a half-mile. READY REB tired in the stretch. SEAVOY, in contention between horses to the turn, gradually tired thereafter.

Owners— 1, Kelly & Christianson; 2, J K Houssels Sr Estate; 3, Hemet Hills Farm; 4, Ridder B J; 5, Spelling A; 6, Sorenson Heather D; 7, Eklund R L; 8, Fanning & Harrison; 9, Campanelli-Meyer-Murphy-Thomas.

Overweight: Shantin 1 pound; War House 1; Message To Garcia 4.

4th Hollywood

7 FURLONGS. (1.19⅗) ALLOWANCE. Purse $26,000. 3-year-olds and upward which have not won $2,500 three times other than maiden, claiming or starter. Weights, 3-year-olds, 114 lbs.; older, 122 lbs. Non-winners of two such races since March 1 allowed 3 lbs.; such a race since then, 6 lbs.

B. Rich George

Ch. c. 3, by Don B—Patch It Up, by My Host
Br.—Trickett B H (Cal) 1982 10 1 2 1 $28,180
Own.—Solar Stable 111 Tr.—Webb George H 1981 12 1 3 3 $35,475
Lifetime 22 2 5 4 $63,655 Turf 2 0 1 0 $6,800

21May82-7Hol 7f :221 :45 1:223ft 4½ 114 11 11 2hd 33½ Olivares F6 Aw26000 80 Jet Travel, Dena Jo, B. RichGeorge 6
15May82-8Hol 1⅛ ⓣ:47 1:11 1:403fm 13 114 2½ 1hd 42½ 815 Olivares F3 W Rgrs H 81 GiveMeStrength,AskMe,Accousticl 8
15May82—Run in two divisions, 8th and 9th races.
15Apr82-8SA a6½f ⓣ:214 :4341:144fm 17 119 2½ 2hd 2hd 2hd Mena F7 Aw30000 85 ChuliStreet,B.RichGeorge,Spiritino 9
3Apr82-5SA 6f :22 :452 1:093ft 5½ 120 42½ 2½ 1hd 1¾ Mena F8 Aw28000 90 B.RichGeorg,Polly'sRulr,Accousticl 9
21Mar82-4SA 6½f :212 :44 1:152ft 13 120 32 21 23 47½ Mena F4 Aw20000 85 RemembrJohn,ClticSbr,EstrSrmon 6
7Mar82-2SA 6½f :212 :44 1:144ft 11 120 62¾ 66½ 66 47¾ Mena F3 Aw20000 88 AdvanceMan,GeneralJimmy,L'Ntty 9
10Feb82-7SA 6f :214 :45 1:114sy 3½ 120 2hd 23 39 59 Mena F3 Aw19000 70 JtPirt,HowNowDow,StndupComdin 7
30Jan82-7SA 6f :212 :44 1:091ft 3½ 120 21½ 1½ 2½ 66 ValenzuelPA5 Aw19000 86 TimeToExplode,JourneytSe,SrdSpy 8
14Jan82-5SA 6f :213 :443 1:091ft 5 120 1½ 11 2hd 22½ AsmussenCB2 Aw19000 90 Jet Travel, B. RichGeorge,Rise'nFly 9
8Jan82-5SA 6f :213 :444 1:102gd 2½ 120 33 45½ 715 827 McCarronCJ4 Aw19000 59 Unpredictable,Fanjet,HowNowDow 8
May 7 Hol ⓣ 1 fm 1:47 h (d) Apr 26 Hol 4f ft :49 h

*Some Lute

B. h. 5, by Luthier—Some Dame, by Vieux Manoir
Br.—Secd'Elvs&ExploitationAgr (Fra) 1982 2 0 0 0
Own.—Vanian Souken S 116 Tr.—Perkins Larry 1981 8 1 0 2 $21,313
Lifetime 21 2 1 4 $51,265 Turf 21 2 1 4 $51,265

13May82-8Hol 1 ⓣ:4521:10 1:34 fm 81 114 1½ 2hd 86½1015 ValenzuelPA9 Aw30000 84 Table Torch, Guarantee, Dhausli 10
29Apr82-8Hol 6f :22 :443 1:082ft 37 115 76 78½ 712 713 Pierce D6 Aw26000 82 LaughingBoy,BeachWalk,Redoutble 7
27Sep81♦4Longchamp(Fra) a1 1:471gd 1-5 126 ⓣ 1010 BdelA Pr du Rond Pt(Gr3) Deltwn,DimondProspect,Redoutbl 10
8Aug81♦7Deauville(Fra) a1 1:422fm 14 127 ⓣ 54½ Badel A Pr de Varaville Tarrago, Wild Idea, Bookman 9
23Jly81♦4MLafitte(Fra) a1 1:361gd 17 121 ⓣ 13 Badel A Pr Messidor(Gr3) Ya Zaman, Daeltown, Spoleto 16
4Jly81♦4Longchamp(Fra) a7f 1:271gd 35 128 ⓣ 76¾ BadelA Pr Porte Maillot(Gr3) Gosport, Mistra, Manjam 13
9Jun81♦5Chantilly(Fra) a1 1:411gd 26 126 ⓣ 31½ BdlA PrChmndFrdNrd(Gr3) Gosport, Moon Ingraver,SomeLute 8
19May81♦5StCloud(Fra) a1 1:474sf 7 121 ⓣ 1nk Badel A Pr Lovelace Some Lute,Thisman,NewGrandame 8
1May81♦4StCloud(Fra) a1 1:411sf 9 119 ⓣ 79¾ StMrtY Pr du Muguet(Gr3) North Jet, Joberan, Confetti 9
12Apr81♦6Longchamp(Fra) a1 1:422gd 12 123 ⓣ 31½ StMrtin Pr Butte Mrtmrt Daeltown, Roll of Power,SomeLute 8
May 26 Hol 4f ft :462 h May 20 Hol 4f ft :473 h May 7 Hol 1 ft 1:403 h Apr 26 Hol 4f ft :483 hg

Chapel Creek

B. c. 4, by Our Native—Spanked, by Cornish Prince
Br.—Conners Mary E (Conn) 1982 6 0 0 1 $4,950
Own.—Loblolly Stable 116 Tr.—Cleveland Gene 1981 10 2 1 1 $47,526
Lifetime 22 3 4 2 $73,896 Turf 1 0 0 0

8May82-3Hol 6f :221 :444 1:084ft 27 115 62½ 55 44 32½ McHrgueDG1 Aw26000 90 BeachWlk,MsterWrrior,ChpelCreek 8
29Apr82-8Hol 6f :22 :443 1:082ft 10 115 43 42 53½ 66¾ Hawley S3 Aw26000 88 LaughingBoy,BeachWalk,Redoutble 7
31Mar82-8OP 6f :222 :464 1:14 ft 3 114 88½ 89½ 711 75½ Snyder L6 Aw20000 69 HerefordMan,TryMac,MyDerChrlie 8
20Mar82-8OP 170:47 1:132 1:432ft 6 111 2hd 2hd 716 720 Kaenel J L9 Aw17500 59 VodikaCollins,Dr.Spnky,Rckensck 10
10Mar82-9OP 6f :213 :453 1:123ft 3½ 113 99¾ 710 54 42½ Kaenel J L3 Aw17500 79 BinABttle,Miromn,AvngingGossip 12
4Mar82-9OP 6f :23 :473 1:123ft *6-5 113 95½ 83 75½ 77 Kaenel J L7 Aw20000 75 Lind'sLughin,JoK.Jr.,Contorsionst 10
2Aug81-5Sar 6f :214 :442 1:082ft 19 112 68¾ 66½ 57 69 Maple E4 Aw23000 89 Maudlin, Khartoum, Will Of Iron 7
8Jly81-6Bel 6f :224 :451 1:084ft 15 111 46½ 37 46½ 47½ MacBeth D2 Aw23000 90 Miswaki, Khartoum, Fly North 6
12Jun81-8Bel 1 ⓣ:45 1:09 1:34 fm 24 113 89 1014101610121 Vasquez J4 Aw25000 74 WrofWords,Bucksplshr,ExplosvBd 11
9May81-8Bel 1 :451 1:10 1:364ft 9½ 126 56 78 710 713 Maple E4 Withers 71 Spirited Boy, Willow Hour, A Run 7
●May 22 Hol 7f ft 1:25 h May 16 Hol 5f ft 1:004 h ●Apr 20 SA 6f ft 1:103 h Apr 14 SA 4f ft :461 h

Surprise George

B. c. 4, by Pleasure Seeker—Porterville Bay, by Nigret
Br.—Achterberg G (Cal) 1981 10 2 0 1 $52,800
Own.—Achterberg G 116 Tr.—Brooks L J 1980 2 1 1 0 $10,237
Lifetime 12 3 1 1 $63,037 Turf 7 1 0 1 $36,900

9Jly81-9Hol 1 ⓣ:4621:1031:35 fm 3½ 114 66½ 41 3½ 63½ Lipham T4 Westwood 91 Lemhi Gold,RockSoftly,IslandWhirl 7
9Jly81—Run in two divisions, 8th & 9th races.
26Jun81-4Hol 1⅛ⓣ:4731:1141:413fm 6½ 117 63¾ 64 77 77½ Lipham T4 Aw30000 83 MinnsotChif,IslndWhirl,MstrThtch 7
7Jun81-8Hol 1⅛ⓣ:4511:0931:403fm 15 114 913 45½ 44 44¾ Lipham T7 Cinema H 91 MinnsotChf,Stnchrry,SplnddSpruc 12
23May81-8Hol 1⅛ⓣ:4611:1041:412fm 11 115 65½ 62¾ 42½ 32½ LiphamT5 Wl Rgers H 89 SplendidSpruce,Sfood,SurprisGorg 8
1May81-8Hol 1 ⓣ:4641:1041:351fm 4½ 117 99½ 53¾ 33 1nk Lipham T9 Aw28000 93 SurprisGorg,WtrwyDriv,QuntumLp 10
15Apr81-8SA 1⅛ⓣ:46 1:0931:464fm 8½ 114 43½ 32 23 54½ Lipham T3 La Puente 89 Axe House, Mehmet, Flying Gene 13
1Apr81-8SA a6½f ⓣ:211 :4331:143fm 12 114 87½ 79 65¾ 4nk Lipham T8 Baldwin 86 Descaro, Motivity, Steelinctive 13
21Mar81-6SA 1⅛:461 1:111 1:433gd 4½ 115 2hd 1hd 2hd 42½ DelhoussyeE7 Aw28000 80 Seafood, Partez, Table Torch 8
13Mar81-6SA 6½f :212 :441 1:154ft 7 117 611 69½ 46 47½ Lipham T1 Aw30000 84 Litigator, Scotts Bar, Steelinctive 6
28Feb81-2SA 6½f :214 :451 1:173sy 7 114 85 3½ 13 11 Lipham T8 ⓈAw21000 82 SurprisGorg,Ultrchrg,SunshinSwg 11
May 19 Hol 6f ft 1:152 h May 14 Hol 6f ft 1:14 h May 9 Hol 5f ft 1:001 h May 4 Hol 4f ft :473 h

```
Sali's Royal Dream                    B. g. 4, by Blood Royal—Sali Sara, by Nagea
                                      Br.—Gaylord Ann (Ky)                   1982  2  0  0  0     $2,600
Own.—Merton Mr–Mrs H D          116   Tr.—Whitby Steve M                     1981  9  3  1  2    $45,675
                                Lifetime   11  3  1  2   $48,275             Turf  1  0  0  0
29Apr82-8Hol  6f  :22  :443 1:082ft    4  114  64½ 65½ 66½ 55½  Guerra W A4   Aw26000 90 LaughingBoy,BeachWalk,Redoutble 7
11Apr82-5SA   6½f :22  :451 1:17 sy    8¼ 114  710 76  54  41½  McCarronCJ3   Aw26000 83 Tellround,Redoutble,He'sSomthing 7
9Dec81-7Hol   6½f :221 :45  1:154ft    8¼ 114  87¾ 77½ 69½ 58½  Ramirez O5    Aw25000 82 PompeiiCourt,KngrooCourt,Dorcro 8
27Nov81-7Hol  6½f :223 :453 1:183sy    4¼ 113  76½ 75½ 36½ 33¼  Hawley S1     Aw25000 74 DndyWit,PompiiCourt,Sli'sRoylDrm 8
15Nov81-5Hol  1 1/16 T:4711:1121:414fm  4 112  54  42½ 46  69   McCarronCJ9   Aw28000 81 Krassawitz, Vorlaufer, Lucullus 9
6Nov81-9SA    6f  :22  :443 1:09 ft   19  119  77  610 56½ 31½  Ramirez O1    Aw30000 92 ShrpHoofer,Inception,Sli'sRoylDrm 7
24Oct81-8SA   1 1/16 :46 1:10 1:414ft   7¾ 112  76½ 77¾ 89¼ 611  McCrronCJ1  Alibhai H 81 Native Tactics, Rock Softly, Damas 9
24Aug81-8Dmr  1   :452 1:101 1:363ft    3  113  42½ 33½ 45  21½  McCarronCJ3   Aw30000 83 AtYourPlesure,Sli'sRoylDrem,Dscro 6
30Jly81-7Dmr  6f  :224 :452 1:102ft    4  115  65¾ 43½ 32½ 1hd  McCarronCJ8   Aw18000 86 Sli'sRoylDrem,BondRullh,BronzStr 8
1Jly81-9Hol   6f  :213 :45  1:103ft   *2¾ 116  75½ 74¾ 53½ 1no  McCarronCJ6   Aw20000 84 Sl'sRoylDrm,SchoolHr,RllySmbdy 12
    May 25 Hol 6f ft 1:131 h       May 18 Hol 5f ft 1:00 h       May 11 Hol 3f ft :36 h       Apr 24 SA 4f ft :47 h

Perry Cabin                           B. g. 5, by Arts and Letters—Hester Prynne, by Dedicate
                                      Br.—Headley D A (Ky)                   1982  7  2  2  0    $43,450
Own.—Baumbach & King            116   Tr.—Fanning Jerry                      1981 21  3  4  3    $91,010
                                Lifetime   56 10 12  7   $206,198            Turf 15  5  1  0    $82,435
15May82-3Hol  7f  :221 :442 1:22 ft    5  119  612 68  45  2¾   Olivares F1     62500 86 No No, Perry Cabin, Philip E. 6
29Apr82-7Hol  1 1/16 T:4641:1031:411fm  4¼ 116  48½ 33  52¾ 1no  Olivares F7     62500 93 Perry Cabin, Val De Roi, Chriserik 9
11Apr82-3SA   1⅛  :474 1:121 1:494sy  15  116  43  31  11½ 12½  Toro F3         50000 80 Perry Cabin, Three Bits, HeartBeat 6
14Mar82-9SA   1 1/16 :464 1:12 1:452sy 11  116  712 714 717 518  Lipham T5       62500 56 TheArgyleKid,BeauMoro,Stingingly 7
24Feb82-5SA   1⅛ T:4631:1041:474fm  5¼ 116  67½ 66  89½ 812  Lipham T10      62500 76 BadRascal,BeauSoleil,BlueDncerII 10
31Jan82-9SA   1 1/16 :462 1:103 1:421ft  6  116  67½ 62¾ 32  2nk  Lipham T1       50000 90 Three Bits, Perry Cabin, Geshes 7
1Jan82-5SA    1 1/16 :48 1:133 1:471hy  5¾ 116  55½ 65½ 45½ 59½  Lipham T3       50000 55 Alshurouk, Three Bits, Dogo 9
6Dec81-9Hol   1   T:4621:1121:354fm  5¼ 116  67  63¾ 56¾ 42½  Lipham T2       65000 87 Sosegdo,MisterWilder,DissiptdDollr 8
21Nov81-9Hol  1   :454 1:10 1:351ft    4  118  87½ 68½ 511 510  Harris W3       65000 80 Black Sulphur, Dogo, Hard to Lee 8
9Nov81-8LA    1 1/16 :441 1:10 1:431ft  2  116  58½ 53¾ 3½  2½   Harris W2     Aw28000 92 DancynTim,PerryCbin,BlckSulphur 5
    May 29 Hol 3f ft :371 b        May 23 Hol 5f ft 1:021 h      May 14 Hol 3f ft :363 b      Apr 26 Hol 5f ft 1:012 h

Master Warrior                        Ch. g. 4, by Native Charger—Mia Mood, by Crozier
                                      Br.—Hooper F W (Fla)                   1982  7  0  2  0    $14,950
Own.—Hooper F W                 116   Tr.—Fenstermaker L R                   1981 11  3  0  2    $44,700
                                Lifetime   20  3  2  2   $59,650             Turf  4  0  0  0       $650
8May82-3Hol   6f  :221 :444 1:084ft   22  115  31  21½ 2½  2½   Sibille R6    Aw26000 92 BeachWlk,MsterWrrior,ChpelCreek 8
29Apr82-8Hol  6f  :22  :443 1:082ft   16  115  53½ 52  33  44½  Sibille R7    Aw26000 90 LaughingBoy,BeachWalk,Redoutble 7
14Mar82-7SA   6½f :213 :443 1:182sy  *2½ 117  47½ 36  25  21½  McCarronCJ6   Aw26000 76 Trrsto'sSngr,MstrWrror,H'sSmthng 6
26Feb82-7SA   6f  :22  :444 1:084ft   14  116  2½  2hd 41¾ 46   McCarronCJ4   Aw26000 88 MisterWilder,LughingBoy,Tllround 7
14Feb82-5SA   1 1/16 :46 1:10 1:414ft  16  113  2½  3½  86¾ 911  Hansen R D1   Aw30000 81 Egg Toss,EarlySettler,MisterWilder 9
28Jan82-7SA   6½f :212 :434 1:153ft   47  116  67½ 68  53  53   Hansen R D4   Aw26000 89 Tooovrprim,MistrWildr,Cloonwillin 7
15Jan82-5SA   6f  :22  :443 1:082ft   44  116  65½ 67  69¼ 611  Hansen R D7   Aw26000 85 Maxistar, Bond Rullah, Tellaround 8
22Nov81-7Hol  7f  :213 :442 1:223ft   18  116  67½ 53½ 57½ 63   Hansen R D4   Aw30000 81 ImportntMmo,KnndyRidg,DustyHul 9
2Nov81-10LA   7f  :222 :461 1:242ft  *4-5 112  1½  1hd 11  1hd  Hansen R D4   Aw24000 87 MasterWarrior,Who'sLeder,Prmetti 7
21Oct81-5SA   a6½f T:212 :4411:142fm 10  116  42½ 33½ 64¼ 65½  ValenzuelPA3  Aw25000 81 StrRoute,MisterWilder,Prodigious 10
  ●May 29 Hol 3f ft :34 h          May 23 Hol 6f ft 1:15 h       May 7 Hol 3f ft :364 h       Apr 27 Hol 4f ft :491 h
```

In the fourth race, one of the consensus favorites and the favorite of the betting crowd was Perry Cabin. Perry Cabin was ridden by Frank Olivares, who had guided him to a first- and a second-place finish in two recent races at Hollywood Park. The expected value for a show bet on Perry Cabin was about 1.05, with a final tote board of

	Totals	#6 Perry Cabin
Odds		2—1
Win	192,676	50,523
Show	40,661	9,824

Perry Cabin won the race and paid $3 to show. This was quite a reasonable payoff for a 2–1 shot with only seven horses and a 1.01 final expected value. The payoff was improved when the second favorite finished out of the money. My $50 bet returned $75, for a $25 profit. The chart of the race was as follows:

FOURTH RACE
Hollywood
MAY 30, 1982

7 FURLONGS. (1.19⅗) ALLOWANCE. Purse $26,000. 3–year–olds and upward which have not won $2,500 three times other than maiden, claiming or starter. Weights, 3–year–olds, 114 lbs.; older, 122 lbs. Non–winners of two such races since March 1 allowed 3 lbs.; such a race since then, 6 lbs.

Value of race $26,000, value to winner $14,300, second $5,200, third $3,900, fourth $1,950, fifth $650. Mutuel pool $319,342. Exacta Pool $427,407.

Last Raced	Horse	Eqt.A.Wt	PP	St	¼	½	Str	Fin	Jockey	Odds $1
15May82 ^{3}Hol^{2}	Perry Cabin	b 5 116	6	5	6^{5}	5^{2}	3^{1}	1^{nk}	Olivares F	2 20
29Apr82 ^{8}Hol^{5}	Sali's Royal Dream	4 116	5	4	5^{1½}	3^{1}	1^{½}	2^{3}	McCarron C J	6.50
21May82 ^{7}Hol^{3}	B. Rich George	3 117	1	6	1^{1½}	1^{1}	2^{½}	3^{1½}	Pincay L Jr	4.00
8May82 ^{3}Hol^{2}	Master Warrior	4 116	7	1	4^{1½}	2^{hd}	4^{2½}	4^{1}	Sibille R	2.30
9Jly81 ^{9}Hol^{6}	Surprise George	b 4 116	4	7	7	7	6^{8}	5^{¾}	Delahoussaye E	17.00
8May82 ^{3}Hol^{3}	Chapel Creek	4 116	3	2	2^{hd}	4^{1}	5^{hd}	6^{10}	McHargue D G	5.90
13May82 ^{8}Hol^{10}	Some Lute	5 116	2	3	3^{hd}	6^{3}	7	7	Valenzuela P A	23.90

OFF AT 3:14 Start good. Won driving. Time, :22⅕, :44⅗, 1:09⅖, 1:22 Track fast.

$2 Mutuel Prices:			
6–PERRY CABIN	6.40	3.40	3.00
5–SALI'S ROYAL DREAM		5.60	4.20
1–B. RICH GEORGE			3.80

$5 EXACTA 6–5 PAID $92.50

B. g, by Arts and Letters—Hester Prynne, by Dedicate. Trainer Fanning Jerry. Bred by Headley D A (Ky).

PERRY CABIN, unhurried early, saved ground around the turn, found room to rally on the rail through the stretch and was up in the closing yards. SALI'S ROYAL DREAM, never far back, moved to contention inside horses at the far turn, got the lead in the upper stretch but could not quite last. B. RICH GEORGE sprinted to the lead in the opening quarter-mile, but weakened in the final sixteenth. MASTER WARRIOR, in contention while far wide into the far turn, tired in the final furlong. CHAPEL CREEK, in contention between horses to the far turn, gradually weakened after a half-mile. SOME LUTE had only brief early speed.

Owners— 1, Baumbach & King; 2, Morton Mr-Mrs H D; 3, Solar Stable; 4, Hooper F W; 5, Achterberg G; 6, Loblolly Stable; 7, Vanian Souken S.

Overweight: B. Rich George 6 pounds.

The fifth race was for three-year-olds over 6 furlongs for an $18,000 purse. The top choices were Insearchof, Jet Pirate, Extra Quick, Spectacular Bee, and Distant Gem. Insearchof had finished in the money in three of the last four races against similar-quality horses. Jet Pirate was out of the money in the last four races. However, he had run in faster time against higher-quality opposition. Today he was dropping in class. Extra Quick was moving up in class and appeared too weak for this opposition. Spectacular Bee was never in the money in eight 1982 starts and did not impress me. Distant Gem had a similar record. My preference was for Insearchof, and his show bet expected value was 1.08, making it close to a Dr. Z system bet. At post time the tote board stood as follows:

	Totals	#3 In Search Of
Odds		5—2
Win	174,928	41,682
Show	45,568	8,539

5th Hollywood

6 FURLONGS. (1.07⅗) CLAIMING. Purse $18,000. 3-year-olds. Weight, 122 lbs. Non-winners of two races since March 28 allowed 3 lbs.; a race since then, 6 lbs. Claiming price $40,000; for each $2,500 to $35,000 allowed 2 lbs. (Races when entered for $32,000 or less not considered.)

Ramble on John *

B. g. 3, by Speak John—Hicksville, by Tudor Grey
Br.—Palmer R (Ky) 1982 6 1 0 0 $12,120
Own.—Priddy R or Ann **116** **Tr.—Priddy Ann** **$40,000** 1981 2 M 0 0
Lifetime 8 1 0 0 $12,120

8Apr82-9SA	1	:46	1:103	1:36 ft	25	118	52¾	1017	1019	1022	Valenzuela P A8	50000	67	BisonBy,FortyEightFcts,Rconfirm	10
26Mar82-9SA	1	:46	1:103	1:354ft	8	115	63¾	53½	77½	712	Valenzuela P A3	55000	78	Tell Don, Bison Bay, King Darius	9
18Mar82-9SA	6f	:214	:452	1:12 m	8¾	1155	69½	65½	52¾	42¾	Steiner J J1	50000	75	Shantin, Daily Report, Il Paladino	7
7Mar82-6SA	6½f	:213	:442	1:151ft	8¼	120	45	48½	514	818	ValenzuelPA2	Aw20000	76	TexsCommerce,LeSmirk,Buckohoy	9
10Feb82-7SA	6f	:214	:45	1:114sy	14	120	58½	58½	410	44½	Byrnes D5	Aw19000	74	JtPirt,HowNowDow,StndupComdin	7
3Jan82-6SA	6½f	:23	:473	1:224hy	4¾	118	53¾	21	1½	1no	Byrnes D6	Mdn	56	Ramble on John,Supron,BlueJester	7
26Dec81-4SA	6f	:213	:443	1:104ft	57	118	32	22½	44½	73	Byrnes D9	Mdn	81	Fanjet, Supron, Berbereau	12
8May81-4Hol	5f	:222	:461	:584ft	5¾	116	54½	76	711	79¾	Valenzuela P A6	Mdn	75	VagabondSong,KhalDve,RpidRebel	8

May 27 Hol 4f ft :472 h   May 20 Hol 6f ft 1:143 h   May 14 Hol 5f ft :59 h   May 8 Hol 4f ft :472 h

Familiar Tune

Dk. b. or br. c. 3, by Prove It—Harpsichord, by Dr Kacy
Br.—Ellsworth Kim R & R C (La) 1982 5 1 0 2 $8,460
Own.—Sugich D or Jane **112** **Tr.—Hop Michael D** **$35,000** 1981 0 M 0 0
Lifetime 5 1 0 2 $8,460

22May82-3Hol	6f	:214	:45	1:103ft	14	119	33	32	31	31	Sibille R6	32000	83	Michelle'sDrem,Insrchof,FmilirTun	7
25Apr82-9Hol	1$\frac{1}{16}$	:463	1:111	1:443ft	53	116	42	76¼	815	721	Ortega L E4	50000	51	‡IndinO.,FrenchCommnder,Cn'tBBt	8
16Apr82-7SA	6f	:214	:443	1:10 ft	4½	116	44	55	47	69½	Asmussen CB8	c40000	79	DlwrExprss,IndnO.,HomCourtRulng	9
7Apr82-6SA	6f	:221	:451	1:102ft	3	118	2hd	1hd	12½	15½	Asmussen CB7	M32000	86	FamilirTune,King'sPlot,RoringJet	11
12Mar82-9TuP	5½f	:222	:47	1:072m	21	110	67	64½	44½	34	Snyder D3	Aw3100	67	Solid Charge, BayTay,FamiliarTune	8

May 29 Hol 3f ft :344 h   ●May 20 Hol 3f ft :334 h   May 8 Hol 5f ft :593 h   Apr 24 Hol 3f ft :384 h

Insearchof

Dk. b. or br. c. 3, by Windy Sands—Gaelic Toot, by Gaelic Dancer
Br.—Gaskill Lynn & Arlene (Cal) 1982 6 1 2 1 $14,975
Own.—Gaskill-Lewis et al **116** **Tr.—Stute Warren** **$40,000** 1981 8 M 1 1 $8,325
Lifetime 14 1 3 2 $23,300

22May82-3Hol	6f	:214	:45	1:103ft	3	119	22	22	2½	2nk	McHargue D G4	32000	84	Michelle'sDrem,Insrchof,FmilirTun	7
9May82-5Hol	6f	:22	:444	1:09 ft	10	116	52½	32½	57	613	McHargue D G3	50000	79	L'Cap, Shantin, Can't Be Beat	6
30Apr82-5Hol	6f	:214	:444	1:10 ft	5½	116	2hd	1hd	11	23	Pierce D7	40000	84	Cn'tBeBet,Inserchof,BetterWithAg	7
20Apr82-4SA	6f	:22	:444	1:094ft	*9-5	118	11	1½	12½	13½	McHrguDG12	[S]M32000	89	Insearchof, Leckie, Susanne's Boy	12
15Apr82-3SA	6f	:214	:444	1:101ft	12	118	32½	43	54½	55¼	Asmussen C B6	[S]Mdn	82	Konewah, Prince Channon,FastAxe	6
24Mar82-6SA	6f	:22	:45	1:103ft	4½	118	1½	11	1½	32	Asmussen CB6	M50000	83	Stream Side, Kanui, Insearchof	8
25Oct81-3SA	1	:454	1:111	1:38 ft	19	118	1hd	3½	46½	816	Olivares F8	Mdn	63	Bison Bay, Berbereau, Crystal Star	8
11Oct81-4SA	1	:463	1:114	1:374ft	5½	118	32½	32	35	48¾	Olivares F2	[S]Mdn	71	RacingIsFun,CrystlStr,AlmoStrnger	7
30Sep81-3SA	6f	:214	:451	1:10 ft	13	118	2hd	2½	31½	56½	Ortega L E4	[S]Mdn	82	Gaelic'sSport,Shntin,DesertEnvoy	12
9Sep81-8Dmr	1	:453	1:111	1:372ft	100	114	76½	73¼	61¾	87¼	Ortega L E3	Dmr Fut	74	GatoDelSol,TheCaptain,RingProud	10

May 29 Hol 3f ft :374 h   May 16 Hol 5f ft 1:023 h   May 7 Hol 4f ft :503 h   Apr 27 Hol 4f ft :491 h

Jet Pirate *

Dk. b. or br. g. 3, by Tri Jet—Be Victorious, by Stevward
Br.—Schwietert F C (Fla) 1982 6 2 0 0 $21,775
Own.—Cavanagh Mr-Mrs T M **116** **Tr.—Carno Louis R** **$40,000** 1981 7 1 1 0 $11,950
Lifetime 13 3 1 0 $33,725

9May82-5Hol	6f	:22	:444	1:09 ft	10	116	21	22	34½	46¼	Sibille R5	50000	85	L'Cap, Shantin, Can't Be Beat	6
14Apr82-3SA	6f	:214	:443	1:094ft	6	120	51¾	43	43	53¾	Castaneda M6	62500	85	SkiRacer,Smuggler'sGold,ImSizzler	6
7Apr82-3SA	6f	:22	:442	1:084ft	21	120	46	34½	44½	55¾	Sibille R3	Aw23000	88	Spiritino, Art Director, Le Smirk	6
25Feb82-7SA	6½f	:221	:45	1:152ft	9	120	1½	1½	22½	612	Sibille R3	Aw22000	81	LuckyLegend,RcingIsFun,GtoDlSol	6
10Feb82-7SA	6f	:214	:45	1:114sy	7¼	115	1hd	13	16	14½	Sibille R2	Aw19000	79	JtPirt,HowNowDow,StndupComdin	7
15Jan82-2SA	7f	:22	:444	1:232ft	3½e	116	1½	11½	13	14	Sibille R7	40000	83	JetPirte,CptinTuffy,OutBeforDwn	12
30Dec81-4SA	6½f	:222	:46	1:193m	2¼e	116	1hd	15	12½	2¾	Ortega L E1	40000	71	CapturetheSpirit,JetPirate,JamMan	7
25Nov81-5Hol	6f	:221	:452	1:104ft	5½	114	1hd	11	2½	74¾	Ortega L E6	40000	78	Jet Travel, JamMan,MoodyCaptain	9
30Oct81-3SA	6½f	:22	:451	1:173ft	*9-5	118	1hd	12½	14	12¾	Ortega L E4	M25000	82	JetPirte,CptinTuffy,OneBoldReson	8
27Aug81-3Dmr	6f	:223	:461	1:12 ft	6½	118	3nk	42	66	912	Ortega L E11	M40000	66	Dena Jo, Smuggler's Gold,SirBoss	12

May 27 Hol 3f ft :361 h   May 22 Hol 4f ft :484 h   May 17 Hol 5f ft 1:003 h   May 7 Hol 4f ft :50 h

Extra Quick

Ro. g. 3, by Messenger of Song—Trishlyn, by Performance
Br.—Humes Mr-Mrs W A (Cal) 1982 5 1 0 0 $6,950
Own.—Four D Stables **116** **Tr.—Hartstone George D** **$40,000** 1981 4 1 1 0 $8,900
Lifetime 9 2 1 0 $15,850

15May82-2Hol	1$\frac{1}{16}$	:464	1:113	1:44 ft	*2¼	116	2½	31	33	109¼	McCarron C J1	c32000	66	Jam Man, Carrie's Ten, ClubFlush	11
29Apr82-5Hol	6f	:22	:443	1:094ft	3¼	115	2½	2hd	1½	14½	Guerra W A4	20000	88	ExtrQuick,OleKingTuck,Jo'sTribut	10
8Apr82-2SA	6f	:214	:45	1:092ft	35	117	44½	46	46½	46	Guerra W A1	[S] 20000	85	Chris's Lad,Vavavavoom,BrightIsle	9
5Mar82-1SA	6f	:214	:444	1:103ft	13	118	54	1215	1219	1212	Sibille R2	20000	73	Mchll'sDrm,Prt'sOvr,Chcr'sOrphn	12
12Feb82-1SA	6f	:222	:453	1:114gd	13	116	41¾	813	817	925	Sibille R1	32000	54	L'Cap, Ima Sizzler, Supercede	9
11Dec81-2Hol	6½f	:222	:454	1:183ft	3½	117	3nk	2hd	12	11¼	Sibille R7	M25000	77	ExtrQuick,ARoylWlcom,ToughTim	12
27Aug81-3Dmr	6f	:223	:461	1:12 ft	5½	118	1hd	2½	76	1116	Lipham T4	M40000	62	Dena Jo, Smuggler's Gold,SirBoss	12
19Jun81-4Hol	5f	:22	:464	:593ft	3	116	21	23	2hd	22¼	Lipham T2	Mc32000	79	Subdivide,ExtraQuick,Cpt'nArphy	10
6Jun81-6Hol	5f	:214	:454	:581ft	8¾	116	3½	34	47½	511	Lipham T4	[S]Mdn	77	DistntHrt,B.RichGorg,SwtndNturl	10

May 25 Hol 4f ft :48 h   May 10 Hol 5f ft 1:03 h   Apr 25 Hol 4f ft :47 h   Apr 20 Hol tr.t 4f ft :52 h

Distant Gem Ch. c. 3, by Distant Day—Gypsy Gem, by Aegean Isle
Br.—Marshall F (Cal) 1982 2 0 0 0 $400
Own.—Marshall Mr-Mrs F 116 Tr.—Tinsley J E Jr $40,000 1981 5 1 0 1 $11,400
Lifetime 7 1 0 1 $11,800
20Feb82-2SA 6f :214 :442 1:10 ft *2 118 31 23 47 511 McHargue D G6 40000 77 L'Cap,FrenchCommander,ImSizzler 7
21Jan82-6SA 6f :221 :453 1:11 m 4½ 120 69 612 615 619 McHrgueDG1 Aw19000 64 Speed Broker, Breen, HowNowDow 6
29Dec81-2SA 6f :212 :441 1:101ft 3½ 120 1½ 12½ 11½ 74 Pincay L Jr9 Aw18000 83 WorldRuler,Gelic'sSport,CrystlStr 12
12Dec81-5Hol 6f :213 :443 1:094ft 6½ 118 46 44½ 37½ 516 Ortega L E1 Aw18000 72 Irisher,Unpredictable,CaptainTuffy 6
28Nov81-3Hol 6f :222 :46 1:123m 2¾ 118 11½ 1hd 21 35 Ortega L E3 Aw18000 69 ArtDirector,RedCurrent,DistntGem 5
14Nov81-2Hol 6f :22 :45 1:102ft 8½ 118 1½ 1½ 11 11½ Ortega L E5 [S]Mdn 85 DistntGem,FleetEric,NoHoldsBrrd 12
4Sep81-6Dmr 6f :221 :453 1:11 ft 10 118 11 11 52½ 813 Lipham T5 [S]Mdn 70 PrinceSpellbound,CrystlStr,Shntin 12
May 28 Hol 3f ft :344 h May 16 Hol 5f ft :591 h May 9 Hol 6f ft 1:133 hg May 4 Hol 5f ft 1:013 h

Murtazz B. c. 3, by Exclusive Native—Privileged, by Flying Fury
Br.—Cashman E C (Ky) 1982 2 0 0 0 $400
Own.—Cashman E C 116 Tr.—Sullivan John $40,000 1981 4 1 1 0 $10,356
Lifetime 6 1 1 0 $10,756 Turf 5 1 1 0 $10,756
28Apr82-8GG 1 (T):4721:1211:374fm 5 114 52½ 42½ 44½ 55 Baze R A1 Aw16000 73 TheBrginHunter,ThreeDocs,Cvllrizzo 7
17Apr82-2SA 6f :212 :444 1.10 ft 79 114 96½ 96¾ 87¾ 97½ Diaz A L9 Aw19000 80 Polly's Ruler, L'Natty,WindyScott 12
28Sep81♦5StCloud(Fra) a6½f 1:213gd 38 119 (T) 9 SamaniH Pr Eclipse(Gr3) Pas de Seul, Rollins, Dear Patrick 10
11Sep81♦1Evry(Fra) a5½f 1:044gd 9¾ 128 (T) 13 Gibert A Pr de Lamballe Murtazz, Moondreamer, Valrant 7
19Aug81♦3Vichy(Fra) a5f 1:01 gd 8 118 (T) 21½ Hassine L Pr Tripolette Goulaine, Murtazz, Rolling Mado 10
21Jly81♦7Evry(Fra) a6f 1:114gd 5½ 123 (T) 612 SamaniH Pr Pensbury African Joy, King's Envoy, Cinto 8
May 27 Hol 5f ft 1:014 h May 21 Hol 5f ft 1:04 h Apr 24 SA 3f ft :362 h Apr 15 SA 4f ft :482 h

Nat's Penny Ch. g. 3, by L'Natural—Quinto Penny, by Catchpenny II
Br.—Warwick G M (Cal) 1982 6 0 2 0 $5,070
Own.—Warwick G M 114 Tr.—West Ted $37,500 1981 9 2 2 1 $23,540
Lifetime 15 2 4 1 $28,610
4May82-6GG 6f :223 :461 1:122ft 15 115 2hd 2hd 3½ 74½ Burkes T7 Aw14000 72 PublicTrdition,SirMcmllon,Pt'sDud 8
31Mar82-6GG 6f :224 :46 1:114sy 11 115 41½ 41½ 22 23 Burkes T1 Aw13000 77 SirMacmillion,Nt'sPenny,Pet'sDude 6
10Mar82-8GG 6f :222 :453 1:102ft 6¾ 115 43 53½ 55½ 77½ Burkes T3 Aw14000 80 ThBrginHuntr,WlkPst,HonorblLook 7
9Feb82-8GG 6f :221 :453 1:111ft 16 117 55 77 812 89½ Lawless G5 Gldn Bear 73 DustyTrader,JetTravel,CousinJosh 11
4Feb82-8BM 6f :224 :461 1:111ft *1 114 21 1½ 11 22 Lawless G4 Aw13000 82 SeniorCitizen,Nt'sPnny,CountMrsll 6
9Jan82-8BM 6f :223 :46 1:12 gd 8½ 115 61¾ 54 68 88 Burkes T3 Athtn 72 DominntRoni,Shilling,RoylMmory 12
11Dec81-8BM 6f :223 :453 1:11 ft 4½ 115 2½ 42½ 31½ 2¾ Burkes T4 Aw12000 84 Walk Past, Nat's Penny, Ace King 9
15Nov81-10AC 6f :22 :434 1:084ft 6 122 3½ 44½ 64¾ 611 Munoz J4 A C Fut 84 Sari'sDreamer,Tular,B.RichGeorge 12
7Nov81-9AC 6f :22 :44 1:093ft 2½ 120 41¾ 41 42 44½ Munoz J2 Aw5000 87 DlwrExprss,FltPlAllsn,TwStrAdmrl 6
7Aug81-11SR 5½f :22 :443 1:043ft 4½ 122 32 31½ 31 11½† Levine C3 Rdwd Empr 90 ‡Nat'sPenny,Demarday,Tohottocari 9
† 7Aug81—Disqualified and placed fifth
May 27 Hol 3f ft :361 h May 22 Hol 3f ft :37 h May 3 GG 3f ft :371 h Apr 28 GG 5f ft 1:011 h

Gringo Jim * Dk. b. or br. c. 3, by Gallant Romeo—Zonta, by Dr Fager
Br.—Tartan Farms Corp (Fla) 1982 4 1 0 0 $9,350
Own.—Tartan Stable 116 Tr.—Lukas D Wayne $40,000 1981 0 M 0 0
Lifetime 4 1 0 0 $9,350
3Apr82-5SA 6f :22 :452 1:093ft 42 120 75½ 812 717 818 Lipham T5 Aw20000 72 B.RichGeorg,Polly'sRulr,Accousticl 9
31Jan82-2SA 1 1/16 :454 1:102 1:432ft 28 116 2hd 3½ 79¾ 918 ValenzuelPA9 Aw20000 66 Turbulation, Ask Me, Keno Hill 10
20Jan82-6SA 6½f :22 :454 1:192sy 10 118 21 1½ 12½ 12 McCarron C J5 Mdn 73 Gringo Jim, Idaho, Sir Pele 8
10Jan82-6SA 6f :214 :451 1:094ft 17 118 83¾ 1011 1015 1022 McCarron C J3 Mdn 67 JournytS,Htmoto,ConsciousEffort 10
May 27 Hol 4f ft :512 h May 21 Hol 4f ft :492 h May 14 Hol 3f ft :364 h

Checker's Orphan Ch. g. 3, by Raise an Orphan—Checker's Honey, by Orbit Ruler
Br.—Downey J (Cal) 1982 6 1 1 1 $13,525
Own.—Crowley & Downey 116 Tr.—Jordan James $40,000 1981 3 1 1 0 $7,500
Lifetime 9 2 2 1 $21,025
16May82-1Hol 1 1/16 :471 1:113 1:431ft 5 116 32½ 3nk 53 69 Pierce D3 50000 70 Duntlss,FltPulAllison,SultnofSwing 8
1May82-1Hol 1 :454 1:104 1:364ft 5¾ 116 11 12½ 15 14 Pierce D1 32000 82 Chckr'sOrphn,ClubFlsh,Ed'sDynsty 9
16Apr82-4SA 1 :452 1:103 1:361ft *3-2 116 22½ 11 1hd 22½ McCarron C J4 25000 85 WestCostNtive,Checkr'sOrphn,Bgly 8
5Mar82-1SA 6f :214 :444 1:103ft 7 116 2½ 22 32 32 McHargue DG4 c20000 83 Mchll'sDrm,Prt'sOvr,Chcr'sOrphn 12
12Feb82-1SA 6f :222 :453 1:114gd 7½ 116 62½ 510 411 516 McHargue D G7 32000 63 L'Cap, Ima Sizzler, Supercede 9
14Jan82-5SA 6f :213 :443 1:091ft 61 114 73½ 913 916 824 Black K3 Aw19000 68 Jet Travel, B. RichGeorge,Rise'nFly 9
19Aug81-4Dmr 6f :224 :463 1:123ft *2 118 31 4¾ 12½ 12½ Pincay L Jr7 Mc32000 75 Checker'sOrphn,TrvlingPul,Ris'nFly 9
7Aug81-6Dmr 6f :23 :464 1:123ft 5½ 118 96½ 87¾ 47 25 Pincay L Jr6 M32000 70 Michll'sDrm,Chckr'sOrphn,Grnnng 11
17Jly81-4Hol 6f :221 :454 1:113ft 14 117 1213 1111 1012 913 Pincay L Jr5 M45000 66 AntiquRulr,Kll'sBoy,GillgnsPurchs 12
May 25 Hol 5f ft 1:004 h Apr 24 SA 5f ft 1:00 h ●Apr 9 SA 7f ft 1:24 h

Spectacular Bee B. c. 3, by Nose for Money—Bee Cane, by Tumble Turbie
Br.—Ball & Newman (Fla) 1982 8 0 0 0 $3,150
Own.—Twin W Stable 116 Tr.—Calascibetta Joseph $40,000 1981 4 1 1 0 $7,490
Lifetime 12 1 1 0 $10,640
12May82-5Hol 6f :214 :44 1:091ft 35 115 54 55 65 54¾ Toro F6 Aw20000 86 JettingPlesure,TellFib,VgbondSong 8
30Apr82-5Hol 6f :214 :444 1:10 ft 19 116 53½ 41¼ 53½ 45½ Guerra W A1 40000 82 Cn'tBeBet,Inserchof,BetterWithAg 7
13Mar82-7GP 7f :221 :452 1:24 ft 12 117 31 3½ 65½ 68¾ Soto S B7 Aw12000 75 HauntedLad,Pavarotti,RoiMusique 11
3Mar82-5Hia 6f :223 :453 1:111ft 10 116 21½ 45 58½ 512 Soto S B1 75000 75 Mr. B. B., DirectAnswer,PeterOwen 7
13Feb82-6Hia 6f :222 :452 1:11 ft 14 116 53 55½ 46½ 55¾ Soto S B10 Aw13000 82 Richness, Pathline, Chan Balum 12
30Jan82-5Hia 6f :22 :45 1:103ft 31 116 86¾ 68½ 47¼ 44½ Soto S B8 Aw13000 86 ThrAStrw,Compo'sTmpo,GlfordRd 10
23Jan82-5Hia 6f :214 :443 1:10 ft 50 116 32 52¾ 67½ 811 Soto S B1 Aw13000 82 Cut Away,FrankGomez,StarChoice 12
9Jan82-5Hia 6f :222 :46 1:112ft 22 116 2½ 4¾ 76½ 78¾ Smith A Jr7 Aw13000 77 Angel Bike, Cut Away,CourtScene 12
8Jly81-9Crc 5½f :223 :471 1:071ft 3½ 116 2hd 3nk 34 511 Cohen G6 Aw9500 78 SmrtAli,VictorinLine,IntrepidChrgr 6
12Jun81-5Crc 5f :223 :462 :593ft *3-2 117 1hd 2hd 22½ 44½ Beuviere J L2 Aw9500 89 Center Cut, SmartAli,VictorianLine 6
May 25 SA 4f ft :49 h Apr 12 Crc 5f ft 1:032 b Apr 6 Crc 5f ft 1:022 b Apr 1 Crc 4f ft :50 h

Two long shots, Nat's Penny and Gringo Jim, dominated the race and finished one-two when both Insearchof and Jet Pirate, who were vying for the lead at the stretch, faded. Luckily, Insearchof held on for third and paid \$3.80 for show. Jet Pirate finished fourth. The \$3.80 payoff for show on the 5–2 shot Insearchof was again a combination of two factors: At a 1.08 expected value it was a reasonably good bet, and the 1–2 finishers in the race went off at 28–1 and 26–1 odds, respectively. My \$50 bet returned \$95, for a profit of \$45. The chart of the race was as follows:

FIFTH RACE
Hollywood
MAY 30, 1982

6 FURLONGS. (1.07$\frac{4}{5}$) CLAIMING. Purse \$18,000. 3-year-olds. Weight, 122 lbs. Non-winners of two races since March 28 allowed 3 lbs.; a race since then, 6 lbs. Claiming price \$40,000; for each \$2,500 to \$35,000 allowed 2 lbs. (Races when entered for \$32,000 or less not considered.)

Value of race \$18,000, value to winner \$9,900, second \$3,600, third \$2,700, fourth \$1,350, fifth \$450. Mutuel pool \$294,266. Exacta Pool \$454,047.

Last Raced	Horse	Eqt.	A.	Wt	PP	St	¼	½	Str	Fin	Jockey	Cl'g Pr	Odds \$1
4May82 ^{6}GG^{7}	Nat's Penny	b	3	115	8	2	8^{hd}	4^{hd}	$3^{1\frac{1}{2}}$	1^{hd}	Delahoussaye E	37500	28.10
3Apr82 ^{5}SA^{8}	Gringo Jim		3	117	9	1	6^{hd}	6^{3}	5^{3}	2^{nk}	Pincay L Jr	40000	26.80
22May82 ^{3}Hol^{2}	Insearchof	b	3	116	3	10	1^{hd}	$2^{\frac{1}{2}}$	$1^{\frac{1}{2}}$	$3^{3\frac{1}{2}}$	McHargue D G	40000	2.50
9May82 ^{5}Hol^{4}	Jet Pirate	b	3	116	4	4	3^{hd}	$3^{2\frac{1}{2}}$	2^{hd}	$4^{1\frac{1}{2}}$	Sibille R	40000	2.30
22May82 ^{3}Hol^{3}	Familiar Tune		3	112	2	9	2^{hd}	$1^{\frac{1}{2}}$	$4^{\frac{1}{2}}$	$5^{1\frac{1}{2}}$	Ortega L E	35000	17.60
8Apr82 ^{9}SA^{10}	Ramble on John	b	3	116	1	7	10	$7^{\frac{1}{2}}$	7^{4}	$6^{\frac{1}{2}}$	Ramirez O	40000	56.70
15May82 ^{2}Hol^{10}	Extra Quick	b	3	116	5	8	9^{7}	5^{3}	$6^{2\frac{1}{2}}$	7^{3}	Castaneda M	40000	8.00
12May82 ^{5}Hol^{5}	Spectacular Bee	b	3	116	10	3	$7^{\frac{1}{2}}$	9^{7}	9^{8}	8^{7}	McCarron C J	40000	3.50
28Apr82 ^{8}GG^{5}	Murtazz	b	3	116	7	5	$4^{\frac{1}{2}}$	8^{hd}	$8^{\frac{1}{2}}$	9	Lipham T	40000	48.00
20Feb82 ^{2}SA^{5}	Distant Gem	b	3	116	6	6	5^{hd}	10	10	—	Valenzuela P A	40000	8.40

Distant Gem, Eased.

OFF AT 3:46 Start good. Won driving. Time, :22$\frac{1}{5}$, :45$\frac{4}{5}$, :58$\frac{1}{5}$, 1:11$\frac{4}{5}$ Track fast.

\$2 Mutuel Prices:			
8–NAT'S PENNY	58.20	20.60	10.60
9–GRINGO JIM		20.00	8.40
3–INSEARCHOF			3.80

\$5 EXACTA 8–9 PAID \$1,433.00

Ch. g, by L'Natural—Quinto Penny, by Catchpenny II. Trainer West Ted. Bred by Warwick G M (Cal).

NAT'S PENNY, never far back, rallied between horses on the turn, challenged outside the leaders in the upper stretch and outfinished rivals in the final sixteenth. GRINGO JIM, in contention while forced to stay wide early, rallied strongly in the middle of the track through the stretch but missed. INSEARCHOF vied for the lead from the outset, continued to respond in the final drive but could not get up. JET PIRATE forced the pace between horses to the final furlong, drifted slightly in behind INSEARCHOF in the stretch and steadied momentarily. The stewards lit the inquiry sign but after reviewing the videotapes of the stretch run, allowed the finish to stand. FAMILIAR TUNE set or forced the early pace inside INSEARCHOF and weakened in the final furlong. RAMBLE ON JOHN, awkward gaining stride after the start, did not reach contention. EXTRA QUICK saved ground to no avail. SPECTACULAR BEE forced to stay wide into the turn, lacked a rally. DISTANT GEM was eased in the final sixteenth.

Owners— 1, Warwick G M; 2, Tartan Stable; 3, Gaskill-Lewis et al; 4, Cavanagh Mr-Mrs T M; 5, Sugich D or Jane; 6, Priddy R or Ann; 7, Four D Stable; 8, Twin W Stable; 9, Cashman E C; 10, Marshall Mr-Mrs F.

Overweight: Nat's Penny 1 pound; Gringo Jim 1.

Distant Gem was claimed by Winning Ways Stable; trainer, Mitchell Mike.

Scratched—Checker's Orphan (16May82 ^{1}Hol^{6}).

The sixth race was among lightly raced maidens, including several horses making their first start. Since there were no standouts (for example, a horse that consistently finished in the money and had done so recently), I decided to avoid the risk and skip this race.

The seventh race was on the turf. The consensus picks were Fast, Pirate Law, and Moonball. However, my preference was for Patti's Triumph, who was the public's fourth choice at 4–1. Patti's Triumph had finished in the money in four of the last five races against similar-quality opposition. His only finish out of the money was in a major handicap race at a longer distance. He had been leading the race, then faded to fourth at the finish. This fading was typical of most of Patti's Triumph's races. Normally, his lead was sufficiently good to compensate for his late fading so that he still finished well. The odds were quite good, with an expected value of 1.12, or nearly a Dr. Z system bet, when I bet with one minute to post time. The final tote board was as follows:

	Totals	#6 Patti's Triumph
Odds		4—1
Win	¹82,509	28,241
Show	48,202	5,171

indicating an expected value per dollar bet of 1.14.

Patti's Triumph got a poor start and was in the race in second or third position until the stretch. He then faded to fourth. The three favorites finished in the money. I had a $50 loss on this race. The chart of the race was as follows:

SEVENTH RACE
Hollywood
MAY 30, 1982

1 $\frac{1}{16}$ MILES.(turf). (1.39⅘) ALLOWANCE. Purse $40,000. 4-year-olds and upward. Non-winners of $18,000 twice since July 20. Weight, 121 lbs. Non-winners of $22,000 at a mile or over since April 1 allowed 3 lbs.; such a race of $19,500 since December 5, 5 lbs.; such a race since July 20, 7 lbs. (Claiming and starter races not considered.)

Value of race $40,000, value to winner $22,000, second $8,000, third $6,000, fourth $3,000, fifth $1,000. Mutuel pool $305,904. Exacta Pool $482,464.

Last Raced	Horse	Eqt.A.Wt	PP	St	¼	½	¾	Str	Fin	Jockey	Odds $1
22May82 ^{5}Hol^2	Pirate Law	b 5 114	3	4	$4^{\frac12}$	$5^{1\frac12}$	4^{hd}	$2^{1\frac12}$	1^{hd}	Valenzuela P A	a-3.00
28Dec80 ^{8}SA^3	Fast	b 6 114	5	6	6^5	6^6	$5^{2\frac12}$	1^{hd}	$2^{1\frac14}$	McCarron C J	2.60
14May82 ^{8}Hol^1	Moon Ball	6 115	7	8	8^3	$8^{\frac12}$	8^{10}	$5^{\frac12}$	$3^{\frac34}$	Castaneda M	4.20
22May82 ^{5}Hol^3	Patti's Triumph	b 5 118	6	5	5^3	3^{hd}	$2^{1\frac12}$	3^{hd}	4^2	Hawley S	4.40
16May82 ^{8}Hol^7	Sunny Winters	b 5 116	4	9	9	9	6^{hd}	6^{hd}	$5^{3\frac12}$	Delahoussaye E	16.20
14May82 ^{8}Hol^4	Confetti	5 117	9	7	7^2	7^1	7^2	7^5	6^1	Pincay L Jr	10.30
22May82 ^{5}Hol^6	Haughty But Nice	4 115	1	1	$1^{\frac12}$	1^{hd}	1^{hd}	4^2	7^{10}	McHargue D G	11.90
23May82 ^{8}GG^6	Golden Flak	b 4 114	8	2	$3^{\frac12}$	$4^{1\frac12}$	3^{hd}	8^{15}	8^{17}	Hansen R D	a-3.00
25Apr82 ^{7}Hol^7	Another Realm	b 4 114	2	3	$2^{\frac12}$	2^{hd}	9	9	9	Gilligan L	15.90

a-Coupled: Pirate Law and Golden Flak.

OFF AT 4:48. Start good. Won driving. Time, :22, :45⅘, 1:10⅕, 1:34⅘, 1:41 Course firm.

$2 Mutuel Prices:			
1-PIRATE LAW (a-entry)	8.00	3.20	2.20
5-FAST		4.00	2.60
7-MOON BALL			3.00

$5 EXACTA 1-5 PAID $73.50.

B. h, by Ruffled Feathers—Patio II, by Court Martial. Trainer Barrera Lazaro S. Bred by M Pelinger Estate (Fla).

PIRATE LAW saved ground in good position to the far turn, remained on the rail to lodge his bid in the stretch and outfinished FAST in the final sixteenth. The latter lacked early speed, rallied outside horses around the final turn, got the lead a furlong out but could not outfinish the winner. MOON BALL, outrun for six furlongs, rallied wide into the stretch but finished strongly. PATTI'S TRIUMPH, in contention between horses to the stretch, weakened in the final furlong. CONFETTI, never a factor, appeared lame pulling up following the finish. HAUGHTY BUT NICE set or forced the pace to the final furlong and faltered. GOLDEN FLAK was forced wide at the clubhouse turn, remained in contention on the outside to the stretch but tired quickly thereafter. ANOTHER REALM lugged out on both turns.

Owners— 1, Barrera & Jones Mmes; 2, Hunt & Pascoe III; 3, Perdomo & Pulliam; 4, Grutman D S; 5, Tresvant Stable; 6, Mirkin-Mirkin-Pacifica; 7, Daniels Mrs T L; 8, Barrera & Saiden; 9, Goldstein Margaret.

Overweight: Moon Ball 1 pound; Confetti 3; Haughty But Nice 1.

The eighth race was the featured race of the day: the Los Angeles Handicap. The field was headed by Never Tabled and Remember John. Never Tabled had not raced until he was a five-year-old. But in his four career races, all at Santa Anita and Hollywood Park in April and May of 1982, he had had three wins and a second against strong competition with fast times. Remember John had performed brilliantly in his two-year career. This year he had had four wins and a second with speed ratings from 92 to 99. He was coming to the Los Angeles Handicap with four consecutive wins and post position 1. The race also featured such strong horses as Shanekite, and Petro D. Jay. Pompeii Court was scratched.

The *Daily Racing Form* consensus and the crowd favored Never Tabled, with Remember John second. My preference was for Remember John if the odds were good. He seemed more proven and reliable. Never Tabled was running with a longer time between starts than he had before. This, plus the post-position disadvantage and Never Tabled's brief four-race career, gave the nod to Remember John.

8th Hollywood

6 FURLONGS. (1.07⅘) 30th Running of THE LOS ANGELES HANDICAP (Grade III). $75,000 added. 3-year olds and upward. By subscription of $100 each, which shall accompany the nomination, $750 additional to start, with $75,000 added, of which $15,000 to second, $11,250 to third, $5,625 to fourth and $1,875 to fifth. Weights Tuesday, May 25. Starters to be named through the entry box by closing time of entries. A trophy will be presented to the owner of the winner. Closed Wednesday, May 19, 1982 with 13 nominations.

Remember John — **B. g. 3, by The Irish Lord—Yoweee, by Crozier**
Own.—Sheridan Mr-Mrs J **115** **Br.—Valenti P (Cal)** 1982 5 4 1 0 $113,100
Tr.—Vienna Darrell 1981 6 1 2 1 $52,900
Lifetime 11 5 3 1 $166,000

16May82-6Hol	5f	:21^{2}	:44	:56 ft	6-5	116	1^{hd}	1½	1½	1¾	DelhoussyeE^{1}	Aw37000	99	RemembrJohn,Unlklt,Trrsto'sSingr	7
1May82-7Hol	6f	:22	:44^{2}	1:08^{3}ft	*3-5	122	2^{hd}	1^{hd}	1^{1}	1½	McCrronCJ^{4}	Debonair	94	RemmbrJohn,ArtDirctor,RingProud	5
31Mar82-8SA	6½f	:21^{3}	:44^{1}	1:15^{1}ft	3	117	1½	1^{hd}	1½	1¾	DelhoussyeE^{1}	Baldwin	94	RmmbrJohn,TmToExplod,CrystlStr	7
21Mar82-4SA	6½f	:21^{2}	:44	1:15^{2}ft	*2-3	115	1½	1^{1}	1^{3}	1^{5}	DelhoussyeE^{1}	Aw20000	93	RemembrJohn,CIticSbr,EstrSrmon	6
17Feb82-8SA	6f	:21^{2}	:43^{4}	1:08^{3}ft	20	117	1^{hd}	2^{1}	2^{2}½	2^{3}	DlhoussyE^{6}	Blsa Chca	92	TmToExplod,RmmbrJohn,JornytS	10
9Sep81-8Dmr	1	:45^{3}	1:11^{1}	1:37^{2}ft	10	117	1^{hd}	1^{hd}	5^{1}¾	9^{7}½	McCarronCJ^{8}	Dmr Fut	73	GatoDelSol,TheCaptain,RingProud	10
26Aug81-8Dmr	1	:45^{4}	1:10^{3}	1:36^{4}ft	6½	117	1½	1^{1}½	2^{hd}	5^{5}½	Toro F^{6}	Balboa	78	TheCaptain,DistantHeart,GtoDelSol	9
12Aug81-8Dmr	6f	:22	:45	1:11 ft	*4-5	120	1^{hd}	1½	1^{hd}	3^{1}	McCarronCJ^{5}	De Anza	82	King'sFinder,Heln'sBu,RmmbrJohn	5
29Jly81-8Dmr	6f	:22^{1}	:45^{2}	1:10^{4}ft	*4-5	114	1½	1½	1^{2}½	1^{1}¾	McCrrCJ^{5}	[S]Gradution	84	RemmbrJohn,King'sFindr,DistntHrt	9
18Jly81-8Hol	6f	:21^{3}	:44^{4}	1:10^{2}ft	19	115	2^{hd}	2^{hd}	1½	2^{hd}	Toro F^{10}	Hol Juv	85	TheCptin,RememberJohn,Hln'sBu	12

May 28 Hol 3f ft :35^{2} h May 23 Hol 5f ft :59^{3} h May 14 Hol 3f ft :35^{3} h May 9 Hol 4f ft :47^{3} h

Shanekite — **B. c. 4, by Hoist Bar—Win Shane, by Anyoldtime**
Br.—Udko Selma (Cal) 1982 6 0 3 0 $40,925
Own.—Udko Selma **117** **Tr.—Landers Dale** 1981 10 6 0 0 $161,000
Lifetime 22 8 5 0 $224,050 Turf 1 0 1 0 $12,000

16May82-6Hol	5f	:21^{2}	:44	:56 ft	*6-5	119	5^{7}½	5^{7}½	5^{6}½	5^{5}¾	Hawley S^{6}	Aw37000	93	RemembrJohn,Unlklt,Trrsto'sSingr	7
8May82-8Hol	7f	:21^{4}	:44	1:21 ft	*1	117	6^{7}½	5^{4}½	3^{1}½	2^{2}	HwleyS^{7}	Trple Bend H	90	NeverTbled,Shnekite,PompeiiCourt	7
17Apr82-8SA	a6½f Ⓣ	:21	:43^{1}	1:13 fm	7½	118	6^{5}½	6^{2}¾	3½	2^{1}½	Hawley S^{1}	Sn Simn H	92	Shagbark, Shanekite, Belfort	8
24Mar82-8SA	5½f	:21^{3}	:44^{2}	1:02^{1}ft	4½	118	—	—	—	—	HawleyS^{6}	El Conejo H	—	ToB.OrNot,Belfort,Terresto'sSinger	8
24Mar82—Lost rider															
9Jan82-8SA	7f	:21^{3}	:43^{4}	1:20^{4}ft	3½	119	4^{3}½	4^{1}½	8^{9}	8^{12}	Hawley S^{6}	Sn Crlos H	84	Solo Guy,‡King Go Go, Smokite	8
3Jan82-8SA	7f	:22^{1}	:45^{4}	1:26 hy	*8-5	120	5^{1}½	1½	2½	2^{6}	Hawley S^{6}	Malibu	64	Island Whirl, Shanekite, It'stheOne	8
19Dec81-8Hol	7f	:21^{2}	:43^{4}	1:21^{3}ft	*4-5	117	4^{1}½	4^{1}½	1^{1}	1^{2}½	Hawley S^{4}	Yuletide H	89	Shanekite, FlyingChick,IslandWhirl	5
28Nov81-8Hol	1	:48	1:13	1:38^{4}m	3½	113	1^{hd}	1½	3½	4^{2}½	Hawley S^{4}	Ntv Dvr H	69	Syncopate, King Go Go, Wickerr	6
11Nov81-8Hol	6f	:21^{3}	:44^{1}	1:08^{1}ft	2¾	114	5^{2}½	1^{1}	1^{4}	1^{2}½	HawleyS^{8}	Sprnt Chmp	96	Shanekite,Syncopte,BigPresenttion	8
11Nov81—Run in two divisions, 8th & 9th races.															
29Oct81-7SA	6f	:22	:44^{3}	1:09 ft	*4-5	118	2^{2}½	2^{2}½	2^{hd}	1^{5}	Hawley S^{1}	Aw34000	93	Shnekite,ImportntMemo,NtivFishr	7

May 22 Hol 4f ft :47^{3} hg Apr 30 Hol 6f ft 1:14^{2} h Apr 24 SA 4f ft :49^{4} h Apr 13 SA Ⓣ 5f yl 1:04 h (d)

Pompeii Court B. h. 5, by Tell—Port Damascus, by Damascus
Br.—Keck H B (Ky) 1982 5 2 0 2 $54,300
Own.—Lewyk & Crowe 116 Tr.—Anderson Laurie N 1981 16 5 5 3 $45,954
Lifetime 25 9 7 5 $105,134

8May82-8Hol 7f :214 :44 1:21 ft 3½ 116 3½ 21 21½ 32 ShmrW6 Trple Bend H 90 NeverTbled,Shnekite,PompeiiCourt 7
7Mar82-3SA 1 :443 1:083 1:342ft *2½ 116 2½ 1½ 1½ 1hd Hawley S1 Aw40000 97 PompCort,KngrooCort,SonofDodo 7
18Feb82-7SA 1 :451 1:09 1:333ft 11 114 1½ 11 13 14½ Hawley S2 Aw32000 101 PompeiiCourt,QuntumLep,Western 8
5Feb82-7SA 6½f :212 :433 1:15 ft 11 115 42½ 42½ 43 33¾ Sibille R5 Aw32000 91 VictorySmpl,BondRullh,PompCourt 8
20Jan82-5SA 7f :214 :45 1:244sy 4½ 115 2hd 1hd 1hd 42 Sibille R1 Aw32000 74 Gristle,QuntumLep,AnswertoMusic 5
18Dec81-7Hol 6f :214 :443 1:093ft 9 115 3nk 3nk 32 55 Sibille R6 Aw30000 84 Hacwind,BennyBob,CrestoftheWve 7
9Dec81-7Hol 6½f :221 :45 1:154ft 5½ 116 1hd 1½ 12 11½ Sibille R2 Aw25000 91 PompeiiCourt,KngrooCourt,Dorcro 8
27Nov81-7Hol 6½f :223 :453 1:183sy *3 115 1hd 11½ 21½ 2¾ Sibille R4 Aw25000 76 DndyWit,PompiiCourt,Sli'sRoylDrm 8
13Nov81-7Hol 6f :22 :443 1:084ft 15 115 1hd 2½ 2½ 34½ Sibille R1 Aw26000 89 Hcwind,KngrooCourt,PompiiCourt 8
17Oct81-8StP 6f :222 :451 1:101ft *9-5 118 55½ 54½ 35 44 Garcia C1 Aw6500 94 Kinlin, Flashys Champ,ThreeforYou 7
May 21 Hol 5f ft 1:004 h May 3 Hol 6f ft 1:131 h Apr 23 SA 6f ft 1:121 h Apr 16 SA 4f ft :483 h

Petro D. Jay Dk. b. or br. g. 6, by Tudor Grey—Mucho Petre, by Distillate
Br.—Synhorst W (Neb) 1982 5 2 1 0 $13,410
Own.—Ottley R 116 Tr.—Bradshaw Randy K 1981 13 6 2 2 $53,210
Lifetime 29 11 4 2 $85,755

9May82-9TuP 6f :213 :432 1:071ft *1-5 120 11½ 13 16 112 Renteria S4 Aw3325 101 Petro D. Jay, Pelemise, Jared Fox 5
4Apr82-10TuP 6f :211 :431 1:091ft *2-5 120 11 1hd 11 1nk Powell J P1 Express H 91 Petro D. Jay, No Pomp, Maui Star 7
13Mar82-7SA 6f :221 :452 1:103gd 12 114 1hd 31½ 68 711 Hulet L6 Aw35000 74 Belfort, Mad Key, A Run 10
21Feb82-10TuP 6f :212 :433 1:091ft 6½ 112 86½ 67 36 47 Hulet L3 Phx Gd Cp 84 Imperial Lass, Mad Key, Bold Ego 9
6Feb82-10TuP 6f :212 :431 1:08 ft *1-2 114 11 11 11 2¾ Hulet L2 Aw3900 96 Mad Key, Petro D. Jay, Bobby Ben 7
13Sep81-11Pom 6f :211 :442 1:102ft *8-5 117 2hd 2hd 31 55½ Rosales R4 Gov Cp H 86 MrblCourt,Murrthblurr,AmnBrothr 5
5Sep81-8Sac 5½f :213 :434 1:021ft *2-3 119 1½ 2hd 2½ 34¾ Hamilton M2 HcpO 94 SrPortRulr,GryMoonRnnr,PtroD.Jy 4
1Aug81-11SR 6f :22 :442 1:083ft *7-5 118 2hd 1½ 1hd 1hd SrnsnJJ5 Ernst Fnly H 101 PetroD.Jy,RomnOblisk,SirPortRulr 7
19Jly81-11Sol 5½f :212 :433 1:022ft *1-2 116 1hd 1½ 11 2½ Sorenson J J4 Aw12000 100 SirPortRuler,PetroD.Jay,BeauBlade 6
4Jly81-11Pln 6f :22 :442 1:091ft *6-5 121 1hd 2hd 44½ 611 SrnsJJ4 Whtng Mm H 87 ThnkYoWlkr's,KnConty,ImSdwndr 6
●May 27 Hol 4f ft :453 h ●May 6 TuP 4f ft :45 h

Cool Frenchy Dk. b. or br. h. 7, by French Policy—Cool Persian, by Persia
Br.—Lichlyter Mary Ada (Cal) 1982 1 0 0 0
Own.—Lichlyter Dr or Mrs F E 112 Tr.—Lichlyter Mary A 1981 13 3 2 3 $79,930
Lifetime 45 10 8 5 $201,924 Turf 3 0 0 0 $2,200

16May82-6Hol 5f :212 :44 :56 ft 8½ 1095 33½ 33 44 78½ Garcia J J3 Aw37000 90 RemembrJohn,Unlklt,Trrsto'sSingr 7
4Jly81-11Pln 6f :22 :442 1:091ft 8-5 122 3½ 31½ 34 45¼ BzeRA5 Whtng Mm H 92 ThnkYoWlkr's,KnConty,ImSdwndr 6
20Jun81-7Hol 6f :214 :444 1:093ft 3½ 114 1hd 1hd 31 35½ Olivares F5 Aw36000 84 Rb'sGoldnAl,GrndAllnc,CoolFrnchy 6
11Jun81-8Hol 6f :214 :443 1:09 ft 3½ 114 1½ 1½ 11 2½ Olivares F7 Aw36000 91 FlyingChick,CoolFrenchy,ThCrpntr 8
25May81-7Hol 5f :212 :44 :56 ft 10 113 1½ 2hd 22½ 43½ Lipham T7 Aw40000 95 I'm Smokin,Back'nTime,Syncopate 9
20May81-7Hol 6f :214 :442 1:084ft 2½ 114 1½ 12 2½ 54¾ Mena F2 Aw36000 88 Destroyer, Shady Fox, Rich Doctor 6
25Apr81-8GG 7½f Ⓣ:224 :46 1:28 fm 5½ 117 1hd 1½ 2½ 54¾ Toro F2 Tly Pp Inv H 95 His Honor, Police Inspector,Josher 9
7Apr81-8GG 6f :222 :443 1:091ft *2-3 120 1hd 1½ 11½ 1½ Mena F5 Aw20000 93 CoolFrenchy,‡LotoCnd,ChrlySutton 5
25Mar81-8SA 5½f :214 :441 1:022ft 11 115 12 12 2hd 31½ Mena F9 El Conejo H 100 ToBOrNot,SmmrTmGy,ColFrnchy 11
10Mar81-8GG 6f :22 :442 1:083ft 2½ 122 11½ 11 13 15 Mena F2 Aw20000 96 CoolFrenchy,MightyMixup,Mrketti 5
May 26 Hol 6f ft 1:152 h May 12 Hol 5f ft :593 hg ●May 7 Hol 4f ft :461 h May 2 Hol 4f ft :472 h

Beach Walk * Ro. g. 5, by Windy Sands—Squishie, by Gaelic Dancer
Br.—Old English Rancho (Cal) 1982 10 2 5 1 $52,890
Own.—Knapp P R 113 Tr.—Villagomez Jaime 1981 7 3 1 1 $28,950
Lifetime 32 7 9 3 $100,405

23May82-7Hol 6f :22 :444 1:092ft 5½ 1095 2hd 1½ 1½ 2½ Steiner J J5 Aw32000 89 ShadyFox,BeachWalk,AmenBrother 7
8May82-3Hol 6f :221 :444 1:084ft 3 1095 11 11½ 1½ 1½ Steiner J J4 Aw26000 93 BeachWlk,MsterWrrior,ChpelCreek 8
29Apr82-8Hol 6f :22 :443 1:082ft 3 1095 11 1½ 2½ 22½ Steiner J J5 Aw26000 92 LaughingBoy,BeachWalk,Redoutble 7
18Apr82-3SA 6½f :212 :441 1:142ft 7½ 1095 1½ 1hd 2hd 21¾ Steiner J J5 45000 96 NaynoBay,BeachWalk,Incorporator 6
11Apr82-1SA 6f :214 :451 1:094sy 7 116 11 1½ 1hd 2nk Ortega L E4 40000 89 NaynoBay,BechWlk,SupremeGlow 12
21Mar82-1SA 6f :214 :444 1:091ft 13 114 2hd 2hd 22 34½ Asmussen C B4 45000 87 Fingal, Incorporator, Beach Walk 8
12Mar82-6SA 6f :224 :47 1:13 sl 3 1115 12 11½ 2½ 1nk Steiner J J3 32000 73 BeachWalk,Chnnon'sBrother,I'vPet 4
6Mar82-4GG 6f :22 :443 1:093ft 3½ 114 1hd 2hd 3½ 42½ Meza R Q4 35000 88 Cross Flags, Ono Bret, Johnny Iver 5
26Feb82-8GG 6f :221 :443 1:092ft 3 115 1hd 32 66 710 Burkes T3 Aw15000 82 Ineffble,FerlessBedeux,TudorGrove 7
5Feb82-8BM 6f :214 :441 1:09 ft 13 114 21½ 23 23 23½ Meza R Q7 Aw16000 91 Coyotero,BeachWalk,PleasntPower 7
May 16 Hol 4f ft :483 h Apr 26 Hol 4f ft :494 h Apr 5 SA 5f ft :593 h Apr 1 SA tr.t 4f sy :51 h

Never Tabled Dk. b. or br. h. 5, by Never Bend—Table Flirt, by Round Table
Br.—Wygod M J (Ky) 1982 4 3 1 0 $55,950
Own.—Wygod M J 116 Tr.—Mandella Richard 1980 0 M 0 0
Lifetime 4 3 1 0 $55,950

8May82-8Hol 7f :214 :44 1:21 ft 5 112 1½ 11 11½ 12 McCrrCJ1 TrpleBendH 92 NeverTbled,Shnekite,PompeiiCourt 7
2May82-3Hol 6f :223 :444 1:084ft *2-5 120 31½ 22 22½ 2no McCarronCJ2 Aw22000 93 Jenny'sDvid,NeverTbled,StrikItBig 5
15Apr82-7SA 6f :214 :444 1:09 ft *1 120 2½ 2hd 12 15½ McCarronCJ7 Aw19000 93 Never Tabled, Santir,TonysLanding 9
2Apr82-6SA 6f :214 :45 1:101ft 2½ 118 32 31 12½ 18 Pincay L Jr2 Mdn 87 NeverTbled,Hwkire,SpnishNugget 10
May 28 Hol 3f ft :35 h May 24 Hol 6f ft 1:134 h ●Apr 26 SA 6f ft 1:112 h Apr 11 SA 5f ft 1:021 h

Terresto's Singer *   **Dk. b. or br. g. 5, by Terresto—Sweet Canary, by No Robbery**
Br.—Valenti P (Cal)   **1982 8 1 1 3 $34,600**
Own.—Tschudi & Wong   **113**   **Tr.—Goodwin Floyd C**   **1981 3 1 0 0 $4,975**
Lifetime 18 3 3 4 $52,300   **Turf 1 0 0 0**

16May82-6Hol	5f	:21^{2}	:44	:56 ft	21	115	$4^{5\frac{1}{2}}$	$4^{3\frac{1}{2}}$	3^{3}	$3^{4\frac{1}{2}}$	McHrgueDG^{4}	Aw37000	95	RemembrJohn,Unlklt,Trrsto'sSingr	7
8May82-3Hol	6f	:22^{1}	:44^{4}	1:08^{4}ft	$8\frac{1}{2}$	116	$4^{1\frac{1}{4}}$	$3^{1\frac{1}{2}}$	$5^{5\frac{1}{2}}$	5^{6}	Jin D^{8}	Aw26000	87	BeachWlk,MsterWrrior,ChpelCreek	8
17Apr82-8SA	a$6\frac{1}{2}$f Ⓣ	:21	:43^{1}	1:13 fm	47	115	2^{hd}	2^{hd}	7^{5}	8^{19}	Jin D^{4}	Sn Simn H	75	Shagbark, Shanekite, Belfort	8
24Mar82-8SA	$5\frac{1}{2}$f	:21^{3}	:44^{2}	1:02^{1}ft	29	115	3^{nk}	2^{hd}	3^{nk}	$3^{4\frac{3}{4}}$	Jin D^{8}	El Conejo H	96	ToB.OrNot,Belfort,Terresto'sSinger	8
14Mar82-7SA	$6\frac{1}{2}$f	:21^{3}	:44^{3}	1:18^{2}sy	$6\frac{1}{2}$	115	1^{1}	$1^{3\frac{1}{2}}$	1^{5}	$1^{1\frac{1}{2}}$	Jin D^{4}	Aw26000	78	Trrsto'sSngr,MstrWrror,H'sSmthng	6
25Feb82-4SA	6f	:21^{2}	:44^{1}	1:09^{1}ft	26	116	$3^{2\frac{1}{2}}$	3^{2}	2^{hd}	$2^{\frac{1}{2}}$	Jin D^{4}	25000	91	Devon, Terresto's Singer,NaynoBay	7
16Jan82-1SA	6f	:21^{4}	:44^{1}	1:09^{2}ft	21	118	1^{hd}	1^{3}	$2^{2\frac{1}{2}}$	3^{4}	Jin D^{8}	20000	87	Ggntc,Truxton'sDobl,Trrsto'sSngr	12
9Jan82-1SA	6f	:21^{3}	:44^{4}	1:09^{2}ft	25	118	3^{1}	$6^{1\frac{1}{4}}$	$7^{7\frac{1}{2}}$	8^{15}	Jin D^{1}	25000	76	WnwoodHost,Dcodd,ConslorCoony	9
5Dec81-1Hol	6f	:22	:45^{3}	1:11 ft	18	119	1^{2}	1^{hd}	2^{3}	4^{11}	Jin D^{9}	25000	71	Decoded, GummoJoe,AlwaysProper	9
7Nov81-9LA	6f	:21^{3}	:44^{3}	1:10^{3}ft	9	120	1^{hd}	$1^{1\frac{1}{2}}$	3^{1}	$8^{9\frac{1}{2}}$	Jin D^{8}	Aw24000	82	Now and Then,BronzeStar,Graben	10

May 28 Hol 3f ft :34^{4} h   **May 23 Hol 6f ft 1:13^{3} h**   **May 6 Hol 3f ft :35 h**   **Apr 25 Hol 6f ft 1:14 h**

The show odds on Remember John were quite good throughout the betting period. With one minute to post time the expected value was 1.15, qualifying it as a Dr. Z system bet. The tote board was:

	Totals	#1 Remember John
Odds		2—1
Win	386,787	105,775
Show	50,581	9,430

Instead of making my $50 bet, I made a Dr. Z system bet. I had brought $2,000 with me to the track. Of this I reserved $250 for my $50 bets, so my betting fortune was $1,750. The optimal Dr. Z system bet was $121. There was some last-minute betting on Remember John. However, his show odds were nearly the same at post time, with an expected value of 1.12. The tote board at post time read:

	Totals	#1 Remember John
Odds		2—1
Win	439,354	121,364
Show	56,794	11,311

It was a very consistent race, as the following chart indicates. Remember John ran a creditable race, always in second position, but he could not catch the long shot, Terresto's Singer. With Never Tabled out of the money, the payoff to show on the Dr. Z system bet on Remember John was a handsome $3.40. My $121 bet returned $205.70, for a profit of $84.70.

EIGHTH RACE
Hollywood
MAY 30, 1982

6 FURLONGS. (1.07⅘) 30th Running of THE LOS ANGELES HANDICAP (Grade III). $75,000 added. 3-year olds and upward. By subscription of $100 each, which shall accompany the nomination, $750 additional to start, with $75,000 added, of which $15,000 to second, $11,250 to third, $5,625 to fourth and $1,875 to fifth. Weights Tuesday, May 25. Starters to be named through the entry box by closing time of entries. A trophy will be presented to the owner of the winner. Closed Wednesday, May 19, 1982 with 13 nominations.

Value of race $81,550, value to winner $47,800, second $15,000, third $11,250, fourth $5,625, fifth $1,875. Mutuel pool $647,017.

Last Raced	Horse	Eqt.	A.	Wt	PP	St	¼	½	Str	Fin	Jockey	Odds $1
16May82 ^{6}Hol^{3}	Terresto's Singer		5	113	7	1	$1^{\frac12}$	$1^{2\frac12}$	1^{2}	1^{nk}	Valenzuela P A	46.60
16May82 ^{6}Hol^{1}	Remember John		3	115	1	4	$2^{1\frac12}$	$2^{2\frac12}$	$2^{3\frac12}$	2^{3}	Delahoussaye E	2.00
9May82 ^{9}TuP^{1}	Petro D. Jay		6	116	3	5	4^{3}	4^{3}	3^{hd}	3no	Castaneda M	7.20
16May82 ^{6}Hol^{5}	Shanekite	b	4	117	2	7	7	7	5^{hd}	$4^{\frac12}$	Hawley S	5.10
23May82 ^{7}Hol^{2}	Beach Walk	b	5	113	5	3	$6^{1\frac12}$	5^{hd}	$4^{2\frac12}$	5^{1}	Steiner J J	27.70
8May82 ^{8}Hol^{1}	Never Tabled		5	116	6	6	5^{hd}	$6^{\frac12}$	6^{3}	6^{8}	McCarron C J	1.00
16May82 ^{6}Hol^{7}	Cool Frenchy		7	113	4	2	$3^{\frac12}$	$3^{\frac12}$	7	7	Aragon J	49.00

OFF AT 5:19. Start good. Won driving. Time, :21, :43⅘, :55⅘, 1:09⅕ Track fast.

$2 Mutuel Prices:			
8-TERRESTO'S SINGER	95.20	18.00	5.00
1-REMEMBER JOHN		4.20	3.40
4-PETRO D. JAY			4.20

Dk. b. or br. g, by Terresto—Sweet Canary, by No Robbery. Trainer Goodwin Floyd C. Bred by Valenti P (Cal).

TERRESTO'S SINGER outsprinted REMEMBER JOHN from the gate, drew well clear on the turn, then gamely held that one safe through the final sixteenth. REMEMBER JOHN, unable to keep pace with the winner on the turn, rallied gamely under strong handling in the final furlong and was getting to the winner at the end. PETRO D. JAY went evenly and without apparent mishap, SHANEKITE passed tired horses in the stretch. NEVER TABLED stumbled a stride out of teh gate and failed to mount a threat. COOL FRENCHY tired in the stretch.

Owners— 1, Tschudi & Wong; 2, Sheridan Mr-Mrs J; 3, Ottley R; 4, Udko Selma; 5, Knapp P R; 6, Wygod M J; 7, Lichlyter Dr or Mrs F E.

Overweight: Cool Frenchy 1 pound. **Scratched**—Pompeii Court (8May82 ^{8}Hol^{3}).

The final race of a day's card often contains a good bet—a top horse who is heavily bet to win but is overlooked to place or show. With the cumulative losses of the day mounting for most bettors, a show bet on such a horse provides little hope of salvaging the day. Heart Beat was such a horse in the ninth race. He was the top choice of all the *Daily Racing Form*'s consensus experts and their best bet of the day, with a rating of 29 out of a possible 35. The next-rated horse had a 5! Heart Beat had run recently at Hollywood, finishing second. With Laffit Pincay, Jr., on board again, he looked like an excellent prospect. The crowd bet Heart Beat down to a 6–5 favorite. His show odds were good, with an expected value in the 1.10–1.15 range throughout the betting period—not quite a Dr. Z system bet, but it was close, so I decided to compromise and bet $100 to show on Heart Beat.

9th Hollywood

1⅛ MILES. (TURF). (1.46) CLAIMING. Purse $28,000. 4-year-olds and upward. Weight, 122 lbs. Non-winners of two races at a mile or over since March 28 allowed 3 lbs.; such a race since then, 6 lbs. Claiming price $50,000; for each $2,500 to $45,000 allowed 2 lbs. (Races when entered for $40,000 or less not considered.)

Fabulous Reason *

B. h. 5, by Le Fabuleux—Hail to Nurse, by Hail to Reason
Br.—Brookmeade Stable (Ky) — 1982 9 1 0 1 $15,050
Own.—Stepp J C **116** **Tr.—Moreno Henry** **$50,000** — 1981 6 1 0 1 $9,550
Lifetime 25 2 0 4 $31,825 — Turf 7 0 0 1 $4,050

16May82-9Hol	1⅛Ⓣ:46^{2}1:10^{2}1:47^{1}fm	74	109^{5}	9^{21}	9^{17}	9^{17}	8^{13}	Steiner J J^{9}	Aw24000	81	PetrJons,PrinclyVrdict,MdlofHonor	9
1May82-5Hol	$1\frac{1}{16}$Ⓣ:46 1:09^{4}1:40^{4}fm	54	117	$7^{9\frac12}$	8^{13}	7^{13}	7^{12}	Black K^{8}	Aw24000	83	CllMeMister,Essenbee,MdlofHonor	8
21Apr82-2SA	1⅛Ⓣ:46^{1}1:10^{2}1:47^{3}fm	41	118	$7^{4\frac14}$	$9^{3\frac34}$	$10^{9\frac34}$	$8^{8\frac12}$	ValenzuelPA^{5}	Aw25000	80	Disclaim, LordCarnavon,Essenbee	12
8Apr82-5SA	1⅛Ⓣ:46^{2}1:10^{3}1:48^{1}fm	65	120	$7^{7\frac14}$	$7^{5\frac12}$	$8^{7\frac34}$	$6^{5\frac34}$	CastanedaM^{1}	Aw26000	80	‡Rostropovich,Tom'sSerend,Islndr	12
21Mar82-5SA	1⅛ :46^{1} 1:10^{2} 1:48^{1}ft	24	118	6^{8}	5^{6}	7^{12}	7^{14}	AsmussenCB^{5}	Aw27000	74	DurbanDeep,Rostropovich,Disclaim	7
7Mar82-7SA	1⅛Ⓣ:45^{4}1:10^{4}1:47^{4}fm	21	118	$7^{5\frac34}$	$8^{5\frac12}$	5^{11}	$3^{7\frac12}$	CastanedaM^{2}	Aw27000	80	RasPenng,Essenbee,FbuiousReson	10
7Feb82-5SA	1¼Ⓣ:47 1:36^{2}2:00^{4}fm	34	121	$5^{4\frac12}$	$6^{1\frac12}$	$6^{4\frac12}$	6^{5}	AsmussenCB^{6}	Aw27000	78	Jurisconsult,CptnGnrl,PrnclyVrdct	11
23Jan82-4SA	$1\frac{1}{16}$:47^{2} 1:12 1:44^{4}gd	16	121	$6^{5\frac34}$	$7^{6\frac34}$	$7^{7\frac14}$	$6^{6\frac14}$	Gallitano G^{5}	Aw25000	71	BrillintDouble,CllMeMistr,PocktMn	7
1Jan82-9SA	$1\frac{1}{16}$:49^{1} 1:14 1:47^{1}hy	16	118	$3^{\frac12}$	$1^{2\frac12}$	1^{3}	$1^{\frac12}$	Gallitano G^{3}	Aw20000	65	FabulousReason,Stingingly,Clbong	8
8Dec81-6BM	$1\frac{1}{16}$:45^{3} 1:09^{4} 1:42^{1}ft	9¾	117	8^{14}	8^{13}	7^{16}	7^{16}	GonzalezRM^{4}	Aw11000	72	Cinnpo, Invective, Court Leader	8

May 22 Hol 6f ft 1:14^{3} h **May 14 Hol 4f ft :50 h** **May 8 Hol 4f ft :51^{3} h** **Apr 27 Hol 4f ft :51^{2} h**

*Kundalini

B. h. 7, by Snow Track—Karen, by Maporal
Br.—Haras Curiche (Chile) 1982 2 0 0 1 $5,730
Own.—Wright W J 116 Tr.—Brinson Clay $50,000 1981 19 1 2 6 $47,350
Lifetime 61 7 14 11 $96,574 Turf 50 7 11 10 $93,374
20May82-9Hol 1 1/16 Ⓣ:4621:1041:413fm 21 116 75 75¾ 55 33½ Valenzuela P A6 50000 87 Ultracharge, Giriama, Kundalini 8
8May82-3GG 1 Ⓣ:4731:1141:364fm 5½ 113 59 57½ 58 49¾ Anderson JR5 Aw17000 74 KneCounty,UncleBrrydown,MstrAc 7
3Dec81-8Hol 1 Ⓣ:4821:1241:362fm 6½ 116 54 3½ 22 32 ValenzuelPA2 Aw19000 85 First Blade,SpringDigger,Kundalini 9
7Nov81-8BM 1 1/16 Ⓣ:4721:1231:452fm 38 111 1020 1019 1022 1023 CblleroR2 Sbsct Inv H 58 LsAsprs,PolicInspctor,Dggr'sPont 10
17Oct81-8BM 1⅛Ⓣ:47 1:1111:48 fm 51 112 913 88¼ 88½ 79 Caballero R1 Tan H 99 TheBart,TahitianKing,Dgger'sPoint 9
3Oct81-8BM 1 1/16 Ⓣ:4721:1211:45 gd 16 112 710 79 67½ 35½ CblleroR2 Sn Jqn Iv H 77 Borrego Sun, Les Aspres,Kundalini 7
26Sep81-6BM 1 :454 1:101 1:353ft 6½ 115 58¾ 58½ 411 412 Howell W C5 Aw15000 79 FleetTempo,HeadHawk,BlackSaber 5
19Sep81-11Bmf 1 1/16 Ⓣ:4621:1041:434fm 17 112 811 66½ 67 36 Meza R Q8 Sn Mtn H 83 Hoedown'sDy,BorregoSun,Kundlini 8
7Sep81-9Dmr 1 1/16 Ⓣ:4641:1121:424fm 7½ 116 721 713 57½ 44½ Pierce D3 50000 91 GreatGrndson,Spinoz,HostileKnight 8
27Aug81-8Dmr 1⅛Ⓣ:5021:1411:502fm 5 117 76 76 56½ 55¼ CastanedaM2 Aw18000 81 PocketMn,ChncyBiddr,MusicIBoyII 7
May 19 SA 3f ft :353 h May 6 GG 4f ft :494 h Apr 28 SA 7f ft 1:274 h Apr 21 SA 7f ft 1:261 h

Buffalo Hart *

B. c. 4, by Buffalo Lark—To My Lady, by Amber Morn
Br.—Madden P (Ky) 1982 8 1 0 0 $21,625
Own.—Rogers Red Top Farm 116 Tr.—Sullivan John $50,000 1981 17 1 0 1 $15,878
Lifetime 28 3 0 2 $44,613 Turf 6 0 0 0 $2,964
20May82-8Hol 1 Ⓣ:4641:1011:333fm 110 118 85½ 88 811 813 Pierce D7 Aw35000 88 Piperhill, Faiz, Quantum Leap 8
4Apr82-7SA 1 :452 1:094 1:344ft 57 1155 21 66 79½ 712 Steiner J J6 Aw35000 83 Maxistar, Son of a Dodo, A Run 7
28Mar82-7SA 1 1/16 :451 1:084 1:411ft 44 119 23 48 713 812 AsmussenCB5 Aw35000 83 Sunshine Swag, A Run, RockSoftly 8
21Mar82-3SA 1 1/16 :46 1:10 1:411ft 28 118 611 59½ 510 516 McHrgueDG4 Aw35000 79 Mehmet, Native Tactics, A Run 6
12Mar82-5SA 1¼ :471 1:40 2:074sl 12 114 1hd 13 13½ 1½ AsmussenCB1 Aw32000 50 Buffalo Hart, Pettrax, Lucullus 5
6Mar82-6SA 1 :442 1:083 1:343ft 34 114 714 79½ 78½ 58¼ Lipham T4 Aw30000 88 Mehmet, Western, Notable Axe 7
13Feb82-7SA 6½f :22 :45 1:152ft 26 114 63½ 65¾ 611 619 Lipham T3 Aw32000 74 KngrooCort,Arstocrtcl,AnswrtoMsc 6
5Feb82-7SA 6½f :212 :433 1:15 ft 70 114 67 65½ 55½ 44¼ Lipham T3 Aw32000 91 VictorySmpl,BondRullh,PompCourt 8
27Dec81-5SA 1 1/16 :454 1:093 1:413ft 37 115 89¾ 812 1011 1021 Pierce D1 Aw30000 72 KngrooCourt,PierrLMont,EggToss 10
26Nov81-5Hol 1 1/16 Ⓣ:4641:1031:41 fm 25 113 67 63½ 88 87¾ Hawley S5 Aw27000 86 Truckload, Vorlaufer, Early Settler 8
May 28 Hol Ⓣ 4f fm :482 h (d) May 13 Hol Ⓣ 7f fm 1:31 h (d) May 7 Hol Ⓣ 7f fm 1:294 h (d) May 2 Hol 5f ft 1:034 h

*El Pancho Angel

Ch. h. 6, by Tantoul—Doninda, by Cardanil II
Br.—Haras Dadinco (Chile) 1982 5 0 0 0 $2,900
Own.—T 9 0 Ranch 116 Tr.—Fanning Jerry $50,000 1981 11 1 5 1 $56,050
Lifetime 28 6 8 2 $85,686 Turf 22 6 7 2 $77,536
8May82-9Hol 1 Ⓣ:4611:1011:34 fm 6¾ 116 43½ 31 42½ 65½ Olivares F6 80000 93 RghtofLght,Jursconsult,SonofDodo 7
30Apr82-7Hol 1⅛Ⓣ:47 1:1111:47 fm 3½ 114 511 66 54 66½ Guerra W A9 Aw30000 88 HemphillCounty,TbleTorch,Disclim 9
21Apr82-5SA a6½f Ⓣ:211 :4331:13 fm 6½ 116 86½ 88¼ 47 43 McHargue DG12 80000 91 Fingal, Tellaround, Gray Dandy 12
11Apr82-5SA 6½f :22 :451 1:17 sy 10 114 53¾ 43 3½ 51½ Lipham T1 Aw26000 83 Tellround,Redoutble,He'sSomthing 7
21Mar82-7SA 6½f :214 :443 1:151ft 18 114 52 41¾ 67¾ 69 Olivares F6 Aw35000 85 DoubleDiscount,Aristocrticl,PirtLw 7
5Sep81-8Dmr 1 1/16 Ⓣ:4811:1211:42 fm 21 114 77¼ 76¼ 87¼ 86 Lipham T1 Escndo H 93 Advocatum,ReglBering,MjorSport 10
3Aug81-8Dmr 1⅛Ⓣ:4731:1141:494fm 10 119 611 55 41 2¾ Olivares F8 Aw24000 88 Wild Surf, El Pancho Angel, Idyll 9
17Jly81-8Hol 1 1/16 :462 1:10 1:42 ft 6½ 122 68 66½ 55¼ 58¾ Lipham T5 200000 S 76 Joleg, Fingal, Sham's Fool 7
1Jly81-7Hol 1 Ⓣ:4511:0921:342fm 6¾ 115 615 67½ 42 1hd Lipham T2 Aw40000 97 ElPnchoAngel,Lif'sHop,SonofDodo 8
3Jun81-5Hol 1 1/16 Ⓣ:4631:1041:412fm 6¾ 114 57 44½ 1½ 2¾ Lipham T7 Aw24000 91 Bnfctor,ElPnchoAngl,MstrSurgon 10
May 19 Hol 4f ft :503 h Apr 19 SA 4f ft :471 h Apr 10 SA 3f ft :38 h Apr 4 SA 5f ft :593 h

*Heart Beat

Dk. b. or br. g. 5, by Hard to Beat—Wampum, by Warfare
Br.—Guest R (Fra) 1982 7 1 2 1 $30,650
Own.—Bacharach B 116 Tr.—Frankel Robert $50,000 1980 9 2 2 2 $28,057
Lifetime 16 3 4 3 $58,707 Turf 10 2 3 2 $33,657
12May82-7Hol 1⅜Ⓣ:4731:3842:16 fm 3½ 117 37 52½ 31 2no Pincay L Jr3 50000 75 Phillipic, Heart Beat, Nar 8
11Apr82-3SA 1⅛ :474 1:121 1:494sy *6-5 116 1hd 1hd 21½ 33¾ Shoemaker W1 50000 77 Perry Cabin, Three Bits, HeartBeat 6
2Apr82-5SA 1⅛ :482 1:131 1:512gd 2½ 115 54 64¾ 44 41¾ Shoemaker W2 60000 70 TheArgyleKid,Ultrchrge,Stingingly 7
20Mar82-5SA 1 1/16 :454 1:10 1:411ft 4 114 32½ 32 43½ 47¼ ShoemkerW1 Aw30000 88 Tell Again, Lucullus, Chriserik 7
14Feb82-9SA 1 :464 1:11 1:354ft 4½ 116 2hd 11 12 11¼ DelahoussayeE5 40000 90 HertBet,AnHeirAboutHim,Decodd 10
24Jan82-4SA 1⅛ :462 1:112 1:504ft 3¼e 116 22½ 21½ 11½ 21½ Ortega L E3 32000 73 Denali Ridge,HeartBeat,PortVelate 6
17Jan82-9SA 6½f :221 :442 1:151ft 6¼e 116 96¼ 912 915 813 Ortega L E3 50000 81 MrblCourt,ThArgylKid,AmnBrothr 12
4Nov80♦4MLaffitte(Fra) a1⅝ 3:04 gd 3-2 123 Ⓣ 32 Head F Px Merlin Multicolore, Vald'Amain,HeartBeat 6
11Oct80♦5CrLaroche(Fra) a1½ : sf — 121 Ⓣ 22 StMrtY Px Rene Wattinne Eternity, HeartBeat,FlingDutchman 8
11Oct80—No time taken.
14Sep80♦6Compiegne(Fra) a1⅛ : gd *1 126 Ⓣ 1hd BtblD Px Imperatrice Eugenie Heart Beat, Bold Gold, Pontois 9
14Sep80—No time taken. Race for lady riders.
May 26 Hol 5f ft 1:003 h May 20 Hol 4f ft :491 h May 9 Hol 6f ft 1:134 h May 3 Hol 6f ft 1:17 h

***Ingres**
B. h. 6, by Djakao—Insulaire, by Aureole
Br.—LaComtesse Orazio Sanjust (Fra) 1982 7 0 0 0 $1,450
Own.—Yauk A 116 Tr.—Perkins Larry $50,000 1981 10 1 1 0 $33,932
Lifetime 33 2 4 4 $86,229 Turf 30 2 4 4 $85,479
12May82-7Hol 1⅜Ⓣ:4731:3842:16 fm 9¾ 116 815 810 78¾ 54¾ McHargue D G2 50000 71 Phillipic, Heart Beat, Nar 8
21Apr82-9SA 1¼Ⓣ:4441:3421:593fm 55 108 716109½105¾1011 StinrJJ2 Sn Jacinto H 78 Durban Deep, Monarch, Kilty 10
21Apr82—Run in two divisions, 8th & 9th races.
2Apr82-5SA 1⅛:482 1:131 1:512gd 20 116 78 76¾ 66¼ 54¾ Pierce D4 62500 68 TheArgyleKid,Ultrchrge,Stingingly 7
24Mar82-5SA 1⅛:452 1:092 1:472ft 56 116 819 815 718 721 Ontiveros J A7 62500 71 Chriserik, BeOnTime,TheArgyleKid 8
10Mar82-5SA 1⅛Ⓣ:4521:1011:474fm 79 112 10171011107½ 711 Ontiveros J A7 70000 77 RightofLight,Monico,NoblTrdition 10
24Feb82-5SA 1⅛Ⓣ:4631:1041:474fm 54 116 91410101012 914 Gilligan L6 62500 74 BadRascal,BeauSoleil,BlueDncerII 10
13Feb82-5SA 6½f:213 :442 1:161ft 73 114 1017101910211020 Ontiveros JA2 Aw26000 69 Kearney,LaughingBoy,Mari'sBook 10
18Oct81♦4Longchamp(Fra) a1⅞ 3:434sf 9 120 Ⓣ 817 BarelliE Pr Jouvence H Santa Aquila, Jete Battu, SoMisty 14
13Sep81♦3Longchamp(Fra) a1⅞ 3:293gd 6¾ 113 Ⓣ 21½ BarelliE Pr de Dangu H Val d'Ajol, Ingres, Veneziano 14
15Aug81♦4Deauville(Fra) a2¼ 4:002fm 6¼ 102 Ⓣ 13 BrlliE Grand de la Manche H Ingres, ‡Hartwood, Grey Imperial 23
May 26 Hol 6f ft 1:184 h May 11 Hol 3f ft :371 h May 6 Hol 1 ft 1:45 h Apr 30 Hol 6f ft 1:15 h

Wantazee
Ch. g. 4, by Orbit Ruler—Princess Scott, by Doc Scott J
Br.—Coffman R (Cal) 1982 6 3 1 0 $35,075
Own.—Giacoppuzzi G 119 Tr.—Cofer Riley S $50,000 1981 4 1 1 0 $2,570
Lifetime 10 4 2 0 $37,645
8May82-7Hol 1 1/16:46 1:103 1:43 ft *1 114 41¾ 31½ 21 21¼ McCarronCJ3 Aw22000 79 ‡LittleShah,Wantazee,RomnMjesty 8
8May82—Placed first through disqualification
28Apr82-9Hol 1 1/16:463 1:103 1:422ft 3 114 2½ 1hd 2½ 21 McCarronCJ1 Aw22000 82 Fager'sBid,Wantzee,FriendlyRoylty 7
4Apr82-9SA 1 1/16:463 1:104 1:414ft 15 114 2½ 2hd 32 43¼ ValenzuelPA7 Aw21000 89 Pal's Lad, Peter Jones,RamBoldly 10
4Mar82-3SA 1 1/16:451 1:094 1:422ft 9-5 117 36 22 53½ 53¾ Pincay L Jr3 c32000 85 CptinOrient,EgleTost,PriorApprovl 6
14Feb82-1SA 1 :451 1:094 1:36 ft 5¼ 115 34 21½ 2½ 1¾ ValenzuelaPA5 c20000 89 Wantazee, Embermatic,Bandelaire 10
29Jan82-9SA 1 1/16:463 1:104 1:43 ft 24 115 1hd 1hd 2hd 1nk Valenzuela P A1 16000 86 Wantazee,ElGtoGrnde,OnYourWy 11
19Dec81-3Hol 1 :464 1:121 1:39 ft 25 114 41¼ 52¾ 66 57¼ Valenzuela P A7 22500 64 MjstcCourt,FoxyQllo,AttBoyBrook 7
9Dec81-3Hol 6f :22 :452 1:104ft 23 119 76¾ 76¼ 68½ 612 Ontiveros JA3 Ⓢ 20000 71 GrfieldCounty,ImmnntIssu,Ws'sRb 9
15Nov81-3AC 6f :223 :443 1:101ft *1 116 1hd 1½ 13 12½ Ontiveros J A3 AlwM 88 Wantazee,SirDvidR.,RhythmRunner 6
8Nov81-4AC 6f :222 :451 1:102ft *1 1097 64¼ 64¾ 24 24 Cervantes J L1 AlwM 83 Eds Novel, Wantazee, Valley Flash 7
May 26 Hol 5f ft 1:00 h May 20 Hol 5f ft 1:02 h May 5 Hol 5f ft 1:003 h Apr 22 Hol 4f ft :484 h

Pierre La Mont
B. g. 8, by Great Mystery—Two Su Sis, by Andys Glory
Br.—Amlung R (Fla) 1982 8 1 1 1 $30,275
Own.—Giddings & Wilson 116 Tr.—Landers Dale $50,000 1981 19 4 5 3 $85,875
Lifetime 74 16 15 8 $250,911 Turf 46 8 10 8 $135,719
12May82-7Hol 1⅜Ⓣ:4731:3842:16 fm 6¾ 116 2hd 2hd 44½ 79½ Castaneda M5 50000 66 Phillipic, Heart Beat, Nar 8
20Apr82-5SA 1⅛Ⓣ:45 1:0911:473fm 5 120 24 22½ 1hd 31¼ Castaneda M7 50000 88 NightLegue,SoftMrket,PirrLMont 11
14Mar82-9SA 1 1/16:464 1:12 1:452sy 7 120 49 614 616 620 Castaneda M7 62500 54 TheArgyleKid,BeauMoro,Stingingly 7
24Feb82-5SA 1⅛Ⓣ:4631:1041:474fm 4¼ 120 22½ 22½ 33 45½ Castaneda M9 62500 82 BadRascal,BeauSoleil,BlueDncerII 10
15Feb82-5SA 1⅛Ⓣ:4731:1221:493gd 10 118 1hd 1hd 45½ 78½ ValenzuelaPA10 75000 70 Ptti'sTriumph,RightofLight,Gmmt 12
31Jan82-5SA 1⅛Ⓣ:4721:1141:493gd 2½ 116 11 11 1hd 44 Valenzuela P A3 75000 75 Serang, Lanarkland, Mr. Mud 9
17Jan82-7SA 1 :451 1:093 1:344ft *7-5 115 1hd 2hd 1hd 12¾ ValenzuelPA4 Aw30000 95 PierreLaMont,SirDancer,Mr.Metaxa 9
6Jan82-4SA 1⅛:49 1:14 1:532m *2-3 115 11½ 1½ 25 29½ Valenzuela PA6 A40000 52 TellAgain,PierreLaMont,DenliRidge 6
27Dec81-5SA 1 1/16:454 1:093 1:413ft 7¾ 115 11 12 2hd 2½ ValenzuelPA6 Aw30000 92 KngrooCourt,PierrLMont,EggToss 10
16Dec81-7Hol 1 1/16Ⓣ:4841:1241:424fm 4¾ 115 11 11 1½ 22 ValenzuelPA3 Aw27000 83 LeDucdeBar,PierreLMont,Lucullus 7
May 24 Hol 4f ft :50 h May 3 Hol 4f ft :50 h Apr 13 SA 3f ft :373 h Apr 8 SA 5f ft 1:014 h

At post time the expected return per dollar bet on Heart Beat to show was 1.12 and the tote board was as follows:

	Totals	#5 Heart Beat
Odds		6—5
Win	171,124	64,610
Show	26,958	7,465

Heart Beat won the race easily. The payoff of $2.60 to show was reasonable, given the fact that Heart Beat did go off as a 6–5 favorite, that the third and fourth picks came in the money, and that there was a substantial breakage. Again, it is clear that the bet on Heart Beat was a reasonable one but not good enough to be a Dr. Z system bet. My $100 bet returned $130, for a $30 profit.

NINTH RACE
Hollywood
MAY 30, 1982

1 ⅛ MILES.(turf). (1.46) CLAIMING. Purse $28,000. 4-year-olds and upward. Weight, 122 lbs. Non-winners of two races at a mile or over since March 28 allowed 3 lbs.; such a race since then, 6 lbs. Claiming price $50,000; for each $2,500 to $45,000 allowed 2 lbs. (Races when entered for $40,000 or less not considered.)

Value of race $28,000, value to winner $15,400, second $5,600, third $4,200, fourth $2,100, fifth $700. Mutuel pool $252,477. Exacta Pool $518,984.

Last Raced	Horse	Eqt.	A.Wt	PP	St	¼	½	¾	Str	Fin	Jockey	Cl'g Pr	Odds $1
12May82 ^{7}Hol^{2}	Heart Beat		5 117	5	2	$5^{2\frac{1}{2}}$	3^{hd}	3^{1}	$1^{1\frac{1}{2}}$	1^{2}	Pincay L Jr	50000	1.20
20May82 ^{9}Hol^{3}	Kundalini		7 116	2	6	$6^{\frac{1}{2}}$	7^{1}	6^{hd}	4^{2}	$2^{2\frac{1}{2}}$	Valenzuela P A	50000	7.90
12May82 ^{7}Hol^{7}	Pierre La Mont	b	8 116	8	1	1^{hd}	1^{hd}	2^{2}	3^{1}	$3^{\frac{1}{2}}$	Hawley S	50000	5.60
8May82 ^{7}Hol^{1}	Wantazee		4 119	7	3	$2^{2\frac{1}{2}}$	$2^{2\frac{1}{2}}$	1^{hd}	2^{hd}	$4^{2\frac{1}{2}}$	Delahoussaye E	50000	11.10
16May82 ^{9}Hol^{8}	Fabulous Reason		5 116	1	4	4^{hd}	6^{1}	$7^{1\frac{1}{2}}$	6^{hd}	5no	Castaneda M	50000	28.70
12May82 ^{7}Hol^{5}	Ingres	b	6 116	6	8	8	8	8	7^{4}	$6^{3\frac{1}{2}}$	Sibille R	50000	12.70
8May82 ^{9}Hol^{6}	El Pancho Angel	b	6 116	4	7	7^{1}	5^{hd}	$5^{1\frac{1}{2}}$	$5^{3\frac{1}{2}}$	7^{5}	Lipham T	50000	3.20
20May82 ^{8}Hol^{8}	Buffalo Hart		4 116	3	5	3^{hd}	4^{3}	4^{hd}	8	8	Pierce D	50000	21.80

OFF AT 5:50. Start good. Won ridden out. Time, :23⅕, :46⅘, 1:10⅘, 1:34⅘, 1:47⅗ Course firm.

$2 Mutuel Prices:

5-HEART BEAT	4.40	3.40	2.60
2-KUNDALINI		6.80	3.80
8-PIERRE LA MONT			3.60

$5 EXACTA 5-2 PAID $62.00.

Dk. b. or br. g, by Hard to Beat—Wampum, by Warfare. Trainer Frankel Robert. Bred by Guest R (Fra).

HEART BEAT, just outside the leaders while reserved off the early pace, rallied to take command from outside entering the stretch and drew off. KUNDALINI, unhurried for six furlongs, rallied willingly in the middle of the course through the final quarter-mile but did not menace the winner. PIERRE LA MONT outsprinted WANTAZEE for the early lead, then weakened in the final furlong. WANTAZEE lacked the needed rally. EL PANCHO ANGEL failed to threaten.

Owners— 1, Bacharach B; 2, Wright W J; 3, Giddings & Wilson; 4, Giacoppuzzi G; 5, Stepp J C; 6, Yank A; 7, T 9 0 Ranch; 8, Rogers Red Top Farm. **Overweight:** Heart Beat 1 pound.

Summary of betting

Race	Bet ($)	Payoff per $2 Bet ($)	Profit ($)
3	50	3.60	40.00
4	50	3.00	25.00
5	50	3.80	45.00
7	50	0	−50.00
8	113	3.40	84.70
9	100	2.60	30.00
			174.70

In summary, there was only one Dr. Z system bet: Remember John in the eighth. Insearchof in the fifth and Heart Beat in the ninth were close, as was the loser Patti's Triumph in the seventh.

All my bets were to show. Six of the seven horses actually came in the money, so I had a pleasant afternoon with a nice profit. This performance was better than what you can expect on average. Since about two thirds of all favorites finish in the money, one would expect to win about four or five races out of seven. For this reason, it is best to bet when the odds are good. The payoffs will then be higher to compensate for the bets you lose.

PLAYING THE DR. Z SYSTEM AT LOUISIANA AND CHURCHILL DOWNS

Since the first edition of *Beat the Racetrack* was published in the fall of 1984, numerous people have been using the Dr. Z system at racetracks across North America. We have received hundreds of letters, and in general the feedback has been very positive. The following results were obtained by Rusty P. Ford at Louisiana Downs and Churchill Downs in October and November of 1986. Rusty used a number of modifications to the Dr. Z system rules discussed in Chapter 5 to account for his special circumstances, and they have worked well for him. He used the Kelly bet when the expected return at the one-minute mark was 1.14 or more, and a half Kelly in the range 1.10–1.14. When the return was in the range 1.05–1.10 he used flat bets whose size depended upon the odds in the following way:

1–1 or less	$100
6–5	90
7–5	80
3–2	70
8–5	60
9–5	50
2–1	40
5–2	30
3–1 or above	20

That is, the more favored the horse, the more he bet, as the Kelly method would suggest. When the track was not fast he bet the smaller wager of one-quarter Kelly, or $20. He also rounded the Kelly, one-half Kelly, and one-quarter Kelly bets down to common betting amounts.

During the course of twenty-one days, he made 138 show bets and 6 place bets. Ninety-five of the 144 bets, or 66%, were in the money for a profit of 24.5%. Using an initial wealth of $5,000, he bet $16,230 to make $3,973 over this period, or about $190 per day. He had a small gain of $84 on the flat bets. Only three of the wagers that were good at one minute to post time dropped to an expected return of less than 1.00. The bet sizes ranged from $20 to $1,220. His longest losing streak was four races, and he also lost three in a row twice. His longest winning streak was ten races on October 31 and November 1 at Churchill Downs. His largest payoff was $7 to show on a 5–1 shot, and his lowest was $2.20 to show. Churchill Downs now pays a minimum of $2.10, however, Louisiana Downs still pays a minimum of $2.20. Tables 14.3 and 14.4 summarize his results.

TABLE 14.3 ***Rusty P. Ford's Results Using the Dr. Z System at Louisiana and Churchill Downs in 1986***

Date	*Track*	*Wealth*	*Horse # Show, Place Odds*	*Expected Return with 1 Minute to Post Time*	*Expected Return at Post Time*	*Optimal Kelly Bet ($)*
10/16	4-LD	5,000	6-s-2–1	1.27	1.38	108
	5-LD	5,080	11-s-6–5	1.20	1.06	418
	7-LD	5,200	5-p-1–1	1.10	1.02	254
	8-LD	5,080	12-s-2–1	1.18	1.10	223
	10-LD	5,256	7-s-3–2	1.23	1.05	402
10/17	10-LD	5,416	3-s-3–1	1.11	1.13	10
10/18	2-LD	5,411	3-s-1–2	1.20	1.17	1,229
	3-LD	5,771	1-s-5–2	1.17	1.13	207
	6-LD	5,831	3-s-6–5	1.29	1.21	964
	10-LD	5,591	1-s-1–1	1.18	1.12	623
10/19	1-LD	5,711	4-s-3–1	1.21	1.08	113
	2-LD	5,611	6-s-4–5	1.26	1.18	815
	6-LD	5,851	3-s-5–2	1.11	1.05	128
	10-LD	5,821	7-s-1–1	1.45	1.29	1,113
10/30	1-CD	6,301	10-s-3–1	1.19	1.10	37
	2-CD	6,325	10-s-7–2	1.23	1.26	45
	3-CD	6,355	3-s-2–1	1.19	1.06	146
	4-CD	6,285	3-s-7–2	1.19	1.07	21
	7-CD	6,307	9-s-2–1	1.22	1.09	83
	9-CD	6,355	7-s-3–2	1.12	1.01	197
10/31	1-CD	6,255	1-s-3–2	1.22	1.07	148
	2-CD	6,339	4-s-2–1	1.16	1.09	79
	3-CD	6,387	4-s-2–1	1.13	1.00	131
	4-CD	6,429	10-s-5–2	1.54	1.28	159
	5-CD	6,685	4-s-2–1	1.15	1.17	48
	6-CD	6,705	3-s-1–2	1.07	1.10	0
	7-CD	6,709	2-s-2–1	1.32	1.02	186
	8-CD	6,725	3-s-2–1	1.16	1.14	131
	9-CD	6,733	2-s-2–1	1.18	1.20	86
11/1	1-CD	6,751	11-s-5–1	1.13	1.12	0
	2-CD	6,779	8-s-2–1	1.18	1.06	151
	1-SA	6,739	1-s-5–1	1.34	1.05	70
	4-CD	6,699	2-s-8–5	1.21	1.14	356
	6-CD	6,339	9-s-1–1	1.11	1.02	391
	8-CD	6,379	8-s-4–5	1.27	1.15	848
	9-CD	6,715	11-s-2–1	1.15	1.06	125
	7-SA	6,775	2-s-8–5	1.23	1.10	413
11/2	1-CD	6,895	8-s-7–2	1.16	1.14	7
	2-CD	6,875	2-s-9–5	1.30	1.11	269
	3-CD	6,953	1-s-2–1	1.14	1.13	105
	4-CD	6,965	3-s-2–1	1.07	1.15	0
	5-CD	6,945	9-s-4–5	1.36	1.26	717

Size	Bet ($)	Total of Wagers ($)	Payoff Per $2 Wager	Profit	Cumulative Profit ($)	Cumulative Profit (%)
K	100	100	3.60	80	80	80.0
K	400	500	2.60	120	200	40.0
$\frac{1}{2}$K	120	620	0	−120	80	12.9
K	220	840	3.60	176	256	30.5
K	400	1,240	2.80	160	416	33.5
$\frac{1}{2}$K	5	1,245	0	−5	411	33.0
K	1,200	2,445	2.60	360	771	31.5
$\frac{1}{2}$*	100	2,545	3.20	60	831	32.7
$\frac{1}{2}$*	240	2,785	0	−240	591	21.2
K	600	3,385	2.40	120	711	21.0
K	100	3,485	0	−100	611	17.5
K	800	4,285	2.60	240	851	19.9
$\frac{1}{2}$*	30	4,315	0	−30	821	19.0
$\frac{1}{2}$*	600	4,915	3.60	480	1,301	26.5
$\frac{1}{2}$*	20	4,935	4.40	24	1,325	26.8
$\frac{1}{2}$*	20	4,955	5.00	30	1,355	27.3
$\frac{1}{2}$*	70	5,025	0	−70	1,285	25.6
K	20	5,045	4.20	22	1,307	25.9
K	80	5,125	3.20	48	1,355	26.4
$\frac{1}{2}$K	100	5,225	0	−100	1,255	24.0
K	140	5,365	3.20	84	1,339	25.0
K	80	5,445	3.20	48	1,387	25.5
$\frac{1}{2}$K	70	5,515	3.20	42	1,429	25.9
K	160	5,675	5.20	256	1,685	29.7
$\frac{1}{2}$*	20	5,695	4.00	20	1,705	29.9
f	20	5,715	2.40	4	1,709	29.9
$\frac{1}{2}$*	40	5,755	2.80	16	1,725	30.0
$\frac{1}{2}$*	40	5,795	2.40	8	1,733	29.9
$\frac{1}{4}$*	20	5,815	3.80	18	1,751	30.1
f	20	5,835	4.80	28	1,779	30.5
$\frac{1}{2}$*	40	5,875	0	−40	1,739	29.6
$\frac{1}{2}$*	40	5,915	0	−40	1,699	28.7
K	360	6,275	0	−360	1,339	21.3
$\frac{1}{2}$K	200	6,475	2.40	40	1,379	21.3
K	840	7,315	2.80	336	1,715	23.4
K	120	7,435	3.00	60	1,775	23.9
K	400	7,835	2.60	120	1,895	24.2
f	20	7,855	0	−20	1,875	23.9
$\frac{1}{2}$*	130	7,985	3.20	78	1,953	24.5
$\frac{1}{4}$*	20	8,005	3.20	12	1,965	24.5
f	20	8,025	0	−20	1,945	24.2
$\frac{1}{4}$*	180	8,205	0	−180	1,765	21.5

F = flat bet, R = rain (off track), * = anticipate loser and K = Kelly bet.

Date	Track	Wealth	Horse # Show, Place Odds	Expected Return with 1 Minute to Post Time	Expected Return at Post Time	Optimal Kelly Bet ($)
	6-CD	6,765	2-s-7–5	1.19	1.07	324
	7-CD	6,893	5-s-8–5	1.11	1.09	140
11/4	2-CD	6,921	3-s-3–1	1.16	1.06	36
	3-CD	6,953	4-s-2–1	1.16	1.12	132
	5-CD	7,044	8-s-9–2	1.26	1.16	53
	6-CD	7,024	4-s-7–2	1.12	1.02	0
	7-CD	7,044	3-s-5–2	1.12	1.09	7
	8-CD	7,060	1-s-9–2	1.20	1.11	27
	9-CD	7,098	10-p-9–2	1.14	1.16	32
11/5	1-CD	7,088	6-s-3–1	1.28	1.16	54
	2-CD	7,118	9-s-3–1	1.12	1.07	18
	3-CD	7,098	2-s-2–5	1.26	1.05	1,072
	4-CD	7,124	7-s-7–2	1.09	1.14	0
	5-CD	7,104	6-s-2–1	1.12	1.14	61
	6-CD	7,084	3-s-7–5	1.06	1.01	0
	7-CD	7,092	8-s-5–2	1.38	1.09	244
	8-CD	7,152	2-s-2–1	1.13	1.06	86
	9-CD	7,127	1-s-5–2	1.11	1.03	20
11/6	1-CD	7,135	12-s-9–5	1.07	.97	0
	3-CD	7,141	1-s-4–1	1.06	1.10	0
	4-CD	7,155	4-s-9–5	1.25	1.07	291
	5-CD	7,187	10-s-3–1	1.14	1.20	4
	6-CD	7,167	10-s-4–5	1.05	.99	0
	7-CD	7,147	6-s-4–5	1.19	1.15	584
	8-CD	7,207	8-s-9–2	1.30	1.33	54
	9-CD	7,187	4-s-4–5	1.07	1.08	0
11/7	1-CD	7,167	6-p-1–1	1.06	1.11	0
	2-CD	7,183	1-s-7–5	1.09	1.15	0
	3-CD	7,197	4-s-1–1	1.18	1.09	437
	4-CD	7,230	10-s-4–1	1.16	1.12	7
	5-CD	7,220	5-s-7–5	1.16	1.10	247
	6-CD	7,160	2-s-3–2	1.53	1.13	393
	7-CD	7,220	4-s-3–1	1.24	1.16	110
	8-CD	7,244	4-s-4–5	1.08	1.04	0
11/8	1-CD	7,246	3-s-5–1	1.12	1.09	0
	2-CD	7,226	2-s-3–1	1.06	1.03	0
	3-CD	7,206	4-s-3–1	1.07	1.05	0
	4-CD	7,186	4-s-4–1	1.10	1.09	0
	5-CD	7,166	4-s-1–1	1.17	1.15	556
	6-CD	7,256	3-s-2–1	1.12	1.11	127
	7-CD	7,274	5-s-5–2	1.20	1.15	173
	8-CD	7,234	9-s-7–2	1.16	1.04	0
11/9	1-CD	7,214	9-s-7–2	1.18	1.12	9
	2-CD	7,194	3-s-5–1	1.10	1.07	0
	3-CD	7,212	8-s-9–5	1.13	1.14	186
	4-CD	7,227	1-s-5–1	1.07	1.00	0

Size	*Bet ($)*	*Total of Wagers ($)*	*Payoff Per $2 Wager*	*Profit*	*Cumulative Profit ($)*	*Cumulative Profit (%)*
K	320	8,525	2.80	128	1,893	22.2
$\frac{1}{2}$K	70	8,595	2.80	28	1,921	22.4
K	40	8,635	3.60	32	1,953	22.6
K	130	8,765	3.40	91	2,044	23.3
$\frac{1}{2}$*	20	8,785	0	−20	2,024	23.0
f	20	8,805	4.00	20	2,044	23.2
f	20	8,825	3.60	16	2,060	23.3
f	20	8,845	5.80	38	2,098	23.7
$\frac{1}{4}$*	10	8,855	0	10	2,088	23.6
Rf	20	8,875	5.00	30	2,118	23.9
Rf	20	8,895	0	−20	2,098	23.6
R$\frac{1}{4}$	260	9,155	2.20	26	2,124	23.2
Rf	20	9,175	0	−20	2,104	22.9
Rf	20	9,195	0	−20	2,084	22.7
Rf	20	9,215	2.80	8	2,092	22.7
R$\frac{1}{4}$	60	9,275	4.00	60	2,152	23.2
R$\frac{1}{4}$	25	9,300	0	−25	2,127	22.9
Rf	20	9,320	2.80	8	2,135	22.9
Rf	20	9,340	2.60	6	2,141	22.9
Rf	20	9,360	3.40	14	2,155	23.0
R$\frac{1}{4}$	80	9,440	2.80	32	2,187	23.2
Rf	20	9,460	0	−20	2,167	22.9
Rf	20	9,480	0	−20	2,147	22.6
R$\frac{1}{4}$	150	9,630	2.80	60	2,207	22.9
Rf	20	9,650	0	−20	2,187	22.7
Rf	20	9,670	0	−20	2,167	22.4
Rf	20	9,690	3.60	16	2,183	22.5
Rf	20	9,710	3.40	14	2,197	22.6
R$\frac{1}{4}$	110	9,820	2.60	33	2,230	22.7
R*	10	9,830	0	−10	2,220	22.6
R$\frac{1}{4}$	60	9,890	0	−60	2,160	21.8
R$\frac{1}{4}$	100	9,990	3.20	60	2,220	22.2
R$\frac{1}{4}$	30	10,020	3.60	24	2,244	22.4
Rf	20	10,040	2.20	2	2,246	22.4
Rf	20	10,060	0	−20	2,226	22.1
Rf	20	10,080	0	−20	2,206	21.9
Rf	20	10,100	0	−20	2,186	21.6
Rf	20	10,120	0	−20	2,166	21.4
R$\frac{1}{2}$	150	10,270	3.20	90	2,256	22.0
R$\frac{1}{4}$	30	10,300	3.20	18	2,274	22.1
R$\frac{1}{4}$	40	10,340	0	−40	2,234	21.6
Rf	20	10,360	0	−20	2,214	21.4
Rf	20	10,380	0	−20	2,194	21.1
Rf	20	10,400	3.80	18	2,212	21.3
Rf	50	10,450	2.60	15	2,227	21.3
Rf	20	10,470	0	−20	2,207	21.1

Date	Track	Wealth	Horse # Show, Place Odds	Expected Return with 1 Minute to Post Time	Expected Return at Post Time	Optimal Kelly Bet ($)
	6-CD	7,207	6-s-9–2	1.18	1.20	7
	7-CD	7,221	3-s-4–5	1.06	1.05	0
	8-CD	7,225	5-s-4–5	1.05	1.00	0
	9-CD	7,227	9-s-5–1	1.23	1.21	23
11/14	2-LD	7,277	11-s-8–5	1.22	1.14	200
	3-LD	7,347	4-s-5–2	1.11	1.03	50
	4-LD	7,322	9-s-7–5	1.05	1.07	80
	5-LD	7,328	4-s-2–1	1.05	1.05	40
	6-LD	7,318	9-s-3–2	1.06	1.06	70
	7-LD	7,342	1-s-2–1	1.07	1.09	40
	8-LD	7,348	2-s-5–1	1.23	1.12	50
	9-LD	7,366	7-s-6–5	1.12	1.13	280
	10-LD	7,216	3-s-7–2	1.09	1.07	20
11/15	2-LD	7,234	9-s-6–5	1.14	1.08	300
	3-LD	7,324	12-s-2–1	1.11	1.13	60
	4-LD	7,360	2-p-4–5	1.08	1.04	100
	6-LD	7,410	6-s-5–2	1.13	1.02	70
	7-LD	7,340	11-s-6–1	1.05	1.01	20
	8-LD	7,320	2c-s-1–1	1.26	1.17	1,220
	9-LD	8,400	8-s-5–1	1.07	1.10	20
	10-LD	8,380	2-s-3–5	1.07	1.13	100
11/16	2-LD	8,390	9-s-4–5	1.13	1.12	540
	3-LD	8,444	6-s-9–5	1.10	1.12	540
	5-LD	8,458	6-s-7–1	1.16	1.06	20
	6-LD	8,448	6-s-9–2	1.08	1.11	20
	8-LD	8,438	1-s-4–5	1.19	1.15	1,200
	9-LD	8,618	1-s-3–1	1.12	1.18	20
11/20	1-CD	8,624	4-s-5–1	1.08	1.05	20
	2-CD	8,632	1-s-5–2	1.08	.95	30
	3-CD	8,640	1-s-1–1	1.17	1.09	380
	4-CD	8,690	9-p-7–5	1.11	1.00	80
	5-CD	8,640	7-s-5–2	1.23	1.16	140
	6-CD	8,540	3-s-5–2	1.06	1.11	30
	7-CD	8,558	2-s-6–1	1.21	1.16	20
	8-CD	8,548	1-p-7–5	1.27	1.12	440
	9-CD	8,248	11-s-2–1	1.09	1.08	40
11/21	1-CD	8,266	2-s-7–2	1.11	1.10	20
	2-CD	8,268	9-s-2–1	1.09	1.08	40
	3-CD	8,286	7-s-7–2	1.24	1.15	110
	4-CD	8,374	5-s-9–5	1.31	1.14	340
	5-CD	8,509	11-s-6–5	1.20	1.06	440
	6-CD	8,620	9-s-4–1	1.10	1.09	20
	8-CD	8,635	1-s-2–1	1.14	1.08	50
	9-CD	8,659	1-s-5–2	1.26	1.23	120
11/22	1-CD	8,743	5-s-7–2	1.07	1.10	20
	2-CD	8,733	12-s-8–5	1.09	1.07	50

Size	Bet ($)	Total of Wagers ($)	Payoff Per $2 Wager	Profit	Cumulative Profit ($)	Cumulative Profit (%)
Rf	20	10,490	3.40	14	2,221	21.2
Rf	20	10,510	2.40	4	2,225	21.2
Rf	20	10,530	2.20	2	2,227	21.1
Rf	20	10,550	7.00	50	2,277	21.6
K*	100	10,650	3.40	70	2,347	22.0
$\frac{1}{2}$K*	25	10,675	0	−25	2,322	21.8
F*	20	10,695	2.60	6	2,328	21.8
F*	10	10,705	0	−10	2,318	21.7
F*	35	10,740	3.40	24	2,342	21.8
F*	10	10,750	3.20	6	2,348	21.8
K*	20	10,770	3.80	18	2,366	22.0
$\frac{1}{2}$K*	150	10,920	0	−150	2,216	20.3
f	20	10,940	3,80	18	2,234	20.4
$\frac{1}{2}$K	300	11,240	2.60	90	2,324	20.7
$\frac{1}{2}$K	60	11,300	3.20	36	2,360	20.9
F	100	11,400	3.00	50	2,410	21.1
$\frac{1}{2}$K	70	11,470	0	−70	2,340	20.4
F	20	11,490	0	−20	2,320	20.2
K	1,200	12,690	3.80	1,080	3,400	26.8
F	20	12,710	0	−20	3,380	26.6
F	100	12,810	2.20	10	3,390	26.5
$\frac{1}{2}$K*	270	13,080	2.40	54	3,444	26.3
F*	20	13,100	3.40	14	3,458	26.4
F*	10	13,110	0	−10	3,448	26.3
F*	10	13,120	0	−10	3,438	26.2
K*	600	13,720	2.60	180	3,618	26.4
f*	10	13,730	3.20	6	3,624	26.4
Rf*	10	13,740	3.60	3	3,632	26.4
Rf*	20	13,760	2.80	8	3,640	26.4
R*	250	14,010	2.40	50	3,690	26.3
$\frac{1}{2}$R*	50	14,060	0	−50	3,640	25.9
R*	100	14,160	0	−100	3,540	25.0
Rf*	20	14,180	3.80	18	3,558	25.1
Rf*	10	14,190	0	−10	3,548	25.0
R*	300	14,490	0	−300	3,248	22.4
Rf*	30	14,520	3.20	18	3,266	22.5
F*	10	14,530	2.40	2	3,268	22.5
F*	30	14,560	3.20	18	3,286	22.6
K*	80	14,640	4.20	88	3,374	23.0
K*	270	14,910	3.00	135	3,509	23.5
K*	370	15,280	2.60	111	3,620	23.7
f*	10	15,290	5.00	15	3,635	23.8
$\frac{1}{2}$K*	30	15,320	3.60	24	3,659	23.9
K*	60	15,380	4.80	84	3,743	24.3
F*	10	15,390	0	−10	3,733	24.3
F*	20	15,410	0	−20	3,713	24.1

Date	*Track*	*Wealth*	*Horse # Show, Place Odds*	*Expected Return with 1 Minute to Post Time*	*Expected Return at Post Time*	*Optimal Kelly Bet ($)*
	3-CD	8,713	7-s-6–5	1.06	1.06	80
	4-CD	8,731	10-s-3–1	1.20	1.20	130
	6-CD	8,661	1-s-5–2	1.08	1.02	40
	7-CD	8,676	9-s-9–5	1.14	1.13	100
	8-CD	8,711	8-s-6–1	1.09	1.15	20
	9-CD	8,701	10-s-4–5	1.14	1.14	410
11/23	2-CD	8,851	5-s-3–1	1.08	1.10	20
	5-CD	8,859	2-s-7–5	1.13	1.06	140
	6-CD	8,909	2-s-8–5	1.13	1.05	120
	8-CD	8,923	5-s-1–1	1.39	1.21	660

Size	Bet ($)	Total of Wagers ($)	Payoff Per $2 Wager	Profit	Cumulative Profit ($)	Cumulative Profit (%)
F*	60	15,470	2.60	18	3,731	24.1
K*	70	15,540	0	−70	3,661	23.6
F*	30	15,570	3.00	15	3,676	23.6
$\frac{1}{2}$K*	70	15,640	3.00	35	3,711	23.7
F*	10	15,650	0	−10	3,701	23.6
K*	300	15,950	3.00	150	3,851	24.1
F*	10	15,960	3.60	8	3,859	24.2
$\frac{1}{2}$K*	100	16,060	3.00	50	3,909	24.3
$\frac{1}{2}$K*	70	16,130	2.40	14	3,923	24.3
K*	100	16,230	3.00	50	3,973	24.5

F = flat bet, R = rain (off track), * = anticipate loser and K = Kelly bet.

TABLE 14.4 ***Rates of return versus expected value. Results from 21 days and 144 wagers at Churchill Downs and Louisiana Downs***

Expected Value of a $1 Bet at Post Time	*# of Bets*	*Total Wager ($)*	*Total Profit ($)*	*Rate of Return (%)*
below 1.05	24	1,105	−236	−21.4
1.05–1.09	45	3,990	946	23.7
1.10–1.14	42	4,185	403	9.6
1.15–1.19	19	5,320	2,328	43.8
1.20–1.24	8	550	−114	−20.7
1.25–1.29	4	960	586	61.0
1.30+	2	120	60	50.0
overall	144	16,230	3,973	24.5

15

Minus Pools

ELIMINATING POSSIBLE MINUS POOLS: THE KENTUCKY OAKS AT CHURCHILL DOWNS, MAY 1, 1981

The payoffs for win, place, and show bets reflect the individual pools, the amounts bet on the in-the-money horses, the track take, and breakage. By law, tracks must always pay a minimum amount on any winning bet. This is generally $2.10 for a $2 bet.* A minus pool occurs when the return to bettors, after the track take has been calculated in, is less than this minimum. Such a pool can occur when a horse (or group of horses coupled as an entry) looks unbeatable. The bet is so large on this one possibility that the track must forego some of its profit or actually lose money in order to pay the $2.10. When such a situation appears likely in a given pool, management is likely to disallow certain betting to avoid a minus pool. Such a situation occurred during the running of the 1981 Kentucky Oaks at Churchill Downs in Louisville, Kentucky. The entry of Heavenly Cause and De La Rose was bet down to 3–2 as the second favorite. Since there were only five alternative bets and two extreme favorites (the entry and the even-money favorite, Truly Bound), there would likely be a minus pool in the show mutuels. Management, therefore, disallowed show betting.

Heavenly Cause and De La Rose finished 1-2 and returned $5 to win and also $5 to place. The favorite, Truly Bound, finished fourth, out of the money.

The identical payoffs to win and place meant that, after adjusting for breakage, the percentages bet on the entry in the win and place pools were

*An exception was Kentucky, where the minimum payment was $2.20. See the discussion of the Kentucky Oaks in Chapter Six and further comments made later. While Kentucky's minimum payment has been recently lowered to $2.10, there is still a $2.20 minimum payoff in Louisiana.

Kentucky Oaks

EIGHTH RACE
Churchill
MAY 1, 1981

1 1/16 MILES. (1.41⅗) 107th Running THE KENTUCKY OAKS (Grade I). $100,000 Added. (Plus $10,000 KTDF). 3-year-old fillies. By subscription of $100 which covers nomination for borth The Kentucky Oaks and the La Troienne. All nomination fees to Kentucky Oaks. $200 to pass entry box, $500 additional to start, $100,000 added, of which with the subscription fees and all starting fees to be divided 65% to the winner, 20% to second, 10% to third and 5% to fourth. Weight 121 lbs. Starters to be named through the entry box Wednesday, April 29 at usual time of closing. If race is divided entries or couplings will be divided. The owner of the winner to receive a silver trophy.
Value of race $124,000, value to winner $79,300, second $26,400, third $12,200, fourth $6,100. Mutuel pool $685,768.

Last Raced	Horse	Eqt.A.Wt	PP	St	¼	½	¾	Str	Fin	Jockey	Odds $1
25Apr81 ^{8}CD^{1}	Heavenly Cause	3 121	4	4	4^{3}	4^{4}	1½	$1^{1½}$	1no	Pincay L Jr	a-1.50
8Apr81 ^{7}Kee^{4}	De La Rose	3 121	3	6	6	5^{1}	5^{4}	2^{1}	2^{5}	Day P	a-1.50
18Apr81 ^{7}Kee^{2}	Wayward Lass	3 121	1	1	3½	3^{1}	$2^{1½}$	3^{1}	3^{3}	Asmussen C B	8.40
18Apr81 ^{7}Kee^{1}	Truly Bound	3 121	2	3	2½	2^{hd}	4^{1}	4^{5}	4^{4}	Shoemaker W	1.00
17Apr81 ^{8}Aqu^{4}	Real Prize	3 121	6	5	5½	6	6	5^{2}	$5^{8½}$	Fell J	23.00
4Apr81 ^{9}OP^{2}	Nell's Briquette	3 121	5	2	1^{hd}	1½	3^{hd}	6	6	Lively J	5.00

a–Coupled: Heavenly Cause and De La Rose.

OFF AT 5:30 EDT. Start good, Won driving. Time, :25, :48⅘, 1:13, 1:37⅘, 1:43⅗ Track fast.

$2 Mutuel Prices:			
1–HEAVENLY CAUSE (a–entry)	5.00	5.00	—
1–DE LA ROSE (a–entry)	5.00	5.00	—
2–WAYWARD LASS		—	—

(No Show Wagering)

Ro. f, by Grey Dawn II—Lady Dulcinea, by Nantallah. Trainer Stephens Woodford C. Bred by Ryehill Farm (Md).

HEAVENLY CAUSE, allowed to settle early, took command on the outside leaving the backstretch, drew clear in upper stretch but was all out to withstand DE LA ROSE with pressure from both sides. The latter, unhurried early, launched a bold bid in the extreme outside when set down for the drive, was also under pressure from both sides in the final furlong and just missed at the wire. WAYWARD LASS just behind the early leaders, had no rally. TRULY BOUND prompted the pace for a half and weakened along the rail leaving the backstretch. REAL PRIZE never launched a serious bid. NELL'S BRIQUETTE made the early pace and gave way.

Owners— 1, Ryehill Farm; 2, deKwiatkowski H; 3, Flying Zee Stable; 4, Windfields Farm; 5, Buckland Farm; 6, Triple L Stables.

Trainers— 1, Stephens Woodford C; 2, Stephens Woodford C; 3, Martin Jose; 4, Delp Grover G; 5, Campo John P; 6, Van Berg Jack.

the same. Hence the entry was not a Dr. Z system bet to place. Indeed, its expected value per dollar bet to place was about 90¢ (amounting to the track's payback plus the adjustment for the entry). Techniques for the selection of Dr. Z system bets with entries are discussed in Chapter Sixteen. When the favorite finished out of the money, the 1-2 finish provided a good payoff.

AN EXTRAORDINARY SHOW POOL: THE COACHING CLUB AMERICAN OAKS AT BELMONT, JUNE 27, 1981

The entry of Heavenly Cause and De La Rose was also entered the next month in the Coaching Club American Oaks at Belmont. Their strong 1-2 finish in the Kentucky Oaks made them a 2–5 favorite. The entry was bet even more heavily for show, so that a minus pool was likely.

Management decided not to eliminate the show pool. The betting public believed that a show bet on the entry of Heavenly Cause and De La Rose was virtually a sure thing. It seemed that at least one of these top horses would beat two of the other four horses in the race and finish in the money. The chart of the race speaks for itself:

Coaching Club American Oaks

EIGHTH RACE
Belmont
JUNE 27, 1981

1 ½ MILES. (2.24) 65th Running COACHING CLUB AMERICAN OAKS (Grade I). Purse $125,000 added. Fillies. 3-year-olds. Weight 121 lbs. By subscription of $250 each, which should accompany the nomination; $1,000 to pass the entry box, with $125,000 added. The added money and all fees to be divided 60% to the winner, 22% to second, 12% to third and 6% to fourth. Starters to be named at the closing time of entries. Trophies will be presented to the winning owner, trainer and jockey and mementoes to the grooms of the first four finishers. A special permanent trophy will be presented to the owner of the winner of the Coaching Club American Oaks if the filly has also won the Acorn and the Mother Goose. (Nominations close Wednesday, June 10, 1981). Closed with 17 nominations.

Value of race $136,250, value to winner $81,750, second $29,975, third $16,350, fourth $8,175. Mutuel pool $469,774, OTB pool $305,150.

Last Raced	Horse	Eqt.A.Wt	PP	¼	½	1	1¼	Str	Fin	Jockey	Odds $1
5Jun81 ^{8}Bel^{4}	[D]Real Prize	3 121	1	$5\frac{1}{2}$	6	$5\frac{1}{2}$	2^{hd}	$1^{1\frac{1}{2}}$	$1^{2\frac{1}{4}}$	Velasquez J	9.80
5Jun81 ^{8}Bel^{1}	Wayward Lass	3 121	2	3^{4}	3^{1}	2^{hd}	3^{4}	$2\frac{1}{2}$	$2^{2\frac{1}{4}}$	Asmussen C B	5.00
5Jun81 ^{8}Bel^{3}	Banner Gala	3 121	5	1^{hd}	1^{1}	1^{2}	$1^{1\frac{1}{2}}$	3^{10}	3^{13}	Cordero A Jr	3.20
5Jun81 ^{8}Bel^{2}	Heavenly Cause	3 121	4	4^{4}	4^{6}	4^{4}	4^{5}	4^{3}	$4^{1\frac{3}{4}}$	Pincay L Jr	a-.40
5Jun81 ^{8}Bel^{5}	Autumn Glory	b 3 121	6	$2^{1\frac{1}{2}}$	$2\frac{1}{2}$	$3\frac{1}{2}$	5^{5}	5^{8}	$5^{7\frac{1}{2}}$	Martens G	35.60
13Jun81 ^{8}Mth^{1}	De La Rose	3 121	3	6	$5\frac{1}{2}$	6	6	6	6	Maple E	a-.40

[D]-Real Prize Disqualified and placed second.
a-Coupled: Heavenly Cause and De La Rose.
OFF AT 4:55 EDT. Start good, Won ridden out. Time, :24⅕, :47⅘, 1:11⅘, 1:36⅕, 2:01⅘, 2:28⅕, Track fast.

$2 Mutuel Prices:			
3-(B)-WAYWARD LASS	12.00	7.20	35.40
2-(A)-REAL PRIZE		8.60	61.60
5-(F)-BANNER GALA			51.20

Wayward Lass—Dk. b. or br. f, by Hail the Pirates—Young Mistress, by Third Martini. Trainer Martin Jose. Bred by Luro H A (Fla).

REAL PRIZE, unhurried while outrun to the far turn, settled suddenly after going a mile, angled out to continue her rally approaching the stretch, lugged in interfering with WAYWARD LASS near the final furlong and drew away under intermittent urging. REAL PRIZE was disqualified and placed second following a stewards inquiry and foul claim by the rider of WAYWARD LASS. WAYWARD LASS, close up early while under light restraint, made a run between horses leaving the far turn, was checked behind REAL PRIZE near the final furlong and continued on with good courage to best the others. BANNER GALA took over from AUTUMN GLORY at the first turn, made the pace under good handling, saved ground after sprinting away to a clear lead at the far turn, held a narrow advantage into the stretch and weakened. HEAVENLY CAUSE moved up outside horses to reach contention after entering the backstretch, raced within striking distance for nine furlongs and had nothing left. AUTUMN GLORY saved ground while racing forwardly for a mile and tired badly. DE LA ROSE showed nothing.

Owners— 1, Buckland Farm; 2, Flying Zee Stables; 3, Phipps O; 4, Ryehill Farm; 5, Ruiz E; 6, de Kwiatkowski H.

Trainers— 1, Campo John P; 2, Martin Jose; 3, Penna Angel; 4, Stephens Woodford C; 5, Barrera Guillermo S; 6, Stephens Woodford C.

Scratched—Outlaw Native (13Jun81 ^{8}Pim^{3}).

The possible minus pool from the extremely heavy betting to show on the entry led to two possible show outcomes: (1) $2.10 for all horses finishing in the money if at least one of the entry horses was in the money and (2) very large payoffs for the in-the-money finishers if both of the entry horses were out of the money. Indeed, when both of the entry horses finished out of the money, the show payoffs were astronomical! The winner, Wayward Lass, paid three times as much to show as to win. The second-place finisher, Real Prize, paid about seven times as much to show as he did to place, and five times as much as he would have paid to win if he had won. The third-place finisher, Banner Gala, who was the second favorite in the race at 3–1, paid $51.20 to show.

At first glance, you would think that all these horses were good bets to show. It turns out that only Banner Gala was a Dr. Z system bet; she had an expected value of about $1.24 per dollar bet. Bets on Real Prize and Wayward Lass in fact had expected values *less* than $1; for Real Prize it was 89¢. How could this be? With a possible minus pool, there were three possible outcomes for a show bet on Banner Gala, Real Prize, or Wayward Lass: (1) Our horse and at least one of the entry horses would be in the money—result: $2.10; (2) our horse finished out of the money—result: 0; and (3) our horse was in the money and both entry horses were not—result: a high payoff. The difficulty is that possibilities (1) and (2) were the most likely ones, and (3) had a very small chance of occurring. Thus even though the payoff in (3) would be high, it might still be that, on average, you would lose with such a bet. For example, with Real Prize these probabilities were (1) 0.260, (2) 0.720, and (3) 0.020. Hence the expected value per $2 bet on Real Prize was

$$\underbrace{(0.260)(\$2.10)}_{\substack{\text{Real Prize and at least}\\ \text{one of the entry horses}\\ \text{in the money}}} + \underbrace{0.720(0)}_{\substack{\text{Real Prize}\\ \text{out of the money}}} + \underbrace{0.020(\$61.60)}_{\substack{\text{Real Prize}\\ \text{in the money and}\\ \text{both of the entry}\\ \text{horses out of}\\ \text{the money}}} = \$1.78$$

or 89¢ per dollar bet!

The situation was better with Banner Gala. The probabilities were (1) 0.617, (2) 0.360, and (3) 0.023. The expected value per $2 bet on Banner Gala was 0.617($2.10) + 0.360(0) + 0.023($51.20) = $2.47, or about $1.24 per dollar bet. Thus an extraordinarily high payoff of $51.20 to show on a relative favorite—recall that Banner Gala was a 3–1 shot—was required to make the bet profitable. The reason for the advantageous bet on Banner Gala was her relatively high odds to win and the extraordinary low amount bet on her to show.

The Coaching Club American Oaks illustrates that an occasion may arise where it is advisable to bet in a possible minus pool. However, we feel it is a rare instance indeed and that, in general, bets should not be made in a possible minus pool. This example also demonstrates that the favorite should generally not be bet in a possible minus pool. Table 15.1 shows that even with a 98% probability of being in the money, the expected value per dollar bet to show is only 1.03, a return that certainly does not justify the risk. In fact, the best situation to imagine for a possible minus pool is a horse with a probability of 1 of finishing in the money; this would return an expected value per dollar bet to show of 1.05. But by the very nature of the event, no horse can ever have a probability of 1 of finishing in the money. For example, John Henry, horse of the year in 1981, had ten starts. Although he won eight of them, he was out of the money in the other two races. So he was in the money only 80% of the time.

TABLE 15.1 ***Probabilities of various outcomes and expected value of show bets in the Coaching Club American Oaks***

Horse	Win Odds	Probability of Winning	Probability of Finishing Second	Probability of Finishing Third	Probability of Finishing in the Money	Probability of Finishing out of the Money	Percentage of Money Bet to Show	Probability of Finishing in the Money When Both Entry Horses Are out of the Money	Probability of Finishing in the Money with at Least One of the Entry Horses	Expected Value per dollar Bet to Show
Wayward Lass	5.00	0.13	0.15	0.20	0.48	0.52	1.91	0.022	0.458	0.87
Real Prize	9.80	0.07	0.09	0.12	0.28	0.72	1.07	0.020	0.260	0.89
Banner Gala	3.20	0.19	0.20	0.25	0.64	0.36	1.30	0.023	0.617	1.24
Entry	0.40	0.59	0.53	0.39	0.98[a]	0.02	95.22	—	—	1.03
Autumn Glory	35.60	0.02	0.03	0.04	0.09	0.81	0.50	0.008	0.082	0.53
		1.00	1.00	1.00						

Note: The calculations of the probabilities were made using the assumptions described in Chapter Five.
[a]At least one horse.

The point of all this is clear: In a possible minus pool, where the minimum payoff is \$2.10, *do not bet to place or show on any horse.**

As a rough rule of thumb, you will have a minus pool at a \$2.10 minimum payoff track when 70% or more of the show pool is wagered on a single betting interest. For example, suppose the show pool has $S = \$100{,}000$ and $S_1 = \$70{,}000$ is wagered on the standout horse #1. The show pool has \$30,000 bet on the other horses. Suppose there are nine others and that the two next show favorites have \$5,000 each wagered on them and that the track payback is $Q = 0.83$ as in New York. Then the track has to pay out 1.05(\$70,000 + \$5,000 + \$5,000) or \$80,000, which is more than their usual payout of $QS = 0.83(\$100{,}000)$, even before breakage. This creates the minus pool.

Generally, there will be a minus pool whenever $1.05(S_1 + S_2 + S_3) \geqslant QS$, where horse #1 is the big favorite and #2 and #3 have the most show money wagered on them. If $Q = 0.83$ and S_1 and S_2 each have 5% as much wagered to show on them as is wagered to show on #1, then we have the minus pool when

$$\frac{S_1}{S} \geqslant 0.72.$$

Hence the rough 70% guideline. Since breakage will be rounding down the payoffs to \$2.10 even if you do not have a true minus pool but are close, the cutoff of when you should bet is even a little lower. Using the 1.095 level that is truncated to 1.05 gives a cutoff of 69%.

AN EXCEPTION TO THE RULE TO NOT BET ON MINUS POOLS

A minus pool to show occurs when at least 80% or so of the show pool is bet on one horse. We have recommended that you do not bet to place or show on any horse in a minus pool. However, a rare exception to this rule occurs when well above 90% of the show pool is on one horse. In this case the minus pool can actually be exploited to devise a "lock," or a guaranteed profit. This sure thing is not achieved by betting on just one horse but rather

*An *exception* is when the minimum payoff is \$2.20, as it is, in Louisiana. Then a bet is worth making to show on any horse going off at 1–2 or less. At 1–2, the chance of winning the show wager is about 95.5% (see Table 6.2) for an edge of about 5%. The odds are 1–10 for a \$2.20 payoff. Hence the optimal Kelly wager, namely the edge divided by the odds, is a staggering 50% of one's fortune. With such a large risk we recommend a fractional Kelly wager of a quarter to a half of this amount because of the risks involved. As the odds become lower, the wager becomes even better and the Kelly criterion would suggest an even larger bet.

by properly betting on all the horses. Locks were described in *Sports Illustrated* (September 10, 1979) and *Fortune* (October 22, 1979 and October 6, 1980).

The 1979 *Fortune* article illustrated the lock with the following example, the Alabama Stakes at Saratoga on August 11, 1979:

Horse	*Show Bet ($)*	*% of Show Pool*
Davona Dale	435,825	95.5
It's in the Air	7,901	1.7
Mairzy Doates	4,518	1.0
Poppycock	4,417	1.0
Croquis	3,873	0.8
Totals	456,534	100.0

Davona Dale's 95.5% share of the show pool is unusually high and clearly has created a minus pool; if Davona Dale finishes in the money, then the show payoff on each of the first three finishers will be \$2.10. By betting a large sum on Davona Dale and properly chosen smaller amounts on the other four horses, a profit can be guaranteed. To see how this might happen, note that if Davona Dale is in the money then we will receive 5% of the money wagered on her plus 5% on the money wagered on the other two of the top three finishers. If this adds up to more than the lost wagers on the fourth- and fifth-place horses, then we are ahead. If, as well, the amounts wagered on the four long shots are such that if Davona Dale finishes out of the money, our return covers both the bet on her and on the other out-of-the-money horse, then we have a profit regardless of the outcome of the race. What conditions are necessary for a lock, and how can we wager on the horses to develop a lock?

We will suppose our bettor wishes to receive approximately the same profit regardless of who are the in-the-money finishers. To simplify the analysis, it will also be supposed that (1) except for the favorite, the public has wagered the same amount on each horse to show, and (2) our bets do not affect the odds. The example above obviously does not satisfy the first of these two assumptions (show bets range from \$3,873 to \$7,901), and the second assumption will only hold if our wagers are relatively small. Despite these difficulties the following variables can be used to develop a system for wagering: n = number of horses in the race, k = fraction of the show pool that is on the favorite, Q = track's payback proportion, and S = show pool. For our example, $n=5$, $k=.955$, $Q=.85$ and $S=\$456,534$. The show bet on the favorite is kS and, by assumption 1, the show bet on each of the other horses is $(1-k)S/(n-1)$. Let x represent our wager on the favorite and y represent our show bet on each of the other horses. This leads to a total wager of $x+(n-1)y$. If the favorite is in the money then we are returned 5% on x and two of the y bets, but lose $(n-3)y$ on the $(n-3)$ losers. Thus, the profit in this case is $.05(x+2y)-(n-3)y$. Suppose now that the favorite is out of the money. Then our profit will be

$$3[QS-3(1-k)\,S/(n-1)]y/[3(1-k)S/(n-1)] - x - (n-4)y.$$

The first term is the profit on each of the in-the-money horses times three of them. The next two terms are the losses on the favorite and the $(n-4)$ other horses.

To get the same profit regardless of the finish, these two profit functions must be equal. This equality means that x and y must satisfy the following ratio:

$$x/y = -2 + Q(n-1)/[1.05(1-k)] \tag{15.1}$$

So, if x and y are kept in this ratio and do not grow so large as to affect the odds, then the first profit equation above gives profit as

$$.05(x+2y)-(n-3)y = .05yQ(n-1)/[1.05(1-k)] - (n-3)y.$$

For a lock to exist, this last expression must be positive. This holds when

$$.05Q(n-1)/[1.05(1-k)] > -3,$$

$$\text{or} \quad k > 1 - Q(n-1)/[21(n-3)]. \tag{15.2}$$

For $Q=.85$ and $n=5$, as in our example, equation (15.2) indicates a lock will exist if k exceeds 0.919. Davona Dale's $k=0.955$ is well above the 0.919 cutoff, so we can devise a lock. Equation (15.1) tells how to choose the relative amounts of x and y. It says $x/y = 69.96$. Thus, if we had \$2,500 to wager, we would wager $x=\$2,364$ on the favorite and $y=\$34$ on each of the other four horses.

If Davona Dale finished at least third (in fact, she came second and Poppycock and It's in the Air were first and third, respectively), then our profit would be \$53.60. If the public's show bets on the other four horses had been the same, then the profit would have also been \$53.60, even if Davona Dale finished fourth or fifth. Thus, a guaranteed 2.1% on our money in, roughly, two minutes! In fact, the show bets on the four other horses are not equal. This will not affect our profit of \$53.60 if Davona Dale finished at least third. However, if Davona Dale finished fourth or fifth, our profit would depend on which of the four horses were the top three finishers. Table 15.2 lists the possible top three horses if Davona Dale were to finish fourth or fifth and the profit that would be realized with that trio.

TABLE 15.2

Top Three Finishers (order does not matter)	*Profit*
It's in the Air, Mairzy Doates, Poppycock	$12.60
It's in the Air, Mairzy Doates, Croquis	148.60
It's in the Air, Poppycock, Croquis	172.40
Mairzy Doates, Poppycock, Croquis	597.40

The odds of the horses would suggest that the first trio is the most likely of the four trios. If the four profits are weighted by their likelihoods, the average profit should be on the order of $53.60.

This analysis has supposed our bets do not affect the payoffs. For this example and a total wager of $2,500, this assumption has been fine. In fact, accounting for the effect of our wagers on the payoffs would reduce each of the profits in Table 15.1 by less than $7. The effect on the payoffs of a much larger total wager is much more serious though, e.g., betting a total of $25,000 cannot be expected to guarantee a profit of about $536.00.

Equation 15.2 shows that the condition for a lock is more easily met when n, the number of horses, is small and/or Q, the track payback proportion, is large. Unlike the minimum payoff of $2.10 in most states, Louisiana has a minimum of $2.20. Equation 15.2, revised for Louisiana, would show a less restrictive lock condition.

The lock condition is rarely met, and to get a large return one needs a large bankroll. However, the times when it is met should not be complete surprises; it happens when there is an extreme favorite that the crowd figures cannot be out of the money. The adjective "extreme" cannot be overemphasized though. For example, even Princess Rooney, the heavy favorite in the 1983 Kentucky Oaks (see Chapter Six), had only 84% of the show pool on her. Davona Dale, however, allowed another lock in the 1979 Coaching Club American Oaks at Belmont. She won that race with 97.8% of the show pool on her! Two years after Davona Dale won that race, the entry of Heavenly Cause and De La Rose had 95.2% of the 1981 Coaching Club American Oaks show pool. This race was mentioned earlier in this chapter; recall the astronomical show payoffs when neither of these two was in the money. Spectacular Bid ran thirty races and finished out of the money only once, and that was as a two-year-old. He was such a standout that he often went off at 1–20 odds, a good sign that a lock may exist. One lock on him was the 1980 Amory Haskell Handicap, where he had 96.0% of the show pool. In the 1985 Jersey Stakes, Spend A Buck, in his $2.6-million race, went off at 1–20 odds and created a minus show pool of $22,492. It would seem that a lock existed there too.

The lock strategy is very different from the Kelly strategy we advocate in this book. The Kelly strategy's goal is the maximization of the growth of one's bankroll. The lock strategy requires a guaranteed positive return

TABLE 15.3

Top Three Horses (order does not matter)	*Probability of These Being the Top Three Horses*	*Respective Show Payoffs*
Davona Dale, It's in the Air, Mairzy Doates	0.31998	2.10, 2.10, 2.10
Davona Dale, It's in the Air, Poppycock	0.24539	2.10, 2.10, 2.10
Davona Dale, It's in the Air, Croquis	0.27893	2.10, 2.10, 2.10
Davona Dale, Mairzy Doates, Poppycock	0.04670	2.10, 2.10, 2.10
Davona Dale, Mairzy Doates, Croquis	0.05324	2.10, 2.10, 2.10
Davona Dale, Poppycock, Croquis	0.04054	2.10, 2.10, 2.10
It's in the Air, Mairzy Doates, Poppycock	0.00473	33.20, 56.60, 58.00
It's in the Air, Mairzy Doates, Croquis	0.00538	33.20, 56.80, 65.80
It's in the Air, Poppycock, Croquis	0.00413	33.20, 58.00, 66.00
Mairzy Doates, Poppycock, Croquis	0.00098	57.20, 58.60, 66.40
	1.00000	

TABLE 15.4

Horse	*Expected Return on a Show Bet*
Davona Dale	1.034
It's in the Air	1.123
Mairzy Doates	0.758
Poppycock	0.635
Croquis	0.737

and, thus, it will trade off some growth for some reduction in risk. That is, to reduce the risk, the lock strategy makes wagers on every horse despite the negative expected returns to some of the horses. We can employ the Kelly strategy in this extreme minus pool setting though; it requires going beyond the results in Tables 15.1 through 15.4 to determining how to wager on several horses simultaneously and uses the B6 formulation in Appendix B. While not necessary for determining the Kelly bets on each horse, it will be instructive to determine the possible payoffs on each horse and the likelihoods of those payoffs. And then, with those figures, the expected return to a show bet on each horse can be determined. Tables 15.3 and 15.4 show the results of these calculations using the public's win odds to determine each horse's win probability, the Harville formulas to calculate show probabilities, and the public's show bets to determine show payoffs.

Only the show bets on Davona Dale and It's in the Air have positive expected profits. With an initial wealth of $2,500, the B6 formulation recommends the following wagers:

Davona Dale	$2273
It's in the Air	221
Mairzy Doates	0
Poppycock	0
Croquis	6

Notice that the entire $2,500 is wagered, and regardless of the three top horses, the bettor does not go bankrupt. Also, there is a wager on Croquis despite an expected return of $0.737 on the dollar. The explanation for this wager is diversification—it is unlikely that both Davona Dale and It's in the Air will finish out of the money, but in that case Table 15.3 shows that Croquis has the best payoff of the other three horses.

Table 15.5 presents the possible profits from these wagers (accounting for their effect on the payoffs) and their likelihood.

TABLE 15.5

Top Three Horses (order does not matter)	*Probability of These Being the Top Three Horses*	*Profit*
Davona Dale, It's in the Air, Mairzy Doates	0.31998	$118.70
Davona Dale, It's in the Air, Poppycock	0.24539	118.70
Davona Dale, It's in the Air, Croquis	0.27893	125.00
Davona Dale, Mairzy Doates, Poppycock	0.04670	−113.35
Davona Dale, Mairzy Doates, Croquis	0.05324	−107.50
Davona Dale, Poppycock, Croquis	0.04054	−107.50
It's in the Air, Mairzy Doates, Poppycock	0.00473	1,102.30
It's in the Air, Mairzy Doates, Croquis	0.00538	1,300.90
It's in the Air, Poppycock, Croquis	0.00413	1,300.90
Mairzy Doates, Poppycock, Croquis	0.00098	−2,299.60

The expected profit can be calculated to be $101.93, or 4.1% on the bankroll. Notice that while this is significantly greater than the lock's profit of $53.60, the lock strategy had no risk while the Kelly bets have substantial risk—the bettor has only an 85.9% chance of a positive profit, and there is a 0.098% chance of losing $2299.60! But as mentioned earlier, from the standpoint of maximizing the rate of growth of one's bankroll, the additional expected return to the Kelly bets compensates their additional risk. The actual finish, Poppycock—Davona Dale—It's in the Air, would have returned a profit of $118.70.

A TYPICAL MINUS POOL: THE SAN JUAN CAPISTRANO INVITATIONAL HANDICAP AT SANTA ANITA, APRIL 18, 1982

The final example in this chapter indicates that in a typical minus pool for place or show: (1) it is not advisable to bet any horses to place or show regardless of how promising they might appear to be on the basis of either their past performance (the overbet) or their odds (the underbet); and (2) the only bets that are worth considering are win or features bets on horses other than the extreme favorite.

The San Juan Capistrano Invitational Handicap was run as the eighth race on Santa Anita's card. The race featured the dynamite entry of Exploded ridden by Bill Shoemaker, Captain General with Chris McCarron, and Perrault with Laffit Pincay, Jr., in the irons. Perrault was the consensus best bet of the day, with Exploded a major contender. The chief competition to this seemingly unbeatable field was provided by Lemhi Gold ridden by Walter Guerra. The 15–1 shot, Rainbow Connection, was scratched and the remaining five horses were rated at 20–1 or more in the morning line. The field looked unbeatable to the crowd, which immediately installed it as a 1–5 favorite, the same as its morning line. The place and show betting were even more intense, with about three-quarters of these pools being bet on the entry. The tote board indicated a likely minus pool, with a $2.10 place and show payout for all the horses finishing in the money, as long as at least one of the field came in the money.

Throughout the betting period, about a fifth of the win pool was bet on Lemhi Gold, consistent with his 5–2 or 3–1 odds. But only about one sixteenth of the show pool was bet on Lemhi Gold. After correction for the track take of 15%, one minute before post time the expected value of a dollar bet to show on Lemhi Gold was a whopping 1.97! (This expected value was about the same throughout the betting period.) This would normally be an outstanding Dr. Z system bet on a very top horse, a most enviable position to be in. Further analysis, however, showed this to be a smoke screen. The minus-pool betting on the field made a show bet on Lemhi Gold or any other horse an unattractive proposition.

To establish this conclusion we utilized the data with one minute to post time, when one would normally be doing the final calculations concerning a possible bet. The probability that Lemhi Gold would win the race was about 0.221, and the probability that he would come in second 0.204, and third 0.182. At these odds he would be in the money about 60.7% of the time.

There were three possible outcomes: (1) Lemhi Gold and at least one of the entry horses would finish in the money with a show payoff of $2.10; (2) Lemhi Gold would finish out of the money with a show payoff of zero,

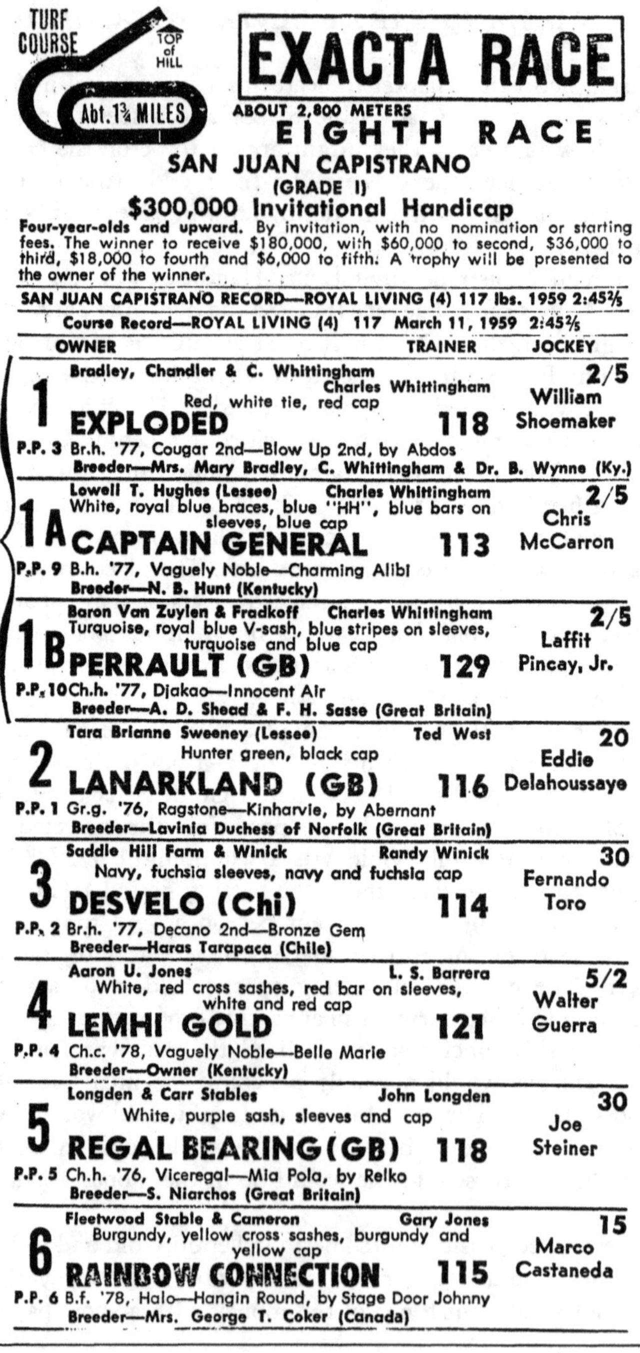

EXACTA RACE

ABOUT 2,800 METERS

EIGHTH RACE

SAN JUAN CAPISTRANO

(GRADE I)

$300,000 Invitational Handicap

Four-year-olds and upward. By invitation, with no nomination or starting fees. The winner to receive $180,000, with $60,000 to second, $36,000 to third, $18,000 to fourth and $6,000 to fifth. A trophy will be presented to the owner of the winner.

SAN JUAN CAPISTRANO RECORD—ROYAL LIVING (4) 117 lbs. 1959 2:45⅖

Course Record—ROYAL LIVING (4) 117 March 11, 1959 2:45⅖

	OWNER	TRAINER	JOCKEY
1 P.P. 3	Bradley, Chandler & C. Whittingham Red, white tie, red cap **EXPLODED** 118 Br.h. '77, Cougar 2nd—Blow Up 2nd, by Abdos Breeder—Mrs. Mary Bradley, C. Whittingham & Dr. B. Wynne (Ky.)	Charles Whittingham	2/5 William Shoemaker
1A P.P. 9	Lowell T. Hughes (Lessee) White, royal blue braces, blue "HH", blue bars on sleeves, blue cap **CAPTAIN GENERAL** 113 B.h. '77, Vaguely Noble—Charming Alibi Breeder—N. B. Hunt (Kentucky)	Charles Whittingham	2/5 Chris McCarron
1B P.P. 10	Baron Van Zuylen & Fradkoff Turquoise, royal blue V-sash, blue stripes on sleeves, turquoise and blue cap **PERRAULT (GB)** 129 Ch.h. '77, Djakao—Innocent Air Breeder—A. D. Shead & F. H. Sasse (Great Britain)	Charles Whittingham	2/5 Laffit Pincay, Jr.
2 P.P. 1	Tara Brianne Sweeney (Lessee) Hunter green, black cap **LANARKLAND (GB)** 116 Gr.g. '76, Ragstone—Kinharvie, by Abernant Breeder—Lavinia Duchess of Norfolk (Great Britain)	Ted West	20 Eddie Delahoussaye
3 P.P. 2	Saddle Hill Farm & Winick Navy, fuchsia sleeves, navy and fuchsia cap **DESVELO (Chi)** 114 Br.h. '77, Decano 2nd—Bronze Gem Breeder—Haras Tarapaca (Chile)	Randy Winick	30 Fernando Toro
4 P.P. 4	Aaron U. Jones White, red cross sashes, red bar on sleeves, white and red cap **LEMHI GOLD** 121 Ch.c. '78, Vaguely Noble—Belle Marie Breeder—Owner (Kentucky)	L. S. Barrera	5/2 Walter Guerra
5 P.P. 5	Longden & Carr Stables White, purple sash, sleeves and cap **REGAL BEARING (GB)** 118 Ch.h. '76, Viceregal—Mia Pola, by Relko Breeder—S. Niarchos (Great Britain)	John Longden	30 Joe Steiner
6 P.P. 6	Fleetwood Stable & Cameron Burgundy, yellow cross sashes, burgundy and yellow cap **RAINBOW CONNECTION** 115 B.f. '78, Halo—Hangin Round, by Stage Door Johnny Breeder—Mrs. George T. Coker (Canada)	Gary Jones	15 Marco Castaneda

7	Kjell H. Qvale — Bruce Headley Flame orange, green oak tree on back, orange bars on green sleeves, orange cap **SILVEYVILLE** **118** P.P. 7 B.c. '78, Petrone—Zurina, by Successor Breeder—Tanaka & Tanaka (California)	20 Danny Winick
8	Cimarron Stable — R. W. Mulhall White, green hoops and bars on sleeves, white and green cap **RANKIN (Fr)** **117** P.P. 8 Ch.h. '77, Owen Dudley—Cup Cake, by Dan Cupid Breeder—Mrs. Eric Loder (France)	20 Sandy Hawley

Nos. 1, 1A & 1B—Bradley, Chandler & C. Whittingham—Lowell T. Hughes (Lessee)—Baron Van Zuylen & Fradkoff entry.

8th Santa Anita

ABOUT 1¾ MILES. (TURF). (2.45⅘) 43rd running of THE SAN JUAN CAPISTRANO INVITATIONAL HANDICAP (Grade I). Purse $300,000. 4-year-olds and upward. By invitation, with no nomination or starting fees. The winner to receive $180,000, with $60,000 to second, $36,000 to third, $18,000 to fourth and $6,000 to fifth. Weights to be published Wednesday, April 7. The Los Angeles Turf Club will invite a field of the highest weighted horses to accept. In the event that one or more of these decline, those weighted below them will be invited in weight order to replace them. The field will be drawn by the closing time of entries, Friday, April 16. A trophy will be presented to the owner of the winner.

Coupled—Exploded, Captain General and Perrault.

***Lanarkland** — Gr. g. 6, by Ragstone—Kinharvie, by Abernant
Own.—Sweeney Tara (Lessee) **116** Br.—Lavinia Duchess of Norfolk (Eng) 1982 5 2 1 0 $70,925
Tr.—West Ted 1981 8 0 1 1 $2,677
Lifetime 25 7 3 2 $92,057 Turf 25 7 3 2 $92,057

28Mar82-8SA 1½(T):4622:00 2:24 fm 32 126 58½ 57½ 513 520 CastanedM1 Sn Ls Ry 75 Perrault, Exploded, John Henry 5
13Mar82-9SA 1½(T):4832:0342:29 gd 5 118 77¾ 42½ 1hd 13½ GuerrWA4 Sn Mrno H 70 Lanarkland, Desvelo,SunshineSwag 8
13Mar82—Run in two divisions, 8th & 9th races.
27Feb82-8SA 1½(T):4812:0222:271fm 4¾ 115 98½ 32 43 75 GrrWA10 Sn Ls Obs H 74 RegalBearing,LeDucdeBar,Goldiko 10
14Feb82-7SA 1⅛(T):4641:1131:50 gd 6½ 114 65¾ 62½ 2hd 12¾ Guerra W A7 Aw35000 77 Lanarkland,Gonzales,YellowMrmlde 8
31Jan82-5SA 1⅛(T):4721:1141:493gd 41 112 55 54 4nk 2½ Guerra W A2 70000 78 Serang, Lanarkland, Mr. Mud 9
6Oct81◆5Brighton(Eng) 1 1:413gd*3-2 118 (T) 7 Reid J Bramber TowerWin,MnInThMiddl,Smckovr 13
21Sep81◆4Bath(Eng) a1¼ 2:133gd 20 125 (T) 53½ Perks S Langridge H Aventura,Blakenor,LadyofCornwll 19
31Aug81◆4Epsom(Eng) 1½ 2:394gd 20 160 (T) 59½ BsttlJ Gntlmn Amtr Rdrs H No Bombs, Gay George, GetStoned 8
27Aug81◆6Brihgton(Eng) 1½ 2:293fm 6½ 140 (T) 616 Reid J Rottingdean H BuncBoy,SkrryDnc,FoolsTstimony 11
5Aug81◆4Brighton(Eng) 1½ 2:263fm 10 133 (T) 38½ Reid J Brghtn Chllng Cp Bunce Boy, Lohengrin, Lanarkland 9
Apr 17 SA (T) 3f fm :35 h (d) ●Apr 13 SA (T) 1 yl 1:424 h (d) Apr 7 SA (T) 4f fm :48 h (d) Mar 24 SA 7f ft 1:263 h

***Desvelo** — Dk. b. or br. h. 5, by Decano II—Bronze Gem, by Tobin Bronze
Br.—Haras Tarapaca (Chile) 1982 5 3 1 1 $58,450
Own.—Saddle Hill Farm & Winick **114** Tr.—Winick Randy 1981 4 0 0 1 $4,725
Lifetime 13 4 2 4 $71,393 Turf 10 4 1 3 $67,087

26Mar82-8SA 1¼(T):4641:3622:004fm*7-5 122 55½ 42 3½ 2½ Toro F7 Aw32000 82 ‡CaptainGeneral,Desvelo,NotbleAxe 7
26Mar82—Placed first through disqualification
13Mar82-9SA 1½(T):4832:0342:29 gd 2½ 116 1hd 11 2hd 23½ ShomkrW7 Sn Mrno H 66 Lanarkland, Desvelo,SunshineSwag 8
13Mar82—Run in two divisions, 8th & 9th races.
20Feb82-5SA 1¼(T):4731:36 2:003fm 3½ 121 11½ 12 14 13¾ Toro F3 Aw27000 84 Desvelo, Chancey Bidder, Dip 8
6Feb82-7SA 1¼(T):4521:3522:002fm 4½ 115 47½ 12½ 12½ 11½ Toro F5 Aw20000 85 Desvelo, Padirac, Flying Gene 9
29Jan82-7SA 1$\frac{1}{16}$:472 1:112 1:423ft 7 115 52½ 42¼ 43 36 Toro F8 Aw20000 82 DurbanDeep,Parson'sLeder,Desvelo 8
18Dec81-5Hol 1⅛(T):4811:1211:482fm 3½e 116 1½ 1½ 31 42¾ Hawley S3 Aw19000 85 ‡BlueDncerII,SpringDiggr,Amrpour 8
4Nov81-7SA 1⅛(T):47 1:1041:473fm 21 117 42½ 31½ 44 34½ Gallitano G5 Aw22000 85 Caesr'sProfile,HomeBound,Desvelo 6
21Oct81-2SA a6½f (T):212 :44 1:14 fm 48 116 64½ 79½ 79½ 89½ Gallitano G8 Aw25000 80 AlwysAChnc,NowndThn,MdnghtMn 8
7Oct81-7SA 6½f :22 :443 1:152ft 87 1125 64¾ 79¾ 1012 1117 Schoeller CF1 Aw20000 76 StarRoute,NowndThen,Cloonwillin 11
30Nov80◆9ClubHipico(Chile a1⅛ 2:01 fm 11 123 (T) 34½ EscbrO ClFernandoFantiniB Rasputin, Chalotin, Desvelo 7
●Apr 15 SA (T) 4f fm :482 h (d) Apr 10 SA (T) 1 fm 1:422 h (d) Apr 4 SA 4f ft :482 h Mar 23 SA 4f ft :50 h

Exploded — Dk. b. or br. h. 5, by Cougar II—Blow Up II, by Abdos

Own.—Bradley-Chandler-Whttnghm 118 — Br.—Bradley-Whittinghm-Wynne (Ky) 1982 4 0 3 0 $64,875

Tr.—Whittingham Charles 1981 16 1 4 2 $213,750

Lifetime 29 3 8 5 $377,375 Turf 18 1 6 3 $234,425

28Mar82-8SA 1½Ⓣ:4622:00 2:24 fm 8-5e 126 45¾ 43¼ 21 23¼ Sibille R2 Sn Ls Ry 92 Perrault, Exploded, John Henry 5

13Mar82-8SA 1½Ⓣ:4842:0222:272gd *3-2 119 22½ 22½ 25 25 Sibille R3 Sn Mrno H 73 LemhiGold,Exploded,ChnceyBidder 8

13Mar82—Run in two divisions, 8th & 9th races.

28Feb82-3SA 1⅛Ⓣ:4731:1211:471fm *7-5 115 65 63¾ 44 21¾ Sibille R1 Aw40000 89 Patti's Triumph, Exploded, Isopach 6

15Feb82-8SA 1¹⁄₁₆:462 1:10 1:41 ft 4e 114 75¼ 41¾ 44 42¾ McCrronCJ7 El Monte 93 WoodlandLad,SirDncer,LemhiGold 10

8Nov81-8SA 1½Ⓣ:4721:5932:232fm 7¾e 126 54 65¼ 57¾ 59¼ McCrronCJ2 Oak Tree 80 John Henry, Spence Bay, The Bart 7

25Oct81-8SA 1¼Ⓣ:48 1:3632:003fm 3e 116 85¾108 108¼ 812 McHrDG5 C F BurkeH 72 SpencBy,ProvidntilII,SuprMomnt 10

9Oct81-8SA 1¼Ⓣ:4841:37 2:014fm 4 115 75¼ 42 43 23¼ CastanedaM7 Aw40000 74 SuperMoment,Exploded,BeechGrov 8

7Sep81-8Dmr a1¼:463 1:352 1:572ft 2¾e 115 812 86¾ 89 811 Toro F4 Dmr Inv H 79 Wickerr, Tahitian King,GalaxyLibra 8

16Aug81-8Dmr 1⅛Ⓣ:4931:14 1:494fm 6 114 78¼ 74¼ 74½ 52½ CastanedM4 E Read H 86 Wickerr,SuperMoment,MikeFogrty 7

2Aug81-8Dmr 1¹⁄₁₆:46 1:10 1:41 ft 3½ 115 67½ 44¼ 36 34¾ CstnedM7 Sn Diego H 90 SummerTimeGuy,Shmgo,Exploded 7

Apr 14 SA Ⓣ5f fm :594 h (d) Apr 10 SA Ⓣ7f fm 1:292 h (d) Apr 5 SA Ⓣ5f gd 1:024 h (d) Mar 21 SA 5f ft 1:003 h

Lemhi Gold — Ch. c. 4, by Vaguely Noble—Belle Marie, by Candy Spots

Own.—Jones A U 121 — Br.—Jones A U (Ky) 1982 4 2 1 1 $73,675

Tr.—Barrera Lazaro S 1981 7 2 1 0 $50,070

Lifetime 11 4 2 1 $123,745 Turf 3 3 0 0 $81,305

13Mar82-8SA 1½Ⓣ:4842:0222:272gd 2¼ 119 12½ 12½ 15 15 GuerrWA4 Sn Mrno H 78 LemhiGold,Exploded,ChnceyBidder 8

13Mar82—Run in two divisions, 8th & 9th races.

25Feb82-8SA 1⅛Ⓣ:4641:1111:48 fm *8-5 113 42 41½ 1½ 11¼ Guerra W A8 Aw35000 87 LemhiGold,Fingal'sCave,Essenbee 10

15Feb82-8SA 1¹⁄₁₆:462 1:10 1:41 ft 3½ 114 43 31½ 33½ 31½ Guerra WA1 El Monte 95 WoodlandLad,SirDncer,LemhiGold 10

6Feb82-6SA 1¹⁄₁₆:462 1:094 1:41 ft *4-5 114 53½ 33½ 23½ 25½ Guerra W A4 Aw25000 90 Shashy, Lemhi Gold, Call MeMister 7

29Aug81-8Bel 1 :444 1:082 1:331ft 12 117 108¼ 913 913 915 VelsquezJ11 Jerome H 87 Noble Nashua, Maudlin, Sing Sing 11

15Aug81-8Sar 1¼:463 1:372 2:034sy 17 126 811 911 923 726 Vasquez J6 Travers 55 WillowHour,PlesntColony,LordAvi 10

2Aug81-8Sar 1⅛:47 1:103 1:491ft 3½ 117 53 33 31½ 2½ CordroAJr6 Jim Dandy 88 WillowHour,LemhiGold,SilvrSuprm 8

9Jly81-9Hol 1 Ⓣ:4621:1031:35 fm 2¼ 114 44 62¼ 4¾ 1½ McCrrnCJ6 Westwood 94 Lemhi Gold,RockSoftly,IslandWhirl 7

9Jly81—Run in two divisions, 8th & 9th races.

28Mar81-8SA 1¹⁄₁₆:46 1:10 1:42 ft *3-2 119 57½ 68 711 58 Pincay LJr6 Sn Flpe H 83 Stnchrry,SplndidSpruc,FlyingNshu 12

19Mar81-7SA 1 :452 1:093 1:351ft *1-5 120 44 44½ 46½ 49 Pincay L Jr5 Aw22000 84 Torso, Native Tactics, El Jebel 5

Apr 15 SA Ⓣ4f fm :492 h (d) ●Apr 9 SA Ⓣ1 fm 1:39 h (d) Mar 28 SA 4f ft :482 b Mar 23 SA 3f ft :363 h

***Regal Bearing *** — Ch. h. 6, by Viceregal—Mia Pola, by Relko

Own.—Longden & Carr Stables 118 — Br.—Niarchos S (Eng) 1982 6 2 0 0 $155,225

Tr.—Longden John 1981 6 2 1 0 $52,400

Lifetime 30 11 3 0 $309,426 Turf 22 8 3 0 $209,716

3Apr82-8GG 1¹⁄₁₆:483 1:13 1:46 m 5¾ 117 46½ 41¾ 12 13½ Baze R A4 G G H 73 ReglBring,VisiblPol,ScorTwntyFour 5

20Mar82-8GG 1 Ⓣ:48 1:1221:364yl *2¾ 121 96¾ 75¾ 78¾ 811 Steiner JJ4 S F Mle H 72 Silveyville, Visible Pole, ASureHit 10

27Feb82-8SA 1½Ⓣ:4812:0222:271fm 3¾e 114 43 2hd 12½ 13½ SteinrJJ5 Sn Ls Obs H 79 RegalBearing,LeDucdeBar,Goldiko 10

15Feb82-8SA 1¹⁄₁₆:462 1:10 1:41 ft 26 114 95¾ 85½ 912 814 Gilligan L10 El Monte 82 WoodlandLad,SirDncer,LemhiGold 10

7Feb82-7SA a6½f Ⓣ:213 :4341:133fm 5e 118 74½ 65¾ 712 813 Steiner J J2 HcpO 78 Mr.PrimMinistr,TrmmlLuck,PirtLw 8

31Jan82-7SA 6f :213 :442 1:084ft 13 1115 68 68 67½ 57½ Steiner J J3 Aw35000 86 Mr.PrmMnstr,Emprr'sKy,FlngChck 6

9Oct81-8SA 1¼Ⓣ:4841:37 2:014fm 3½ 122 11 2hd 2½ 45½ ShoemkerW5 Aw40000 73 SuperMoment,Exploded,BeechGrov 8

2Oct81-8SA 6½f :22 :45 1:152ft 9-5 122 66½ 67 511 411 ShoemkerW5 Aw34000 82 BigPrsnttion,TonUp,ExcutivCounsl 6

5Sep81-8Dmr 1¹⁄₁₆Ⓣ:4811:1211:42 fm *3½ 121 55½ 63¾ 54½ 22 ShomkrW10 Escndo H 97 Advocatum,ReglBering,MjorSport 10

26Aug81-7Dmr 1¹⁄₁₆:464 1:104 1:414ft *2-3 117 1hd 2hd 1hd 1nk ShoemkerW3 Aw32000 91 Regal Bearing, Damas, I'llStandPat 6

Apr 14 SA Ⓣ7f fm 1:264 h (d) Mar 29 GG 5f sy 1:063 b (d) Mar 17 SA tr.t 5f sy 1:01 h Mar 13 SA 6f sl 1:151 h

Silveyville — B. c. 4, by Petrone—Zurina, by Successor

Own.—Qvale K H 118 — Br.—Tanaka & Tanaka (Cal) 1982 5 1 1 0 $76,875

Tr.—Campbell E L 1981 11 6 1 2 $207,130

Lifetime 17 7 3 2 $285,155 Turf 7 4 1 0 $243,250

3Apr82-8GG 1¹⁄₁₆:483 1:13 1:46 m 8-5 122 2½ 1hd 47 414 Winick D5 G G H 59 ReglBring,VisiblPol,ScorTwntyFour 5

20Mar82-8GG 1 Ⓣ:48 1:1221:364yl 3 121 11½ 12 13 16 Winick D6 S F Mle H 83 Silveyville, Visible Pole, ASureHit 10

21Feb82-8SA 1¼Ⓣ:4341:34 1:591fm 11 120 31½11151127 — OlivresF11 Sra Nvda H — HighCounsel,HndsomeOn,IrishHrt 11

21Feb82—Eased

10Feb82-8SA 1¼Ⓣ:4731:3812:043yl 8½ 117 11½ 2½ 21½ 25 Olivares F6 Arcadia H 59 Perrault, Silveyville, Le Duc de Bar 7

17Jan82-8SA 1⅛:452 1:092 1:473ft 17 123 77½ 89 911 715 Winick D7 Sn Frndo 76 It's the One, Princelet, Rock Softly 9

12Dec81-8BM 1⅛Ⓣ:4841:3411:533sf 7½ 120 14 1hd 31½ 43 Winick D8 B M H 69 SuperMoment,TahitianKing,TheBrt 8

28Nov81-8BM 1¹⁄₁₆Ⓣ:4821:1321:481sf 3½ 120 12 1½ 11½ 1¾ Winick D5 B M Dby H 67 Silveyvill,SunshinSwg,Tmpo'sTigr 10

15Nov81-9Hol 1⅛Ⓣ:4621:1031:481fm 27 122 11 11½ 11 1no Winick D1 Hol Dby 89 Silveyville,FrenchSssfrs,WtrwyDriv 8

15Nov81—Run in two divisions, 8th & 9th races.

24Oct81-8BM 1¹⁄₁₆Ⓣ:4711:1241:451fm 19 111 13 21 2½ 1nk Winick D7 Ascot H 82 Silveyville,LordTrendy,WterwyDriv 7

9Oct81-8BM 1¹⁄₁₆:451 1:101 1:412ft 3 114 1hd 31½ 48½ 512 Winick D1 Rnd Tbl H 80 Chiaroscuro,FairShast,Productivity 7

●Apr 14 GG Ⓣ7f fm 1:31 b (d) ●Mar 13 GG 6f gd 1:12 h Mar 6 GG 6f ft 1:134 h Feb 18 SA 4f ft :474 h

***Rankin**
Ch. h. 5, by Owen Dudley—Cup Cake, by Dan Cupid
Br.—Leder Mrs E (Fra) 1982 3 1 0 0 $23,000
Own.—Cimarron Stable 117 Tr.—Mulhall Richard W 1981 4 0 1 0 $14,532
Lifetime 17 4 3 1 $152,286 Turf 17 4 3 1 $152,286
4Apr82-8SA 1⅛Ⓣ:4721:1131:483gd 21 117 44½ 41½ 2½ 1½ Pincay L Jr5 Aw40000 84 Rankin, Patti's Triumph, Glenorum 8
27Mar82-3SA 1⅛Ⓣ:46 1:0941:462fm 8¼ 117 2½ 31½ 43 57½ Pincay L Jr2 Aw40000 87 Falamoun, Pirate Law,CaptainNick 9
24Feb82-7SA a6½f Ⓣ:22 :4431:14 fm 11 115 86¾ 97½ 911 99¾ McCarronCJ3 Aw35000 79 Kangroo Court, Belfort, Jimsel 9
4Jun81♦3Epsom(Eng) 1½ 2:442gd 33 126 Ⓣ 5 StrkG Coronation Cup(Gr1) Master Willie, Prince Bee, Vielle 5
1May81♦4Newmarket(Eng) 1½ 2:38 gd 4 119 Ⓣ 422 StrkyG Jockey Club(Gr3) MasterWillie,KingsRide,FenneyMill 6
25Apr81♦3Sandown(Eng) 1¼ 2:112gd 2½ 120 Ⓣ 21½ StrkeyG Westbury(Gr3) Hard Fought, Rankin, Vielle 7
15Apr81♦2Newmarket(Eng) 1⅛ 1:542gd 3 122 Ⓣ 49 StrkyG Earl of Sefton(Gr3) HrdFought,Moryshire,PlyboyJubile 9
18Oct80♦2Newmarket(Eng) 1¼ 2:053gd 14 122 Ⓣ 42½ StrkyG Champion(Gr1) Cairn Rouge, Master Willie,Nadjar 13
29Jly80♦4Goodwood(Eng) 1½ 2:38 gd 2¾ 128 Ⓣ 413 StrkeyG Gordon(Gr3) PrinceBee,FingalsCave,LightCavlry 6
28Jun80♦3Curragh(Ire) 1½ 2:434yl 12 126 Ⓣ 79½ StrkG Irish Sweeps Dby(Gr1) Tynavos, Prince Bee, Ramian 13
Apr 12 SA 1 gd 1:413 h ●Mar 25 SA 4f ft :452 h Mar 20 SA 7f ft 1:264 h Mar 6 SA Ⓣ 1 fm 1:421 h (d)

Captain General
B. h. 5, by Vaguely Noble—Charming Alibi, by Honeys Alibi
Br.—Hunt N B (Ky) 1982 5 0 1 0 $11,775
Own.—Hughes L T (Lessee) 113 Tr.—Whittingham Charles . 1981 5 1 1 0 $40,225
Lifetime 17 2 3 1 $75,425 Turf 8 1 1 0 $54,625
8Apr82-5SA 1⅛Ⓣ:4621:1031:481fm*4-5 114 99¾ 87 54½ 42½ McCarronCJ3 Aw26000 83 ‡Rostropovich,Tom'sSerend,Islndr 12
26Mar82-8SA 1¼Ⓣ:4641:3622:004fm 9-5 114 67½ 31 4¾ 1½ † McCarronCJ5 Aw32000 83 ‡CaptainGeneral,Desvelo,NotbleAxe 7
†26Mar82—Disqualified and placed fourth
27Feb82-8SA 1½Ⓣ:4812:0222:271fm 4¾ 113 1016 1016 89 86 VlnzlPA7 Sn Ls Obs H 73 RegalBearing,LeDucdeBar,Goldiko 10
20Feb82-5SA 1¼Ⓣ:4731:36 2:003fm*4-5 115 814 67½ 57½ 46¾ ValenzuelPA4 Aw27000 77 Desvelo, Chancey Bidder, Dip 8
7Feb82-5SA 1¼Ⓣ:47 1:3622:004fm*9-5 115 1010 51¾ 31 2hd ValenzuelPA9 Aw27000 83 Jurisconsult,CptnGnrl,PrnclyVrdct 11
9Apr81-8SA 1¼Ⓣ:4641:35 1:591fm 5 116 713 76½ 78½ 64½ VlenzulPA7 Grg Ryl H 86 RustyCanyon,BeechGrove,Catermn 7
14Mar81-8SA 1½Ⓣ:4622:0022:244fm 22 113 97¾ 94½ 55 1no VlnzulPA6 Sn Mrno H 91 CaptainGeneral,Aliyoun,‡Catermn 12
25Feb81-7SA 1⅛:47 1:104 1:483ft *9-5 117 711 77½ 76½ 56 ShoemkerW2 Aw23000 80 Defince,RoyllyTrue,MsterCermonis 7
12Feb81-9SA 1⅛:464 1:103 1:484ft 3½ 117 717 613 51½ 22 ShoemkerW3 Aw24000 83 ChuckyBby,CptinGenerl,HerbgerLd 7
16Jan81-5SA 1⅛Ⓣ:4531:1031:482fm 8¼ 117 819 87½ 85 52 Pierce D10 Aw22000 83 Viking, Macdon, ‡Benefactor 10
16Jan81—Placed fourth through disqualification
Apr 16 SA 3f ft :352 h Apr 5 SA 6f ft 1:134 h Mar 21 SA 6f ft 1:134 h Mar 8 SA Ⓣ 5f fm 1:004 h (d)

***Perrault**
Ch. h. 5, by Djakao—Innocent Air, by Court Martial
Br.—Sasse & Shead (Eng) 1982 3 2 1 0 $263,900
Own.—Baron de Zuylen & Fradkoff 129 Tr.—Whittingham Charles 1981 8 3 2 1 $203,566
Lifetime 20 7 5 3 $556,442 Turf 19 7 4 3 $456,442
28Mar82-8SA 1½Ⓣ:4622:00 2:24 fm 8-5e 126 11½ 11½ 11 13½ Pincay L Jr5 Sn Ls Ry 95 Perrault, Exploded, John Henry 5
7Mar82-8SA 1¼:45 1:342 1:59 ft 4½e 126 57 41½ 1½ 1no† Pincay L Jr4 S A H 94 ‡Perrault, John Henry, It'stheOne 11
† 7Mar82—Disqualified and placed second
10Feb82-8SA 1¼Ⓣ:4731:3812:043yl *8-5 124 44½ 1½ 11½ 15 Pincay LJr7 Arcadia H 64 Perrault, Silveyville, Le Duc de Bar 7
8Nov81-8SA 1½Ⓣ:4721:5932:232fm 7¾e 126 42½ 55½ 711 715 St Martin Y5 Oak Tree 83 John Henry, Spence Bay, The Bart 7
4Oct81♦4Longchamp(Fra) a1½ 2:351sf 27 130 Ⓣ 42¾ SmnH Arc de Triomphe (Gr1) Gold River, Bikala, April Run 24
30Aug81♦4Deauville(Fra) a1⅝ 2:583fm*6-5 131 Ⓣ 1hd StMrtY GrndPrixdeDeuville(Gr2) Perrault, Castle Keep, Glenorum 11
14Jly81♦6StCloud(Fra) a1⅝ 2:382gd*6-5 130 Ⓣ 12½ StMrtY PrixMuricedeNieul(Gr2) Perrault,RoiGuillume,DomMenotti 10
23May81♦5Evry(Fra) a1½ 2:423gd 6½ 124 Ⓣ 2hd StMrtY Gr Pr d'Evry (Gr2) Lancastrian, Perrault, Kelbomec 12
10May81♦6Longchamp(Fra) a1½ 2:492sf *2½ 123 Ⓣ 1hd StMrtY La Coupe(Gr3) Perrult,SonofLove,MonsiurDgobrt 10
20Apr81♦2Longchamp(Fra) a1½ 2:332gd 2¾ 121 Ⓣ 31½ StMrtnY Prix d'Hedouville Lancastrian, En Calcat, Perrault 10
●Apr 14 SA Ⓣ 5f fm :59 h (d) Apr 10 SA Ⓣ 1 fm 1:464 h (d) Apr 5 SA Ⓣ 5f gd 1:073 h (d) Mar 27 SA Ⓣ 3f fm :361 h (d)

Analyst's Comment

EIGHTH RACE

1—Perrault
2—Lemhi Gold
3—Exploded

PERRAULT has done just about everything asked of him this winter and won't have arch rival John Henry to battle today. This import ran a winning race at just about this distance in France under 131 pounds, which suggests he'll have no problems with 129 pounds, although this race has been a jinx for topweights. LEMHI GOLD has found his calling on the turf and has won all three of his grass starts in good style. However, this is an exacting distance and he's second topweight at 121. EXPLODED loves a distance and was second to Obraztsovy in this fixture last year. LANARKLAND is better than his last and he could be the upsetter under 116 pounds and leading rider Eddie D.

SWEEP'S Santa Anita Graded Handicaps

EIGHTH RACE ***Probable Post, 4:45***

ABOUT 1 ¾ MILES.(turf) 43rd running of THE SAN JUAN CAPISTRANO INVITATIONAL HANDICAP (Grade I). 4-Year-Olds and Up.. Purse $300,000.

10	PERRAULT	Pincay L Jr	129	Field at his mercy	1-5
4	LEMHI GOLD	Guerra W A	121	Going great for Laz	5-1
3	EXPLODED	Shoemaker W	118	Runs best against best	1-5
5	REGAL BEARING	Steiner J J	118	Won Golden Gate 'Cap	12-1
7	SILVEYVILLE	Winick D	118	Dangerous early speed	15-1
9	CAPTAIN GENERAL	McCrrnCJ	113	Flopped at odds-on	1-5
1	LANARKLAND	Delahoussaye E	116	Last in San Luis Rey	20-1
8	RANKIN	Hawley S	117	Rang bell at 21-1	20-1
6	RAINBOW CONNECTION	CstdM	115	Look for improvement	20-1
2	DESVELO	Toro F	114	Good try to easier	20-1

Coupled—Perrault, Exploded and Captain General.

EXPERTS' SELECTIONS

Consensus Points: 5 for 1st (best 7), 2 for 2d, 1 for 3d. Best in CAPITALS.

Trackman, Warren Williams | **SANTA ANITA** | Selections Made for Fast Track

	TRACKMAN	HANDICAP	ANALYST	HERMIS	SWEEP	CONSENSUS	
8	PERRAULT EXPLODED LEMHI GOLD	PERRAULT EXPLODED LEMHI GOLD	PERRAULT LEMHI GOLD EXPLODED	PERRAULT REGAL BEARING LEMHI GOLD	PERRAULT LEMHI GOLD EXPLODED	PERRAULT LEMHI GOLD EXPLODED	27 7 6

The tote board was as follows:

	#1 Entry of Exploded, Captain General, and Perrault	#4 Lemhi Gold	Totals
With nine minutes to post time			
Odds	1—5	3—1	
Win pool	86,716	26,684	138,011
Place pool	76,728	13,277	103,643
Show pool	68,451	4,796	83,830
With seven minutes to post time			
Odds	2—5	5—2	
Win pool	92,620	31,028	152,377
Place pool	88,450	14,921	118,856
Show pool	73,009	5,954	91,464
With three minutes to post time			
Odds	2—5	5—2	
Win pool	107,936	41,934	189,118
Place pool	95,831	17,551	134,935
Show pool	84,990	6,994	109,578
With one minute to post time			
Odds	2—5	5—2	
Win pool	117,171	45,591	205,973
Place pool	101,114	18,762	143,313
Show pool	97,604	7,483	124,437
After the last-minute surge of betting			
Odds	1—2	5—2	
Win pool	141,334	50,790	238,741
Place pool	108,593	19,610	153,673
Show pool	107,094	8,643	136,568
At post time			
Odds	2—5	3—1	
Win pool	154,169	52,104	253,952
Place pool	116,750	19,820	157,537
Show pool	112,441	8,753	142,689

which would occur with a probability of 0.393;* and (3) Lemhi Gold would finish in the money and all the entry horses would finish out of the money, in which case the payoff for show would be quite high.

If Lemhi Gold came in without any of the entry horses, he would have to pay \$23.80 to show for the bet to be a fair proposition. In fact, from the final tote-board values, Lemhi Gold would have paid only \$9.80.† The \$9.80 would have been quite a good payoff in its own right, given that Lemhi Gold went off at 3–1.

Thus the minus pool makes all show bets poor betting opportunities, regardless of how good they might look.

The only bet in this race that made any sense was Lemhi Gold to win.

---

*The probability that Lemhi Gold would win was $q_{LG} = W_{LG}/W = 45{,}591/205{,}973 = 0.221$. The probability that each of the three entry horses would win was about $q_E = 117{,}171/(205{,}973)/3 = 0.190$. The probabilities that the other five long-shot horses would win were about $q_{LS} = 0.210/5 = 0.0420$. The probability that Lemhi Gold would be second was then about

$$q_{LG} \times \left\{ \frac{3q_E}{1 - q_E} + \frac{5q_{LS}}{1 - q_{LS}} \right\} = 0.204$$

and third,

$$q_{LG} \times \left\{ 3\frac{2q_E^2}{(1 - q_E)(1 - 2q_E)} + \frac{5q_E q_{LS}}{(1 - q_E)(1 - q_{LS} - q_E)} + 5\frac{2q_E q_{LS}}{(1 - q_{LS})(1 - q_{LS} - q_E)} + \frac{4q_{LS}^2}{(1 - q_{LS})(1 - 2q_{LS})} \right\} = 0.182.$$

Thus the place probability was 0.425, the show probability 0.607, and the probability that Lemhi Gold would be out of the money was $1 - 0.607 = 0.393$.

†The probability that Lemhi Gold would be in the money with none of the triple entry horses was

$$\underbrace{\frac{q_{LG}(5)(4)q_{LS}^2}{(1 - q_{LS})(1 - 2q_{LS})}}_{\text{Lemhi Gold third}} + \underbrace{\frac{q_{LG}(5)(4)q_{LS}^2}{(1 - q_{LS})(1 - q_{LS} - q_{LG})}}_{\text{Lemhi Gold second}} + \underbrace{\frac{q_{LG}(5)(4)q_{LS}^2}{(1 - q_{LG})(1 - q_{LS} - q_{LG})}}_{\text{Lemhi Gold first}} = 0.0335.$$

The probability that Lemhi Gold would be in the money was 0.607. Thus the probability that Lemhi Gold would be in the money with at least one of the entry horses was $0.607 - 0.0335 = 0.574$.

To break even on a show bet on Lemhi Gold, the expected profit must be equal to zero:

$$0 = -1(0.393) + 0.05(0.574) + O_{LG}(0.0335).$$

Solving for the show odds, $O_{LG} = 10.875$, or a payoff of \$23.75 or \$23.80 with breakage. The actual O_{LG} was

$$\frac{QS - (S_{LG} + 2S_{LS})}{3S_{LG}} = \frac{(1 - 0.15)(142{,}689) - [8{,}753 + 2(4{,}299)]}{3(8{,}753)} = 3.958,$$

which yielded a payout after breakage of \$9.80.

If Lemhi Gold's chances of winning were 25% or better, then the bet was reasonable. I thought so and bet it accordingly. It turned out to be a wise investment.

The final result was an easy victory for Lemhi Gold. Perrault, heavily weighted at 129, was unable to mount a late charge and finished third. Exploded took second. The chart of the race was as follows:

San Juan Capistrano Handicap

EIGHTH RACE
Santa Anita
APRIL 18, 1982

ABOUT 1 ¾ MILES.(turf). (2.45⅗) 43rd Running THE SAN JUAN CAPISTRANO HANDICAP (Grade I). Purse $300,000. Invitational Handicap. 4-year-olds and upward. By invitation, with no nomination or starting fees. The winner to receive $180,000, with $60,000 to second, $36,000 to third, $18,000 to fourth and $6,000 to fifth. Weights to be published Wednesday, April 7. The Los Angeles Turf Club will invite a field of the highest-weighted horses to accept. In the event that one or more of these decline, those weighted below them will be invited in weight order to replace them. The field will be drawn by the closing time of entries, Friday, April 16. A trophy will be presented to the owner of the winner.

Value of race $300,000, value to winner $180,000, second $60,000, third $36,000, fourth $18,000, fifth $6,000. Mutuel pool $554,178, Minus place pool $4,378.03, Minus show pool $5,968.06. Exacta Pool $401,828.

Last Raced		Horse	Eqt.	A.	Wt	PP	St	1	1¼	1½	Str	Fin	Jockey	Odds $1
13Mar82	^{8}SA^{1}	Lemhi Gold		4	121	4	4^{2}	$3^{2\frac{1}{2}}$	2^{4}	1^{hd}	$1^{2\frac{1}{2}}$	1^{7}	Guerra W A	3.10
28Mar82	^{8}SA^{2}	Exploded		5	118	3	9	8^{1}	6^{hd}	4^{1}	3^{2}	$2^{1\frac{3}{4}}$	Shoemaker W	a-.40
28Mar82	^{8}SA^{1}	Perrault	b	5	129	9	2^{1}	$2^{\frac{1}{2}}$	$1^{\frac{1}{2}}$	2^{1}	2^{6}	$3^{2\frac{1}{2}}$	Pincay L Jr	a-.40
8Apr82	^{5}SA^{4}	Captain General		5	113	8	8^{1}	$7^{\frac{1}{2}}$	7^{1}	$6^{1\frac{1}{2}}$	$5^{1\frac{1}{2}}$	4^{nk}	McCarron C J	a-.40
4Apr82	^{8}SA^{1}	Rankin		5	117	7	6^{1}	$5^{1\frac{1}{2}}$	5^{1}	$3^{1\frac{1}{2}}$	4^{3}	$5^{3\frac{1}{2}}$	Hawley S	19.60
28Mar82	^{8}SA^{5}	Lanarkland		6	116	1	7^{hd}	9	9	7^{2}	6^{7}	6^{13}	Delahoussaye E	14.00
3Apr82	^{8}GG^{4}	Silveyville		4	118	6	$1^{1\frac{1}{2}}$	1^{5}	$3^{\frac{1}{2}}$	8^{hd}	8^{1}	$7^{\frac{1}{2}}$	Winick D	36.70
26Mar82	^{8}SA^{1}	Desvelo		5	115	2	3^{1}	$4^{2\frac{1}{2}}$	4^{1}	5^{1}	7^{2}	8^{nk}	Castaneda M	27.10
3Apr82	^{8}GG^{1}	Regal Bearing		6	118	5	5^{5}	$6^{\frac{1}{2}}$	$8^{1\frac{1}{2}}$	9	9	9	Steiner J J	21.80

a-Coupled: Exploded, Perrault and Captain General.

OFF AT 5:23 Start good, Won easily. Time, :23, :46, 1:09⅕, 1:33⅘, 1:58⅘, 2:45⅗, Course firm.

$2 Mutuel Prices:			
4-LEMHI GOLD	**8.20**	**2.10**	**2.10**
1-EXPLODED (a-entry)		**2.10**	**2.10**
1-PERRAULT (a-entry)		**2.10**	**2.10**

$5 EXACTA 4-1 PAID $33.00.

Ch. c, by Vaguely Noble—Belle Marie, by Candy Spots. Trainer Barrera Lazaro S. Bred by Jones Aaron U (Ky).

LEMHI GOLD, taken in hand after the start, raced in good position while reserved off the pace through the first mile, moved to closer contention outside of PERRAULT on the front stretch, was roused a bit to stay alongside that one when PERRAULT moved strongly to the lead on the backstretch, got the advantage on the stretch turn and quickly drew off when set down in the upper stretch. EXPLODED, unhurried until after 10 furlongs, rallied when set down but could not reach close contention. PERRAULT, reserved off the early pace and moved strongly to the lead early on the backstretch, matched strides with the winner to the stretch then weakened in the final furlong. CAPTAIN GENERAL failed to threaten.

Owners— 1, Jones Aaron U; 2, Bradley & Chandler & Whittingham; 3, Fradkoff & Van Zuylen; 4, Hughes L T; 5, Cimarron Stable; 6, Sweeney Tara Brianne; 7, Qvale K H; 8, Savoca & Winick; 9, Longden-Carr Stable.

Trainers— 1, Barrera Lazaro S; 2, Whittingham Charles; 3, Whittingham Charles; 4, Whittingham Charles; 5, Mulhall Richard W; 6, West Ted; 7, Headley Bruce; 8, Winick Randy; 9, Longden John.

Overweight: Desvelo 1 pound.

Scratched—Rainbow Connection (3Apr82 ^{8}SA^{5}).

My win bet provided a handsome payoff, and the rest of the tote board's $2.10s reflected the minus pools. An even more outstanding bet was the 4–1 exacta, which paid $33 for a $5 bet, or $6.60 per dollar bet, considerably more than the $4.10 per dollar bet in the win pool.

The conclusion of the analysis is this: When there is a minus pool with a minimum payoff of $2.10, do not bet to place or show on any horses, regardless of how attractive a bet on one of them appears to be. The only bets that are of possible interest are in the win or features pools. The decision to bet on such latter situations should be based on handicapping estimates that the probability of winning exceeds the odds estimate of the horses' chances. In localities such as Louisiana where the minimum payoff is $2.20, it may on occasion be advantageous to bet in a race with a minus pool. In this case, you should use an analysis like that described in Chapter Six for the Kentucky Oaks to determine the expected value per dollar bet.

16

Refinements to the Basic Dr. Z System

DANGERS TO LOOK FOR, WHEN NOT TO BET AND HORSES TO AVOID, CONSERVATIVE VERSUS RISKY USE OF THE DR. Z SYSTEM, AND HINTS ON GOOD BETTING TECHNIQUES AT THE RACETRACK

In Chapter Five we discussed the steps needed to apply the Dr. Z system. There we considered such important topics as horses to avoid and dangers to look for. Now that you have gone through our various applications of the Dr. Z system to real races, let us consider these matters again. Reread that section. Remember not to bet on off tracks, in minus pools, on long shots, and on "Silky Sullivans." Be careful betting on horses coming off a long layoff and on first-time starters. Bet them only if you feel very confident about their prospects of being in the money. Be sure you can both watch the tote board and wager near the end of the betting period. Don't bet too early! Also try to estimate if there are many Dr. Z system bettors at your track and if their presence is greatly affecting the quality of your bets. If so, read the appropriate section in Chapter Seventeen. Learn how to quickly use the tables in this book to determine when and how much to bet by practicing before you bet, both at home and at the track. Or get one of the calculators discussed in Chapter Five. Decide in advance if you are a strict Dr. Z system bettor or if you prefer to bet most races. If you want to stick closely to the Dr. Z system, then keep your betting fortune for these bets separate from your fun bets or those based on other systems. Don't bet unless the horse in question really does meet the suggested cutoffs: 1.10 (for the very best races), 1.14 for top tracks, and 1.18 for other tracks. If you want to increase your chances of being sure to come out ahead, bet less than the optimal Kelly amount by using one of the fractional Kelly strategies discussed in Chapter Five. By chopping the bet to half you will still get about 73%

of the maximum growth and you will substantially increase your chances of doubling, tripling, or quadrupling your initial betting fortune before losing half of it. If you want to bet every race, then follow the advice in Chapter Fourteen. Try more or less to break even on your non–Dr. Z system bets by betting small amounts and by wagering more as the bet becomes more advantageous, with higher expected value per dollar bet and higher probability of winning. Wager the optimal amount for your Dr. Z system bets out of your Dr. Z system betting wealth, reserving your additional betting wealth for your other bets. If you think you can handicap better than $q_i = W_i/W$, then modify your betting by using the analysis later in this chapter and in Chapter Seven. Learn how to use the Harville formulas if you do this. Above all, be careful and enjoy the sport!

REGRESSION EQUATIONS BASED ON DIFFERING WEALTH LEVELS AND TRACK HANDLE

Betting-wealth level and track handle are both very important factors in determining the optimal bet size. Certainly the larger our betting wealth, the more we will tend to bet, and since our bets affect the odds more at a small track than at a large one, we will generally bet less at the small track. Table 16.1, on optimal place betting, accounts for these factors by reporting optimal-place-bet regression equations for four different wealth levels ($50, $500, $2,500, $10,000) and three different place pools ($2,000, $10,000, $150,000). By averaging these equations, we can determine the optimal place bet for *any* wealth level and place pool. This is accomplished in Table 16.2, which indicates which equation from Table 16.1 to use and its corresponding weights for any wealth level and place pool. Tables 16.3 and 16.4 perform the same tasks for show betting. One further qualification: These regression equations were calibrated for a track payback proportion Q of 0.829. For Q's other than 0.829, a correction factor in the optimal bet size must be included. This factor is discussed in the following section.

To illustrate the use of these equations, let us study the Triple Bend Handicap at Hollywood Park on May 8, 1982, which was presented in Chapter Six. The tote board one minute before post time was:

	Totals	#8 Shanekite	Expected Value per Dollar Bet on Shanekite
Odds		1—1	
Win	398,851	155,321	
Show	59,163	14,585	1.18

TABLE 16.1 ***Optimal place bets for various betting-wealth levels and place-pools sizes***

Place Pool ($)	w_0 = \$50	w_0 = \$500	w_0 = \$2,500	w_0 = \$10,000
2,000		$P2 = 261q + 256q^2 + 180q^3 - \left(\frac{199qP_i}{qP - 0.70P_i}\right)$	$P5 = 426q + 802q^2 - \left(\frac{459qP_i}{qP - 0.60P_i}\right)$	$P8 = 487q + 901q^2 - \left(\frac{521qP_i}{qP - 0.60P_i}\right)$
10,000	$P1 = 39q + 52q^2 - \left(\frac{25qP_i}{qP - 0.75P_i}\right)$	$P3 = 375q + 525q^2 - \left(\frac{271qP_i}{qP - 0.70P_i}\right)$	$P6 = 1{,}307q + 1{,}280q^2 + 902q^3 - \left(\frac{993qP_i}{qP - 0.70P_i}\right)$	$P9 = 2{,}497q + 1{,}806q^2 + 2{,}073q^3 - \left(\frac{2{,}199qP_i}{qP - 0.60P_i}\right)$
150,000		$P4 = 505q + 527q^2 - \left(\frac{386qP_i}{qP - 0.60P_i}\right)$	$P7 = 2{,}386q + 2{,}668q^2 - \left(\frac{1{,}877qP_i}{qP - 0.60P_i}\right)$	$P10 = 7{,}072q + 10{,}470q^2 - \left(\frac{5{,}273qP_i}{qP - 0.70P_i}\right)$

TABLE 16.2 ***Weighting factors to determine the optimal place bet for any betting-wealth level and place-pool size***

Place Pool (\$)	w_0 = \$50	w_0 = \$51–\$500	W_0 = \$501–\$2,500
0–2,000	$\left(\frac{w_0}{50}\right)\left(\frac{P}{2{,}000}\right)[P1]$	$\left(\frac{500-w_0}{450}\right)\left(\frac{P}{2{,}000}\right)[P1]$ $+\left(\frac{w_0-50}{450}\right)\left(\frac{P}{2{,}000}\right)[P2]$	$\left(\frac{2{,}500-w_0}{2{,}000}\right)\left(\frac{P}{2{,}000}\right)[P2]$ $+\left(\frac{w_0-500}{2{,}000}\right)\left(\frac{P}{2{,}000}\right)[P5]$
2,001–10,000		$\left(\frac{500-w_0}{450}\right)[P1]$ $+\left(\frac{w_0-50}{450}\right)\left(\frac{10{,}000-P}{8{,}000}\right)[P2]$ $+\left(\frac{w_0-50}{450}\right)\left(\frac{P-2{,}000}{8{,}000}\right)[P3]$	$\left(\frac{2{,}500-w_0}{2{,}000}\right)\left(\frac{10{,}000-P}{8{,}000}\right)[P2]$ $+\left(\frac{2{,}500-w_0}{2{,}000}\right)\left(\frac{P-2{,}000}{8{,}000}\right)[P3]$ $+\left(\frac{w_0-500}{2{,}000}\right)\left(\frac{10{,}000-P}{8{,}000}\right)[P5]$ $+\left(\frac{w_0-500}{2{,}000}\right)\left(\frac{P-2{,}000}{8{,}000}\right)[P6]$
10,001–150,000	$\left(\frac{w_0}{50}\right)[P1]$	$\left(\frac{500-w_0}{450}\right)[P1]$ $+\left(\frac{w_0-50}{450}\right)\left(\frac{150{,}000-P}{140{,}000}\right)[P3]$ $+\left(\frac{w_0-50}{450}\right)\left(\frac{P-10{,}000}{140{,}000}\right)[P4]$	$\left(\frac{2{,}500-w_0}{2{,}000}\right)\left(\frac{150{,}000-P}{140{,}000}\right)[P3]$ $+\left(\frac{2{,}500-w_0}{2{,}000}\right)\left(\frac{P-10{,}000}{140{,}000}\right)[P4]$ $+\left(\frac{w_0-500}{2{,}000}\right)\left(\frac{150{,}000-P}{140{,}000}\right)[P6]$ $+\left(\frac{w_0-500}{2{,}000}\right)\left(\frac{P-10{,}000}{140{,}000}\right)[P7]$

TABLE 16.2 *(continued)*

Place Pool (\$)	w_0 = \$2,501–\$10,000	w_0 = \$10,001+
150,001+	$\left(\frac{500 - w_0}{450}\right)[P1] + \left(\frac{w_0 - 50}{450}\right)[P4]$	$\left(\frac{2{,}500 - w_0}{2{,}000}\right)[P4] + \left(\frac{w_0 - 500}{2{,}000}\right)[P7]$
0–2,000	$\left(\frac{10{,}000 - w_0}{7{,}500}\right)\left(\frac{P}{2{,}000}\right)[P5] + \left(\frac{w_0 - 2{,}500}{7{,}500}\right)\left(\frac{P}{2{,}000}\right)[P8]$	$\left(\frac{P}{2{,}000}\right)[P8]$
2,001–10,000	$\left(\frac{10{,}000 - w_0}{7{,}500}\right)\left(\frac{10{,}000 - P}{8{,}000}\right)[P5] + \left(\frac{10{,}000 - w_0}{7{,}500}\right)\left(\frac{P - 2{,}000}{8{,}000}\right)[P6] + \left(\frac{w_0 - 2{,}500}{7{,}500}\right)\left(\frac{10{,}000 - P}{8{,}000}\right)[P8] + \left(\frac{w_0 - 2{,}500}{7{,}500}\right)\left(\frac{P - 2{,}000}{8{,}000}\right)[P9]$	$\left(\frac{10{,}000 - P}{8{,}000}\right)[P8] + \left(\frac{P - 2{,}000}{8{,}000}\right)[P9]$

TABLE 16.2 ***(continued)***

Place Pool ($)	w_0 = \$2,501–\$10,000	w_0 = \$10,001+
10,001–150,000	$\left(\frac{10{,}000 - w_0}{7{,}500}\right)\left(\frac{150{,}000 - P}{140{,}000}\right)[P6]$ $+ \left(\frac{10{,}000 - w_0}{7{,}500}\right)\left(\frac{P - 10{,}000}{140{,}000}\right)[P7]$ $+ \left(\frac{w_0 - 2{,}500}{7{,}500}\right)\left(\frac{150{,}000 - P}{140{,}000}\right)[P9]$ $+ \left(\frac{w_0 - 2{,}500}{7{,}500}\right)\left(\frac{P - 10{,}000}{140{,}000}\right)[P10]$	$\left(\frac{150{,}000 - P}{140{,}000}\right)[P9]$ $+ \left(\frac{P - 10{,}000}{140{,}000}\right)[P10]$
150,001+	$\left(\frac{10{,}000 - w_0}{7{,}500}\right)[P7]$ $+ \left(\frac{w_0 - 2{,}500}{7{,}500}\right)[P10]$	[*P*10]

TABLE 16.3 ***Optimal show bets for various betting-wealth levels and show-pool sizes***

Show Pool ($)	w_0 = \$50	w_0 = \$500	w_0 = \$2,500	w_0 = \$10,000
1,200		$S2 = 9 + 994q^2 - 464q^3 - \left(\frac{150qS_i}{qS - 0.80S_i}\right)$	$S5 = 13 + 1{,}549q^2 - 901q^3 - \left(\frac{303qS_i}{qS - 0.60S_i}\right)$	
6,000	$S1 = 10 + 183q^2 - 135q^3 - \left(\frac{11S_i}{qS - 0.80S_i}\right)$	$S3 = 86 + 1{,}516q^2 - 968q^3 - \left(\frac{90.7S_i}{qS - 0.85S_i}\right)$	$S6 = 53 + 5{,}219q^2 - 2{,}513q^3 - \left(\frac{934qS_i}{qS - 0.70S_i}\right)$	$S8 = 58 + 7{,}406q^2 - 4{,}211q^3 - \left(\frac{1{,}359qS_i}{qS - 0.65S_i}\right)$
100,000		$S4 = 131 + 2{,}150q^2 - 1{,}778q^3 - \left(\frac{150S_i}{qS - 0.70S_i}\right)$	$S7 = 533 + 9{,}862q^2 - 7{,}696q^3 - \left(\frac{571S_i}{qS - 0.80S_i}\right)$	$S9 = 1{,}682 + 28{,}200q^2 - 16{,}880q^3 - \left(\frac{1{,}769S_i}{qS - 0.85S_i}\right)$

TABLE 16.4 **Weighting factors to determine the optimal show bet for any betting-wealth level and show-pool size**

Show Pool ($)	w_0 = \$0–\$50	w_0 = \$51–\$500	w_0 = \$501–\$2,500
0–1,200	$\left(\frac{w_0}{50}\right)\left(\frac{S}{1{,}200}\right)[S1]$	$\left(\frac{500-w_0}{450}\right)\left(\frac{S}{1{,}200}\right)[S1]$ $+\left(\frac{w_0-50}{450}\right)\left(\frac{S}{1{,}200}\right)[S2]$	$\left(\frac{2{,}500-w_0}{2{,}000}\right)\left(\frac{S}{1{,}200}\right)[S2]$ $+\left(\frac{w_0-500}{2{,}000}\right)\left(\frac{S}{1{,}200}\right)[S5]$
1,201–6,000		$\left(\frac{500-w_0}{450}\right)[S1]$ $+\left(\frac{w_0-50}{450}\right)\left(\frac{6{,}000-S}{4{,}800}\right)[S2]$ $+\left(\frac{w_0-50}{450}\right)\left(\frac{S-1{,}200}{4{,}800}\right)[S3]$	$\left(\frac{2{,}500-w_0}{2{,}000}\right)\left(\frac{6{,}000-S}{4{,}800}\right)[S2]$ $+\left(\frac{2{,}500-w_0}{2{,}000}\right)\left(\frac{S-1{,}200}{4{,}800}\right)[S3]$ $+\left(\frac{w_0-500}{2{,}000}\right)\left(\frac{6{,}000-S}{4{,}800}\right)[S5]$ $+\left(\frac{w_0-500}{2{,}000}\right)\left(\frac{S-1{,}200}{4{,}800}\right)[S6]$

TABLE 16.4 *(continued)*

Show Pool (*$*)	w_0 = \$0–\$50	w_0 = \$51–\$500	w_0 = \$501–\$2,500
6,001–100,000	$\left(\frac{w_0}{50}\right)[S1]$	$\left(\frac{500 - w_0}{450}\right)[S1]$	$\left(\frac{2{,}500 - w_0}{2{,}000}\right)\left(\frac{100{,}000 - S}{94{,}000}\right)[S3]$
		$+ \left(\frac{w_0 - 50}{450}\right)\left(\frac{100{,}000 - S}{94{,}000}\right)[S3]$	$+ \left(\frac{2{,}500 - w_0}{2{,}000}\right)\left(\frac{S - 6{,}000}{94{,}000}\right)[S4]$
		$+ \left(\frac{w_0 - 50}{450}\right)\left(\frac{S - 6{,}000}{94{,}000}\right)[S4]$	$+ \left(\frac{w_0 - 500}{2{,}000}\right)\left(\frac{100{,}000 - S}{94{,}000}\right)[S6]$
			$+ \left(\frac{w_0 - 500}{2{,}000}\right)\left(\frac{S - 6{,}000}{94{,}000}\right)[S7]$
100,001 +		$\left(\frac{500 - w_0}{450}\right)[S1]$	$\left(\frac{2{,}500 - w_0}{2{,}000}\right)[S4]$
		$+ \left(\frac{w_0 - 50}{450}\right)[S4]$	$+ \left(\frac{w_0 - 500}{2{,}000}\right)[S7]$

TABLE 16.4 *(continued)*

Show Pool (*$*)	w_0 = \$2,501–\$10,000	w_0 = \$10,001+
0–1,200	$\left(\frac{S}{1{,}200}\right)[S5]$	
1,201–6,000	$\left(\frac{6{,}000 - w_0}{4{,}800}\right)[S5]$ $+ \left(\frac{10{,}000 - w_0}{7{,}500}\right)\left(\frac{S - 1{,}200}{4{,}800}\right)[S6]$ $+ \left(\frac{w_0 - 2{,}500}{7{,}500}\right)\left(\frac{S - 1{,}200}{4{,}800}\right)[S8]$	$\left(\frac{6{,}000 - S}{4{,}800}\right)[S5]$ $+ \left(\frac{S - 1{,}200}{4{,}800}\right)[P8]$
6,001–100,000	$\left(\frac{10{,}000 - w_0}{7{,}500}\right)\left(\frac{100{,}000 - S}{94{,}000}\right)[S6]$ $+ \left(\frac{10{,}000 - w_0}{7{,}500}\right)\left(\frac{S - 6{,}000}{94{,}000}\right)[S7]$ $+ \left(\frac{w_0 - 2{,}500}{7{,}500}\right)\left(\frac{100{,}000 - S}{94{,}000}\right)[S8]$ $+ \left(\frac{w_0 - 2{,}500}{7{,}500}\right)\left(\frac{S - 6{,}000}{94{,}000}\right)[S9]$	$\left(\frac{100{,}000 - S}{94{,}000}\right)[S8]$ $+ \left(\frac{S - 6{,}000}{94{,}000}\right)[S9]$
100,001+	$\left(\frac{10{,}000 - w_0}{7{,}500}\right)[S7]$ $+ \left(\frac{w_0 - 2{,}500}{7{,}500}\right)[S9]$	[S9]

Suppose our betting wealth is \$400. We refer to the show Table 16.4 with w_o = \$400 and S = \$59,163. This indicates that the show regression equations needed from Table 16.3 are $S1$, $S3$, and $S4$. The $S1$ equation is weighted by $(500 - w_o)/450 = (500 - 400)/450 = 0.222$, and the $S3$ equation is weighted by

$$\left(\frac{w_0 - 50}{450}\right)\left(\frac{100{,}000 - S}{94{,}000}\right) = \left(\frac{400 - 50}{450}\right)\left(\frac{100{,}000 - 59{,}163}{94{,}000}\right) = 0.338,$$

and the $S4$ equation is weighted by

$$\left(\frac{w_0 - 50}{450}\right)\left(\frac{S - 6{,}000}{94{,}000}\right) = \left(\frac{400 - 50}{450}\right)\left(\frac{59{,}163 - 6{,}000}{94{,}000}\right) = 0.440.$$

The sum of the weights is one: $0.222 + 0.338 + 0.440 = 1.000$. From Table 16.3 with w_o = \$400, S = \$59,163, S_i = \$14,585, and $q = W_i/W = 155{,}321/398{,}851 = 0.389$, equation $S1$ is

$$10 + 183q^2 - 135q^3 - \frac{11S_i}{qS - 0.80S_i} = 10 + 183(0.389)^2 - 135(0.389)^3$$

$$- \frac{11(14{,}585)}{(0.389)(59{,}163) - (0.80)(14{,}585)}$$

$$= 10 + 27.7 - 7.9 - 14.1 = \$16.$$

For simplicity, we write q rather than q_i in these formulas.

Similarly, equation $S3$ is

$$86 + 1{,}516q^2 - 968q^3 - \frac{90.7S_i}{qS - 0.85S_i}$$

$$= 86 + 229.4 - 57.0 - 124.6 = \$134,$$

and equation $S4$ is

$$131 + 2{,}150q^2 - 1{,}778q^3 - \frac{150S_i}{qS - 0.70S_i}$$

$$= 131 + 325.3 - 104.7 - 170.9 = \$181.$$

From the calculated weightings, the optimal show bet is

$$(0.222)(16) + (0.338)(134) + (0.440)(181) = \$128.$$

Since California has $Q = 0.85$, we must include a correction factor for Q different from 0.829. We will return to our example after discussing this correction factor.

ADJUSTING THE OPTIMAL BET SIZE FOR DIFFERING TRACK PAYBACKS

An increase in the track payback Q is beneficial to the bettor, since it will mean larger payoffs on winning tickets. This is illustrated in Figure 9.4, which shows how a change in Q can have a surprisingly large effect on long-run profits. To account for differing Q's, we must be able to calculate expected values per dollar bet and optimal bet sizes for any Q. Equations (4.5) and (4.6) accomplish the former, and in this section we discuss how to adjust the optimal betting results of Tables 16.1–16.4, since they were calibrated for $Q = 0.829$. The adjustment steps follow:

1. Use Tables 16.1 and 16.2 to calculate the optimal place bet p^* or Tables 16.3 and 16.4 to calculate the optimal show bet s^* for a track payback of 0.829.
2. To p^* add the adjustment factor

$$(Q - 0.829)(3.16p^* + 0.0351w_o), \qquad (16.1)$$

or to s^* add the adjustment factor

$$(Q - 0.829)(3.16s^* + 0.0351w_o). \qquad (16.2)$$

These steps result in the correct optimal bet size. For Q larger than 0.829, the adjustment factor is positive; for Q less than 0.829, it is negative.

To illustrate, let's return to the Triple Bend Handicap example. Step 1 gave $s^* = \$128$. Since $w_o = \$400$ and $Q = 0.85$ in California, step 2 indicates that the correct optimal show bet is

$$128 + (0.85 - 0.829)[(3.16)(128) + (0.0351)(400)] = 128 + 9 = \$137.$$

ADJUSTMENTS FOR COUPLED ENTRIES

Occasionally, two or more horses are run as a single coupled entry, or simply as an entry, because (1) an owner or a trainer has two or more horses in the same race, or (2) there are more horses than the tote board can accommodate. The latter case is more commonly called a field. The entry wins, places, or shows if any of the horses wins, places, or shows. If the horses in the entry come first and second, all the place pool goes to the place tickets on the entry. If two of three of the in-the-money horses are from the entry, then two/thirds of the show pool goes to the tickets on the entry (rather than the usual third).* Finally, if all the in-the-money horses are from the entry, then the entire show pool goes to the show tickets on the entry.

*In some locales the split is 50-50, as each betting opportunity shares the profit equally.

Because of the possibility that the entry will collect the whole place pool or a major portion, or even all, of the show pool, the expected value per dollar bet to place or show on the entry is higher than if the entry were just one horse. Equations (4.7) and (4.8) indicate how to adjust the expected-value formulas for coupled entries. Here we describe the steps we took to adjust the optimal betting for coupled entries:

Place betting on horse i

1. Set $q = W_i/W$.
2. Let $\tilde{q} = 0.991q + 0.1378q^2 + 3.47 \times 10^{-7} w_o$. (16.3)
3. Use $\tilde{q}$, w_o, P, P_i in Tables 16.1 and 16.2.

Show betting on horse i

1. Set $q = W_i/W$.
2. Let $\tilde{q} = 1.07q + 4.13 \times 10^{-7}w_o - 0.00663$. (16.4)
3. Use $\tilde{q}$, w_o, S, S_i in Tables 16.3 and 16.4.

This method does not attempt the difficult task of setting up a new set of tables similar to Tables 16.1–16.4, but specifically designed for coupled entries. Rather, it simply increases q to $\tilde{q}$, where $\tilde{q}$ is the single-horse entry probability that leads you to bet the optimal amount when q is a two-horse entry probability.

There is still greater advantage to a three-or-more-horse entry or field. The additional benefits, however, become very small once you move beyond accounting for the entry as two horses. For this reason we suggest the simplification of considering all coupled entries or fields as two-horse entries.

Also, if the Dr. Z system underestimates the value of a bet on an entry (before we perform the adjustments), then it stands to reason that it overestimates the value of a bet on a single horse running against an entry. While this is true, tests have shown that this overestimation is very small and that for all practical purposes we may ignore it.

ADJUSTMENTS FOR MAKING MORE THAN ONE BET

The optimal-bet equations assume that you are making only one place bet or one show bet in a race. If the expected-value equations indicate that there is more than one Dr. Z system bet in the race, then it is *not* correct to calculate each of the optimal bets using the regression equations and then wager those amounts. If you did, you would often be overbetting—although often, for diversification reasons, you would be underbetting. This should indicate why accounting mathematically for multiple bets is difficult. The most common multiple bet is a Dr. Z system place bet and a Dr. Z system show bet on the same horse. We have carefully analyzed this situation.

If the expected-value formulas from Chapter Four, accounting for any necessary adjustment factors, indicate making a Dr. Z system bet to both place and to show on a horse, then the recommended procedure is as follows:

1. Use Tables 16.1 to 16.4 to determine the suggested place bet p^* and show bet s^*.
2. Make any necessary adjustments on p^* and s^* for $Q \neq 0.829$ or for a coupled entry.
3. Let the *true* optimal place bet $\tilde{p}^*$ be
$$\tilde{p}^* = \min\{p^*, 1.59p^* - 0.639s^*\} \tag{16.5}$$
and the true optimal show bet $\tilde{s}^*$ be
$$\tilde{s}^* = 0.907s^* - 0.134p^*. \tag{16.6}$$
4. Wager the amounts $\tilde{p}^*$ and $\tilde{s}^*$.

As an example, consider the 1984 Breeder's Cup Sprint. The six-furlong contest was run as the third race at Hollywood Park on November 10, 1984. The feeling was the Eillo would dominate if he did not break down. This son of Mr. Prospector had bandages on all four legs and ran in a very dangerous style. He was a Dr. Z system bet both to place and show.

With three minutes to go:

	Totals	*#5 Eillo*	*Expected Value Per Dollar Bet*	*Optimal Bet*
Odds		6-5		
Win	310,679	114,405		
Place	123,682	30,439	1.19	263
Show	87,548	20,666	1.18	413

With one minute to go:

	Totals	*#5 Eillo*	*Expected Value Per Dollar Bet*	*Optimal Bet*
Odds		7-5		
Win	415,309	146,279		
Place	162,447	40,278	1.14	223
Show	113,462	25,230	1.18	423

The optimal bets of $223 to place and $423 to show were each based on making only one bet. Since both wagers were Dr. Z system bets it would be too risky and overbetting to make both of these wagers at these levels.

Using formulas (16.5) and (16.6) yields the optimal wagers of $351 to show and $84 to place. The place bet is minimum $(p^*, 1.59p^* - 0.639s^*)$

*Flow Chart of the Betting Rules for a Single Bet to Place or Show**

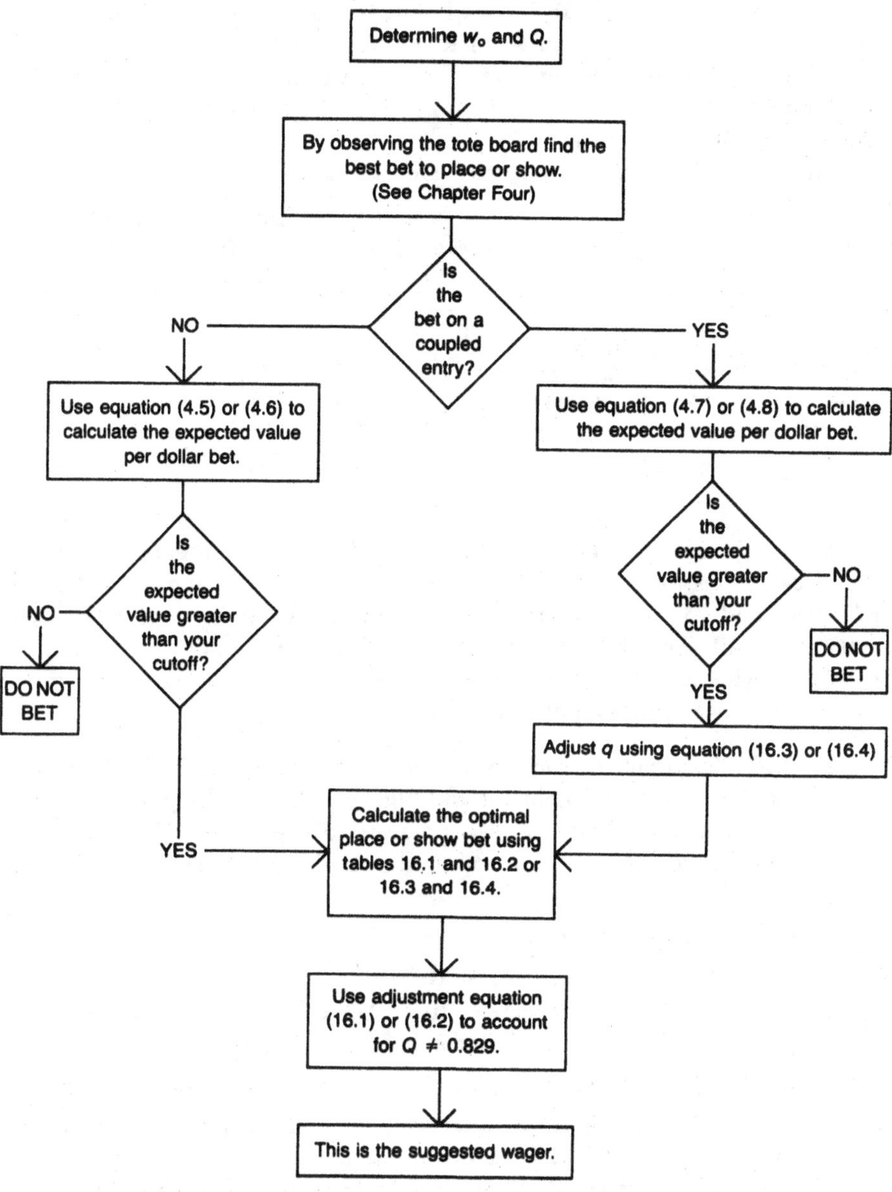

*For place and show bets on the same horse, follow this flow chart for each bet and then adjust the place- and show-betting amounts using equations (16.5) and (16.6).

= minimum [223, 1.59(223) − 0.639(423)] = minimum (223, 84.20) = $84.20. Here p* = 223 and s* = 423. The show bet is 0.907s* − 0.134p* = 0.907(423) − 0.134(223) = $351. So the optimal bets at one minute to post were $84 to place and $351 to show.

Eillo won the race leading wire to wire just nipping the charging Commemorate at the finish. He paid $4.60 to win, an excellent $3.80 to place and a respectable $2.80 to show.

The final tote board and payoffs were as follows:

	Totals	*#5 Eillo*	*Expected Value Per Dollar Bet*	*Optimal Bets (not considering both wagers)*	*Optimal Bets (considering both wagers)*
Odds		6-5			
Win	457,470	163,868			
Place	180,253	46,216	1.13	215	48
Show	125,282	27,584	1.19	460	388

Warning: The equations in Tables 16.1 and 16.3 are the result of statistical regressions using data with (1) q between 0.1 and 0.7; and (2) EX Place and EX Show (equations [4.3] and [4.4], respectively) between 1.05 and 1.40. Therefore the equations in Tables 16.1 and 16.4 should be used only when these conditions are met. However, we can deal with cases that do not meet these conditions as follows:

1. If q is less than 0.1 we recommend no wagering since the long-shot bias, presented in Table 3.1 and Figure 3.2, is working against you. If q is greater than 0.7 it is possible to use Tables 16.1–16.4 by pretending q is 0.7 and scaling down the other data inputs. The procedure is:

   If $q > 0.7$ then let (i) $\tilde{q} = 0.7$
   (ii) $\tilde{P}_i = (0.7/q)P_i$
   (iii) $\tilde{S}_i = (0.7/q)S_i$
   (iv) input $\tilde{q}, \tilde{P}_i$, P, $\tilde{S}_i$, and S.

2. If EX Place or EX Show is less than 1.10, we recommend no wagering; even with corrections for differing Q it is unlikely that the adjusted expected value would meet the suggested cutoffs.

   If EX Place or EX Show is greater than 1.40, another scaling-down procedure is suggested using Tables 16.1–16.4.

   Let (i) $\tilde{P}_i = qP/1.93$
   (ii) $\tilde{S}_i = qS/2.32$
   (iii) input q, $\tilde{P}_i$, P, $\tilde{S}_i$, and S.

An example of this procedure is Viendra in the Matinee Handicap at Hollywood Park discussed in Chapter Six. Both of the scaling-down procedures indicate a lower bet than is optimal, but usually it is close to optimal.

One final warning: For horses with a very low probability of winning and a very low expected value per dollar bet, the betting equations will indicate a negative bet. Obviously in these cases the optimal bet is zero.

USING FUNDAMENTAL INFORMATION TO IMPROVE THE DR. Z SYSTEM

Throughout this book we have emphasized that the win market is efficient: That is, a good estimate of the probability of horse i to win is $q_i = W_i/W$. However we have also mentioned that there are some expert handicappers who have the ability, over the long run, to calculate better win probabilities than the crowd. That is, they can determine their own q_i values. Can you, as such a handicapper, use the Dr. Z system? The answer is yes and the adjustments are very easy:

1. In the expected-value formulas of Chapter Four, use your estimated win probability q_i instead of W_i/W.
2. In the optimal-bet-size equations of this chapter use your q_i instead of the crowd's $q = W_i/W$.

What we are suggesting here is very similar to what we discussed in Chapter Seven. There we looked at the 1982 Belmont Stakes, which provided for other-track betting at many tracks across the United States. While each track had its own q_i estimates, we believed that since the home-track Belmont crowd had access to more information, their q_i estimates were the best. That meant that if we were at one of the other tracks, we would prefer to use the Belmont track win odds over our own track's win odds when calculating expected values and optimal bet sizes. This would be possible if our track presented the betting mutuels at Belmont on the infield screen or over the closed-circuit televisions, and this is sometimes actually done. Handicappers with their own q_i estimates would use them in a similar way.

In Appendix C we discuss the dosage theory and its remarkable predictive record for the Kentucky Derby. Hausch, Winkler and Ziemba (1987, forthcoming) have attempted to combine dosage values with the public's wagers to generate more accurate probabilities of success than the odds board provides. The idea is to lower the true odds and hence increase the probability of winning for horses with good dosage values and do the reverse for those with bad dosage values. For example, consider the wager of Sunny's Halo in the 1983 Kentucky Derby. With his excellent dosage values a handicapper might argue that the true win odds on Sunny's Halo should be about 2–1 instead of the 5–2 track odds. According to Table 3.5, this gives a win probability of about 28%. So we have:

	Totals	#8 Sunny's Halo	Expected Value per Dollar Bet	Optimal Kelly Wager with a bankroll of $1,494.70
Odds				
Win	1	0.28		
Show	1,098,076	175,643	1.28	$360

The 1.28 expected value and wager of $360 compare with 1.14 and $87 which we used; see the discussion in Chapter Eleven. Obviously, such a handicapper would have raised the odds on Althea, Chief's Crown, Snow Chief and other Kentucky Derby horses with poor dosage figures.

RECOMMENDED HANDICAPPING BOOKS

The raw material of handicapping is contained in the past-performance pages, official result charts, jockey and trainer standings, workout reports, and columns of news and commentary published in the *Daily Racing Form*. Individual methods of interpreting and evaluating this material vary widely, but the substance of handicapping is far more significant than the procedures devised by its practitioners. No matter what his school of thought may purport to be, and no matter how elaborate the gadgetry, graphs, tabulations, and worksheets he or she may use, the handicapper's effectiveness remains below par until his or her skills are applied to the full range of available information (see *American Racing Manual*, 1986 p. 716).

Handicapping is still, and perhaps will remain, an art. Statistical and computer methods that combine the myriad factors that make up a race to generate the probability of a given horse's winning have, so far, met with limited success. The difficulty is that there are so many relevant factors, and these factors interact in different ways as circumstances change. The *American Racing Manual*'s statement on the fundamentals of handicapping considers the most important basic factors to be class, form, consistency, distance, pace, speed, weights, rider, mud, turf, post position and paddock, and post parade. Each of these basic factors are compositions of a number of subfactors. Trying to put them together is a stimulating challenge. Good advice to help you in this regard can be found in the following: Ainslie (1986), Beyer (1975, 1983), Davidowitz (1979), Ledbetter and Ainslie (1980), Mitchell (1985a, b), Quinn (1986a, 1987b), and Quirin (1984, 1986) and especially Quirin (1979).

Each of these authors is an extremely knowledgeable and successful handicapper with over twenty years of experience. Their books are also written in a very lucid style. They are all active as handicappers and have written other books or are currently writing new books.

In Quinn (1987a) the author provides compact "abstracts" to give you the main ideas of many of the important contributions made to handicapping since 1965.

Finally, a bibliography listing many of the existing handicapping books through 1979 with brief comments on their contents is Gardner (1980). These books are probably available at your local library.

Good luck! Remember that to break even on bets to win, you will need to be at least 15% better than the average bettor, who establishes probabilities of winning for horse i or W_i/W.

17 Epilogue

WHY ARE WE MAKING THE DR. Z SYSTEM PUBLIC?

I am frequently asked why I don't quit my job as a university professor and make more money betting on the horses full time. People are shocked that I give lectures, often without honoraria, to academics and others on the Dr. Z system and its development. They believe that I should have a whole army of Dr. Z system players betting at major North American racetracks and reap a substantial share of the profits. You may be wondering about this as well, so here's my explanation.

Academics by their very nature are inquiring people. I have more interests and demands on my time than I ever dreamed possible. For me, it's exciting to be involved in research in various areas, such as portfolio theory and management and other areas of finance, optimization under uncertainty—my true academic love, how to make decisions in an uncertain world, energy policy, and my special hobbies of Oriental rugs and the mathematics of gambling. Professors like to share their findings with colleagues all over the world—that's the academic way.

This academic jet-setting life style aside, why are Don and I making the Dr. Z system public? I'm convinced that the benefits of doing so exceed the satisfaction and profits from keeping the Dr. Z system secret. First, we shall still be able to play the Dr. Z system when we wish to join in with all the others. Second, a best-selling book brings a number of attendant benefits to the authors. Besides the royalties, it opens doors to new books, consulting and lecture activities, and other useful contacts. The exposure and attention are fun and rewarding as well. Third, the process of developing the Dr. Z system and writing this book taught us a lot about the subject of horse-racing and efficient betting markets. This will certainly be useful to us. Fourth, it is a supreme intellectual challenge to beat the races, and we wanted to present our full evidence to our critics, as well as to the general public. We believe that the evidence is quite convincing. The Dr. Z system actually works. Obviously, more evidence will be forthcoming. Many academics and serious horse players will be skeptical at first. Among other things, our whole approach of exploiting the inefficiencies in betting markets is very likely to be new to many, if not most, people. We hope this book is thorough enough to allay such skepticism. Fifth, there is a great threat of rediscovery. Several articles that we mentioned in Chapter One had ideas that are consistent with our approach. After publishing the paper "Efficiency of the Market for Racetrack Betting" in *Management Science* in November 1981, and after giving numerous talks to academic groups, as well as appearing on radio and television talk shows, we found that our ideas are getting around. If we had not written this book, someone else probably would have. We felt it should be us.

WILL THE MARKET BECOME EFFICIENT: HOW MUCH CAN BE BET BY ALL DR. Z SYSTEM BETTORS?

Naturally, as more people learn about and utilize the Dr. Z system, the place- and show-betting markets will tend to become more efficient. We would like to know the answers to two basic questions: How many people can play the Dr. Z system and still allow it to provide the kind of profits we have obtained in this book? and How many people need to be playing before their bets make the place- and show-betting markets so efficient that the profit margins of all Dr. Z systems players will shrink to virtually zero? We also need to ask how likely is the latter situation to occur, how can you recognize it, and what should you do about it?

Let's look first at the initial question and try to assess how many people can play the Dr. Z system and have it still provide the 10%–20% return on investment we have described. One way to analyze this is to determine how much additional money can be bet on a particular horse to place or show before the expected value per dollar bet reaches the suggested cutoffs for good betting opportunities. Figures 17.1, 17.2, and 17.3 give you the information to calculate this amount for place bets for cutoffs of 1.10, 1.14, and 1.18, respectively. Similarly, Figures 17.4, 17.5, and 17.6 provide this same information for show bets. Recall that 1.10 was suggested when the very highest-quality horses and large pools were available at events such as the Kentucky Derby Day, 1.14 for top-quality tracks on ordinary days, and 1.18 at other tracks. These figures are based on a track take of 17.1%. To use these figures, determine the present expected value per dollar bet using equations (4.5) for place bets and (4.6) for show bets. Then, using the probability of winning for the horse in question, read off the additional fraction of the current place or show pool that can be bet on the vertical axis.

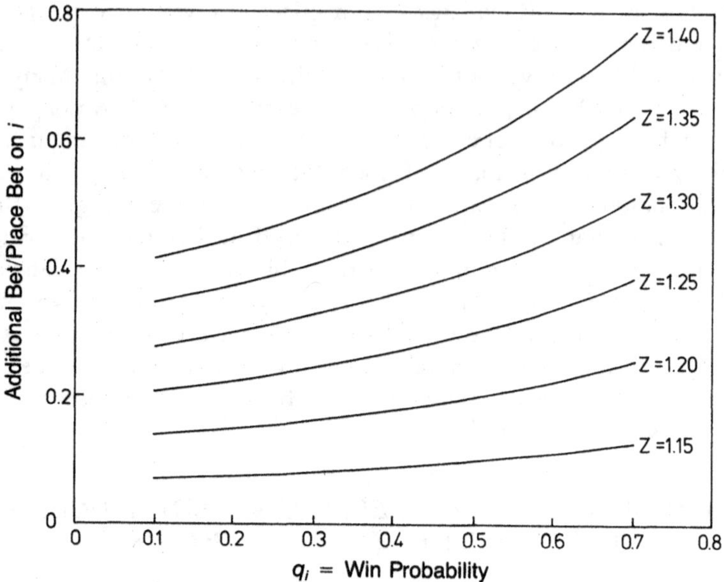

Figure 17.1 How much can be bet, B, by Dr. Z system bettors relative to the crowd's place bet P_i on horse i to lower the expected value to place i from Z to 1.10 when the track take is 17.1%

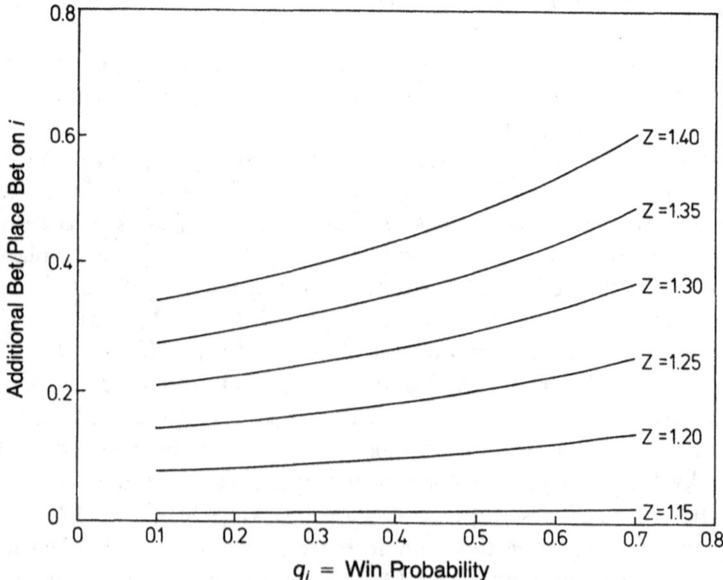

Figure 17.2 How much can be bet, B, by Dr. Z system bettors relative to the crowd's place bet P_i on horse i to lower the expected value to place on i from Z to 1.14 when the track take is 17.1%

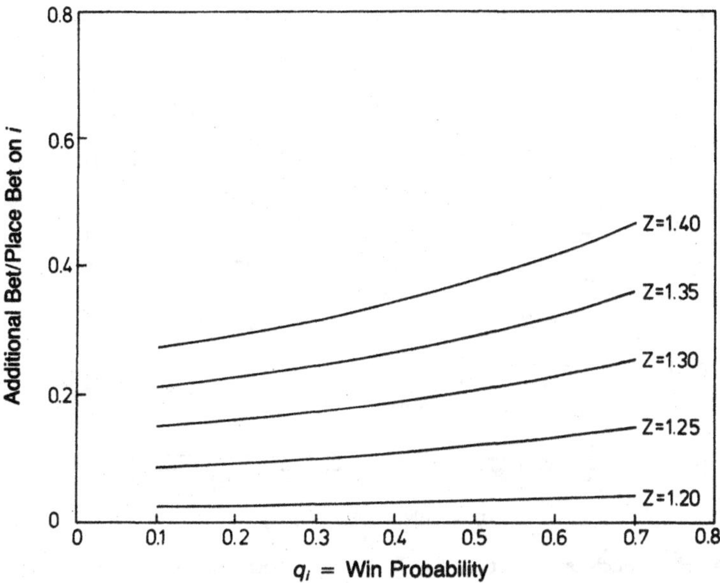

Figure 17.3 How much can be bet, B, by Dr. Z system bettors relative to the crowd's place bet P_i on horse i to lower the expected value to place on i from Z to 1.18 when the track take is 17.1%

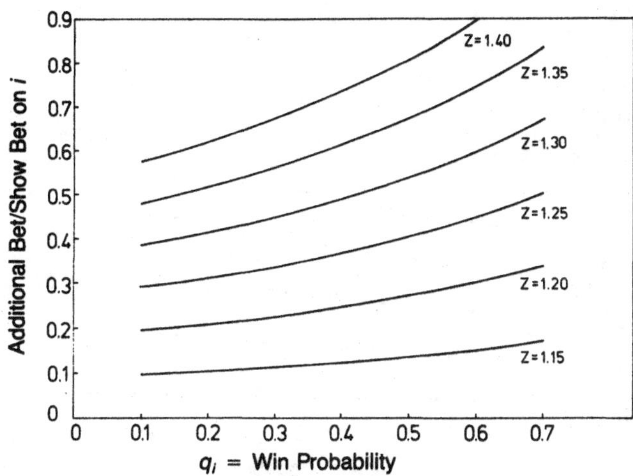

Figure 17.4 How much can be bet, B, by Dr. Z system bettors relative to the crowd's show bet S_i on horse i to lower the expected value to show on i from Z to 1.10 when the track take is 17.1%

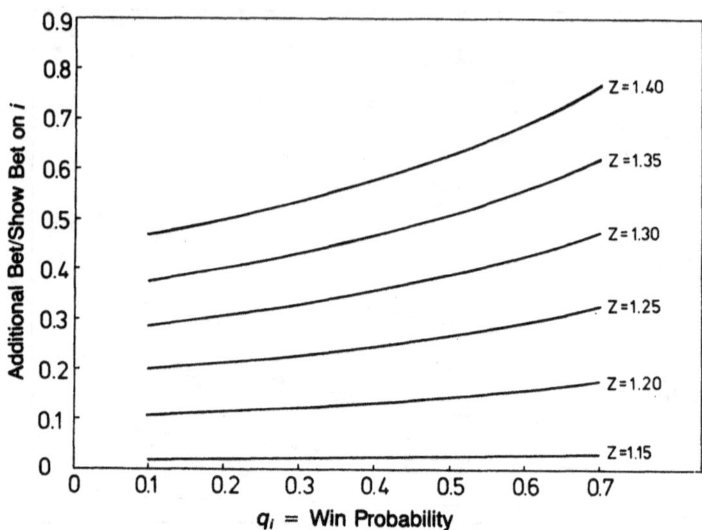

Figure 17.5 How much can be bet, B, by Dr. Z system bettors relative to the crowd's show bet S_i on horse i to lower the expected value to show on i from Z to 1.14 when the track take is 17.1%

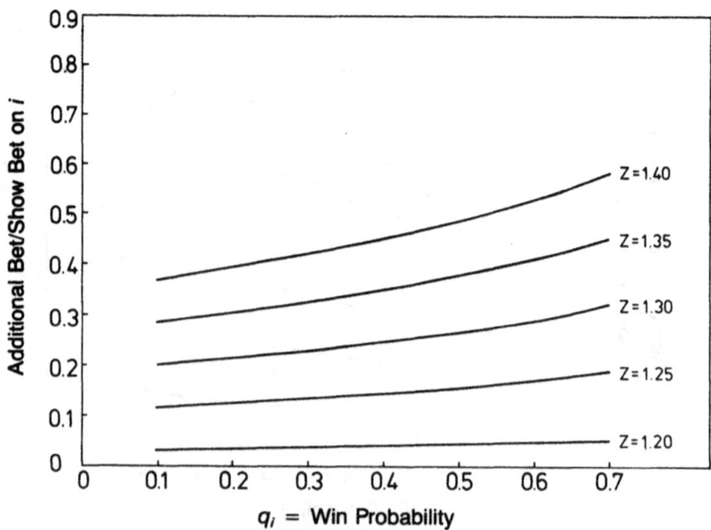

Figure 17.6 How much can be bet, B, by Dr. Z system bettors relative to the crowd's show bet S_i on horse i to lower the expected value to show on i from Z to 1.18 when the track take is 17.1%

Table 17.1 provides guidance concerning our two basic questions and addresses an additional point. In this table we made the following experiment: For each potential Dr. Z system bettor, we posited that his or her optimal bet is computed about one minute to post time. Then, using the final tote-board values, we can compute how many Dr. Z system bettors there can be before the expected value per dollar bet drops to the suggested cutoff, or to 1.06, or to 1.02. At an expected value of 1.06, we still should expect to make a rate of return on our bets of about 5% based on the data in Table 5.2. Finally at 1.02, we would expect simply to break even. This experiment is close to what might happen in practice, except for the fact that we or any other Dr. Z bettors who now bet on these races would not be counted, so to be fair one might add these bettors to those in Table 17.1. Also, Dr. Z system bettors following the Kelly criterion make hefty bets, so if many bettors are following a fractional Kelly criterion, even more people can bet.

The number of Dr. Z bettors that you can have depends upon four factors: the size of the place- or show-betting pools, the expected value per dollar bet, the probability that the horse wins the race, and the betting wealth of the Dr. Z system players. We have used examples with expected-value cutoffs of 1.10 and 1.14. They have a variety of expected values per

TABLE 17.1 ***Amount that can be bet by and number of Dr. Z system bettors to drop the expected value per dollar bet to the Dr. Z system bet cutoff, to a 5% - return-on-investment level, or the break-even point***

Name of Horse	Type of Bet	Expected Value per Dollar Bet at Post Time	Win Pool at Post Time ($)	Win Bet on *i* at Post Time ($)	Probability of Winning	Show or Place Pool at Post Time ($)
C'est Moi Cheri Hollywood Park Chapter Five, pp. 122–125	Show	1.29	335,698	136,125	0.406	56,841
Sunny's Halo Churchill Downs Chapter Twelve, pp. 257–269	Show	1.14	3,143,669	745,524	0.237	1,099,990
John Henry Santa Anita Chapter Eight, pp. 194–199	Place	1.22	425,976	149,879	0.352	122,847
	Show	1.34	425,976	149,879	0.352	79,645
Viendra Hollywood Park Chapter Six, pp. 162–166	Show	1.47	129,233	16,353	0.127	27,488

TABLE 17.1 ***(continued)***

Show or Place Bet on *i* at Post Time ($)	Recommended Expected-Value Cutoff	Total Amount That Can Be Bet by All Dr. Z System Bettors before the Expected Value per Dollar Bet Reaches the Cutoff ($)	Optimal Dr. Z System Bets with Betting Wealths (using data up to one minute to post time) of			
			$200	$500	$1,000	$2,000
12,284	1.14	4,814	91	227	383	694
179,758	1.10	19,323	11	31	52	96
27,894	1.14	3,909	14	33	70	143
14,007	1.14	6,916	68	173	311	587
1,149	1.14	1,411	22	56	72	106

Number of Dr. Z System Bettors Who Can Make the Usual Gains with Betting Wealths of				Total Amount That Can Be Bet by All Dr. Z System Bettors before the Expected Value per Dollar Bet Becomes 1.06 ($)	Number of Dr. Z System Bettors Needed to Drop the Expected Value per Dollar Bet to 1.06, so All Bettors Will Still Have Modest Profits with Betting Wealths of			
$200	$500	$1,000	$2,000		$200	$500	$1,000	$2,000
53	21	13	7	9,229	101	40	24	13
1,757	623	372	201	41,175	3,743	1,328	792	429
279	118	56	27	8,925	637	270	127	62
102	40	22	12	12,029	177	70	39	20
64	25	20	13	1,923	87	34	27	18

Total Amount That Can Be Bet by All Dr. Z System Bettors before the Expected Value per Dollar Bet Becomes 1.02 ($)	Number of Dr. Z System Bettors Needed to Drop the Expected Value per Dollar Bet to 1.02, so All Bettors Will Simply Break Even with Betting Wealths of			
	$200	$500	$1,000	$2,000
12,417	136	54	32	18
68,409	6,219	2,207	1,316	713
12,077	862	366	173	84
15,654	230	90	50	27
2,264	103	40	31	21

dollar bet to place or show, ranging from a low of 1.14 to a high of 1.47. They also have various probabilities of winning that vary from 0.127 to 0.406. The total amount that can be bet in the three categories, based on likely average rates of return of 10%–20%, 5%, and 0%, ranges from $1,411 to $19,323, $1,923 to $41,175, and $2,264 to $68,409, respectively. At the 10%–20% level, the number of Dr. Z system bettors ranges from 53 to 1,757 bettors with $200 fortunes down to 7 to 201 bettors with $2,000 fortunes. At the 5% level, the ranges are 87 to 3,743 bettors with $200 and 13 to 429 bettors with $2,000. Finally, we reach the 0% level, where there are between 103 and 6,219 bettors with $200 and 18 to 713 bettors with $2,000.

ADVICE AND CONCLUSIONS

1. When the bet is good and the track mutuels are large, it will usually take quite a few Dr. Z system bettors to make the market efficient.
2. A few very big bettors can certainly do the others in, so you must keep an eye out for them.
3. If you think such bettors are at your track, simply watch the tote board and either don't bet or bet modestly. If the bet has an expected value of 1.20 with two minutes to post time, and it's 1 at post time, your worst fears have been realized.
4. Don't despair. Take a few weeks' holiday, then try it again; the big bettors may have gone away.
5. Remember that at tracks with small mutuel pools the effect of large bettors will be even greater. At such tracks, however, there are proportionally fewer people betting, and any Dr. Z system bettor bets less as well, since his or her bets will influence the odds.
6. Our experience with inefficiences in other areas, such as blackjack and options markets, shows that it takes quite a while before the inefficiency is wiped out; the same will probably be true here.
7. People are greedy and like to brag. That will not change! Sooner or later, they will go back to their old bets and you will be able to apply the Dr. Z system successfully again, even if the market does become efficient temporarily.

USING THE DR. Z SYSTEM FOR HARNESS RACING

Although this book has been concerned with thoroughbred racing, the Dr. Z system can be used in the same way at harness races. As we saw in Figure 3.5 and Table 3.4, the win market at harness tracks is efficient. It shows the usual favorite–long-shot bias. You can make profitable place and show bets.

To test the Dr. Z system, I went to Cloverdale Raceway near Vancouver on Saturday, February 12, 1983. The program contains the past performances, driver standings, post-position statistics, percentage of winning favorites, etc. The track take for straight bets is 16.1%; it's 3% higher, or 19.1%, for the features. The driver standings report the in-the-money finishes and win-place percentages. But you need to compute the in-the-money percentages, as I have done below. Harness races generally have eight or fewer horses and standouts dominate, so top jockeys have very high in-the-money percentages. A guide for reading the racing information and a list of the major harness racing tracks in North America appear as well.

TABLE 17.2 ***Driver standings up to and including Saturday, February 5, 1983; minimum 1 drive per day (75 drives to qualify)***

Up to and Including Saturday, February 5/83
Minimum 1 Drive per Day (75 drives to qualify)

	Starts	First	Second	Third	Win and Place (%)	In the Money (%)
1. Keith Linton	281	83	45	43	45.6	60.9
2. Joe Hudon	339	90	59	50	44.0	58.7
3. John Glen	95	22	20	8	44.2	52.6
4. Mike Evans	112	24	21	16	40.2	54.5
5. Bill Davis	171	38	26	23	37.4	50.9
6. Dave Jungquist	171	25	21	37	26.9	48.5
7. Mike Stymest	86	16	20	18	41.9	62.8
8. Paul Megens	236	34	37	26	30.1	41.1
9. Sten Ericsson	202	30	27	26	28.2	41.1
10. Jim Wiggins	243	28	42	27	28.8	39.9
11. Bill Babineau	81	10	7	7	21.0	29.6
12. Bob Cameron	85	7	12	19	22.4	44.7
13. Keith Quinlan	300	29	48	44	25.7	40.3
14. Brent Beelby	206	23	25	32	23.3	38.8
15. Howard Portelance	176	22	14	31	20.5	38.1
16. Denis Linford	174	19	22	24	23.6	37.4
17. Ed Stewart	86	8	13	12	24.4	38.4
18. Phil Coleman	138	11	22	22	23.9	39.9
19. Clark Beelby	99	13	11	7	24.2	31.3
20. Al Bowman	82	9	11	8	24.4	34.1
21. Leonard Hill	113	12	14	13	23.0	34.5

WINNING POST POSITIONS

Up to and including Sat., Feb. 5, 1983 – 75 Race Days, 751 Races

	1	2	3	4	5	6	7	8
No. of Starts	751	751	751	751	748	723	635	630
No. of Wins	134	108	97	145	84	60	43	82
	dead heat	dead heat		dead heat		dead heat		

% OF WINNING FAVORITES

Up to and including Sat., Feb. 5, 1983 – 75 Race Days, 751 Races

Order of finish of favorite	1	2	3	4	5	6	7	8
No. of Wins of Favorite	286	140	108	62	48	49	28	30
% of Wins of Favorite	38%	19%	14%	8%	6%	6%	4%	5%

71% in the money

OF EVERY $1 WAGERED AT CLOVERDALE RACEWAY . . .

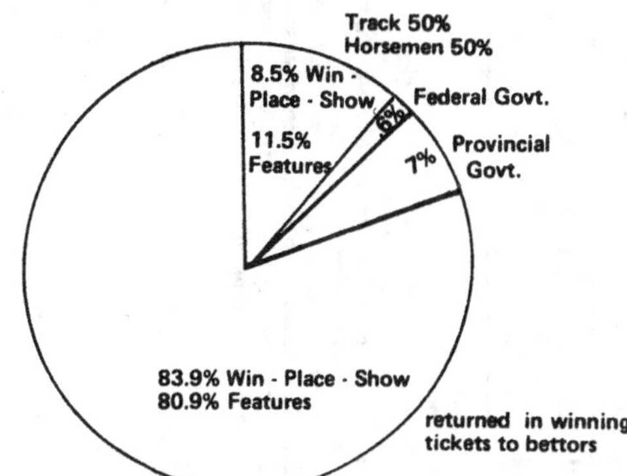

HORSEMEN'S SHARE:
Distributed in the form of purses.

TRACK'S SHARE:
Used for operating costs and capital improvements.

FEDERAL GOVERNMENT SHARE:
Used to defray supervision costs.

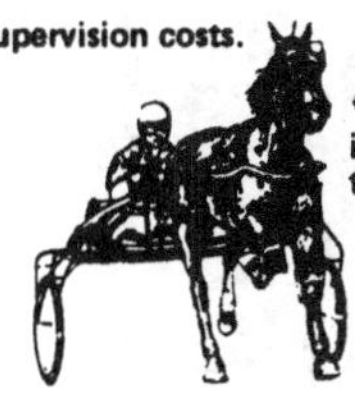

PROVINCIAL GOVERNMENT SHARE:
3.5% General Revenue
3.5% horse racing improvement fund, as follows:
1.0% B.C. Bred Purse Suppl.
.9% Purse & Stake Suppl.
.6% Sire Stakes
.5% Broodmare program
.4% Filly & Mare program
.1% Reserve Fund
*Note: These supplements are NOT included in the advertised purse in the program.

HOW TO READ THE RACING INFORMATION

1	2	3	4		
BARON NUFF	B. g.	1976,	Goodnuff — Baroness Brenna — Baron Hanover		
	5 Hudon Stables, Surrey, B. C.			1983 1 0 0 1 $ 600	8
Joe Hudon, A, 165, blue, orange 11	10 Tr. J. Hudon	Time 1:59^{3}M,5, (6)	Earn. to 1983 $87,300 (7)	1982 2:02^{3}H 4 2 1 0 $ 6,150	9

1. BARON NUFF. This is the name of the horse.
2. B. g. This indicates the color and sex of the horse. Here the "B" is an abbreviation for Bay and the "g" means he is a gelding.
3. 1976. This is the year the horse was foaled. He is now a seven year old.
4. Goodnuff – Baroness Brenna – Baron Hanover. In order these are the names of the horse's father (sire), mother (dam), and the sire of the dam.
5. Hudon Stables, Surrey, B. C. This is the owner and his address.
6. Time 1:59.4F,4. This is the best winning time ever for Baron Nuff. His mark of 1:59.4 was taken on a five-eights track as a four-year old.
7. Earnings to 1983 $87,300. This is a record of the total amount he has won in purses to December 31, 1982.
8. 1983 1 0 0 1 $600 . This is his performance recap from this year (to Jan.20). He started once and finished third for total earnings of $600.
9. 1982 2:02.3H 4 2 1 0 $6,150. This is his performance recap from last year. His best winning time was 2:02.3 and he started 4 times, had 2 wins and 1 second for earnings of $6,150.
10. Tr. J. Hudon. J. Hudon trains the horse.
11. JOE HUDON, A, 165, BLUE, ORANGE. This the name of the driver, his license classification, weight and the color of his silks.

PAST PERFORMANCE LINE

Date of Race	Track	Race Number	Track Condition	Condition	Purse	Distance	Leader's time at ¼	Leader's time at ½	Leader's time at ¾	Winner's time	Post Position	Pos. & lengths at ¼	Pos. & lengths at ½	Pos. & lengths at ¾	Pos. & lengths at Stretch	Pos. & lengths at Finish	Horse's actual time	Dollar Odds	Driver	Winner	Second Horse	Third Horse	Temperature	No. of starters
Mr21^{1}Clv^{6}			ft	Inv	6000	m	:29^{2}	1:01	1:31^{3}	2:00^{4}	3	$1^{1\frac{1}{2}}$	$1^{1\frac{1}{2}}$	1^{1}	1^{2}	$1^{3\frac{1}{2}}$	2:00^{4}	*.45	J.Hudon	BaronNuff	SengaRoly	Jodana	15	4

Track ratings are determined from individual times made by horses at one track compared with times made by the same horses at other tracks during comparable seasons of the year, over tracks rated "fast", without breaks or parkouts and at the standard mile distance.

AC (5/8)	Atlantic City, N.J.	2:03.2
AP (1)	Arlington Park	2:04.1
Aur (1/2)	Aurora Downs, Ill.	2.07
Bal (1/2)	Balmoral Park, Ill.	2:03.1
BaR (1/2)	Barrie Raceway, Ont.	2:05.3
Bat (1/2)	Batavia Downs, N.Y.	2:05.1
BB (5/8)	Blue Bonnets, Que.	2:03.1
BgR (1/2)	Bangor Raceway, Main.	2.07.1
Blm (1/2)	Bloomsburg, Pa.	2:06.1
Blv (1/2)	Belleville, Que.	2:06.4
BM (1)	Bay Meadows, Calif.	2:04
BR (1/2)	Buffalo Raceway, N.Y.	2:05.1
Brd (5/8)	Brandywine Raceway, Del	2:02.3
Cen (1/2)	Centennial Park, Colo	2.05.2
Cls (1/2)	Carlisle, Pa.	2.05.
Cka (3/4)	Cahokia Downs, Ill.	2:04.1
Cltn (1/2)	Clinton Raceway, Ont	2:06
Col (1/2)	Columbus, Ohio	2:05.1
Clv (1/2)	Cloverdale Raceway, B.C.	2.06.2
Cum (1/2)	Cumberland Raceway	2:06.1
Conn (1/2)	Connaught Park, Que.	2:05.3
DD (5/8)	Dover Downs, Del.	2:04.2
Del (1/2)	Delaware, Ohio	2:04.3
Dres (1/2)	Dresden Raceway, Ont.	2:05.3
DuQ (1)	Du Quoin, Ill	2:01.1
Elm (1/2)	Elmira Raceway, Ont.	2:05.4
FD (5/8)	Frontenac Downs, Ont	2:04.2
Fhld (1)	Freehold Raceway, N.J.	2:04.
FlmD (1/2)	Flamboro Downs, Ont	2:04.4
FP (1)	Fairmount Park, Ill.	2:03.3
GCy (5/8)	Garden City, Ont.	2:03.3
GG (1)	Golden Gate Fields, Calif	2:03.1
Gor (1/2)	Gorham Raceway	2:06.1

Gos (1/2)	Goshen N.Y.	2.05
GMP (1)	Green Mountain Park	2:04.3
GrR (5/8)	Greenwood Raceway, Ont.	2:04.2
Har (1/2)	Harrington Raceway, Del.	2.05.2
Haw (1)	Hawthorne Park, Ill.	2:03.4
Haz (5/8)	Hazel Park, Mich.	2:04
Hin (1/2)	Hinsdale Raceway, N.H.	2:06.1
Hnvr (1/2)	Hanover Raceway, Ont.	2.05.5
HP (1)	Hollywood Park, Calif.	2:01.4
Ind (1)	Indianapolis, Ind.	2:01.4
Jac (1/2)	Jackson Raceway, Mich	2:05.
KD (5/8)	Kawartha Downs, Ont.	2:04.3
LA (5/8)	Los Alamitos, Calif.	2.03.4
Lat (1/2)	Latonia-Kentucky	2.03
Lau (5/8)	Laurel Raceway, Maryland.	2.03.1
LB (5/8)	Liberty Bell, Penn.	2:02.3
Lea (1/2)	Leamington Raceway, Ont.	2:05.1
Leb (1/2)	Lebanon Raceway, Ohio	2:06.2
Lew (1/2)	Lewiston Raceway, Me.	2:05.2
Lex (1)	Lexington Trots, Kentucky	2:01.2
Lon (1/2)	Western Fair Raceway, Ont	2:05.1
LouD (1/2)	Louisville Downs, Kentucky	2:05.2
May (1/2)	Maywood Park, Ill.	2:04
Mea (5/8)	The Meadows, Penn.	2:03.
Mid (1/2)	Midwest Raceway, Kty.	2.05.3
Mlds (1)	Meadowlands, N.J.	2:01.2
Moh (5/8)	Mohawk Raceway, Ont.	2:04.
MqD (5/8)	Marquis Downs, Sask.	2:04.2
MR (1/2)	Monticello Raceway, N.Y.	2:03.1
NEn (5/8)	New England, Mass.	2:03.
Nfld (1/2)	Northfield Park, Ohio	2:04.3
Nor (1/2)	Northville Downs, Mich.	2.05
NP (5/8)	Northlands Park, Alta.	2:04.2

OcD (1/2)	Ocean Downs, Md.	2:04.3
Orn (1/2)	Orangeville Raceway, Ont.	2:06.2
OwnS (1/2)	Owen Sound, Ont.	2:06.4
PcD (5/8)	Pocono Downs, Penn.	2:03.1
PPk (5/8)	Pompano Park, Fla.	2:03.2
PVR (5/8)	Pre Vert Raceway, Que.	2:06.
QcD (5/8)	Quad City Downs, Ill.	2:04.
Que (1/2)	Quebec City, Que.	2:04.4
RC (5/8)	Rideau Carlton, Ont.	2:04
Reg (1/2)	Exhibition Track, Sask	2:05.3
Ric (1/2)	Richelieu Park, Que	2:04.
Roc (1/2)	Rockingham Park, N.H.	2:04.4
RoR (1/2)	Rosecroft Raceway, Md.	2:03.3
RP (5/8)	Raceway Park, Ohio	2:03.3
RR (1/2)	Roosevelt Raceway, N.Y.	2:03.2
Sac (1)	Cal Expo, Sacramento, Calif.	2:03.2
Sca (1/2)	Scarborough Downs, Me.	2:05.3
San (5/8)	Sandown Raceway, B.C.	NR
ScD (5/8)	Scioto Downs, Ohio	2:02.2
Sem (1)	Seminole Downs, Fla	2:03.2
Spk (5/8)	Sportsman's Park, Ill.	2:02.4
Spr (1)	Springfield, Ill.	2.01
Stga (1/2)	Saratoga Raceway, N.Y.	2:03.2
StP (5/8)	Stampede Park, Alta.	2:04.2
Sud (1/2)	Sudbury Downs, Ont.	2:05.3
TrR (1/2)	Hippodrome Trois-Riv., Que.	2:05.
VD (3/4)	Vernon Downs, N.Y.	2:01.4
Was (1)	Washington Park, Wash.	2:03.1
Wdsk (1/2)	Woodstock Raceway, Ont.	2:06.1
Wol (1)	Wolverine Raceway	2:01.2
WR (5/8)	Windsor Raceway, Ont.	2:04.
YR (1/2)	Yonkers Raceway, N.Y.	2:03.3

3rd race

BLACK SADDLE CLOTH

1 MILE PACE
VIP Tavern Feature

EXACTOR

SUPER 6

EXACTOR

PURSE $2300 — Claiming Handicap — Claiming Prices $3500 to $4000 plus allowances.

HANDICAP SELECTIONS: 5 – 1 – 6

ASK FOR HORSE BY THIS NUMBER

1 DECK HAND

$3500 — 7-2

B. g. 1972, Shadow Wave — Rhonda Byrd — Poplar Byrd
S. Petrachuk, Surrey, B. C.
Steve Petrachuk, A, 160, blue, white — Tr. S. Petrachuk — Time 2:01M,4, Earn. to 1983 $81,417

1983 6 0 1 1 $ 950
1982 2:03^{3}F 51 6 9 10 $10,068

Date Tk. Cond. Class	Purse Dis.	Leaders Times	Post	1/4	1/2	3/4	Str.	Fin.	Time	Odds	Driver	1st/2nd/3rd	Temp./Starters
Fb10^{3}Clv^{6} sy 3500	2000	m:32^{3}1:05^{3}1:38^{1}2:10^{1}	7	8^{10}	7^{6}	7$^{5\frac14}$	6$^{5\frac12}$	6^{5}	2:11^{1}	34.00	S.P'chuk	Moore.Dick Marg.Misty PilotFrost	8^{8}
Fb2^{3} Clv^{7} ft 3500	2000	m:31^{1}1:02^{4}1:34^{3}2:07	3	4^{4}	6$^{4\frac14}$	^{o}5$^{3\frac14}$	4^{5}	4$^{3\frac14}$	2:07^{2}	15.65	S.P'chuk	NorLeaSue JimTheBear Rad.General	6^{7}
Ja26^{3}Clv^{2} gd 3500hp	2200	m:31^{1}1:03^{3}1:36^{3}2:08^{3}	2	5^{4}	5$^{2\frac12}$	^{o}5^{3}	7^{7}	7^{5}	2:09^{3}	11.35	S.P'chuk	Beth.Blazet Rad.General PilotFros.	9^{8}
Ja19^{3}Clv^{5} gd 3500	2000	m:32^{1}1:06^{3}1:39^{1}2:10^{4}	8	6^{7}	6^{5}	^{o}6^{4}	6$^{5\frac12}$	3^{2}	2:11	6.50	S.P'chuk	BraveBullet GypsyBlue DeckHand	9^{8}
Ja13^{3}Clv^{6} ft 3000	1800	m:31^{1}1:02^{1}1:34^{4}2:05^{4}	5	7^{11}	6^{6}	^{o}5$^{2\frac12}$	2^{4}	2$^{3\frac14}$	2:06^{2}	13.25	S.P'chuk	GypsyBlue DeckHand Wint.PrinceA	6^{8}
Ja7^{3} Clv^{2} sy 3500hp	2000	m:31^{2}1:04^{1}1:37 2:08^{4}	5	7^{6}	^{o}6^{4}	^{o}7^{4}	3^{3}	5^{7}	2:10^{1}	19.65	S.P'chuk	DustyBreeze PanawaBay Sen.Lytton	13^{8}

2 GYPSY BLUE

$3500 — 6-1

Ch. g. 1970, Thor Hanover — Koala Red — Flight Commander
J. Palmer, Vancouver, B. C.
Glen White, C, 150, red, white — Tr. D. Linford — Time 2:04F,10, Earn. to 1983 $81,552

1983 2:05^{4}H 6 2 2 1 $ 3,055
1982 2:04^{4}F 45 6 10 7 $10,988

Date Tk. Cond. Class	Purse Dis.	Leaders Times	Post	1/4	1/2	3/4	Str.	Fin.	Time	Odds	Driver	1st/2nd/3rd	Temp./Starters
Fb5^{3} Clv^{4} ft c3000	1800	m:32^{3}1:04^{2}1:36^{1}2:07^{2}	4	4$^{4\frac12}$	^{o}3^{2}	^{oo}3$^{1\frac14}$	4^{4}	5^{6}	2:08^{3}	3.10	K.Quinlan	Moore.Dick CooksChas. JimTheBear	7^{7}
Ja29^{3}Clv^{7} ft 3000	1800	m:30^{2}1:02^{3}1:34^{3}2:06^{2}	4	6$^{5\frac12}$	5^{4}	^{o}2$^{1\frac12}$	1^{k}	1$^{\frac12}$	2:06^{2}	2.20	K.Quinlan	GypsyBlue MrKeith AndysDean	10^{8}
Ja24^{3}Clv^{9} gd 3500hp	2000	m:31^{2}1:04 1:36^{1}2:09	7	8^{11}	8$^{6\frac12}$	^{o}8^{5}	6$^{3\frac12}$	3^{2}	2:09^{1}	9.25	P.Megens	BethanyOdd Shad.D'less GypsyBlue	10^{8}
Ja19^{3}Clv^{5} gd 3500	2000	m:32^{1}1:06^{3}1:39^{1}2:10^{4}	2	5^{6}	4$^{3\frac12}$	^{o}4^{2}	3$^{2\frac12}$	2$^{\frac12}$	2:10^{4}	2.40	P.Megens	BraveBullet GypsyBlue DeckHand	9^{8}
Ja13^{3}Clv^{6} ft 3000	1800	m:31^{1}1:02^{1}1:34^{4}2:05^{4}	3	5^{4}	5$^{4\frac12}$	^{o}2$^{\frac12}$	1^{4}	1$^{3\frac14}$	2:05^{4}	3.55	K.Quinlan	GypsyBlue DeckHand Wint.PrinceA	6^{8}
Ja6^{3} Clv^{2} sy 3000	1700	m:30^{3}1:01^{4}1:33^{4}2:07	2	3^{2}	^{o}3^{1}	^{o}1^{hd}	1^{1}	2^{ns}	2:07^{1}	*2.60	K.Quinlan	Hol.Hero GypsyBlue SimplyGrand	7^{8}

3 SHADOWS DAUNTLESS

$3500 — 10-1

Br. g. 1978, Invincible Shadow — Lucinda Goose — Brown Prince
A.Gatey,M.Lebaron,W.Terry, Prince George,B.C.Alta.
Dave Smith, A, 180, red, white — Tr. N. Clarkson * — Time 2:03F,4, Earn. to 1983 $17,163

1983 2:08^{1}H 6 1 2 1 $ 1,889
1982 2:03F 53 3 8 7 $ 9,935

Date Tk. Cond. Class	Purse Dis.	Leaders Times	Post	1/4	1/2	3/4	Str.	Fin.	Time	Odds	Driver	1st/2nd/3rd	Temp./Starters
Fb9^{3} Clv^{6} sy 4500	2400	m:33 1:05^{3}1:37^{1}2:09	7	6$^{7\frac12}$	5^{5}	5^{5}	x7$^{8\frac12}$	7^{17}	2:12^{2}	16.80	D.Smith	RomanJoe T'tahiRidge Ch.Dominion	10^{8}
Fb3^{3} Clv^{6} ft 4000	2200	m:30^{3}1:03^{4}1:36^{1}2:08^{4}	6	8$^{10\frac12}$	^{o}5$^{3\frac14}$	^{o}3$^{1\frac12}$	3$^{2\frac14}$	3^{1}	2:08^{4}	16.35	D.Smith	Yarver RomanJoe ShadowsDauntless	4^{8}
Ja28^{3}Clv^{9} ft 4500hp	2600	m:30^{4}1:02^{1}1:34 2:07^{1}	5	6$^{8\frac12}$	6^{7}	^{o}5^{3}	6$^{4\frac14}$	6$^{4\frac12}$	2:07^{4}	15.60	D.Smith	Mich.Hall Chel.Domin. Blk.StormA	8^{7}
Ja24^{3}Clv^{9} gd c3000hp	2000	m:31^{2}1:04 1:36^{1}2:09	3	^{o}2$^{1\frac12}$	^{o}2^{1}	^{o}2^{nk}	2^{hd}	2^{1}	2:09	12.65	C.Sibiga	BethanyOdd Shad.D'less GypsyBlue	10^{8}
Ja20^{3}Clv^{3} ft c2500	1500	m:32 1:04^{4}1:36^{3}2:08^{1}	4	1$^{1\frac12}$	1$^{1\frac12}$	1$^{\frac12}$	1^{2}	1$^{1\frac12}$	2:08^{1}	*1.55	D.Smith	Shad.D'less SurdaleAlex Ch.Poncho	9^{8}
Ja14^{3}Clv^{1} ft 2500	1500	m:30^{3}1:02^{1}1:35^{2}2:08^{1}	6	5$^{6\frac12}$	^{o}5^{8}	^{o}3$^{1\frac12}$	2$^{2\frac12}$	2^{2}	2:08^{3}	9.25	D.Smith	Damuraz Shad.Dauntless KingKoil	4^{8}

4 FERR CHER

$3500 — 10-1

Br. m. 1976, Ferric Hanover — Lassie Tar — Cole Tar
D. Weinert, B. White, Vancouver, Surrey, B. C.
Bruce White, B, 170, red, white — Tr. B. White — Time 2:05H,4, Earn. to 1983 $19,376

1983 2:07^{4}H 6 1 2 0 $ 1,855
1982 2:06^{1}H 47 1 9 8 $ 6,432

Date Tk. Cond. Class	Purse Dis.	Leaders Times	Post	1/4	1/2	3/4	Str.	Fin.	Time	Odds	Driver	1st/2nd/3rd	Temp./Starters
Fb5^{3} Clv^{4} ft 3000	1800	m:32^{3}1:04^{2}1:36^{1}2:07^{2}	7	7^{8}	6^{6}	^{o}6$^{4\frac12}$	5$^{4\frac12}$	4^{5}	2:08^{1}	18.35	B.White	Moore.Dick CooksChas. JimTheBear	7^{7}
Fb3^{3} Clv^{10}ft 3000	1800	m:30^{3}1:02 1:34^{2}2:07^{1}	5	6$^{6\frac12}$	^{o}7$^{4\frac12}$	^{o}2^{1}	2$^{1\frac12}$	2^{nk}	2:07^{1}	14.05	G.White	AndysDean FerrCher PanawaBay	4^{8}
Ja29^{3}Clv^{7} ft 3000	1800	m:30^{2}1:02^{3}1:34^{3}2:06^{2}	3	5^{4}	^{o}4^{3}	7$^{4\frac12}$	6$^{7\frac12}$	6^{7}	2:07^{4}	6.25	B.White	GypsyBlue MrKeith AndysDean	10^{8}
Ja21^{3}Clv^{4} ft 2500	1500	m:31 1:03^{2}1:35^{4}2:07^{4}	2	3$^{2\frac12}$	3$^{1\frac12}$	^{o}1$^{\frac12}$	1^{3}	1^{3}	2:07^{4}	*1.45	B.White	FerrCher Assin.Brave HustlingHall	5^{8}
Ja10^{3}Clv^{1} gd c2500	1500	m:33 1:06^{1}1:37^{2}2:09^{1}	4	5^{6}	^{o}6^{5}	^{o}4$^{3\frac12}$	4^{3}	2^{1}	2:09^{2}	3.25	S.P'chuk	GunsmokeN FerrCher ReyOGrattan	12^{8}
Ja3^{3} Clv^{9} sy 3000	1700	m:31^{4}1:04^{3}1:37^{1}2:09^{4}	2	3$^{2\frac12}$	4$^{3\frac12}$	6^{4}	5^{4}	4$^{3\frac12}$	2:10^{2}	14.40	S.P'chuk	MicroH'over BudsChamp Fr.Memory	10^{8}

$3500 **5** 3-1

CEFFYL DU

Blk. g. 1971, Toreador Hanover — Black Maggie — Johnny Globe
B. Ashcroft, Surrey, B. C.
1983 2:07^2H 4 1 0 3 $ 1,572
Mike Evans,A,170,white,brown,orange Tr. J. Richards Time 2:01M,10, Earn. to 1983 $35,802
1982 2:05^2F 42 3 5 2 $ 5,715

Fb5^3 Clv^3 ft c3000 1800 m:31 1:03^2 1:36^2 2:09^1 7 °4^3½ 4^3½ °3^2 3^2 3^2 2:09^3 3.30 P.Coleman CountForce BraveBullet CeffylDu 7^8
Ja27^3 Clv^6 gd c3000 1800 m:31^7 1:02^4 1:34^4 2:07^1 3 6^8½ °5^7 °5^3 5^3½ 3^3¼ 2:07^4 *.95 M.Evans W.PrinceA PanawaBay CeffylDu 9^8
Ja10^3 Clv^6 gd 3000 1800 m:31^4 1:04^2 1:35^2 2:07^2 8 3^2½ °2½ 1^2 1^3 1^3 2:07^2 *1.05 M.Evans CeffylDu CavalierN JimTheBear 12^8
Ja6^3 Clv^6 sy 4000 2000 m:31^3 1:04^1 1:36^1 2:08 5 6^6½ °5^4½ °6^3 6^4¼ 3^1 2:08^1 2.45 M.Evans DandyCola SatinSatan CeffylDu 7^8
Dc31^2 Clv^6 ft 4000hp 2000 m:30^3 1:02^4 1:35^1 2:07^4 7 °6^4¼ °4^2¼ °3^2 3^1¼ 2½ 2:07^4 17.45 M.Evans Kings.Hanover CeffylDu Dus.Breeze 1^8
Dc22^2 Clv^1 gd 4000 2000 m:31^2 1:03 1:34^2 2:06^2 8 3^2¾ °3^2 °3^2 3^2¼ 1^1 2:06^2 3.45 M.Evans CeffylDu Kings.Hanover Ethnic 6^7

$4000 **6** 9-2

HUGGY

Blk. m. 1976, Brother Christie — Richalon Scott — Dr. Scott Hal Volo
G. Phair and C. Salamanchuk, High River and Calgary, Alta.
1983 5 0 0 0 $ 421
Todd Beelby,C,150,lt.blue,dk.blue Tr. C. Beelby Time 2:03^3F,5, Earn. to 1983 $20,756
1982 2:06^4F 39 2 11 6 $13,686

Ja31^3 Clv^7 ft 4000hp 2400 m:30^2 1:02^2 1:34^2 2:06^1 8 4^5 °3^2½ °2^1½ 3^3 5^3½ 2:06^4 9.50 B.Beelby DustyBreeze ArdenBret SatinSatan 8^8
Ja24^3 Clv^6 gd 4000 2200 m:32 1:03 1:35^4 2:08^1 3 °1^k °2^1 °2^hd 3^2 4^4 2:08^4 4.65 C.Beelby Spec.Game MichiganHall JimTheB. 10^8
Ja21^3 Clv^6 ft 4000cd 2500 m:31 1:03^3 1:36 2:08 5 2^1 2^1 4^3 5^6 5^7 2:09^3 8.75 C.Beelby Dus.Breeze Rad.General PilotFrost 5^6
Ja14^3 StP^2 ft 4000 1700 m:30^1 1:03^3 1:33^3 2:05^4 2 1^1 1^1½ 2½ 2^1½ 6^5¼ 2:06^4 7.15 R.Hennessy Spring.Crocus Kara.Beau Su.Adios -3^8
Ja2^3 StP^3 ft 5500 2200 m:29^1 1:01^2 1:32^4 2:05^3 7 2^1 2^1 3^3 6^7½ 7^18¼ 2:09^1 22.95 G.McQuaid Lilloet SepoyNatel MarubaPicky 2^8
Dc12^2 StP^3 ft 5500 2400 m:29^2 1:00^2 1:32 2:05 5 1^1 1^1 1½ 3^1½ 8^6¼ 2:06^1 9.15 EdTracey SepoyNatel WarCloud TedTheGreat 10^8

$4000 **7** 6-1

KINGSLEY HANOVER

B. g. 1971, Hondo Hanover — Little Kim — Hundred Proof
P. Megens, Surrey, B. C.
1983 2:07^3H 5 1 0 0 $ 1,516
Paul Megens, A, 160, red, white Tr. P. Megens Time 2:00^4M,10, Earn. to 1983 $49,052
1982 2:00^4M 33 10 6 3 $14,047

Fb3^3 Clv^6 ft 4000 2200 m:30^3 1:03^4 1:36^1 2:08^4 2 x4^4 °3^2 °2^1 2^2 4^3 2:09^2 *1.95 P.Megens Yarver RomanJoe ShadowsDauntless 4^8
Ja26^3 Clv^2 gd 4000hp 2200 m:31^1 1:03^3 1:36^3 2:08^3 6 °3^2 °3^1¼ °4^2 5^6 6^4½ 2:09^2 3.25 P.Megens Beth.Blaze† Rad.General PilotFros.9^8
Ja21^3 Clv^9 ft 5000cd 2800 m:32^2 1:05 1:36^3 2:07^4 5 6^6½ °5^4 6^5 7^13 7^13 2:10^1 3.90 P.Megens MightyTyrosA PerleBlue Keesno 5^7
Ja14^3 Clv^6 ft 5000hp 2800 m:31^3 1:02^1 1:34^2 2:05^2 3 °1^1 2^1 4^1½ 5^5½ 5^5 2:06^2 *2.10 P.Megens Beth.Pegas. Hol.GoSkip LTWohcaz 4^8
Ja7^3 Clv^7 sy 5000 2400 m:31^3 1:04^2 1:35^4 2:07^3 1 2^1½ 2^2½ 3^1½ 2^1½ 1^k 2:07^3 2.95 P.Megens Kings.Hanover Daub.Comm. Ethnic 13^8
Dc31^2 Clv^6 ft 4000hp 2000 m:30^3 1:02^4 1:35^1 2:07^4 6 °5^3¼ °2^1 °2^1 1^k 1½ 2:07^4 6.25 P.Megens Kings.Hanover CeffylDu Dus.Breeze 1^8

$3500 **8** 8-1

HOLRIDGE HERO

Br. g. 1977, Skip Away — Du Du Byrd — Du Boy *B.C. Bred*
W. Waples, Surrey, B. C.
1983 2:07H 6 2 0 0 $ 1,990
Wendell Waples, A, 150, gold, blue Tr. W. Waples Time 2:02^2F,4, Earn. to 1983 $15,922
1982 2:07^1H 25 4 4 3 $ 6,923

Ja29^3 Clv^7 ft 3000 1800 m:30^2 1:02^3 1:34^3 2:06^2 8 3^2½ 3^2½ 3^2½ 5^5½ 5^6½ 2:07^3 8.30 W.Waples GypsyBlue MrKeith AndysDean 10^8
Ja24^3 Clv^9 gd 3000hp 2000 m:31^2 1:04 1:36^1 2:09 5 7^9 6^4 6^3 7^4½ 5^4 2:09^3 6.00 W.Waples BethanyOdd Shad.D'less GypsyBlue 10^8
Ja19^3 Clv^5 gd 3500 2000 m:32^1 1:06^3 1:39^1 2:10^4 4 1^k 1^1½ 1^k 1^1 5^2½ 2:11 3.35 W.Waples BraveBullet GypsyBlue DeckHand 9^8
Ja13^3 Clv^6 ft c3000 1800 m:31^1 1:02^1 1:34^4 2:05^4 6 °2^hd °2^1 °3^1½ 5^7 6^8 2:07^2 2.95 S.Ericsson GypsyBlue DeckHand Wint.PrinceA 6^8
Ja6^3 Clv^2 sy 3000 1700 m:30^3 1:01^4 1:33^4 2:07 7 °4^2¼ °1^hd 2^hd 2^1 1^ns 2:07 15.65 S.Ericsson Hol.Hero GypsyBlue SimplyGrand 7^8
Ja1^3 Clv^4 gd 3000 1700 m:32^1 1:06 1:39^2 2:12^1 2 2^1 °2^1 2^k 1^2 1^4 2:12^1 *2.15 S.Ericsson Hol.Hero SimplyGrand SallyStreak. 4^8

*Denotes Assistant Trainer

In the third race, horse number 3, Shadows Dauntless, was a Dr. Z system bet. Near post time the tote board was as follows:

	Totals	#3 Shadows Dauntless	Expected Value per Dollar Bet on Shadows Dauntless
Odds		4—1	
Win	6,257	1,065	
Show	2,147	202	1.24

The mutuel pools at Cloverdale are quite small, so I used a betting fortune of $200. The optimal bet was then $8. It proved very easy to bet just before post time. The favorite, Ceffyl Du, won the race, Shadows Dauntless took second, and Gypsy Blue was third. Shadows Dauntless's $4.20 show payoff returned $16.80 on my $8 bet, for an $8.80 profit. The mutuel payoffs were as follows:

5	6.60	4.10	2.70
	3	5.50	4.20
		2	3.20

Pardner Jove, the number 6 horse, was a Dr. Z system bet in the eighth race. Pardner Jove was the favorite for his seventh race in succession, this time at 6–5 odds.

With one minute to post time the tote board was as follows:

	Total	#6 Pardner Jove	Expected Value per Dollar Bet on Pardner Jove
Odds		6—5	
Win	9,093	3,264	
Show	2,476	560	1.16

I bet $33. At post time the odds were:

	Total	#6 Pardner Jove	Expected Value per Dollar Bet on Pardner Jove
Odds		6—5	
Win	9,410	3,387	
Show	2,609	621	1.13

Chatter won the race. Pardner Jove took second, followed by Here By Chance. Pardner Jove paid $2.80, so my $33 bet returned $46.20, for a $13.20 profit. The mutuel payoffs were as follows:

4	14.00	5.20	3.20
	6	3.30	2.80
		1	3.30

USING THE DR. Z SYSTEM AT STAMPEDE PARK'S HARNESS-RACING TRACK

Since the first edition of *Beat the Racetrack* was published, many people have used the Dr. Z system for harness racing. Very consistent horses, the fact that the drivers are often the owners and hence do their utmost to win, and many odds-on favorites lead to a large number of Dr. Z wagers. My visits to Cloverdale invariably yield four or more good wagers on each card. Track conditions are less important than with thoroughbreds because of the hard track surface. Post-position bias is very strong and is apparently well reflected in the odds. Barry Meadow, the harness-racing editor of *Gambling Times,* has been using the approach and has written about it in several columns including his review of *Beat the Racetrack*, Meadow (1985). A colleague in Calgary has been using the Dr. Z system at Stampede Park there and his results follow. He has been using a 1.15 cutoff and an initial bankroll of $1,500. The results indicate a profit of $2,063.60 during the period of July 1–August 10, 1986 for a rate of return of 15% on money wagered. The final expected returns, including the effect of his bets, averaged a 12% edge, so the 15% profit is a good outcome, statistically speaking. The 12% edge reflects some late betting on the Dr. Z horses but the wagers were still good. On nine occasions the final expected return was less than 1.00. There were 113 wagers on sixteen days, or 7 wagers on an average day. The least number of wagers was two—a place and show bet on the same horse—and the greatest number was sixteen wagers on August 23. Very frequently there were place and show wagers on the same horse. He used an approximate Kelly betting system with adjustments to account for the multiple wagers. He lost twenty-eight wagers and won eighty-five for a 75% winning percentage. His longest losing streak was five wagers on three horses, and he had a winning streak of twenty-one wagers on August 17–23. The wagers were all on short-odds horses with the largest payoff being $6.20 on a place wager on August 13. The $8.20 payoff on August 5 was on the only win bet that was made. One handicapping observation he related to me was that the top five drivers rarely finish third in claiming races. They tend to win, place, or finish out of the money in these races. Assuming this tendency persists, it suggests a movement toward place bets and away from show wagers in such situations.

The detailed results appear in Table 17.3. Table 17.4 relates the results

8th race BLUE SADDLE CLOTH — 1 MILE PACE

EXACTOR SUPER 6 — **SUPER 6** EXACTOR

PURSE \$3200 — Claiming — Claiming Price \$7000 plus allowances.

HANDICAP SELECTIONS: 6 — 4 — 8

ASK FOR HORSE BY THIS NUMBER

1 HERE BY CHANCE — \$7000 — 8-1

B. g. 1975, Adios Pick — Actress Abbe — Actor Abbe — *B.C. Bred*
F. Rasmussen, C. Pedersen, Vanc., B. C. — 1983 8 0 1 3 \$ 2,684
Howard Portelance,A,140,grey,bl,orange Tr. T. Brown * Time 2:03F,7, Earn. to 1983 \$31,901 — 1982 2:03F 40 1 10 4 \$ 9,534

Date Tk. Cond. Class	Purse	Dis. Leaders Times	Post	1/4	1/2	3/4	Str.	Fin.	Time	Odds	Driver	1st/2nd/3rd	Temp./Starters
Fb5^3 Clv^5 ft 7000hp	3200	m:30^{2}1:02^{2}1:33^{3}2:05^1	1	$4^{4\frac{1}{2}}$	4^4	7^5	$4^{7\frac{1}{2}}$	$3^{6\frac{1}{2}}$	2:06^2	5.70	H.P'lance	HHClipper MacLobellA HereByChance	7^8
Ja29^{3}Clv^5 ft 7000hp	3200	m:30^{1}1:02^{1}1:34 2:06^2	4	$6^{7\frac{1}{2}}$	$6^{4\frac{1}{2}}$	8^4	$7^{3\frac{1}{2}}$	2^{nk}	2:06^2	18.80	H.P'lance	Wind.Andy H.ByChance TakeAStar†	10^8
Ja26^{3}Clv^{10}sy 7000	3000	m:31^{3}1:03^{4}1:36^{1}2:08^1	6	$6^{7\frac{1}{2}}$	$7^{7\frac{1}{2}}$	$^o7^6$	$7^{4\frac{1}{2}}$	4^2	2:08^2	14.75	H.P'lance	Rich.Dauber Nor.Roddy Daub.Com.	9^8
Ja22^{3}Clv^6 ft 7000hp	3200	m:31^{1}1:03^{1}1:34^{1}2:06^3	2	$2^{1\frac{1}{2}}$	$^o2^{nk}$	$^o1^{hd}$	3^2	5^3	2:07^1	6.15	H.P'lance	SengaPayne Nor.Roddy Com.Osborne	8^8
Ja15^{3}Clv^{10}gd 7000hp	3000	m:32 1:05 1:37^{4}2:09^2	4	6^6	$8^{6\frac{1}{2}}$	$^o7^{4\frac{1}{2}}$	$7^{4\frac{1}{2}}$	4^2	2:09^4	3.45	H.P'lance	Wind.Andy Nor.Roddy Com.Osborne	6^8
Ja12^{3}Clv^7 gd 7000	3000	m:31^{1}1:02^{3}1:34^{3}2:06^2	3	$4^{4\frac{1}{2}}$	$4^{3\frac{1}{2}}$	$^o3^{1\frac{1}{2}}$	$4^{2\frac{1}{2}}$	$3^{1\frac{1}{2}}$	2:06^4	3.85	H.P'lance	Inv.Strip Daub.Comm. H.B.Chance	10^7

2 HICRIDGE APOLLO † — \$7000 — 6-1

B. g. 1972, Army Hanover — Bertha Breeze — Mighty Medium
W. Dobie, Surrey, B. C. — 1983 2:06^{2}H 5 1 0 1 \$ 2,098
Mike Evans,A,170,white,brown,orange Tr. J. Richards Time 2:02F,6, Earn. to 1983 \$91,230 — 1982 2:05^{3}F 35 9 3 7 \$14,495

Date Tk. Cond. Class	Purse	Dis. Leaders Times	Post	1/4	1/2	3/4	Str.	Fin.	Time	Odds	Driver	1st/2nd/3rd	Temp./Starters
Fb5^3 Clv^5 ft 7000hp	3200	m:30^{2}1:02^{2}1:33^{3}2:05^1	4	$7^{8\frac{1}{2}}$	$7^{6\frac{1}{4}}$	$^o8^{5\frac{1}{2}}$	$7^{8\frac{1}{2}}$	4^9	2:06^4	5.55	M.Evans†	HHClipper MacLobellA HereByChance	7^8
Ja28^{3}Clv^{10}ft 6000cd	2800	m:30^{4}1:01^{4}1:34 2:06^2	1	$1^{1\frac{1}{2}}$	1^{hd}	$1^{1\frac{1}{2}}$	1^2	1^5	2:06^2	*2.10	M.Evans†	Hic.Apollo† FracoDoc Sur.Princess	8^8
Ja19^{3}Clv^6 gd 5000	2600	m:31^{1}1:02^{2}1:34^{2}2:06	3	$3^{1\frac{1}{4}}$	3^3	$5^{3\frac{1}{2}}$	$4^{4\frac{1}{2}}$	$3^{1\frac{1}{4}}$	2:06^1	2.90	M.Evans†	JohnHanoverN Hol.GoSkip H.Apollo†	9^8
Ja7^3 Clv^6 sy 6000	2600	m:30^{1}1:00^{4}1:33^{1}2:05^2	7	7^{13}	7^{15}	$7^{8\frac{1}{2}}$	7^{13}	6^{13}	2:08^1	7.85	M.Evans†	Rich.Dauber HippocampusC Chatter	13^8
Ja3^3 Clv^5 sy 6000hp	2600	m:32^{1}1:05^{3}1:36^{2}2:07^3	5	6^7	$^o6^{4\frac{1}{2}}$	$^o4^5$	$4^{6\frac{1}{2}}$	$5^{7\frac{1}{4}}$	2:09	*2.35	M.Evans†	Com.Osborne Rich.Daub. Daub.Comm.	10^8
Dc27^{2}Clv^7 gd 6000	2600	m:30^{3}1:03 1:35^{2}2:06^3	1	4^3	$^o3^2$	$^o1^{\frac{1}{2}}$	1^2	1^{hd}	2:06^3	4.20	M.Evans†	Hic.Apollo† MarkDoc LTWohcaz	3^8

3 UFLEX — \$7000 — 10-1

Blk. g. 1972, Springflex — U Love — U Scott
M. Graham, D. Tough, G. Lum, Surrey, Vancouver, B. C. — 1983 6 0 0 1 \$ 856
Paul Megens, A, 160, red, white Tr. G. Abbott Time 2:00^{1}M,7, Earn. to 1983 \$107,139 — 1982 2:05^{4}H 34 9 4 4 \$18,444

Date Tk. Cond. Class	Purse	Dis. Leaders Times	Post	1/4	1/2	3/4	Str.	Fin.	Time	Odds	Driver	1st/2nd/3rd	Temp./Starters
Fb5^3 Clv^5 ft 7000hp	3200	m:30^{2}1:02^{2}1:33^{3}2:05^1	6	3^3	$3^{2\frac{1}{2}}$	3^3	5^8	$7^{10\frac{1}{2}}$	2:07^1	43.65	P.Megens	HHClipper MacLobellA HereByChance	7^8
Fb2^3 Clv^2 ft 7000	3000	m:30^{4}1:03^{1}1:34^{2}2:05^4	4	2^1	$3^{1\frac{1}{4}}$	$7^{3\frac{1}{4}}$	$5^{6\frac{1}{2}}$	4^6	2:07	6.75	P.Megens	Rich.Dauber Com.Osborne J.Indigo	6^8
Ja27^{3}Clv^9 gd 8000	3200	m:31 1:03 1:34 2:06^2	1	$4^{3\frac{1}{2}}$	$^o4^{2\frac{1}{4}}$	$^o6^3$	$7^{3\frac{1}{2}}$	5^3	2:06^4	11.00	P.Megens	S.Chettsal Lang.Charm Nor.Martin	9^8
Ja20^{3}Clv^9 ft 8000	3200	m:30^{1}1:01^{3}1:34^{2}2:06	7	8^7	7^7	$^o7^5$	7^9	7^{10}	2:08	11.30	P.Megens	Pard.Jove Sw.Angie LangleyCharm	9^8
Ja14^{3}Clv^9 ft 10000hp	4000	m:29^{3}1:01^{2}1:33 2:05	3	4^5	$4^{4\frac{1}{2}}$	$5^{4\frac{1}{2}}$	6^5	$6^{7\frac{1}{4}}$	2:06^3	9.65	P.Megens	CallNRaise HHClipper RossN	4^6
Ja7^3 Clv^9 sy 10000hp	3800	m:31^{4}1:05^{1}1:36^{2}2:08	2	$2^{1\frac{1}{2}}$	$2^{1\frac{1}{2}}$	$3^{1\frac{1}{4}}$	$3^{1\frac{1}{2}}$	3^2	2:08^2	17.35	P.Megens	GritN PrairieJean Uflex	13^6

4 CHATTER — \$7000 — 7-2

Blk. h. 1976, Speedy Count — Noccalula — Spectator
B. Hirsch, Surrey, B. C. — 1983 2:07H 4 1 0 2 \$ 2,048
Jim Wiggins, A, 150, green, gold Tr. B. Hirsch Time 2:01F,4, Earn. to 1983 \$23,605 — 1982 2:01^{2}F 37 12 3 4 \$13,044

Date Tk. Cond. Class	Purse	Dis. Leaders Times	Post	1/4	1/2	3/4	Str.	Fin.	Time	Odds	Driver	1st/2nd/3rd	Temp./Starters
Fb4^3 Clv^7 ft 6000	2800	m:30^{2}1:02^{1}1:34^{2}2:07	7	8^{10}	$8^{6\frac{1}{2}}$	$^o8^6$	7^4	1^2	2:07	22.90	J.Wiggins	Chatter Invinc.Strip Spec.Game	4^8
Ja28^{3}Clv^{10}ft 6000cd	2800	m:30^{4}1:01^{4}1:34 2:06^2	7	7^7	$^o6^{5\frac{1}{4}}$	$^o7^{4\frac{1}{2}}$	$8^{8\frac{1}{4}}$	8^{17}	2:09^3	3.35	K.Linton	Hic.Apollo† FracoDoc Sur.Princess	8^8
Ja17^{3}Clv^7 gd 6000cd	2800	m:31^{2}1:02^{1}1:33^{4}2:05^2	5	6^5	$^o5^{6\frac{1}{2}}$	$^o5^{4\frac{1}{4}}$	5^7	$3^{5\frac{1}{2}}$	2:06^3	3.80	J.Wiggins	FortDean DantePatch Chatter	10^8
Ja7^3 Clv^6 sy 6000	2600	m:30^{1}1:00^{4}1:33^{1}2:05^2	6	6^{11}	6^{10}	$^o5^{2\frac{1}{2}}$	3^4	$3^{4\frac{1}{4}}$	2:06^2	3.05	K.Linton	Rich.Dauber HippocampusC Chatter	13^8
Dc29^{2}Clv^8 ft 7000	2800	m:31^{4}1:03^{2}1:35^{3}2:06^4	3	$6^{6\frac{1}{2}}$	$6^{5\frac{1}{2}}$	$^o5^5$	$5^{4\frac{1}{2}}$	$5^{3\frac{1}{4}}$	2:07^2	9.00	J.Wiggins	CannyBretN BwanaByrd North.Martin	0^8
Dc20^{2}Clv^{10}sy 6000	2600	m:31^{2}1:03^{2}1:35^{2}2:07^2	2	2^1	$^o1^1$	1^1	$1^{1\frac{1}{2}}$	$1^{1\frac{1}{2}}$	2:07^2	3.20	J.Wiggins	Chatter Com.Osborne RedBerryN	6^8

```
$7000 FLASH FIRE          B. m. 1976, Dexter Hanover — Stonegate Taretta — Tarport Count
5                         J. and L. Kositsky and J. Plottel, Vancouver, B. C.    1983        6  0  1  0 $ 1,245
10-1  Wendell Waples, A, 150, gold, blue   Tr. J. Kositsky.   Time 2:03F,4, Earn. to 1983 $44,661   1982 2:06^2H 31 3 2 6 $ 9,013
Fb5^3 Clv^5 ft 7000hp   3200 m:30^2 1:02^2 1:33^3 2:05^1 5  2^1½  2^1  2^2  3^6  8^11  2:07^1 17.25 D.J'quist  HHClipper MacLobellA HereByChance 7^8
Ja29^3Clv^5 ft 7000hp   3200 m:30^1 1:02^1 1:34 2:06^2 1  2^1½  3^1¼  3^1½  3^1¼  5^2¼  2:06^4  6.80 D.J'quist  Wind.Andy H.ByChance TakeAStart 10^8
Ja19^3Clv^7 gd 8000hp   3200 m:31^3 1:04 1:35^2 2:05^4 5  5^6  5^5  5^5  5^7½  5^8¼  2:07^3 *1.75 D.J'quist  Nor.Martin Jam.Indigo Rich.Dauber 9^5
Ja13^3Clv^10ft 8000     3200 m:30 1:03^2 1:35^3 2:05^3 4  1^1  1^1  1^nk  2^4  6^7½  2:07  3.15 D.J'quist  Jim.N'nuff Lang.Charm Nor.Martin 6^8
Ja8^3 Clv^7 gd 8000hp   3000 m:29^4 1:02^3 1:34^2 2:06^3 6  2^1½  2^1½  °2^hd  1½  2½  2:06^3  3.35 D.J'quist  PrimaGavel FlashFire H.ByChance 6^8
Ja3^3 Clv^7 sy 9000hp   3500 m:31^1 1:05^3 1:38^3 2:09^2 3  1^1  1^1  1½  2^2  5^3½  2:10^1  5.15 S.Ericsson  Booz.Delight Comm.Jove Pr.Jean 10^7

$7000 PARDNER JOVE        B. g. 1974, Tar Duke — Lady Jane Grey — Lon Tass                        *B.C. Bred*
6                         Hudon Stables, Surrey, B.C.                            1983 2:06H   4  1  1  0 $ 2,791
3-1   Joe Hudon, A, 165, blue, orange   Tr. J. Hudon   Time 2:02^3F,8, Earn. to 1983 $61,734   1982 2:02^3F 39 10 8 7 $23,397
Ja28^3Clv^6 ft 10000    3700 m:29^3 1:00^4 1:32^2 2:04^3 2  4^5½  4^4½  6^4¼  6^7  5^5  2:05^2 *2.40 J.Hudon  LaurelWayGB ServingYou JamesGem 8^7
Ja20^3Clv^9 ft 8000     3200 m:30^1 1:01^3 1:34^2 2:06 2  4^3  3^2½  °1^1  1^1½  1^1  2:06 *1.30 J.Hudon  Pard.Jove Sw.Angie LangleyCharm 9^8
Ja13^3Clv^10ft 8000     3200 m:30 1:03^2 1:35^3 2:05^3 3  6^4½  °2^1  °2^nk  3^5½  4^7  2:07 *1.45 J.Hudon  Jim.N'nuff Lang.Charm Nor.Martin 6^8
Ja6^3 Clv^10sy 8000     3000 m:30^1 1:01^3 1:33^2 2:05^3 8  4^3½  °4^2½  °2^2½  2^2  2^2  2:06 *1.95 J.Hudon  Sen.Chettsal Pard.Jove Nor.Martin 7^8
Dc27^2Clv^10gd 9000cd   3300 m:31^3 1:04^3 1:36^2 2:08^2 7  i4^4½  °3^1½  °2½  3^2  4^3  2:09 *1.50 J.Hudon  Uflex JustDuke PrimaGavel 3^8
Dc17^2Clv^8 sy 10000hp  3800 m:30^2 1:02^1 1:36 2:08^2 5  6^5½  °5^9  5^5½  6^6½  6^8  2:10 *1.65 J.Hudon  Prair.Jean Wing.Lead.† S.Chettsal 6^8

$7000 MAC LOBELL A        B. g. 1977, Smart Lobell — Narooma Gift — Free Fight
7                         A. Peterson, R. Acheson and J. Glen, Surrey, B. C.     1983        3  0  1  0 $   950
8-1   Mike Stymest,A,150,orange,green,white   Tr. J. Glen   Time 2:00^4F,4, Earn. to 1983 $24,743   1982 2:02^2F 15 1 4 3 $ 6,685
Fb5^3 Clv^5 ft 7000hp   3200 m:30^2 1:02^1 1:33^3 2:05^1 8  5^5½  5^5  5^3½  2^2  2^3  2:05^3  9.25 J.Glen  HHClipper MacLobellA HereByChance 7^8
Fb2^3 Clv^2 ft 7000     3000 m:30^4 1:03^1 1:34^2 2:05^4 3  8^8  °6^3  °3^1¼  3^3  5^6¼  2:07  5.50 J.Glen  Rich.Dauber Com.Osborne J.Indigo 6^8
Ja21^3Clv^8 ft 10000hp  4000 m:31^4 1:04 1:35^4 2:06^3 1  3^2  5^3  6^3¼  7^5½  8^8¼  2:08^1  7.80 J.Glen  RossN GritN KawarthaOshawa 5^8
Ja13^3Clv^1 ft Qua       Nil m:30^3 1:01^4 1:34^3 2:05^4 5  4^7½  4^13  3^3¼  3^3  3^2¼  2:06^2  NB J.Glen  Hol.Iroqua BaronNuff MacLobellA 5^5
Ja6^3 Clv^4 sy Qua       Nil m:34 1:08 1:41^3 2:13^2 6  6^7  7^7½  5^4  4^2  2½  2:13^2  NB J.Glen  GunsmokeA MacLobellA BabyKhan 7^7
Ag21^2Reg^8 gd wo1000L6 1500 m:31^3 1:03^3 1:35^2 2:06^3 5  °1^1  2^2  2^2  2^1½  5^12  2:09  2.55 J.Glen  SirMedicine M.Majestic IrishCom. 28^6

$7000 BWANA BYRD          B. g. 1976, Baron Duane — Birdie Bright Eyes — Tar Duke
8                         B. Babineau, Surrey, B. C.                             1983 2:07^3H 5  1  0  1 $ 1,932
9-2   Bill Babineau,A.160,r.bl,lt.bl,white   Tr. B. Babineau   Time 2:02F,5, Earn. to 1983 $26,427   1982 2:03^1F 50 14 11 7 $18,283
Fb7^3 Clv^6 gd 5000hp   2600 m:30^2 1:02^2 1:35 2:07^3 6  fog  8^8  fog  3^2  1^1  2:07^3  4.60 B.Babineau  BwanaByrd RedBerryN Yarver 5^8
Fb3^3 Clv^7 ft 8000     3200 m:30^1 1:02^1 1:35^2 2:06^4 7  8^14  8^6  °7^3  7^6  7^5¼  2:07^3 21.35 B.Babineau  Lang.Charm FortDean North.Martin 4^8
Ja13^3Clv^8 ft 8000cd   3400 m:30^1 1:01^3 1:33^2 2:04^3 4  5^4½  °5^4  °4^3½  4^6  3^7¼  2:06  5.10 B.Babineau  TributeN Hoatu BwanaByrd 6^7
Ja8^3 Clv^7 gd 7000hp   3000 m:29^4 1:02^3 1:34^2 2:06^3 2ix°4^4½  °3^2½  8^8  8^12  8^18  2:09^3 *2.15 B.Babineau  PrimaGavel FlashFire H.ByChance 6^8
Ja1^3 Clv^7 sl 7000cd   2800 m:32^2 1:06^2 1:39 2:11^2 6  7^8½  °6^5i  °6^4  7^5½  4^4½  2:12^1  3.25 B.Babineau  TributeN BaronsLass Hoatu 4^7
Dc29^2Clv^8 ft 7000     2800 m:31^4 1:03^2 1:35^3 2:06^4 2  5^4  5^4  °4^4  2^1  2^ns  2:06^4  3.15 B.Babineau  CannyBretN BwanaByrd North.Martin 0^8

ALSO ELIGIBLE: THIS HORSE WILL ONLY START IN THE EVENT OF A SCRATCH

$7000 DAUBERS COMMAND     Br. h. 1978, Hank The Dauber — Gladys Command — Take Command              *B.C. Bred*
9                         W. and T. Smith, Surrey, B. C.                         1983        7  0  2  2 $ 2,448
(P.P. .....) Dave Smith, A, 180, red, white   Tr. N. Clarkson *   Time 2:03^4F,4, Earn. to 1983 $19,226   1982 2:03^4F 31 8 8 2 $11,169
Fb9^3 Clv^7 sy 7000cd   3000 m:31^4 1:03^3 1:35^4 2:06^4 2  1^1  1^nk  4^2¼  7^10  7^15  2:09^4  5.55 D.Smith  Jim.N'nuff Arm.Almond B'sFancy† 10^8
Ja31^3Clv^10ft 6000cd   3400 m:30^3 1:02 1:33^4 2:05^1 1  2^1½  2^1¼  3^1¼  3^2  5^3  2:05^3  6.00 D.Smith  DiabloN KinaJ EastwindStar 8^8
Ja26^3Clv^10sy 7000     3000 m:31^3 1:03^4 1:36^1 2:08^1 2  1^1½  1^1½  1^1  1½  3^1½  2:08^2 10.10 D.Smith  Rich.Dauber Nor.Roddy Daub.Com. 9^8
Ja19^3Clv^7 gd 7000hp   3200 m:31^3 1:04 1:35^2 2:05^4 2  1^1½  1½  2½  3^4  4^7½  2:07^2  3.15 J.Wiggins  Nor.Martin Jam.Indigo Rich.Dauber 9^5
Ja12^3Clv^7 gd 7000     3000 m:31^1 1:02^3 1:34^3 2:06^2 2  1^1  1^1½  1½  1^1½  2^1  2:06^3  8.75 J.Wiggins  Inv.Strip Daub.Comm. H.B.Chance 10^7
```

*Denotes Assistant Trainer

TABLE 17.3 ***Results of using the Dr. Z System on 113 wagers on 16 days at Stampede Park in Calgary, July 1–August 10, 1986***

Date	Race	Final Expected Return	Amount ($)	Type of Bet/Horse Number	Finish	Net Return ($)	Payoff per $2 Wager ($)	Cumulative Wager ($)	Profit ($)	Cumulative Return (%)	Cumulative Final Expected Return (%)
7/25	1	1.01	30	P/2	4-2-3	6.50	2.40	22	6.50	22	1
		1.03	30	S/2		3.00	2.30	15	9.50	15	2
(MUD)	7	1.20	10	S/2	7-1-5	−10.00		−1	−0.50	−1	4
	8	1.16	50	P/2	5-4-2	−50.00		−42	−50.50	−42	9
		1.20	100	S/2		20.00	2.40	−14	−30.50	−14	14
	9	1.13	15	S/3	8-2-5	15.75	4.10	−6	−14.75	−6	14
	10	1.35	50	P/3	1-8-3	−50.00		−23	−64.75	−23	18
		1.38	50	S/3		32.50	3.30	−10	−32.25	−10	21
7/26	1	1.17	50	S/6	8-2-5	−50.00		385	−82.25	−21	20
	8	1.03	100	P/4	3-4-5	55.00	3.10	485	−27.25	−6	17
		1.12	100	S/4		25.00	2.50	585	−2.25	0	16
7/27	1	1.17	50	S/3	1-3-8	17.50	2.70	635	15.25	2	16
	4	1.23	50	P/3	7-5-6	−50.00		685	−34.75	−5	16
(MUD)	7	1.31	130	S/3	4-3-1	45.50	2.70	815	10.75	1	19
	8	1.14	20	S/1	2-3-4	−20.00		835	−9.25	−1	19
7/30	6	1.12	123	S/6	5-6-2	12.30	2.20	958	3.05	0	18
	10	1.10	50	S/7	5-2-7	47.50	3.90	1,008	50.55	5	17
8/1	1	1.14	20	S/7	7-4-6	5.00	2.50	1,028	55.55	5	17
	4	1.09	300	S/1	1-4-6	15.00	2.10	1,328	70.55	5	15
	6	1.10	30	P/1	4-6-1	−30.00		1,358	40.55	3	15
		1.22	50	S/1		22.50	2.90	1,408	63.05	4	16
	7	1.16	100	S/2	2-3-8	90.00	3.80	1,508	153.05	10	16
	8	1.16	81	P/3	3-1-5	44.55	3.10	1,589	197.60	12	16
		1.00	25	S/3		1.25	2.10	1,614	198.85	12	15
8/2	1	1.13	150	P/1	1-6-3	60.00	2.80	1,764	258.85	15	15

	5	1.08	120	P/3	3-5-4	72.00	3.20	1,884	330.85	18	15
	6	1.18	50	P/6	5-4-1	−50.00		1,934	280.85	15	15
		1.12	100	S/6	5-4-1	−100.00		2,034	180.85	9	15
	7	1.06	80	P/2	4-3-2	−80.00		2,114	100.85	5	14
	10	1.06	30	P/3	3-6-7	33.00	4.20	2,144	133.85	6	14
8/3	1	1.20	230	P/3	8-3-6	69.00	2.60	2,374	202.85	9	15
		1.17	174	S/3	8-3-6	26.10	2.30	2,548	228.95	9	15
	2	1.41	86	P/5	5-4-2	107.50	4.50	2,634	336.45	13	16
		1.16	20	S/5	5-4-2	8.00	2.80	2,654	344.45	13	16
	7	1.17	30	P/4	4-3-2	27.00	3.80	2,684	371.45	14	16
8/5	1	1.09	100	S/4	4-5-6	40.00	2.80	2,784	411.45	15	16
	3	1.20	40	W/5	5-?-?	124.00	8.20	2,824	535.45	19	16
	7	1.10	100	S/3	6-7-4	−100.00		2,924	435.45	15	15
	8	1.05	304	P/7	7-5-4	121.60	2.80	3,228	557.05	17	14
		1.13	190	S/7	7-5-4	47.50	2.50	3,418	604.55	18	14
	10	1.07	50	S/5		−50.00		3,468	554.55	16	14
8/13	1	1.03	200	P/4	4-6-5	30.00	2.30	3,668	584.55	16	14
		1.10	100	S/4	4-6-5	5.00	2.10	3,768	589.55	16	14
	2	1.01	70	P/9	4-9-8	28.00	2.80	3,838	617.55	16	13
		1.20	70	S/9	4-9-8	31.50	2.90	3,908	649.05	17	13
	3	1.18	50	P/8	8-4-3	105.00	6.20	3,958	754.05	19	14
	4	1.09	275	P/3	3-7-1	82.50	2.60	4,233	836.55	20	13
		1.14	250	S/3	3-7-1	37.50	2.30	4,483	874.05	19	13
	5	1.04	26	P/3	3-4-2	36.40	4.80	4,509	910.45	20	13
	6	0.92	20	S/1	5-1-4	2.00	2.20	4,529	912.45	20	13
	7	1.16	300	S/3	3-1-2	45.00	2.30	4,829	957.45	20	13
	10	1.01	100	S/5	2-4-7	−100.00		4,929	857.45	17	13
8/15	1	1.10	56	S/1	4-6-7	−56.00		4,985	801.45	16	13
	2	0.92	82	P/1	5-1-4	57.40	3.40	5,067	858.85	17	13
	4	1.34	10	S/7	4-3-5	−10.00		5,077	848.85	17	13
	7	1.23	100	S/5	7-5-2	80.00	3.60	5,177	928.85	18	13
	8	1.09	100	S/1	2-3-5	−100.00		5,277	828.85	16	13
	10	1.04	50	S/3	6-4-8	−50.00		5,327	778.85	15	13

Date	Race	Final Expected Return	Amount ($)	Type of Bet/Horse Number	Finish	Net Return ($)	Payoff per $2 Wager ($)	Cumulative Wager ($)	Profit ($)	Cumulative Return (%)	Cumulative Final Expected Return (%)
8/16	1	0.98	230	P/5	1-5-7	11.50	2.10	5,557	790.35	14	12
		1.18	136	S/5	1-5-7	13.60	2.20	5,693	803.95	14	12
	4	1.06	164	P/7	6-5-2	−164.00		5,857	639.95	11	12
		1.07	47	S/7	6-5-2	−47.00		5,904	592.95	10	12
	5	1.15	20	P/1	8-4-1	−20.00		5,924	572.95	10	12
		1.07	20	S/1	8-4-1	20.00	4.00	5,944	592.95	10	12
	6	1.12	120	P/4	4-3-2	12.00	2.20	6,064	604.95	10	12
		1.19	120	S/4	4-3-2	6.00	2.10	6,184	610.95	10	12
	7	1.21	40	S/2	4-6-2	10.00	2.50	6,224	620.95	10	12
	9	1.12	20	S/2	6-1-8	22.00	4.20	6,244	642.95	10	12
8/17	1	1.10	215	S/2	2-1-3	32.25	2.30	6,459	675.20	10	12
	4	1.11	100	P/6	6-?-?	20.00	2.40	6,559	695.20	11	12
		1.26	270	S/6	6-?-?	40.50	2.30	6,829	735.70	11	13
	5	1.26	70	P/3	?-?-3	−70.00		6,899	665.70	10	13
		1.26	50	S/3	?-?-3	42.50	3.70	6,949	708.20	10	13
	6	1.25	100	S/1	1-?-?	75.00	3.50	7,049	783.20	11	13
8/20	1	1.16	43	P/7	2-7-1	30.10	3.40	7,092	813.30	11	13
	2	1.13	150	S/3	3-4-2	37.50	2.50	7,242	850.80	12	13
	3	0.96	83	P/4	1-4-3	74.70	3.80	7,325	925.50	13	13
		1.37	10	S/4	1-4-3	7.00	3.40	7,335	932.50	13	13
	6	1.00	310	P/9	9-2-4	62.00	2.40	7,645	994.50	13	12
		1.11	320	S/9	9-2-4	48.00	2.30	7,965	1042.50	13	12
	7	1.05	150	P/2	4-2-6	127.50	3.70	8,115	1170.00	14	12
	8	0.93	20	S/1	1-7-6	13.00	3.30	8,135	1183.00	15	12
	10	1.11	150	S/2	2-3-4	45.00	2.60	8,285	1228.00	15	12

8/22	1	1.15	110	S/3	3-1-6	44.00	2.80	8,395	1272.00	15	12
	2	1.12	60	S/7	7-2-1	21.00	2.70	8,455	1293.00	15	12
	5	1.08	200	P/5	5-9-1	50.00	2.50	8,655	1343.00	16	12
		1.18	500	S/5	5-9-1	50.00	2.20	9,155	1393.00	15	12
	8	1.02	200	P/4	7-4-3	110.00	3.10	9,355	1503.00	16	12
	10	1.13	50	S/1	3-1-6	20.00	2.80	9,405	1523.00	16	12
8/23	1	1.14	50	S/4	2-4-1	22.50	2.90	9,455	1545.50	16	12
		1.11	100	P/2	2-4-1	25.00	2.50	9,555	1570.50	16	12
		1.14	270	S/2	2-4-1	54.00	2.40	9,825	1624.50	17	12
	2	1.11	250	P/1	1-5-6	200.00	3.60	10,075	1824.50	18	12
	3	1.10	21	P/7	5-3-4	−21.00		10,096	1803.50	18	12
		1.03	50	S/7	5-3-4	−50.00		10,146	1753.50	17	12
	4	1.09	50	S/7	6-5-1	−50.00		10,196	1703.50	17	12
	5	0.98	50	P/6	2-5-3	−50.00		10,246	1653.50	16	12
		1.15	100	S/6	2-5-3	−100.00		10,346	1553.50	15	12
	6	1.08	400	P/2	2-6-4	80.00	2.40	10,746	1633.50	15	12
		1.20	300	S/2	2-6-4	15.00	2.10	11,046	1648.50	15	12
	7	1.10	20	S/1	7-2-5	−20.00		11,066	1628.50	15	12
	8	0.99	193	P/3	5-3-4	38.60	2.40	11,259	1667.10	15	12
		1.11	134	S/3	5-3-4	13.40	2.20	11,393	1680.50	15	12
	10	1.15	50	P/4	4-5-7	30.00	3.20	11,443	1710.50	15	12
		1.11	150	S/4	4-5-7	37.50	2.50	11,593	1748.00	15	12
8/24	1	1.15	300	S/?		60.00	2.40	11,893	1808.00	15	12
	2	0.97	150	P/1	1-2-3	97.50	3.30	12,043	1905.50	16	12
	3	0.94	120	P/1	1-4-6	42.00	2.70	12,163	1947.50	16	12
	4	1.09	337	P/3		101.10	2.60	12,500	2048.60	16	12
		1.13	400	S/3		60.00	2.30	12,900	2108.60	16	12
	7	1.21	200	S/2	2-?-?	20.00	2.20	13,100	2128.60	16	12
	8	1.11	200	S/2	7-3-6	−200.00		13,300	1928.60	15	12
	10	1.04	150	S/6		135.00	3.80	13,450	2063.60	15	12

TABLE 17.4 ***Rate of return versus expected value. Results from 16 days and 113 wagers at Stampede Park***

Expected Value of a $1 Bet at Post Time	*Number of Bets*	*Total Wager ($)*	*Total Profit ($)*	*Rate of Return (%)*
below 1.05	22	2,289	553.85	24.2
1.05–1.09	17	2,727	251.70	9.2
1.10–1.14	33	4,084	378.70	9.3
1.15–1.19	20	2,334	326.85	14.0
1.20–1.24	11	1,190	332.00	27.9
1.25–1.29	4	490	88.00	18.0
1.30+	6	336	132.50	39.4
overall	113	$13,450	$2,063.60	15.3

TABLE 17.5 ***Rate of return versus expected value. Combined results of tables 14.3 and 17.4***

Expected Value of a $1 Bet at Post Time	*Number of Bets*	*Total Wager ($)*	*Total Profit ($)*	*Rate of Return (%)*
below 1.05	46	3,394	317.85	9.4
1.05–1.09	62	6,717	1,197.70	17.8
1.10–1.14	75	8,269	781.70	9.5
1.15–1.19	39	7,654	2,654.85	34.7
1.20–1.24	19	1,740	218.00	12.5
1.25–1.29	8	1,450	674.00	46.5
1.30+	8	456	192.50	42.2
overall	257	$29,680	$6,036.60	20.3

to the expected value at post time. The results are quite reasonable. The one surprising aspect is how well the bets that were 1.15 at bet time and fell to 1.05 or less did: these twenty-two wagers made 24.2%. Whether these latter results are small sample based or real is not clear. The Stampede Park and Churchill Downs and Louisiana Downs results from Table 14.3 are combined in Table 17.5.

USING THE DR. Z SYSTEM IN ENGLAND

The parimutuel system of betting utilizing electric totalizator boards is the dominant method of betting at North American racetracks. Las Vegas and the other legal sports books may set odds on particular betting situations,

TABLE 17.6 ***Rates of return for different odds ranges in British flat racing before taxes***

	Rate of Return				
Odds Ranges	1950	1965	1973	1975	1976
1—100 to 2—5	97.2	108.1	108.5	112.1	107.0
4—9 to 2—5	98.8	89.4	109.7	108.4	107.8
8—11 to 1—1	94.8	88.4	93.6		
21—20 to 3—2	96.5	87.2	88.6		
13—8 to 9—4	90.4	95.9	83.6		
95—40 to 4—1	95.5	95.0	95.5		
9—2 to 9—1	90.1	89.5	89.1		
19—2 to 18—1	64.5	64.9	66.5		
larger than 18—1	23.8	37.3	23.2		

Sources: Figgis (1974) and Rothschild (1978).
Note: Taxes on course of 4% and off course of 8.5% must be subtracted to determine the actual net rate of return. These rates of return are based on the assumption that every horse in each odds range was bet to return 100.

but these fixed odds are not available at racetracks. In England and in other Commonwealth countries, such as Australia and Hong Kong, and in other European countries, such as Italy and France, odds betting against bookies is the prevalent wagering scheme. The bookies set odds that you can *lock in* by buying a ticket. These odds do change over time, largely so that the bookies can balance their books to ensure themselves of a profit no matter which horse wins. You therefore have the chance to bet on different horses at different times, so you can hedge your bets. If you play it right, you either never or rarely lose, while making a sizable return all or most of the time.*

Table 17.6 lists the rates of return in British flat racing for thoroughbreds for different odds levels set by the bookmakers. As you can see, to get action on the favorites, they have to set the odds at levels that allow you to make a profit betting on these horses. Notice also, that they have the usual favorite-long-shot bias. They make their profits on the medium- and longer-priced horses, in particular on the long shots over 18–1, where they return an average of only about 20%–40% of the amount bet. The total average take by the bookies, including government taxes of 4% on course and 8.5% off course, is 10% on course and 19% off course. You have the option of paying the tax when you bet or when you win. For example, with a bet of £100

*Lest you think we've just invented a method for shaking the money out of the trees, let me tell you that this is pretty tricky. But see Lane and Ziemba (1985) for some preliminary research on this problem in the context of Mexican team Jai Alai, whose odds are set in a similar fashion.

on course, you can pay the £4 in advance, or pay 4% of your winnings. Suppose the payoff is £3 per pound bet. The tax is then £4 if paid in advance, but £12 if you win and have not prepaid the tax. In the long run, if you are more or less breaking even on your bets, the tax collected is about the same by either method. However, if you are winning on average, it is better to prepay the tax. If you are losing on average, it is better to pay the tax only when you win.

A parimutuel betting system using the tote board, although less popular in England, is available for betting on course as well as off course. As in North America, the odds are flashed periodically, but the betting pools are not shown. The odds are quoted on the payoff per £1 bet with a minimum payoff of £1. Forget about betting on superhorses—all you will get is your money back. Also the odds are quoted in terms of total return, so if the odds are shown as 3.1–1, you get £3.1 per pound bet if the horse wins, not £4.1 as would be the case in North America.

Instead of the North American parimutuel system of win, place, and show, the bets are to win and place. By "place" the British mean "finish in the money." This is much like what North Americans call show. There is, however, one important difference. The number of horses that can place in a particular race is dependent on the number of starters. This works as follows:

NUMBER OF HORSES THAT PLACE	NUMBER OF STARTERS
one: the winner	four or fewer
two: winner and second	five, six, or seven
three: winner, second, and third	eight to fifteen
four: winner, second, third, and fourth	sixteen or more

The place pools are not shown on the tote board, but the current payoffs for place bets for each horse are flashed on the screen. Bookies, on the other hand, simply pay a percentage of the win odds, as shown in Table 17.7.

There are many types of exotic bets as well, as shown on page 455. The tote jackpot corresponds to what North Americans call the pick six or sweep six. The tote placepot bet has no analogue in North America. The average rates of return on the various bets on and off course against a bookmaker or the tote are listed in Table 17.8. Of particular interest to us is the fact that the track take is 5% larger in the place pool than in the win pool. The tote take is larger than what the bookies make on average, and on-course betting takes are much less than off-course takes.

In June 1983, I was in Europe participating in conferences on risk and capital and Oriental rugs and finishing up a project at a research institute. I had a free day in London on Thursday, June 9, and took the special train from Paddington to the Newbury Race Course, where six races were being featured that day. The races in England are on the turf for distances of

TABLE 17.7 *Bookmakers payoff for place bets*

Number of Runners	Type of Race	Fraction of Win Odds Paid on Place Element	Horses Regarded
Two to five		No place betting	
Six or seven	Any	$\frac{1}{4}$	First and second
Eight or more	Any except handicaps involving twelve or more runners	$\frac{1}{5}$	First, second, and third
Twelve to fifteen	Handicaps	$\frac{1}{4}$	First, second, and third
Sixteen to twenty-one	Handicaps	$\frac{1}{5}$	First, second, third, and fourth
Twenty-two or more	Handicaps	$\frac{1}{4}$	First, second, third, and fourth

Source: Rothschild (1978).

generally at least a mile, except for some shorter races for two-year-olds. The season in southern England is unique in that races are run for about three days at each race course. The jockeys, trainers, and so forth then move on to a new course. After a month or so they return to the same course. Handicapping is very sophisticated in England. It has to be, with little information easily accessible (they have no analogue of the *Daily Racing Form*, although some past performances are available in newspapers) and all that moving from course to course. The first race in the program is shown on page 458. It featured twenty-one horses.* The mutuel payoffs to win and place were

1	7.80	1.80
	25	2.00
	88	2.00
	28	1.00

*The second race had twenty-seven starters. These are huge fields compared to the typical six to twelve in North America.

Your tote Betting Guide

MINIMUM STAKE: £1 on Win, Place, Dual Forecast and Daily Double pools; 50p for Jackpot, Placepot and Daily Treble pools, but 10p Jackpot lines accepted for permutations of not less than £5 in value.

HOW TO BET: Win, Place and Dual Forecast tickets on sale at all windows marked 'SELL' or 'BET HERE' Please use racecard numbers when placing your bet, e.g. "£1 each way number four". At some meetings SELL AND PAY will be handled at the same window. Special windows in each enclosure sell Jackpot, Placepot, Daily Double and Treble tickets.

WIN: In the Win pool, payout is on the first horse subject to the 'weighed-in'.

PLACE: Place dividends are paid on the first, second, third and fourth in handicaps of 16 or more runners coming under starter's orders; on the 1,2,3 in other races of 8 or more runners coming under orders and on the 1 and 2 in races of five, six or seven runners coming under orders. When a place pool is operating and the number of runners is reduced to four or less before coming under starter's orders, a place dividend will be declared on the winner only.

DUAL FORECAST: Dual Forecasts in which you nominate the first and second to finish in either order are available in every race with three or more runners.

PLEASE RETAIN YOUR TICKETS UNTIL THE 'WEIGHED-IN' HAS BEEN ANNOUNCED

TOTE DAILY DOUBLE: Pick the winners of the third and fifth races on the card. Winning tickets on the first leg must be exchanged for tickets on the second leg of the Double.

TOTE DAILY TREBLE: Pick the winners of the second, fourth and sixth races on the card. Winning tickets must be exchanged after each of the first two legs.

TOTE JACKPOT: Pick the winners of races 1,2,3,4,5 and 6. If there is no all-correct entry, the gross pool is carried forward.

TOTE PLACEPOT: To win the Placepot you must nominate a horse on which a place dividend is declared in Races 1,2,3,4,5 and 6 (see PLACE paragraph above). If there are 4 or less runners you must name the winner.

NON-RUNNERS: If a horse is withdrawn without coming under starter's orders a refund is made to holders of tickets nominating a non-runner in the Win, Place and Forecast pools. In the Jackpot, Placepot, Daily Double and Daily Treble, non-runners are put on the S.P. favourite. If there is more than one favourite, the backer is on the one with the lowest racecard number. Winning tickets in any one leg of the Double or Treble which have not been exchanged for a selection in the next leg will be invested on the favourite.

LATE PAY: Pay windows will remain open until 30 minutes after the last race. Tickets can be cashed on any subsequent day of the same meeting or sent for payment by post to Horserace Totalisator Board (Dept T), Tote House, 74 Upper Richmond Road, London SW15 2SU.

TABLE 17.8 ***Rates of return on different types of bets in England on thoroughbred and greyhound racing***

Type of Bet	Rate of Return (%)
On-course bookmaker	90
Off-course bookmaker	81
Single bet to win with off-course bookmaker	85
Double bet to win with off-course bookmaker	78
Treble bet to win with off-course bookmaker	72
ITV Seven bet to win with off-course bookmaker	70–75
Computer straight forecast with off-course bookmaker	65
Greyhound forecast with off-course bookmaker	76
Greyhound forecast double with off-course bookmaker	58
Place element of each-way with off-course bookmaker	80
Ante-post betting with off-course bookmaker	96
Horse race tote win pool (on course)	80
Horse race tote win pool (off course)	77
Horse race tote place pool (on course)	75
Horse race tote place pool (off course)	72
Horse race tote daily double pool (on course)	74
Horse race tote daily double pool (off course)	71
Horse race tote daily treble pool (on course)	70
Horse race tote daily treble pool (off course)	67
Horse race tote daily forecast pool (on course)	70
Horse race tote daily forecast pool (off course)	67
Horse race tote jackpot pool (on course)	70
Horse race tote jackpot pool (off course)	67
Horse race tote placepot pool (on course)	70
Horse race tote placepot pool (off course)	67
Greyhound tote pool betting, average	83.5

Source: Rothschild (1978).

With more than sixteen starters, four horses placed. Horse number 28, Tower Win, at 3.90–1 to win paid £1 for a fourth in-the-money place finish, namely a return of one's money. Since I bet on Tower Win, that was one feature of English betting learned the hard way.

The method of computing the place payoffs in England differs from that used in North America. In both locales, the net pool is the total amount wagered minus the track take. In North America, the cost of the winning in-the-money tickets is first subtracted to form the profit. This profit is then shared equally among the in-the-money horses. Holders of winning tickets receive a payoff consisting of the original stake plus their proportionate share of the horse's profits. This means that the amount of money wagered on the other horses in the money greatly affects the payoff. In England, the total net pool is divided equally among the horses that finish in the money. This means that the payoff on a particular horse depends upon how much is bet on this horse to place but *not* on how much is bet on the other horses. Since the minimum payoff is £1 per £1 wager, management is able to keep a control on betting for particular favorites. Once this minimum level is reached, it does not pay to wager on a given horse. This occurs whenever the percentage of the place pool that is bet on a given horse becomes as large as Q_p, which is the track take for place, divided by m, which is the number of in-the-money horses. In a race with 8–15 starters, if Q_p is about 0.735, and $m = 3$, the just-get-your-money-back point is reached when the bet on a particular horse to place becomes 24.5% of the total place pool: 0.735/3 = 24.5%. Hence in England you will often see horses whose place payoffs are £1 or just slightly higher. This method of sharing the place pool tends to favor longer-priced horses at the expense of the favorites.

The current track take to win is about 20.6% and to place is 26.5%, and the breakage is of the 10¢ variety, or more properly 10p, for pence.* These track takes are much higher than those in North America.

---

*We can calculate these track takes as follows: The payoff on horse i if it wins is $Q_w W/W_i$, but the pools are not made public. So let $q_i = W_i/W$, the efficient-market assumption. Let B be the average breakage, namely, 4.5p. Since breakage can be 0,1,2, . . . ,9 pence, its average is 4.5p. Then the payoff on i is $Q_w/q_i - B$, which equals the odds O_i, since the odds are based on total return (not return plus original stake as in North America). So $q_i = Q_w/(B + O_i)$. Summing over all n horses gives

$$\sum_{i=1}^{n} q_i = 1 = Q_w \sum_{i=1}^{n} \left(\frac{1}{B + O_i}\right),$$

since some horse must win. Hence

$$Q_w = \frac{1}{\sum_{i=1}^{n} (B + O_i)}.$$

For place, there are one, two, three, or four horses that are in the money, depending upon the number of starters. So

$$Q_p = \frac{m}{\sum_{i=1}^{n} (B + O_i)},$$

where $m = 1, 2, 3$, or 4.

Since the track paybacks to win and place are different, we call the former, $Q_w = 0.794$, and the latter, $Q_p = 0.735$.

It is easy to apply the Dr. Z system in Great Britain, although with its much higher track takes, there may not be as many Dr. Z system bets. We will utilize the simple substitution that

$$q_i = \frac{Q_w}{O_i} \tag{17.1}$$

where Q_w is the track payback to win and O_i are the odds to win on the horse under consideration.

At Newbury, $Q = 0.794$, so equation (17.1) becomes

$$q_i = \frac{0.794}{O_i} \tag{17.2}$$

We developed new equations and figures to compute the expected value per pound bet to place, which may be used with your cutoff to determine when to bet.

The expected value per pound bet to place on horse i is

$$\begin{aligned}\text{EX Place} &= \text{(probability of placing) (place odds)} \\ &= (\text{Prob})(PO_i).\end{aligned} \tag{17.3}$$

In the third race, the eight starters had win odds O_i and place odds PO_i as follows:

Horse Number	O_i	$1/(O_i + B)$	PO_i	$1/(PO_i + B)$
1	2.80	0.35149	1.10	0.87336
3	10.00	0.09955	1.50	0.64725
4	6.60	0.15049	1.90	0.51414
6	2.70	0.36430	1.60	0.60790
7	6.50	0.15279	1.80	0.54201
8	17.70	0.05635	3.10	0.31797
9	22.10	0.04516	3.30	0.29895
12	23.80	0.04194	3.50	0.28209
		1.25922		4.08367

Hence $Q_w = 1/1.25922 \cong 0.794$, and $Q_p = 3/4.0836 \cong 0.735$.

First Race One Mile, Straight Course, for Three Yrs Old and Upwards

2.00 The Polar Jest Apprentice Stakes (Handicap)

1 MILE, STRAIGHT COURSE START

£2000 added to stakes
Distributed in accordance with Rule 194 (iii) (b)
for three yrs old and upwards — Rated 0-35
ONE MILE, Straight Course
£4 to enter, **£16** extra if declared to run

Lowest weight 7st 7lb
Penalties, after May 18th, a winner 7lb
To be ridden by Apprentices who have not ridden more than 3 winners
Allowances: Riders who have not ridden a winner 3lb
(Apprentice races in all cases included)
THE BILLY HIGGS MEMORIAL WHIP will be presented to the winning rider
This is given in his memory by his son, Mornington I. Higgs

A **SS**

Weights raised 1lb and Rule 94 (iii) (c) complied with where applicable

98 entries, 65 at £4 and 33 at £20. — Closed 18th May, 1983.

Owners Prize Money. Winner £1556; Second £476; Third £228.
(Penalty Value £2024.00)

Form	No.	Horse / Owner (Trainer)	Age	st	lb	Draw	Jockey
24640-2	**1**	**SOCKS UP** Ch g Sharpen Up — Mrs Moss **Mr R.F. Johnson Houghton (R.F. Johnson Houghton, Didcot)** **BUFF, BLUE sleeves, MAUVE cap.**	6	9	10	(17)	D. Price
041210-	**2**	**MASSINO** B c Blakeney — Never a Fear **Mr Peter S. Winfield (P.D. Cundell, Newbury)** **ROYAL BLUE and RED (quartered), WHITE sleeves, BLACK cap.**	4	9	8	(12)	J. Kennedy
4030-	**5**	**SMILING LAUREL** Ch c Young Emperor — Tom's Delight (USA) **Mr P. Terry (Mrs Barbara Waring, Malmesbury)** **RED and WHITE check, DARK BLUE sleeves, RED and BLUE quartered cap.**	4	9	2	(19)	S. Keightley
6-0400	**8**	**SWIFT PALM** B g Some Hand — March Stone **Nimrod Company (P.D. Cundell, Newbury)** **YELLOW, BLACK seams, BLACK cap with YELLOW star.**	6	8	0	(7)	
34360-4	**9**	**WESTGATE STAR** B g He Loves Me — Sea Swallow (FR) **Mr G. Harwood (P. Calver, Ripon)** **YELLOW and RED (halved horizontally), BLACK 'H', BLACK and RED halved sleeves, quartered cap.**	4	8	8	(16)	
4650-00	**10**	**ON THE SPOT** Gr g Town Crier — Creolina **Mrs G.E. Maloney (C.E. Brittain, Newmarket)** **Mrs C.E. Brittain** **BLACK and ORANGE stripes.**	4	8	6	(11)	S. Gilmour
6003-60	**11**	**POLO BOY** Ch g Red Alert — Bermuda **Mrs A. Herbage (G.B. Balding, Weyhill)** **GREEN and ORANGE (quartered), ORANGE sleeves, GREEN cap.**	3	8	5	(14)	
0560-42	**15**	**OPTIMISTIC DREAMER** B g Full of Hope — La Crima **Mr Jeff Goodman (A. Bailey, Newmarket)** **MAROON, GREY spots.**	4	8	3	(18)	
46/0050	**16**	**COFFEE HOUSE** Br g Silly Season — Village Gossip **Mrs I.A. Balding (I.A. Balding, Kingsclere)** **GREEN and GOLD stripes**	8	8	2	(10)	A. Watkins

Form		Trainer	Age	st	lb	Draw
17	**SOLEROF**		**5**	**8**	**2**	**(1)**
	B g Averof — Solhoon					
03460/0-	**Mr M.C. Lawrence**	**(J. Thorne, Bridgwater)**				
	LIGHT and DARK GREEN (halved), sleeves reversed, LIGHT GREEN cap, DARK GREEN star.					
18	**NO SALE**		**4**	**8**	**1**	**(5)**
	B c Nonoalco (USA) — Salote (USA)					
5606-00	**Mr J.D. Riddell**	**(R.A.L. Atkins, Elstead)**				
	RED, BLACK star, BLACK cap, RED star.					
20	**MARDI GRAS**		**4**	**8**	**0**	**(15)**
	Gr g Martinmas — Miss Pimm					
00450-0	**Mrs H.G. Cambanis**	**(B. Hobbs, Newmarket)**				J. Brown
	BLACK, WHITE spots on body and sleeves.					
21	**MATCH MASTER**		**4**	**8**	**0**	**(8)**
	Ch g Roman Warrior — Giglet					
325325-	**Mr J.B. Stafford**	**(C.R. Nelson, Upper Lambourn)**				
	Mrs N.G. Stafford					
	DARK BLUE, LIGHT BLUE sleeves, YELLOW cap with DARK BLUE stripes.					
22	**ACUSHLA MACREE**		**6**	**8**	**0**	**(20)**
	Ch m Mansingh (USA) — Cannie Cassie					
2140-00	**Mr R.F. Johnson Houghton**					
		(R.F. Johnson Houghton, Didcot)				Sherry Cooper
	BUFF, BLUE sleeves, MAUVE cap.					
25	**DANCER'S EMULATION**		**3**	**7**	**10**	**(13)**
	Gr c Dancer's Image (USA) — Mossinella					
0000-6	**Mr Jim Horrocks**	**(M.J. Masson, Lewes)**				
	PURPLE and BEIGE stripes.					
26	**SCOTTISH GREEN**		**5**	**7**	**10**	**(3)**
	Ch g Scottish Rifle — Nuque (CHI)					
50/5020-	**Mr B.E. Green**	**(P.J. Makin, Marlborough)**				
	BROWN, LIGHT GREEN hoop, YELLOW cap.					
28	**TOWER WIN**		**6**	**7**	**8**	**(4)**
	Ch h Tower Walk — Takawin					
64130-4	**Mr D. Turner**	**(C.J. Benstead, Epsom)**				
	BROWN and EMERALD GREEN diamonds, GREEN sleeves, YELLOW cap.					
29	**SWEET DIPPER**		**6**	**7**	**7**	**(9)**
	Br g Golden Dipper — Sharp And Sweet					
000000-	**Mrs Andrew Normand**	**(W.G.R. Wightman, Upham)**				
	PINK, BLACK sleeves and cap, PINK spots.					
30	**DARTCAN**		**4**	**7**	**7**	**(21)**
	Ch f Streak — Canamour					
0400-0	**Mr W.N. Pooley**	**(D.C. Tucker, Frome)**				
	ROYAL BLUE and MAUVE (quartered), WHITE sleeves, MAUVE hoops, WHITE cap, ROYAL BLUE hoops.					
31	**LADY CYNARA**		**5**	**7**	**7**	**(6)**
	B m Starch Reduced — Golden Perch					
000/045	**Mr William Ivin**	**(C.P. Wildman, Salisbury)**				
	YELLOW, RED diamond, RED cap, YELLOW star.					
33	**RIVERHILL BOY**		**5**	**7**	**7**	**(2)**
	B g Manacle — My Grace					
030/0-00	**Mr A.G. Marriott**	**(C.P. Wildman, Salisbury)**				
	PINK, LIGHT GREEN sash, armlets and cap.					

NUMBER OF DECLARED RUNNERS 21 **(DUAL FORECAST)**

BLINKERS WILL BE WORN BY No. 11,17,18,22,26 30,33

1st .... 2nd .... 3rd .... 4th ....

Time: .... Distance: ....

Standard Time: 1 min. 38.2 secs.

1982 Winner: **Fandangle**, 4-9-6, M. Rogan, 11-4 (fav), A. J. Tree 11 ran

In equation (17.1), PO_i refers to the odds to place on horse i. Prob, the probability of placing is determined as follows:*†

With n = 5 to 7 horses, the first 2 horses place and

$$\text{Prob} = 0.0667 + 2.37q - 1.61q^2 - 0.0097n. \qquad (17.5)$$

With n = 8 to 15 horses, the first 3 horses place and

$$\text{Prob} = 0.0665 + 3.44q - 3.47q^2 - 0.0049n. \qquad (17.6)$$

With n = 16 or more horses, the first 4 horses place and

$$\text{Prob} = 0.0371 + 4.47q - 6.29q^2 - 0.00164n. \qquad (17.7)$$

You may use Figures 17.7, 17.8, and 17.9 to determine Prob directly using only O_i, the win odds on the horse in question. You read off the graph corresponding to the number of horses in the race. Figure 17.7 corresponds to equation (17.5) and applies when there are five, six, or seven horses. Figure 17.8 corresponds to equation (17.6) and applies when there are eight to fifteen horses. Finally, Figure 17.9 corresponds to equation (17.7) and applies when there are sixteen or more horses.

The optimal Kelly-criterion bet is then‡

$$\textbf{Optimal bet} = \left(\frac{\text{Prob } PO_i - 1}{PO_i - 1}\right)\textbf{(betting wealth)}. \qquad \textbf{(17.8)}$$

So you wager (Prob PO_i − 1)(PO_i − 1) percent of your betting wealth.

You can determine the optimal fraction of your wealth to bet indicated by equation (17.8) using Figure 17.10.

The fourth race was the Kingsclere Stakes for two-year-old fillies over 6 furlongs. The field had seven starters, which meant that only two horses could place. The favorite of the crowd at odds of 2.20–1 to win was Valkyrie.

*These equations were developed using the 1981–82 Aqueduct data to relate probability of in-the-money finishes to q, the probability of winning and n, the number of horses. Equations (17.5), (17.6), and (17.7) had R^2's of 0.991, 0.993, and 0.998, respectively. These equations are valid when q ranges from 0 to 0.6 for (17.5), from 0 to 0.45 for (17.6), and 0 to 0.3 for (17.7), which should be the case in most instances. However, Figures 17.7, 17.8, and 17.9 are valid for any q.

†In a race with n = 2, 3, or 4 horses, only one horse places, the winner. Such races are rare. Also, it is unlikely that the win and place pools would then become so unbalanced as to yield a Dr. Z system bet. However, one would occur when PO_i/O_i was at least 1.44, for a track payback of 0.794 and an expected-value cutoff of 1.14, since 1.14/0.794 is 1.44. In such a case, one would have a good bet.

‡We have assumed that your bets will be small and hence will not affect the odds very much. Thus to determine the optimal bet b for betting wealth w_O, you maximize Prob log $[w_O + (PO_i - 1)b]$ + $(1 - \text{Prob})\log(w_O - b)$, whose solution is equation (17.8).

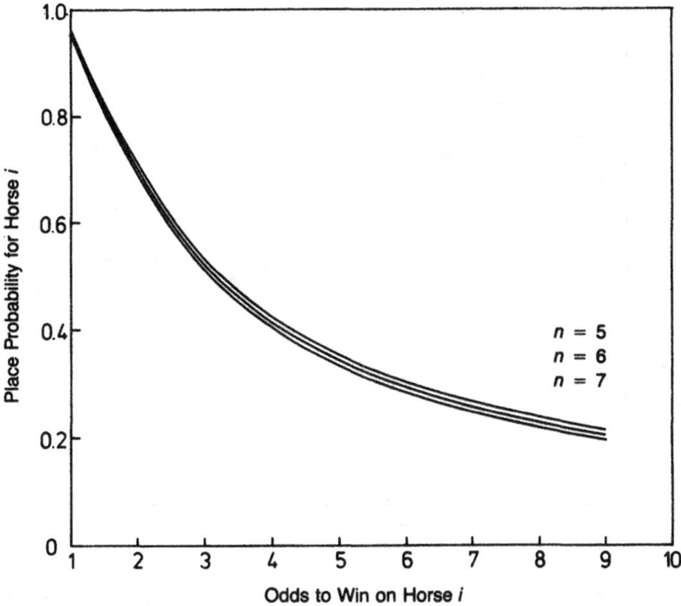

Figure 17.7 Probabilities of placing for different odds horses when the race has five to seven starters

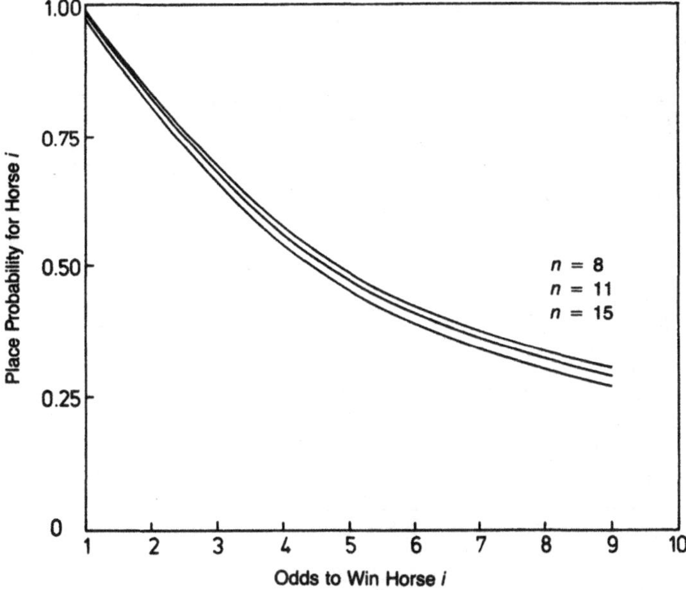

Figure 17.8 Probabilities of placing for different odds horses when the race has eight to fifteen starters

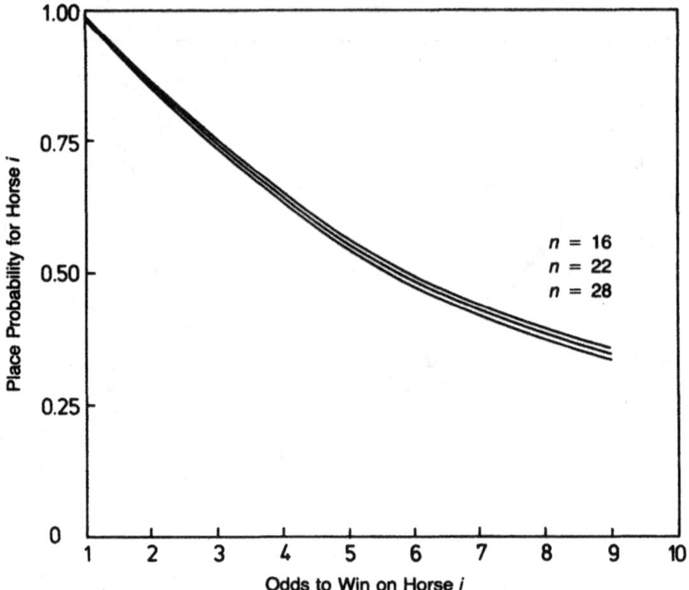

Figure 17.9 Probabilities of placing for different odds horses when the race has sixteen or more starters

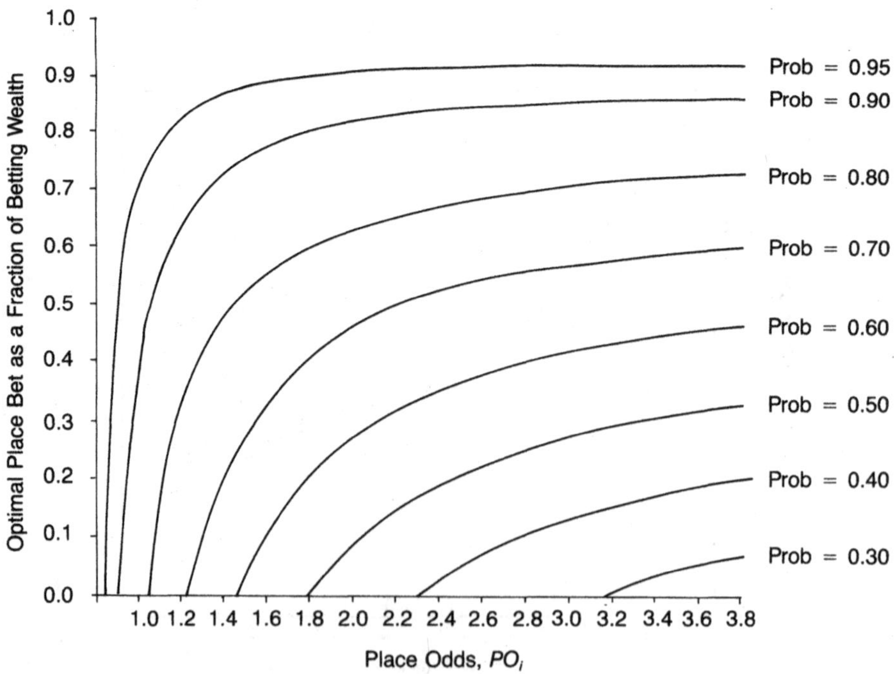

Figure 17.10 Optimal bets when the probability of placing is Prob and the place odds of the horse in question is PO_i

She was ridden by the legendary jockey Lester Piggot, England's answer to America's Bill Shoemaker. Near post time, the place odds on Valkyrie were 1.90–1. Hence by equation (17.2),

$$q = \frac{0.794}{2.20} = 0.361.$$

So Valkyrie had a 36.1% chance of winning the race. Her chance of placing, using equation (17.5) or Figure 17.7, was

$$\begin{aligned} \text{Prob} &= 0.0667 + 2.37(0.361) - 1.61(0.361)^2 - 0.0097(7) \\ &= 0.646. \end{aligned}$$

Hence, Valkyrie's chance of placing was 64.6%. The expected value per pound bet to place on Valkyrie from equation (17.3) was

$$\begin{aligned} \text{EX Place} &= (\text{Prob})(PO_i) \\ \text{EX Place} &= (0.646)(1.90) = 1.23. \end{aligned}$$

Thus we should expect to make a 23% profit betting on Valkyrie to place.

My betting fortune was £100, so from Figure 17.10 or equation (17.8), my optimal bet was £25. Pebbles won the race, followed by Refill, with Valkyrie taking third. I lost my £25 bet (see pages 464 and 465). Pebbles later became a very top horse; she won the $2 million Breeder's Cup Turf at Aqueduct in 1985.

The fifth race was the Kenneth Robertson Stakes for three-year-olds over 1 mile and 3 furlongs. There were eight starters, so three horses would place. With three minutes to post time the tote board read as follows:

	Horse							
	#1	*#2*	*#4*	*#8*	*#9*	*#10*	*#11*	*#12*
Win odds	7.20	4.70	3.50	5.50	5.90	7.70	15.40	18.30
Place odds	1.70	2.70	1.40	1.20	1.60	1.80	3.60	6.20

Near the end of the betting period the tote board was

	Horse							
	#1	*#2*	*#4*	*#8*	*#9*	*#10*	*#11*	*#12*
Win odds	7.30	4.80	3.60	4.30	6.90	9.10	17.20	17.80
Place odds	1.90	1.80	1.70	1.20	2.00	1.90	3.40	6.10

Fourth Race
TOTE TREBLE

Six Furlongs, for Two Yrs Old Fillies Only

3.30 The Kingsclere Stakes

£6000 added to stakes
Distributed in accordance with Rule 194 (iii) (a)
(Includes a fourth prize)
for two yr old fillies only
SIX FURLONGS
£12 to enter, **£48** extra if declared to run
Weights: 8st 8lb each

6 FURLONG START

Penalties, a winner of a race value £2500 .... 4lb
Maidens allowed 3lb

The winner of this race, if qualified under Rule 195, will receive a Fillies' Premium of £2400

FP **A** **SS**

72 entries, 54 at £12 and 18 at £60. — Closed 18th May, 1983.

Owners Prize Money. Winner £3817; Second £1253; Third £596; Fourth £268.
(Penalty Value £4963.20)

Form	No.	Horse / Breeding / Owner / Colours	Trainer	Age	st	lb	Draw	Jockey
1	1	**BLANCHE NEIGE** .... Gr f Forlorn River — La Magna **Mrs Paulette Meynet** **PINK, PURPLE diamonds, PURPLE sleeves, hooped cap.**	**(M.A. Jarvis, Newmarket)**		**8**	**8**	**(3)**	B. Raymond
41	2	**VALKYRIE** .... B f Bold Lad (IRE) — Sarissa **Lord Howard de Walden** **APRICOT.**	**(H. Cecil, Newmarket)**		**8**	**8**	**(4)**	L. Piggott
32	5	**DAMKINA** .... Gr f Hittite Glory — Charter Island **Mrs Peter Hastings** **PRIMROSE, BLACK hoop, armlets and cap.**	**(R. Sheather, Newmarket)**		**8**	**5**	**(6)**	
	8	**ISLAND MILL** .... B f Mill Reef (USA) — Siliciana **Mrs I.A. Balding** **GREEN and GOLD stripes.**	**(I.A. Balding, Kingsclere)**		**8**	**5**	**(2)**	J. Matthias
0	10	**PEBBLES** .... Ch f Sharpen Up — La Dolce **Capt M. Lemos** **ROYAL BLUE, WHITE hoop on body, striped cap.**	**(C.E. Brittain, Newmarket)**		**8**	**5**	**(5)**	P. Robinson
2450	11	**POUSDALE-TACHYTEES** .... B f Tachypous — Teesdale **Lord Oakley Ltd** **DARK GREEN, YELLOW chevron and armlets, hooped cap.**	**(Mrs C.J. Reavey, Wantage)**		**8**	**5**	**(7)**	
	13	**REFILL** .... Br f Mill Reef (USA) — Regal Twin (USA) **Mr E.N. Kronfeld** **DARK BLUE, WHITE cross-belts and sleeves, PINK cap.**	**(I.A. Balding, Kingsclere)**		**8**	**5**	**(1)**	Pat Eddery

NUMBER OF DECLARED RUNNERS 7 **(DUAL FORECAST)**

1st .... 2nd .... 3rd .... 4th ....

Time: .... Distance: ....

Standard Time: 1 min. 12.6 secs.

1982 Winner: **Bright Crocus (USA)**, 8-5, L. Piggott, 4-9, H. Cecil 9 ran

---

The Horserace Betting Levy Board Prize Money Scheme provides for the inclusion of £486,810 added money at this racecourse of 1983

Fifth Race
DAILY DOUBLE

One Mile and Three Furlongs, for Three Yrs Old Only

4.00 The Kenneth Robertson Stakes (Handicap)

£3000 added to stakes
Distributed in accordance with Rule 194 (iii) (b)
for three yrs old only – Rated 0-50
ONE MILE AND THREE FURLONGS
£6 to enter, **£24** extra if declared to run

1 MILE, 3 FURLONG START

Lowest weight 7st 7lb
Penalties, after May 18th, a winner 6lb
SS

Weights raised 7lbs and Rule 94 (iii) (c) complied with where applicable

55 entries, 43 at £6 and 12 at £30. — Closed 18th May, 1983.
Owners Prize Money. Winner £1923; Second £585; Third £277.
(Penalty Value £2502.60)

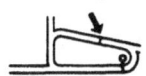

Form			Trainer	Age	st	lb	Draw
	1	**ORANGE REEF**			**9**	**7**	**(5)**
		Ch c Mill Reef (USA) — Carrot Top					
515		**Beckhampton Ltd**	**(A.J. Tree, Marlborough)**		Pat Eddery		
		PINK, BLACK and WHITE striped sleeves, WHITE cap.					
	2	**EQUANAID**			**9**	**7**	**(2)**
		B c Dominion — Jungle Queen					
010-12		**Mr V. Kilkenny**	**(C.R. Nelson, Upper Lambourn)**				
		DARK GREEN and YELLOW (quartered), YELLOW sleeves, check cap.					
	4	**GAELIC JEWEL**			**9**	**3**	**(8)**
		Br f Scottish Rifle — Red Ruby					
0-13		**Lavinia Duchess of Norfolk**	**(J.L. Dunlop, Arundel)**				
		SKY BLUE, SCARLET quartered cap.					
	8	**MOON JESTER**			**8**	**11**	**(4)**
		Gr c Comedy Star (USA) — Castle Moon					
41-2622		**Mr T.C. Marshall**	**(M.D.I. Usher, Lambourn)**		D McKay		
		ORANGE and WHITE (halved), sleeves reversed, striped cap.					
	9	**MISINSKIE (USA)**			**8**	**11**	**(6)**
		B f Nijinsky (CAN) — Kankakee Miss (USA)					
4233-		**Mr S.S. Niarchos**	**(P.T. Walwyn, Lambourn)**		J Mercer		
		DARK BLUE, LIGHT BLUE cross-belts, striped sleeves, WHITE cap.					
	10	**HARBOUR BRIDGE**			**8**	**8**	**(7)**
		B c Blakeney — Solar					
030-015		**Mrs R.B. Kennard**	**(W.G.R. Wightman, Upham)**		B. Rouse		
		PALE BLUE and ORANGE stripes, BLUE cap, ORANGE diamond.					
	11	**CAPTAIN WEBSTER**			**8**	**2**	**(3)**
		Ch c Sandford Lad — Maynooth Belle					
01-6416		**Mr J. Woodman**	**(S. Woodman, Chichester)**		W. Newnes		
		Mr S.R. Deveson					
		BROWN, YELLOW seams, hooped cap.					
	12	**KWA ZULU (USA)**			**7**	**11**	**(1)**
		Ch c Naskra (USA) — Sweet Nothings (USA)					
055-5		**Mr D.I. Scott**	**(G.H. Hunter, East Ilsley)**				
		Mr G.H. Hunter					
		BLACK, WHITE Maltese cross and cap, RED sleeves.					

NUMBER OF DECLARED RUNNERS 8 **(DUAL FORECAST)**

1st .... 2nd .... 3rd .... 4th ....

Time: .... Distance: ....

Standard Time: 2 mins. 18 secs.

1982 Winner: **Khairpour,** 9-1, J. Reid. 11-10, R F Johnson.Houghton 9 ran

The best bet was on Gaelic Jewel, the number 4 horse. From equation (17.2)

$$q = \frac{0.794}{3.60} = 0.221.$$

So Gaelic Jewel's chance of winning was 22.1%. His chance of placing, using equation (17.6) or Figure 17.8, was

$$\begin{aligned} \text{Prob} &= 0.0665 + 3.44(0.221) - 3.47(0.221)^2 - 0.0049(8) \\ &= 0.616. \end{aligned}$$

Hence, Gaelic Jewel would be in the money 61.1% of the time. The expected value per pound bet to place on Gaelic Jewel from equation (17.3) was then

$$\text{EX Place} = (0.616)(1.70) = 1.05.$$

This low expected value signaled caution. A bet of £5 was suggested from Figure 17.10 or equation (17.8).

$$\begin{aligned} \text{Optimal bet} &= \frac{(0.616)(1.70) - 1}{(1.70 - 1)} \text{(betting wealth)} \\ &= (0.07)(£75) \\ &= £5. \end{aligned}$$

Moon Jester won the race. Gaelic Jewel took second, and Orange Reef was third. My £5 bet returned £8.50, for a £3.50 profit.

In summary, the Dr. Z system is easy to apply in England, France, Italy, Germany, Australia, Hong Kong, and the other countries that utilize a win-and-place betting scheme. First determine Prob using one of Figures 17.7, 17.8, or 17.9. Then multiply Prob by PO_i to determine the expected value per pound bet to place. If this value exceeds the cutoff—we recommend 1.14—then use O_i in Figure 17.10 to determine the optimal bet. We have not done enough research to determine how often Dr. Z system bets will occur in England. With the higher track take, however, it is likely that there are fewer than in North America.

APPENDIX

Thoroughbred Racetracks in North America: Seasons, Purses, Betting, and Track Takes

Toward the end of this appendix is a map that shows you the location of the major thoroughbred racetracks in North America. More detailed information on the typical seasons, days, attendance, mutuel handles, races run, and number and percentage of winning crowd favorites at these racetracks in 1985 appears in Table A.1. Information about thoroughbred racing in North America appears in Tables A.2–A.5. Table A.2 shows the number of racing days by state in 1985 for the thirty-two states that have thoroughbred racing as well as for Canada and Mexico. California, with 619, had the most racing days in the United States with large purses at Del Mar, Hollywood Park, and Santa Anita, medium purses at Bay Meadows and Golden Gate Fields, and small purses at the fair meetings.

The daily average gross purses by state in 1985 are shown in Table A.3. New York, which features Aqueduct, Belmont, and Saratoga and both on-track and off-track betting, has the largest purses, averaging $216,000 per racing day. California, New Jersey, and Arkansas have purses that are nearly as large. Arkansas rates high because the only racing is at Oaklawn Park, one of the nation's top tracks.

In 1985, purses in the United States averaged 6.8% of the money bet. The daily average betting in 1985, by state, appears in Table A.4. California had the highest figure, followed by Arkansas, New York, New Jersey, Florida, Illinois, Maryland, and Minnesota, each of which averaged more than $1 million per day. The total betting per year appears in Table A.5. California and New York swamp the other states with totals of $1.9 and $1 billion, respectively. Surprisingly, Louisiana is fourth, higher than such wealthier states as Florida, New Jersey, Pennsylvania, and the famous racing state of Kentucky.

Track takes are listed by state for the United States, by province for Canada, and for Mexico in Table A.6. Finally, the current racing results of the highest-priced yearlings appear on page 480. So far, these multimillionaires' performances have not lived up to their initial promises.

TABLE A.1 ***Typical seasons, attendance, mutuel handle, and percentage of winning favorites of the crowd at major North American racetracks in 1985***

Track	Dates	Days	Attendance	Mutuel Handle	Races Run	Winning First Choices	% Winning Favorites	Total Gross Distribution ($)	Total Net Distribution ($)	Aver. Net per Race ($)	Aver. Net per Day ($)
Agua Caliente Mexico	Jan 1 to June 30	52	200,000	19,855,627	621	194	.30	2,176,900	2,176,900	3,505	41,863
	Jly 6 to Dec. 29	52	145,000	14,552,291	596	201	.32	1,842,101	1,834,351	3,077	35,275
Aiken Hunt	Mar 23	1	8,755	—	4	†	†	18,500	18,500	4,625	18,500
Ak-Sar-Ben	May 1 to Aug 25	86	1,305,753	154,159,067	811	264	.31	9,952,975	9,643,515	11,890	112,133
Albuquerque	Mar 15 to Apr 28	27	127,764	15,167,983	210	70	.32	918,050	896,500	4,269	33,203
	Sep 6 to Oct 6	25	192,779	21,349,657	222	59	.25	1,724,785	1,537,100	6,923	61,484
Aqueduct	Jan 1 to Mar 11	57	656,998	157,377,984	506	157	.30	11,878,650	11,407,500	22,544	200,131
	Mar 13 to May 6	48	646,370	154,166,959	432	143	.33	10,744,400	10,157,000	23,511	211,604
	Oct 23 to Dec. 31	60	725,065	174,956,813	539	177	.32	25,879,600	24,829,000	46,064	413,816
Arlington Park	May 19 to Jly 30	66	671,051	125,929,035	594	228	.37	7,648,415	7,315,830	12,396	110,846
	Aug 25	1	35,651	3,674,448	10	3	.30	1,236,425	1,224,000	154,553	1,224,000
Assiniboia Downs	May 3 to Oct 15	108	393,032	39,427,949	1,008	328	.32	3,874,935	3,650,578	3,621	33,801
Atlanta Hunt	Apr 6	1	—	—	6	†	†	92,000	92,000	15,333	92,000
Atlantic City	Jly 26 to Aug 31	32	209,047	19,796,076	292	96	.31	2,473,850	2,408,600	8,248	75,268
Atokad Park	May 4 to Jly 21	26	36,998	2,859,421	286	106	.35	344,550	341,900	1,195	13,150
Balmoral	Jun 26 to Aug 18	40	135,099	14,111,815	360	132	.35	1,687,576	1,647,105	4,575	41,177
Bay Meadows	Jan 1 to Feb 4	26	267,044	56,274,383	250	82	.32	2,845,100	2,813,000	11,252	108,192
	Sep 17 to Oct 14	21	176,442	35,878,497	197	77	.38	2,326,550	2,251,650	11,429	107,221
	Oct 17 to Dec 31	55	547,004	136,103,898	526	175	.32	7,460,000	7,096,000	13,490	129,018
Bay Meadows Fair	Aug 31 to Sep 14	13	111,291	21,584,757	117	35	.29	1,306,275	1,269,000	10,846	97,615
Belmont Park	May 8 to Jly 29	72	1,160,668	245,990,512	648	223	.33	20,707,250	18,941,500	29,230	263,076
	Aug 28 to Oct 21	47	678,123	143,765,674	423	150	.35	16,084,050	14,422,500	34,095	306,861
Billings	Aug 7 to Oct 6	36	113,606	5,197,400	377	120	.31	698,979	694,179	1,841	19,282
Blue Ribbon Downs	Feb 8 to Jly 7	64	170,000	22,532,501	239	74	.30	531,450	507,600	2,123	7,931
	Aug 8 to Dec 8	59	138,468	19,305,561	258	86	.32	728,647	564,700	2,188	9,571
Boise	May 8 to Aug 18	51	161,567	7,543,053	403	154	.37	545,273	471,200	1,169	9,239

Bowie	Jan 1 to Jan 19	15	99,451	14,221,244	127	37	.29	995,300	980,500	7,720	65,366
	Jun 3 to Jly 13	36	220,490	32,741,689	324	97	.29	2,714,700	2,658,000	8,203	73,833
Calder	Jan 1 to Jan 7	6	74,156	11,518,939	60	24	.38	1,365,381	1,131,900	18,865	188,650
	May 4 to May 28	20	181,995	23,123,719	177	53	.29	1,966,725	1,853,200	10,470	92,660
	May 31 to Nov 9	121	978,614	137,074,544	1,210	373	.29	14,475,778	14,079,200	11,635	116,357
	Nov 11 to Dec 31	43	359,712	53,499,745	432	122	.27	4,722,925	4,566,800	10,571	106,204
Camden Hunt	Mar 30 & Nov 17	2	69,000	—	11	†	†	144,500	144,500	13,136	72,250
Canterbury Downs	Jun 26 to Oct 15	83	1,092,529	84,210,804	781	278	.34	7,067,630	6,894,725	8,828	83,068
Charles Town	Jan 4 to Mar 31	59	179,845	21,005,565	566	173	.29	1,777,240	1,776,340	3,138	30,107
	Apr 1 to Jun 30	64	253,266	27,774,615	634	216	.33	2,078,030	2,070,780	3,266	32,355
	Jly 1 to Sep 29	66	272,510	28,736,869	658	250	.37	2,262,420	2,259,320	3,433	34,232
	Oct 1 to Dec 15	54	162,105	18,072,357	534	183	.33	2,014,210	1,953,260	3,657	36,171
Churchill Downs	Apr 27 to Jun 30	57	678,371	80,092,805	534	200	.37	7,340,035	6,690,705	12,529	117,380
	Oct 27 to Nov 30	30	283,327	34,943,530	272	76	.27	3,539,304	3,192,000	11,735	106,400
Clemmons Hunt	May 11	1	18,000	—	5	†	†	35,000	35,000	7,000	35,000
Columbus	Jly 26 to Sep 11	25	92,166	8,248,346	240	83	.34	1,062,575	1,056,700	4,402	42,268
Darby Downs	Apr 5 to Jly 14	61	213,298	23,527,122	595	173	.28	2,497,250	2,468,700	4,149	40,470
	Nov 1 to Dec 16	29	81,040	9,593,432	276	88	.31	1,228,475	1,202,900	4,358	41,479
Delaware Park	Apr 27 to Oct 14	99	418,653	51,691,306	813	269	.32	4,104,600	4,044,700	4,975	40,855
Del Mar	Jly 24 to Sep 11	42	830,605	150,115,233	378	135	.34	8,886,270	8,337,000	22,055	198,500
Delta Downs	Jan 1 to Mar 31	48	121,224	19,860,556	507	149	.28	1,816,400	1,421,400	2,803	29,612
	Sep 20 to Dec 31	52	120,741	17,824,090	539	175	.31	1,592,900	1,534,900	2,847	29,517
Detroit	Mar 29 to Nov 10	181	748,647	119,668,162	1,740	610	.34	10,102,716	9,896,616	5,687	54,677
Ellis Park	Jun 27 to Sep 2	59	304,960	36,738,546	590	177	.29	3,580,198	3,497,448	5,927	59,278
Evangeline Downs	Apr 12 to Sep 15	103	323,337	34,036,041	1,027	334	.31	3,040,800	2,793,250	2,719	27,118
Exhibition Park	Apr 7 to Oct 27	140	1,038,969	143,954,097	1,261	392	.30	7,301,850	6,951,600	5,512	49,654
Fair Grounds	Jan 1 to Apr 14	68	497,964	87,654,328	751	279	.36	6,822,775	6,538,000	8,705	96,147
	Nov 23 to Dec 31	26	197,509	31,628,467	286	102	.35	2,658,035	2,453,000	8,576	94,346
Fair Hill	May 27 to Jun 8	2	19,747	316,543	16	2	.15	83,500	83,500	5,218	41,750
	Oct 12	1	8,632	117,906	8	2	.25	33,000	33,000	4,125	33,000
Fairfax	Sep 21	1	5,400	—	5	†	†	20,000	20,000	4,000	20,000
Fairmount Park	Mar 15 to Nov 3	167	782,639	89,088,871	1,664	512	.30	7,297,869	7,114,394	4,275	42,601
Far Hills	Oct 26	1	33,000	—	6	†	†	75,000	75,000	12,500	75,000

TABLE A.1 *(continued)*

Track	Dates	Days	Attendance	Mutuel Handle	Races Run	Winning First Choices	% Winning Favorites	Total Gross Distrbution ($)	Total Net Distribution ($)	Aver. Net per Race ($)	Aver. Net per Day ($)
Ferndale	Aug 8 to Aug 17	9	37,308	1,478,126	52	24	.44	84,775	83,572	1,607	9,285
Finger Lakes	Mar 29 to Apr 27	16	40,350	4,547,815	144	39	.26	729,600	729,600	5,066	45,600
	Apr 28 to Jun 30	46	134,519	14,705,515	424	133	.31	2,220,950	2,213,200	5,219	48,113
	Jly 1 to Aug 31	45	142,661	15,026,736	426	137	.31	2,526,030	2,474,500	5,808	54,988
	Sep 1 to Nov 12	54	129,625	14,631,573	482	162	.33	2,526,114	2,380,300	4,938	44,079
Fonner Park	Feb 21 to Apr 27	42	226,425	26,482,824	398	144	.35	1,589,216	1,552,476	3,900	36,963
Fort Erie	Apr 28 to Sep 30	71	325,855	34,908,300	706	253	.35	2,678,800	2,667,200	3,777	37,566
Foxfield	Apr 27 to Sep 29	2	38,487	—	12	†	†	71,000	71,000	5,916	35,500
Fresno	May 3 to Jun 17	27	84,329	11,868,117	196	62	.31	805,575	785,200	4,006	29,081
	Oct 7 to Oct 20	13	66,755	8,247,590	117	49	.40	502,250	488,800	4,177	37,600
Garden State Park	Apr 1 to Jun 15	66	791,145	83,228,661	619	202	.32	14,163,850	13,605,750	21,980	206,147
	Jun 17 to Jly 25	34	337,340	35,259,233	317	83	.25	4,075,375	4,029,325	12,710	118,509
Genesee Valley	Oct 12	1	2,000	—	1	†	†	2,500	2,500	2,500	2,500
Glyndon	Apr 27	1	—	—	1	†	†	15,000	15,000	15,000	15,000
Golden Gate	Feb 5 to May 5	65	641,862	130,943,321	630	196	.30	7,608,200	7,380,000	11,714	113,538
	May 8 to Jun 23	35	365,606	76,223,303	329	104	.31	4,332,550	4,189,500	12,734	119,700
Grand Nat'l (Butler)	Apr 20	1	—	—	3	†	†	19,000	18,000	6,333	19,000
Grants Pass	May 24 to Jly 7	23	31,165	2,425,580	144	45	.30	132,675	126,800	880	5,513
Great Falls	May 18 to Aug 4	30	73,211	3,216,030	323	111	.31	363,150	363,150	1,124	12,105
Greenwood	Mar 18 to Apr 27	29	234,697	44,733,129	277	103	.37	2,695,050	2,648,100	9,559	91,313
	Oct 28 to Dec 5	28	195,233	42,794,847	260	68	.26	3,220,325	3,129,000	12,034	111,750
Green Meadow	May 4 & Oct 19	2	41,600	—	13	†	†	80,200	80,200	6,169	40,100
Gulfstream Park	Jan 8 to Mar 6	50	695,375	114,940,056	509	148	.28	9,193,775	8,366,000	16,436	167,320
Harbor Park	Jly 20 to Jly 29	6	—	183,687	27	13	.44	14,870	13,520	500	2,253
*Hawthorne	Aug 5 to Sep 30	51	367,349	68,455,602	459	173	.36	6,794,535	5,760,460	12,550	112,950
	Oct 1 to Dec 31	84	491,813	97,690,274	756	246	.31	7,110,965	6,869,840	9,087	81,783
Hialeah	Mar 7 to May 3	50	439,706	71,485,620	508	152	.29	6,591,150	6,048,800	11,907	120,976

Hollywood Park	Apr 24 to Jly 22	67	1,722,264	367,573,583	606	206	.33	18,240,800	17,322,000	28,584	258,537
	Nov 13 to Dec 24	30	633,876	135,851,498	271	95	.33	9,306,900	8,757,850	32,316	291,928
Jefferson Downs	Apr 18 to Sep 28	106	459,996	55,316,455	1,062	357	.33	4,402,200	4,247,200	3,999	40,067
	Oct 2 to Nov 22	30	110,805	14,163,750	303	113	.35	1,273,550	1,125,500	3,714	37,516
Juarez	May 19 to Sep 29	20	45,895	2,254,844	166	60	.33	307,107	294,015	1,771	14,700
Keeneland	Apr 6 to Apr 26	15	200,996	19,210,935	120	50	.41	2,357,725	2,213,900	18,449	147,593
	Oct 5 to Oct 26	16	205,261	19,492,003	128	45	.34	2,773,940	2,634,245	20,580	164,640
La Mesa Park	Apr 27 to Sep 29	61	87,536	11,275,253	412	157	.37	800,741	527,600	1,280	8,649
Latonia	Jan 1 to Apr 4	69	272,474	38,593,353	674	195	.28	4,426,253	4,289,580	6,364	62,167
	Sep 4 to Oct 4	27	127,190	18,501,827	312	74	.23	1,728,000	1,678,200	5,378	62,155
	Nov 24 to Dec 31	31	102,481	15,371,364	309	91	.29	1,624,580	1,604,880	5,193	51,770
Laurel	Jan 22 to Mar 10	41	324,091	49,025,075	369	105	.28	3,607,650	3,439,000	9,319	83,878
	Sep 22 to Dec 31	81	621,652	91,779,610	730	223	.30	9,086,119	8,496,594	11,639	104,896
Lexington	Apr 28	1	—	—	5	†	†	47,500	47,500	9,500	47,500
Lincoln State Fair	Sep 3 to Nov 11	41	177,377	19,728,259	376	131	.34	1,301,924	1,245,614	3,312	30,380
Longacres	Apr 3 to Oct 14	133	1,133,266	158,034,744	1,330	386	.28	10,789,015	10,060,200	7,564	75,640
Malvern	May 18	1	8,000	—	7	†	†	43,500	43,500	6,214	43,500
Marquis Downs	May 10 to Jun 22	25	25,904	2,413,492	225	84	.37	327,488	323,950	1,439	12,958
	Aug 30 to Oct 14	27	27,719	3,061,208	255	96	.37	472,399	466,150	1,828	17,264
Marshfield Fair	Aug 16 to Aug 24	8	43,439	3,461,827	81	32	.37	162,800	162,800	2,009	20,350
Meadowbrook	Sep 22	1	—	—	4	†	†	62,500	62,500	15,625	62,500
Meadowlands	Sep 2 to Dec 31	93	1,160,948	178,160,199	925	311	.32	14,382,055	13,592,155	14,694	146,157
Middleburg	Apr 21 & Oct 5 & 6	3	16,115	—	19	†	†	65,000	65,000	3,421	21,666
Monkton	Apr 13	1	—	—	2	†	†	15,000	15,000	7,500	15,000
Monmouth Park	May 24 to Aug 31	86	987,142	139,321,867	832	288	.34	12,329,110	11,795,575	14,177	137,157
Montpelier	Nov 2	1	7,122	—	5	†	†	20,500	20,500	4,100	20,500
Morven Park	Oct 12	1	—	—	6	†	†	29,000	29,000	4,833	29,000
Mt Pleasant	Jly 6 to Oct 5	5	—	—	5	3	.60	3,200	3,200	640	640
Northampton Fair	Aug 30 to Sep 7	9	50,000	4,866,630	93	24	.25	210,900	210,900	2,317	23,433
Northlands Park	May 24 to Sep 2	75	374,976	49,447,832	683	228	.33	3,109,417	3,108,7271	4,551	41,449
Nuevo Laredo	Jan 19 to Dec 14	49	53,194	3,213,608	288	131	.45	334,450	306,200	1,063	6,248
Oaklawn Park	Feb 8 to Apr 20	62	1,367,371	165,123,545	606	165	.26	8,964,950	8,309,350	13,711	134,021
Oxmoor	Apr 13	1	—	—	5	†	†	15,500	15,500	3,100	15,500

TABLE A.1 *(continued)*

Track	Dates	Days	Attendance	Mutuel Handle	Races Run	Winning First Choices	% Winning Favorites	Total Gross Distribution ($)	Total Net Distribution ($)	Aver. Net per Race ($)	Aver. Net per Day ($)
Palm Beach	May 9	1	5,750	—	4	†	†	50,000	50,000	12,500	50,000
Penn National	Jan 4 to Apr 10	46	174,147	22,784,673	447	133	.28	1,699,400	1,699,400	3,801	36,943
	Apr 12 to Jly 3	60	235,381	28,055,753	579	179	.30	2,581,853	2,575,853	4,448	42,930
	Jly 4 to Dec 30	103	399,955	48,426,395	1,018	334	.32	4,927,325	4,881,300	4,794	47,391
Percy Warner	May 11	1	—	—	5	†	†	70,000	70,000	14,000	70,000
**Philadelphia Park	Jan 1 to Jan 30	21	122,038	17,576,548	184	55	.29	1,563,645	1,544,845	8,395	73,564
	Feb 1 to Mar 31	47	335,710	48,721,432	436	133	.29	4,273,825	4,179,500	9,586	88,925
	Sep 1 to Nov 12	64	427,131	61,104,170	597	206	.33	7,457,900	7,192,000	12,046	112,375
	Nov 13 to Dec 31	39	230,678	36,960,901	365	101	.27	3,879,275	3,779,000	10,353	96,897
Pimlico	Mar 11 to Jun 1	72	637,230	81,319,339	649	215	.32	7,396,100	6,935,000	10,685	96,319
	Jly 15 to Aug 23	32	220,655	27,897,136	288	89	.30	2,715,900	2,604,000	9,041	81,375
	Sep 3 to Sep 21	17	110,154	13,518,406	153	43	.27	1,391,900	1,373,000	8,973	80,764
Pine Mountain	Nov 3	1	7,520	—	4	†	†	85,000	85,000	21,250	85,000
Playfair	May 1 to Oct 21	101	324,697	27,322,423	1,014	311	.30	2,429,867	2,278,100	2,246	22,555
Pleasanton	Jun 21 to Jly 7	13	134,485	19,557,297	117	38	.31	1,185,625	1,156,000	9,880	88,923
Portland Meadows	Jan 1 to Apr 28	65	242,449	24,023,784	579	217	.36	1,204,150	1,188,500	2,052	18,284
	Oct 25 to Dec 31	27	108,562	9,319,266	253	95	.36	572,420	543,100	2,146	20,114
Pomona	Sep 12 to Sep 29	18	264,840	45,029,323	162	43	.25	2,452,730	2,357,500	14,552	130,972
Prescott Downs	May 25 to Sep 2	35	73,741	4,408,671	229	92	.38	271,528	266,793	1,165	7,622
Prospect	May 25	1	—	—	5	†	†	73,400	73,400	14,680	73,400
Red Bank	Oct 19	1	25,103	—	5	†	†	61,000	61,000	12,200	61,000
Regina	Jun 28 to Aug 24	30	31,809	3,241,538	286	107	.36	436,880	428,450	1,498	14,281
River Downs	Apr 20 to Jun 23	56	241,045	32,401,355	564	190	.32	3,223,770	3,159,700	5,602	56,423
	Jun 24 to Nov 18	91	375,311	52,204,817	919	291	.31	5,268,140	5,175,450	5,631	56,873
Rockingham Park	Apr 19 to Nov 26	165	786,390	90,910,710	1,665	551	.32	8,577,450	8,428,800	5,062	51,083
Ruidoso	May 17 to Sep 2	59	316,194	33,781,719	412	117	.27	1,912,248	1,488,000	3,611	25,220
Sacramento	Aug 20 to Sep 2	13	101,550	11,040,287	116	46	.38	678,750	654,100	5,638	50,315

Salem	Aug 23 to Oct 20	36	101,200	6,289,433	314	111	.34	346,005	334,800	1,066	9,300
San Juan Downs	May 4 to Sep 2	56	71,522	4,602,398	291	92	.30	351,229	329,996	1,134	5,892
Sandown Park	Oct 26 to Nov 18	12	24,876	1,826,198	102	39	.37	223,500	223,500	2,191	18,625
Santa Anita Park	Jan 1 to Apr 22	84	2,750,563	502,494,688	755	243	.31	23,697,550	22,353,250	29,606	266,110
	Oct 2 to Nov 11	32	858,652	157,504,086	288	97	.32	8,598,750	8,035,000	27,899	251,093
	Dec 26 to Dec 31	5	181,979	31,865,906	45	13	.27	1,297,450	1,246,000	27,688	249,200
Santa Fe	May 3 to Sep 2	71	252,244	30,419,047	606	170	.27	2,942,197	2,157,850	3,560	30,392
Santa Rosa	Jly 22 to Aug 4	13	128,614	15,431,935	117	29	.24	891,375	870,700	7,441	66,976
Saratoga	Jly 31 to Aug 26	24	649,883	107,946,092	216	71	.32	8,147,250	7,197,000	33,319	299,875
Solano	Jly 9 to Jly 21	13	110,282	15,450,663	117	32	.26	844,950	826,600	7,064	63,584
Southern Pines	Apr 13	1	35,000	—	5	†	†	31,000	31,000	6,200	31,000
Sportsman's Park	Feb 25 to May 18	75	563,768	122,668,290	675	209	.30	9,361,165	9,107,315	13,492	121,430
Stampede Park	Apr 5 to May 20	31	106,316	15,504,428	310	111	.35	1,087,021	1,071,086	3,455	34,551
	Sep 6 to Nov 11	41	129,760	20,397,075	410	117	.28	1,884,245	1,825,125	4,451	44,515
Stockton	Aug 6 to Aug 18	12	71,088	10,252,453	108	40	.36	513,981	506,501	4,689	42,208
Strawberry Hill	Apr 13	1	—	—	6	†	†	23,000	23,000	3,833	23,000
Suffolk Downs	Jan 1 to Dec 29	251	1,279,553	204,569,210	2,517	896	.34	13,877,240	13,681,300	5,435	54,507
Sun Downs	Mar 2 to Mar 31	10	—	747,833	23	7	.41	15,300	15,300	665	1,530
	Jun 21 to Jun 30	6	—	301,854	20	7	.31	13,700	13,700	685	2,283
	Sep 21 to Oct 20	6	—	540,992	9	2	.22	5,700	5,700	633	950
Sunland Park	Jan 1 to May 5	53	160,082	17,712,209	416	138	.32	1,503,876	1,058,200	2,543	19,966
	Oct 12 to Dec 31	35	95,044	9,883,415	262	100	.37	708,037	580,000	2,213	16,571
Tampa Bay	Jan 1 to Apr 9	72	281,318	29,586,449	723	219	.29	3,207,450	3,056,100	4,226	42,445
	Dec 3 to Dec 31	20	63,591	7,022,343	200	58	.28	757,770	732,500	3,662	36,625
Thistledown	Mar 15 to May 19	47	222,945	31,846,381	444	151	.33	2,658,660	2,636,300	5,937	56,091
	May 22 to Jly 28	50	257,643	33,883,085	474	155	.31	3,291,200	3,248,740	6,853	64,974
	Jly 31 to Oct 6	50	238,579	31,371,522	471	154	.32	2,967,380	2,931,600	6,224	58,632
	Oct 8 to Dec 9	44	186,345	25,861,878	419	142	.33	2,424,965	2,391,300	5,707	54,347
Timonium	Aug 24 to Sep 2	10	66,572	5,999,070	91	26	.27	446,900	443,500	4,873	44,350
Tryon	Apr 20	1	12,750	—	5	†	†	27,000	27,000	5,400	27,000
Turf Paradise	Jan 1 to Feb 17	40	193,798	21,189,716	442	125	.27	1,830,350	1,793,350	4,057	44,833
	Feb 18 to May 12	63	283,421	29,361,624	656	203	.30	2,493,716	2,417,400	3,685	38,371
	Oct 4 to Dec 31	55	268,623	28,330,985	593	176	.28	2,311,546	2,104,410	3,548	38,262

TABLE A.1 *(continued)*

Track	*Dates*	*Days*	*Attendance*	*Mutuel Handle*	*Races Run*	*Winning First Choices*	*% Winning Favorites*	*Total Gross Distribution ($)*	*Total Net Distribution ($)*	*Aver. Net per Race ($)*	*Aver. Net per Day ($)*
Unionville	Nov 9	1	4,500	—	6	†	†	17,000	17,000	2,833	17,000
Uranium Downs	Aug 24 to Sep 29	11	—	—	20	11	.55	22,278	19,897	994	1,808
Waterford Park	Jan 1 to Mar 31	51	87,706	10,046,616	521	153	.28	1,100,700	1,100,700	2,112	21,582
	Apr 1 to Jun 30	64	138,344	14,721,384	673	206	.29	1,367,000	1,361,800	2,023	21,278
	Jly 1 to Sep 29	60	140,750	13,858,949	636	187	.28	1,282,500	1,282,500	2,016	21,375
	Oct 3 to Dec 31	59	90,753	10,175,314	611	191	.30	1,124,300	1,124,300	1,840	19,055
Woodbine	Apr 28 to Oct 27	136	1,145,816	210,971,643	1,274	384	.30	20,273,696	18,707,600	14,684	137,555
Wyoming Downs	May 25 to Sep 2	42	131,332	5,961,479	275	91	.32	364,561	292,308	1,062	6,959
Yakima Meadows	Mar 2 to Apr 1	15	27,564	2,954,143	150	54	.35	198,450	176,800	1,178	11,786
	Apr 6 to Jun 10	30	42,693	4,329,158	181	67	.35	190,900	189,100	1,044	6,303
	Aug 31 to Oct 6	15	24,457	1,903,037	92	34	.36	93,150	91,800	997	6,120
	Oct 12 to Dec 1	23	25,664	3,115,988	230	83	.34	318,805	261,800	1,138	11,382
Totals		8,143	54,998,805	8,254,612,623	75,687	24,674	.32	$652,475,303	$619,515,147	8,185	76,079

†No Wagering
*Includes dates for Arlington Park Aug. 5 to Sep. 30
**Includes dates for Keystone Park Jan. 1 to Mar. 31
Source: The American Racing Manual, 1986: Daily Racing Form.

TABLE A.2 ***Thoroughbred racing days in the United States, Canada, and Mexico in 1985***

1.	California	619	18.	New Hampshire	165
2.	Louisiana	558	19.	Oregon	151
3.	Illinois	484	20.	Oklahoma	123
4.	West Virginia	477	21.	Delaware	99
5.	New York	471	22.	Minnesota	83
6.	Ohio	428	23.	Montana	66
7.	Kentucky	397	24.	Arkansas	62
8.	New Mexico	387	25.	Idaho	51
9.	Florida	383	26.	Wyoming	42
10.	Pennsylvania	382	27.	Colorado	11
11.	Washington	345	28.	Virginia	11
12.	New Jersey	313	29.	North Carolina	3
13.	Maryland	310	30.	South Carolina	3
14.	Massachusetts	268	31.	Georgia	2
15.	Nebraska	233	32.	Tennessee	1
16.	Arizona	193		Canada	753
17.	Michigan	186		Mexico	173
				Total	8143

Source: The American Racing Manual 1986: Daily Racing Form

TABLE A.3 ***Daily average gross purses at all thoroughbred tracks in the United States, Canada, and Mexico in 1985 in thousands of dollars***

1.	New York	216	18.	Massachusetts	53
2.	California	169	19.	New Hampshire	52
3.	New Jersey	152	20.	Delaware	41
4.	Arkansas	145	21.	Washington	41
5.	Florida	110	22.	Arizona	36
6.	Maryland	92	23.	North Carolina	31
7.	Georgia	88	24.	New Mexico	28
8.	Minnesota	85	25.	Virginia	28
9.	Illinois	85	26.	West Virginia	27
10.	Tennessee	70	27.	Montana	16
11.	Kentucky	69	28.	Oregon	15
12.	Pennsylvania	69	29.	Idaho	11
13.	Louisiana	68	30.	Oklahoma	10
14.	Nebraska	62	31.	Wyoming	9
15.	Ohio	55	32.	Colorado	2
16.	Michigan	55		Canada	63
17.	South Carolina	54		Mexico	27
				Average	80

Source: The American Racing Manual 1986: Daily Racing Form

TABLE A.4 ***Average daily mutuel handles at all thoroughbred tracks in the United States, Canada, and Mexico in 1985 in dollars***

1.	California	3,154,735	18.	Delaware	522,134
2.	Arkansas	2,663,282	19.	Arizona	431,559
3.	New York	2,212,239	20.	New Mexico	372,588
4.	New Jersey	1,465,485	21.	Oklahoma	340,146
5.	Florida	1,173,433	22.	West Virginia	302,707
6.	Illinois	1,077,723	23.	Oregon	278,530
7.	Maryland	1,041,123	24.	Idaho	147,903
8.	Minnesota	1,014,588	25.	Wyoming	141,939
9.	Nebraska	915,003	26.	Montana	127,476
10.	Louisiana	877,892	27.	Colorado	DNA
11.	Kentucky	864,948	28.	Virginia	DNA
12.	Massachusetts	794,394	29.	North Carolina	DNA
13.	Pennsylvania	693,762	30.	South Carolina	DNA
14.	Michigan	661,150	31.	Georgia	DNA
15.	Washington	578,069	32.	Tennessee	DNA
16.	Ohio	562,358		Canada	813,654
17.	New Hampshire	550,974		Mexico	230,499

Source: The American Racing Manual 1986: Daily Racing Form

TABLE A.5 ***Thoroughbred mutuel handles in the United States, Canada, and Mexico in 1985 in dollars*** **(Numbers in parentheses indicate the actual racing days used in the calculations due to missing data values)**

1.	California	1,952,780,968	18.	New Hampshire	90,910,710
2.	New York (467)	1,033,115,673	19.	Minnesota	84,210,804
3.	Illinois	521,618,335	20.	Arizona	83,290,996
4.	Louisiana	489,863,833	21.	Delaware	51,691,306
5.	New Jersey (311)	455,766,036	22.	Oregon	42,058,063
6.	Florida (382)	448,251,415	23.	Oklahoma	41,838,062
7.	Maryland (304)	316,501,569	24.	Montana	8,413,430
8.	Pennsylvania (380)	263,629,872	25.	Idaho	7,543,053
9.	Kentucky (304)	262,944,363	26.	Wyoming	5,961,479
10.	Ohio	240,689,592	27.	Colorado	DNA
11.	Nebraska	213,195,842	28.	Virginia	DNA
12.	Massachusetts	212,897,667	29.	North Carolina	DNA
13.	Washington	199,433,859	30.	South Carolina	DNA
14.	Arkansas	165,123,545	31.	Georgia	DNA
15.	West Virginia	144,391,669	32.	Tennessee	DNA
16.	New Mexico	144,191,681		Canada	612,681,736
17.	Michigan (181)	119,668,162		Mexico	39,876,370

Source: The American Racing Manual 1986: Daily Racing Form

TABLE A.6 ***Track takes in percentage for the United States, Canada, and Mexico in 1985***

United States		*United States*	
Arizona	18	Nebraska	15
Arkansas	16	New Hampshire Harness	19
California	15.33	New Jersey	17
Harness and fair track	16.75	New Mexico	18.75
Colorado	17	New York	17
Florida	17.6	Harness	17
Harness	19	Ohio	17.50
Quarter horse	18	Oregon	16
Idaho	17	Pennsylvania	17
Illinois	17	South Dakota	18.25
Kentucky	15	Washington	16
Harness	18	West Virginia	17.25
Quarter horse	17	*Canada*	
Louisiana	17		
Maryland	15	Alberta	15.1
Fair tracks	16	British Columbia	15.8
Steeplechase	18	Manitoba	17.6
Massachusetts	19	Ontario	14.8
Michigan	16.25	Saskatchewan	22.1
Montana	20	*Mexico*	24.76

Source: Daily Racing Form. Your local Jockey Club can advise you of any changes in these rates.

Locations of North American Thoroughbred Tracks

MAP KEYS

1 Ak Sar-Ben
2 Albuquerque
3 Aqueduct
4 Arlington Park
5 Assiniboia Downs
6 Atlantic City
7 Atokad Park
8 Balmoral
9 Bay Meadows
10 Belmont Park
12 Beulah Race Track
14 Bowie Race Course
16 Calder Race Course
17 Caliente
18 Centennial Race Track
19 Charles Town
20 Churchill Downs
21 Coeur D'Alene
22 Columbus
23 Commodore Downs
25 Delaware Park
26 Del Mar
27 Delta Downs
28 Detroit Race Course
29 James C. Ellis Park
30 El Comandante
31 Evangeline Downs
32 Exhibition Park
33 Fair Grounds
34 Fairmount Park
35 Ferndale
36 Finger Lakes
38 Fonner Park
39 Fort Erie
40 Fresno
41 Golden Gate Fields
42 Great Barrington
44 Greenwood
45 Gulfstream Park
46 Hawthorne
47 Hazel Park
48 Hialeah Park
49 Hipodromo de las Americas
50 Hollywood Park
51 Jefferson Downs
52 Juarez Race Track
53 Keeneland
54 Keystone Race Track
55 La Mesa Park
56 Latonia
57 Laurel Race Course
58 Les Bols Park
59 Lethbridge
60 Lincoln State Fair
61 Longacres
62 Los Alamitos
63 Louisiana Downs
64 Marquis Downs
65 Marshfield Fair
66 The Meadowlands
67 Monmouth Park
68 Northampton
69 Northlands Park
70 Oaklawn Park
71 Park Jefferson
72 Penn National Race Course
73 Pimlico Race Course
74 Playfair
75 Pleasanton
76 Pocono Downs
77 Pomona
78 Portland Meadows
79 Prescott Downs
80 Regina
81 Rillito Race Track
82 River Downs
83 Rockingham Park
84 Ruidoso Downs
85 Sacramento
86 Salem Fairgrounds
87 Sandown Park
88 Santa Anita Park
89 Sante Fe
90 Santa Rosa
91 Saratoga
93 Solano
94 Sportsman's Park
95 Stampede Park
96 Stockton
97 Suffolk Downs
98 Sunland Park
99 Tampa Bay Downs
100 Thistledown
101 Timonium
102 Turf Paradise
103 Waterford Park
104 Woodbine
105 Yakima Meadows

MOUNTAIN STANDARD TIME
CENTRAL STANDARD TIME
EASTERN STANDARD TIME
CANADA
WINNIPEG
NORTH DAKOTA
MINNESOTA
SOUTH DAKOTA
WYOMING
NEBRASKA
IOWA
SIOUX CITY
OMAHA
COLORADO
DENVER
KANSAS
MISSOURI
ST LOUIS
ILLINOIS
CHICAGO
INDIANA
EVANSVILLE
HENDERSON
LOUISVILLE
LEXINGTON
KENTUCKY
WISCONSIN
MICH
MICHIGAN
DETROIT
WINDSOR
TORONTO
ROCHESTER
BUFFALO
ERIE
CLEVELAND
AKRON
OHIO
COLUMBUS
CINCINNATI
PENNSYLVANIA
PITTSBURGH
HARRISBURG
WILKES BARRE
PHILADELPHIA
BALTIMORE
MD
WASHINGTON
WEST VIRGINIA
VIRGINIA
NORTH CAROLINA
S CAROLINA
TENNESSEE
GEORGIA
ALABAMA
MISSISSIPPI
ARKANSAS
HOT SPRINGS
LOUISIANA
SHREVEPORT
BEAUMONT
NEW ORLEANS
FLORIDA
TAMPA
HALLANDALE
MIAMI
NEW MEXICO
SANTA FE
ALBUQUERQUE
OKLAHOMA
TEXAS
EL PASO
MEXICO
MEXICO CITY
NEW YORK
ALBANY
VT
NH
MAINE
MASS
SALEM
BOSTON
CONN
RI
PAWTUCKET
NEWARK
WILMINGTON
DEL
PUERTO RICO
SAN JUAN

Matters Of Fact: Leading Earners Sold As Yearlings

Of the 167 yearlings sold for $1 million or more at public auction in North America, none earned as much as $1 million. Of the 105 Thoroughbreds which have earned $1 million or more while making at least one start in North America, 27 were sold at public auction as yearlings. The following list represents the 10 leading millionaires sold at public auction as yearlings in North America.

Horse	Earnings	Yearling Price
John Henry	$6,591,860	$1,100
Creme Fraiche	$2,401,379	$160,000
Life's Magic	$2,255,218	$310,000
Wild Again	$2,204,829	$50,000
Desert Wine	$1,618,043	$165,000
Temperence Hill	$1,567,650	$80,000
Dancing Brave	$1 534,537	$200,000
Skip Trial	$1,522,491	$25,000
Tank's Prospect	$1,355,645	$625,000
Princess Rooney	$1,343,339	$38,000

Source: The Blood-Horse of January 31, 1987

Matters Of Fact: Highest-Priced Yearlings

In 1976, the first million-dollar yearling was sold at a public auction. Blue Meadows Farm paid $1.5 million for the colt Canadian Bound (Secretariat—Charming Alibi), a half-brother to champion Dahlia. Racing one year in North America and France, Canadian Bound was unplaced in four starts and earned $1,050. He is owned by a syndicate and stands at stud in Kentucky.

Since then, 167 yearlings have been sold for $1 million or more. Northern Dancer is the sire of seven of the 10 highest-priced yearlings. Two of the 10 yearlings are by Northern Dancer's son, Nijinsky II, and one, a filly, is by Alydar.

Following is a list of the five highest-priced yearlings of each sex, showing price, name, sire and dam, year sold, purchaser, and race record.

Colts

1. $13,100,000, Seattle Dancer (Nijinsky II—My Charmer), purchased in 1985 by Robert Sangster and partners. Unraced at two in Great Britain.
2. $10,200,000, Snaffi Dancer (Northern Dancer—My Bupers), 1983, Shaikh Mohammed bin Rashid al Maktoum. Unraced.
3. $8,250,000, Imperial Falcon (Northern Dancer—Ballade), 1984, Shaikh Mohammed (lessee). Raced two years in Great Britain, three starts, two wins, earned $14,318.
4. $7,100,000, Jareer (Northern Dancer—Fabuleux Jane), 1984, Shaikh Mohammed. Raced two years in Great Britain, five starts, one win, $3,996.
5. $7,000,000, Laa Etaab (Nijinsky II—Crimson Saint), 1985, Shaikh Maktoum bin Rashid al Maktoum. Unraced at two in Great Britain.

Fillies

1. $2,700,000, Milliardaire (Alydar—Priceless Fame), 1985, Mike Rutherford. Unraced at two in North America.
2. $2,500,000, Ma Petite Jolie (Northern Dancer—Ballade), 1983, Shaikh Mohammed. Raced two years in Great Britain, 10 starts, one win, $8,627.
3. $2,500,000, Moon Light Miracle (Northern Dancer—Blue Tepee), 1985, D. Wayne Lukas. Unraced at two in North America.
4. $2,500,000, Yaqut (Northern Dancer—Christmas Bonus), 1985, Shaikh Maktoum. In 1986 in Great Britain, three starts, one win, $4,419.
5. $2,500,000, Savannah Dancer (Northern Dancer—Valoris), 1983, Allen Paulson. Raced two years in North America, 16 starts, six wins, $360,000. Won Del Mar Oaks (gr. II), Santa Ysabel Stakes, Los Cerritos Stakes, The Very One Stakes; 2nd Hollywood Derby (gr. I); 3rd Senorita Stakes.

Source: The Blood-Horse of January 10, 1987

APPENDIX

B

Mathematics of the Dr. Z System*

The basic assumptions of the Dr. Z model are (1) the efficiency of the win market; (2) the validity of the Harville formulas, which along with (1) provide good estimates of the probability of all possible in-the-money finishes; and (3) the Kelly-criterion capital-growth model for determining the optimal bet size.

If q_i is the probability that horse i wins, then assumption (1) is

$$q_i = \frac{W_i}{W} \qquad \text{(B1)}$$

where $i = 1, \ldots, n$ horses and W_i is the amount bet to win on horse i out of a total win pool of W.

The Harville formulas then estimate the probability that horse i is first and j is second as

$$q_{ij} = \frac{q_i q_j}{1 - q_i} \qquad \text{(B2)}$$

for all i and j running from 1 to n. Similarly, the probability that horse i is first, j is second, and k is third is

$$q_{ijk} = \frac{q_i q_j q_k}{(1 - q_i)(1 - q_i - q_j)} \qquad \text{(B3)}$$

for all i, j, and k running from 1 to n.

Equations B1–B3 can be used to calculate the expected value per ad-

*This appendix is highly mathematical and is intended for those readers who would like a more detailed development of the Dr. Z system. The results given here were adapted from Hausch, Ziemba, and Rubenstein (1981) and Hausch and Ziemba (1985).

ditional dollar bet to place, EXP_l, and show, EXS_l on any given horse l as follows:

$$\text{EXP}_l =$$

$$\sum_{\substack{j=1\\ j\neq l}}^{n}\left(\frac{q_l \times q_j}{1-q_l}\right)\left\{1+\frac{1}{20}\text{INT}\left[\left(\frac{Q(P+1)-(1+P_l+P_j)}{2}\right)\left(\frac{1}{1+P_l}\right)20\right]\right\}$$

$$+\sum_{\substack{i=1\\ i\neq l}}^{n}\left(\frac{q_i q_l}{1-q_i}\right)\left\{1+\frac{1}{20}\text{INT}\left[\left(\frac{Q(P+1)-(1+P_i+P_l)}{2}\right)\left(\frac{1}{1+P_l}\right)20\right]\right\} \tag{B4}$$

$$\text{EXS}_l =$$

$$\sum_{\substack{j=1\\ j\neq l}}^{n}\sum_{\substack{k=1\\ k\neq l,j}}^{n}\frac{q_l q_j q_k}{(1-q_l)(1-q_l-q_j)}$$

$$\times\left\{1+\frac{1}{20}\text{INT}\left[\left(\frac{Q(S+1)-(1+S_l+S_j+S_k)}{3}\right)\left(\frac{1}{1+S_l}\right)20\right]\right\}$$

$$+\sum_{\substack{i=1\\ i\neq l}}^{n}\sum_{\substack{k=1\\ k\neq i,l}}^{n}\frac{q_i q_l q_k}{(1-q_i)(1-q_i-q_l)}$$

$$\times\left\{1+\frac{1}{20}\text{INT}\left[\left(\frac{Q(S+1)-(1+S_i+S_l+S_k)}{3}\right)\left(\frac{1}{1+S_l}\right)20\right]\right\}$$

$$+\sum_{\substack{i=1\\ i\neq l}}^{n}\sum_{\substack{j=1\\ j\neq l,i}}^{n}\frac{q_i q_j q_l}{(1-q_i)(1-q_i-q_j)}$$

$$\times\left\{1+\frac{1}{20}\text{INT}\left[\left(\frac{Q(S+1)-(1+S_i+S_j+S_l)}{3}\right)\left(\frac{1}{1+S_l}\right)20\right]\right\} \tag{B5}$$

In these formulas Q is the track payback; P_i and S_i are the place and show bets on horse i, respectively; $P = \sum_{i=1}^{n} P_i$ and $S = \sum_{i=1}^{n} S_i$ are the place and show pools, respectively; and INT(Y) means the largest integer not exceeding Y. The expressions involving INT assume here that the breakage is of the 5¢ variety. For 10¢ breakage replace 20 with 10 in equations (B4) and (B5). These equations were used to compute the expected values per dollar bet in Table 5.2.

The Kelly criterion is equivalent to maximizing the expected logarithm of final wealth after the public's bets in each race are known. Considering the effect of all possible i,j,k finishes on the possible payoffs and the fact that our bets influence these odds, we have the following model for determining our optimal place and show bets, which we denote by p_l and s_l.

$$\underset{\{p_l\}\ \{s_l\}}{\text{Maximize}} \sum_{i=1}^{n} \sum_{\substack{j=1 \\ j\neq i}}^{n} \sum_{\substack{k=1 \\ k\neq i,j}}^{n} q_{ijk} \log \left[\begin{array}{l} \dfrac{Q(P + \Sigma_{l=1}^{n} p_l) - (p_i + p_j + P_i + P_j)}{2} \\ \times \left(\dfrac{p_i}{p_i + P_i} + \dfrac{p_j}{p_j + P_j} \right) \\ + \dfrac{Q(S + \Sigma_{l=1}^{n} s_l) - (s_i + s_j + s_k + S_i + S_j + S_k)}{3} \\ \times \left(\dfrac{s_i}{s_i + S_i} + \dfrac{s_j}{s_j + S_j} + \dfrac{s_k}{s_k + S_k} \right) \\ + w_0 - \displaystyle\sum_{\substack{l=1 \\ l\neq i,j,k}}^{n} s_l - \sum_{\substack{l=1 \\ l\neq i,j}}^{n} p_l \end{array} \right] \tag{B6}$$

such that

$$\sum_{l=1}^{n} (p_l + s_l) \leqslant w_0, \qquad p_l \geqslant 0, s_l \geqslant 0, \ l = 1, \ldots, n.$$

Model (B6) assumes that any horse i can win, followed by any horse j (except i), and any horse k can finish third (except i or j). This event has probability q_{ijk}. The expression inside the brackets has three parts: returns received from possible place bets; returns received from possible show bets; and money left over because the place and show bets made are less than the bettor's fortune w_0.

The only data needed to compute the optimal place and show bets in any given race using (B6) are Q, the track payback; the place and show bets P_i and S_i, respectively, on each horse i; the total place and show pools P and S, respectively; and the investor's wealth w_0.

Although model (B6) lacks some desirable concavity properties—see Kallberg and Ziemba (1981)—it is easy to solve on a computer. Calculations for thousands of races have routinely been made on the University of British Columbia's AMDAHL 470V6 Model II computer, using a code for the generalized reduced gradient algorithm.

DEVELOPMENT OF THE DR. Z SYSTEM FOR USE AT THE TRACK

Since phones are not generally available at racetracks and since even portable computers are cumbersome, and the time you have to act is so short, we have used multiple regression approximations to the solutions to (B6). These equations, such as the expected-value-per-dollar-bet equations in Chapter Four and the optimal-betting-amount equations in Chapters Five and Sixteen, were developed by solving (B6) for many many races and then regressing the results on the variables of interest. In all cases, the regression's independent variables are functions of only the simplest input data, namely, Q, w_0, W, W_i, P, P_i, S, and S_i for horse i.

In developing the Dr. Z system for very general use, several factors had to be considered: different track sizes, different betting-wealth levels, different track paybacks, coupled entries, and multiple betting. These factors are discussed below.

Track Size and Betting-Wealth Level

Track size and wealth level do not affect the expected-value equations, since (B4) and (B5) involve only the relative size of the public's bets and the track take. However, track size and wealth level are both important factors in determining the optimal bet sizes in (B6). To account for them, (B6) was solved for a broad range of wealths and track sizes. Regressions were determined for four different wealth levels ($50, $500, $2,500, $10,000), three different place pools ($2,000, $10,000, $150,000), and three different show pools ($1,200, $6,000, $100,000). These twelve pairs of wealth and place pools resulted in the twelve optimal place regressions in Table 16.1, and these twelve pairs of wealth and show pools resulted in the twelve optimal show regressions in Table 16.3. Then Tables 16.2 and 16.4 used interpolation of these 24 regressions to account for *any* betting wealth and place- or show-pool size. The R^2 values for these regressions were extremely good, varying from 0.982 to 0.995.

Track Payback

Both the expected-value equations (B4) and (B5) and the optimal bet sizes from (B6) are nondecreasing functions of Q, the track payback. As was demonstrated in Figure 9.4, a change in Q can have a very large effect on long-run profits. This section therefore develops modifications of the basic regression equations for use at tracks with differing paybacks.

Regression equation (4.3) for the expected value per dollar bet to place was calculated with $Q = 0.829$. Equation (B4) gives the exact expected value. If we neglect breakage for simplicity, it is

$$\mathbf{EXP}_i = \sum_{j \neq i} \left(\frac{q_i q_j}{1 - q_i} + \frac{q_i q_j}{1 - q_j} \right) \left[1 + \frac{QP - (P_i + P_j)}{2P_i} \right].$$

Note that EXP_i is linear in Q and

$$\frac{\partial \mathbf{EXP}_i}{\partial Q} = \frac{q_i P}{2P_i} \left[1 + \sum_{j \neq i} \left(\frac{q_j}{2 - q_j} \right) \right]. \qquad \text{(B7)}$$

Thus the appropriate adjustment factor for equation (4.3) to account for a $Q \neq 0.829$ should involve an approximation to (B7). From 124 Exhibition Park races with EXP_i in the range 1.16 and greater, the true $a\text{EXP}_i/aQ$ was regressed against q_i

$$\frac{\partial \mathbf{EXP}_i}{\partial Q} = 2.22 - 1.29 q_i \qquad R^2 = 0.861, \quad SE = 0.0548, \qquad \text{(B8)}$$

and both coefficients are highly significant.

Therefore when the track payback is Q, the expected value per dollar bet to place can be approximated by adjusting equation (4.3) to

$$\mathbf{EXP} = 0.319 + 0.559 \left(\frac{W_i / W}{P_i / P} \right) + \left[2.22 - 1.29 \left(\frac{W_i}{W} \right) \right] (Q - 0.829).$$

This is equation (4.5). A similar procedure for expected value to show results in equation (4.6) from equation (4.4).

The regression equations in Chapter Sixteen were calibrated for $Q = 0.829$. Since the optimal bet size is nondecreasing in Q, which will vary from track to track, we must adjust the optimal bets at tracks with $Q \neq 0.829$. To study this effect, the optimization model (B6) was run on a number of Exhibition Park examples to compute the optimal place or show bets at several different initial wealths, several track sizes, and several different Q's (from 0.809 to 0.859). The results indicated that $\Delta p^*/\Delta Q$ and $\Delta s^*/\Delta Q$ were independent of Q over this short range of Q's. Therefore with a ΔQ of 0.01, $\Delta p^*/\Delta Q$ and $\Delta s^*/\Delta Q$ were regressed on p^*, w_o, P_i, P, and s^*, w_o, S_i, S respectively. The analysis for $\Delta p^*/\Delta Q$ showed that p^* and w_o were very significant independent variables but that neither P_i nor P was significant; similar results for $\Delta s^*/\Delta Q$ were observed.

The regressions were

$$\frac{\Delta p^*}{\Delta Q} = 0.0316 p^* + 0.000351 w_0$$

$$R^2 = 0.948, SE = 2.23, n = 56.$$

$$\frac{\Delta s^*}{\Delta Q} = 0.0316s^* + 0.000351w_0$$

Therefore, if p^* and s^* are the optimal place and show bet sizes from Tables 16.1 to 16.3, then the true optimal place bet $\tilde{p}^*$ and true optimal show bet $\tilde{s}^*$ for a racetrack with a track payback Q are

$$\tilde{p}^* = p^* + (Q - 0.829)(3.16p^* + 0.0351w_o) \tag{B9}$$

and

$$\tilde{s}^* = s^* + (Q - 0.829)(3.16s^* + 0.0351w_o). \tag{B10}$$

Coupled Entries

As mentioned in Chapter Sixteen, because of the possibility that an entry will collect the whole place pool or a major portion of the show pool, the expected value per dollar bet to place or show is underestimated, as is the optimal bet size. The formula for correcting this underestimation is presented here.

Suppose the coupled entry has number 1 and let $q_1 = W_1/W$. Then q_1 estimates the probability that one of the horses in the entry will win the race. Suppose further that q_{1A} and q_{1B} (with $q_{1A} + q_{1B} = q^1$) are the correct winning probability estimates of the two horses in the entry. Calculating the probability to place using q_1 for one horse, and using q_{1A} and q_{1B} for two horses, results in the same probabilities. This suggests that the only reason the one-horse expected-value equations are underestimates of the true two-horse expected-value equations is the possibility of 1A-1B and 1B-1A finishes. To make a correction for this, the true expected value per dollar bet was calculated for the one-horse case of q_1 and for the two-horse case of q_{1A} and q_{1B}.* The difference between these two expected values, call it ΔC_i, was then regressed on (W_i/W) and (P_i/P). Again, Exhibition Park† data were used and

$$\Delta C_i = 0.867(W_i/W) - 0.857(P_i/P). \tag{B11}$$

Adding this correction factor for coupled entries changes equation (4.5) to (4.7). A similar procedure yields equation (4.8) from (4.6).

The regression equations in Chapter Sixteen underestimate the true optimal bets on a coupled entry. To understand this phenomenon (1) many

*It is generally the case that the two horses in the entry are not of equal ability. It is assumed that $q_{1A} = (\frac{2}{3})q_1$ and $q_{1B} = (\frac{1}{3})q_i$. The results are quite robust to the weighting, however.

†The data used were for cases where the expected value was at least 1.16, that is, the cases of interest. For instances with a low expected value, the correction factor is not accurate.

Exhibition Park examples were run on the optimization model (B6) assuming the data were for one horse, then (2) the same examples were run again using (B6) supposing the entry was two horses (the formulation was adjusted to consider the possibility of the two horses finishing first and second and then receiving a high payoff), but the win bet on the entry was lowered, using an iterative scheme, until the optimal bet was the same as the optimal bet from (1). This procedure gave pairs of $\tilde{q}_i^P$ and q_i, where $\tilde{q}_i^P$ was the probability of entry i's winning in (1), that is, thinking of the entry as one horse; and q_i was the adjusted probability that gave the same optimal bet in (2) as was observed in (1), that is, thinking of the entry as two horses. Since the regression equations in Chapter Sixteen give the optimal place bet when the horse's probability of winning is q_i, then using the slightly higher $\tilde{q}_i^P$ in those regressions would give the approximate optimal place bet when the entry's probability of winning is q_i.

The regression relating $\tilde{q}_i^P$ and q_i is

$$\tilde{q}_i^P = 0.991q_i + 0.137q_i^2 + 3.471 \times 10^{-7}w_o \quad (R^2 = 0.9998,\ SE = 0.00161). \qquad \text{(B12)}$$

The examples from which the data were derived spanned many wealth levels and pool sizes. While the wealth level was a very significant independent variable, the pool size was found to be statistically insignificant. Therefore, to compute the optimal place bet on coupled entry i use the following procedure:

1. Set $q_i = W_i/W$.
2. Determine $\tilde{q}_i^P$
3. Use $\tilde{q}_i^P$ w_o P, and P in regression equations in Tables 16.1 and 16.2.

Use the same procedure for the optimal show bet on coupled entry i:

1. Set $q_i = W_i/W$.
2. Determine
   $\tilde{q}_i^s = 1.07q_i + 4.13 \times 10^{-7}\, w_o - 0.00663$
   $R^2 = 0.999, SE = 0.00298$, all coefficients highly significant.
3. Use $\tilde{q}_i^s$, w_o, S, and S_i in the regression equations in Tables 16.3 and 16.4.

Multiple Betting

The optimal bet equations in Tables 16.1 and 16.3 were calibrated assuming only one place bet or one show bet in a race. Sometimes, however, there is more than one Dr. Z system bet in a race (see Chapter Sixteen). It is not correct to calculate each of the optimal bets using the regression equations and then wager those amounts. In some instances it would result in overbetting; in others, for reasons of diversification, it would result in underbetting.

In what follows we have accounted for the most common multiple-betting situation—Dr. Z system bets to place and show on the same horse. Ninety-eight cases of place and show betting on the same horse were analyzed over a wide range of track handles, q_i's, and w_o's. Using the optimization model (B6) resulted in the quadruples $(p_T^*, s_T^*, p_A^*, s_A^*)$. The p_T^* and s_T^* are the optimal pair of place and show bets when they are considered together. The p_A^* is the optimal place bet assuming it is the only good bet in the race and s_A^* is the optimal show bet supposing it is the only good bet in the race—namely, the values obtained using the regressions in Tables 16.2 and 16.4. Then p_T^* was regressed on p_A^*, s_A^*, w_o, P_i, P, and q_i. The only statistically significant independent variables were p_A^* and s_A^*, leading to the regression equation

$$\tilde{p}_T^* = 1.59p_A^* - 0.639s_A^*.$$

(R^2 = 0.967, SE = 73.7, and all coefficients are highly significant.)

A similar procedure for s^* yields

$$\tilde{s}_T^* = 0.907s_A^* - 0.134p_A^*.$$

(R^2 = 0.992, SE = 72.6 and all coefficients are highly significant.)

These are equations (16.5) and (16.6), respectively.

Exploitation of Inefficiencies or Chance?

An important question concerns the reliability of the results: Are the results true exploitations of market inefficiencies or could they be obtained simply by chance? This question is investigated utilizing the following simple model. The first application is concerned with an estimate of the probability that the Dr. Z system's theory is vacuous and, indeed, the observations conform to specific favorable samples from a random betting population. The second application estimates the probability of not making a positive profit. The calculations utilize the 1980 Exhibition Park data; those appear in Table 9.3.

Let π be the probability of winning a bet in each trial and

$$X_i = \begin{cases} 1 + w & \text{if the bet is won,} \\ 0 & \text{otherwise} \end{cases}$$

be the return from a \$1 bet in trial i. In n trials, the probability of winning at least $100y\%$ of the total bet is

$$\Pr\left[\frac{1}{n}\left(\sum_{i=1}^{n} X_i\right) - 1 > y\right]. \qquad \text{(B13)}$$

Assume that the trials are independent. Since the X_i are binomially distributed, (B13) can be approximated by a normal probability distribution as

$$1 - \phi\left\{\frac{\sqrt{n}\,[y - (1 + w)\pi + 1]}{(1 + w)\pi\sqrt{(1 - \pi)/\pi}}\right\} \qquad \text{(B14)}$$

where ϕ is the cumulative distribution function of a standard $N(0, 1)$ variable. The observed probability of winning a bet, weighted by size of bet made from the 1980 Exhibition Park bets according to Table 9.5, yields 0.771 as an estimate of π. If the system's theory were vacuous and random betting were being made, then $(1 + w)\pi$ would equal 0.83, since the track's payback is approximately 83%. The twenty-two bets made totalled \$5,304 and resulted in a profit of \$1,216, for a rate of return of 22.9%. Using the equation with $n = 22$, gives 3×10^{-5}, which is negligible, as the probability of making 22.9% through random betting.

Suppose that the 1980 Exhibition Park results represent typical Dr. Z system behavior, then $\pi = 0.771$ and $(1 + w)\pi = 1.229$. In n trials the probability of making a nonpositive net return is

$$\Pr\left[\frac{1}{n}\left(\sum_{i=1}^{n} X_i\right) - 1 < 0\right]$$

which can be approximated as

$$\phi\left[\frac{\sqrt{n}(1 - (1 + w)\pi)}{(1 - w)\pi\sqrt{(1 - \pi)/\pi}}\right] = \phi(-0.342\sqrt{n}).$$

For $n = 22$, this probability is only 0.054. Thus after twenty-two races, the chance is only 5.4% that you are behind. For $n = 50$ or 100, the probabilities are 0.008 and 0.0003, respectively. Thus it is reasonable to suppose that the results from the 1980 Exhibition Park data (as well as the 1978 Exhibition Park, 1973–74 Santa Anita, 1981–82 Aqueduct data and our 1981–86 Kentucky Derby Day, Rusty P. Ford's Churchill and Kentucky Downs, and our colleagues' Stampede Park results, with their larger samples) represent true exploitation of a market inefficiency.

APPENDIX

C

Dosage Analysis: How to Pick the Winner of the Kentucky Derby*

A horse's chance for success surely depends to a large extent on his or her pedigree. But how much? How can one evaluate the combined effects of all the sires and dams in a horse's heritage? When is such an analysis useful? Does it point to horses to consider or to eliminate?

A most interesting and useful theory is that of dosage. It has provided us with the winner of the Kentucky Derby the last four years, and its performance in this race over the years has been nothing short of remarkable.

The theory of dosage began with Lt. Col. J.J. Vullier in his *Les Croisements Rationnels dans la Race Pure*, written in the 1920s. Vullier found that within a particular time frame of approximately twenty years, very few stallions appear with great frequency in pedigreed bloodlines. These stallions can be said to be fixing the breed since the percentage of blood attributable to them was roughly constant in this time period. He called them chefs de race. Vullier argued that matings should be made to keep these percentages in balance. His ideas were used in the very successful breeding program of the H.H. Aga Khan.

Dr. Franco Varola in his *Typology of the Race Horse* in 1974 added to the dosage theory. He considered classifications of speed and endurance that were passed on by the chef-de-race sires. The character of the offspring horse then resulted from the total number of appearances in each classification regardless of the generation of the sire. We could say that this offspring had a probability distribution that would describe its probable running behavior.

In the last few years Dr. Steven A. Roman, following additional work by Mr. Abram S. Hewitt, has modified and extended the Vullier-Varola theory to its current useful state. The ideas are simple. First, only the sires

*Thanks are due to James Quinn, Leon Rasmussen, and Ross Stewart for helpful comments on an earlier draft of this appendix.

are counted, because mares produce too few numbers to permit reliable generalizations. The past four generations are evaluated, with each succeeding generation becoming twice as important. Nonchefs do not count since they have not been known to generate consistent racing qualities in their offspring—we can call their effect "noise." The current chef-de-race sires are listed in Tables C.1 and C.2. The categories brilliant, intermediate, classic, solid, and professional refer to admixtures of speed and stamina. Brilliant is prepotent speed, professional is prepotent stamina, and the others are more relative mixtures of these qualities. According to Dr. Roman, the categories are defined as follows:

1. *Brilliant:* characterized by great speed and early maturity, little propensity for distance.
2. *Intermediate:* characterized by speed and early maturity, but capable of being a runner of classic potential.
3. *Classic:* characterized by a balance of speed and stamina, well suited to classic distances and often capable of expressing each quality separately.
4. *Solid:* characterized by less speed and later maturity than the first three categories; also capable of classic potential.
5. *Professional:* characterized by lack of speed, enormous endurance, and late maturity; runners tend to be plodders.

The designation of a chef is a quantitative but judgmental exercise of determining that the sire does indeed breed a consistent characteristic, that is, he is prepotent. By studying a large population of a sire's offspring one can empirically determine whether a sire is prepotent and also assign him into one or more aptitude classes to make his population consistent with the entire population. Dr. Roman and collaborators Abram S. Hewitt and Leon Rasmussen of the *Daily Racing Form* have developed the designated chefs in Tables C.1 and C.2.

Using only the sires in a horse's pedigree to determine its running style may sound sexist, but there is a reason for it. A horse can be put into one or two of the five categories only after analyzing the running styles of many offspring. A sire may service fifty or more mares a year, and thus, after several years, there are many offspring racing. For a mare, however, the five to fifteen lifetime offspring is not enough to classify her with any degree of statistical significance.

To use these ideas one can construct statistical distributions that reflect the basic characteristics. To compute these so-called "dosage profiles," a chef-de-race sire appearing in the first generation is assigned 16 points, which is split 8–8 if the sire has influence in two classes. Second-generation chef-de-race sires receive 8 points, third-generation sires receive 4 points, and fourth-generation sires get 2 points. Notice that each generation is allocated 16 points. Each sire becomes less influential the further back he

TABLE C.1 ***Chef-de-race sires alphabetized within aptitudinal class***

		Brilliant	
Abernant	Gallant Man*	Never Bend*	Raise a Native
Black Toney*	Grey Sovereign	Noholme II*	Reviewer*
Bold Ruler*	Habitat	Northern Dancer*	Roman*
British Empire	Heliopolis	Olympia	Royal Charger
Bull Dog	Hyperion*	Orby	Sir Cosmo
Cicero	Intentionally*	Panorama	Spy Song
Court Martial	Mr. Prospector*	Peter Pan	Tudor Minstrel
Double Jay	My Babu	Phalaris	Turn-to*
Fair Trial	Nasrullah	Pharis	Ultimus
Fairway	Nearco*	Pompey	What a Pleasure
		Intermediate	
Ben Brush	Eight Thirty	Nashua	Sir Ivor*
Big Game	Equipoise*	Native Dancer*	Star Kingdom*
Black Toney*	Full Sail	Never Bend*	Star Shoot
Bold Ruler*	Gallant Man*	Petition	Sweep
Broomstick	Havresac II	Pharos	The Tetrarch
Colorado	Intentionally*	Polynesian	Tom Fool*
Congreve	Khaled	Princequillo*	Traghetto
Damascus*	King Salmon	Roman*	Turn-to*
Djebel	Mahmoud*	Sir Gaylord*	T.V. Lark
		Classic	
Alibhai	Forli	Nearco*	Rock Sand*
Aureole	Gainsborough	Never Say Die	Sicambre
Bahram	Graustark*	Noholme II*	Sideral
Blandford	Gundomar	Nijinsky II*	Sir Galahad III
Blenheim II*	Hail to Reason	Northern Dancer*	Sir Gaylord*
Blue Larkspur	Herbager*	Persian Gulf	Sir Ivor*
Brantome	Hyperion*	Pilate	Star Kingdom*
Buckpasser	In Reality	Prince Bio	Swynford
Bull Lee	Lyphard	Prince Chevalier	Ticino*
Clarissimus	Mahmoud*	Prince John	Tom Fool*
Count Fleet	Midstream	Prince Rose	Tom Rolfe*
Damascus*	Mossborough	Reviewer*	Tourbillon*
Equipoise*	Mr. Prospector*	Ribot*	Tracery
Exclusive Native	Native Dancer*	Roberto	Vieux Manoir
	Navarro		War Admiral
		Solid	
Asterus	Discovery	Oleander	Sea-Bird
Bachelor's Double	Fair Play*	Princequillo*	Sunstar
Ballymoss	Graustark*	Relko	Tantieme
Blenheim II*	Herbager*	Right Royal	Teddy
Bois Roussel	Man o' War	Rock Sand*	Ticino*
Chaucer	Nijinsky II*	Round Table	Vatout
			Worden
		Professional	
Admiral Drake	Dark Ronald	Mieuxce	Spearmint
Alcantara II	Donatello II	Ortello	Sunny Boy
Alizier	Fair Play*	Precipitation	Tom Rolfe*
Alycidon	Foxbridge	Rabelais	Tourbillon*
Bayardo	Hurry On	Ribot*	Vaguely Noble
Bruleur	La Farina	Sardanapale	Vandale
Chateau Bouscaut	Le Fabuleux	Solario	Vatellor
Crepello	Massine	Son-in-Law	Wild Risk

NOTE: An asterisk following a sire's name indicates he has been placed in two separate classes. Therefore, his influence in any generation is divided equally between two classes.

TABLE C.2 ***An alphabetical listing of chef-de-race sires***

Horse Name	*Class*	*Horse Name*	*Class*	*Horse Name*	*Class*	*Horse Name*	*Class*
Abernant	B	Donatello II	P	Native Dancer	I, C	Sardanapale	P
Admiral Drake	P	Double Jay	B	Navarro	C	Sea-Bird	S
Alcantara II	P	Eight Thirty	I	Nearco	B, C	Sicambre	C
Alibhai	C	Equipoise	I, C	Never Bend	B, I	Sideral	C
Alizier	P	Exclusive Native	C	Never Say Die	C	Sir Cosmo	B
Alycidon	P	Fair Play	S, P	Nijinsky II	C, S	Sir Gallahad III	C
Asterus	S	Fair Trial	B	Noholme II	B, C	Sir Gaylord	I, C
Aureole	C	Fairway	B	Northern Dancer	B, C	Sir Ivor	I, C
Bachelor's Double	S	Forli	C	Oleander	S	Solario	P
Bahram	C	Foxbridge	P	Olympia	B	Son-in-Law	P
Ballymoss	S	Full Sail	I	Orby	B	Spearmint	P
Bayardo	P	Gainsborough	C	Ortello	P	Spy Song	B
Ben Brush	I	Gallant Man	B, I	Panorama	B	Stage Door Johnny	S, P
Blenheim II	C, S	Graustark	C, S	Persian Gulf	C	Star Kingdom	I, C
Big Game	I	Grey Sovereign	B	Peter Pan	B	Star Shoot	I
Black Toney	B, I	Gundomar	C	Petition	I	Sunny Boy	P
Blandford	C	Habitat	B	Phalaris	B	Sunstar	S
Blue Larkspur	C	Hail to Reason	C	Pharis	B	Sweep	I
Bois Roussel	S	Havresac II	I	Pharos	I	Swynford	C
Bold Ruler	B, I	Heliopolis	B	Pilate	C	Tantieme	S
Brantome	C	Herbager	C, S	Polynesian	I	Teddy	S
British Empire	B	Hurry On	P	Pompey	B	The Tetrarch	I
Broomstick	I	Hyperion	B, C	Precipitation	P	Ticino	C, S
Bruleur	P	In Reality	B, C	Prince Bio	C	Tom Fool	I, C
Buckpasser	C	Intentionally	B, I	Prince Chevalier	C	Tom Rolfe	C, P
Bull Dog	B	Khaled	I	Prince John	C	Tourbillon	C, P
Bull Lea	C	King Salmon	I	Princequillo	I, S	Tracery	C
Chateau Bouscaut	P	La Farina	P	Prince Rose	C	Traghetto	I
Chaucer	S	Le Fabuleux	P	Rabelais	P	Tudor Minstrel	B
Cicero	B	Lyphard	C	Raise a Native	B	Turn-to	B, I
Clarissimus	C	Mahmoud	I, C	Relko	S	T.V. Lark	I
Colorado	I	Man o' War	S	Reviewer	B, C	Ultimus	B
Congreve	I	Massine	P	Ribot	C, P	Vaguely Noble	C, P
Count Fleet	C	Midstream	C	Right Royal	S	Vandale	P
Court Martial	B	Mieuxce	P	Roberto	C	Vatellor	P
Crepello	P	Mill Reef	C, S	Rock Sand	C, S	Vatout	S
Damascus	I, C	Mossborough	C	Roman	B, I	Vieux Manoir	C
Dark Ronald	P	Mr. Prospector	B, C	Round Table	S	War Admiral	C
Discovery	S	My Babu	B	Royal Charger	B	What a Pleasure	B
Djebel	I	Nashua	I, C	Run the Gantlet	P	Wild Risk	P
		Nasrullah	B			Worden	S

NOTE: Brilliant = B, Intermediate = I, Classic = C, Solid = S, and Professional = P.

appears in the pedigree but the number of sires increases to compensate. Summing the points in each of the five classes then gives the dosage profile. While these profiles shed much light on a horse's possible performance, two indices have been developed that are easier to work with and understand, as they summarize the profile as a single number. The first is the dosage index (DI), which is computed by dividing the speed component (brilliant and intermediate points plus half the classic points) by the stamina component (half the classic points plus the solid and professional points). Thus the DI can vary from 0 (all stamina) to ∞ (all speed). Brilliant and professional points receive the same attention as intermediate and solid points. Future refinements of this measure might use different weightings, although it may be argued that equal importance is the most appropriate weighing. More attention is paid to the polar attributes in the second index, the center of distribution (CD), which multiplies the brilliant points by two, adds in the intermediate points, subtracts the solid points, and subtracts twice the number of professional points. Dividing by the total number of points gives the CD. Table C.3 shows these calculations for four of the standouts in the 1985 Kentucky Derby.

What is striking about these measures is that they are very helpful in predicting actual winners, or, more precisely, pointing out probable losers. Dr. Roman has found in his research on the Kentucky Derby and Belmont Stakes races over the past forty-eight years, since 1940, that no Derby winner has ever had a dosage index above 4.00 or a CD above 1.25 (see Table C.4) and only three Belmont Stakes winners—Creme Fraiche, Damascus, and Conquistador Cielo—had dosage indices above 4.00. Only Conquistador Cielo and Creme Fraiche had CDs above 1.25. Since Conquistador Cielo's and Creme Fraiche's victories in 1982 and 1985, respectively, were in the mud, these exceptions are a bit suspect. The fact is that horses with high-dosage indices and CDs simply do not win the classic three-year-old distance races—even if they are favored by the betting public. Additional research shows no winners of the Kentucky Derby with DIs above 4.00 since at least 1929. Roman (1984) has also studied stakes races from 6 to 12 furlongs worth $25,000 or more. As the distances become longer, the percentage of winners with dosage indices above 4.00 diminishes in a continuous fashion from 7 to $8\frac{1}{2}$ furlongs, drops significantly at 9 furlongs ($1\frac{1}{8}$ miles), and it drops dramatically between 9 and 10 furlongs. Figure C1 shows the average dosage index versus distance for the 1983 $25,000-plus open stakes: at $1\frac{1}{4}$ miles, the average winner has a dosage index of 2.58, well below 4.00. Hence the last quarter and especially the last eighth of a mile in the Kentucky Derby presents, according to Dr. Roman, "a significantly greater barrier than encountered at any other distance." It is thus one of the great difficulties in actually winning a Kentucky Derby. Indeed at $1\frac{1}{4}$ miles or more, only 3.8% of the winners, or less than 1 in 25, have dosage indices above 4.00. This compares with 31.4% and 42.9% winners with dosage indices above

TABLE C.3 ***Sample dosage profiles, dosage indices, and centers of distribution***

Chief's Crown Sires	*Brilliant*	*Intermediate*	*Classic*	*Solid*	*Professional*
1st Generation (16 pts)					
Danzig					
2nd Generation (8 pts)					
Northern Dancer	4		4		
Secretariat					
3rd Generation (4 pts)					
Nearctic					
Admiral's Voyage					
Bold Ruler	2	2			
Swoon's Son					
4th Generation (2 pts)					
Nearco	1		1		
Native Dancer		1			
Crafty Admiral					
Petition		2			
Nashrullah	2				
Princequillo		1		1	
The Doge					
T.V. Lark		2			
Dosage Profile	9	8	6	1	0

$$\text{Dosage Index} = \frac{9 + 8 + \frac{1}{2}(6)}{\frac{1}{2}(6) + 1} = \frac{20}{4} = 5.00$$

$$\text{Center of Distribution} = \frac{2(9) + 8 - 1}{24} = 1.04$$

Tank's Prospect Sires[a]	*Brilliant*	*Intermediate*	*Classic*	*Solid*	*Professional*
1st Generation (16 pts)					
Mr. Prospector					
2nd Generation (8 pts)					
Raise A Native	8				
Pretense					
3rd Generation (4 pts)					
Native Dancer		2	2		
Nashua		4			
Endeavour II					
Rough N' Tumble					
4th Generation (2 pts)					
Polynesian		2			
Case Ace					
Nasrullah	2				
Count Fleet			2		
British Empire	2				
Hyperion	1		1		

TABLE C.3 ***(continued)***

Tank's Prospect Sires[a]	*Brilliant*	*Intermediate*	*Classic*	*Solid*	*Professional*
Free For All					
War Relic					
Dosage Profile	13	8	5	0	0

$$\text{Dosage Index} = \frac{13 + 8 + \frac{1}{2}(5)}{\frac{1}{2}(5)} = 9.40$$

$$\text{Center of Distribution} = \frac{2(13) + 8}{26} = 1.31$$

Stephan's Odyssey Sires	*Brilliant*	*Intermediate*	*Classic*	*Solid*	*Professional*
1st Generation (16 pts)					
Danzig					
2nd Generation (8 pts)					
Northern Dancer	4		4		
Gallant Man	4	4			
3rd Generation (4 pts)					
Nearctic					
Admiral's Voyage					
Migoli					
Ribot			2		2
4th Generation (2 pts)					
Nearco	1		1		
Native Dancer		1	1		
Crafty Admiral					
Petition		2			
Bois Roussel				2	
Mahmoud		1	1		
Tenerani					
Cosmic Bomb					
Dosage Profile	9	8	9	2	2

$$\text{Dosage Index} = \frac{9 + 8 + \frac{1}{2}(9)}{\frac{1}{2}(9) + 2 + 2} = \frac{21\frac{1}{2}}{8\frac{1}{2}} = 2.53$$

$$\text{Center of Distribution} = \frac{2(9) + 8 - 2 - 2(2)}{30} = \frac{20}{30} = 0.67$$

TABLE C.3 ***(continued)***

Spend A Buck Sires	*Brilliant*	*Intermediate*	*Classic*	*Solid*	*Professional*
1st Generation (16 pts)					
Buckaroo					
2nd Generation (8 pts)					
Buckpasser			8		
Speak John					
3rd Generation (4 pts)					
Tom Fool		2	2		
No Robbery					
Prince John			4		
Jaipur					
4th Generation (2 pts)					
Menow					
War Admiral			2		
Swaps					
Prince Bio			2		
Princequillo		1		1	
Tronado					
Nasrullah	2				
Battlefield					
Dosage Profile	2	3	18	1	0

$$\text{Dosage Index} = \frac{2 + 3 + \frac{1}{2}(18)}{\frac{1}{2}(18) + 1} = \frac{14}{10} = 1.40$$

$$\text{Center of Distribution} = \frac{2(2) + 3 - 1}{24} = 0.25$$

[a]In 1986, Mr. Prospector was designated as a brilliant-classic chef. With this change Tank's Prospect has a dosage profile of (21-8-13-0-0), a DI of 5.46, and a CD of 1.19.

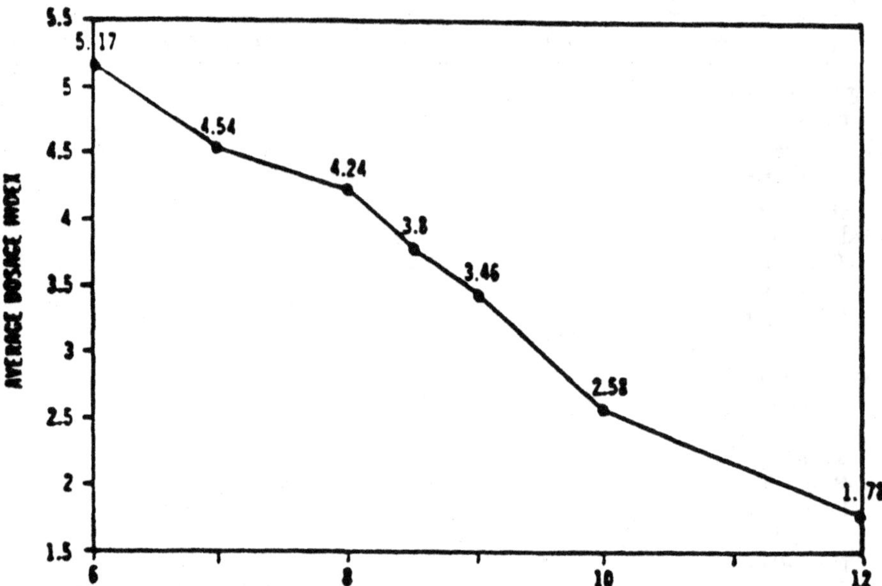

Figure C.1 Average dosage index of winners of 1983 open stakes of value $25,000 or more. *Source:* Roman (1984).

4.00 for middle distances of 8–10 furlongs and sprints of less than a mile, respectively. The fact that the horses have never run $1\frac{1}{4}$ miles before in the Derby and $1\frac{1}{2}$ miles in the Belmont is an important and perhaps crucial aspect of the theory. Tables C.5–C.8 give dosage analyses of the 1984 to 1987 Kentucky Derbys, respectively. To win the race, a balance of speed and stamina is needed. Sprinters burn out. In 1984, Althea, the favorite and a 107-rated winner in her previous race—a smashing victory in the Arkansas Derby against the "boys"—was leading nearing the 1 mile pole. She finished nineteenth! The last eighth of a mile of the Derby is one of the great tests of thoroughbred stamina. Tank's Prospect, the Arkansas Derby winner, had a similar fate in 1985. So did Snow Chief in 1986.

We became acquainted with Dr. Roman's research in time for the 1984 Derby. His previous results for the 1972 and subsequent Derbys appear in Table C.9. Naturally, one needs quality in addition to proper dosage to win. Hence one needs a "filter rule" to eliminate all but the strongest classic contenders: The rule is needed to relate pedigree and performance in a strong positive way. The suggested rule is that to be a contender a horse must have been rated within ten pounds of the two-year-old champion on the experimental free handicap. (An alternative rule suggested by James Quinn is that for horses lightly raced as two-year-olds, they should have won at least one

TABLE C.4 ***Winners of the Kentucky Derby Since 1940***

Year	*Horse*	*Dosage Profile*	*Dosage Index*	*Center of Distribution*
1987	Alysheba	12-14-6-2-0	3.80	1.08
1986	Ferdinand	14-2-16-8-0	1.50	0.55
1985	Spend A Buck	2-3-18-1-0	1.40	0.25
1984	Swale	8-1-11-2-0	1.93	0.68
1983	Sunny's Halo	4-5-13-2-0	1.82	0.46
1982	Gato Del Sol	6-3-5-2-2	1.77	0.50
1981	Pleasant Colony	7-1-9-1-4	1.32	0.27
1980	Genuine Risk	14-10-23-2-0	2.57	0.72
1979	Spectacular Bid	9-6-2-3-0	4.00	1.05
1978	Affirmed	8-6-26-0-0	2.08	0.55
1977	Seattle Slew	7-6-4-5-0	2.14	0.68
1976	Bold Forbes	11-4-9-4-0	2.29	0.79
1975	Foolish Pleasure	27-10-11-4-2	3.70	1.04
1974	Cannonade	9-6-6-3-4	1.80	0.46
1973	Secretariat	20-14-7-9-0	3.00	0.90
1972	Riva Ridge	19-4-7-2-2	3.53	1.06
1971	Canonero II	5-0-7-2-2	1.13	0.25
1970	Dust Commander	9-4-3-3-1	2.64	0.85
1969	Majestic Prince	27-11-12-4-2	3.67	1.02
1968	Forward Pass	22-2-17-1-0	3.42	1.07
1967	Proud Clarion	11-8-26-4-3	1.60	0.38
1966	Kauai King	0-22-18-8-0	1.82	0.29
1965	Lucky Debonair	2-0-15-3-0	0.90	0.05
1964	Northern Dancer	8-16-15-3-0	3.00	0.69
1963	Chateaugay	4-16-6-0-4	3.29	0.53
1962	Decidedly	2-2-17-6-3	0.71	−0.20
1961	Carry Back	4-2-12-6-0	1.00	0.16
1960	Venetian Way	5-9-4-2-0	4.00	0.85
1959	Tomy Lee	20-2-26-0-4	2.06	0.65
1958	Tim Tam	10-11-17-4-0	2.36	0.64
1957	Iron Liege	8-2-28-11-3	0.86	0.02
1956	Needles	4-2-10-2-2	1.22	0.20
1955	Swaps	4-18-14-4-8	1.53	0.13
1954	Determine	4-4-41-3-2	1.12	0.09
1953	Dark Star	8-2-0-4-8	0.83	−0.09
1952	Hill Gail	8-0-26-9-3	0.84	0.02
1951	Count Turf	8-0-16-0-2	1.60	0.46
1950	Middleground	6-0-4-0-2	2.00	0.67
1949	Ponder	4-0-22-10-4	0.60	−0.25
1948	Citation	12-0-24-6-8	0.92	0.04
1947	Jet Pilot	0-0-29-13-2	0.49	−0.39
1946	Assault	6-6-8-1-3	2.00	0.46
1945	Hoop, Jr.	0-4-16-8-4	0.60	−0.38
1944	Pensive	8-0-16-8-8	0.67	−0.20
1943	Count Fleet	0-2-1-1-0	1.67	0.25
1942	Shut Out	4-14-9-3-6	1.67	0.19
1941	Whirlaway	0-12-20-8-0	1.22	0.10
1940	Gallahadion	0-0-16-8-8	0.33	−0.75
		Averages	1.84	0.37

TABLE C.5 ***Dosage analysis of the 1984 Kentucky Derby***

Post Position	Horse	Odds[a]	Dosage Profile[b]	Dosage Index[b]	Center of Distribution[b]		Finish
	Classic Contenders Eligible by Weight[c]						
5	Life's Magic	2.80a	10-4-6-0-6	1.89	0.90		8
7	Fali Time	18.70	6-6-3-3-0	3.00	0.83		5[d]
15	Swale	3.40	8-1-11-2-0	1.93	0.68		1
	Classic Contenders Not Eligible by Weight						
3	Bear Hunt	57.40	6-0-8-0-0	2.50	0.86		18
4	So Vague	9.9f	3-3-5-5-8	0.55	−0.50		11
6	Fight Over	78.90	10-8-9-5-0	2.37	0.72		7
8	Bedouin	9.90f	4-6-15-3-0	1.67	0.38		15
11	Silent King	4.80	2-6-9-2-1	1.67	0.30		9
14	At the Threshold	32.70	3-3-18-1-0	1.40	0.25		3
17	Biloxi Indian	9.90f	5-8-14-1-0	2.50	0.61		12
18	Pine Circle	6.00b	8-9-3-4-0	3.36	0.86		6
19	Coax Me Chad	9.90f	6-4-16-0-0	2.25	0.62		2
20	Gate Dancer	18.90	13-4-16-2-0	2.50	0.80		4[e]
	Sprinters						
1	Althea	2.80a	19-8-7-2-0	5.55	1.22	OU[f]	19
2	Raja's Shark	59.10	13-7-1-3-0	5.86	1.25	OU	14
9	Rexson's Hope	9.90f	9-6-0-0-1	15.00	1.37	OO	10
10	Taylor's Special	6.80	12-2-0-0-0	—	1.86	OO	13
12	Vanlandingham	6.00b	8-2-0-0-0	—	1.80	OO	16
13	Secret Prince	9.90f	13-8-7-2-0	4.45	1.08	OU	17
16	Majestic Shore	9.90f	13-6-7-0-0	6.43	1.23	OU	20

[a]a, b = entries, f = field
[b]Data from article by Leon Rasmussen, *Daily Racing Form*, May 5, 1984.
[c]Classic means DI of less than 4.00, CD less than 1.25. Eligible by weight means within 10 pounds of the two-year-old champion.
[d]Placed 4th after disqualification.
[e]Placed 5th after disqualification.
[f]The first O means over the 4.00 dosage-index criterion; second O means over the 1.25 center-of-distribution criterion; and U means under the same center-of-distribution criterion.

of eleven major Grade I races* as a two- or three-year-old. This rule has not yet been systematically investigated.)

In 1984, the theory pointed to Swale at odds of 3.4–1, Fali Time at 18.7–1, and the co-entry filly Life's Magic running with the favorite Althea

*The proposed races are as follows: for two-year-olds the Champagne Stakes, Laurel Futurity, Young America Stakes, Hollywood Futurity, and Remsen Stakes; and for three-year-olds the Flamingo Stakes, Florida Derby, Santa Anita Derby, Arkansas Derby, Wood Memorial, and Blue Grass Stakes.

TABLE C.6 ***Dosage analysis of the 1985 Kentucky Derby***

Post Position	*Horse*	*Odds*[a]	*Dosage Profile*[b]	*Dosage Index*[b]	*Center of Distribution*[b]		*Finish*
			Classic Contenders Eligible by Weight				
5	Stephan's Odyssey	13.40	9-8-9-2-2	2.53	0.67		2
9	Spend A Buck	4.10	2-3-18-1-0	1.40	0.25		1
			Classic Contenders Not Eligible by Weight				
1	Rhoman Rule	7.50a	10-8-14-0-0	3.57	0.87		9
7	I Am the Game	101.30	10-9-5-3-1	3.31	0.86		13
8	Floating Reserve	134.80	1-10-3-3-3	1.67	0.05		8
10	Proud Truth	4.90	7-1-18-10-4	0.74	0.075		5
12	Fast Account	92.40	7-9-14-0-0	3.29	0.77		4
			Sprinters				
13	Eternal Prince	7.50a	23-4-0-0-0	7.00	1.39	OO	12
2	Irish Fighter	40.90	—	7.00	1.25	OU	11
3	Chief's Crown	1.20	9-8-6-1-0	5.00	1.04	OU	3
4	Tank's Prospect	11.30	13-8-5-0-0	9.40	1.31	OO	7
6	Encolure	103.50	18-7-6-3-0	4.67	1.18	OU	10
11	Skywalker	17.70	6-11-5-0-0	7.80	1.05	OU	6

[a]a, b = entries, f = field.
[b]Data from articles by Leon Rasmussen, *Daily Racing Form*, May 4, 1985.
[c]The first O means over the 4.00 dosage-index criterion; second O means over the 1.25 center-of-distribution criterion; and U means under the same center-of-distribution criterion.

at 2.8–1. Swale was an obvious choice to concentrate your betting on. All of the high finishers were classic contenders. None of the sprinters was among the top ten finishers, including three that were heavily favored by the betting public.

In 1985 the theory pointed to Spend A Buck at 4.1–1 and Stephan's Odyssey at 13.4–1. Proud Truth at 4.9–1, although not qualified as a lightly raced two-year-old, did win the Flamingo Stakes and the Florida Derby and could be considered a legitimate contender. These were the suggested bets. The result was a 1–2 finish for the two qualifying horses. Spend A Buck paid $10.20 to win and the $2 exacta paid a whopping $118.20. Four of the top five finishers—all but the 6–5 favorite Chief's Crown—were classic contenders. Chief's Crown had a brilliant record and was the choice of a vast majority of the professional handicappers. With a dosage index of 5.00, he was above the 4.00 cutoff. Hence he was a legitimate threat to the theory's record. However, his fading from second to third was just as expected—his Belmont race was similar.

TABLE C.7 ***Dosage analysis of the 1986 Kentucky Derby***

Post Position	*Horse*	*Odds*[a]	*Dosage Profile*[b]	*Dosage Index*[b]	*Center of Distribution*[b]		*Finish*
	Classic Contenders Eligible by Weight						
1	Ferdinand	17.70	14-2-16-8-0	1.50	0.55		1
14	Groovy	57.30	4-2-16-0-0	1.75	0.45		16
	Classic Contenders Not Eligible by Weight						
10	Badger Land	2.60	0-2-2-0-2	1.00	−0.33		5
9	Broad Brush	14.40	8-5-5-1-3	2.38	0.64		3
8	Rampage	9.00	13-2-10-5-8	1.11	0.18		4
7	Vernon Castle	12.20	6-3-15-4-0	1.43	0.39		15
16	Fobby Forbes	16.00f	8-4-5-11-0	1.07	0.32		7
11	Wheatley Hall	47.70	2-2-14-0-0	1.57	0.33		6
15	Zabaletta	16.00f	4-3-12-1-0	1.86	0.50		12
5	Icy Groom	16.00f	10-3-15-0-4	1.78	0.47		8
3	Wise Times	16.00f	4-7-9-0-0	3.44	0.75		9
6	Southern Appeal	16.00f	6-3-16-1-0	1.89	0.54		13
	Sprinters						
12	Snow Chief	2.10	0-4-2-0-0	5.00	0.67	OU[c]	11
2	Mogambo	8.80	23-9-15-1-0	4.64	1.13	OU	10
4	Bold Arrangement[d]	9.10	6-2-0-0-0	∞	1.75	OO	2
13	Bachelor Beau	60.00	18-7-5-0-2	6.11	1.22	OU	14

[a]a, b = entries, f = field.
[b]Data from articles by Leon Rasmussen, *Daily Racing Form*, May 3, 1986.
[c]The first O means over the 4.00 dosage-index criterion; second O means over the 1.25 center-of-distribution criterion; and U means under the same center-of-distribution criterion.
[d]See the footnote on page 15.

In 1986 the theory pointed to Ferdinand at 17.7−1 and Groovy at 57.3−1. They were the only horses with dosage indices of 4.00 or less who were within ten pounds of the top-rated horse in the experimental free handicap. Snow Chief, with a dosage index of 5.00, was the favorite at 2.1−1. The significance of his dosage index was somewhat suspect because it was based on only three chefs. With his suspect DI and his brilliant record, he, like Chief's Crown in 1985, was a threat to the theory's record. He finished eleventh, though. Ferdinand won the race, and Groovy, who led early, finished last. Ferdinand's win preserved the unblemished dosage record, that a dosage index of 4.00 or less has been characteristic of the winner since 1940, and his win also upheld the ten-pound rule for the winner, which had been applicable since 1972. Except for the British invader Bold

TABLE C.8 ***Dosage analysis of the 1987 Kentucky Derby***

Post Position	Horse	Odds[a]	Dosage Profile[b]	Dosage Index[b]	Center of Distribution[b]		Finish
Classic Contenders Eligible by Weight[c]							
3	Alysheba	8.40	12-4-6-2-0	3.80	1.08		1
14	Bet Twice	10.10	10-3-6-9-0	1.50	0.50		2
5	Capote	6.30a	8-1-3-2-0	3.00	1.07		eased
15	Conquistarose	52.80	12-5-12-9-0	1.53	0.53		9
10	Demon's Begone	2.20	5-3-8-0-0	3.00	0.81		bled
7	Masterful Advocate	6.20	11-6-10-3-2	2.20	0.66		12
Classic Contenders Not Eligible by Weight							
12	Candi's Gold	48.50	13-8-15-0-0	3.80	0.94		8
1	Cryptoclearance	6.50	8-3-13-1-3	1.67	0.43		4
9	On the Line	6.30a	1-6-8-1-0	2.20	0.44		10
2	War	6.30a	6-1-3-0-2	2.43	0.58		13
13	Shawklit Won	50.20	2-2-3-2-1	1.22	0.20		11
17	No More Flowers	55.30	8-7-5-2-0	3.89	0.95		15
4	Templar Hill	24.50f	3-4-5-0-0	3.80	0.83		5
11	Momentus	24.50f	6-13-12-1-0	3.57	0.75		14
Sprinters							
6	Gulch	4.90b	19-7-14-0-0	4.71	1.13	OU[d]	6
8	Leo Castelli	4.90b	17-8-9-0-0	6.56	1.23	OU	7
16	Avies Copy	24.50f	7-9-4-0-2	4.50	0.86	OU	3

[a]a,b = entries, f = field.
[b]Data from articles by Leon Rasmussen, *Daily Racing Form*, May 2, 1987.
[c]Classic means DI less than 4.00, CD less than 1.25. Eligible by weight means within 10 pounds of the two-year-old champion.
[d]O means over the 4.00 dosage index criterion; U means under the 1.25 center-of-distribution criterion.

Arrangement—who had an infinity dosage index but was possibly bred for distance and not by chefs—all the sprinters finished tenth or worse.*

In 1987 there were six horses that were classic contenders eligible by

*According to Leon Rasmussen, writing in *Bloodlines* in the October 31, 1986, *Daily Racing Form*, "Since the Derby research has shown that Relko, the damsire of Persian Bold and the sire of Bold Arrangement, deserves recognition—long overdue—as a solid chef de race. Therefore, Bold Arrangement with his DP of: 6-2-0-4-0 has a DI of 2.00 and a CD of 0.83." With this change, Bold Arrangement becomes a classic contender not eligible by weight, and the sprinters finished 10th, 11th and 14th. Bold Arrangement was co-third-topweight on the international classifications as a two-year-old, which suggests that he did have considerable class and was near being a champion two-year-old in Europe. This reclassification of Relko after the fact is not a juggling by the dosage proponents to make the theory look better. Rather unexpected performance is studied to learn more about the way the breed is evolving. Pedigree evolution and the resulting dosage numbers are tied to racetrack performance. The breed evolves from its best performers who are also prepotent. The researchers are not juggling the numbers, just trying to interpret and understand performance in terms of pedigree.

weight: Alysheba, Bet Twice, Capote, Conquistarose, Demon's Begone and Masterful Advocate. In addition, Cryptoclearance, who had the best dosage profile for the race, had won the Florida Derby and could qualify on Jim Quinn's guidelines. Alysheba had won only one of ten races, and had a borderline 3.80 DI. So even though he was coming into the Derby from having crossed the finish line first in his last race (he had been disqualified in the Blue Grass Stakes at Keeneland the previous Saturday), others looked better. Bet Twice was my choice. He had a 1.50 DI, a 0.50 CD, a good dosage profile and 6 wins in 10 starts. Capote, the four-year-old champion, had a reasonable DI and CD but his dosage profile was skewed to speed. Also, he performed badly in his only two starts in 1987, although both were on off tracks. He was a definite question mark. Conquistarose had excellent DI, CD and dosage profiles but had a poor record against the other top contenders. His trainer, Woody Stephens, had indicated that his main hope was an off track. At over 50–1 he seemed doubtful as a major contender. Masterful Advocate had an excellent DI, CD and dosage profile plus a strong 1987 record in California.

Demon's Begone was the Derby favorite. He came into the race with three outstanding wins, including a strong performance in the Arkansas Derby. Critics said his competition was weak. His DI and CD were 3.00 and 0.81, respectively, which were within the guidelines but a little on the high side.

The theory then pointed to Bet Twice, Demon's Begone, Cryptoclearance and Masterful Advocate as the top choices, with Alysheba, Capote and Conquistarose as secondary picks. I wagered on all these horses, concentrating on Bet Twice across the board.

Alysheba in a show of great courage won the race, even though he nearly collided with Bet Twice on two occasions. The Preakness, which dosage theory is pretty silent on, produced the same one-two finish with Alysheba beating Bet Twice by a short margin.

The dosage theory was again vindicated, although the outcome was a little surprising. I had to bet thrice on Bet Twice before I was fully vindicated when he romped to a 14-length victory at 8–1 in the Belmont. There the obvious exacta of Bet Twice and Cryptoclearance came in 1–2 exactly according to the dosage script. Charts of the Derby and Belmont races follow.

An interesting question is how much to wager on the various horses with favorable dosage indices. Studies such as those summarized in Chapter Three indicate that on average, the odds do represent very closely the real chances that each horse will win. Figure C.2 shows a similar graph for the Kentucky Derby for 1903–86. Even with this many Derbies, the data is small, and it is hard to draw conclusions. However, the usual favorite–long-shot bias does not appear. In fact, the favorites and the long shots seem to have relatively little bias at all. Many racing novices use the strategy of "bet the favorite." This and the large number of novices at the Kentucky Derby

EIGHTH RACE
Churchill
MAY 2, 1987

1 ¼ MILES. (1.59⅖) 113th Running THE KENTUCKY DERBY (Grade I). $350,000 added. 3-year-olds with an entry fee of $10,000 each and a starting fee of $10,000 each. All fees will be paid to the winner. $350,000 added shall be paid by Churchill Downs Incorporated as the Added Purse. Second place shall receive $100,000, third place shall receive $50,000 and fourth place shall receive $25,000 from the Added Purse (the Added Purse and fees to be divided equally in the event of a dead-heat). Starters shall be named through the entry box on Thursday, April 30, 1987, at the usual time of closing (the "Closing"). The maximum number of starters shall be limited to twenty (20) and each shall carry a weight of 126 pounds. In the event that more than twenty entries pass through the entry box at the Closing, the starters shall be determined at the Closing with preference given to those horses that have accumulated the highest earnings in Graded Sweepstakes, including all moneys paid for performance in such Graded Stakes.

Last Raced	Horse	Eqt.	A.	Wt	PP	¼	½	¾	1	Str	Fin	Jockey	Odds $1
23Apr87 7Kee1	Alysheba	b	3	126	3	14^{2}	$13^{2\frac{1}{2}}$	$7^{\frac{1}{2}}$	3^{1}	$2^{1\frac{1}{2}}$	$1^{\frac{3}{4}}$	McCarron C J	8.40
4Apr87 10GP5	Bet Twice		3	126	14	$5^{\frac{1}{2}}$	6^{1}	4^{1}	1^{hd}	1^{1}	$2^{2\frac{1}{2}}$	Perret C	10.10
23Apr87 7Kee5	Avies Copy	b	3	126	16	10^{hd}	10^{2}	$8^{\frac{1}{2}}$	4^{hd}	3^{1}	3^{nk}	Solomone M	f-24.50
4Apr87 10GP1	Cryptoclearance		3	126	1	$16^{1\frac{1}{2}}$	$15^{1\frac{1}{2}}$	$14^{\frac{1}{2}}$	$7^{\frac{1}{2}}$	$4^{\frac{1}{2}}$	$4^{\frac{1}{2}}$	Santos J A	6.50
18Apr87 10GS2	Templar Hill	b	3	126	4	9^{hd}	$11^{1\frac{1}{2}}$	9^{2}	$9^{\frac{1}{2}}$	$6^{\frac{1}{2}}$	$5^{\frac{1}{2}}$	Hutton G W	f-24.50
18Apr87 8Aqu1	Gulch		3	126	6	$15^{1\frac{1}{2}}$	16^{hd}	$15^{\frac{1}{2}}$	12^{1}	7^{3}	$6^{\frac{1}{2}}$	Shoemaker W	b-4.90
23Apr87 7Kee3	Leo Castelli	b	3	126	8	7^{hd}	$4^{\frac{1}{2}}$	5^{1}	6^{1}	$5^{1\frac{1}{2}}$	7^{5}	Vasquez J	b-4.90
11Apr87 7Kee2	Candi's Gold		3	126	12	$3^{\frac{1}{2}}$	3^{hd}	$6^{1\frac{1}{2}}$	8^{hd}	$8^{2\frac{1}{2}}$	$8^{2\frac{1}{2}}$	Hawley S	48.50
16Apr87 7Kee3	Conquistarose	b	3	126	15	17	17	16	16	13^{4}	9^{2}	Bailey J D	52.80
25Apr87 9CD1	On The Line	b	3	126	9	$1^{\frac{1}{2}}$	$2^{2\frac{1}{2}}$	$1^{\frac{1}{2}}$	$2^{1\frac{1}{2}}$	$9^{\frac{1}{2}}$	10^{2}	Stevens G L	a-6.30
18Apr87 8Aqu3	Shawklit Won	b	3	126	13	$11^{\frac{1}{2}}$	$9^{\frac{1}{2}}$	11^{1}	$11^{\frac{1}{2}}$	$12^{\frac{1}{2}}$	11^{nk}	Migliore R	50.20
4Apr87 5SA2	Masterful Advocate		3	126	7	6^{hd}	$7^{\frac{1}{2}}$	$10^{\frac{1}{2}}$	$13^{\frac{1}{2}}$	$11^{\frac{1}{2}}$	12no	Pincay L Jr	6.20
23Apr87 7Kee1	War	b	3	126	2	$8^{1\frac{1}{2}}$	$5^{\frac{1}{2}}$	$3^{\frac{1}{2}}$	$5^{\frac{1}{2}}$	10^{1}	13^{7}	McCauley W H	a-6.30
11Apr87 7Kee3	Momentus	b	3	126	11	$12^{1\frac{1}{2}}$	12^{1}	13^{2}	15^{3}	14^{3}	$14^{2\frac{1}{2}}$	Brumfield D	f-24.50
25Apr87 9CD2	No More Flowers		3	126	17	$4^{1\frac{1}{2}}$	$8^{\frac{1}{2}}$	12^{2}	14^{2}	$15^{1\frac{1}{2}}$	15	Guerra W A	55.30
18Apr87 8Aqu4	Capote		3	126	5	$2^{2\frac{1}{2}}$	$1^{1\frac{1}{2}}$	2^{hd}	10^{1}	16	—	Cordero A Jr	a-6.30
18Apr87 9OP1	Demons Begone		3	126	10	13^{1}	$14^{1\frac{1}{2}}$	—	—	—	—	Day P	2.20

Capote, Eased; Demons Begone , Bled.
a-Coupled: On The Line, War and Capote; b-Gulch and Leo Castelli.
f—Mutuel field.

OFF AT 5:35. Start good. Won driving. Time, :22⅘, :46⅗, 1:11, 1:36⅘, 2:03⅖ Track fast.

$2 Mutuel Prices:				
	4-ALYSHEBA	18.80	8.00	6.20
	9-BET TWICE		10.00	7.20
	14-AVIES COPY (f-field)			6.80
	$2 EXACTA (4-9) PAID $109.60.			

B. c, by Alydar—Bel Sheba, by Lt Stevens. Trainer Van Berg Jack C. Bred by Preston Madden (Ky).

ALYSHEBA, carefully handled when caught in close quarters between horses just after the start, advanced steadily to reach contention approaching the stretch, stumbled when he clipped the heels on BET TWICE just inside the final three-sixteenths, came out to avoid that rival again leaving the furlong grounds and proved best under strong handling. BET TWICE, never far back, rallied from the outside approaching the end of the backstretch, caught ON THE LINE soon after starting the final turn, then swerved repeatedly under pressure during the drive bothering ALYSHEBA a couple of times and continued on gamely. AVIES COPY moved within easy striking distance from the outside nearing the far turn, remained a factor to midstretch and finished with good energy. CRYPTOCLEARANCE lacked room along the inside after the start, moved fast from the outside leaving the far turn but wasn't good enough. TEMPLAR HILL rallied approaching the stretch and was going well at the finish. GULCH, eased back between horses soon after the start, raced very wide into the stretch but failed to seriously menace with a mild late reponse. LEO CASTELLI, caught in tight quarters between horses racing into the first turn, moved up along the inside entering the backstretch, raced within easy striking distance to the upper stretch but lacked the needed response. CANDI'S GOLD raced forwardly until near the stretch and tired. CONQUISTAROSE was without speed. ON THE LINE raced outside CAPOTE while vying for the lead, held on well for a mile and flattened out. SHAWKLIT WON tired. MASTERFUL ADVOCATE, caught in close quarters racing into the first turn, was finished before reaching the far turn. WAR lacked room between horses following the start and again along the inside at the first turn, continued to save ground while making a run approaching the end of the backstretch but was finished after going a mile. MOMENTUS failed to be a serious factor. NO MORE FLOWERS showed some early foot while racing wide. CAPOTE raced well out from the rail while vying for the lead to the far turn, gave way suddenly and was eased through the final 70 yards. DEMONS BEGONE, outrun early, bled after entering the backstretch.

Owners— 1, Scharbauer Dorothy & Pamela; 2, Cisley Stable & Levy Blanche P; 3, Badgett Brown; 4, Teinowitz P; 5, Kowitz E J; 6, Brant P M; 7, Brant P M; 8, Royal Lines lessee; 9, de Kwiatkowski H; 10, Klein E V; 11, Anchel E; 12, Belles (Lessee) & Leveton; 13, Gentry T; 14, Duckett et al; 15, Appleton A I; 16, French, Beal & Klein; 17, Loblolly Stable.

Trainers— 1, Van Berg Jack C; 2, Croll Warren A Jr; 3, Kassen David C; 4, Schulhofer Flint S; 5, Seefeldt Paul D; 6, Jolley Leroy; 7, Jolley Leroy; 8, Gregson Edwin; 9, Stephens Woodford C; 10, Lukas D Wayne; 11, LaBoccetta Frank; 12, Manzi Joseph; 13, Lukas D Wayne; 14, Dollase Wallace; 15, Alter Happy; 16, Lukas D Wayne; 17, Hauswald Philip.

EIGHTH RACE
Belmont
JUNE 6, 1987

1 ½ MILES. (2.24) 119th Running THE BELMONT (Grade I). $350,000 Added. 3-year-olds. By subscription of $200 each, which should accompany the nomination if made on or before January 15, 1987, or $1,000 if made on or before March 17, 1987, $5,000 to pass the entry box, $5,000 to start with $350,000 added. The added money and all fees to be divided 60% to the winner, 22% to second, 12% to third and 6% to fourth. Colts and geldings, 126 lbs. Fillies, 121 lbs. Starters to be named at the closing time of entries. The Belmont field will be limited to sixteen (16) starters. In the event that more than 16 entries pass through the entry box at the closing, the starters will be determined at the closing with 50% of the field (8 starters) given preference by accumulating the highest earnings in Graded Stakes (lifetime), including all money paid for performance in such Graded Stakes. The next five (5) starters (approximate 30%) will be determined by accumulating the highest earnings (lifetime) in all races except restricted races (i.e., any stake containing eligibility conditions other than sex and age). The remaining 3 starters (approximate 20%) shall be determined by accumulating the highest earnings (lifetime) in all races. Should this preference produce any ties the additional starter(s) shall be determined by lot. If the rules described result in the exclusion of any horse, the $5,000 entry fee will be refunded to the owner of said horse. The winning owner will be presented with the August Belmont Memorial Cup, to be retained for one year, as well as a trophy for permanent possession and trophies will be presented to the winning trainer and jockey.

Value of race $1,548,600; value to winner $1,329,160; second $120,692; third $65,832; fourth $32,916. Mutuel pool $1,409,970, OTB pool $1,782,395. ExPl$672,681OTB ExPl$1,150,263TriPl$358,887.OTBTriPl$864,852

Last Raced	Horse	Eqt.	A.	Wt	PP	¼	½	1	1¼	Str	Fin	Jockey	Odds $1
16May87 9Pim2	Bet Twice		3	126	4	$3^{\frac{1}{2}}$	3^{3}	$1^{1\frac{1}{2}}$	1^{5}	1^{7}	1^{14}	Perret C	8.00
16May87 9Pim3	Cryptoclearance		3	126	6	$5^{\frac{1}{2}}$	6^{2}	5^{4}	2^{hd}	2^{2}	2no	Pincay L Jr	4.50
25May87 8Bel1	Gulch		3	126	9	6^{hd}	8^{4}	$8^{\frac{1}{2}}$	8^{7}	4^{2}	3^{nk}	Day P	b-7.70
16May87 9Pim1	Alysheba	b	3	126	3	4^{1}	4^{2}	4^{hd}	4^{1}	$3^{2\frac{1}{2}}$	$4^{9\frac{1}{2}}$	McCarron C J	.80
24May87 8Bel3	Shawklit Won	b	3	126	8	$8^{3\frac{1}{2}}$	5^{hd}	$6^{2\frac{1}{2}}$	6^{1}	7^{3}	5^{hd}	Cordero A Jr	20.10
24May87 8Bel2	Gone West		3	126	1	$1^{1\frac{1}{2}}$	2^{2}	2^{hd}	3^{2}	$5^{2\frac{1}{2}}$	$6^{1\frac{1}{2}}$	Maple E	5.40
25May87 10GS1	Avies Copy	b	3	126	2	$2^{1\frac{1}{2}}$	1^{2}	$3^{2\frac{1}{2}}$	5^{4}	6^{1}	7^{9}	Solomone M	30.70
25May87 12Suf2	Manassa Jack	b	3	126	5	9	9	9	9	9	8^{nk}	Delgado A	46.70
24May87 8Bel1	Leo Castelli	b	3	126	7	7^{1}	7^{2}	7^{7}	$7^{2\frac{1}{2}}$	8^{5}	9	Santos J A	b-7.70

b–Coupled: Gulch and Leo Castelli.

OFF AT 5:33. Start good. Won ridden out. Time, :24$\frac{2}{5}$, :49$\frac{3}{5}$, 1:13$\frac{4}{5}$, 1:38$\frac{3}{5}$, 2:03, 2:28$\frac{1}{5}$, Track fast.

$2 Mutuel Prices:			
5–(E)–BET TWICE	18.00	5.00	3.80
7–(G)–CRYPTOCLEARANCE		4.80	3.80
2–(J)–GULCH (b–entry)			4.40

$2 EXACTA 5–7 PAID $77.80. $2 TRIPLE 5–7–2 PAID $472.00.

B. c, by Sportin' Life—Golden Dust, by Dusty Canyon. Trainer Croll Warren A Jr. Bred by Farish W S III & Hudson E J (Ky).

BET TWICE, allowed to follow the early leaders, moved fast from the outside to gain a clear lead before going a mile, drew off quickly when roused after entering the stretch and continued to increase his advantage under a hand ride. CRYPTOCLEARANCE, allowed to drop well back around the first turn, commenced to rally approaching the end of the backstretch, continued his bid into the stretch but was no match for the winner and just lasted for the place. GULCH, away alertly, was unhurried while dropping far back around the first turn, raced wide into the stretch and finished with good energy. ALYSHEBA, reserved into the backstretch, moved with CRYPTOCLEARANCE approaching the far turn, was steadied looking for room between horses nearing the five sixteenths pole, then checked sharply behind GONE WEST nearing the stretch. After recovering, he altered course to the outside and finished with good courage between horses. SHAWKLIT WON, stoutly restrained around the first turn, failed to be a serious factor. GONE WEST sprinted clear racing to the first turn then was unhurried when outrun for the lead by AVIES COPY, made a run between horses racing into the far turn but was finished entering the stretch. AVIES COPY opened a clear lead nearing the backstretch, saved ground while making the pace to the end of the backstretch and tired badly. MANASSA JACK was never close. LEO CASTELLI saved ground to no avail.

Owners— 1, Cisley Stable & Levy Blanche P; 2, Teinowitz P; 3, Brant P M; 4, Scharbauer Dorothy & Pamela; 5, Anchel E; 6, Hickory Tree Farm; 7, Badgett T B; 8, Gavegnano R J; 9, Brant P M.

Trainers— 1, Croll Warren A Jr; 2, Schulhofer Flint S; 3, Jolley Leroy; 4, Van Berg Jack C; 5, LaBoccetta Frank; 6, Stephens Woodford C; 7, Kassen David C; 8, Downing Michael W; 9, Jolley Leroy.

Scratched—Conquistarose (17May87 8Bel4).

may account for the favorite not being underbet. All of the efficiency studies deal with returns on average over many, many races. The key here are the words "on average." In any particular race the odds may be off. For horses with dosage indices above 4.00 they certainly are in the Derby. It's clear that in 1985 such horses as Chief's Crown at 6–5 and Tank's Prospect at

11.3–1 were overbet, and horses like Spend A Buck at 4.1–1 and Stephan's Odyssey at 13.4–1 were underbet. Mitchell (1985) has reminded us of the 80–20 rule. In this case the "good population" are the classic contenders. Give them 80% of the probability, and assign the high-dosage horses the remaining 20%. Assume that within these classes, the horses chances are related to their odds. You can then generate the probability of all possible finishes using Harville formula equations (5.2) and (5.3). These probabilities will generate overlays on the classic contenders. You can use the Kelly criterion or a related modification to compute the suggested win, place, show, and exacta bets. It's a bit of an exercise, but it is well worth it. See Hausch, Winkler, and Ziemba (1987).

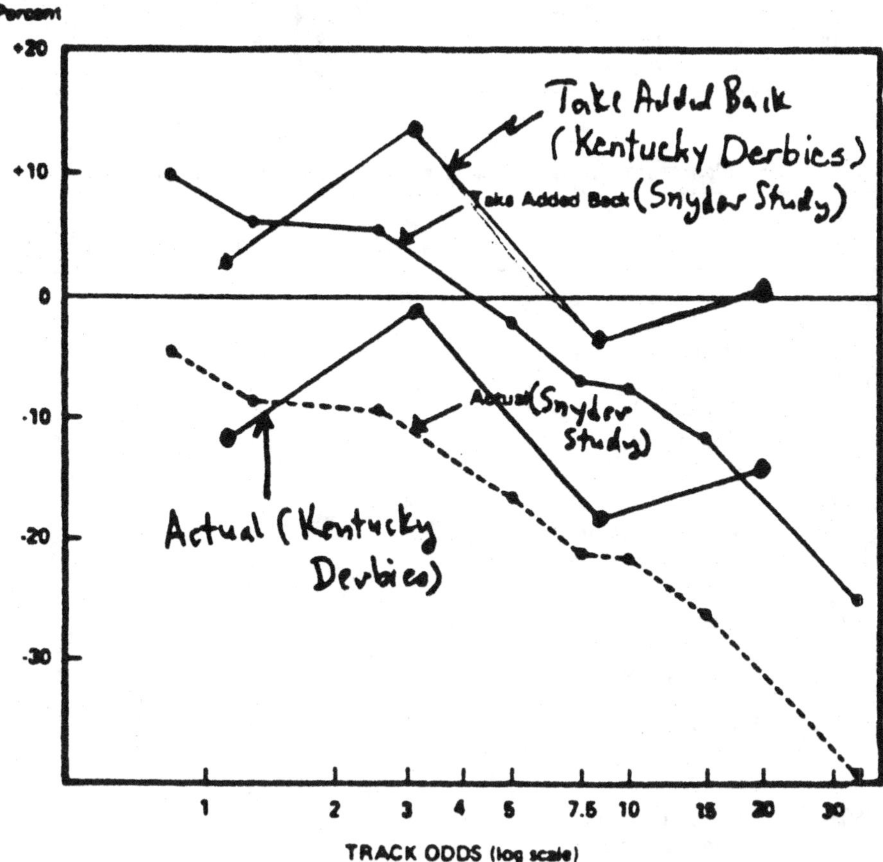

Figure C.2 Expected return per dollar bet with and without the track take deducted for different odds levels in the Kentucky Derby 1903–1986, and in 35,285 races run during 1947–1975 from data in Snyder (1978).

The data for Figure C.2 are as follows:

Win Probability	*Odds*	*# of Wagers*	*Average Return*	*Grouping for Figure C.1*
0.000–0.049	16.1 –	358	0.00	0.00 on 358 Wagers
0.050–0.099	7.5 –16.0	188	0.26	−0.059 on 286 Wagers
0.100–0.149	4.7 –7.4	98	−0.67	
0.150–0.199	3.3 –4.6	47	0.31	+0.149 on 107 Wagers
0.200–0.249	2.37–3.2	39	−0.09	
0.250–0.299	1.81–2.36	21	0.23	
0.300–0.349	1.41–1.80	22	0.39	+0.030 on 63 Wagers
0.350–0.399	1.11–1.40	16	−0.32	
0.400–0.449	0.87–1.10	9	−0.20	
0.450–0.499	0.69–0.86	4	−0.49	
0.500–0.549	0.53–0.68	6	0.28	
0.550+	0.20–0.52	6	0.08	

TABLE C.9 ***Dosage analysis and the Kentucky Derby Winners: 1972–1987***

Year	*Classic Contenders*[a]	*Number of Other Horses*	*Finish*	*Odds of Winner*
1972	Riva Ridge	10	1	3–2
	Hold Your Peace		3	
	Freetex		out	
1973	Secretariat	11	1	3–2
	Angle Light		out	
1974	Cannonade	22	1	3–2
1975	Foolish Pleasure	14	1	1.9–1
1976	Bold Forbes	5	1	3–1
	Honest Pleasure		2	
	Elocutionist		3	
	Cojak		out	
1977	Seattle Slew	11	1	1–2
	For the Moment		out	
	Get the Axe		out	
	Nostalgia		out	
1978	Affirmed	8	1	9–5
	Alydar		2	
	Believe It		3	
1979	Spectacular Bid	5	1	3–5
	General Assembly		2	
	Golden Act		3	
1980	Genuine Risk	8	1	13.3–1
	Rumbo		2	
	Rockhill Native		out	
	Plugged Nickle		out	
	Execution's Reason		out	

TABLE C.9 ***(continued)***

Year	*Classic Contenders*[a]	*Number of Other Horses*	*Finish*	*Odds of Winner*
1981	Pleasant Colony	17	1	9–2
	Pass the Tab		out	
	Noble Nashua		out	
	Cure the Blues		out	
1982	Gato Del Sol	16	1	21.2–1
	Laser Light		2	
	Cassaleria		out	
1983	Sunny's Halo[b]	17	1	5–2
	Caveat		3	
	Pax In Bello		out	
1984	Swale	17	1	3.4–1
	Fali Time		out	
	Life's Magic		out	
1985	Spend A Buck	11	1	4.1–1
	Stephen's Odyssey		2	
1986	Ferdinand	14	1	17.7–1
	Groovy		16	
1987	Alysheba	11	1	8.4–1
	Bet Twice		2	10.1–1
	Capote		out	6.3–1
	Conquistarose		out	52.8–1
	Demon's Begone		out	2.2–1
	Masterful Advocate		out	6.2–1

[a]Dosage index of 4.00 or less plus two-year-old form with weighting within ten pounds of the two-year-old champion on the experimental free handicap.
[b]Sunny's Halo was the two-year-old champion in Canada and weighted there at 126 pounds within the 10-pound guideline.

Information on the dosage profiles, dosage indices, and centers of distribution for specific horses can be obtained from services that advertise in publications such as *The Blood-Horse*. However, as shown in Table C.3, these quantities are very easy to compute once you have a four-generation pedigree. For Derby Day, the *Daily Racing Form* runs miniarticles on all the entrants written by Leon Rasmussen so the information and his summary is readily available.* The number of nonclassic contenders in the Derby has fallen over the last several years. In 1987 there were only three of seventeen starters. This suggests that the horse owners have accepted dosage theory. However, despite the detailed coverage in the *Daily Racing Form* by Leon Rasmussen, and the impressive evidence, the dosage theory has not influenced the odds that much, to the great pleasure of its followers. We look forward to next year's Derby.

*Capps (1986) for the *Thoroughbred Record* discusses a dosage theory that uses all the stallions rather than just the chef-de-race stallions. It results in somewhat different values, such as those shown for the 1986 Derby:

Horse	*Record Dosage Index*	*Roman Dosage Index*
Ferdinand	1.93	1.50
Bold Arrangement (GB)	5.74	∞
Broad Brush	2.00	2.38
Rampage	2.20	1.11
Badger Land	3.96	1.00
Wheatly Hall	1.50	1.57
Fobby Forbes	1.84	1.07
Icy Groom	3.13	1.78
Wise Times	5.53	3.44
Mogambo	5.59	4.65
Snow Chief	6.29	5.00
Zabaleta	5.59	1.86
Southern Appeal	3.41	1.89
Bachelor Beau	5.40	6.11
Vernon Castle	2.18	1.43
Groovy	3.57	1.75

It remains to be seen, when research is done, if this dosage theory provides some value added to the Roman theory. The approach seems to inflate the dosage indices almost capriciously and the evidence for what these values mean and can predict is missing.

Bibliography

Ainslie, Tom. *Ainslie's Complete Guide to Thoroughbred Racing*. 3rd edition. New York: Simon & Schuster, 1986.

A revised edition of an early guide to handicapping fundamentals.

———. *Ainslie's Encyclopedia of Thoroughbred Handicapping*. New York: Morrow, 1978.

Brief abstracts about many horseracing topics.

Ali, Mukhtar M. "Probability and Utility Estimates for Racetrack Bettors." *Journal of Political Economy*, 85 (August 1977), pp. 803–15.

A technical article concerned with the efficiency of win markets and the favorite–longshot bias in harness racing.

American Racing Manual. Chicago: Triangle Publications, published annually.

The definitive year-by-year sources of information concerning all aspects of racing.

Arvesen, James. Review of *Beat the Racetrack*, *Journal of the American Statistical Association* (June 1986), p. 564.

A review of the Dr. Z method by a well-known statistician, who practices the art of gambling as well.

Asch, Peter, Burton G. Malkiel, and Richard E. Quandt. "Racetrack Betting and Informed Behavior." *Journal of Financial Economics*, 10 (1982), pp. 187–94.

A demonstration that late bettors are better informed than the general public.

———. "Market Efficiency in Racetrack Betting." *Journal of Business*, 57 (1984), pp. 165–75.

———. "Market Efficiency in Racetrack Betting: Further Evidence and a Correction." *Journal of Business* 59 (1986), pp. 157–60.

This and their previous paper are on exposition of a place and show betting strategy based on the dynamics of late betting.

Asch, Peter, and Richard E. Quandt. *Racetrack Betting: The Professor's Guide to Strategies*. Dover, Mass.: Auburn House, 1986.

A highly readable account of the difficulties and possibilities of winning at the racetrack along with the authors' late-money place and show system.

Bell, Robert M., and Thomas M. Cover. "Competitive Optimality of Logarithmic Investment." *Mathematics of Operations Research*, 5 (May 1980), pp. 161–66.
They show that the Kelly criterion is optimal even for single bets.

Beyer, Andrew. *Picking Winners*, New York: Houghton Mifflin Co., 1975.
An excellent source of information on speed handicapping.

———. *My $50,000 Year at the Races*. New York: Harcourt, Brace, Jovanovich, Inc., 1978.
Colorful story of this well-known handicapper's attempts to beat the races over a full season.

———. *The Winning Horseplayer*. New York: Houghton Mifflin Co., 1983.
An introduction to trip handicapping written in an entertaining style.

———. "Computer Wagering: Shows the Way." *Washington Post* (19 February 1985).
A review of the Dr. Z system by one of the game's top handicappers and racetrack writers.

Bolton, Ruth N., and Randall G. Chapman. "Searching for Positive Returns at the Track: A Multinomial Logit Model for Handicapping Horse Races." *Management Science*, 32 (1986), pp. 1040–1060.
A method for estimating win probabilities with a statistical model.

Canfield, Brian, Bruce Fauman, and William T. Ziemba. "Efficient Market Adjustment of Odds Prices to Reflect Track Biases." Faculty of Commerce Working Paper No. 973, Vancouver: University of British Columbia (November 1986). Forthcoming in *Management Science*.
A look at the wisdom of betting on favorable post positions.

Capps, Timothy T. "Dosages: Right and Wrong." *The Thoroughbred Record* (10 May 1986), pp. 2355–2378.
An exposition of a theory of dosage using all stallions rather than only the chef-de-race stallions.

Chernoff, Herman. *An Analysis of the Massachusetts Numbers Game*. Department of Mathematics, MIT, Technical Report Number Twenty-three. Cambridge, Mass. (November 1980).
A clever analysis of how statistical methods can be used to attempt to isolate numbers sufficiently unpopular so that they are profitable bets. The conclusions are easy to follow despite the highly mathematical analysis.

Cootner, Paul, ed. *The Random Character of Stock Market Prices*. Cambridge, Mass.: MIT Press, 1964.
Important collection of papers dealing with random walk ideas in security markets.

Copeland, Thomas E., and J. Fred Weston. *Financial Theory and Corporate Policy*. 2d ed. Reading, Mass.: Addison-Wesley, 1982.
Standard business-school textbook describing modern financial analysis.

Daily Racing Form. Chicago: Triangle Publications, published daily.
The definitive source of current racing information.

Davidowitz, Steven. *Betting Thoroughbreds*. Revised edition. New York: Dutton, 1979.
Informative and entertaining tips by one of the nation's top handicappers.

Doig, Stephen K. "Professor Has Horse Betting Down to a Science." *The Miami Herald* (27 October 1986), p. B-1.
A report of a day studying the Dr. Z system at a seminar and its successful use at Calder.

Dowie, Jack. "On the Efficiency and Equity of Betting Markets," *Economica*, 43 (May 1976), pp. 139–50.
Shows that the win market in England is efficient.

Epstein, Richard A. *Theory of Gambling and Statistical Logic*. 2d ed. New York: Academic Press, 1977.
The definitive source of information on the mathematics of gambling.

Ethier, Stuart, and Steve Tavare. "The Proportional Bettor's Return on Investment." *Journal of Applied Probability* (1983).
Win rates using the Kelly criterion.

Fabricand, Burton F. *Horse Sense*. New York: McKay, 1965.
This and the author's other book present an interesting theory of horse-race betting based on rules of similarity.

———. *The Science of Winning*. New York: Van Nostrand Reinhold, 1979.

Fama, Eugene F. "Efficient Capital Markets: A Review of Theory and Empirical Work." *Journal of Finance*, 25 (May 1970), pp. 383–417.
Survey of research on random walks of security prices.

Figgis, E.L. "Rates of Return from Flat Race Betting in England in 1973." *Sporting Life*, 11 (March 1974).
Estimates of track takes by bookies and totalizator betting.

Finkelstein, Mark, and Robert Whitley. "Optimal Strategies for Repeated Games." *Advances in Applied Probability*, 13 (1981), pp. 415–428.

Friedman, Joel H. "Understanding and Applying the Kelly Criterion." Mimeograph, 1981.
The article that introduced fractional Kelly strategies to a wide audience.

Gardner, Jack. *Gambling: A Guide to Information Sources*. Detroit: Gale Research Co., 1980.
A bibliography listing many of the existing handicapping books through 1979 with brief comments on their contents. Write to Gale Research Co., Book Tower, Detroit, Mich. 48226.

Griffin, Peter A. "Different Measures of Win Rate for Optimal Proportional Betting." *Management Science* 30:12(December 1984), pp. 1540–1547. Analysis of alternative ways to measure win rates.

Griffith, R.M. "Odds Adjustment by American Horse Race Bettors." *American Journal of Psychology*, 62 (April 1949), pp. 290–294.
An early study of the favorite–long-shot bias.

Harville, David A. "Assigning Probabilities to the Outcomes of Multi-Entry Competitions." *Journal of American Statistical Association*, 68 (June 1973), pp. 312–16.

Presentation of the formulas that bear author's name for computing the probabilities of all possible in-the-money finishes.

Hausch, Donald B., Robert L. Winkler, and William T. Ziemba. "How to Bet on the Kentucky Derby." Forthcoming, 1987.

An attempt to combine the dosage and Dr. Z theories to obtain accurate probabilities of finish in the Derby and how the Kelly criterion can then be used to compute the optimal wagers.

Hausch, Donald B. and William T. Ziemba. "Transactions Costs, Extent of Inefficiencies, Entries and Multiple Wagers in a Racetrack Betting Model." *Management Science*, 31 (April 1985), pp. 381–94.

———. "Optimal Strategies for Multiple Track Betting on Major Stakes Races." Faculty of Commerce Working Paper No. 975, Vancouver: University of British Columbia (February 1987).

A mathematical article concerned with cross-track hedging and Kelly betting on races such as the Triple Crown, which are bet on at many tracks with the aid of closed-circuit TV simulcasts.

Hausch, Donald B., William T. Ziemba, and Mark Rubinstein. "Efficiency of the Market for Racetrack Betting." *Management Science*, 27 (December 1981), pp. 1435–52.

This and the April 1985 study by Hausch and Ziemba are the technical articles that form the basis of the Dr. Z system.

Herbert, Ivor. *Horse Racing: The Complete Guide to the World of the Turf*. New York: St. Martin's Press, 1980.

Lavish pictorial book with useful information concerning the sport of kings.

Humber, Larry. "You Don't Have to Lose at the Races," in *The Big Winner's System Book*, edited by L. Miller. Hollywood, Calif.: Gambling Times Publications (1981).

Argues that place and show betting may be profitable.

Isaacs, Rufus. "Optimal Horse Race Bets." *American Mathematical Monthly* (May 1983), pp. 310–315.

A mathematical article accounting for the effect of bet sizes on the win odds when determining the optimal bet size.

Kallberg, Jerry G., and William T. Ziemba. "Generalized Concave Functions in Stochastic Programming and Portfolio Theory." In *Generalized Concavity in Optimization and Economics*, edited by S. Schaible and W.T. Ziemba. New York: Academic Press, 1981, pp. 719–767.

A technical article concerned with mathematical properties of the Dr. Z system.

Kelly, John, L., Jr. "A New Interpretation of the Information Rate." *Bell System Technical Journal* (July 1956), pp. 917–926.

The article where the Kelly criterion system of wagering was first presented.

King, A. P. "Market Efficiency of a Multi-Entry Competition." M.B.A. Essay, Graduate School of Business, University of California, Berkeley: June 1978.
An early analysis of the predictive effect of the Harville formulas.

Lane, Daniel, and William T. Ziemba. "Jai Alai Hedging Strategies." In the *Fifth Conference on Gambling and Risk Taking*, edited by W. Eadington. University of Nevada, Reno, 1985, pp. 276–299.
The development of exact and approximate winning hedge strategies for the game of Mexican team jai alai.

Ledbetter, Bonnie, and Tom Ainslie. *The Body Language of Horses*. New York: Morrow, 1980.
An exposé of methods to evaluate the fitness of horses to perform well in a given race based on their personal appearance and comformation.

Malkiel, Burton G., *A Random Walk Down Wall Street*. 4th ed. New York: W.W. Norton and Co., 1985.
Lucid account of modern financial theories and their use in evaluating stocks and other securities.

McCleary, James. "Blue Chip Investments in Horse Racing" and "Blue Chip Investments in Horse Racing: An Update," in *The Big Winner's Systems Book*, edited by L. Miller. Hollywood, Calif.: Gambling Times Publications, 1981.
Shows that betting on overwhelming favorites in major stakes and futurity races can be profitable.

McDonald, Archie. "Dr. Z Good Bet at Windows." *The Vancouver Sun* (1 February 1986).
Discussion of the Dr. Z methods.

McGlothlin, W.H. "Stability of Choices Among Uncertain Alternatives." *American Journal of Psychology*, 69 (December 1956), pp. 604–15.
An early article on the favorite–long-shot bias.

MacLean, Leonard, William T. Ziemba, and George Blazenko. "Growth Versus Security in Dynamic Investment Analysis." Mimeograph, Vancouver: University of British Columbia (February 1987).
A technical article concerned with fractional Kelly betting strategies and their role in the evaluation of investment strategies for favorable games such as blackjack, horseracing, lottos, and futures trading.

McNeill, Stuart. "This Math Whiz Knows How to Pick the Winners." *Vancouver Sun* (6 January 1983), p. B4.
This and the Miller article give an account of how I showed that you can beat the Quebec Hockey sports pool to the tune of $70,000.

Meadow, Barry. "Harness Betting." *Gambling Times* (October 1985), pp. 46, 77.
Meadow reviews the first edition of *Beat the Racetrack* and relates his positive experiences with the Dr. Z system at harness racetracks.

Miller, David, "Successful Bets a Sure Thing for B.C. Professor." *Toronto Sunday Star* (16 January 1983), p. A14.

Mitchell, Dick. *A Winning Thoroughbred Strategy*, Los Angeles: Cynthia Publishing Co., 1985a.

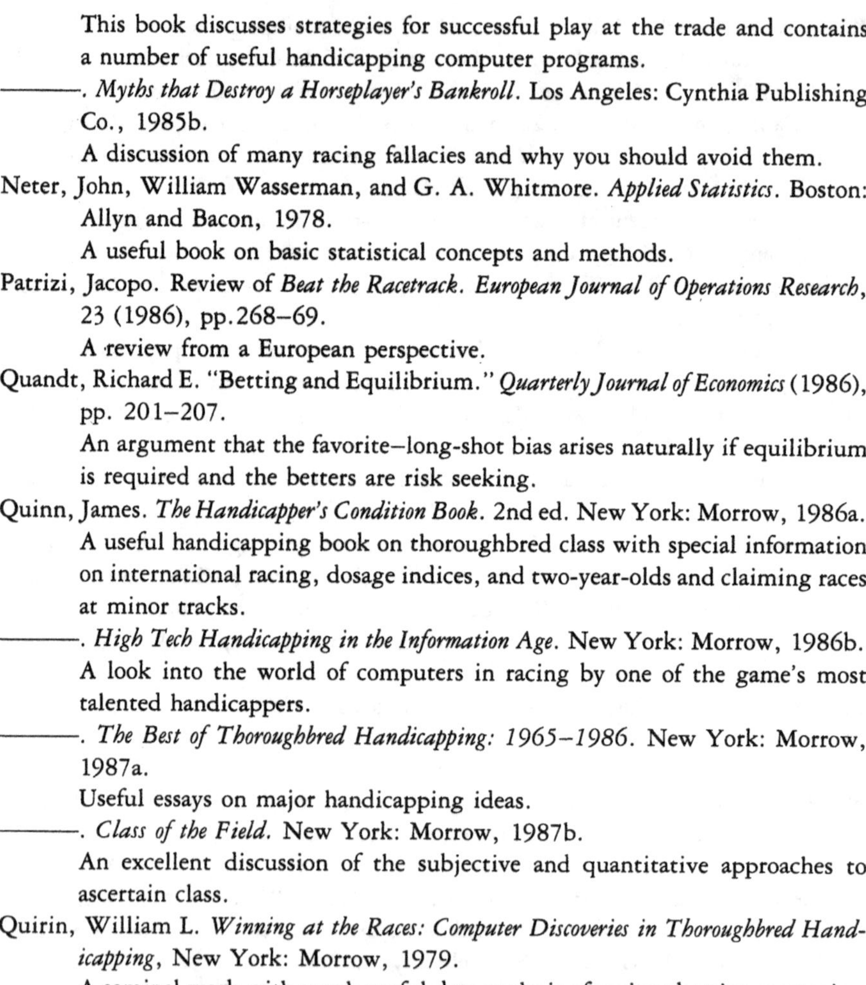

This book discusses strategies for successful play at the trade and contains a number of useful handicapping computer programs.

———. *Myths that Destroy a Horseplayer's Bankroll.* Los Angeles: Cynthia Publishing Co., 1985b.

A discussion of many racing fallacies and why you should avoid them.

Neter, John, William Wasserman, and G. A. Whitmore. *Applied Statistics.* Boston: Allyn and Bacon, 1978.

A useful book on basic statistical concepts and methods.

Patrizi, Jacopo. Review of *Beat the Racetrack. European Journal of Operations Research,* 23 (1986), pp.268–69.

A review from a European perspective.

Quandt, Richard E. "Betting and Equilibrium." *Quarterly Journal of Economics* (1986), pp. 201–207.

An argument that the favorite–long-shot bias arises naturally if equilibrium is required and the betters are risk seeking.

Quinn, James. *The Handicapper's Condition Book.* 2nd ed. New York: Morrow, 1986a.

A useful handicapping book on thoroughbred class with special information on international racing, dosage indices, and two-year-olds and claiming races at minor tracks.

———. *High Tech Handicapping in the Information Age.* New York: Morrow, 1986b.

A look into the world of computers in racing by one of the game's most talented handicappers.

———. *The Best of Thoroughbred Handicapping: 1965–1986.* New York: Morrow, 1987a.

Useful essays on major handicapping ideas.

———. *Class of the Field.* New York: Morrow, 1987b.

An excellent discussion of the subjective and quantitative approaches to ascertain class.

Quirin, William L. *Winning at the Races: Computer Discoveries in Thoroughbred Handicapping*, New York: Morrow, 1979.

A seminal work with much useful data analysis of various betting strategies.

———. *Thoroughbred Handicapping: State of the Art.* New York: Morrow, 1984.

A followup to the 1979 book emphasizing recent handicapping developments.

———. *Handicapping by Example.* New York: Morrow, 1986.

Forty-one races are analyzed, each to bring out a handicapping point or angle.

Ritter, Jay R. "Racetrack Betting: An Example of a Market with Efficient Arbitrage." Term Paper, Finance 432–433, University of Chicago (3 March 1978).

Early paper on the wisdom of wagering on overlooked place and show bets.

Roman, Steven A. "Dosage: A Practical Approach." *Daily Racing Form* (May 1981).

A discussion of the principles of dosage in a three-part article, which is available from the *Daily Racing Form* as a $3 reprint.

———. "An Analysis of Dosage." *The Thoroughbred Record* (April 1984).

Further findings on dosage, especially related to distance of races and the classic races.

Rosecrance, John D. *The Degenerates of Lake Tahoe*. New York: Peter Lang, 1985.

A sociological study of the persistence in the social world of horse-race gambling.

Rothschild, Lord. *Royal Commission on Gambling, Vols. I and II*. Presented to Parliament by command of the Queen (July 1978).

The definitive source of information on gambling activities and practices in England.

Scott, William L. *How Will Your Horse Run Today?* Baltimore: Amicus, 1984.

A handicapping theory developed by careful study of 433 races at four Eastern racetracks in 1981.

Seligman, Daniel. "The Two Minute Sprint." *Fortune* (24 June, 1985), p. 114.

A discussion of the Dr. Z system in connection with the efficient-market hypothesis.

Sharpe, William, F. *Investments*. 3rd ed. Englewood Cliffs, N.J.: Prentice Hall, 1985.

A leading business-school text discussing modern investment ideas by the coinventor of the capital asset pricing model.

Synder, Wayne W. "Horse Racing: Testing the Efficient Markets Model." *Journal of Finance*, 33 (September 1978), pp. 1109–1118.

A summary of research on the favorite–long-shot bias for win bets.

Thorp, Edward O. *Beat the Dealer*. New York: Random House, 1966.

The book that changed the rules of blackjack by presenting the first winning card-counting system.

———. "Portfolio Choice and the Kelly Criterion." In *Stochastic Optimization Models in Finance*, edited by William T. Ziemba and Raymond G. Vickson. New York: Academic Press, 1975, pp. 599–619.

A lucid technical account of the major properties of the Kelly system of betting.

Thorp, Edward O., and Sheen T. Kassouf. *Beat the Market*, New York: Random House, 1967.

The development of a profitable strategy for warrant hedging.

Vergin, R.C. "An Investigation of Decision Rules for Thoroughbred Race Horse Wagering." *Interfaces*, 8 (1977), pp. 34–45.

Shows that sets of ad-hoc filter rules may lead to profitable betting schemes.

Yass, Jeffrey. "An Econometric Strategy for Winning at the Track." *Gambling Times* (January 1980), 46–48.

Argues that place and show bets may be advantageous if they are sufficiently underbet.

Ziemba, William T. "The Favorite–Long-shot Bias in Hockey: Betting on the 1982 Stanley Cup Playoffs." Mimeograph, Vancouver: University of British Columbia, Faculty of Commerce (March 1984).

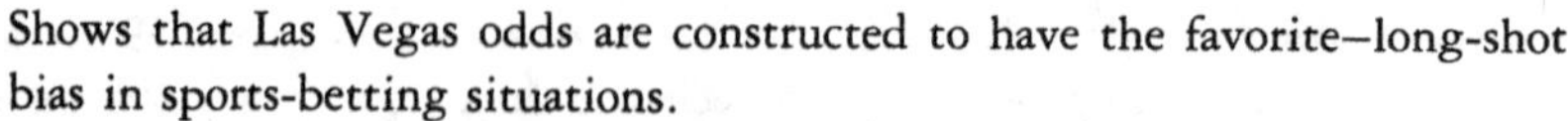

Shows that Las Vegas odds are constructed to have the favorite–long-shot bias in sports-betting situations.

———. "Mathematics of Gambling and Investment." Monthly column in *Gambling Times* (March 1987ff.).

I discuss topics of current interest, with the emphasis on turning wagers into investments with positive expectations.

———. *Strategies for Making Excess Returns in the Stock Market*, forthcoming, 1988.

An exposition of various security-market anomalies that have consistently provided edges in the sense that their risk-adjusted returns exceed that of the general market averages.

Ziemba, William T., Shelby L. Brumelle, Antoine Gautier, and Sandra L. Schwartz. *Dr. Z's 6/49 Lotto Guidebook*. Los Angeles, Dr. Z Investments, Inc., 1986.

An analysis of Lotto games, including the chances of winning the various prizes and strategies that have edges using unpopular numbers. Write to Dr. Z Investments, Inc., Box 35334, Los Angeles, Calif, 90035.

Ziemba, William T. and Donald B. Hausch. *Betting at the Racetrack*. Los Angeles: Dr. Z Investments, Inc., 1985.

An extension of the ideas of this book to the exotic wagers of the exacta, the quinella, the daily double and the triactor.

Ziemba, William T. and Raymond G. Vickson, eds. *Stochastic Optimization Models in Finance*. New York: Academic Press, 1975.

Technical articles concerned with the mathematics of the Kelly criterion and other financial topics.

Index

www.ingramcontent.com/pod-product-compliance
Lightning Source LLC
Chambersburg PA
CBHW070819250426
43671CB00036B/482

* 9 7 8 1 6 3 5 6 1 7 4 9 8 *